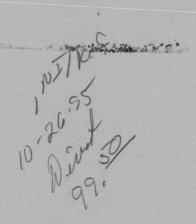

The McGraw-Hill
Encyclopedia
of
Economics

The McGraw-Hill Encyclopedia of Economics

Second Edition

Douglas Greenwald

Editor in Chief

McGraw-Hill, Inc.

New York   San Francisco   Washington, D.C.   Auckland   Bogotá
Caracas   Lisbon   London   Madrid   Mexico City   Milan
Montreal   New Delhi   San Juan   Singapore
Sydney   Tokyo   Toronto

Library of Congress Cataloging-in-Publication Data

The McGraw-Hill encyclopedia of economics / Douglas Greenwald, editor
in chief. -- 2nd ed.
     p.   cm.
  Rev. ed. of: Encyclopedia of economics. c1982.
  Includes indexes.
  ISBN 0-07-024410-3
   1. Economics—Encyclopedias. I. Greenwald, Douglas.
  II. Encyclopedia of economics. III. Title: Encyclopedia of
economics.
  HB61.E55 1994
  330'.03—dc20

                         93-9805
                             CIP

  2 3 4 5 6 7 8 9 0 DOC/DOC 9 9 8 7 6 5 4

ISBN 0-07-024410-3

*The sponsoring editor for this book was Betsy N. Brown, the editing
supervisor was Frank Kotowski, Jr., and the production supervisor was
Donald F. Schmidt. It was set in Melior by North Market Street Graphics.*

Printed and bound by R. R. Donnelley & Sons Company.

Contents

Contributors

Name and Affiliation	Articles
Alan Abouchar Professor of Economics, University of Toronto; former Economist, International Bank for Reconstruction and Development.	Decline of the Soviet Economy; Perestroika
Rex A. Ahene Associate Professor of Economics and Business, Lafayette College.	Coauthor, Infrastructure; coauthor, Stages theory of economic development
Bruce T. Allen Professor of Economics, Michigan State University; author, *Managerial Economics*.	Concentration of industry
Clopper Almon, Jr. Professor of Economics, University of Maryland and Director of its Inter-industry Forecasting Project; author, *Matrix Methods in Economics*.	Distributed lags in economics; Input-output analysis
Edward I. Altman Max L. Heine Professor of Finance, Stern School of Business, New York University; author of recently published books on Corporate Financial Distress, Recent Advances in Corporate Finance, Investing in Junk Bonds.	Junk (high-yield) bond market

Name and Affiliation	Articles

Henry C. F. Arnold
Senior Faculty Associate, Seton Hall University; coauthor, *McGraw-Hill Dictionary of Modern Economics*.

Bond; Bond rating agencies; Price-earnings ratio; Securities and Exchange Commission; Stock; Stock exchange; Stock price averages and indexes; Yield curve

David A. Aschauer
Elmer W. Campbell Professor of Economics, Bates College; former Senior Economist, Federal Reserve Bank of Chicago.

Public capital

Richard Aspinwall
Senior Vice President and Chief Economist, Chase-Manhattan Bank; coauthor, *Handbook for Banking Strategy*.

Commercial banks: problems and solutions

Irving M. Auerbach
Retired; former Senior Vice President and Economist, Aubrey G. Lamson & Co., Inc.; former Manager, Statistics Department, Federal Reserve Bank of New York.

Monetary policy

Lawrence M. Ausubel
Professor of Economics, University of Maryland; author, "The Failure of Competition in the Credit Card Market," *American Economic Review*, March 1991.

Credit cards

Roger E. Backhouse
Senior Lecturer in Economics, University of Birmingham, England; author, *A History of Modern Economic Analysis*.

Gresham's law

Theodore Bakerman
Professor of Business, Emeritus, Indiana State University; author, *Anthracite Coal: A Study in Advanced Industrial Decline*.

Fringe benefits

Sam Barone
Dean, School of Business, Towson State College; former Dean, College of Business and Administration, University of Detroit.

Collective bargaining; Labor-management relations

Name and Affiliation	Articles

Thomas A. Barthold
Staff Economist, Joint Committee on Taxation, U.S. Congress; former Assistant Professor, Dartmouth College.

Capital gains

James R. Baumgardner
Assistant Professor of Economics, Duke University.

Division of Labor

William J. Baumol
Joseph Douglas Green '95 Professor of Economics, Princeton University; Professor of Economics, New York University; coauthor, *Contestable Markets and the Theory of Industry Structure.*

Contestable market

John H. Beck
Associate Professor of Economics, Gonzaga University.

State and local government finance

Jere Behrman
William R. Kenan, Jr. Professor of Economics, University of Pennsylvania; Co-Director, Center for Household and Family Economics, University of Pennsylvania.

Coauthor, Human capital

Anita M. Benvignati
Economic Consultant; author, "Industry Determinants and Differences in U.S. Intrafirm and Arms-Length Exports," *Review of Economics and Statistics.*

Barriers to trade; Dumping

Peter L. Bernstein
President, Peter L. Bernstein Inc.; founder and Consulting Editor, *The Journal of Portfolio Management*; author, *Capital Ideas: The Improbable Origins of Wall Street.*

Mutual funds

Stanley W. Black
George Lurey Professor of Economics, University of North Carolina; author, "Transactions Costs and Vehicle Currencies, *Journal of International Money and Finance.*

Foreign exchange rates

Name and Affiliation	Articles
Roger D. Blair Huber Hurst Professor of Economics, University of Florida, coauthor, *Antitrust Economics.*	Integration, Antitrust policy; Restraint of trade
Mark Blaug Consultant Professor, University of Buckingham, England; Professor Emeritus, Economics of Education, University of London, Institute of Education; author, *Economic History and the History of Economics.*	Cambridge school; Comparative advantage theory; Labor theory of value; Manchester school
David M. Blitzer Vice President and Chief Economist, Standard and Poor's Corporation; former corporate staff economist, McGraw-Hill, Inc.	Profits measurement
Arthur I. Bloomfield Professor Emeritus of Economics, University of Pennsylvania; former Senior Economist, Federal Reserve Bank of New York.	Gold standard
Marshall E. Blume Howard Butcher III Professor of Finance and Director of the Rodney L. White Center for Financial Research at the Wharton School, University of Pennsylvania, coauthor, "The Theory of Security Pricing and Market Structure," *Journal of Financial Markets, Institutions and Instruments.*	Portfolio management theories
Michael J. Boskin Chairman, Council of Economic Advisers; former Professor of Economics, Stanford University.	Council of Economic Advisers
John E. Bregger Assistant Commissioner, Office of Current Employment Analysis, Bureau of Labor Statistics; former Chief, Division of Employment and Unemployment Analysis, Bureau of Labor Statistics.	Coauthor, Employment and unemployment; coauthor, Labor force

Name and Affiliation	Articles

William J. Brown
Edgerton Professor of Business Administration and Head, Department of Business and Economics, Berry College; former Senior Financial Economist, Office of the Controller of the Currency.

Banking system; Debt; Debt management; Deposits; Federal Trade Commission; Financial institutions; Financial instruments

Brian C. Brush
Associate Dean, College of Business Administration, Marquette University; author, "Market Power and Cyclical Wage Flexibility in U.S. Manufacturing Industries," *Review of Business and Economic Research.*

Economies of scale

Barbara Everitt Bryant
Director, Bureau of the Census; former Senior Vice President, Market Opinion Research.

Bureau of Census

William R. Buechner
Senior Economist, Joint Economic Committee of Congress.

Joint Economic Committee of Congress

M. L. Burstein
Professor of Economics, York University, Ontario; author, *The New Art of Central Banking.*

Business inventory; Stock-flow analysis

James L. Burtle
Senior Adviser, Foreign Exchange Service, Wharton Economic Forecasting Associates; Professor of Economics, Iona College; Managing Editor, *International Country Risk Guide.*

Exports; Foreign exchange management; Imports

Colin D. Campbell
Professor of Economics Emeritus, Dartmouth College; coauthor, *Money, Banking and Monetary Policy.*

Chicago school

Carol Carrado
Chief, Industrial output section, Division of Research and Statistics, Board of Governors of the Federal Reserve System.

Coauthor, Industrial production index

Name and Affiliation	Articles

Carol S. Carson
Director, Bureau of Economic Analysis; United Nations contributing expert on revision of the System of National Accounts.

Bureau of Economic Analysis; System of National Accounts

Phillip A. Cartwright
Director of Econometric Analysis and Senior Economist, A. C. Nielsen; former Associate Professor of Economics and Director of Georgia Economic Forecasting Project, University of Georgia.

Marketing research and business economics; Sampling in economics

Benjamin Chinitz
Fellow, A. Alfred Taubman Center for State and Local Government, Harvard University; former Senior Fellow, Lincoln Institute of Land Policy.

Regional economics; Urban economics

John S. Chipman
Regents Professor of Economics, University of Minnesota; Humboldt Research Award for Senior U.S. Scientist, 1992.

Acceleration principle

Gregory C. Chow
Class of 1913 Professor of Political Economy and Director, Econometric Research Program, Princeton University; author, *Econometrics.*

Simulations in economics and business

Robert W. Clower
Hugh C. Lane Professor of Economic Theory, College of Business Administration, University of South Carolina; former Professor of Economics, University of California, Los Angeles.

Economics; Factors of production; Money illusion; Scarcity

Warren Coats
Adviser, International Monetary Fund; former Assistant Professor of Economics, University of Virginia.

Coauthor, Special drawing rights

Willard W. Cochrane
Professor Emeritus, Center for International Food and Agricultural Policy, University of Minnesota; coauthor, *Reforming Farm Policy: Toward A National Agenda.*

Agricultural economic policy

Name and Affiliation	Articles

Richard N. Cooper
Mauritz C. Boas Professor of International Economics, Harvard University; Chairman, Federal Reserve Bank of Boston; coauthor, *International Financial Integration: the Policy Challenges.*

Value of the dollar

John Cornwall
McCulloch Professor of Economics, Dalhousie University, Halifax; author, *The Theory of Economic Breakdown: An Institutional Analysis.*

Capitalism

Bernard Corry
Professor of Economics and Dean of the Faculty of Social Studies, Queen Mary and Westfield College, University of London; coeditor, *Essay in Honour of Lord Robbins.*

Consumers' surplus; Marshallian economics

Camilo Dagum
Professor of Economics, University of Milan, Italy; Professor Emeritus, University of Ottawa; former Guest Scholar, Brookings Institution.

Coauthor, Index numbers; coauthor, Secular trend

Estela Bee Dagum
Director, Time Series Research and Analysis Division, Statistics, Canada; Editor, *International Journal of Forecasting*; former Senior Adviser to Bureau of Census and Bureau of Labor Statistics.

Coauthor, Index numbers; Seasonal adjustment methods; Seasonal variations; coauthor, Secular trend

Michael R. Darby
Professor of Economics, John E. Anderson Graduate School of Management, U.C.L.A.; former Undersecretary for Economic Affairs, U.S. Department of Commerce; former Assistant Secretary of the Treasury for Economic Policy.

Consumption function; Dynamic analysis; Dynamic macroeconomic models; *IS-LM* model; Permanent income hypothesis; Static analysis

Paul Davidson
Fred Holly Chair of Political Economy, University of Tennessee; author, "The Dual Nature of the Keynesian Revolution," *Journal of Post-Keynesian Economics.*

Post Keynesian economics

Name and Affiliation	Articles
Thomas F. Dernburg Chair of Excellence in Free Enterprise, Austin Peay State University; former Professor of Economics, American University; author, *Macroeconomics*.	Automatic stabilizers; Macroeconomics
Ronald W. Dickey Director, the Center for Real Estate Studies and Professor of Real Estate Finance and Economics, Fairleigh Dickinson University.	Coauthor, Small business
Dudley Dillard Deceased; former Professor of Economics, University of Maryland; author, *The Economics of John Maynard Keynes*.	Keynesian economics
E. I. Doukas Manager, Options and Equities Group, Department of Economic Analysis, Chicago Board of Trade; former Research Analyst, Dean Witter Reynolds.	Commodity exchange
M. Kathryn Eickhoff President, Eickhoff Economics; former Vice President, Townsend-Greenspan & Co., Inc.	Anticipation surveys, business
Robert Eisner William R. Kenan Professor of Economics, Northwestern University; author, *The Total Income Systems of Accounts*; Past President, American Economic Association.	Business investment in new plants and equipment; Capital formation; Debt and deficits; Investment function; Profits in economic theory
Adel I. El Ansary Eminent Scholar and First Chairholder of the Paper and Plastics Education and Research Foundation Endowed Research Chair in Wholesaling, College of Business Administration, University of North Florida; former Professor and Chairman of Business Administration, George Washington University.	Channels of marketing

Name and Affiliation	Articles
Holgar L. Engberg Professor of Finance and International Business, Stern School of Business, New York University; completing manuscript on index numbers and international trade.	Money markets
Joshua Feinman Economist, Division of Monetary Affairs, Board of Governors of the Federal Reserve System.	Federal Reserve System
Martin Feldstein President, National Bureau of Economic Research Inc.; former Chairman, Council of Economic Advisers.	National Bureau of Economic Research
Wayne Ferson Graduate School of Business, University of Chicago; author, "Theory and Empirical Testing of Asset Pricing Models," Chap. A6 of *The Finance Handbook*.	Asset pricing models
Stanley Fischer Professor of Economics, M.I.T.; former Chief Economist, World Bank; author, "Indexing and Inflation," *Journal of Monetary Economics*.	Indexation
Robert J. Flanagan Professor of Labor Economics, Graduate School of Business, Stanford University; coauthor, *Unionism, Economic Stabilization and Income Policies*.	Income policy
Karl A. Fox Distinguished Professor of Economics and Statistics, Emeritus, Iowa State University; author, *Econometric Analysis for Public Policy*.	Coauthor, Cross-sectional analysis in business economics; coauthor, Game theory, economic applications; coauthor, Regression analysis in business and economics; coauthor, Simultaneous equation estimates in business and economics
Bernard S. Friedman Senior Research Fellow, Agency for Health Care and Policy Research; former Vice President for Research, Hospital Research and Education Trust, Northwestern University.	Health economics; Medicare program; Subsidies

Name and Affiliation	Articles
A. Blake Friscia Adjunct Professor of Economics, New York University; former Vice President, and International Economist, Chase-Manhattan Bank.	Less-developed country debt
John Kenneth Galbraith Paul M. Warburg Professor of Economics Emeritus, Harvard University; author, *The Affluent Society and the New Industrial State.*	Affluent society; Countervailing power; New industrial state
Nicholas Georgesau-Roegen Distinguished Professor of Economics Emeritus, Vanderbilt University; author, "Utility and Value in Economic Thought," *Dictionary of the History of Ideas.*	Utility
Margaret S. Gordon Research Economist Emeritus, Institute of Industrial Relations, University of California, Berkeley; author, *Social Security Policies in Industrial Countries, A Comparative Analysis.*	Negative income tax
Peter T. Gottschalk Professor of Economics, Boston College; former Project Associate, Research Institute on Poverty, University of Wisconsin.	Poverty
John P. Gould Dean and Distinguished Service Professor of Economics, Graduate School of Business, University of Chicago; coauthor, *Microeconomic Theory.*	Price theory
Edward M. Graham Senior Fellow, Institute for International Economics; former Associate Professor, Fuqua School of Business Administration, Duke University; coauthor, *Foreign Direct Investment in the United States.*	Foreign direct investment; General agreement on tariffs and trade; Joint venture; Multinational corporation; Nationalization of industry; Protectionism

Name and Affiliation	Articles
Melvin L. Greenhut Abell Professor of Liberal Arts and Distinguished Professor of Economics, Texas A&M University; author, *Plant Location in Theory and Practice*.	Location theory
Douglas Greenwald Editor-in-chief, *McGraw-Hill Encyclopedia of Economics* and *McGraw-Hill Dictionary of Modern Economics*; former Vice President, Economics, McGraw-Hill Publications Company; Fellow of the National Association of Business Economics and the American Statistical Association.	Coauthor, Anticipation surveys, consumer; Distribution theory; Mercantilism; coauthor, Monopoly and oligopoly
Jeanne L. Hafstrom Associate Professor of Family and Consumer Economics, University of Illinois; Editor, *Compendium of Quality of Life Research*.	Family budgets; Standard of living
Robert W. Hahn Resident Scholar, American Enterprise Institute; Adjunct Research Fellow, John F. Kennedy School of Government, Harvard University.	Coauthor, Economic incentives for environmental protection
Thomas W. Hamilton Teaching Assistant, University of Wisconsin.	Coauthor, Real estate investment trusts
David G. Hartman Managing Director and Chief International Economist, D.R.I./McGraw-Hill; former Executive Director, National Bureau of Economic Research.	Economic blocs; J curve
Robert W. Hartman Assistant Director for Special Studies, Congressional Budget Office, U.S. Congress.	Congressional Budget Office

Name and Affiliation	Articles

Steven Haugen
Economist, Division of Labor Force Statistics, Bureau of Labor Statistics.

Coauthor, Employment and unemployment

William J. Hausman
Professor of Economics, College of William and Mary; Editor, *Business and Economic History.*

Industrial revolution

H. Robert Heller
Vice President, Visa Corporation; former Governor, Board of Governors, Federal Reserve System; former Senior Vice President and Director, International Economics, Bank of America.

International Monetary Fund; Special drawing rights

James M. Henderson
Professor of Economics, Duke University; former Professor of Economics, University of Minnesota; coauthor, *Microeconomic Theory; A Mathematical Approach.*

Isoquant; Microeconomics; Production function

Walter G. Hoadley
Senior Research Fellow, Hoover Institution; former Executive Vice President and Chief Economist, Bank of America.

International economics, an overview

Mary A. Holman
Professor of Economics, George Washington University; author, *The Political Economy of the Space Program.*

Cobweb theorem; Demand; Elasticity; Supply

Francis Horvath
Economist, Division of Labor Force Statistics, Bureau of Labor Statistics.

Coauthor, Labor force

James Horvath
John A. Arbuckle Professor of Economics and Research Scholar, Holcombes Research Institute, Butler University; author, *Chinese Technology Transfer to the Third World: A Grants Economy Analysis.*

Grants economics

Name and Affiliation	Articles
Charles R. Hulten Professor of Economics, University of Maryland; author, many articles on depreciation.	Depreciation allowance
Thomas M. Humphrey Vice President and Economist, Federal Reserve Bank of Richmond; author, *Essays on Inflation.*	Banking school; Currency school
Walter Isard Professor of Economics, Emeritus, Cornell University; Adjunct Professor, University of Pennsylvania; Founder, fields of Regional Science and Peace Science.	Peace economics
A. J. Jaffe Senior Research Scholar, retired, Columbia University; coauthor, *Misused Statistics.*	Malthusian theory of population
David Jansen Assistant Professor of Economics, Texas A&M University.	Rational expectations
Robert A. Jarrow Ronald P. and Susan E. Lynch Professor of Investment Management, S. C. Johnson Graduate School of Management, Cornell University; Associate Editor, Advances in Futures and Options Research; Associate Editor, *The Review of Futures Markets.*	Futures
D. Gale Johnson Professor of Economics, University of Chicago; coauthor, *The Measurement of Productivity.*	Agricultural productivity
Robert W. Johnson Professor of Management, Krannert Graduate School of Management, Purdue University; Senior Research Associate, Credit Research Center; author, "The Consumer Bankruptcy Problems: Causes and Cures," *Journal of Retail Banking.*	Consumer credit

Name and Affiliation	Articles

F. Thomas Juster
Director, Institute for Social Research and Professor of Economics, University of Michigan; author, *Anticipations and Purchases: An Analysis of Consumer Behavior.*

Consumer theory; Expectations; Income

George Katona
Deceased; a founder of and Research Coordinator of Survey Research Center, Institute for Social Research, University of Michigan.

Coauthor, Anticipation surveys, consumer

Bernard S. Katz
Professor of Economics, Lafayette College; editor of numerous economics books.

Coauthor, Bretton Woods Conference; coauthor, Infrastructure; coauthor, Smithsonian Agreement; coauthor, Stages theory of economic development.

Tej J. Kaul
Chairperson and Professor, Department of Management Information Resources School of Business, Western Illinois University; coauthor, *Intermediate Economic Statistics.*

Coauthor, Cross-sectional analysis in business and economics; coauthor, Game theory, economic applications; coauthor, Regression analysis in business and economics; coauthor, Simultaneous equation estimates in business and economics

Irwin L. Kellner
Chief Economist, Chemical Banking; past President of Forecasters Club of New York and New York Association of Business Economists; former Assistant Business Outlook Editor, *Business Week.*

U.S. business obsession with short-term performance

John W. Kendrick
Professor of Economics Emeritus, George Washington University; coauthor, *New Developments in Productivity Measurement and Analysis, Studies in Income and Wealth;* author, *The Formation of Stocks and Total Capital.*

Productivity; Wealth

Name and Affiliation	Articles
John J. Klein Professor of Economics, Georgia State University; author, *Money and the Economy*.	Interest, economic theory; Real balance effect theory
Lawrence R. Klein Benjamin Franklin Professor of Economics Emeritus, University of Pennsylvania; past President, American Economic Association and Econometrics Society; Nobel Laureate in Economics, 1980.	Computers in economics; Econometrics; Economic models
Philip A. Klein Professor of Economics, Pennsylvania State University.	German historical school; Institutional economics; Kuznets cycles
Robert E. L. Knight Associate Professor of Economics, University of Maryland; author, Industrial Relations in the San Francisco Bay Area.	Zero population growth
Alexander J. Kondonassis David Ross Boyd Professor of Economics and Director of Advanced Program in Economics, University of Oklahoma, past President, International Executive Board of International Honor Society in Economics.	German unification: problems and prospects
Finn E. Kydland Professor of Economics, Carnegie-Mellon University; coauthor, "Time to Build and Aggregate Fluctuations," *Econometrics*.	Real business cycles
Kelvin J. Lancaster John Bates Clark Professor of Economics, Columbia University; author, *Modern Consumer Theory*.	Second best
Walther Lederer Statistical Consultant, Flow of Funds Section of the Federal Reserve Board; former Senior Adviser for Balance of Payments Analysis, U.S. Department of Treasury.	Balance of international payments; Balance of international trade; International investment position

Name and Affiliation	Articles
Brian Leverich Information Systems Scientist and Project Leader, Rand Corporation.	Linear programming; Operations research
Richard Levich Professor of Finance and International Business, Stern School of Business, New York University; author, *The Capital Market Effects of International Accounting Diversity.*	Eurodollar market
Mickey D. Levy Senior Vice President and Chief Economist, CRT Government Securities; former Chief Economist, First Fidelity Bancorp.	Fiscal policy
Herman I. Liebling Economic Consultant; former Professor of Economics, Lafayette College; former Chief Economist, U.S. Department of Treasury.	Economic forecasts; Gross domestic product; Phillips curve; Stagflation
Fabian Linden Executive Director, Consumer Research Center, the Conference Board; author of "Midlife and Beyond" and "Baby Boomers in Mid-Passage."	Demographics and economics
John Llewellyn Head of the Secretary General's Private Office, OECD, former Director, Social Affairs Manpower and Education, OECD.	Organization of Economic Cooperation and Development
Peter Ludlow Director, Center for European Policy Studies; author and editor, *CEPS Annual Review of EC Affairs.*	European Community
Hugh Macauley Alumni Professor of Economics Emeritus, Clemson University; coauthor, *Environmental Use and the Market.*	Externalities
Fritz Machlup Deceased; former Professor of Economics, New York University; past President, American Economic Association.	Coauthor, Austrian economics; coauthor, Marginal revenue

Name and Affiliation	Articles

Edwin Mansfield
Director, Center for Economics and Technology and Professor of Economics, University of Pennsylvania; Member of the Academy of Arts and Sciences.

Automation

Stephen Martin
Professor and Head of Department of Economics, European University Institute, Florence, Italy; former Professor of Economics, Michigan State University.

Cartel

G. H. Mattersdorff
Professor of Economics and Public Administration, Lewis and Clark College; former economist, 13th National Bank Region, Comptroller of the Currency.

Diminishing returns law; Economic rent; Physiocrats

Peggy May
Retired; former Economist, Federal Reserve Bank of New York.

Data banks

Edward Mayers
Deceased; coauthor, *McGraw-Hill Dictionary of Modern Economics*; Former Senior Economist, McGraw-Hill Publications Company's Department of Economics.

Coauthor, Monopoly and oligopoly

E. Scott Maynes
Professor, Department of Consumer Economics and Housing, Cornell University; Editor, *The Frontier of Research in the Consumer Interest*.

Consumerism

Martin C. McGuire
Heinz Economics Professor for Global Peace and Security, University of California, Irvine; former Professor of Economics, University of Maryland.

Normative economics

Robert L. McLaughlin
Publisher, *Turning Points*; former Director, Corporate Commercial Research, Scoville Manufacturing Corp; member of the McGraw-Hill Informal Conference of Economists.

Leading indicator approach to forecasting

Name and Affiliation	Articles

A. James Meigs
Economic Consultant to Eastern European Banks and Mutual Funds; former Senior Vice President and Chief Economist, First Interstate Bancorp; author, *Money Matters, Economics, Markets, Politics.*

Money supply; Quantity theory of money; Velocity of circulation of money

Robert C. Merton
George Fisher Baker Professor of Business Administration, Harvard Business School; author, *Continuous Time Finance.*

Options

Ann-Marie Meulendyke
Manager and Senior Economist, Federal Reserve Bank of New York; author, *U.S. Monetary Policy and Financial Markets.*

Coauthor, Open-market operations

Paul A. Meyer
Professor of Economics, University of Maryland; author, *Money, Financial Institutions and the Economy.*

Say's law of markets

Geoffrey H. Moore
Director, Center for International Business Cycle Research, Graduate School of Business, Columbia University; author, *Leading Industries for the 1990s.*

Business cycles; Diffusion indexes

Arnold X. Moskowitz
Chairman, Moskowitz, Capital Consulting Inc.; former Senior Vice President and Director, Investment Strategy, County Nat-West USA.

Closed-end investment companies; Random walk hypothesis

Laurence S. Moss
Professor of Economics and International Business, Babson College; author of numerous articles on economics and its history in *History of Political Economy, Eastern Economic Journal, Economic Appliquee, Journal of Economic Literature.*

Classical liberalism; Classical school; Laissez-faire; Liberalism; Neoclassical economics

R. Charles Moyer
Integon Chair of Finance, Babcock Graduate School of Management, Wake Forest University; author, *Managerial Economics.*

Opportunity cost

Name and Affiliation	Articles
John G. Myers Professor of Economics, Southern Illinois University, Carbondale; coauthor, *Saving Energy in Manufacturing.*	Energy costs
Egon Neuberger Leading Professor of Economics, State University of New York, Stony Brook; past President, Association for Comparative Economic Studies.	Comparative economic systems, an overview
Janet L. Norwood Senior Fellow, Urban Institute; former commissioner of the Bureau of Labor Statistics.	Bureau of Labor Statistics
James J. O'Leary Economic Consultant; former Vice Chairman of the Board, United States Trust Co.	Capital markets and money markets
Robert W. Oliver Professor of Economics Emeritus, California Institute of Technology; author, International Cooperation and the World Bank.	World Bank
Janusz A. Ordover Professor of Economics, New York University; Deputy Assistant Attorney General, Antitrust Division, U.S. Justice Department.	Marginal cost; coauthor, Marginal revenue
Rudolph Oswald Director, Department of Economic Research, AFL-CIO; past President of Industrial Relations Research Association.	Labor unions
Rudolph G. Penner National Director, Economic Studies, Policy Economics Group, Peat Marwick; former Senior Fellow, Urban Institute; former Director, Congressional Budget Office.	Federal budget; Federal budget process
Henry M. Peskin President, Edgevale Associates; former Senior Fellow, Resources for the Future; coauthor, *Cost-Benefit Analysis and Water Pollution Policy.*	Pollution abatement costs

Name and Affiliation	Articles
William H. Peterson Lundy Professor of Business Philosophy, Campbell University; Adjunct Scholar, Heritage Foundation and Ludwig von Mises Institute.	Capital intensive industry; Government regulation business; Return on investment; Right-to-work law
Solomon W. Polochek Professor of Economics, State University of New York at Binghamton; coauthor, *The Economics of Earnings.*	Discrimination economics
Joel Popkin President, Joel Popkin and Company; former Assistant Commissioner for Prices; Bureau of Labor Statistics; former Senior Staff Economist, President's Council of Economic Advisers.	Consumer price index; Cost of living; Escalator clause; Implicit price deflator; Price measurement; Producer price index; Rigid prices
Louis Putterman Professor of Economics, Brown University; author, "Theory of the Firm under Capitalism, Socialism and Labor Management," *Handbook of Comparative Economics.*	Firm theory
Richard Raddock Economist, Industrial Output Section, Board of Governors of the Federal Reserve System; former Assistant Professor of Economics, Guilford College.	Coauthor, Industrial production index
Roger L. Ranson Professor of Economics and History, University of California, Riverside; coauthor, *One Kind of Freedom: the Economic Consequences of Emancipation.*	Great Depression
Martin Regalia Executive Vice President, Policy Development and Chief Economist, National Council of Community Bankers; former Principal Analyst, Fiscal Analysis Division, Congressional Budget Office.	Thrift institutions: problems and challenges; Mortgage credit

Name and Affiliation	Articles
Vincent Reinhart Chief, Banking and Money Market Analysis, Board of Governors of the Federal Revenue System; former Senior Economist, International Research Department, Federal Reserve Bank of New York.	Federal Reserve policy
Paul Craig Roberts William E. Simon Chair in Political Economy, Center for Strategic and International Studies; Chairman, Institute for Political Economy; author, *The Supply Side Revolution*.	Supply-side economics
Joshua Ronen Professor of Accounting, Graduate School of Business Administration, New York University.	Break-even analysis
Nancy Ruggles Deceased; coauthor, *National Income Accounting and Income Analysis*; coauthor, *The Design of Economic Accounts*.	Coauthor, National income accounting
Richard Ruggles Professor of Economics, Emeritus, Yale University; coauthor, *National Income Accounting and Income Analysis*.	Coauthor, National income accounting
Peter G. Sassone Associate Professor of Economics and Management Technologies, Georgia Tech's Ivan Allen College of Management, Policy and International Affairs; Consultant to major corporations and governmental agencies on measurement of white collar productivity and on economic impact of information technology.	Cost-benefit analysis; Welfare economics
Raymond J. Saulnier Professor of Economics Emeritus, Barnard College, Columbia University; former Chairman, Council of Economic Advisers to the President.	Credit, an overview; Selective credit controls

Name and Affiliation	Articles
Shiva Sayeg Assistant Professor of Economics, Lafayette College; former Senior Lecturer, Towson State College.	Coauthor, Bretton Woods Conference; coauthor, Smithsonian Agreement
Francis H. Schott Economics and Finance Consultant, former Senior Vice President and Chief Economist, Equitable Life Assurance Society.	Disintermediation; Interest rates; Variable annuity; Social security
Eli Shapiro Alfred P. Sloan Professor of Management Emeritus, M.I.T.; former Vice Chairman of the Board, Travelers Corporation.	Business credit
Howard J. Sherman Professor of Economics, University of California, Riverside; author, *The Business Cycle: Growth and Crisis under Capitalism.*	Communism, Marxism; Radical economics; Socialism
Robert J. Shiller Stanley B. Resor Professor of Economics, Yale University; member of the Cowles Foundation for Research in Economics; author, *Market Volatility.*	Stock market crashes
James D. Shilling Associate Professor, Graduate School of Business, University of Wisconsin.	Coauthor, Real estate investment trusts
Herbert S. Simon Professor of Computer Science and Psychology, Carnegie-Mellon University; Prize in Economic Science in memory of Alfred Nobel.	Satisficing
Eugene Smolensky Dean, Graduate School of Public Policy, University of California, Berkeley; former Professor of Economics, University of Wisconsin.	Income distribution; Lorenz curve

Name and Affiliation	Articles

Ira Sohn
Professor of Finance, Montclair State College; author of articles and books on input-output techniques and natural resources.

Economic planning

Robert Solomon
Guest Scholar, The Brookings Institution; former Director, Division of International Finance, Federal Reserve Board.

Liquidity, international

Hugo Sonnenschein
Provost, Princeton University; former Dean and Thomas S. Gates Professor, School of Arts and Sciences, University of Pennsylvania.

General equilibrium

Joseph A. Starshak
Managing Director, Starman, Starshak, Welnhofer & Co.; former Vice President, Corporate Finance Division, Northern Trust Co.

Risk premium on investment

Robert N. Stavins
Assistant Professor of Public Policy and Senior Research Associate, Center for Science and International Affairs, John F. Kennedy School of Government, Harvard University; University Fellow, Resources for the Future.

Coauthor, Economic incentives for environmental protection

Peter D. Sternlight
Executive Vice President, Federal Reserve Bank of New York in charge of open-market operations; former Deputy Undersecretary for Monetary Affairs, U.S. Treasury Department.

Coauthor, Open-market operations

C. Eugene Steuerle
Senior fellow and Acting Director, Changing Domestic Priorities Project, Urban Institute; author, *The Tax Decade: How Taxes Came to Dominate the Public Agenda.*

Taxation, an overview

Name and Affiliation	Articles

Theodore Suranyi-Unger, Jr.
Professor of Economics, Department of Resources Management, Industrial College of the Armed Forces, National Defense University; former Research Professor of Economics, George Washington University.

Innovation; Research and development; Technology

Alan Sweezy
Retired; former Professor of Economics, California Institute of Technology.

Multiplier

Alan A. Tait
Deputy Director, Fiscal Affairs Department, International Monetary Fund.

Value-added tax

Paul Taubman
Professor of Economics, University of Pennsylvania; coauthor, *Education as an Investment and as a Screening Device.*

Coauthor, Human capital

Lester G. Telser
Professor of Economics, University of Chicago; Fellow of Econometrics Society and American Statistical Association.

Advertising, economic aspects; Arbitrage; Competition

Bernard H. Tenenbaum
Founding Director, George Rothman Institute of Entrepreneurial Studies and first George Rothman Clinical Professor of Entrepreneurship, Fairleigh Dickinson University; former Associate Director, Sol C. Snyder Entrepreneurial Center, Wharton School.

Coauthor, Small business

Albert Teplin
Chief, Flow of Funds Section, Division of Research and Statistics, Board of Governors, Federal Reserve System; former teacher of Economics, School of Business, Indiana University and University of Maryland.

Flow of funds; Savings

Nestor E. Terleckyj
President, National Planning Association Data Services Inc.; former Vice President and Director, Domestic Research Centers, National Planning Association.

Economic growth

Name and Affiliation	Articles
George C. Tiao W. Allen Wallis Professor of Statistics, Graduate School of Business, University of Chicago; coauthor, "Model Specification in Multivariate Time Series," *Journal of the Royal Statistical Society.*	Time series analysis
James Tobin Sterling Professor of Economics, Emeritus, Yale University; Prize in Economic Science in Memory of Alfred Nobel, 1981.	Inflation
Lloyd M, Valentine Professor of Economics, Emeritus, University of Cincinnati; coauthor, *Business Cycles and Forecasting.*	Juglar cycle; Kitchen cycle; Kondratieff cycle
C. Edward Weber Professor of Policy and Management, School of Business Administration, University of Wisconsin; Founding Dean, School of Business Administration, University of Wisconsin at Milwaukee.	Decision making in business: a behavioral approach
J. Fred Weston Cordner Professor of Money and Financial Markets, Anderson Graduate School of Management, University of California, Los Angeles; past President, American Finance Association, Financial Management Association, and Western Economic Association.	Capital budget process; Conglomerate; Financial distress; Going private and leveraged buyouts; Liquidity, corporate; Mergers, takeovers, and restructuring
William E. Wetzel, Jr. Forbes Professor of Management, Whitemore School of Business and Economics and Director of the Center for Venture Research, University of New Hampshire; former Paul T. Babson Visiting Professor of Entrepreneurial Studies, Babson College.	Venture capital
Gunther Wittich Deputy Treasurer, International Monetary Fund.	Coauthor, International Monetary Fund

Name and Affiliation	Articles

David Wyss
Vice President and Research Director, DRI/McGraw-Hill; former Senior Staff Economist, Council of Economic Advisers.

Economic forecasting methods

Victor Zarnowitz
Professor of Economics and Finance, Graduate School of Business, University of Chicago; author, *Business Cycles Theory, History, Indicators, and Forecasting.*

Accuracy of economic forecasts

Arnold Zellner
H.G.B. Alexander Distinguished Service Professor of Economics and Statistics, Graduate School of Business, University of Chicago; past President, American Statistical Association.

Bayesian inference; Statistical methods in economics and business, an overview

Preface

The purpose of the second edition of the *McGraw-Hill Encyclopedia of Economics* is to bring together the expertise of distinguished contributors from academic, business, and government sectors in order to provide an up-to-date reference book of highest-quality authorship. In this book, we are providing meaningful and useful articles, written by the experts, on the most important subjects in economics and related fields.

Unfortunately—maybe fortunately—for editors and authors of economic encyclopedias and economic dictionaries, economic terms change with changing times and societies. The period from 1981, when our first edition of the *Encyclopedia* was published, to when we completed our second edition has been one of evolution or revolution in economics throughout the world. We have seen the collapse of communism in the Soviet Union, the rebirth of capitalism in most of Eastern Europe, the unification of capitalistic and communistic Germany, and a setback in the European Community's movement toward a single central bank and a single currency.

The recent presidential election campaign in the United States has once again emphasized economic growth, or the lack of it, productivity, or the lack of it, saving, or the lack of it, the peace dividend, or the lack of it, lower taxes, or the need for them, reduced entitlements, or the need for them, the importance or unimportance of federal debt and deficits, as currently measured, the relative importance of fiscal and monetary policy, and, finally, the problems and solutions of commercial banks and thrift institutions. All of these major international and domestic issues are discussed thoroughly in this edition of the *Encyclopedia*.

The second edition of the *McGraw-Hill Encyclopedia of Economics* is significantly different from the first edition. Thirty subjects were dropped from the first edition while 37 new subjects were added. New authors have prepared 69 new articles on subjects previously included in the earlier edition, and contributors to both the first and second editions of the *Encyclopedia* have significantly revised an additional 65 articles. Finally, most of the remaining articles were updated.

The first step in organizing the contents of the second edition of the *Encyclopedia* was to decide which subjects in the first edition should be eliminated and which new subjects should be added. I did this through a survey of a small group of business and academic economists. Members of this panel were as follows: Henry Arnold (Seton Hall University), Peter Bernstein (Peter Bernstein, Inc.), David Blitzer (Standard & Poor's), William Brown (Berry College), James L. Burtle (Advisor, the WEFA Group), Morris Cohen (Morris Cohen & Associates), Robert J. Eggert (Eggert Economic Enterprises), Robert Eisner (Northwestern University), Walter E. Hoadley (Hoover Institution), John Kendrick (George Washington University), Herman I. Liebling (Consultant), Paul W. McCracken (University of Michigan), Edmund A. Mennis (Consultant), Joel Popkin (Joel Popkin & Co.), Paul A. Samuelson (M.I.T.), Francis H. Schott (Consultant), Eli Shapiro (M.I.T.), A. Gary Shilling (A. Gary Shilling & Co.), and Murray L. Weidenbaum (Washington University of St. Louis).

At the end of this phase of the project, a consensus developed with 31 articles eliminated and 37 new subjects added.

The second step was to decide who should prepare articles for these new subjects and who should be selected to prepare new articles on subjects previously included in the *Encyclopedia* but whose original authors were no longer available or able to update, revise, or rewrite their original articles.

In order to carry out this phase of the organization of the second edition of the *Encyclopedia,* I surveyed a large number of business, academic and government economists, econometricians, statisticians, and marketing experts, who, in turn, provided names of potential authors for the list of new and old subjects to be included in this edition of the *Encyclopedia.* The list of people who provided names of qualified potential authors for subjects in the *Encyclopedia* follows: Kenneth J. Arrow (Stanford University), Peter L. Bernstein (Peter L. Bernstein, Inc.), Henry B. Biesdorf (Cornell University), David Blitzer (Standard & Poor's), George E. P. Box (Stanford University), James L. Burtle (Advisor, the WEFA Group), Joe Cobb (Joint Economic Committee), Morris Cohen (Morris Cohen & Associates), Donald Dewey (Columbia University), Joseph W. Duncan (Dun and Bradstreet), Robert Ekelund (Auburn University), Robert J. Eggert (Eggert Economic Enterprises), Robert Eisner (Northwestern University), Holgar Engberg (New York University), Edgar T. Fiedler (the Conference Board), John K. Galbraith (Harvard University), John I. Griffin (Consultant), James L. Hamilton (Wayne State University), Walter E. Hoadley (Hoover Institution), John W. Kendrick (George Washington University), Israel M. Kirzner (New York University), Saul Klaman (Retired), Walther Lederer (Consultant), Herman I. Liebling (Consultant), Gunther H. Mattersdorff (Lewis & Clark College), Todd May (*Fortune Magazine*), Edward Mayers (Retired), Paul W. McCracken (University of Michigan), Edmund A. Mennis (Consultant), Robert C. Merton (M.I.T.), Richard Musgrave (University of California, Santa Cruz), John Neter (University of Georgia), Mancur Olson (University of Maryland), William N. Parker (Retired), Joel Popkin (Joel Popkin & Co.), Alice Rivlin (Brookings Institution), Paul A. Samuelson (M.I.T.), Francis H. Schott (Consultant), Eli Shapiro (M.I.T.), William Shepherd (Amherst), A. Gary Shilling (A. Gary Shilling & Co.), Charles W. Smithson (Chase Manhattan Bank), Louis W. Stern (Northwestern University), Murray L. Weidenbaum (Washington University of St. Louis), Thomas E. Wieskopf (University of Michigan), and Howell H. Zee (International Monetary Fund).

This survey provided at least two names of qualified authors for each new subject and for the rewrites of earlier articles. I selected the name of the expert to whom the panel had given the most votes for a specific subject. I then wrote to these people plus the authors of articles in the first edition of the *Encyclopedia* who, for the most part, were still willing and happy to update or revise their articles.

There are 191 authors for the 306 articles in the *Encyclopedia* and each of the contributors is an expert or is extremely knowledgeable about the subject or subjects for which he or she prepared articles for the *Encyclopedia*. A listing of authors with a bit more biographical material than just current affiliation follows the table of contents.

Both new and previous authors took their assignments seriously. Several asked about the level of the audience which the *Encyclopedia* was expected to reach. I suggested that for this edition, the articles should be aimed at the graduate level or even higher. Other authors asked how the article or articles they were preparing would fit in with related articles covered in the second edition of the *Encyclopedia*. I provided these authors with lists of related articles.

The subjects and written articles in the *Encyclopedia* vary widely in degree of complexity or in the amount of mathematics used. No matter how they try, experts cannot make very complex subjects simplistic without distorting some of the meaning.

First drafts of some articles, prepared by academic, business, and government economists, were circulated within their departments as working papers with staff comments incorporated into the final draft. Specifically, three contributors to the *Encyclopedia*, John Chipman, Charles Hulton, and Louis Putterman, wished to thank Paul Samuelson, Drew Lyon of the University of Maryland, and Gil Skillman of Brown University for their comments. In addition, some professors tried out their articles on students in their classes.

All 306 articles were edited and reviewed by myself. The articles were edited primarily for clarity and for the appropriateness of content. Since the articles were prepared by experts on the subjects or knowledgeable people in their specific fields, my editing was generally minor. Virtually all of my suggestions for revisions were agreed upon by the authors.

As in the first edition, we continue to arrange the subject matter in alphabetical order. We have tried to list the articles by the subject we believe the reader would look up. However, other guides to the location of articles in the *Encyclopedia* are provided. For example, an alternative entry to "Accuracy of economic forecasting" is the entry "Economic forecasting accuracy."

In addition it is thoroughly cross-referenced and indexed with extensive bibliographical references to guide the reader who wants to know more about the subject and how it relates to other subjects.

Thus the *McGraw-Hill Encyclopedia of Economics* is an indispensible tool for practitioners, teachers, and graduate and undergraduate students in economics, econometrics, statistics, and marketing. In addition, many business economics articles included in the *Encyclopedia* should prove useful to business executives who, perhaps, need information on subjects such as "Capital budgeting," "Capital gains," "Depreciation allowance," "Financial distress," "Fiscal policy," "Going private and leveraged buyouts," "Junk (high-yield) bond market," "Mergers, takeovers, and corporate restructuring," "Monetary policy," "Mutual funds," "Stock market crashes," "Taxation, an overview," "U.S. business obsession with short-run performance," and "Venture capital."

In my correspondence with authors of articles in the *Encyclopedia*, they suggested that the first edition was very useful to them, to their colleagues, and to their students. Many of the authors indicated they were pleased to revise or prepare new articles for such a prestigious book. One author indicated that there was a feeling of immortality that goes with writing for an *Encyclopedia*.

I would like to acknowledge exceptional secretarial help, in the course of organizing and preparing the *McGraw-Hill Encyclopedia of Economics* for publication, from Nancy Barbie, Karen Peel, Thomas Peel, Patricia Nebel of Office Services in Sarasota, and Joan McCabe Moore of Letter Perfect on Siesta Key.

First I would like to thank the economists, econometricians, statisticians, and marketing experts who helped in providing new subjects for the *Encyclopedia* and those who provided names of qualified contributors.

I must also thank my wife Mickey for her support and encouragement while I was organizing and editing the *Encyclopedia*. In her capacity as psychologist and author she also read and made some insightful comments on several of the articles.

Finally I thank all the authors of the excellent articles that make up this encyclopedia. Although their financial rewards were relatively small, their contribution in terms of time and effort was very large.

Douglas Greenwald

Acceleration principle

The acceleration principle, which evolved in writings of Cassel, Bouniatian, Aftalion, Bickerdike, Clark, and Frisch, states that since there is a basic productive relationship between the stock of capital and the flow of output of consumer goods, a rise in consumption expenditures will bring about a more than proportionate rise in investment in fixed capital, and a fall in the rate of increase of consumption expenditures is enough to bring about an absolute fall in net, and possibly gross, investment. Since the principle is able to explain turning points in the business cycle, and is consistent with the observed greater volatility of investment than consumption, it has come to form an important component of the leading business-cycle theories such as those of Harrod, Haberler, Hansen, Samuelson, Hicks, and Goodwin. It is also at the basis of theories of long-run growth developed by Cassel, Harrod, Domar, and others.

While it has been applied to real income and capital formation, and by Metzler to inventory investment, the acceleration principle can also be applied in the financial sphere. If investors hold shares of stock for appreciation, then when the rate of appreciation of shares begins to fall, investors will have an incentive to switch to other financial assets, and this may cause share prices to actually fall.

Historical Evolution of the Concept

Cassel (1904, pp. 76–77) observed that "it does not require a fall in the freight market for the shipyards to suffer from unemployment; all that is needed is that the demand for tonnage cease to increase and stay at the point it has reached. . . . [demand] has only to fall slightly or assume a horizontal level for a terrible fall in shipbuilding employment to result." The same analysis reappeared in Cassel (1918, Section 70, pp. 510–511; 1932, Section 69, pp. 596–598). Cassel (1918, Section 6; 1932, Section 6) also showed how the relation between capital and output could support balanced growth.

Bouniatian (1908, pp. 109–110; 1922, p. 236; 1930, p. 266) held that demand for producer goods depends on demand for consumer goods, and "in the case of constant or insufficiently increasing consumption, any augmentation of capital must . . . lead to . . . overproduction of consumer goods."

A quite precise formulation was given by Aftalion (1909, pp. 219–220; 1913, vol. II, pp. 371–373). Citing Marshall's (1891) theory of derived demand, as well as a paper by Carver (1903), Aftalion observed that fluctuations in consumption would lead to magnified fluctuations in investment. His argument may be interpreted as follows. Denoting consumption by C, gross investment by I, and capital stock by K, Aftalion supposed that replacement investment was a small proportion δ of the capital stock and that output of consumer goods C required capital in the proportion $K = \kappa C$; gross investment is then

$$I = \delta K + \Delta K = \kappa(\delta C + \Delta C) \tag{1}$$

He observed that, starting from constant consumption and assuming a depreciation rate of $\delta = \frac{1}{10}$, a 10-percent increase in consumption would lead to a doubling of gross investment; that is, if gross investment is initially equal to replacement, the proportionate rise in gross investment following from an increase in consumption is

$$\frac{\Delta I}{I} = \frac{\kappa(\delta C + \Delta C) - \kappa \delta C}{\kappa \delta C} = \frac{1}{\delta} \frac{\Delta C}{C} \tag{2}$$

Thus (Aftalion, 1909, p. 219; 1913, vol. II, p. 372): "A slight expansion of the consumption-good industries will result in a much greater expansion of the capital-good industries." The 1909 version cited Carver (1903) in support of this statement.

Carver (1903) had noted that a small percentage rise in a firm's revenues could lead to a large percentage rise in its profits—an observation already made by Marshall (1891, p. 657) and used by Aftalion (1909, p. 249) in another part of his theory. Capitalizing the stream of profits at a given discount rate, Carver noted that a proportionate rise in the price of the product would lead to a magnified proportionate rise in the value of the firm, the elasticity being the reciprocal of the profit margin $(p - c)/p$ (where p = price and c = unit cost)—a formula much like Equation (2); according to Paul Samuelson, this effect used to be known as the Carverian "lever." Carver went on to argue that the rise in the value of the firm would raise the prices of producers' goods and that this in turn would "lead to larger investment in producers' goods" (p. 499). Despite the analogies, however, this lever does not describe the same mechanism as the acceleration principle, although it evidently stimulated Aftalion into developing the principle.

Bickerdike (1914), citing suggestive comments by Pigou (1912, p. 144) and Robertson (1914) regarding durability of capital as a source of business fluctuation, independently discovered the magnification effect of final demand on investment, using a numerical example of shipping and shipbuilding. Robertson had discussed Aftalion's theory of the effect of the gestation period, but not his analysis of the magnification effect. Robertson subsequently (1915, pp. 122–123) discussed Aftalion's and Carver's magnification effects.

Clark (1917), presumably unaware of all the preceding developments, was the first to formulate the acceleration principle explicitly as a relationship between derived demand for new capital goods and the rate of change of consumption (p. 220): "The demand for maintenance and replacement of existing capital varies with the amount of the demand for finished products, while the demand for new construction or enlargement of stocks depends upon whether or not the sales of the finished product are growing"—which is what is stated by Equation (1). Again: "If demand be treated as a rate of speed . . . , maintenance varies roughly with the speed, but new construction depends upon the acceleration." He obtained formula (2) for the elasticity of "demand for new construction" with respect to "previous demand for maintenance" (p. 223n), where $1/\delta$ is the length of life of the capital equipment, from which he concluded that a slackening in the rate of increase of consumption *may* bring about a fall in *gross* investment. Rather incautiously, Clark subsequently (1923, p. 390) replaced "may" by "will"—a mistake that was later corrected by Frisch (1931).

Frisch (1931, p. 648) explicitly provided the above model in the continuous form

$$I = \delta K + \dot{K} = \kappa(\delta C + \dot{C}) \qquad \text{hence } \dot{I} = \kappa(\delta \dot{C} + \ddot{C}) \tag{3}$$

showing that a slowing down of consumption growth need not lead to a fall in *gross* investment unless δC is sufficiently small. He also provided a numerical example illustrating this, built upon the examples Hansen (1927, p. 113) had introduced to illustrate Clark's thesis, extending and elaborating those of Aftalion and Bickerdike. He also made the important point with regard to the first equation of (3) that "we have two variables but only one equation" (p. 649); hence the theory was incomplete. This led to a synthesis of the acceleration principle with the theory of the multiplier suggested by Clark (1932) and subsequently developed by Clark (1935), Harrod (1936), Tinbergen (1937), Haberler (1937), and Hansen (1938), culminating in the model of Samuelson (1939a, 1939b).

Samuelson worked in terms of net investment, which he assumed proportional to current-period consumption minus previous-period consumption, and he assumed consumption in turn to be a linear function of the previous period's net income. He found fields of values of the two parameters leading to (1) monotone convergence, (2) damped oscillations, (3) explosive oscillations, and (4) exponential growth. He remarked that nonlinear functional relationships would be needed to generate limit cycles; such a program was subsequently carried out by Hicks (1950) and Goodwin (1951). These models did not take account of replacement investment, and so Frisch's problem of whether one could generate fluctuations in gross national product remained unaddressed.

Harrod (1939) and Domar (1946) developed their growth models on the basis of the accelerator and multiplier and found that the equilibrium rate of growth would be s/κ, where s is the (constant) propensity to save. This "warranted" rate of growth need not correspond to the rate of increase of the labor force—a contradiction that has given rise to models of economic growth with less rigid assumptions; see Hahn and Matthews (1964) and Samuelson (1988).

Limitations, Extensions, and Empirical Verification

The acceleration principle, as expressed by the model (3), has obvious limitations. As Aftalion (1909, 1913) stressed, production takes time, and one cannot expect capital to adjust to consumption instantaneously. Moreover, capacity limitations impose an upper limit on the rate of gross investment at any one time, and this rate cannot be negative; that is, $0 \le I \le \bar{I}$. Combined with (3), this implies that the acceleration principle cannot hold in the strict sense except when the proportional rates of change of consumption and capital stock are confined to the interval

$$-\delta \le \frac{\dot{C}}{C} = \frac{\dot{K}}{K} \le \frac{\bar{I}}{K} - \delta = \frac{\bar{I}}{\kappa C} - \delta \tag{4}$$

Further, the principle in its simplified form rests on an implicit assumption that changes in consumption will be permanent and not temporary, as pointed out by Kuznets (1935, pp. 229–231); it thus rests on primitive foundations for the formation of expectations.

These considerations led Tinbergen (1938) to conclude that the acceleration principle could be valid only under limited conditions and during certain phases of the business cycle. In linear (and apparently nonhomogeneous) regressions of $\Delta K/K$ on $\Delta C/C$ lagged one year, he obtained regression coefficients of approximately 0.5 instead of 1, concluding that "the acceleration principle cannot help very much in the explanation of real investment fluctuations, with the possible exception of railway rolling stock" (p. 176). Manne (1945) found a regression coefficient of 0.3, which increased to 0.6 when idle capacity was removed from capital stock. Manne also brought out—as had Metzler (1941) previously in the case of the inventory accelerator—the implicit assumption of a unitary elasticity of expectations, and found an improved fit when a single lag was replaced by a 3-year moving average. Manne also investigated the constancy of the capital-output ratio κ but concluded that it was relatively insensitive to the relative price of capital and labor.

Goodwin (1948, p. 120) introduced a "flexible accelerator" which replaced the assumption $K = \kappa C$ by one such as $\dot{K} = \alpha(\kappa C - K)$, so that if $K \neq \kappa C$, then capital increases or decreases in proportion to the difference between desired and actual capital stock. Subsequently Goodwin (1951) introduced a nonlinear accelerator such that capital increases at a certain capacity rate if $K < \kappa C$ and decreases at a certain scrapping rate if $K > \kappa C$. Neither of these formulations takes account of replacement investment. Goodwin calibrated both of his models to time series data. Mechanisms somewhat similar to Goodwin's were posited by Hicks (1950) and Chenery (1952).

Kaldor (1951) was sharply critical of the acceleration principle, stressing the gestation period, capacity limitations, and the formation of expectations. The investment function of his own (1940) model of the business cycle is, however, quite close to Goodwin's flexible accelerator.

Koyck (1954) developed a method of estimating distributed lags in order to better capture the formation of expectations of future consumption in the investment decision. He pointed out (pp. 72–73) that this formulation made it possible to encompass Kaldor's investment function and the strict acceleration principle as special cases. This work, together with Goodwin's and Chenery's formulations of the "flexible accelerator," has strongly influenced subsequent empirical studies of investment behavior; these have been reviewed in comprehensive surveys by Eisner and Strotz (1963) and Jorgenson (1971). The original simplicity of the acceleration principle has been sacrificed for greater realism, but the basic idea has survived.

References

Aftalion, Albert, "La réalité des surproductions générales," *Revue d'économie politique,* vol. 22, October 1908, pp. 696–706; vol. 23, February 1909, pp. 81–117; vol. 23, March 1909, pp. 201–229; vol. 23, April 1909, pp. 241–259 (collected as *Essai d'une théorie des crises périodiques de surproduction, La réalité des surproductions générales,* Larose, Paris, 1909); Aftalion, Albert, *Les crises périodiques de surproduction* (2 vols.), Marcel Rivière et Cⁱᵉ, Paris, 1913; Bickerdike, C. F., "A Non-Monetary Cause of Fluctuations in Employment," *Economic Journal,* vol. 24, September 1914, pp. 357–370; Bouniatian, Mentor, *Wirtschaftskrisen und Ueberkapitalisation,* Ernst Reinhardt, Munich, 1908, 2d ed.; *Ekonomicheskie krizisy,* Tip. Mysl', Moscow, 1915; French translation of 2d ed., *Les crises économiques,* Marcel Giard, Paris, 1922; 2d

French ed., Marcel Giard, Paris, 1930; Carver, T. N., "A Suggestion for a Theory of Industrial Depressions," *Quarterly Journal of Economics,* vol. 17, May 1903, pp. 497–500; Cassel, Gustav, "Om kriser och dåliga tider" ("On Crises and Bad Times"), *Ekonomisk Tidskrift,* vol. 6, 1904, pp. 21–35, 51–81; Cassel, Gustav, *Theoretische Sozialökonomie,* C. F. Wintersche Verlagshandlung, Leipzig, 1918; 5th ed., 1932; English translation of 5th ed., *The Theory of Social Economy,* Harcourt, Brace, New York, 1932; Chenery, Hollis B., "Overcapacity and the Acceleration Principle," *Econometrica,* vol. 20, January 1952, pp. 1–28; Clark, J. Maurice, "Business Acceleration and the Law of Demand: A Technical Factor in Economic Cycles," *Journal of Political Economy,* vol. 25, March 1917, pp. 217–235; Clark, J. Maurice, *Studies in the Economics of Overhead Costs,* University of Chicago Press, Chicago, 1923; Clark, J. M., "Capital Production and Consumer-Taking—A Reply," *Journal of Political Economy,* vol. 39, December 1931, pp. 814–816; "A Further Word," vol. 40, October 1932, pp. 691–693; Clark, J. Maurice, *Strategic Factors in Business Cycles,* National Bureau of Economic Research, New York, 1935; Domar, Evsey D., "Capital Expansion, Rate of Growth, and Employment," *Econometrica,* vol. 14, April 1946, pp. 137–147; Eisner, Robert, and Robert H. Strotz, "Determinants of Business Investment," in *Impacts of Monetary Policy,* prepared for the Commission on Money and Credit, Prentice-Hall, Englewood Cliffs, N.J., 1963, pp. 59–337; Frisch, Ragnar, "The Interrelation between Capital Production and Consumer-Taking," *Journal of Political Economy,* vol. 39, October 1931, pp. 646–654; "A Rejoinder," vol. 40, April 1932, pp. 253–255; "A Final Word," vol. 40, October 1932, p. 694; Goodwin, Richard M., "Secular and Cyclical Aspects of the Multiplier and the Accelerator," in *Income, Employment and Public Policy, Essays in Honor of Alvin H. Hansen,* Norton, New York, 1948, pp. 108–132; Goodwin, Richard M., "The Nonlinear Accelerator and the Persistence of Business Cycles," *Econometrica,* vol. 19, January 1951, pp. 1–17; Haberler, Gottfried, *Prosperity and Depression,* League of Nations, Geneva, 1937; Hahn, F. H., and R. C. O. Matthews, "The Theory of Economic Growth: A Survey," *Economic Journal,* vol. 74, December 1964, pp. 779–902; Hansen, Alvin H., *Business-Cycle Theory,* Ginn, Boston, 1927; Hansen, Alvin H., *Full Recovery or Stagnation?,* Norton, New York, 1938; Hansen, Alvin H., with a chapter by Richard M. Goodwin, *Business Cycles and National Income,* Norton, New York, 1951; Harrod, R. F., *The Trade Cycle,* Clarendon Press, Oxford, 1936; Harrod, R. F., "An Essay in Dynamic Theory," *Economic Journal,* vol. 49, March 1939, pp. 14–33; Hicks, J. R., *A Contribution to the Theory of the Trade Cycle,* Clarendon Press, Oxford, 1950; Jorgenson, Dale W., "Econometric Studies of Investment Behavior: A Survey," *Journal of Economic Literature,* vol. 9, December 1971, pp. 1111–1147; Kaldor, Nicholas, "A Model of the Trade Cycle," *Economic Journal,* vol. 50, March 1940, pp. 78–92; Kaldor, Nicholas, "Hicks on the Trade Cycle," *Economic Journal,* vol. 61, December 1951, pp. 833–847; Koyck, L. M, *Distributed Lags and Investment Analysis,* North-Holland Publishing Co., Amsterdam, 1954; Kuznets, Simon, "Relation between Capital Goods and Finished Products in the Business Cycle," in *Economic Essays in Honor of Wesley Clair Mitchell,* Columbia University Press, New York, 1935, pp. 209–267; Manne, A. S., "Some Notes on the Acceleration Principle," *Review of Economic Statistics,* vol. 27, May 1945, pp. 93–99; Marshall, Alfred, *Principles of Economics,* 2d ed., Macmillan, London, 1891; Metzler, Lloyd A., "The Nature and Stability of Inventory Cycles," *Review of Economic Statistics,* vol. 23, August 1941, pp. 113–129; Pigou, A. C., *Wealth and Welfare,* Macmillan, London, 1912; Robertson, D. H., "Some Material for a Study of Trade Fluctuations, *Journal of the Royal Statistical Society* [A], vol. 77, January 1914, pp. 159–173; Robertson, D. H., *A Study of Industrial Fluctuation,* King, London, 1915; Samuelson, Paul A. (a), "Interactions between the Multiplier Analysis and the Principle of Acceleration," *Review of Economic Statistics,* vol. 21, May 1939, pp. 75–78; Samuelson, Paul A. (b), "A Synthesis of the Principle of Acceleration and the Multiplier," *Journal of Political Economy,* vol. 47, December 1939, pp. 786–797; Samuelson, Paul A., "The Keynes-Hansen-Samuelson Multiplier-Accelerator Model of Secular Stagnation," *Japan and the World Economy,* vol. 1, no. 1, 1988, pp. 3–19; Tinbergen, Jan, Review of R. F. Harrod, *The Trade Cycle, Weltwirtschaftliches Archiv,* vol. 45, 1937, I, Schrifttum, pp. 89*–91*; Tinbergen, Jan, "Statistical Evidence on the Acceleration Principle," *Economica,* N.S., vol. 5, May 1938, pp. 164–176.

(*See also* Investment function)

John S. Chipman

Accuracy of economic forecasts

That forecasts be verifiable is an essential requirement of evaluating their accuracy. Some predictions are so vague, broad, or hedged as to be trivial. Some have the opposite fault of being pretentious—spuriously precise, given the quality of the measurements to which they refer. Still others rely on entirely improbable conditions, which render them meaningless. But such gross defects are no longer widely ignored or tolerated, and they seem to be relatively uncommon among present-day economic forecasts.

The main purpose of economic forecasts is to help formulate and improve public and private plans and decisions. Ideally, the decision maker would know the cost of acquiring and using the forecast and the returns attributable to it, as well as his or her own needs and preferences that determine the relevant "loss function." This would enable the decision maker to evaluate the quality of the forecast exactly, at least in retrospect. However, the costs and returns associated with forecasting are typically difficult to estimate and unknown to the outside analyst. The loss functions of the users differ and are also as a rule unknown. The size of forecasting errors may not be sufficient to assess their consequences for the decisions based on the forecasts. But it is the size of the errors that can be most readily measured once the actual outcomes become known. Thus it seems reasonable to evaluate the forecasts principally by their relative accuracy. It seems natural to most people to discriminate among forecasting sources, methods, or models according to past accuracy: the lower the errors, the higher the given set of predictions is ranked. In effect, the accuracy of a set of predictions is frequently viewed as the principal single aspect of its quality.

In any event, it is clear that forecasts must be properly evaluated if the makers of forecasts are to learn from past errors and if the users of forecasts are to choose intelligently among the available sources and methods. Without dependable accuracy assessments, informed comparisons of costs and returns associated with forecasting are impossible.

Types of Forecasts and Assessments

The forecasting procedures that are most widely used can be broadly classified as follows:

1. Various types of extrapolation of past values or behavior of time series, ranging from simple projections of levels, changes, or trends to sophisticated stochastic models

2. Observations from the evidence of series with systematic properties of timing in the business cycle, particularly the leading indicators in relation to others that tend to move more sluggishly

3. Econometric models, that is, single-equation regression and multiequation simulation models designed to represent certain quantitative relationships among the pertinent economic variables and estimated primarily with time series or other statistical data

4. Surveys of intentions and anticipations by units making economic decisions

These methods and techniques serve different purposes but may often complement each other; for example, regressions with distributed lags may be used to predict the coincident from the leading indicators; indexes based on anticipation surveys may be incorporated in econometric models; a time series model may be developed to explain the residuals, i.e., error terms, in a regression equation. Forecasters may favor one or another of these approaches, depending on their purposes, interests, etc.; forecasters typically use various combinations of them in a more or less judgmental fashion. Judgment, of course, enters the forecasting process at several stages, in the choice of data, models, and methods as well as in the assessment and use of the results.

Depending on the type of forecast, different appraisals of the predictive process and its results can be made. These include (1) ex ante and ex post model evaluations; (2) checks on the data inputs and estimation procedures; (3) monitoring, measurement, and analysis of errors of forecasts; (4) comparisons with a hierarchy of standards of predictive performance; and (5) combinations of different predictors and assessment of their respective contributions to the joint forecasts.

Econometric and Time Series Models   If a forecast is based on a model of relations among economic variables, it is desirable and usually possible to assess that model in the light of economic theory. However, the forecaster probably will have selected the model specifications after experimentation with alternatives. This is because the clues from theory and prior beliefs of the forecaster seldom are sufficient for the forecaster to choose a model that could not be improved upon with the aid of the available and potentially relevant data. But the experimentation creates the danger of choosing an incorrect model that for accidental reasons happens to fit the data well. For this reason, it is important to keep a record of the various steps taken in developing the model. The same applies to any subsequent model changes and also to any approximations and ad hoc procedures that may have been used, particularly the adjustments of constant terms that are typically applied to equations in econometric forecasting models in efforts to reduce the size and interdependence of errors. The information is, of course, valuable to forecast users and reviewers as well, and is increasingly provided to them by the forecasters.

In addition to the model's logical consistency, theoretical adequacy, and residual properties, it is well to check the statistical estimation procedures and the inputs used. It is important to keep in mind that the reported (ex ante) forecasts of econometric variety involve judgmental predictions of the exogenous inputs, recurrent revisions of the model, and frequent adjustments of the constant terms ("fine-tuning")—all subject to modifications in the light of whatever current information is available to the forecaster. Such results, therefore, tell us something about how well the forecaster uses the model, other information, and judgment rather than about how well the model per se forecasts. To examine the forecasting performance of both the models and their operators, and how the two interact, it is necessary to analyze not only the ex ante forecasts but also the ex post forecasts which use the actual historical values for the exogenous variables; also, one must take into account the adjustments of the constant terms.

Although the widest range of such tests and evaluations is available for econometric models (provided they are well documented and accessible), some of the above or similar assessments can be applied to other forecasting approaches. Thus, there are established methods for the specification, estimation, and diagnostic checking of linear stochastic time series models. Different forms of such models can be used to predict a given variable, and the results can be compared in the light of their relative accuracy. Predictions from such models have been used as standards against which to compare genuine ex ante forecasts, with the models being fitted ex post to currently available data. These are not fair tests, but it is possible (though laborious) to revise and reestimate the time series models to produce benchmark predictions comparable to the actual forecasts (i.e., fitted to the data that were available at the time the forecasts were made).

Where costs matter, as in forecasting sales and managing inventory systems, simple mechanical techniques such as moving averages or exponential smoothing are widely used. Such projections are akin to the naive models often employed as minimal standards of forecast evaluation in that they are not grounded in economic and statistical theory, but they may well be useful when properly applied and monitored. The selection and updating of the models are roughly guided by the properties of the series to be predicted and the accumulated error records, but they are made as automatic as possible in the interest of keeping the costs acceptably low.

Surveys and Indicators   Periodic surveys of economic agents are the source of basic data on micropredictions, plans, or intentions, and sometimes, as in the case of business expenditures for plant and equipment, also of the corresponding realizations. Such data have manifold uses—in studies of errors and changes in economic expectations, in tests of hypotheses on the formation and properties of expectations, and in analyses of predictive performance of aggregate series of business investment anticipations and consumer attitudes and buying plans. Presumably, expectations incorporate elements of extrapolation of past behavior of the given series and inferences from observed relations with other series; however, they may also include some additional information as a result of insider knowledge, expert insight, or mere hunches. Hence, even where an anticipations series is not very efficient as a single direct predictor, it may make a significant net contribution as an ingredient in a forecasting process that combines expectational with other inputs.

Similarly, the net predictive value of a leading indicator can be assessed by using that series as one of the explanatory variables in an econometric model; e.g., contracts and orders for plant and equipment may help determine and forecast nonresidential fixed investment. However, the task to which these indicators are put in the first place is to signal business-cycle turning points—recessions and recoveries. The selection of series for this purpose is based on a system of scoring for such characteristics as economic significance, statistical adequacy, cyclical conformity and timing, smoothness, and currency. Composite indexes are constructed which incorporate the best-scoring series from different economic-process groups (e.g., employment, production, consumption, investment, money and credit) and combine those with similar timing behavior, using as weights their overall performance scores. Such indexes outperform the individual indicators because of their greater smoothness and diversified economic coverage. In addition to comprehensive historical studies of the behavior of indicators, some tests of their predictive performance or value are available. These include evaluations of forecasts that relied on this approach and measures of types of error ("missed turns" and "false warnings") that would have been made under certain prespecified rules of using the indexes or the individual indicators to predict business-cycle turns.

Criteria and Measures of Accuracy

The computational simplicity of measuring the accuracy of forecasts, given comparable data on actual values, hides a number of conceptual and practical problems.

1. Isolated successes or failures can be due to chance; hence, they do not prove that a source or type of forecast is (or is not) accurate with a fair degree of reliability. Thus, the average performance of a predictor should be examined over sufficient time to include different economic developments; the longer and the more varied the period covered, the more informative the analysis of forecast errors. Unfortunately, few forecasters have produced long, consistent series of verifiable predictions, and the evaluation of forecasts suffers considerably from small sample problems for which no good statistical solutions are available.

2. The period covered should be varied because different types of economic change confront the forecaster with problems of differing nature and degree of difficulty. If a business expansion has taken hold and is gathering speed, it is safe and easy to predict that the expansion will continue, but a reasonably accurate forecast of the end of such a movement (of peaks in real gross national product, industrial production, employment) is much more difficult even over short spans. Many forecasters and users of predictions recognize this, which explains why they pay much attention to turning-point errors.

3. Individual predictions can suffer from excusable errors in assumptions about exogenous, often noneconomic, events; or, conversely, they can be relatively accurate in spite of being based on wrong assumptions (i.e., they are correct for the wrong reasons because of offsetting errors). Thus, forecasting assumptions should be reported and their analysis included in the process of forecast evaluation. However, if, over time, a forecaster's record is poor on the average, it is unlikely to be so only because of consistently wrong assumptions.

4. Conceivably, the effectiveness of forecasts could seriously complicate their evaluation. Forecasts may influence economic behavior and, in particular, the variables being predicted; to the extent that this happens, the forecasts may validate or invalidate themselves. For example, universally optimistic predictions and expectations would presumably contribute to a high growth rate for the economy. Conversely, widespread recession forecasts may act as a depressant and prompt the government to adopt policies designed to avert or postpone the apprehended downturn. The interaction of expectations, behavior, and policies (which are themselves in part anticipated) is an intricate subject about which there is little knowledge, but it is easy to exaggerate or misjudge such feedback effects. In particular, the macroeconomic forecasts in the United States are probably too numerous and differentiated to have strong effects of this kind, which indeed are seldom documented.

5. Feedback effects should be distinguished from direct controls; a forecaster is not concerned with plans for fully controlled variables. However, true forecasts refer not only to variables over which the forecaster has no control but also to variables over which the forecaster has some control or influence. Other things being equal, the more controlled a variable is, the better the chance that it is well predicted (business short-term anticipations of plant and equipment expenditures would be expected to have a better record than business sales anticipations with the same spans, and they have).

6. For many economic variables, forecast errors appear to be small when compared with the levels of the series concerned but are actually large in terms of

the more meaningful comparisons with the changes to be predicted. Some performance measures such as correlations of the predicted with the actual values are much more meaningful for change forecasts than for level forecasts. For aggregates with strong trends and where rates of growth are of particular interest, it is well to define the errors as differences between the predicted and actual percentage changes (or changes in logarithms).

7. Although knowledge of the decision maker's loss function may not be available or complete, the choice of the measure of average forecast accuracy can be linked to the assumed form of the loss function. For example, if a quadratic loss criterion is adopted, the appropriate measure is the root-mean-square error. This measure, based on the variance of the errors around zero, has the advantages of mathematical and statistical tractability, and it gives more than proportionate weights to the large errors, which may be desirable. Nevertheless, other measures, e.g., the mean absolute error, may sometimes be preferred.

8. Ideally, forecasts should be unbiased; that is, their average errors should be approximately zero (no systematic underestimation or overestimation). They should also be efficient; that is, their errors should not be correlated either with the forecast values or with each other serially over time. (All this is to be interpreted in terms of the appropriate statistical tests of significance.) The method(s) of decomposing the mean-square error into bias, inefficiency, and residual variance elements is often used. The larger the residual variance component, given the size of the total measured error, the better the quality of the forecast is deemed to be. This is because the forecaster should ascertain the correct model or learn from past errors how to avoid bias and inefficiency, whereas random errors are largely unavoidable. In practice, however, many economic forecast series are not long enough or consistent enough to permit successful measurement of, let alone ex ante correction for, the systematic error components.

9. The standard of perfection (zero errors) is obviously unrealistic, but any other criterion for evaluating the absolute accuracy of forecasts is arbitrary. It is, therefore, necessary to measure the relative accuracy of forecasts by comparing summary error measures across sets of authentic economic predictions and benchmark projections from some objective formulas or models. The extrapolations used as yardsticks range from the simplest models to statistically sophisticated autoregressive integrated moving average (ARIMA) and multivariable vector autoregressive (VAR) models. In principle, there is an optimal extrapolation for each time series with a known and stable statistical structure, but the available economic data often do not satisfy the required conditions. Benchmarks based on objective applications of other (nonextrapolative) models or methods of forecasting can be used in many cases.

10. Accuracy is a relative and multidimensional concept, and conclusive discrimination between forecasters is often difficult even where their products are sufficiently comparable: the differences may not be significant, or forecast set X is better in one respect and forecast set Z is better in another respect. Moreover, even if one source or type of forecast outperforms the others, it does not follow that it alone merits consideration since two or more of the sets may have net predictive values. Many forecasts are products of an informal combi-

nation of different elements and techniques. The relative accuracy analysis can help in inferring the structure of such forecasts, that is, the shares of informative content that they have in common with extrapolations or other benchmark models. Formal methods of combining predictors have been proposed, which are optimal under certain restrictive assumptions, and the evaluation of the results suggests that the overall forecasts are frequently superior to each of their components.

A Summary of Evidence

Annual Forecasts Table 1 is based on the longest available series of predicted annual rates of change in aggregate demand (nominal GNP), output (real GNP), and price level (IPD). It covers a large number of forecasts from a great variety of sources: business economists and others employed by private companies in manufacturing, finance, trade, and consulting; some academic and research institutions; and the Council of Economic Advisers to the President (CEA), which prepared the principal government forecasts. Predominantly judgmental predictions are represented along with predictions made by econometricians working with large models. The included forecasts differ in many respects but are sufficiently comparable for the purpose of considering the broad trends over time in forecasting accuracy. All the predictions covered are made around the end of the year for the year ahead.

The mean absolute errors (MAEs), in percentage points, average 1.2 for GNP, 1.2 for RGNP, and 1.0 for IPD (column 4). Averaging over individuals has the effect of reducing the dispersion of these measures across the forecasts sets, so that even the ranges between the extreme values are moderate (0.4, 0.4, and 0.1 for GNP, RGNP, and IPD, respectively). The figures for the successive (mostly overlapping) subperiods suggest that the MAEs may have decreased somewhat for GNP, increased for IPD, and remained remarkably stable for RGNP. But the errors of inflation forecasts increased on average over time much less than the actual inflation did, so the accuracy of these forecasts improved greatly in relative terms (compare columns 4 and 8). Such comparisons also suggest a definite reduction in the relative errors for GNP, but a small increase in those for RGNP. In general, the forecasts are definitely superior to extrapolations from naive models selected for relative efficiency, as shown by comparisons of the corresponding MAEs (columns 6 and 7). All the MAE forecast/extrapolation ratios fall in the range of 0.3 to 0.8, except the one for IPD in 1959–1967 (a period of unusually low and stable inflation).

In the 1950s and 1960s forecasters tended to underpredict both the nominal and real GNP growth rates in years of cyclical expansion, that is, most of the time (see the negative mean errors, MEs, in column 5). The early postwar period enjoyed more real growth than had been expected on the basis of historical experience. Gradually and somewhat belatedly, forecasters learned to be more optimistic. Real GNP increases were strongly underestimated in 1959–1967 but overestimated in 1962–1976, particularly in 1969–1976. In the 1980s, as before, growth was generally overpredicted in years of downturns and slowdowns and underpredicted in years of recovery and expansion. Meanwhile, the IPD forecasts had little or no bias in the period of relative price stability, 1959–1967; but when inflation was rising and high, it was clearly underestimated, as in 1962–1976 and again especially in 1969–1976. After inflation peaked in 1980–1981, predicted rates moved down with a lag, thus tending to overstate the actual rates.

TABLE 1   Annual Forecasts of Percentage Changes in Aggregate Income, Output, and the Price Level: Mean Absolute Errors and Mean Errors, 1956–1989*

Line (1)	Period covered (2)	Forecast sets and sources[§] (3)	Measures of forecast error[+] MAE (4)	ME (5)	Extrapo- lations[‡] MAE (6)	Relative error[§] (7)	Preliminary data[π] MAE (8)	ME (9)	MA%Δ (10)
			Gross National Product (GNP)						
1	1956–1963	1,2,4	1.6	−0.4	1.9	0.8	0.5	−0.3	5.0
2	1963–1976	1,2,6,7,8	1.0	−0.5	1.8	0.6	0.3	−0.3	7.9
3	1969–1976	1,2,5,6,7,8	0.9	−0.1	2.0	0.5	0.3	−0.3	8.4
4	1969–1989	5,6	1.1	0.1	2.0	0.6	0.5	−0.5	8.4
			GNP in Constant Dollars (RGNP)						
5	1959–1967	3,7	1.2	−0.7	1.7	0.7	0.5	−0.2	4.3
6	1962–1976	6,7	1.2	0.4	2.6	0.5	0.4	−0.1	4.1
7	1969–1976	5,6,7,8	1.2	0.7	3.6	0.3	0.3	0.1	3.6
8	1969–1989	5,6	1.1	−0.2	2.6	0.4	0.6	0.0	3.2
			GNP Implicit Price Deflator (IPD)						
9	1959–1967	3,7	0.6	0.1	0.3	2.0	0.3	−0.3	1.9
10	1962–1976	6,7	1.0	−0.5	1.3	0.8	0.4	−0.3	4.2
11	1969–1976	5,6,7,8	1.4	−0.8	2.0	0.7	0.4	−0.4	5.9
12	1969–1989	5,6	1.1	−0.1	1.3	0.8	0.6	−0.4	5.6

* CODE   (1) Livingston Survey, mean; (2) mean of eight private forecasts (Harris Bank, National Securities and Research Corp., Conference Board Economic Forum, University of Missouri School of Business, UCLA Business Forecasting Project, *Fortune* magazine, IBM Economic Research Department, Prudential Insurance Co.); (3) mean of five forecasts (the first five listed under set 2 above); (4) New York Forecasters Club, mean; (5) ASA-NBER Economic Outlook Survey, median; (6) Council of Economic Advisers to the President (CEA); (7) Research Seminar in Quantitative Economics of the University of Michigan (RSQE); (8) Wharton School Economic Forecasting Unit, University of Pennsylvania (Wharton).
[+] MAE (mean absolute error) = $1/n \ \Sigma |E_t|$, where $E_t = P_t − A_t$; P_t = predicted value; A_t = actual value (first estimate for year t published in year $t + 1$). ME (mean error) = $1/n \ \Sigma \ E_t$.
[‡] For GNP and RGNP: projections of the moving average of the last four observed percentage changes $(1/n \ \Sigma \ A_{t−i}, i = 1, \ldots , 4)$. For IPD: projections of the last observed percentage change $(A_{t−1})$. MAE = mean absolute error of these extrapolations, based on preliminary data (see note π below).
[§] Ratio, column 4 divided by column 6.
[π] First estimates for year t published in year $t + 1$ (as a rule in January). Errors based on comparisons of preliminary data with the latest revised data. MA%Δ = mean absolute percentage change.

Quarterly Multiperiod Forecasts   It is much more ambitious and difficult to predict sequences of quarterly changes within the year ahead and, *a fortiori*, beyond than to predict annual changes. Forecasts for the years as a whole can be satisfactory when based on a good record for the first two quarters; they tend to be more accurate than forecasts with longer spans. The average accuracy of forecasts typically decreases as their horizon increases; for example, GNP is predicted with larger MAEs and larger RMSEs (root-mean-square errors) one quarter ahead $(t + 1)$ than two quarters ahead $(t + 2)$, etc. However, the margins by which the absolute or squared errors cumulate over the forecast span tend to decrease, and beyond a certain point (often $t + 4$ or $t + 5$) the errors often flatten or vary irregularly around some high plateau. Current information and knowledge may help us forecast $t + 1$ better than $t + 4$, but we may be equally ignorant about $t + 8$ and $t + 10$, for example. Much of the time, the errors are found to increase less than in proportion to the horizon; e.g., semiannual predictions are less than twice as accurate as the annual ones. However, in some highly turbulent periods, such as the first half of the 1970s, errors for real growth and inflation cumulated rapidly beyond the spans of two or four quarters.

Surveys of multiperiod quarterly predictions for the principal economic variables can serve as rich sources of diversified forecasting data. The National Bureau of Economic Research (NBER) and the American Statistical Association (ASA) jointly conducted a survey each quarter in 1968–1990, producing several thousand of individual time series of forecasts defined by source, variable, and horizon (more than 100 respondents; 86 consecutive surveys each covering two annual and five quarterly spans; 21 variables; continued since 1990 by the Federal Reserve Bank of Philadelphia). The NBER-ASA survey data were used in a number of studies that extend our understanding of the potential and limitations of macroeconomic forecasting.

In Table 2, the absolute and relative errors of forecasts from the NBER-ASA surveys are compared by span and subperiod for the rates of change in GNP, RGNP, and IPD. The median RMSEs were larger in 1979–1990 than in 1968–1979 for GNP but smaller for IPD; for RGNP the differences between the two periods were small and mixed (compare columns 1 and 5). The group mean forecasts (g), calculated by averaging all predictions in each survey for a given variable and span, were generally more accurate than the median individual respondent (i). This is shown by the RMSE ratios i/g, which all exceed 1.00, mostly by substantial margins (columns 2 and 6). These ratios differ little between 1968–1979 and 1979–1990 in most cases.

Bayesian vector autoregressions (BVAR) predict each in a group of selected variables by regression on its own lagged values and those of the others. There are no exogenous variables here and little use of economic theory and judgment, but, to avoid overfitting, constraints on the coefficients are imposed with the aid of the model builder's prior distributions concerning the stochastic properties of the processes and lags involved. This is a recent and relatively sophisticated approach to extrapolative prediction, and a not-so-easy standard for the forecasters to exceed. The BVAR used here is a five-variable, six-lag quarterly model (with RGNP, IPD, broad money supply M-2, the Commerce index of leading indicators, and the 3-month Treasury bill rate). On average and in general, the NBER-ASA survey forecasts outperformed the BVAR forecasts, except for RGNP in 1979–1990 (see the i/bv RMSE ratios in columns 3 and 7). The group mean predictions from the surveys were more accurate throughout than BVAR (note that the ratios $g/bv < 1$ in all cases, columns 4 and 8).

There is no evidence that the forecasts on the whole either improved or deteriorated significantly in the 1980s as compared with the 1970s. (The two periods covered, of about equal length, have been economically very different. The period 1968:4–1979:3 witnessed rising and volatile inflation and unemployment, a stressful war, price controls, and huge oil price hikes. The period 1979:4–1990:1 saw an abrupt monetary tightening, sharp peaks and declines in inflation and interest rates, and steep rises in government and trade deficits. Each period included two recessions and sequences of growth speedups and slowdowns.)

Further Assessments Macroeconomic variables differ greatly in forecastability. The smoother (more autocorrelated) time series are easier to predict, and they are in gen-

TABLE 2   Individual, Group Mean, and BVAR Forecasts of Percent Changes in GNP, RGNP, and IPD, Selected Comparisons by Span and Subperiods, 1968–1979 and 1979–1990

		Forecasts for 1968:4–1979:3				Forecasts for 1979:4–1990:1			
		Median RMSE$_i$*	RMSE ratios[†]			Median RMSE$_i$*	RMSE ratios[†]		
			i/g	i/bv	g/bv		i/g	i/bv	g/bv
Line	Span (Qs)	(1)	(2)	(3)	(4)	(5)	(6)	(7)	(8)
		Gross National Product (GNP)							
1	0–1	0.60	1.34	0.53	0.48	0.86	1.15	0.79	0.71
2	0–2	1.13	1.20	0.58	0.50	1.56	1.17	0.78	0.69
3	0–3	1.68	1.18	0.60	0.51	2.23	1.18	0.81	0.70
4	0–4	2.04	1.21	0.60	0.49	3.08	1.15	0.81	0.71
5	0–5	2.24	1.19	0.51	0.47	3.80	1.18	0.82	0.70
		Gross National Product in Constant Dollars (RGNP)							
6	0–1	0.69	1.29	0.62	0.57	0.80	1.20	0.88	0.76
7	0–2	1.25	1.18	0.78	0.69	1.34	1.15	1.01	0.82
8	0–3	1.87	1.17	0.85	0.76	1.80	1.15	1.03	0.86
9	0–4	2.59	1.14	0.99	0.84	2.30	1.16	1.16	0.94
10	0–5	3.13	1.13	1.04	0.92	2.84	1.15	1.24	0.99
		Implicit Price Deflator (IPD)							
11	0–1	0.50	1.29	0.90	0.73	0.37	1.22	0.87	0.74
12	0–2	1.00	1.14	0.90	0.80	0.64	1.31	0.70	0.56
13	0–3	1.57	1.08	0.89	0.84	0.93	1.28	0.60	0.51
14	0–4	2.25	1.04	0.92	0.89	1.37	1.26	0.64	0.50
15	0–5	3.06	1.05	0.99	0.95	1.94	1.25	0.63	0.49

* Median of the root-mean-square errors of the individual forecasts from the quarterly NBER-ASA surveys.
[†] Ratio of the median RMSE of the individual forecasts (i) to the RMSE of the corresponding group mean forecast (g) in columns 2 and 6. Ratio of the median RMSE of the individual forecasts (i) to the RMSE of the corresponding BVAR model forecast (bv) in columns 3 and 7. Ratio of the RMSE of the group mean forecast (g) to the RMSE of the corresponding BVAR model forecast (bv) in columns 4 and 8.

eral more accurately predicted than the volatile series with large random components. Thus, forecasts of real GNP and consumption have smaller percentage-change errors than investment forecasts, particularly for residential construction and change in business inventories. Some forecasting methods (e.g., the monetarist approach) deal more effectively with changes in the economy at large than with changes in particular processes and sectors. Also, there is a partial cancellation of errors in predictions of components of GNP.

Inflation has been greatly underestimated and poorly predicted by more forecasters most of the time. Negative correlations between forecast errors for IPD and RGNP (and some other real variables) are often observed in studies of methods and results of economic prediction.

It is difficult to compare macroeconomic forecasts, if only because the models vary in scale and choice of exogenous variables and the predictions vary in timing (those released late enjoy advantages of additional and more current information). Nevertheless, there have been several independent attempts at comparative assessments of forecasts from well-known private and public sources, and the results agree on two basic points.

1. The rankings of forecasters vary considerably depending on the variables, periods, and spans covered; they vary also, but much less, with the criteria and measurements applied.

2. At least for the predictions of the principal aggregates, the summary measures of accuracy do not show the differences among the forecasters to be both large and systematic.

Not surprisingly, then, the search for a consistently superior forecaster is fruitless and unpromising (and economic forecasting remains competitive).

Different forecasting methods and techniques serve different purposes and are often complementary, which is why they are used in various combinations. Econometric model forecasts with judgmental adjustments are on the average as accurate as the corresponding noneconometric forecasts from professional sources—actually often better, but not systematically so and mostly by slight margins. Without the adjustments, the econometric-model predictions are on the whole considerably worse. Thus, mechanical uses of the existing models cannot be relied upon to produce good forecasts.

There is a great deal of disenchantment with macroeconomic forecasting, but much of it is due to unrealistically high prior expectations rather than to unacceptably poor performance. Also, forecasting economic change, as a practical activity with recorded and tested results, is very young by any standard, and it probably can be developed well beyond its present stage. However, it is clear that there are limits to the potential accuracy of economic (and other social) forecasts, which may prove much narrower than the early enthusiasts thought. Such forecasts concern inherently uncertain future events that are not nearly as "knowable" as the data of history and science.

Progress in forecasting will chiefly require better data and models, but also will require improvements in time series analysis, econometric methods, cyclical indicators, and anticipations surveys. These are essentially complementary tools and should be used efficiently as such, not as competitors or substitutes.

The predictive needs of decision makers who are necessarily future-oriented are not reduced by the perceived shortcomings of past forecasts. However, policymakers can to a degree reduce their dependence on forecasts by increasing their ability and readiness to respond promptly and flexibly to the unforeseen changes. Stable government policy rules may have positive stabilizing effects on private expectations and self-disciplining effects on the authorities. The main defects of macro forecasts from the point of view of policy are the errors of missing cyclical turning points and shifts in the average rates of inflation. Major reductions in such errors should rank high on the agenda of economics.

References

Butler, W. F., R. A. Kavesh, and R. B. Platt (eds.), *Methods and Techniques of Business Forecasting,* Prentice-Hall, Englewood Cliffs, NJ, 1974; Hickman, B. G. (ed.), *Econometric Models of Cyclical Behavior,* 2 vols., Columbia University Press for the National Bureau of Economic Research, New York, 1972; Klein, L. R., and E. Burmeister (eds.), *Econometric Model Performance, Comparative Simulation Studies of the U.S. Economy,* University of Pennsylvania Press,

Philadelphia, 1976; McNees, S. K., "How Accurate Are Macroeconomic Forecasts?", *New England Economic Review*, July/August, 1988, pp. 15–36; Mincer, J. (ed.), *Economic Forecasts and Expectations: Analyses of Forecasting Behavior and Performance*, Columbia University Press for NBER, New York, 1969; Moore, G. H., *Business Cycles, Inflation, and Forecasting*, 2d ed., Ballinger for NBER, Cambridge, Mass, 1983; Pindyck, R. S., and D. L. Rubinfeld, *Econometric Models and Economic Forecasts*, 2d ed., McGraw-Hill, New York, 1981; Theil, H., *Applied Economic Forecasting*, Rand McNally, Chicago, 1966; Zarnowitz, V., *An Appraisal of Short-Term Economic Forecasts*, NBER, New York, 1967; Zarnowitz, V. (ed.), *The Business Cycle Today*, NBER, New York, 1972; Zarnowitz, V., *Business Cycles: Theory, History, Indicators, and Forecasting*, University of Chicago Press for NBER, Chicago, 1992.

(*See also* Anticipation surveys, business; Anticipation surveys, consumer; Econometrics; Economic models; Economic forecasting methods; Statistical methods in economics and business, an overview)

Victor Zarnowitz

Acquisitions (*see* Mergers, takeovers, and corporate restructuring)

Administered prices (*see* Rigid prices)

Advertising, economic aspects

Any system or method of attracting attention to and inducing the purchase or sale of goods or services may be defined as advertising. However, in practice the definition is usually confined to those methods of persuasion in which an advertising message is conveyed along with other information or entertainment in a variety of media.

Classification of Advertising Expenditures

Expenditures on advertising are usually classified in two ways: first, in terms of the area within which the advertiser sells the product, and, second, in terms of the medium used by the advertiser. The first classification divides advertising into local and national categories, with retailers as the dominant local advertisers and national business firms as the dominant national advertisers.

Since the 1970s the dichotomy between local and national advertising has remained remarkably constant. In the late 1980s, out of total advertising outlays of over $110 billion, about 55 percent was spent by national advertisers and the remainder by local advertisers.

The second way to classify advertising is by the media that carry the advertising. The main ones are print media (newspapers, magazines, and business papers), broadcasting (television and radio), outdoor advertising, and direct mail. Most of these media carry both national and local advertising (for example, newspapers, television, and radio).

In recent years, newspapers have accounted for 27 percent of all advertising outlays and direct mail for 17 percent. The broadcast media, television and radio, have accounted for about 22 percent and 7 percent, respectively, of the total advertising. Magazines have accounted for under 5 percent. The remaining 22 percent of the total advertising outlay is spread among outdoor advertising, business papers, classified telephone directories, and so on. It should be noted that certain outlays are not included in these figures such as the cost of displays and signs in retail establishments.

This distribution changes when the individual media shares are broken into national and local categories, because some media are more concentrated in one category than the other. Newspapers, for example, account for only 6 percent of total national advertising but for nearly 53 percent of local advertising. The situation in television is more complicated owing to the rising importance of cable television and the accompanying rise in the number of channels that viewers of television now have available to them. While national advertising still predominates in television, local advertising is of growing importance. Advertising in radio is primarily local.

Advertising and Economic Theory

Economic theory can study how advertising affects the behavior of buyers and sellers without judging whether advertising is desirable or undesirable. The judging of the desirability or undesirability of advertising has to do with whether advertising weakens competition, how much advertising is deceptive, and whether too much is spent on advertising.

Advertising is generally assumed to come from sellers because it is most familiar to consumers in this form. However, buyers of products may also find that advertising serves their interest, and sometimes both buyers and sellers advertise. With this in mind, an explanation for who does the advertising emerges. That party to a transaction finances the advertising for whom it is the cheapest way of conveying the advertising message to the other. With few buyers and many dispersed sellers who are costly to contact, it is the buyers who will advertise; similarly, with many widely dispersed buyers and few sellers, the sellers will advertise. When there are few of each and it is costly for them to contact each other face-to-face, both may advertise (classified advertising is the leading example). Generally, the most suitable candidate for advertising is a standardized commodity or service.

The content of the advertising message must somehow advance the interest of the one who pays for it. In the simplest cases, the message gives information about the identity and location of the seller, the nature of the product, the terms of sale, and so on. In other cases, it attempts to obtain the patronage of a potential customer by demonstrating that highly admired people (celebrities) use the product, by showing that people similar to the potential customer use the product, by claiming that the product is bought by many people, or by asserting that the product has been sold on the market for a long time. Because the advertiser has a self-interest in focusing on the good aspects of the product, a reasonably prudent potential customer cannot accept these claims unreservedly. The more credible claims are those that the potential customer can accept or verify eventually. For instance, the buyer may indeed wish to associate with a segment of the population that is supposed to use the product such as personable, active young people. The fact that the seller has been in business for a long time and has an investment in his or her reputation to protect may also be a verifiable claim. For these reasons, some economists, notably Nelson (1970), argue that advertising focuses on those aspects of a product that cannot be ascertained before its actual purchase or use.

The relation between advertising and competition is a popular area of economic research. One line studies the relation between advertising intensity and the concentration of sales. It is claimed that the higher the concentration of sales among the four leading sellers, the less competition among them. Hence finding that advertising intensity, as measured by the ratio of advertising outlays to sales, goes up with the four-firm concentration ratio is taken as evidence that advertising and competition vary inversely. Although it is true that many have found a positive association between concentration and advertising intensity, it does not follow that this shows advertising reduces competition. It is a question not only of whether the four-firm concentration ratio is higher for more highly advertised consumer products but also of whether the same four firms maintain high market shares by means of their large advertising outlays. A second line of research relates the profit rate to advertising intensity. A typical finding is a positive relation between the two. However, it does not follow that advertising outlays are a means to high profits. Often the measured profit rates reflect accounting conventions more than the pertinent profit rates. This reason is the failure to capitalize advertising outlays so that the long-lasting effects are correctly measured. It is necessary to include this capital together with the tangible capital on which to reckon the profit rate. Accounting conventions allow advertising outlays to be treated as a current expense. This biases the estimates of the relevant profit rate in various ways that throw doubt on nearly all the empirical studies of the relation between profit rates and advertising intensities.

References

Bain, Joe S., *Barriers to New Competition,* Harvard University Press, Cambridge, Mass., 1956; Comanor, William, and Thomas Wilson, *Advertising and Market Power,* Harvard University Press, Cambridge, Mass., 1974; Ferguson, James M., *Advertising and Competition: Theory, Measurement, Fact,* Ballinger, Cambridge, Mass., 1974; Nelson, Phillip, "Information and Consumer Behavior," *Journal of Political Economy,* vol. 78, March/April 1970, pp. 311–329; Nelson, Phillip, "Advertising as Information," *Journal of Political Economy,* vol. 81, July/August 1974, pp. 729–754; Stigler, George J., "The Economics of Information," *Journal of Political Economy,* vol. 69, June 1961, pp. 213–225; Telser, Lester G., "Advertising and Competition," *Journal of Political Economy,* vol. 62, December 1964, pp. 537–562.

(*See also* Economic growth; Economies of scale; Marketing research and business economics)

Lester G. Telser

Affluent society

The economics of affluence holds that there is a definitive change in the controlling economic context with advanced well-being. The flow of goods and services that once had a firm basis in physical survival and elementary well-being is now greatly expanded and diversified and meets much less compelling needs. There is a wide range of choice, which, very specifically, is subject through advertising and salesmanship to the influence of the producing firm. In substantial measure that firm, once faced with an externally determined demand function, now shapes and creates the demand for what it produces, and demand creation thus becomes an intimate part of the economic process. Affirming this is the evident and often decisive role of modern advertising and marketing activity. Accepted microeconomic theory with its externally determined demand function is sadly obsolescent.

There are larger effects of affluence. Persuasion extends to consumer debt creation. Production becomes important less for the goods and services it produces or renders than for the income that it provides. Consumption taxes, falling as they do directly or indirectly on less urgent or contrived consumption, become less regressive.

There is also a problem of social balance between strongly and even strenuously promoted private goods and less effectively promoted public services. There is a new world of excellent television sets, expensive television programming, and poor public schools.

Further, there is the unsolved problem of why, in a general environment of affluence, some parts of the larger community—in the United States the central cities, the Appalachian plateau, much of the rural South—remain poor. On this matter in recent times, the 1980s and the 1990s, the political economy of affluence has taken a somewhat different form. Poverty in the rural areas, always less visible, has, on balance, become less acute. That of the central cities, on the other hand, has become more acute. And so has the resistance to action to alleviate it. In the 1980s, the income of the politically influential middle class ceased to grow; the political voice and influence of a wealthy minority became stronger, as did its claim on income. Both were articulate in political discussion of their new position. The resistance to taxes and services that would benefit the poor, now called the underclass, became stronger, even decisive. This poses one of the major problems for the American economy and polity and one by which future developments, especially those affecting social and political tranquility, will be greatly shaped.

References

Galbraith, John Kenneth, *The Affluent Society,* 4th ed., Houghton Mifflin, Boston, 1984; Galbraith, John Kenneth, *The Culture of Contentment,* Houghton Mifflin, Boston, 1992.

(*See also* Advertising, economic aspects; Consumer credit; Credit cards; Microeconomics; Negative income tax; Poverty; Supply-side economics)

John Kenneth Galbraith

Agricultural economic policy

General agricultural economic policy consists of a body of policies that have been formulated and implemented to influence the economic health, or well-being, of the agricultural sector. In the nineteenth century in the United States such policies were concerned with the distribution of land, tariff protection, and money and credit, and with the improvement of the productive capacity of farmers through education and training. In the twentieth century such policies have been concerned with production control, surplus disposal (both domestic and foreign), market discrimination, demand expansion, price support, income transfers, and commodity stabilization, as well as tariff protection, agricultural credit, education, and training. Finally, economic policy in agriculture in the twentieth century has placed great emphasis on research, technological development, and farm technological advances.

Goals and Policies

The goals of the U.S. general agricultural economic policy throughout the twentieth century have been and continue to be as of the 1990s:

1. A stable, prosperous farming sector
2. A family farming structure
3. An adequate, nutritious supply of food at reasonable prices
4. An efficient agricultural marketing and distribution system, both domestically and internationally, with a minimum of government regulation

Since 1920, farmers, with the assistance of the federal government, have made a major effort to manage, or control, the supply of their products and as a result push up farm prices in the marketplace. Two techniques have been employed: first, control over the input, land, as a means of controlling output; second, the management of the flow of product to different markets through the use of marketing orders. The use of these supply-management devices in adjusting supplies to demand at prices deemed acceptable by farmers has been moderately successful.

Prices of farm products have been supported directly by government action through the use of two types of programs. First, the government has supported the price of storable commodities through the use of the nonrecourse loan mechanism; in this type of action the government makes a loan—a nonrecourse loan—to a farmer on the farmer's commodity (e.g., wheat) at the price-support level; if the market price falls below the price-support level, the farmer keeps the loan and gives the collateral, wheat in this example, to the government; if the market price stays above the price-support level, the farmer sells the commodity in the open market and pays off the loan from the government. Second, the government enters the market and purchases sufficient commodity to drive its price in the marketplace up to the defined price-support level.

The government has sometimes supported the incomes of farmers directly in several ways. It has paid farmers to remove land from production and to undertake desirable conservation measures. But most important, it has made deficiency payments to farmers to increase the return on each unit produced and sold by an amount equal to the difference between the market price and a defined fair price (i.e., the target price).

The government has undertaken a variety of policy measures to expand the demand for farm products and thus act to support or raise the level of farm prices. Most important, the government has taken title to farm commodities acquired through the operation of nonrecourse loan and purchase operations, stored those commodities and thereby held them off the commercial market, and finally disposed of those products through noncommercial channels at home and abroad. At home the government has given those commodities to persons and families living on relief or on welfare, to the Red Cross, and to schools and charitable institutions for their feeding programs. Abroad the government has distributed these surplus commodities to the poor and needy across the less-developed world through Public Law 480. Foreign food aid programs under this law have run at a level of between $1 billion and $2 billion annually since the middle 1950s. Commercial farm exports have been subsidized by an array of programs since the middle 1950s as well.

The federal government has also sought to expand the demand for food through a variety of specialized food programs. It developed and now operates a large food stamp plan to assure the very poor of an adequate supply of food. It has developed and operated special milk programs and lunch programs for schoolchildren and food assistance programs for pregnant and nursing mothers and preschool children. These domestic food assistance programs have become big business—total government expenditures on these programs in 1990 exceeded $20 billion.

The government has fostered and supported the development of special credit institutions and instruments to assist farmers in the purchase of land, the obtaining of production credit, and the financing of their cooperative purchasing and marketing associations.

The government has protected certain industries—dairy, beef cattle, sheep, and sugar—through the imposition of tariffs, import quotas, and public health measures.

Finally, the government has assisted both farm production units and agribusiness service units to reduce costs of operation through the financial support of a research, development, and extension system. This has contributed to a rapid rate of technological development in American agriculture with concomitant increases in resource productivity and reductions in unit costs of production.

The specific set of economic policies and programs adopted by and implemented by the federal government in any given year since 1930 has depended upon a host of circumstances: the economic conditions of the time, the critical problems of the time, the basic politico-economic philosophy of the electorate, the political power of special-interest groups, the budget situation and goals of the government, the interests and commitments of the President, the leadership skills and economic philosophy of the secretary of agriculture, and so on. From this array of political pressures, economic philosophies and goals, and economic conditions, the specific set of agricultural policies and programs that took shape in a particular year represented a compromise among the many and varied contending interests. The policy results were thus acceptable in a political action sense, but many, if not most, of the contending interests were unhappy with the final result. Farmers typically have been dissatisfied with the levels of price and income support realized in their programs; they have felt that they were deserving of higher levels of support. Urban consumers generally have been of the opinion that the farm programs cost too much, and they result in food prices that are higher than they need to be. Agribusiness leaders often view farm programs as too much, or unneeded, government interference with the workings of the market. The President and advisers often view farm programs as involving unnecessarily high expenditures of governmental funds. But each interest group accepted the policy result because it was realized that, in the political process in which policies are forged, it was the best alternative possible.

Economic and Social Consequences

What have been the economic and social consequences of these policies and programs? It is generally agreed that the policies and programs of the 1930s kept many farmers from losing their farms and assisted many others who had gone broke to get started once again, and that they contributed to an increase in a cash flow into the farming sector that was literally starved for cash. It is also generally agreed that the policies and programs in the 1950s and 1960s and again in the 1980s held farm prices and incomes higher than they otherwise would have been in a short-run context, and kept the farming sector from going through as serious an asset deflation as would have been the case without the programs. But many economists argue that if the farming sector had gone through an asset wringing-out process in the 1950s and again in the 1980s, farm prices and incomes would have been higher in the succeeding decades than they were. In other words, the policies and programs were beneficial to the farming sector in the short run, but the implications for the long run are questionable. However, farmers, their representatives, and the rest of society opted for protection and support in the short run.

The argument has been developed and is being increasingly accepted that the general agricultural economic policy of the nation has contributed, and continues to contribute, to a changed structure of American farming—a structure in which there are fewer and fewer and larger and larger farms. The number of farms has declined significantly in recent years—from 5.6 million in 1950 to about 2.1 million in 1989. Commercial agricultural production has been increasingly concentrated in a relatively few large farms; in 1960 some 340,000 farms, each grossing $20,000 or more, accounted for about 51 percent of the total cash receipts from farming; by 1989 some 324,000 farms, each grossing over $100,000 per year, accounted for about 78 percent of the total cash receipts from farming.

The argument runs as follows. Where agricultural policies and programs operate (1) to stabilize farm prices over time and reduce economic risk, (2) to increase the cash flow to the larger farmers via government income payments, and (3) to maintain a flow of new and improved production technologies which reduce unit costs of production, the better, more aggressive managers exploit this set of policy circumstances to expand the size of their operations. They are able to do this only by acquiring the productive assets of their less able, less efficient neighbors, which they have been doing for three decades. Thus, the argument goes, the policies and programs pursued by the United States for the past 30 years in the name of helping the small family farmer have in fact operated to destroy that farmer. The larger, more innovative, more aggressive farmers have cannibalized the smaller, less efficient farmers.

Demand for Change in Policy

The passage of the Agricultural Act of 1981 with high target prices, and the lax administration of its features, led to extraordinarily large government program costs for farm price and income support. In 1986, for example, those program costs exceeded $26 billion. These large program costs in combination with huge federal budget deficits have created strong political pressures to reform farm policies in the direction of lower levels of price and income support. Concurrent with these budget-induced pressures, other demands to reform farm policies have developed.

Environmental concerns regarding the pollution of water supplies, soil erosion, loss of wildlife habitat, and contamination of the food supply have forced their way onto the farm policy agenda. Thus in the agricultural acts of 1985 and 1990, various provisions have been incorporated into those acts that regulate the use of chemicals and that provide incentives to farmers to stop draining wetlands and to place cropland subject to erosion into a conservation reserve. But these provisions would seem to be only the beginning; the environmental movement is gaining strength with each passing year. In future farm legislation there will certainly be efforts to reduce or restrict the use of chemical fertilizers and pesticides, to protect water supplies from pollution, to expand greenbelts and forest lands to serve as wildlife habitat and watershed protection, and to move agricultural production toward a sustainable state.

Consumers are also demanding a food supply that is nutritious, healthful, and protected against injurious practices and ingredients. Thus, the government is expanding its programs of research and education in nutrition, and it is placing greater emphasis on its food inspection services and food regulatory services.

The preceding developments are taking the form of political pressures to reform and redirect farm policy. Some of these reforms were incorporated into the Agricultural Act of 1990. More will be incorporated into the next major piece of farm legislation. Whether these reforms will be modest or revolutionary remains to be seen.

Foreign Trade and Foreign Policies

The role of foreign trade in agricultural products in the national economy is not in itself an issue. The importance of a continued strong foreign demand for many of the products of American agriculture is fully understood and appreciated. Nonetheless, there are policy issues with respect to the agricultural export market that are receiving increased attention. What are the responsibilities of the United States, as a reliable supplier, to its leading and regular foreign national customers? To what extent should fluctuation in export demand be permitted to destabilize the domestic market for food? What should be the commitment of the United States to provide food aid to the less-developed world? The Reagan and Bush administration have pushed hard in GATT negotiations to reduce barriers to trade in agricultural products, as well as domestic production subsidies, in all the important trading nations of the world. As of 1991, there has been much talk about the desirability of moving toward a more open international trading system in agricultural products, but the achievements have been modest.

Some General Conclusions

The general agricultural economic policy of the United States is not unique or atypical. Every developed nation in the world has a comparable and elaborate set of policies and programs to manage and direct in its food and agricultural sector. This is the case because the farming sector of any country is inherently unstable; unpredictable variations in the weather and the extreme inelasticity of demand for food make it so. In addition, the adequacy and the security of the food supply are viewed by the citizenry of each of these nations to be too important to be left to the market. The national government of each nation feels compelled to undertake policies designed to stabilize the farming sector and to guarantee its population an adequate supply of food.

The specific policies and programs adopted and implemented by each developed country do, however, vary importantly. They vary first in accordance with the position of the country as a food importer or food exporter. The policies and programs of Canada, for example, are concerned first and foremost with developing and retaining export markets. The policies and programs of Japan, on the other hand, are concerned with the acquisition of an adequate domestic supply of food through domestic production subsidies and the location of cheap and assured foreign supplies. No foreign developed country and few underdeveloped countries depend entirely on the market to direct the production and distribution of its food supply. Like the United States, each has an elaborate set of policies and programs to guide and direct the production and distribution of its food supply. But as noted already, political pressures are at work in the United States to reform traditional farm policies. These reforms could lead to a more market-oriented domestic farm economy, a more open international trading system, more protection for the environment in rural areas, and stronger measures to ensure a safe, nutritious food supply for consumers.

References

Benedict, Murray R., *Farm Policies of the United States, 1790–1950,* Twentieth Century Fund, New York, 1953; Cochrane, Willard W., and Mary E. Ryan, *American Farm Policy, 1948–1973,* University of Minnesota Press, Minneapolis, 1976; Cochrane, Willard W., and C. Ford Runge, *Reforming Farm Policy: Toward a National Agenda,* Iowa State Press, Ames, 1992; "Farm Commodity Programs and Their Effects," *National Food Review,* ERS, USDA, January–March 1990; Rasmussen, Wayne D., and Gladys L. Baker, *Price-Support and Adjustment Programs from 1933 through 1978: A Short History,* U.S. Department of Agriculture Information Bulletin 424, 1979.

(*See also* Agricultural productivity)

Willard W. Cochrane

Agricultural productivity

Productivity is the ratio of output or product to an input or group of inputs. Frequently used measures in agriculture are the yield of crops per unit of land, output per animal, or output per worker. These are partial productivity measures. Another measure of productivity is that of total, or multifactor, productivity, which is the output per unit of all inputs. The partial productivity measure can be used for a specific time and place, such as the yield of corn in Iowa in 1990 (118 bushels per acre), or it can be used as an index of change over time (the average yield of corn in the United States in 1990 was 1.9 percent greater than in 1989). Total productivity measures are almost always measures of changes in the ratio of output per unit of input over time.

Measuring Agricultural Productivity

The appropriate measure of agricultural productivity depends upon the objective of the measurement. Care must be taken in interpreting yields per unit of land or output per farm worker. A comparison of crop yields across either space or time does not indicate whether the land with the higher yield is inherently more productive than the land with the lower yield. Since it takes more than one input, land, to produce a crop, the land with the higher yield may have had more of other inputs applied to it than the land with the lower yield. The yield per unit of land depends upon seed (amount and quality), fertilizer applied, moisture or rainfall, temperature, land preparation, cultivation, herbicides or insecticides applied, and disease-control measures. Thus, differences in yields per unit of land may measure many factors other than an inherent quality of the land.

An important objective of measuring agricultural productivity is to determine if there has been a change in technology or productivity over time. In other words, can the same resources produce more than before? This seems like a simple question, but the measurement complexities are not simple. The inputs themselves, such as labor, management, machinery, and fertilizer, change over time. The important debate between Griliches and Jorgenson, on the one side, and Denison, on the other, two decades ago (Jorgenson, Griliches, and Denison, 1972) reveals the major complexities and difficulties.

Stated simply, measurement of total factor productivity involves estimating a function such as the following:

$$\text{Log } O = \log C + \alpha \log A + \beta \log L + \eta \log F + \mu \log w + \theta \log t$$

where O is a measure of output; C is a constant; and A, L, and F are measures of specific inputs such as land, labor, and fertilizer. The term w is included as a measure of conditions over which producers have no control; in most cases it would be an index of weather. The data are observations over time, generally on an annual basis. The size of the coefficient t is a measure of the annual rate of change in O per unit of input and is a measure of productivity change. If the coefficient of t has a value of 1.5, it means that output per unit of input is increasing at the rate of 1.5 percent annually.

The particular function used here is known as the Cobb-Douglas production function, and it is only one of many different specifications of the relationships between inputs and output. Examples of other specifications may be found in Kendrick and Vaccara (1980).

Measurement Problems

There are important measurement problems in productivity analysis. Quality changes in both outputs and inputs can present major difficulties, and the importance of the difficulties grows the longer the time period involved. Outputs, such as beef and poultry, do not remain the same over time. Quality changes in inputs have been important in agriculture. Farm tractors today are very different machines than they were in the 1950s or 1960s. Farm operators are significantly better educated than in the past. Major changes have occurred in the quality of seeds.

When changes in input quality are ignored, the change in output attributed to productivity change will be too large. While in many ways the U.S. Department of Agriculture is a leader in producing an annual measure of productivity change in agriculture, the failure to adjust for many changes in input quality, especially for machinery, seeds, and labor, adversely affects the value of its work. In addition, no consideration is given to the effects of climate upon output. The measure of agricultural productivity is often, if not generally, misleading for determining year-to-year comparisons since most of the difference in the productivity measure can be due to differences in weather.

Why does output per unit of measured inputs increase over time? Changes in productivity do not occur at a uniform pace. Evidence indicates that from 1880 to 1930 there was no increase in agricultural productivity in the United States—all of the substantial increase in production was due to increasing inputs. In the subsequent half-century, output per unit of input more than doubled and productivity improvement has continued since 1980. The fundamental sources of the increased productivity were increases in knowledge created primarily through research. Knowledge of the fundamental processes of nature has improved over time; the improved knowledge permits the available human and natural resources to be used more effectively. For example, new crop varieties are made possible by increased understanding of genetics and of techniques of plant breeding. Since there is much that is unknown about nature, the potential for realizable productivity of agriculture remains far from being realized.

References

Ball, V. Eldon, "Output, Input, and Productivity Measurement in U.S. Agriculture, 1948–1979," *American Journal of Agricultural Economics,* vol. 67, 1985, pp. 475–486; Hayami, Yujiro, and Vernon W. Ruttan, *Agricultural Development: An International Perspective,* Johns Hopkins Press, Baltimore, 1985; Jorgenson, Dale W., Zvi Griliches, and Edward F. Dennison, *The Measurement of Productivity,* Brookings, Washington, D.C., 1972; Kendrick, John W., and Beatrice N. Vaccara (eds.), *New Developments in Productivity Measurement and Analysis,* National Bureau of Economic Research, Studies in Income and Wealth, vol. 44, University of Chicago Press, Chicago, 1980; U.S. Department of Agriculture, *Economic Indicators of the Farm Sector: Production and Efficiency Statistics,* Economic Research Service, ECIFS 9-4, April 1991.

(*See also* Agricultural economic policy; Productivity)

D. Gale Johnson

Allocation of resources (*see* Income distribution)

Alternative cost (*see* Opportunity cost)

Anticipation surveys, business

Business anticipation surveys ask participating companies about their plans or expectations of future activity—sales, prices, capital investments, as well as questions regarding past activity. In certain respects these surveys are similar to surveys made of consumers. Both types of survey began after the end of World War II. The best known of the business surveys, the Department of Commerce Survey of New Plant and Equipment Expenditures, was begun in 1945, while the Survey Research Center at the University of Michigan began its work in the consumer area in 1946.

There are, however, major differences between the two types of anticipation survey: consumer and business. Consumer surveys rely on probability sampling to extrapolate conclusions from a relatively small sample of consumers, perhaps 3000 to 4000, to the much larger universe of all consumers.

Business surveys come much closer to being a modified census than a random sample. Fewer than 0.5 percent of the corporations in the United States account for 69 percent of all corporate assets. Within the manufacturing sector at the beginning of 1991, 368 companies out of 155,000 submitting active income tax returns accounted for 71 percent of the manufacturing assets and 57.9 percent of receipts. In business surveys, an attempt is made to include as many of these large companies as possible. A more random sampling is made of the medium- and smaller-sized companies to eliminate any systematic, large-company bias.

Reliability of Business Surveys

The reliability of business anticipation surveys tends to be a direct function of how many of the largest companies have responded. In general, business surveys are more reliable than consumer surveys in predicting the magnitude of expected change in sales or investment, as opposed to direction alone. (Consumer surveys are primarily useful in predicting turning points in consumer behavior.) The reason is that companies, particularly large companies, plan expenditures and a future year's activity to a much greater extent than do consumers.

For the same reason, surveys of investment plans tend to be more reliable than sales expectations. The capital investment process by its nature requires planning. Prospective rates of return on alternative projects must be evaluated. Once viable options have been selected, the expenditures must be approved and the funds appropriated by a board of directors. This decision-making process itself fixes probable capital investment some time into the future. In addition, for many capital projects there is a very long time span between approval of projects, letting of contracts, and completion of the projects. As long as progress on a project is on schedule, the expenditure stream should be predictable within fairly narrow limits. However, there will be some slippage on the "up" side of a capital goods expansion as delivery times slow, and companies may cut plans or stretch out projects during a recession to conserve their cash flow.

Still, under normal conditions, a company will not spend significantly more or less than planned in any given fiscal year. Accordingly, surveys of such plans are good indicators of future investment activity.

Companies also set sales plans. In many cases sales plans could more accurately be described as goals or targets rather than point forecasts. There is rarely a penalty to management for exceeding its sales forecast, while major cost overruns on a capital project could put a company in financial jeopardy. Furthermore, many cyclical companies are vulnerable to factors outside their control. An unexpected contraction in overall economic activity, for example, could make their sales forecast unrealistically high.

Because of the nature of sales planning, surveys of anticipated sales are better indicators of business confidence than predictors of future activity. However, business confidence plays a very important role in capital investment. Thus, if the outlook for sales turns sour, it may mean that planned capital investment is vulnerable to cutbacks.

Although business anticipation surveys focus mainly on the future, they often include a number of questions pertaining to past activity. Provided they are asked regularly, the answers to these questions are often useful in their own right or as a means of determining the probable error in results of the anticipation survey.

Department of Commerce Survey

The best-known and oldest business survey is that conducted by the Department of Commerce and the Securities and Exchange Commission (SEC). Initially, most companies registered with and reporting to the SEC (almost all the large, publicly owned companies) were included, as well as a large sample of unregistered manufacturing companies that reported to the Department of Commerce. The survey is currently conducted solely by the Department of Commerce, and the size of the sample has increased over time to provide more complete coverage in service industries. The companies surveyed report not only their planned capital investments, but also their actual expenditures in the past period.

Over the nearly 46 years that this survey has been conducted, it has become apparent that there is a systematic bias in the response of certain industries both annually and on a quarterly basis. The Department of Commerce attempts to compensate for this through application of a bias adjustment. This adjustment has been the source of some controversy, but it continues to be used. In recent years, the adjustment has tended to improve the results for individual industries, while producing the opposite result for total expenditures. The adjustment in some periods has been large. For example, adjusted plant and equipment expenditures for 1989 reported in November 1989 were $475.2 billion. Before the bias adjustment, expenditures of $473 billion were reported as anticipated by respondents. Inasmuch as more than 10 months of the year had passed at the time the survey was conducted, the discrepancy was quite large. Under normal conditions, such a large adjustment so late in the year would appear highly questionable. In seven of the ten quarters from the beginning of 1989 through mid-1991 for which actual data are available, actual expenditures have been lower than planned expenditures one quarter ahead. The bias adjustment may be partially responsible for this discrepancy. However, since the bias adjustment is reported quarterly only for the annual data, it is not possible to determine from the published data whether or not these discrepancies correlate with the bias adjustment on a quarter-by-quarter basis.

Other Surveys

If one's definition of anticipation survey is not restricted to those which predominantly request information about future business activity, many trade associations' membership surveys could also be included among anticipation surveys. Some of these, such as the National Association of Purchasing Management, predominantly focus on current activity: production, orders, employment, prices, and inventories, but occasionally ask questions regarding the companies' views on the outlook for future activity. Others, such as the American Paper Institute's annual capacity survey, focus on a very narrow range of activity. Some companies, such as Dun and Bradstreet, and some Wall Street firms conduct surveys to take advantage of the proprietary data networks that they have.

All these surveys can be useful to the business analyst provided they are well designed. The longer any given survey is maintained without changes in definitions, the more valuable it tends to become.

References

Eisner, Robert, *Factors in Business Investment,* National Bureau of Economic Research, Ballinger, Cambridge, Mass., 1978; Ferber, Robert (ed.), *Determinants of Investment Behavior,* Universities—National Bureau Conference Series, no. 19, Columbia University Press, New York, 1967; U.S. Bureau of Economic Analysis, *Survey of New Plant and Equipment Expenditures,* U.S. Department of Commerce, published quarterly; *The Dun and Bradstreet Manufacturing Survey* and *The Dun and Bradstreet Construction Survey,* published monthly.

(*See also* Anticipation surveys, consumer; Business investment in new plants and equipment)

M. Kathryn Eickhoff

Anticipation surveys, consumer

Consumer anticipation surveys ask consumers about their intentions to purchase housing, automobiles, and household appliances as well as query the participants about their attitudes and expectations. The measurement of expectations through questioning representative population samples about expected changes in general and personal economic trends has been carried out for nearly half a century. The direct approach of measurement, in place of substituting past for expected trends or of assuming what rational expectations ought to be in the judgment of experts, provides information not only about the average expectations of all Americans but also about the expectations of groups of individuals or families that can be related to their subsequent actions, such as their purchase of consumer durable goods.

Consumer versus Business Anticipation Surveys

In some respects, consumer anticipation surveys are similar to business anticipation surveys. Both types of survey began after the end of World War II when there arose a need for anticipating changing trends in consumption of goods and in investment in new plants and equipment. However, consumer surveys have proved less reliable than business surveys in predicting the magnitude of expected changes as opposed to direction—either up or down. Nevertheless, anticipation data from surveys have become important elements in the forecasting of short-term economic conditions.

History of Consumer Anticipation Surveys

Led by George Katona, the Survey Research Center (SRC) of the University of Michigan began its consumer survey work in 1946–1947, following earlier surveys directed by Katona for the Division of Program Surveys in the U.S. Department of Agriculture. Rapid progress in the development of reliable sampling, particularly in probability sampling, as well as in interviewing methods in the 1940s, made it possible for research organizations to carry out consumer surveys. These surveys are thus able to extrapolate conclusions on attitudes and expectations from a relatively small sample of consumers—at most about 4000—to the universe of all consumers.

After several years of experience with measuring changes in consumer attitudes and expectations, the SRC in 1952 constructed an index of consumer sentiment. It is composed of answers to simple questions about changes in personal financial well-being (both in the recent past and in the near future), about people's general economic outlook (during the next year and 5 years ahead), and an evaluation of market conditions for consumer durable goods (whether it is a good time or bad time to buy them).

For many years, only the SRC collected data on consumer sentiment in the United States. Beginning in the 1960s, several American-based organizations (the Conference Board, Sindlinger, and Gallup) started to survey American consumers on their attitudes and expectations through the use of questions similar to those asked by the SRC and contributed to the dissemination of economic survey data and the prediction of economic trends. In the 1970s the European Common Market arranged for periodic surveys of consumer attitudes and expectations to be carried out in each of its member countries.

How Useful Are the Consumer Anticipation Surveys?

Through repeated surveys—monthly or quarterly—it is possible to determine the presence or absence of, direction or extent of, or changes in optimism or pessimism as well as in confidence or doubt and uncertainty of consumers. Change in these attitudes and expectations indicates change in people's willingness to make expenditures on housing or major consumer durable goods.

Consumer surveys are primarily useful in predicting turning points in consumer behavior, less useful in predicting the number of housing units to be built or sold in the year ahead or the number of automobiles and household appliances expected to be sold over the same period. The strongest test of the predictive value of consumer attitudes and expectations consists of a comparison of the movement of the index of consumer sentiment with the turning points in the business cycle. With regard to recessions, in nearly every instance, the consumer sentiment index proved to be an excellent leading indicator, turning down well before recessions started. Before economic recoveries, the performance of the index of consumer sentiment was not as good as it was before recessions, and the time lag between the attitudinal indicator, on the one hand, and spending and saving, on the other, was significantly shorter than it was for downturns in economic activity. In periods of small economic changes, attitudes tended to fluctuate very little and indicated that major changes in the economic trend were not imminent.

Problems with Consumer Anticipation Surveys

There remain a number of unsolved problems in consumer anticipation surveys. Among them are:

1. The question of who should be surveyed. Should a sample of all families be used or only upper-income families who make most of the purchases of consumer durable goods or only lower-income families who suffer most during economic downturns?

2. The relationship of ability to buy and willingness to buy. Under different circumstances, the relative power of the two has varied. Rising income and savings don't always convert into a willingness to buy new durables.

3. Understanding the origin of changes in consumer sentiment. Studies along this line are continuing. Obviously changes in consumer sentiment depend upon a variety of factors, the relative importance of which vary over time.

Changing times may require change in anticipation surveys. Further development may be needed in methods of conducting these surveys and in ways of evaluating their implications.

References

Katona, George, *Psychological Economics,* Elsevier, New York, 1975, chaps. 5, 6, 7; Strumpel, Burkhard, *Economic Means for Human Needs: Social Indicators of Well-Being and Discontent,* Institute for Social Research, Ann Arbor, Mich., 1976; Strumpel, Burkhard, James N. Morgan, and Ernest Zahn (eds.), *Human Behavior in Economic Affairs,* Elsevier, New York, 1972, chaps. 15, 16, 18.

(*See also* Anticipation surveys, business; Consumer theory; Marketing research and business economics; Sampling in economics)

George Katona and Douglas Greenwald

Antitrust policy

Fundamentally, antitrust policy in the United States is an expression of Americans' preference for competition as a means of allocating scarce resources. Alternatively, antitrust can be viewed as an expression of hostility toward monopoly. This latter attitude reflects an understanding of the economic problems caused by monopoly and a distrust of concentrations of wealth for the viability of political democracy.

Historical Background

In spite of inadequacies in transportation and accurate market information, it is safe to say that there were very few monopoly problems before the Civil War. Industries were relatively unconcentrated and, for the most part, populated by small firms. Following the Civil War, however, a few industries began to exhibit monopolistic tendencies as economies of large-scale production were exploited. Some large firms seemed to be adopting predatory business practices to cripple their smaller rivals. In addition, there were reports of political corruption linked to big business.

In other industries that appeared to be structured competitively, organized restraints of trade increased substantially. For the most part, these took the form of price-fixing agreements or pools, but some were more formal trusts or mergers. These noncompetitive agreements surfaced in many industries that were vital to the bulk of society: petroleum, railroads, coal, lumber, iron, ice, tile, oatmeal milling, steel, and beer.

The combination of economic and political abuse created a hostile atmosphere for the business community. In the final years before the passage of antitrust legislation, there seemed to be a great deal of truth in the charges that trusts (1) corrupted public employees and legislators, thereby threatening political democracy; (2) enjoyed the insulation of protective tariffs; (3) hurt consumers by charging higher prices; (4) engaged in questionable financial practices like watering stock; and (5) caused serious dislocations by suddenly closing plants. The American public felt abused by the trusts and wanted a law that would curtail the power of the trusts. Any law that prohibited the worst abuses of the most visible trusts would be satisfactory. What Americans got was the Sherman Act.

The Sherman Antitrust Act

The Sherman Antitrust Act, which was passed on July 2, 1890, is the cornerstone of antitrust policy in the United States. Its two main provisions are:

> Sec. 1. Every contract, combination in the form of trust or otherwise, or conspiracy, in restraint of trade or commerce among the several States, or with foreign nations, is hereby declared to be illegal.

and

> Sec. 2. Every person who shall monopolize, or attempt to monopolize, or combine or conspire with any other person or persons, to monopolize any part of the trade or commerce among the several States, or with foreign nations, shall be deemed guilty of a felony, . . .

The sanctions for violating the Sherman Act have stiffened over the years. Originally, antitrust violations were misdemeanors, but now they are felonies. Corporate fines can reach $10 million, while personal fines can total $350,000. Perhaps more importantly, an antitrust felon can be imprisoned for up to 3 years.

The vague and general prohibitions of trade restraints and monopolization provided in Sections 1 and 2 of the Sherman Act have caused much mischief. Due to the lack of specificity, the Sherman Act was little more than a legislative command that the judiciary develop the law of antitrust. Since the statute did not provide much guidance, the courts would have to be guided by the apparent legislative intent of Congress.

Legislative Intent   There have been many arguments about the proper goals of antitrust policy, but the goal most palatable to economists is the promotion of consumer welfare through the allocative efficiency of the competitive process. Robert Bork made a compelling argument for this view based upon his thorough review of the Sherman Act's legislative history and its structure.

Early Enforcement   The early enforcement of the Sherman Act was consistent with the promotion of consumer welfare. During the 1897–1899 period, Justice Peckham wrote five major opinions that reflect an appreciation for the economic benefits of competition. For example, in his *U.S. v. Joint Traffic Association* (1898) opinion, Peckham wrote:

> *The natural, direct and immediate effect of competition is, however, to lower rates, and to thereby increase demand for commodities, the supplying of which increases commerce, and an agreement, whose first and direct effect is to prevent this play of competition, restrains instead of promoting trade and commerce.*

Thus, it is clear that Justice Peckham understood that competition reduced price and expanded output. A direct restraint upon the forces of competition would result in higher prices and reduced output. Consequently, Justice Peckham established that any business practices designed primarily to restrict output would be illegal. This is certainly consistent with the economist's theory of allocative efficiency and thereby consistent with a legislative aim of promoting consumer welfare.

In spite of the fact that the early Sherman Act decisions were consistent with promoting consumer welfare, there was almost immediate dissatisfaction with the statute. Some critics contended that its vague standards were unfair because no bright line was drawn between legal and illegal business behavior. Others were concerned about the extent of judicial discretion as some feared that the act would be interpreted too severely while others feared a lax interpretation. These fears were galvanized by Justice White's opinion in *Standard Oil Co. v. U.S.* (1911), which enunciated the rule of reason. White ruled that the Sherman Act's language prohibiting every contract in restraint of trade should be read to prohibit every contract that unduly or unreasonably restrained trade. White explained that while the Sherman Act's language was broad so that offenders could not slip through loopholes, the broad language required the exercise of judgment on the part of the judiciary in applying the act. White ruled that the act did not preclude a firm from being the only seller of a commodity, but it did prohibit all firms from using exclusionary practices to preclude others from selling that commodity. Contracts that tended to exclude rival firms were illegal. Life, however, is not simple—a judge is required to exercise discretion, i.e., to use reason, in determining whether any particular contract unduly (i.e., unreasonably) restrained someone's freedom to compete. If it did, it was illegal.

White's rule of reason confirmed the fears of all Sherman Act opponents. Additional legislation was demanded. While some groups wanted absolute prohibitions for certain business practices, other groups were more inclined to favor unbridled laissez-faire. The final result was compromise legislation, the Clayton Act, which was supposed to provide greater specificity.

The Clayton Act

The Clayton Act, which was enacted on October 15, 1914, was an expression of Congress's desire to outlaw specific business practices that were thought to be anti-competitive. The practices that were condemned fall into three main categories: (1) price discrimination, (2) exclusionary practices, and (3) mergers.

Price Discrimination   Section 2 of the Clayton Act, as amended by the Robinson-Patman Act of 1936, bans price discrimination where it is likely to have anticompetitive consequences:

Sec. 2 (a). That it shall be unlawful for any person engaged in commerce, . . . either directly or indirectly, to discriminate in price between different purchasers of commodities of like grade and quality, . . . where the effect of such discrimination may be substantially to lessen competition or tend to create a monopoly in any line of commerce, . . .

Since Congress did not want to penalize efficiency where the consequent cost savings were passed on to the consumer in the form of lower prices, there is a provision in Section 2(a) that permits price differences that reflect cost differences. There is also a meeting-competition defense, which allows a seller to protect himself or herself against rival offers of low prices to selected customers by cutting prices to those customers without having to cut the price to all customers. The language of Section 2(b) allows a threatened seller to meet—but not beat—a low-price offer of a rival irrespective of the effect upon competition among the customers.

Exclusionary Practices   Section 3 of the Clayton Act prohibits conditional sales where such sales have an adverse effect on competition:

Sec. 3. That it shall be unlawful for any person engaged in commerce . . . to lease or make a sale of goods, wares, merchandise, machinery, supplies, or other commodities, whether patented or unpatented, . . . on the condition, agreement, or understanding that the lessee or purchaser thereof shall not use or deal in the goods, wares, merchandise, machinery, supplies, or other commodities of a competitor or competitors of the lessor or seller, where the effect . . . may be to substantially lessen competition or tend to create a monopoly in any line of commerce.

This section has been used to forbid tying arrangements, where the purchaser can buy product A only if he or she also buys product B; requirements contracts, where the buyer agrees to purchase all his or her requirements for a particular commodity from a single seller; exclusive dealing, where the buyer agrees not to handle competing lines of merchandise; and imposition of territorial confinement, where a buyer is not allowed to resell the product outside a carefully delineated territory.

Mergers   Most of the antitrust laws deal with competitive problems in a remedial fashion. In contrast, Section 7 of the Clayton Act, which was amended by the Cellar-Kefauver Act of 1950, provides some preventive measures. More specifically, Section 7 forbids a merger where a possible substantial lessening of competition or tendency toward monopoly would accompany the merger:

Sec. 7. That no corporation engaged in commerce shall acquire, directly or indirectly, the whole or any part of the stock or other share capital and no cor-

poration subject to the jurisdiction of the Federal Trade Commission shall acquire the whole or any part of the assets of another corporation engaged also in commerce, where in any line of commerce in any section of the country, the effect of such acquisition may be substantially to lessen competition, or tend to create a monopoly.

The language of Section 7 applies to horizontal mergers between direct competitors, vertical mergers between buyers and their suppliers, and conglomerate mergers between firms that do not interface in the market. The prophylactic aspect of Section 7 can be a useful tool of public policy to prevent the sort of market structure that is conducive to collusive behavior or single-firm dominance.

The Federal Trade Commission Act

In addition to the Sherman Act's broad prohibitions, there was another feature that disturbed some people: the lack of an agency specifically designed to implement and enforce the act.

Dissatisfaction with the performance of the Department of Justice in enforcing the Sherman Act resulted in a growing sentiment for some form of interstate trade commission to supplement the Department of Justice's efforts. As a result, such an enforcement agency was created by the Federal Trade Commission Act, which was enacted on September 26, 1914. The major provision of the act empowers the FTC to discipline business behavior:

Sec. 5. (a)(1) Unfair methods of competition in or affecting commerce, and unfair or deceptive acts or practices in or affecting commerce, are hereby declared unlawful.

The primary economic rationale for a prohibition of unfair methods of competition resided in the belief that monopoly power was transitory without the exercise of unfair business practices. Accordingly, by outlawing such unfair methods of competition, society would be free of entrenched monopolies. Additionally, a specialized agency with delegated rule-making authority can respond more effectively than Congress to new abuses and new unfair practices. Moreover, a specialized agency can shape remedies with greater flexibility than the judiciary. It can employ experts to advise the commissioners on a continuing basis during both the rule-making and adjudicative phases of the proceedings.

Antitrust Enforcement

Enforcement of the antitrust laws is shared among two federal enforcement agencies, the attorneys general of the individual states and private plaintiffs.

Federal Enforcement   There are two federal antitrust enforcement agencies—the Antitrust Division of the Department of Justice and the Federal Trade Commission. Only the Department of Justice can prosecute the criminal provisions of the Sherman Act. The Federal Trade Commission, along with the Department of Justice, is empowered to enforce the Clayton Act by issuing cease and desist orders that carry no civil or criminal penalties.

Private Enforcement   Supplementing the public enforcement sanctions is Section 4 of the Clayton Act, which provides an incentive for private enforcement. This provision allows anyone who has been injured by an antitrust violation to sue in federal court and recover treble damages plus the costs of the suit, including a reasonable attorney's fee.

Parens Patriae Suits The "private attorney general" feature of the antitrust laws was bolstered in 1976 by the Hart-Scott-Rodino Antitrust Improvement Act, which added a *parens patriae* provision to the Clayton Act. Under that provision, a state attorney general may file an action under the Sherman Act on behalf of the residents of his or her state. In these instances, the remedies available are the same as those available in a suit by an individual but any monetary recovery is reduced by the amount recovered in other private actions.

Modern Interpretation of Antitrust

Section 1 of the Sherman Act has been used to attack collusive restraints of trade in their various guises. Price fixing is the prototypical restraint and has been condemned almost from the inception of the act. There are, of course, many ways to restrain trade and thereby elevate price above the competitive level. As variations arise and are recognized, their anticompetitive purposes and effects are revealed and the practice is condemned. Bid rigging and customer allocation schemes were condemned in *U.S. v. Addyston Pipe & Steel* (1898). A similar fate awaited market division or territorial allocation in *U.S. v. Topco Associates, Inc.* (1972), boycotts or concerted refusals to deal in *U.S. v. General Motors Corp.* (1966), minimum-fee schedules in *Goldfarb v. Virginia State Bar* (1975), information exchanges in *U.S. v. Container Corporation of America* (1969), maximum-fee schedules in *Arizona v. Maricopa County Medical Society* (1982), agreements to refrain from competitive bidding in *National Society of Professional Engineers v. U.S.* (1978), and an agreement to end interest-free credit in *Catalano, Inc. v. Target Sales, Inc.* (1980).

Section 2 of the Sherman Act has not condemned the structural condition of monopoly. It has, however, condemned the act of monopolizing. A two-prong test for illegal monopolization is summarized succinctly in *U.S. v. Grinnell Corp.* (1966):

> *The offense of monopoly under § 2 of the Sherman Act has two elements: (1) the possession of monopoly power in the relevant market and (2) the willful acquisition or maintenance of that power. . . .*

During the last 20 years, there have been very few monopoly cases. A major reason for this is that the enforcement of Section 7 of the Clayton Act has prevented market structure from approaching monopoly dimensions.

Clayton Act interpretation has been somewhat peculiar. Section 2's prohibition of price discrimination has been vilified as anticompetitive and protectionist. This, however, is not much of a current problem since there is little interest at the Federal Trade Commission or the Department of Justice in pursuing these cases. Similarly, it is difficult to say what the law is with respect to mergers. Since the 1960s when a series of harsh decisions were rendered, the Supreme Court has become far more conservative and the antitrust agencies have filed very few cases. Finally, the prohibitions under Section 3 of the Clayton Act usually can be prosecuted under Section 1 of the Sherman Act as well. Many of these prohibitions are quite controversial. These include resale price maintenance, maximum resale price fixing, tying arrangements, territorial confinement, and exclusive dealing.

References

Blair, Roger D., and David L. Kaserman, *Antitrust Economics,* Irwin, Homewood, Ill., 1985; Bork, Robert H., "Legislative Intent and the Policy of the Sherman Act," *Journal of Law and Economics,* vol. 9, April 1966, pp. 7–48; Bork, Robert H., *The Antitrust Paradox,* Basic Books, New York, 1978; Letwin, William, *Law and Economic Policy in America,* Random House, New York, 1965; Thorelli, Hans B., *The Federal Antitrust Policy,* Allen & Unwin, London, 1954.

(*See also* Cartel; Competition; Concentration of industry; Economies of scale; Mergers, takeovers, and corporate restructuring; Monopoly and oligopoly; Restraint of trade)

Roger D. Blair

Arbitrage

Arbitrage refers to purchases in one market and sales in another market that have the effect of maintaining prices of comparable commodities traded in these markets within limits set by the cost of buying the commodity in one market and selling it in another. The effect of arbitrage is to establish limits within which the price of a given commodity traded in a given market must lie. A tendency for the price to move outside these limits which depend on the transaction costs induces arbitrage, forcing the price back into the limits.

Arbitrage occurs among markets in foreign exchange. Between any pair of currencies there is an exchange rate. In a system where individuals may trade foreign currencies, arbitrage ensures that a sequence of transactions starting in one currency and going through several others will result in the same quantity of the starting currency less transaction costs. For instance, trading U.S. dollars for French francs, French francs for Japanese yen, and, finally, Japanese yen for U.S. dollars results in a final quantity of U.S. dollars equal to the initial quantity less transaction costs.

Arbitrage also occurs across markets in which the same commodity is traded, if an individual can make transactions in all these markets or if pairs of markets can be linked by trades of the same individual. Thus, the price of silver in New York cannot differ from the price of silver in Chicago by more than the cost of transporting a given quantity of silver from one market to the other. A tendency for the price of silver to go outside these bounds would induce arbitrage operations that would have the effect of lowering the price in the market to which the commodity is shipped and raising it in the market from which it comes until it is no longer possible to obtain a positive net return from such pairs of transactions.

Although the main effect of arbitrage is to bring about a relation among prices of similar commodities according to the cost of converting the commodity from one form to another, uncertainty may be present. For example, there may be an announcement of a merger proposed between two companies such that company A will acquire all the stock of company B at a given ratio, say two shares of stock of company A for one share of stock of company B. If the merger is certain to occur, then the price per share of company B stock must equal twice the price per share of company A stock as a result of arbitrage, assuming trade is possible in the shares of both companies. Until the merger is certain, however, the price ratio of shares of stock in the two companies need not be 2 to 1 because of the risk that the merger will not occur. Trades that take the form of selling shares of one company's stock and buying shares of the other company's stock owing to a departure of the current price ratio from that which will prevail when the merger is certain are a form of arbitrage even though an element of risk is present.

A form of arbitrage occurs when a merchant acquires a stock of a commodity at a given spot price, the merchant sells an equal quantity forward, and, because of these and similar transactions, the forward price does not exceed the spot price by more than the cost of storing the commodity until delivery is called for by the terms of the forward contract. Arbitrage establishes price relations among commodities for delivery at different times such that the price of later delivery cannot exceed the price for earlier delivery by more than the marginal cost of storage between the two dates.

Program trading is a recent kind of arbitrage. In program trading, for example, the price of a bundle of shares of stock on the New York Stock Exchange is brought into approximate equality with the price of a futures contract traded on another exchange, in this case the Chicago Mercantile Exchange, for that bundle of shares in the form of a futures contract based on the Standard & Poor's 500 Index. Traders transact simultaneously in both markets depending on the profitable opportunities for arbitrage between them. It is an error to say that trades in the financial futures contract cause opposite movements in the share prices on the stock exchange because the two are mutually related.

References

Einzig, Paul A., *A Dynamic Theory of Forward Exchange,* 2d ed., St. Martins Press, New York, 1967; Einzig, Paul, *The Eurodollar System,* 5th ed., St. Martins Press, New York, 1973; Stoll, Hans, "Portfolio Trading," *Journal of Portfolio Management,* vol. 14, Summer 1988, pp. 20–24.

(*See also* Commodity exchange)

Lester G. Telser

Arbitrage pricing theory (*see* Asset pricing models)

Asset pricing models

Asset pricing models describe the prices or expected rates of return of financial assets, which are claims traded in financial markets. Examples of financial assets are common stocks, bonds, options, and futures contracts. Asset pricing models are based on two central concepts. The first is the no-arbitrage principle, which states that market forces tend to align the prices of financial assets so as to eliminate arbitrage opportunities. An arbitrage opportunity arises when assets can be combined in a portfolio by buying and selling such that the portfolio has zero cost, no chance of a loss, and a positive probability of gain. Arbitrage opportunities tend to be eliminated by trading in financial markets since prices adjust as investors attempt to exploit them. The second central concept is financial market equilibrium. Investors' desired holdings of financial assets derive from an optimization problem. In financial market equilibrium the first-order conditions of an optimization problem must be satisfied. Equilibrium asset pricing models follow from the first-order conditions.

General Asset Pricing Models

Virtually all asset pricing models are a special case of the expression

$$P_t = E_t \left[m_{t+1} \left(P_{t+1} + D_{t+1} \right) \right] \tag{1}$$

where P_t is the price of the asset at time t and D_{t+1} is the amount of any dividends, interest, or other payments received at time $t + 1$. The marketwide random variable m_{t+1} is known as a benchmark pricing variable, stochastic discount factor, equivalent martingale measure, or intertemporal marginal rate of substitution. The notation $E_t[.]$ denotes the conditional expectation, given a marketwide information set.

Repeated substitution in Equation (1), assuming that the limiting expression is finite, produces

$$P_t = E_t \left[\sum_{j>0} \left(\prod_{k=1,\ldots,j} m_{t+k} \right) D_{t+j} \right] \tag{2}$$

Equation (2) is called the present-value model. In early work m_{t+j} was often taken to be a fixed discount factor [i.e., $m_{t+j} = (1+r)^{-1}$]. More recently, the present-value model with a fixed discount factor has been used to study the relation between the variance of aggregate stock prices and dividends (Campbell and Shiller, 1987; Kleidon, 1986; LeRoy and Porter, 1981; Shiller, 1981; and others). See Cochrane (1991) and Grilles and LeRoy (1991) for reviews. Asset pricing models are more typically used to study the rates of return of financial assets. Equation (1) is equivalent to

$$E_t(m_{t+1} R_{t+1}) = 1 \tag{3}$$

where $R_{t+1} = (P_{t+1} + D_{t+1})/P_t$ is the gross return and $R_{t+1} - 1$ is the rate of return.

Without more structure, Equations (1) to (3) have no content because it is always possible to find a random variable m_{t+1} for which the equations hold. However, with the restriction that m_{t+1} be a strictly positive random variable, Equation (1) becomes equivalent to the no-arbitrage principle (Beja, 1971, Hansen and Richard, 1987; Harrison and Kreps, 1979; Ross, 1977; Rubenstein, 1976).

The return difference $R_{i,t+1} - R_{0,t+1}$ is the excess return of asset i relative to a reference return, $R_{0,t+1}$. Asset pricing models have traditionally focused on relations between expected excess returns and risk. The models therefore attempt to explain the expected excess return as a risk premium. The reference asset $R_{0,t+1}$ is often chosen to be one that is relatively free of risk, such as a short-term Treasury bill. With some algebraic substitutions, Equation (3) implies

$$E_t(R_{i,t+1} - R_{0,t+1}) = \mathrm{Cov}_t(R_{i,t+1} - R_{0,t+1}; -m_{t+1})/E_t(m_{t+1}) \qquad \text{for all } i \tag{4}$$

where $\mathrm{Cov}_t(.;.)$ is the conditional covariance. The conditional covariance with a benchmark pricing variable m_{t+1} is a general measure of systematic risk. Risk is systematic if it cannot be eliminated by portfolio diversification, in the sense that the risk would be present in an aggregate market portfolio of all traded assets. If the conditional covariance with m_{t+1} is zero for a particular asset, the expected risk premium for that asset should be zero. At this level of generality we can think of the returns and of the m_{t+1} as being either real or nominal. Any common unit of measurement is legitimate.

In an equilibrium asset pricing model, Equation (1) arises as a first-order condition for a consumer-investor's optimization problem. The investor maximizes a lifetime utility function, denoted by $V(.)$, allocating resources to consumption and investment assets each period. If the allocation is optimal, the marginal utility cost at time t of the consumption forgone to buy any asset must equal the expected marginal utility gain of selling the asset and consuming the proceeds at time $t + 1$: $P_t (\delta V/\delta C_t) = E_t[(P_{t+1} + D_{t+1}) (\delta V/\delta C_{t+1})]$, which is equivalent to Equation (1), with

$$m_{t+1} = (\delta V/\delta C_{t+1})/(\delta V/\delta C_t) \qquad (5)$$

When Equation (5) defines m_{t+1}, it is the intertemporal marginal rate of substitution (IMRS) of the consumer, and Equation (1) is the consumer's intertemporal Euler equation. Equilibrium asset pricing models focus on the relation of security returns to aggregate quantities, and follow from aggregating the Euler equations of individual consumers. Assumptions that justify aggregating the Euler equations are discussed by Constantinides (1982), Gorman (1953), Rubinstein (1974), Wilson (1968), and others.

When m_{t+1} is defined by (5), Equation (4) says that an asset earns a positive expected risk premium if its return is negatively correlated with the IMRS. This means that the asset is likely to return more than expected when the marginal utility in the future period $t + 1$, relative to the current period t, is lower than expected. The more negative the covariance with the IMRS, the less desirable the distribution of the random return and the larger the expected compensation for holding the asset.

Asset pricing models often measure risk using beta coefficients. The beta is the regression coefficient of the asset return on one or more portfolios or risk factors. For example, $Cov_t(R_{i,t+1}; R_{p,t+1})/Var_t(R_{p,t+1})$ is the conditional beta of $R_{i,t+1}$ relative to $R_{p,t+1}$. Consider a projection of the benchmark pricing variable m_{t+1} on the vector of returns R_{t+1}, and form $R_{p,t+1}$ as the portfolio that is proportional to the fitted values. Form excess returns relative to a zero beta portfolio for $R_{p,t+1}$, denoted as $R_{z,t+1}$ and satisfying the condition $Cov_t(R_{z,t+1}; R_{p,t+1}) = 0$. With some algebraic substitution, the following beta pricing model can be derived from Equation (4):

$$E_t(R_{i,t+1} - R_{z,t+1}) = [Cov_t(R_{i,t+1}; R_{p,t+1})/Var_t(R_{p,t+1})] E_t(R_{p,t+1} - R_{z,t+1}) \text{ for all } i \qquad (6)$$

Equation (6) is equivalent to the statement that the portfolio $R_{p,t+1}$ is a conditional minimum variance portfolio. A portfolio is a minimum variance portfolio if it has the smallest variance of any portfolio with the same expected return. A portfolio $R_{p,t+1}$ is mean variance efficient if it satisfies Equation (6) and if also $E_t(R_{p,t+1} - R_{z,t+1}) > 0$ (Black, 1972; Fama, 1976; Roll, 1977).

The Capital Asset Pricing Model

The first equilibrium asset pricing model was the capital asset pricing model (CAPM) of Sharpe (1964), Lintner (1965), and Black (1972). The model assumes that investors allocate their funds to maximize an expected utility function which depends only on the expected return and variance of the portfolio. The first-order conditions state that investors desire to hold mean variance efficient portfolios. The aggregate demand for assets is a portfolio of the investors' portfolios. Since a linear combination of mean variance efficient portfolios is mean variance efficient, the CAPM concludes that the aggregate portfolio that is demanded and supplied in equilibrium must be mean variance efficient. The CAPM is equivalent to the statement that the market portfolio of all traded assets is mean variance efficient and therefore can replace $R_{p,t+1}$ in Equation (6).

Consumption-Based Asset Pricing Models

Breeden (1979) and Lucas (1978) derived consumption-based asset pricing models in which the consumers' preferences are of the form $V = \Sigma_t \beta^t u(C_t)$, where β is a time preference parameter, C_t is consumption, and the function $u(.)$ is increasing and concave in consumption. An example assumes a power function:

$$u(C) = \frac{C^{1-\alpha} - 1}{1 - \alpha} \tag{7}$$

where $\alpha > 0$ is the concavity parameter that governs risk aversion and intertemporal substitution. The IMRS in Equation (5) becomes $\beta(C_{t+1}/C_t)^{-\alpha}$. Epstein (1990), Ferson and Campbell (1992), and Singleton (1990) provide reviews of the theory and empirical tests of consumption-based pricing models.

Multiple-Beta Asset Pricing Models

Multiple-beta asset pricing models are derived by Connor (1984), Cox, Ingersoll, and Ross (1985), Long (1974), Merton (1973), Ross (1976), and others. These models express the expected excess return of an asset as the sum of K terms:

$$E_t(R_{it+1}) = \lambda_{0t} + \sum_{j=1}^{K} b_{ijt} \, \lambda_{jt} \qquad i = 1, \ldots, N \tag{8}$$

The $b_{i1t}, \ldots, b_{iKt}$ are the betas of asset i relative to K risk factors. λ_{0t} is the expected return of any zero beta security, conditionally uncorrelated with all the risk factors (that is, $b_{0jt} = 0$, $j = 1, \ldots, K$). The $\lambda_{j,t}$, $j = 1, \ldots, K$, are marketwide prices of risk, represented as increments to the expected return per unit of type j beta. The betas are the multiple regression coefficients of the asset with respect to the risk factors $F_{j,t+1}$, $j = 1, \ldots, K$, in a factor model regression:

$$R_{it+1} = a_{it} + \sum_{j=1}^{K} b_{ijt} \, F_{jt+1} + u_{it+1} \text{ for all } i \tag{9}$$

where $E_t(u_{i,t+1} F_{j,t,+1}) = 0$ for all i and j. The important assumption of a multiple-beta equilibrium model is that the risk factors capture the risk in the sense that the security-specific components of the returns, the $u_{i,t+1}$ in (9), are uncorrelated with marginal utility: $E_t(u_{i,t+1}, m_{t+1}) = 0$. Substituting the factor model (9) into the right-hand side of (4) implies

$$E_t(R_{i,t+1}) = \lambda_{0t} + \Sigma_{j=1,\ldots,K} \, b_{ijt} \, [\text{Cov}_t(F_{j,t+1}, -m_{t+1})/E_t(m_{t+1})] \tag{10}$$

which is the same as Equation (8) with $\lambda_{jt} = [\text{Cov}_t(F_{j,t+1}, -m_{t+1})/E_t(m_{t+1})]$ for $j = 1, \ldots, K$.

The multiple-beta asset pricing model has no empirical content until the factors are specified. As it generalizes Equation (6), there will always be a minimum variance portfolio that satisfies (8). There have been three approaches for specifying the risk factors to operationalize multiple-beta asset pricing models. The first uses factor analytic or principal components methods to extract factors from the covariance matrix of security returns. This approach is motivated by the arbitrage pricing model (APT), which is described herein after. In the second approach the risk factors are chosen economic variables (e.g., Chen, Roll, and Ross, 1986). A third approach uses cross-sectional regressions of common-stock returns on firms' attributes (see Ferson, 1992, for a review).

The risk premiums λ_{jt} can be identified as the conditional expected excess returns on factor-mimicking portfolios. A mimicking portfolio is one whose return can be used in place of the factors, both in the factor model (9) and in the identification of risk premiums. An example of a mimicking portfolio for a risk factor j is one that minimizes conditional variance, has a beta on factor j equal to 1.0, and has betas on the other factors equal to zero. (For further characterizations of mimicking portfolios, see Grinblatt and Titman, 1987; Huberman, Kandel, and Stambaugh, 1987; Lehmann and Modest, 1988; and Shanken, 1987.) When mimicking portfolios are used, Equation (8) is equivalent to saying that a combination of these portfolios is of minimum variance and therefore satisfies Equation (6).

Asset pricing models are usually stated in terms of the conditional expectations, given information at time t. However, empirical tests examine unconditional expected returns or use instruments that are a subset of the available information. Therefore, empirical work examines whether particular portfolios are unconditionally minimum variance or are minimum variance conditional on a subset of the information. The set of conditionally minimum variance portfolios is (weakly) larger than the set of unconditionally minimum variance portfolios. If a particular portfolio is unconditionally minimum variance, then it must be conditionally minimum variance; but if it is conditionally minimum variance, it is not necessarily unconditionally minimum variance (Hansen and Richard, 1987).

Arbitrage Pricing Theory

The arbitrage pricing theory of Ross (1976) assumes that the factors in (9) represent the important comovements in the asset returns, so that the error terms are diversifiable, as opposed to systematic risk. The no-arbitrage principle is applied asymptotically as the number of assets, N, becomes infinite, and Equation (8) is obtained as an approximation. The model is refined by Chamberlain and Rothschild (1983), Huberman (1982), and Reisman (1992) among others. Chamberlain and Rothschild (1983) assume that the $N \times N$ covariance matrix of the errors u_{it+1} in Equation (9) has bounded eigenvalues as N increases and the eigenvalues of the $N \times N$ matrix of the factor loadings bb' are exploding. With these assumptions, proxies for the risk factors can be obtained using factor analysis or principal components methods (Connor and Korajczyk, 1986, 1988; Roll and Ross, 1980). The factor scores are interpreted as the returns of mimicking portfolios for the risk factors, and the expected excess returns of these portfolios are the risk premiums $\lambda_{jt}, j = 1, \ldots, K$.

References

Beja, A., "The Structure of the Cost of Capital under Uncertainty," *Review of Economic Studies,* vol. 4, 1971, pp. 359–369; Black, F., "Capital Market Equilibrium with Restricted Borrowing," *Journal of Business,* vol. 45, 1972, pp. 444–454; Breeden, D., "An Intertemporal Asset Pricing Model with Stochastic Consumption and Investment Opportunities," *Journal of Financial Economics,* vol. 7, 1979, pp. 265–296; Campbell, John Y., and R. J. Shiller, "Cointegration and Tests of Present Value Models," *Journal of Political Economy,* vol. 95, 1987, pp. 1062–1088; Chamberlain, Gary, and M. Rothschild, "Arbitrage, Factor Structure and Mean Variance Analysis on Large Asset Markets," *Econometrica,* vol. 51, 1983, pp. 1281–1304; Chen, N., R. Roll, and S. Ross, "Economic Forces and the Stock Market," *Journal of Business,* vol. 59, 1986, pp. 383–403; Cochrane, John H., "Volatility Tests and Market Efficiency: A Review Essay," *Journal of Monetary Economics,* vol. 27, 1991, pp. 463–485; Connor, Gregory, "A Unified Beta Pricing Theory," *Journal of Economic Theory,* vol. 34, 1984, pp. 13–31; Connor, Gregory, and Robert A. Korajczyk, "Performance Measurement with the Arbitrage Pricing Theory: A New Framework for Analysis," *Journal of Financial Economics,* vol. 15, March 1986, pp. 373–394; Connor, G., and R. Korajczyck, "Risk and Return in an Equilibrium APT: Application of a New Test Methodology," *Journal of Financial Economics,* vol. 21, 1988, pp. 255–290; Constantinides, George M., "Intertemporal Asset Pricing with Heterogeneous Consumers and without Demand Aggregation," *Journal of Business,* vol. 55, 1982, pp. 253–267; Cox, John C., Jonathan E. Ingersoll, and Stephen A. Ross, "A Theory of the Term Structure of Interest Rates," *Econometrica,* vol. 53, 1985, pp. 385–408; Epstein, Larry G., *Behaviour under Risk: Recent Developments in Theory and Applications,* working paper, University of Toronto Department of Economics, 1990; Fama, Eugene F., *Foundations of Finance,* Basic Books, New York, 1976; Ferson, Wayne E., "Theory and Empirical Testing of Asset Pricing Models," chap. A6 in Robert E. Jarrow, William T. Ziemba, and Vojislav

Maksimovic (eds.), *The Finance Handbook,* North-Holland Publishers, Netherlands, 1992; Ferson, Wayne E., and R. Harvey Campbell, "Seasonality and Consumption-Based Asset Pricing Models," *Journal of Finance,* vol. 47, 1992, pp. 511–552; Gilles, Christian, and Stephen F. LeRoy, "Econometric Aspects of Various Bounds Tests: A Survey," *Review of Financial Studies,* vol. 4, 1991, pp. 1303–1314; Gorman, W. M., "Community Preference Fields," *Econometrica,* vol. 21, 1953, pp. 63–80; Grinblatt, Mark, and Sheridan Titman, "The Relation between Mean-Variance Efficiency and Arbitrage Pricing, *Journal of Business,* vol. 60, 1987, pp. 97–112; Hansen, Lars P., and Scott F. Richard, "The Role of Conditioning Information in Deducing Testable Restrictions Implied by Dynamic Asset Pricing Models," *Econometrica,* vol. 55, 1987, pp. 587–613; Harrison, M., and D. Kreps, "Martingales and Arbitrage in Multi-Period Securities Markets," *Journal of Economic Theory,* vol. 20, 1979, pp. 381–408; Huberman, Gur, "A Simple Approach to Arbitrage Pricing Theory," *Journal of Economic Theory,* vol. 28, 1982, pp. 183–191; Huberman, Gur, Shmuel A. Kandel, and Robert F. Stambaugh, "Mimicking Portfolios and Exact Arbitrage Pricing," *Journal of Finance,* vol. 42, 1987, pp. 1–10; Kliedon, Allan W., "Variance Bounds Tests and Stock Price Valuation Models," *Journal of Political Economy,* vol. 94, 1986, pp. 953–1001; Lehmann, B., and D. Modest, "Empirical Foundations of the Arbitrage Pricing Theory: Basis Portfolios," *Journal of Financial Economics,* vol. 21, 1988, pp. 213–254; LeRoy, S. F., and R. D. Porter, "The Present Value Relation: Tests Based on Implied Variance Bounds," *Econometrica,* vol. 49, 1981, pp. 555–574; Lintner, John, "The Valuation of Risk Assets and the Selection of Risky Investments in Stock Portfolios and Capital Budgets," *Review of Economics and Statistics,* vol. 47, 1965, pp. 13–37; Long, J., "Stock Prices, Inflation, and the Term Structure of Interest Rates," *Journal of Financial Economics,* vol. 1, 1974, pp. 131–170; Lucas, Robert E., Jr., "Asset Prices in an Exchange Economy," *Econometrica,* vol. 46, 1978, pp. 1429–1445; Merton, Robert C., "An Intertemporal Capital Asset Pricing Model," *Econometrica,* vol. 41, 1973, pp. 867–887; Reisman, Haim, "Reference Variables, Factor Structure, and the Approximate Multibeta Representation," *Journal of Finance,* vol. 47, 1992, pp. 1303–1314; Roll, Richard, "A Critique of the Asset Pricing Theory's Tests—Part 1: On Past and Potential Testability of the Theory," *Journal of Financial Economics,* vol. 4, 1977, pp. 129–176; Roll, Richard R., and Stephen A. Ross, "An Empirical Examination of the Arbitrage Pricing Theory," *Journal of Finance,* vol. 35, 1980, pp. 1073–1103; Ross, S. A., "The Arbitrage Pricing Theory of Capital Asset Pricing," *Journal of Economic Theory,* vol. 13, 1976, pp. 341–360; Ross, S., "Risk, Return and Arbitrage," in I. Friend and J. Bicksler (eds.), *Risk and Return in Finance,* Ballinger, Cambridge, Mass., 1977; Rubinstein, Mark, "An Aggregation Theorem for Securities Markets," *Journal of Financial Economics,* vol. 1, 1974, pp. 225–244; Rubinstein, Mark, "The Valuation of Uncertain Income Streams and the Pricing of Options," *Bell Journal of Economics and Management Science,* vol. 7, 1976, pp. 407–425; Shanken, Jay, "Multivariate Proxies and Asset Pricing Relations: Living with the Roll Critique," *Journal of Financial Economics,* vol. 18, 1987, pp. 91–110; Sharpe, W. F., "Capital Asset Prices: A Theory of Market Equilibrium under Conditions of Risk," *Journal of Finance,* vol. 19, 1964, pp. 425–442; Shiller, R. J., "Do Stock Prices Move Too Much to Be Justified by Subsequent Changes in Dividends?" *American Economic Review,* vol. 71, 1981, pp. 421–436; Singleton, K., "Specification and Estimation of Intertemporal Asset Pricing Models," in B. Friedman and F. Hahn, (eds.), *Handbook of Monetary Economics,* North-Holland, Netherlands, 1990; Wilson, Robert B., "The Theory of Syndicates," *Econometrica,* vol. 36, 1968, pp. 119–131.

(*See also* Arbitrage; Portfolio management theories, Random walk hypothesis; Risk premium on investment)

Wayne E. Ferson

Austrian economics

The Austrian school of economics is not an academic institution but a way of reasoning, technique of analysis, program of research, and theoretical system distinct from other schools of economic thought. It differs in essential respects from classical economics, from the historical school, and from Marxian, institutional, and mathematical economics. On the other hand, many of the principles of Austrian economics have been incorporated into neoclassical and modern economics.

Although derived from the writings of the recognized founder of the school—Carl Menger's *Principles of Economics* (1871) and *Problems of Economics and Sociology* (1883)—Austrian economics is not a completely uniform system accepted in every detail by all members of the group. Even the second generation—chiefly Eugen von Böhm-Bawerk and Friedrich von Wieser, often regarded as the cofounders of the school—disagreed with one another and with Menger on several issues; variants and deviations have become more conspicuous over time. This makes it difficult to define the school by a set of doctrines shared by all its members. In the 1890s the following four tenets were given as characteristic: marginalism, diminishing marginal utility, costs as forgone utility, and imputation of value to complementary factors. In later years major emphasis was placed on methodological individualism and subjectivism as most typically Austrian. If one speaks, not of Austrian economics as a whole, but instead of an Austrian approach to methodology, an Austrian theory of value, an Austrian theory of capital, an Austrian theory of the trade cycle, and an Austrian theory of economic freedom, one finds the Austrian school united only on the first two aspects but divided on the rest.

Precursors, Coevals, and Followers

Several of the Austrian tenets regarding value theory had been anticipated by earlier economists. Among the precursors of the notion of utility combined with scarcity had been Galiani (1750), de Condillac (1776), Auguste Walras (1831), Lloyd (1834), Dupuit (1844), and especially Gossen (1854). The last three, and perhaps also Galiani, fully understood the law of diminishing marginal utility. Marginalism not applied to utility had been expounded by many writers, most explicitly by von Thünen (1826) and Cournot (1838). The chief difference between the precursors and Menger was that none of the former had built an integrated theoretical system on the fundamental hypotheses in question.

There were, however, contemporaries of Menger who independently built a hypothetical-deductive system on the same fundamental assumptions: William Stanley Jevons (1862, 1870) and Léon Walras (1873). A major difference between them and Menger was that their exposition employed mathematical notations while Menger's was verbal. This probably explains why for the last decades of the nineteenth century the Viennese had a much larger following than his colleagues in London and Lausanne, and why the Austrian school is generally regarded as nonmathematical.

The writings of Böhm-Bawerk and Wieser contributed greatly to the worldwide spread of Austrian economics. Austrians of later generations, such as Ludwig von Mises and Friedrich A. von Hayek, lived and taught for many years in England and America and exerted great influence on their audiences.

The Main Tenets of the Austrian School

The following brief propositions may be offered as statements of positions held by many, perhaps most, adherents of the Austrian school:

1. *Methodological Individualism.* In the explanation of economic phenomena we have to go back to the actions (or inaction) of individuals; groups or collectives cannot act except through the actions of individual members.

2. *Methodological Subjectivism.* In the explanation of economic phenomena we have to go back to judgments and choices made by individuals on the basis of whatever knowledge they have or believe to have and whatever expectations

they entertain regarding external developments and especially the consequences of their own intended actions.

3. *Marginalism.* In all economic decisions, the values, costs, revenues, productivity, etc., are determined by the significance of the last unit, or lot, added to or subtracted from the total.

4. *Tastes and Preferences.* Subjective valuations (utility) of goods and services determine the demand for them, so that their market prices are influenced by (actual and potential) consumers; diminishing marginal utility of each good or service consumed affects the allocation of consumers' incomes among various uses.

5. *Opportunity Costs* (first called Wieser's law of costs). These costs, which producers or other economic actors calculate, reflect the most important of the alternative opportunities that have to be forgone if productive services are employed for one purpose rather than for the (sacrificed) alternatives.

6. *Time Structure of Consumption and Production.* Decisions to save reflect "time preference" regarding consumption in the immediate, distant, or indefinite future, and investments are made in view of larger outputs to be obtained from given inputs by means of processes taking more time.

The last of these propositions states the two basic principles of Böhm-Bawerk's theory of capital. "Perspective undervaluation of the future" (or "impatience" in Irving Fisher's terminology) induces consumers to discount the expected utility of future consumption (or the importance of future needs); hence, saving (nonconsumption of income) and the supply of capital are scarce. "Roundaboutness of production," that is, the use of productive services (labor, land) over longer periods of production (investment), makes these services more productive, which explains the demand for capital. This theory of capital and interest was rejected by Menger and Wieser, but its main ideas were accepted by many other Austrians.

Controversies within the School

Highly controversial were two additional tenets, proposed by the Mises branch of Austrian economists:

7. *Consumer Sovereignty.* The influence consumers have, directly, on the effective demand for goods and services and, indirectly, through the prices that result in free competitive markets, on the production plans of producers and investors is not merely a fact but also an important objective, attainable only by complete avoidance of governmental interference with the markets and of restrictions on the freedom of sellers and buyers to follow their own judgment regarding quantities, qualities, and prices of products and services. (In a way this tenet is an equivalent of Pareto's optimum. The proposition amounts to a value judgment.)

8. *Political Individualism.* Only when individuals are given full economic freedom will it be possible to secure political and moral freedom. Restrictions on economic freedom lead, sooner or later, to an extension of the coercive activities of the state into the political domain, undermining and eventually destroying the essential individual liberties that the capitalistic societies were able to attain in the nineteenth century. (This is less a proposition of economics than of politics.)

These two added tenets were rejected by other Austrian economists. Joseph Schumpeter (1954) protested against "an association between . . . marginalism and capitalist apologetics." In the United States, nevertheless, the label "Austrian economics" has come to imply a commitment to the libertarian program.

There have been numerous controversies among Austrians. Menger regarded Böhm-Bawerk's theory of capital and interest as a grave error. Böhm-Bawerk and Wieser debated whether total utility (to whom? for what?) was equal to marginal utility (or price) times quantity or to the integral of marginal utility. Related to this was the problematic significance of surplus utility (equivalent to Marshall's consumer surplus). There was an argument about whether a progressive income tax can be justified by diminishing marginal utility of income. The disagreement on cardinal versus ordinal utility, and on measurability of utility, has continued to this day.

Still unresolved is the question of to what extent Austrian economics is equilibrium economics, though the answer obviously depends on what is meant by equilibrium. (Surely the equalization of marginal utilities of expenditures on different goods implies equilibrium of the household, and the notion of opportunity cost implies even more comprehensive equilibration.) That Menger rejected certain notions of equilibrium, especially some of the market equilibriums implied in the Walrasian conception of general equilibrium, need not make him an opponent of the use of the idea of equilibrium in the explanation of mere tendencies interpreted as adjustments to change. The Austrians attached great importance to the path toward equilibrium, but did not formulate precise conditions that must be satisfied at a point of equilibrium (least of all in instances when more than two goods are involved). The list of intraschool squabbles could easily be extended.

Austrian Economists

Not every economist born or residing in Austria was a member of the Austrian school, but there is wide agreement about those who qualify. The second generation included, besides Böhm-Bawerk and Wieser, Eugen von Philippovich, Emil Sax, Robert Zuckerandl, Johann von Komorzynski, Robert Meyer, and Richard Schüller. They all started publishing before the turn of the century. Two Viennese economists of the same period, Rudolph Auspitz and Richard Lieben, ought to be mentioned, though they have sometimes been relegated to the mathematical school and regarded as "un-Austrian Austrians." The same designation has been applied to Joseph Schumpeter, though despite his stronger allegiance to Walras, he is usually counted among the third generation of Austrian economists. Most of them had been members of the Böhm-Bawerk seminar and began publishing after 1900. The most important members of this group were Mises, Schumpeter, Hans Mayer, Alfred Amonn, Richard von Strigl, and Leo Schönefeld-Illy. Austrians who began publishing in the 1920s are regarded as the fourth generation. With the exception of Alexander Mahr, virtually all of them had been members of the private seminar that Mises conducted in Vienna from 1922 to 1934. They included Friedrich A. von Hayek, Gottfried Haberler, Fritz Machlup, Oskar Morgenstern, and Paul N. Rosenstein-Rodan; all had left Vienna before 1938, most of them before 1935. A fifth generation of the Austrian school is still active in Vienna; Erich Streissler is its representative.

Non-Austrian Austrian Economists

If Austrian economics is characterized by methods of analysis and fundamental hypotheses employed rather than by national origin or residence of those who professes it, one will recognize many non-Austrian Austrian economists. Indeed, Charles Gide and Charles Rist wrote as early as 1909 that "lately the Austrian school has become more American than Austrian," and mentioned the writers who "cultivate it with passion." Among the adherents of Austrian economics on the European continent were Maffeo Pantaleoni and later Augusto Graziani of Italy; Nicolas Gerard Pierson and G. M. Verrijn-Stuart of the Netherlands; Paul Leroy-Beaulieu, Adolphe Landry, and Gaëtan Pirou of France; Laurits Vilhelm Birck of Denmark; and most important, Knut Wicksell of Sweden. In England the most eminent of the early Austrian economists was Philip Wicksteed. One may add William Smart and William Robert Scott, and, among our contemporaries, Lionel Robbins and John R. Hicks as the most hospitable to the teachings of the Austrian school.

In the United States at least five economists who began publishing in the last decades of the nineteenth century may be mentioned for their "Austrian connection." John Bates Clark developed his theory of marginal productivity independently, but it converges with the work of the Austrians. Irving Fisher was a Walrasian in value theory, an Edgeworthian in refining indifference curve analysis, but a Böhm-Bawerkian in much of his theory of capital and interest. David J. Green contributed to Wieser's law of costs the term "opportunity cost." Herbert J. Davenport, an institutionalist in some respects, taught the Austrian theory of cost and value. Finally, Frank A. Fetter in his value theory was more Austrian than some real Austrian economists, and he created the concept of "psychic income."

A few years after Mises moved to the United States in 1940, a Mises seminar started in New York. Among his American students one may single out Israel M. Kirzner for his theory of entrepreneurship and Murray N. Rothbard for his espousal of libertarian anarchism. Finally, Ludwig Lachmann, a native of Germany with degrees from Berlin and London, has become a prolific author of American-Austrian economics.

References

Böhm-Bawerk, Eugen von, *Capital and Interest,* 3 vols., Libertarian Press, South Holland, Ill., 1959, first published as *Kapital und Kapitalzins,* 1884, 1889, and 1912; Hayek, Friedrich A. von, *The Pure Theory of Capital,* Macmillan, London, 1941; Hayek, Friedrich A. von, *Individualism and Economic Order,* University of Chicago Press, Chicago, 1948; Hayek, Friedrich A. von, "Economic Thought, VI: Austrian School," *International Encyclopedia of the Social Sciences,* vol. 4, Macmillan and Free Press, New York, 1968, pp. 458–462; Hicks, John R., and Wilhelm Weber, *Carl Menger and the Austrian School of Economics,* Clarendon Press, Oxford, 1978; Kauder, Emil, *A History of Marginal Utility Theory,* Princeton University Press, Princeton, N.J., 1965; Kirzner, Israel M., *Perception, Opportunity, and Profit: Studies in the Theory of Entrepreneurship,* University of Chicago Press, Chicago, 1979; Menger, Carl: *Principles of Economics,* Free Press, Glencoe, Ill., 1950, first published as *Grundsätze der Volkswirtschaftslehre,* 1871; Menger, Carl, *Problems of Economics and Sociology,* University of Illinois Press, Urbana, 1963, first published as *Untersuchungen über die Methode der Socialwissenschaften und der Politischen Okonomie Insbesondere,* 1883; Mises, Ludwig von, *The Theory of Money and Credit,* Yale University Press, New Haven, Conn., 1953, first published in German, 1912; Mises, Ludwig von, *Socialism: An Economic and Sociological Analysis,* Jonathan Cape, London, 1969, first published in German, 1922; Mises, Ludwig von, *Human Action: A Treatise on Economics,* Regnery, Chicago, 1966, 1st ed., 1949; Rosenstein-Rodan, Paul N., "Marginal Utility," *International Economic Papers,* vol. 10, pp. 71–106, first published, with bibliography, as "Grenznutzen," *Handworterbuch der Staatswissenschaften,* vol. 4, 1927; Schumpeter, Joseph A., *The Theory of Economic Development,* Harvard University Press, Cambridge, Mass., 1934, first published in German, 1912; Schumpeter, Joseph A., *History of Economic Analysis,* Oxford University Press, New York, 1954, p. 870; Spadaro, Louis M. (ed.), *New Directions in Austrian Economics,* Sheed, Andrews and McMeel, Kansas City, Mo., 1978; Wieser, Friedrich von, *Natural Value,* Kelley and Millman, New York, 1956, first published as *Der Natürliche Wert,* 1889.

(*See also* General equilibrium; German historical school; Institutional economics; Neoclassical economics; Opportunity cost; Utility)

Fritz Machlup

Automatic stabilizers

Automatic or built-in stabilizers are those components of the federal budget whose magnitudes automatically contract or expand with movements in the economy, thereby adding to or subtracting from the federal deficit. Examples are unemployment compensation, the individual income tax, the corporate income tax, and social security payroll taxes. Between 1989, a prosperous year, and the recession year 1991, federal transfer payments increased $87.6 billion. Nearly all of this increase was an automatic expenditure response to rising unemployment.

In the past, fluctuations in tax receipts represented more important stabilizers than those on the expenditure side. However, legislated tax changes during the Reagan administration removed much of the responsiveness of the individual income tax to fluctuations in the economy. In addition, the payroll taxes that finance social insurance programs have grown sharply in relative importance. They now, and for the first time, yield nearly as much revenue as the individual income taxes. Such taxes are flat-rate taxes applied to a maximum taxable base and are not as responsive as income taxes to the ups and downs in the economy. Indeed the only federal revenue component that appeared to be a significant automatic stabilizer during the 1980s was the corporation income tax. Rough estimates suggest that a one percentage point increase in the unemployment rate now automatically raises the federal deficit by roughly $50 billion—$45 billion in increased expenditures and about $5 billion in reduced revenues.

Many economists believe that the automatic stabilizers are highly beneficial inasmuch as they help to stabilize aftertax incomes. They thereby help to prevent large fluctuations in consumer spending and, therefore, in the economy. For example, if a laid-off worker loses his or her entire income, this will necessitate a drastic reduction in his or her spending. However, if a substantial portion of the worker's lost income is replaced by unemployment compensation as well as a reduction in tax liabilities, this helps to maintain the worker's disposable (aftertax spendable) income and consumption expenditures.

Because of the importance of the automatic stabilizers in helping to moderate fluctuations in the economy, it is important to separate the budget deficit into a cyclical and a so-called structural component. The cyclical component of the deficit is that portion of the deficit that measures the automatic effect of fluctuations in the economy. The structural component measures the magnitude of the deficit that would be observed if the economy were at full employment. It is important to maintain a clear distinction between the two. If, for example, an automatic widening of the deficit due to a recession were to provoke fiscal measures such as tax increases and/or expenditure reductions, this would further remove purchasing power from the economy and worsen the recession. By the same token, legislation that pre-scribes phased deficit reduction to achieve budgetary balance at some time in the future should target the structural budget deficit so as to permit the stabilizers to continue their beneficial role.

References

Blinder, A. S., and R. N. Solow, "Analytical Foundations of Fiscal Policy," *The Economics of Public Finance,* Brookings, Washington, D.C., 1974; Dernburg, T. F., *Macroeconomics,* 7th ed., McGraw-Hill, New York, 1985, chaps. 5, 18; Lewis, Wilfred, Jr., *Federal Fiscal Policy in the Post-war Recessions,* Brookings, Washington, D.C., 1962; U.S. Committee on the Budget, "Long Range Fiscal Strategy," U.S. Senate, October 1975.

(*See also* Employment and unemployment; Federal budget; Fiscal policy; Debt and deficits)

Thomas F. Dernburg

Automation

While automation has meant different things to different people, it generally has referred to processes designed to mechanize the human cognitive, conceptual, and informational processes. For example, there are automatic control mechanisms, which introduce the closed-loop feedback principle and permit the creation of an automatic remote-controlled, self-contained production system. Feedback is a con-cept of control by which the input of a machine is regulated by the machine's own output, the consequence being that the output meets the conditions of a predeter-mined objective—as in a thermostatically controlled heating system. Process-control machines have found use in oil refineries and chemical plants. In addition, there are transfer machines, commonly called "Detroit automation," which have been employed in the automobile industry. There also are a variety of uses of computer technology in metalworking, such as numerically controlled machine tools and industrial robots, as well as in many other industries.

Automation and Unemployment

Does automation necessarily result in increases in aggregate unemployment? Con-trary to much popular opinion, the answer is no. Changes in aggregate unemploy-ment are governed by the growth in the aggregate demand for goods and services and the growth in the labor force, as well as the growth in output per hour of labor. If the rate of increase of aggregate demand equals the rate of increase of productivity plus the rate of increase of the labor force, there should be no increase in aggregate unem-ployment, regardless of how high the rate of increase of productivity may be.

Consequently, rapid technological change need not result in increased aggregate unemployment, so long as aggregate demand increases at the proper rate. If aggre-gate demand increases too slowly, increases in aggregate unemployment will take place. If aggregate demand increases too rapidly and resources are already fully employed, inflation will result. Unfortunately, there is nothing that ensures that aggregate demand will grow at the right pace—as witnessed by the fact that it grew too slowly in the 1930s and too rapidly during the years of double-digit inflation.

However, monetary and fiscal policies, if properly formulated, should help in this regard.

In the 1950s and 1960s, there was concern that workers and jobs were becoming more mismatched. According to the "structuralists," new methods and equipment were increasing the skill and educational requirements of available jobs, and making it more likely that shortages of highly educated workers would coexist with pools of unemployed unskilled workers. Other economists denied that there was a substantial increase in the amount of structural unemployment—unemployment that exists because the workers available for employment do not possess the qualities that employers with unfilled vacancies require. An important and lively debate took place, both inside and outside the government.

In 1987, a National Academy of Sciences panel concluded as follows:

> *Technological change is an essential component of a dynamic, expanding economy. The modern U.S. economic system, in which international trade plays an increasingly important role, must generate and adopt advanced technologies rapidly, in both the manufacturing and nonmanufacturing sectors, if growth in employment and wages is to be maintained. Recent and prospective levels of technological change will not produce significant increases in total unemployment, although individuals will face painful and costly adjustments. Rather than producing mass unemployment, technological change will make its maximum contribution to higher living standards, wages, and employment levels if appropriate public and private policies are adopted to support the adjustment to new technologies.[1]*

Flexible Manufacturing Systems: A Major Type of Automation

Perhaps the best way to understand modern automation is to look in some detail at flexible manufacturing systems (FMS), widely regarded as among the most important types of automation in the 1990s. According to the U.S. Department of Commerce, flexible manufacturing systems allow "a wide variety of parts [to] be manufactured in random order with few or no people involved, while the system provides monitoring for correction of deviation from design requirements. The FMS concept has provided the ability to respond to product variation in lower volume production runs while remaining in a position to manufacture in a cost-effective and competitive manner."

Flexible manufacturing systems tend to be built around a core of machine tools. Automation of the system occurs through the integration of materials handling and inspection. A numerical or programmable controller controls each work station, and a supervisory control oversees management at the systems level. Central computer control over real-time routing, production scheduling, and load balancing distinguishes flexible manufacturing systems from flexible manufacturing cells.

Most metalworking manufacturing is done in batch production. Flexible manufacturing systems are best suited for firms with mid-volume production of a family of related parts. An important advantage of FMS is flexibility, which enables the firm to respond quickly to frequent changes in product design and production requirements.

---

[1] Permission granted by the editor of *Technology and Unemployment.*

Also, FMS can increase machine utilization and reduce work-in-process inventories. Computer control can help to organize the production system so that the proper amount of output is produced at the right time to meet demand. Fewer machines and less floor space may be required, and direct labor costs may be cut. Also, lead times may be reduced, and product quality may be enhanced by FMS.

How FMS Has Spread

First introduced in 1970, flexible manufacturing systems have gained widespread acceptance. In Japan, the United States, and Western Europe (defined for present purposes as France, Italy, the United Kingdom, and West Germany combined), over 40 percent of the firms with more than 10,000 employees in the automobile, electrical equipment, machinery, and aerospace industries began using such systems by 1987. The percentage using such systems seemed to be substantially higher in Japan than in the United States or Western Europe, and in the aerospace and automobile industries than in the machinery or electrical equipment industries.

Nonetheless, the rate of diffusion of flexible manufacturing systems seems to have been relatively slow. From the date of first use in a particular industry, it has taken about 5 years, on the average, for one-quarter of the major firms in these industries to begin using such systems. Compared with other significant recent industrial innovations, the rate of imitation for flexible manufacturing systems seems low. For example, about half of the major potential users of numerically controlled machine tools had begun using them within 5 years after the date of first use in a particular industry. Even the industrial robot, which has spread more slowly than most innovations for which we have data, seems to have had a higher rate of imitation in many industries than flexible manufacturing systems.

Users of flexible manufacturing systems tend to be much larger firms than nonusers. This was true as well for numerically controlled machine tools, industrial robots, and many other innovations. Large firms would be expected to begin using flexible manufacturing systems more quickly than small firms because they have more resources and are better able to take the risks involved than their smaller rivals. Since a typical flexible manufacturing system costs several million dollars, it is obvious that many small firms are not able to introduce them.

Based on data obtained from a substantial sample of Japanese, American, and Western European users, it appears that flexible manufacturing systems are generally a success. (The percentage of firms reporting FMS was not a success was higher in the automobile industry than in the electrical equipment, machinery, or aerospace industries.) Nonetheless, according to these users, estimated rates of return from their investments in their first flexible manufacturing systems have tended to fall short of anticipations; and although, on the average, these investments seem to have yielded more than the minimum required rate of return, this has not been true for many individual users. However, as so frequently occurs, learning has improved the situation: as firms have learned how to operate these systems more effectively, these estimated rates of return have tended to increase.

Automation in the United States and Japan

The United States has traditionally been the leader in many areas of automation, but it is being challenged on a wide front by other countries, notably Japan. For example, although the industrial robot was largely an American invention, the rate of diffusion of robots was much higher in Japan than in the United States. According to data I gathered, the number of robots used per 10,000 employees in 1985 was about four to eight times as great (depending on the industry) in Japan as in the United States. In considerable part, this observed difference in robot use between Japan and the United States seems to be due to differences in the minimum rate of return required to justify investing in robots. Whereas the Japanese often invested in robots yielding returns of 20 percent, U.S. firms frequently insisted on 30 percent or more.

Data for 1988 for flexible manufacturing systems indicate that it took American firms, on average, almost 3 years—and about 20,000 hours of labor—to develop a flexible manufacturing system. When these figures for system development time and cost are compared with those found by Jaikumar (1986), whose figures pertained to 1984, it appears that between 1984 and 1988 American firms may have been able to reduce their investment in labor and time to develop such a system. However, system development time and labor-hours still seemed to be higher in the United States than in Japan or West Germany. Jaikumar found that the Japanese took about 1.5 years and 6000 hours of labor to develop a system, and unpublished data from a German machine tool builder estimated that West German firms took about 14,000 hours of labor.

Jaikumar and others have charged that "U.S. companies used FMS the wrong way—for high-volume production of a few parts rather than for high-variety production of many parts at low cost per unit." Results for 1988 indicate that U.S. firms produced, on average, about 15 types of parts on an FMS, which is greater than the figure (10) Jaikumar obtained in 1984, but less than the figure (82) that the West German machine tool builder reported for West German firms. Thus, American firms seemed to be increasing the variety of parts produced but were still not producing as wide a variety of parts as their German or Japanese rivals. Moreover, although the annual volume per part (775) was lower than Jaikumar reported, it still was far higher than his estimate (258) for Japanese firms.

However, as one might expect, questions have arisen concerning Jaikumar's charges. Ayres and Ranta (1989) have suggested that "it seems possible that he was inadvertently comparing apples and oranges," since his Japanese sample was heavily weighted toward machine tool production, whereas his U.S. sample was heavily weighted toward high-volume producers of standardized items of heavy equipment. Because of the difficulties in obtaining comparable data in studies of this sort, one must be cautious about interpreting differences as evidence of relative inefficiency.

Effects of Automation on Productivity and Economic Growth

In conclusion, it must be emphasized that automation has had a notable effect on productivity and economic growth in the United States and other countries. Automation has transformed the production of many goods and services and has improved the efficiency of a wide variety of production processes. It has contributed to the increase of output per hour of labor and thus has helped to boost living standards in many parts of the world.

References

Ayres, R., and J. Ranta, "Factors Governing the Evolution and Diffusion of CIM," in J. Ranta (ed.), *Trends and Impacts of Computer Integrated Manufacturing,* IIASA, Laxenburg, 1989; Cyert, R., and D. Mowery (eds.), *Technology and Employment,* National Academy Press, Washington, D.C., 1987; Jaikumar, R., "Postindustrial Manufacturing," *Harvard Business Review,* 1986; Mansfield, Edwin, "Flexible Manufacturing Systems: Economic Effects in Japan, United States, and Western Europe," *Japan and the World Economy* (forthcoming); Mansfield, Edwin, "Industrial Innovation in Japan and the United States," *Science,* September 30, 1988.

(*See also* Computers in economics; Innovation; Productivity; Research and development; Technology)

Edwin Mansfield

Balance of international payments

Compilations of the balance of international payments (or better, of the international transactions) of a country present a systematic account of the monetary values, usually in the country's currency, of goods, services, investment income, gifts, taxes, and pensions and similar payments, and of financial assets and obligations transferred between domestic and foreign residents during a specified time period.

Each of the international transactions of domestic residents, in accordance with the principles of a double-entry accounting system, is deemed to consist of two offsetting transactions of equal size: (1) a credit transaction, usually represented by a +, indicating the receipts of domestic residents for the transfer to foreign residents of goods and services, receipts of investment incomes, gifts, taxes, pensions, and receipts for the transfers to foreign residents of financial assets or obligations; and (2) a debit transaction, usually represented by a –, indicating the payments by domestic residents for the same kinds of items transferred from foreign residents. Thus, if exports of merchandise by country A to country B are paid by checks drawn on country B banks, the compilations of the balance of international transactions for A would show the value of the exports as credits and the equal value for the acquisition of financial assets, in the form of deposits in foreign banks, as debits. Country B would show the value of imports as debits and the increase in deposit liabilities to foreign residents (the equivalent of a loan received from abroad) as a credit. If the exports by country A were paid by a check drawn by the B importers on banks in country A, the debit transaction for A would be a decline in its banking liabilities to foreign residents. In the compilations of the international transactions of country B, the credit part of the transaction would be a reduction of its holdings of foreign assets (deposits in foreign banks).

The balance of international transactions includes not only data on transactions in which the credit and debit components are the result of many unrelated decisions, but also data on transactions in which the credit and debit sides of the transactions are linked. This particularly applies to the inclusion in the compilations of reinvested earnings of majority-owned foreign affiliates. The country of the parent companies would consider these earnings as receipts of income from foreign investments (credits) and as capital outflows through direct investments (debits). The country in which the affiliates are located would consider these earnings as income payments on foreign investments (debits) and as capital inflows through direct investments (credits).

Another type of transaction for which data are included in the compilation of balance of international transactions is official and private aid in kind, which may consist of goods and services transferred to foreign countries. The values of such transfers are based on valuations in commercial markets or on budget expenditures by distributing organizations. The debit transaction is deemed to be the transfer of the gift or aid to a foreign country as if it were in the form of cash (e.g., deposits in a bank of the donor country). The credit transaction is deemed to be the return of that cash from the foreign country as payment for the exports of goods and services.

Compilations of the balance of international transactions are now an integral part of the system of national accounts (SNA) that has been developed under the auspices of several international agencies. Compliance with the principles of these accounts assures not only that data on international transactions are compatible with, and can be used in, the compilations of other parts of national accounts, such as income and output, savings and investments, and the flow of funds, but also that they are comparable with the national accounts of other countries.

In some of the major countries the compilations of the international accounts were started as a continuing statistical program soon after the end of World War I, several years earlier than programs to prepare the domestic production and income accounts were initiated. Reports of the principal international transactions also became mandatory for members of the International Monetary Fund (IMF) soon after the end of World War II.

The adoption of the SNA makes it necessary for some countries to adjust their reports on international transactions. The major item that may require adjustment is capital gains and losses, both those reflected in reinvested earnings and those reflecting actual monetary transfers. Since, in the national accounts, capital gains or losses do not reflect increases or decreases in the value of current production, they are not a component of current incomes on investments. That applies also to income on international investments paid out or received. Capital gains or losses thus have to be treated in the international accounts as capital transactions.

Most countries collect the data on international transactions (with a few exceptions for large and special types of transactions) from surveys or estimates for specific types of transactions, such as merchandise trade, various types of services, investment income, acquisitions, and sales of various types of securities and from reports by banks and other business enterprises on changes in other outstanding claims on, or liabilities to, foreign residents. The totals of all credits and of all debits for reported and estimated transactions usually are not equal. To achieve a balance, the smaller amount of either credits or debits is supplemented by an entry with the same sign, which is designated as a balance on unrecorded transactions, a statistical discrepancy, or errors and omissions.

The size of the statistical discrepancy in the compilation of the international transactions is not necessarily a good indicator of the reliability of the presented data. Data based on records of exchange control authorities may not need significant amounts to balance their reported transactions; but this would not indicate the amount of transactions that escape the exchange control authorities. In general, it is very difficult to associate statistical discrepancies with specific categories of data, but large fluctuations in the discrepancy over short time periods usually are associated with unreported capital movements. In the 1980s and the early 1990s, the compilations of some of the major countries have shown large amounts of unrecorded transactions. This may reflect in part capital transactions that bypassed the channels that were used as sources for statistical data, in part the development of new types of capital transactions that have not been included among those that had to be reported, and in part unreported movements of currency or illicit transactions. The rise in unreported transactions may be reversed again, as statistical reporting systems are broadened and the motivations for international transfers of currencies, and perhaps also for some transactions outside the usual channels, subside.

Purpose of Balance of International Payments Compilations

Compilations of balances of international transactions were made initially to aid in the analysis of pressures on the international exchange rates of a country's currency, and of changes in that country's holdings of internationally accepted media of exchange, particularly gold and certain currencies that were convertible into gold at fixed exchange rates. The maintenance of the stability of the value of a country's currency relative to those internationally accepted media of exchange, and thus to the value of other countries' currencies, was usually the responsibility of the country's central bank.

To facilitate an analysis of developments that contributed to the pressures on the exchange rate of the country and to the changes in the holdings of internationally accepted media of exchange by the central banking authorities, the compilations of the balances of international transactions were divided into two parts: (1) the net acquisitions or net disposals of internationally accepted media of exchange by the central monetary authorities in order to maintain the exchange value of their country's currency and (2) all other international transactions. The balance on international transactions was considered to be positive when credits on these transactions exceeded debits, and acquisitions exceeded disposals of internationally accepted media of exchange.

After the conclusion of World War II, and the establishment of the IMF, the value of the U.S. dollar and the values of gold and of the quotas in the IMF were linked. Consequently, the U.S. dollar became an internationally accepted trading and reserve currency. (In later years, the use of other currencies in these roles was also accepted by some countries.) This meant that central monetary authorities in countries other than the United States held deposits in U.S. banks and other U.S. obligations that could, with a minimum chance for losses in value, be sold for dollar deposits, and changes in their holdings were considered in the compilations of the international transactions of the United States to reflect monetary transactions that were required to settle the excesses of either credits or debits on all other U.S. transactions.

The monetary authorities in countries other than the United States could hold dollar deposits not only in banks in the United States but also in banks located outside the United States, including foreign branches of U.S. banks, banks chartered in countries other than the United States, and even banks domiciled in their own countries.

Generally, the banks outside the United States balanced their dollar liabilities with assets denominated in dollars.

Private banks in foreign countries could hold dollar deposits in U.S. banks as part of their own reserves so long as they were assured that their own central banks could purchase these dollar deposits at prices within very narrow exchange rate ranges when such deposits were offered for sale. Central banks in some foreign countries used dollar deposits as a medium in open-market operations to change the reserves of their private banks and thus to expand or contract the money supply and thereby business activity in their country. These operations did not directly change the aggregate amount of dollar deposits held in countries outside the United States, but it did shift holdings among foreign monetary authorities, banks, and sometimes other foreign organizations.

The measure of monetary transactions—called "official reserve transactions balance"—did not reflect changes in foreign official holdings of dollar assets in the form of deposits in banks outside the United States, including banks located in the same country as the monetary authorities. The counterpart to these deposits were deposits held by these banks (or other foreign residents to whom the dollars may have passed through loans) in U.S. banks. The measure may also have attributed changes in foreign official dollar holdings resulting from foreign internal monetary policy operations to U.S. international transactions.

To avoid potential misinterpretations of the data, the official reserve transactions balance was adjusted in the United States by a broader definition of monetary transactions that included also changes in deposits in domestic banks and in other "liquid liabilities" held by foreign private banks and enterprises. That broader definition of the monetary balance also had the advantage that the statistical balance on the other transactions was not affected by the shifts of dollar assets between central and private banks resulting from operations of the central banks to achieve internal economic policy goals.

This broader definition of the monetary balance did not take into account, however, the rising use of dollar deposits and other liquid dollar assets by foreign financial organizations and business enterprises either as a transaction currency or as a medium for private cash holdings and investments. To some extent, therefore, a rise in foreign holdings of dollar funds thus may have resulted from a rise in the demand for dollar funds and not from dollar purchases by official agencies to compensate for a weakness in the balance on other international transactions of the United States.

After the convertibility of the dollar into gold at a fixed exchange rate was suspended in March 1973, it became virtually impossible to separate the compilations of the international transactions of most countries, but particularly of the United States, into those that could be classified as monetary transactions undertaken to offset imbalances in the other international transactions, and thus to provide a measure of surpluses or deficits in these other transactions. This difficulty was accentuated by the opportunities created by the flexibility in exchange rates for central monetary authorities to pursue domestic economic policy goals by actively intervening in the foreign exchange markets of their currencies rather than limiting such activities to meet imbalances in other international transactions.

The distinction among the international transactions that received increased attention was that between current and capital transactions. Current transactions include the transactions between domestic and foreign residents in goods, services, and earnings on investments. The data on net receipts from these transactions with foreign countries, added to estimates for goods, services, and investment incomes that are absorbed within the domestic economy, provide a measure of total domestic production in the national income and product account (NIPA).

Net receipts from transfers to foreign countries of goods and services and from investment incomes plus net receipts of transfer payments (gifts, taxes, pensions, etc.) from foreign countries compose the balance on all current transactions. That balance equals (with opposite sign) the balance on capital transactions plus the balance on unrecorded transactions. (It is usually assumed that unrecorded transactions are more likely to be capital transactions than current transactions.) The balance on current transactions equals net foreign investment in NIPA and thus is an important component of the measure of total investment by domestic residents.

The capital items in the international transactions account also indicate the domestic funds that have been invested abroad, the foreign funds that have been invested in the domestic economy, and the kinds of investments that were involved. The composition of the data in the capital account may indicate whether such investments are largely influenced by shifts in relative yields or reflect long-term business considerations, including loans and participations in the management of business enterprises through the acquisition of a major part of their equities.

The data that are used in the compilations of the capital account of the international transactions are also used in flow of funds compilations to measure transfers of funds from and to the foreign sector by each of the various domestic economic sectors, and thus facilitate the computation of the balance of net transfers of funds among these domestic sectors.

The procedure used to measure domestic production by adding to domestic expenditures on goods and services the balance on the international transactions in goods, services, and investment incomes is frequently assumed to reflect the economic effects of all international transactions on domestic economic activity.

Specifically, a positive balance on goods, services, and investment incomes is often assumed to increase the purchases of goods and services from domestic producers and thus to expand domestic employment and incomes. This interpretation does not take into account that a rise in the positive balance on these current transactions is associated with a rise in the negative balance on capital transactions. This means that capital outflows have to occur that provide the funds to the foreign countries to pay the net receipts on these current account transactions. If the rise in exports is not financed by the exporting country's central monetary authority, which would expand that country's money supply, the outflow of capital would reduce domestic funds that are available for either consumption or investment. This negative effect on the domestic demand for domestic products would offset the positive effect of the rise in net exports, so that the aggregate direct effect of the international transactions is likely to be very minor.

Similarly, compilations of international transactions that show positive current account balances and negative balances on capital transactions may be evaluated as indications of very healthy economies with rising investments abroad. Vice versa, negative current account balances and positive balances on capital transactions may be viewed as indications of economic weaknesses that cannot be sustained for long. These judgments may not be valid when net capital outflows occur while domestic investments are reduced. The shift in investments from the domestic to foreign economies may reflect conditions that have made investments in the domestic economy relatively less attractive than abroad and may indicate a corresponding lag in the growth of domestic incomes relative to those earned in other countries. It is also possible, however, that net capital inflows reflect the development of favorable investment opportunities in the domestic economy and stimulate even larger domestic investments and increases in the productivity of domestic factors of production. These examples are intended to suggest that an accurate evaluation of the effects of changes in international investments on the economy can be made only on the basis of an analysis of the associated changes in the aggregate domestic savings and investments, and, indeed, the aggregate business activity.

Thus, the compilations of all the international transactions, including the balances of the current as well as the capital account, have to be taken into account when the effects of the international transactions on the domestic economy are analyzed.

References

The Balance of Payments Statistics of the United States, Hearings before the Subcommittee on Economic Statistics of the Joint Economic Committee, 89th Cong., 1st Sess., May 11, June 8, and June 9, 1965; International Monetary Fund, *Balance of Payments Manual,* 4th ed., 1977; International Monetary Fund, *Balance of Payments Statistical Yearbook,* published annually; International Monetary Fund, *Report on the World Current Account Discrepancy,* September 1987; Machlup, Fritz, *International Payments, Debts and Gold,* Scribner's, New York, 1964; "Report of the Review Committee for Balance of Payments Statistics," *The Balance of Payments Statistics of the United States, A Review and Appraisal, 1985;* Statistical Policy Division, Office of Management and the Budget, "Report of the Advisory Committee on the Presentation of Balance of Payments Statistics," *Statistical Reporter,* June 1976; *Survey of Current Business,* quarterly data for U.S. international transactions in March, June, September, and December issues; U.S. Department of Commerce, Bureau of Economic Analysis, *The Balance of Payments of the United States, Concepts, Data Sources, and Estimating Procedures, 1990.*

(*See also* Balance of international trade; Exports; Foreign exchange rates; Imports; International economics, an overview; Mercantilism; Value of the dollar)

Walther Lederer

Balance of international trade

The balance of international trade of a country is the difference between its exports and imports. A narrow definition of exports and imports includes only tangible goods. A broader definition would cover products of factors of production in all forms, such as services related to international transportation and travel, insurance, the planning and supervision of construction projects, management assistance, the work performed by migratory workers, and incomes from royalties and from international investments.

Basis for Trade Statistics

The statistics for trade in tangible goods are usually based on documents filed by exporters and importers with customs officials at the time, or shortly after, the goods move across a country's border. Some countries, including the United States and Canada, which have extensive trade with each other over land borders, are now using the import data of their trade partners in their own export statistics. Since border authorities usually pay more attention to the collection and verification of import than of export documents, this procedure not only improves the trade statistics of both countries, but also reduces administrative costs and inconveniences. The basic documents indicate a classification of the goods (most countries use uniform international coding systems), the values of the goods, and the destination of exports or the country of origin of imports. The trade statistics of most countries show the movements of goods regardless of whether or when payments are received or made. (Some countries whose trade statistics are based on exchange control documents are exceptions.) Payments may be made before or after the goods cross the border; in the case of gifts or government grants, payments are not required. Shipments across the border may, but do not necessarily, coincide with the transfers of ownership.

The value of exports usually includes transportation costs to the border (or alongside sea and air carriers), but not beyond that point, even if transportation is provided by companies of the exporting country. Most countries value their imports c.i.f., that is, the *costs* of the goods and the charges for *insurance* and *freight* to bring these goods to their border or port of entry. This valuation improves the comparability of the total or average values of goods that are imported with those that are produced domestically, but there are many other considerations that have to be taken into account in such comparisons. The United States and several other countries value their imports f.a.s., that is, *free alongside ship* or other carrier, excluding the cost of loading. More rarely the imports are valued f.o.b.—*free on board* the carrier, which includes the cost of loading.

Import data incorporated into the compilations of the balance of international transactions are based on f.a.s. values. International transportation transactions are estimated separately. This procedure is necessary to avoid showing transportation and insurance payments to the country's own companies as a part of the imports. Import data based on f.a.s. valuations are also required when exports and imports of different countries are compared.

Export and import statistics usually reflect the values indicated in the invoices. There can be exceptions, however, when the valuations of imports are adjusted to conform with customs regulations affecting the computation of import duties. This applies particularly to goods that are believed to be valued below costs of production and may affect shipments from affiliated companies, goods produced abroad by government-owned and -operated enterprises, and goods whose exports are promoted through government subsidies.

The geographic breakdown of the export and import data is subject to problems that affect the trade balances with individual countries more than the trade balance with the total of all foreign countries. Particularly in the case of standardized commodities, shipped in bulk, the export documents indicate only the immediate destinations, which are not necessarily the countries where the goods are finally used. Import documents usually show the country of origin, which is the country from which the goods are shipped. When goods are imported from a country where they were assembled from components produced elsewhere, the import statistics are likely to attribute the entire value of such imports to the country where the goods were assembled. In the United States, statistics of international merchandise trade are assembled and published monthly by the Bureau of the Census. These figures are adjusted, mainly for coverage, for use in the compilations of the accounts covering all international transactions, published quarterly by the Bureau of Economic Analysis, U.S. Department of Commerce. Transactions by U.S. defense agencies and their personnel, which include transfers of goods as well as services, are shown separately in these accounts.

A Broader Concept of Trade

The broader concept of the balance of trade, except for minor adjustments, is used in the computation of gross national product (GNP). Exports are considered purchases by foreign residents which are added to purchases of domestic residents, and imports are deducted to obtain the total output of the economy.

The balance of trade, even with its broader coverage, does not adequately indicate its impact on the domestic economy. Imports of certain commodities are required in domestic production, while some of the exports may reduce domestic purchases. Furthermore, the trade balance does not reflect flows of monetary funds because to a large extent such flows are reversed through capital transactions, which affect domestic investments and consumption expenditures.

The balance of trade in goods and services is used sometimes to evaluate the competitive position of a country in international business and to indicate the strength of its balance of payments in general. A rise in imports relative to exports may reflect, however, a country's ability to attract foreign capital and the need for resources required by the rise in its domestic investments. Only when a country has to borrow abroad, or use its international reserves to finance its net imports of goods and services (and when these conditions are not due to temporary or reversible developments), so that the increase in its foreign debt is not associated with at least an equal increase in its domestic productive assets, can the net imports of goods and services be interpreted as a sign of an economic weakness, and as an indication that adjustments are required in its economy and/or in the exchange rate of its currency.

References

Commodity Trade Statistics, Statistical Office of the United Nations, New York (provides data on the distribution of exports and imports by commodity categories for as many countries as possible); International Monetary Fund, *Direction of Trade,* Washington, D.C., published monthly (provides data for exports of all countries and imports of partner countries); International Monetary Fund, *International Financial Statistics,* Washington, D.C., published monthly (provides data on total exports and imports of merchandise and of goods and services for as many countries as possible); Organization for Economic Cooperation and Development, *Trade by Commodities,* Series B, Paris; U.S. Bureau of the Census, *Highlights of U.S. Export and Import Trade,* U.S. Department of Commerce (provides data on U.S. exports and imports of merchandise, by country and by major commodity groups).

(*See also* Balance of international payments; Exports; Foreign exchange rates; Imports; International economics, an overview; Mercantilism; Value of the dollar)

Walther Lederer

Balance of international settlements (*see* Balance of international payments)

Banking school

The banking school was a group of influential British economists who opposed the rival currency school in the celebrated mid-nineteenth-century bank charter debate over the regulation of the bank note issue. Led by Thomas Tooke, John Fullarton,

James Wilson, and J. B. Gilbart, the banking school disapproved of all forms of monetary regulation except the requirement that banks convert notes into coin upon demand. In particular, the banking school rejected the currency school's plan for a 100 percent gold reserve requirement for notes, a plan embodied in the Bank Charter Act of 1844. Unlike the currency school, which feared that inflationary monetary overexpansion would occur unless convertible banknotes were backed 1 for 1 with gold, the banking school argued that the volume of convertible notes is automatically regulated by the needs of trade and, therefore, requires no further limitation. This conclusion stemmed directly from the real bills doctrine and the law of reflux, which together posited guaranteed safeguards to overissue, obviating the need for monetary control.

The real bills doctrine states that the stock of money can never be excessive as long as notes are issued on loans made to finance real transactions in goods and services. Similarly, the law of reflux asserts that overissue is impossible because any excess notes will be returned immediately to the banks for conversion into coin or for repayment of loans. Both doctrines embody the notions of a passive, demand-determined money supply and of reverse causality running from prices to money rather than vice versa as in the quantity theory. According to the reverse causality hypothesis, changes in the level of prices and economic activity induce corresponding shifts in the demand for bank loans which the banks accommodate via variations in the note issue. In this manner prices determine the money stock, the expansion of which is the result, not the cause, of price inflation. As for the price level itself, the banking school attributed its determination to factor costs (wages, interest, rents, etc.), thus establishing the essentials of a cost-push theory of inflation.

Nonmonetarist Ideas

The concepts of cost inflation, reverse causality, and passive money are the hallmarks of an extreme nonmonetarist view of the monetary mechanism to which the banking school adhered. Its list of nonmonetarist ideas included the propositions (1) that international gold movements are absorbed by idle balances and have no effect on the volume of money in circulation, (2) that an efflux of specie stems from real shocks to the balance of payments and not from domestic price inflation, (3) that changes in the stock of money tend to be offset by compensating changes in the stock of money substitutes, leaving the total circulation unaltered, and (4) that discretion is preferable to rules in the conduct of monetary policy.

In its critique of the monetarist doctrines of the currency school, which contended that monetary overexpansion is the sole or primary cause of domestic inflation and external specie drains, the banking school argued as follows. First, overissue is impossible since the stock of notes is determined by the needs of trade and cannot exceed demand; therefore, no excess supply of money exists to bid up prices. Second, in any case, causation runs from prices to money rather than vice versa. Third, specie drains stem from real rather than monetary disturbances to the balance of payments and occur independently of domestic price-level movements.

These arguments severed all but one of the links in the currency school's monetary transmission mechanism running from money to prices to gold flows and back again to money. The final link was broken when the banking school asserted that gold flows come from idle hoards and cannot affect the volume of money in circulation. To ensure that these hoards would be sufficient to accommodate gold drains, the banking school recommended that the Bank of England hold larger metallic reserves. As for the currency school's claim that the entire stock of money and money substitutes can be controlled through the bank note base, the banking school flatly rejected it. The banking school asserted the impossibility of controlling the monetary circulation via the note component alone since limitation of notes would simply induce the public to use money substitutes (i.e., checking deposits and bills of exchange) instead. More generally, the banking school questioned the efficacy of attempts to control the stock of money in a financial system that can produce an endless variety of money substitutes. With regard to the currency school's prescription that discretionary policy be replaced by a fixed rule, the banking school rejected it on the grounds that rigid rules would prevent the banking system from responding to the needs of trade and would hamper the central bank's power to deal with financial crises.

In retrospect, the banking school rightly stressed the importance of checking deposits as a medium of exchange. But it was wrong in believing that the real bills doctrine, which tied note issues to loans made for productive purposes, would prevent inflationary money growth. Henry Thornton in 1802 exposed this flaw when he pointed out that rising prices would require an ever-growing volume of loans just to finance the same level of real output. In this way inflation would justify the monetary expansion necessary to sustain it and the real bills criterion would not limit the quantity of money in existence. Furthermore, Thornton, and later Knut Wicksell, convincingly demonstrated that an insatiable demand for loans results when the loan rate of interest is below the expected rate of profit on capital. In such cases the real bills criterion provides no bar to overissue.

Radcliffe Report

Today the term "banking school" is closely associated with the British *Radcliffe Report* (1959). Indeed, the principal ideas of the banking school, i.e., the notions (1) of a passive, demand-determined money supply, (2) of reverse causation running from economic activity to money, (3) of cost-push inflation, (4) of new money entering idle balances rather than active circulation, (5) of a large and variable volume of money substitutes, (6) of a high degree of substitutability between money and near moneys, (7) of the futility of attempts to control the total stock of money and money substitutes (liquidity) via control of a narrowly defined monetary base, (8) of nonmonetary as opposed to monetary causes of trade balance disequilibrium, and (9) of the desirability of discretion over rules in the conduct of monetary policy, all have exact counterparts in the *Radcliffe Report*.

References

Committee on the Working of the Monetary System, *A Report to the Radcliffe Committee,* HMSO, London, 1959; Humphrey, T., "Rival Notions of Money," *Economic Review,* Federal Reserve Bank of Richmond, no. 75, September/October 1988, pp. 3–9; Robbins, L., *Robert Torrens and the Evolution of Classical Economics,* Macmillan, London, 1958, chap. 5; Viner, J., *Studies in the Theory of International Trade,* Kelley, New York, 1965, chap. 5.

(*See also* Currency school)

Thomas M. Humphrey

Banking system

A banking system is an integrated network of commercial banks legally empowered to hold demand and time deposits from any person or organization and to lend for any purpose in any area of the world not specifically prohibited by law. A banking system, as contrasted with a system of financial institutions, consists of commercial banks chartered by either (1) a state or (2) the federal government through the Office of Comptroller of the Currency (a division of the U.S. Treasury Department). Not all institutions with the word "bank" in their name are commercial banks. In certain areas of the country there are many savings banks which are more akin to savings and loan associations than to commercial banks. Commercial banks have the broadest powers for accepting deposits and making loans of any financial institutions.

System Functions

Commercial banks perform three major functions: (1) lending money, (2) holding demand and time deposits, and (3) facilitating the transfer of funds by performing a variety of other activities. All three functions involve close cooperation among banks. For example, individual banks often receive loan requests from commercial firms larger than the bank would prudently accept. Each bank wants to diversify its portfolio of loans widely to reduce risk, and it therefore avoids making very large loans to any one person or organization. Laws and regulations also govern maximum loan sizes and the stated purpose for which loans may be made. To provide the funds needed to a large creditworthy customer, a bank wishing to make a very large loan to a single firm will seek cooperation from other banks, each of which will own a portion of the loaned amount. In the event a customer cannot repay a loan, no single bank is exposed to a disastrously large loss.

Another example of bank cooperation has to do with finance of international trade. If, for example, a firm in Springfield, Illinois, wishes to import goods from abroad, it can go to its local bank for financial assistance. The Springfield firm does not know the character of the selling firm, and the selling firm does not know the buying firm. The purchaser is unwilling to pay before the goods are loaded on a ship or airplane, and the seller is unwilling to load on a transportation vehicle without being paid. The Springfield bank does not have facilities for financing and expediting international trade, but it does have a correspondent relationship with a larger bank that regularly does such business. Through that correspondent bank, the Springfield bank can provide as good international service as that received by the largest firms in the country.

The same correspondent network is useful to banks in another way. Smaller banks in rural areas often have a period of the year when they have more funds on deposit than they can prudently lend in their own community, but those small banks know that within a few months at most, they will have large demands for loans, so they cannot put the surplus funds into permanent investments. Small banks regularly send excess funds to their correspondent banks because the larger banks have a wider variety of short-term loan opportunities than do small banks. The large correspondent bank borrows the excess funds, say, $5 million, usually on an overnight basis, and will either lend the funds somewhere else, invest the funds overnight, or use the funds itself as reserves. As bankers work together in such arrangements, they come to know in advance which banks will have surplus funds at particular times of the year and which banks will need to borrow at given seasons of the year, so they can plan their funds utilization effectively.

The banking system also performs essential functions for the clearing of checks: the presentation of checks to the institution on which they were drawn for payment. When a bank in Spokane, Washington, receives a check from a depositor on a bank in Atlanta, Georgia, the check must travel to Atlanta to be presented for credit to the Spokane bank. The more rapidly the Spokane bank can get the check to Atlanta, the sooner it receives its money. There are two ways to proceed: (1) the Spokane bank can arrange to have the check sent to Atlanta, or (2) the Spokane bank can give the check to the Federal Reserve System for transportation to Atlanta. The sending bank will choose the quickest and least expensive route. If the bank elects not to send the check via the Federal Reserve System, it will send the check to one of its correspondents, probably in Seattle. That bank will receive checks from banks all over the Pacific Northwest, and it may operate a check-clearing operation for its correspondent banks. The checks might be sent as cargo in commercial passenger airliners or in private aircraft hired by the bank, or the Seattle bank may use the services of yet another correspondent bank.

Competition

In the past 15 years, individual banks have encountered tremendous competition for deposits from savings and loan associations, savings banks, and money-market mutual funds, among others. Foreign banks, pension funds, insurance companies, and other entities have provided competition to individual banks in the market for loans. Among lending institutions, however, only commercial banks have a close-knit relationship among themselves constituting a system. Indeed, the commercial banks often form a vital link to the broader financial system for some of their most important competitors. Pension funds purchasing U.S. government securities, for example, pay in immediately available funds (federal funds), available from commercial banks.

Foreign banks have their own networks of interrelationships among one another, and they pose the greatest competitive challenge to the commercial banking system outside the United States. Within the United States, foreign banks use the U.S. banking system. In the past 15 years, a number of foreign banks have grown larger than the largest U.S. banks, and individually and collectively, they seriously challenge U.S. commercial banks.

Regulation

Because financial institutions have a fiduciary relationship to their depositors, they have long been regulated. For example, persons seeking a bank charter must be free of criminal records and be otherwise suited to the position of responsibility required of bank directors and officers. Many of the regulations on commercial banks stemmed from the Great Depression of the 1930s, when many banks failed, causing great hardship to depositors. Today, most banks are part of the deposit insurance protection system provided by the Federal Deposit Insurance Corporation, but many banks have failed, imperiling the deposit insurance fund. There are many reasons for those failures, but one thing seems clear: regulation was inadequate to prevent a large number of failures. The result has been that a rather substantial group of scholars have called for substantial relaxation of current bank regulations, while others suggest the need for greater or more detailed regulation.

While the operations of individual banks are subject to many regulations and restrictions, the scope of activities that banks may engage in with one another has not been heavily regulated. The large flows of deposits from smaller banks to larger correspondents are not subject to heavy regulation, nor are many of the other interbank financial relationships.

References

Kidwell, David S., and David L. Peterson, *Financial Institutions, Markets, and Money,* 4th ed., Dryden Press, Hinsdale, Ill., 1990; Rose, Peter S., and Donald R. Fraser, *Financial Institutions,* 3d ed., Irwin, Homewood, Ill., 1988.

(*See also* Commercial bank problems and solutions; Deposits; Federal Reserve System; Financial institutions; Money supply)

William J. Brown

Barriers to trade

Barriers to trade are national government policies or actions that interfere with free-market buying and selling of goods and services internationally. Free trade, and its welfare benefits, is sacrificed in some fashion and to varying degree by such barriers. Consequently they are often the focus of international trade controversies and negotiations.

International trade talks under the General Agreement on Tariffs and Trade (GATT) have vastly reduced the most common form of trade barrier, namely, tariffs. However, many other types of barriers continue to exist, if not thrive. These others, called "non-tariff barriers" (NTBs), include quotas, export subsidies, antidumping duties, international cartels, voluntary export restraints, economic intergration, and certain national laws and regulations discriminating against foreign imports from one or more countries. With the exception of a few industries where tariffs remain high in industrialized countries—textiles, apparel, footwear, and agricultural products—NTBs now present the primary threat to open world markets and efficiency gains from trade. More recent rounds of GATT, including the ongoing Uruguay Round, have therefore focused on NTBs rather than tariffs.

An overwhelming conclusion in the economics of international trade is that free trade yields the greatest welfare gains to all participating nations. Only then are national and worldwide resources allocated to their most productive uses and is output maximized. As an example of how a barrier to trade can deny this outcome and lead to inefficient uses of resources, Figure 1 shows a nation's supply and demand curve for a particular product, and the consequent welfare effect of a fixed tariff on this product, in the circumstance where foreign prices are initially lower than domestic prices. If all foreign imports were excluded, the domestic equilibrium price would be $Pd,$ that is, the intersection of the supply and demand curves. By contrast, if the nation was completely open to trade, and the foreign price was $Pf,$ then the domestic market would produce Qd and import M quantities of the good.

Now suppose a fixed tariff, $t,$ is imposed on each unit imported, making the imported price $Pf + t.$ When import prices rise to $Pf + t,$ the quantity of imports would fall to $M2,$ domestic production would rise to $Qd2,$ and government revenues would rise by the amount of tariff t times the amount imported, $M2.$ While producer welfare increases by area A and government revenues increase by area $C,$ consumer welfare

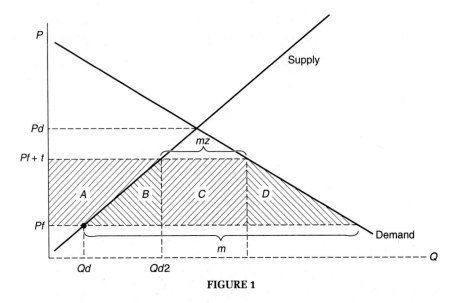

FIGURE 1

declines by areas $A + B + C + D$, leaving a "net" welfare *loss* of $B + D$ to the economy overall. The sources of this net loss are the higher prices consumers must now pay for the good as well as greater production now occurring domestically by the less efficient producers. A similar, though not identical, analysis accompanies all NTBs, for similar reasons, although the specifics and magnitude of impact vary depending on the type of instrument employed and specific market conditions in existence.

If a nation's welfare is diminished by trade barriers, why do nations adopt them as part of their foreign trade policy? The answer in early times was (1) nations had isolationist views of the world, and thereby sought to support and protect domestic production, the essential ingredient to independent survival, and (2) young nations and governments needed tax revenues (tariffs) to support their consolidation efforts and national existence. More recently, the reasons expand to include (1) a response to political hostilities during wars, (2) protection of an "infant industry" until it takes off, and (3) political logrolling between politicians to protect different industries whose economic interests they represent. While the reasons and policy options have broadened over time, they are, for the most part, no more justified from the standpoint of economic welfare than those of earlier times.

References

Baldwin, Robert E., "The Changing Nature of U.S. Trade Policy since World War II," in R. E. Baldwin and J. D. Richardson (eds.), *International Trade and Finance: Readings,* 3d ed., Scott, Foresman, Glenview, Ill., 1986, chap. 11; Husted, Steven, and Michael Melvin, *International Economics,* Harper & Row, New York, 1990; Salvatore, Dominick, *International Economics,* 3d ed., Macmillan, New York, 1990.

(*See also* Comparative advantage theory; Competition; General Agreement on Tariffs and Trade; International economics, an overview; Protectionism)

Anita M. Benvignati

Bayesian inference

Bayesian inference is a collection of concepts, principles, and procedures designed to assist scientific investigators in learning from their data. Such learning is conceived of as changes in beliefs induced by new data. In particular, new data may change beliefs about the adequacy of particular hypotheses or models, about the probable values of parameters, and about the values of as yet unconfirmed observations; that is, new data may help in dealing with the problems of confirming hypotheses or models, estimation, and prediction, respectively. In addition, Bayesian inference techniques are useful in designing surveys and experiments, control problems, and other decision problems. These inference and decision problems are solved in a systematic and unified fashion in the Bayesian approach for which axiomatic support has been provided in the works of Burks (1977), de Finetti (1972), DeGroot (1970), Jeffreys (1957, 1967), Raiffa and Schlaifer (1961), Savage (1954), and others.

Use of Numerical Probabilities

In most forms of Bayesian inference, numerical probabilities are employed to represent degrees of belief. For example, the degree of belief that a particular hypothesis accounts for the variation in a given set of data is assumed measurable by a numerical probability in much the same fashion that one states that the probability that it will rain tomorrow in a particular area is 0.75. Similarly, it is assumed that a degree of belief that a parameter's value lies between, say, 0.7 and 1.0 can be represented by a numerical probability in the interval 0 to 1, where 0 and 1 represent complete certainty and intermediate values represent various degrees of uncertainty. While the assumption that degrees of belief can be represented by cardinal probabilities is a strong one, and some have sought to relax it, its use does permit use of the standard inductive calculus to measure changes in degrees of belief, that is, learning in a logically consistent way for statistical problems encountered in quantitative economics.

Bayes' Theorem

Central in Bayesian inference is Bayes' theorem, a noncontroversial theorem from the probability calculus. Let $p(y, \theta \mid I_0)$ be the joint probability density function (PDF) for an observation vector y and a parameter vector θ, both considered random, given prior or initial information, denoted by I_0. The joint PDF can be expressed in terms of its marginal and conditional PDFs to obtain Bayes' theorem:

$$p(y, \theta \mid I_0) = p(\theta \mid I_0)p(y \mid \theta, I_0)$$
$$= p(y \mid I_0)p(\theta \mid y, I_0) \tag{1}$$

or

$$p(\theta \mid D) = p(\theta \mid I_0)p(y \mid \theta, I_0)/p(y \mid I_0) \tag{2a}$$

where $D = (y, I_0)$, the given sample and prior information. Equation (2a) is often expressed as

$$p(\theta \mid D) \propto p(\theta \mid I_0)p(y \mid \theta, I_0) \tag{2b}$$

where $\propto$ denotes proportionality and the proportionality constant is the reciprocal of

$$p(y \mid I_0) = \int_{R_\theta} p(\theta \mid I_0)p(y \mid \theta, I_0) \, d\theta$$

In (2b), $p(\theta \mid D)$ is the posterior PDF for θ, $p(\theta \mid I_0)$ is the prior or initial PDF for θ, and $p(y \mid \theta, I_0)$ is the likelihood function. Thus, (2b) states Bayes' theorem as

$$\text{Posterior PDF} \propto \text{prior PDF} \times \text{likelihood function} \tag{2c}$$

Our initial beliefs regarding the parameters' values are represented by $p(\theta \mid I_0)$, the prior PDF. By use of (2), the information in the data, incorporated in the likelihood function $p(y \mid \theta, I_0)$, is combined with the information in the prior PDF to yield the posterior PDF, $p(\theta \mid y; I_0)$, which generally differs from the prior PDF. This difference is the change in beliefs regarding values of the parameters induced by the information in the data y. Applications of Bayes' theorem in analyses of many models encountered in economics and statistics are provided in Box and Tiao (1973), DeGroot (1970), Fienberg and Zellner (1975), Jeffreys (1967), Leamer (1978), and Zellner (1971).

Application of Bayes' Theorem

To use Bayes' theorem it is necessary to introduce and formulate a prior PDF, $p(\theta \mid I_0)$, to represent initial beliefs. When there is little prior or initial information about parameters' values, that is, when initial information is vague or diffuse, a prior PDF that represents "knowing little," or ignorance, is employed. Such prior PDFs have been employed in analyses of many problems. Their use has enabled Bayesian analysts to produce many estimation results that are technically similar to those provided by non-Bayesian methods but that have a completely different interpretation. On the other hand, if some initial information about parameters' values is available from past studies and/or subject-matter considerations, a prior PDF can be formulated to represent it and employed in Bayes' theorem.

Thus, prior or initial information is formally introduced by use of a prior PDF, a distinctive feature of Bayesian inference. In applied non-Bayesian analyses of data, prior information is extensively employed but usually in an informal manner. Attempts to obtain posterior PDFs without introducing prior PDFs, as in R. A. Fisher's fiducial inference, have not been successful. By use of a prior PDF, it becomes possible to represent and use all information, including prior and sample information, in a logically consistent fashion, a major objective of Bayesian inference. Much controversy has centered on the extent to which prior PDFs adequately represent initial prior information and on the kinds of prior information which should be introduced. If the prior information and the information embodied in the form of the likelihood function taken together are considered to be a hypothesis or model, it is possible to use data, as will be shown, to compute posterior probabilities associated with such models. These posterior probabilities reflect the degree to which the data support or fail to support alternative models.

The posterior PDF, $p(\theta \mid D)$, in (2) can be employed to make posterior probability statements. For example, one can compute the probability that θ lies in a particular region, $P_r(\theta \subset R \mid y, I_0)$ by integrating the posterior PDF over R. Also, if θ is partitioned, $\theta' = (\theta_1', \theta_2')$, the marginal posterior PDF for θ is

$$
\begin{aligned}
p(\theta_1 \mid D) &= \int_{R_{\theta_2}} p(\theta_1, \theta_2 \mid D)\, d\theta_2 \\
&= \int_{R_{\theta_2}} p(\theta_1 \mid \theta_2, D) p(\theta_2 \mid D)\, d\theta_2
\end{aligned}
\tag{3}
$$

where $D \equiv (y, I_0)$ and R_{θ_2} is the region for θ_2. The second integral in (3) shows that the integration with respect to θ_2 can be interpreted as an averaging of the conditional posterior PDF for θ_1 given θ_2 with $p(\theta_2 | D)$, the marginal posterior PDF for θ_2 serving as the weighting function. The integration in (3) is a convenient way of removing nuisance parameters, that is, parameters that are not of special interest to an investigator.

With regard to point estimation, a measure of central tendency, for example, the modal value or mean of the posterior PDF, $p(\theta | D)$, can be employed. If a convex loss function $L(\theta,\hat{\theta})$, where $\hat{\theta} = \hat{\theta}(D)$, is available, the Bayesian point estimate is the value of $\hat{\theta}$ which minimizes expected loss, that is, the solution to the following problem:

$$\min_{\hat{\theta}} EL(\theta,\hat{\theta}) = \min_{\hat{\theta}} \int_{R_\theta} L(\theta,\hat{\theta})p(\theta | D) \, d\theta \tag{4}$$

The solution to (4), $\hat{\theta}^*$, is the Bayesian estimate for θ. It is known that $\hat{\theta}^*$ viewed as an estimator is consistent. Also, when average risk

$$\int_{R_\theta} r(\theta)p(\theta | I_0) \, d\theta$$

where

$$r(\theta) = \int_{R_y} L(\theta,\hat{\theta}^*)p(y | \theta) \, dy$$

is finite, Bayesian estimators are admissible and minimize average risk. For quadratic loss functions, θ^* is the posterior mean vector. In large samples, under general conditions $p(\theta | D)$ approaches a normal form with mean equal to the maximum likelihood estimate and variance-covariance matrix equal to the inverse of the estimated Fisher information matrix.

With respect to prediction, Bayesians employ the predictive PDF to make probability statements about as yet unobserved values of variables and to calculate prediction intervals and point predictions. The predictive PDF, for y_f, a vector of as yet unobserved values of a variable, is given by

$$p(y_f | D) = \int_{R_\theta} p(y_f | \theta)p(\theta | D) \, d\theta \tag{5}$$

where $p(y_f | \theta)$ is the PDF for y_f given θ, and $p(\theta | D)$ is the posterior PDF for θ given by (2). The predictive PDF in (5) can be viewed as an average of the conditional PDF, $p(y_f | \theta)$, with the posterior PDF for θ, $p(\theta | D)$, serving as the weighting function. Probability statements regarding y_f or particular elements of y_f can be made using the predictive PDF in (5). Also, if a convex loss function $L(y_f, \hat{y}_f)$, where $\hat{y}_f = \hat{y}_f(D)$ is a point prediction, is available, a Bayesian point prediction is obtained by solving the following problem:

$$\min_{\hat{y}_f} EL(y_f, \hat{y}_f) = \min_{\hat{y}_f} \int_{R_{y,f}} L(y_f \hat{y}_f)p(y_f | D) \, dy_f \tag{6}$$

The solution to the problem in (6), $\hat{y}_f^*$, is the Bayesian point prediction, which has similar desirable properties as Bayesian parameter estimates or estimators. In the special case that $L(y_f, \hat{y}_f)$ is a quadratic loss function, it is easily shown that the mean of the predictive PDF is the Bayesian point prediction.

In connection with comparing and testing hypotheses, Bayes' theorem is employed to model the transformation of prior or initial probabilities associated with alternative hypotheses. If H_1 and H_2 are two mutually exclusive hypotheses with prior or initial probabilities π_1 and π_2, respectively, application of Bayes' theorem yields

$$K = \frac{\pi_1}{\pi_2} \frac{p_1(y | D_1)}{p_2(y | D_2)} \tag{7}$$

where K is the posterior odds ratio, π_1/π_2 is the prior odds ratio, y is a vector of observations, and

$$p_i(y \mid D_i) = \int_{R_{\theta,i}} p_i(y \mid \theta_i, H_i) p(\theta_i \mid H_i, I_0)\, d\theta_i, \qquad i = 1,2$$

is the averaged likelihood function with the prior PDF, $p(\theta_i \mid H_i, I_0)$, serving as the weighting function. The ratio $p_i(y \mid D_i)/p_2(y \mid D_2)$ is called the Bayes factor. In the case of two simple hypotheses $\theta_1 = \theta_2^0$ and $\theta_2 = \theta_2^0$, where θ_1^0 and θ_2^0 are given values, the Bayes factor is exactly equal to the likelihood ratio. As (7) indicates, the prior odds ratio π_1/π_2 is modified by the Bayes factor, which reflects the impact of sample and prior information to yield the posterior odds ratio K. If, for example, $\pi_1/\pi_2 = 1$, a value of $K = 3$ would indicate increased support for H_1 relative to H_2. If H_1 and H_2 are mutually exclusive and exhaustive (as would be the case if H_2 is the negation of H_1), $K = P_1/(1 - P_1)$, where P is the posterior probability associated with H_2 and $1 - P_1$ is the posterior probability associated with H_2. The posterior probabilities P_1 and $1 - P_1$ can be employed to choose between hypotheses H_1 and H_2 if losses associated with incorrect decisions are available.

Bayesian concepts, principles, and procedures have been applied to many statistical problems in a variety of areas. (See, e.g., Poirier, 1991.) Current research is directed toward formulating broader ranges of prior PDFs and developing computational techniques for using them. Further study is being done on analyses of random-parameter models, time series models, posterior odds ratios for hypotheses relating to parameters of multivariate models, computational problems, and applications.

References

Box, G. E. P., and G. C. Tiao, *Bayesian Inference in Statistical Analyses,* Addison-Wesley, Reading, Mass., 1973; Burks, A. W., *Chance, Cause and Reason: An Inquiry into the Nature of Scientific Evidence,* University of Chicago Press, Chicago, 1977; de Finetti, B., *Probability, Induction and Statistics: The Art of Guessing,* Wiley, New York, 1972; DeGroot, M. H., *Optimal Statistical Decisions,* McGraw-Hill, New York, 1970; Fienberg, S. E., and A. Zellner (eds.), *Studies in Bayesian Econometrics and Statistics in Honor of Leonard J. Savage,* North-Holland, Amsterdam, 1975; Jeffreys, H., *Scientific Inference,* 2d ed., Cambridge University Press, Cambridge, 1975; Jeffreys, H., *Theory of Probability,* 3d ed., Oxford University Press, London, 1967; Leamer, E. E., *Specification Searches: Ad Hoc Inference with Nonexperimental Data,* Wiley, New York, 1978; Poirier, D. J. (ed.), "A Report from the Battlefront," *Journal of Business and Economic Statistics,* January 1989, pp. 137–139; Poirier, J. (ed.), "Bayes' Empirical Studies in Economics and Finance," *Journal of Econometrics, Annuals,* vol. 49, 1991, pp. 1–304; Raiffa, H., and R. Schlaifer, *Applied Statistical Decision Theory,* Graduate School of Business Administration, Harvard University, Boston, 1961; Savage, L. J., *The Foundations of Statistics,* Wiley, New York, 1954; Zellner, A., *An Introduction to Bayesian Inference in Econometrics,* Wiley, New York, 1971.

(*See also* Economic forecasting methods; Statistical methods in economics and business, an overview; Time series analysis)

Arnold Zellner

Bond

A bond is a debt instrument, which represents a financial claim that the holder (creditor) has against the issuer (debtor). It is a written promise to pay a certain sum of money (principal) at a definite date in the future or periodically over the course of the loan. In most cases the issuer promises to pay the holder fixed money amounts (interest) on specified dates while the bond is outstanding.

History

Who issued the first bonds and when that occurred is uncertain. The best evidence suggests that the Republic of Venice floated the first issue (called *prestiti*) in the late twelfth century. But debt as a means of finance predates that event by at least four millennia. Records of contracts describing interest-bearing loans date back to the Sumerian civilization—around 3500 B.C. Hammurabi's Code, compiled about 1800 B.C., indicates that mortgages and promissory notes were used to facilitate commerce at that time. But these instruments, and those that Greek, Roman, and medieval money lenders and merchant bankers used, were not bonds. They all involved one creditor lending money to one debtor, while a bond issue implies the existence of many creditors, that is, hundreds or today even thousands of bondholders who have lent money to the issuer.

Although Venice floated the first issue nearly eight centuries ago, bonds became a popular debt instrument much more recently. In the eighteenth and nineteenth centuries, nation-states developed and many issued bonds to finance their operations—in many cases associated with military endeavors. And the nineteenth century saw the rapid development of the corporate form of business organization, many of which used bonds to finance their growth. Consequently, today virtually all industrial nations, many publicly held corporations, and, in the United States, most state and local governments have issued bonds.

Federal Debt Obligations

The U.S. government issues several kinds of debt obligations, which are classified as marketable or nonmarketable. At the end of 1990 about 65 percent of the nearly $3.4 trillion of Treasury securities outstanding were marketable. The remaining obligations were issued directly to individuals, U.S. government agencies, and foreign, state, and local governments. For example, U.S. government agencies held nearly $830 billion of nonmarketable Treasury securities, while individuals held roughly $125 billion of series EE and HH U.S. savings bonds.

Of the marketable Treasury securities outstanding at the end of 1990, bonds accounted for nearly 18 percent and notes for more than 57 percent. (Treasury bills made up the remaining one-quarter. Even though they represent a debt obligation of the federal government, they are not classified as bonds because they are short-term, maturing in 1 year or less.) Treasury notes and bonds are virtually the same, except for the length of time from date of issue to maturity: notes mature between 1 and 10 years, while bonds usually mature in more than 10 years.

State and Local Government Debt Obligations

State and local governments, as well as other political subdivisions, such as school districts, water authorities, and so on, issue debt obligations to finance capital investment projects in most cases. The data show that they have borrowed extensively. In 1902, local government debt outstanding totaled under $2 billion and state government debt was about $230 million. By the end of 1990, state and local government obligations outstanding had soared to more than $840 billion. Most of this increase in state and local government debt outstanding has occurred since World War II, when the population boom, the movement to the suburbs, and other factors compelled states and municipalities to finance schools, highways, water and sewerage systems, and so forth.

State and local government bonds, which are exempt from federal income taxes, fall into one of two categories: general or limited obligation bonds. The former rest on the "full faith and credit" of the issuer for payment of interest and repayment of principal, which simply means the issuing government's power to tax. The latter, frequently called revenue bonds, depend on revenues gained from whatever asset—e.g., a bridge, tunnel or turnpike—they financed for payment of interest and repayment of principal. Other things being equal, the risk of default is obviously greater for limited obligation bonds.

Corporate Bonds

Corporations, the third major issuer of bonds in the United States, have relied heavily on debt for expansion since World War II, because it is a less expensive method of raising funds than equity financing. The chief reason is that interest payments are tax deductible, while dividend payments are not, making the effective cost of debt capital lower than the cost of equity capital. During the 1980s, the tax advantages of debt, the economic expansion, and the explosion in the issuance of "junk bonds" (those with ratings below BBB) led to a total of approximately $975 billion of corporate bonds outstanding at the end of 1990—more than double the level at the beginning of the decade.

Corporate bonds can be classified as secured (mortgage bonds) or unsecured (debentures). In the former case, the corporation executes either a mortgage pledging specific assets as security or a blanket mortgage, which established a lien as security against all the real property owned by the corporation. In the latter case, although specific assets are not pledged, debentures are secured by all the corporation's unpledged assets and the holder is in the same position as any other general creditor. In both cases, the real safety of a corporate bond essentially rests on the corporation's earning ability.

Bonds are issued under indentures, which are agreements between issuers and trustees that govern the bond issue. For example, an indenture would specify the amount of the issue, any assets pledged as security, the method of extinguishing the bonds, and so on. The trustee, who may legally be any person but is usually a commercial bank, has three major responsibilities: (1) to certify that the bond contract and indenture meet legal requirements, (2) to make sure the issuer performs the responsibilities set forth in the indenture, and (3) to act on the bondholders' behalf if the issuer defaults on either interest or principal payments.

Types of Bonds and Means of Redemption

The different kinds of provisions that a bond can include are limited only by the issuer's ingenuity. Some of the more popular features include the following: Some bonds, like U.S. savings bonds, are registered, while other are not. The latter type is referred to as a bearer or coupon bond, a term that refers to the attached coupons that are clipped when interest payments are due. (Since August 1986, U.S. Treasury notes and bonds, as well as Treasury bills, are issued in "book-entry" form. That is, they are computer entries—no pieces of paper exist and, thus, no coupons can be clipped.) Most corporate and municipal bonds contain a call provision, which gives the issuer the right to redeem the bonds before maturity. If the issuer exercises this right and calls the bonds, the issuer usually must pay an amount greater than the face value, or principal—the call premium—to the holders. Obviously a corporation or other issuer will call bonds only if interest rates have declined enough to at least cover the premium and other expenses. Convertible debentures are bonds that the holder may convert into the preferred or common stock of the same corporation at the holder's option. The terms of the conversion privilege are specified at the outset of the issue and include the conversion ratio—how many shares of stock the holder will receive for each bond that is converted.

Bonds may be extinguished in three ways. First, they may be redeemed in cash, either at maturity or over the course of the loan. State and local governments frequently issue serial bonds, which provide for the redemption of a portion of the issue each year it is outstanding. And some corporate bonds carry a sinking fund provision, which requires the company to purchase and retire some bonds each year. Second, bonds may be refunded at maturity with a new issue, a technique that the U.S. government has used in its debt management operations. Finally, with convertibles, a debt is extinguished every time holders decide to convert their debentures into stock.

Economic Function of Bonds

Bonds are important to a growing economy because they represent an instrument used to bring savers and investors together. Advanced economies typically have a high degree of specialization. Thus, the people and institutions that save (consume less than their incomes) are usually different from those who desire to invest (produce capital goods that will increase the output of consumer goods and services). To bring these savers and investors together in the financial sense, several financial institutions, such as commercial banks and investment banks, have developed. They use various legal instruments such as common stock, commercial paper, and bonds to transfer funds from the savers to the investors. Given the number of bond issuers and the amount of this kind of debt outstanding, bonds are one of the more important, if not the most important, instruments boosting investment and, therefore, increasing the U.S. economy's output.

References

Brigham, Eugene F., and Louis C. Gapenski, *Financial Management Theory and Practice,* 6th ed., Dryden Press, Hinsdale, Ill., 1991; Stigum, Marcia, and Frank J. Fabozzi, *Bond and Money Market Instruments,* Dow-Jones-Irwin, Homewood, Ill., 1987.

(*See also* Bond rating agencies; Financial instruments; Junk, high-yield, bonds; State and local government finance; Stock)

Henry C. F. Arnold

Bond rating agencies

Bond rating agencies are private business firms that provide informed judgments on the quality of corporate, municipal, and other bonds to those (including issuers, investors, and regulatory agencies) interested in the merits of particular issues. But as the rating agencies emphasize, bond ratings are not recommendations to buy. Since the value of ratings depends on agency credibility, the rating agencies are independent organizations—they do not sell bonds and they are not connected with either issuers or investors.

History and Importance

Until the early part of this century, there was little need for rating agencies because most borrowers and lenders had close personal relationships and the creditor could judge the quality of the debt instrument. But the number of corporations and governments that issue bonds grew so large that it became impossible for most investors to assess the thousands of debt issues outstanding. To fill this need some financial publishing firms began rating bonds. The first such firm was that of John Moody, who published security ratings in his 1909 *Analyses of Railroad Investments.* Moody's has grown since then and today rates the bonds of some 4000 corporations and has outstanding around 17,000 ratings of municipal general obligation and revenue bonds. Standard & Poor's began rating corporate bonds in 1923 and municipal bonds in 1940. Today that firm has more than 13,000 municipal bond ratings outstanding and has rated the issues of approximately 5600 corporations.

Basis for Ratings

The ratings essentially constitute a ranking of bond issues according to the probability of default—the failure of the issuing entity to make interest or sinking fund payments on time or to repay the principal at maturity. To determine the likelihood that a state or local government will default on a general obligation bond issue, the agencies consider many factors. The most important one is the strength of the local economy, because economic forces strongly affect the financial health of state and local governments and their ability to meet debt obligations. Questions that must be answered include: What taxes are relied on for revenues? What local and regional population, employment, and income trends prevail? And how vulnerable are the local and regional economies to adverse economic conditions? The rating agency also investigates the form of government involved and how efficiently it operates. It checks how well the issuer has handled past debt obligations and examines accounting procedures and budgetary factors.

When rating revenue bonds, the analytical focus shifts to determining whether the facility financed by the proceeds from the issue will be able to provide enough revenues above operating costs to meet debt service requirements. Finally, many considerations are taken into account when rating corporate bonds, but the key measure is how many times the corporation's earnings, before interest and taxes, cover its fixed charges. Since interest payments usually constitute the major part of fixed charges, the higher the "times interest earned," other things being equal, the safer the bond and the higher its rating.

Although the probability of default is the principal criterion used in determining the rating of a given bond issue, the agencies also consider the specific provisions of the obligation and the relative position of the bondholders as creditors if default, reorganization, or any other event covered by bankruptcy and other laws occurs.

Similarity of Rating Categories

Standard & Poor's and Moody's rating categories are quite similar—even to the letter symbols used. For example, a triple-A rating (S&P's AAA and Moody's Aaa) signifies the highest-quality bonds, whose issuers have the strongest capacity to meet their obligations. The chance of a triple-A bond defaulting is extremely small. These agencies' other ratings are listed in the table.

Rating Categories

S&P's	Moody's	Comments
AA	Aa	The issuers of these bonds have a very strong capacity to meet interest and principal payments when due, and their quality is only slightly below triple-A's. The two top ratings include bonds that are usually labeled "high grade."
A	A	Bonds rated A have a strong capacity to pay interest on time and repay principal when due, but are vulnerable to adverse changes in economic conditions. They are regarded as upper-medium-grade obligations.
BBB	Baa	This rating applies to medium-grade bonds that have adequate capacity to meet obligations, so long as economic conditions remain healthy.
BB, B CCC and CC	Ba, B Caa and Ca	All these ratings indicate that, on balance, the bonds are predominantly speculative as far as the issuer's ability to pay interest and principal on time. BB and Ba bonds are the least speculative, while CC and Ca are the least secure. Moody's Ca rating includes bonds that have defaulted.
C	C	S&P's C rating is reserved for income bonds on which no interest is being paid. Moody's applies the C rating to the lowest-quality bonds, those which have little possibility of attaining investment standing. Most have defaulted.
D		S&P uses a D rating for bond issues in default.

It has been estimated that some 70 to 80 percent of the bonds rated by the agencies are placed in the same category. Those bonds that are not are rarely more than one category apart. Although this might hint at collusion, this is not the case. The analysts at the rating agencies have been trained similarly, avail themselves of the same data, and use similar rating techniques, and so it is not surprising that they come up with comparable ratings.

Reference

Cohen, Jerome B., Edward D. Zinberg, and Arthur Zerkel, *Investment Analysis and Portfolio Analysis,* 5th ed., Irwin, Homewood, Ill., 1987.

(*See also* Bond)

Henry C. F. Arnold

Break-even analysis

The break-even point represents the volume of sales at which revenues equal expenses—that is, at which profit is zero. Computationally, the break-even volume is arrived at by dividing fixed costs (costs that do not vary with output) by the contribution margin per unit, that is, selling price minus variable costs (costs that vary directly with output). In certain situations, and especially in the consideration of multiproducts, break-even volume is measured in terms of sales dollars rather than units. This is done by dividing the fixed expenses by the contribution margin ratio (contribution margin divided by selling price). Often, in such computations, the desired profit is added to the fixed costs in the numerator in order to ascertain the sales volume necessary for producing the target profit.

Break-Even Chart

Other than as a rough indicator of the changes in volume which the company might experience before suffering losses or making profit, the break-even point is in itself of little relevance to managerial decision making. More broadly, however, break-even analysis refers to a crude initial evaluation of the impact on profits of small, short-run changes in volume, in fixed costs, and in the per-unit price and variable cost. Typically, this is achieved by use of break-even charts or graphs which represent linear approximations of the economist's curves of total cost and revenue. These linear approximations are drawn up by assuming both a given decision on output and input level and a given selling price. Thus, they are to be considered reasonable only within a narrow range around the given output; outside such a range, different break-even charts would be called for.

The break-even chart allows management to visualize the sensitivity of profit to such contemplated policy changes as would affect the four operating variables (volume, fixed costs, per-unit price, per-unit variable cost), or the sensitivity to errors in forecasting these variables. The indicated sensitivity guides management with respect to the degree of care and effort required in analyzing its plans or in refining its forecasts.

Historical Development

The notion of zero profit and the distinctions between fixed and variable costs evolved early in the nineteenth century but gained momentum only during the century's final quarter. The first known break-even chart (also referred to later as a crossover chart or profit graph) is attributed to a publication by the American engineer Henry Hess in 1903. Further development of break-even concepts and their application to forecasting and cost control throughout the first half of the twentieth century is credited to C. E. Knoeppel, and also to Walter Rautenstrauch, who was the first to actually publicize the term "break-even point chart." But while Knoeppel stressed the functional classification of the sources of the costs and the uses of profits, Rautenstrauch—in what later became the popular version of the chart—highlighted only the fixed-cost–variable-cost distinction.

Usefulness of Break-Even Analysis

Beyond linearity, other simplifying assumptions limit the usefulness of break-even analysis; actual costs incurred (fixed and variable) are substituted for opportunity costs; the environment is depicted as static; that is, factors other than volume affecting revenues and costs, such as demand and technology, are assumed to be insignificant; still more importantly, uncertainty is ignored.

However, some simplistic assumptions are relaxed in certain extensions of break-even analysis: in a multiproduct, multiconstrained production environment, linear programming can be used to identify such product mixes as would allow the firm either to break even or to maximize profits. Moreover, nonlinear revenue and costs including semifixed costs (discontinuous, stepwise cost functions) and semivariable costs (costs that vary with output but that are partly fixed, even if no output is produced) can be introduced into the analysis by using piecewise linear approximations.

Uncertainty has been incorporated into break-even analysis by allowing sales volume, together with prices and costs, to be random variables and then computing the probability of achieving various profit levels and expected profits. Break-even analysis under uncertainty must incorporate a risk measure. Since any production alternative under consideration is only one among many in the portfolio of projects within a firm, and since stockholders possess portfolios of firms, the use of systematic risk (covariance with a market rate of return) has been suggested in lieu of merely variance of profits. However, from the standpoint of understanding and predicting behavior, it is to be recognized that a manager will act so as to maximize expected utility, instead of shareholders' wealth; thus a risk measure pertinent to the manager's personal portfolio rather than systematic risk is likely to be considered appropriate.

Break-even analysis evolved as an attempt to enable management to use the economic model of the firm by processing cost and revenue data compiled by the accountants. The assumptions and approximations required for this purpose drew criticisms of the tool as too simplistic. But apparently it has been judged that, on balance, costs of accumulating data for the use of the more realistic models are in excess of any possible losses from use of the simpler model. Thus, the use of break-even analysis continues.

References

Harris, Clifford, *The Breakeven Handbook: Techniques for Profit Planning and Control,* Prentice-Hall, Englewood Cliffs, N.J., 1978; Meigs, Walter B., Charles E. Johnson, and Robert F. Meigs, *Accounting, The Basis for Business Decisions,* 4th. ed., McGraw-Hill, New York, 1977.

(*See also* Linear programming)

Joshua Ronen

Bretton Woods Conference

In the short period covering July 1–20, 1944, 45 nations meeting at Bretton Woods, New Hampshire, agreed to a comprehensive arrangement that would govern the world trade and payments system for 28 years. The world depression and the accompanying trade warfare involving narrow bilateral trade agreements, tariffs, and competitive devaluations of the years between World Wars I and II underlined the urgency of postwar international economic cooperation. Nevertheless, the unsuccessful interwar attempts at trade and monetary agreements boded poor prospects for cooperation. If a post–World War II agreement were to be achieved, it would require mutual recognition of benefits, a reasonable international payments system, and the acceptance of mutual dependence.

Creation of the Regime

Planning for the international arrangement began in 1942 as Britain initiated discussions with the United States with the objective of securing employment and exchange rate stability. The British proposal was the outcome of concern over Britain's declining economic power. Its postwar trade position was expected to be in deficit, and it believed that returns on prior overseas investments would decline. With anticipated high levels of domestic unemployment, the British favored an expansive international monetary system, one that permitted aggressive domestic monetary and fiscal policy. The United States, as the emerging world economic and political power, was also wary of a postwar recession.

The two nations, aided by the common cause of wartime camaraderie, cleared much of the necessary groundwork in advance of the meeting so that rapid progress was made at the 1944 meetings. Discussions at Bretton Woods touched on national and regional problems, but accumulated war debts and the volatile export earnings of raw material–producing nations were not allowed to present roadblocks.

The participating nations agreed upon an international payments system to be administered by the creation of the International Monetary Fund (IMF) and a support-ing institution, the International Bank for Reconstruction and Development (IBRD), whose function was to promote international investment. The IMF, on the other hand, was designed to promote international exchange rate stability, multilateral trade, and currency convertibility. With the creation of the IMF, signatory nations gained access to consultative groups and monetary resources which would facilitate these objectives.

Under the arrangement, nations defined their currency in terms of gold, with only the United States pledging convertibility. Consequently a system of fixed cross rates was established where adjustments could be made only in cases of fundamental dis-equilibrium and only under the guidance of the IMF. The exact conditions under which a nation could exercise such a privilege, however, were never specified.

All IMF signatory nations were to contribute both gold and currency, and each nation was expected to promote exchange rate stability. Members were then permit-ted to borrow those currencies necessary to maintain stability in the foreign exchange market. In this fashion, currency borrowing and corrective domestic policies would maintain a self-equilibrating international payments system.

The Fund would also provide liquidity to member countries in the form of SDRs, or special drawing rights. SDRs, which were created as an international reserve cur-rency to be used for international debt settlements, replaced "bancors," the alterna-tive proposed by Keynes, but one that never came to be.

Whereas the IMF was charged with supporting fixed exchange rates, the IBRD was intended to have a limited role of primarily guaranteeing private short- and long-term loans for investment in the war-torn nations. It was believed that private interna-tional investors would be few and hesitant in the immediate postwar period. More-over, the Bretton Woods conferees had no desire to usurp the role of private investment throughout the free world.

The Demise of the Bretton Woods Agreement

The Bretton Woods regime appeared to function fairly well through the late 1960s as it facilitated the eventual expansion of world trade and incomes. As the first world agreement explicitly stipulating the rules of an international monetary system as well as the means to execute and maintain its principles, the agreement was a remarkable achievement in international cooperation.

However, the uneven growth of world incomes, divergent monetary and fiscal policies among the rapidly growing industrial nations, and international liquidity constraints laid the foundation for the eventual demise of the system. Of special significance in that process was the conflict faced by the United States. Since the dollar was the currency used by other central banks in foreign exchange interventions, the United States had the responsibility of creating sufficient dollars to ensure adequate liquidity. This goal, however, conflicted with the requirement that the number of dollars in the hands of foreign central banks should not exceed the U.S. gold stock, lest there be a loss of confidence in the U.S. commitment to hold the price of gold at $35 per ounce.

It was in fact the excess of the U.S. dollar liabilities over its gold stock which ultimately forced the United States into initiating a devaluation of the dollar in August 1971, triggering a rapid breakdown of the system. The international state of turmoil caused by the decision of the major industrialized countries to float their currencies against the dollar lasted until March 1973, when the Bretton Woods Agreement was abandoned in favor of the official recognition of a system of flexible exchange rates.

The float inherent in the new set of exchange rates, as defined by the Smithsonian Agreement, was considered temporary. Yet the effects of this shift in the exchange rate regime, combined with the large drawings on the International Monetary Fund by both developed and developing countries during the first oil shock, undermined any attempts to return to a system of fixed exchange rates. As such, the basic mission of the Bretton Woods Agreement, the commitment to a system of stable exchange rates, was no longer valid. The role of the agreement was further undermined by the creation of the European Monetary System, which allowed member countries to stabilize their exchange rates and rely on the associated credit facilities instead of utilizing the Fund's resources.

The Legacies Left Behind

Since the 1970s, membership in the IMF has risen from the original 50 to 150. This growth came about as the Fund expanded the scope of its activities beyond the members' quota contributions and offered additional financing through its own borrowing. As a result, in the 1970s and early 1980s the Fund was instrumental in financing the deficits of the oil-importing countries by channeling the balance of payments surplus of the oil exporters to the former. Later, with the advent of the international debt crisis, it played a significant role in encouraging lending by commercial banks through making its own resources available to troubled debtor nations.

The International Bank for Reconstruction and Development, the IMF's sister institution, started from a less favorable position, as its inception lacked the lively discussions afforded the IMF. From the beginning, the IBRD was relegated to a secondary position, which was later reinforced by a coupling of at best modest contributions from member states and the natural bankers' conservatism in using borrowed funds. Since the 1980s, however, the original sharp distinctions between the functions of these two institutions has become less obvious as countries, especially Third World nations, have increasingly come to face chronic finance and development problems simultaneously. Consequently, both institutions extend conditional medium-term loans for balance of payments deficits with the conditions targeting structural and macroeconomic variables.

Today the organizations remain active, though there have been calls for an end to the role of the IMF. Some believe that the current prevalence of flexible exchange rates renders the original function of the IMF as a lender for short-term balance of payments problems unnecessary. However, the abolition of the IMF remains very unlikely since the institution continues to play a crucial role with regard to both small developing countries that maintain fixed exchange rates and struggling debtor countries.

References

Gwin, Catherine, Richard Feinberg, et al., *The International Monetary Fund in a Multipolar World: Pulling Together,* Transaction Books, New Brunswick, 1989; Kennen, Peter, B., *Financing, Adjustment, and the International Monetary Fund,* Brookings, Washington, D.C., 1986; Williamson, John, *The Failure of World Monetary Reform, 1971–74,* New York University Press, New York, 1977; Yarbrough, Beth V., and Robert M. Yarbrough, *The World Economy: Trade and Finance,* Dryden Press, Chicago, 1991.

(*See also* Foreign exchange rates; International Monetary Fund; Smithsonian Agreement; Special drawing rights)

Bernard S. Katz and Shiva Sayeg

Bureau of the Census

The Commerce Department's Bureau of the Census is the agency of the federal government responsible for conducting a census of the United States population and housing every 10 years. Additionally, the Census Bureau conducts 10 other censuses—agriculture, governments, retail, wholesale, services, transportation/communication/utilities, manufactures, minerals, finance/insurance/real estate, and construction industries—every 5 years.

The Census Bureau also conducts numerous annual, quarterly, and monthly surveys. These include:

- Current Population Survey, which generates the nation's official measures of employment, unemployment, income, and poverty
- Survey of Income and Program Participation, which measures changes in economic and social well-being in the United States
- American Housing Survey, which details the types and costs of housing available across the United States

In the economic arena, the Census Bureau conducts over 100 surveys for the Current Industrial Reports. These reports include 14 routinely released economic indicators on subjects such as retail trade, wholesale trade, housing starts and completions, foreign trade, and plant and equipment. The Census Bureau has placed additional emphasis in the last few years on developing reports on enterprise statistics, minority-owned and women-owned businesses, and the characteristics of business owners.

Uses of Census Data

The information gathered by these censuses and surveys is used for a wide variety of purposes. The best-known use of the population census information is the apportionment of the U.S. House of Representatives. However, the population census information also is used to determine the allocation of billions of dollars of federal, state, and local funds. Almost all federal social service programs use census or survey information to determine eligibility. Additionally, the allocation of funds for transportation and other industrial programs are based on census and survey data.

Census Bureau data are a major source for national product and income accounts, the balance of payments, and the index of industrial production. Private companies use Census Bureau data to help in marketing and plant-siting decisions.

History

Article I, Section 2, of the U.S. Constitution calls for a census of population every 10 years. The Constitution leaves to Congress the details of how censuses are to be taken and what they should cover.

The first U.S. Census was conducted in 1790 by federal marshals who went door-to-door and counted a population of approximately 4 million people. The 1990 census enumerated a population of over 249 million people.

The Census Bureau came into being in 1902 when Congress decided to establish a permanent organization to collect and publish statistics on the country's population and economy. In 1903, the Census Bureau became part of the Department of Commerce.

The 1810 population census was the first to collect economic data. Questions on manufacturing, mining, agriculture, and fisheries followed in 1840. The 1850 census added questions about taxes.

In 1905, economic censuses were separated from the population census with the first census of manufactures. From 1930 to 1965, the economic census program expanded to cover retail trade, wholesale trade, construction, and selected services. In 1963, the economic censuses were coordinated so that they would occur in years ending in "2" and "7." The 1987 economic censuses covered nearly 12 million establishments.

Technology and Censuses

The censuses and surveys conducted by the Census Bureau require collection, tabulation, and publication of data on a grand scale. For instance, the long-form questionnaire of the 1990 population and housing census is a sample of 17.7 million households.

To effectively handle these massive amounts of information, the Census Bureau has pioneered many processing technologies. In 1890, Dr. Herman Hollerith installed his recently patented system of punch cards and punches, electric tabulating machines, and sorters in the census office to tabulate the results of the 1890 census. By the 1900 census, use of Hollerith's tabulating equipment allowed the processing of up to 15,000 census cards a day, per machine, instead of the typical 7000 to 8000 cards a day. An individual keyer could punch about 850 cards a day using this system.

In 1930, the Census Bureau began using Remington Rand keypunch machines. This system was complicated, but with typical Census Bureau initiative, employees simplified the system so that an experienced keyer could punch about 1800 cards a day.

The Census Bureau also began using IBM machines about this same time. By the peak of census tabulating in 1941, the Census Bureau had 4600 people involved in processing 550 million punch cards using 1400 punching machines, 900 verifying machines, and a host of other equipment.

In 1951, the Census Bureau had the world's first commercial UNIVAC-1 computer installed to process the 1950 census. This computer was so large that it had to be barged from Philadelphia to the Census Bureau's Suitland, Maryland, offices.

Then in 1953, the Census Bureau developed a film optical sensing device for input to computers (FOSDIC) that electronically scanned microfilmed questionnaires. These developments allowed the 1960 census to be tabulated by computer.

The Census Bureau continued improving the census to meet the changing American scene by using a mail-out/mail-back procedure for the 1970 census. This was in response to fewer Americans being at home during the day for a census worker to call upon.

The major technological advance for the 1990 census was the development and use of a computer-readable map database, called the topologically integrated geographic encoding and referencing system, or TIGER. This is the first coast-to-coast computer-readable map. It was developed through close teamwork between the U.S. Geological Survey and the Census Bureau. This technology is now being used and adapted by public and private organizations across the country.

Census Products

Technology also is playing a major role in how census information is distributed. The data produced by the various demographic and economic censuses and surveys are available in a variety of forms.

The most popular form for census data remains the written report. However, the computer-readable compact disc (CD-ROM) is quickly catching up with written reports as more organizations and individuals are using personal computers.

The computer disc allows the user to have thousands of pieces of information in a very small space. The user can then create tabulations that meet specific needs.

Census data also are available on computer tapes and cartridges, on floppy discs, on microfiche, and through on-line computer transmission of CENDATA. Users can reach CENDATA through either CompuServe or DIALOG information services.

The most popular Census Bureau information product is the annual *Statistical Abstract of the United States.* This invaluable reference tool contains over 1500 tables and graphs on the social, political, and economic conditions of the United States. *Statistical Abstract* contains information from both public and private organizations. It has been published by the Census Bureau since 1902 and, before that, by other federal organizations from 1878 to 1902.

Printed Census Bureau products can be ordered from the nearest Government Printing Office. Computer-related products can be ordered directly from the Census Bureau by calling 301-763-4100.

References

Eckler, A. Ross, *The Bureau of the Census,* Praeger, New York, 1972; U.S. Bureau of the Census, *Statistical Abstract of the United States,* published annually.

(*See also* Sampling in economics; Statistical methods in economics and business, an overview)

Barbara Everitt Bryant

Bureau of Economic Analysis

The Bureau of Economic Analysis (BEA) is an operating unit within the Economics and Statistics Administration of the U.S. Department of Commerce. Before 1972, it was known as the Office of Business Economics. BEA provides basic information on such key issues as economic growth, inflation, regional development, and the nation's role in the world economy in the framework of the nation's economic accounts, of which it is the keeper and developer.

Economic Accounts and Economic Activity

BEA's national economics program encompasses the national income and product accounts (NIPAs) and the input-output accounts. The NIPAs—the most widely used branch of the economic accounts—show the value and composition of the nation's output and the distribution of incomes generated in its production. The accounts include estimates of gross domestic product (GDP) and gross national product (GNP), which are the market values of goods and services produced within the United States and produced by residents of the United States, respectively. They also include estimates of the goods and services that make up GDP, associated prices, national income, personal income, corporate profits, and stocks of inventories and fixed capital. The accounts also provide a consistent framework within which other estimates, such as of government expenditures and the surplus or deficit and of expenditures to protect the environment, are prepared.

The input-output accounts show how industries interact—providing input to, and taking output from, each other—to produce the nation's output. Benchmark tables, at the 500 industries-commodities level of detail, are prepared every 5 years. Annual tables are prepared at a more summary level.

BEA's regional economics program provides estimates and analyses at subnational levels. Personal income and related estimates are available by region, state, metropolitan area, and county. Gross state product estimates are the counterpart of gross domestic product at the national level. BEA provides long-term projections of personal income, employment, and earnings by industry and maintains a midterm econometric model to forecast economic activity and to analyze the impacts of projects and programs.

BEA's international economics program encompasses the international transactions accounts (balance of payments accounts) and the direct investment estimates. The balance of payments accounts provide a detailed and comprehensive view of economic transactions between the United States and foreign countries. The accounts include estimates of merchandise exports and imports; travel, transportation, and other services; foreign aid, and private and official capital flows, including direct investment. Estimates of the international investment position of the United States are prepared consistent with the balance of payments.

The estimates of U.S. direct investment abroad and of foreign direct investment in the United States include the direct investment position and flow of capital, income, royalties and license fees, and other service charges between parent companies and affiliates. The estimates also cover capital expenditures by majority-owned affiliates of U.S. companies, the financial structures and operations of U.S. parent companies and their foreign affiliates and of U.S. affiliates of foreign companies, and U.S. business enterprises acquired or established by foreign direct investors.

BEA maintains a system of economic indicators to track and to evaluate cyclical movements in aggregate economic activity. This system features the composite indexes of leading, coincident, and lagging indicators.

BEA's Work

In developing and maintaining the economic accounts, BEA makes adjustments to the underlying source data and fills in gaps to conform the estimates to the definitions and timing called for by the accounts. This process is necessary because the data come from a multitude of sources, almost none of which developed their information to dovetail with the requirements of the economic accounts. Most of the data underlying BEA's estimates are obtained from other government agencies—such as the Bureau of the Census, Bureau of Labor Statistics, Department of Agriculture, and Internal Revenue Service—and from private sources such as trade associations. The only area in which BEA collects data is international transactions, mainly direct investment.

Although BEA provides policy-oriented analysis, it does not provide policy advice. This distinction helps to preserve BEA's reputation for objectivity and professional integrity.

Development of Economic Accounts

Work within the federal government on economic accounts started with balance of payments accounting in 1921, and the first report was issued in 1923. The development of estimates of national income—including its industrial origin and its distribution in the form of wages, profits, and other types of payments—was called for in a 1932 Senate resolution. The initial report was published in 1934 as a Senate document. Subsequent income reports were published by the Department of Commerce. Monthly personal income first became available in 1938. State-by-state income payments to individuals were first published in 1939. National estimates of disposable personal income became available in 1942. The first report on the size distribution of income was issued in 1953; size distributions were published for selected years from 1944 to 1971 and then were discontinued in 1981. Regional personal income estimates were disaggregated further in 1967, when estimates were published for the metropolitan statistical areas, and in 1974, when estimates became available for counties.

The measurement of product flows—consumer purchases, investment, imports and exports, and government purchases—became important during World War II in mobilizing economic resources. These measurements resulted in the preparation of the GNP in 1941. GNP by quarters first became available in 1942. In 1947 the Commerce Department used an "accounting approach" in its revision of the national income and product estimates. This approach divides the economy into groups of transactors and pictures the economic process in terms of their transactions.

Constant-dollar (real) GNP estimates became a regular feature for annual estimates in 1951 and for quarterly estimates in 1958. Real GNP originating by industry was introduced in 1962.

BEA took on input-output work in 1959 and has published input-output benchmark tables for 1958, 1963, 1967, 1972, 1977, and 1982. Annual updates have been published for most nonbenchmark years from 1968 to 1986.

In the area of tangible wealth, estimates of the stock of nonresidential fixed business capital were first published in 1962. In 1982, BEA first published a complete set of series for the stocks of privately owned and government-owned equipment and structures and of durable goods owned by consumers in the United States.

Estimates of spending for pollution abatement and control by consumers, business, and government were made available within the framework of the NIPAs in 1975. The most recent addition to BEA's estimates was gross state product. The estimates, which were introduced in 1988, provide the most comprehensive measures of state production now available.

Updating the Economic Accounts

In 1990 BEA announced a plan to modernize and extend its national and international accounts. The national accounts will move toward the revised System of National Accounts, the international guidelines followed by most countries. A 1991 move to emphasize GDP, rather than GNP, as the primary measure of production anticipated other steps to be taken in the mid-1990s. The international accounts will be in line with the revised guidelines to be published by the International Monetary Fund.

References

Carson, Carol S., "The History of the United States National Income and Product Accounts: The Development of an Analytical Tool," *Review of Income and Wealth,* June 1975; *Survey of Current Business,* U.S. Department of Commerce, published monthly; *A User's Guide to BEA Information,* U.S. Department of Commerce, 1991.

(*See also* Anticipation surveys, business; Balance of international payments; Business investment in new plants and equipment; Gross domestic product; Input-output analysis; System of national accounts)

Carol S. Carson

Bureau of Labor Statistics

The Bureau of Labor Statistics (BLS) is the principal data-gathering agency of the federal government in the broad field of labor economics. Most of the Bureau's data come from voluntary responses to surveys of businesses or households conducted by BLS staff, by the Bureau of the Census (on a contract basis), or in conjunction with cooperating state and federal agencies. The Bureau adheres to a rigorous confidentiality policy, which ensures that the data collected will only be used for statistical purposes and that the identity of individual respondents will not be disclosed. This tradition of safeguarding the privacy of those who furnish data has helped sustain a high degree of voluntary cooperation with BLS surveys.

The Bureau of Labor Statistics produces objective and accurate data that are relevant to user needs. Outside reviews of BLS programs by professional social scientists began early in the history of the agency. In 1933, the Bureau called on the Social Science Research Council and the American Statistical Association for advice on methods and programs. Other reviews have been conducted by the National Bureau of Economic Research, President Kennedy's Committee to Appraise Employment and Unemployment Statistics, and the National Academy of Sciences. The Bureau established permanent Business and Labor Research Advisory Councils in 1947; these councils function through standing committees that correspond to the major BLS program areas. From time to time, special advisory groups are convened, such as the State Advisory Committee for Occupational Safety and Health Statistics. In addition, formal user surveys are designed and fielded for BLS programs on an ongoing basis.

Historical Highlights

On June 27, 1884, President Chester A. Arthur signed a bill establishing the Bureau of Labor in the Department of the Interior. Creation of the Bureau was a response to the appeals of reformers and organized labor for government agencies that would help end exploitation of labor and industrial strife by making known the facts about wages, prices, and working and living conditions. Carroll Davidson Wright, chief of the Massachusetts Bureau of the Statistics of Labor, became the Bureau of Labor's first commissioner. Over the next 20 years he guided the Bureau, publishing a series of innovative reports on the rapidly changing social and economic conditions. Wright initiated much of the work on wages and prices which was continued over the years by the Bureau, and he established the traditions of objectivity, nonpartisanship, and impartiality that have guided BLS activities ever since. In 1913, President Taft signed into law the act that established the Department of Labor. Renamed the Bureau of Labor Statistics, the Bureau became a unit of the new agency.

Major Programs

Employment and Unemployment The Bureau of Labor Statistics analyzes and publishes data from the Current Population Survey (CPS) on the labor force, employment, unemployment, and persons not in the labor force. Studies based on CPS data cover a broad range of topics, including annual analyses of labor-market developments; occupational analyses; characteristics of special worker groups, such as minorities and women maintaining families; and displaced workers.

The Bureau also collects, analyzes, and publishes detailed industry data on employment, wages, hours, and earnings of workers on payrolls of nonfarm business establishments. It publishes monthly estimates of state and local unemployment for use by federal agencies in allocating funds as required by various federal laws. In addition, the Bureau provides current data on occupational employment in most industries for economic analysis and for vocational guidance and education planning.

Prices and Living Conditions The Bureau develops information on prices in retail and primary markets and conducts research to improve the measurement of price change. The consumer price indexes (CPI) program provides measures of price change for a specified market basket of consumer goods and services. A continuing annual survey of consumer expenditures and income is the basic source of data for revising items and weights to be priced for the CPI market basket. The producer price indexes program measures changes in prices received by domestic producers at the level of the first commercial transaction for many products and some services. The international prices and price indexes program measures changes in the prices of commodities exported from or imported into the United States. Price and index number research covers various aspects of price measurement, such as adjustment for quality change and cost-of-living indexes.

Compensation and Working Conditions These Bureau programs cover two broad subject-matter areas: (1) compensation levels and trends and (2) safety, health, and working conditions. BLS conducts three major types of occupational compensation surveys: area surveys, industry surveys, and a national survey. Nonwage compensation is covered in a comprehensive survey of the incidence and characteristics of employee benefit plans. The Bureau's broadest measure of changes in compensation is the employment cost index, which covers the total private nonfarm economy and state and local governments. Studies in labor-management relations include analyses of wage and benefit changes in major collective bargaining agreements, statistics on work stoppages, and reports on pending labor-management negotiations in major bargaining units.

The Bureau conducts an annual survey, in cooperation with state agencies, of employer records for job-related injuries and illnesses and analyzes the results. This survey provides injury and illness information by industry. Supplementary surveys of work injury reports examine data from employees on the characteristics of selected kinds of injuries or accidents.

Productivity and Technology   The Bureau's programs of productivity measurement and technology studies measure productivity trends in the economy, major sectors, individual industries, and government. Labor productivity measures are developed for the business, nonfarm business, and manufacturing sectors of the economy as well as for nonfinancial corporations. The multifactor productivity program develops indexes of productivity based on output of combined labor and capital inputs. The program for analysis of technological trends focuses on the projected impact of major impending changes in equipment, products, materials, and production methods in selected industries. BLS also conducts comparative research in international economic data covering labor force and unemployment, hourly compensation costs, and various other economic indicators, in addition to productivity comparisons.

Employment Projections   The Bureau develops 10- to 15-year economic projections based upon certain specific assumptions that include projections of aggregate labor force, potential GNP, industrial output, and employment by industry and occupational detail. These projections provide a comprehensive and integrated framework for analyzing the implications of likely economic growth trends for the national economy and for employment in each industry and occupation. BLS also furnishes occupational projections and descriptive information for use in career guidance and education planning.

The Bureau's major programs are supported by a staff dedicated to research in statistical and economic methods and techniques. Work of this staff includes administration of the National Longitudinal Survey of Labor Market Experience—the oldest longitudinal data collection effort in the United States. BLS programs also benefit from a collection procedures research laboratory, which uses the techniques of cognitive psychology to improve survey design and response. In addition, Bureau programs are enhanced by the work of in-house experts who use computer technology for survey processing and database management.

The Bureau's program of information dissemination includes a national publications office and economic analysis and information staffs in eight regional locations. The Bureau's statistics and analyses are issued regularly in both print and electronic format; the agency also furnishes information by telephone, letter, and personal visit. BLS publishes six major periodicals and makes data available on diskette, on tape, through an electronic news service, and by 24-hour recorded messages. The Bureau's statistics and analyses have been published in an authoritative labor economics journal, the *Monthly Labor Review,* since 1915.

References

Major Programs of the Bureau of Labor Statistics, Report 793, 1991; *BLS Centennial Album,* June 1984; Goldberg, Joseph P., and William T. Moye, "The First Hundred Years of the Bureau of Labor Statistics," *Bulletin* 2235, 1985.

(*See also* Consumer price index; Employment and unemployment; Labor force; Producer price index; Statistical methods in economics and business, an overview)

Janet L. Norwood

Business anticipation surveys (*see* Anticipation surveys, business)

Business credit

The term "credit" refers to a deferred exchange, i.e., a transaction in which the contribution of one of the parties is postponed until some time in the future. Definitions of credit are legion. Some writers stress the uses to which credit is put. A distinction is made between business credit and consumer credit. Thus, loans secured to finance consumption are distinguished from loans employed to finance business. Business credit is considered here.

One way to view business credit is to portray the combined balance sheet of all business firms, i.e., proprietorships, partnerships, and corporations. The sum of all assets in this imaginary balance sheet would be financed by an ownership interest or net worth composed of initial sales of stock plus new issues of stock, together with earnings that were retained by the businesses after payments of taxes and dividends. The difference between the sum of all assets minus the net worth of these firms represents the amount of credit extended to these businesses. An alternative but identical way to present this information is to suggest that the assets of all business firms are financed by equity plus debt. The debt as viewed by the businesses is precisely the same quantity as the credit extended to these businesses by the lenders.

Needs for Business Finance

Before focusing on the sources of business credit, we examine the forces giving rise to a need for business financing and look at the way these needs are met. Total financing needs of business result from increases in the following types of assets:

Increases in short-term assets
  Inventories
  Net trade credit
  Consumer credit
  Net miscellaneous financial assets

Plus

Increases in long-term assets

   Plant and equipment

   Residential construction

   Direct foreign investment

Plus

Increases in liquid financial assets

Equal

Total financing needs

Inventories   A substantial portion of the cyclical variability in total financing needs arises from the variability of inventory investments.

Net Trade and Consumer Credit   In the ordinary course of events, the business firm buys its supplies and materials on credit from other firms, recording the debt as an account payable. Accounts payable, trade credit, or trade debt is the largest single category of short-term debt, representing about 40 percent of the current liabilities of nonfinancial corporations. Trade credit is both a source of credit for financing purposes and a use of funds to the extent that the firm finances credit sales to customers. As a rule, large corporations extend substantial amounts of trade credit, especially to smaller corporations, single proprietorships, and partnerships. Corporations also extend credit to their retail customers in the form of consumer credit. In its role as a supplier of trade and consumer credit, the nonfinancial corporate sector functions to some extent as a financial institution by channeling funds to other economic sectors. As with inventories, there has been a cyclical component to the increase in this class of financial assets, which in turn has contributed to the cyclicality in total financing demands.

Plant and Equipment, Other Long-Term Assets   For the corporate sector as a whole, the largest financing demands arise from investment in new plant and equipment. Expenditures on new capacity are critically dependent upon the current rate of market demand and the expectation of business of the growth in these demands. As capacity utilization rises from the cyclical trough, there is often substantial slack capacity within an industry. Thus, rising demands generate relatively little need for plant and equipment additions. As industry approaches full capacity, however, small increases in market demand can generate relatively large percentage increases in the desired investment in new production capability. This process generates a clear cyclical component in the demand for plant and equipment additions.

Liquid Financial Assets   Corporations have traditionally accumulated and reduced liquid asset holdings. These liquid assets have served as a buffer in the financial process. When in periods of declining economic activity financing demands fell, liquid assets were run down, thereby providing a source of incremental finance.

Sources of Business Finance

Corporations meet some fraction of their financing demands from the cash flow generated by their own operations. These funds are called internal funds or internal cash flow. Internal cash flow is defined as being equal to retained profits after tax, plus depreciation. In addition, the rundown of liquid assets would augment internal sources. If total financing demands exceed internal funds, then corporations must obtain the remainder from external sources. Thus, externally raised funds are the difference between total financing demand and internal funds.

In the late 1960s and early 1970s, the rate of growth of internal funds decreased, while investment as measured by total financing demands continued to grow. This increased investment could be financed only with an increase in external funds. Whereas externally raised funds had been on average one-third of internal funds in the 1950s and 1960s, they increased substantially through the mid-1970s. Since 1975 internal financing continued to increase relative to external finance. By the very late 1980s external financing on average was about 10 percent of internal finance.

Sources of Externally Raised Funds   New external funds can be raised in financial markets by issuing financial promises, in the form of either increased short-term debt, increased long-term debt, or new equity issues. The principal source of short-term debt for corporations has been the commercial banking system. The principal sources of long-term debt for corporations are corporate bonds and mortgages acquired largely by life insurance companies and pension funds. Corporate bonds, the general long-term debt obligations of corporations, have generally been the dominant source of long-term debt for manufacturing and public utility corporations. Mortgages have been an important source of funds for financing real property such as office buildings, shopping centers, and apartment buildings.

In addition, commercial banks have often made term loans to corporate business. Indeed, more than one-third of all bank loans in recent years have been term loans. Term loans are generally considered to be intermediate-term finance, being longer than 1 year, the arbitrary breakpoint for most definitions of short-term debt, and yet shorter than the typical 15- to 30-year maturities of long-term debt. They are usually unsecured and are typically repaid in level installments over the period of the loan. Beginning in the 1970s, insurance companies competed with banks in providing term loans to business.

The Historical Pattern of New Funds Raised in Financial Markets   In addition to the cyclicality in the total of externally raised funds, there also appears to be a clear cyclicality in the composition of these funds. In the early phases of a business cycle, long-term sources of funds, particularly long-term debt, are the principal sources of new funds. Toward the middle of each cycle, as total new funds are usually accelerating rapidly, the increase in long-term debt declines. In this period, short-term debt becomes the principal source of funds raised in financial markets. And, finally, toward the end of each cycle in the economic recession or slowdown, the increase in short-term debt declines rapidly and long-term debt resumes its role as the principal source of external funds.

Alternative Strategies for Raising New Funds   The clear cyclical pattern of raising new funds is attributable to corporate financial decision making. To a large extent corporate financial managers attempt to match the maturity of their liabilities to the maturity of their assets. Thus, other things being equal, they attempt to fund increases in short-term assets with short-term debts and increases in long-term assets with long-term funds.

But corporate financing decisions do not always follow a policy of relatively passive maturity matching. As interest rates in financial markets fluctuate, aggressive corporate financial managers may attempt to time their long-term debt issues to avoid periods of relatively high long-term interest rates and exploit periods of relatively low long-term rates. The typical cycle of corporate finance in recent years has been a heavy reliance on short-term debt during the peak of an expansion, corporate concern about the financial imbalances thus generated, and a refunding of short-term debt with long-term funds in the subsequent recession.

The Impact of Inflation on Net External Financing Demands   Inflation increases the financial demands of corporations by raising the current nominal cost of any new plant and equipment, inventory, or financial assets investment needed to support business growth. In addition, inflation leads to higher wage rates, to higher unit labor costs, and thus to increased production costs. If prices expand commensurately, then profit margins can be maintained and the dollar value of internal funds can be expanded proportionately. In several recent inflations, corporations have not maintained their profit margins. As a result, operating profits fell sharply, and internal funds were unable to increase with inflation. Further, the pace of inflation in several key investment areas such as inventories and plant and equipment was often faster than the general pace of inflation.

The corporate income tax system compounded these difficulties until the passage of the Revenue Act of 1981 which permitted accelerated depreciation. In earlier years, when computing income for tax purposes, corporations were allowed to choose depreciation mainly on the basis of historical costs. Thus, income tax payments were based on an overstated level of income. These increased corporate tax payments seriously eroded aftertax internal cash flow during inflationary periods. While reported profits grew throughout, the portion of these reported profits that arose from understatement of the replacement costs of inventory and plant and equipment grew to be very large. As more of the funds represented by reported profits were necessary to replace existing inventory and plant and equipment, less was available to finance new investment in these areas. The Revenue Act of 1981 substantially altered the earlier years' experience.

The Increased Leverage of U.S. Business

A noteworthy feature of the 1980s was the rapid growth of business credit (or debt). The leveraging of business occurred not only among nonfinancial corporations, but also among other nonfinancial business.

Between 1980 and 1990 the corporate sector increased its market debt relative to the size of the economy by about one-third. Over this same period noncorporate business market debt grew relative to GNP by almost 40 percent.

Over the 1980s corporate assets declined by about 10 percent compared with the size of the economy; holdings of tangible assets fell by somewhat more. Corporations were borrowing not to invest in either financial or physical assets, but to reduce their own or other corporations' equity. Thus, from 1984 through 1990 about $641 billion of common stock was retired.

Unlike the mergers of the 1960s which were financed by an exchange of securities, acquisitions in the 1980s relied heavily on borrowed funds to pay cash to selling shareholders. Leveraged buyouts (LBOs), the most highly leveraged transactions, grew rapidly. In addition to financing LBOs and other mergers and acquisitions, debt was also used by corporations to discourage unsolicited or unfriendly takeovers, as well as to repurchase their own common stock outstanding.

Short-Term Debt

While corporations attract funds from a number of financial markets, short-term debt has played a particularly important role among their sources of external funds. Bank loans are by far the largest source of short-term business debt. Finance companies are an important source of supplementary lending, generally to the smaller companies whose working capital needs they finance. United States government agencies also extend short-term credits to business. In addition, the largest corporations also use commercial paper—short-term, unsecured promissory notes sold in the open market—to fund some of their short-term needs.

Bank Debt   Because bank loans are the dominant source of corporate short-term finance, their cost and availability play a pivotal role in corporate short-term markets. Unlike most external funds that are raised by the sale of securities, bank loans are negotiated privately between a corporation and its banker. While the terms of each bank loan are tailored to the particular needs of a business, these terms have certain common characteristics. In particular, most bank loans are priced by setting their interest rate at some spread above the bank's prime rate, the interest rate reserved for the bank's most creditworthy borrowers. The prime rate itself tends to be an industrywide rate, with most banks quoting the same prime at any given time. Actually, the total cost of bank borrowing is more complex and varies according to several provisions of a loan agreement, particularly the compensating deposit balances that businesses are implicitly required to hold with the bank.

The prime rate in recent years has become much more responsive to open-market interest rates. Indeed, several large money-center banks have explicitly tied their quoted prime rate to open-market rates, specifically to the rates obtained on commercial paper. Thus the cost of business loans has become more closely related to the market-determined costs of short-term credit in the financial system.

Banks provide different types of loan arrangements for corporations, which for classification purposes can be divided into lines of credit, revolving credit agreements, and term loans. Both lines of credit and revolving credit agreements are generally classified as short-term credit arrangements.

With a line of credit the bank assures its customers that (if called upon) it will provide short-term funds up to some specified limit, with the interest rate generally set at some spread over the bank's prime rate and which thus floats with the prime rate. The customer is generally required to keep certain compensating deposit balances with the bank as a part of the line of credit. While these lines of credit do not appear to be legally binding, banks invariably attempt to stand behind the implied commitments barring an altogether unforeseen and unmanageable set of circumstances. The lines of credit are, of course, periodically reviewed to make sure that they appropriately serve the interests of both the borrower and the bank.

A revolving credit agreement, on the other hand, is a written contractual agreement to provide short-term funds; it is binding upon the bank. The credit agreement provides the assurance of short-term funds, up to some specified limit, for a specified period of time, at an interest rate generally tied to the prime rate. The customer is often charged a commitment fee for this credit agreement in addition to the compensating deposit balances which are generally required by the agreement.

The bank is essentially guaranteeing to its customers the availability of short-term funds either implicitly or explicitly. Business corporations enter into these agreements to ensure that their expected and, for that matter, unexpected short-term needs can be met. The compensating balance requirements and fees that are involved in the arrangements are the cost of this insurance.

Commercial Paper Market as an Alternative Source of Short-Term Debt   While large banks are the dominant source of short-term business credit, many large corporations also use the commercial paper market to fund some of their short-term needs. Commercial paper issued by nonfinancial corporations, which amounted to $95 million outstanding in 1945, had risen to $116 billion by year-end 1990.

The commercial paper market provides a means for borrowers to obtain short-term funds from money-market investors without the direct services of the commercial banks. Commercial paper refers to short-term, unsecured, promissory notes issued by both financial and nonfinancial corporations. Traditionally, the commercial paper market has been divided into two segments: the directly placed market and the dealer-placed market.

Direct paper is sold directly to money-market investors by the issuing corporation through its own selling organization supplemented by regional banks that may solicit orders. Dealer paper is sold to investors through an investment banking or brokerage house.

The primary requirement for borrowing in the money markets is that the borrower possess an excellent credit standing. Since money-market lending is conducted on an unsecured and impersonal basis, financial strength and viability are necessary to ensure minimal default risk and investor confidence. It is for this reason that only large, financially strong corporations, sometimes referred to as prime credits, have usually been able to issue commercial paper. Credit rating appears to be influential in assessing credit standing and determining whether a corporation would be able to sell commercial paper in the money markets.

While commercial paper notes are sold in a wide range of denominations, the dealer-placed notes of nonfinancial corporate issuers are generally available in denominations from $100,000 to $5 million. The exact times to maturity for commercial paper notes are primarily influenced by the needs of borrowers and the preference of investors, but they generally have quite short maturities—between 35 and 270 days.

Another important aspect of commercial paper financing is the use of backup lines of credit. It is customary for a commercial paper issuer to secure a line of credit at a commercial bank. The backup line provides an additional measure of safety and liquidity to the borrowing corporation in the event that adverse money-market conditions or a temporary cash flow problem threatens the borrower's ability to redeem its notes at maturity. Although the granting of backup lines may facilitate corporate use of commercial paper financing instead of bank debt, commercial bankers are willing to engage in this business for several reasons. First, because of competition among the banks, it is sensible for each bank to provide its prime-credit corporate customers with a high level of service including such services as backup lines. Furthermore, granting these backup lines may be viewed as a profitable business, for the bank can earn a return consisting of either compensating balances or commitment fees without normally investing any assets.

Eurodollar Financing   Our domestic financial markets are now augmented by external markets for dollar-denominated loans. Foreign bank lending to U.S. corporations in the Eurodollar market differs from most lending in the domestic market. The borrowers among U.S. corporations are almost always large, well-known corporations that have the alternatives of borrowing in the domestic loan market and possibly the domestic commercial paper market as well as the Eurodollar loan market. Eurodollar loans are usually individually arranged. Banks do not offer Eurodollar lines of credit under which they ensure continuous availability of funds up to a predetermined limit. The Eurodollar loan market is a wholesale market, and these lending banks have no legally imposed reserve requirements or deposit insurance fees. For all these reasons, lending costs in the Eurodollar bank loan market tend to be lower than in the U.S. market. Interest rates in the Eurodollar bank loan market float with open-market rates, as does the prime rate on U.S. bank loans. The Eurodollar borrowing rate is based on the London interbank offer rate (LIBOR), which measures the rate at which banks in the foreign market will lend dollars to each other.

During the 1980s, many firms changed from borrowing through Eurodollar loans to borrowing via note issuance facilities (NIF). An NIF is a line of credit that allows the borrower to issue a series of short-term Euronotes generally over a period of 5 to 7 years. These notes are marketed on behalf of the borrower by one or more banks or investment banks. Often a different group of banks underwrites the issue by promising to absorb any unsold notes. The borrower usually pays an initial fee and an annual underwriting fee. The Euronotes issued under a note issuance facility commonly have a 3- to 6-month maturity, although longer maturities and a choice of the currency in which the debt is issued are available.

Long-Term Debt

Corporate bonds are the dominant form of long-term corporate debt. Other forms of long-term debt play important supplementary roles. Commercial mortgages, for example, are important to real estate corporations in the financing of office buildings, shopping centers, and other commercial projects. Bank term loans are used as supplementary forms of intermediate-term finance by many companies. Special forms of tax-exempt financing are used to fund some industrial development projects as well as pollution-control equipment. In addition, leasing arrangements are often used as substitutes for long-term financing.

Suppliers of Long-Term Debt   The long-term corporate bond market has a very broad range of institutional suppliers of funds. Life insurance companies hold more than one-half of the outstanding corporate bonds. Private and public pension funds also hold about a third of the outstanding bonds. The remaining third is divided among mutual savings banks, casualty insurance companies, mutual funds, broker dealers, foreign investors, and others, including individuals and endowments of various educational, religious, and charitable institutions.

There are many different types of corporate bonds and many different segments of the corporate bond market. There are long-term and intermediate-term bonds, high-quality and low-quality bonds, utility bonds and industrial bonds, callable bonds, sinking fund bonds, and many other types of such instruments. Among the more important distinctions is the distinction between privately placed bonds and publicly issued bonds. Privately placed bonds are relatively illiquid and are sold to a small number of purchasers through private negotiations. Typically, the purchasers are large, sophisticated financial institutions. Publicly issued bonds are sold to a large number of purchasers through a public sale or underwriting. They are accompanied by a wider dissemination of investor information and wider access to potential purchasers.

Before the late 1970s, companies that did not qualify for investment-grade ratings (BBB/Baa or higher) were unable to issue debt in the public bond market. They were restricted, for the most part, to incurring bank debt, usually with short-term maturity, or to selling private placements to insurance companies, which usually imposed severely restrictive loan covenants. At that time Drexel, Burnham, Lambert, an investment banking house, concluded that issues of high yield (or junk bonds as they are unfortunately called) should be salable. Initially, the buyers were individuals or high-yield mutual funds; they were subsequently joined by pension funds, insurance companies, banks, and savings and loans.

The high-yield features of these issues suggest that attached to their ownership is a substantial probability that the interest payments and principal repayment will not occur as promised. As institutional investors in the public bond market became convinced that the high yields attached to these issues more than compensated for their risks, especially when held in a diversified portfolio, the high-yield bond market grew rapidly. The economic expansion of the 1980s added to the favorable environment for issuance of these bonds. Thus, following a relatively slow start, high-yield issues burgeoned; by 1990 about 25 percent of all corporate bonds outstanding comprised these issues.

There are important differences in the market for privately placed and publicly issued bonds. Among other things, the suppliers differ, the terms of the debt securities differ, and the purchasers of these securities differ. Typically, life insurance companies supply 90 percent of the private placements. In contrast, pension funds, both private and public, generally dominate the public issue market. Individuals participate almost exclusively in the public issue market. In the public market the terms of the debt instruments reflect prevailing norms and tend to be standardized. They vary relatively little from issue to issue and tend to be inflexible in terms of any special needs of the issuer and/or the investor. Conversely, the terms of a private placement can be extremely flexible. Special provisions are often created to meet particular financing problems that the borrower may encounter. Also, special protections are often included to meet the interests of the lender or lenders. On average, private placements tend to have a shorter lifetime than publicly issued bonds. Private placements are in many ways the long-term equivalent of bank loans. They are privately negotiated, specifically tailored debt financings which are not traded in the financial markets. On the other hand, publicly issued bonds can be compared to the bond market equivalent of short-term market instruments, namely open-market commercial paper. While the privately negotiated form of financing bank loans has dominated the short-term corporate market, the open-market form of bond financing, public issues, dominates the longer-term bond markets. However, since 1987, the volume of privately placed bonds exceeded that of publicly offered issues.

References

Brealey, R. A., and S. C. Meyers, *Principles of Corporate Finance,* 4th ed., McGraw-Hill, New York, 1991, chaps. 14, 17, 18, 24, 29–32; Brigham, E. F., and L. C. Gapenski, *Financial Management, Theory and Practice,* 6th ed., Dryden Press, Hinsdale, Ill., 1991, chap. 19; Crabbe, L. E., M. H. Pickering, and S. D. Prowse, "Recent Developments in Corporate Finance," in R. W. Kolb (ed.), *Corporate Finance: A Reader,* Kolb Publishing Company, Miami, Fla., 1991; Friedman, B. (ed.), *Corporate Capital Structure in the United States,* National Bureau of Economic Research, University of Chicago Press, Chicago, 1985; Friedman, B., "The Risks of Financial Crisis," in M. Feldstein, *The Risk of Economic Crisis,* National Bureau of Economic Research, University of Chicago Press, Chicago, 1991; Helfert, E. A., *Techniques of Financial Analysis,* 5th ed., Irwin, Homewood, Ill., 1982, chap. 5; Kopcke, R. A., and E. S. Rosengren (eds.), *Are the Distinctions between Debt and Equity Disappearing?,* Federal Reserve Bank of Boston, October 1989; Korswick, W. J., and C. O. Marberg, *The Loan Officers Handbook,* Irwin, Homewood, Ill., 1986; Marsulis, R. A., *The Debt Equity Choice,* Ballinger, Cambridge, Mass., 1988; Warshawsky, M. J., "Is There a Corporate Debt Crisis? Another Look," in R. G. Hubbard (ed.), *Financial Markets and Financial Crises,* National Bureau of Economic Research, University of Chicago, Chicago, 1991.

(*See also* Banking system; Bond; Capital markets and money markets; Consumer credit; Credit, an overview; Debt; Eurodollar market; Financial institutions; Financial statements; Interest rates; Money markets)

Eli Shapiro

Business cycles

The definition of business cycles that underlies the widely accepted chronology of cycles in the United States was formulated by Wesley C. Mitchell in 1927. In 1946 Mitchell and Arthur F. Burns revised the definition in certain respects but left its major import intact, and it has continued to be used by the National Bureau of Economic Research in establishing business-cycle peak and trough dates.

According to the definition:

Business cycles are a type of fluctuation found in the aggregate economic activity of nations that organize their work mainly in business enterprises: a cycle consists of expansions occurring at about the same time in many economic activities, followed by similarly general recessions, contractions, and revivals which merge into the expansion phase of the next cycle; the sequence of changes is recurrent but not periodic; in duration business cycles vary from more than one year to ten or twelve years; they are not divisible into shorter cycles of similar character with amplitudes approximating their own.

Using this definition, the National Bureau has identified business-cycle peaks and troughs by months, quarters, and years in the United States, Great Britain, France, and Germany. Table 1 (see page 98) gives the U.S. chronology, starting in 1790 on an annual basis, and in 1854 on a monthly and quarterly basis. Monthly and quarterly figures on economic activity were less plentiful than annual data in the early 1800s. During the entire 200-year period from 1790 to 1990 there were 44 cycles, with an average duration of 53 months. The expansion phases, running from a business-cycle trough to the peak, averaged 34 months. The contraction, or recession, phases lasted 20 months on average. The shortest contraction, 6 months, occurred in 1980; the longest, 65 months, was in 1873 to 1879. The longest recorded expansion, 106 months, ran from 1961 to 1969; the shortest expansion, 10 months, came in 1919 to 1920.

Over the long stretch of history covered in Table 1, business-cycle expansions in the United States have become somewhat longer relative to contractions. This is true even when one excludes the extraordinarily long expansion from 1961 to 1969. The typical expansion is now something like 3 to 4 years; the typical contraction about 1 year.

Since the definition of business cycles, and the corresponding chronology, has come to be widely used in the United States over a period of more than half a century, it is evident that the definition can be applied objectively and with relatively little controversy. It is also evident that the phenomenon of the business cycle has not changed its character so completely as to make it impossible to apply the concept throughout the period.

No single measure of aggregate economic activity is called for in the definition because several such measures appear relevant to the problem, including output, employment, income, and trade. Also, no single measure either is available for a long period or possesses all the desired attributes. Quarterly figures for gross national product (GNP) became available only in the 1940s in the United States and even later, if at all, in other countries. Since monthly peak and trough dates are desired, quarterly figures are not sufficient in any case. Furthermore, GNP has always been measured in two different ways, which yield different estimates, one from the income side of the accounts and the other from the product or expenditure side. Another choice involves gross national product or gross domestic product. The U.S. Department of Commerce recently opted for the latter, as have many other countries. In the case of employment, two different measures of employment are often available, one based upon a survey of households, the other upon a survey of employers. Income and sales can be expressed in current prices or in constant prices, and output can be measured in physical units or in value terms. Virtually all economic statistics are subject to error, and hence are often revised. Use of several measures necessitates an effort to determine what is the consensus among them, but it avoids some of the arbitrariness of deciding upon a single measure that perforce could be used only for a limited time with results that would be subject to revision every time the measure was revised. For these reasons the procedure adopted has been to employ a dozen or more measures of activity that were in common use during the period under review or became available later.

Since the definition refers not only to aggregate activity but also to widespread movements in many activities, it is necessary to have some measure of the scope of the fluctuations that are being considered. For this purpose diffusion indexes have been constructed. They show how many types of activity within some group, or how many industries within one aggregate, are experiencing expansion or contraction. Such indexes, usually expressed in terms of the percentage of components that are expanding, reach high levels during the upward phase of the business cycle and low levels during the downward phase (when a majority are contracting rather than expanding).

Table 2 (see page 100) contains a selection of measures of duration, depth, and diffusion of recessions in the United States between 1920 and 1991. It shows that business-cycle contractions have varied widely in length, severity, and scope. The biggest depression was that of 1929–1933, while one of the smallest recessions occurred in 1980. The various measures show some degree of correlation, though it is far from perfect.

TABLE 1 A Two-Hundred-Year History of Business Cycles in the United States, 1790–1990

Dates of peaks and troughs						Duration in months*			
By months		By quarters		By calendar years				Cycle	
Trough	Peak	Trough	Peak	Trough	Peak	Contraction (peak to trough)	Expansion (trough to peak)	Trough to trough	Peak to peak
				1790	1796	—	72	—	—
				1799	1802	36	36	108	72
				1804	1807	24	36	60	60
				1810	1812	36	18	72	54
				1812	1815	6	36	24	42
				1821	1822	72	12	108	84
				1823	1825	12	24	24	36
				1826	1828	12	24	36	36
				1829	1833	12	48	36	60
				1834	1836	12	24	60	36
				1838	1839	24	12	48	36
				1843	1845	48	24	60	72
				1846	1847	12	12	36	24
				1848	1853	12	60	24	72
Dec. 1854	June 1857	4Q 1854	2Q 1857	1855	1856	24	30	84	54
Dec. 1858	Oct. 1860	4Q 1858	3Q 1860	1858	1860	18	22	48	40
June 1861	Apr. 1865	3Q 1861	1Q 1865	1861	1864	8	46	30	54
Dec. 1867	June 1869	1Q 1868	2Q 1869	1867	1869	32	18	78	50
Dec. 1870	Oct. 1873	4Q 1870	3Q 1873	1870	1873	18	34	36	52
Mar. 1879	Mar. 1882	1Q 1879	1Q 1882	1878	1882	65	36	99	101
May 1885	Mar. 1887	2Q 1885	2Q 1887	1885	1887	38	22	74	60
Apr. 1888	July 1890	1Q 1888	3Q 1890	1888	1890	13	27	35	40
May 1891	Jan. 1893	2Q 1891	1Q 1893	1891	1892	10	20	37	30
June 1894	Dec. 1895	2Q 1894	4Q 1895	1894	1895	17	18	37	35
June 1897	June 1899	2Q 1897	3Q 1899	1896	1899	18	24	36	42
Dec. 1900	Sept. 1902	4Q 1900	4Q 1902	1900	1903	18	21	42	39
Aug. 1904	May 1907	3Q 1904	2Q 1907	1904	1907	23	33	44	56
June 1908	Jan. 1910	2Q 1908	1Q 1910	1908	1910	13	19	46	32

Trough	Peak								
Jan. 1912	Jan. 1913	1913	1Q 1913	4Q 1911	1911	24	12	43	36
Dec. 1914	Aug. 1918	1918	3Q 1918	4Q 1914	1914	23	44	35	67
Mar. 1919	Jan. 1920	1920	1Q 1920	1Q 1919	1919	7	10	51	17
July 1921	May 1923	1923	2Q 1923	3Q 1921	1921	18	22	28	40
July 1924	Oct. 1926	1926	3Q 1926	3Q 1924	1924	14	27	36	41
Nov. 1927	Aug. 1929	1929	3Q 1929	4Q 1927	1927	13	21	40	34
Mar. 1933	May 1937	1937	2Q 1937	1Q 1933	1932	43	50	64	93
June 1938	Feb. 1945	1944	1Q 1945	2Q 1938	1938	13	80	63	93
Oct. 1945	Nov. 1948	1948	4Q 1948	4Q 1945	1945	8	37	88	45
Oct. 1949	July 1953	1953	2Q 1953	4Q 1949	1948	11	45	48	56
May 1954	Aug. 1957	1957	3Q 1957	2Q 1954	1953	10	39	55	49
Apr. 1958	Apr. 1960	1960	2Q 1960	2Q 1958	1957	8	24	47	32
Feb. 1961	Dec. 1969	1969	4Q 1969	1Q 1961	1961	10	106	34	116
Nov. 1970	Nov. 1973	1973	4Q 1973	4Q 1970	1970	11	36	117	47
Mar. 1975	Jan. 1980	1979	1Q 1980	1Q 1975	1975	16	58	52	74
July 1980	July 1981	1981	3Q 1981	3Q 1980	1980	6	12	64	18
Nov. 1982	July 1990	1990	3Q 1990	4Q 1982	1982	16	92	28	108
Averages									
14 cycles	1790–1854					24	31	56	53
14 cycles	1854–1913					23	25	49	48
8 cycles	1913–1948					17	36	51	54
8 cycles	1948–1990					11	52	56	63
44 cycles	1790–1990					20	34	53	53

* Entries from 1790 to 1855 are based upon calendar-year dates.

NOTE: For a basic statement of the method of determining business-cycle peaks and troughs, see Arthur F. Burns and Wesley C. Mitchell, *Measuring Business Cycles*, National Bureau of Economic Research, New York, 1946, chap. 4. Some of the dates shown there (p. 78) have since been revised. For a review of the chronology, including the dates back to 1790, see Geoffrey H. Moore and Victor Zarnowitz, "The Development and Role of the National Bureau of Economic Research's Business Cycle Chronologies," in Robert J. Gordon (ed.), *The American Business Cycle: Continuity and Change*, University of Chicago Press, Chicago, 1986. For a description of how the National Bureau method has been applied more recently, see Zarnowitz and Moore, "The Timing and Severity of the 1980 Recession," in Moore, *Business Cycles, Inflation and Forecasting*, 2d ed., Ballinger, Cambridge, Mass., 1983.

SOURCE: Center for International Business Cycle Research, Columbia University, New York, July 1991.

TABLE 2 Selected Measures of the Duration, Depth, and Diffusion of Recessions, 1920–1991

	Duration (months)	Depth Percent change in real GNP	Depth Unemployment rate, maximum	Diffusion, Percent of industries with declining employment, maximum
Three depressions				
January 1920–July 1921	18	n.a.	11.9	97
August 1929–March 1933	43	−32.6	24.9	100
May 1937–June 1938	13	−18.2	20.0	97
Six sharp recessions				
May 1923–July 1924	14	−4.1	5.5	94
November 1948–October 1949	11	−1.5	7.9	90
July 1953–May 1954	10	−3.2	6.1	87
August 1957–April 1958	8	−3.3	7.5	88
November 1973–March 1975	16	−4.9	9.0	88
July 1981–November 1982	16	−2.6	10.8	72
Five mild recessions				
October 1926–November 1927	13	−2.0	4.4	71
April 1960–February 1961	10	−1.2	7.1	80
December 1969–November 1970	11	−1.0	6.1	80
January 1980–July 1980	6	−2.5	7.8	63
July 1990–May 1991*	10	−1.2	6.9	73
Averages				
1920–1938 (5)	20	−14.2	13.3	92
1948–1991 (9)	11	−2.4	7.7	80

* Tentative.

SOURCE: Based on Table A-2 in G. H. Moore, *Business Cycles, Inflation and Forecasting*, 2d ed., Ballinger, Cambridge, Mass., 1983. Note that the brief and mild recession of 1945 is omitted here.

If there are uncertainties about identifying business cycles historically, they are far greater when it is done contemporaneously. How soon a peak or trough can be recognized depends partly upon how rapidly the economy descends from the peak or rises from the trough. It also depends upon one's ability and willingness to make forecasts, for example, that a decline in the several measures of aggregate activity will last as long and go as deep as in previously recognized recessions, and that the declines will be widespread. As a result, most turns in the business cycle have been recognized only with a lag. The most recent peak, July 1990, was determined by the National Bureau of Economic Research in April 1991, some 9 months after the peak. At this writing (January 1992) the trough date has not been selected by the NBER, and it is unlikely to differ from the tentative May 1991 date shown in Table 2.

In recent years a concept of a business cycle known as the growth cycle has come into use, especially for international comparisons. It represents a fluctuation around the long-run growth trend of a nation's economy, i.e., a trend-adjusted business cycle. Chronologies based upon this concept, using the definition cited earlier but applying it to data from which long-run trends have been eliminated, are shown in Table 3 (see page 102). The dates mark the approximate time when aggregate economic activity was farthest above its long-run trend level (peak) or farthest below its long-run level (trough). The number of growth cycles during a given period usually exceeds the number of business cycles, because slowdowns that sometimes occur during long business-cycle expansions become actual contractions in the trend-adjusted figures. In the United States, for example, such slowdowns occurred in 1962–1964, 1966–1967, and 1984–1985. Another difference is that peaks in the growth cycle usually occur some months before the corresponding peaks in the business cycle, because activity usually slows before a business-cycle peak is reached. Growth-cycle and business-cycle troughs tend to be more nearly simultaneous, but sometimes the growth-cycle trough lags. As a result of these differences, expansions and contractions are more symmetrical, in both duration and amplitude, in growth cycles than in business cycles.

References

Bronfenbrenner, Martin, *Is the Business Cycle Obsolete?*, Wiley, New York, 1969; Burns, Arthur F., *The Business Cycle in a Changing World*, National Bureau of Economic Research, New York, 1969; Burns, Arthur F., and Wesley C. Mitchell, *Measuring Business Cycles*, National Bureau of Economic Research, New York, 1946; Fels, Rendigs, and C. Elton Hinshaw, *Forecasting and Recognizing Business Cycle Turning Points*, National Bureau of Economic Research, New York, 1968; Friedman, Milton, and Anna Schwartz, *A Monetary History of the United States, 1867–1960*, National Bureau of Economic Research, New York, 1963; Gordon, Robert J., *The American Business Cycle: Continuity and Change*, University of Chicago Press, Chicago, 1986; Haberler, Gottfried, *Prosperity and Depression*, League of Nations, Geneva, 1937; Joint Economic Committee, *The Business Cycle and Public Policy, 1929–80*, Congress of the United States, November 28, 1980; Klein, Philip A. (ed.), *Analyzing Modern Business Cycles*, Sharpe, Armonk, N.Y., 1990; Klein, Philip A., and Geoffrey H. Moore, *Monitoring Growth Cycles in Market-Oriented Countries*, Ballinger, Cambridge, Mass., 1985; Lahiri, Kajal, and Geoffrey H. Moore (eds.), *Leading Economic Indicators: New Approaches and Forecasting Methods*, Cambridge University Press, Cambridge, Mass., 1991; Mintz, Ilse, *Dating Postwar Business Cycles: Methods and Their Application to Western Germany, 1950–67*, National Bureau of Economic Research, New York, 1970; Mitchell, Wesley C., *Business Cycles: The Problem and Its Setting*, National Bureau of Economic Research, New York, 1927; Mitchell, Wesley C., *Business Cycles and Their Causes*, University of California Press, 1941; Moore, Geoffrey H., *Business Cycle Indicators*, National Bureau of Economic Research, New York, 1961; Moore, Geoffrey H., *Business Cycles, Inflation and Forecasting*, Ballinger, Cambridge, Mass., 1983; Moore, Geoffrey H., *Leading Indicators for the 1990s*, Dow Jones-Irwin, Homewood, Ill., 1989; Schumpeter, Joseph A., *Business

TABLE 3 Growth-Cycle Peak and Trough Dates, 11 Countries, 1948–1990

Peak or trough	North America		Europe				Pacific region					North America	4 countries Europe	5 countries Pacific	10 countries excl. U.S.	G-7 countries	11 countries
	United States	Canada	United Kingdom	West Germany	France	Italy	Japan	Australia	Taiwan, R.O.C.	South Korea	New Zealand						
P	7/48																
T	10/49	5/50										10/49					
P	3/51	4/51	3/51	2/51				4/51				4/51					
T	7/52	12/51	8/52					11/52				7/52					
P	3/53	3/53					12/53					3/53					
T	8/54	10/54		2/54			6/55					8/54					
P	2/57	11/56	12/55	10/55	8/57	10/56	5/57	8/55				2/57	5/57		5/57	3/57	3/57
T	4/58	8/58	11/58	4/59	8/59	7/59	1/59	1/58				4/58	3/59	1/59	2/59	5/58	5/58
P	2/60	10/59						8/60				2/60				2/60	2/60
T	2/61	3/61						9/61				2/61				2/61	4/61
P	5/62	3/62	3/61	2/61			1/62					4/62	3/61	3/61	3/61	2/62	2/62
T	10/64	5/63	2/63	2/63			1/63		6/63			11/63	2/63	1/63	2/63	2/63	2/63
P					2/64	9/63	7/64							9/64	2/64		
T					6/65	3/65	2/66							3/66			
P	6/66	3/66	2/66	5/65	6/66			4/65	4/65	9/66	6/66	3/66	3/66			6/66	3/66
T	10/67	2/68	8/67	8/67	5/68			1/68	8/67		4/68	10/67	5/68		5/68	10/67	10/67

P	3/69	2/69	6/69	5/70	11/69	8/69	6/70	5/70	11/68	10/69	7/70	8/69	4/70	6/70	6/70	10/69	10/69
T	11/70	12/70	2/72	12/71	11/71	9/72	1/72	3/72	1/71	3/72	11/72	11/70	2/72	1/72	2/72	11/71	11/71
P	3/73	2/74	6/73	8/73	5/74	4/74	11/73	2/74	12/73	10/73	2/74	11/73	11/73	10/73	11/73	11/73	11/73
T	3/75	10/75	8/75	5/75	6/75	5/75	3/75	10/75	2/75	6/75	3/75	5/75	8/75	2/75	8/75	5/75	5/75
P		5/76				12/76		8/76	6/76		12/76						
T		12/77				10/77		10/77	7/77		2/78						
P	12/78	10/79	6/79	2/80	8/79	2/80	2/80		8/78	2/79	1/80	12/78	11/79	2/80	2/80	2/80	2/80
T		5/80			8/81*					10/80	11/80	6/80					
P	12/82	6/81	6/83	7/83	3/83*	6/83	6/81	10/82		7/81	7/81	7/81	6/84	5/83	5/83	12/82	2/83
T		11/82			1/85*		5/83			5/83	5/83	12/82	8/84		5/85	5/85	5/87
P	6/84*	11/85*	5/85*	7/86*		6/85*	5/85*	5/84*	2/84	8/84					5/85	5/85	5/85
T	1/87*	11/86*	1/87*	10/88*		8/88*	5/87*	8/85*	10/85	1/87					5/87	5/87	5/87
P	2/89*	12/89*			6/90*	6/89*											

NOTE: The chronologies for groups of countries are based on composite indexes of output, income, employment, and trade, weighted by each country's GNP in 1980, expressed in U.S. dollars. The chronologies begin at different dates because appropriate data are not available earlier. Since the chronologies are not updated frequently, the absence of a recent date does not necessarily mean that a turn has not occurred. The G-7 country group includes the United States, Canada, United Kingdom, West Germany, France, Italy, and Japan.

* Based on trend-adjusted coincident index.

SOURCE: For the United States through 1982, National Bureau of Economic Research. For other countries, Center for International Business Cycle Research.

Cycles: A Theoretical, Historical and Statistical Analysis of the Capitalist Process, McGraw-Hill, New York, 1939; Thorp, Willard L., *Business Annals,* National Bureau of Economic Research, New York, 1926; U.S. Department of Commerce, *Business Conditions Digest,* monthly; Zarnowitz, Victor (ed.), *The Business Cycle Today,* National Bureau of Economic Research, New York, 1972.

(*See also* Diffusion indexes; Economic growth; Great Depression; Kitchin cycle; Kondratieff cycle; Kuznets cycle; Leading indicator approach to forecasting; National Bureau of Economic Research)

Geoffrey H. Moore

Business inventory

Business inventory—the supply of various goods kept on hand by a business firm—has been intensely studied from both microeconomic and macroeconomic angles.

Any firm obviously wants to be able comfortably to fill orders uninterruptedly and to offer prompt delivery of a large menu of products. And any firm reacts to a trade-off between the profitability of attaining such objectives and their cost; the "just-in-time" inventory techniques of various Japanese firms are cited for their perspicacious adaptations to the trade-off's stringencies.

On the macroeconomic side, Maccini (1987) cogently remarks that "interest in inventories among economists stems primarily from the [role] of inventory fluctuations . . . in business cycles" (p. 970). (See the seminal work by Abramowitz, 1950.)

Another macroeconomic theme concerns the influence of monetary policy—through effects on interest rates and availability of credit—on inventory decisions and so on business fluctuations. This empirically problematical azimuth owes much to Hawtrey (1928, 1932, 1950).

Three facets of business inventory will be probed.

1. Turnover of inventories, a counterpart to circulating capital, is described.

2. The microeconomic foundations of business inventory behavior are sketched out. This work suggests that inventory is an inelastic function of sales, relative to expectations of prices and interest rates—all the more so if expectations are formed "rationally."

3. Finally, the "inventories and macroeconomic fluctuations" theme is developed. Maccini's (1987) caveat should be heeded: "Inventories appear to be a propagating mechanism, not a causal force, in business cycles. There is no evidence that exogenous shifts in inventory investment are an underlying cause of fluctuations in GNP" (p. 970).

Turnover of Inventories

The so-called period of production (associated with Böhm-Bawerk) is one of the most intractable knots in economics. But if the data can be transformed into turnover statistics, serious perplexities can, at the least, be bypassed. Thus calculate the ratio of the value of circulating capital to annual sales in some sector of the economy; call the reciprocal of this ratio T. The circulating capital is said to turn over T times a year: turnover of grocers' stocks will be high; that of jewelers' stocks low.

Anticipating later macroeconomic discussion, say that fiscal restraint or anticipated higher interest rates are expected to curtail final demand: final sales are expected to fall. What will be the impact on gross investment in inventories, neglecting finer points of microeconomic theory? By choice of measure, initial annual sales are to be unity. Say that final sales are expected to fall by 1 percent; and naively assume that desired inventories also fall by 1 percent. It would take $365/100T$ days to fall by 1 percent, at the initial rate of final sales: (3.65) $(1/T)$ (1.01) days are required at the new (lower) rate of final sales. More generally, if the rate of final sales falls by v percent, it takes (3.65) (v/T) $[(1 + v)/100]$ days to accomplish a v percent reduction in inventory. If final sales fall by 2 percent per annum and inventories typically turn over 40 times a year, it would take 0.186 day to accomplish the adjustment. For $T = 0.5$, 14.89 days are required: suppliers experience a bleak fortnight, although their "permanent" sales fall by only 2 percent. Suppliers' share prices would be little affected. And production would *not* be suspended for 2 weeks: suppliers would produce for stock, so that the adjustment would be spread out over many weeks.

The acceleration principle does not much affect inventory expenditure: replacement demand bulks too large in expenditure on circulating capital for that to happen. What is more, theoretical inventory cycles are generated by properties of the adaptive expectations that are typically stipulated—so that higher-order differential equations are generated in typically simplistic modeling. (See Allen, 1967, as well as Evans, 1969. This line of development was begun by Metzler, 1941, 1965.)

Now consider a product like American cars, governed by a model year. Whether or not output is placed with dealers on consignment, the product does not fit into standard inventory theory: the bulk of what is measured as inventory is unsold stock that is not to be replaced; one observes, within a model year, not so much inventory control as time profiles of sales.

Microeconomic Foundations

Two problems are solved. One concerns inventory criteria for a distributor; the other, inventory criteria for a manufacturer. Following Baumol:

> A retailer . . . confidently expects to sell . . . Q^* units . . . over the next year at a predetermined price, with demand spread evenly over the year. How much inventory should he keep on hand? . . . He can meet his demand by having the entire amount delivered to his warehouse at the beginning of January . . . ; alternatively, he can have 50,000 units delivered to him right after the first of the year and [an] equal amount on July 1.[1]

The first approach avoids reordering cost and entails substantial carrying cost; the second reduces carrying cost. (Carrying cost may be negative: inventories can increase in value over holding periods because of price inflation or enhancement through aging—as, for example, of wine.) The solution reduces to an especially useful optimality calculation:

$$D = \sqrt{\frac{2a^*Q^*}{k^*}} \tag{1}$$

Equation (1) determines the average inventory level, $D/2$: one-half of the regular intake, sales being spread evenly over the year; if 100,000 units are in stock on January 1, average inventory for the year is 50,000. The variable D is the optimal

---

[1]Baumol (1977, p. 6). Reprinted by permission of Prentice-Hall, Inc., Englewood Cliffs, N.J.

reorder quantity corresponding to sales volume Q^*; k^* is the unit carrying cost; and a^* is a fixed reorder cost. Baumol explains that "inventory should increase only in proportion to the *square root* of sales"—a famous result, especially interesting to the general reader, and confirming the thrust of this article: inventory holdings are less sensitive to sales than the literature may suggest.

A rather simplistic model of a manufacturer entails a number of points ably developed by Schlaifer (1959):

Two kinds of uncertainty may enter into an inventory problem . . . (1) There may be uncertainty concerning the quantity which will be demanded during any given time period. (2) There may be uncertainty concerning the lead time which will elapse between the date on which an order is placed and the date on which the new lot of product will actually arrive.[2]

In elementary inventory analysis, each decision is assumed to be independent of previous ones; and implications for the future are neglected. This is where stochastic and dynamic programming (or optimal control theory) come in—subject to a chilling reminder from Kydland and Prescott (1977) about intertemporal inconsistency of "optimal" plans. Hadley's (1964) observations remain pertinent:

Once storage is possible . . . the time required to dispose of any number of units depends . . . on the distributions for demand in a whole series of periods. . . . Analysis of costs is extremely complex if the probability distribution for demand is changing with time.

Pressure of space mandates that these themes be developed rather impressionistically—relying on a model of Dorfman, Samuelson, and Solow (1958).

A producer is to optimize relative to known demands $x_1, x_2, \ldots, x_n$ over periods $1, 2, \ldots, n$. The amount of stock (inventory) taken into the first period Y_1^* is given, as is the amount to be taken out of the nth period, Y_{t+1}^*. Productions are $y_1, y_2, \ldots, y_n$. The rate of interest over the tth period is r_t. The interest rate used for discounting from the beginning of the first period through the tth period is r_{1t}. Unit carrying costs in the tth period are a_t. The problem is to

$$\text{Maximize} \sum_{t-1}^{t=n} \frac{p_t x_t - i_t}{(1 + r_t)^t}$$

subject to Eqs. (2), (3), and (4):

$$\sum_{t=1}^{t-n} y_t + Y_1^* = \sum_{t=1}^{t-n} x_t + Y_{n+1}^* \tag{2}$$

$$c_t = f(y_t) + (r_t + a_t) Y_t \tag{3}$$

$$Y_{t+1} = Y_t = y_t - x_t \tag{4}$$

The problem's shape stresses intertemporal dependence of stocks and outputs. Two remarks are in order.

1. The solution is invariant against a scaling up of all nominal prices and costs together with nominal rates of interest. High nominal interest rates should not be confused with high real ones.

---

[2]R. Schlaifer, *Probability and Statistics for Business Decisions*, 1959, McGraw-Hill. Reproduced by permission of McGraw-Hill.

2. Higher real short-term interest rates need not cause a crescendo in the production plan. (The concepts of "crescendo" and "diminuendo" were developed by Hicks, 1946, 1965.) If plants are being operated near levels of minimum-cost production, discounted incremental costs of producing more later may dwarf interest savings from carrying less stock.

Inventories and Macroeconomic Fluctuations

The theory of rational expectations goes far to explain why "inventory" phenomena do not contribute as much to business fluctuations as, say, Metzler's (1941/1965) seminal work—based on adaptive expectations—suggests.

Inventory holdings are obviously affected by sales expectations. And for many years such expectations were modeled adaptively, so that sales experience would provoke a knee-jerk reaction (described by exponential decay, for example). If inventory investments typically hinge on "rational" forecasts of future sales, unanticipated changes in sales are properly attributed to random shock, to "established errors" in variables or equations, or to changes in policy regimes (à la Lucas, 1976, 1983) or some such thing. Then inventory cycles are apt to be chimerical—although intrinsically random shocks may induce speciously "regular" processes in the following way. Effects of properly identified random shocks may persist: e.g., replacement of inventories unexpectedly run off will be times with due attention to costs of more rapid adjustment. Such shocks may dissipate "linearly," or they may induce oscillations. What is more, effects of past shocks are modeled by wave mechanics, featuring diffraction. Waves generated by successive shocks may cancel, or phase coincidence may provoke resonance; cancellation is likely to predominate if there are many firms and industries—at a given time, there is unlikely to be much net effect from past shocks; "inventory cycles" are highly unlikely.

Induction of Inventory Fluctuations by Monetary Policy

Squeezes on the availability of credit may strongly influence decisions on inventories and other circulating capital in ways not captured by formal modeling: much of such capital is fungible and quasi-liquid, so that it becomes a prime candidate for attempted disposal under pressures of forced liquidation—and, of course, such pressures to liquidate intensify illiquidity! Appreciating this point, Japanese authorities squeezed credit from time to time (in the past) in order to promote the Japanese current account. It should, however, be noted that in 1992, importantly because of computer-driven controls, business inventories are very lean: the potential influence of monetary and credit policies on inventory accumulation is now quite slight.

Bagehot (1915) explained how the Bank of England, when menaced by external drains, reduced its discounts, clamping down on the ability of British importers to maintain their stocks. Nonlinear dynamics, including "chaos" theory, probably must be deployed for the factors just described to be integrated into formal theory—to the extent that induced inventory fluctuations still matter.

References

Abramowitz, Moses, *Inventories and Business Cycles with Special Reference to Manufacturers' Inventories,* National Bureau of Economic Research Studies in Business Cycles No. 4, National

Bureau of Economic Research, New York, 1950; Allen, R. G. D., *Macro-Economic Theory,* Macmillan, London, 1967; Arrow, K. J., S. Karlin, and H. Scarf, *Studies in the Mathematical Theory of Inventory and Production,* Stanford University Press, Stanford, Calif., 1958; Bagehot, W., *Lombard Street,* John Murray, London, 1915 (first published in 1873); Baumol, W. J., *Economic Theory and Operations Analysis,* 4th ed., Prentice-Hall, Englewood Cliffs, N.J., 1977; Dorfman, R., P. Samuelson, and R. Solow, *Linear Programming and Economic Analysis,* McGraw-Hill, New York, 1958, chap. 12; Evans, M. K., *Macroeconomic Activity,* Harper & Row, New York, 1969; Hadley, G., *Nonlinear and Dynamic Programming,* Addison-Wesley, Reading, Mass., 1964, p. 238; Hawtrey, R. G., *Trade and Credit,* Longmans, Green, London, 1928; Hawtrey, R. G., *The Art of Central Banking,* Longmans, Green, London, 1932; Hawtrey, R. G., *Currency and Credit,* 4th ed., Longmans, Green, London, 1950; Hicks, J. R., *Value and Capital,* 2d ed., Clarendon Press, Oxford, 1946; Hicks, J. R., *Capital and Growth,* Clarendon Press, Oxford, 1965; Hirsch, A. A., and M. Lovell, *Sales Anticipations and Inventory Behavior,* Wiley, New York, 1969; Hobbs, J. A., *Control over Inventory and Production,* McGraw-Hill, New York, 1973; Holt, C., F. Modigliani, J. Muth, and H. Scarf, *Planning Production, Inventories and Work Force,* Prentice-Hall, Englewood Cliffs, N.J.; Lovell, Michael, "Determinants of Inventory Investment," in E. P. Denison and L. R. Klein (eds.), *Models of Income Determination,* Princeton University Press (for the NBER), Princeton, N.J., 1964; Lovell, M., "Inventory Cycles," in *The New Palgrave: A Dictionary of Economics,* vol. 2, Stockton Press, New York, 1987, pp. 972–975; Lucas, R. E., "Econometric Policy Evaluation," *Journal of Monetary Economics,* vol. 2, Supplement, 1976, pp. 19–46; Lucas, R. E., *Studies in Business Cycle Theory,* MIT Press, Cambridge, Mass., 1983; Maccini, L. J., "Inventories," in *The New Palgrave: A Dictionary of Economics,* vol. 2, Stockton Press, New York, 1987, pp. 969–972; Metzler, L. A., "The Nature and Stability of Inventory Cycles, *Review of Economic Statistics,* vol. 23, 1941—reprinted in AER, *Readings in Business Cycles,* Irwin, Homewood, Ill., 1965; Schlaifer, R., *Probability and Statistics for Business Decisions,* McGraw-Hill, New York, 1959, p. 237; U.S. Department of Commerce, Office of Business Economics, *A Survey of Current Business* and supplements thereto; Whitin, T. M., *The Theory of Inventory Management,* Princeton University Press, Princeton, N.J., 1957.

(*See also* Acceleration principle; Economic growth; Expectations; Interest rates; Rational expectations; Stock-flow analysis)

M. L. Burstein

Business investment in new plants and equipment

Business investment in new plants and equipment is a major component of gross private domestic investment. As defined by the Bureau of Economic Analysis (BEA) of the U.S. Department of Commerce, it includes expenditures for plant, machinery, and equipment for which companies maintain depreciation accounts. Purchases of capital goods and maintenance and repair expenditures charged to current account as well as purchases of land, used plant or equipment, and facilities for installation outside the country are excluded.

Business investment in new plants and equipment, some $530 billion in 1991, was about 71 percent of the gross private domestic fixed investment of the national income and product accounts; the balance consisted of residential investment and a modest amount of investment by nonprofit institutions. Generally excluded from "private investment" are tangible investments by government, household investment in durable goods, and all intangible investment such as investment in research and development, education, and health. Specifically excluded from business investment in new plants and equipment is investment in residential structures and equipment and in agriculture and by professional persons, real estate operators, and nonprofit institutions. Also excluded are oil-well drilling costs charged to current expense, net purchases of used capital goods from government, and dealers' margins on purchase of used capital goods. Correspondingly, the new plant and equipment totals are not reduced by receipts from the sales of used capital to foreigners or to dealers in scrap material.

Investment Anticipations Surveys

Business plant and equipment expenditures and plans are surveyed four times a year by the Census Bureau. The survey is of companies, not establishments, with expenditures allocated to industries on the basis of the primary industry of all of each company's production. Firms are asked in forms mailed at the beginning of each quarter to report on their actual, current-dollar expenditures during the previous quarter and their planned expenditures for the current and two subsequent quarters. The third- and fourth-quarter surveys ask for anticipations of annual expenditures for the next calendar year. The Census Bureau then applies the implicit price deflator for nonresidential fixed investment, and its anticipations of that deflator, to convert current-dollar to constant-dollar figures (now on a 1987 base). Figures in percent changes and billions of dollars are reported for individual manufacturing and nonmanufacturing industries and in aggregates.

New structures and additions include all nonresidential construction and major alterations, land improvements, and exploratory and development expenditures chargeable to fixed-asset accounts. New machinery and equipment include "automobiles, trucks, tractors, etc., furniture and fixtures, office machinery, and all other new equipment." Where motor vehicles or other capital is purchased both for personal and for business use, only the portion allocated to business is included. Expenditures for all items charged off as current operating expense, including costs of maintenance and repairs, new facilities owned by the federal government but operated under contract by private companies, and plant and equipment furnished by communities and organizations, are excluded.

Expenditures are generally reported as payments are made, and on an ownership rather than a use basis. In airlines and railroads where there is extensive leasing of equipment, however, the total value of the equipment is counted as expenditure at the time it is leased.

Despite the fact that business investment in new plants and equipment is a lagging indicator, it is closely watched by economic analysts and forecasters as a particularly important and sensitive cyclical indicator as well as for its relation to long-term growth. It is somewhat influenced, especially in the short run, by liquidity considerations and the availability of internal funds from profits as well as external sources of finance, and in the long run by the relative cost of capital and other inputs to production. Investment in new plants and equipment is also influenced by needs to modernize and, in recent years, by government standards related to environmental protection. A major portion of business investment in new plants and equipment generally involves the replacement of old capital that has worn out or outlived its usefulness; some 60 percent tends to be classified as replacement and modernization as opposed to 40 percent for expansion. Investment in new plant and equipment is thought to "embody" technological change which adds to productivity and lowers costs.

Investment and the Economy

An overwhelming influence on business investment is the general state of the economy and, particularly, the pressure of demand on existing capacity and the rate of growth of output. The substantial business investment related to expansion clearly depends upon the rate at which demand and output are growing and are expected to grow in the future. Even a modest slowing of the rate of growth of final product, as from 4 to 3 percent, might thus in principle generate a reduction in expansion investment of 25 percent; 3 percent growth requires one-fourth less in the way of additional plant and equipment than does 4 percent growth. At the extreme, an actual decline in output in a recession can be devastating to business investment. Thus, from the beginning of 1974 to the third quarter of 1975, while the unemployment rate rose from 5.2 to between 8½ and 9 percent, real, nonresidential business fixed investment (in constant 1987 dollars) fell 17.5 percent. In current dollars, business spending for new plant and equipment fell from $146.79 billion in the fourth quarter of 1974 to $141.04 billion in the third quarter of 1975, a drop of 3.9 percent. The decline in constant (1987) dollars, from a peak of $308.47 billion in the second quarter of 1974 to a trough of $262.26 billion in the fourth quarter of 1975, was no less than 15 percent. In the recession of the early 1980s, from a third-quarter 1981 peak of $367.54 billion, in 1987 dollars, business fixed investment fell to $320.76 billion in the first quarter of 1983, a drop of 12.7 percent; the total of real nonresidential fixed investment fell 12.8 percent over roughly the same period. In our latest recession that investment fell 9.3 percent from the third quarter of 1990 to the fourth quarter of 1991.

Inflation, perhaps paradoxically, does not have a generally negative effect on business plant and equipment spending. Indeed, there is some reason to believe that businesses seek to buy more plant and equipment in periods of rising prices with the intention of making their purchases before costs get higher as well as with the expectation that proceeds to be realized from higher selling prices of the product of new capital will be greater.

Investment Incentives

There have been various efforts on the part of government to increase business plant and equipment spending. These have generally involved acceleration of depreciation for tax purposes and a so-called investment tax credit, at 10 percent at the time of its elimination in 1986, but limited chiefly to equipment. This credit reduced business income taxes by up to 10 percent of equipment expenditures. It is argued by some that accelerated tax depreciation and the equipment tax credit increased business investment by reducing its aftertax cost relative to that of other business expenditures. Just how much this did so, however, is open to doubt. Both responses by business and the results of various econometric studies suggest that these tax incentives to spur business investment may cost more in the way of lost tax revenues to the Treasury than the amount of new plant and equipment expenditures that they induce. They would also seem to be least effective in periods of recession when business investment falls and most likely to stimulate more business investment in booms where investment is already high and the dangers of the stimuli contributing to inflation may be greater.

References

Eisner, Robert, *Factors in Business Investment,* Ballinger, Cambridge, Mass., 1978; Eisner, Robert, and R. H. Strotz, "Determinants of Business Investment," in Commission on Money and Credit, *Impacts of Monetary Policy,* Prentice-Hall, Englewood Cliffs, N.J., 1964, pp. 59–223; Ferber, Robert (ed.), *Determinants of Investment Behavior,* Universities—National Bureau Conference Series, no. 19, Columbia University Press, New York, 1967; Fromm, Gary (ed.), *Tax Incentives and Capital Spending,* Brookings, Washington, D.C., 1971.

(*See also* Anticipation surveys, business; Capital formation; Investment function)

Robert Eisner

Cambridge school

Cambridge school is a convenient term for a body of somewhat discordant ideas associated with a number of economists at the University of Cambridge, England. These economists either worked with John Maynard Keynes or were deeply involved in the Keynesian revolution of the 1930s, and they included Nicholas Kaldor, Joan Robinson, and Piero Sraffa. Members of the Cambridge school see themselves as developing Keynes's theories to deal with the long-run problems of growth and income distribution that Keynes himself largely neglected. For that reason, the ideas of the Cambridge school also travel under the name of "post Keynesian economics," and indeed the U.S. wing of the Cambridge school, once led by Sidney Weintraub and now by Paul Davidson, cluster around the *Journal of Post-Keynesian Economics,* promoting an approach to economic issues similar to, but not identical with, those of British Keynesians.

Antineoclassical Microeconomics

The Cambridge or post Keynesian economists are more united by what they are against than by what they are for. They are against any and all versions of so-called neoclassical microeconomics—maximizing economic agents, rapid response to price changes, emphasis on competitive equilibrium outcomes, Pareto optimality, and so on—and to what they scathingly refer to as "bastard Keynesianism," namely, the income-expenditure, 45°-diagram interpretation of Keynesian macroeconomics familiar to all students of elementary economics around the world. What the Cambridge economists are for, however, is more difficult to describe, because different members of the school have different views as to how to proceed in constructing the edifice of post Keynesian economics.

Sraffa's Role

Piero Sraffa's book, *Production of Commodities by Means of Commodities* (1960), is concerned with the classic problem of how relative prices are determined. Sraffa constructs a model of production in which demand plays no role in the determination of prices, and he concentrates his efforts on demonstrating that we cannot determine prices at all unless we start either with a predetermined wage rate or with a predetermined rate of profit. How these are themselves determined is left open to question. This controversial model is seen by some Cambridge economists as forming the basis of a wholly new microeconomics. Other post Keynesian economists, however, prefer the ideas of Michael Kalecki, a Polish economist who developed a theory of markup pricing under conditions of oligopoly. Sraffa's book has also attracted much attention from Marxist economists, some of whom are keen to reformulate Marx in the light of Sraffa; these Marxist members of the Cambridge school are frequently known as neo-Ricardians because of the links between some of Sraffa's arguments and those of Ricardo.

Whether favoring Sraffa or not, Cambridge economists are united in believing that the neoclassical model of pricing contains a fatal flaw: In general drawing a negatively inclined demand curve for capital as a function of the rate of profit or rate of return on capital is impossible because of the phenomenon of reswitching. *Reswitching* refers to the possibility that a given technique may be the most profitable one for business firms to adopt at two different rates of profit but unprofitable at rates in between these two. If reswitching of techniques is possible, then so is *capital reversing*, meaning that the capital-labor ratio in an economy may not necessarily continue to rise indefinitely as the rate of profit falls. Thus, the widespread neoclassical notion that capital intensity is always uniquely related to the rate of return on capital has to be abandoned.

The point at issue has been conceded by all the leading neoclassical economists, who nevertheless continue to deny the empirical importance of capital reversing in actual economies. The Cambridge economists, however, are convinced that capital reversing is a general and indeed common phenomenon in a capitalist economy, and they argue, therefore, that neoclassical economics has to be scrapped as logically inconsistent.

Progrowth Models Based on Investment

Apart from such problems of microeconomics, the Cambridge school firmly believes that fruitful theorizing in economics will have to take the form of growth models that are squarely based on the Keynesian primacy of investment, itself the product of business confidence or "animal spirits," rather than on prices and the returns to factors of production. The Cambridge school goes beyond Keynes in operating with two saving functions, one for capitalists and a different one for workers. Around these central ideas, both Nicholas Kaldor and Joan Robinson have developed distinct growth models, that is, abstract formulations of the steady-state conditions required for an economic system to reproduce itself, unchanged in all essential aspects "from here to eternity." Both models have the common property that the respective shares of income received by capitalists and workers are determined simultaneously with the rate of profit, the capital-output ratio, and the overall growth rate of the economy. They give rise to such elegant results as the Pasinetti theorem: The equilibrium rate of profit in steady-state growth is uniquely determined by the growth rate of the economy and the saving propensity of capitalists, completely independent of the saving behavior of workers as well as the underlying technology of production. The import of the Pasinetti theorem is unclear; equally unclear is the importance of theorems that flow from certain alternative neoclassical growth models, such as "the golden rule of accumulation," which tells us that consumption per head is only maximized in an economy growing at a steady state when the rate of return on capital is equalized with the growth rate. However, no economy has ever been observed in steady-state growth, and actual growth is unsteady and unbalanced for deep, inherent reasons. It cannot be argued, therefore, that growth theory is as yet capable of throwing much light on actual economies growing over time, which no doubt accounts for the failure to resolve the now 30-year-old debate between Cambridge, England, and Cambridge, Massachusetts. The Cambridge school continues to gain adherents, but only time will tell whether it has the capacity to provide an alternative framework, a new paradigm that is as fertile as that furnished by the orthodox mainstream of neoclassical economics.

References

Blaug, M., *The Cambridge Revolution: Success or Failure?*, Institute of Economic Affairs, London, 1975; Eichner, A. S. (ed.), *A Guide to Post-Keynesian Economics*, M. E. Sharpe, White Plains, N.Y., 1979; Eichner, A. S., and J. A. Kregel, "An Essay on Post-Keynesian Theory: A New Paradigm in Economics," *Journal of Economic Literature*, vol. 13, December 1975, pp. 1293–1314; Harcourt, G. C., *Some Cambridge Controversies in the Theory of Capital*, Cambridge University Press, New York, 1972; Kregel, J. A., *The Reconstruction of Political Economy: An Introduction to Post-Keynesian Economics*, Macmillan, London, 1973; Sraffa, Pierre, *Production of Commodities by Means of Commodities: Prelude to a Critique of Economic Theory*, Cambridge University Press, Cambridge, 1960; Weintraub, S. (ed.), *Modern Economic Thought*, University of Pennsylvania Press, Philadelphia, 1977.

(*See also* Economic growth; Keynesian economics; Post Keynesian economics)

Mark Blaug

Cameralism (*see* Mercantilism)

Capacity, industrial (*see* Industrial production index)

Capital budgeting

The planning and analysis processes conducted when evaluating outlays whose benefits flow beyond a short period is called *capital budgeting*. Capital budgeting is significant because: (1) the consequences of the decisions continue over an extended period, involving a loss of flexibility; (2) the commitments represent an implicit sales forecast which, if incorrect, will cause overinvestment or underinvestment in fixed assets; (3) financial distress can be caused by too much investment in fixed assets or too little; (4) fixed asset expansion may involve substantial expenditures whose financing must be arranged in advance; (5) good capital budgeting will improve the timing of asset acquisitions and their quality. The importance of capital budgeting decisions is demonstrated by studies which report that the stock prices of firms react favorably to announcements of the expansion of investment programs and negatively to contractions.

Administration of Capital Budgeting

Different categories of investment require somewhat different evaluation and analysis. Replacement decisions usually involve small uncertainty. Expansion decisions that involve adding capacity in an existing product line are also based on prior experience. Growth investments into new product lines and/or new geographic markets generally involve greater risk because experience may be less applicable. Mandatory investments such as pollution control equipment must be made whether or not they add value to the firm, because their social externalities make them desirable. Intangible investments include facilities which may improve employee morale but whose effects on revenues may be difficult to estimate.

Another grouping of investment types is based on their degree of interdependence. Independent projects have little or no influence on one another. Mutually exclusive investments involve alternative methods of performing the same function—gas powered versus electric forklift trucks. Complementary investments may enhance one another—adding computers may lead to investments to improve quality control, materials handling, inventory control, etc. Some projects may involve product substitutes which may use existing facilities but reduce revenues in other lines.

The administration of capital budgeting involves formulating proposals, reviewing and evaluating them and their financing, controlling the release of funds in relation to completion, and evaluating performance against forecasts. Larger dollar amounts require higher levels of final approval. An important function of the top executive group and of the board of directors is approval of major outlays and of total capital budgeting programs. The planning horizon varies with the durability of the investment, visibility of the future, competitive pressures, etc.

Alternative Project Ranking Methods

The net present value (NPV) decision rule meets economic criteria for making sound investment decisions. The NPV of an investment is the present value of expected cash inflows less the present value of expected cash outflows, using a market-determined applicable (risk-adjusted) discount factor (cost of capital). Independent projects with a positive NPV should be accepted. If projects are mutually exclusive, choose the one with the highest NPV. The NPV rule meets four criteria: (1) It considers all relevant cash flows; (2) it discounts cash flows at a market-determined opportunity cost of capital; (3) it satisfies the value-additivity principle—decisions on combinations of projects cannot contradict decisions that would be made viewing the projects independently; (4) it selects the projects which maximize the value of the firm.

Unlike the NPV, the profitability index (PI) uses a ratio of the present values of inflows to outflows instead of their difference. PI is similar to Tobin's q ratio in macroeconomics—the ratio of the market value of the firm to the current replacement costs of its assets. For Tobin's q, a ratio above one stimulates investment activity since greater values are generated than their costs. When Tobin's q is below 1, investment activity will be slowed so that capacity utilization will be improved. Tobin's q is applicable at the level of the firm, industry, or economy so it avoids a limitation of the

PI, which does not account for the scale or size of investments. Thus the PI would rank a $1 investment with a gross present value (GPV) of $5 above a $100,000 investment with a GPV of $300,000 over the same time horizon.

Another alternative to the NPV criterion is the internal rate of return (IRR) decision rule. The IRR is the interest rate (or discount rate) at which the NPV of the project is zero. The IRR rule selects those independent projects for which the IRR is greater than the applicable cost of capital. For mutually exclusive projects, select the highest IRR. Although the NPV and IRR methods are similar, they can produce contradictory decisions. The NPV rule is the only one which is always correct. The IRR makes a faulty reinvestment rate assumption that intermediate fund flows during the life of the project can be reinvested at the project's IRR. Projects of equal risk should have the same opportunity cost but may have different IRRs; therefore, discounting at the IRR is inappropriate. The IRR criterion can violate the value-additivity principle. The NPV rule obeys value additivity. Using NPV, the value of the firm is the sum of the values of the separate projects which comprise the firm. Finally, the IRR results in meaningless multiple rates of return whenever cash flows change direction more than once during the life of the project.

Foreign Capital Investments

Foreign capital investments can be analyzed using the NPV rule. Potential advantages of foreign investment include: (1) larger markets; (2) increased utilization of capabilities (fixed factors); (3) risk reduction if changes in foreign economic conditions are imperfectly correlated with changes in domestic economic conditions. Potential disadvantages include: (1) complex government regulations, possibly discriminatory against foreign firms; (2) differences in consumer tastes and needs; (3) differences in worker and manager attitudes and sensitivities; (4) instability in political conditions.

Capital Budgeting under Uncertainty

Capital budgeting under certainty is an exercise in decision making across time with known discount rates. Under uncertainty, cash flows and even discount rates may change, and management may or may not have flexibility in the timing of investment decisions. Decision trees and option pricing have provided models for aiding investment decisions under uncertainty.

Every investment project may be described as a decision tree that requires five kinds of information: (1) cash flows along branches of the decision tree; (2) timing of the cash flows; (3) probabilities of the cash flows; (4) types of decisions that can be made at nodes in the decision tree; (5) appropriate risk-adjusted discount rates. Decision trees explicitly recognize flexibility that can be represented by future actions that are contingent on future states of nature. Decision trees provide no advice on which risk-adjusted discount rate should be used or how it may change over time. However, the investment project under uncertainty may be priced by utilizing a perfectly correlated security which is priced and whose pattern of payoffs is perfectly correlated with the payoffs depicted by the decision tree for the investment project.

Another approach is to apply option pricing. NPV analysis is augmented to incorporate the flexibility provided by decisions that can be made in the future. Decision makers can take into account asset option opportunities such as deferral of the decision, expansion (growth), shrinkage, abandonment, or switching. These options are equivalent to the purchase or sale of call or put options. NPV analysis that does not account for the option alternatives will undervalue investments under uncertainty. Asset options are a promising area for further development because they show promise in enabling managers to place numerical values on the flexibility provided by future decisions.

References

Brennan, M., and E. Schwartz, "Evaluating Natural Resource Investments," *Journal of Business,* April 1985, pp. 135–157; Fama, E., "Risk-Adjusted Discount Rates and Capital Budgeting under Uncertainty," *Journal of Financial Economics,* August 1977, pp. 3–24; Gehr, A., "Risk-Adjusted Capital Budgeting Using Arbitrage," *Financial Management,* Winter 1981, pp. 14–19; Howe, Keith M., and H. Lapan, "Inflation and Asset Life: The Darby Versus the Fisher Effect," *Journal of Financial and Quantitative Analysis,* June 1987, pp. 249–258; Weingartner, H. M., *Mathematical Programming and the Analysis of Capital Budgeting Problems,* Prentice-Hall, Englewood Cliffs, N.J., 1963; Weston, J. Fred, and Thomas E. Copeland, *Managerial Finance,* 9th ed., Dryden, 1992, chaps. 9 and 13.

(*See also* Business investment in new plants and equipment)

J. Fred Weston

Capital formation

Capital formation is the development of means of future production. In classical economics the means of production was divided into three categories: land, labor, and capital. Land comprised all the endowments of nature, including resources under the ground, and in the water and air. These shared with labor the characteristics that they did not come out of the process of production itself. They were also thought, somewhat inaccurately, never to be exhausted in production. Capital was distinguished as both produced by the economy and subject to consumption or depreciation in the productive process.

Concepts of Capital

In terms of business enterprises, capital comprises buildings, structures or plants, machinery or equipment, and inventories. Somewhat more broadly, capital also includes residential housing, whether rented or owner-occupied; transportation facilities and equipment, including highways and airports, whether owned by private industry or government; and, still more broadly, all physical or tangible producible facilities, whether owned by government, households, nonprofit institutions, or government.

A still wider concept, increasingly used in recent years, embraces human and nonphysical capital as well. Capital would thus include the knowledge produced by research and development expenditures, the skills derived from education and training, improvement in productivity brought on by investment in the health of workers, and increases in the value of land and natural resources such as might be achieved by clearing forests, improving the quality of soil, exploring for minerals, and investing in the preservation and improvement of the water and air of the environment.

Capital formation in any of these forms is characterized by the devotion of current production to the creation of something which is not consumed or enjoyed now but is utilized in future production, either of consumption services or of more capital. Capital formation is less widely perceived to have a price or cost—loss of the opportunity to produce something else for immediate enjoyment. In return, however, capital formation offers a reward of increased future production which can make possible more future consumption.

Although capital formation may generally be expected to increase the capacity for future output, it will not necessarily increase on a permanent basis the opportunities for future consumption. For a given technology, more capital is likely to imply greater productive capacity, but, as capital formation proceeds, the return to capital diminishes, as does the return to any factor of production which is used more and more, whereas the use of other factors does not increase in proportion. This, indeed, is a facet of the law of diminishing returns. Thus, picks and shovels will enable ditchdiggers to dig much more rapidly than with their bare hands. But eventually, when all the ditchdiggers have picks and shovels to suit every possible need, both for replacement and a variety of possible kinds of soil, additional utensils will only get in the way and will add no more to productive capacity, let alone cover their own costs.

Similarly, investment in human or nonphysical capital is likely to be subject to diminishing marginal returns. At some point, additional education or additional research and development spending or additional investment in health will not offer sufficient benefits to return their costs.

When Is Capital Formation Worthwhile?

If we were all indifferent as to the enjoyment of consumption now and consumption in the future, that is, if our marginal rate of time preference were zero, and if we were starting with an economy in stationary equilibrium, that is, with no growth, capital formation would be worthwhile if its net marginal product were positive. This is to say, for example, that it would pay to produce an additional $100 machine if it would add to future output anything more than $100. Since the machine will eventually break down or become obsolete and have no further value, in order to be worth acquiring, it must over its lifetime produce enough to cover its depreciation or return its original cost.

In an economy without growth but with a positive rate of time preference (or positive real rate of interest), where for reasons of impending mortality, general uncertainty, or some other factor, people would prefer to have more now even if this means less later, new capital formation should be undertaken only if it can produce more in the way of additional goods and services in the future than what the resources devoted to the production of capital could otherwise produce in the present. Put another way, utilizing the rate of interest and rate of discount which reflects this preference of the present over the future, the present value of expected future returns from additional capital must be at least equal to its cost.

In a growing economy where noncapital inputs, say labor, are growing, net capital formation, that is, a growth in the stock of capital, will be necessary merely to keep factor proportions constant. If all factors of production, including capital, grow at some constant rate, we may presume, technological change aside, that total production, consumption, and capital formation can and will grow at that same rate. Given the positive marginal rate of time preference, we may then also presume a positive marginal net product of capital, such that additional saving or capital formation will raise the rate of output.

But a higher rate of capital formation, implying a higher capital-labor ratio, implies that more capital will be needed in the future merely to meet increased replacement requirements and increased requirements for additional capital to maintain the higher capital-labor ratio as labor services continue to grow.

For example, if the number of workers is growing by 1 million per year and each worker produces with the aid of $10,000 capital, the net capital formation necessary to maintain this ratio is $10 billion, i.e., 1 million times $10,000. If increased capital formation brings us to a ratio of $11,000 per worker, then $11 billion, which equals 1 million times $11,000, will be necessary in the way of net capital formation to provide the additional capital for each additional worker.

Additional capital formation will increase output. But if that increase is not enough to meet the requirements both for reproducing itself as it wears out and for providing enough additional capital for the additional workers to maintain the labor force at its higher capital intensity, this higher capital intensity and higher production can be maintained only by reducing consumption.

We are thus left finally with the conclusion that in most economies, including that of the United States, with a positive rate of economic growth and a positive rate of time preference, more capital formation will lead to more future output but will not necessarily lead to more future consumption. To maximize future consumption, we should proceed with capital formation only to the critical point where the diminishing net marginal product of capital has fallen to the marginal investment requirement necessary to maintain the capital-labor ratio. If we proceed to this point, we will be operating according to the "golden rule" and maximizing consumption. If we have less capital formation or more capital formation, we will have less consumption.

Of course, the real economies of the world have many different types of capital, each of which will add to production and more than pay for its cost and more than maintain itself up to that critical point. For those forms of capital where, by these criteria, we do not have enough capital formation, increased capital formation will add to both output and consumption in the long run. Where, however, we already have enough or too much capital formation, the attempt to increase the rate of capital formation will only reduce the possible stream of future consumption and possibly future output as well.

Profit Motive and Capital Formation

In a freely competitive economy where capital is owned by private producers who themselves enjoy the returns from their capital, we may expect that the owners, with appropriate information, will arrive at optimal amounts of capital formation. Government intervention to encourage more capital formation, unless it is merely countering other government interventions that have held down capital formation, runs the risk of raising capital formation beyond its optimal levels.

Even in the most free-enterprise, private-profit-oriented economies, the formation of much capital, including both government capital and vast amounts of human capital, is not determined by its private owners. Although we may expect the profit motive to lead business to acquire appropriate amounts of plant, equipment, and inventories, the profit motive does not readily operate to ensure an optimal amount of capital formation in the form of research and development, education, health, and social overhead or government capital generally. And in the case of business capital formation, the general failure of aggregate demand and macroeconomic breakdown associated with depressions and severe recessions bring on enormous reductions in capital formation. Thus government and the political process must both provide a general climate of prosperity in which private-profit-oriented business capital formation can reach its optimum and see to it that nonbusiness capital formation also reaches its optimum.

References

Denison, Edward, *Accounting for Economic Growth 1929–1969,* Brookings, Washington, D.C., 1974; Eisner, Robert, *The Total Incomes System of Accounts,* University of Chicago, Chicago, 1989; Kendrick, John W., *The Formation and Stocks of Total Capital,* National Bureau of Economic Research, New York, 1976; Marx, Karl, *Capital,* Kerr, Chicago, 1906, especially vol. 1, part 8, "The Accumulation of Capital"; Phelps, Edmund S. (ed.), *The Goal of Economic Growth,* Norton, New York, 1969; Shapiro, Eli, and William L. White (eds.), *Capital for Productivity and Jobs,* Prentice-Hall, Englewood Cliffs, N.J., 1977.

(*See also* Business investment in new plants and equipment; Economic growth; Human capital; Productivity)

Robert Eisner

Capital gains

Owners of invested capital generally earn returns on their investment in one of four forms: profits, receipt of interest or dividend payments, receipt of rental or royalty payments, or appreciation in value of the asset representing that invested capital. The appreciation in value of an asset represents a capital gain to the owner of the asset.

Although fluctuations in market values continually lead to accrued gains and losses, for income tax purposes a capital gain (or loss) is the gain (or loss) from the sale or exchange of a capital asset. That is, income tax principles generally only measure capital gains when they are realized rather than as they accrue. The term "capital asset" generally includes any property held by an individual or business except inventory, business accounts receivable, depreciable or real property used in a trade or business, and certain other property.

Tax data indicate the largest source of capital gains realized by individuals to be gains on the sale of corporate stock, followed by gains on the sale of a principal residence, the sale of partnership interests and S-corporations, the sale of residential rental property, the sale of depreciable business real property, the sale of real estate other than farm land, the sale of commodities and futures contracts and options, the sale of bonds and notes, the sale of depreciable business personal property, the sale of livestock, the sale of mutual fund shares, the sale of farm land, and the sale of standing timber.

The Theory and Practice of Taxing Capital Gains

Because capital gains result from the change in value of assets, capital gains do not necessarily result from the increased flow of goods and services to the economy. Hence, in national income accounting capital gains are not income. The theory of taxing capital gains as part of an income tax rests on the net accretion principle. The net accretion principle holds that increases in real wealth represent increases in the command over real resources and thereby represent income to the individual. Thus, any increase in net real wealth during a period is income, regardless of whether this increase in net wealth is realized. Similarly, reductions in net wealth represent negative income.

The net accretion principle implies that theoretically correct income taxation of capital gains would tax only real capital gains, would tax capital gains as they accrue, and would permit the taxpayer to write off losses against other income. No major western economy taxes capital gains in this manner. Only Great Britain and Australia tax real capital gains.

The United States does require accrual taxation of certain traders in futures contracts; however, this represents a very small percentage of total capital gains. The commonly held view is that accrual taxation, also known as "marking-to-market" taxation, is impractical for all assets but readily tradable securities. Instead, countries which tax capital gains tax the gains upon realization.

Primarily as a consequence of the decision to tax upon realization rather than accrual, no country provides full loss offset of capital losses against other income. Taxation upon realization affords taxpayers the opportunity to select whether it is in their best interests to pay tax. If full loss offset were provided, the rational taxpayer always would choose to realize losses immediately and defer as long as possible the recognition of gains. The result would be substantial revenue loss to the government as losses shield other income from tax.

In theory, income from capital gains should be treated no differently for tax purposes than income from interest, dividends, or wages. In practice, most western countries provide special taxation of capital gains, either at lower rates than other income or not at all. However, such preferential treatment generally is not consistent across all forms of capital gains. Between 1988 and 1990, the United States alone taxed capital gains at the same rates as wages, interest, and dividends. In Germany, some short-term capital gains are taxed as ordinary income, and all long-term capital gains are untaxed. In Japan, capital gains on corporate securities are taxed more lightly than capital gains on real estate. Almost from the inception of the income tax in the United States until 1987, long-term capital gains (generally 1 year or more) were taxed at rates below that of ordinary income.

Economic Issues in the Taxation of Capital Gains

Deferral Effect   Taxing capital gains upon realization rather than accrual permits the taxpayer to defer payment of tax. Deferring tax lowers the present value of tax liability. As a result the effective real rate of tax on realized capital gains is lower than the statutory rate.

Lock-In Effect   Taxing capital gains upon realization rather than accrual discourages sales of assets. In particular, taxation upon realization discourages selling one asset to reinvest the proceeds in another asset. Because of the opportunity for deferral, the alternative asset must offer a higher future rate of appreciation than the current asset to make such asset switching worthwhile. Taxpayers who find it not in their interest to switch assets even though alternative assets offer a higher expected future return are said to be locked in to their current investments. Lock-in imposes an efficiency loss as investors will hold suboptimal portfolios. Lock-in is exacerbated by permitting the basis of an asset to be stepped up to its current market value upon transfer of the asset at death, without recognizing any of the accrued gain to the decedent. Holding assets until death effectively creates a zero tax rate on accrued capital gains.

Revenue from Tax Changes   If the lock-in effect is economically important, a reduction in tax rates theoretically could induce substantial asset switching, or "unlocking." Upon such realizations, taxes would be paid, and, theoretically, government revenues could increase as a result of the tax cut. This possibility has been an important point of debate among academic and government economists and policymakers in recent years.

"Conversion" Opportunities   Preferential taxation of the income from capital gains enables taxpayers to convert other, ordinary, income to capital gains income, creating tax shelters. For example, if a taxpayer borrows $100 at 10 percent annual interest to acquire a capital asset that is sold for $110 one year later, and repays the borrowing with sales proceeds, the taxpayer has an interest deduction of $10 that can reduce, or "shelter," ordinary income as a business expense and a capital gain of $10 subject to a preferential tax. The taxpayer has created a net aftertax positive cash flow even though on a pretax basis the transaction was not profitable.

Cost of Capital   As a tax on the return to capital, taxation of capital gains should increase the cost of capital. How taxes on capital gains affect the cost of capital depends on the effective tax rate (after accounting for deferral and step up) and the extent to which taxpayers, as opposed to tax-exempt sources, are the marginal suppliers of investment capital.

Risk Taking   An accrual tax on capital gains with full loss offset theoretically should increase risk taking by investors. With less than full loss offset, preferential taxation of capital gains may be necessary to encourage risk taking.

Inflation   Taxing nominal capital gains upon realization increases the effective tax rate on real capital gains. Partial exclusion from tax of income from capital gains is sometimes advocated as a simpler solution than indexing for avoiding the taxation of inflationary gains. As exclusions do not generally vary with holding periods or inflation rates, at best they provide a very crude offset for inflation.

Distribution of the Tax Burden   To the extent that taxes on the returns to capital are borne by the owners of capital, the distribution of the burden of taxes on capital gains is borne primarily by higher-income individuals, as higher-income individuals own proportionately more capital assets than lower-income individuals. The distributional benefit of a reduction in taxes on capital gains has been an important point in the debate over the proper tax policy toward capital gains.

Reference

Joint Committee on Taxation, *Proposals and Issues Relating to the Taxation of Capital Gains and Losses* (JCS-10-90), Mar. 23, 1990.

(*See also* Taxation, an overview)

Thomas A. Barthold

Capital-intensive industry

In a capital-intensive industry the ratio of plant and equipment costs, essentially as measured by depreciation costs, to total costs is higher than the average such ratio for all industries. The capital intensity of an industry can also be inferred from the relationship of its capital input to its labor input. Hence, more capital input than labor input connotes a capital-intensive industry; conversely, more labor input than capital input indicates a labor-intensive industry. Thus, a labor-intensive industry requires a high proportion of labor compared with the other factors employed, especially capital. Intensities of capital or labor input are relative or comparative terms of measurement.

Examples of capital-intensive industries include petroleum, tobacco, chemicals, utilities, and primary metals. Examples of labor-intensive industries include textiles, leather products, furniture, and the production of services. Among the latter, for example, the U.S. Postal Service is about 85 percent labor intensive (1991).

Measurement of Capital Intensity

Ambiguities in the concept of capital and, hence, in the concept of capital-intensive industries exist. In the eighteenth century Adam Smith dichotomized capital into fixed capital and circulating capital, the latter to include financial resources and work in process. In 1977 the Conference Board in its Road Maps of Industry series broadened its definition of capital invested to include land and inventory as well as plant and equipment. However, the board did not include financial capital, such as treasury bills or cash on hand, as capital invested. According to this broadened definition, an industry with a high inventory investment, such as the gold- or diamond-working industry, would also be regarded as a capital-intensive industry.

Another example would be agriculture, in which the costs of land as well as plant and equipment, especially equipment, take the largest share of total costs. Agriculture's capital share has risen, while the farm labor share has fallen. Figures reveal that 24.9 percent of the civilian labor force depended on farming for its livelihood in 1930 compared with only 2.7 percent in 1991.

The Conference Board's research suggests rising capital intensity over time for virtually all industries in the United States, even for those still regarded as labor intensive. Work by John W. Kendrick and others substantiates this observation.

Capital intensity, therefore, can be measured not only on an industry-by-industry basis but also from one period to another in the same industry. So also can capital intensity or labor intensity be measured from one period to another for the same economy.

Capital and Productive Efficiency

Capital is usually employed as a means of increasing productive efficiency, i.e., productivity improvement, whatever the industry. Using improved or new technology also increases productivity. These factors help to explain the trend of rising capital intensity in the U.S. economy over time. In the steel industry, for example, the process of converting iron into steel has steadily improved over the past 100 years as evidenced by the progressive switch from Bessemer furnaces to open-hearth furnaces to electric and oxygen furnaces. The development of continuous strip-rolling mills turning out flat-rolled sheets is another example of technology leading to rising capital intensity in the steel industry.

Whatever the industry, almost all technological advances tend to lead to substitutions of more efficient capital equipment for less efficient capital equipment. But in a larger sense, these substitutions amount to factor substitution—the replacement of labor by capital with a decline in unit labor costs usually resulting. This phenomenon is especially the case in decreasing-cost industries. Such industries as well as their customers are the beneficiaries of economies resulting from large-scale production. Manufacturing in general is a decreasing-cost industry, depending on the degree of capital intensity.

Given high intensity, volume is the key to decreasing costs, as in the automobile industry. Assembly-line production, automatic multiple boring of engine blocks, giant body-stamping equipment, and the like all demand intensive, almost full-time use for the heavy capital investments to pay off. When the investments do pay off, unit costs tend to fall. Economies of scale also usually apply to automotive supplier industries, such as aluminum, plastics, rubber, glass, battery, headlamp, and spark plug.

Implications of Rising Capital Intensity

The implications of rising capital intensity are many and far-reaching. National economic development or economic growth, for example, is generally held to be a function of capital investment. Hence, countries have been classified as capital-rich and capital-poor, e.g., the United States is said to be capital-rich and Third World countries such as India capital-poor. Indeed, for the most part the entire Third World is capital-poor. Economic development, according to Walt W. Rostow (*The Stages of Economic Growth,* 1960), proceeds through five stages: the traditional society, the preconditions for takeoff, the takeoff, the drive to maturity, and the age of high mass consumption. The takeoff stage is critical because it is in this stage that capital intensity rises and thus economic development becomes virtually assured. In the nineteenth century the United States was in the takeoff stage because of an infusion of private foreign capital, mainly British and French.

Another implication of the historical proclivity to substitute capital for labor and encourage capital intensity is the role of interest rates. The interest rate is, in a sense, the cost of capital. A falling interest rate, with constant or rising labor costs, other things being equal, tends to induce capital investment and intensity—for capital is then the relatively cheaper input and labor the dearer. Conversely, as the interest rate rises, with constant or falling labor costs, the tendency is the other way around—a pull toward a substitution of labor for capital.

References

Ackley, Gardner, *Macroeconomics: Theory and Policy,* 4th ed., Macmillan, New York, 1978, p. 619ff; Feldstein, Martin, *Taxes and Capital Formation,* University of Chicago, Chicago, 1987; Kendrick, John W., *Productivity Trends in the United States,* National Bureau of Economic Research, New York, 1961, especially pp. 85–94; Kuznets, Simon, *Capital in the American Economy,* National Bureau of Economic Research, New York, 1961; Layard, P. R. G., and A. A. Walters, *Microeconomic Theory,* McGraw-Hill, New York, 1978, p. 68ff; Rostow, Walt W., *The Stages of Economic Growth,* Cambridge University Press, Cambridge, 1960.

(*See also* Capital formation; Productivity.)

William H. Peterson

Capital markets and money markets

The highly efficient capital and money markets of the United States are largely a product of the twentieth century. The United States' financial system began its tremendous development around the turn of the century, and it has been the catalyst in the rapid real growth of this country since that time.

The capital and money markets in the United States include the total sources and uses of credit and equity funds in the U.S. economy. The markets include both long-term (capital markets) and short-term (money markets) sources and uses of funds, because these two markets merge closely into one another and at many points are interchangeable. The behavior of interest rates can be understood only within the context of the total market for credit. The available data do, however, permit a rough separation of long-term and short-term sectors.

The Principal Sources of Data

As is true of so much basic economic data, much of the knowledge about the U.S. capital and money markets stems from research by the National Bureau of Economic Research (NBER). Morris Copeland's *A Study of Money Flows in the United States* (1952) is the seminal study. Simon Kuznets' report, *Capital in the United States, Its Formation and Financing,* (1961), also contributed enormously to our knowledge of the subject. Raymond W. Goldsmith has also done invaluable work on the capital markets; his monumental three-volume report, *A Study of Saving in the United States* (1955), provides a comprehensive account of the growth of our savings and investment markets during the period 1897 to 1949, an account which he later brought up to date in his NBER studies.

The Federal Reserve Board (FRB) is today the basic source of statistics on the U.S. capital and money markets through the flow-of-funds accounts which it has maintained for many years as the outgrowth of Copeland's work. The FRB staff has over the years developed the flow-of-funds accounts into the financial system's counterpart of the GNP accounts. The two tables provided in this article illustrate the richness of the data supplied by the Federal Reserve. Table 1 shows a summary of total funds raised by various users in the capital and money markets during the period 1983 to 1990, and Table 2 presents a summary of total funds advanced from various sources. These two tables are supported by a wealth of detail on individual components of credit used and supplied. The data supplied by the FRB are available annually going back to 1946, and they are currently supplied quarterly on a seasonally adjusted annual rate basis. These data are keyed into the national income and product accounts so that the two systems of basic economic statistics can be reconciled.

The flow-of-funds data are net figures; for example, in Table 1 the estimate of $662.1 billion of borrowing by domestic nonfinancial sectors in 1990 is the net increase in outstanding credit to the nonfinancial sector for that year, and the individual components are also net figures. For example, the $264.4 billion figure for U.S. Treasury issues in 1990 is the net increase in such issues. Similarly, the figures in Table 2 also are net lending by the various sources of funds. The distinction between net and gross is an important one. For example, in 1990 the net funds advanced by the life insurance companies amounted to $122.9 billion. Actually, the gross cash flow for investment by life insurance companies (including not only new saving through life insurance companies but also repayments from past loans and investments) probably was nearly double the net increase. Unfortunately, however, the state of the art does not yet permit the flow-of-funds data to be prepared on a gross basis because of unavailability of such data from most sources. Although better knowledge of gross flows would be very helpful to understanding the behavior of the capital and money markets, the current net data are nonetheless most useful and are widely used by analysts of the money and capital markets.

The data are in nominal dollars—that is, they are not corrected for inflation. It would, of course, be possible to portray the flow of funds in real terms, but it can be argued that the financial markets behave in nominal-dollar terms so that there is no great need or advantage to correct them for inflation.

Trends from 1983 to 1990

Trends in the capital and money markets from 1983 to 1990, a long period of economic expansion after the recession of 1980 to 1982, contain some interesting developments. The flow-of-funds data show that total outstanding debt of domestic nonfinancial sectors of the U.S. economy exploded from $4.7 trillion at the end of 1982 to $10.6 trillion at the end of 1990, an increase of 125 percent in only 8 years. All forms of debt participated in this explosion. U.S. government debt held by the public rose from $991.4 billion at the end of 1982 to $2,568.9 billion at the end of 1990, or by 159 percent. Household debt (home mortgages and consumer credit) rose from $1.6 trillion to $3.8 trillion, or by 137.5 percent; nonfinancial business debt jumped from $1.7 trillion to $3.5 trillion, or by 106 percent; and state and local government debt increased from $334.1 billion to $648.8 billion, or by 94 percent. The rate of increase in total outstanding debt of the nonfinancial sectors was especially high during 1983 to 1986 when it averaged 13.1 percent per annum, far in excess of the increase in current dollar GNP. The flow-of-funds data also show, however, that private financial assets expanded from $3.3 trillion at the end of 1982 to $6.8 trillion at the close of 1990, or by 106 percent.

As seen in Table 1, the annual net increase in one- to four-family home mortgages rose from $120.4 billion in 1983 to $234.9 billion in 1987 before declining to $214.4 billion in 1990. As seen in Table 2, however, the net increase in "mortgage pools" (Fannie Mae, Ginnie Mae, and Freddie Mac) became the dominant vehicle for supplying home mortgage credit, as the pools' net increase rose from $44.4 billion in 1984 to $148 billion in 1990. This was particularly evident, as shown in Table 2, with the huge net reduction in funds available from the mutual savings and loan associations in 1989–1990, totalling $247.5 billion as these traditional home mortgage lenders fell into virtual demise.

Another very interesting trend from 1983 to 1990 has been the huge net increase in foreign funds invested in the U.S. credit markets and into the equities of U.S. business firms as well as direct investments. As seen in Table 2, the net increase in foreign funds invested here rose from $23.7 billion in 1983 to $97.6 billion in 1988 and since then has slackened to $66.4 billion in 1990. This trend has been, of course, the product of the huge deficit buildup in this period in the U.S. current account balance of payments with the rest of the world. The result is that, although in 1983 the total foreign holdings of U.S. credit instruments (U.S. government securities, corporate bonds, loans to U.S. nonbank borrowers, and open-market paper) exceeded U.S. holdings of foreign credit instruments by only $16.4 billion, the excess had risen to $483.8 billion by the end of 1990.

Finally, of interest in the bottom of Table 1, is the steady and massive net reduction since 1983 in corporate equity funds raised in U.S. markets. The figures show that the total funds raised by nonfinancial corporations fell by $552.3 billion from 1984 to 1990 and that the total funds raised by financial corporations declined by

TABLE 1 Summary of Net Funds Raised in Credit and Equity Markets

				Annual flows, $ billions				
	1983	1984	1985	1986	1987	1988	1989	1990
			Net Credit Market Borrowing by Nonfinancial Sectors					
Total net borrowing by domestic nonfinancial sectors	538.1	752.3	848.1	836.9	687.0	760.8	678.2	662.1
U.S. government	186.6	198.8	223.6	215.0	144.9	157.5	151.6	272.5
Treasury issues	186.7	199.0	223.7	214.7	143.4	140.0	150.0	264.4
Agency issues & mortgages	-.1	-.2	-.1	.4	1.5	17.4	1.6	8.2
Private domestic nonfinancial sectors	351.5	553.5	624.5	621.9	542.1	603.3	526.6	389.6
Debt capital instruments	247.1	319.9	451.2	465.8	453.2	459.2	379.8	309.6
Tax-exempt obligations	43.3	51.0	135.4	22.7	49.3	49.8	30.4	19.4
Corporate bonds	16.0	46.1	73.5	126.8	79.4	102.9	73.7	61.5
Mortgages	187.9	222.8	242.2	316.3	324.5	306.5	275.7	228.7
Home mortgages	120.4	136.7	156.8	218.7	234.9	231.0	218.0	214.4
Multifamily residences	14.1	25.2	29.8	33.5	24.4	16.7	16.4	-.7
Commercial	51.0	62.2	62.2	73.6	71.6	60.8	42.7	14.8
Farm	2.4	-1.2	-6.6	-9.5	-6.4	-2.1	-1.5	.2
Other debt instruments	104.4	233.6	173.3	156.1	88.9	144.1	146.8	80.0
Consumer credit	48.9	81.7	82.5	58.0	33.5	50.2	39.1	18.4
Bank loans n.e.c.	25.0	68.0	40.6	66.9	10.0	39.8	39.9	-3.0
Commercial paper	-.8	21.7	14.6	-9.3	2.3	11.9	20.4	9.7
Other loans	31.3	62.2	35.6	40.5	43.2	42.2	47.4	54.9
By borrowing sector:	351.5	553.5	624.5	621.9	542.1	603.3	526.6	389.6
State & local governments	23.6	28.1	90.9	36.2	48.8	45.6	29.6	14.6
Households	185.6	231.8	284.5	293.0	302.2	314.9	285.0	260.1
Nonfinancial business	142.3	293.6	249.1	292.7	191.0	242.8	211.9	114.9
Farm	3.9	-.4	-14.5	-16.3	-10.6	-7.5	1.6	3.0
Nonfarm noncorporate	81.9	123.2	129.3	99.2	77.9	65.7	50.8	14.3
Corporate	56.5	170.8	134.3	209.7	123.7	184.6	159.5	97.6
Foreign net borrowing in the United States	17.3	8.4	1.2	9.7	4.5	6.3	10.9	23.3
Bonds	3.1	3.8	3.8	3.1	7.4	6.9	5.3	21.1
Bank loans n.e.c.	3.6	-6.6	-2.8	-1.0	-3.6	-1.8	-.1	-2.8
Commercial paper	6.5	6.2	6.2	11.5	2.1	8.7	13.3	12.3
U.S. government & other loans	4.1	5.0	-6.0	-3.9	-1.4	-7.5	-7.5	-7.4
Total domestic plus foreign	555.4	760.6	849.3	846.6	691.5	767.1	689.1	685.4

	Net Credit Market Borrowing by Financial Sectors							
Total net borrowing by financial sectors	100.3	150.7	201.3	285.1	300.2	247.6	205.5	199.4
U.S. government-related								
Sponsored credit ag., sec.	67.8	74.9	101.5	154.1	171.8	119.8	151.0	170.6
Mortgage pool securities	1.4	30.4	20.6	15.2	30.2	44.9	25.2	22.6
Loans from U.S. government	66.4	44.4	79.9	139.2	142.3	74.9	125.8	148.0
	—	—	1.1	-.4	-.8	—	—	—
Private financial sectors	32.5	75.9	99.7	131.0	128.4	127.8	54.5	28.8
Corporate bonds	18.6	34.3	50.9	82.9	78.9	51.7	36.8	44.1
Mortgages	"	.4	.1	.1	.4	.3	"	.7
Bank loans n.e.c.	-.4	1.4	2.6	4.0	-3.2	1.4	1.8	.7
Open-market paper	21.3	24.0	32.0	24.2	27.9	54.8	26.9	8.0
Federal Home Loan Bank loans	-7.0	15.7	14.2	19.8	24.4	19.7	-11.0	-24.7
Total by sector	100.3	150.7	201.3	285.1	300.2	247.6	205.5	199.4
Sponsored credit agencies	1.4	30.4	21.7	14.9	29.5	44.9	25.2	22.6
Mortgage pools	66.4	44.4	79.9	139.2	142.3	74.9	125.8	148.0
Private financial sectors	32.5	75.9	99.7	131.0	128.4	127.8	54.5	28.8
Commercial banks	5.0	7.3	-4.9	-3.6	6.2	-3.0	-1.4	-1.1
Domestic affiliates	13.3	16.1	16.6	15.2	14.3	5.2	6.2	-27.7
Savings and loan associations	-6.2	17.2	17.3	20.9	19.6	19.9	-14.1	-32.4
Mutual savings banks	-.4	1.2	1.5	4.2	8.1	1.9	-1.4	-.1
Finance companies	17.5	24.3	57.7	54.7	40.8	67.7	46.3	50.9
REITs	-.3	.5	-.1	.8	.3	3.5	-1.9	-.3
SCO issuers	3.6	9.3	11.5	39.0	39.1	32.5	20.8	39.5
External Corporate Equity Funds Raised in U.S. Markets								
Total net share issues	54.6	-40.5	17.2	86.8	10.9	-124.2	-63.7	17.2
Mutual funds	27.2	29.3	84.4	159.0	73.9	1.1	41.3	66.9
All other	27.3	-69.8	-67.2	-72.2	-63.0	-125.3	-105.1	-49.7
Nonfinancial corporations	20.0	-79.0	-84.5	-85.0	-75.5	-129.5	-124.2	-63.0
Financial corporations	3.6	8.2	13.6	11.6	14.6	3.3	2.4	6.1
Foreign shares purchased in the United States	3.7	.9	3.7	1.2	-2.1	.9	16.7	7.2

SOURCE: Federal Reserve Board, Flow-of-Funds Section.

TABLE 2 Total Net Lending in Credit Markets, 1983–1990

	1983	1984	1985	1986	1987	1988	1989	1990
	Total Net Borrowing and Lending in Credit Markets*							
Total net lending in credit markets	655.7	911.4	1050.6	1131.7	991.7	1014.7	894.5	884.8
Private dom. nonfin. sectors	145.6	163.2	270.5	121.5	214.6	241.7	195.9	212.0
Households	103.3	125.0	178.6	68.2	182.0	250.8	196.0	203.9
Nonfarm noncorp. business	7.8	9.9	5.3	4.2	-.7	-.7	-1.2	-1.2
Corporate business	16.7	9.5	-.6	13.2	14.6	-12.5	2.2	15.9
State & local governments	17.9	18.9	87.3	35.9	18.7	4.2	-1.1	-6.6
Foreign	23.7	57.9	62.3	97.8	62.7	97.6	72.1	66.4
U.S. government	9.7	17.1	17.8	9.7	-7.9	-9.4	-2.4	34.0
Financial sectors	476.8	673.2	699.9	902.7	722.4	684.8	629.0	572.3
Sponsored credit agencies	3.4	29.8	23.7	14.1	27.0	37.1	-.5	22.2
Mortgage pools	66.4	44.4	79.9	139.2	142.3	74.9	125.8	148.0
Monetary authority	14.7	8.4	18.4	19.4	24.7	10.5	-7.3	8.1
Commercial banking	143.3	174.0	188.4	198.1	135.4	156.3	177.3	119.9
U.S. commercial banks	136.5	158.7	165.6	162.5	99.2	126.4	146.0	92.2
Bank affiliates	1.5	.9	3.7	-.3	2.0	-.1	2.8	-1.4
Foreign banking offices	3.7	12.9	16.4	35.0	34.2	29.4	26.7	29.0
Banks in U.S. poss.	1.6	1.5	2.7	.9	.1	.6	1.8	.2

Annual flows, $ billions

Private nonbank finance	249.0	416.6	389.6	531.9	393.0	406.0	333.8	274.2
Savings institutions	134.2	154.7	87.9	107.6	136.8	120.4	-90.9	-141.0
Savings & loans	103.3	129.3	64.8	75.2	93.3	86.3	-93.8	-135.0
Mutual savings banks	18.8	10.1	9.7	17.4	25.6	17.8	-4.8	-13.9
Credit unions	12.1	15.3	13.4	15.0	17.8	16.3	7.7	7.9
Insurance sector	100.1	121.8	150.1	160.1	179.7	198.7	177.9	226.1
Life insurance cos.	52.5	54.1	74.4	86.9	91.7	103.8	90.7	122.9
Private pension funds	29.9	21.3	26.6	-.8	22.2	31.4	7.2	9.1
St. & loc. govt. rtr. funds	16.0	34.7	22.9	31.3	26.3	34.6	49.1	65.4
Other insurance cos.	1.7	11.7	26.1	42.6	39.5	28.9	30.8	28.7
Finance n.e.c.	14.7	140.1	151.6	264.2	76.6	86.9	246.8	189.1
Finance companies	26.8	38.3	49.5	54.8	39.4	39.2	39.2	53.4
REITs	.1	.8	2.4	"	1.0	.9	-.3	-.8
Mutual funds	9.8	17.9	68.7	123.1	25.8	11.9	23.8	38.2
Money market funds	-17.7	45.0	13.9	34.1	1.8	10.7	67.1	81.5
Brokers and dealers	-7.7	28.8	5.6	13.2	-30.6	-8.2	96.3	-22.7
SCO issuers	3.6	9.3	11.5	39.0	39.1	32.5	20.8	39.5

* Excludes corporate equities.

SOURCE: Federal Reserve Board, Flow-of-Funds Section.

$640.7 billion. This was the result of retirement by corporations of their equities and the replacement of equities with debt, much of which was "junk bonds."

References

Board of Governors of the Federal Reserve System, *The Flow of Funds in the United States,* 1955; Copeland, Morris, *A Study of Money Flows in the United States,* National Bureau of Economic Research, New York, 1952; Goldsmith, Raymond W., *A Study of Saving in the United States,* Princeton University, Princeton, N.J., 1955; Kuznets, Simon, *Capital in the United States, Its Formation and Financing,* Princeton University, Princeton, N.J., 1961.

(*See also* Banking system; Bond; Business credit; Consumer credit, Credit, an overview; Debt; Debt management; Disintermediation; Federal Reserve policy; Federal Reserve System; Financial institutions; Financial instruments; Flow of funds; Inflation; Interest rates; Monetary policy; Money markets; Mortgage credit; Saving; Stock; Thrift institutions: problems and challenges)

James J. O'Leary

Capital stock (*see* Wealth)

Capitalism

Economic systems are often classified according to whether the factors of production are privately owned, publicly owned, or some mixture of the two. If private ownership prevails, the system is considered capitalistic; if public ownership prevails, socialistic or communistic is deemed an appropriate description. The term "mixed economy" is retained for those systems that reveal ownership features of capitalism and socialism, although where capitalism becomes a mixed system and the latter turns into socialism is never clear-cut.

Classifying economic systems solely on the basis of one criterion fails to capture some very important economic (and political) differences between capitalist economies, especially as they have evolved in the post–World War II period. However important as these differences might be, it seems more important to define capitalism in such a way that it can be used to denote a wide variety of real world economies that are distinguishable from a group of other economies that do not share the basic political and cultural as well as the economic institutions that are the essence of capitalism.

The Perfectly Competitive Market System

To sharpen the analysis, it is useful to begin with a favorite tool of those economists concerned with the manner in which economic activities are organized under capitalism—the model of the perfectly competitive market system. In this model, the economy is viewed as a system of markets in each of which a homogeneous good is traded. Moreover, in each market buyers and sellers of the good are so numerous that no single buyer or seller can influence the price at which the good is exchanged. (The notion of a market in this model later was extended to include that market for factors of production as well as goods.) Furthermore, this price, or the price mechanism, acts as a signal that provides all the information necessary to distribute output and factors throughout the economy in such a way that an optimal situation results. In other words, given the initial distribution of resource endowments among the population—human skills, ownership of physical and financial capital and land—the resulting production and distribution of that production will be such that no member of the society can be made better off in some material sense without making someone else worse off.

This outline of the perfectly competitive capitalist economy was first popularized by Adam Smith. It was Smith's view that not only could such a decentralized decision-making system effectively organize itself but also that the system would do so even though each individual acted according to self-interest, for there was an "invisible hand" at work coordinating the decisions of buyers and sellers in such a way as to promote the common good. So powerful and enduring was the influence of Smith's view of capitalism as a system functioning like the perfectly competitive model of the economists' textbooks that it was not until the Great Depression of the 1930s that economists and public officials (outside of Marxist circles) seriously challenged Smith's doctrines.

However, the inability of capitalist economies in so many countries to right themselves during the 1930s soon brought into question Smith's views. This questioning was strengthened by the writings of John Maynard Keynes, whose book, *The General Theory of Employment, Interest and Money,* provided a systematic explanation of why it might be the natural outcome of an unregulated, decentralized market system to periodically break down. His solution suggested a need for direct intervention from time to time by central governments in the form of tax and spending policies to offset destabilizing fluctuations in private spending.

Dominant Market Forms

The invisible-hand parable and the economist's model underlying it were challenged from another direction at about the same time. During the interwar period, economists developed models of capitalist economies that incorporated various forms of market structure other than the perfectly competitive one. For some time economists and public officials had been aware of the existence of monopolies, i.e., the dominance of a single seller in a market, which allowed the monopolist to exert varying degrees of control over prices. But throughout the interwar period, economists and others increasingly viewed the perfectly competitive model as less and less relevant for explaining how real economies operate. Rather than markets being made up of numerous buyers and sellers in which homogeneous goods are exchanged (along with an occasional monopoly), it became increasingly clear that the dominant market form under capitalism was not the perfectly competitive one but rather was one of monopoly, oligopoly (a few sellers), or monopolistic competition (many sellers who are likely to be selling similar, but not identical or homogeneous, goods).

Today, there is widespread acceptance of the fact that almost from their inception, capitalist economies have borne little resemblance to the world of perfect competition and that over time the economies have moved further from the competitive form. In spite of this, the model of a perfectly competitive economy continues to play an influential role in the economics literature.

Separation of Ownership from Control

What has become increasingly clear in the evolution of capitalism is the increased separation of ownership from control of the modern corporation. By common agreement capitalism requires that private ownership of the factors of production be widespread. However, with the rise of the modern corporation, stockholders, although technically the owners of the corporation, have become a group that does little more than rubber-stamp the decisions of management. This trend suggests that while any definition of capitalism requires private ownership of the factors of production, it should also encompass economies where the authority conferred by ownership can and has been delegated to a managerial class.

This conclusion suggests an additional consideration. The separation of ownership from control has led to an increased inclination on the part of government to provide a supervisory role over the private sector, reinforcing the tendency toward government intervention stemming from the Great Depression. But not only has there been an increased tendency toward government intervention and control, the evolution of capitalism also has been marked by a rising trend in government expenditures as a percentage of total expenditures in the economy and, to a much lesser extent, outright nationalization of certain industries until recently. In the post–World War II period especially, the production and distribution of output have become less the outcome of the working markets, and the mixed economy has become the rule rather than the exception.

It is difficult to generalize about the causes and patterns of public ownership, even in the postwar period, when nationalization of existing industries and the formation of government-owned or -controlled industries reached a peak. In some cases, nationalization was essentially a "bailing out" of private industry, a situation in which the industry could not maintain solvency and the government was not willing to let the industry "go under." In other cases government-controlled or -owned industries were established deliberately so that they would act as catalysts for other sectors of the economy. However, it would be difficult to conclude that there has been any dramatic shift toward increased public ownership of the factor of production. More recently the earlier trend toward nationalization has even reversed with privatization programs in which government-owned industries have been sold back to private investors.

Increased Role of Government

One of the outstanding developments under capitalism has been the increased role played by government in determining the composition of output. Government expenditures and tax revenues as a percentage of total output have been rising fairly steadily throughout most of the twentieth century, and consumption of nondurable goods and services as a percentage of output has declined. The rise of the role of government within the context of a system of predominant private ownership of the factors of production is largely the reflection of the rise of the so-called welfare state. The spread of public education, public medical and dental systems, pension and welfare schemes, and retraining programs along with retirement and unemployment benefit programs has been one of the outstanding features of post–World War II capitalist development. The rise of the welfare state and increase in public ownership indicate a shift in economic decision making in capitalist economies away from the private sector. This trend leads to a final consideration in the definition of capitalism. Capitalism as used here denotes an economic system in which the owners of the factors of production and those making economic decisions concerning such things as production, savings, and investment are *predominantly* private individuals. Although somewhat vague, such a definition allows the analysis to incorporate some important historical developments as part of the definitive features of capitalism, features which are useful in distinguishing it from other forms of economic organization.

The increased significance of the government sector, especially during the post–World War II period, in determining the composition of output was accomplished without a decline in private consumption levels. Thus, although consumption of nondurable goods and services as a percentage of total output fell in capitalist economies during this period, the absolute level of per capita consumption rose. Moreover, this took place at a time when investment by businesses in plant and equipment in each country as a share of total output was at an all-time historical high, at least outside North America. The key to this seemingly paradoxical series of developments lay in the fact that never in the past had so many capitalist economies grown so rapidly for such sustained periods. The one exception was the United States. Thus, during the postwar period from, say, the early 1950s up through the early 1970s, in almost every capitalist economy rates of growth of total output and output per worker were outstanding compared with each country's previous performance. From the mid-1970s on, a definite slowdown in the growth of total output and output per worker occurred throughout the developed capitalist world. Consumption levels continued to rise but at a much reduced rate.

Growth and Development

The similarities in the patterns of growth and development of the different economies are of interest. In every developed capitalist economy, as levels of per capita incomes rose, there was an absolute (and relative) decline in employment in agriculture and an absolute (and relative) increase in employment in the service or tertiary sector. Employment patterns in industry followed a different path. From relatively low per capita incomes (for developed capitalist countries), relative and absolute employment in industry rose. After higher levels of per capita incomes were realized (those attained in most economies by the mid-1960s), employment in industry as a share of total employment began to drop off. In contrast, in absolute terms employment in industry rose continuously in the majority of the developed capitalist economies until the early 1970s, when stagnation set in.

A simple way of characterizing this process of growth and development in the postwar period is to envisage a situation of high rates of growth of productivity and low rates of growth of demand in agriculture interacting to release labor for industry and the service sector. The high rates of business investment mentioned earlier enabled the expanded labor force in the nonagricultural sectors to be equipped with the most productive capital plant and equipment available. This was especially so for those economies starting from relatively low levels of per capita incomes, since these economies were in a position to borrow the most advanced technology from the high-income economies such as the United States. Thus, an outstanding characteristic of the Japanese postwar modernization process was the widespread purchases of licenses from the United States of process technologies. These required modifications and adaptation to suit the Japanese needs, to be sure, but Japanese industrialists (and others) clearly were able to skip some of the research and development stages involved in implementing a technology and thereby reduce costs of production. These industrialists were also in a better position to borrow and install only the best technologies available. As a result of these and other factors, the period from the early 1950s to the early 1970s saw a strong tendency for countries with relatively low levels of per capita income at the beginning of the period to grow relatively rapidly. For all the developed capitalist economies, the same period marked (in terms of its duration and pervasiveness) capitalism's greatest boom in history.

The period since the early 1970s has been termed a period of "stagflation" for capitalism, characterized by stagnation (slow growth, low investment, and high unemployment) together with inflation. Growth rates (and inflation rates) have continued to diverge from one country to the next during the current period, but there has been a general scaling-down of the pace of growth and development in all the developed capitalist economies. The primary factor involved in the collapse of the worldwide postwar boom has been a fear of inflation engendered by an acceleration in the rate of inflation beginning in the late 1960s and lasting into the mid-1970s. The response of governments to inflation in the majority of the capitalist economies has been to pursue anti-inflationary demand policies coupled at times with some form of incomes policy. This approach has led to higher rates of unemployment and lower rates of profits and utilization of capital by business. The latter has definitely depressed business investment and has contributed to the decline in growth rates. Whether such recession-induced anti-inflationary policies will work eventually is still a matter of heated discussions among economists. If the policies do not work and if efforts by governments to restore prosperity through stimulative aggregate demand policies accelerate inflation rates, one of two responses is likely. Either new forms of increased government intervention will occur or the authorities will choose to restrict aggregate demand and maintain high rates of unemployment on a long-run basis in order to contain inflation. In either case, an entirely new concept defining the essential features of capitalism will become appropriate.

References

Cornwall, John, *Modern Capitalism: Its Growth and Transformation,* Martin Robertson, Oxford, 1977; Cornwall, John, *The Theory of Economic Breakdown: An Institutional Analytical Approach,* Blackwell, Oxford, 1990; Keynes, J. M., *The General Theory of Employment, Interest and Money,* Macmillan, London, 1936; Svennilson, I., *Growth and Stagnation in the European Economy,* Economic Commission for Europe, Geneva, 1954.

(*See also* Comparative economic systems, an overview; Competition; Monopoly and oligopoly; Nationalization of industry)

John Cornwall

Cartel

A cartel is a group of producers who coordinate price and output decisions to increase combined and individual output. If all producers of a good combine, the cartel may seek to imitate the behavior of a monopoly supplier. Commonly, however, a fringe of smaller producers will operate outside the cartel. The presence of such a fringe will interfere with the ability of firms in the cartel to exercise control over prices.

Cartels and the Exercise of Market Power

A cartel must deal with all the problems that would be faced by a monopolist operating in the same industry. A cartel will attempt to increase profit by raising price, but any such increase in price confronts the trade-off between higher price and lower sales along the industry demand curve. As the cartel price rises, consumers switch to other products, and sales decline. A cartel faces the additional problem that different firms in the cartel are likely to disagree on the best price for the cartel.

At the same time, a cartel must confront the possibility of defection by member firms. As the cartel price rises, the cartel must allocate reductions in output among its members. Since cartel agreements are ordinarily illegal, they cannot usually be enforced in a court of law. Rather, cartel stability requires that individual cartel members be willing to voluntarily accept the reduction in output implied by their membership in the cartel.

Much of the recent game-theoretic literature on noncooperative collusion analyzes strategies that could be used by cartels to induce individual cartel members to adhere to the cartel agreement. Typically, such strategies involve some sort of threat. If a single firm produces more than the cartel plan calls for it to produce, other firms are committed to expand output in a way which leaves the defector worse off than it would be if it adhered to the cartel strategy. There is, however, no evidence that strategies of this kind allow real-world industries to get much closer to joint profit maximization than would independent (Cournot) behavior.

A cartel must also deal with the threat of entry by new firms into the industry. For a complete cartel to exercise long-term control over price, some impediment or barrier to entry must prevent new firms from entering and eroding market power. Industrial economists have traditionally emphasized structural barriers to entry and barriers to entry imposed by government—patents, regulations that raise the cost of entry, control of high-quality inputs, product differentiation, and economies of large-scale production. Recent work highlights imperfect information as a condition that will allow incumbent firms to build a reputation for predatory, entry-discouraging behavior.

The Success of Cartels

A cartel is more likely to be successful in an industry for which demand is relatively insensitive to price increases. If demand does not fall very much when prices rise, the gains from successful cartelization will be large. The incentive of individual cartel members to reach and maintain an agreement will be correspondingly large.

A cartel is more likely to succeed when entry is difficult. If entry requires access to scarce mineral resources or a large initial sunk investment, it is less likely to occur, whatever the price set by the cartel. This reduces the danger that noncooperative outsiders will enter the industry.

It will be easier to enforce an agreement if it is easy to discover cheating and if retaliation can be rapid. If sales and prices are publicly and promptly reported, price cheaters will be subject to quick counteraction. Where sales are small and frequent, the gain from cutting price on any particular sale will be small. The potential loss, if other cartel members respond in kind so that price falls on all later sales, will be great. Reaching and enforcing collusive agreements will be easier when a product is standardized than when each customer receives a slightly different product.

If a cartel is successful, it will create the same adverse welfare effects which accompany any exercise of market power. Price will be raised above the cost of product. Profit will exceed the normal level; income will be transferred from consumers to producers. Output will be restricted, so that less than the optimal amount of the product will be available for society.

References

Friedman, James W., "A Non-cooperative Equilibrium for Supergames," *Review of Economic Studies,* vol. 38, no. 1, January 1971, pp. 1–12; Kreps, David M., and Robert Wilson, "Reputation and Imperfect Information," *Journal of Economic Theory,* vol. 27, 1982, pp. 253–279; Milgrom, Paul, and J. Roberts, "Predation, Reputation, and Entry Deterrence," *Journal of Economic Theory,* vol. 27, no. 2, August 1982b, pp. 280–312; Slade, Margaret E., "Interfirm Rivalry in a Repeated Game: An Empirical Test of Tacit Collusion," *Journal of Industrial Economics,* vol. 35, no. 4, June 1987, pp. 499–516.

(*See also* Competition; Concentration of industry; Monopoly and oligopoly)

Stephen Martin

Census Bureau (*see* Bureau of the Census)

Channels of marketing[1]

Individual consumers and corporate/organizational buyers are aware that thousands of goods and services are available through a very large number of diverse channel outlets. What they may not be well aware of is the fact that the *channel structure,* or the set of institutions, agencies, and establishments through which the product must move to get to them, can be amazingly complex.

Usually, combinations of institutions specializing in manufacturing, wholesaling, retailing, and many other areas join forces in marketing channel arrangements to make possible the delivery of goods to industrial users or customers and to final consumers. The same is true for the marketing of services. For example, in the case of health care delivery, hospitals, ambulance services, physicians, laboratories, insurance companies, and drugstores combine efforts in an organized channel arrangement to ensure the delivery of a critical service. All these institutions depend on each other to cater effectively to consumer demands. Therefore, marketing channels can be viewed as *sets of interdependent organizations involved in the process of making a product or service available for use or consumption.* From the outset, it should be recognized that not only do marketing channels *satisfy demand* by supplying goods and services at the right place, quantity, quality, and price, but they also *stimulate demand* through the promotional activities of the units (e.g., retailers, manufacturers' representatives, sales offices, and wholesalers) comprising them. Therefore, the channel should be viewed as an orchestrated network that creates value for the user or consumer through the generation of form, possession, time, and place utilities.

A major focus of marketing channel management is on *delivery.* It is only through distribution that public and private goods can be made available for consumption. Producers of such goods (including manufacturers of industrial and consumer goods, legislators framing laws, educational administrators conceiving new means for achieving quality education, and insurance companies developing unique health insurance coverage) are individually capable of generating only form or structural

[1]Permission to use specific passages from pages 1, 3, 10, 37, 40, and 41 of chap. 1 of Louis W. Stern and Adel I. El-Ansary, *Marketing Channels* (4th ed.), 1992, was granted by Prentice-Hall.

utility for their "products." They can organize their production capabilities in such a way that the products they have developed can, in fact, be seen, analyzed, debated, and, by a select few perhaps, digested. But the actual large-scale delivery of the products to the consuming public demands different types of efforts which create time, place, and possession utilities. In other words, consumers cannot obtain a finished product unless the product is transported to where they can gain access to it, stored until they are ready for it, and eventually exchanged for money or other goods or services so that they can gain possession of it. In fact, the four types of utility (form, time, place, and possession) are inseparable; there can be no "complete" product without incorporating all four into any given object, idea, or service.

Manufacturers, wholesalers, and retailers, as well as other channel members, exist in channel arrangements to perform one or more of the following generic functions: carrying of inventory; demand generation, or selling; physical distribution; after-sale service; and extending credit to customers. In getting its goods to consumers or end users, a manufacturer must either assume all these functions or shift some of them or all to channel intermediaries.

The above discussion underscores three important principles in the structure of marketing channels:

1. One can eliminate or substitute institutions in the channel arrangement.

2. However, the functions these institutions perform cannot be eliminated.

3. When institutions are eliminated, their functions are shifted either forward or backward in the channel and are therefore assumed by other members.

It is a truism that "you can eliminate an intermediary, but you cannot eliminate its functions."

To the extent that the same function is performed at more than one level of the marketing channel, the work load for the function is shared by members at these levels. For example, manufacturers, wholesalers, and retailers may all carry inventory. This duplication may increase distribution cost. However, the increase in cost is justifiable to the extent that it may be necessary to provide goods to customers at the right quantity, quality, time, and place.

A *flow* in the marketing channel is identical to a *function*. However, the term "flow" is somewhat more descriptive of movement, and, therefore, we tend to prefer it. Physical possession, ownership, and promotion are typically forward flows from producer to consumer. Each of these flows moves "down" the distribution channel—a manufacturer promotes a product to a wholesaler, who in turn promotes it to a retailer, and so on. The negotiation, financing, and risking flows move in both directions, whereas ordering and payment are backward flows.

In every marketing channel, the members that do business together have some kind of working relationships. On the extreme ends on the continuum of these relationships, there are purely transactional relationships on one side and purely collaborative ones on the other. Transactional relationships occur when the customer and supplier focus on the timely exchange of basic products for highly competitive prices. Collaborative relationships, or *partnerships,* occur through partnering, which is a process where a customer and supplier form strong and extensive social, economic, service, and technical ties *over time.* The intent in a strategic partnership or alliance is to lower total costs and/or increase value for the channel, thereby achieving mutual benefit. A strategic alliance can also denote horizontal partnerships that develop between two organizations at the same marketing level. Partnerships capitalize on the notion that marketing channels are *vertical value-adding chains* that create *competitive advantage.*

A trend that is an outgrowth of partnerships is the *seamless channel.* This concept is related to the concept of the seamless organization, which has all departments working together to serve the customer, thereby blurring the organizational lines that separate departments within the organization. The seamless channel blends the borders of channel members by having multiple levels in each organization work together with their counterparts in other channel organizations to deliver quality service to the customer. Partnerships contribute to the seamless channel by giving channel members a sense of being on the same *team.* The adversarial role that is so prevalent is replaced with one built on trust and cooperation.

Viewing channels as competitive units is significant for all companies, including those that market their products through a number of different channels and those that develop assortments of goods and services by purchasing from a variety of suppliers. How individual manufacturers coordinate their activities with the various intermediaries and vice versa will determine the viability of one type of channel alignment versus other channel alignments made up of different institutions and agencies handling similar or substitutable merchandise.

If, within a given marketing channel, an institution or agency does not see fit to coordinate effectively and efficiently with other members of the same network but rather pursues its own goals in an independent, self-serving manner, one can predict the eventual demise of the channel alignment of which it is a part as a strong competitive force. Ideally, then, channel members should attempt to coordinate their objectives, plans, and programs with other members in such a way that the performance of the total distribution system to which they belong is enhanced. However, it has been argued that such integrated action up and down a marketing channel is actually a rarity.

Channel participants are often not concerned with all the transactions that occur between each of the various links in the channel, however. Intermediaries, in particular, are most concerned about the dealings that take place with those channel members immediately adjacent to them from whom they buy and to whom they sell. In this sense, channel intermediaries are not, in fact, functioning as enlisted member components of a distribution system, but rather are acting individually as *independent markets,* choosing those products and suppliers that best help them serve the target groups for whom they act as purchasing agents. From this perspective, the intermediary's method of operation—the functions it performs, the clients it serves, and the objectives, policies, and programs it adopts—is the result of its own independent decisions.

This notion of each channel intermediary acting as an independent market must be qualified and analyzed with regard to *total channel performance.* Although an "independent" orientation on the part of any channel member may indeed be operational at times, it is put into effect only at the risk of sacrificing the levels of coordination necessary for overall channel effectiveness, efficiency, growth, and long-run survival. Thus, a high degree of independent, suboptimizing behavior on the part of individual channel participants serves as a detriment to the viability of the total channel network. The goal for actors within any distribution network is, therefore, to cooperate in developing an interorganization system that will minimize suboptimization so that a high degree of channel coordination is still attainable. The need for channel management is to coordinate the activities in the channel to ensure that *total quality management* is pervasive throughout the channel and quality customer service is the product delivered by the entire channel.

As marketers continue to face hostile, unstable, and competitive environments, distribution will play an increasingly important role. Companies are already adapting to move into new distribution channels that match up with market segments more precisely and effectively. Future executives will pay more attention to their selection of distribution channels to obtain a competitive advantage over companies who copy their product designs and quality and undercut their prices. For example, new channels of distribution, such as wholesale clubs, factory outlets, electronic shopping channels, franchises of all sorts, direct marketing operations, and hybrid channels, are emerging.

Distribution channels will be a major factor in the effective development of market share, particularly internationally. Retrofitting and adjustment of channels will occur, allowing more flexibility. To maintain quality and ensure service, more direct distribution may be undertaken by many manufacturers. Also, the use of multiple channels will expand and include telemarketing, direct response marketing, mail order, and computer-assisted buying.

References

Lazer, William, Priscilla LaBarbara, James MacLachlan, and Allen Smith, *Marketing 2000 and Beyond,* American Marketing Association, Chicago, 1990; Stern, Louis W., and Adel I. El-Ansary, *Marketing Channels* (4th ed.), Prentice-Hall, Englewood Cliffs, N.J., 1992.

Adel I. El-Ansary

Chicago school

The Chicago school refers to the philosophy, policy preferences, view of the economic system, and methodology associated with the department of economics at the University of Chicago. Recognition of a distinctive Chicago school arose in the 1950s. Milton Friedman, who became a member of the Department of Economics at the University of Chicago in 1946, is more closely identified with the Chicago school than any other economist.

The principal characteristic of the philosophy of the Chicago school is its emphasis on freedom rather than equality. The interest in individual freedom stems primarily from the work of Frank H. Knight, who was appointed a professor at the University of Chicago in 1928 and was active until the late 1960s. Two of his books that combine the study of economics with social philosophy are *The Ethics of Competition and Other Essays* and *Freedom and Reform.*

The following are important policy positions associated with economists of the Chicago school:

1. They believe that competitive markets are the best way to organize economic activity among business firms.
2. They are critical of most types of government regulation of the economy.
3. They believe that the kind of monetary system a country has is important.

Competitive Markets

To Chicagoans, the teaching of economics is viewed largely as the explanation of how it is possible to organize economic activity through a system of competitive markets. The preference for competitive markets rather than overall economic planning is based primarily on the predominant role given to freedom as a social goal. As stated by Milton Friedman (1974), competitive markets are viewed as "the only means so far discovered of enabling individuals to coordinate their economic activities without coercion." In addition, competitive markets are believed to be efficient—scarce resources tend to be used to produce those goods and services in greatest demand. A principal difference between Chicagoans and others is that Chicagoans view the market system as basically stable, provided there is an appropriate monetary system. They attribute economic instability primarily to large swings in the rate of growth in the money supply. Non-Chicagoans usually insist that business fluctuations are the result of the instability of investment spending and the development of maladjustments in an unplanned economy.

Government Regulation

Chicagoans are critical of most types of governmental regulation of the economy. Their attitude is one of skepticism about the relationship between the intent and the actual effects of such regulation. They believe that instead of benefiting the public, government regulation usually benefits certain industries, property owners, or persons with relatively high incomes. The development of the public choice approach to government—initially at the University of Virginia in the 1960s—has reinforced the Chicago rejection of government regulation.

Monetarist Theory

The most important empirical work supporting the point of view that "money matters" is the study by Milton Friedman and Anna J. Schwartz, *A Monetary History of the United States, 1867–1960,* published in 1963. The monetarist theory of inflation differs from the cost-push theory that attributes inflation primarily to excessively rapid increases in wages or to increases in commodity prices. Chicagoans believe that the acceleration in the rate of inflation in the United States from 1965 to 1980 would not have occurred if the Federal Reserve System had not permitted the money supply to increase at an excessively rapid rate.

In Friedman's monetarist theory of business cycles, a major cause of recessions is a decline in the rate of expansion in the money supply. He believes that it was the Federal Reserve's tight money policy in 1928 and 1929, designed to combat stock market speculation, that led to the beginning of the Great Depression. He also believes that the Federal Reserve System could have prevented the sharp decline in the money supply during the Great Depression if it had wanted to do so. Friedman's interpretation of business cycles is different from that of his teacher, Henry C. Simons. Simons's explanation of recessions emphasized the decline in business confidence and the fall in the velocity of money rather than the decline in the quantity of money. The countercyclical policies proposed by Simons—stabilization of a price level, fiscal policy, government antimonopoly programs, and reform of the financial structure to differentiate sharply between money and other types of financial assets—have been rejected by Friedman.

Chicago School and the Economic System

An important outcome of the research of the Chicago school is the change that occurred in the view toward monopoly. Simons believed that labor unions had excessive monopolistic power over wages. After World War II, the empirical work of H. Gregg Lewis supported the point of view that union power over wages is significantly restrained by competition. At the same time, research by Aaron Director, George J. Stigler, Sam Peltzman, Harold Demsetz, and Lester Telser led to a sharp decline in the role assigned to monopoly in explaining a wide range of activities in industrial and financial markets. Chicagoans also rejected the belief that the managers of large corporations are very powerful—that they can control consumer demand through advertising, that they do not need to maximize profits because they are not selected by the stockholders, and that they have great control of the prices and kinds of products they produce.

The Chicago concept of wage flexibility also differs from the conventional view. Chicagoans usually assume that in the long run wages are sufficiently flexible to equate the demand and the supply of labor. In the conventional view, even during periods of prosperity there is typically a large pool of workers who cannot find jobs. It is believed that this results from both the tendency for the growth of the labor force to exceed the growth of aggregate demand and the inflexibility of wages. Research on the theory of rational expectations by Robert E. Lucas at Chicago provides a basis for believing that prices and wages may be more flexible than was formerly believed even in the short run. In both Keynesian theory and the research of Friedman, wages and prices are assumed to respond slowly to changes in aggregate demand. The theory of rational expectations has led to major revisions in traditional macroeconomic theory.

Empirical Testing

A distinctive characteristic of the methodology of the Chicago school is the emphasis on the empirical testing of theoretical generalizations. Empirical testing, especially the work of Friedman and Stigler with the National Bureau of Economic Research, was influenced by Wesley C. Mitchell of Columbia University. From the point of view of this methodology, early economists at Chicago who were influential were Paul H. Douglas and Henry Schultz.

Competitive Price Theory

The most important characteristic of the Chicago school is the use of competitive price theory as a tool for analyzing a wide range of concrete problems. The roots of this characteristic go back to the two great teachers at the University of Chicago in the 1930s, Frank H. Knight and Jacob Viner.

After World War II, when theories of monopolistic competition and oligopoly were predominant at other universities, at Chicago Friedman taught that the theory of perfect competition is the most useful approach to understanding economic activity. As stated by Friedman in his essay entitled "The Methodology of Positive Economics," the test of a good theory is "its ability to predict much from little" rather than the realism of its assumptions. Critics of the Chicago school often reject the results of analyses using competitive price theory because they believe that the theory's assumptions of individual choice and maximizing behavior are unrealistic.

Competitive price theory has been extended by economists influenced by the Chicago school—many are not at the University of Chicago—to problems traditionally viewed as outside economics. Neoclassical economic analysis has been applied by Ronald H. Coase to the role of managerial coordination within the firm and the effect of transactions costs on individual bargaining; by Gary S. Becker to the analysis of human capital, marriage, and family planning; by Merton H. Miller to corporate finance; and by Richard A. Posner to law.

The most remarkable extension of neoclassical economic theory has been to the analysis of the government sector of the economy. This type of analysis has mushroomed into a major field of economics known as public choice. The leaders in this field include James M. Buchanan and Gordon Tullock. The public choice approach to government is very different from the traditional approach in which the economist assumes that he or she is offering advice to an all-wise and benevolent government. Instead, the public choice approach assumes that public policies reflect the self-interest of those involved and attempts to explain how the political process shapes public policies.

The Chicago School and Keynes

There has been some discussion among historians of economic thought of the relationship between the Chicago school and the economics of John Maynard Keynes. J. Ronnie Davis has shown that during the Great Depression, Chicago economists recommended the use of budget deficits, and they were opposed to cutting money wages as a method of stimulating the economy. These are the same as the basic policies of the Keynesian revolution. Despite this, Chicagoans were not as enthusiastic about Keynes's *General Theory* as economists at other universities. There are some differences between Keynes and the economists at Chicago who influenced the development of the Chicago school. To Keynes, the purpose of fiscal deficits was to increase government expenditures and thus to increase aggregate demand. To Chicago economists, the purpose of the fiscal deficit was to increase the money supply, and their solution was called "fiscal inflation." In addition, although Keynes was pessimistic about the long-run prospects for full employment in capitalist economies, Chicagoans were not. There has also been some discussion of the relationship between Friedman's monetary theories and policies and those of his teachers at the University of Chicago. Don Patinkin maintains that Friedman's reformulation of the quantity theory of money is more closely related to the Keynesian theory of liquidity preference than to the quantity theory of money held by Friedman's teachers.

The Future

The uniqueness of the Chicago school has diminished in recent years partly because of the wider acceptance of ideas associated with the school. Also, much of the research now done at Chicago is similar to the mathematical economics done at other universities. Despite these changes, economists at Chicago still have a more positive attitude toward competitive price theory than usually found elsewhere.

References

Friedman, Milton, "The Monetary Theory and Policy of Henry Simons," *The Journal of Law and Economics,* vol. 10, October 1967, pp. 1–13; Friedman, Milton, "Schools at Chicago," *The University of Chicago Magazine,* August 1974, pp. 11–16; Miller, H. Laurence, "On the 'Chicago

School of Economics,' " *The Journal of Political Economy*, vol. 70, February 1962, pp. 64–69; Reder, M. W., "Chicago School," *The New Palgrave, A Dictionary of Economics*, Macmillan, London, 1987, pp. 413–418; Samuels, Warren J. (ed.), *The Chicago School of Political Economy*, Michigan State University, East Lansing, Mich., 1976; Shils, Edward (ed.), *Remembering the University of Chicago, Teachers, Scientists, and Scholars*, University of Chicago, Chicago, 1991; Stigler, George J., *Memoirs of an Unregulated Economist*, Basic Books, New York, 1988.

(*See also* Business cycles; Competition; Federal Reserve policy; Federal Reserve System; Government regulation of business; Indexation; Keynesian economics; Monetary policy; Money supply; Monopoly and oligopoly; Permanent income hypothesis; Price theory; Quantity theory of money; Velocity of circulation of money)

Colin D. Campbell

Classical liberalism

Classical liberalism may be defined simply as the social philosophy that recognizes the need for open markets and for decentralized control of the means of production for individual liberty. John Locke, the celebrated philosopher of the so-called glorious revolution, is considered to be the father of classical liberalism, although elements of his teachings can be located in Roman stoic thought as early as the fourth century B.C. In his *Second Treatise on Government* (1690), Locke developed three important notions about the relationship between the individual and government: first, that individuals existed in cooperative social groupings prior to the creation of civil government; second, that individuals enter into political society with certain natural rights that cannot be legitimately traded away in commercial exchange or eliminated by government; and third, that when government is no longer able (or willing) to protect these rights, the members of society are justified in overthrowing their government and replacing it with a more effective one. Of these three notions, the second and third are frequently cited by intellectual historians, especially because they formed the antiauthoritarian ideologies of both the U.S. and French Revolutions. Locke's first notion, that society existed prior to government, encouraged a search for the factors promoting order and organization among individuals and in this way served as an important formative influence on social scientific thought in the eighteenth century.

Classical Liberals as Foes of Socialists

The eighteenth-century British philosophers, Bernard Mandeville, David Hume, Adam Smith, C. L. de Montesquieu, Edmund Burke, John Millar, Adam Ferguson, and later writers, such as Sir Henry Maine, Carl Menger, Ludwig von Mises, and Friedrich A. von Hayek, explored the actual social processes by which custom, business law, private property, money and banking institutions, and so on came into existence and have been maintained. Frequently, those institutions most useful to humanity evolved as an unintended consequence of self-interested behavior in the market. By way of contrast, those arrangements brought about by government planners often fail to meet their objectives and are chaotic and oppressive to individual liberty. For these reasons, modern classical liberals join company with traditional conservatives (followers of Burke) and warn of the dangers of damaging through government intervention in business the wisdom of the ages as contained in established customs and business practices. Classical liberals are the arch-foes of socialists who propose centralized control of the means of production and the substitution of central planning for impersonal market mechanisms.

In the eighteenth and nineteenth centuries, economists explained how markets contain a variety of self-regulating devices that move resources (constantly) toward their most highly valued uses and thereby promote economic development. The role of open markets in eliminating waste and responding rapidly to changing consumer wants left classical liberals opposed to all those monopolization schemes that would restrict entry into markets and limit competition. Classical liberals generally oppose the creation of public utilities, the issuance of licenses and entry requirements into professions, the imposition of restrictions on international trade, immigration quotas, and the use of state power to restrict competition. Still, classical liberals are not advocates of strict laissez-faire. They offer a long agenda of duties and responsibilities for the state to perform such as national defense, police protection, regulation of public health and industrial safety, provision of large-scale capital projects such as harbors and dams, patents to encourage innovation, and the creation of a sound and secure currency. As constitutionalists, classical liberals believe the purpose of the law is to provide a framework or rule of law within which individuals may freely associate and interact for their mutual benefit. Law must be designed to create broad incentives for individuals to take one course of action rather than another and be applied to all individuals regardless of race, religion, or personal wealth. At all times the political system must avoid substituting a rule of human beings for the rule of law because discretionary behavior on the political level can open the way toward abuses of state power in the form of political favoritism and corruption.

Fiscal Conservatism

As supporters of representative government, classical liberals wish to make the politicians responsible to the voters in the most obvious and basic ways possible. That is why they favor fiscal conservativism, that is, the creation of a close connection between government projects and the actual economic cost of those projects in the minds of the voters. If every dollar of government money spent in a fiscal year is financed by a dollar of current taxes, the voters would be informed of the economic cost of government programs quickly and dramatically. When, however, the state issues bonds and the banking system uses them as a basis for creating bank money (checking accounts), then the politicians choose to finance their spending by monetizing new debt rather than by raising taxes. Politicians prefer to increase the money supply rather than to raise taxes even when this policy results in severe inflation. That is because the voting population is generally unable to connect their loss of wealth through inflation with the successive bouts of government spending. The voters blame the rise of prices on scapegoats such as foreigners, unions, multinational corporations, or simple private greed, allowing the otherwise unacceptable public projects to escape voter scrutiny. Unexpected inflations produce great anxiety among the civilian population as wealth becomes redistributed in a mysterious manner. This fosters a general distrust for the market economy, which is blamed for the inflation and the economic uncertainty that accompanies it. Discouraged by inflation, many citizens support national economic planning and with it severe modification of capitalist institutions. With national planning, politicians are better able to pursue costly government projects.

Classical liberals view these trends as a threat to prosperity and political liberty. For this reason classical liberals such as Ludwig von Mises favored the international gold standard. The plan was to remove the size of the various national money supplies from the hands of the politicians. Contemporary classical liberals such as Milton Friedman also want to limit the money-issuing powers of the state but by means of a constitutional amendment limiting by law the rate of growth of the money supply. Classical liberals understand that individual liberty and open-market processes cannot survive during an escalating inflation when the majority of voters demand and willingly elect totalitarian parties that promise stability at the expense of liberty.

References

Baumgarth, William P., "Hayek and Political Order: The Rule of Law," *Journal of Libertarian Studies,* vol. 2, Winter 1978, pp. 11–28; Benson, Bruce L., *The Enterprise of Law: Justice without the State,* Pacific Research Institute, San Francisco, 1990; Buchanan, James M., and Richard E. Wagner, *Democracy in Deficit,* Academic Press, New York, 1977; Friedman, David, *The Machinery of Freedom: Guide to Radical Capitalism,* Open Court, La Salle, Ill., 1990; Nozick, Robert, *Anarchy, State and Utopia,* Basic Books, New York, 1974; Rothbard, Murray N., *For a New Liberty,* Macmillan, New York, 1973; Tame, Chris R., "The Revolution of Reason: Peter Gay, The Enlightenment, and the Ambiguities of Classical Liberalism," *Journal of Libertarian Studies,* vol. 1, Summer 1977, pp. 217–228.

(*See also* Austrian economics; Laissez faire)

Laurence S. Moss

Classical school

Ever since Karl Marx referred to all those economists with a less-than-perfect vision of how the economy operated as belonging to the classical school, it has been usual for historians to speak of the classical school as representing a naive or even primitive understanding of the economic system. This label is commonly attached to the group of predominantly British economists who followed Adam Smith in the search for the laws regulating the production, distribution, and consumption of wealth. The group of classical writers includes David Ricardo (*Principles of Political Economy and Taxation,* 1817); James Mill (*Elements of Political Economy,* 1821); John R. McCulloch (*Principles of Political Economy,* 1825, 1836); Robert Torrens (*An Essay on the Production of Wealth,* 1821); Mountifort Longfield (*Lectures on Political Economy,* 1834); John Elliot Cairnes (*Some Leading Principles of Political Economy,* 1874); John Stuart Mill (*Principles of Political Economy,* 1848); and several French writers, including Jean Baptiste Say (*A Treatise on Political Economy; or the Production, Distribution, and Consumption of Wealth,* 1821).

It is usual to date the end of the classical school sometime before the publication of Alfred Marshall's *Principles of Economics* (1890)—an event that marks the ascendancy of the Cambridge school of economics—but there is a major disagreement on this point. John Maynard Keynes described most of the economic work that predated his *General Theory of Employment, Interest and Money* (1936) as classical because it accepted what he called the erroneous doctrine that the economy naturally tends to a position of full employment of labor and other resources. If we follow Keynes, we would have to include nearly the entire early Cambridge school as part of the classical school.

Smith's Influence

Disagreement about definitions stems from the fact that there was no classical school in the sense of a well-defined group of economists drawing intellectual sustenance from a single great master and acting in combination for a given purpose. In many cases the label "classical school" has served mostly as a polemical device to make one writer's personal theories seem superior to earlier points of view. This is unfortunate, because the period following Adam Smith's *Wealth of Nations* (1776) is bubbling with analytic contributions and suggestive controversies that reappear in different form with every new generation of writers. Institutions change, but the substantive issues of social and political organization retain a permanence that time has difficulty erasing. We need only point to the similarities between the monetary-fiscal debate of recent years and the older nineteenth-century controversy between the currency and banking schools following the Napoleonic wars.

Still, there is something to be said for grouping these writers together under the heading "classical." They shared a great respect for and profound intellectual debt to Smith's *Wealth of Nations.* This is not to say that they revered the work or swore allegiance to every doctrine of the old master—quite the contrary. The classical writers used Smith's writing as a springboard for their own analyses of economic problems. Often a single chapter, paragraph, or even sentence in the *Wealth of Nations* launched an enormously rich and lively secondary literature full of doctrinal innovation.

Consider the impact of Smith's casual remark that the profits of the capitalists represent a deduction from the worker's wages. Karl Marx used the deduction theory of profit to explain the origin of surplus value. Furthermore, Marx declared that one fundamental task of scientific socialism was to explain how this surplus value gets extracted from the working class when the entire market process is based on voluntary exchange. Ricardo molded the deduction theory into his inverse profit-wage theorem. According to Ricardo, a general rise in real wages will lower profits—the two always vary inversely. Government-imposed taxes affect the allocation of resources, but unless these taxes also alter the general rate of wage, they will have no effect on the rate of profit and the distribution of income. Ricardo went on to explain how diminishing returns in agriculture result in a rise in food prices and wages, ultimately lowering profits and propelling the economy toward the stationary state in which both capital accumulation and population growth end.

The Irish economist Mountifort Longfield readily admitted Smith's point that profits represent a deduction from the worker's wage, but he explained with considerable optimism that the worker is not exploited because net wages are considerably greater than what could be earned by working unaided without any capital at all. Longfield went on to develop this idea into a marginal productivity account of how capital goods are priced. Finally, in the famous wage-fund controversy that raged during the latter part of the nineteenth century between W. Thornton, J. S. Mill, and others, the issue was whether or not organized labor could negotiate a larger share of the national income at the expense of the capitalists.

Deductions from the laborer's wage can be arbitrary or necessary; they can result from outmoded institutions or correspond to important psychological determinants of economic action. N. W. Senior implied that the latter was the case in his abstinence theory of profit, which later influenced both J. S. Mill's and Alfred Marshall's thinking about profit and its relationship to wages. Senior insisted that profit was needed to compensate the capitalists for the inconvenience of waiting for repayment of their loans.

This thumbnail sketch of the impact that just one of Adam Smith's remarks has had on generations of writers illustrates in what form a classical school existed in the history of economic thought. Essentially, the classical school consisted of a diverse number of talented writers who developed ideas and corrected alleged errors found in the *Wealth of Nations* and in so doing improved the analytic foundations of the nascent science of economics.

References

Hollander, Samuel, *Classical Economics,* Basil Blackwell, New York, 1988; Moss, Laurence S., *Mountifort Longfield: Ireland's First Professor of Political Economy,* Green Hill, Ottawa, Ill., 1976; O'Brien, D. P., *The Classical Economists,* Clarendon, Oxford, 1975; Schwartz, Pedro, *The New Political Economy of J. S. Mill,* Duke University, Durham, N.C., 1972; Sowell, Thomas, *Classical Economics Reconsidered,* Princeton University, Princeton, N.J., 1974; Staley, Charles E., *A History of Economic Thought,* Basil Blackwell, Cambridge University, 1989.

(*See also* Cambridge school; Economics; Laissez faire; Marshallian economics; Neoclassical economics)

Laurence S. Moss

Closed-end investment companies

Investment companies obtain funds from individuals and buy financial assets. Closed-end funds are investment companies whose shares are purchased by investors. Closed-end funds do not redeem their shares at prices that reflect the day-by-day value of their security holdings as do open-end funds. Instead, closed-end fund share prices fluctuate according to supply and demand, often selling at deep discounts from their per-share net asset values.

These funds are called "closed-end" because the number of shares is not likely to be reduced unless such funds buy in their own shares in the open market. The number of closed-end shares is also more or less fixed in terms of new offerings. Like other corporations, closed-end funds may sell to new or existing stockholders through rights or under prospectus. But closed-end funds do not support sales organizations by paying high commissions, and the same lack of commissions means less support for the shares from brokers, especially when the nation's largest broker began to offer open-end shares. As a result, this route to equity capital expansion is restricted if not closed.

The number of closed-end shares can be reduced, however, if closed-end companies purchase their own shares in the open market. The investment companies have an incentive to do so when their shares are selling at a deep discount to the market value of their assets, since this would increase net asset value per share—a chief index of management's performance. In practice, however, most closed-end funds have failed to take advantage of this long-run opportunity to attract new investors because, in the short run, such policies reduce the amount of net assets under management, which usually determines fund management's remuneration. This occurs because some assets must be sold to buy in the funds' shares, and only the amount representing the discount can be reinvested.

The opportunity to buy securities at substantial discounts from the current market prices of closed-end funds' underlying assets is an example of an imperfection in modern capital asset pricing and efficient market theory, according to Burton G. Malkiel (1977), who, through regressions, attempts to explain closed-end funds' discounts. Tax liability on unrealized capital gains in closed-end funds in particular has not been sufficient to account for the discounts. Malkiel also attempts to measure the impact of other more subjective factors such as past performance in terms of net asset per share and investment policies that permit funds to purchase relatively illiquid foreign and letter stock. He finds that adding these factors to built-in tax liability to explain wide discounts does not add significantly to the power of his equation. Variations in the level of management fees are also found to be insignificant in Malkiel's regressions.

Malkiel and Firstenberg (1978) have suggested that the risk of a wider discount can be hedged in part by the purchase of a special kind of closed-end fund, namely, the dual fund. Dual funds allow one class of shareholders to collect all the dividends while an equal number of shareholders receive the value of all assets after income shares have been redeemed at their purchase price. Since dual funds have a fixed expiration date, any widening of the discount between the underlying assets of both income and capital shares will be reduced as liquidation approaches. Moreover, upon redemption, any discount will be eliminated. Malkiel therefore suggests the purchase of equal amounts of income and capital shares of dual funds to create an investment that is equivalent to a closed-end fund with this additional advantage: Liquidation (and hence the elimination of the discount) is assured by a certain date.

Malkiel also notes that average discount of selected closed-end dual funds (with matched income and capital shares) appears to decline when the funds' share prices are declining and to rise when funds' share prices rise. It follows that the risk of such investments is reduced in line with the negative covariance of these funds' discount and their market prices. For this reason the average beta (a measure of market-adjusted risk) on closed-end funds' shares is lower than the average beta on shares held in the same closed-end's portfolio—dramatically so for pairings of dual fund capital and income share investments. This results in higher returns from the same investment with lower risk. As indicated, this is in apparent conflict with current capital asset pricing theory, which, with restrictive assumptions, is based on the theory of efficient markets.

A number of nondiversified (and generally smaller) closed-end funds did not transform themselves into diversified funds after the passage of the Investment Company Act in 1940. Unlike diversified closed-end funds, these corporations may continue to hold securities of particular issuers (including the U.S. government and other investment companies) in excess of 5 percent of their total assets, and they may hold more than 10 percent of the voting securities of particular issuers. Because of the lack of restrictions on such companies and because they may hold large blocks of individual securities for long-term control purposes, unrealized capital gains (and hence built-in capital gains tax liability) is often substantial. For this reason and others most nondiversified closed-end funds sell at deeper discounts from their net asset value per share than diversified funds.

In general, original prospectuses for dual fund share offerings promised both classes of shareholders that investments would be made in common stocks providing somewhat below-average current yields, with the expectation that cash dividends for such securities would rise (or commence) after a reasonable period. The inherent conflict of interest between the two classes of shareholders was also addressed in some cases with a promise to include investments affording above-average yields if there was an expectation of capital appreciation within the holding period.

Income Shareholders

Income shareholders in most dual funds are entitled to cumulative dividends, whether or not earned, up to some stipulated nominal amount, payable quarterly, with any excess net investment income in any fiscal year being distributed in the form of an extra dividend. In general, such "extras" do not apply against minimum dividend payments in the future, however. Thus, in the event that the minimum dividend is not earned and is in arrears, net investment income distributed in any year is applied first to cover such arrearages.

As a rule, income shares are noncallable prior to the date on which the liquidation of the dual fund is called for, and on that date income shareholders are entitled to receive out of the assets of the dual fund then on hand a specified par value for each of their shares—generally close to or equal to their purchase price—plus accumulated and unpaid dividends through that date. Since income shares have 200 percent of their initial asset coverage, it is generally assumed that there would be sufficient capital to pay off the income shareholders.

Net investment income distributable to income shares is generally interest, dividends, and other income received or accrued less management fees, bank custodian fees, taxes (except federal and foreign capital gains taxes), and all other expenses that might be properly charged against income. However, capital gains, stock dividends, distributions designated as return of capital, and transfer taxes and brokerage commissions do not enter into the computation of net investment income. Moreover, to the extent that there are dividend arrearages in the income shares at the time of redemption, management fees and other current expenses are generally borne by the capital shareholders.

Capital Shareholders

All net capital gains accrue to the capital shares, but they are also the first to bear capital losses with the fund reinvesting all long-term capital gains. Capital shareholders are entitled to credits for taxes paid by the dual fund on such gains. Therefore: (1) the capital shareholder includes as his or her own long-term capital gain the pro rata share (determined without reference to income shares) of the dual fund's long-term capital gain on which the fund has paid the applicable tax; (2) the capital shareholder will therefore be entitled to a credit on the return or a refund of this tax; (3) the capital shareholder will be allowed to increase the adjusted tax basis of the capital shares by 75 percent of the amount so included in the return.

If short-term capital gains are distributed to the holder of capital shares to entitle the dual fund to tax treatment as a regulated investment company, such distributions will be reportable as ordinary income. Finally, the amount paid upon redemption by the fund for the shares of the capital shareholder will constitute a long-term capital gain (or loss) to the extent that such amount is greater (or less) than the adjusted tax basis for the shares, provided that the holding period is greater than 6 months.

References

Malkiel, Burton G., "The Valuation of Closed-End Investment Company Shares," *Journal of Finance,* June 1977; Malkiel, Burton G., and Paul B. Firstenberg, "A Winning Strategy for the Efficient Market," *Journal of Portfolio Management,* Summer 1978, pp. 20–25; Pratt, Eugene J.,

"Myths Associated with Closed End Investment Company Discounts," *Financial Analysts Journal,* July–August, 1966; Snyder, Linda, "The Closed End Funds May Be Opening Up," *Fortune,* February 1978, p. 137; Stoll, Hans, "Discounts and Premium on Shares of Diversified Closed End Investments Funds," Working Paper 11-73, Rodney L. White Center for Financial Research, University of Pennsylvania, Philadelphia, 1973; Thompson, Rex, "Capital Market Efficiency and the Information Content of Discounts and Premiums of Closed End Shares: An Empirical Analysis," Working Paper 30, Graduate School of Industrial Administration, Carnegie-Mellon University, Pittsburgh, February 1978.

(*See also* Mutual funds)

Arnold X. Moskowitz

Cobb-Douglas production function (*see* Production function)

Cobweb theorem

The cobweb theorem is an analytical product of the 1930s that attempts to explain the lack of an adjustment process that results in a Marshallian equilibrium price and quantity between consumers and producers in competitive markets. The fluctuations take on cyclical patterns with prices and quantities moving up and down in opposite directions. Such fluctuations, which have long been observed, occur in many agricultural products. For example, when prices are high, growers expand their outputs so that after a while they drive prices down. The lower prices in turn cause cutbacks in production, which bring a later upswing in prices. The name "cobweb" comes from the appearance of one of the diagrams that can be drawn to illustrate the theorem.

Applied to competitive markets, demand is a function of current price. However, supply is a function of the price in the previous period. The period can be 1 year, as with annual crops; the period can be 2, 3 or more years, as with hogs, beef cattle, fruit trees, etc. The period of time, in fact, could be a whole generation. Alfred Marshall (*Principles of Economics,* 1890) said that the supply of labor in an occupation in any one generation, "tends to conform to its earnings not in that but in the preceding generation."

Three simple models illustrate the essentials of the cobweb theorem. In the models, demand is a linear function of price in each period of time. That is, $D = f(p_t)$. Supply, however, is lagged, being a linear function of price in the preceding period. That is, $S = f(p_t - 1)$. In the three models, both the demand and supply functions remain constant for several periods.

Perpetual Oscillation Model

The model of perpetual oscillation has demand and supply curves, the slopes of which, disregarding the sign, are equal. If the price is at its equilibrium level, it will stay there indefinitely, under the assumption of constant demand and supply. Suppose, however, that the price in period 1 is above equilibrium. Then in period 1 the producers will, under the lagged-supply assumption, produce and offer for sale a quantity larger than the equilibrium amount. But the same quantity has to sell in period 2 for less than the equilibrium price. Believing that this low price will prevail in period 3, the producers cut back to a smaller quantity in period 3. The smaller quantity sells for a higher price in period 3. This higher price is exactly the same as the price in period 1, owing to the assumed equality of the slope of the linear demand and supply curves. Then the cycle begins anew.

Economists investigating the ramifications of the cobweb theorem support the notion that Muth's (1961) work on rational expectations is an offshoot of the cobweb theorem. Consumers, but especially producers, would be extremely naive to believe that perpetually oscillating prices are the norm. Muth suggests that when producers have concise information about the parameters that affect demand and supply functions, to include elasticities, they would calculate the equilibrium price and cause the cobweb fluctuations to cease. These "rational" producers, of course, would not be faced with any exogenous or random factors that could affect supply and demand functions.

Damped Oscillation Model

In the damped oscillation model of the cobweb theorem, the slope of the supply curve is greater (less elastic) than that of the demand curve. The producers' quantity adjustments in response to variations in price are relatively smaller than the buyers' adjustments. Suppose again that the price in period 1 is above equilibrium. Then in period 2, the producers will produce and offer for sale more than the equilibrium quantity. This sells in period 2 for a price below equilibrium. Then in period 3, the producers reduce the quantity they produce. The resulting price in period 3 is not as high as was the price in period 1. The cause is the lesser slope of the demand curve. But the price in period 3 is still above the equilibrium, and so in period 4 the amount produced causes the price to drop but not to as low a level as in period 2. What happens in this model then is that the oscillations about equilibrium are dampened, becoming ever smaller. The cycle attenuates, and, as eventual equilibrium is reached, the cycle ceases to exist.

Explosive Oscillation

The third of the simple cobweb models yields explosive oscillations. This model has a supply curve with a slope less (more elastic) than that of the demand curve. In their ever wider divergences from equilibrium, the quantities sold by the producers in successive periods cause ever wider movements of prices. Prices plunge and soar as quantities shrink and swell. It seems indeed as if this particular demand-supply-price mechanism must fly apart.

Theory and data do not necessarily bear out explosive oscillations. Indeed, some data on agricultural products show that the price elasticity of demand is less than the price elasticity of supply. Such conditions call for explosive oscillation. But other data, observed cycles, do not show such explosive behavior. In 1958, and with some success, Nerlove tried to adapt theory to fact by using the notion that producers do, in fact, employ adaptive expectations that prevent explosive oscillations in the agricultural sector.

Significance of the Cobweb Theorem

First, the rigidity of the lagged-supply response makes the models work. Modification of the assumption to allow for differences in the behavior of producers brings formidable complexities. However commodity cycles persist and are real. It appears that lagged-supply response continues as a pattern of producers' behavior. Second, the theoretical significance of the cobweb theorem is its holding the kernel of a dynamic theory. Third, the cobweb theorem draws attention to one more of the imperfections of actual competitive markets. Although efficiency embraces more than equilibrium in competitive markets, equilibrium is its *sine qua non*. Finally, perusal of the literature in economic journals, and also of undergraduate and graduate text books on microeconomic theory, shows that the cobweb theorem has been of relatively minor concern to economists in recent years.

References

Ezekiel, Mordecai, "The Cobweb Theory," *Quarterly Journal of Economics,* February 1938, reprinted in American Economic Association, *Readings in Business Cycle Theory,* Blakiston, Philadelphia, 1944, chap. 21; Muth, John, "Rational Expectations and the Theory of Price Movements," *Econemetrica,* July 1961, pp. 315–335; Nerlove, Mark, "Adaptive Expectations and Cobweb Phenomena," *Quarterly Journal of Economics,* May 1958, pp. 227–240; Nicholson, Walter, *Intermediate Microeconomics and Its Applications* (5th ed.), Dryden, Chicago, 1990, pp. 405–408; Pashigian, B. Peter, "Rational Expectations and the Cobweb Theory," *Journal of Political Economy,* March–April 1970, pp. 338–352; Samuelson, Paul A., "Dynamic Process Analysis," in Howard S. Ellis (ed.), *A Survey of Contemporary Economics,* Blakiston, Philadelphia, 1948, chap. 10.

(*See also* Competition; Demand; Dynamic analysis; Expectations; General equilibrium; Rational expectations; Supply)

Mary A. Holman

Colbertism (*see* Mercantilism)

Collective bargaining

The many views regarding collective bargaining depend on whether one is a trade union member; an employer of labor represented by a trade union; an employer of nonunion workers; a practitioner of collective bargaining such as a labor lawyer, labor relations consultant, union business agent or representative, labor arbitrator or mediator; or a scholar or educator in the field. These varied views are difficult to distill into a neat and precise definition, but some common threads weave through the various viewpoints and approaches to the subject, allowing for a cohesive definition, though imprecise, of collective bargaining.

The term "collective bargaining" originated in the 1890s in the scholarly works of Sidney Webb and Beatrice Webb, who were members of England's Fabian Society. The term was first introduced in the United States at the turn of the century by the Industrial Commission, which was created by an Act of Congress in 1898. Hence, collective bargaining is a relatively new process and thus has only rather recently engaged the interest of economists, historians, and other social scientists. Although no neat and precise body of principles renders collective bargaining a science, as an important human endeavor it occupies the interests of economists, historians, political scientists, sociologists, social psychologists, legal scholars, and practitioners from a variety of backgrounds.

Labor Agreement

Collective bargaining is a dynamic process of trade union representation of employees to employers for the fundamental purpose of negotiating wages, hours, and other terms or conditions of employment into a written labor agreement, and for the purpose of establishing a system of industrial jurisprudence to resolve any grievances which may arise thereunder. Thus collective bargaining provides a representative function to serve the interests and welfare of trade union members. It is a bilateral means toward achieving ends, the latter being generally wages, hours, and other terms or conditions of employment. The labor agreement defines the terms and conditions of the employment contract between the employer and the individual employee. Adopting a political analogy, we may say that collective bargaining can be described by three functions:

1. A legislative function which culminates into a private law—a labor agreement which is enforceable in legal tribunals and the process of labor arbitration

2. An executive function which requires the administration of the employment relationship between employer and employee in accordance with the labor agreement

3. A judicial function wherein third-party neutral labor arbitrators resolve differences regarding conflicting interpretations of specific language of the labor agreement and adjudicate any grievances that may arise thereunder

Fair Treatment

Collective bargaining provides the means toward affording fair treatment in the processing of employee grievances through the grievance machinery incorporated into the labor agreement without the necessity of incurring the huge time-consuming expense of litigation. Some authorities refer to this procedure as the "absolute law of fair treatment." Collective bargaining also provides a means of equal treatment of equals in that as the employer-union relationship matures, and as experience is gathered in dealing with day-to-day routine matters, a common body of shop law evolves which may or may not be incorporated with the formal labor agreement or may be mutually accepted as common practice binding both employers and employees. A fundamental aim of collective bargaining is to provide a system of relative claims to available work. A variety of techniques are used to achieve this goal, but all have the common characteristic of providing individual job security through a system of recognizing years of service to the employer as a principal means of determining promotability, order of layoff when economic and/or technological conditions necessitate a reduction in force, and a recall to work from layoff status. Very often, however, strict seniority or job tenure is modified or qualified by skill and ability to perform available work and/or eligibility conditions reflecting one's training and experience.

All the above refers to the micro aspects of the employer-employee relationship—that between the individual employer and the union which represents employees of that employer. There is, however, another dimension of collective bargaining which is more aggregative and involves the trade union organization as a political institution to achieve economic security and welfare needs of constituents through political action. Such activity transcends collective bargaining in the conventional sense but is still an important raison d'être of the trade union movement. This is true of large national union organizations and is a particularly important function of federations of trade unions. Thus, trade unions and trade union movements engage in activities which go beyond collective bargaining as described above.

Industrial Jurisprudence

In the absence of collective bargaining, the fundamental questions between employers and employees regarding wages, hours, and other terms or conditions of employment are left to the parties themselves functioning within the broad parameters of their relevant labor market. Under the latter circumstances, the employer and employee determine substantive terms of the employment relationship subject to market forces. These market forces provide the important economic function of allocating scarce labor resources through the pricing mechanism; however, in this case, the important dimension of industrial jurisprudence is left to the good offices of the employer. Consequently, any grievances that may arise between the employer and employee are resolved by the employer unilaterally and, of course, without any provision that unresolved matters between the parties may be adjudicated by a third-party neutral.

Under collective bargaining the employer does not have unilateral authority to make ultimate decisions regarding an employee. A system of industrial jurisprudence prevails that provides bargaining members due process in resolving disputes with employers, which provides a check on the power of employers. That is, the employee is provided an assurance of equitable treatment and, in fact, has an absolute claim to fair treatment through the grievance procedure negotiated in virtually all labor agreements. The collective bargaining agreement provides for individual job security or job rights based on some form of seniority which undergirds a system of relative claims to available work determined by seniority rights on the job. Thus, it is important to recognize that the collective bargaining agreement transcends the mere determination of the wage and effort bargain by providing for an individual's relative job security and assurance of fair treatment. In this respect, these characteristics of collective bargaining are unique to the United States in that they reflect the constitutional system of governance. If collective bargaining provided for nothing else but relative job security and fair treatment for employees, it would still be a worthy institution to preserve in the absence of alternative means toward these ends.

References

Beal, Edwin, F., E. D. Wickersham, and P. K. Kienast, *The Practice of Collective Bargaining* (5th ed.), Irwin, Homewood, Ill., 1976; Davey, Harold W., *Contemporary Collective Bargaining* (3d ed.), Prentice-Hall, Englewood Cliffs, N.J., 1972; Perlman, Selig, "The Principles of Collective Bargaining," in E. Wight Bakke and Clark Kerr (eds.), *Unions, Management and the Public* (2d ed.), Harcourt, Brace, New York, 1960; Sturmthal, Adolph (ed.), *Contemporary Collective Bargaining in Seven Countries,* Institute of International Industrial and Labor Relations, Cornell University, Ithaca, N.Y., 1957; Trotta, Maurice, *Collective Bargaining,* Simmons-Boardman, New York, 1962; Windmiller, John P., *Collective Bargaining in Industrialized Market Economies: A Reappraisal,* International Labor Organization, Geneva, 1987.

(*See also* Labor-management relations; Labor unions)

Sam Barone

Commercial banks: problems and solutions

A bank is a vehicle for the delivery of financial services. Broadly speaking, financial services may be classified along five lines: (1) transacting, including funds transfer and clearing; (2) issuance of deposits and interest-bearing nondeposit instruments; (3) extension of credit to be held in portfolio as well as origination for distribution to other investors; (4) insurance against financial and nonfinancial risk; and (5) performance of fiduciary activities such as trust, custody, and advice. Some services fall into more than one category. For example, a credit card used to facilitate purchases where balances are liquidated promptly is a transacting vehicle. It may also provide access to credit.

In the United States banks and their affiliates and subsidiaries are authorized to perform most of these services. Only two classes of activities remain subject to major proscription: the underwriting of life (except credit life), casualty, and fidelity insurance and the sponsorship and distribution of open-end mutual funds. Two further constraints to the exercise of powers should be identified. First, bank branching is not now permitted across state lines. Second, certain securities powers must be undertaken in separate subsidiaries and often are limited as a percentage of total activity.

Commercial bank problems are of two general forms. First, for many institutions capital in place has been insufficient to cover valuation losses which, in turn, largely have reflected excessive credit concentrations, most recently in real estate. At the same time, inroads by nonbank sources of financial services have compressed returns in many traditional loan and deposit markets. Indeed, these competitive pressures played a role in the increased real-estate-related lending by many banks.

A second general problem entails reforms necessitated by the first. Two major components may be identified: (1) the distribution of cleanup costs for resolving insolvent banks between other banks as a group and the taxpaying public and (2) the implementation of regulatory reform that, at the same time, affords reasonable operating latitude to "healthy" entities while eliminating undercapitalized ones before losses result.

Problems

Bank competitive positions have eroded dramatically because of the introduction and development of substitutes. These substitutes have been facilitated by information technology available to new entrants at steadily falling prices as well as by barriers to adaptiveness on the part of the banks themselves. Disadvantages in funding costs relative to major nonbank entities have furthered the erosion of bank positions in credit extensions, especially for businesses.

Overall, bank shares of credit extended to nonfinancial sectors dropped from 31 percent in 1982 to 25 percent in 1991. The bank share of business lending fell from 33 to 24 percent over that period. This decline has reflected pricing disadvantages attaching to bank loans as well as borrower balance sheet restructuring, where greater emphasis has been accorded to long-term debt. Banks also have facilitated less recourse to bank borrowing by promotion of "off-balance-sheet" letters of credit and commitments. In a similar vein, the share of deposits at banks and thrifts in a broad measure of money (M_3) fell from 92 percent in 1970 to 76 percent in 1991.

Another factor in the decline of share has been actions by banks to securitize and sell portions of asset holdings. The securitization development has enhanced liquidity management and has made loan markets—even relatively smaller ones—more sensitive to national pricing patterns.

During the 1980s many banks increased their allocations to those credit sectors where they believed information asymmetries to exist. Commercial real estate is a prime example. Between 1982 and 1988, the net increase in commercial real estate lending by banks comprised 32 percent of the total net increase in bank lending. This ratio was almost three times the 12 percent share of commercial real estate loans in loan portfolios at the beginning of the period. The overbuilding to which this lending contributed—encouraged by laxity in credit judgment and in administrative practices—subjected banks concentrating in this activity to major earnings and capital problems.

The dimensions of bank performance erosion are indicated by industry averages. From the 1960s through the mid-1980s returns on equity for all banks averaged about 11 percent and asset returns about 74 basis points. Over the period 1986 to 1990, however, asset returns averaged 52 basis points and returns on equity about 8¼ percent. Generally speaking, banks located in the central states performed well above national averages, and those in the northeast and some western states performed worse.

Problems: Cleanup Costs

The legacies of the higher and more volatile interest rates of the 1970s and early 1980s followed by the adversities associated with disinflation and, in some cases (e.g., commercial real estate) deflation, were widespread failures of thrift institutions and commercial banks, with the consequent exhaustion of reserves of the Federal Savings and Loan Insurance Corporation and the Federal Deposit Insurance Corporation. Improper accounting practices combined with managerial ineptness and forbearance on the part of regulatory agencies resulted in both delay in the recognition of the magnitude of losses and improper managerial incentives leading to riskier practices. These added materially to eventual recognized losses.

The magnitude of eventual losses cannot be estimated with precision until asset dispositions are completed. In the case of savings and loan (S&L) failures, the present value of public disbursements may reach at least $250 billion. Reserves held by the Bank Insurance Fund approximated a negative $7 billion at year-end 1991, representing an absorption in excess of $25 billion over a period of 4 years. In 1990 and 1991 the Fund was charged with an estimate of future losses, in addition to outlays during the current year. The Fund's deposit insurance premium rose from a rate of 0.08 to 0.23 percent by year-end 1991 and undoubtedly will rise further. As of year-end 1991, problem banks—both commercial and savings—numbered 1069, about one-third less than the recent peak in 1987. The assets of those problem institutions, however, approximated $611 billion in 1991, about 70 percent higher than in the mid-1980s and almost 50 percent greater than 1 year earlier. In consequence, there is widespread concern that costs of resolving failing or failed banks will require recourse to public funds.

New Strategies at Banks

Strategies for improving bank positions fall into five general categories. One of the most important is the application of securitization to a wide range of customer loan categories. As capital constraints have become more binding, some of the intermediation function has been replaced by that of origination for distribution. Loans may be syndicated immediately or—especially if of smaller denomination—packaged and securitized. Some of this activity, e.g., in residential mortgages, has been shifted to nonbank affiliates within bank holding companies.

A second development has been the use of a bank's balance sheet on which to generate risk management services for others. These include swaps, caps, futures, and options covering interest rates, commodity prices, and currency prices. In this, U.S. banks appear to have attained recognition for innovative pricing and product development.

A third strategy has entailed expanded product offerings. On the business side, larger wholesale-oriented banks have attained authority (generally in separate affiliates under so-called Section 20 approval) to engage in public debt and equity underwriting and advisory functions. So far, with few exceptions, market penetration by banks has tended to be limited. On the consumer side, constraints on insurance underwriting and mutual fund sponsorship have impaired bank efforts to increase their share of customer asset positions. Some services, such as annuities and mutual funds, have been sold through banks acting as agents for others. In short, given the wide range of alternatives facing users, banks have found it difficult to differentiate their services, and they have not been able to convince customers of the virtues of bundling or services with a single source.

A fourth strategy, extending from the third, entails expansion of shares of more traditional deposit and loan services in present and contiguous markets. Efforts are aimed at capturing efficiencies in marketing, distribution, and processing costs. This has involved a substantial amount of merger activity. Recent analyses in the United States question the amount and permanence of savings from eliminating redundant expense in within-market or contiguous-market consolidations.

Beginning in 1990 acquisitions of parts of failed banks and thrifts on a "clean" basis attained increased importance. Although the customer base of failed entities often eroded during the firm's decline, acquisitions of this kind typically avoided exposure to the serious asset valuation risks which afflict whole-bank amalgamations. Another feature of the amalgamation process has been acquisitions of portfolios of credit card receivables and mortgage servicing. Valuations are subject to less error than with whole banks, and operational integration is more readily achieved.

In this context the term "excess capacity" is often used to characterize the impetus for banking amalgamation. This term misleadingly suggests that pressures from an overpopulation of competing institutions would be eased by a smaller number of entities. In an environment where virtually all markets are contestable, however, improved profitability is likely to encourage new competition from banks as well as nonbank entities.

Finally, a fifth strategy has entailed greater sensitivity to the need to exit specific product, customer, or geographic positions. U.S. banks have closed branches in Europe and Asia. Many have reduced commitments to corporate finance in general and business lending in particular. Other moves have included dispositions of branch clusters and bank affiliates with small market shares, credit card businesses, investment management functions, and mortgage banking. In short, candidates for divestiture have been virtually as broad as the powers accorded to banks.

Capital as Centerpiece of Regulatory Reform

Forbearance in the regulatory resolution of capital-short banks and S&Ls eventually increased the costs borne by insurance agencies and the public at large. These costs were increased in two ways. First, assets of impaired quality tend to depreciate with time and under conditions of inadequate oversight. Second, managers of weak institutions have incentives to undertake new and risky operating tactics in an effort to recoup capital or earnings positions. On average, these efforts further deplete capital.

The Federal Deposit Insurance Corporation Improvement Act of 1991 (FDICIA) provided for the most sweeping regulatory changes since the 1930s. The central element of this Act is the requirement that regulatory agencies (1) define capital positions in five categories, or tranches: well capitalized, adequately capitalized, undercapitalized, significantly undercapitalized, and critically undercapitalized; (2) apply more restrictive operating constraints on banks having lower capital positions in this hierarchy and require the formulation of programs to raise new capital; and (3) take prompt corrective action—including appointment of a receiver or conservator—for those institutions critically undercapitalized.

Although the legislation did not stipulate how capital should be measured, it did provide that in order to qualify for any category an institution had to meet all minimum criteria established for that category. Regulatory agencies are required to establish during 1992 the number of capital measures to be employed, calculations by which capital is measured, and the thresholds corresponding to the first four categories. The only ratio contained in FDICIA is that of a minimum of 2 percent tangible equity to total assets as the upper limit of critically undercapitalized.

Other provisions of the Act extend other aspects of regulatory oversight. These include risk-based deposit insurance assessments (to replace the flat-rate system now in place), provision for capital against interest rate risk and loan concentrations, and disclosure of supplemental market value information. The latter may lead eventually to capital requirements having greater sensitivity to changes in market values applying to all aspects of bank operations. The Act made no provision for expanded powers.

Further reduction in the shares of banks relative to other financial intermediaries is in prospect by virtue of continued competitive pressures and the contractive pressures likely to be associated with the new capital standards. The future profitability of banks will reflect the economic vitality of the markets they serve, the net burdens of regulatory policies, the strength of competition, and the effectiveness of bank management itself.

References

Aspinwall, Richard, "The Erosion of the Banking Franchise," *The Journal of Commercial Bank Lending,* January 1992; Benston, George J., Robert A. Eisenbeis, Paul M. Horvitz, Edward J. Kane, and George G. Kaufman, *Perspectives on Safe and Sound Banking,* MIT, Cambridge, Mass., 1986; Federal Deposit Insurance Corporation, "Quarterly Banking Profile," various issues; Humphrey, David Burras, "The Likely Effects of Interstate Branching on Bank Costs and Service Prices," paper prepared for the Congressional Budget Office, October 1991; Kane, Edward J., *The S&L Insurance Mess: How Did It Happen?,* Urban Institute, Washington, D.C., 1989; Kaufman, George G., "Capital in Banking: Past, Present, and Future," *Journal of Financial Services Research,* April 1992; Litan, Robert E., *The Revolution in U.S. Finance,* Brookings, Washington, D.C., 1991; Sinkey, Joseph F., *Commercial Bank Financial Management in the Financial Services Industry,* 3d ed., Macmillan, New York, 1989; U.S. Department of the Treasury, *Modernizing the Financial System,* February 1989.

(*See also* Banking system; Financial institutions; Less-developed country debt; Thrift institutions: Problems and challenges)

Richard Aspinwall

Commodity exchange

A commodity exchange is a voluntary association of individuals who provide a physical marketplace for the purchase or sale of various commodities. The commodities traded on these exchanges vary widely and include products such as grains, energy, metals, interest rates, stock indexes, foreign currencies, and livestock. Some of these commodities are traded on a cash basis, but the vast majority are traded in the form of futures contracts and futures options contracts.

A *futures contract* is a standardized, legally binding agreement to deliver or take delivery of a specified quantity and quality of a commodity during a specific month under terms established by the federally designated contract market in which trading is conducted. The price for the commodity is agreed upon in the trading pit or trading ring for that commodity at the exchange it is traded on at the time the contract is executed. The terms of the futures contract provide the seller (the short) the option to deliver the underlying commodity to the buyer (the long) at any time during a specified delivery period. The delivery price is adjusted for variations in the quality of the commodity actually delivered.

The standardization of the contract terms (deliverable grade, unit of trading, delivery procedures, etc.) is a key factor in the success and usefulness of futures contracts. Standardization makes all futures contracts of a specific delivery month identical and completely interchangeable. The buyers or sellers of the contracts can readily liquidate or offset their positions at any time prior to delivery. The buyer would offset the obligation to take delivery of the underlying commodity by selling an equal number of the specified contracts. The seller would eliminate the obligation to deliver the commodity by buying an equal number of the contracts. Through this process, futures market participants can readily utilize the contracts to protect against adverse market movements in the underlying market without having to make or take delivery.

A *futures option contract* is a standardized, legally binding agreement which gives its owner the right (but not the obligation) to buy or sell a particular futures contract at a specified price at any time on or before a given date. Two types of options are traded: call options and put options. A futures call option grants the buyer the right to buy the underlying futures contract at a predetermined price (referred to as the "exercise price" or "strike price"), on or before a predetermined date. The seller of the call option is obligated to sell the underlying futures contract to the call option buyer if the option is exercised. A futures put option grants the buyer the right to sell the underlying futures contract at a predetermined price on or before a predetermined date. The seller of the put option is obligated to buy the underlying futures contract from the option buyer if the option is exercised. All futures option contracts of the same delivery month, type (call or put), and strike price are completely identical and interchangeable. Futures option contracts are also widely used as a risk reduction mechanism for participants in the underlying markets.

Role of the Exchange

Most commodity exchanges are not-for-profit membership associations incorporated in the states in which they are located. Commodity exchanges themselves are not involved in the actual trading of or setting the prices of commodities listed for trading. The major role of a commodity exchange is to provide a centralized facility where members of the exchange can trade futures and futures option contracts. In addition, commodity exchanges have the responsibility of establishing trading rules and standards of conduct and to enforce these rules and standards.

The exchanges are self-governing associations with various member committees and a board of directors having the responsibility of enforcing the various rules and regulations and setting the policies of the exchange. Memberships are limited to individuals, and only members of the exchange are allowed to trade contracts on the trading floor. The actual number of memberships or "seats" available at one time is typically set by each exchange at a fixed number. The value of these seats is determined through a bid and offer negotiation process which is administered by exchange officials.

In order to become a member of an exchange, an applicant must meet certain good character and financial requirements. In addition, members must adhere to an extensive set of exchange rules and regulations which involve all aspects of trading floor procedures. Members who fail to comply with these rules and regulations face the possibility of fines, suspension, and/or the loss of membership. These standards play an important role in ensuring the integrity of transactions executed on the exchange floor. Through the adherence of these rules and regulations, commodity exchanges are able to maintain liquid, efficient, and openly competitive markets.

Commodity exchanges in the United States are regulated by and must receive designation as an approved contract market by the Commodity Futures Trading Commission (CFTC). The CFTC is an independent, federally regulated agency charged by and empowered under the Commodity Futures Trading Commission Act of 1974 with the regulation of futures trading in all commodities. The CFTC is headed by a chair and four commissioners. Each has been appointed by the president of the United States, and all are subject to U.S. Senate confirmation.

Exchanges seeking to trade new futures and futures option contracts must first receive approval by the CFTC. To receive approval, an exchange is required to provide and justify in a written submission the specific trading regulations for the proposed contract. In addition, the exchange must demonstrate that the proposed contract satisfies an "economic purpose test." To satisfy this test, evidence must be provided that (1) the new contract market will be a basis for determining prices and that these prices will be generally disseminated and/or (2) the new contract will provide a viable mechanism for and be used as a risk transference (hedging) vehicle.

All futures and option transactions on an exchange are processed and cleared by the clearinghouse of that exchange. Clearinghouses are either fully separate chartered corporations or a division of the exchange itself. The role of the clearinghouse involves the matching and reconciling of all futures and option transactions, and the assuming of the responsibility as a guarantor to every contract traded, hence ensuring financial integrity.

Ten designated commodity exchanges currently exist in the United States which presently trade futures and/or futures option contracts. These exchanges include the Chicago Board of Trade; the Chicago Mercantile Exchange; the Coffee, Sugar, & Cocoa Exchange; the Commodity Exchange, Inc.; the Kansas City Board of Trade; the MidAmerica Commodity Exchange (an affiliate of the Chicago Board of Trade); the Minneapolis Grain Exchange; the New York Cotton Exchange; the New York Futures Exchange (an affiliate of the New York Stock Exchange); and the New York Mercantile Exchange.

History of Futures Trading and Markets

The fundamental principles that underlie commodity futures trading date back to the Greek and Roman empires. In those times, structured marketplaces existed which provided a fixed time and location for trading, common currency and barter systems, and the ability to contract for future delivery. The Agora in Athens and the Forum in Rome were both originally established as marketplaces.

The principles of a marketplace continued through the Dark Ages and developed in feudal times in the form of local markets. The number of these markets and the variety of commodities traded multiplied rapidly from the eleventh to fourteenth centuries. These markets typically took the form of a medieval fair that traveled from city to city. These fairs provided preannounced markets at fixed places and times and had a key role in the formalization and institutionalization of trading rules and practices. Although the majority of trading at these fairs involved the immediate delivery of the cash (spot) commodity, the practice of contracting for the future delivery of a commodity did exist.

The importance of these medieval fairs declined as improvements in transportation and communication occurred. Market centers at specific locations developed in their place. These "exchanges," as they were known, provided a formalized gathering place for local commerce. In many instances, the trading practices and standards of conduct developed by the medieval fairs served as the foundation for the rules established by the exchanges. A number of these centralized exchanges came into existence in the sixteenth through eighteenth centuries in locations ranging throughout Europe, Japan, and the United States. Examples of these exchanges include the Royal Exchange in London, which opened in 1570; the Osaka Rice Exchange, which was established in 1730; and an exchange for domestic produce that existed in New York in the 1750s.

A major factor in the continued development of these markets and the emergence of futures contracts as the main trading vehicle involved the growth in the nineteenth century of Chicago as a key commercial center. Chicago's geographical location provided important advantages for both rail and water transportation and allowed Chicago to become a major grain terminus. Typically, merchants would purchase grain from local farmers after harvest, store it through the winter, and bring it to Chicago in the following spring. However, due to variable supply and demand situations, the price the merchants would be able to receive for their stored grain was always an uncertainty. This uncertainty was especially heightened by the lack of adequate transportation routes and storage facilities.

To overcome these difficulties, merchants began the process of making contracts during harvest time for forward delivery of grain in Chicago in the spring. Both the standard grade of the commodity to be delivered and its price were agreed upon in the contract. These contracts allowed grain merchants to effectively shift the risks of adverse price changes to buyers in Chicago willing to assume the risks.

This system of forward trading evolved in the United States during the nineteenth century and spanned markets for commodities such as grains, cotton, tobacco, and sugar. In 1848, the Chicago Board of Trade was formed. Developed by a group of 82 businessmen, the Chicago Board of Trade initially provided a centralized marketplace for the trading of both cash and forward delivery commodities.

Although this forward contract system continued to develop, trading was limited by the lack of standardization and the resulting difficulties in the ability to readily trade specific contracts. These difficulties led to the development and trading of futures contracts at the Chicago Board of Trade during the 1860s. Unlike forward contracts, futures contracts were standardized contracts in which all contract features except the price were specified. The price was determined on the trading floor of the exchange. Standardization included standard delivery grades (quality and quantity) and allowable delivery procedures. In addition, the contracts were subject to specific exchange rules and regulations. In the late 1800s, futures markets continued to mature as clearing and settlement procedures were established by exchanges and the practice of offsetting a contract before delivery became routine.

Other exchanges emerged in the nineteenth and twentieth centuries as futures trading developed in such cities as New York, New Orleans, London, and Minneapolis. Commodities traded on these exchanges included grains, metals, livestock, foodstuffs, and fibers. In the 1970s, futures contracts on interest rates and currencies were developed. These contracts effectively provided financial market participants the ability to transfer risk in the similar manner as grain dealers. In the 1980s, energy and stock index futures contracts were introduced. Futures contracts on financial instruments, stock indexes, energy, and currencies have become so popular and widely used they now comprise by far the largest volume of exchange activity. In 1990, 340.6 million futures and futures option contracts were traded on U.S. exchanges. Of this total, 254.1 million contracts (approximately 75 percent) involved interest rate, energy, stock index, and currency contracts.

In 1981, the CFTC initiated a pilot program to allow the trading of certain commodity option contracts on U.S. exchanges. Prior to this program, trading in regulated commodity options was prohibited due to widespread abuses that existed, especially during the 1930s. The reintroduction of option contracts on exchanges proved to be successful as significant marketplace interest emerged for these products. The CFTC subsequently expanded the program to include other allowable commodity options, and by 1987 futures option trading on exchanges was established on a permanent basis. Exchanges have embraced option trading and in most cases have listed for trading the companion futures option contract for each of its successful futures contracts.

Futures and options trading has also developed rapidly outside the United States. In the past decade, a number of new commodity exchanges have opened in the Far East and Europe. Products on these exchanges generally span similar agricultural and financial products offered by U.S. exchanges, and the aggregate rate of growth by these foreign markets has been particularly impressive. The Chicago Board of Trade as the largest futures exchange in the world experienced approximately an 84 percent increase in volume between 1985 and 1990. Nevertheless, the Board of Trade's share of world futures market volume decreased from 39.0 percent to 27.5 percent over this same period.

Hedging

The standardized, homogenous features of futures and option contracts enhance the usefulness of these instruments for risk management and hedging purposes. Hedging is generally defined as the initiation of a position in the futures or option market that provides a temporary substitute for the future purchase or sale of the underlying commodity. Futures contracts are sold in advance of future sales of the actual commodity to protect against possible price declines. Futures contracts are purchased in advance of future purchases of the actual commodity to insulate against possible price increases before the actual purchase.

In the mid-1800s, hedging activities gained prominence in a number of the various grain markets. Today, for a wide range of cash market participants, hedging with futures and/or futures option contracts is an indispensable part of normal business activities to better manage price volatility and protect profit margins. Commercial firms, commodity producers, commodity merchandisers, commodity processors, investment companies, corporations, pension funds, banks, security dealers, and insurance companies are all exposed to price risks and are active hedgers in the futures and/or options markets.

Hedging cash positions with futures and/or options contracts can be a successful strategy largely because over time movements in cash market prices correlate closely with movements in futures market prices. This parallel price relationship is mainly due to the fact that the same economic and fundamental factors affect both markets. In addition, the futures delivery process reinforces this close correlation between the markets. The ability to deliver the cash commodity against the futures contract ensures that an economic relationship exists between the two markets and that during the delivery period the cash and futures price will converge.

This relationship between the cash and futures markets provides cash market participants the incentive to establish equivalent positions in futures contracts opposite to their positions in the underlying commodities. To illustrate, a farmer in the spring might have expectations that the price of corn will likely fall by harvest time. In order to protect against a decline in price, the farmer sells the appropriate quantity of corn futures contracts. By placing this hedge, the farmer has effectively insulated his targeted selling price from a market downturn. Over the duration of the hedge, if corn prices decrease (increase), the losses (gains) on the selling price in the cash market will be approximately offset by the gains (losses) in the futures position.

The above "short" hedge is typically used by the owner or producer of a commodity to ensure against a potential decrease in price before the commodity can be sold. Alternatively, processors, merchandisers, and users of commodities often face the risk of prices rising and costs increasing before the commodity can be purchased. In these situations, futures contracts will be bought ("long" hedge) to "lock-in" a buying price.

Speculating

Hedgers in commodity markets looking to insulate against risk need to be able to readily transfer that risk to other participants who are willing and able to accept it. Speculators provide this risk-shifting mechanism and in the process provide the liquidity (ongoing presence of both buyers and sellers) needed for hedgers to easily buy or sell futures and/or option contracts. Speculators in these markets look to use their capital to establish market positions in line with their forecasts of future price movements. The interchangeability of futures and option contracts allows speculators to establish market positions and readily offset the positions (typically before the actual delivery period).

Through their activities, speculators ensure that sufficient liquidity exists to allow hedgers to buy or sell the desired quantity of contracts with minimal price impacts. Related to this, academic studies have indicated that active speculation tends to dampen price volatility and hence foster price stability.

References

Black, Fischer, "The Pricing of Commodity Contracts," *Journal of Financial Economics,* vol. 3, 1976, pp. 161–179; Chicago Board of Trade, "Commodity Trading Manual," Education and Marketing Services Department, Chicago Board of Trade, 1989; Figlewski, Stephen, *Hedging with Financial Futures for Institutional Investors: From Theory to Practice,* Ballinger, Cambridge, Mass., 1985; Hieronymus, Thomas A., *Economics of Futures Trading,* Commodity Research Bureau, New York, 1977; Leuthold, Raymond M., Joan C. Junkus, and Jean E. Cordier, *The Theory and Practice of Futures Markets,* Lexington Books, Lexington, Mass., 1989; Peck, Anne E. (ed.), *Futures Markets: Their Economic Role,* American Enterprise Institute for Public Policy Research, Washington, D.C., 1985; Schwarz, Edward W., Joanne M. Hill, and Thomas Schneeweis, *Financial Futures Fundamentals, Strategies, and Applications,* Irwin, Homewood, Ill., 1986.

(*See also* Arbitrage; Futures; Options; Stock exchange)

E. Ted Doukas

Communism

Communism refers to (1) an ideology, (2) a group of political parties, and (3) a proposed economic system. As an ideology or a coherent system of ideas, communism has ancient roots in various proposed utopias. Karl Marx formulated communism as a critique of the existing capitalist economic system and as a vision of a possible future economic system. Marx divided future systems into socialism and communism. *Socialism* referred to collective ownership of the means of production, but with continued inequality in wages, paid according to the amount of an individual's work. *Communism* referred to an advanced stage of socialism in which the means of production—including all factories and land—would continue to be collectively owned, but with equal distribution of goods according to need.

A Group of Political Parties

Communism was a unified political movement from 1917 till the end of World War II. Following World War II, however, when Communist parties achieved independent political power, international solidarity gave way to violent conflicts between different parties, based on their differing interpretations of the Marxist message.

Some factions of Communist parties still follow, to some degree, the views of Joseph Stalin. The Chinese Communists follow the teachings of Mao Tse-tung, since his death emphasizing the pragmatic aspects of these teachings over the dogmatic. The West European Communist parties have their own concepts, designated "Eurocommunism" (which advocates socialism plus democracy), and some are even dropping the name "Communist." The Communist regimes of Eastern Europe have all fallen, having been ousted in 1989 or 1990.

Proposed Economic System

Communism as a proposed economic system (collective ownership of the means of production and equality of income distribution) remains an ideal yet to be realized, even though Communist parties have ruled some countries for a long time. But political parties do not necessarily advocate the economic system from which they take their name. Most Socialist parties advocate mixed capitalism and socialism, with perhaps an all-socialist economy years later. Most Communist parties advocate immediate socialism, with communism relegated to the far future. As the regimes of Eastern Europe collapsed, their economies moved toward capitalism.

Free Goods and Services: The Goal

Although communism remains unrealized anywhere, many people through the years have dreamed the utopian idea of a system where labor is given freely by all workers, accompanied by freely available goods and services. Critics of this egalitarian proposal generally argue: (1) workers will get lazy because they can live without working; (2) there will be an infinite demand for each of the free goods and services; and (3) it would be impossible to plan rationally an economy where there are no changing prices in the marketplace to signal changes in the demand for different goods and services.

The first point, that workers would get lazy if they could live without working, may have some validity, at least in some societies, but if availability of free goods and services was extended slowly, workers would easily find other things on which to spend their money, so that the incentive to work would not materially decline.

The second point has a high degree of validity: Wants tend to be unlimited, and some rationing process is necessary. But this is not true of all goods and services. For education or health care, for example, there is a finite demand, a saturation point beyond which no further increased supply would be required. There is also a finite demand for many basic necessities such as bread and potatoes. Of course there is an infinite demand for luxuries such as yachts and expensive vacations, for which some form of rationing would be required.

The third point, that rational economic planning requires price signals, has no validity. Economic planning can be done rationally, without price data, if certain information is known. Planners would need to know what resources, both of labor and of capital, are available; what technologies exist for combining resources into desirable outputs; and how much of each free good will be desired at a zero price. The data exist on availability of most resources; engineers, even in a capitalist society, must calculate what technologies are possible; and market surveys and questionnaires can give a good estimate of how much of a good will be desired at a zero price.

The issue, therefore, is how difficult this conceptually possible planning would be and whether the resulting system would be a great improvement in equity and in human behavior over the capitalist system.

Free Goods and Services: The Reality

In communist countries, many goods and services are sold on the market to consumers, but a wide range of goods and services are available at no cost. For example, in the former Soviet Union, all education and medical care were free.

But availability of free goods and services is not limited to communist countries. Even in the present United States, some goods and services are available at no cost; for example, primary and secondary education, and even some higher education. In terms of recreation, there are many national, state, and municipal parks where admission is free.

These goods and services are not free in the sense that no labor is required to produce them. They are free in that the federal, state, and local governments give them, free of charge, to anyone who wants them.

Health Care

A major argument in the United States today concerns the extension of free services to the health sector, with some members of Congress advocating a completely free and comprehensive health care system. The arguments against expansion of free goods and services to include health care are: (1) It will destroy workers' incentive to work, since they will have less use for money; (2) people will have no choice of doctors; and (3) people may seek health care they do not need. (Points (1) and (3) are, of course, very similar to the arguments cited earlier against making any goods and services available without charge.)

The answers to these arguments are: (1) workers will still have many other things to buy but will be healthier so they can work better; (2) the present situation in which the poor cannot get any doctor will change, and there will be some freedom of choice of doctors within each clinic; and (3) doctors can exclude patients who do not need health care because the government, not the patient, is paying for the service.

The Goal of Income Equality

Any extension of free goods and services automatically means a more nearly equal income distribution, since everyone gets these goods and services equally. Anyone in favor of income equality (in terms of real goods and services available to each individual) supports this extension of the free goods sector as one tool of greater equality. Such an extension of free goods and services also implies that a political commitment has been made by the community to ensure that every person—regardless of money income—be educated and healthy. Finally, it is argued that free education and health care will reduce the spirit of dog-eat-dog commercialism found in all capitalist societies and foster a spirit of cooperation.

References

Claudin, Fernando, *The Communist Movement,* Monthly Review, New York, 1977; Engels, F., *Anti-Duhring, Part III,* International Publishers, New York, 1939; Sherman, Howard, "Economics of Pure Communism," *Soviet Studies,* July 1970, pp. 24–36; Wiles, Peter, *Political Economy of Communism,* Blackwell, Blackwood, N.Y., 1964.

(*See also* Comparative economic systems, an overview; Marxism; Socialism)

Howard J. Sherman

Comparative advantage theory

Early in the eighteenth century, a common doctrine was that it pays a country to import those goods which it is unable to produce at all or which it cannot produce at home at a lower absolute cost than the goods are produced abroad. A few writers advanced the still wider rule that it even pays a country to import goods which it can actually produce more cheaply than another country, provided it can pay for them with exports that are still more cheaply produced at home. It was not generally recognized that this meant that freely traded goods are not necessarily produced in countries where their total cost of production is lowest: What governs the profitability of buying at home or abroad is not the absolute but the relative or comparative advantage of countries in the production of different goods. Furthermore, when all countries specialize in the production of those goods in which they have a comparative advantage, obtaining whatever else they need by foreign trade, the net result is a larger world output than could have been obtained by a universal policy of national self-sufficiency. Thus, the theory of comparative advantage not only accounts for the commodity composition of foreign trade under conditions of free competition between nations but also demonstrates the mutual advantages of such a "territorial division of labor."

Modern textbooks in economics invariably credit David Ricardo not only with the first explicit formulation of the theory of comparative advantage but also with the first attempt to spell out the implications of the theory for trade policies. But recent research has shown that it was James Mill rather than Ricardo who first formulated the theory and explained its practical meaning in terms of cost ratios, and that it was his son, John Stuart Mill, who completed the theory by taking account of the role of reciprocal demands. It was from John Stuart Mill, and not from Ricardo, that later economists learned the theory of comparative advantage as the foundation of the pure theory of international trade.

Ricardo's Example of Comparative Advantage

In Ricardian theory, free trade is important primarily as an offset to diminishing returns in agriculture. To Ricardo free trade meant a policy appropriate to an advanced manufacturing nation seeking to import cheap wheaten bread for its workers and raw materials for its industry from backward agrarian countries. The thrust of his famous chapter on foreign trade was to show that the import of luxuries had no influence either on the rate of profit or on the rate of wages at home and therefore had no influence on the growth path of the economy. But the numerical example of Ricardo's comparative advantage was in terms of England exporting cloth in exchange for the importation of wine, not wheat, from Portugal. The purpose of the example was to show that, although one country had an absolute cost advantage in both products, it paid both countries to specialize in the production of one and to import the other. The notion of Portugal having an absolute cost advantage over England in the production of textile clothing must have struck contemporary readers as peculiar; besides, since England at that time produced no wine at all, the example was certainly ill-designed to illustrate the principle of comparative advantage.

Ricardo supposed that Portugal could produce a given quantity of wine with 80 worker-years (all other inputs being ignored) and a given quantity of cloth with 90 worker-years. England, on the other hand, would require as much as 120 worker-years to produce the same amount of wine and as much as 100 worker-years to produce the same amount of cloth. In Portugal, wine will exchange for cloth at the rate of 80/90, or 0.88; in England 1 unit of wine will buy 120/100, or 1.2 units of cloth. It is clearly to Portugal's advantage to export wine to England as long as 1 unit of wine can be traded with England for more than 0.88 unit of cloth; likewise, it is to England's advantage to export cloth if less than 1.2 units of cloth must be given for 1 unit of wine. Hence, the theory of comparative advantage states the upper and lower limits within which exchange can take place between countries to their mutual benefit. Ricardo assumed that wine would exchange for cloth at a rate of 1:1. Thus, as a result of free trade, Portugal obtains cloth for 80 worker-years which would have cost 90 worker-years to produce at home, and England obtains wine for 100 worker-years which would have cost 120 worker-years to produce domestically. Before trade, it took 80 + 90 + 120 + 100, or 390, worker-years for Portugal and England each to produce 1 unit of wine and 1 unit of cloth; after trade, these 4 units require only 80 + 80 + 100 + 100, or 360, worker-years. The "gains of trade" equal 30 worker-years, which are divided between the two countries depending on where the barter terms of trade between wine and cloth will lie between the upper and lower limits, which in turn depends on the pattern of demand in the two countries, an aspect of the problem which Ricardo ignored.

International Implications

Ricardo recognized that the phenomenon of comparative advantage has definite implications for international wage and price differences between countries, although it was Nassau William Senior, not Ricardo, who first stated classical theory of international prices. Given the situation depicted by Ricardo's example, foreign trade is possible only if Portuguese money wages and hence prices in terms of gold are higher than they are in England. If they were the same, Portugal would never import cloth because its consumers would insist on obtaining cloth more cheaply from domestic suppliers. In consequence, England would have to ship gold to Portugal to pay for wine imports, which would raise wages and prices in Portugal to the point where it would become profitable for Portuguese consumers to import English cloth. In general, then, the low-cost country has the higher gold wage and hence the higher money price for similar goods. There is, as Ricardo said, a "natural distribution of specie" among the trading nations of the world that not only tends to balance each country's exports and imports but also results in such relative price levels between countries as to induce each country to produce those goods in which it has a comparative advantage. Although the world no longer uses the gold standard, this result of the classical theory of international prices still holds: A high level of wages and prices in a country may be the result of higher efficiency and by no means prevents that country from competing successfully in international trade.

Despite all the changes in economics since the days of Ricardo and Mill, the theory of comparative advantage still stands today as a pillar of sound economic reasoning about international trade. Both Ricardo and John Stuart Mill explained the pattern of trade in terms of underlying productivity differences between countries, but they left these differences themselves unexplained. The modern Heckscher-Ohlin theory of international trade explains these productivity differences themselves in terms of the relative factor endowments of countries and consequently incorporates the principle of comparative advantage of a more fundamental theorem: A country will tend to have a comparative advantage in those goods which use intensively the country's relatively abundant factor of production and will therefore import goods which use intensively the country's relatively scarcer factor.

References

Blaug, M., *Economic Theory in Retrospect* (4th ed.), Cambridge University, New York, 1985, chaps. 4, 6; Thweatt, W. O., "James Mill and the Early Development of Comparative Advantage," *History of Political Economy,* vol. 8, no. 2, Summer 1976, pp. 207–234.

(*See also* Exports; Factors of production; Imports; International economics, an overview)

Mark Blaug

Comparative economic systems, an overview

Comparative economic systems (CES) is a venerable field in the throes of a revolution. The distinguishing characteristic of the field is that it places the economic system and its institutions at the center of the analysis and makes it the variable to be analyzed. In contrast, most other fields in economics generally ignore systemic considerations altogether or presume, on an ad hoc basis, a particular institutional framework. There have been many definitions of the economic system, all agreeing that it is a socially established mechanism for resolving economic decisions as to what to produce, how to produce, and for whom to produce.

The focus on the economic system as the variable, subject to analysis and the comparison of alternative systems, makes CES an important field within economics. As Jan Tinbergen (1954) stated, "the problem of comparing alternative forms of economic life constitutes the problem par excellence of economic science; its real raison d'être." The dramatic changes in the Soviet Union and Eastern Europe at the end of the 1980s and beginning of 1990s have added strong impetus to interest in economic systems, and particularly in system change. The problems of transition from central planning to the market ("transition economics") challenges students of CES as well as other social scientists.

In the past, CES has relied primarily on institutional description. In the 1970s and 1980s, a new comparative economic systems emerged, stressing the theory of economic systems and the application of modern econometric techniques to comparative systems analysis, thereby moving the field toward the frontiers of economics.

CES has antecedents as far back as Plato, Thomas More, and the mercantilists. From the mercantilists, it inherited the emphasis on the rules and institutions governing the conduct of economic affairs and, therefore, concern about the key role played by the government in this process. The utopian socialists and economic liberals in the late eighteenth and early nineteenth centuries fought against this critical role given to government by the mercantilists. They developed models of economic systems which placed the government in an ancillary role—the liberals by promoting free-market capitalism, the utopians like Proudhon and Fourier by emphasizing decentralized communal organizations. These early contributors to CES were followed by Karl Marx, who hypothesized that class struggle led to a sequence of economic systems (slaveholding, feudal, capitalist, socialist, communist).

A Changing Field

The field has changed drastically in nature, scope, and approach, dramatically changing how the field is viewed both by comparative systems specialists (comparativists) and by economists in general. It is significant that the *International Encyclopedia of the Social Sciences,* published in 1968, did not include a survey of the field or even a single index entry dealing with CES, although the work included several surveys and 21 index entries on comparative methods in political science, law, psychology, and anthropology. The fact that the present encyclopedia, as well as the latest *Encyclopedia Britannica* each include a major survey of CES represents recognition of the important changes in the field. The major series on *Fundamentals of Pure and Applied Economics* edited by Jacques Lesourne and Hugo Sonnenschein, and published by Harwood Economic Publishers, has devoted a whole section with several monographs to the field, with J.M. Montias as editor of this section. On the other hand, the new *Palgrave Encyclopedia* has, surprisingly, retrogressed by neglecting CES completely.

CES has moved closer to both the mainstream and the frontiers of economics and has thereby expanded significantly the scope of economics. In this process, CES has become much more analytical and less political and ideological, and a start has been made on important empirical treatments of the subject. This change, which has gathered momentum in the past two decades, moved the scholars in the field (under the auspices of the Association for Comparative Economic Studies) to initiate in the mid-1970s the *Journal of Comparative Economics,* and then in the 1980s to convert the *ACES Bulletin* into a second major journal, *Comparative Economic Studies.* In 1991, a third journal devoted completely to CES was initiated in Europe, the *Journal of International and Comparative Economics.*

The earliest modern analyses of economic systems are Enrico Barone's analysis in the first decade of the twentieth century of collectivist central planning and the analysis of socialism by Vilfredo Pareto, who viewed various types of socialism as organizations ruled by different elites. These were followed by debates in the 1920s and 1930s between Ludwig von Mises and Friedrich A. von Hayek who questioned the economic rationality of socialism, and Oskar Lange and Abba Lerner who defended it. Lange (1938) gave an excellent example of systems analysis, in which he responded to the criticisms of socialism by developing a carefully constructed model of an economic system combining social ownership of the means of production with a market for inputs and outputs. This so-called socialist controversy was a major event in the history of CES. It increased the theoretical and technical level of discourse, substituting analysis of economic models for descriptions of actual economic systems, and it raised many of the important issues that are still of central concern in CES: centralization and decentralization in decision making and information, the compatibility of various incentive schemes with the decision-making and information structures, the comparisons of the relative efficiencies of different system models, the true nature of price and market systems, and potential combinations of plan and market.

A Shift from the "Isms" Approach

While this important debate was being conducted primarily at the level of models of economic systems, most of the textbooks of that period, indeed until the 1970s, concentrated on what might be called the grand "isms" approach, describing capitalism, socialism, communism, fascism, and similar overall social, political, ideological, and economic systems, in imitation of the comparative government approach. This approach was based on the attempt to understand the newly formed Soviet communist system, the Italian fascist and German national socialist systems, and then the communist systems in Eastern Europe, Asia, and Latin America. More recently, emphasis in the professional CES literature shifted from these general, comprehensive approaches to CES to somewhat narrower, economically based, more technical approaches. The modern literature utilizes the advances in economic theory, game theory, econometrics, and organization theory to throw light on the functioning of economic systems at the macro level of the whole economy, at the micro level of individual economic sectors, and at the micro-micro level of economic organizations. It engages in comparisons of the structure and behavior of the economic system at each of these levels. In this approach, the noneconomic components of the earlier approach, such as ideology and political and social systems, are treated in the same light as technology, resource endowment, or level of development, i.e., as crucial exogenous variables influencing the various features of the economic system and its ability to perform its tasks.

A third important approach to CES, which forms a bridge between the "isms" approach and the technical approach, concentrates on property or ownership relations as the most important feature of economic systems. Ownership is considered the sole source of decision-making authority, and systems of private, public, or mixed ownership are distinct. If ownership is viewed as a mechanism for providing the owner with a bundle of decision-making rights, including the rights to control the use of the owned object, its disposal, and the distribution of income generated by it, then this approach, if stripped of its ideological content, may be regarded as part of the decision-making approach to systems analysis.

Systems Theory

The decision-making approach to CES, which is being developed jointly by economic theorists and comparativists, views the economic system as a set of rules, laws, and procedures determining the allocation of decision-making authority, the channels and content of informational messages, and the mechanisms applied to motivate participants (the decision-making, information, and motivation structures). The economic system is one of the critical variables operating on the economic environment to produce outcomes to be evaluated by norms or weighting functions. This approach forms the emerging paradigm of the new comparative economics systems.

The most complete, rigorous early treatment of the new approach to CES is provided by J. M. Montias (1976), while a less technical development of the paradigm is found in Egon Neuberger and William Duffy (1976), a textbook that attempts to provide a coherent decision-making theoretical framework, based on the Tjalling Koopmans and J. M. Montias (1971) view of the place of the economic system in the total analysis of an economy's performance. David Conn (1977) formalized the Neuberger-Duffy framework and wrote a useful survey of the CES literature, distinguishing the contributions of theorists and comparativists in this endeavor. A leading textbook in the field by Paul Gregory and Robert Stuart (1992) follows in the footsteps of these earlier works, and provides an updated version of the new approach, while the most recent and complete updating of the new comparative systems is found in J. M. Montias, Avner Ben-Ner, and Egon Neuberger (1993).

Within this emerging paradigm of comparative economics, Koopmans and Montias view the outcomes of economic activities as determined by the environment, the economic system, and government policies. Performance is measured by these outcomes, weighted by a norm (in effect, a social welfare or preference function). Probably the most difficult aspect of this approach is the question of what norm to use in evaluating outcomes. Edward Ames (1973) has stressed the importance of the social preference function in the emerging theory of economic systems, and the problems raised by Kenneth Arrow and others in developing nondictatorial functions of this type. Social preference functions, such as Abram Bergson's famous social welfare functions, are the choice of most CES students, despite the well-known problems associated with these functions. Economic theorists, however, tend to start from the postulates of new welfare economics. According to David Conn in "Economic Theory and Comparative Economic Systems, A Partial Literature Survey," *Journal of Comparative Economics* (December 1978):

> *A basic distinction of emphasis exists, however, between the groups of scholars (the comparativists and the theorists) working in this field. The comparativists (Neuberger and Duffy, Koopmans and Montias, etc.) are primarily concerned with the development of a general theory suitable for positive analysis of a variety of economic systems, whereas the theorists (Hurwicz, Mount, and Reiter,*

etc.) have more of a welfare orientation and hence emphasize the possibility of designing systems that satisfy, among other things, welfare criteria, such as the Pareto criterion.[1]

Given the role of the economic system in partially determining the outcome of economic activity, the new paradigm proceeds to analyze the three component structures of the economic system. Here again, a difference in emphasis has developed, with economic theorists stressing the information structure and, more recently, the incentive structure, while comparativists have stressed the decision-making structure, i.e., the allocation of decision-making authority among economic agents, and the concept of the economic system as an organic entity involving the complex interrelations among the three structures. Two important examples of these interrelations are: (1) the requirements placed by different decision-making structures on the information structure, e.g., the much greater burden placed by a centralized planning system than by a decentralized market system, and (2) the impact of the incentive structure on the extent to which information transmitted by agents is withheld, filtered, or biased; this forms a critical part of the moral hazard and adverse selection problems (or, more generally, of the principal-agent problem).

A major difference between comparativists and theorists is the tendency of theorists to try to provide ostensibly institution-free models while actually depending on concepts derived from a particular economic system. Both Janos Kornai (1971), a leading East European contributor to CES and particularly to the disequilibrium approach to systems analysis, and Koopmans and Montias (1971) stress the danger in using system-bound terminology as though it were system-free. They attempt to provide a system-free terminology for systemic comparisons constructed from "primitives" (undefined terms that may be considered common knowledge).

However, we should not exaggerate the differences between these two groups of scholars. Their common agreement on the nature of the economic system and their mutual interaction are much more important. At least three important conferences—in Berkeley in 1967, in Ann Arbor in 1968, and at Wayne State in 1978—have brought together leading theorists and comparativists. Thus, it is no accident that a common view on economic systems emerged by the end of the 1970s.

Regional and Other Emphases

For the past 50 years or so, work in CES has tended to have a very strong regional concentration, primarily on the former Soviet Union, and secondarily on what used to be called the "Soviet bloc" (China, Eastern Europe, and Cuba, in particular). The emphasis on the former Soviet Union and other centrally planned economies was not at all surprising. The introduction of a centrally planned system in Russia in the late 1920s, which was the polar opposite of the western market economy, played a major role in the development of CES as a recognized special field of study within economics, concentrating on the comparison of this new economic system with the existing capitalist market systems. The emergence of the Soviet Union as a major power during and

---

[1]Permission for David Conn quote granted by publisher of *Journal of Comparative Economics.*

after World War II, and the availability of financial support in the United States for the study of its institutions and performance, combined to encourage the growth of Soviet studies, including the study of Soviet and Soviet-type economics. The same factors spurred the development of Chinese studies about a decade later.

During the 1970s and 1980s the scope of CES broadened beyond this focus. For example, a special issue of the *Journal of Comparative Economics* (1990) was devoted to the analysis of French, Japanese, Indian, Korean, and Yugoslav versions of indicative planning. Then, in the early 1990s, the former Soviet Union and Eastern Europe again acquired pride of place because of the tremendous interest in the revolutionary economic reforms undertaken by some of the Eastern European countries and the paralysis and disintegration of the Soviet economy. A complete special issue of *The Journal of Economic Perspectives,* a journal of the American Economic Association (1991), was devoted to an analysis of "transition economics" in the Soviet Union and Eastern Europe.

In addition to the changes in the geographical emphasis of CES, there has been a shift toward more explicitly comparative macroeconomic studies on one hand, and comparative microlevel studies on the other, and a greater use of econometric approaches.

Other Important Contributions

The field of CES also encompasses important studies of specific economies, e.g., the path-breaking work by Abram Bergson in calculating real national income accounts for the Soviet Union, and the work by Abram Bergson, Alec Nove, Edward Ames, and others on the Soviet centrally planned economy. There is also the work by Alexander Eckstein, Robert Dernberger, Dwight Perkins, and others on the Chinese economy; theoretical and econometric analyses, particularly contributions to index number theory, by Alexander Gerschenkron and Richard Moorstein; analysis of the communist international system by Paul Marer, Peter Wiles, and Thomas Wolf; analysis of the property rights approach to economic systems by Eirik Furubotn, Svetozar Pejovich, Frederic Pryor, and others; econometric models of various countries, such as the econometric model of the Soviet Union by Donald Green; aggregate production function analysis by Martin Weitzman, Yasushi Toda, and others; cross-country comparative econometric analyses within the disequilibrium macroeconomic framework by Richard Portes and David Winter; as well as the comparative empirical studies by the Economic Commission for Europe, the Organization for Economic Cooperation and Development (OECD), the European Economic Community, the World Bank, and the many university-based centers of CES in the United States, Europe, and other regions.

In addition, important work has been done on analyzing economic systems in contexts other than national economies. There has been some development of the analysis of international organizations, such as the European Economic Community or the Council of Mutual Economic Assistance, but much greater emphasis has been placed on analyzing sectors of economies, such as foreign trade, banking, agriculture, energy, and primary economic units, such as enterprises, associations of enterprises, collective farms, communes. Some of the literature on enterprises, such as the output-maximizing firm under central planning by Edward Ames, the worker-managed firm by Benjamin Ward and Jaroslav Vanek, the life-cycle approach by Avner Ben-Ner, the numerous empirical studies of cooperatives by Derek Jones, the economics of cooperation and the labor-managed economy by John P. Bonin and Louis Putterman, as well as the monograph by Estelle James and Susan Rose-Ackerman on nonprofit organizations are all very close in spirit to the newly developing decision-making approach to economic systems.

The study of CES has retained some of its interdisciplinary commitment, as, for example, in Frederic Pryor's study of primitive economies (1977), which tests quantitatively many hypotheses found in the anthropological literature. In addition, the strong connection between economics and politics manifest in the East European transition, requires enlisting ideas from public choice and political science, as was done in a special issue of the *Journal of Comparative Economics* (1991).

Finally, mention must be made of the important work of scholars who are not normally included in the field of CES but whose contributions are important to the progress of the field. A very partial list would include works of the following scholars: Joseph Schumpeter on the framework within which innovation takes place and participants group and regroup themselves in response to changes in the environment and norms; Herbert Simon, Ronald Coase, and Oliver Williamson on organization theory and industrial organization; Tjalling C. Koopmans, Guillermo A. Calvo, and Stanislaw Wellisz on hierarchies; Richard Nelson and Sidney Winter on evolutionary economics; Jacob Marschak and Roy Radner on the theory of teams; Kenneth Boulding, Janos Horvath, Alan Brown, and Martin Pfaff on the grants economy; and finally Ragnar Frisch, L. V. Kantorovich, Henri Theil, and Jan Tinbergen on optimal economic policy, based on the application of operations research methods.

The Future

In conclusion, the field of comparative economic systems has come of age and is beginning to achieve its logical position as one of the central fields in economics. The next 10 years should witness further dramatic progress. With continuing cooperation between theorists and comparativists, the emerging paradigm will yield important new results at the theoretical level in analyzing the interaction of the decision-making, information, and incentive structures. This approach will be enriched by the combination of the decision-making approach with developments in industrial organizations, game theory, public choice, grants economics, evolutionary economics, and other fields. The rapidly developing econometric cross-country comparisons will provide the essential final ingredient—the ability to test hypotheses on the role of the economic system and its structures in determining performance.

References

Ames, Edward, "The Emerging Theory of Comparative Economic Systems," *The American Economist,* Spring 1973, pp. 22–28; Barone, Enrico, "The Ministry of Production in the Collectivist State," *Giornale degli economisti,* 1905, translated in F. A. von Hayek (ed.), *Collectivist Economic Planning,* Routledge, London, 1935; Ben-Ner, Avner, "The Life Cycle of Worker-Owned Firms in Market Economies: A Theoretical Analysis," *Journal of Economic Behavior and Organization,* October 1988, pp. 287–313; Bergson, Abram, *The Real National Income of Soviet Russia since 1928,* Harvard University, Cambridge, Mass., 1961; Bonin, John P., and Louis Putterman, *Economics of Cooperation and the Labor-Managed Economy,* in J. Lesourne and H. Sonnenschein (eds.), *Fundamentals of Pure and Applied Economics,* Harwood Economic Publishers, Chur, Switzerland, 1987; Conn, David, "Toward a Theory of Optimal Economic Systems," *Journal of Comparative Economics,* December 1977, pp. 325–350; Conn, David, "Economic Theory and Comparative Economic Systems, A Partial Literature Survey," *Journal of Comparative Economics,* December 1978, pp. 355–381; Gregory, Paul R., and Robert C. Stuart,

Corporative Economic Systems (4th ed.), Houghton-Mifflin, Boston, 1992; Hare, Paul G., *Central Planning in Fundamentals of Pure and Applied Economics,* Harwood Economic Publishers, Chur, Switzerland, 1991; Hurwicz, Leonid, "The Design of Mechanisms for Resource Allocation," *American Economic Review,* May 1973, pp. 1–30; James, Estelle, and Susan Rose-Ackerman, *The Nonprofit Enterprise in Market Economics in Fundamentals of Pure and Applied Economics,* Harwood Economic Publishers, Chur, Switzerland, 1986; Koopmans, Tjalling C., and John Michael Montias, "On the Description and Comparison of Economic Systems," in A. Eckstein (ed.), *Comparison of Economic Systems: Theoretical and Methodological Approaches,* University of California, Berkeley, Calif., 1971; Kornai, Janos, *Anti-Equilibrium: On Economic Systems Theory and the Tasks of Research,* North Holland, Amsterdam, 1971; Lange, Oskar, "On the Economic Theory of Socialism," in B. E. Lippencott (ed.), *On the Economic Theory of Socialism,* University of Minnesota, Minneapolis, 1938, originally published in *Review of Economic Studies,* Longman Group, Edinborough, 1936 and 1937; Montias, John Michael, *The Structure of Economic Systems,* Yale University, New Haven, Conn., 1976; Montias, John Michael, Avner Ben-Ner, and Egon Neuberger, *Comparative Economics in Fundamentals of Pure and Applied Economics,* Harwood Economic Publishers, Chur, Switzerland, 1993; Neuberger, Egon, and William Duffy, *Comparative Economic Systems: A Decision-Making Approach,* Allyn & Bacon, Boston, 1976; Pareto, Vilfredo, *Complete Works,* vol. 5: *Les Systemes Socialistes,* 1902–1903, Librarie Droz, Geneva, 1965; Portes, Richard, "Internal and External Balance in a Centrally Planned Economy," in E. Neuberger and L. D. Tyson (eds.), *The Impact of International Economic Disturbances on the Soviet Union and Eastern Europe: Transmission and Response,* Pergamon, Elmsford, N.Y., 1980; Pryor, Frederik, *The Origins of the Economy: A Comparative Study of Distribution in Primitive and Peasant Economies,* Academic Press, New York, 1977; Tinbergen, Jan, *Centralization and Decentralization in Economic Policy,* North Holland, Amsterdam, 1954, p. 47; Wolf, Thomas A., *Foreign Trade in the Centrally Planned Economy in Fundamentals of Pure and Applied Economics,* Harwood Economic Publishers, Chur, Switzerland, 1988.

(*See also* Capitalism; Communism; Marxism; Mercantilism; Socialism)

Egon Neuberger

Competition

Competition refers to the nature of the conditions under which individuals may trade property rights. It assumes a definition of property rights that individuals may trade among themselves as well as a description of the trading process. A competitive equilibrium is the outcome of competition. The very existence of such an equilibrium depends on the nature of the property rights. These aspects of competition are especially important in connection with the development of new technology and new products and with the use of low-cost, large-scale methods of production and distribution.

The simplest situation in an analysis of competition is a market where individuals have initial endowments of commodities that they own and that they may trade among themselves. All trades occur at the same time and place. The essential characteristics remain valid when trades do not all occur at the same time and place. However, individuals would have incomplete knowledge relevant for their decisions. This complication changes the nature of the outcome of competition. Incomplete knowledge is inevitable partly because the future is unknown. Even so, it is often less costly to take current actions that will have future consequences without knowing what these will be than to respond only to momentary events of the present. The advantages of planning and the resulting exposure to hazards that may occur alter the effects of competition. These basic considerations help explain the nature of production and why the quantities of goods offered will change over time in response to the expectations and information firms have. They also explain why some common notions about competition are inadequate. Among the inadequate notions about competition is the belief that a necessary condition for competition is a lack of power by any firm to affect the prices of its products. Sometimes this is put in another form, that competition can exist in an industry only if the demand curves facing the individual firms in that industry are infinitely elastic so that changes in the quantities sold by a single firm cannot affect the product price. This condition is not necessary for competition. Nor is it necessary for competition that the number of firms be so large that each one is of negligibly small size relative to the total market for the commodities made by firms in the industry. Finally, it may be consistent with competition that some or all firms in an industry have obtained very high profit rates.

Pure Exchange

Assume there is a market where there are individuals, each of whom starts with given amounts of various commodities. Each one would like to make trades that will result in the acquisition of goods preferred to those goods to be exchanged. The theory assumes that for each trader the purpose of trade is to improve the trader's position. Hence, the trader would not willingly leave the market with a bundle of goods worth less than his or her initial holdings. The theory also assumes that each trader owns the commodities to be traded, that they can be traded on terms that are mutually acceptable to the parties directly involved in an exchange, and that each trader may accept or reject the terms offered. Underlying the possibility of exchange is the existence of property rights in the goods. Competition requires voluntary exchange so that no trader is compelled to accept or reject offers without freely given consent. The very notion of exchange implies, therefore, a voluntary agreement among those who are directly involved in the transaction on the terms that each one willingly accepts. In pure exchange, although the total quantities of the commodities exchanged among the parties is constant, each one must regard the obtained goods as worth more than the exchanged goods. If the parties can reach agreement on mutually beneficial terms of exchange, the result is an allocation of the commodities among the individuals that must make at least one of them better off than before and cannot make anyone worse off than before.

The theory assumes that no individual accepts terms that would leave that individual in a worse position than if no trades at all were made. In the latter case the individual retains the initial endowment of goods and attempts to improve the situation by seeking others in the market with whom mutually beneficial exchanges can be arranged. The process of improvement applies to groups of traders as well as to individuals. Assume that groups of traders as well as individuals are free to reach agreements among themselves on mutually beneficial terms of trade. Assume there are no restrictions on their choice of trading partners with whom they can arrange multilateral exchanges. Further assume that each individual is free to accept or reject offers unilaterally. The trades that result from these conditions form a competitive equilibrium.

The existence of a state of competition in pure exchange allows the participants to seek the best terms that they can obtain from the others. Competition does not require the presence of a very large number of traders nor does it require that each of the individual traders in the market must be of such a small relative size that none can affect the terms of trade. Traders can make tentative agreements with each other subject to the condition that these agreements become binding only if none can obtain better terms from others. The final outcome is a set of exchanges among the traders such that no individual or group of individuals can obtain better terms. The set of outcomes with these attributes need not be unique. All possible outcomes with these attributes represent the state of competition. The set of all possible trades that can satisfy these conditions is known as the core of a market. Therefore, the set of trades induced by competition in a market is in the core of a market.

Auction Markets—Competition in Practice

Actual markets exist that closely approximate the theoretical model. An auction market in which the buyers and sellers submit sealed bids to the auctioneer is a leading example. The commodities go to the highest bidders from the sellers who submit the lowest offers. Nor is this all. Rules exist capable of inducing the participants in the market to give their true valuations in the sealed message they submit to the auctioneer. All successful bidders pay the same price per unit, and all successful sellers receive the same price per unit. Therefore, the price paid by a successful bidder never exceeds his or her bid and is just high enough to exclude enough buyers to enable the quantity demanded to equal the quantity offered at the market clearing price. Similarly, the price received by a successful seller may be above the minimum that a seller would be willing to accept. With respect to the sellers the price is low enough to exclude enough sellers to enable the quantity offered to equal the quantity demanded. The outcome is an allocation of the goods to those who value them the most. These rules for conducting a sealed-bid auction are equivalent to the equilibrium determined by the intersection of supply and demand curves.

Spatial and Temporal Competition

The simplest theoretical model of competition assumes that all trades occur at the same time and place because all traders gather at one time in the same place. However, competition also exists even though the traders are not in the same place and do not all trade at the same time.

Trades dispersed in space (that is, over a distance) need not occur at a common price. This is partly because shipping goods from one place to another is costly, so that prices at different locations may differ but not by more than the marginal cost of transportation. Also, prices can differ because traders at one point may not know what prices prevail elsewhere. Because it is costly to acquire information about conditions prevailing in other markets, traders have incomplete knowledge. A trader has that stock of knowledge about market conditions that is optimal taking into account the cost of acquiring information, the cost of maintaining the stock of knowledge, and the probable benefit derived from the information. Owing to these factors less than complete information is optimal. Consequently, prices can differ among the markets although there is competition. Instead of a single price, competition induces a distribution of prices among the markets consistent with the cost of acquiring information about market conditions and the probable benefit derived from the information.

Somewhat similar considerations generate the distribution of prices over time as a result of competition. Individuals make current transactions and plan for later ones on the basis of current conditions and on the basis of what they believe will occur in the future. They differ in the extent of their knowledge about prevailing conditions and in their ability to predict what is likely to happen later. A distribution of prices over time is consistent with competition, the cost of knowledge, and ignorance of future events.

Competition and Production

The conditions of production affect the competitive equilibrium. Although a more elaborate theory is required to embrace the consequences of production, the main aspect of competition in pure exchange remains valid. Assume firms can buy inputs or can hire the services of factors of production in order to make commodities for sale to other firms or to households of consumers. The description of this process involves transactions in related goods, services, and commodities in different places and at different times. The firm will buy some inputs before it knows the terms on which it can sell the goods that will use these inputs. For instance, a firm buys machinery and builds factories which it can use to make commodities over some duration of time. The firm must expect to obtain enough revenue from the sale of these commodities to cover the cost of the machinery and the factory and receive a return on its capital commensurate with its best alternatives. The firm acts as an intermediary between the suppliers of inputs at an earlier time and the customers for its outputs at a later time. In effect there are transactions among all these participants although they are separated in space and in time. Hence the basic forces of competition described in pure exchange remain valid.

To complete the analogy with pure exchange, it would be necessary for all the participants simultaneously to have agreements for a whole sequence of transactions that will not all be finally consummated until a considerable time has elapsed. Although such forward transactions happen, it is less costly for individuals not to tie their hands so completely. Even so, some firms suffer the consequence of error and incur losses while others benefit from good fortune and make profits. Loss and profit are consistent with competition and are the result of incomplete knowledge of the future, differences of ability among those who make decisions, and the necessity as well as the propensity of individuals to act now and expose themselves to future events. Success brings profit, and failure brings loss.

Rates of Return

Some firms may obtain large profits, but this does not invite others to emulate them by entering into the production of similar or closely related commodities. What induces investment is the expectation of future profit, not the current profit. The latter results from past decisions and good fortune. Past and current profit are not always a reliable predictor of future profit. Therefore, firms in an industry may have high profits, and yet new firms do not enter the industry, which is compatible with competition in the industry.

Under competition firms may obtain different rates of return. The explanation closely resembles that given by David Ricardo to explain why the rent on land may differ from one farm to another although all produce and sell the same agricultural commodity at the same price. Land differs in quality. The better-quality land gives a larger output for a given amount of purchased inputs than the poorer-quality land. The owner of the better-quality land can obtain a higher return, i.e. higher rent, because competition among the farmers for the use of the land bids up the rent to the point where all farms will yield the same rate of return to the farmers who till the soil.

Similarly, in the case of firms, owners of the more productive inputs can obtain a higher return owing to the competition among those who wish to hire their services. A satisfactory explanation of these differences of ability and quality among firms in the same industry does not yet exist. The differences in the returns among firms in the same industry that result from the differences in their abilities is easily mistaken for the effects of a lack of competition among the firms. In the case of musicians, artists, novelists, lawyers, surgeons, entertainers, sports stars, and so on, it seems that the large differences in income among those in the same occupation result from forces like those that explain differences in the rent of land. It is the scarcity of these great abilities and the active demand for those with these abilities that explains the high income. All this is consistent with competition.

Scarcity

Classical economists distinguish between "natural" and "contrived" scarcity. The supply of a naturally scarce factor is perfectly inelastic, and its owners receive rents. The supply of a factor that is artificially restricted is not completely inelastic. The owner of this factor receives a monopoly return. The former is consistent with competition, and the latter is not.

This raises the question of what can contrive scarcity. Legal restrictions are often the source of a contrived scarcity. The state may confer a patent to an inventor or a copyright to an author. Hence none may use the patent or publish a copyrighted item without meeting the terms set by its owner. The government may control entry into certain occupations and professions. This may cause a contrived scarcity and furnish a monopoly return to those who can control entry.

Trademarks and brand names enable a firm to distinguish its products. The government confers property rights to firms by allowing them the exclusive use of this means of identification. Yet this is not a means of contrived scarcity nor a departure from competition. Without these property rights, no competitive equilibrium is possible.

Competition and Product Differentiation

Property rights are essential for competition. No one would be willing to produce without the assurance of ownership of the output. No one would be willing to buy without secure property rights to the purchased goods. Competition requires clearly defined property rights so that individuals can decide what to buy and sell, what to make, what offers to make, and what bids to accept. A failure of markets to function is often the result of an inadequate assignment of property rights. Experience leads to remedies and to new forms of property rights so that a competitive equilibrium can occur.

Although a firm can make a product closely resembling one made by another so that customers may regard the two as nearly equivalent, a firm cannot make a literal copy of another firm's product and claim it is exactly the same as the other's. (This issue arises in acute form in the semiconductor, computer, and software industries with respect to clones of well-known products.) Product differentiation is ubiquitous. Without this product differentiation, there would be no incentive for a firm to offer something different that customers would find more appealing than the existing alternatives. Competition often occurs by means of offering goods with new attributes or new combinations of attributes on terms that customers will find more attractive than the existing varieties.

Competition among different products is often more important than the simple textbook case of competition among products that are perfect substitutes. Indeed, owing to the ability and desire of firms to distinguish their products so that customers can easily repeat the purchase of satisfactory items, the concept of perfect substitutes can have no basis in reality. Competition can exist without perfect substitutes. Customers can choose among alternatives composed of different attributes according to which offers the most value for the price.

This analysis implies that it is not necessary for competition that a firm face an infinitely elastic demand for its product at the prevailing market price. A firm can be in a highly competitive environment and face vigorous challenges from resourceful and innovative rivals, although changes in its rate of output have a perceptible effect on the price at which it can sell its product.

Incomplete knowledge, the cost of acquiring information, and the existence of property rights explain why sellers of new products must struggle for success. The difficulty of success and the ease of failure do not imply the absence of competition. Advertising outlays and promotional expenses are readily understood as means of competition, although some economists view these expenditures as anticompetitive. The lower the real cost of contacting customers in order to inform them about what is available and on what terms, the more vigorous is competition.

Competition and the Number and Size of Firms in an Industry

Owing to the costs of coordinating activities or to the economies of large-scale production, the optimal size of firms may be large relative to the quantity demanded of the product. Therefore, an industry may have a few large firms. Some conclude that this is a structural indicator of a lack of competition in the industry. This argument asserts that there is monopoly with only one firm in an industry and competition with many firms in an industry. With an intermediate number, there is something between monopoly and competition, often described by the terms "monopolistic competition," "imperfect competition," or "oligopoly."

The main argument for the belief that collusion is more likely when there is a small number of firms in the industry is the contention going back to Adam Smith that it is easier for a few than for many to agree on a common purpose. Numbers alone do not settle matters. Other factors include similarity in the interests of the firms, stability of the underlying supply and demand conditions, and the costs of policing and enforcing collusion. Even if collusive agreements were legally enforceable, which they are not in the United States, it does not follow that competition would be less profitable than collusion and, therefore, dominated by it. The costs of maintaining collusion may outweigh the gains so that a firm obtains a higher expected return under competition than by collusion.

Under some circumstances the least costly way of satisfying the demand requires a single firm to do so. The natural monopoly as described by Alfred Marshall is an example. More general conditions for natural monopoly are now known. These arise when bargains struck between groups of buyers and sellers must be inconsistent with overall efficiency. In the terminology for the description of pure exchange, the core is empty. An efficient equilibrium can exist only if there are suitable restrictions on individual freedom to make bids and accept offers. Thus, some overall coordination is necessary to get an efficient outcome. An efficient equilibrium cannot exist without some constraints that are equivalent to an assignment of property rights among the market participants. Some industries seem to illustrate these conditions, including public utilities, airlines, railroads, ocean shipping, and some of the communications industries.

References

Bohm-Bawerk, Eugen von, *Positive Theory of Capital,* G. D. Hencke and H. F. Sennholz (trans.), Libertarion, South Holland, Ill., 1959 (1st ed. in German, 1889); Debreu, Gerard, *Theory of Value,* Yale University, New Haven, Conn., 1959; Edgeworth, Francis Y., *Mathematical Psychics,* Keegan-Paul, London, 1881; Knight, Frank H., *Risk, Uncertainty and Profit,* Houghton Mifflin, Boston, 1921; Telser, Lester G., *Competition, Collusion and Game Theory,* Aldine, Chicago, 1972; Telser, Lester, G., *Economic Theory and the Core,* University of Chicago, Chicago, 1978; Telser, Lester G., *A Theory of Efficient Cooperation and Competition,* Cambridge University, Cambridge, 1987; Telser, Lester G., *Theories of Competition,* North-Holland, New York, 1988.

(*See also* Antitrust policy; Cartel; Concentration of industry; Mergers, takeovers, and corporate restructuring; Monopoly and oligopoly; Price theory; Scarcity)

Lester G. Telser

Competitive price theory (*see* Chicago school)

Computers in economics

Much of economics concerns quantitative analysis. Since economics is data intensive, the electronic computer plays a very important role in economics today. In some form or other, computers—slide rule, desktop mechanical calculator, voltage-analog machines, punched-card tabulators—were in use during the flowering of quantitative economics during the 1920s and 1930s. But heavy computational burdens were always a restraining factor. Research organization and assistants were required to implement major quantitative studies dealing with economic trends, business cycle classifications, early econometrics, national income accounting, sample surveys, and censuses.

During the late 1940s and especially during the 1950s, researchers began to use electronic computation in economic research. It had already been used in the natural sciences. The first cases were for data processing of census and sample survey materials. The analysis of economic time series for business-cycle studies made early use of the computer, and several centers of econometric research began to use electronic computers for separate phases of their work.

A revolution took place at this time in quantitative economics. Now, the computer is a common tool in both teaching and research. It is absolutely necessary in applied econometrics and is widely used in many branches of economics outside formal econometrics. As universities began to relax foreign language requirements for higher degrees, students began to learn new languages—the languages of computer programming. It is possible to take advanced degrees in economics without using the computer, but it is very common for research students to learn elementary computer programming.

The computer has greatly lightened the burden of data-intensive economics, enabling the investigator to accumulate, use, or tap vast data sources. Computers are often used for primary or source data analysis and even more frequently for secondary data sources. Large data banks are now available that store in computer files long statistical series of thousands and thousands of economic variables. The computer also stores census and survey materials for analytical work. The economist can tap these data files from remote computer terminals all over the world in only seconds. In the computer data files, statistical series are corrected, revised, adjusted, ready for use. Traditional printed delivery of data usually gives only limited amounts of data in this form, and many sources for each series must be spliced or compiled. Data are ready to use without such further processing in stored files on the computer. This is of enormous advantage. In its present form, this kind of facility became available only in the 1960s and is under continuous development. Stores of data are shared now between private and public sources, but in some countries, the central statistical bureau places the whole array of economic statistics in one set of computer files, available through electronic or other distribution, sometimes even for remote-entry withdrawal. In addition, networks of researchers can communicate, interchange data files, and share information through computer-assisted teleconferencing. These computer-based activities are not tied to economics; they are used in many scholarly and business fields, but they play increasing roles in economics because the quantitative side of the subject relies increasingly on use of the computer.

An Experimental Tool

Experimentation in econometrics and other quantitative branches of economics has been greatly opened up by the computer. In searching for regularities in economic life, the economist can experiment with many relationships almost simultaneously, until one is found that satisfies the theoretical and other criteria. If several statistical series—10, 20, 30, or more—are simultaneously withdrawn from a computer data file, the investigator, in seconds, can obtain estimates of relationships among many combinations of these, as many as the human eye can carefully scrutinize, before going on to the next experimental stage. These can be linear or nonlinear relationships. The sample span can be split into components. Graphical displays and many diagnostic statistics can be obtained. Enormous flexibility far surpasses the former methods of examining one single case at a time, each case requiring up to an hour's calculating effort, and with much less accuracy.

Not only is searching experimentally over a wide range of alternative specifications of economic relationships possible now, but experimenting with different estimation procedures of varying degrees of sophistication or complication is also an option.

After the stage of estimation of economic relationships, the investigator will usually be concerned with testing and applications. The computer is an invaluable experimental tool here, too. Most economic relationships are dynamic, meaning that they show motion of the economy, or parts of it, over time. Most economic relationships are also probabilistic because of uncertainty about the true state of the economy, either from the viewpoint of the knowledge of the true relationships or of the external factors affecting the relationships. That the relationships are nonlinear, in most cases, poses numerical problems in obtaining solutions for economic magnitudes, given the initial state of the economy and the external factors affecting the economy. The computer, however, handles these complications in a very direct and manageable way through the technique of simulation. This technique can be used to cut through all these problems and generate time paths of economic variables, given the inputs for initial and external magnitudes. The uncertainty aspect can be handled by computer generation of random numbers and adding them to the economic relationships. This would be called a "probabilistic simulation." Otherwise, the result would be called a "deterministic situation."

The great advantages of the computer for this type of analysis are:

1. Alternative formulations of economic relationships can be tested in a dynamic mode against historical reality. These are validation experiments.

2. Alternative projections for future possibilities can be examined with a variety of assumptions about input values, which are unknown.

3. Drawings of random numbers for probabilistic simulations and solutions of nonlinear equations can be approximated by the computer. The probabilistic simulations allow the estimation of numerical probabilities of alternative economic outcomes, such as the probability of onset of recession or recovery.

4. Large-scale systems of economic relationships for many periods in a dynamic simulation can be handled very quickly and economically by computers.

Computers are indispensable for simulation studies in economics. A wide range of alternatives can be explored; this was never possible in economics before the 1960s. Nowadays many important public policies and private business decisions are investigated by the means of alternative computer simulations. This has become a standard tool for quantitative economics.

The calculations produced by the computer are often meaningful only to the primary investigator, but the computer also has been harnessed for interpretation of findings through programming for informative tabular displays and graphics. Through appropriate preprogramming, the results of the solution of an economic exercise can be automatically transformed for information display.

Software (programs) packages have been developed that are capable of doing all the following tasks separately or in regular sequence:

1. Assembly of data in a data bank

2. Withdrawal of data for analysis

3. Estimation of relationships from data

4. Simulation testing of relationships against historical data

5. Simulation projections of economic data, given initial values and external input values

6. Display of tables, summary measures, and graphs of results

From beginning to end, it is possible to go through this series of steps entirely within the computer system, automatically and without manual intervention, although for economic understanding it is generally necessary to have human intervention at various stages.

The computer is not only an important research tool in economic analysis; it is also valuable as a teaching tool. Computer-based numerical examples of the type of tabular presentation that has always been found in economics textbooks can be generated in the classroom or by the student, independently, to analyze various economic calculations that involve alternative sets of quantitative conditions. With large screens for an entire class or with individual terminals for each student, the economics teacher can take students step-by-step through many economic problems and make graphical displays of the outcome. Many textbooks now package data and software diskettes for the student to use in a microcomputer as a teaching supplement.

Some Trends

Although the computer has made possible a revolution in economic teaching and research, it has not yet reached the limits of development, and evolutionary process is presently at work. A number of trends indicate the way of the future.

In an early generation of computers, networks of users were served from centralized mainframe computers that were accessed by terminals in time-sharing mode. This is still being done but is increasingly being replaced by versatile workstations, distribution of information by diskette (or similar small device), and direct electronic distribution over telecommunication systems around the world. The microcomputer is now so capable of large-scale computation and so inexpensive that nearly all economic researchers can have access to huge amounts of data, software for interpreting the data, and up-to-the minute information about economic affairs. Except for storage of large data files and for the most intricate of econometric type calculations, there are few, if any, quantitative issues in economics that pose insurmountable computational problems. Progress is always being made, and economic computation is becoming faster, cheaper, and easier to execute.

More governments will probably make their statistical services available to public files than can readily be accessed by telephone or other simple communication devices. And more and more information will be found in these files. More international statistics will be available, possibly through the efforts of several national bodies to make public information available more broadly through direct satellite communications systems.

At present most economic data are collected at sources—the enterprise, the market, the household, or the individual—and then transferred manually to the computer for processing and storage for potential use. The manual steps of data collection and transfer can potentially be eliminated through direct logging of economic transactions from the point of occurrence to the computer file. This is already done for sales and inventory statistics of large commercial establishments.

References

Berndt, Ernst R., *The Practice of Econometrics*, Addison-Wesley, Reading, Mass., 1991, esp. chap. 1; IBM Corporation, *APL Econometric Planning Language, Program Description/Operations Manual* (3d ed.), IBM Form Sh 20-1620, Armonk, New York, 1977; Klein, L. R., "A History of Computation in Econometrics," Ronald G. Bodkin, Lawrence R. Klein, Kant Marwah, and Edward Elgar, (eds.), *A History of Macroeconometric Model Building*, Aldershot, England, 1991, 509–525; Kuh, Edwin, "An Interactive Econometric Environment: The TROLL System," in F. Schohr and H. D. Plotzeneder (eds.), *Okonometrische Modelle und Systemme*, Oldenbourg, Munich, 1978, pp. 107–123; Norman, Morris, *Software Package for Economic Modelling*, IIASA, no. RR721, Laxenburg, November 1977; Schleicher, Stephen, "Design Principles for Econometric Software," in F. Schohr and H. D. Plotzeneder (eds.), *Okonometrische Modelle und Systemme*, Oldenbourg, Munich, 1978, pp. 63–75.

(*See also* Data banks; Econometrics; Economic forecasting methods; Operations research; Simulation in business and economics)

Lawrence R. Klein

Concentration of industry

A concentrated industry is one in which a few sellers account for a large share of the industry's output. An industry's concentration level is of interest because of its implications for the following:

1. The existence of noncompetitive pricing and monopoly profits via tacit collusion

2. The existence of noncompetitive pricing and monopoly profits even when sellers act independently (as in Cournot or Stackelberg theories of oligopoly)

3. A traditional political suspicion that, in industry as in government, "concentration of power" is incompatible with democracy and decentralized decision making

Quantitatively, concentration measures "how much business is done by how few." Qualitatively, concentrated markets can be expected to have some of the structural and behavioral characteristics described in economic theories of oligopoly.

At (usually) 5-year intervals since 1947, the U.S. Bureau of the Census has published concentration ratios. These show the combined market shares of the top 4 (CR$_4$), or of the top 8, 20, and 50 firms in manufacturing industries defined at the 4- and 5-digit levels of the Standard Industrial Classification. In 1982, the Bureau began publication of the Herfindahl-Hirschman Index (HHI), which is the sum of the squared market shares of the industry's top 50 firms.

Concentration is an imperfect joint measure of two important market characteristics. It varies inversely with the number of sellers in an industry (and directly with their "fewness"); it varies directly with the inequality of their sizes. Both characteristics are often hypothesized to assist the maintenance of tacitly (or even explicitly) collusive behavior. In addition, inequality is associated with domination of an industry by its largest firm, whose strategic choices between cooperation and aggressive competition can determine the nature and extent of rivalry among all its firms.

For industries whose definitions do not change, measured concentration is normally stable over time. Moreover, the ranking of industries by degree of concentration tends to be similar across national economies, suggesting that concentration has predictable economic determinants. However, attempts to explain concentration levels have been only partly successful. Economies of scale at the plant or firm level account for only a fraction of observed concentration levels. For some consumer-product industries, high advertising intensity and high concentration tend to occur together, with the causal connection running in both directions.

The most tantalizing research question associated with concentration concerns whether it leads to monopolistic prices and profits. The usual research design was to take a cross-section of industries and (since price comparisons among diverse industries are not meaningful) to look for a positive relation between concentration and profits, after controlling for other profit determinants. In studies conducted between 1951 and 1981, such a positive relation almost always appeared. The obvious conclusion was that concentration facilitated tacit collusion (which was not directly observed) which in turn led to monopolistic profits. Studies searching for a "critical concentration level" at which an industry's profits become significantly higher have not been uniformly successful, but some have placed this level at a CR$_4$ value between 40 and 60.

This "collusion hypothesis" found challenges from 1970 on. Most centered on the truism that an industry's concentration is high when its leading firms have high market shares. In studies where industry-specific concentration effects can be distinguished from firm-specific market-share effects, market share is usually the better predictor of profits. One interpretation of these results is that large firms in concentrated industries enjoy economies of scale that lead to lower costs and higher profits. Another interpretation is that concentration and profits are both the result of cost-decreasing productivity changes or even good luck. In these and similar interpretations, the concentration-profits relation does not imply a role for collusion or monopoly. Although these revisionist views enjoy wide acceptance, they are silent about why entry or within-industry competition doesn't eventually eliminate the relationship between concentration and profits. A more promising line of inquiry since 1980 has found a direct and significant relation between concentration and *price* across different geographic markets for identical products such as cement, gasoline, or advertising rates.

On other issues, there is really no clear consensus on the effects of concentration. Many studies have investigated an implication of Schumpeter's claim that innovation is more likely when the profits of the innovating firm are protected by monopoly. These studies have proceeded by looking for an empirical relation between some measure of innovation or progressiveness on the one hand, and concentration or other indicia of market structure on the other. As a result of such studies, there is little support for the Schumpeterian claim as a generally valid proposition.

References

Martin, S., *Industrial Economics,* Macmillan, New York, 1988; Scherer, F. M., and D. Ross, *Industrial Market Structure and Economic Performance* (3d ed.), Random House, New York, 1990; Schmalensee, R., "Inter-Industry Studies of Structure and Performance," in R. Schmalansee and R. Willig (eds.), *Handbook of Industrial Organization,* North-Holland, Amsterdam, 1989, chap. 16; U.S. Bureau of the Census, U.S. Department of Commerce, *1982 Census of Manufactures: Concentration Ratios in Manufacturing,* Washington, D.C., 1986; Weiss, L. W. (ed.), *Concentration and Price,* M.I.T., Cambridge, Mass., 1989.

(*See also* Competition; Monopoly and oligopoly)

Bruce T. Allen

Conglomerates

In general, a conglomerate is a corporation formed by many mergers and acquisitions in which the acquired companies are engaged in activities that may have little or no relation to the activities of the acquiring company. The acquiring company may be engaged in manufacturing, or it may be an investment company seeking a controlling interest in nonfinancial firms. Conglomerates of this latter type are known as "financial conglomerates."

The Federal Trade Commission classifies three types of conglomerate mergers: (1) product extension mergers—firms which have some degree of functional relationship in either product or distribution; (2) market extension mergers—firms which are in the same product line, but sell in different geographic markets; and (3) unrelated combinations which would include financial conglomerates or concentric conglomerates. In a concentric conglomerate, a firm combines activities with similar specific management functions such as research, engineering, production, marketing. Specialist counsel is provided by corporate staff, and a carry-over of the general or generic management functions of planning, organizing, directing, controlling, etc., is emphasized.

Finance is a specific management function, but since it is the language for recording the activities of all operations, it is also a pervasive or generic management function. Some conglomerate firms achieved interactions between financial information flows and operating activities so effectively that substantial synergies resulted. In practice, most conglomerates had activities related in some respects.

Three Economic Functions of Financial Conglomerates

Financial conglomerates may achieve three possible economic functions: (1) portfolio effects, (2) financial responsibility, and (3) resource allocations. The portfolio effects refer to investment diversification. However, homemade diversification by individual investors can substitute for corporate or business diversification. In addition, investment companies can achieve diversification more efficiently than conglomerates because of greater flexibility in buying and selling financial instruments.

A second economic function of conglomerates is the avoidance of bankruptcy of one of its segments because of a temporary adverse run of losses. If the long-run prospects for a division are favorable, it will be sustained through a period of losses until demand conditions or managerial performance improves. In this respect a financial conglomerate is clearly distinguished from an investment company which simply buys and sells securities.

A third possible function of conglomerates is to redeploy assets. If the potentials for a product line are favorable but the individuals managing assets in these product market areas are not achieving their potentials, those managers may be redeployed. In addition, assets may be redeployed as the prospects in some product market areas become more favorable than in others.

Thus, even in "pure conglomerates" some economic functions may be performed. In addition, multiproduct firms whose activities are related concentrically may achieve economies of scale or scope and lower cost functions by combining complementary business activities.

Three Categories of Empirical Studies

A critical issue is therefore raised as to the actual performance of conglomerate firms. Empirical studies dealing with conglomerates have been of three categories. The first type of study was concerned with conglomerates' accounting performance. Some studies in the early 1960s concluded that conglomerate mergers satisfied managers' desires for larger firms but did not increase earnings or market prices. Later studies found that conglomerates as a group raised the return on total assets up to the average for all firms. Other studies indicated that conglomerates acquired more profitable firms than did nonconglomerate acquirers and increased the utilization of latent debt capacity.

The second type of empirical study focused on conglomerate performance within the context of the capital asset pricing model. Studies through 1969 found that conglomerates provided higher ratios of return to systematic risk than did mutual funds. However, other studies through the 1970s found that conglomerates exhibited higher levels of systematic risk but not significantly different risk-adjusted rates of return or other performance measures.

A third type of empirical study utilized residual analysis to remove market and industry effects, thereby testing for possible gains from mergers. In conglomerate mergers and acquisitions (M&As), acquired firms on average gained while acquiring firms probably experienced small negative returns—about the same results as for M&As generally.

Early Concerns about Conglomerate Firms

As conglomerate merger activity increased during the 1960s, a number of antitrust issues were raised. One was that conglomerate mergers permit the extension of market power of one firm into other industries. However, the opposite conclusion seems equally plausible. Conglomerate diversification by the acquisition of firms in other industries increases potential competition. The threat of potential entry becomes stronger.

A cross-subsidization criticism argued that in the large conglomerate various types of predatory behavior can occur because activities that are less profitable can be subsidized by the profitable segments of the business. However, this argument lacks plausibility because if some activities are unprofitable, it is better to dispose of them rather than to subsidize them. A related argument is that a "deep pocket" policy may be followed. This refers to the ability of large firms to engage in heavy advertising and product differentiation which smaller firms may not be able to afford. However, this argument can also be extended to other clearly socially desirable forms of competition, such as quality improvements and research and development expenditures.

Another concern with conglomerate firms is the possibility of increased reciprocity. This is the practice of a conglomerate basing its purchasing policy on projected sales rather than on prices and product quality. But with the broadened application in recent years of decentralized management responsibility and accountability, reciprocity would conflict with established management policies. Managers must be free to follow the most economic and efficient policy if they are to be fairly evaluated.

Another concern was whether conglomerate mergers increased industrial concentration. The share of the largest 200 manufacturing firms in 1956 was 53 percent of total manufacturing assets. This share rose to 61 percent in 1977. However, much of this apparent rise results from diversification by manufacturing firms into nonmanufacturing activities. When the calculation is based on the 200 largest nonfinancial assets, this ratio has remained stable from 1958 through 1990 at about 40 percent. Conventional four-firm concentration ratios in individual industries, on average, have remained essentially flat at the same 40 percent figure in recent decades.

Later Criticisms of Conglomerate Merger Activity

With the recognition of increased competition in many dimensions, particularly with internationalization of markets, antitrust policies beginning in the late 1970s became less restrictive. A higher proportion of mergers in the 1980s represented horizontal and vertical relationships. New criticisms emerged: (1) Conglomerate mergers represented unrelated acquisitions. (2) Unrelated acquisitions did not increase profitability, so were inefficient. (3) Acquisitions in the 1980s mainly reversed and corrected the unsound, unrelated M&As of the 1960s. (4) Since the mergers of the 1960s were mistakes, the positive returns in the event studies of the mergers of the 1960s represented market miscalculations and were, therefore, not to be trusted in evaluating long-term effects. (5) The mergers of the 1980s reversed the excess diversification of the 1960s and refocused corporations to their core activities.

Counterarguments have also been made: (1) Other studies find that profitability did, in fact, improve. (2) Divesting 46 to 50 percent of acquisitions by numbers is also evidence that 50 percent or more of the acquisitions were successful in the sense that they were not divested. (3) Recent studies show that the divested activities were sold for more on average than their purchase price. If the investments should have earned the returns of the Standard & Poor's (S&P) 500 stocks while they were held, deducting these market returns makes the net amount received less than the amounts paid. However, the net figure is still greater than the preacquisition market prices of the target firms. (4) Acquisitions and divestitures represent only a portion of the overall strategies of firms. A sample of the most active acquirers and divestors finds that 70 percent of the firms achieved returns to shareholders in excess of the market return measured either by the S&P 500 or broader measures of the "market."

Policy proposals have shifted from new government rules to prevent conglomerate mergers to recommendations to corporate managements to avoid unrelated diversification. However, the concept of "related" remains ambiguous and subjective. Divestitures may represent learning as well as mistakes. Many "unrelated" acquisitions have been spectacularly successful. Decisions on acquisitions should go beyond the single "related" versus "unrelated" criterion.

References

Kaplan, Steven, and Michael S. Weisbach, "The Success of Acquisitions: Evidence from Divestitures," *Journal of Finance,* vol. 47, March 1992, pp. 107–138; Mueller, Dennis C., "The Effects of Conglomerate Mergers: A Survey of the Empirical Evidence," *Journal of Banking and Finance,* vol. 1, December 1977, pp. 315–348; Porter, Michael, "From Competitive Advantage to Corporate Strategy," *Harvard Business Review,* May–June 1987, pp. 43–59; Shleifer, Andrei, and Robert W. Vishny, "Takeovers in the '60s and the '80s: Evidence and Implications," *Strategic Management Journal,* vol. 12, 1991, pp. 51–59; Smith, Keith V., and J. Fred Weston, "Further Evaluation of Conglomerate Performance," *Journal of Business Research,* vol. 5, March 1977, pp. 5–14; Weston, J. Fred, "The Nature and Significance of Conglomerate Firms," *St. John's Law Review,* vol. 44, Spring 1970, pp. 66–80; Weston, J. Fred, "Divestitures: Mistakes or Learning," *Journal of Applied Corporate Finance,* vol. 2, Summer 1989, pp. 68–76; Weston, J. Fred, and Surenda K. Mansinghka, "Tests of the Efficiency Performance of Conglomerate Firms," *Journal of Finance,* vol. 26, September 1971, pp. 919–936.

(*See also* Integration; Mergers, takeovers, and corporate restructuring)

J. Fred Weston

Congressional Budget Office

The Congressional Budget Office (CBO) was created by the Budget and Impoundment Control Act of 1974 to be a nonpartisan support staff to both Houses of Congress in carrying out newly established congressional budget responsibilities. The director of CBO is appointed for a 4-year term by the congressional leaders. Three economists have served as directors of the CBO: Alice Rivlin (1975–1983), Rudolph Penner (1983–1987), and Robert Reischauer (1989–).

From a beginning level of about 175 people, the CBO staff grew to about 220 by the mid-1980s and has since remained at that level. The staff is recruited on a strictly nonpolitical basis, mostly from professionals with a social science background. CBO's largest unit, the Budget Analysis Division—responsible for spending estimates and projections—generally draws younger analysts, often recent recipients of Masters degrees from public policy or business administration graduate schools. The program divisions, which write policy analyses, and the fiscal analysis and tax divisions, responsible for economic forecasts and revenue estimates, are staffed largely by more senior level Ph.D. economists.

Economic Forecasts

A major task of CBO since its inception has been to produce macroeconomic forecasts that are independent of the administration's. These independent forecasts have deviated from those of various administrations, most notably in 1981 when the Reagan administration put forward its most overly optimistic forecast (the "Rosy Scenario"). CBO forecasts tend to be similar to the consensus of private forecasts.

Until the mid-1980s, the CBO forecast was usually the basis for congressional budget resolutions, which set out a fiscal plan for the upcoming fiscal year. With the advent of the Gramm-Rudman-Hollings (GRH) procedures, however, the budget resolution's fiscal stance was predetermined: GRH set in advance the maximum allowable deficit over a multiyear period. Similarly, the laws enacted to enforce the Summit agreements between the Bush administration and the Congress intentionally tied the government's hands at the outset by specifying maximum spending levels and constraining tax cuts or entitlement liberalizations. As a result, the economic forecast of CBO plays a lesser role in guiding legislation; it now mainly serves as an objective standard of what is likely to happen.

Cost Estimates and Projections

Many of CBO's products are of a technical nature, used to support the Congress's budget and legislative processes. The report accompanying each bill passed out of a committee must by law contain a CBO cost estimate showing the spending effects of the legislation over a 5-year period (the Joint Committee on Taxation furnishes kindred information on tax bills). Similar 5-year projections are developed for all existing budget lines and for the elements of the tax code. These are aggregated into the CBO baseline, a measure of where the budget is heading in the absence of policy changes. CBO also keeps track of legislation as it passes through committees and sends scorekeeping reports to the House and Senate budget committees. These reports constitute the basis for the budget committees to challenge committee actions that may be out of line with the budget resolution's limits.

As the enforcement procedures for the congressional budget became more sharply defined after the GRH procedures were instituted, CBO's cost estimates became more important. Many measures were killed in committee because CBO advised that the costs were inconsistent with the Congress's budget plan.

The importance of these CBO cost estimates is all the more remarkable in that the 1990 Budget Enforcement Act made the administration's Office of Management and

Budget (OMB) the ultimate arbiter of the numbers. Under the 1985 version of GRH, an average of OMB's and CBO's numbers—after an audit by the General Accounting Office (GAO)—was to be used to determine whether budget goals were met. If not met, there would be an automatic across-the-board spending cut—called a "sequestration"—in a host of defense and domestic spending lines. The Supreme Court in 1986 ruled out the GAO's (and, consequently, the CBO's) direct hand in such an "executive"—as opposed to legislative—activity. Subsequent budget process legislation explicitly stated that only OMB's estimates could trigger sequestration; the Congress, nonetheless, uses CBO's scoring of bills as it develops them.

Policy Studies

CBO communicates with the committees of the Congress in a number of ways. Formally published studies (in 1991, 18 volumes) and less formal CBO papers and staff memoranda (27 in 1991) are prepared at the request of committee chairs or ranking minority members. These studies usually present an analysis of options for changing some element of federal policy, with an emphasis on alternative budgetary outcomes. Thus, for example, as interest in lowering defense spending increased with the dissolution of the Soviet military, CBO prepared analyses of the budgetary and economic effects of alternative defense postures. Similar work is done on virtually all government programs in which major legislative changes are contemplated. For example, in 1991, CBO published major studies of medical care programs, deposit insurance, and unemployment compensation.

With few exceptions, CBO studies do not take a position on the legislation under discussion. In keeping with the agency's nonpartisan charter, the studies instead try to explain both sides of an issue in an objective manner. Such an approach does not always insulate CBO studies from criticism, as might be expected, given the politically charged Capitol Hill atmosphere.

Testimony before congressional committees, usually by the director of the CBO, is probably the most effective way that CBO's voice is heard. Early in each calendar year, the budget and tax committees hold hearings on the economic outlook, where CBO's economic forecast is presented. The appropriations committees usually invite CBO to comment on the president's budget proposal. And, increasingly, congressional committees have found it useful to start a series of hearings by having CBO present an "overview." These testimonies set out the issues and provide a balanced background for the Congress as it tries to sort out the competing views represented in subsequent presentations.

(*See also* Congressional Budget Office; Council of Economic Advisers; Joint Economic Committee of Congress)

Robert W. Hartman

Constant utility price (*see* Index numbers)

Consumer anticipation surveys (*see* Anticipation surveys, consumer)

Consumer credit

Consumer credit is defined by the Federal Reserve Board as "short- and intermediate-term credit extended to individuals through regular business channels, usually to finance the purchase of consumer goods and services or to refinance debts incurred for such purposes." Among the financial transactions excluded by this definition are loans secured by real estate, leases of automobiles and other consumer durables, and borrowings against the cash value of life insurance policies or generally against savings accounts.

Two Classes of Consumer Credit

There are two main classes of consumer credit: noninstallment credit and installment credit. Noninstallment credit is consumer credit that is scheduled to be repaid in a lump sum and includes single-payment loans, 30-day charge accounts provided by retailers and travel and entertainment card issuers (American Express and Diners Club), and service credit, principally amounts owed to doctors and hospitals and public utilities. Installment credit represents all consumer credit that is scheduled to be repaid (or with the option of repayment) in two or more installments. Consumer installment credit greatly exceeds noninstallment credit. At the end of 1990, amounts outstanding (seasonally adjusted) of these two types of credit were $735.1 billion and $59.3 billion, respectively.

Consumer credit may also be classified as sales credit or cash credit. Consumer credit for the purchase of goods and services (sales credit) began in Colonial times with the granting of open-book credit. The installment purchase of automobiles created an explosion of consumer installment credit in the 1900s. Cash loans were also available to consumers in the 1800s from unregulated lenders who devised various schemes for evading the state usury statutes. Beginning in 1916, states enacted exceptions to their usury laws in order to permit consumers to obtain small amounts (initially $300) of legal cash credit. Rate ceilings on small cash loans were initially fixed at 42 percent per year. Most states now limit rates on small loans to 36 percent, with lower rate ceilings for large loans. Rate ceilings on consumer credit are set by the states, and the trend in recent years has been to relax or eliminate rate ceilings on various types of consumer credit in order to allow competition in the market to set the rates.

The Federal Reserve classifies consumer installment credit by major holder and by major type of credit. The four major types of credit are automobile, revolving, mobile home, and "other." Determining market shares by major holder of revolving credit and other types of credit is difficult because many large credit grantors have transferred their receivables to securitized portfolios, which are classified as one of the major holders of installment credit.

For many years, the most rapidly growing form of consumer credit has been revolving credit. Originating in the late 1930s, revolving credit, or open-end credit, has three distinctive features. Typically, it is a plan whereby the creditor (1) permits the consumer to make purchases or obtain loans from time to time, either directly from the creditor or indirectly by means of a credit card; (2) permits the customer to pay amounts owed in full or to make minimum monthly payments; and (3) may compute a periodic finance charge on the outstanding balance. Many issuers of bank credit cards also assess an annual fee. The convenience or low transactions cost involved with this type of credit explains in large part its growing acceptance by consumers.

Economic Function

The basic economic function of consumer credit is to move consumers' consumption of goods and services forward in time. Although some have argued that the payment of finance charges represents a nonproductive expenditure, consumers' willingness to pay such charges is evidence that there is a time utility in consumption. A refrigerator today has greater value than a refrigerator 24 months from now.

Consumers use credit for the same reasons that business and government use credit. A large portion of consumer credit is for investment purposes and is economically productive in the same sense that business firms use credit to acquire machinery. Thus, the installment purchase of a washing machine may provide a (nontaxable) return on the investment by permitting a consumer to avoid the time and outlays required to travel to the laundromat. Although the credit purchase of a dress or suit may not directly earn a return on the investment, it is justified by providing immediate, rather than delayed, satisfaction.

Consumers also use credit to meet emergencies, such as hospital and doctors' bills—just as governments turn to credit to meet the crises of wars and depressions. Finally, in a manner similar to the use of open-book credit by a business, consumers use credit as a matter of convenience to pay for multiple purchases. For example, telephone bills are paid monthly, and many consumers use revolving credit plans as a convenient means of summing small purchases into one or more monthly payments.

Macro and Micro Effects of Consumer Credit

Legislators and economists are concerned with the macro and micro effects of consumer credit. At the macroeconomic level, some have argued that consumer credit is destabilizing and, therefore, should be controlled directly through requiring minimum down payments and limiting contract maturities. Although such controls are presently used in a few other nations, they have been employed in the United States only during World War II and the Korean intervention. Since consumer credit makes up only about 6 percent of total credit market debt, other forms of credit may have more influence on the business cycle.

Some have also been concerned about the quality of consumer credit, arguing that when consumers become overextended their inability to repay their debts will further depress the economy. Frequently, these fears are generated by comparing outstanding consumer installment credit to consumers' disposable personal income. This measure of "debt burden" is faulty for several reasons. First the comparison is of a "stock" (outstandings) to a "flow" (income). Second, maturities on many types of closed-end loans have lengthened over time, thereby keeping monthly payments in check, even though the stock of debt rises. Finally, revolving credit has become an increasing portion of outstanding debt, but much of revolving credit is merely postponed cash payments, or convenience credit, which consumers pay off in 30 to 45 days. A proper measure of debt burden is a comparison of monthly payments on consumer installment credit to income. Data from the Federal Reserve from surveys since 1970 show that payments in relation to income have remained remarkably stable, averaging about 10 percent of income among those families having such debts. Concerns about the microeconomic effects of consumer credit upon the family have led to a great quantity and variety of state and federal legislation. Some has been directed at better informing the consumer, such as requiring that finance charges be disclosed in a uniform manner (Truth-in-Lending Act) and that consumers have access necessary to correct their credit reports if necessary (Fair Credit Reporting Act). Other laws intend to protect consumers: restrictions on levels of finance charges, limits on collection remedies, bans on discrimination in the granting of credit, and ready access to bankruptcy courts to eliminate or reduce debts. Much of current economic research in the area examines whether the actual effects of these laws and regulations match the intended effects.

References

Avery, Robert B., Gregory E. Elliehausen, and Arthur B. Kennickell, "Changes in Consumer Installment Debt: Evidence from the 1983 and 1986 Surveys of Consumer Finances, *Federal Reserve Bulletin,* vol. 73, October 1987, pp. 761–778; Canner, Glenn B., and Charles Luckett, "Payment of Household Debts," *Federal Reserve Bulletin,* vol. 77, April 1991, pp. 218–229; A household Credit Data Handbook and a series of working papers and monographs concerning consumer credit are available from the Credit Research Center, Purdue University, West Lafayette, IN 47907-1310.

(*See also* Business credit; Credit, an overview; Debt; Interest rates; Mortgage credit; Selective credit controls)

Robert W. Johnson

Consumer price index

The consumer price index (CPI) is the name typically applied in both the United States and other countries to the statistic that measures the price changes of the vast number of goods and services purchased by households. The broad concept underlying the CPI is that it measures the purchasing power of money with respect to a fixed market basket of consumer goods and services.

The CPI for the United States was first published in 1921 and contained data going back to 1913. Indexes for food and some U.S. cities are available prior to that. The CPI is compiled and released monthly by the Bureau of Labor Statistics (BLS).

Laspeyres Index Formula

The mathematical formula used to calculate the U.S. CPI is basically the Laspeyres index formula. That formula is:

$$I_t = \frac{\Sigma p_t q_o}{\Sigma p_o q_a} \times 100$$

where I = index

p = price

q = quantity

Σ = the summation of the products of price and quantity for all the items in the index

t = the time period to which the index refers

a = the base period to which the quantity weights refer

o = the base period to which the prices refer

If the base period to which prices refer is identical with that to which the quantity weights refer, the formula is exactly equivalent to a Laspeyres index. In any event, the quantities are fixed in some base period, and changes in the index therefore reflect changes only in the prices consumers must pay for that fixed market basket of goods.

Since it is difficult to measure quantities in a consistent way for use in the above formula, it is recast to permit the index to be calculated without having to determine quantities directly. That reformulation is:

$$I_t = I_{t-1} \left[\frac{\Sigma(p_{t-1}q_a)(p_t/p_{t-1})}{\Sigma p_{t-1}q_a} \right]$$

For each item, its product, the first term of the numerator divided by the denominator, represents the proportion of the consumer's dollar that would be spent on each item in the market basket if the consumer purchased the base quantities. This ratio is called a "relative importance" and may change from period to period if the price of the item changes relative to all other prices. It is the relative importances that are usually, though inaccurately, referred to as "quantity weights." The relative importances may be used to calculate special indexes for particular time periods from among the component price series comprising the CPI.

Consumer Expenditure Surveys

The relative importances required to calculate the index based upon the formula derived above are usually obtained through a periodic survey called the "consumer expenditure survey." Weights reflected in the index since January 1987 are those obtained in the consumer expenditure survey for the period 1982 to 1984. This survey obtains information about the various amounts spent on the full spectrum of foods and services purchased by the population of consumers represented in the index. Such surveys may also include questions designed to obtain information on savings and, in some cases, even on assets and liabilities. But the consumer price index measures only prices associated with expenditures on goods and services.

The decision about how frequently weights are to be revised depends both on resource availability and other considerations. The frequency of weight revisions is, however, an important matter because it is generally thought that as base periods become more and more out of date the calculation of the CPI through the use of the Laspeyres formula yields an upward bias.

The population covered by the consumer price index varies from country to country. In the United States, indexes are calculated for two consumer groups, all-urban consumers and urban wage earners and clerical workers. The index for the first group was initiated in 1978.

The 1982–1984 base period to which CPI weights currently apply is also the period for which the index equals 100, its reference base. The selection of a reference base is arbitrary—any time period can be selected without affecting the rate of change of the index. Traditionally, however, the reference bases of U.S. government statistics are changed about once every 10 years.

Two Criteria for Price Data

The other major ingredient of a price index is, of course, prices. There are two major criteria which the price data must meet. One is that data are a sample representative of the items purchased by the population group covered by the index and of the outlets in which that group makes those purchases. The second criterion is that every attempt is made to ensure the comparability of what is being priced from one time period to the next. The first criterion is usually met by drawing a probability sample of items from the consumer expenditure survey. However, such a survey rarely gives details on the outlets where these items were purchased. In practice, the data on outlets are mostly derived from a separate survey of households called a point-of-purchase survey.

The second criterion is usually met by drawing up a precise specification of the item to be priced and the outlet in which the price is to be collected, and following that item in that store over time. In practice this may be difficult, and other methods must be relied on to compare prices of items for which the specification has changed.

Use of the CPI

CPIs have several important uses. Early in this century, changes in economic conditions required new data related to industrialization, in addition to data already collected for agricultural and external trade. Industrialization was often accompanied by collective bargaining for setting wages. Thus, in the United States, the need arose for a CPI to be used in labor-management negotiations, especially when inflation accelerated during World War I.

As economic conditions changed, the use and the design of CPIs changed. During the 1930s, CPIs were used to measure real income flows of families. The CPI was being used as a deflator, but during a time of price decline it actually inflated incomes. With the advent of Keynesian economics and government short-run policies to stimulate employment and stabilize prices, the CPI grew in importance as an input for policymaking. In recent years, when worldwide inflation has accelerated, the CPI has become a closely watched statistic. It is widely used to compensate for inflation. Such uses include adjustments to wage contracts, social security and other transfer payments, and income tax brackets.

CPI Detail

In the United States, the aggregate CPI and component detail are published monthly. The item detail for the United States includes the major components: food and beverages, housing, apparel and upkeep, transportation, medical care, entertainment, and other goods and services. These are broken down further into a large number of subindexes.

CPIs are also available on a monthly, bimonthly, or semiannual basis for 27 major urban areas. Monthly indexes are also prepared for four regions of the country and for five size classes of cities. Some indexes for selected size classes of cities in particular regions are also prepared.

Currently, the CPI is based on about 100,000 monthly price quotations. Rents and property tax rates are collected from other sources. The sources are located in 91 primary sampling units which are geographical areas.

In the United States and many other countries the statistical agencies make data available on both nonadjusted and seasonally adjusted bases. The former estimates are usually used in the escalation of contracts, the latter by policymakers in assessing the short-run course of inflation.

Conceptual and Measurement Problems

Like all economic statistics, the CPI has conceptual and measurement problems which are potential sources of error. The food and clothing components are examples of the problem of pricing items that are seasonal in nature and are found in markets only during particular months. The medical care component is an area in which measuring quality change is difficult. The use of the Laspeyres index formula as an approximation to a cost-of-living index is another issue raised about the index.

References

U.S. Department of Labor, *The Consumer Price Index: Concepts and Content over the Years,* U.S. Bureau of Labor Statistics Report 517, 1977.

(*See also* Bureau of Labor Statistics; Cost of living; Index numbers; Inflation; Price measurement; Statistical methods in economics and business, an overview; Value of the dollar)

Joel Popkin

Consumer theory

The theory of consumer behavior has evolved over the last several decades from a set of statements about how consumers allocate a given income among a set of purchased goods and services to a theory incorporating concerns about the division of income between saving and spending, the supply of labor services to the market, and the way in which consumers allocate their time generally between market production, home production, and consumption or leisure activities.

Marshallian Demand Analysis

The standard theory of the consumer is represented by Marshallian demand analysis and the Hicks-Slutsky analysis of indifference functions. In Marshall's classical treatment, consumers face a set of prices for various goods and services and hold a set of demand functions for these goods and services. The demand functions picture the amount that consumers are willing to buy at each hypothetical price. Generally, the lower the price of the product, the greater the quantity consumers will wish to obtain—the familiar downward-sloping demand curve, based on diminishing marginal utility in the consumption of individual goods and services.

In Marshallian analysis, many things besides price affect quantity consumed, but these are thought of as shifting the location of the entire demand function. An increase in income, for example, normally means that people would be willing to buy more of the product at each price than previously; hence the entire demand function shifts outward and to the right. A rise in the price of a commodity that is complementary in consumption would shift the demand function inward and to the left—for example, a rise in the price of bacon would mean that people would be less willing to buy eggs at each particular price for eggs, because the demand for eggs depends partly on the price of bacon.

Marshallian demand theory contains two other aspects of technical interest. The first is the proposition that a unique demand curve, defined as the relation between the amount people are willing to buy of any product and different hypothetical prices for that product, does not really exist in theory, for Marshallian demand curves are based on the underlying assumption that nonprice forces affecting demand are unchanged as the price changes. But one of those factors is real income, and real income must be changing as the price of any single product changes, because real income is represented by money income adjusted by an index of price change. Thus, if the price of housing services were to fall, consumer real income would rise because the same money income would be able to buy more total goods and services owing to the fall in the price of housing services. Thus, in Marshallian terms, any movement along a demand curve due to a decline in the price of a product will result in a (miniscule) rise in real income, which would move the demand curve to the right. Hence, a Marshallian demand curve does not actually hold real income constant but holds it constant only to the extent that real income is affected by factors other than the decline in price of the product under consideration.

The second aspect is the idea of consumers' surplus. In Marshallian analysis, consumers will buy a product up to the point where the marginal utility from purchasing the last dollar's worth is equal to the marginal utility of money income generally. But the total utility from consuming a particular product is obviously not represented by the marginal utility of the last dollar's worth multiplied by the number of dollar-equivalent units acquired: All units but the marginal one must have yielded greater utility, assuming that marginal utility declines with increased quantities consumed. Hence, total consumer utility from purchase of any commodity must be greater than the product of marginal utility times units consumed (which is equivalent to price times quantity consumed). The difference between those two measures is called "consumers' surplus," and for purposes of analyzing social welfare is an important concept.

Indifference Function Analysis

The indifference function analysis developed by Hicks and Slutsky asks how consumers should allocate a fixed budget between various purchasable commodities. The usual strategy is to define one commodity (y) as "all other commodities taken together," the other as a particular commodity (x) under investigation. Thus, if all income were spent on commodity x, nothing of all other commodities y could be acquired; if no x at all were purchased, an amount of all other commodities y equal to income divided by the price index could be acquired. The line connecting these two opportunity points is called a "budget constraint," and under assumptions that consumers cannot affect price by buying more or less, the budget constraint is a straight line. Movements in income would shift the budget line outward, while movements in the prices of either x or y would rotate the budget line around one or the other point.

To go along with the budget line or opportunity locus, functions relating consumer preferences toward purchasing alternative sets of commodities are constructed as follows. Given consumption of any particular amount of commodity x, say quantity a, and an amount of commodity y (all other commodities) equal to b, consumers would be at a certain level of total satisfaction. (The purchase of a and b exhausts consumer income.) If people were to acquire more of commodity x, how much y would have to be taken away to keep total satisfaction at the same level as before? Creating a set of alternative combinations of commodities x and y—points of equal total satisfaction— leads to creation of an indifference function, a locus of points where consumer satisfaction is identical throughout. Other indifference curves can be constructed, involving more of both x and y, or less of both x and y, than in the first illustration, and thus we have a family of indifference curves.

Indifference functions have certain properties. They will generally be convex to the origin, suggesting that consumers would be less and less willing to give up commodity x as they got to hold smaller and smaller amounts of x (and larger and larger amounts of y). Convexity holds so long as the marginal rate of substitution between x and y declines as more x (and thus less y) is consumed. Interestingly enough, the implied marginal utility conditions are a little less stringent than would be true of Marshallian demand analysis, which is based on the assumption of declining marginal utility. Indifference curves are convex to the origin so long as the ratio of marginal utilities (x/y) declines, a condition consistent with decreasing, constant, or increasing marginal utility for any one product. And indifference curves cannot intersect, since otherwise consumers would be both indifferent to sets of commodities and simultaneously hold preferences for equivalent sets of the same commodities—a logical impossibility.

The basic theory underlying both Marshallian demand analysis and indifference function analysis is, of course, exactly the same, and one can easily move from one analysis to the other. Indifference curve construction allows easier observation of certain kinds of relationships in consumer choice theory than does with Marshallian demand functions—for example, whether a demand function is of elastic, inelastic, or unitary elasticity can be seen at a glance with indifference curves but is more complicated to observe with the Marshallian apparatus.

Both the Marshallian and Hicks-Slutsky analyses of consumer behavior are concerned entirely with the way in which consumers allocate income among a set of goods and services purchased in the market. Neither has much in the way of empirically refutable content unless particular restrictions are applied to the utility function, e.g., the linear expenditure restrictions of Stone-Geary, or the separability restrictions of Deaton-Muellbauer).

Although this analytical apparatus technically can be used to examine the allocation of consumer income between spending and saving (more precisely, between current consumption and future consumption), that problem is of little concern to theorists in the Marshallian or Hicks-Slutsky tradition. It was of concern to Irving Fisher, whose interest was in the role of time preference in determining the choice between present and future consumption, but even Fisher was not concerned with cyclical variability in consumer saving and spending patterns. In general, classical consumer theory pays little attention to aggregate movements in consumer spending or saving relative to income, although much modern macroeconomics has that flavor.

Observation of data for the U.S. economy since World War II suggests the reason for the modern interest in aggregate consumer spending and saving behavior. Since World War II, consumers appear to have been the driving force behind most business-cycle contractions and expansions in the United States, largely reflecting changes in expenditure rates on houses, cars, and other durable or discretionary items (Juster, 1966). In part, this finding relates to issues of definition: We conventionally treat consumer expenditures on durable goods as current consumption rather than as investment, hence as reducing consumer saving. In contrast, consumer purchases of owner-occupied housing are treated as business investment.

It is now widely recognized that consumer expenditures are highly volatile cyclically, that phenomena which cause consumers to speed up their rates of acquisition of housing, cars, durables, and other large items will generate increased demand for goods and services in the aggregate and are likely to fuel cyclical expansions, and that a collapse of spending on such discretionary items is apt to be associated with periods of economic recession.

Consumption Function

Although a voluminous literature analyzes the so-called consumption function, i.e., the relation between consumer income and consumer spending, little actually addresses the cyclical characteristics of consumer behavior. A substantial part of the consumption function literature relates to the permanent income theory developed by Milton Friedman, theory which treats consumption decisions as based on a longer-run concept of income than receipts during some arbitrary accounting-run period such as a year. But in the Friedman model, consumption (defined as the using up of goods and services, not their acquisition) is being analyzed, not consumer expenditures. Thus, the permanent income literature has little to say directly about the causes of cyclical variation in consumer spending unless permanent income is itself affected by cyclical change—in which case the desired stock of durables will change, and net investment or disinvestment in durables will occur.

The life-cycle model developed by Modigliani, Ando, and Brumberg represents an attempt to deal with the way in which consumers dispose of their income over time, and in that model wealth is assigned a crucial role in consumption decisions. In the life-cycle model, wealth includes not only property (houses, stocks, bonds, savings accounts, etc.) but also the value of future earnings. Thus, consumers visualize themselves as having a stock of initial wealth, a flow of income generated by that wealth over their lifetime, and a target (which may be zero) for their end-of-life wealth. Consumption decisions are made with that whole series of financial flows in mind. Thus, changes in wealth, as reflected by unexpected changes in earnings profiles or unexpected movements in asset prices, would have an impact on consumer spending decisions because they would enhance future earnings from property or labor or both. The theory has empirically testable implications for the age pattern of saving, and for the role of wealth in influencing aggregate consumer spending. Empirical estimates (Modigliani Papers, 1980) suggest that the propensity to consume out of wealth change is small—of the order of 0.03 to 0.06. Thus the 1987 stock market crash had little impact on consumption.

Another approach to cyclical variations in consumer spending and saving behavior relies more on the movement of waves of optimism and pessimism growing out of consumers' perceived improvement or deterioration in present and prospective financial position. One can trace the elements of this back at least to Keynes, who noted that the relation between consumption and income depends on, among other factors, expectations, optimism, and other psychologically related phenomena. Keynes downgraded the empirical importance of such phenomena for consumers, essentially arguing that they tended to cancel out, although psychological factors played a major role in Keynes's investment theory.

In the United States, the canceling-out presumption does not hold up. The work of Katona and his colleagues at the University of Michigan documents the quantitative importance of consumer optimism and pessimism in influencing consumer spending and saving decisions, and in recent years many analyses of cyclical movements in the U.S. economy have relied on measures of changes over time in the way consumers perceive the general economy, their own personal financial prospects, market conditions, etc.

There is little agreement even now among students of consumer spending behavior about the relative importance of factors such as income change, asset holdings, expectations about lifetime income, and psychological factors with labels like "optimism" or "pessimism." The empirical data that might be used to test alternative explanations for the cyclical variability of consumer saving and spending are not sufficiently detailed to allow one to distinguish between competing explanations, and the empirical data at the level of individual households are too dominated by measurement error to permit strong tests of competitive theories.

Consumer Theory of Labor Supply and Time Allocation

A second important modern development in consumer theory concerns analysis of consumer choices about labor supply and the allocation of time and between production and consumption activities. Most of the consumer theory discussed previously focuses on how consumers allocate income among various goods and services or how they allocate income between spending and saving. But both analyses presume that consumer income is a given and do not recognize that income reflects a choice about participation in the market.

The basic idea underlying this broadening of consumer theory is that consumer decisions about how to spend time represent choices, an idea which is especially important in multiperson households where it is possible to have a complex division of labor between market and nonmarket activities. Moreover, focusing on how consumers allocate their time over various activities—market production, home production, and consumption or leisure—forces us to recognize that the real budget constraint facing consumers is not income but time.

Recent developments in consumer theory that focus on how consumers allocate time take the view that households are best thought of as miniature firms providing labor services to the market, purchasing goods and services from the market, providing services to each other within the framework of the household itself, and generally deciding how much time to spend in a set of activities that exhaust the total time budget of 24 hours per day.

The seminal theory in this area is attributable to Becker (1965), who developed the notion of households as firms producing commodities with a combination of goods purchased from the market and their own time. Thus, households produce a commodity called "child quality" which is obtained by acquiring food, clothing, music lessons, schooling, etc., from the market and combining it with time spent by parents in various activities involving children—feeding, teaching, training, disciplining, playing games, etc. How people choose to spend their time depends on their productivity in various activities open to them—market work, home production of various sorts, etc. How much of market goods they choose to combine with their own time depends on the value of their time and the price of market goods and, in multiperson households, on the relative values of time spent in the market and time spent in home production by the several household members. The Becker framework is related to an earlier idea suggested by Kelvin Lancaster—that consumer utility is derived from the characteristics of products, and that new products are essentially new combinations of characteristics.

This relatively new idea in economic thinking has both advocates and critics. The proponents would argue that treating time as the basic currency reflecting choice is bound to provide a much more comprehensive picture of how individuals choose to pursue the maximization of well-being and that economists' notions of prices and productivity can be applied with appropriate analytical modifications to virtually all decisions made by consumers. (For a recent review of both theory and applications in this area, see Juster and Stafford, 1991.) Skeptics would argue that economic analysis is best applied to situations in which objective economic actors buy and sell products at defined prices, not to situations where the choice of activities is influenced by personal commitments of a continuing nature, where the commodities produced are often unobservable, frequently perceptual, and rarely measurable, and where there is neither a price at which transactions can take place nor a market where transactors gather together.

Other Modern Developments

Important recent work in consumer theory is concerned with decision making under uncertainty—the maximization of expected utility subject to a budget constraint with a stochastic element. The idea of expected utility originated with Von Neumann-Morgenstern (1980). Hall (1978) produced a modern version of the permanent income theory incorporating a random walk, with consumption determined by unpredictable changes in permanent income. The analysis was extended to expenditures or durable goods by Mankiw (1982). Flavin (1981) and Deaton (1980) examined whether the time-series responsiveness of consumption to income is larger or smaller than predicted by a random walk theory.

References

Abel, Andrew, Collected Papers of Franco Modigliani, vol. 2, M.I.T., Cambridge, Mass., 1980; Ando, Albert, and Franco Modigliani, "The 'Life-Cycle' Hypothesis of Saving," American Economic Review, vol. 53, no. 1, part 1, March 1963, pp. 55–84; Becker, Gary S., "A Theory of the Allocation of Time," Economic Journal, vol. 75, no. 299, September 1965, pp. 493–517; Deaton, Angus, Measurement of the Welfare Theory and Practical Guidelines, ISMS Working Paper, Series No. 7, World Bank, Washington, D.C., 1980; Fisher, Irving, The Theory of Interest, as Determined by Impatience to Spend Income and Opportunity to Invest It, Macmillan, New York, 1930; Flavin, Marjorie A., "The Adjustment of Consumption through Changing Expectations about the Future Income," Journal of Political Economy, vol. 89, 1981, pp. 974–1009; Friedman, Milton, A Theory of the Consumption Function, National Bureau of Economic Research General Series, no. 63, Princeton University Press, Princeton, N.J., 1957; Hall, Robert E., "Stochastic Implications of the Life Cycle–Permanent Income Hypothesis: Theory and Evidence," Journal of Political Economy," vol. 86, April 1978; Hicks, T. R., "A Reconsideration of the Theory of Value: Part I," Economica, no. 1, February 1934, pp. 52–76; Juster, F. Thomas, Household Capital Formation and Financing, 1897–1962, National Bureau of Economic Research General Series, no. 83, Columbia University Press, New York, 1966; Juster, F. Thomas, and Frank P. Stafford, "The Allocation of Time: Empirical Findings, Behavioral Models, and Problems of Measurement," Journal of Economic Literature, vol. 29, June 1991, pp. 471–522; Katona, George, Psychological Analysis of Economic Behavior, McGraw-Hill, New York, 1951; Keynes, John M., The General Theory of Employment, Interest and Money, Harcourt, Brace, New York, 1936; Mankiw, N. Gregory, "Hall's Consumption Hypothesis and Durable Goods," Journal of Monetary Economics, vol. 10, 1982, pp. 417–425; Marshall, Alfred, Principles of Economics: An Introductory Volume (8th ed.), Macmillan, London, 1938; Mincer, Jacob, "Labor Supply, Family Income, and Consumption," American Economic Review, vol. 50, no. 2, May 1960, pp. 574–583; Slutsky, Eugen, "Sulla Teoria del Bilancia del Consumatore," Giornali Degli Economisti, vol. 51, July 1915, pp. 1–26; Von Neumann, John, and Oscar Morganstern, *Theory of Games and Economic Behavior,* Princeton University Press, Princeton, 1980.

(*See also* Anticipation surveys, consumer; Consumers' surplus; Consumption function; Demand; Keynesian economics; Marshallian economics; Money illusion; Permanent income hypothesis; Saving; Utility; Wealth)

F. Thomas Juster

Consumerism

Three views of consumerism are extant—those of activists, scholars, and moralists. The scholars' views are exemplified by Maynes (1973), who defines consumerism as "the articulation of consumer discontent and the furtherance of corrective measures," and by Mayer (1989), who sees consumerism as "a diverse and evolving social movement seeking to enhance the economic wellbeing and political power of consumers."

By contrast, activists, such as Ralph Nader, have a narrower focus, tending to restrict consumerism to efforts directed toward government intervention on behalf of consumers. Thus, many activists would exclude from the consumer movement such consumer information and education organizations as Consumers Union.

Finally, moralists interpret consumerism as "an obsessive interest in goods, akin to materialism." When Pope John Paul II decried "consumerism," he was using the term in this pejorative sense (Mayer, 1989, p. 3). Our discussion will focus on the first two main interpretations.

Consumerism and the Price Mechanism

Consumerism merits the attention of economists because it responds to the failures and helps improve the functioning of the price mechanism that lies at the heart of a market economy.

Fundamentally, the price mechanism is a system of motivation and error correction. A price rise signals that the agent is performing well and should do more of it; a price fall, the opposite. The motivation for responding to the signal? Self-interest in the former of higher wages, profits, interest, rent. Over time, the market economy is a system of error correction. For a business, a continuing fall in demand signals that the firm is doing something wrong. Further errors will result in losses, then a loss of control (a takeover), and ultimately to the end of the firm. But the price signal is crude: It communicates failure, not its causes.

The organizations of the consumer movement improve the functioning of the price mechanism in several ways. First, they provide information that helps consumers make better choices—be they for basic necessities, stereo equipment, insurance choices, or consumer policy proposals. Consumer information organizations now have considerable clout. *Modern Maturity,* the magazine of the American Association of Retired Persons (AARP), has 22.4 million subscribers, and *Consumer Reports* has 4.7 million. There are "*Consumer Reports*" magazines in all the advanced countries. Their circulation is impressive with 5 percent of British and German households subscribing and 10 percent of the Dutch. Many follow their advice, some religiously.

Second, consumer organizations can voice discontent in a commanding way. Ralph Nader's *Unsafe at Any Speed* (1965) led to the demise of the Chevrolet Corvair and ultimately to seat belts in the 1970s and air bags in 1990. The Consumer's Guidance Society in India seeks to gain protection against food and drug adulteration. Similar efforts abound in many countries.

Third, within businesses, consumer affairs professionals seek to anticipate and avoid consumer problems and to respond quickly and effectively to problems that occur. The nature of the business response is indicated by the activities in which the consumer affairs professionals engage: complaint resolution (their dominant activity); consumer education; employee training; monitoring consumerism, their firm's response to consumerism, their firm's advertising and consumer policies. The informational feedback to firms from these activities clarifies the market signal and thus improves the functioning of markets.

The Causes of Consumerism

Consumerism can be more than just widely shared feelings of consumers that they are ill-served by their economy. In its most vigorous form, it produces outrage, sometimes stemming from the abuse of power by sellers, a situation that still holds in many developing countries. Often this discontent arises from market failures: (1) unsafe products; (2) dishonored promises, misrepresentation, deceptive advertising, fraud, failures of communication between buyer and seller; (3) performance failures ("it doesn't work" or doesn't work as it should, repairs that are done badly or not at all), delivery failures (not delivered, delivered late, not delivered as specified); (4) price gouging; (5) all these, amplified by the rising expectations of consumers. Even this list of causes is incomplete when we recognize the frustrations arising from the information problems consumers face in assessing quality, understanding complex products and services (e.g., life insurance), even in conceptualizing their problems as consumers. Finally, most consumers have yet to recognize and learn to deal with the near-zero correlation of price and quality in local consumer markets (Geistfeld, 1988).

Two national surveys—the 1976 Sentry Survey (Harris, 1977) and the 1982 ARCO Survey (Harris, 1983) have convincingly documented extensive consumer discontent and widespread support for the consumer movement. No recent surveys have been taken. But the similar results of the two surveys, one conducted at the peak of consumerist influence in the 1970s and the other in the first flush of enthusiasm for deregulation in the Reagan administration, suggest that consumerism rests on a robust foundation. Our knowledge and understanding of consumer grievances has been insightfully analyzed by Andreasen (1988).

It is difficult to organize consumers, because consumer interest is a "thin" interest, approved by many while primary to hardly anyone. It stands in strong contrast to the producer interest of, say, farmers, which is primary, commanding strong support. Even so, there is enough smoldering consumer discontent to ignite consumer activism. Key leadership in advancing the consumer interest and in articulating outrage has been provided by Consumers Union, Ralph Nader, and the Consumer Federation of America in the United States and by the International Organization of Consumers Unions worldwide.

History

Consumerism began earlier than one might expect. In the 1700s, common distress over the adulteration of food and drink led several European countries to take action against these practices. U.S. consumerism, according to Herrmann (1982), has come in three eras. The first occurred in the first decade of this century and was focused by such muckrakers as Upton Sinclair on unsanitary treatment of food and such non-consumer issues as child labor and sweatshops. This era culminated in the birth of two organizations—the National Consumers' League in 1898 and the Food and Drug Administration in 1906.

The second era occurred in the 1920s and 1930s. It saw the founding of two consumer product-testing organizations, Consumers' Research in 1927 followed in 1936 by its more influential successor, Consumers Union with its *Consumer Reports.* During the New Deal, the federal government first recognized the need for formal representation of consumers with the creation of a Consumer Advisory Committee for the National Recovery Administration.

The third era started with President John F. Kennedy's assertion of four consumer "rights" in 1962 (to safety, to be informed, to choose, to be heard) and was given thrust and leadership by Ralph Nader (*Unsafe at Any Speed,* 1965). This surge of consumer activism reached its peak in 1976 and came within an eyelash of creating a cabinet level "Department of Consumers" in the federal government. This third era brought with it two new consumer organizations outside government—the Consumer Federation of America and the Nader Network—important safety regulations (seat belts), new government regulatory agencies (Consumer Safety Product Commission, National Highway Safety Transportation Administration), a revitalized Federal Trade Commission, a flood of product liability lawsuits, and laws mandating information (truth-in-lending, labeling etc.). At the same time, Consumers Union, the oldest and most influential consumer organization, greatly increased its influence and scope.

The Organizations of the Consumer Movement

Over six decades Consumers Union (CU) has been the largest and most influential consumer organization. CU is a consumer interest conglomerate. Its chief activity is the dissemination of quality ratings of nationally distributed products through *Consumer Reports.* The revenues from *Consumer Reports* finance CU's other activities. Besides *Consumer Reports,* CU publishes *Zillions* for children, the *CR Travel Letter* and *CR Health Letter,* and a broad array of how-to books; it undertakes lobbying and litigation from offices in Washington, San Francisco, and Austin; it offers syndicated news to newspapers, radio, and television. The number of subscribers of *Consumer Reports* mirrors the growth of consumerism: 1937—0.04 million; 1947—0.18; 1957—0.78; 1967—1.10; 1977—1.80; 1987—2.80; 1992—4.80.

A major contribution by CU to the consumer movement has been the organizations it has helped spawn. The American Council on Consumer Interests, Consumer Federation of America, the International Organization of Consumer Unions, and Consumers' Association (the Consumers Union of the United Kingdom) were all helped into being by CU. In 1957 CA of the United Kingdom and the Association des Consommateurs of Belgium became the first foreign consumer product-testing organizations; now all 40 industrially advanced countries have such CUs, all in a sense copies of the U.S. CU.

The American Council on Consumer Interests is a professional organization for consumer economists/educators. It publishes the *Journal of Consumer Affairs* and *Advancing the Consumer Interest.*

To the extent that it is a consumer organization, the American Association of Retired Persons is a special interest consumer organization, catering to older people, generously defined as 50 or older. Through its magazine *Modern Maturity* (circulation: 22.4 million), AARP dispenses advice and information to and organizes discounts for older consumers. In addition, it seeks to influence government policy affecting older persons.

The business response to consumerism was institutionalized in the 1970s in the most progressive businesses by the designation of company directors or vice presidents of consumer affairs. Their primary function has been to deal effectively with consumer complaints and positively with customers and the consumer movement. Their professional organization, the Society for Consumer Affairs Professionals in Business, is a natural successor to that earlier, still extant institution, the Better Business Bureaus (1912).

The advocacy organizations, the Consumer Federation of America and the Nader Network, came into being in the late 1960s to articulate consumer discontent and to press aggressively for corrective measures, primarily by the federal government. These organizations call attention to abuses of consumers, engage in issue-oriented research, formulate and promulgate consumer policies through lobbying, litigation, publications, news generation, media appearances. Without the advocacy organizations, there would have been no Consumer Product Safety Commission, no National Highway Traffic Safety Administration, no revitalized Federal Trade Commission. It is to the advocacy organizations that we owe seat belts, air bags, other safety measures, and information disclosure measures such as the Truth-in-Lending legislation.

The regulatory agencies of the federal government which are part of the consumer movement are the Food and Drug Administration, Federal Trade Commission, Office of Consumer Affairs, and Consumer Products Safety Commission. These agencies were characterized by an interventionalist ardor in the 1970s, particularly during the Carter administration, and the dampening of this ardor during the Reagan years.

The nongovernment consumer organizations registered remarkable growth during the third era of consumerism, in contrast to the relative nongrowth of the regulatory organizations over the entire 1970 to 1990 period. In addition to growth, the nongovernment consumer organizations experienced an increased professionalization of their staffs, a stabilization and broadening of their financial support, an increasing breadth of interests, activities, and influence. The consumer movement has not been confined to the United States. The umbrella organization of the world consumer movement, the International Organization of Consumers Unions founded in 1960, now has 180 member organizations in 64 countries.

Consumerism and Economics

Despite unanimous acceptance of Adam Smith's dictum that "consumption is the end purpose of all production," mainstream economics has taken little note of consumerism and its highly visible institutions. The few exceptions would include a new literature on the economics of information, informationally imperfect markets, issues of regulation and deregulation, the economics of safety.

More or less in step with the growth of consumerism has developed a new, applied discipline, consumer economics. Now doctoral, master's, and undergraduate programs in consumer economics (or family economics, family resource management, consumer studies, consumer affairs) are offered in a number of universities, often in former colleges of home economics. Consumer economics now has its own professional association, the American Council on Consumer Interests and its own journals—the *Journal of Consumer Affairs, Journal of Consumer Policy* (European), *Journal of Consumer Research* (shared with marketing), *Advancing the Consumer Interest* (consumer education), *Journal of Home Economics and Consumer Studies* (British), *Consumer Review* (British). Will consumer economics grow? We do not know. Its support is uncertain because, unlike colleges of agriculture or business schools, it lacks a highly focused, strongly supportive constituency. See Maynes 1988 and Mayer 1991 for the topics that concern contemporary consumer economists.

The Future of Consumerism

Will consumerism last? Will it grow? Most assuredly yes. Consumerism will inexorably gain in resources, influence, and visibility. Periodically, it will be given a new burst of life by a new consumer problem or disaster. We do not know whether it will be discontent with the delivery of health care, the issue of the privacy of consumer records, concern about the safety and environmental consequences of some product or service, or frustration stemming from an inability to obtain and use relevant consumer information. But we can be confident that from time to time consumer discontent will focus on some problem or concern. Periodically, these new concerns will restart the growth of consumerism and consumer organizations.

We cannot be sure precisely what new consumer organizations will arise. Who in 1970 would have foreseen AARP as the largest consumer organization? Who in 1970 anticipated the Society of Consumer Affairs Professionals in Business? Who could imagine that by 1992 IOCU would have full members in 64 different countries plus vigorous associate members emerging in nearly every country in Eastern Europe? Thus it seems certain that some new consumer organizations will arise to deal with some newly discovered consumer needs.

References

Andreasen, Alan R., "Consumer Complaints and Redress: What We Know, What We Don't Know," in E. Scott Maynes, ed., *The Frontier of Research in the Consumer Interest,* American Council on Consumer Interests, Columbia, Mo. 1988, pp. 675–722; Brobeck, Stephen J., *The Modern Consumer Movement, References and Resources,* G. K. Hall, Boston, 1990; Geistfeld, Loren V., pp. 143–172, in Maynes, op. cit.; Louis Harris and Associates, *Consumerism at the Crossroads: A National Opinion Research Survey of Public, Activist, Business, and Regulator Attitudes toward the Consumer Movement,* Sentry Insurance Company, Boston, 1977; Louis Harris and Associates, *Consumerism in the Eighties,* Atlantic Richfield, Los Angeles, 1983; Herrmann, Robert O., "The Consumer Movement in Historical Perspective," in David A. Aaker and George S. Day (eds.), *Consumerism: Search for the Consumer Interest* (4th ed.), Free Press, New York, 1982, pp. 23–32; Mayer, Robert N., *The Consumer Movement, Guardians of the Marketplace,* G. K. Hall, Boston, 1989; Mayer, Robert N. (ed.), *Enhancing Consumer Choice,* American Council on Consumer Interests, Columbia, Mo., 1991; Maynes, E. Scott, "Consumerism: Origin and Research Implications," in Eleanor B. Sheldon (ed.), *Family Economic Behavior: Problems and Prospects,* Lippincott, Philadelphia, 1973, pp. 270–294; Maynes, E. Scott, (ed.), *The Frontier of Research in the Consumer Interest,* American Council on Consumer Interests, Columbia, Mo., 1988; Nader, Ralph, *Unsafe at Any Speed,* Simon & Schuster, New York, 1965.

(*See also* Government regulation of business; Monopoly and oligopoly)

E. Scott Maynes

Consumers' surplus

Consumers' surplus was introduced into economics by Alfred Marshall, although the use of the concept goes back at least to the French economist Dupuit writing in the first half of the nineteenth century. Current evaluation to the usefulness of the concept is subject to much controversy: Two Nobel Prize winners in economics disagree fundamentally about the utility of the concept; John Hicks saw great use for the concept as a cornerstone of welfare economics, whereas Paul Samuelson believes that we may discard the concept without loss. There is also the question of whether we can talk of *consumers'* surplus or only of *consumer's* surplus—whether we can use the concept for a whole group of consumers of a product or only for an individual household.

Demand and Demand Curve

The meaning and use of consumer's surplus may be seen from the following example. Suppose that it is agreed that a certain commodity should be produced if the benefits exceed the provision costs. The problem is that the measurement of benefits would seem to be practically an impossible task. Economists, however, thought that they had found a simple way to estimate consumer benefits. The method involves the concepts of demand and the demand curve.

Imagine a household's demand per week for a particular commodity x as a function of the price per unit of that commodity. If all other influences on the demand for the commodity are constant, the relationship between the price of x and the quantity of x demanded per week will be inverse. Specifically let it be as follows:

Price of x	Quantity of x demanded per week
$1.00	0
0.90	1
0.80	2
0.70	3
0.60	4
0.50	5
0.40	6
0.30	7
0.20	8
0.10	9
0	10

If the price is 40 cents per unit, the household purchases 6 units and spends $2.40. Is the household in fact prepared to pay more than $2.40 for six units? According to the demand schedule, the answer is yes! The household is prepared to pay 90 cents for one unit, 80 cents for the second unit, and so on; thus it follows that for 6 units the household will pay a maximum of $3.90, i.e., $1.50 more than it actually has to pay. It is this difference between the amount actually paid and the maximum that would be offered that Marshall called consumer's surplus.

We are sometimes concerned with a change that alters the price of a product, that is, not with the total benefits derived from the existence of a particular commodity but with the change in benefit due to a change in the price of the commodity. Equally, the concept of consumer's surplus may be applied to such changes. In terms of a demand curve, consumer's surplus may be restated as follows: The benefit derived from the provision of a commodity or service at a particular price is the area under the demand curve at that price, and the consumer's surplus is that benefit minus the sum of money the consumer actually pays; the change in benefit is the change in the area due to a price change; and the change in consumer surplus is the change in benefit minus the change in the money sum paid.

Suppose we were to aggregate all individual demand curves for a commodity to obtain the market demand curve; could we also aggregate the consumer's surpluses to get consumers' surplus? If we could, we have a powerful way of estimating consumer benefits from, say, an innovation that will lower the price of a good. All that appears to be required is the statistical estimation of demand functions. Suppose, for example, that an authority is contemplating building a river bridge that will be free to users; then its estimate of consumer benefit from the bridge will be the area under the demand curve, and this can be compared with the cost.

Consumers' surplus, therefore, would appear to be a powerful tool in the evaluation of proposed public projects, and it is indeed regarded by some commentators as a central tool in cost-benefit analysis.

Doubts about Use and Validity of Consumers' Surplus

Other economists are much more doubtful about the use and validity of the concept. The main concern is that once the assumptions under which Marshall originally drew up his measure of consumer's or consumers' surplus are relaxed, the area under the demand curve will not be an accurate measure of benefits. There are two main reasons for this skepticism.

First, changes in the price of the good will alter real income, the extent to which will depend on the proportion of total expenditure that is spent on the good, and this in turn will shift the original demand curve. Thus one of the initial assumptions required to measure consumers' surplus is violated. Using a method developed by Slutsky, whereby the effects of a price change are broken down into income and substitution effects, it can be shown that there are several measures of consumers' surplus and they will coincide only under very restrictive conditions.

Second, there is the problem of the interrelationships between the demand for different commodities. Suppose the price of x falls and more money is now spent on the commodity; the extra purchases result in an increase in consumers' surplus. But the net benefit will be less because there will have been a reduction in the purchases of other goods, and this will lower the sums of consumers' surplus arising from the purchase of them.

Whether the concept of consumers' surplus will continue to be used in economic inquiry remains to be seen. It is certainly an issue that continues to be strongly debated.

References

Marshall, A., in C.W. Guillebaud (ed.), *Principles of Economics* (9th ed.), Macmillan, New York, 1961, Book III, chap. 6; Pearce, D. W., *Cost-Benefit Analysis* (2d ed.), St. Martin, New York, 1983, chap. 3; Varian, H. R., *Intermediate Microeconomics* (2d ed.), Norton, New York, 1990, chap. 15.

(*See also* Cost-benefit analysis; Demand; Marshallian economics; Normative economics; Welfare economics)

Bernard A. Corry

Consumption function

The consumption function relates total consumption to the level of income or wealth and perhaps other variables. Consumption functions are sometimes defined for individual households, but their major role is determining total national consumption in a macroeconomic model.

One characteristic of the consumption function, the marginal propensity to consume (MPC), is an important determinant of the stability of the economy in simple models of the multiplier type. The MPC measures the responsiveness of consumption to assumed changes in income and is the ratio of the change in consumption to the change in income, other things being equal. In general, the smaller the MPC, the more stable is the economy with respect to changes in government spending, investment, net exports, or money.

Introduced by Keynes

The consumption function was introduced by John Maynard Keynes (1936) as a major element in his model of income determination. Although Keynes catalogued many of the factors discussed below, he argued that consumption depends mainly on the total net income of consumers and that the MPC would be less than the ratio of consumption to income (the average propensity to consume, or APC). The latter assertion was justified by reference to the decreased marginal utility of current consumption at higher levels of income.

The simple Keynesian consumption function can be expressed as

$$c = a + by$$

where c is consumption, b the MPC, and y net income. If a is greater than zero, the APC exceeds the MPC (by a/y). In Keynesian analysis, consumption and net income are measured in real (deflated) terms. This consumption function was widely used until the early 1950s, when more data and improved statistical techniques demonstrated its inadequacy.

Optimizing Hypothesis

A number of hypotheses were proposed as alternatives to the Keynesian absolute income hypothesis, but only variants of the optimizing hypothesis have withstood the test of time. The optimizing hypothesis states that current consumption will be determined as part of an optimal lifetime allocation of current and future income to current and future consumption and bequests. An increase in current or future income increases the total wealth to be allocated and so generally increases current and future consumption and bequests. Thus, factors which cause a persistent or permanent increase in income would have a much greater effect on wealth and current consumption than a temporary or transitory increase in income. In this way, the optimizing hypothesis suggests that the short-period changes in current net income considered by Keynes should have relatively small effects on consumption; that is, the MPC for transitory variations in income is small.

If income were permanently increased by some factor, then wealth would rise proportionately. The simplest assumption would be that this increase in wealth would be allocated proportionally among current and future consumption and bequests. Whether this in fact happens in the optimizing model depends on whether the ratios of marginal utilities of current and future consumption and bequests are unchanged as their levels are increased proportionally. If they are, an increase in wealth will result in a proportional increase in current consumption. Keynes's belief that consumption would fall relative to income as wealth increased was based on looking at only the falling marginal utility of current consumption. But the marginal utility of future consumption and bequests also falls as wealth increases, and a rational plan compares the marginal utility of consumption given up now with the marginal utility of future consumption or bequests obtained. No general theoretical statement can be made as to whether current consumption rises more or less than in proportion to wealth. Since the empirical data dating from the 1800s reveal a roughly constant APC for the United States, proportionality of consumption and wealth is widely used as a working hypothesis.

Permanent Income and Life-Cycle Hypotheses

Three forms of the optimizing hypothesis are widely used: the permanent income hypothesis; the life-cycle hypothesis; and the rational expectations hypothesis. Although they are equivalent in their most general forms, different simplifying assumptions have been used in empirical work.

The permanent income hypothesis of Milton Friedman (1957) attempts to divide current net income into two components termed "permanent income" and "transitory income." Permanent income is real perpetuity yield from total current wealth. On the assumptions that there is a constant long-term real interest rate and that consumption is proportional to wealth, consumption is a constant fraction of permanent income, and permanent income is that interest rate times wealth. Wealth increases over time owing to normal saving from permanent income plus the (positive or negative) windfall effect of transitory income. Transitory fluctuations in income thus have relatively small effects on permanent income and consumption.

The life-cycle hypothesis of Franco Modigliani and Richard Brumberg (1954) has made use of direct estimates of nonhuman wealth and substitutes for human wealth based on variables such as current labor income and this income times the unemployment rate. The life-cycle approach has been most popular in analyzing survey data on individual households in which age, marital status, and other demographic variables play an important role.

It has been usual in applications of the life-cycle approach to assume that bequests are zero. Although all income is consumed over an individual's life, aggregate saving results in a growing economy, because youthful savers are richer and more numerous than retired savers. Recent evidence indicates that bequests are a much larger source of aggregate saving in the United States. As with retirement saving, bequests are a source of aggregate saving only in a growing economy so that individuals accumulate to leave a larger estate than they inherit. The assets which are eventually bequeathed serve as a general reserve during life, so precautionary motives as well as concern for heirs explain their size.

Robert Hall (1978) nearly turned the permanent income hypothesis around by arguing that current consumption is proportional to current permanent income, so changes in consumption can occur only if there are changes in permanent income. Leaving aside planned changes in permanent income and consumption due to planned saving, Hall emphasized that variability in consumption growth must reflect unexpected changes in wealth over the period of concern. Although the hypothesis proved analytically appealing, the rational expectations hypothesis has been less successful empirically. (See, e.g., Campbell 1982.) This difficulty is probably explained by a more general difficulty in applying the basic optimizing hypothesis to explaining actual consumer expenditures over any given period.

In principle, the optimizing hypothesis is strictly applicable only to the consumption of service flows, that is, to purchases of nondurable goods and services plus the rental value (not purchases) of durable and semidurable goods and services. This differs from Keynes's consumption concept (consumer expenditures for all goods and services) which is of interest in macroeconomic models. The National Income and Product Accounts (NIPA) reflect Keynes's concept, and thus changes in NIPA consumption reflect variations in household investment in durable and semidurable goods as well as changes in permanent income. The intractability of this problem may explain the limited success in practical application of the rational expectations version of the permanent income hypothesis.

The distinction between consumption and consumer expenditures is a problem of long standing. Some earlier analysts have applied permanent income and life-cycle models of consumption of service flows directly to consumer expenditures data. The results can be characterized as inconsistent and misleading. Others (including Friedman, Modigliani, and their associates) have applied the optimizing models to data on consumption flows. Other models are used to explain consumer expenditures on durable goods. Accounting identities are then used to derive implied estimates of total consumer expenditures. Michael Darby (1977–1978) combined the consumption flows and durable goods models into a single consumer expenditure function. Because consumer durable goods purchases are quite responsive to transitory income, the estimated value of the MPC is substantial—about 0.4 or 0.5. This MPC estimate is rather less than indicated initially by the Keynesian absolute income hypothesis but is much greater than would be supposed from the effect on consumption flows alone.

Controversy

A source of some controversy has been which concept of net income to use. It was once popular to use only cash receipts of households as measured by disposable personal income. Much recent work has shown that undistributed corporate profits (or business saving) seems to be treated by households in large part as income. Other things being equal, higher business saving increases consumer expenditures and reduces personal saving. Also, some increases in income are supposed to be intermediate between temporary and permanent, and others, such as a temporary tax decrease to be paid for by a future tax increase, leave wealth unchanged. Various methods have been proposed to improve wealth estimates by taking account of these differences, but none has been generally accepted. In most aggregate work, permanent income or life-cycle measures are used for total wealth.

The major unresolved issue is the empirical importance of the real balance effect. The real balance effect refers to higher levels of real money balances causing higher consumer expenditures for given values of other variables. Some economists have argued that this would occur because money (at least government-issued money) is a component of wealth missed in permanent income and other measures of wealth. Others have explained the real balance effect in terms of substitution from money to consumers' durable goods during the adjustment to an unexpected change in the money supply. Traditional Keynesian economists have been skeptical of both views. This is a topic requiring substantially more empirical research.

In sum, the consumption function has developed from little more than a rule of thumb to a sophisticated empirical model of aggregate consumer expenditures.

References

Campbell, John Y., "Does Saving Anticipate Declining Labor Income?" *Econometrica,* vol. 55, November 1987, pp. 1249–1274; Darby, Michael R., "The Consumer Expenditure Function," *Exploration in Economic Research,* no. 4, Winter–Spring 1977–1978, pp. 645–674; Friedman, Milton, *A Theory of the Consumption Function,* Princeton University Press, Princeton, N.J., 1957; Hall, Robert E., "Stochastic Implications of the Life Cycle-Permanent Income Hypothesis: Theory and Evidence," *Journal of Political Economy,* vol. 86, April 1978; Keynes, John Maynard, *The General Theory of Employment, Interest, and Money,* Harcourt, Brace, New York, 1936; Modigliani, Franco, and Richard Brumberg, "Utility Analysis and the Consumption Function: An Interpretation of Cross-Section Data," in K. E. Kurihara (ed.), *Post-Keynesian Economics,* Rutgers University, New Brunswick, N.J., 1954.

(*See also* Consumer theory; Investment function; Keynesian economics; Microeconomics; Permanent income hypothesis; Real balance effect theory)

Michael R. Darby

Contestable markets

A market is defined to be *perfectly contestable* if exit from it and entry into it are perfectly free. Both of these conditions will be satisfied if entry does not require any sunk investments, because then the entrant can, if it wishes, leave with all its outlays recouped, and its entry decision will have cost it nothing. The concept also requires that the entrant be able to open for business instantly, before incumbent rivals can undertake strategic retaliation. This is, of course, not possible literally. But it can be achieved through quickly signed contracts between the entrant and the incumbents' customers, specifying prices and other terms for the future transactions that the entrant will carry out.

A perfectly contestable market is a theoretical construct that is a generalization of the concept of perfect competition, since it is defined by the free entry and exit feature of perfect competition but adopts none of the other assumptions of the latter. The two concepts have similar purposes: to facilitate theoretical analysis and to guide the design of policy related to the economic behavior of business firms and industries.

The assumption that a market is either perfectly competitive or perfectly contestable eliminates a number of analytic difficulties, because in either case the firm becomes a "price taker" (i.e., forced to accept the price dictated by the market), thus precluding both strategic interdependence among the pricing decisions of rival enterprises as well as the need to incorporate a demand function for the firm into any study of the company's decisions. Where government intervention is justified, both perfect competition and perfect contestability are useful theoretical archetypes, serving as the ideal models of behavior which regulatory policy may force firms to emulate. However, perfect competition is usable as a guide only where scale economies are absent, so that a large number of rival firms can survive and prosper. Contestability can encompass a broader range of circumstances, notably markets containing only a few large firms—the only case where, normally, government intervention is considered appropriate. Not that such markets are usually perfectly contestable, or even approximately so. Rather, only in markets where competition is impotent is it reasonable for government to intervene, using the contestable market model as its guide.

The theory of perfect contestability goes back to the mid-1970s and is the work of Robert Willig, John Panzar, Elizabeth Bailey, William Baumol, Dietrich Fischer, Thijs ten Raa, and others. But its origins are much earlier, notably in Joe S. Bain's writings, shortly after World War II, on the role of entry.

Perfect Contestability and the Public Welfare

The reason perfect contestability can serve as a model of socially desirable firm behavior is that, except in the case of pure monopoly, such a market can be shown, in equilibrium, to enjoy all the welfare benefits usually associated with perfect competition. Even a contestable pure monopoly can be shown to have an incentive to behave in a manner compatible with the public interest and to be prevented from most forms of monopolistic misbehavior. Specifically, perfect contestability: (1) precludes excess profits, that is, total revenues which exceed total costs (including the current competitive cost of capital); (2) rules out any form of inefficiency, including sheer waste, misallocation of resources, or poor organization of the industry (for example, firms inefficiently large or small); (3) except in the case of pure monopoly, requires the price of each product to equal its marginal cost—just as the goal of Pareto optimality calls for; and, finally, (4) precludes cross-subsidy in multiproduct firms (i.e., losses on some products made up by overcharges on other products)—a matter of great concern to government regulators.

One can illustrate the logic that leads to these conclusions with the case in which an incumbent firm earns excess profits. In this circumstance an entrant can make a profit by signing contracts with the incumbent's customers which cut prices below their current excess levels. Thus, punishment for excess profits will be meted out by entrants, who can make money by luring away customers of the overcompensated firm. Exactly the same logic shows why inefficiency cannot last in a perfectly contestable market, because any excess costs enable efficient entrants to undercut the wasteful incumbents. Similarly, cross-subsidy is prevented by the preclusion of excess profits on any product or group of products, because if the firm earns no excess profits anywhere, it would go bankrupt if it were to sell any of its products at prices that do not cover its costs. All these intuitive arguments have also been carried out in rigorous terms, but the substance of the proofs is the same as that just described. See Baumol, Panzar and Willig (1988, chap. 12), where the rather more difficult proof of the marginal-cost-pricing theorem is examined in detail.

In short, it follows from this analysis that a contestable market offers the (theoretical) benefits that perfect competition provides, although it is applicable to a far greater range of circumstances. Thus, the contestable market has all the qualifications for an ideal that one can rationally seek to induce real firms to approximate in their behavior.

Some Unsettled Issues

Despite some heated debate soon after the appearance of contestability theory, the unsettled issues seemed to narrow rather quickly. Moreover, most of the participants in the debate apparently agree upon the identity of the issues and the fact that they are not yet resolved.

The first unresolved issue is whether, in reality, few or many markets approximate perfect contestability; if some do, do they approximate it very closely? There seems some reason to believe that the truck and barge transport industries come fairly close, although passenger aviation is less close than it had been believed to be soon after deregulation, and heavy industries with large sunk investments have few, if any, of the required attributes of perfect contestability. However, no systematic study of industries from this point of view has so far been carried out.

The second unsettled issue is the consequence of mild departures from the requirements of perfect contestability. Do even small deviations weaken the market's control of monopoly power drastically, or does a reasonably close approximation to contestability ensure good market performance? These important unresolved questions indicate that the subject is still a promising research arena.

Applications

In economic theory the concept of contestable market has yielded a variety of results. It has been used in international trade analysis and in the study of firm and industry equilibria, and it has opened up the analysis of the determination of industry structure. This last refers primarily to the influences that determine whether an industry will turn out to be a monopoly, an oligopoly, perfectly competitive, or of some other variety.

In a perfectly contestable market, that issue can be decided directly. Because any of the possible market forms may or may not be contestable (depending on ease of entry), it is possible to construct a model of perfect contestability in which it has not been assumed in advance that the industry is, say, an oligopoly. Once such a model has been built, one can examine which of the forms the forces of the market dictate. How those forces will make their decision and impose it upon the industry follows from the theorem that, in perfectly contestable equilibrium, production will always be carried out at minimum cost. Thus, depending on the technology of the industry, the number of firms needed to produce the industry's products at a minimum cost can be determined. The calculation is sometimes complex, but in principle it can always be carried out. This approach seems to have elicited a considerable number of studies of particular industries which have provided much illumination on their cost structure and the ways in which it affects their number of firms.

Contestable market theory continues to be used in the design of policy for economic regulation. Using the criterion proposed earlier—that the public interest role of economic regulation is to serve as a substitute for the forces of competition—the theory has been employed to derive rules for pricing, economic depreciation, valuation of invested assets, investment policy, and other related issues that have long been subjects of regulatory attention. These rules are designed to prevent business managements from adopting decisions that effective competition would have prevented. But, beyond this, these rules have undertaken to preserve maximum scope for the freedom of decision making that allows the business firm to respond quickly and effectively to changing market conditions, as is necessary for the free-market system to yield its vaunted efficiency and productivity results. Already, the contestable market principles have profoundly affected the regulation of railroads and telephones in the United States, and they are making inroads in the regulation of pipelines. The principles have also influenced the pattern of telecommunications regulation in the United Kingdom.

This type of application is likely to receive renewed attention with the surge of privatization of industry in Eastern Europe, Latin America, and elsewhere, because a number of the newly private firms are likely not to be constrained effectively by the forces of competition, at least initially, and regulation is likely to follow. If the acts of privatization are to achieve their purpose by substituting the market mechanism for the central planner, the market will have to be allowed to do its work. But regulation will be compatible with that goal only if the regulatory rules adopted replicate the workings of the market, rather than undermine them, and that is precisely what the contestable market model is designed to do.

References

Bailey, Elizabeth E., and Ann F. Friedlaender, "Market Structure and Multiproduct Industries," *Journal of Economic Literature,* vol. 20, September 1982, pp. 1024–1048; Bain, Joe S., *Barriers to New Competition,* Harvard University, Cambridge, Mass., 1956; Baumol, William J., John C. Panzar, and Robert D. Willig, *Contestable Markets and the Theory of Industry Structure,* (rev. ed.), Harcourt Brace Jovanovich, San Diego, 1988; Spence, A. Michael, "Contestable Markets and the Theory of Industry Structure: A Review Article," *Journal of Economic Literature,* vol. 21, 1983, pp. 981–990.

(*See also* Competition; Monopoly and oligopoly)

William J. Baumol

Convertible debentures (*see* Bond)

Corporate income taxation (*see* Taxation, an overview)

Corporate liquidity (*see* Liquidity, corporate)

Corporate restructuring (*see* Mergers, takeovers, and corporate restructuring)

Correspondence principle (*see* Static analysis)

Cost-benefit analysis

Cost-benefit analysis is a generic term applied to any systematic, quantitative appraisal of a public sector project to determine whether or to what extent that project is worthwhile. In this context, a "project" may range from conventional public investments in flood control or transportation through social programs in the health or education areas to the passage of public laws or regulations. Essentially, a cost-benefit analysis attempts to determine whether the benefits of a public project justify the costs. Ordinarily, cost-benefit studies are prospective—evaluating proposed projects—although there are also retrospective studies. In all cases, the hallmark of a cost-benefit analysis is the systematic comparison of alternative courses of action. Cost-benefit analyses are best considered aids to decision makers rather than directives. Cost-benefit analysis is sometimes described as applied welfare economics and draws much of its theoretical basis from that discipline.

Five Steps in a Cost-Benefit Analysis

There are five steps in the performance of a cost-benefit analysis.

Identification of Effects. First, all the effects of the project are identified. Typically, such effects might include changes in output levels, prices, income distribution, environmental parameters, and social parameters. The effects are identified both for the present and for all relevant future periods. This involves forecasting trends and events about which little may be known with certainty. The key in this step is estimating as accurately as possible what difference the project will make.

Quantification of Effects. The second step is the development of quantitative estimates, in physical units, of the effects identified in the first step. For example, changes in output of a certain good might be specified as so many tons per year for each year of the project. Some effects, such as contributions of a project to social harmony, democracy, aesthetics, or culture, may be difficult to quantify. Such intangible effects, although meriting description within the cost-benefit study, often remain outside the quantitative aspects of the study.

Monetary Quantification. The third step is the valuation, or monetary quantification, of the effects identified in the first step and physically quantified in the second. For example, for an increase in output of so many tons per year of some good, a monetary value for that change in output is developed. The rule governing the determination of monetary values is social willingness to pay, which refers to the valuation of items according to what society, if perfectly informed, would be willing to pay to gain a benefit or avoid a cost. Under certain conditions market prices reflect social willingness to pay, and these prices can be used to accomplish this step of the study. Under other conditions, principally those involving situations in which the real world differs markedly from the model of perfect competition, market prices either do not exist or are not adequate measures of social willingness to pay. Cases involving public goods or externalities typify such situations. In these cases, the monetary values often used are shadow prices, that is, estimated prices of social willingness to pay. Effects amenable to physical quantification, but which are difficult to translate into monetary terms (such as lost lives or cases of cancer), are often called incommensurables.

Aggregation. The fourth step is aggregation of all effects within each time period and then across all time periods. The purpose of aggregation is to reduce costs and benefits over the span of the project to a single number which captures the overall worth of the project. Of the many approaches to aggregation, the three most popular involve the calculation of the project's internal rate of return, its benefit-cost ratio, and its net present value. Each of these measures has advantages and disadvantages, although among the three the net present value is usually the preferred approach. All reasonable aggregation schemes involve discounting future costs and benefits, that is, placing less weight on an effect the further into the future it is expected to occur. Discounting is accomplished by employing a discount rate, and assigning weights to time periods by the formula

$$w_t = 1/(1 + d)^t$$

where t is the index of time periods (usually in years), d is the discount rate, and w_t the weight assigned to all effects in period t. By convention the current time period is designated as $t = 0$, so its weight w_o equals 1. All future years have weights less than 1, declining from 1, and eventually nearing 0 as t becomes large. For example, the weight for effects expected 20 years from now using a discount rate of 10 percent is roughly 0.15. This means a $100 benefit 20 years from now would be counted as having the same value as a $15 benefit this year. Experience has shown that the results of cost-benefit studies tend to be quite sensitive to the discount rate employed. Economists continue to debate the proper choice of a discount rate for cost-benefit studies.

Sensitivity Analysis. The final step is sensitivity analysis, which involves calculations to determine how sensitive the results of the study are to changes in the values of the variables and parameters used in the study, and to changes in the probability of their occurrence. This provides an indication of the validity of any conclusions and allows (through tabular and/or graphic displays, and recently through interactive computer models) the decision maker to insert chosen parameter values and to determine how the results of the study would thereby change.

History and Importance

The inception of cost-benefit analysis occurred in 1844 with the publication of an essay, "On the Measurement of the Utility of Public Works," by Jules Dupuit, a French engineer. Dupuit developed the concept of consumers' surplus, an idea which today is a cornerstone of cost-benefit analysis. However, Dupuit's ideas lay dormant until the passage of the U.S. Flood Control Act of 1936, which decreed that flood control projects should pass the test that "the benefits to whomsoever they may accrue are in excess of the estimated costs." This act stimulated work in both the theory and application of cost-benefit analysis, first only in the area of water resources, but, by the 1950s, in defense analysis, and, since the 1960s, in virtually all areas of public expenditure. Today, cost-benefit analyses are routinely carried out throughout the federal bureaucracy and sometimes at the state and local levels as well. Such studies often play a prominent role in the debates over public projects, but because such project decisions are made in the political arena, it is difficult to establish the degree to which the results of cost-benefit studies actually influence those final decisions. Certainly, there are many examples of public decisions running counter to the results of cost-benefit studies.

International Considerations

Cost-benefit analysis has found acceptance outside the United States, both in advanced and lesser-developed countries. In particular, Great Britain has produced many significant contributions to the field. Under the leadership of international organizations such as the United Nations and the Inter-American Development Bank, cost-benefit analysis is being brought to bear on the development programs of the Third World. In these applications, cost-benefit analysis faces more than its usual complement of difficulties due to the multiple (often conflicting) objectives and chronic disequilibrium conditions of the host countries.

Relation to Other Terms

The field of project appraisal abounds with terms similar in appearance or intent to cost-benefit analysis. Capital-budgeting analysis is the private sector equivalent of cost-benefit analysis. It is project appraisal from the firm's point of view. Cost-effectiveness analysis is a special case of cost-benefit analysis in which, among the alternatives under consideration, either the cost of each or the benefit of each is the same, and the purpose of the study is to identify the alternative with the greatest effectiveness (benefit) or the least cost. Social impact assessment, economic impact assessment, environmental impact assessment, and technology assessment can all be considered partial cost-benefit analyses in the sense that each typically considers only a subset of the whole range of project effects and typically progresses only through the second step (and perhaps partially into the third step) of the five steps described above.

Positive and Negative Views

Criticisms of the field are both general and specific. One general criticism is that cost-benefit analysis attempts to reduce everything to the common denominator of money and that this is simply not possible. Another general criticism is that public project decisions are, and should be, political decisions, and that economic substitutes for the political process are insidious. Another such criticism is that cost-benefit analysis feigns an objectivity it indeed lacks, and that cost-benefit results are hopelessly biased by the subjective attitudes of those performing the study. Criticisms often revolve around effects allegedly erroneously included or excluded as benefits or costs, as valuation procedures, or as aggregation procedures.

Even proponents of cost-benefit analysis admit some criticisms are justified. They point, however, to the continuing evolution of cost-benefit analysis: Over time researchers and practitioners have worked to eliminate glaring deficiencies. For example, although in earlier years the only project effects included in cost-benefit studies were those affecting gross national product, today many studies attempt to treat environmental and social factors, regional factors, and income redistribution factors as well. But the real justification advanced by proponents is summed up by their query, "What is the alternative?" At the very least, cost-benefit analysis forces assumptions, projections, estimates, and reasoning to be laid open to scrutiny. It is, in this sense, a scientific procedure.

References

Dasgupta, P., A. Sen, and S. Marglin, *UNIDO Guidelines for Project Evaluation,* United Nations, New York, 1972; Gramlich, E. M., *A Guide to Benefit-Cost Analysis,* Prentice-Hall, Englewood Cliffs, N.J., 1990; Harberger, Arnold (ed.), *Cost-Benefit and Policy Analysis,* vols. 1–4, Aldine, Chicago, 1972–1975; Little, I. M. D., and J. Mirrlees, *Project Appraisal and Planning for Developing Countries,* Basic Books, New York, 1974; Mishan, E. J., *Cost Benefit Analysis,* Praeger, New York, 1976; Pearce, Cost-Benefit Analysis, 2d ed., St. Martin's Press, New York, 1983; Sassone, P. G., and W. A. Schaffer, *Cost-Benefit Analysis: A Handbook,* Academic Press, New York, 1978; Stiglitz, J., *Economics of the Public Sector,* 2d ed., Norton, New York, 1988.

(*See also* Consumers' surplus; Normative economics; Utility; Welfare economics)

Peter G. Sassone

Cost of living

The cost of living is a term loosely used to refer to the cost of purchasing a basket of consumer goods at today's prices compared with what the same basket would have cost in some previous or base period. In its general usage, the term is viewed as synonymous with the consumer price index (CPI). However, in a more technical sense, an index of the cost of living is quite different from that of consumer prices. When reference is made to such a cost-of-living index as distinct from a consumer price index, that distinction is generally heralded by the use of the phrase "true cost-of-living index."

A True Cost-of-Living Index

A true cost-of-living index introduces the notion that there may be more than one bundle of goods or market basket that affords the consumer a given level of satisfaction. Thus, a consumer may consider that he or she is equally well off when consuming 6 pounds of beef and 3 pounds of pork as when consuming 3 pounds of beef and 8 pounds of pork. Note that the foregoing example of equivalence is predicated on a 50 percent reduction in beef consumption and a greater than 50 percent increase in pork consumption to achieve equivalence. The inference is that, on balance, consumers prefer beef to pork. But, some circumstances, i.e., those in which the consumer gets more than 1 pound of pork for each pound of beef given up, yield equivalent satisfaction.

In fact, if the consumer viewed beef and pork as yielding equivalent satisfaction, pound for pound, then one would expect that a 50 percent reduction in beef would be offset by a 50 percent increase in pork if the consumer satisfaction were to remain unchanged. Under those circumstances, beef and pork are not really different products, but are the same product, meat.

If equivalent market baskets exist, then the consumer is free to choose among them. On what will the selection be predicated? The unique market basket that will be selected among all equivalents will be determined, according to economic theory, by relative prices. That is, if the price of beef rises relative to the price of pork, the consumer will pick a basket from among the equivalent baskets; it will be a basket that contains more pork relative to the basket that would have been selected had the price of beef not risen. In other words, given the consumer's tastes, reflected by the rate at which the consumer is willing to substitute beef for pork, the consumer will select the unique equivalent market basket that yields the greatest possible satisfaction given the relative prices of the items in the market basket and given the consumer's income. In a second period, relative prices may have changed, leading the consumer to select a different market basket. To calculate the change in the true cost of living, it is necessary to calculate the expenditure necessary to purchase the new market basket compared with the expenditure on the market basket of the previous time period, subject to the constraint that both baskets yield identical satisfaction. The ratio of the former to the latter will be an index of the true cost of living.

The Equivalent Market Basket Problem

In a consumer price index the same market basket is priced in every period. For a true cost-of-living index, an equivalent market basket, not necessarily the identical market basket, is priced in every period. The logical question is whether the true cost of living will rise faster or slower than a consumer price index based on a fixed market basket in the base year. The answer is that if consumer tastes and real income are unchanged from one period to another, then a true cost-of-living index will rise less than an index such as the CPI, calculated by using the Laspeyres formula. However, in the real world, such conditions are rarely met, so it is not really possible to know whether a true cost-of-living index would rise faster or slower than a Laspeyres index or a Paasche index.

Some studies suggest that the difference between the Laspeyres index and the true cost-of-living index might be of the order of magnitude of about 0.2% a year in terms of rates of change, the true cost-of-living index rising more slowly than the CPI. But such studies, although they have improved vastly, particularly through increasing the number of items among which substitution effects can be quantified, are still in the pioneering stage.

Other Differences

Some think that there are other differences between the consumer price index and the true cost-of-living index than merely the notion of equivalent market baskets. However, most such differences could be relevant to either a CPI or cost-of-living index. For example, some think that taxes and saving and the benefits derived from government purchases belong rightfully in a true cost-of-living index but not in a consumer price index. However, it is possible to formulate both indexes to answer the question of what level of income is required at today's market prices to maintain the base-period living standard. The present CPI and its true cost-of-living analog described above were intended to answer the question of what level of expenditure is required in today's market prices to maintain the base-period living standard. Thus, both indexes can be framed in terms of either expenditures or income. In fact, both can be framed even more broadly to encompass total wealth rather than income. Such an index would address the issue of what is the change in wealth required to leave an individual equally well off in two price situations. So the main difference between the technical use of the true cost-of-living index and the consumer price index has to do with the fact that even for two period comparisons, the former may include more than one market basket that would yield equivalent satisfaction, whereas the CPI is based on only one market basket.

References

Manser, Marilyn E., and Richard J. McDonald, "An Analysis of Substantial Bias in Measuring Inflation, 1959–85," *Econometrics,* July 1988, pp. 909–930; Pollak, Robert A., *The Theory of the Cost of Living Index,* Oxford University Press, New York, 1989.

(*See also* Consumer price index; Index numbers; Price measurement)

Joel Popkin

Council of Economic Advisers

The mission of the President's Council of Economic Advisers (CEA), which was established by the Employment Act of 1946, is to provide the President with the best possible economic advice, to develop and recommend economic policies to the President, and to appraise programs and activities of the federal government as they pertain to the health of the nation's economy. In addition to the Council's role in directly advising the President, the Council is represented, usually by the chair, at Cabinet meetings, meetings of the Economic Policy Council, the Domestic Policy Council, and the Council on Competitiveness, and at National Security Council meetings on issues of economic importance.

Throughout its history, the Council has stressed the importance of maximizing sustainable economic growth to raise U.S. living standards, of setting ambitious but realistic long-term economic goals, and of removing barriers to market forces. In its interactions with various outside groups—the Congress, the business community, international organizations, and the press—the Council emphasizes the administration's fiscal, monetary, regulatory, and trade policy principles.

Following closely macroeconomic developments, the Council briefs the President and participates in regular discussions on macroeconomic policy issues with the Department of Treasury, the Office of Management and Budget (OMB), and other members of the President's economic team. The Council also regularly exchanges information and meets with the Federal Reserve Board on monetary policy issues and the economic outlook.

The Council also participates in discussions on a wide range of macroeconomic issues with officials of the World Bank and the International Monetary Fund and government and other representatives from other countries. The Council often leads U.S. delegations to the Organization for Economic Cooperation and Development (OECD). For some years, the CEA chair has been the chair of the OECD Economic Policy Committee.

The Council and the other members of the "Troika"—Treasury and OMB—produce the administration's economic forecasts and projections. Usually two official forecasts are published annually: one at the start of the year, which is used as part of the President's budget, and one as part of the midsession review in July. The Troika's forecasting group is chaired by the Council.

In its work in the area of microeconomics, the Council stresses that government regulation must pass careful cost-benefit tests and that where government regulation is appropriate, it should be formulated to allow workers and firms maximum flexibility and to provide incentives to meet social goals in the least costly manner.

The Council works to improve economics education and the quality of economic information through a comprehensive series of memoranda and briefing papers on economic events for the President and the White House senior staff; through regular briefings for the White House press on major economic news; and through meetings with outside economists, forecasters, financial analysts, and businesspeople. The chair and Council members regularly testify before the Congress on the administration's economic principles, policies, and outlook. The chair and the other Council members also give speeches before numerous other organizations.

The Council produces two publications a year for the public. The Council's *Economic Report of the President* is the principal medium through which the Council informs the public of its work and its views. It is an important vehicle for presenting the administration's domestic and international economic policies. Annual distribution of the *Report* in recent years has averaged about 45,000 copies. The Council also assumes primary responsibility for the monthly *Economic Indicators,* which is issued by the Joint Economic Committee of the Congress and has a distribution of approximately 10,000.

Although the small size of the Council permits the chair and the Council members to work as a team on most policy issues, the chair is responsible for communicating the Council's views on economic developments to the President through personal discussions and written reports. The chair also represents the Council at daily White House senior staff meetings; at budget review group meetings with the President; and at many other formal and informal meetings with the President and White House senior staff, as well as with other senior government officials. The chair guides the overall work of the Council and exercises ultimate responsibility for directing the work of the professional staff.

The Council members are responsible for the full range of issues within the Council's purview and for the direct supervision of the work of the professional staff. Members represent the Council at a wide variety of interagency and international meetings and assume major responsibility for selecting issues for Council attention.

(*See also* Congressional Budget Office; Joint Economic Committee of Congress)

Michael J. Boskin

Countervailing power

Economists in both the classical and Marxist traditions in economics are fully agreed on the socially damaging character of unchecked economic power. *Countervailing power* is the force by which such power is checked. The damage that can be done by the monopoly (or monopsony) in enhancing its profits at the expense of those to whom it sells or from whom it buys is common ground in both traditions. A principal difference lies in the conclusion that is drawn. In the classical/neoclassical tradition, monopoly or monopoly power is exceptional, and in the common textbook view of economic policy it can be made more exceptional by well-considered policy. Antitrust action and lower tariffs are other steps to promote competition and are an effective antidote to monopoly and market power. In the Marxist tradition this, of course, is not the case. Capitalist concentration of monopoly power increases along with the attendant exploitation until the inevitable end.

Curbing Economic Power

The concept of countervailing power does not deny the role of competition as a solvent for economic power. It does argue against efforts to dissolve positions of economic power as the principal remedy. It is the curious tendency of much economic instruction to disguise everyday reality, and countervailing power is a case in point. Specifically, when sellers and buyers are faced with the practical consequences of monopoly power, they are usually more successful in organizing opposing and neutralizing positions of power than in dissolving the original concentration. The clearest case is the labor market. In theory it is open to the seller of labor to hope that through public policy buyers or employers of labor will be made as numerous and as weak in the market as they are themselves. In practice no one thinks this possible. And in consequence the trade union comes into existence to develop an equalizing or countervailing power. And, although the trade union is the outstanding manifestation of countervailing power, it is by no means the only one. Farmers faced with the strong monopolistic or oligopolistic position of the buyers of their products have in all modern countries organized themselves into selling cooperatives. Or they have sought the support of the state in enhancing their bargaining power. And faced with strong sellers of fertilizer, petroleum, and other farm supplies, farmers have similarly organized themselves into buying cooperatives. Such organization has also been the common recourse of consumers. And within the framework of capitalist markets the large mass-market retailers develop and deploy their buying power to negate the market power of manufacturers and other suppliers—the practical deployment of countervailing power. As a device against economic power it is far more effective and much more used than action through the antitrust laws to dissolve such power.

The concept of countervailing power was developed in Galbraith's *American Capitalism: The Concept of Countervailing Power* (1952). On the whole, it has survived the ensuing discussion. However, not all the argument originally put forward can be sustained. For example, the argument concerning the inevitability of countervailing power or its tendency to an equilibrium in which all or most market power is dissolved no longer seems valid.

Time has revealed another flaw. Galbraith argued in the initial version that countervailing power did not work well under conditions of excess demand or inflation—that it could dissolve into a coalition against the larger public. But it was not then foreseen that inflation would become a normal circumstance in the modern industrial economy. And to the extent that it has become normal, the role of countervailing power has been reduced. This reduction has not been complete; the rise of consumerism in the 1960s and 1970s was obviously a powerful manifestation of the phenomenon. But inflation is assuredly inimical to a socially benign deployment of countervailing power.

References

Galbraith, John Kenneth, *American Capitalism: The Concept of Countervailing Power*, Houghton Mifflin, Boston, 1952 (rev. ed., 1956).

(*See also* Competition; Monopoly and oligopoly)

John Kenneth Galbraith

Credit, an overview

Credit and its opposite, debt, involve transactions in which command over resources is obtained in the present in exchange for a promise to repay in the future, normally with a payment of interest as compensation to the lender—activities that were a part of life in the earliest and simplest societies and are today more crucial to the economic process than ever before. Credit appears wherever capital is used, and thus wherever savings are required—as much in economies in which the production process is socialized and centrally directed (where credit extension becomes a major arm of the planning process) as in market-oriented, enterprise economies built on the institution of private property. Because its use has at times been marked by extravagant excesses, credit has been at the bottom of some of the most spectacular crises of commercial history, not least of which has been the spate of financial difficulties experienced in the 1980s and continuing into the 1990s. This makes credit and the credit-extending process of great interest to governments, economists, businesses, and consumers alike.

Credit transactions occur in many forms—at one extreme as simple personal arrangements between individuals, as when money is loaned by one friend to another; at the other extreme, when funds are raised under carefully drawn legal contracts in financial markets of the highest technical development. The parties involved, the kind of instruments used, and the terms on which funds are advanced are in virtually continuous evolution, with changes occurring at an especially rapid rate in recent years. Among recent changes the issuance of "junk bonds" and the "securitization" of debt have been of particular importance, the former involving securities of "less than investment grade," the latter the issuance for public sale of debt securities backed by a collection of smaller obligations, e.g., home mortgages, that would not command a market of equal breadth. Brought on in large part by recession and a collapse of real estate values, defaults on these two types of securities, and on many loans made in conventional form, were responsible for most of the failures of financial institutions in the 1980s and 1990s, creating conditions reminiscent of the 1930s. Indeed, the Resolution Trust Corporation that was established to deal with these problems was designed to perform a function similar to that performed by the Home Owners Loan Corporation in the 1930s.

Institutional arrangements for the extension of credit vary greatly from country to country, yet the essentials are the same everywhere: A present value is transferred by a creditor (investor) to a debtor (borrower) who undertakes to repay in the future on terms specified in a credit agreement, with the debtor promising also to pay interest or other fees as compensation to the creditor. The extent of the activity is now immense. Based on research that began in the United States at the National Bureau of Economic Research in the 1940s and has been continued at the Board of Governors of the Federal Reserve System, data are published quarterly in the flow-of-funds accounts that show the volume of credit raised in U.S. credit markets by all groups of borrowers, and the sources from which it is obtained. The excess of credit extended in any period over repayments in the same period results, of course, in an increase in the volume of debt outstanding. This total (credit market debt) is estimated to have grown by the end of 1989 in the United States to $12.4 trillion.

Range of Credit Instruments and Agreements

Having evolved to serve the needs of a great variety of borrowers seeking credit for widely different purposes under varying conditions from creditors with different investment objectives, credit instruments and the agreements underlying them naturally exhibit a wide range of features.

Promise to Repay   The obligation to repay (found everywhere except in the unusual case of perpetual debt, as in British consols—consolidated annuities with no maturity date) is usually supported by some form of security. This may be only the promise of the debtor, attested to by his or her signature or by the signature of a designated "signing official" for a business concern. Such a credit is typically called "unsecured," but the borrower's promise allows claims to be entered against his or her income or assets, or that of a business concern, in the event of default. Security may be provided also by additional names (cosigners), by a lien on specific assets (home mortgages on real property; trust receipts on railroad equipment, etc.), by an assignment of accounts receivable, or by claims to inventory. Alternatively, there may be an assignment of rights to a flow of income, as in revenue bonds used frequently to finance public improvements, or by a pledge of the "full faith and credit" of a government, in effect a reliance on the government's ability to raise revenue through taxation or other means. Also, loans are often made under some insurance arrangement, public or private, as when the Federal Housing Administration insures home mortgage loans made by private lending institutions. In all these arrangements, the purpose of whatever is serving as security is to give the lender or investor something of value to fall back on if the loan contract is not fulfilled.

Time to Repay   Credits vary also according to maturity, i.e., according to the length of time the advance will be permitted to remain outstanding. At one extreme, transactions may be entered into to borrow only overnight, which is common between commercial banks; at the other, the credit may be allowed to remain outstanding for a long period—30 years is common in corporate, government, and home mortgage financing in U.S. credit markets. Consumer installment credit, however, typically requires full repayment within 1 to 5 years. In some instances, and typically in consumer installment credit, the loan balance must be paid down in equal amounts in regularly spaced installments, but repayment may be due only at final maturity. Although this is rarely now the case, it was common in the United States before 1929 for commercial banks to write mortgages for short periods, often for only a year, to require no reduction of principal in the interim and at maturity to allow the loan to remain indefinitely in a technically defaulted status as long as interest was paid. Not surprisingly, it was a practice that proved disastrously unwise when personal incomes and property values collapsed, as they did in the 1930s. A multitude of loans went into default at that time, embarrassing large numbers of banking institutions. In some respects the number of loan defaults and failures of financial institutions has been even greater in recent years than in the 1930s, involving immense costs to the Federal Treasury as well as to individuals and businesses.

Means of Transfer   Debt instruments may differ also with respect to their transferability. Some are nonnegotiable, but others may be transferred readily from one investor to another by sale, a process which constitutes the daily business of bond markets associated with national securities exchanges. Direct transfers between investors are also numerous. Since interest on a security is normally fixed at origination, the market value of the instrument varies inversely with subsequent fluctuations in interest rates, a feature which makes bonds a potential vehicle for speculative investment. In addition, markets exist for trading in futures contracts on financial instuments (i.e., rights to buy a specified instrument at a specified price at some future date).

Interest   The interest payable on a credit instrument is usually fixed, but variable (adjustable) rates are used more widely now than formerly, especially in home mortgage financing. Such advantage to the parties to the loan—the lender and the borrower—as there proves to be in an adjustable rate contract depends, of course, on how interest rates move over the life of the loan.

Usually, interest is paid at regular intervals, normally by transfer of cash, but sometimes only on presentation of a coupon attached to the credit instrument itself (giving rise to the expression "coupon clipper"); alternatively, interest may be taken in the form of a face value of the debt at maturity that is greater than the amount originally advanced (as in a "zero coupon" bond). There is also the use in home mortgage financing of "points," in which the proceeds to the borrower are less by one or more percentage points than the amount for which the borrower is ultimately liable. Obviously, this means that the effective cost to the borrower will be greater than the stated interest rate.

Transaction   Finally, credit may be extended in a single transaction, as when a bond is sold or a loan is made, or the proceeds may be advanced at intervals at the discretion of the debtor, under an "open credit" agreement. Credit cards, used widely now in purchase transactions, are a leading example of the latter. The amount of open credit extended is subject to limitation, however, if repayment obligations are not respected according to schedule.

In contrast to credit cards, which involve an extension of credit by the card-issuing institution to the cardholder, there is increasing use nowadays of "debit cards." When used in a purchase transaction, these make possible an immediate transfer of funds to the bank account of the vendor by debit to the cardholder's deposit account, making a cash transaction out of what would otherwise involve an extension of credit.

It is, of course, the availability of electronic data-processing equipment that has made credit (and cash) transactions of these types possible. It has greatly facilitated the use of credit cards, and the use of the debit card would be totally impossible without it. It has expanded the use of "registered" securities, where ownership is registered with a trustee while the security itself is held by a financial institution acting for the investor, and payments of interest and principal are made by electronic transfer directly to the investor's deposit account. The handling of investment transactions is being further simplified by the use of "book entry" accounts, which make a thing of the past of the large, handsomely engraved bond (coupons attached) that had to be held by the investor under whatever safekeeping arrangement could be devised.

Extension of Credit

Determining whether credit can be extended safely may be casual or highly formal, as when the loan committee of a bank must act on a loan application or when a public offering of bonds is underwritten by an investment banking syndicate. To service these activities, private agencies have been formed that rate bonds, and companies are found in most markets that provide information on the credit standing of individuals and businesses. Also, some lending institutions have developed a sophisticated credit-scoring system, under which various characteristics of the credit and the debtor are used in a statistical formula designed to separate acceptable from unacceptable risks.

Along with other features of the credit agreement, the interest rate will, naturally enough, vary according to the creditor's judgment of the risk involved in the transaction. But since some losses (failures of judgment) are inevitable, sound management of a credit-extending institution dictates regular charges against income to accumulate a loss "reserve" against which losses, when they do occur, can be charged. Should the loss reserve be inadequate, invading the institution's capital becomes necessary, perhaps to an extent that creates bankruptcy.

Credit Regulation

Few areas of enterprise are regulated and supervised by government more closely than the extension of credit. Commercial codes in the legal system of all countries specify the rights and obligations of debtors and creditors; interest rate ceilings are specified in the "usury" statutes of many states; loans to individuals are commonly subject to limitations as to maximum amount and maximum interest rate in state small loan legislation; and, to protect depositors, shareholders, or policy owners, most types of lending or investing institutions are subject to regular examination by state or federal authorities, or both. Where home mortgage loans have been insured or guaranteed by government, as by the Federal Housing Administration, not only the mortgage but the property that secures it, and the purposes for which the loan is advanced, are subject to federal regulation. Given the immense credit losses incurred in the late 1980s and 1990s, these precautions and guarantees clearly have been grossly inadequate.

At times, controls have been imposed directly on specific types of credit, as in the control of consumer credit and home mortgage credit during World War II and the Korean conflict. For example, the Federal Reserve Board has issued regulations, under a series of laws, designed to protect the consumer in credit transactions:

1. The Consumer Credit Protection Act of 1968 (Truth-in-Lending Act) specifies what information must be provided on the cost of borrowing or of buying on credit.

2. The Equal Credit Opportunity Act prohibits discrimination in the extension of credit on grounds of age, race, sex, or marital status, and certain other factors.

3. The Fair Credit Reporting Act established procedures for correcting mistakes on an individual's credit record.

4. The Fair Credit Billing Act established procedures for correcting errors in billing disputes arising particularly from the use of credit cards.

5. The Community Reinvestment Act is designed to prevent so-called red-lining, a practice alleged to involve arbitrary limitations on lending in specified areas of a community.

Fractional Reserve System

The involvement of government in credit markets in the 1990s has centered mainly on the "rescue" of financial institutions that, because of credit losses, needed assistance to stay afloat and the reimbursement (under deposit insurance agreements) of depositors in failed financial institutions, and legislation since the 1960s has been concerned increasingly with the "fairness" aspect of credit extension. However, the major continuing public interest in credit arises from the use in the United States of a fractional reserve banking system in which a commercial bank is required to hold reserves only up to a specified fraction of its deposit liabilities and the connection between this system and changes in the size of the nation's money supply. Because a commercial bank commonly advances loan proceeds by crediting the borrower with a deposit that becomes part of the nation's money supply, and because economic studies show a connection between changes in money supply and changes in the level of prices, there is at all times a keen public interest in controlling these credit-extending and deposit-generating processes.

In the U.S. banking system, the instruments for exercising this control are in the hands of the Federal Reserve System, which can influence the volume of bank reserves and thus the degree to which deposit volume can be expanded. If need be, these powers can be used also to force a contraction of deposit volume. It was once a widely held view that no harm would be done by credit expansion and deposit creation so long as credits were limited to loans for self-liquidating purposes (e.g., where credit was extended for the accumulation of inventory and repaid from sales receipts as inventory was turned over), but the conventional view currently is that what is crucial is the quantity of credit extended, regardless of purpose or quality, and the corollary expansion of deposit liabilities and money supply.

References

Board of Governors of the Federal Reserve System, *Flow of Funds Accounts, Financial Assets and Liabilities, Year-End 1966–1989,* Washington, D.C., September 1990; Federal Reserve Bank of Richmond, *Instruments of the Money Market,* 1986; Federal Reserve Bank of New York, *U.S. Monetary Policy and Financial Markets,* December 1989; Lawrence, Colin, and Robert Shay (eds.), *Technological Innovation, Regulation and the Monetary Economy,* Ballinger, Cambridge, Mass., 1986; *The Report of the President's Commission on Financial Structure and Regulation* (the Hunt Commission), U.S. Government Printing Office, Washington, D.C., December 1971; Young, Ralph A., *Instruments of Monetary Policy in the United States,* International Monetary Fund, Washington, D.C., 1973, chap. 2.

(*See also* Business credit; Consumer credit; Credit cards; Debt, Federal reserve policy; Federal Reserve System; Interest rates; Monetary policy; Mortgage credit; Selective credit controls)

Raymond J. Saulnier

Credit, business (*see* Business credit)

Credit, consumer (*see* Consumer credit)

Credit, mortgage (*see* Mortgage credit)

Credit cards

A credit card is an instrument, usually made of plastic, which authorizes the holder to purchase goods and services (and, often, to obtain advances of cash) against a line of credit. Credit cards differ from other financial instruments in that they dually serve a transaction function and a credit function; that is, the same devices are used both to charge and to borrow. And each role for credit cards has dramatically expanded in the past decade. The U.S. charge volume on Visa, MasterCard, and American Express cards reached $322.1 billion in 1990, up from $67.4 billion in 1980. (Worldwide charge volume on these three cards and their affiliates reached $657.2 billion in 1990, up from $98.3 billion in 1980.) Hundreds of billions of dollars per year more are charged on proprietary retail cards. Meanwhile, credit card debt has been the fastest-growing component of consumer credit in the United States. Total outstanding bank revolving credit (primarily on MasterCard and Visa cards) reached $232.4 billion, out of $748.3 billion in all consumer installment credit, at year-end 1990. This compared to only $54.9 billion, out of $313.5 billion in all consumer installment credit, at year-end 1980.

Partially removing the credit function from a credit card—by requiring the card-holder to pay each monthly bill in full—yields a "charge card" or "travel and entertainment card" (such as the American Express green card, Carte Blanche, or Diners Club). Entirely removing the credit function from a credit card yields a "debit card," which operates similarly to a checking account (but is also typically made of plastic). Entirely removing the transaction function from a credit card yields a simple line of credit.

History

The term "credit card" apparently originated in Edward Bellamy's 1887 utopian socialist novel, *Looking Backward*. Providing a futuristic account of the year 2000, the American author wrote of a pasteboard card with which individuals charged all purchases against their current year's income. The fictional cards also permitted a limited facility for borrowing against next year's income, at a "heavy discount." Charge cards made their practical emergence as an outgrowth of the older practice of retailers extending credit to their customers. In the early twentieth century, some U.S. department stores, hotels, and oil companies began to issue cards made of paper or metal (known as "shoppers' plates") to identify their credit customers. The first general purpose credit card was issued in 1947 by the Flatbush National Bank, enabling customers of the bank to charge purchases at establishments in a two-square-block area of Brooklyn, New York. The first travel and entertainment card was introduced by Diners Club in 1950, initially allowing customers to charge meals at Manhattan restaurants. The American Express Company followed with its own travel and entertainment card in 1958 and Carte Blanche in 1959. The Franklin National Bank was the first, in 1951, to issue bank cards to other than its own depositors and outside a local area.

By the mid-1950s, more than 100 American banks had established their own credit card plans, which operated only on regional bases; by the late 1950s, banks began to offer revolving terms of credit on their cards. However, the growth of bank credit cards was hampered during this period by the lack of reciprocity among different banks. Incompatibilities were resolved in 1966, as the two dominant national and international networks of bank credit cards formed: Bank of America began to franchise its successful BankAmericard (now Visa), while several other large banks formed a second competing system called the Interbank Card Association (now MasterCard). Nonbank institutions began to offer close facsimiles of bank credit cards on a large scale in the second half of the 1980s. Sears introduced its Discover card in 1986, American Express introduced its Optima card in 1987, and AT&T began to offer MasterCard and Visa cards in 1990.

Organization and Regulation of the Industry

If Visa and MasterCard were the relevant levels of business to examine, then two firms would control a substantial part of the United States credit card market. However, most relevant business decisions are made at the level of the issuing bank. Individual banks own their cardholders' accounts and determine the interest rate, annual fee, grace period, credit limit, and other terms of the accounts. (Only charges such as the "interchange fee" from the merchant's bank to the cardholder's bank are standardized, and the cardholder's bank appears to only break even on such charges. Moreover, there is absolutely no indication that the MasterCard and Visa organizations serve to facilitate collusion on other prices.) In essence, each of MasterCard and Visa is operated as a joint venture, licensing individual banks (and some other institutions) to issue credit cards bearing its trademark and to utilize its interchange network. The relevant levels of business to think of as "firms" are the issuing banks.

Thus, the correctly defined market for bank credit cards is relatively unconcentrated. The top ten firms control only about half of the market and the next ten firms little more than one-tenth of the market. Moreover, the market is exceptionally broad. A bank which ranked number 100 in 1991 still had approximately 155,000 active accounts and $120 million in outstanding balances.

Unlike most aspects of U.S. banking, the credit card business has historically operated free of interstate banking and branch banking restrictions, and the largest issuers today conduct truly national businesses. In the past, credit card issuers were constrained by state usury laws. However, the U.S. Supreme Court's December 1978 decision in *Marquette National Bank v. First of Omaha Service Corporation* paved the way for the practical elimination of price regulations. The Court held that only the usury ceiling of the state in which the bank is located, and not that of the state in which the consumer is located, restricts the interest rate the bank may charge. This gave banks the option of shifting their credit card operations to wholly owned subsidiaries situated in states without usury laws. By 1982, amid *Marquette*-created bank pressure and historically high market interest rates, most leading banking states had relaxed or repealed their interest rate ceilings. Meanwhile, South Dakota and Delaware had established themselves as attractive homes-away-from-home for credit card issuers. Although a number of states maintain binding usury laws at this writing (most notably, Arkansas, with a ceiling of five percentage points above the Federal Reserve discount rate), essentially all major issuers can pursue business in those states free of restriction. It is fair to say that the bank credit card market in the United States was functionally deregulated in 1982.

The "Failure of Competition"

From an economist's perspective, the most interesting aspect of the credit card market is its failure to adhere to anything remotely resembling the model of perfect competition, despite the unconcentrated and unregulated state of the industry. The cost of funds is generally the largest single component of the marginal cost of lending via credit cards, and it is usually the only component of marginal cost which varies widely from week to week and quarter to quarter. Thus, a model of continuous spot market equilibrium would predict a substantial degree of connection between the interest rate charged on credit cards and the banks' cost of funds. A competitive model would also predict that all credit card issuers earn zero long-run economic profits. (Many models of imperfect competition which preserve the free entry assumption would also yield the zero-profits prediction.)

The empirical experience of the U.S. bank credit card market stands in stark contrast to these competitive predictions. Visa and MasterCard interest rates in the United States were highly sticky during the period 1982 through 1989. When the credit card interest rate (taken at quarterly intervals) was regressed on its own lagged value, the lagged cost of funds, and a constant, the coefficient on cost of funds was found to be only about 0.05, meaning that a 1.00 percent movement in the cost of funds translated to only about a 0.05 percent movement in the credit card interest rate one quarter later. By comparison, analogous regressions on other consumer credit products, such as unsecured personal loans, auto loans, and mortgages, as well as on the prime rate, produce much larger coefficients, indicating that credit card interest rates have been uncannily rigid.

Credit cards were also extremely profitable for banks. During the years 1983 to 1988, the 50 largest American issuers of MasterCard and Visa cards typically earned three to five times the ordinary rate of return from banking activities. In some of the years, many large issuers earned pretax returns on equity exceeding 100 percent per year. Over the longer period of 1976 to 1988, smaller issuers still appear to have earned roughly twice the ordinary rate of return in banking.

The interest-rate rigidity (and the high profits in years that the cost of funds was low) has been attributed in part to an adverse selection argument. Suppose that there are three classes of consumers in the market: consumers who do not intend to borrow on their accounts, but find themselves doing so anyway; consumers who fully intend to borrow on their credit card accounts (and do so); and consumers who never borrow. Then a credit card issuer which unilaterally cuts its interest rate is likely to draw disproportionately many customers from the second class, who are the worst credit risks, and to draw disproportionately few customers from the first class, who are more likely to repay their debts.

The adverse selection theory is consistent with the observed fact that noninterest fees such as annual fees are relatively low and sometimes zero and that issuers often provide transaction bonuses such as collision damage waivers, frequent flyer miles, and rebates. There is no adverse selection associated with competing on those terms of the credit card account which are independent of borrowing behavior.

Public Attention

Any time that the level of market interest rates attains a cyclical low, and given the stickiness of credit card rates, a large spread clearly will develop between credit card rates and the cost of funds. Given the visibility and preponderance of credit cards, this situation sets the stage for public attention, both in the United States and elsewhere. Such a circumstance has developed at least twice in the recent past: in 1986, and again in 1991.

In Great Britain, credit cards have been the subject of investigations by the Monopolies and Mergers Commission, which found that credit card profitability has been higher than might have been expected under normal competition. In Australia, a Parliament committee observed in November 1991 that, despite considerable declines in other interest rates over the previous 2 years, there had been no reduction in credit card interest rates, concluding that "there is an appearance of a lack of price competition in the credit card market."

And in the United States, credit card interest rates created a major political flap. In a November 1991 speech, President George Bush said, "I'd frankly like to see the credit card rates down. I believe that would help stimulate the consumer and get the consumer confidence moving again." The U.S. Senate responded on the following day by voting 74 to 19 to impose a national ceiling on credit card interest rates of about 7 percentage points above the yield on Treasury securities with less than 3-year maturities. The episode was widely blamed for triggering a 120-point stock market plunge and leading to the resignation of White House Chief of Staff John H. Sununu. The legislation was never voted on by the House of Representatives and was abandoned 2 weeks later.

References

Ausubel, Lawrence M., "The Failure of Competition in the Credit Card Market," *American Economic Review*, March 1991, pp. 50–81; Bellamy, Edward, *Looking Backward: 2000–1887*, Ticknor, Boston, 1888 (reprinted, Penguin Books, New York, 1982); Mandell, Lewis, *The Credit Card Industry: A History*, Twayne, Boston, 1990.

(*See also* Consumer credit; Credit, an overview; Financial instruments; Interest rates)

Lawrence M. Ausubel

Credit controls, selective (*see* Selective credit controls)

Cross-sectional analysis in business and economics

Cross-sectional analysis is the study of relationships between two or more variables which measure the situations of different households, firms, or geographical entities at the same point in time. This analysis contrasts with time series analysis, which measures the changing situations of a single entity (e.g., a national economy) at successive points in time. Since the 1950s, interest has developed in the possible ways of pooling information from cross-sectional and time series studies.

The statistical technique generally used in cross-sectional studies is least-squares regression analysis. Some of the problems involved are the same as in time series analysis: choosing the form of the function to be fitted, allowing for the biasing effects of errors in the independent variables, and recognizing the probable effects of excluded variables.

If the observations are listed according to some ordering principle, the Durbin-Watson statistic used to test for autocorrelation in time series may also be helpful in cross-sectional studies. For example, if the successive observations in a cross-sectional study refer to geographically contiguous areas, positive autocorrelation in the residuals may disclose systematic effects of climate, large-region food habits, or other omitted variables. Prais and Houthakker (1955) listed households in order of total expenditure and used the Durbin-Watson statistic to determine whether the residuals from linear regressions indicated significant departures from linearity; if so, they proceeded to fit appropriate nonlinear functions.

Random errors in the independent variable of a simple least-squares regression equation bias the regression coefficient toward zero in cross-sectional as well as in time series studies. Friedman created an elaborate economic theory to explain why the regression coefficients of family expenditures upon family income in (ungrouped) cross-sectional data were lower than those obtained from time series of national income and consumption expenditures. However, Houthakker maintained that errors of measurement in the family income data were sufficient to account for the lower cross-sectional coefficients and that Friedman's economic theory, right or wrong, was logically independent of the statistics on which he based it.

In cross-sectional studies, as in time series studies, it is important to be clear about what is being measured. For example, the gross outputs of different farms in a given year may be strongly influenced by weather. If we regress gross output on gross input, positive deviations may or may not indicate greater managerial efficiency. If we have data on each farm for several successive years, weather effects may be largely eliminated by fitting a regression equation based on several yearly average values of the variables for each farm; the residuals from this equation should give a much clearer indication of differences in efficiency.

History

The earliest type of cross-sectional analysis was the study of household expenditures upon different categories of goods. The first and most famous empirical relationship based on such a study was Engle's law, proposed in 1857: "The poorer a family, the greater the proportion of its total expenditure that must be devoted to food."

Household expenditure studies increased in number and improved in quality from the 1870s on. William F. Ogburn, known primarily as a sociologist, was (in 1916) among the first to fit multiple regression equations to such data, expressing expenditures on each category as a function of family income and family size. Stigler (1954) calculated income elasticities of expenditure from Ogburn's equations.

In the early 1950s, several economists tried grafting cross-sectional estimates of income elasticities into time series regressions of per capita food consumption upon food prices and per capita income. Thus, if the original time series demand function were $q_t = a + bp_t + cy_t + u_t$ and the regression coefficient of q on y in the cross-sectional data were c^*, these economists would compute an adjusted consumption variable $q_t^* = (q_t - c^*y_t)$ and fit the equation $q_t^* = a + bp_t + u_t$ to estimate the net relationship between consumption and price. This procedure was criticized by other economists on the allegation that cross-sectional data should reflect long-run adjustments of family consumption patterns to family incomes, whereas time series of annual observations should reflect short-run adjustments only. This allegation is probably not true for food, but the possibility that cross-sectional and time series regressions may reflect different types of behavior must be carefully considered in each particular case.

As more time series data for individual firms became publicly available, combining cross-sectional and time series data for identical firms became possible. The first major study of this sort was published by Kuh in 1959 using annual data for 73 firms over a period of 17 years. Averaging values of the variables over the 73 firms in each year gave him 17 times series observations, and averaging values of the variables over the 17 years for each firm gave him 73 cross-sectional observations. He fitted equations of the same form to the two sets of observations and obtained substantially different regression coefficients. He also demonstrated more powerful methods based on variance and covariance analysis of all 1241 (73 firms times 17 years) observations.

Maddala (1971) asserted that the use of analysis of covariance techniques in the pooling of cross-sectional and time series data had become a common practice in econometric work.

References

Kuh, Edwin, "The Validity of Cross-Sectionally Estimated Behavior Equations in Time Series Applications," *Econometrica*, vol. 27, 1959, pp. 197–214; Maddala, G. S., "The Use of Variance Components Models in Pooling Cross Section and Time Series Data," *Econometrica*, vol. 39, 1971, pp. 341–358; Nerlove, Marc, "Further Evidence on the Estimation of Dynamic Economic

Relations from a Time Series of Cross Sections," *Econometrica,* vol. 39, 1971, pp. 359–382; Prais, S. J., and H. S. Houthakker, *The Analysis of Family Budgets,* Cambridge University, Cambridge, 1955, 1971; Stigler, George J., "The Early History of Empirical Studies of Consumer Behavior," *The Journal of Political Economy,* vol. 62, 1954, pp. 95–113.

(*See also* Elasticity; Regression analysis in business and economics; Time series analysis)

Tej K. Kaul and Karl A. Fox

Currency school

The *currency school* refers to a group of influential British economists who wrote about monetary regulation in the middle decades of the nineteenth century. Led by Lord Overstone (Samuel Jones Lloyd), George Warde Norman, and Robert Torrens, the currency school advocated 100 percent gold reserve backing for banknotes to ensure that the volume of notes varied identically with changes in the nation's monetary gold stock. This prescription was derived from the principle of metallic fluctuation, the cornerstone of the school's analysis. According to the metallic principle, a mixed currency of paper and coin should be made to behave exactly as if it were wholly metallic, automatically expanding and contracting dollar for dollar with inflows and outflows of gold. Departure from this rule would permit inflationary overissue of paper, forcing an efflux of specie through the balance of payments, which in turn could endanger the gold reserve, threaten the gold convertibility of the currency, compel the need for sharp contraction, and thereby precipitate financial panics. No such consequences would ensue if the currency conformed to the metallic principle, however. Forced to behave like gold (regarded by the currency school as the stablest of monetary standards), the currency would be spared those sharp fluctuations in quantity that constitute the main source of economic disturbances.

Strict Regulation

Given the desirability of making banknotes behave like gold, by what means was this result to be achieved? Earlier writers, notably David Ricardo, had found the answer in convertibility. If the currency were convertible, they reasoned, any excess issue of notes, which raised British prices relative to foreign prices, would be converted into gold to make cheaper purchases abroad. The resulting loss in specie reserves would force banks to contract their note issue, thus eliminating the excess.

A series of monetary crises in the 1820s and 1830s, however, convinced the currency school that mere convertibility was not enough to safeguard the currency. Convertibility was an insufficient safeguard because it allowed banks too much discretion in the management of their note issue. Banks could and did continue to issue notes even as gold was flowing out, delaying contraction until the last minute when reserves were almost depleted, and then contracting with a violence that sent shock waves throughout the economy. What was needed, the currency school thought, was a law removing the note issue from the discretion of bankers and placing it under strict regulation. To be effective, this law should require banks to contract their note issues one for one with outflows of gold, thereby putting an early and gradual stop to specie drains.

The currency school scored a triumph when its ideas were enacted into legislation. The famous Bank Charter Act of 1844 embodied its prescription that, except for a small fixed fiduciary issue, notes were to be backed by an identical amount of gold. In modern terminology, the act established a marginal gold reserve requirement of 100 percent to back notes. With notes rigidly tied to gold in this fashion, external gold drains would be accompanied by a domestic reduction of a like amount of notes, as required by the metallic principle.

Banking School's Arguments

The currency school's prescription, however, was not universally endorsed. The rival banking school flatly denied the need for statutory note control, arguing that the note issue was automatically regulated by the needs of trade. Indeed, the banking school rejected the entire analytical framework underlying the act. Comprising the quantity theory of money and the classical price-specie-flow mechanism, that framework postulated a causal chain running from note overissue to domestic inflation to specie drains. By contrast, the banking school contended (1) that overissue is impossible because the supply of notes is demand determined, (2) that causation runs from prices to money rather than vice versa, and (3) that specie drains stem from nonmonetary shocks to the balance of payments rather than from domestic price inflation. Finally, the banking school asserted the impossibility of controlling the monetary circulation via the note component alone, since limitation of notes would simply induce the public to use checking deposits and bills of exchange instead. In other words, the total circulation is like a balloon; when squeezed at one end, it expands at the other.

The currency school, however, rejected this criticism on the grounds that the volume of deposits and bills is rigidly constrained by the volume of notes and therefore can be controlled through notes alone. In short, the total circulation is like an inverted pyramid resting on a banknote base, with variations in the base inducing equiproportional variations in the superstructure of money substitutes. In counting deposits as part of the superstructure, the currency school excluded them from its concept of money. It did so on the grounds that deposits, unlike notes and coin, were not generally acceptable in final payments during financial panics.

Shortcomings of the Currency School

In retrospect, the currency school erred in failing to define deposits as money to be regulated like notes. This failure enabled the Bank of England to exercise discretionary control over a large and growing part of the money stock, contrary to the intentions of the currency school. The school also erred in not recognizing the need for a lender of last resort to avert liquidity panics and domestic cash drains. With regard to cash drains, the currency school refused to distinguish between domestic and foreign ones. As far as policy was concerned, both drains were to be handled the same way, i.e., by monetary contraction. By the end of the century, however, it was widely recognized that the two drains required different treatment and that the surest way to arrest an internal drain was through a policy of liberal lending. The currency school nevertheless remained opposed to such a policy, fearing it would place too much discretionary power in the hands of the central bank. These shortcomings, it should be noted, in no way invalidated the school's contention that convertibility is an inadequate safeguard against monetary overexpansion and therefore must be reinforced by positive regulation. Nor did they undermine the school's monetary theory of inflation, which was superior to any explanation its critics had to offer.

Currency School and Monetarism

Today the term "currency school" is closely associated with monetarism. The school's principal conclusions—(1) that rules are preferable to discretion in the conduct of monetary policy, (2) that inflation is largely or solely produced by excessive monetary growth, (3) that monetary shocks are the primary source of economic disturbances, and (4) that the entire stock of money and money substitutes can be governed via control of a narrowly defined base—constitute the core of monetarist doctrine.

References

Humphrey, T., "Rival Notions of Money," Federal Reserve Bank of Richmond, *Economic Review,* no. 75, September–October 1988, pp. 3–9; Robbins, L., *Robert Torrens and the Evolution of Classical Economics,* Macmillan, London, 1958, chap. 5; Viner, J., *Studies in the Theory of International Trade,* Kelley, New York, 1965, chap. 5.

(*See also* Banking school)

Thomas M. Humphrey

Data banks

In this era of the ubiquitous personal computer, pouring over books and press releases to collect and post data is as old-fashioned as wearing bustles. Economists wanting to move out of the esoteric world of theory to test their hypotheses or to keep up with what's actually happening in the economy need to feed their computers with gobs of data that are continually being updated and revised. As a result, data banks have sprouted up to bring data collection into the PC mode. What is a data bank? It is a service devoted to the maintenance and rapid dissemination of information. This involves centralized collection, upkeep, documentation, and access facilities for a community of users. The terms "data bank" and "database" are somewhat distinguishable. A bank can consist of one or more bases. A database is used primarily for a focused collection of information: a particular study, economic model, accounting system, or some other special purpose. Economists are primarily concerned with numeric or statistical data banks, but they may also encounter textual data banks which consist of bibliographies, abstracts, indexes, or other reference material. Numeric data banks may include internal company accountings, cross-sectional microdata, macroeconomic time series, or any variation and combination of these. We must also define a couple of terms the user may stumble across. Collections stored for preservation and future use are called data archives. Individual machine-readable volumes (tapes, cassettes, disks, etc.) containing data resulting from a particular survey or enumeration are called data files.

Many economists use microdata banks to analyze public policy questions, test theories, or set up marketing programs. The term "microdata" refers to information on individual reporting units—families, individuals, companies, establishments, etc. Machine-readable microdata banks consist of files containing a number of items of information (variables) about each unit at one point in time (or over one period of time). A collection of cross-sectional data files, each of which refers to the same unit at successive points in time, is called a longitudinal microdata bank. Microdata can be generated as the by-product of an administrative process. More often, however, they result from a specific sample survey or an entire census enumeration. Advances in computer technology, sophisticated programming, and data organization have made it possible to retrieve and manipulate large masses of microdata for economic, political, and sociological analysis. They are indispensable for analyzing the behavior of classes of individual economic units and the relationships among different variables and activities. Also, by providing the smallest possible building blocks for the aggregation of statistical information, microdata make it possible to compute, for example, income distributions or aggregations of consumer expenditures by category.

Until recently, microdata sets often entered the public domain insufficiently documented and unedited for errors, inconsistencies, and unreadable codes. This made their use costly and of dubious value. In recent years, however, considerable progress has been made toward improving documentation standards and manipulatory software. These developments facilitate editing and documenting microdata before their release and greatly enhance their usefulness.

The proliferation of computer-accessible records and the advances of computer technology have increased the ease with which privacy and confidentiality can be violated. The concept of microdata banks has thus aroused considerable controversy. The very term "data bank" is often treated in a pejorative fashion, synonymous with "dossier," to describe any "collection of information about individuals assembled in one place for easy access by a number of users" (Westin and Baker, 1972). However in this respect it is information on criminal activities, sources of income, medical records, credit ratings, etc., which represents the greatest threat to the citizen's privacy. By contrast, the microdata banks used for economic-statistical analysis are usually well safeguarded. Not only do they carry no recognizable identification (except with the consent of the individual respondent), but their administrators are very careful in their analysis to avoid possible disclosure. The Census Bureau's 1980 public use sample, for instance, was released in six different versions, each containing somewhat different variables, in order to avoid the possibility of identification through detailed cross-classification searches. Statistics Canada stores all its data using a random-number-generated code.

Printed collections of economic time series have existed for a long time. *The Statistical Abstract of the United States* was begun over 110 years ago, and the *Survey of Current Business* was started in 1920. Theoretically, computer-readable data banks became possible around 1963 when computers were first employed for economic analysis. There were many private collections of data (on cards), but data banks were not actually practical until the advent of commercially available time sharing around 1966. Before that time, the only generally available macroeconomic data bank was maintained by the Brookings Institution on magnetic tape; it was updated only annually.

However, a group of New York City business economists engaged in short-term forecasting and business conditions analysis shared programs as a loosely knit group called Project Economics. Realizing the advantages of sharing the cost of maintaining machine-readable time series, they started as a cooperative venture in 1967, with each participant responsible for a group of time series. The group soon found that professional statisticians and data handlers were needed to ensure the reliability and integrity of the data. Since the National Bureau of Economic Research (NBER) was part of Project Economics, it was decided that its staff would assume responsibility for the upkeep of the data and the further development of the data bank. Subsequently, the number of time series in the bank was greatly increased, as were the number of users and the amount of effort involved. By 1978, NBER bowed out of the data-bank business as many commercial projects (such as DRI, Wharton, and Haver) were ably supplying economists' needs. These data collections had been started to support large econmetric models, but to meet their customers' needs they had been expanded to cover a wide spectrum of information.

The time series data banks available in the United States today contain historical time series at all levels of aggregation. Some carry national data only; others specialize in regional data; and still others carry series for detailed industrial or other classifications. They also vary in accessibility: some are available on magnetic tape only and others through time-sharing systems; some can be used only by purchasers of models, forecasts, or similar services, while others are available independently. Historically, data were collected from published sources, put in standardized computer-readable form, and checked for accuracy, consistency, and continuity before users had access. Presently, already machine-readable data are subject to this same process. Some data banks include estimates projected by econometric models.

Time series data banks are also available for foreign data. They are being maintained in the United States as well as abroad. Data banks of international data are increasingly available within the United States. The International Monetary Fund's *International Financial Statistics* consists of 23,000 historical time series, with monthly updates available. The Organization for Economic Cooperation and Development (OECD) has computerized its *Main Economic Indicators* and presents conceptually comparable data on many aspects of the real economy for 25 countries. The United Nations makes available an extensive collection of data by 4-digit ISIC code for over 100 countries. It also collects and releases details on the gross domestic product of 177 countries—now including the United States. The Bureau of Labor Statistics provides machine-readable (but mostly unpublished) data for 15 countries adjusted to U.S. definitions of employment, unemployment, productivity, and labor costs. Fifty developing countries are covered by the Institute of International Finance. Although these data banks are available on various formats of magnetic tape, they are more easily accessible via a commercial time-sharing company such as Haver Analytics based in New York City.

To get an idea of how to use a database, it is advisable to pick an example and describe the procedure. Haver Analytics is one with which I am familiar. It specializes in data banks and software products for economic analysis and business decision making. Begun in the mid-1970s, Haver Analytics gathers data and forecasts from government agencies and private organizations all over the world, including more than a million time series. It adds time series and databases at a client's request and in response to changing marketplace demands. Databases are updated within hours, usually no more than 2, of the release time of data. Internal quality-control checks ensure data accuracy. There are three ways that clients can get to and analyze Haver's data. Clients choose the one that is best for them: (1) on-line, (2) diskette, or (3) PC database manager. A menu-driven system enables clients to peruse the databases and find the data that they need; check data availability, sources, and updates; and download data directly into Lotus 1-2-3 worksheets or other PC files. Economic consultants who are knowledgeable about Haver's data and software cover the service hotline during working hours to answer clients' questions about the data, databases, and software. Technical support is available 24 hours a day, 7 days a week, to solve communications or other problems. A monthly newsletter informs clients about all manner of changes: new databases and data series, changes in concepts, revisions to existing series, etc.

Many federal agencies are making their current data available in machine-readable form. The Department of Commerce maintains several on-line facilities: The Electronic Bulletin Board and Cendata are both available by modem and at modest cost. The National Trade Data Bank, on the National Institute of Health Computer, is an excellent example of careful data editing. The Bureau of Labor Statistics not only makes its current statistical releases available via modem, but also makes available historical data of its labor-force series—and in more detail than is published. The Board of Governors of the Federal Reserve System, an independent agency, releases its data on magnetic tape through the National Technical Information Service.

Data banks are a great convenience to the user, but they do not eliminate the necessity for careful examination of the data. Many times concepts change, and it is difficult for the agencies to provide consistent series over long periods of time. In 1983, for example, the Bureau of Labor Statistics modified the consumer price index by changing its measure of the price of owner-occupied housing. A data-bank user unaware of this change could have skewed his or her analysis. Ergo, documentation of the data in a data bank is of the utmost importance. It is possible to comment on each data point in a time series, on-line. The Bank for International Settlements maintains an international database that provides this facility, but only central banks have access to this valuable material. International trade data are particularly prone to these difficulties, and the U.S. government has made large efforts to present the data consistently. In early 1992, President Bush recommended a $30 million statistical initiative to improve the U.S. data in many ways, but improved data are likely also to lead to breaks in the historical series. (See Economic Report of the President, 1992, pp. 239–246.)

References

Bisco, Ralph L. (ed.), *Data Bases, Computers & the Social Sciences,* Wiley-Interscience, New York, 1970; Boschan, Charlotte, "The NBER Timeseries Data Bank," *Annals of Economic and Social Measurement,* National Bureau of Economic Research, New York, April 1972; Capretta, Claire (ed.), *The Federal Data Base Finder,* 1991, a directory of free and fee-based databases and files available from the federal government, Information, USA, P.O. Box 15700, Chevy Chase, Md. 20815; Darrow, Joel W., and James R. Belilove, "The Growth of Databank Sharing," *Harvard Business Review,* November–December 1978, pp. 180–194; Data Use and Access Laboratories, *1970 Census Data Finder,* Rosslyn, Va. 1973; Frachet, Y., "Issues for Official Statistical Systems in Democratic Market Societies," *Business Economics,* July 1991, pp. 59–62; Harrigan, F. J., "The Reconciliation of Inconsistent Economic Data: The Information Gain," *Economic Systems Research,* vol. 2, no. 1, 1990, pp. 17–25; McGuckin, R. H., and S. V. Nguyen, "Public Use Macrodata; Disclosure and Usefulness," *Journal of Economic and Social Measurement,* vol. 16, no. 1, 1990, pp. 19–35; Meyer, Kenneth R., and D. S. Schmidt (eds.), "Computer Aided Proofs in Analysis," The Institute for Mathematics and Its Applications, *Volumes in Mathematics and Its Applications,* vol. XXVIII, Springer, New York, 1991; Michalewicz, Z. (ed.), Proceedings of the Fifth International Conference on Statistical and Scientific Database Management, V SSDBM, Charlotte, N.C., April 3–5, 1990, *Lecture Notes in Computer Science,* vol. IV, Springer, New York, 1990; Ostenso, J., "The Statistics Corner: New Products from the Census Bureau," *Business Economics,* April 1991, pp. 60–62; Westin, Allen F., and Michael A.

Baker, *Data Banks in a Free Society; Computer Record-Keeping and Privacy,* Report of the Project on Computer Data Banks of the Computer Science and Engineering Board, National Academy of Sciences, Quadrangle, New York, 1972.

(*See also* Bureau of the Census; Computers in economics; Regression analysis in business and economics; Time series analysis)

Peggy M. May

Debt

Debt is an obligation by one person or entity to another person or entity. In business, a debt is normally a money debt, in which case an obligation is created by voluntary contract between a lender, or creditor, and a borrower, or debtor. Typically, a lender transfers money to a borrower in return for a promise by the borrower to either (1) repay the entire amount on a given future date or (2) repay principal periodically during the life of the loan.

Evidence of debt is typically given by an instrument in writing, such as a promissory note, a bond, a debenture, a certificate of deposit, or other written document. Such documents may be payable only to the named individuals or entities in the document, or the debt may be freely transferable to others. For example, a debenture is an unsecured obligation of a business to pay to its creditors on the terms specified in the indenture. (Bonds are similar, but secured.) Debentures and bonds of many corporations are traded on the New York Stock Exchange and over the counter. Similarly, the obligations of the U.S. government and of state and local governments are widely traded among owners (creditors).

In addition to the promissory note evidencing debt, there are often terms and conditions accompanying the promissory note that are agreed to by the lender and the borrower. For example, a mortgage specifies what rights and obligations the creditor and the debtor have over the life of the loan evidenced by the promissory note the borrower signed. Bonds and debentures are accompanied by indentures which, like mortgages, specify the rights and obligations of the borrowing business and of the bond or debenture owners. Such documents may become longer and more detailed when banks or insurance companies lend to corporations for long periods of time, because of the possibility of unforeseen future events. The difficulties, and therefore the documentation, are increased when loans are made across national boundaries, as they often are today.

Reasons for Debt

In the normal course of their economic activities, some firms and individuals accumulate surplus funds, while others need more funds than they have available. We might say that the economy has surplus funds units and deficit funds units. Lending by surplus funds units to deficit funds units allows the surplus funds units—the savers—to earn interest on their money. Loans permit borrowers to spend more than they have received in cash flow during the time period involved or have accumulated.

Consumers may borrow to achieve a higher standard of living earlier than they could if they were reliant solely on their own resources. Business firms typically borrow when the present value of the use of the money exceeds the present value of the borrowing. In the past decade, business managers have become acutely aware that they must increase the value of the shareholders' holdings with the actions they take or else face the threat of a hostile takeover. Governments frequently borrow in anticipation of receipt of tax collections, or for the purpose of building useful infrastructure in their areas of jurisdiction, such as bridges, hospitals, roads, public buildings, and water or sewer services.

Credit Quality

During the 1980s, one aspect of debt which became of paramount importance was the ability of borrowers to repay their obligations—credit quality—and the effect it had on the business firms that had granted credit. Banks and savings and loan associations saw what seemed like sound loans become nonperforming (interest payments cease) and greatly devalued. Some of those problems resulted from changes in regional economic conditions, others from incorrect judgments by lenders, and some from dishonesty by lending officials. In the case of savings and loan associations and banks, the federal insurance funds were exhausted, and taxes replenished the funds, using resources that could have been productively used for other projects.

Furthermore, the safety of some insurance companies was jeopardized by loans that had deteriorated, and payments by insurance companies to annuitants were threatened. Endowment funds by colleges and universities were adversely affected in some cases. The result of these problems was hardship for taxpayers, for annuitants, and for many other persons in the economy.

The 1980s were characterized by extremely active merger and corporate takeover activity. Such activities require large sums of money, and especially in the early part of the decade, funds for takeovers, mergers, or leveraged buyouts were often financed with sales of bonds below investment grade (below the top four rankings as rated by Standard & Poor's or Moody's). Those bonds paid higher interest than other bonds because of the risk involved, and savings and loan associations and insurance companies were heavy purchasers. When business conditions deteriorated later in the decade, defaults occurred, the value of bonds not in default fell drastically, and the purchaser's existence sometimes was threatened. These bonds of less than investment grade are often referred to derisively as "junk bonds." Some weathered the recession; others did not.

The Burden of Private Debt

While credit quality was one aspect of debt, another was the burden of interest and principal payments on debtors. U.S. tax laws strongly encourage businesses to use debt as permanent capital because interest payments are deductible as expenses of normal operation, while dividend payments must be made from aftertax dollars. For example, a firm needs $1 of pretax income to pay interest, but if the firm has a combined corporate tax rate of 37 percent, it needs

$$\$1/(1 - \text{tax rate}) = \$1/(1 - 0.37) = \$1.59$$

of pretax income to pay $1 of dividends.

Debt, however, involves a firm promise to pay, whereas equity involves faith that managers of a firm will try to earn profits—nothing more. Should business conditions deteriorate, dividends can be cut or eliminated, and some of the nation's largest firms did so in the recession of 1991. Some firms with heavy debt became bankrupt or were forced to sell assets to satisfy creditors, and many tried to repay debt by selling equity. Debt can be a great benefit when sales are strong, but a heavy burden when business conditions deteriorate.

The Burden of Government Debt

The burden of debt is often thought of in the context of governments, particularly the federal government. In total, state and local governments have more debt outstanding than does the federal government, but attention seems focused much more on Washington, D.C., than on state capitals or on local units of government.

Government borrowing abroad increases the volume of goods or services available to the domestic economy. Attempts to purchase more from abroad without foreign borrowing would result in a decline in a nation's foreign exchange reserves, or in a change in the price of its currency compared with that of other countries, or both. Interest paid to foreigners and repayment of debt sold abroad mean less availability of goods or services in the borrowing country. External debt, therefore, represents a real future burden for a country, involving foregone consumption.

Borrowing by a government from its own citizens does not change the productive resources available to the country, but at full employment, it can reallocate resources from the private sector to the government unit (federal, state, or local). The borrower—the government—obtains money with which to purchase services or physical goods, and those lending to the government obtain financial assets. Those financial assets are very safe if they are U.S. government obligations, pay interest, are required to be held by some financial institutions, and are highly liquid. Obviously, borrowing by a government requires the payment of interest to purchasers of the bonds. That interest may be paid semiannually (or otherwise), or it may be deferred to the maturity of the bond issue (zero coupon bonds).

If the government body uses proceeds of a bond issue to build public assets such as roads, bridges, sanitation plants, water plants, or school buildings, or uses the money to purchase other valuable public services, such as freedom from war, the contribution to total economic productivity in the nation may exceed the cost of taxes paid to service the debt. In some instances, governments may create toll highways or bridges, charge fees for parks, or collect other types of user fees for goods or services, obviating the necessity for collecting taxes. In such a case, those who benefit and those who pay may be loosely matched, and the public good may greatly benefit many others as well.

When governments borrow, they do so on the same basis as other borrowers. They compete with all other borrowers. If an economy is already at full employment, government borrowing attracts funds that would have been devoted to private capital formation. At times, such a result is viewed as desirable. For example, war finance is consciously designed to put the nation's resources in the hands of the federal government to provide for the survival of the nation. If there are idle resources in the nation, spending from government borrowing can stimulate production which otherwise would not have taken place.

References

Boskin, Michael J., "Federal Government Deficits: 'Some Myths and Realities,' " *American Economic Review,* vol. 72, no. 2, May 1982, pp. 296–303; Eisner, Robert, "That (Non) Problem, the Budget Deficit," *The Wall Street Journal,* June 19, 1990, p. A15; Eisner, Robert, and Paul Pieper,

"A New View of the Federal Debt and Budget Deficits," *American Economic Review,* vol. 74, no. 1, March 1984, pp. 11–29; Federal Reserve System, Board of Governors, *Flow of Funds Statistics,* various issues; Lacker, Jeffrey M., "Why Is There Debt?" *Economic Review,* Federal Reserve Bank of Richmond, July/August 1991, pp. 3–19; Rose, Peter S., and Donald R. Fraser, *Financial Institutions,* 3d ed., Irwin, Homewood, Ill., 1988.

(*See also* Business credit; Consumer credit; Credit, an overview; Debt and deficits; Debt management; Interest rates; Mortgage credit)

William J. Brown

Debt and deficits

Everybody talks about the debt and deficits, but very few, literally, know what they are talking about. Presidential candidates, journalists, and network television anchors cannot even keep straight the difference between debt and deficits.

The deficit, all should know, is in principle the increase in the debt. Thus, if the government has a public debt of $3000 billion at the end of 1992 and runs a deficit of $200 billion in 1993, the debt by the end of 1993 will have risen to $3200 billion. The $200 billion of borrowing to finance the deficit, the excess of outlays over income, constitutes the increase in debt.

This relation—that the deficit is the addition to debt—applies, of course, to households, businesses, and government, but there is one fundamental qualification for the federal government. It does not really have to borrow to finance any excess of spending over income. It can in effect simply print more money. In fact, strictly speaking, for an economist the total debt of the federal government can be broken into interest-bearing debt—all the Treasury bonds, notes, and bills and all the U.S. savings bonds we know well—and non-interest-bearing debt. This latter consists of Treasury coin and currency and, indirectly, that part of our cash and bank deposits that is matched by Federal Reserve holdings of government securities. The interest paid by the government to the Federal Reserve on its holdings of securities essentially goes right back to the Treasury, as the Federal Reserve Banks cannot retain profits in excess of 6 percent of their invested capital.

In one sense it does not matter whether the federal debt is interest-bearing or not—in the form of securities or money—because in both cases the debt is an asset for those who hold it. It would be an aid to thinking if, before remarks about debt, every speaker would repeat out loud the ditty, "For every debtor there must a creditor be." The federal debt is then the assets of its holders who, perhaps also contrary to popular myths, are overwhelmingly American; the proportion of the gross public debt held by foreigners is in the neighborhood of 13 percent, and has not generally been rising.

The economic significance of the debt is to be found largely in this fact that it is an asset of its holders. The larger the debt, the larger these assets; and according to most economic theory and analysis, the larger these assets, other things equal, the richer people feel and hence the more they spend.

The relevant debt, it may be pointed out, is the debt owed to the public, that is, held outside the government itself. The total "gross public debt" at the end of the 1991 fiscal year was $3599 billion, but subtracting the amounts held within the government, chiefly by trust funds such as those for social security, brought the debt held by the public to $2687 billion. Indeed a further subtraction may well be in order for the $265 billion held by the Federal Reserve; these are counted as part of the holdings outside the government since the Federal Reserve Banks are technically private corporations. Inasmuch as the interest received goes back to the Treasury, though, the securities held by the Fed may well be excluded from the interest-bearing debt of the government.

There is, it should be confessed, a body of economic thought that argues that the federal debt is not properly viewed as a net asset of the private sector. Given the label "Ricardian equivalence," after the great classical English economist, David Ricardo, who presented—and rejected—the idea, it argues that financing spending by borrowing—deficits—and financing spending by taxes are essentially equivalent because people know that if they are spared taxes now they will only have to pay them later to pay off the debt. Hence, if we find that we have $200 billion more in government securities, we will not run out and spend any of these assets but will rather save them to be used eventually to pay the taxes that will pay the debt off. To the argument that we may fail to spend more because the debt payoff and increase in taxes may not take place until after we die, the counterargument is made that we still want to save the assets for our children—or grandchildren—for them to pay off.

Ricardian equivalence, which argues that debt, and deficits, largely do not matter, has many enthusiastic adherents among economic theorists, following the lead of Robert Barro, its original modern protagonist. Most economists, however, feel that, what with liquidity considerations and all the other differences between government and private finance, issues of risk and uncertainty, and, indeed, the probability that debt will never be paid off but rather rolled over and repeatedly increased in line with the growth of the economy, people will feel richer when they hold more government securities. Hence they will spend more, and so debt and deficits do matter.

How debt and deficits matter is something else. If the main effect of a deficit, increasing the public wealth in the form of government securities, is to increase spending, the question is, Is that increase in spending good or bad? That comes down to two issues: is more spending in general good or bad, and what is the increase in spending for?

Clearly, if the economy is at full employment, with no idle resources, more spending cannot bring forth more output. It can only raise prices and hence add to inflation. We thus may properly object to a deficit as too large if it brings about too much spending. This excess of spending would in the first instance raise prices. If the Federal Reserve seeks to hold inflation in check, as it probably would, the consequence will be higher real interest rates and thus less investment. And this is the essential argument against deficits that are too large. They bring about a decrease in investment—and hence of saving—and thus hold back growth in productivity and put a burden on the future. Deficits, we are frequently told, entail too much government or private consumption and "crowd out" investment.

For this argument to be applicable, however, the economy must be at, or pretty close to, full employment. Otherwise the increased public or private spending resulting from a deficit can and will bring forth more production to meet the demand. Employment and income will rise, and we will end up with more consumption and more investment and saving. Too many forget that more goods going to consumption must mean less goods going to investment only if the total amount of production is fixed. If there are idle resources, deficits that put them to work increase total output and can well increase all its components.

In fact, over at least most of the decades since World War II, real structural deficits were associated with subsequent increases in output, consumption, and investment. It would appear that much of the furor about deficits contributing to a shortfall of capital and future decline is without foundation. It may well be argued, to the contrary, that with unemployment 2 to as much as 8 percentage points above the roughly 3 percent level achieved at the peak of the high-spending Vietnam war years, deficits were too small over most of this period. We would have had more output, consumption, and investment, along with higher employment, if the deficits had been larger.

We cannot know whether deficits are larger or smaller, too large or too small, however, unless we measure them right. The measures that receive most public attention, those relating now to what Congress and the administration, Democrats and Republicans, spend most of their time arguing about, are utterly arbitrary, are inconsistent with customary business practice, and make little economic sense. Some items are decreed "off-budget." These now include the vast outlays and receipts of the social security trust funds, so that the off-budget total was in surplus in 1991 to the amount of $52 billion. Many ignore this surplus and hence count the "deficit," including only the "on-budget" items, as $52 billion more.

A fundamental, major problem in attempting to evaluate the deficit is that the conventional federal budget of the Office of Management and Budget (OMB) and the Treasury makes no distinction between current and capital spending. Of course, every private business, along with state and local governments, does. If private businesses included their current capital spending in their profit and loss statements, rather than only the depreciation charges on past investment, the bulk of those growing and most profitable would show accounting losses—or deficits.

The OMB and congressional budgets not only make no distinction between current and capital expenditures; they count acquisition of assets, financial or real, as outlays, adding to the deficit, and sales of assets as negative outlays and hence reductions in the deficit! If some $70 billion of net investment and $67 billion for acquisition of savings and loan assets were excluded from outlays, the consolidated 1991 fiscal year deficit, put at $269 billion, would be cut by half, to a current account deficit of $132 billion, as shown in Table 1. (It might be mentioned that the Bureau of Economic Analysis of the U.S. Department of Commerce, in its national income and product accounts, does at least exclude purchases and sales of assets and hence does not count the savings and loan bailout.) The addition of state and local government surpluses, which would hardly exist without federal grants-in-aid well in excess of $100 billion, would then bring the total government budget deficit down by $30 billion more, to $102 billion.

TABLE 1 Adjusted and Unadjusted Deficit, Fiscal Year 1991 (in Billions)

Federal consolidated budget	− $269
Deposit insurance	− 67
Budget excluding deposit insurance	− 202
Net investment (estimated)	− 70
Federal budget, current account	− 132
State and local budgets	+ 30
Total government budget	− 102
Inflation tax: 3.345% of $2550	+ 85
Total government, adjusted	− $17

A further important correction relates to inflation. It has been pointed out that the deficit is significant in that in adding to the debt held by the public it makes people feel richer and hence spend more. But surely, the public will not long feel richer if its holdings of debt go up by 2 percent while inflation reduces by 4 percent the real value of the debt it holds initially. It is the real debt, the debt adjusted for inflation or this inflation tax on its holders, that should matter. With the debt held by the public in fiscal 1991 averaging $2550 billion, the 3.345 percent rate of inflation entails an inflation tax of $85 billion, bringing us to a bottom line of a deficit of only $17 billion. And that deficit is more than accounted for by the shortfall of government revenues and increase of outlays for unemployment compensation related to the recession. The real, structural, current budget was thus not in deficit but in surplus!

Much is made of the importance of a balanced budget, that is, a deficit that is zero. A proper measure of balance, however, for households, business, or government, would be one in which debt is growing, but only in line with income. For the federal government this may be taken to be the ratio of debt to gross national product. It is instructive to note that this ratio stood at 0.47 at the end of the 1991 fiscal year (September 30, 1991), $2687 billion debt to $5720 billion GNP, as shown in Table 2. If there were no recession and GNP were to grow at its more normal rate of 7 percent, a similar 7 percent growth in the debt would be necessary to keep the ratio at 0.47. But 7 percent of $2687 comes to $188 billion, the amount the debt must increase, or the amount of the deficit necessary to keep the debt-GDP ratio constant. If we add to that the some $80 billion of deficit accountable to the recession, we have a total deficit of $268 billion, almost identical to the actual 1991 deficit. We find again that, except for the recession, the budget is in economically relevant balance; it is, in a growing economy, keeping the debt-income ratio from either growing or declining.

TABLE 2   Deficit with Constant Debt-to-GDP Ratio

	Debt (in billions)	GNP (in billions)	Ratio
1991	$2687	$5720	0.47
7% growth	188	400	0.47
1992	$2875	$6120	0.47

Deficit = increase in debt = $188 billion
Estimated cyclical deficit, if recession continues, $80 billion
"Balance" adjusted for recession, $268 billion
Total deficit, 1991 fiscal year, $269 billion

Of course, the United States' budget has not generally been in balance in this sense. But the debt-GNP ratio has been much higher than it is now. Immediately after World War II it was no less than 1.2, or 120 percent of gross national product. By 1980 the debt was in fact larger, but because of real growth and inflation, the ratio had sunk to 0.24, Then, with the large deficits of the 1980s the ratio doubled, but it is still much less than half of what it was in 1946.

What should be done with the debt and deficit? In a recession, one should certainly refrain from efforts to reduce the deficit (except to the extent easier money and lower interest payments would lower outlays). These, by decreasing spending, public or private, would only make the recession worse.

But even at relatively full employment, efforts to reduce the deficit, presumably in the interest of reducing public or private consumption and hence increasing national saving, may be injurious. If these efforts imply a reduction in government investment for the tangible capital of roads, bridges, airports, and infrastructure in general, or for the intangible capital of research, education, training and retraining, and the health of the population, they will mean a reduction of a relevant, comprehensive measure of national investment and saving. This would imply an increased, rather than decreased, burden on future generations. Reduction of the deficit by increases in taxes may, in similar fashion, bring reduced investment by households in new houses, durable goods, and the education and health of their children.

The conclusion then is that debt and deficits do matter. Deficits can be too small as well as too large. You cannot tell which unless you measure them right. And deficits and increases in debt may be good or bad for our tomorrows—and indeed for today—dependent on what we use them for.

References

Eisner, Robert, *How Real Is the Federal Deficit?* Free Press, New York, 1986; Eisner, Robert, "Budget Deficits: Rhetoric and Reality," *Journal of Economic Perspectives,* vol. 3, no. 2, Spring 1989, pp. 73–93; French version, "Les Déficits Budgétaires: De La Rhétorique à la Réalité," in *Économie Appliquée,* tome XLII, nos. 1–2, 1989, pp. 135–159; Rock, James M. (ed.), *The Debt and the Twin Deficits Debate,* Bristletone Books/Mayfield, Mountain View, Calif., 1991, pp. 81–107.

(*See also* Debt; Debt management; Fiscal policy)

Robert Eisner

Debt management

Any economic entity that has debt outstanding has a debt management problem. Debt issuers find themselves in one of two separate sets of circumstances which largely determine the type of debt management problem they will have. First, there are debtors who have some debt outstanding, and they may have more or less debt outstanding in the future. Usually, these are corporations or local governments that have issued some debt to finance a specific activity. Second, some debtors have a large volume of debt outstanding all the time with the intention of maintaining or increasing such debt indefinitely in the future. States, major cities, large corporations, and the federal government all experience this situation.

Infrequent Debt Issues

For debtors in the first category above, the problem of debt management normally is confined to the question of when to redeem the debt. If a corporation has issued debt in the past, for example, it may wish to buy back some of that outstanding debt in the market if it can do so at a discount to the par value of the securities. That is normally the case when market interest rates are higher than the coupon rates on the debt. With that rate situation, it is not easy for a business or government to buy back its own debt at a discount, but those with cash reserves may wish to do so. Firms with sinking funds for refunding their debt will have cash reserves even when interest rates are high.

Frequently, bonds are callable at various times at varying call premiums. For example, a bond issued some time ago may be callable very soon at 103 (1.03 times the par value), with declining premiums at future dates. Use of the concept of the time value of money allows a business or a government to determine whether paying the premium is profitable if the outstanding issue can be financed by a new bond issue at a lower coupon rate of interest. The incentives to redeem outstanding high coupon debt issues are very strong and can therefore lead to ethical dilemmas. Several years ago, *The Wall Street Journal* (Asinoff and Herman, 1991) detailed concerns of municipal bond traders that issuers might be using "staged defaults" to trigger required repayments of outstanding high-yield issues. By defaulting, an issuer became liable for repayment of the full amount immediately. That obligation could be satisfied by a new issue of bonds at a lower interest rate than that paid by the old issue. In at least one case, where a municipality financed certain improvements through a developer, there was a default followed by a new bond issue at lower interest rate to repay the original issue, and the developer who built the original improvement was still managing the improvement.

Another aspect of debt management in corporations involves the relationship between debt and equity. Debt provides financial leverage (the relationship of changes in operating earnings to changes in net income), which is desirable when sales and earnings are rising. Optimal debt will maximize stock prices, permitting equity sales at the highest price and excellent protection against undesirable takeovers. Because equity is being regularly increased through additions to retained earnings, it may be necessary for a corporation to have periodic debt issues to keep the debt-equity ratio at its optimal value.

Periodic Debt Issues

An entirely different problem is faced by debtors who need to keep outstanding a large volume of debt. The problem is particularly visible for the U.S. Treasury Department. With a huge volume of debt outstanding and issues from prior years coming due regularly, Treasury officials have a choice of maturity and type of every new issue. One consideration affecting the decisions made involves the maturity of the federal debt. Decisions to either lengthen or shorten the average maturity of the federal debt depend upon the need for either expansion or contraction of the economy. Shortening of the average maturity of the federal debt could reduce long-term rates and thus encourage investment, and at the same time provide a larger supply of short-term securities that would raise the liquidity of federal debt holders. Scott (1965) found a 34-basis-point change in long versus short yields with a 1-month change in the average maturity of the federal debt. While such changes are minor compared with fiscal or monetary policy changes, they contribute to the overall effect of stabilization policies.

While keeping stabilization policy goals in mind, the Treasury officials must also deal with the practical problem of refinancing a huge volume of debt on a regular basis. That means offering to the public the types of securities it wants to purchase. For two decades before 1991, Treasury officials regularly consulted with U.S. government bond dealers in New York and with bankers in order to determine what type of security they most wanted to purchase. When bidding irregularities by Salomon Brothers, Inc., on U.S. government bonds came to light in 1991, Treasury Department practices concerning sales of bonds came under much closer scrutiny. David Wessel (1991) detailed some of the long-standing elements of the close relationship between the Treasury Department and large customers for U.S. securities.

Corporations with a large volume of debt outstanding which they intend to roll over continually have the same type of problems the U.S. government or a state government has. The issuer of securities wants to sell the type of securities most popular in the market at that time so the price will be the highest possible. When interest rates are historically high, corporations would prefer not to issue long-term debt which will burden them for years to come. But short-term rates may be very high also, and there is always uncertainty at such a time about whether a disruption of the credit markets will occur which would preclude rolling over short-term notes. Therefore, the decision many corporations have made is to issue the long-term securities and pay a slight premium for a call provision in the debt issue. Some organizations have been successful in issuing floating-rate notes, thus relieving some of the worry that the issuer will be forced to carry high-rate debt for a long period of time when interest rates have fallen to more comfortable levels.

Other considerations for corporations issuing debt involve the nature of restrictive covenants the issuer is willing to grant to win a slightly lower interest rate. Repayment plans also figure into the cost of debt. Sinking funds offer protection to bondholders, but they increase the risk that bondholders will be repaid when they least want repayment. Call provisions allow issuers to repay debt when debt holders least wish such repayment without the added security of a sinking fund. Large corporations may borrow abroad in the Eurodollar market, and they may sell debt denominated in foreign currencies as well.

References

Henning, Charles N., William Pigott, and Robert Haney Scott, *Financial Markets and the Economy,* 5th ed., Prentice-Hall, Englewood Cliffs, N.J., 1990; Scott, R. H., "Liquidity and the Term Structure of Interest Rates," *Quarterly Journal of Economics,* vol. 79, February 1965, pp. 135–145; Wessel, David, "The Bond Club," *The Wall Street Journal,* September 25, 1991, p. A1; Asinoff, Lynn, and Tom Herman, " 'Staged' Bond Defaults May Send Holders through a Trapdoor," *The Wall Street Journal,* October 24, 1991, p. C1.

(*See also* Debt; Debt and deficits; Federal Reserve policy; Fiscal policy; Monetary policy)

William J. Brown

Decision making in business: a behavioral approach

Behavioral decision theory explains, predicts, and prescribes decisions in business and elsewhere. A decision is a choice, a commitment to action. Decision making is the set of processes culminating in choices: these processes involve environmental stimuli, perceptions, beliefs, thoughts, and actions, as well as the interactions of people, and sometimes computers and other technical systems, in organizational contexts. The domain of behavioral decision theory encompasses choice about such matters as strategy, technology, prices, resource allocation, acquisitions, divestitures, markets, organization, and staffing. It includes choice situations at the interfirm level and the intrafirm level as well as at the firm level. The emphasis has been on descriptive theory, but it has been applied normatively as well.

History and Criticism of Behavioral Decision Theory

The term "behavioral" distinguishes this theory from economic marginalism and emphasizes the importance of human behavior in the collective making of decisions, beyond the behavior described by marginalism. The founders of behavioral decision theory viewed economic marginalism as inadequate both as an explanation and as a means to predict business decisions. They argued that ambiguity in choice situations causes administrators to make decisions different from those predicted by economic marginalism. The concept of ambiguity is delineated hereinafter: it includes the notions of cognitive limitations, uncertainty, complexity, and conflict.

Business practitioners and management scholars had been discussing how decisions are made and critiquing marginalism, but not proposing a systematic framework to replace marginalism. Rather, they articulated what they called management principles: norms for "right" management. Ground-breaking work was done by Chester I. Barnard, who published *The Functions of the Executive* in 1938 after his retirement as chief executive of the American Telephone Company. Barnard incorporated behavioral hypotheses into the theoretical structure describing organizations' decisions. His work, which contrasted the administrative individual with the economic one, had an important impact within the academic community and especially at Carnegie Mellon University, the locus for early development of behavioral decision theory.

The work of H. A. Simon converted this initial interest by the academic community into a well-developed conceptual framework and stimulated extensive research. Simon laid the interdisciplinary conceptual bases for decision making in business. Research has drawn heavily upon his book *Administrative Behavior,* published in 1947. This work emphasized that administrators operate under conditions that limit and shape their decisions. Simon argued that assumptions attributable to economic marginalism are inappropriate and should be replaced by behavioral assumptions about cognitive and organizational limitations. From these new assumptions, he inferred general patterns that make administrative decisions predictable.

Another important root of behavioral decision theory is the study by R. L. Hall and C. J. Hitch which was first published in 1939. They proposed that prices are set by full-cost (markup) rules under certain conditions rather than by marginalism.

The view that behavioral decision theory better predicts business decisions than does economic marginalism was widely criticized. Fritz Machlup (1967) argued that the assumptions made within behavioral decision theory can be incorporated within a revised theory of marginalism. He delineated models of firms' decisions which incorporated behavioral constraints.

Business strategy—building on industrial economics—emerged more recently and competes with behavioral decision theory in the domain of strategic decisions. Business strategy seeks to explain and prescribe actions leading to optimal performance under various industrial structures and degrees of competition. The framework includes decisions at the levels of the intrafirm, the firm, and the interfirm as well as at the national and international levels. Michael E. Porter created widespread interest within the academic and business communities by providing a systematic framework for this line of thought in *Competitive Strategy* (1980).

The resolution of these controversies is not a matter of logical consistency. Each theoretical approach can account for decision making within its framework. The issue is a matter of use: which approach will scientists and practitioners use to explain, predict, and prescribe business decisions? The issue remains moot: and although there were fierce debates among followers of these approaches, they mostly ignore each other today to work in diverse directions.

Major Concepts and Hypotheses

A central concept of behavioral decision theory is the program: a set of activities patterned into sequences. The activities are evoked by stimuli, and alternative sequences depend on consequences of the activities and on additional stimuli. For example, a decrease in inventory (stimulus) can evoke the ordering (program) of material. The program can incorporate simple or complex decision rules. A simple rule may be the calculation of the amount to reorder, assuming a fixed amount is used in a future period; a more complex rule may involve just-in-time procedures.

Programs can be conceived to fall on a continuum from well-defined, structured decision processes to ill-defined, unstructured ones. A well-defined program is one that occurs in the same form repeatedly so that patterns can be readily recognized and exact sequences specified. An ill-defined program does not occur repeatedly; or if it does, any sequence is infrequent because of the multiplicity of branches. Patterns are obscure for ill-defined programs and described by rough rules of thumb (heuristics). Simon (1987) reasoned that intuition and judgment are ill-structured programs, based on hierarchies of paired situations and solutions, and so hunches and nonanalytical judgments have a logical basis. Accordingly, the assumption of nonrationality can be less restrictive than some models of behavioral decision theory would require.

Behavioral decision theory assumes that even though the participants may not perceive it, much of their decision behavior is standardized and follows well-defined programs. Thus, business decision making can be modeled and predicted by delineating the programs used by firms. Models have been formulated to describe and predict decision behavior in diverse situations. These models range from ones which portray decision making as highly structured programs to ones in which ambiguity makes choice seem fortuitous.

A landmark model was designed by R. M. Cyert and J. G. March in *A Behavioral Theory of the Firm* (1963). The model categorizes programs according to their associations with goals, expectations, and choices, and hypothesizes how these goals, expectations, and choices are determined. For example, the goals of a firm depend on which coalition controls the firm and on the needs of the participants in this coalition. In addition, operational goals depend upon what sequences of activities are evoked by problems and what people are associated with these sequences. The model does not assume that profit is the only goal of a business firm, or even one of several goals, nor does the model assume that a goal is maximized; rather the decision makers try to surpass some level of aspiration that depends on past goals, past performances of the firm, and past performances of comparable firms. The levels of aspiration represent an application of Simon's concept of "satisficing"—being satisfied by performances that are good enough to first reach the minimally acceptable levels of competing goals.

Other key concepts are the allocation of attention, the quasiresolution of conflict, adaptive rules, and ambiguity (March, 1988). The concept of allocation of attention is inferred from the premise that decision makers are limited by their cognitive capacity to attend simultaneously to their goals and potential information. Some information is developed by their search; other information is ignored; while still other information is unknown. Search by the firm depends on their rules for allocating attention. Transaction costs are a subject for decision rules, but their calculation is not a primary consideration in behavioral decision theory. Emphasis is given to rules that shape responses to gaps between performance and aspiration levels. For example, search may not be triggered if performance exceeds aspiration levels, while a large gap may induce a change in aspiration levels as well as second-order search. Other rules guide the path toward innovation and can depend on the availability of slack. An example of this is the "bootlegging" of experimental programs from budgets authorized for other purposes.

The quasiresolution of conflict has been a continuing focus of behavioral decision theory. A premise of behavioral decision theory is that goals and preferences of the firm are often inconsistent and remain so despite institutional arrangements for their resolution. Conflicting goals mean that the achievement of one goal impedes achieving another. Conflict may persist indefinitely, but programs can be formulated which make choices despite conflicting goals. These programs act as buffers among conflicting goals. For example, some divisions of a firm can hold goals inconsistent with other divisions. Each division can make choices based on its goals without resolving the inconsistency with the goals of other divisions. Slack can be a buffer to ameliorate goal conflicts. Another kind of buffer is time: the programs guiding activities now may be pursuing goals that conflict with those pursued previously.

Adaptive rules, another concept, entails processes for modifying rules. Rules and programs are altered to adapt them to changes in the situation. Firms learn and unlearn as a consequence of their decisions and the results of these decisions. Consequently, rules and programs are modified over time: they may be modified in small steps or involve cataclysmic change; they may be changed in the wrong direction or oscillate; or they may remain unchanged despite needed change. Learning is not assured.

Ambiguity is central for explaining and predicting choice behavior in behavioral decision theory. March (1988) saw ambiguity from sources in addition to the probability of outcomes and the uncertainty of what other "players" do. Decision makers also experience ambiguity over what are their preferences, over what are the causal connections in the situation, over what happened in the history of the firm, and over how events are to be interpreted.

The problem of ambiguity is handled in various ways. The Cyert and March model assumes that programs avoid confronting the issue of uncertainty. For example, only short-run commitments are made, and these commitments are adjusted on the basis on information feedback about outcomes. Also participants absorb uncertainty as they process information, with the consequence that the information is characterized by greater certainty when it is received by the decision makers.

A model—poetically described as a garbage can—was proposed by March and Olsen (1976) to account for the diverse ways that organizations handle ambiguity. The model provides a locus for the continuing development of behavioral decision theory. It is a general model in the sense that more specific models can be derived by modifying one or more of its assumptions. For example, work on interpreting the environment would constitute a subset of the family of models encompassed by the garbage can model.

The garbage can model conceives of organizations providing occasions for decision, with these occasions likened to garbage cans. Figuratively, problems and solutions are tossed into various garbage cans, and participants crawl in and out. Problems, solutions, and participants all flow separately from each other into occasions, and organizational and social structures direct these flows. Choices depend on what problems, solutions, and participants are present at the occasion of decision.

Prescriptions for Decision Making

In addition to explaining choices, behavioral decision theory has sought to improve the effectiveness of choice behavior. However, the emphasis is not on normative theory; and prescription focuses on specific issues rather than providing a systematic framework.

An example of a prescription is one aimed to improve the flow of participants. B. L. Hedberg, P. C. Nystrom, and W. H. Starbuck (1976) advocated minimal structures (tents instead of palaces) to permit free flows of participants. Participants have weak constraints on their abilities to change decision programs. Tents are said to be better than palaces if environments are changing rapidly, because bureaucratic structures prevent participants from perceiving changes.

Another example dealt with the question of how firms survive despite the apparent disorder of the garbage can model. M. Masuch and P. LaPotin (1989) simulated the model. They found that participants bootlegged enough rational decisions to keep the organization afloat, depending on the participants' cognitive capacity and commitment. These examples present a paradox that the assumption of nonrationality must be relaxed for those implementing normative applications.

Still other prescriptions promote playfulness, myths and storytelling, conflict and bargaining, games, and judgment. For example, commitment to organizational values is induced by stories about the founders and other charismatic figures in the firm's history.

References

Barnard, C., *The Functions of the Executive,* Harvard University Press, Cambridge, Mass., 1938; Beyer, J. M., "Ideologies, Values and Decision Making in Organizations," in P. C. Nystrom and W. H. Starbuck (eds.), *Handbook of Organizational Design,* Oxford University Press, London, 1980; Cowan, D. A., "Developing a Process Model of Problem Recognition," *Academy of Management Review,* vol. 2, 1986, pp. 763–776; Cyert, R. M., and J. G. March, *A Behavioral Theory of the Firm,* Prentice-Hall, Englewood Cliffs, N.J., 1963; Dutton, J. E., and E. Ottensmeyer, "Strategic Issue Management Systems: Forms, Functions, and Contexts," *Academy of Management Review,* vol. 12, 1987, pp. 355–365; Fredrickson, J. W., and A. L. Iaquinto, "Inertia and Creeping Rationality in Strategic Decision Processes," *Academy of Management Journal,* vol. 32, 1989, pp. 516–542; Hall, R. L., and C. J. Hitch, "Price Theory and Business Behavior," in T. Wilson and P. W. S. Andrews (eds.), *Oxford Studies in the Price Mechanism,* Oxford University Press, Oxford, 1951; Hedberg, B. L. T., P. C. Nystrom, and W. H. Starbuck, "Camping on Seesaws: Prescriptions for a Self-Designing Organization," *Administrative Science Quarterly,* vol. 21, 1976, pp. 41–65; Huff A. S., "Industry Influence on Strategic Reformulation," *Strategic Management Journal,* vol. 3, 1982, pp. 119–131; MacCrimmon, K. P., and R. N. Taylor, "Decision Making and Problem Solving," *Handbook of Industrial and Organizational Psychology,* Rand, Chicago, 1976; Machlup, F., "Theories of the Firm: Marginalist, Behavioral, Managerial," *American Economic Review,* vol. 57, 1967, pp. 1–33; March, J. G., *Decisions and Organizations,* Basil Blackwell, Oxford, 1988; March, J. G., and J. P. Olsen, *Ambiguity and Choice in Organizations,* Universitetsforlaget, Bergen, 1976; March, J. G., and H. A. Simon, *Organizations,* Wiley, New York, 1958; Masuch, M., and P. LaPotin, "Beyond Garbage Cans: An A1 Model of Organizational Choice," *Administrative Science Quarterly,* vol. 34, 1989, pp. 38–67; Porter, M. E., *Competitive Strategy: Techniques for Analyzing Industries and Competitors,* Free Press, New York, 1980; Simon, H. A., *Administrative Behavior,* Free Press, New York, 1947; Simon, H. A., "Making Management Decisions: The Role of Intuition and Emotion," *Academy of Management Execu-*

tive, February 1987, pp. 57–64. Weick, K. E., and R. L. Daft, "The Effectiveness of Interpretation Systems," in K. S. Cameron and D. A. Whetten (eds.), *Organizational Effectiveness: A Comparison of Multiple Models,* Academic Press, New York, 1983, pp. 71–93.

(*See also* Economic models; Firm theory; Satisficing; Simulation in business and economics)

C. Edward Weber

Decline of the Soviet economy

After a long period of national economic growth (starting in 1928) which was unprecedented historically in spite of the calamitous economic cost and suffering of World War II, the Soviet economy began a decline in the early 1970s. This decline led to the perestroika policies of Mikhail S. Gorbachev in the years 1985 to 1991 which were aimed at improving the political, social, and economic life of the consumer while retaining the fundamental features of socialism. Gorbachev was criticized variously for going too far, for stopping too short, and, by those who agreed with the basic policies, for standing too still and not moving faster. The differences in goals and means for achieving the policies espoused by Gorbachev and his critics on both the right and the left and their incessant debate destroyed confidence and engendered chaotic conditions in the supply and production of basic consumer goods; ethnic separatist pressures built up in the constituent Soviet republics and undermined the role of the central government; and other group interests impeded implementation of Gorbachev's pursuit of a more consumer-oriented but still socialist economy. These factors led to the final breakup of the U.S.S.R. in December 1991 and its replacement by the Commonwealth of Independent States (*Sodruzhestvo nezavisimykh gosudarstv,* or SNG).

This article starts with a look at independent Western estimates of Soviet growth (necessitated by deficiencies in Soviet macroeconomic statistical methodology which preclude meaningful analysis of growth) and other important socioeconomic measures of development. The second section concentrates in greater detail on the statistical outlines of the pre-Gorbachev economic decline, and the third section presents various evidence bearing on possible explanations for this decline, mainly, increasing fragmentation and the consequent reduced productivity of capital investment.

1. Statistical Measures of Growth

In 1988, Soviet statistical practice introduced Western-style gross national product for inclusion with the macroeconomic measures traditionally reported to measure Soviet national economic performance, presenting summary data for selected years back to 1980. But the traditional growth statistics presented previously are very poor measures of economic development for three main reasons: (1) consumer services, which normally account for an important part of every nation's total economic activity, are excluded (physical production services are included, however); (2) the prices used to weight output for the critical 1928–1950 period are not constant, their designation as "unchanged (*neizmenennye*) prices of 1926/7" notwithstanding; and (3) in any event, use of fixed early-year price weights, which relate to preindustrialization relative scarcities, seriously exaggerates measured growth since it becomes ever easier (cheaper) to produce industrial products although they continue to be valued at preindustrialization prices (the Gerschenkron effect).

Besides these defects, an important set of macroeconomic measures (gross social product and similarly calculated measures such as gross industrial production) have the additional drawback of representing total sales rather than value-added; they double-count extensively those outputs that serve as intermediate inputs for other producers. Some Westerners have also expressed concern about the non–market conditioning of Soviet prices, presumably impugning their acceptability as reflections of social well-being, although this problem arises wherever there is a large sector of prices which are not determined by strictly market forces, including those parts of Western capitalist economies which are heavily subsidized or influenced by government policy.

In any event, it is clear that independent estimation of Soviet performance was necessary. While many scholars participated in various partial studies, such as industrial production, the pioneering work in total GNP estimation was done by Abram Bergson (1961). Bergson's work continues to represent the main source for analysis of the pre-1960 economy, and his methods continue to provide guidance to the efforts of others in this field for the post-1960 period (Becker, 1969; CIA: Schroeder and Denton, 1982; numerous CIA scholars, 1982; Greenslade, 1976; and others).

Given the great shift in relative scarcities and prices which quite properly must be expected to accompany industrialization, the most appropriate measure of growth over this 47-year period is the geometric average of the growth experienced over subperiods for each of which a constant set of prices is employed. This index-linking procedure is typical standard practice when computing indexes over long time periods and is employed, for example, in consumer price indexes. Economic theory suggests that the prices used within each subperiod be those of the end year of the period. (This is a Paasche index of output and corresponds to division of the ratio of nominal GNP levels by a Laspeyres price index.) The result of using Bergson's calculations for three subperiods (1928–1937, 1937–1950, and 1950–1955, together with Greenslade's calculation for 1955–1970) gives a total GNP annual rate of growth of 5.4 percent from 1928 to 1970.

Naturally it is more meaningful to put this growth into per capita terms. This is complicated by the numerous gaps in published Soviet population statistics, especially in the prewar period. A Western consensus view for 1928 population is 151.5 million, which, when related to the official 1970 population of 241.7 million, represents an annual increase of 1.1 percent and gives a per capita GNP growth rate of 4.3 percent, astounding for such a long period. However, to gauge overall Soviet performance since its beginning requires pushing back the starting date to 1918 (but since 1918 population figures are not reported, we may use 1917 as the threshold year). While the economy was operating far below capacity, the Bolsheviks' efforts in their first decade merely brought it back to the 1913 levels, i.e., did no more than might have been hoped for from a continued tsarist regime. Adding 10 years to the length of the period but continuing with the 1928 production levels, we find a per capita GNP growth rate of 3.5 percent. This is again very high by comparative historic standards of other industrialized countries and in relation to economies with socio-economic conditions similar to those of tsarist Russia (limited social mobility, illiteracy, income polarization), such as Brazil, which constitute a more appropriate comparison. It is an especially notable achievement when improvements in life expectancy, income distribution, and educational attainment are taken into account. For example, the rate of literacy rose from around 35 percent to virtually 100 percent, contrasting with a continuing illiteracy rate of 40 percent or so in Brazil.

2. Decline in Growth since 1970

CIA estimates of annual GNP growth during the 1970s was 3.2 percent on average (with a decline between the first and second quinquennia from 3.7 percent to 2.7 percent), making for annual per capita growth of 2.3 percent overall. Sharpest declines were experienced in agriculture, which was marked by several drought years, but other consumer-related industries were among the hardest hit with per capita growth rates during the 1970s as follows: light industry, 1.7 percent; food industry, 1.4 percent; housing, 1.5 percent; recreation, 1.7 percent. Total per capita consumption growth during the 1970s fell to 2.6 percent from 3.8 percent in the preceding decade and 4.2 percent in the 1950s according to CIA estimates (CIA: Shroeder and Denton, 1982). And despite the high rate of consumption growth in earlier years, Soviet consumption levels were still less than one-third those in the United States and less than half those in Western Europe when Gorbachev was chosen as general secretary in 1985.

This deteriorating performance is surprising at first glance, coming as it does after the institution of the so-called Liberman reforms of the mid-1960s (first bruited under General Secretary and Prime Minister Nikita S. Khrushchev) which introduced more businesslike practices into the planning process; and, indeed, there was a small improvement in GNP growth between the first and second halves of that decade. The subsequent decline beginning in the 1970s is best explained through the increasing bureaucratization of the government and the economic planning process under the prolonged stay in office of Leonid Brezhnev and Alexei Kosygin, who deposed Khrushchev in 1964. Ministerial assertiveness and self-interest, which Khrushchev had tried to break by reorganizing the planning and economic structure from sectoral to regional lines—which proved ineffective in the event—led to fragmentation of investment and excessive delays in capital assimilation. One indicator of this is the declining share of construction work in progress which was actually put on stream—from 31 percent in 1965 to only 9 percent in 1979, recovering somewhat to 22 percent in 1985.

3. The Final Years, 1985–1991

Against the background of declining growth in GNP and consumption and still low consumption levels, Gorbachev took the reins of office on March 11, 1985, after the successive deaths in office of Yuri Andropov (February 1984) and Konstantin Chernenko (March 1985) following the death of Brezhnev in November 1982. Gorbachev attempted to reshape the economy within the basic ideals of socialism, especially promoting consumer welfare through such policies as reduction of military tensions and expenditures; encouragement of new forms of business organization, risk taking, and rewards; and increased personal responsibility and more businesslike behavior in state-owned enterprises. But the new political freedoms that he instituted raised resistance by opponents to change as well as by proponents of much greater change, all compounded by centrifugal regional and ethnic aspirations, leaving his government floundering and the state ultimately foundering on the rocks of separation, with almost all the former Soviet republics declaring independence by December 1991, whereupon 11 of them became loosely affiliated in a new Commonwealth of Independent States.

References

Becker, Abraham, *Soviet National Income 1958–1964,* University of California Press, Berkeley, 1969; Bergson, Abram, *The Real National Income of Soviet Russia since 1928,* Harvard University Press, Cambridge, Mass., 1961; CIA, *USSR: Measures of Economic Growth and Development,*

1950–80, U.S. Congress Joint Economic Committee, 1982, especially Part 1: John Pitzer, "Gross National Product of the USSR, 1950–80," and Part IV: Gertrude E. Shroeder and M. Elizabeth Denton, "An Index of Consumption in the USSR,"; Gerschenkron, Alexander, *A Dollar Index of Soviet Machinery Output, 1927–8 to 1937,* Rand, Santa Monica, Calif., 1951; Greenslade, Rush, "The Real Gross National Product of the USSR, 1950–1975," in *Soviet Economy in a New Perspective,* U.S. Congress Joint Economic Committee, 1976, pp. 269–300; Jasny, Naum, *The Soviet Economy during the Plan Era,* Stanford University Press, Palo Alto, Calif., 1951; *Narodnoe khozyaystvo SSSR* (*National Economy of the USSR*—statistical yearbook), various years.

(*See also* Communism; Marxism; Perestroika; Socialism)

Alan Abouchar

Demand

Demand is a key concept in both macroeconomics and microeconomics. In the former, consumption is mainly a function of income; whereas in the latter, consumption or demand is primarily, but not exclusively, a function of price. This analysis of demand relates to microeconomic theory.

The theory of demand was mostly implicit in the writings of classical economists before the late nineteenth century. Current theory rests on the foundations laid by Marshall (1890), Edgeworth (1881), and Pareto (1896). Marshall viewed demand in a cardinal context, in which utility could be quantified. Most contemporary economists hold the approach taken by Edgeworth and Pareto, in which demand has only ordinal characteristics and in which indifference or preferences become central to the analysis.

Much economic analysis focuses on the relation between prices and quantities demanded, the other variables being provisionally held constant. At the various prices that could prevail in a market during some period of time, different quantities of a good or service would be bought. Demand, then, is considered as a list of prices and quantities, with one quantity for each possible price. With price on the vertical axis and quantity on the horizontal axis, the demand curve slopes downward from left to right, signifying that smaller quantities are bought at higher prices and larger quantities are bought at lower prices. The inverse relation between price and quantity is usually called the law of demand. The law rests on two foundations. One is the theory of the consumer, the logic of which shows that the consumer responds to lower prices by buying more. The other foundation is empirical, with innumerable studies of demand in actual markets having demonstrated the existence of downward-sloping demand curves.

Exceptions to the Law of Demand

Exceptions to the law of demand are the curiosa of theorists. The best-known exception is the Giffen effect—a consumer buys more, not less, of a commodity at higher prices when a negative income effect dominates over the substitution effect. Another is the Veblen effect—some commodities are theoretically wanted solely for their higher prices. The higher these prices are, the more the use of such commodities fulfills the requirements of conspicuous consumption, and thus the stronger the demand for them.

Changes in Consumer Demand

Increases or decreases in demand are changes in the quantities that would be bought at any of the possible array of prices. Changes in demand are shifts or movements of the entire demand curve. A shift to the right means an increase in demand. It can come from any one or a combination of the following: a change in consumer desire or taste, sometimes augmented by volumes of advertising; a rise in consumers' income; a rise in the prices of substitutes; or a fall in the prices of complements. Of course, opposite changes in these factors cause a decrease in demand, i.e., a leftward shift of the entire demand curve. An exception here applies to inferior goods, which are defined as those goods and services bought in smaller amounts as consumer incomes rise.

In an uncertain economy, especially an inflationary one, price expectation can affect demand. For storable commodities, when consumers believe that expected future prices will be higher, buyers tend to increase their current demand and thus tend to make their expectations self-fulfilling.

The demands for durable goods can fluctuate widely over time, as consumers' incomes vary. A durable good has both a stock demand and a flow demand. The stock demand is for the amount that consumers want to hold over a period of years. The flow demand in a given year consists of replacement demand, i.e., for purchases to maintain the stock at some level, and of expansion demand, i.e., for purchases to increase the stock.

Income-Compensated Demand

Income-compensated demand curves indicate how consumers' welfare can change in response to decreases or increases in price. Compensated demand curves explain only the substitution effect. Statistically, the gains or losses in income, resulting from price changes, are removed from the demand equations by estimating the relative share of the item in the consumers' income. For normal goods, the income-compensated demand curve is above the noncompensated demand curve when price rises and below the noncompensated demand curve when price falls. These differences tend to make the income-compensated demand curve less elastic than the noncompensated demand curve and accordingly make the size of consumers' surplus larger.

Utility Produced by the Consumer

The Marshallian individual demand function is taken directly from the marginal utility function of the individual, on the assumption that the individual derives utility from the commodity demanded. In the 1960s Becker and Lancaster (1965) devised an individual demand function, hypothesizing that utility is produced by the consumer, using commodities or commodity characteristics as inputs, rather than as direct sources of utility.

Private versus Collective Demand

The demand for pure private goods is both exclusive and rival. When a good is bought by one individual, exclusion to others is likely. Purchases of goods are also rival; the consumer must make choices among goods, say, food, clothing, and entertainment. With pure public goods, or collective consumer goods, there is neither exclusion nor rivalry. Once the good, say, a stealth bomber, is produced, it is consumed by everyone in society. Furthermore, for the individual consumer, there is no rivalry among the bomber, food, clothing, and entertainment. The market demand curve for the private sector is the horizontal addition of individual demand curves, and so equilibrium occurs when $MU_A + MU_B = MC = P$. Because of nonexclusion for public goods, individual demand curves are vertically summed and equilibrium occurs when $MU_A + MU_B = MC = P$.

Producers' Demand

The demands of producers for productive services, i.e., for land, labor, and raw materials, have properties like those of consumers' demands. Producers' demand is derived demand, ultimately depending on consumers' demands. The quantities demanded by any one producer for any one service are also inversely related to price, and additional quantities of a productive service yield diminishing marginal products. Because of this, the producer is willing to buy more units only at lower prices. The law of demand, then, holds for producers. For them, too, changes in demand come from changes in the prices of related productive services, as well as from changes in the prices of outputs and in technology.

Sellers' Demand

From the points of view of the sellers of products and services, demand holds another perspective. In markets with many sellers of homogeneous products, the demand for the product of any single seller is infinitely large; that is, the individual producer can sell all the goods at the market price. However, in markets with few sellers, demand appears as a line sloping down to the right. But the demand functions of such sellers are critically interdependent, because in each, the most important variable is the prices charged by other sellers in the same market.

Scarcity and Demand

The concept of demand is essential to the understanding of the meaning of shortages or scarcities. They occur when the quantities demanded at some prices exceed the quantities available at the same prices. At the (too low) prices some able and willing buyers cannot buy what they want. Such low prices usually result from government price controls, and sometimes from lags in market adjustments when demand increases rapidly.

References

Becker, Gary S., "A Theory of the Allocation of Time," *Economic Journal,* vol. 75, 1965, pp. 493–517; Edgeworh, F. Y., *Mathematical Psychics,* Kegan Paul, London, 1881. Friedman, Milton, "The Marshallian Demand Curve," *Journal of Political Economy,* vol. LVII, no. 6, December 1949, pp. 463–495; Lancaster, Kelvin J., "A New Approach to Consumer Theory," *Journal of Political Economy,* vol. 74, 1966, pp. 132–157; Marshall, Alfred, *Principles of Economics,* 8th ed., Macmillan, London, 1920, book III; Pareto, Vilfredo, *Cours d' Economies Politique,* Rouge, Lausanne, 1896; Schultz, Henry, *The Theory and Measurement of Demand,* University of Chicago Press, Chicago, 1938; Veblen, Thorstein, *The Theory of the Leisure Class,* Macmillan, New York, 1908.

(*See also* Competition; Consumer theory; General equilibrium; Marginal cost; Marginal revenue; Monopoly and oligopoly; Scarcity; Stock-flow analysis; Supply)

Mary A. Holman

Demographics and economics

The population of a nation—its size, growth rate, and age composition—significantly affects its economic fortunes. The fact that population in many of the less-developed nations of the world has been increasing more rapidly than its industrial and agricultural output has created severe social and human problems. In such nations, efforts to reduce the birthrate are an important facet of economic policy since a lower birthrate is a prerequisite for improving living standards.

More generally, abrupt changes in fertility or mortality rates have far-reaching economic implications for a nation. A sharp rise or decline in the level of the nation's births during any particular period will eventually determine the size of its labor force, and hence, most likely, its rate of economic development. Similarly, medical advances almost always increase longevity; thus, in most nations of the world today an increasing proportion of the population consists of relatively older and economically dependent individuals.

When changes in the fertility and mortality rates occur slowly, the consequences are generally moderate, but abrupt shifts have ripple effects that are extensive and often persist over a long time period. The relatively recent large drop in infant mortality in many of the less-developed nations of the world has accelerated population growth, making it increasingly difficult to improve living standards.

In the United States, the low level of births during the Great Depression in the thirties was followed by the post–World War II birth boom and then, beginning in the mid-sixties, by a sharp decline in fertility rates. These changes, each following so closely on the other, have had abrupt and pronounced effects on the population age mix and the nation's economic growth rate.

In the late seventies, the U.S. labor force grew by more than 2 percent a year, as the children born in the postwar baby boom came of working age. During the 1990s, the country's labor force will grow by only about 1 percent a year, and make for slower economic growth. However, a labor shortage is likely to result in a more rapid rise in wage rates, which, in turn, could induce more capital investment in labor-saving technology. The United States is also likely to liberalize its immigration laws to encourage immigration. In the 1990s, a larger proportion of the American population will be of working age, a small proportion dependents—a situation that contributes to higher living standards. However, early in the next century, when the baby-boom generation begins to reach retirement age, there will be considerable pressure on retirement funds and the government's social security program.

Governments have occasionally taken measures to encourage a higher or a lower fertility rate. Some governments have given bonuses and special privileges to women who have many children. Conversely, the communist government of China, with its large population, mandated a limit of one child for each married couple. This has helped reduce population growth, but it has also resulted in the disturbing situation in which many more male babies than female babies survived beyond the first year.

The economic destiny of a nation is, of course, determined by innumerable forces other than its demographic history. Nevertheless, at any particular moment the size and structure of a country's population can have a significant effect on its economic growth and its general well-being.

References

Cohen, Wilbur J., and Charles F. Westhoff, *Demographic Dynamics in America*, Free Press, New York, 1977; Fosler, R. Scott, *Demographic Change and the American Future*, published for the Committee for Economic Development, University of Pittsburgh Press, Pittsburgh, 1990; Knodel, J. E., *Demographic Behavior in the Past*, Cambridge University Press, Cambridge, 1988; National Bureau of Economic Research, *Demographic and Economic Change in Developed Countries*, Conference of the Universities–National Bureau Committee for Economic Research,

Princeton University Press, Princeton, N.J., 1960; "The World Fertility Survey," *Demographic Surveys,* Oxford University Press, Oxford, 1987.

(*See also* Economic growth; Employment and unemployment; Labor force; Zero population growth)

Fabian Linden

Deposits

Deposits are obligations (liabilities) of a financial institution owned by a person, firm, or institution. The deposit may be payable immediately, in which case it is known as a demand deposit (the familiar checking account), or it may be payable only after the passage of a period of time, in which case it is known as a time deposit.

Demand Deposits

Demand deposits may be paid to anyone designated by the owner of the deposit account. The most familiar method of paying demand-deposit balances to others is by means of a check, showing the person to whom funds should be transferred, the date, and the signature of the person authorized to withdraw funds from the account, usually the owner. The check is a negotiable instrument that may be transferred by endorsement to another person, and that person may transfer it to another, and so on.

Not all demand-deposit withdrawals are by check, however. Individuals or businesses wishing to make rapid transfers of funds may pay by wire. The sending institution sends a message to the receiving institution concerning the transfer, and the transfer is complete. Wire transfers are usually business transactions of substantial amount, but individuals may wire funds also. Withdrawals may also be made from demand-deposit accounts by electronic teller machines. Such withdrawals may be a transfer from the demand-deposit account to a time-deposit account in the same institution, or a withdrawal of currency. Many financial institutions provide telephone transfer service to their depositors, and so depositors may transfer from their demand-deposit account to their time-deposit account (or vice versa) immediately by making a telephone call.

Time Deposits

Time deposits are placed with the financial institution for a period of time, ranging from one day to years. The deposits typically pay interest at a rate stated when the deposit is made, and that rate is often higher than can be obtained from interest-paying demand deposits, such as NOW accounts. Depositors in time deposits gain higher interest payments than in demand-deposit accounts, but sacrifice the convenience of immediate withdrawals. The financial institution pays higher interest rates, but knows when the deposit is made the date when it must be repaid, which aids the institution in management of its assets and liabilities. Time-deposit certificates may be either negotiable or nonnegotiable. Individuals usually invest less than $100,000, the maximum insured amount, but business firms often invest far more than that in time-deposit accounts. Time deposits of $100,000 and over may be negotiable, and business firms usually seek that feature. If the firm subsequently needs the funds before the maturity of the instrument, the deposit certificate can be sold to someone else, who will ultimately present it for redemption.

Deposit Interest Rates

Until April 1, 1986, banks, savings and loan associations, and mutual savings banks operated under a variety of regulations concerning the interest rates they could pay on deposits. The Depository Institutions Deregulation and Monetary Control Act (DIDMCA) of 1980 gave legal responsibility for setting interest rate ceilings to the Depository Institutions Deregulation Committee. That committee included representatives from the federal financial institutions regulatory agencies and the Treasury Department. The committee operated under a congressional mandate to eliminate deposit interest ceilings by early 1986, and it accomplished its task on April 1 of that year.

Deposit Competition

Only commercial banks provided demand-deposit accounts in 1960. By 1984, such accounts were also available through savings and loan associations, savings banks, credit unions, and a variety of nonfinancial firms through arrangements with banks or savings and loan associations. In addition, individuals could invest their money in money-market mutual funds, and they could withdraw their funds by draft, by wire, or by telephone. Stock brokerage customers may have their idle funds held in a money-market account, and they may transfer the funds to securities purchases within the firm, or elsewhere, with ease. All depository institutions can offer interest-paying demand-deposit accounts. The result is very greatly increased competition among financial institutions of all types for deposit funds. Competition in lending has also increased, but not to the same degree as in the market for deposits because not all lenders have the same broad range of options available to them.

References

Federal Reserve Bulletin, various issues; Kidwell, David S., and Richard L. Peterson, *Financial Institutions, Markets, and Money,* 4th ed., Dryden Press, Hinsdale, Ill., 1990; Rose, Peter S., and Donald R. Fraser, *Financial Institutions,* 3d ed., Business Publications, Homewood, Ill., 1988.

(*See also* Banking system; Money supply)

William J. Brown

Depreciation allowances

Depreciation policy is one of the most volatile areas of the U.S. Internal Revenue Code. Periods of liberalization have been followed by periods in which depreciation methods have been tightened, and this cyclical process culminated in the 1980s with the Tax Acts of 1981 and 1986. These two acts could hardly have been more different in their philosophy and economic effects, and they signal a profound disagreement about the appropriate role of depreciation allowances in the formulation of tax policy.

There is no debate about the need for some system of capital cost recovery. If a taxpayer uses up a capital asset in the process of generating income—e.g., if a $10,000 taxicab is worn out after 1 year of service—this loss of capital value must be allowed as a cost in computing the economic income attributable to the asset. If, for example, the taxicab generated only $10,000 in net revenue after operating expenses, the taxi's owner has realized no economic income, since the entire net revenue is needed to replace the capital value lost when the taxi is retired from service (indeed, the owner has actually lost income, since the $10,000 might have earned interest income if put into an alterative investment). In a pure income tax system, the loss in capital value would be recognized as an expense and allowed as a deduction from revenue. For assets lasting more than 1 year, a pure income tax would allow an annual deduction equal to the true loss in capital value occurring during that year. The true loss in value is termed "economic depreciation."

However, while there is no real disagreement about the definition of economic income, there is a basic debate about the desirability of a tax system based on this concept of income. One source of opposition to pure income taxation comes from those who argue that investment incentives are needed to stimulate capital formation during periods of slow economic growth, to compensate for the adverse effects of inflation in a tax system that limits depreciation allowances to the historical cost of an investment and not the replacement cost, and to improve the international competitiveness of American industry.

One way to achieve these goals is to lower the effective rate of taxation on capital income by establishing a more rapid recovery of capital costs than allowed by economic depreciation: because of the time value of money, a dollar of tax deduction received today is worth more than a dollar next year; the interest income earned on the earlier receipt of depreciation deductions offsets part of the tax liability and lowers the effective rate of taxation, even though the nominal tax rate remains the same and the total amount of depreciation remains the same over the life of the asset. The acceleration in deductions can be achieved by allowing more rapid methods of capital cost recovery—the "accelerated depreciation" forms like sum-of-the-years' digits and double declining balances—or by shortening the write-off period over which the asset is depreciated (the "useful life").

Another source of opposition to a pure income tax comes from those who argue that consumption is a more equitable and efficient base for a tax system than income. One approach to achieving a de facto consumption tax is to assign a marginal effective tax rate of zero to income accruing to capital (i.e., essentially to attempt to shift the burden of the tax system onto labor income). One way to achieve a zero marginal effective tax rate is to allow taxpayers to treat capital expenditures as an immediate expense—that is, to accelerate depreciation allowances to such an extent that they are all realized in the first year.

Finally, there are those who argue that a pure income tax is simply not feasible. A truly pure system would require that every capital asset have a separate economic depreciation schedule reflecting the unique experience of that asset. Such a requirement would impose absurdly high administrative costs and complexity on taxpayers: even if it were possible for taxpayers to measure true depreciation costs—and it is by no means clear that such costs can be measured accurately for all types of capital—the sheer amount of record keeping would be excessive. A similar criticism is leveled at any complex system of guidelines, like the old Bulletin F list of useful asset lives that was initially used by the Internal Revenue Service to determine the appropriateness of depreciation allowances claimed by taxpayers.

Tax Acts of 1968, 1982, and 1986
and Depreciation Allowances

The three strands of opposition came together in the Tax Act of 1981 to produce the accelerated cost recovery system of depreciation allowances. This system essentially put all assets into one of four classes, with useful lives of 3, 5, 10, or 15 years. These write-off periods were considerably shorter for most assets than those in effect under the prior asset depreciation range system, and led to a dramatic reduction in the marginal effective income tax rates. Indeed, when combined with the investment tax credit, the marginal effective tax rate on some assets became negative. Moreover, whereas previous depreciation systems had at least paid lip service to the principle that depreciation allowances should be related to actual taxpayer experience, the 1981 act severed any conceptual link between tax depreciation and actual experience.

The dramatic acceleration of depreciation allowances, combined with other provisions of the tax system, e.g., safe-harbor leasing, stimulated the growth of tax shelters, and combined to create the impression that the system was inequitable and complex. In reaction to this perception, the Tax Act of 1982 began to repeal some of the benefits to capital income enacted in 1981, and this reaction culminated in the Tax Act of 1986. The tax reform of 1986 sought to establish a "level playing field" by removing the special incentives and provisions that eroded the base of the income tax and necessitated a higher tax rate on those sources of income not favored by tax policy. In other words, the 1986 Tax Act represented a shift back toward a pure income tax system with a lower marginal rate and larger tax base. But the shift was only partial. Many sources of income were left untaxed (the implicit income from owner-occupied housing), and special provisions remained (the deduction for state and local income taxes). This tendency was also apparent in the new depreciation system, MACRS, which is essentially a modified version of the asset depreciation range system, with somewhat shorter lives and without the "range."

The new depreciation system established multiple asset classes, generally lengthened write-off periods relative to 1981 law, and provided less generous depreciation methods for some assets (principally structures). The resulting marginal effective tax rates were closer to the nominal tax rates, and so the new system moved closer to economic depreciation. However, the new system stopped short of this objective. Total depreciation deductions were still restricted to the original cost of the investment, with no allowance for the effects of inflation. Moreover, by retaining the concept of "useful economic life" as the basis for classifying assets, rather than moving to a system based more explicitly on the decline in asset values, there was little explicit account of the rapid erosion in capital value due to obsolescence that may occur in those types of capital that are subject to rapid technological innovation. This problem was addressed, in part, by the establishment of a new office in the Treasury Department charged with studying value-based economic depreciation and proposing revision where needed.

References

Hulten, Charles R., and Robert A. Klayman, "Investment Incentives," in H. Aaron, H. Galper, and J. Peckman (eds.), *The Uneasy Compromise: Problems of a Hybrid Income-Consumption Tax,* Brookings, Washington, D.C., 1988, pp. 317–337; Hulten, Charles R., and James W. Robertson, "The Taxation of High Technology Industries," *National Tax Journal,* vol. XXXVII, no. 3,

September 1984, pp. 327–346; Hulten, Charles R., and Frank C. Wykoff, "The Measurement of Economic Depreciation," in Charles R. Hulten (ed.), *Depreciation, Inflation, and the Taxation of Income from Capital,* Urban Institute, Washington, D.C., 1981, pp. 81–175.

(*See also* Capital formation; Taxation, an overview)

Charles R. Hulten

Developing nations (*see* International economics, an overview)

Diffusion indexes

A diffusion index is a time series, usually monthly or quarterly, representing the percentage of items in a given population that are rising over a specified interval. Thus, a diffusion index of 75 means that 75 percent of the items are rising and 25 percent are falling. The index can be as high as 100 and as low as zero. The same information can also be reported in other ways, as explained hereinafter.

Use in Economic Analysis

Diffusion indexes are used in economic analysis in several ways. One is to report information that is available only in the form of directions of change. In some surveys of business enterprises, for example, the respondents may be asked only whether production increased during the past month, remained the same, or declined. No information is obtained about the size of the change. The percentage of respondents reporting an increase is a diffusion index. Another type of index is derived from the components of an aggregate, such as total industrial production or total employment. The figures for the individual industries, for example, are used to determine how many industries have experienced an increase in production, and this number is expressed as a percentage of the total number of industries in the aggregate. The daily stock market report on the number of issues that rose or fell in price is an example of this kind of diffusion index. A third type of diffusion index may be constructed from, say, a list of leading indicators that are not commensurate with one another in terms of units but that behave in a similar way during business cycles. The percentage rising during a given interval shows how widespread the expansion or contraction is among these indicators.

Diffusion indexes of the first type are compiled in many countries from surveys of business executives, purchasing managers, and consumers. Often the questions are directed not only to past changes but also to expected future changes. Since the questions are simple, they can be answered quickly by individuals who are likely to know the answers or to have informed opinions. For the same reason, the answers can be tabulated and released promptly.

Calculating Diffusion

The results of these surveys are often reported in the form of net balances, obtained by subtracting the percentage reporting a decline from the percentage reporting an increase. The percentage reporting no change is left out of the calculation, though it does affect the result. The method is arithmetically equivalent, except for a scaling factor, to the alternative method that is commonly used in the two other types of diffusion indexes, which is to divide the no-change group equally between the increases and the declines. If R, U, and F are the percentages rising, unchanged, and falling, respectively, so that $R + U + F = 100$, then the net balance is $R - F$, while the percentage rising plus half the unchanged percentage is $R + \frac{1}{2}U$. It follows that $R - F = 2(R + \frac{1}{2} U) - 100$.

Diffusion indexes expressed in either of these two ways are influenced by the size of the no-change groups and hence are superior to methods that report simply the percentage rising without regard to how the remaining returns are divided between the no-change and the declining groups or to methods that split the no-change group proportionately between the rising and declining groups. Since diffusion indexes are based upon information about changes over time, they are related to rates of change computed over similar intervals. Thus, a diffusion index showing the percentage of industries reporting a rise in employment during the past month will be related to the rise in total employment reported by those industries during the month. The relation will not be precise because the diffusion index ignores the magnitude of the change in each industry, recording only the direction. It answers a different question—namely, how widespread the increases or decreases are among the several industries. It gives information about employment that cannot be inferred directly from the aggregate figure itself. In many instances diffusion indexes are less affected by erratic movements than are rates of change since an occasional large movement in a single component may have a substantial effect upon an aggregate, whereas in a diffusion index the size of the change doesn't matter.

Diffusion Indexes and the Business Cycle

Studies of business cycles have shown that diffusion indexes act in a characteristic way. As a business-cycle expansion gets under way, the number of companies, industries, geographic areas, and types of activity that participate in the expansion increases. Diffusion indexes rise. But after the expansion has been under way for some time, forces develop that prevent further expansion in one industry or another, or one sector or another. Capacity limitations may become a factor here and there, the cost of holding inventories may become burdensome, competition for business may become more intense, the banking system may begin to restrict further credit expansion, etc. The scope of the expansion begins to recede, and diffusion indexes decline. Aggregate economic activity—output, employment, income, sales—is still likely to continue to expand for a while, however. As recessionary factors take hold, diffusion indexes continue to drop and begin recording a majority of activities declining. The downswing spreads over more and more sectors for some months, but then prospects start to brighten in some areas. Purchases that had been postponed are found more attractive, and new investment projects are revitalized. Hiring picks up. Diffusion indexes reach their lows and start to rise. Soon thereafter the decline in aggregate activity comes to a halt and a new business-cycle expansion gets under way.

Historical studies of this process have shown how diffusion indexes undergo cyclical movements corresponding to the business cycle but also leading it in the manner described. They have shown that severe recessions are generally more widespread than mild recessions. Hence, diffusion indexes compiled currently have become one of the tools that analysts use to appraise the state of the business cycle. In Japan, the Economic Planning Agency has constructed a chronology of business cycles based upon diffusion indexes. Diffusion indexes are also employed to show the extent to which business cycles spread from one country to another.

Diffusion Indexes of Prices and Inflation

Diffusion indexes of prices are of special interest in connection with the study of inflation, since inflation is usually defined as a general rise in prices and since price diffusion indexes measure the degree of generality. As inflation spreads, a larger percentage of prices rise. As it subsides, the percentage of rising prices declines. In 1972, for example, in a survey of business executives conducted by Dun and Bradstreet, the percentage reporting that their selling prices had increased since the year before was about 75 percent. By the spring of 1974, this diffusion index had risen to about 95 percent. Then as a recession developed, the proportion reporting price increases fell and reached about 80 percent early in 1975. A similar swing occurred in price diffusion indexes constructed from commodity price quotations.

Diffusion indexes are often used to report expectations. Expected changes in prices, profits, sales, income, and expenditures are regularly reported in this manner. Changes in the climate of opinion can thus be determined and their potential effect on the economy evaluated.

References

Alexander, Sidney S., "Rate of Change Approaches to Forecasting—Diffusion Indexes and First Differences," *The Economic Journal,* June 1958, pp. 288–301; Broida, Arthur L., "Diffusion Indexes," *American Statistician,* June 1955, pp. 7–16; Burns, Arthur F., "New Facts on Business Cycles," *Thirtieth Annual Report,* National Bureau of Economic Research, New York, May 1950, pp. 3–31, reprinted in Geoffrey H. Moore (ed.), *Business Cycle Indicators,* Princeton University Press, Princeton, N.J., 1961, chap. 2; Burns, Arthur F., and Wesley C. Mitchell, *Measuring Business Cycles,* National Bureau of Economic Research, New York, 1946, pp. 66–71, 96–107; Getz, Patricia, and Mark Ulmer, "Diffusion Indexes: An Economic Barometer," *Monthly Labor Review,* April 1990; Hastay, Millard, "The Dun and Bradstreet Surveys of Businessmen's Expectations," *Proceedings of the Business and Economics Statistics Section,* American Statistical Association, Washington, D.C., 1955, pp. 93–123; Hickman, Bert G., "Diffusion, Acceleration and Business Cycles," *American Economic Review,* September 1959, pp. 535–565; Hultgren, Thor, *Costs, Prices, and Profits: Their Cyclical Relations,* National Bureau of Economic Research, New York, 1965; Klein, Philip A., and Geoffrey H. Moore, "NAPM Business Survey Data: Their Value as Leading Indicators," *Journal of Purchasing and Materials Management,* Winter 1988; Mintz, Ilse, *Cyclical Fluctuations in the Exports of the United States since 1879,* National Bureau of Economic Research, New York, 1967; Moore, Geoffrey H. (ed.), *Business Cycle Indicators,* Princeton University Press, Princeton, N.J., 1961, chaps. 2, 8, 9, 18, 19; Moore, Geoffrey H., *Business Cycles, Inflation and Forecasting,* 2d ed., Ballinger, Cambridge, Mass., 1983, chaps. 1, 9, 12; Moore, Geoffrey H., and John P. Cullity, "An Evaluation of Consumer Confidence Surveys as Leading Indicators," Center for International Business Cycle Research, Columbia University, New York, 1989; Shiskin, Julius, "Business Cycle Indicators: The Known and the Unknown," in John J. Clark (ed.), *The Management of Forecasting,* St. Johns University Press, New York, 1969, pp. 47–88; Strigel, Werner H., *Trade Cycle Indicators Derived from Qualitative Data,* Ifo-Institut fur Wirtschaftsforschung, Munich, 1972; Theil, Henri, "Recent Experiences with the Munich Business Test," *Econometrica,* April 1955, pp. 184–192; U.S. Bureau of Labor Statistics, *Employment and Earnings,* published monthly; U.S. Department of Commerce, *Handbook of Cyclical Indicators,* 1984; U.S. Department of Commerce, *Survey of Current Business,* published monthly.

(*See also* Business cycles; Economic forecasting methods; Leading indicator approach to forecasting; Statistical methods in economics and business, an overview)

Geoffrey H. Moore

Diminishing returns law

The law of diminishing returns is the general notion that the productive process becomes progressively less efficient as it expands. Recognized in the 1760s by Anne Robert Jacques Turgot, who served Louis XVI of France as finance minister, the law of diminishing returns states that adding more of a particular input to a productive process will yield progressively less additional output per unit of input. For instance, if tomatoes are planted by hand on a certain farm, augmenting the number of workers engaged in planting will increase the total output of tomatoes less and less. Indeed, adding more workers might ultimately make this process so inefficient that the harvest might end up being absolutely smaller.

Thomas Malthus provided one of the most famous examples of the law of diminishing returns, though he did not use the term and may not have realized the full significance of his conclusions. In the first edition of his *Essay on the Principle of Population* (1798), he hypothesized that when population grows according to a geometric progression (2, 4, 8, 16, 32, . . .), food production would grow only according to an arithmetic progression (2, 4, 6, 8, 10, . . .). This clearly implies that as population and food production expand, the output per worker will shrink; or seen another way, the input of additional labor required to achieve constant increments of output will need to rise dramatically.

A precise statement of the law of diminishing returns requires several elaborations. One is that the law becomes operative only if at least one input into the productive process becomes relatively scarce. Both of the above examples assume that the supply of land used in production does not increase, so that as production expands, the supply of land becomes scarce relative to the other inputs. In some land-rich countries, this limitation may not apply because more land is available to be brought into production. If all inputs can be augmented in equal proportions (including such intangibles as management skills and transportation facilities), the law of diminishing returns will not operate; some scarcity must develop before it does. Land-rich countries may be subject to the law of diminishing returns if they suffer from relatively limited supplies of labor or capital.

Another elaboration is that the law of diminishing returns may, under certain circumstances, be temporarily replaced by its logical opposite, the law of increasing returns (better known as economies of scale). If the input that is, relatively speaking, scarcest in the production of a certain item can be augmented, output may well rise disproportionately. For example, a large, fully equipped factory may have had to operate inefficiently because of a shortage of workers who could handle the machinery. Breaking this bottleneck, e.g., through immigration or by training more workers, will permit better use of the resources (land and machinery) that are already available, so that the productivity per worker might well increase. But this effect will work only up to a point. When one or another of the inputs becomes relatively scarce, the law of diminishing returns will again come into play.

In sum, the impact of the law of diminishing returns may be disguised or postponed by any development that increases the supply or the productivity of the scarcest input. Increased population, division of labor, better specialization, new inventions or innovations, improved technology, and discovery of new resources all serve, temporarily, to stretch the limits imposed by the relative scarcity of one of the inputs into the productive process. As soon as the impact of such a development has played itself out, however, the law of diminishing returns will, without fail, reassert itself.

References

Fellner, William, *Modern Economic Analysis,* McGraw-Hill, New York, 1960, pp. 62–69; Hamberg, Daniel, *Principles of a Growing Economy,* Norton, New York, 1961, pp. 501–511; Watson, Donald S., and Mary A. Holmes, *Price Theory and Its Uses,* 4th ed., Houghton Mifflin, Boston, 1976.

(*See also* Economies of scale)

G. H. Mattersdorff

Discount rate (*see* Federal Reserve policy; Monetary policy; Open-market operations)

Discrimination economics

Discrimination is often equated with the unequal economic position typically observed between racial, gender, or ethnic groups. To whatever group discrimination applies, economists use the same methodology for measuring differences in economic well-being. One takes wages and occupation to represent economic success, and discrimination is measured as the unexplained difference in these success indexes when productivity differences between demographic groups are held constant.

Whether such a definition is without measurement error is open to question, as is where within society the causes for discrimination lie.

Causes for Discrimination

Theories of discrimination are categorized as either demand- or supply-oriented. The value of contrasting these two theories lies in appropriate governmental policy to achieve economic equality. If discrimination emerges because of demand considerations, then the economy is failing to utilize fully its highly productive work force, so that enforcement of current equal employment opportunity (EEO) legislation may be in order. On the other hand, if unequal economic outcomes result because of supply considerations, then EEO-type governmental intervention could lead to a distorted resource allocation with inefficiencies. In this case, rather than helping the disadvantaged groups, efficiency is hampered so that in the long run all end up suffering. Thus understanding the causes of economic differences within an economy is important.

Demand-oriented theories argue that managers, nonminority workers, or even consumers express preferences regarding workers and coworkers. These preferences may be purely prejudicial or instead be based on "statistical discrimination," whereby a firm merely perceives a minority member's productivity to be low. Demand discrimination leads firms to decrease their willingness to hire minorities in good jobs, thus increasing the supply of minorities to the more menial jobs, which causes lower minority wages and exacerbates minority-nonminority wage differentials.

For the most part, evidence seems to contradict such a demand interpretation. Clearly, direct discrimination in hiring would not be consistent with long-run profit maximization. Wage premiums to nonminorities as well as inefficient hiring practices lead to lower productivity and diminished profits. Nondiscriminating firms would enter the market at a competitive advantage. Either discriminators would be driven out of business, or two types of firms would survive—ones composed of only minority workers and others composed of only majority workers. With the possible exception of the nonprofit sector, such a long-run prognosis is inconsistent with data.

Supply theories argue that differences in economic well-being are more a societal phenomenon. Societal institutions in part induced by government policies lead to differential economic well-being. Marriage taxes, for example, can result in lower incentives for wives to work, giving rise to a division of labor in the home which results in lower lifetime female labor-force participation, less female human capital investment, and lower wages and job opportunities. Similarly, lower-quality education in ghetto schools can lead to poor scholastic performance, a diminished work ethic, and lower productivity. Supply theories thus assert that discrimination takes place well before an individual even enters the work force. Firms do not discriminate, but instead pay lower wages to minorities merely to reflect differential worker productivity.

Evidence indicates strong gender differences in labor-market aspirations long before one begins to work. For example, the average woman spends about 10 years out of the labor force. Expectations of intermittent lifetime labor-force participation lead women to take different subjects in school and to specialize in non-market-oriented fields in college. Accordingly, women tend to be found in jobs that require less training than men. Further, married women with children often forgo good jobs to minimize commuting time.

It should be remembered that not all women follow such labor-force work patterns. Some women work every year after leaving school, and some achieve high-level jobs. In fact, women with the strongest labor-force commitments are the ones most likely to achieve the highest-paying, most prestigious jobs.

Similarly, societal institutions change over time. From 1890 to 1988, U.S. married female labor-force participation skyrocketed from 4.6 percent to 56.5 percent. In part because of these changes, the female-to-male earnings ratio rose from about 0.45 in 1890 to about 0.70 in 1988. Indeed from 1980 to 1988 alone, the female wage ratio rose 1.3 percent per year, and differences in professional education and occupational segregation narrowed despite dramatic decreases in government civil rights expenditures.

For blacks there is a history of governmental discrimination, especially regarding educational inequality. Blacks seem to be achieving more equal schooling and labor-market success than previous generations, especially since the May 1954 *Brown v. Board of Education* Supreme Court decision. Indeed the ratio of black-to-white family income which increased from 0.37 to 0.71 between 1939 and 1988 accelerated since 1960.

Measuring Discrimination

Economists determine the amount of discrimination by computing a discrimination coefficient. This measure represents the proportion, for example, of the wage gap between racial, gender, or ethnic groups unexplained once productivity differences are controlled statistically. The discrimination coefficient d is computed conceptually according to the following formula:

$$d = \frac{Y_f^* - Y_f}{\overline{Y}_m - \overline{Y}_f} \tag{1}$$

where Y = measure of economic success (e.g., earnings)

$\quad\quad Y_m$ = mean economic success of group m

$\quad\quad Y_f$ = mean economic success of group f

$\quad\quad Y_f^*$ = earnings power of group f if group f has m's productivity

Clearly the denominator $\overline{Y}_m - \overline{Y}_f$ is the mean earnings differential between m and f, and $Y_f^* - Y_f$ is the earnings gap unexplained by productivity differences. The discrimination coefficient represents the proportion of the unexplained earnings differential.

Implementing this formula is difficult. Y_f^* is not directly observable, and hence must be estimated by statistical regression analysis. In addition, no direct measures are available for worker productivity, so that socioeconomic variables such as education, age, experience, marital status, industry, union membership, and region must be used as proxies.

Essentially this procedure entails using employee data to relate race, gender, and ethnic group to economic success while holding constant the socioeconomic variables designed to reflect productivity. One commonly used regression has the form

$$Y = \delta G + \beta X + \varepsilon \tag{2}$$

where $Y \equiv$ a measure of economic well-being such as earnings (usually measured in logarithmic form)

$\quad\quad G \equiv$ a dummy variable denoting whether an individual is a member of the particular minority group in question

$\quad\quad X \equiv$ a vector of an individual's sociological characteristics

Studies of discrimination concentrate on estimating the δ coefficient. This coefficient reflects earnings differences between racial, gender, or ethnic groups. It measures the earnings gap remaining between any two groups, holding constant the socioeconomic variables chosen to proxy productivity. For example, when Y is the logarithm of earnings and δ is found to be 0.3, then one group receives approximately a 30 percent wage premium. If the total differential is, say, 50 percent, then the discrimination coefficient is 0.60 (0.30/0.50), implying that 60 percent of the wage gap remains unexplained by socioeconomic factors.

Current computations for the United States as well as other countries using various data yield economywide male-female discrimination coefficients between about 10 and 70 percent. However, these figures diminish often to zero for narrow occupations within firms, leading some to believe that firms may be discriminating by assigning women to low-paying jobs. Despite supply-side evidence concerning occupational distribution, believers in this advocate comparable worth policies that would force firms to base wages not on supply and demand considerations, but instead on the characteristics of job incumbents.

For black men compared with white men, the discrimination coefficient using 1980 data is about 40 percent. This indicates that the 38 percent annual earnings disparity observed in 1980 would be reduced to 14 percent if black males had white male characteristics. On the other hand, there is rough wage parity between black and white women's wages.

Potential Biases

Obviously these discrimination measures may be overestimated or underestimated depending on whether errors are embedded within this procedure. Most crucial are the socioeconomic variables chosen as proxies for worker productivity. As an example, take the case of the marital status adjustment when computing sex discrimination. For the average female, being married means lower lifetime labor-force participation, lower human capital investment, and hence lower on-the-job productivity. For males the opposite is true: being married means greater labor-force attachment, more human capital, and higher on-the-job productivity. Thus assuming that marital status (or other socioeconomic variables) should affect males and females in the same way could lead to biases in estimating the discrimination coefficient. Recent evidence for the United States and other countries indicates that indeed this is the case. Since exact measures of worker productivity are not available, the exact choice of socioeconomic variables is crucial. Much criticism of current discrimination estimates centers on this issue.

In addition, one can question the relevance of productivity adjustments on philosophical grounds. The motive for adjustment is apparent. It is expected that payment schemes be based on worker productivity. Observing equally productive workers receiving different wages constitutes discrimination. Yet it is quite possible that discriminatory practices have led to differential productivity in the first place. For example, if unequal employment practices lead blacks to receive inferior education (or women to frequently drop out of the labor force), then blacks obtaining less schooling (or women having lower job aspirations) may be a result of discrimination. Netting out these factors may lead to an understatement of the discrimination coefficient. Even if firms are not responsible, societal influences may be a factor and should be considered.

Other biases also mar the exact computation of discrimination coefficients. These include errors typical of most econometric studies, and have led to alternative though not widely used specifications, including reverse regression analysis to look at education and experience differences among individuals receiving the same wage, simultaneous-equations models to account for the reverse causality of individuals working less hard because firms pay them lower wages, selectivity correction techniques to adjust the data to account for individuals not at work, and panel data to circumvent population heterogeneity problems. Despite these biases, estimates of intergroup differences appear robust, and as with the simpler techniques appear to be shrinking over time.

References

Becker, Gary, *The Economics of Discrimination,* 2d ed., University of Chicago Press, Chicago, 1971; Bergmann, Barbara, *The Economic Emergence of Women,* Basic Books, New York, 1986; Blau, Francine, and Marianne Ferber, *The Economics of Women, Men, and Work,* Prentice-Hall, Englewood Cliffs, N.J., 1986; Cornwall, Richard, and Phanandra Wunnava, *New Approaches to the Analysis of Discrimination,* Praeger, New York, forthcoming; Goldin, Claudia, *Understanding the Gender Gap,* Oxford University Press, Oxford, 1990; Polachek, Solomon, and W. Stanley Siebert, *The Economics of Earnings,* Cambridge University Press, Cambridge, Mass., forthcoming; Smith, James, and Finis Welch, "Black Economic Progress after Myrdal," *Journal of Economic Literature,* June 1989, pp. 519–564; U.S. Commission on Civil Rights, *Comparable Worth: Issue for the 1980s,* U.S. Commission on Civil Rights, 1984.

(*See also* Demographics and economics; Employment and unemployment; Labor force)

Solomon W. Polachek

Diseconomies of scale (*see* Diminishing returns law)

Disintermediation

Financial institutions serve as intermediaries for individuals and nonfinancial corporations that typically channel the bulk of their investable funds into the credit markets. "Disintermediation" is the term applied to a situation in which the normal flow of funds through financial institutions is disrupted because of sudden switches in the preferences of the nonfinancial sector. For example, instead of augmenting a bank savings account, an individual might buy a U.S. Treasury bill; instead of borrowing from a bank, a corporation may issue commercial paper.

The motivation for such switches is economic—more specifically, interest rates in the open market that differ from rates available at financial institutions by an unusual margin. What is meant by "unusual" is open to question, but it will help to recall that in long-term equilibrium the intermediaries must cover all costs, including a return on capital. Hence, some margin—such as 1 to 1½ percentage points—in favor of open-market rates over institutional rates (in the case of the investor), or in favor of the institution as against the open market (in the case of the borrower) represents the normal compensation the market exacts for the financial intermediation service. As will become clear, the viability of the intermediary function itself can become an open question.

Acute and Chronic Disintermediation

The term disintermediation was coined in 1966 when restrictive monetary policy forced open-market rates above then-controlled institutional rates. The association of disintermediation with monetary restraint continued through the subsequent four cyclical episodes that occurred between the mid-1960s and the mid-1980s (i.e., 1969–1970, 1973–1974, 1979–1980, and 1981–1982). The extent of the problem can be judged by the fact that in normal years (e.g., 1976–1977) up to 95 percent of all funds supplied to credit markets came from institutions, whereas in a heavy disintermediation year (e.g., 1982) that proportion fell to roughly 80 percent.

Repetitive cyclical disintermediation periods had profound secular effects upon the U.S. financial intermediary system. These effects—amounting to a pronounced weakening of the intermediary function per se—became apparent during the 1980s and early 1990s. Although not encompassed in the origin of the term, a redefinition such as "chronic disintermediation" (as distinct from previous acute episodes) would describe the new problem precisely.

Whereas it had been believed until the 1980s that interest rate controls on the intermediaries were responsible for disintermediation, it turned out that lifting these controls (as essentially happened by mid-decade) would lead to new difficulties. Thus, the thrift intermediaries (savings and loan associations, mutual savings banks) turned out to have long-term assets (primarily residential mortgages) with insufficient yield to maintain their deposit base at open-market rates. Liberalized asset rules would permit only gradual adjustment, while market pressures were immediate. Thus, greatly increased risk taking (on the lending or deposit-taking side) appeared inevitable but resulted in losses leading to the demise of one-third to one-half of all thrifts by the early 1990s. Government-sponsored intermediaries (such as the Federal National Mortgage Association, FNMA) took over much of the residential mortgage market, primarily by acquiring such mortgages, packaging them into credit-market instruments (such as collateralized mortgage obligations, CMOs), and selling these through investment bankers and/or directly to the public. The character of both intermediaries and intermediation changed substantively.

Chronic disintermediation also came to affect commercial banks, the largest depository intermediary group. The required margin between lending and deposit rates tended to widen (partly because of stiffening bank capital and reserve rules) while commercial paper issuing techniques and markets broadened nationally and internationally. By the early 1990s, commercial banks had lost much credit-market share and were consolidating among themselves while also seeking to enter nontraditional fields. Because of increased risk associated with intermediaries, federal deposit insurance became vital to the maintenance of a depository intermediary system in the United States.

Disintermediation and Credit

There is considerable dissent about the influence of disintermediation upon total credit availability. It can be shown theoretically that potential credit expansion on the basis of any given liquidity base (such as nonborrowed member-bank reserves) is directly correlated with the degree of financial intermediation in the economy. Thus, disintermediation should curb total credit expansion.

The difficulty with an empirical demonstration of the point is twofold. First, since acute disintermediation has tended to coincide with monetary restraint, the effect of such restraint on total credit has to be separated from disintermediation per se—a major statistical problem.

Second, the concept of disintermediation has become muddled as acute episodes have led to chronic consequences. For example, by the late 1970s heavy flows of funds, disintermediated out of traditional thrift institutions, were going into mushrooming money-market funds (MMFs), which then acquired short-term paper of financial and nonfinancial borrowers. The diversion of credit flows continues to be demonstrated by these facts, but whether or not total credit creation has been impaired by disintermediation importantly depends not only on total credit flows at the time of the rise of MMFs but also on whether the term disintermediation should be applied to shifts of funds among intermediaries, which the MMFs surely are. Similarly, the rising importance of government-sponsored mortgage institutions changes the character of intermediation itself.

Disintermediation was originally a part of inflation pathology. The huge fallout effect of disintermediation can be partly traced to lingering inflation effects. However, disintermediation may also be interpreted as the exposure of structural weaknesses in the U.S. financial system.

References

Kaufman, Henry, *Interest Rates, the Markets and the New Financial World,* Times Books, New York, 1986; Ritter, Lawrence S., and William L. Silber, *Principles of Money, Banking and Financial Markets,* 2d ed., Basic Books, New York, 1977.

(*See also* Commercial bank problems and solutions; Credit, an overview; Federal Reserve policy; Financial institutions; Financial instruments; Inflation; Interest rates; Monetary policy; Mortgage credit; Open-market operations; Thrift institutions: problems and challenges)

Francis H. Schott

Distributed lags in economics

In economics, many causes produce effects not all at once but spread over time. A company appropriates funds for a new plant all at once, but those funds are spent gradually as the construction is carried out and the equipment put in place. A consumer's income increases; at first the consumer saves most of the increase but after a while buys a new car or a bigger house. The value of the dollar falls relative to European currencies, but Americans do not immediately cancel their European vacations or stop buying parts for their European automobiles. Gradually, however, they shift away from European goods.

In each of these cases, a cause—the appropriation, the increase in income, or the change in exchange rates—has effects that appear only with a lag. The effects, when they appear, are usually spread over a period of time. If, for example, all the spending from the appropriation came exactly 6 months after the appropriation, we would call the lag discrete; but since the spending is spread over a number of months or quarters, we say that the lag is distributed. Description of distributed lags forms a major part of the work of explaining quantitatively how the economy works.

If we let x be the time series of observations on the cause and y be the time series of observations on the effect, then one way of expressing a distributed lag between x and y is

$$y_t = \sum_{i=0}^{n} w_i x_{t-i} + z_t \qquad (1)$$

where n = number of periods over which the lag extends

z_t = factors other than x which influence y

In the appropriations case, w_i is the fraction of an appropriation spent during the ith period after it was made.

Equation (1) assumes that y is a linear function with fixed weights of x. Although we will be concerned here with only such distributed lags, it should be pointed out that the w_i might be variable. For example, in the appropriations-expenditure lag, the w_i may depend on the backlogs of orders of the equipment suppliers. Or the whole relationship may be nonlinear, as would be the case if a second devaluation sped up the effects of a first devaluation. However, we will concentrate on how to estimate the w_i of Equation (1).

The approach to the estimation depends upon whether n, the number weights, is finite or infinite.

Finite Lags

The direct way to estimate the w's in (1) is by ordinary least-squares regression. If this method gives satisfactory results, if the successive values of w_i rise and fall in a reasonable pattern, no further analysis is necessary. It will often happen, however, that the pattern of weights that results is irregular, raising the suspicion that it is being influenced by chance correlations. One may then impose linear restrictions on the w's to smooth them out. For example, to impose the requirement that the weights w_1, w_2, and w_3 lie on a straight line, one places on them the restriction

$$w_2 - w_1 = w_3 - w_2 \qquad \text{or} \qquad w_3 - 2w_2 + w_1 = 0$$

With an appropriate regression program, one can specify one's subjective trade-off between closeness of fit of the equation on the one hand and conformity to the restriction on the other. The program will then minimize its user's "displeasure" with misses in the fit and with nonconformity to the restrictions.

Often the requirement that the weights lie on a straight line will seem excessively heavy-handed, and it will seem better to require that they lie on a quadratic, for example,

$$w_4 - 3w_3 + 3w_2 - w_1 = 0$$

or on a cubic by requiring that

$$w_5 - 4w_4 + 6w_3 - 4w_2 + w_1 = 0$$

Again, conformity with these restrictions must be balanced against the desire to have the equation fit the data closely.

This approach of imposing restrictions only where they seem necessary is due, basically, to Robert J. Shiller (1973) and generalizes the method of Shirley M. Almon (1965), which requires that all the weights lie exactly on a polynomial of some specified degree.

Infinite Lags

Another, altogether different, approach stems from the work of L. M. Koyck. Koyck (1954) assumed an infinitely long lag ($n = \infty$) with $w_i = a\lambda^i$.

Thus

$$y_t = a \sum_{i=0}^{\infty} \lambda^i x_{t-i} \tag{2}$$

We may then lag this equation once and multiply both sides of λ to get

$$\lambda y_{t-1} = a \sum_{i=0}^{\infty} \lambda^{(i+1)} x_{t-(i+1)} = a \sum_{i=1}^{\infty} \lambda^i x_{t-i} \tag{3}$$

Subtracting (3) from (2) gives

$$y_t - \lambda y_{t-1} = a\lambda^0 x_{t-0} = ax_t \tag{4}$$

or

$$y_t = \lambda y_{t-1} + ax_t$$

In (4), one just regresses the dependent variable on its own lagged value and on x_t.

The Koyck lag can be written as

$$y_t = \frac{1}{1 - \lambda L} ax_t \tag{5}$$

where L is the lag operator defined by the equations

$$Lx_t = x_{t-1} \quad \text{and} \quad Ly_t = y_{t-1}$$

Synthetic division gives

$$\frac{1}{1 - \lambda L} = 1 + \lambda L + \lambda^2 L^2 + \lambda^3 L^3 + \cdots + \lambda^n L^n$$

and this equation applied to (5) gives (2). If we multiply both sides of (5) by $1 - \lambda L$, we get precisely (4).

The Koyck lag in the form of Equation (5) can be readily generalized to, say,

$$y_t = \frac{1}{1 - \lambda L - \mu L^2} (ax_t + bx_{t-1}) \tag{6}$$

This equation would be estimated in the form

$$y_t = \lambda y_{t-1} + \mu y_{t-2} + a x_t + b x_{t-1} \tag{7}$$

and the weights w_i calculated by synthetic division. Equation (7) incorporates both moving-average ($a x_t + b x_{t-1}$) and autoregressive ($\lambda y_{t-1} + \mu y_{t-2}$) elements. It illustrates, therefore, what is called the autoregressive moving-average (ARMA) method. Obviously, more terms of each type could be included.

There are two principal difficulties with equations that include autoregressive terms.

1. If there is more than one explanatory variable, all of them must have the same pattern of lag weights.

2. Lagged values of the dependent variable pick up the influence of other omitted variables that affect y_{t-1} in about the same way as they affect y_t. Thus, y_{t-1} becomes a proxy not merely for earlier values of x but also for other variables. Thus, the estimate of the lag becomes very sensitive to errors of specification. The estimates of λ tend to be too high, and the lag too long.

Neither of these problems arises with the finite lags. For versatility and reliability, finite methods, therefore, are preferable.

References

Almon, Shirley M., "The Distributed Lag between Capital Appropriations and Expenditures," *Econometrica,* vol. 33, 1965, pp. 178–196; Griliches, Zvi, "Distributed Lags: A Survey," *Econometrica,* vol. 35, 1967, pp 16–49; Koyck, L. M., *Distributed Lags and Investment Analysis,* North-Holland, Amsterdam, 1954; Shiller, Robert J., "A Distributed Lag Estimator Derived from Smoothness Priors," *Econometrica,* vol. 41, 1973, pp. 775–788.

(*See also* Regression analysis in business and economics; Time series analysis)

Clopper Almon, Jr.

Distribution theory

Distribution theory is based on the notion that the optimum allocation of resources is achieved through the workings of the price system in which resources move from less profitable to more profitable uses and from less important to more important uses. A widely accepted definition of economics, which itself points out the importance of distribution theory, is the study of the allocation of scarce resources among unlimited and competing uses and users.

A basic problem of every economic system is the means of achieving an allocation of resources that will result in maximum efficiency. In order to achieve this goal, resources should be channeled into the production of goods that consumers want most and should be prevented from entering the production of goods that consumers want least. Prices affect our decisions as consumers and producers.

Consumers' Preference

In a free enterprise society, wants are usually ranked by the preference of consumers, whether individuals or businesses. Thus, the power of the consumer in the economy is indicated by consumer sovereignty, for it is consumers' decisions about the quantities and qualities of goods and services purchased in the marketplace which determine what is to be produced and in what proportions. Since the expenditures of consumers are reflected in market prices, prices play a key role in the decisions that actually determine the allocation of resources.

When producers do not appraise correctly consumers' preferences, the prices of their goods will fall because they will generate an oversupply of goods. Subsequently, their profits will decline, and unless they alter their policy, they will be unable to pay for the resources they buy and use in the production process. Sooner or later the less-efficient businesses will gradually lose out both in competition for consumers' demands and in competition for resources needed in production. And, finally, these firms will fail and go into bankruptcy.

Scarcity

Resource allocation becomes a major problem when the economy is operating under conditions of full or nearly full employment. It is then that resources become scarce. But economic resources are not usually scarce right across the resource board. Thus, there are degrees of scarcity, with some resources more plentiful than others. When resources are scarce, however, the scarcer they are, the higher the price.

Scarce goods are insufficient to satisfy all the wants for them. Thus society faces the choice among the resource range of wants that are to be satisfied. Hence, when resources are devoted to one segment of production, they are unavailable to other segments of the economy. It is then that we have the problem of distributing scarce resources among different uses and users.

It is to society's interest that production techniques be employed which make the greatest use of plentiful resources or make the least use of relatively scarce resources. Resources that are plentiful relative to total demand for them will be lower in price than resource items that are scarce.

Optimum Resource Allocation

A necessary condition for an optimum allocation of resources is that the marginal product of any resource be the same for all its alternative uses. With price competition in all product and resource markets, an optimum allocation is achieved automatically, but monopoly or monopsony leads to different marginal products with different uses and thus to misallocation.

There are other impediments to optimum resource allocation. Among them are ignorance of profitable opportunities, sociological and psychological factors (e.g., lack of factor mobility), and institutional restraints (e.g., labor unions and patents).

References

Baranzini, M., and R. Scazzieri, *Knowledge of Economics in Foundations of Economic Structures of Inquiry and Economic Theory Base*, Blackwell, Oxford, 1986; Bodenhorn, Diran, *Intermediate Price Theory*, McGraw-Hill, New York, 1961, pp. 261–270; Hamberg, Daniel, *Principles of a Growing Economy*, Norton, New York, 1961; Leftwich, Richard H., *The Price System and Resource Allocation*, 6th ed., Dryden Press, Hinsdale, Ill., 1976; Trescott, Paul B., *The Logic of the Price System*, McGraw-Hill, New York, 1970.

(*See also* Demand; General equilibrium; Price theory; Scarcity)

Douglas Greenwald

Division of labor

Division of labor refers to the splitting of tasks or jobs among the individuals that constitute a firm, a household, or even an entire economy. The classic example of the division of labor is Adam Smith's description of the pin factory, a very productive enterprise in which tasks were divided among workers. Some workers only drew the wire, others only straightened it, others cut it, others sharpened the tip, and still others put on the head. This division of labor resulted in much greater productivity than would be observed if every worker were charged with the manufacture of the entire pin.

Indeed, Smith emphasized that efficiency in production and the wealth of a society depended upon the combination of the division of labor and trade among individuals. An entertaining passage in *The Wealth of Nations* distinguishes between the wealth of human society and that of dogs as owing to the canines' failure to break up tasks to the appropriate species and then engage in trade of these efficiently produced tasks.

Several reasons have been put forward to explain why the division of tasks among different people leads to increased efficiency. Concentration on a single activity may contribute to dexterity and the speed with which one can produce a unit. Any setup costs involved in moving from one activity to another can be reduced by limiting the tasks of each individual. Innovation may occur more frequently when each person's attention is focussed on a particular operation. Also, if a worker's productivity increases with the amount of time the worker has spent training for a particular task, then it follows that for a given length of training period, the productivity of workers will be greater the greater is the segregation of workers into the learning and production of particular tasks. Beyond some point, further division of labor may impede productivity. Boredom may result from endless repetition. Innovative thinking may benefit from breadth of perspective.

The fact that larger-volume markets often exhibit a finer division of labor suggests that the potential gains from such division have not been exhausted. In comparison with rural areas, metropolitan areas have more physicians who concentrate on particular disease groups, more specialty retail stores, and more lawyers who concentrate on particular types of cases. Such examples also illustrate that sufficient demand for a final product (that is, a sufficient market size) is required to spawn a greater division of labor.

Transportation costs interact with the nature of a final product to determine the effective size of a market, the degree of the division of labor, productivity, and, ultimately, the wealth of an economy. In service industries, geographic proximity often limits a market's size. In goods industries, access to transportation networks and available transportation technology determine such limits. Smith noted that a finer division of labor occurred along navigable waterways than at inland locations. Either natural or politically imposed barriers to trade will limit the effective size of a market, the degree of division of labor, the productivity of labor, and the wealth achievable in such economies.

Other applications of these ideas include the division of labor in households— which has largely been sex-based—trade among countries in differentiated versions of similar products, and explanations of economic growth. A consideration of ideas about the division of labor suggests that the relationship between population growth and economic well-being can actually run counter to the Malthusian view. Increases in population may allow increases in productivity due to an even greater division of labor and thus lead to greater per capita incomes.

References

Barzel, Yoram, and Ben T. Yu, "The Effect of the Utilization Rate on the Division of Labor," *Economic Inquiry,* vol. 22, January 1984, pp. 18–27; Becker, Gary S., "Human Capital, Effort, and the Sexual Division of Labor," *Journal of Labor Economics,* vol. 3, January 1985 suppl., pp. S33–S58; Francois, Joseph F., "Trade in Producer Services and Returns due to Specialization under Monopolistic Competition," *Canadian Journal of Economics,* vol. 23, February 1990, pp. 109–124; Rosen, Sherwin, "Specialization and Human Capital," *Journal of Labor Economics,* vol. 1, January 1983, pp. 43–49; Smith, Adam, *An Inquiry into the Nature and Causes of the Wealth of Nations,* 1776, Random House, New York, 1937; Stigler, George, "The Division of Labor Is Limited by the Extent of the Market," *Journal of Political Economy,* vol. 59, June 1951, pp. 185–193; Yang, Xiaokai, and Jeff Borland, "A Microeconomic Mechanism for Economic Growth," *Journal of Political Economy,* vol. 99, June 1991, pp. 460–482.

(*See also* Productivity)

James R. Baumgardner

Dumping

The term "dumping" is used in the field of international trade to refer to goods exported at a price set below the exporting country's domestic price or set below the cost of production. The importing country considers the goods to have been "dumped," i.e., sold at an unfairly low price and one that damages its own producers' ability to compete. Under U.S. trade law, the GATT international dumping code, and trade laws of most other countries, dumping is considered to be an unfair trade practice and is subject to antidumping duties to offset the "dumping margin," i.e., the amount below home price or cost.

U.S. Antidumping Law

U.S. antidumping law has existed since 1916, but the antidumping statute that provides the basis for the current law was passed in 1921. (The extended version of the U.S. antidumping statute is in section 731 of the Tariff Act of 1930.) Implementation of the law has evolved and been made more precise, as experiences with difficulties in determining fair market value have grown and as dumping charges worldwide have increased. Standards now employed in the Department of Commerce (DOC) of the United States to determine the fair market value of foreign imports are (1) the exporting country's home price; (2) a comparable third country's price for the same or similar good, if home price is not available; and, finally, (3) a "constructed-value" price equal to "cost" plus general expense (of at least 10 percent) and a normal profit return (of at least 8 percent), if neither of the previously listed measures is available. The below-cost standard represented in item (3) was only added to U.S. trade law in 1974. Before that time, the United States had no legal response to the circumstance where imported goods, priced identically to those sold in the exporter's market, were at the same time priced below the exporter's costs of production. As the law is stated, however, the below-cost standard is used only as a fallback response.

Even with such standards, implementing the antidumping law can be difficult and time-consuming. By itself the process is considered to be a barrier to trade. Under current U.S. law, complaints of dumping are filed simultaneously with the U.S. International Trade Commission (ITC) for preliminary assessment of injury to domestic producers and with the DOC for a first estimate of the dumping margin. Should these preliminary assessments fall in favor of the plaintiff, temporary antidumping duties may be imposed on all such imports even before any final rulings are made. Should these agencies subsequently reverse their final positions, accumulated duties are rebated. There are those who believe that even aside from the lengthy process and the premature levying of duties, the preliminary charges themselves act as an import barrier since they warn and/or threaten foreign exporters to behave more "fairly" and adjust their prices upward.

Models of Dumping

Economic theory dealing with motivations for dumping has traditionally focused on a third-degree price discrimination model. This theory maintains that a domestic producer with monopoly power and import protection from foreign goods will maximize profits by pricing export sales lower than domestic sales, under the assumption that they face greater demand elasticity in foreign markets than they do in their own protected domestic market. In these circumstances, the domestic firm maximizes profits at an output level where the marginal cost in its home-market production (MCh) equals the marginal revenue received from both its home market (MRh) and its foreign export market (MRf), that is, where $MCh = MRh = MRf$. Figure 1 illustrates this circumstance (Caves, Frankel, and Jones, 1990, pp. 302–304). As assumed, Dh, the home-market demand curve facing the exporting firm, is downward-sloping, and therefore its MRh curve lies below Dh; whereas Df, the foreign demand curve facing the firm, is completely horizontal at price Pf and hence equal to MRf. This indicates a home market where the firm has monopoly power and an export market were it faces perfect competition. From Figure 1 we see that the MRh and MRf curves are equal at their intersection point, point a. In order for MC overall to be equal to both MRh and MRf, it too must lie on the MRf line, hence at point b, from which it is determined that the overall profit-maximizing output level for this firm is $Qh + f$—Qh of which is sold domestically at the price Ph, and the remainder, $[(Qh + f) - Qh]$, sold on foreign markets at the lower world price Pf. These circumstances, then, lead directly to dumping by the exporting firm, an action that can persist if specified conditions endure. Empirical data compiled and analyzed by Kravis and Lipsey (1977) indicate

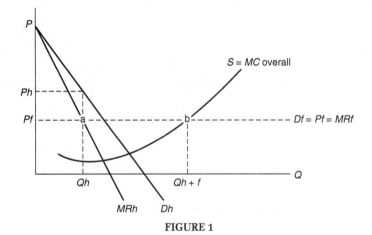

FIGURE 1

that in fact there have been "substantial and prolonged" price discriminations in international markets for the same or similar products.

In addition to the traditional price discrimination model of dumping, other explanations have had textbook exposure. For instance, "sporadic" dumping is said to occur when a monopolistic firm, facing temporary, unforeseen accumulations of inventory in its domestic market, unloads its excess stock onto foreign markets at depressed prices, thereby permitting the firm to sustain its high, home-market price. Another model, referred to as "predatory" dumping, describes the circumstance whereby a firm with monopoly power attempts to enter and capture another country's domestic market by lowering the export prices to well below cost and driving local competitors out of business. At this stage the firm is dumping, assuming it maintains a higher price in its own country. Once the firm eliminates local competition and firmly establishes itself in the foreign market, it is then presumed to raise its export prices back up. As with any predatory behavior, the aggressive firm has a difficult task—it must first have sufficient monopoly profits accumulated to endure the low-price period, and then later, when it raises price, it must be able to count on little or no reentry by local firms or large multinational firms.

More sophisticated dumping theories emerged in the 1980s, about the time the incidence of legal cases substantially increased between industrialized nations. One such theory by Brander and Krugman (1983), referred to as "reciprocal dumping," illustrates how an assumption of greater foreign demand elasticity is not necessary to motivate a nation to dump, and how under certain circumstances the result can be cross dumping of similar or identical products, i.e., intraindustry trade. The circumstances posed are two nations facing *identical* home-market demands that are principally serviced by their own monopolistic firms, and hence together form a world duopoly. Furthermore, it is assumed that the two firms make Cournot decisions and that they face constant marginal costs (*MC*) and relatively low transportation costs (*t*) to the other market. It can be seen in Figure 2 that each duopoly firm will maximize profits by producing at output level *Qh* for the home market at monopoly price *Ph*, and then by exporting further output, *X*, to the other country at price *Pf*, the price just covering marginal cost plus transportation costs. The darkened area represents additional potential gains *per-*

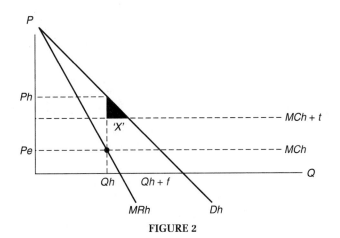

FIGURE 2

ceived by each firm, since in a Cournot equilibrium they each assume the other firm will produce only *Qh*. Of course, if both firms behave in this fashion, they will both be dumping, or cross dumping. For this circumstance to persist, each firm must continue its Cournot response despite lack of confirming rival behavior.

Wilfred Ethier (1982) offers yet another contemporary model that is not dependent on an assumption of monopoly power by either party or nation, and therefore the only theory to unequivocally produce a "below-cost" situation. His theory suggests that firms in industries subject to difficult and expensive entry and exit (e.g., industries with high fixed costs and/or industry-specific inputs) as well as a high sensitivity to business-cycle effects or continually subject to uncertain demand conditions will export their products "below cost" during bad times and export them "above cost" during good times. Assuming equal probability of both good and bad business conditions over the long run, firms in such industries would expect to earn, on average, a normal (competitive) rate of return on all their factors of production. Clearly the exporting nation will be dumping on the importing nation when selling at a below-cost price. Assuming nations have staggered demand cycles and assuming they both produce at a similar long-run equilibrium price, cross dumping is also likely over some period of time. An industry Ethier finds typical of such behaviour is steel, and nations he finds typical of such exchanges are industrialized.

Welfare Effects and Antidumping Policy

Regardless of the trade model applicable, national trade policies have been based on the presumption that any type of dumping is bad. Yet, with the exception of predatory dumping, simple welfare analysis suggests the opposite. Domestic producers lose revenues when foreign goods are dumped on their home market, but such losess are more than compensated for by gains to domestic *consumers* in the form of lower prices. Figure 3 illustrates this net gain to the economy receiving the dumped goods. Price *Pbd* is the nation's "before-dumping" price (domestic equilibrium price before foreign goods are dumped); and price *Pad* is its "after-dumping" price (price of cheaper imports). Area *A* represents the loss in welfare to domestic producers due to competition from lower-priced imports; and areas *A* + *B* + *C* together represent the

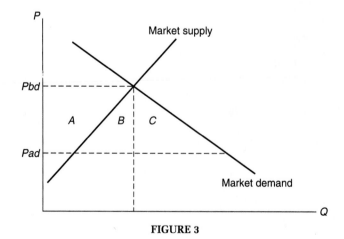

FIGURE 3

gains to consumers from lower prices on imports and domestic goods. Hence, the net gain in welfare to this nation is represented by areas $B + C$.

Despite this favorable welfare conclusion, national trade policies have taken an obstructionist path by laying the legal framework for discouraging, if not preventing, dumping. Legislators have tended to respond to the interests of powerful producer lobbyists, and to fears conjured up by the predatory model, which only if successfully executed has clear undesirable welfare effects. With the exception of predatory dumping, other motivations described by economic theory have no simple welfare justification for antidumping protection. Yet it occurs—in most nations and, of late, rather frequently. In part, it is because the cases are not so simple. Take, for example, charges brought by American industries in the product areas of flat-bed computer screens and minivans (see "Big Three Accuse Japan of 'Dumping,' " 1991, and "Commerce Agency Says Display Screens from Japan Are Being Dumped," 1991). Both are cases where technology for an advanced, or new, product was essentially developed in the United States but then quickly imitated and sold cheaper by Japanese producers. Some might argue that the American inventors were not sufficiently rewarded for their original innovative efforts, and that as part of a longer run, comprehensive policy, antidumping charges are justified to protect and encourage technological innovation, despite short-term welfare losses. The economic issues are clearly more complicated than simple welfare analysis would suggest, though it is interesting to note that overall welfare considerations are not even a part of U.S. antidumping proceedings—only injury to domestic producers and the size of the dumping margin.

References

"Big Three Accuse Japan of 'Dumping,' " *Washington Post,* June 1, 1991; Brander, J. A., and P. R. Krugman, "Reciprocal Dumping Model of International Trade," *Journal of Political Economy,* vol. 15, 1983, pp. 313–332; Caves, Richard E., Jeffrey A. Frankel, and Ronald W. Jones, *World Trade and Payments: An Introduction,* Scott, Foresman/Little, Brown, Glenview, Ill., 1990; "Commerce Agency Says Display Screens from Japan Are Being Dumped," *Wall Street Journal,* February 15, 1991; Ethier, Wilfred J., "Dumping," *Journal of Political Economy,* vol. 90, no. 31, 1982, pp. 487–506; Husted, Steven, and Michael Melvin, *International Economics,* Harper & Row, New York, 1990; Kravis, Irving B., and Robert E. Lipsey, "Export Prices and the Transmission of Inflation," *AER Papers and Proceedings,* vol. 67, no. 1, 1977, pp. 155–163.

(*See also* Arbitrage; Competition; General Agreement on Tariffs and Trade; International economics, an overview)

Anita M. Benvignati

Dynamic analysis

Dynamic analysis refers generally to any analysis in which changes that occur only with the passage of time are explicitly and essentially considered. In economics, these changes frequently involve changes in stock variables due to flows in or out over time. Although dynamic analysis is used in both microeconomic and macroeconomic applications, it has been particularly central to the latter because inflation, business cycles, and economic growth are by their nature inherently dynamic.

A dynamic analysis begins with a compact description of the equilibrium of the system being examined. The existence of such an equilibrium is a sine qua non for the analysis. Usually this equilibrium can be characterized by constant proportional growth rates of the variables in the model, in which case a steady-state equilibrium exists. In dynamic models with explicit random or stochastic elements, this steady-state equilibrium may exist only in an expected-value sense. Two variables with the same steady-state growth rates will have an equilibrium ratio and are said to display balanced growth. If two variables have different growth rates, their ratio approaches zero or infinity over time, a fact that may suggest a problem with the model. Occasionally, the steady-state equilibrium is characterized by zero growth rates so that the equilibrium values are unchanged over time—this is termed a "stationary state." In some cases, the equilibrium is characterized by repeated oscillations that can be described as trigonometric or by other functions of time.

In Paul Samuelson's classic formulation (1947), essentially all dynamic analysis was termed "comparative dynamics." We can now distinguish between comparative dynamics proper and adjustment dynamics. A comparative dynamics analysis would investigate the final effects on the equilibrium of alternative assumed values of initial conditions or on other parameters in the model. If the equilibrium were a stationary state, the analysis would reduce to comparative statics as noted by Samuelson. Adjustment dynamics, on the other hand, studies how and whether the economy converges to equilibrium following a specified permanent or temporary change in the parameters of the model. Stability analysis in comparative statics is, thus, a limited adjustment on dynamics analysis of a stationary state.

In macroeconomics especially, much analysis is devoted to what happens when expectations prove to be incorrect. In the simplest case, this is because of an unpredictable change in the nature of the economy such as a discovery of a new technology or resource. Adjustment dynamics are used to trace the adjustment of the economy from the old equilibrium to the new. More sophisticated analyses consider the evolution of the economy when the economic agents adjust their expectations and hence behavior by learning over time of changes in the basic determinants of the economy.

Besides the important applications to macroeconomics noted above, dynamic analysis is used to address a number of microeconomic questions. One such question is how price and quantity in a particular industry adjust subsequent to a permanent change in a parameter such as a tax rate. An approach suggested by Alfred Marshall (1920) and formalized by John Hicks (1939) examines a sequence of short periods in which supply curves and demand curves shift over time. Supply curves shift as resources in industries producing complements and substitutes adjust. This reduces the analysis to a sequence of comparative statics problems that converge to a specified long-run equilibrium. Recently, more rigorous tools involving the calculus of variations and optimal control theory have been applied to this and other microeconomic problems, such as the firm's investment plan and the use and pricing of exhaustible resources.

References

Hicks, John R., *Value and Capital,* Oxford University Press, Oxford, 1939; Marshall, Alfred, *Principles of Economics,* 8th ed., Macmillan, London, 1920; Samuelson, Paul A., *Foundations of Economic Analysis,* Harvard University Press, Cambridge, Mass., 1947.

(*See also* Dynamic macroeconomic models; Economic models; Macroeconomics; Stock-flow analysis)

Michael R. Darby

Dynamic macroeconomic models

Many macroeconomic questions are inherently dynamic because they involve, in an essential way, changes that occur with the passage of time. Business fluctuations—recessions and depressions—result from changes in underlying conditions to which the economy must adjust. We are primarily interested in the dynamic adjustment process itself rather than the final equilibrium. Both economic growth and secular inflation involve changes over time—in one case, in real output and factors of production, and in the other, in money supply and the price level. For these problems the techniques of comparative dynamics are the natural tools. Even macroeconomic models (such as the *IS-LM* model), which are formulated as static models, are often used for dynamic analysis by applying them to a sequence of short periods.

One of the earliest formal dynamic models was proposed by Irving Fisher (1896) to analyze the relationship between the interest rate and the expected inflation rate. Such a model is inherently dynamic on two counts. First, it involves the rate of inflation, which is the growth rate of the price level. Second, the formulation of expectations of the average future inflation rate over the life of the loan is based on the stock of information which accumulates over time. In Fisher's view, an increase in inflation would not be immediately reflected in the expected inflation rate. This would cause a characteristic transitional dynamic adjustment.

Fisher's classic statement of the equation of exchange (1922) was formulated in a static framework that related the level of prices to the levels of money, transactions, and velocity. However, he applied the model to analysis of both inflation and the transitional period consequent upon an (unexpected) change in money. Similarly, although Keynes accepted the static IS-LM model as an exposition of the main argument of his *General Theory* (1936), his book was necessarily concerned with dynamic applications, particularly with respect to expectations affecting investment and speculation in the bond market. In practice, dynamic elements have been introduced into Keynesian analyses by allowing for period-to-period changes in such variables as the capital stock and holdings of government bonds due to each period's flows, but incorporation of expectations formation has been generally weak.

Milton Friedman (1971) proposed a dynamic model that integrates secular inflation and economic growth with dynamic analysis of the adjustment to unexpected changes in the growth rate of money. This approach has been refined and extended by Darby (1976, 1979) to incorporate the economy's dynamic adjustment to a variety of macroeconomic shocks. These authors view the macroeconomy as fluctuating because of macroeconomic shocks around a (sometimes changing) steady-state equilibrium.

The methodology of the Friedman-Darby approach is first to analyze the comparative dynamic problem to find out how, if at all, the steady-state equilibrium is affected by a specified macroeconomic shock (unexpected change in a parameter of the model). An adjustment dynamic analysis is then used to describe the trajectory of such variables as real income, the price level, and interest rates as the economy moves from the original to the new steady-state equilibrium. This methodology assures that the changes that occur during the adjustment period will be consistent with a movement from the original to the new steady state. For example, this consistency requires that the long-remarked lag in adjustment of the inflation rate to an unexpected increase in money growth implies a catch-up period in which the inflation rate overshoots its new steady-state level.

The Friedman-Darby approach overlaps with a large class of models called rational expectations models or classical models. These models generally are distinguished by two elements:

1. An information lag exists so that macroeconomic expectations are formed based on a stock of information that does not include current information.
2. The economy is displaced from steady-state equilibrium only if the actual value of a driving variable (say, money) differs from its expected value.

Note, however, that once the economy is displaced, an adjustment process may be required to return the economy to steady-state equilibrium. Generally, such models imply that monetary or fiscal policy can stabilize the economy only to the extent that policymakers have an identifiable informational advantage compared with the general public.

These examples of dynamic macroeconomic models could be expanded to include almost all modern macroeconomics. Owing to both increasing professional facility with the required analytical tools and increasing professional appreciation of the empirical relevance of steady-state equilibrium, dynamic analysis is now standard operating procedure for macroeconomic research.

References

Darby, Michael R., *Macroeconomics: The Theory of Income Employment and the Price Level,* McGraw-Hill, New York, 1976; Darby, Michael R., *Intermediate Macroeconomics,* McGraw-Hill, New York, 1979; Fisher, Irving, "Appreciation and Interest," *Publications of the American Economic Association,* vol. 11, no. 4, August 1896; Fisher, Irving, *The Purchasing Power of Money,* 2d ed., Macmillan, New York, 1922; Friedman, Milton, *A Theoretical Framework for Monetary Analysis,* National Bureau of Economic Research Occasional Paper 112, New York, 1971; Keynes, John Maynard, *The General Theory of Employment, Interest, and Money,* Macmillan, London, 1936.

(*See also* Dynamic analysis; Economic models; Macroeconomics)

Michael R. Darby

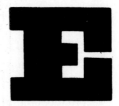

Econometrics

Econometrics is the branch of economic science that applies the methods of mathematics and statistics to measurement of economic relationships and their implications for economic behavior. It means, literally, measurement (-metrics) in economics (econo-). Pure measurement issues or problems in economics that do not come under the heading of econometrics are descriptive measures of the economy that serve as raw material for econometrics. Social accounting measurements of national income, wealth, production, and flow of funds are not, in themselves, econometric work, but they are used extensively in econometric work. The same is true of preparation indexes (prices, wages, interest rates) and other economic statistics. They are all part of the broader subject of quantitative economics, of which econometrics is a branch. Some analytical problems of index construction, depreciation accounting, and wealth measurement may, however, be econometric problems.

The essential feature is that there must be a mathematical formulation of the economics involved and a use of statistical methodology for measurement. The measurement may be hypothetical, in which case it is not actually implemented. Theoretical econometrics usually does not deal with actual measurement, only with what could or should be done in the presence of data. Applied econometrics is concerned with data preparation and use for execution of economic measurement that fits a mathematical specification.

Econometrics must proceed from a mathematical formulation of economic structure. It draws upon statistical inference, which is probability-based. Both inferential and descriptive statistics are used in econometrics.

Examples of Econometric Analysis

Further understanding of the definition of econometrics may be gained from a listing of the more important examples of econometric analysis or practice.

1. Estimation of economic relationships:
   Demand functions
   Engel curves
   Production functions
   Cost functions
   Supply functions
   Market-clearing (supply-demand balance) functions
   Financial instrument pricing equations
2. Estimation of simultaneous systems:
   Cobweb models
   Macro models of cycles and of growth
   International trade models
   Input-output models
   Planning models
   Compatible general equilibrium models
   Exchange rate, capital flows models
3. Distribution:
   Generation of distribution of income, wealth, enterprise size
   Lorenz curves and concentration measures
   Aggregation of micro relationships
4. Econometric method:
   Simultaneous-equation estimation
   Corrections for serial correlation and heteroscedasticity
   Treatment of multicollinearity
   Estimation of distributed lags
   Time series analysis—seasonal and cyclical variations, predictive extrapolations
   Testing economic theory or maintained hypotheses about behavior
   Pooling of cross-sectional and time series data
   Factor analysis and other multivariate methods
   Profit analysis
   Estimation and nonnormal errors
5. Applications:
   Model validation
   Forecasting, with estimates of uncertainty
   Simulation analysis of economic policy and hypothetical scenarios
   Multiplier and scenario analysis
   Probabilistic simulation
   Optimal control for stabilization policy

History

Early work in econometrics began with attempts to estimate demand and supply functions for basic commodities some 70 to 80 years ago, often for agricultural products. Work on Engel curves showing the relationship between family spending and income started more than 100 years ago. Interest grew during the 1930s in estimating behavioral relationships for enterprises in the area of production cost and supply. Macro models of the economy as a whole were first estimated during the 1930s, and much work was done at an earlier stage on income or other distributions. Input-output analysis also was undertaken on a significant scale during the 1930s. After World War II there was a surge in interest in the theory of estimation of simultaneous-equation systems and its implementation in a series of macro models, first of the United States and then of other countries. Input-output analysis also experienced a burst of activity during this time.

During the 1960s the electronic computer became a pervasive tool of econometrics. It was mainly used in applied investigations but was also used in sampling experiments for understanding of small-sample theory and other intractable problems. It also opened the way for new theoretical developments because it showed that many computational bottlenecks could be broken, and thus it gave freer rein to theorists.

During the 1970s large economic data banks and comprehensive computer software (programming) packages tailored for the subject paved the way for widespread application of econometric methods to public and private decision making.

The advent of the microcomputer and associated software generated much more econometric research during the 1980s. Large amounts of inexpensive computer power were put at the disposal of most econometricians.

The Scope of Econometrics

A great deal of effort in econometrics is devoted to the problem of estimating economic relationships. These relationships describe the decision-making behavior, technological limitations, or legal/institutional limitations of the households, enterprises, and public agencies that make up the economy.

Behavioral Decision   A typical economic decision is that associated with household demand. Mathematical theorists may express this as

$$X = f(P_x/P, P_r/P, y/P) + e$$

where X = quantity demanded
  P_x = price of X
   P = general price level
  P_r = price of good related to X
   y = income of consumers
   e = error

This mathematical relationship indicates that demand for a commodity X is a function f of the price of X relative to goods in general, the price of related goods (either substitutes, complements, or both), and the real income of consumers. This relationship is probabilistic because it is assumed to have an additive random error, representing omitted factors that may influence demand. For simplicity, only one variable for P_r is introduced here, but many are often used.

The econometrician would have to specifiy some of the characteristics of this demand function, i.e., whether it is linear or curvilinear, whether demand varies directly or inversely with its own price or related price, whether historical incomes and prices as well as present incomes and prices affect demand.

The econometrics of estimation requires that a sample of data, actual or hypothetical, be defined. Often, the data will consist of aggregate market transactions on volumes purchased and average prices paid. National and related income statistics provide data for y and P. A series of observations at different time points for market aggregates make up the most frequently used samples of data, but sample survey data from individual household reports on purchases and incomes provide microeconomic data sets too. The econometric estimation problem is how best to fit the function f to these data. If the equation were specified to be linear, it would mean estimation of the coefficients in

$$X = a_0 + a_1(P_x/P) + a_2(P_r/P) + e$$

Other (curvilinear) functions define the coefficients differently. Mixtures of mathematical theory of economic behavior and statistical fit to realistic data are used together to choose a best estimate. With present-day computer facilities, this selection process usually involves a great deal of experimental calculation in search for the best.

Technological Limitation   The output of economic product is obtained by using the input of economic factors of production. The inputs are often classified as fixed capital, labor, energy, and materials. The production function is expressed as

$$X = F(K, L, E, M) + u$$

where X = volume of output
   K = amount of capital used in production
   L = amount of labor used in production
   E = amount of energy used in production
   M = amount of materials used in production
   u = error

This relation states that output of good X is a function F of inputs of factors. Omitted factors affect output through the additive error u. A distinguishing feature of this relationship is that the variables are measured in physical units. X should be the number of units of output of a homogeneous product. K should measure the number of equipment or other capital units, L the number of labor units, E the number of energy units, and M the number of material units. If there is a single good and single type of each factor, there is no problem in measurement. Natural units exist for some variables—worker-hours for L and Btu's for E—but even these are approximate. Most production processes have multiple outputs and heterogeneous factor inputs. Approximate index measurement is required for preparing data on each of the variables in most studies. This, in itself, is a first-stage econometric problem. Then assembly of data on time variation for an industry or enterprise-to-enterprise variation in a cross-sectional sample is used to fit the function F to data, and selection of the best-estimated function follows.

The specification of F should take account of the technology of the production process and economic restrictions on the function that are associated with the mathematical theory of economic efficiency.

Legal/Institutional Limitations   The economy is restricted not only by the laws of technology and science but also by the laws of human beings, which vary from place to place, depending on politics, culture, social systems, and other noneconomic factors. A striking example of a legal relationship is a taxation statute:

$$T = g(Y_1, Y_2, \ldots, Y_n) + v$$

where T = tax revenues
Y_1 = income received in the ith tax bracket
v = error

This relation, simply stated, makes tax collection a function g of incomes. If the tax system is progressive, as it is in most advanced countries, the rate will vary with income, going up, to a maximum, as income rises.

Tax laws are written for the individual and have many special allowances or exemptions; therefore, this is only an approximate relationship, and allowance for additive error v must be made. In a simplified case, we would have a linear relationship

$$T = r_1 Y_1 + r_2 Y_2 + \cdots + r_n Y_n + v$$

where r_1 is the rate applicable to income in the ith tax bracket. Published statutory rates could be used as estimates for r_1, if the system is simple, but most complicated legal systems would not admit such a quick and ready estimate. Statistical fitting is then an appropriate procedure for estimating r_1. To use this relationship requires knowledge of the distribution of income among tax classes as well as its aggregate level. This leads to a new dimension of econometrics dealing with income distribution.

Corresponding to income tax relationships, there are other kinds of taxes, related to different variables, subsidies, and welfare payments. There are also institutional relationships for the rules of the banking system, the insurance system, and other supervised parts of the economy.

Distribution   Underlying aggregative measures of the economy such as total income, total wealth, and total employment are corresponding distributions. The distribution of income by tax brackets is one particular example. The striking characteristic of many distributions in economics is their skewness. The distributions of income, wealth, and size of firm (by number of employees) are all skew. They tend to show high concentration in the form of a "hump" at low levels and have a long "tail" for higher levels. In other words, the frequency of occurrence is relatively high for low values and relatively low for high values of income, wealth, or size. Many other economic phenomena are also skew. They lack symmetry.

Econometrics is concerned with fitting types of skew distributions of observed frequencies of occurrence. The names of some of the more familiar skew distributions are the Pareto distribution, the logarithmic normal distribution, and members of the Pearson distribution system. In recent years many new distribution functions have been developed, which describe distribution of economic data more closely.

Characteristics of these distributions are called parameters, and their estimates indicate the degree of inequality of the variable being measured, the degree of dispersion, and average size. Many aggregative econometric relationships depend on such measures as additional explicit variables.

A particular field of econometric study is the generation of such distributions. A problem that is posed to econometricians is to describe analytic processes of income or wealth formation that tend to produce particular forms of income or wealth distributions.

Macroeconometric Systems   The economic system can be conceptualized as a system of simultaneous equations. This idea was introduced by the French economist L. Walras in the nineteenth century. A complete description can be indicated in mathematical theory but cannot be implemented in practice because it is too complicated and detailed. At an aggregative level, approximations to such system have been made. At first, the aggregative approximations were relatively small, no more than about 50 equations and frequently less. In the computer age, such systems run into the hundreds or even the thousands. An equation system of 5000 to 10,000 relations may seem to be complicated and detailed; yet it is still an aggregative approximation to the complete Walrasian system.

Econometricians prepare data for macroeconomic systems from the main social accounts—national income, national product, and flow of funds—supplemented by statistics of prices, labor markets, financial markets, and other sources. These data form the sample from which coefficients are estimated in the relationships of macroeconometric models. Such models explain the interrelationships among spending, production, income payments, price formation, wage formation, interest rate formation, public spending, taxation, welfare systems, and foreign commerce.

These aggregative models are regularly reestimated and revised in making ever-better approximations to the Walrasian ideal. They are kept up to date, in readiness, on computer files for repeated use in analyzing the macroeconomy.

A particular system of the economy as a whole is called an input-output system. In one respect it may be looked upon as a detailed representation of the production process, more detailed than production functions, in showing how intermediate inputs of materials and fuels are transformed into outputs. This method extends the production function concept because it simultaneously treats the entire spectrum of inputs and outputs across industrial sectors of the whole economy. Several hundred (or thousands of) sectors are frequently treated simultaneously.

The equations of the Walrasian-type system have also been estimated for computable general equilibrium models, which interpret the equations of market clearing and optimal behavior of economic agents (households and firms) as closely as possible, with some degree of aggregation. The parameters of such systems are determined partly by methods of statistical inference and partly by judgment.

Solutions of Econometric Systems

A macroeconometric system has three kinds of variables: (1) simultaneous dependent (endogenous) variables, (2) simultaneous independent (exogenous) variables, and (3) prior values (lags) of either dependent or independent variables. For any point of time, present or past, the econometrician, having an estimated system, can insert into the equation prior values of the lagged variables and assumed contemporary values of the independent variables and solve the system for contemporary values of the dependent variables. In this solution procedure, either zero or some specific a priori values may be assigned to the random error terms for deterministic solution. Random numbers may be drawn for use in probabilistic solutions.

After a solution is obtained for one period, the computed values of the dependent variables can be used as new lagged values for the next period, together with assumed values of the prior and new from the (next period) contemporary independent variables. From these values and the solution procedure, a solution for dependent variables in the next period can be obtained, and so on. This provides a dynamic solution, which is called a simulation. The solution procedure is straightforward if the system is linear. Routine iterative methods of successive approximation can be used to solve nonlinear systems of equations. Either for large linear systems or for nonlinear systems of any size, the electronic computer is the factor that makes this kind of analysis possible.

Input-output equations are linear systems and equate a linear function of each sector's output to final demand for the sector. By solving the linear equation system it is possible to express each output as a linear function of the final demands for all sectors. This standardized linear solution forms the basis for the principal uses of input-output analysis. By adding capital accumulation matrix relations to current-flow matrix relations, the input-output analyst can make dynamic simulations.

Time Series Analysis

An econometric approach to the dynamics of the economy that does not work through complete equation systems is the analysis of the time series patterns of individual variables in single equations. Each single equation relates one dependent variable to its own past history; to other variables, both contemporary and historical; and to errors. These errors may also be distributed through historical time.

Best-fitting, dynamic single equations are thus used to project the unlagged dependent variable for this equation in much the same way that it is done for sets of dependent variables in simultaneous systems. Dynamic properties of these equations in terms of cyclical, trend, and probabilistic properties can be established, given estimated values of the coefficients. An obvious generalization is to construct systems of lag relations in which a vector of variables is made a function of each variable's own lags and also lags of the other elements of the vector. This is called a vector autoregressive system (VAR). Its use is gaining in popularity.

The principal difference between the time series approach and the macroeconometric systems approach lies in the fact that the former is not specified to conform to economic behavior or structure in any restrictive way. It allows the data more scope in determining the outcome of projections for dependent variables. It is not so closely guided by a priori economic analysis as are the methods of macroeconometric model building. Some economies can be introduced, however, by classifying different single-equation relationships according to their perceived or institutional role in the economic process.

The Uses of Econometrics

Originally, econometrics was used to illustrate or demonstrate economic theory. The econometric approach gives empirical content to economic theory. At the same time it can be used to test theory or to validate theory. Many theoretical propositions are qualitative:

- Demand for a good varies inversely with its own price, *ceteris paribus.*
- Supply of a good varies directly with its own price, *ceteris paribus.*
- Prices adjust to equate supply and demand.
- Exchange rate depreciation (appreciation) increases (decreases) the value of the trade balance if the absolute values of the export and import elasticities sum to more than 1.0.

It is important to note the *ceteris paribus* condition attached to these statements, requiring that other things remain equal or unchanged. Econometrics, by estimating multivariate relationships, enables one to apply *ceteris paribus* conditions when examining relationships for these qualitative conditions.

Many propositions are more quantitative. Often, in the process of defining economic stability, it is required that certain coefficients lie between −1 and +1 or between 0 and +1. We might examine constancy of returns to scale in production analysis, which requires that some coefficients add to unity or homogeneity of demand relationships, which requires that some coefficients add to zero.

Some relationships might fit the facts better, in a quantitative sense, than others. We might choose the set that agrees more closely, in a quantitative sense, than do others. But in many instances, the econometric method is used simply to lend a quantitative dimension in a descriptive sense. At the time of the energy shocks there was much interest in energy price policy, in which one was required to know, within estimation error, how sensitive energy demand and energy supply are to price changes. In economic stabilization policy, it is important to be able to estimate the employment stimulative effects of a tax reduction, of an easing of credit, or of a combination of both.

Econometrics is used as a decision-making tool by both public and private leaders. Public authorities have to make policy decisions about stabilizing the economy, about improving economic performance, about serving public welfare. All these involve examination of alternatives. It is in this area that the idea of a simulated solution of an estimated econometric equation system is useful. The policymaker can be provided with a wide range of alternative simulation paths, each based on different policy assumptions, and can choose the result that looks best.

The policymaker need not confine the options to those that are generated from econometric systems, but the advantage of this approach is that the computer can generate a number of alternatives quickly. All the alternatives should maintain interrelated consistency for the economy as a whole or that part of it being examined.

That branch of econometrics called optimal-control theory aims to produce the best among feasible alternatives. The best is one that optimizes the policymaker's objective function, that is, that maximizes gain or minimizes loss, while observing all the constraints imposed by the estimated economic system.

What has been said about the public decision maker is also true of the private decision maker, who may be an executive of an enterprise or a business owner. A private decision maker will consider alternative choices open to the firm and select the one that leads to greatest return, minimum cost, or some other desired end based on similar criteria. An optimal decision that observes the model's estimated restraints is then the desired one.

The models and the decision process are both subject to great uncertainty. In order to bring out this aspect of the problem, it is possible to make probabilistic simulations for the choice of alternatives. In some cases, formulas for ranges of decisions can be developed for superposition on deterministic solutions of economic systems.

A principal use or particular simulation that underlies practically all decisions is forecasting. General simulations may be based on hypothetical values for independent variables or coefficients. Simulations can be made after the fact, when observed values of independent variables and initial values of lagged variables are available for use. In forecasting, a careful assessment must be made of possible values for these magnitudes. Some are fixed by statute or custom. Some change gradually and can be assigned values with a high degree of accuracy, while some are difficult to assess for the future. Even initial values for lagged variables are not known with much precision at the beginning of a forecast exercise because there are reporting delays. For many months after a forecast has been prepared, there will be a succession of revisions of main economic magnitudes that are used for initial values.

Careful forecasting is, therefore, usually confined to the near future, say, up to 3 years, often in quarterly or monthly steps. This is the practical range of plausible assessment to typical independent variables in econometric systems, but there is, nevertheless, a great desire and need to plan ahead for longer periods by both private and public decision makers.

Five-year, ten-year, and quarter-century horizons are becoming increasingly relevant in applied econometrics. Simulated projections into the future for horizons in excess of a few years are not, strictly speaking, forecasts. They usually are based on likely trends for independent variables, sometimes adjusted to produce a balanced growth path for the economy. A balanced path would be one that eliminates large chronic surpluses or deficits in savings, profits, trade account, public budgets, labor force, and similar variables. Methods of optimal policy choice can be used in a formal sense to lay out trends for independent variables. The balanced growth path conveniently serves as a baseline case, and alternative future scenarios are then worked out in terms of deviation from the base case.

An excellent test of a theory is its ability to predict. Predictive testing of macroeconometric models is a highly developed practice. Partial models and microeconometric models can also be subjected to predictive tests, but most systematic analysis of prediction errors has been done for macro models that are closed except for the assumed values of independent variables. They are conditional predictions based on the assumptions for values of independent variables. The testing procedures have been carried out on both a conditional and an unconditional basis.

A record of observed values of dependent variables must be established in order to perform predictive tests. This requires the elapse of some years before a sample of cases can be prepared. Some individual-period tests or small sample tests were made during the 1950s and 1960s, but systematic testing has been done on a large scale, covering several different models and several time periods during the past 20 years. For comparative purposes, the tests have also been made for judgmental, time series, sample survey, and other forecasts that do not use the econometric method.

Limitations of the Econometric Method

Econometrics is, to a large extent, based on statistical inference, which, in turn, is based on the laws of probability. There will, therefore, be error in econometrics. Theoretical econometrics analyzes properties and implications of error. Applied econometrics is subject to this error. In contrast with applied mathematics in natural sciences, especially those branches based on controlled experimentation, the error component is relatively large in econometrics.

Econometrics is formulated mathematically; it is often based on large-scale computer calculations, which do not necessarily keep the errors small. The widespread and growing use of applied econometrics by decision makers attests to its usefulness in spite of the presence of significant errors. A subject that is based on sampling of human populations, human behavior, and inability to experiment is bound to be imprecise; yet all approaches to analysis of economic problems—econometric or other—must deal with great uncertainties, and the econometric method is found to have an important contribution to make in spite of its deficiencies.

Omission of Variables   The error term in economic relationships stands for lack of information—an information gap about all the factors that may be at work in the economic process or an inability to quantify and include some variables that are strongly suspected of being relevant but not lending themselves to explicit quantification. These may be subjective, psychological, or personal variables that are significant in the aggregate but not included in the measured relationship. They make up the noise component in the noise-to-signal ratio.

Faulty Measurement   There are errors of behavior, or more broadly, of economic structure, but there are also errors of observation or measurement. Some magnitudes are inherently difficult to measure—income tax evasion, illegal earnings, earnings in kind, inventory changes—and the appropriate variables in economic relationships should consist of two components, the true component and the error component. When this error component is combined with structural or behavioral error, the probability characteristics become considerably more complicated. No matter how the complications are dealt with, there is a significant error component that is due to imprecise measurement.

Misspecification   The various linear, logarithmic, or other curved economic relationships are rarely chosen on the basis of firm knowledge about the form of the relationship. It is generally an empirical choice based on accuracy of fit. There is danger that econometricians may choose an incorrect specification of the relationship that will show up in uses outside the realm of sample experience. Not only the form but the list of relevant variables can be in error. This kind of error is surely present, but it is generally not possible to ascribe a particular amount to it. In computer-based sampling experiments, however, the effects of particular misspecifications can be analyzed. Changing economic structure is a particular form of misspecification and is especially relevant for extrapolation into the future.

Inadequate Sampling   Sampling error is an inherent part of statistical inference in economics. The subject deals with finite samples, which all too often are small. Frequently, in statistical time series analysis of economic relationships, the number of observations is between 50 and 100 (often smaller), while large sample theory of statistics would require more than 200 data points. Not only are errors large in small samples, but their distributions are hard to determine. This is another point where replicated computer sampling experiments have been useful and revealing.

In describing the procedure for simulation and forecasting, it was noted that independent variables had to have assigned values for the whole period of solution. In forecasting applications, this period extends into the future, and there are bound to be errors in the choice of these values. There are, however, repeated experiments in which different econometric model builders make regular forecasts using a common set of assumptions about domestic policy variables and international economic conditions.

References

Dhrymes, P., *Introductory Econometrics,* Springer-Verlag, New York, 1978; Gujarati, Damodar N., *Basic Econometrics,* 2d ed., McGraw-Hill, New York, 1988; Johnston, J., *Econometric Methods,* 3d ed., McGraw-Hill, New York, 1984; Klein, L. R., *An Introduction to Econometrics,* Prentice-Hall, Englewood Cliffs, N.J., 1962; Kmenta, J., *Elements of Econometrics,* 2d ed., Macmillan, New York, 1986; Maddala, G. S., *Econometrics,* McGraw-Hill, New York, 1977; Morgan, Mary S., *The History of Econometric Ideas,* Cambridge University Press, Cambridge, 1990; Theil, H., *Principles of Econometrics,* Wiley, New York, 1971.

(*See also* Economic forecasting methods; Economic forecasts; Economic models; Input-output analysis; Statistical methods in economics and business, an overview; Time series analysis)

Lawrence R. Klein

Economic Analysis Bureau (*see* Bureau of Economic Analysis)

Economic aspects of advertising (*see* Advertising, economic aspects)

Economic blocs

Economic blocs can range from loose confederations with reduced barriers to internal trade all the way to fully integrated units with unified economic policies. Defining a term that applies to the United States, as well as to the 1970s European Community and to the current loose confederation in Southeast Asia, is possible only by focusing on the essential feature of such groups: the freedom of trade.

A definition based on trading relationships, rather than extending, for example, to "policy coordination," highlights substantial and permanent aspects of economic relations. Distinguishing economic blocs from the far more limited "common currency areas" similarly focuses on substantive economic interaction rather than more limited questions such as the way exchange rates are set.

Vitally important global policy questions are raised by the recent push toward formation of regional "trading blocs." The most contentious issue is whether those who are excluded, whether the world as a whole, and even whether the members themselves gain or lose from preferential trading arrangements. The economic analysis of this topic has a long and distinguished history.

Gainers and Losers: The Literature on "Customs Unions"

Largely for historical reasons, much of the literature on trading blocs is found under the rubric of "customs unions." As Jacob Viner (1950) first discussed in his seminal work on the topic, a key issue in assessing the impact of a customs union is whether it is "trade creating" or "trade diverting."

Lowering barriers to trade within a group creates trade, while the preference given to internal trade diverts trade from outsiders. The world as a whole gains efficiency from an economic bloc if the bloc mainly creates trade rather than divert it. For example, fruits and vegetables would be more efficiently produced from a global perspective if a North American Free Trade Agreement resulted in cheap Mexican products substituting for expensive irrigated production in the United States, but not if they merely displaced even cheaper products from Chile, which still bore a tariff.

It is this uncertainty over whether there is even a gain that makes preferential trading arrangements controversial, while at least in principal there is no debate about the wisdom of a generalized lowering of barriers to trade. (As in almost any discussion of trade, there are exceptions even to this rule, depending on one more or less bizarre set of circumstances or another. Rather than repeating "almost always," this discussion will focus on what are believed to be the most realistic situations.)

We will return to current controversies about whether the recent trend toward trading blocs takes time and attention away from the more general barrier-reducing work of the General Agreement on Tariffs and Trade (GATT). But it is important to keep in mind that a loss in world efficiency is possible even without the economic bloc combining freer internal trade with higher barriers to trade to the outside world. A preferential trading area that becomes a fortress, reducing commerce with other nations in violation of GATT article 24, imposes an additional set of costs on the world as a whole, making it more likely that the net result will be negative.

More surprising than the possibility of a global loss is the situation in which an economic bloc is actually harmful to welfare in the member countries. To see how that could happen, suppose that grapes cost $0.50 in Chile but face a 100 percent tariff, while they can be grown for $0.99 in Mexico. Formation of a U.S.–Mexico economic bloc will result in the United States importing $0.99 grapes rather than $0.50 grapes. U.S. residents, as consumers, save $0.01; but they lose, as taxpayers, $0.50 in tariff revenue. The scarce resources Mexico spends producing grapes for $0.99 could be used more productively elsewhere. If examples such as this one predominate, the formation of an economic bloc can harm the members as well, of course, as the "outsiders."

Naturally the world is more complicated than this simple example since prices will change as demand patterns shift. The gains and losses to individual countries, thus, depend on changes in their terms of trade as well as the extent of trade creation/diversion.

Furthermore, recent work in the "new international trade" recognizes such factors as imperfect competition and scale economies and provides a rationale for strategic trade policy to gain an advantage for one country or group. One implication of this literature, surveyed by Corden (1985), is to complicate the analysis of economic blocs. For instance, the potential to isolate a trading area which can then achieve scale economies not available anywhere else in the world is an advantage not readily encompassed within the "trade creation/trade diversion" paradigm. Also, the increased trade with other trade group members holds larger potential gains in an imperfectly competitive situation because a larger group of competitors will be able to contest markets. On a more positive note for analysts, the additional complicating factor of strategic trade policy is probably not so important in this discussion; since economic blocs are defined by their overall reduction in trade barriers, the concept of targeted protection done for strategic reasons has less relevance.

Some Evidence

The measurement of the effect of a preferential trading relationship on member countries and on the rest of the world is obviously a complex matter. Some of the most careful traditional analysis has concerned the European Community (EC).

The widespread conclusion of both casual observation and thorough analysis is that the EC has resulted in large trade creation but little trade diversion overall. Most countries of the Community have long had their dominant trading relations with other countries that are members of the Community, so it is little surprise that trade creation has dominated as barriers to trade have fallen. In fact, trade inside the Community has by most accounts risen only slightly faster than trade with the outside.

The later entry of the U.K. into the EC was also extensively discussed and studied. Here the evidence is mixed. The U.K. had strong historical trade relationships outside Europe, and the possibility of trade diversion was certainly real. Indeed, Miller and Spencer (1977) concluded not only that EC entry resulted in trade diversion but also that the effect was sufficiently large to do harm on net to the U.K. A loss estimated at nearly 2 percent of national income may have resulted, largely from the EC's common agricultural policy (CAP).

At the extreme end of the spectrum is the former Soviet bloc. While a unique example, it does show the consequences of trade diversion; and maximum trade diversion was certainly an explicit goal. In the prewar period, Czechoslovakia, for instance, had practically no trade with the Soviet Union; by the late 1980s, it was dependent on the Soviet Union for nearly half its imports. Isolating the effects of trade policy is difficult in countries where comparative advantage played little role in any decision. Still, it would be hard to believe that establishing an isolated bloc of countries not trading even to remedy some extreme comparative disadvantages was not a severe negative factor in performance. What we know for sure is that these countries are now left with a set of industries, chosen for strategic, not economic, reasons and run for decades without outside competition, virtually none of which is viable in the face of global competition.

Now that a free trade area has been formed in North America, a new major regional bloc may be emerging to rival Europe in size. The initial U.S.-Canada combination has a compelling logic, with 80 percent of Canada's trade having been with the United States even before the agreement. The scope for trade creation relative to trade diversion was obviously very high.

Brown and Stern (1990) consider the evidence on the accord's consequences for Canada and the United States, going far beyond simple notions of trade creation and trade diversion. Specifically, they review other analyses and then perform their own, employing the sophisticated tools of modern international trade research to take into account such market imperfections as cross-border product differentiation, firm-specific product differentiation, and market segmentation.

A conventional analysis shows a relatively small effect of removing the tariffs, which averaged less than 2 percent. But because the Canadian tariffs were by far the higher, a plausible result is a terms-of-trade loss for Canada, confirmed as a 0.3 percent welfare loss in a prior Brown-Stern study. A paper by Hamilton and Whalley, cited by Brown and Stern, includes nontariff barriers, which were higher in the United States, to reverse the conclusion about Canadian welfare, to a 0.7 percent gain. What is more interesting, however, is the effect of incorporating various types of imperfect competition in the analysis. Not only are the welfare gains potentially far higher, but the magnitude is highly sensitive to the specification of the imperfectly competitive situation. The U.S.-Canada competitive environment admittedly provides a tough case study for investigators to reach firm conclusions, with two such similar economies, low prior tariffs, and one country being far larger, but the diversity of results is a bit discouraging.

With freer trade having come to Europe by the end of 1992, the modern tools are again making their contribution. Not surprisingly, the preliminary evidence so far is varied, but it generally points to gains for most participants. Since a major motivation of "1992" was to provide a more competitive business environment, the additional gains found in the "imperfect competition" model conclusions are particularly central to the discussion.

In summary, the "new international trade" literature holds many important lessons for analysts and policymakers. Regarding economic blocs, its most important lesson at this stage of the field's development may be the importance of good evidence on the competitive environment and changes expected as a consequence of freer trade. This evidence is critical to assessing the welfare effects of an economic bloc, even for the participants.

Recent Controversies

The specter of the world dividing into several large economic blocs has been raised by "Europe 1992" and the North American Free Trade Area. Opponents of such a trend believe that a regional focus, even if positive on its own merits, will divert attention from the widely supported multilateral negotiations under GATT. The conventional wisdom has been that GATT would only be supplemented by freer trade within economic blocs, so long as the blocs do not violate article 24 of the GATT by raising external barriers. The evaluation of economic blocs as discussed here follows that precedent by ignoring any trade-off between economic blocs and more general reductions in trade restrictions.

A more sanguine group of observers argues, in fact, that freer trade on a global basis will be enhanced if negotiations can occur among fewer large participants. Indeed, one reason given for discussing a bloc in Asia is to negotiate on an even footing with Europe and North America. It does seem that the reliance of most Asian countries on North American and European markets rules out a "Fortress Asia," as does the diversity of the Asian economies. Further contributing to the pressure against protective measures is the growing dominance of international trade by multinational corporations.

Still others believe that the GATT process holds out little prospect for future success anyway, so the economic blocs could do little damage. Therefore, economic blocs should be evaluated on their own merits, as traditional research has done.

Only time will tell whether multilateral negotiations go forward. This author finds it hard to believe that the regional preferential trading areas will be a net impediment of any significance. But a potential danger to the global trading system cannot be denied, and the possibility that smaller Third World countries left out of the blocs would be disadvantaged should be considered as well.

Whether good or bad, the pull of economic confederation seems inexorable. As this is written we are seeing religious and secular rivalries pull political entities apart even as these same groups simultaneously seek membership in larger economic units. Ethnic rivalries resurfaced in Eastern Europe after years of communist repression; yet most countries are eager to join the EC. Canada joins the United States in a free trade area, while Quebec simultaneously considers leaving the union.

The 1990s have already been a mapmaker's nightmare. In the future, the political boundaries drawn on maps may bear little relation to defining economic units.

References

Branson, William H., Jacob A. Frenkel, and Morris Goldstein (eds.), *International Policy Coordination and Exchange Rate Fluctuations*, NBER, University of Chicago Press, Chicago, 1990; Brown, Drusilla K., and Robert M. Stern, "U.S.-Canada Bilateral Tariff Elimination: The Role of Product Differentiation and Market Structure," in William H. Branson, Jacob A. Frenkel, and

Morris Goldstein (eds.), *International Policy Coordination and Exchange Rate Fluctuations,* NBER, University of Chicago Press, Chicago, 1990; Corden, W. M., "Normative Theory of International Trade," in Ronald W. Jones and Peter B. Kenen (eds.), *Handbook of International Economics,* vol. I, North-Holland, Amsterdam, 1985, chap. 2; Krause, Lawrence B., *European Integration and the United States,* Brookings, Washington, D.C., 1968, chap. 2; Miller, M. H., and J. E. Spencer, "The Static Effects of the U.K. Joining the Common Market: A General Equilibrium Approach," *Review of Economic Studies,* vol. 41, 1977, pp. 71–94; Viner, Jacob, *The Customs Union Issue,* Carnegie Endowment for International Peace, New York, 1950, chap. 4.

(*See also* Barriers to trade; European Community; General Agreement on Tariffs and Trade; International economics, an overview)

David G. Hartman

Economic development stages theory (*see* Stages theory of economic development)

Economic forecasting methods

Forecasting is a fact of business life. Any business plan embodies forecasts of many economic variables—disposable incomes, industry sales, inflation, interest rates, tax policy, and numerous other factors. The question, then, is not whether to forecast, but how to forecast.

There are four principal techniques used to forecast:

- Judgmental forecasting is the oldest and still the most widely used method. This can be as simple as sticking a wetted finger up in the air, or as complicated as various "Delphic" techniques utilizing inputs from people experienced in the market.

- Economic indicators can be used to estimate behavior of related variables. The index of leading indicators published by the Commerce Department is the best-known overall measure, but planners can use many other indicators for their own purposes.

- Time series analysis uses statistical techniques to project trends and cycles in economic or business data. This mechanized pencil-and-straightedge method is especially used for high-frequency (daily or weekly) data.

- Structural models of the economy try to capture the interrelationships between many variables, using statistical analysis to estimate the historic patterns. Large macroeconomic models and small models of individual product lines can be built to provide rigor to forecasts.

These four methods are not mutually exclusive. Combinations of structural modeling and judgmental forecasts are perhaps the most common way of formulating projections today. Univariate and multivariate time series analysis are often used to estimate some parts of a business plan, even while structural techniques are used to project other variables. In the final analysis, all projections must rest on the judgment of the forecaster.

Judgmental Forecasting

Judgment is the oldest and still the most important method of forecasting the future. Experienced managers know what markets are doing and, at least in the short run, can judge fairly well where they are going. Most small-business people still rely on judgment for most of their business planning. Simply knowing what your customers are doing and their plans for the next few years is probably enough for many businesses that do not require detailed long-term investment plans.

Judgmental forecasts can move well past the "hunch" level. Consistency and systematic development can be imposed through several approaches, including the use of spreadsheets to add up sectoral demands or to calculate historically stable ratios to test the plausibility of the forecast.

Judgmental forecasting becomes more complicated as the number of interrelated variables increases. To maintain the internal consistency of the forecast, managers may use spreadsheets or other computer aids to monitor cross relationships. Judgmental forecasting then begins to blend into modeling. In a forecast of gross domestic product (GDP), for example, forecasters would sum up the components of GDP (consumer spending, business investment, residential construction, inventories, government spending, and net exports). They would then calculate the implied incomes and compare their results to projections of personal income, profits, and other variables. In some judgmental models, the implied "multipliers" may be calculated to check the plausibility of the relationship between consumption and investment growth.

Judgmental forecasters often want to blend several forecasters' judgments together to produce a forecast. Bayesian techniques permit a statistical blending of multiple judgmental inputs to produce a single, unified projection. These techniques can become quite elaborate, including feedback from the group consensus back to the individual forecast through Delphi methodologies.

Bayesian techniques allow the statistician to impose a "prior" judgmental estimate on the data. The manager may have a strong opinion about the impact of some variable, and may want his or her opinion given weight along with the historic data. The statistical methodology of Bayesian regression provides a way of combining judgment with data in a more rigorous fashion. The techniques can also be used to combine data from inconsistent sources.

Delphi techniques were worked out originally for Defense Department purposes. These methods allow multiple experts to work together to try to produce a consensus judgmental result. Various implementations are available for Delphi techniques, with most of the more modern ones relying on computer technology.

Indicator Forecasting

Indicator forecasts are nearly as old as judgmental forecasts. An indicator forecast is simply the realization that some event or change in one market can forecast later changes in a related market. The key distinction between indicator forecasts and other methods is that there is no necessary causal link between the indicator and the activity being forecast. Observers simply search for correlations between one economic event and another, and hope that the correlation holds as well in the future as it has in the past.

Many traders operate on such signals. They look for movements in one financial market that seem to presage movements in other markets. For example, a move in the U.S. bond prices often tends to precede a move in the dollar, or in the U.S. stock market. Bond market traders seem to react first to economic events; the sentiment formed in the bond market often extends later to other markets.

At the national level, the most-used business-cycle indicator is compiled by the Bureau of Economic Analysis of the Commerce Department. The index of leading economic indicators is a weighted average of 14 indicators, each of which has been observed to move in advance of the overall economy. The index has a lead of 3 to 6 months on the aggregate economy. In recent years, however, the index appears to be losing its ability to forecast economic developments. The standing joke is that the index has forecast nine out of the last six recessions. In late 1987 and early 1988 the index clearly indicated a coming recession, which never materialized. On the other hand, the index gave no advance warning of the 1990–1991 downturn.

Corporate planners often use indicators in their activities. Many times they find that sales of another product lead demand for their own good. Many manufacturers, for example, feel that orders for cardboard liner, the most commonly used packaging material, are a good leading indicator of overall manufacturing shipments. When factories intend to ship more goods, they have to order the cardboard boxes in advance. Other frequently watched indicators include electricity consumption, freight-car loadings, construction contracts, and consumer confidence.

Sophisticated users of indicators ensure that the economic story behind the correlation makes sense. The story for cardboard liner, for example, is reasonable. There is a clear reason why liner-board orders should lead factory shipments. These indicators are much more reliable than if the historical correlation may be purely accidental.

Sophisticated users will also check the correlation historically to make sure that the story checks out. Checking the timing of movements of troughs in one series versus troughs in the other is one way to do this. Many of the techniques used in time series analysis (see below) are useful, and indicator techniques can thus blend into the multivariate time series approach to forecasting. Notice, however, that statistical tests are, by themselves, fallible. Normally, economists consider a correlation significant if there is less than a 5 percent chance of its being accidental. But even in the case of purely random series, one indicator in twenty will show a statistically significant correlation.

Economic indicators are the most common statistical forecasting method used by corporate planners. Almost all forecasters use indicators to at least some extent, especially in forecasting short-term business developments. To be useful, however, there must be a logic behind the relationship, as well as historical evidence that the correlation is consistent and significant.

Time Series Methods

Time series analysis is a more recent development, based on statistical methodologies for examining the cyclical behavior of individual time series. In its simplest form, the method tries to identify patterns that will repeat in the future. Various forms of moving average, charting, or other techniques are frequently used in constructing these forecasts.

The idea that the past behavior of a series tells you all you need to know about its future is certainly an attractive one, especially to market analysts. It eliminates the drudgery of seeking correlations with other markets and provides simple statistical tools for the analyst. For many time series, these techniques can yield reasonable projections, especially for short-term horizons.

The simplest form is the straightedge-and-pencil method of economic projection. Plot your sales on a chart, lay down a straightedge to best match the data, and use a wide pencil to project the future. Autoregressive moving average (ARMA) techniques allow fancier edges to be used, so that the cyclical as well as trend behavior of the series can be examined.

Most of these techniques are based on the assumption that combinations of sine and cosine waves can accurately portray the past and future of any series. The French mathematician Fourier proved that any continuous series can be portrayed with any desired degree of accuracy by a transformation into trigonometric functions. The concept that the projection of the decomposition is an accurate projection of the series cannot, however, be proved in general.

These simple techniques have a relatively good forecast record for short-term projections. Experience with them suggests that they pick up trends very well, and by examining shorter-term as well as longer-term movements, they can forecast near-term deviations from the trend. The farther out the projection is extended, the less accurate the forecasts become. The forecasts are also, by their nature, useless for asking any kind of "what-if" questions about what would happen in the event of policy or other changes.

In financial-market forecasting, a complicated theory has arisen based on past patterns laid out on charts. Many charting techniques are used to look for recurring patterns in the prices of stocks or other financial assets. These patterns indicate turning points or provide assurance of continuation of trends. This technical analysis, as it is called, has gained wide acceptance in many financial markets. There is evidence that for certain types of patterns, the charting techniques are powerful. Markets do tend to bounce off previous peaks and troughs, and the techniques also appear to indicate breaks in historical trends. The techniques have not, however, proved very useful in projecting future turning points. As with most forecasting techniques, the accuracy tends to deteriorate rapidly as the time horizon is extended. The techniques seem most useful for very high frequency (daily) data, and much less useful for lower-frequency information.

Statistical time series analysis techniques can be extended to multiple variables. Using extended techniques, such as state-space analysis and multivariate ARMA, we can examine historical patterns not only for individual series but for cutting across financial markets and economic data. These techniques have been used most frequently in financial markets, where there is a wealth of very high frequency data to provide an adequate base to construct the correlations. The techniques tend to be data-intensive; that is, many observations are needed to "prove" any significant historical relationship.

Structural Models

Structural models are based more on economic theory than are time series analysis or indicator forecasts. These models can consist of simple correlations of one variable with another, for example, company sales with sales of another industry, or they can be more complicated structures involving multiple equations for an entire economy. The large models of the U.S. economy used by major forecasting firms and the government have up to 1000 interlinked equations. Simple models used by individual firms, however, may have as few as one equation.

Models are based on causality. The distinction between a structural model and an indicator forecast is that the structure of the model is based on economic or business relationships, not simply on observed correlation. Obviously, the two methods blend at the edges, since a good indicator forecast is usually based on causal theory as well.

The distinction becomes more pronounced as the models become more complicated. The more complex models consist of sets of interlocking equations, each one trying to capture the structure of an individual market. When these markets are locked together to form a model of an industry or an economy, they try to capture all the important interrelationships that determine present and future behavior.

One clear advantage of models is that they can address what-if questions about an economy or a business. None of the other forecasting techniques can treat changes in business and government policy explicitly. There is also evidence that detailed models can give the best long-term projections of business developments. There is less evidence that their short-term properties are any better than those of other forecasting techniques. Typically, models are most useful for relatively low frequency data (monthly, quarterly, or annually), and are less useful for extremely high frequency (daily or weekly) data.

The theoretically based structure of economic models also allows forecasters to blend economic knowledge with statistical information. This can be critical in practice, since historical data are scarce. Often, there is reason to believe that the structure of the market has changed dramatically, and thus older data are no longer relevant. Models allow the builder to substitute his or her own judgment for missing data.

Econometric models must be reestimated regularly in order to capture changes in economic behavior. Companies must decide when markets have changed so much that the historical patterns are no longer relevant. The advantage of an econometric model over time series analysis is that the model allows clearer testing for such structural shifts. It also allows the user to look at industry knowledge or economic theory to try to determine what parts of a relationship may have shifted. The business planner may, for example, decide that relative price elasticities have shifted as a result of a technological change but that the income effects should not have altered. A structural model that forecasts sales of a product based on its markets may be altered if a new product takes away one market from your company. The coefficient on that market may shift, but the shift may not affect the rest of the econometric equation. Thus, the econometric model allows the user to blend judgment with the statistical results more precisely than the other forecasting techniques.

Risks and Errors

A good forecast should not only show where sales are headed, but also identify the outstanding risks and their probabilities. Some forecasting techniques are better at determining likely error ranges than others.

In a judgmental forecast, any error range must also be judgmental. The planner should consider not only what the most likely projection is, but where the future could shift and what the implications of alternative futures would be for his or her forecast. The logic structure becomes complicated, since errors in prices, costs, and sales volumes are likely to be correlated.

The strongest advantage of a model-based forecast is that these interrelationships can be taken into account. The forecaster should use the model not only to prepare a base forecast, but also to examine alternative outcomes based on the range of policy and other assumptions.

It is possible to construct a likely error range based on any econometric model. For simple models this is straightforward. The errors of the estimated equations provide an estimated error band for the forecast. For larger models, however, the interrelationships become more complicated, and more complex techniques must be used to calculate error bands.

Time series analysis can provide an estimated error band, based on statistical estimates of the historical performance. Notice that these errors will increase as the number of time periods projected increases, and this error band must be calculated. This is true also of econometric models, although the error bands usually do not expand quite as rapidly.

Indicator forecasts do not provide for easy calculation of error bands. These can be estimated based on the historical performance of the series, but at that point one has really shifted to multivariate time series or modeling techniques.

In any kind of planning exercise, these ranges of errors must be calculated, at least approximately. The planner must consider any likely changes to those bands as well as changes to the forecast.

References

Box, G. E. P., and G. M. Jenkins, *Time Series Analysis,* Holden Day, San Francisco, 1970; Chandler, John, and Paul Cockle, *Techniques of Scenario Planning,* McGraw-Hill, London, 1982; Eckstein, Otto, *The DRI Model of the U.S. Economy,* McGraw-Hill, New York, 1983; Frumkin, Norman, *Guide to Economic Indicators,* Sharpe, Armonk, N.Y., 1990; Granger, C. W. J., and Paul Newbold, *Forecasting Time Series,* Academic Press, New York, 1977; Malkiel, Burton G., *A Random Walk down Wall Street,* Norton, New York, 1985; Pyndyck, Robert S., and Daniel L. Rubinfeld, *Econometric Methods and Economic Forecasts,* McGraw-Hill, New York, 1976.

(*See also* Accuracy of economic forecasts; Anticipation surveys, business; Anticipation surveys, consumer; Business cycles; Computers in economics; Data banks; Econometrics; Economic models; Economic forecasts; Gross domestic product; Index numbers; Input-output analysis; Leading indicator approach to forecasting; Regression analysis in business and economics; Seasonal variations in economic time series; Secular trend; Statistical methods in economics and business, an overview; Time series analysis)

David A. Wyss

Economic forecasts

Economic forecasting in the modern world is widespread, perhaps inescapable, in planning and decision making by business and government, especially with regard to such variables as revenues, costs, prices, employment, debt, and other such parameters. Increasingly, more sophisticated statistical or economic methods are being used despite imperfections of results; in any event, naive or intuitive nonreproducible forecasts, most often, but not always, have been shown as less accurate by McNees (1988). Even guesses made by experts appear more dependable than those made by laypeople. Forecasts and forecasting by sophisticated mathematical methods have proliferated in recent years in part due to increased demand for specified, rationalized procedures and the increased capability and diminishing cost in the use of electronic computers, which have facilitated complicated or mathematical analyses and manipulation of a large number of variables in systems or models.

Short-Term Forecasts

The short-term forecast normally is concerned with readily adjustable and reversible decisions that might be involved in a firm's production, sales, prices, or other such matters. Periodicity in movement during short periods—a day, a week, or a month— might be useful to forecast in order to discern underlying trends unaffected by the season. For example, December retail sales typically represent the high point of the production or merchandising cycle of many consumer products, while construction activity might be lowest in the winter. Well-explored methods exist for calculating seasonal adjustment; the ratio to moving-average procedure in Census II of the U.S. Bureau of the Census is in common usage. In addition, spectral and time series analyses are relatively new developments in seasonal adjustment methods. In brief, the short-term forecast, though sometimes statistically complicated, typically proceeds on the forecast assumption that the seasonal pattern of the past will be repeated, barring exceptional happenings such as strikes or shortages. What constitutes the short term, of course, differs, depending on the product involved. Certainly the short term would be different to a public utility than to a fresh vegetable purveyor—involving a longer period of time than seasonal adjustments in the former case.

Medium-Term Forecasts

The recent hallmarks of medium-term forecasts involve elaborate and sophisticated mathematical methods, largely but not exclusively oriented toward identifying in advance the possible turning points in the business cycle. Among formal methods of forecasting are structural econometric models, which contain empirically derived equations purporting to represent causal structural relationships established by economic theory; barometric or symptomatic measures that depend upon selected time series that typically lead or lag business-cycle turning points; and mathematically elaborated time series models, which extrapolate a variable on the basis of its own past values. This last method reflects the view that causal relationships established by economic theory are considered unknowable or too costly to obtain.

The causally articulated econometric model approach in forecasting beyond 1 year has achieved wide acceptance since the 1960s, especially because computers have made possible easy manipulation of large numbers of equations. Macroeconomic models owe much to the pioneering work of Jan Tinbergen in the 1930s and L. R. Klein and A. S. Goldberger in the 1950s. There are, perhaps, nearly a dozen of such large multiequation macroeconomic models now available for commercial use in the United States. In simple or complex form, they have been much used by governments and business in forecasting such aggregate variables as GNP, prices, and unemployment and in doing economic policy simulations. Business use also has grown in such microeconomic applications as forecasts of market demand, inventory control, and price-cost relations.

Macroeconomic models have experienced mixed success in forecasts of the general economy—the severity of the 1974–1975 and 1981–1982 recessions and the high inflation rates of 1978–1979 were recent misses. In part, such failures can be attributed to the inconstancy in the economic structure that is embodied in the equations, as well as the uncertainty of their causal relationships. For example, the supply of money is considered by some as the principal determinant of overall economic activity and the price level; so-called Keynesians, however, look to a circular aggregate flow of income and expenditures by government, business, and consumers as crucial in the overall economic situation; the dynamics of the total economy are demand-driven, originating from the major sectors rather than the supply side.

A completely different approach is short- and medium-term forecasting that utilizes deterministic models and time series analysis whereby a variable is extrapolated alone by its own past history—eschewing the dictates of economic theory. One such deterministic method is the exponential growth model (whose formula is found in any standard statistics textbook). Because the long-term evolution of the forecasts is completely insulated from new external influences which change the structure of the economy, variables such as shifts in demand and supply conditions, prices, and interest rates make the estimates frequently subject to large errors. Other deterministic methods are weighted or unweighted moving averages of historical values, simple or logarithmic functions relating the movement of a variable to time, and the autoregressive model in which linear or compounded rates of growth of a variable are correlated with earlier values.

In time series analysis, correlating current and past values of a variable is designated as AR, which takes the form

$$X_t = \phi X_{t-1} + \cdots \phi X_{t-2} + \cdots \phi_p X_{t-p} + e_t$$

When combined with moving averages, it is designated as ARMA, with a general form of

$$X_t = \phi X_{t-1} + \cdots \phi X_{t-p} + e_t - \phi\, e_{t-1} \cdots \phi_q e_{t-q}$$

whereby the independent variable X is determined by an autocorrelation coefficient ϕ plus an error term e_t (the AR variables) and by autocorrelation of the error term e (MA variables); p and q refer to the order and number of terms to be included, respectively.

Forecasting by extrapolation of past values of a variable—the so-called Box-Jenkins method—has expanded in use recently. The forecast utilizes a stochastic (probabilistic) value of recent observations and its error of estimate as the basis for future values. Concern centers on past errors of prediction as the most likely basis for a forecast in the succeeding period, and so on. Clearly, this approach is structurally designed to establish a trend or periodicity and to miss turning points in movements. Advocates of this method attribute misses in forecasting turning points to shocks, which, it's argued, also result in forecasting errors made by other methods.

Another perspective in the typology of forecasting is the distinction between judgmental and so-called scientific (or replicative) methods. However, this distinction becomes blurred because, in the scientific method, judgment enters in the selection of variables of the endogenous or determining equations; in the choice of mathematical form; in the forecasted values of the exogenous or predetermined variables; and, finally, in the common use of additive or multiplicative factors, which alters the constant term on the basis of extraneous information in order to account for some missed or unexplained influence that has rendered implausible the forecast of the structural equation.

Cyclical forecasting by barometric or symptomatic means is typified by the so-called indicators approach, originally developed by the National Bureau of Economic Research and subsequently elaborated by the U.S. Department of Commerce. The method depends upon selection of time series that typically lead, coincide, or lag business-cycle turning points. Among the 12-component leading indicator series are those for stock prices, new factory orders, and the real money supply. The method depends heavily on the dubious accuracy of current business statistics. Critics also note that the advance-notice time of the leaders prior to recessions since 1948 usually has varied from 4 to 11 months (and in one case was 23 months); in addition, a decline in the leaders sometimes signals a slowdown in economic growth rather than recession.

Of some significance, in recent years, as barometric measures are the several new indexes of consumer and business sentiment—attitudinal surveys. These supplement other such established and much-used older surveys of household and business intentions to spend (e.g., those of the Survey Research Center of the University of Michigan and the U.S. Department of Commerce, as well as the Conference Board and DRI/McGraw-Hill), which have provided the basis of forecasts of consumer and investment outlays, respectively. The results of such surveys are sometimes incorporated into structural macroeconomic models.

Long-Term Forecasts

Long-term forecasts (sometimes called projections) have been used in planning capital outlays and labor-force requirements, the structure and volume of future markets of goods and services, necessary conditions for overall balanced economic growth as perceived by the government, and so on. In industry, forecasts may be made by a variety of simple or complex methods, from simple extrapolations of growth trends in output or other variables to elaborately developed so-called Delphi procedures, which statistically process successive judgments about the future made by "experts." Special attention usually is given in long-range forecasts to demographic impacts on specific markets such as housing and those resulting from general aspects of growth in GNP, industrial production, and other major economic variables that constitute the forecasting efforts of the major econometric models.

Both private and government econometric models that have been structured to project GNP and related magnitudes for long-range planning purposes have been developed in recent years. As in simpler approaches, assumptions are made regarding (1) the growth of the labor force (with a population already in existence, the participation rate in the work force is the principal unknown); (2) the trend in the workweek; and (3) productivity, or output divided by labor input measured in hours. This calculation yields a supply estimate of GNP at some future date which provides the major planning base for estimation of potential markets and other economic parameters. (In some models, a full-employment assumption is made in calculating the projected GNP, though this need not be done.)

A major methodological development in these econometric procedures is that a demand side of GNP is derived from the incomes that are generated in production, which necessarily equals the calculated value of the supply side. The latter provides a control total within which purchases by consumers, business, and government must reach some reasonable relation to income, by sectors; if not, fiscal or other policy action is introduced to attain a coherent balance of supply and demand under given assumptions of employment, unemployment, and productivity. One major objective of such a model is to test whether a balance can be reached at either economic growth or unemployment rates that are acceptable to policymakers.

Long-range forecasts necessarily involve many assumptions and uncertainties, for example, the state of international relations, international exchange rates of currencies, capital and labor productivity, the effect of environmental and safety requirements on the efficiency of the capital stock, energy composition, and technological discoveries. Frequently, these are exogenously determined variables in an econometric model and subject to increasingly arbitrary resolution as time progresses.

Economists generally conceive of long-range forecasts as useful in broad outline, but only as approximations that need periodic revision. A minority of economists grant only marginal importance to them or regard them suspiciously as aids to unnecessary planning which is potentially dangerous to concepts of a market economy.

Input-output methods frequently have been used as a final step to convert a macroeconomic model projection of the aggregate economy into the demands for intermediate goods and services that the various industries and sectors would be required to supply at a given level of GNP or final demand. For each industry in an interindustry matrix, inputs of current costs of materials plus value added will equal gross output or sales. These are organized into input-output tables, which, in the U.S. Department of Commerce version, show how the output of 162 industries is allocated among intermediate sales to other industries or to final demand sales (which make up the GNP). The coefficients in an interindustry matrix of purchases and sales represent the value of intermediate inputs of purchases made by each industry from one another, in terms of a share of the industry sales dollar that is required to supply a dollar change in final demand. Thus, the quantity of specific inputs plus value added as a percentage of output of each industry is specified and fixed, as of a given time. This has led critics to note that input-output analyses assumes absence of substitution among inputs, even when relative prices and costs change; constant returns per unit in output and revenues when scale of operations changes; fixed technology; etc. Defenders of input-output analysis claim that modifications can be made that resolve these difficulties. The method's grand design appears useful because it enables a conversion of GNP totals and sectors into specific-industry supply requirements of materials, output, work force, and other resources in a system of accounts that compels structural logic and internal consistency.

References

Box, G. E. P., and G. M. Jenkins, *Time Series Analysis,* Holden-Day, San Francisco, 1970; Butler, William F., Robert A. Kavesh, and Robert B. Platt, *Methods and Techniques of Business Forecasting,* Prentice-Hall, Englewood Cliffs, N.J., 1974; Granger, C. W. J., and Paul Newbold, *Forecasting Time Series,* Academic Press, New York, 1977; Klein, Lawrence R., and A. S. Goldberger, *An Econometric Model of the United States, 1929–1952,* North-Holland, Amsterdam, 1955; McNees, Stephen K., "A Critique of Alternative Methods of Comparing Macroeconomic Models," in J. Ramsey and J. Kmenta (eds.), *Methodology of Macroeconomic Models,* North-Holland, Amsterdam, 1980; McNees, Stephen K., "How Accurate Are Macroeconomic Forecasts?," *New England Economic Review,* July/August 1988; Nelson, Charles R., *Applied Time Series Analysis for Managerial Forecasting,* Holden-Day, San Francisco, 1973; Pyndyck, Robert S., and Daniel L. Rubinfeld, *Econometric Models and Economic Forecasts,* McGraw-Hill, New York, 1976; U.S. Department of Labor, *Employment Projections for the 1980's,* Bureau of Labor Statistics Bulletin 2030, 1979; Vaccara, Beatrice N., and Victor Zarnowitz, "How Good Are the Leading Indicators?," *1977 Proceedings,* Business and Economics Section, part 1, American Statistical Association, Washington, D.C., 1977; Zarnowitz, Victor, *An Appraisal of Short-Term Economic Forecasts,* National Bureau of Economic Research, New York, 1967.

(*See also* Accuracy of economic forecasts; Anticipation surveys, business; Anticipation surveys, consumer; Business cycles; Economic forecasting methods; Economic models; Gross domestic product; Input-output analysis; Leading indicator approach to forecasting; Seasonal adjustment methods; Seasonal variations in economic time series; Statistical methods in economics and business, an overview; Time series analysis)

Herman J. Liebling

Economic forecasting accuracy (*see* Accuracy of economic forecasts)

Economic growth

Economic growth is a sustained increase, over a significant period, in the quantity of material goods and services produced in an economy. The economy may encompass a nation or some other geographical, political, or social unit, such as a region, a city, or a population group; it may include a group of nations or the world.

Historically, over the period of which quantitative observation has been possible, growth in the absolute amount of goods and services produced usually has been associated with increases in the average material well-being (i.e., in the quantity produced per person, and with growing population). For that reason the contemporary definitions of economic growth include the concept of rising economic well-being. Thus, according to Simon Kuznets (1973), "Modern economic growth . . . reflects a continuing capacity to supply a growing population with an increased volume of commodities and services per capita." More generally, economic growth may be positive or negative for the total production or for production per capita, and the two need not be in the same direction. This more general concept of absolute growth is also well recognized. "The capacity to sustain rapidly increasing numbers at the same or only slightly lower levels of living, in and of itself, can be viewed as economic growth" (Kuznets, 1966).

Measurement of Economic Growth

Economic growth is measured by comparing the total output of the economy at different times. Because the individual goods and services produced in an economy are not directly comparable with each other, in order to arrive at a measure of their total amount the different outputs are added up in proportion to their value, as reflected in their full cost of production (factor cost) of a given base period. In market economies, the cost of different goods is reflected in their prices. This method of measurement, also called the index numbers method, permits measurement of a total output of different goods and services which is not affected by inflation and other changes in prices of different goods. Hence, it is usually referred to as measurement of the real product of the economy. The most widely known measure of the real output of the economy is the gross national product (GNP), which is a measure of the total volume of goods and services produced in an economy during an accounting period, such as a year. Other related measures of the national output are the gross domestic product (GDP) and the national income. Most often, economic growth is measured in terms of the average annual rates of change in real GNP, total or per capita, which have occurred during a period. Thus, for example, the real GNP of the United States grew at a rate of 3.1 percent a year during the period 1950–1990. Because during the same period, the U.S. population grew at a rate of 1.2 percent a year, the real economic growth per capita was 1.9 percent a year.

While it is a useful construct permitting measurement of the total output of the economy, the GNP is subject to limitations. The measured volume of output and its growth vary with the basis used for valuing the individual products. This index number problem is especially serious in comparing radically different economies, as is the case in comparing successive stages of the same economy over a very long time period, or in comparing two economies at different stages of economic development.

In addition to this problem and apart from frequent difficulties in obtaining adequate statistical data that satisfy the criteria of economic measurement, the concept of economic growth and its statistical indicators are subject to certain substantive limitations. First, considerations of economic growth and its measurement are limited to economic production and economic well-being, leaving out many other aspects of human well-being, such as modern improvements in health care, which have been associated with economic growth. Second, the existing methods of measurement leave out, for the most part, the more narrowly defined economic production, especially production outside the market and government sectors, such as the goods and services produced within the family and household (e.g., home cooking and gardening) and educational and other personal services provided by parents to children. Also, these measures of economic production omit some of the important results of economic growth, such as improvements in working conditions and increases in leisure time, which have occurred as a result of reductions in the workweek, paid vacations, and retirement benefits. Some recently developed analytical approaches attempt to fill some of these gaps by broadening the scope of measurement of well-being to include such social indicators as the state of health. At the same time, measurement of household production seeks to define the economic objectives of families and individuals in more fundamental ways than can be indicated by the quantity of goods and services consumed, and to account for the economic production within households.

Theories of Economic Growth

Theories of economic growth have been concerned with three basic factors and their interactions: population growth, capital formation, and technological change.

Some of the most important interactions between the factors of economic growth, which may enhance or limit it, were identified by the classical economists. Adam Smith saw the realization of the economies of large-scale production as an important source of growing national prosperity. In his view, realization of these economies was made possible by the growth of the markets which permitted progressively more efficient organization of production based on division of labor and the resulting specialization of skills and of methods of production. The principle of diminishing returns, developed by Malthus and Ricardo, identified the limits to economic growth in the limited amount and capacity of land to yield continually increasing produce even with improvements in agricultural techniques and increasing applications of labor and capital in its cultivation.

Later, the neoclassical economists developed theories of industrial production dependent upon available labor and capital and not subject to the limitation of land supply. Within this framework, economic growth was seen primarily as a result of accumulation of sufficient capital to permit use of the economically most efficient combinations of labor and capital. These methods were often thought to involve a deepening of the capital structure and an increase in capital intensity of the economy. Moreover, the available methods of production were often thought to be characterized by increasing returns to scale, a property of the production system which permitted growth in output at rates more rapid than the growth rates of labor and capital inputs.

A radically different theory of the production system and of economic growth was advanced by Joseph A. Schumpeter. This theory made innovations and technological change the prime movers of the economic process, at least in the modern capitalist economies, accounting simultaneously for economic growth and for the business-cycle fluctuations. According to this theory, successful innovators are imitated by a large number of firms attempting to profit from the new production technology. As a result, too much is invested and the ensuing losses cause a depression and a sorting out of surviving firms. Eventually, the new superior technology raises the productivity of the economy to a new higher level.

Beginning with the work of John von Neumann in the 1940s, economists developed mathematical theories of economic growth which were used to investigate the formal requirements for stable growth and other dynamic properties of economic system.

Simon Kuznets developed an approach to the analysis of economic growth over long historical periods which he calls "economic epochs." Each epoch is characterized by a corresponding "epochal innovation" (i.e., "a major addition to the stock of human knowledge which provides a potential for sustained economic growth"—Kuznets, 1973). Exact delineation of these epochs is a matter of judgment, but the innovation defining the epoch should operate throughout its period, providing the main stimulus to growth and to structural change during the epoch. In Kuznets's view, the present scientific epoch of modern economic growth is characterized by a feedback relationship between science and applications of science. It began with the industrial revolution, in particular with the steam engine and the early industrial innovations in production of iron and textiles. This epoch succeeded the earlier epoch of geographic discoveries during which the expansion of land available to the Western world provided the main source of sustained economic growth.

Modern Economic Growth

The period of modern economic growth is characterized by rapid growth in population and in per capita production and by much higher rates of capital formation than those that prevailed in earlier epochs. It is also characterized by an increasingly extensive use of science-based technology. Kuznets estimates that over the 100 years since the mid-nineteenth century, the growth rate in output per capita was about 10 times greater than in the earlier long period from the late Middle Ages to the mid-nineteenth century (2.0 versus 0.2 percent per year) and probably 4 to 5 times more rapid for population (1 versus 0.2 to 0.25 percent). Thus, the growth rate in total output accelerated some 40 to 50 times from that of the earlier period.

In addition to the high growth rates, by historical standards, modern economic growth is characterized, according to Kuznets, by a high rate of growth in productivity (i.e., in output relative to labor, capital, and other inputs); by structural shifts in the economy, most significantly from agriculture to industry and then to services; by social and ideological changes, especially urbanization and secularization; and by much increased international economic linkages. This growth experience, however, has been limited to only some regions of the world, and the gaps in the economic product per person between the economically developed and the less-developed countries have persisted.

While by historical standards the rates of economic growth have been very high in the past 100 years in all countries of the developed world, over shorter periods there were large differences in the growth rates among countries. Also, the economic growth rates in the same countries have varied considerably over shorter periods. Among the larger industrial countries, the economic growth rates experienced over the past 100-year period ranged from 2 percent a year for Great Britain and France to nearly 4 percent for the United States and Japan (Kuznets, 1966).

Sources of Economic Growth

There are indications that during the twentieth century the rate of economic growth in the developed countries has accelerated and that the sources of growth have changed. In the more recent decades, there has been more growth in productivity (increase in output per hour worked) and less growth in labor input (fewer hours worked). The accompanying table gives estimates by Angus Maddison (1979) of the annual growth rates in GDP and in GDP per hour worked, averaged for 16 industrial countries:

Period	GDP, %	GDP per hour, %
1870–1913	2.6	1.7
1913–1950	1.9	1.8
1950–1970	4.9	4.4
1970–1977	3.2	3.8

A number of studies made by American economists in the 1950s established that the rates of economic growth prevailing in the twentieth century were considerably higher than could be explained by the combined growth of labor and capital inputs. Thus, according to estimates by John W. Kendrick (1961), this unexplained residual growth, defined as growth in total factor productivity, continued at an annual rate of 1.7 percent for the private domestic economy in the United States during the period 1900–1950. In the period 1950–1969, this growth rate increased to 2.0 percent a year. After 1969, total factor productivity growth—now called multifactor productivity by the U.S. Bureau of Labor Statistics (BLS), which reports these data regularly—declined sharply. This is brought out in the following analysis of annual growth rates in the business sector based on BLS data:

	1950–1969, %	1969–1970, %
Business-sector output	3.7	2.7
Multifactor input	1.7	2.1
Labor input	0.7	1.5
Capital input	0.9	3.6
Output per unit of input	2.0	0.6

The discovery of the residual growth stimulated interest in technological change as a source of economic growth and gave rise to economic research on innovations, on the effects of research and development activities, and on interindustry and international transfers of technology. It also gave rise to growth accounting, developed by Edward Denison (1974) and others, which attempts to assess quantitatively the contributions made to economic growth during a given period by such basic contributing factors as growth in the quantity of labor and capital inputs and growth in productivity.

Sources of productivity growth and reasons for its changes have not yet been successfully isolated quantitatively, although economic research has produced indications regarding the character of these effects and some of their possible magnitude. In particular, business expenditures for research and development were consistently found to be positively associated with increases in output per unit of input in a large number of studies based on different methods, data, and time periods. Periods of severe recessions or of large variations in prices coincided with periods of slower growth in productivity.

The decline in the growth rate of output per unit of input after 1969 led to reduced growth in earnings per worker. In an unchanging environment, this reduction would also reduce growth in per capita income. However, demographic developments accelerated growth in the number of workers in the United States, postponing the decline in per capita income. Following a large post–World War II baby boom, there was a sharp drop in birthrates in the mid-1960s. Large numbers of women and young workers entered the labor force. The accelerated growth in the labor input compensated for the slowdown in the growth rate in output per unit of input. In 1980, growth in labor input began to diminish. It is likely to cease and even to become negative within the first decade of the twenty-first century. Unless productivity growth accelerates, a prolonged period of slow growth in real earnings and in per capita income may result. With some variations, similar trends are under way in other industrial countries. The main policy approaches for raising future productivity growth concern stimulation of investment in modern fixed capital, training and education, public infrastructure, and development of new technologies as well as maintenance of economic stability (Terleckyj, 1990).

References

Denison, Edward F., *Accounting for United States Economic Growth, 1929–1969,* Brookings, Washington, D.C., 1974; Denison, Edward F., *Trends in American Economic Growth, 1929–82,* Brookings, Washington, D.C., 1985; Kendrick, John W., *Productivity Trends in the United States,* Princeton University Press, Princeton, N.J., 1961; Kuznets, Simon, *Modern Economic Growth: Rate, Structure, and Spread,* Yale University Press, New Haven, Conn., 1966, pp 63–65; Kuznets, Simon, *Population, Capital, and Growth: Selected Essays,* Norton, New York, 1973, pp. 1, 2 ff.; Maddison, Angus, "Long Run Dynamics of Productivity Growth," *Banca Nazionale del Lavoro Quarterly Review,* no. 128, March 1979, pp. 3–43; Schumpeter, Joseph A., *Business Cycles: A Theoretical, Historical and Statistical Analysis of the Capitalist Process,* McGraw-Hill, New York, 1939; Smith, Adam, *The Wealth of Nations,* London, 1776, reprinted by Dent, London, 1960; Terleckyj, Nestor E., *Changing Source of U.S. Economic Growth, 1950–2010: A Chartbook of Trends and Projections,* National Planning Association, Washington, D.C., 1990; von Neumann, John, "A Model of General Economic Equilibrium," *Review of Economic Studies,* vol. 13, no. 1, 1945–1946, pp. 1–9.

(*See also* Business cycles; Capital formation; Classical school; Demographics and economics; Gross domestic product; Human capital; Income; Index numbers; Innovation; Kuznets cycle; Neoclassical economics; Productivity; Research and development; Technology)

Nestor E. Terleckyj

Economic incentives for environmental protection

Public concern over environmental issues has risen dramatically over the last two decades. There has been increasing pressure on the governments of industrialized countries to develop a reasoned response to a variety of problems, such as acid rain, stratospheric ozone depletion, and the cleanup of toxic waste dumps. Partly in response to the growing pressures to address environmental issues, regulators have begun to explore new approaches for addressing environmental problems that use "economic" incentives instead of "command-and-control" regulation.

Under command-and-control regulation, the regulator sets a technical standard or a performance standard for sources that pollute the environment. Command-and-control regulation has been criticized by economists because it does not leave firms and individuals with much choice in how they achieve an environmental target. For example, a law may require that a power plant use a scrubber to reduce air pollution, regardless of whether another technology or group of technologies might be more effective in achieving the same level of air quality.

Economists have argued that many pollution problems can be addressed more effectively through the introduction of economic incentives. The idea behind using economic incentives is to save society resources while achieving a particular environmental goal. For example, in 1990, Congress adopted an economic-incentive approach for limiting acid rain that could save society as much as $1 billion annually in comparison to a conventional command-and-control approach that required the largest polluters to install scrubbers.

There are many different kinds of economic-incentive approaches. They include the use of subsidies, taxes, deposit-refund schemes, marketable permits, and the removal of institutional barriers that lead to price distortions. In the interest of brevity, we focus on taxes and marketable permits, which have received the greatest attention in the academic literature.

Pollution Charges

Charge systems impose a fee, or tax, on pollution. For example, a chemical manufacturer would be charged for every unit of pollutant that it discharged into a river. Pollution charges, by themselves, do not restrict the amount of pollutants that may be emitted; rather, they tax emissions. Such fees ensure that a firm will take pollution costs directly into account in its business decisions. A firm has many options. It might decide that it is in its interest to pay the fee, completely eliminate the discharge, or partially reduce the emission.

Several European nations, including France, the Netherlands, and Germany, currently use water-pollution charge systems. Another potential application discussed frequently is a tax on carbon dioxide production to help address global climate change.

The advantage of the fee system is that all firms face the same incentive to limit pollution at the margin. A firm will control pollution up to the point where the marginal cost of control just equals the fee. The result is that the total costs of pollution control are minimized, as compared with other methods of allocating the pollution-control burden across firms. Charges, like other market-based mechanisms, also provide ongoing incentives for firms to develop and adopt newer, better pollution-control technologies.

One problem with emission charge systems is that governments do not know in advance what level of cleanup will result from any given charge. This problem stems from a lack of knowledge about how firms will respond to a given level of taxation. Governments do not have the information to determine either an individual firm's pollution-control costs or the distribution of costs across firms. This inability to specify a target level of pollution that will be achieved does not, however, alter the reality that charges have the potential to achieve emission reductions at substantially lower cost than command-and-control regulation.

Marketable Permit Systems

Marketable or tradable permits can achieve the same cost-minimizing allocation of the pollution-control burden as a charge scheme, while also avoiding the problem of uncertain responses by firms. Under a tradable permit system, the allowable overall level of pollution is established and then allotted to firms in the form of tradable permits. Firms that keep emission levels below the allotted level may sell or lease their surplus permits to other firms, or use them to offset excess emissions in other parts of their own facilities.

As with a charge system, the marginal cost of control is identical across firms, and thus the total cost of control is minimized for any given level of total pollution control. In the case of local air pollution control, for example, this approach could be substantially more efficient than current regulatory methods, both because its inherent flexibility takes advantage of differences in control costs and because it allows individual firms to decide where and how to make desired emission reductions.

In the event that overall emission targets are viewed as too strict, the government may choose to increase the supply of permits. Likewise, in order to reduce allowable emissions, regulators could take the opposite stance and reduce the supply of permits.

Permit systems have been used primarily in the United States. Examples include the Environmental Protection Agency's Emissions Trading Program; the nationwide lead phasedown in gasoline, which allowed fuel refiners to trade reductions in lead content; and the gradual phaseout of chlorofluorocarbons in the United States, where businesses are allowed to trade the right to produce or import limited quantities of these chemicals. Congress passed legislation calling for a marketable permit system for controlling acid rain. Permit systems might also be applied in other areas, such as local air pollution, point and nonpoint source water pollution, and the control of global climate change through international trading in greenhouse gas permits.

How Charges and Marketable Permit Systems Behave in Practice

An examination of existing charge and marketable permit schemes reveals that they are rarely, if ever, introduced in their textbook form. Virtually all environmental regulatory systems using charges and marketable permits rely on the existing permitting system. This result should not be terribly surprising, since most of these approaches were not implemented from scratch. Rather, they were grafted onto regulatory systems in which permits and standards play a dominant role.

As a result of the way actual charge and marketable permit systems are implemented, the level of cost savings resulting from these approaches is generally far below their theoretical potential. Cost savings can be defined in terms of the savings that would result from meeting a prescribed environmental objective in a less costly manner. Most of the charge systems implemented to date have not had a major incentive effect. We can infer from this that polluters have not been induced to search for a lower-cost mix of meeting environmental objectives as a result of the implementation of charge schemes. Thus, it seems unlikely that charges have performed very well on narrow efficiency grounds. The experience with marketable permits is similar. Only in the case of the lead phasedown do permits appear to perform as well as the theoretical ideal would suggest. In general, different charge and marketable permit systems exhibit wide variation in their effect on cost savings.

While charge systems and marketable permit systems rarely perform near their theoretical potential, it is important to recognize that they have performed as well as, if not better than, command-and-control systems in most cases. In general, the direct effect of both charges and marketable permits on environmental quality appears to be neutral or slightly positive.

The performance of charge systems and marketable permit systems has been broadly consistent with economic theory. For example, where barriers to trading are low, more trading is likely to occur. Where charges are high and more directly related to individual actions, they are more likely to affect the behavior of firms or consumers.

The Future Use of Economic Incentives

Despite the fact that practical political considerations will continue to limit the design and implementation of environmental policy instruments, economic-incentive mechanisms will receive a warmer reception in the years to come. Proponents of incentive-based environmental policies should be guardedly optimistic, precisely because the demand for environmental protection is high and other proposed solutions might result in severe economic dislocation.

The next steps in introducing these approaches will involve the design of market mechanisms that are politically acceptable. Potentially important applications include such diverse problems as global climate change, critical habitat loss, and hazardous waste generation and disposal. While improved policy design and understanding will not necessarily lead to widespread application of economic-incentive approaches, these approaches are destined to remain only a theoretical curiosity without it.

References

Hahn, R., and R. Stavins, "Incentive-Based Environmental Regulations: A New Era from an Old Idea?" *Ecology Law Quarterly*, vol. 18, 1991, pp. 1–42; U.S. Environmental Protection Agency, *Environmental Investments: The Costs of a Clean Environment*, EPA 230-12-90-084, December 1990.

(*See also* Energy costs; Pollution abatement costs; Subsidies)

Robert W. Hahn and Robert N. Stavins

Economic models

A model is an abstract, simplified design of a working system. An economic model is a simplified rendition of economic reality. It could be a diagram, a flowchart, statistical tables, or equation systems. The tendency now in economics is to express models as equation systems. But some economic models are expressed in different ways.

They are, however, hardly ever presented in three-dimensional physical form, as are some scientific, engineering, or medical models. There was, at one time, a brief interest in a hydraulic model of an economic system, but its use was short-lived, and mathematical methods appear to be the most widely used form for presentation.

Classification of Economic Models

Some classifications of economic models are:

- Theoretical versus applied
- Deterministic versus probabilistic (stochastic)
- Particular versus general
- Micro versus macro
- National versus international
- Supranational versus subnational
- Static versus dynamic
- Mainstream versus monetarist

The contrasts among model types reveal the range of consideration.

Theoretical and Applied Models   A theoretical model is an economist's idea of how people behave or ought to behave. Behavior is worked out according to some principle of optimization or equilibrium, and the implied equation system defines a model.

A system of equations expressing

$$\text{Output} = f \quad \text{(factor inputs)} \tag{1}$$
$$\text{Marginal productivity} = \text{real factor rewards} \tag{2}$$
$$\text{Factor supplies} = g \quad \text{(real factor rewards)} \tag{3}$$

may be cast in mathematical form to lay the basis for a model of a producing establishment or an industry. If there are several factors, then there will be several relationships in (2) and (3)—one for each input factor. There could also be models with multiple outputs.

This simple model can be developed from economic principles of profit maximization under conditions of free competitive market structure. It is abstract and theoretical, but if functions f and g are specified according to some particular mathematical forms, we can fit the coefficients of such equations to real-world observations and derive or estimate an applied model of the actual economic situation. A numerical version of this model with statistically estimated coefficients would be an applied model.

Equation (1) would be called a technical relationship. It would be governed by the laws of science and engineering. The next two groups in (2) and (3) are behavioral relationships, showing how economic decisions are made. Two other kinds of economic relationships that are used in models are definitional and legal/institutional. If we had defined

$$\text{Profits} = \text{receipts} - \text{cost}$$

in the above system of profit maximization, we would have had one more equation and one more variable. This relationship is purely one of definition and has no unknown coefficients. If we had introduced a tax or regulatory system, there would have been need for a legal relationship showing how the taxes or regulations were related to the economic variables.

The theoretical system is written as though it were composed of exact relationships. The applied system would be fit to real-world data, and this fit would be only approximate; thus, there would be error, and models are built in economics on the assumption that error follows the laws of probability. Probabilistic or stochastic relationships characterize econometric models, as opposed to those of the deterministic theory of mathematical economics. All numerical models or all applied models are not probabilistic, but those of econometrics are.

Deterministic and Probabilistic Models   In econometric models, the definitional equations are assumed to be exact, that is, without error, but the other relationships are stochastic.

The small economic model in Equations (1) to (3) is only a partial model of a firm or industry. No attention is paid to explanation of demand for the firm's output or to variables from outside the region of operations of the firm. The model represents partial analysis, and to be used in applied work it would have to be based on some assumptions about what is taking place in the rest of the economy.

Micro and Macro Models   Another approach to modeling is to combine the equations from all the different sectors of the economy into one comprehensive and general system. An economywide model is the general type. It can be either a micro or a macro model. A theoretical breakthrough in economic thinking of the nineteenth century was achieved by the French economist Léon Walras, who reasoned that the general economy could be described by a large system of simultaneous equations balancing supplies and demands for all goods and services throughout the economy. His system forms the basis for the model of general equilibrium. It is very large and detailed, covering every conceivable good and service traded in the economy. It is a micro model, as is the model of an individual firm. By contrast, sectors can be aggregated or averaged, and a macro model may be constructed for several combined sectors. A macro model covering behavior, technology, legal relations, and accounting identities for:

- Agriculture
- All nonagricultural firms
- Households
- Banks
- Public authorities
- Average wages, prices, interest rates

could be expressed as an aggregative model. While the Walrasian micro system would consist of billions of equations, a macro system could have as few as 2 to 20 equations. In a practical sense, however, applied macroeconometric models now have as many as several hundred equations. They are still classified as macro models because a few hundred is small relative to billions.

A macro model may differ from a micro model in two important formal characteristics. Variables that describe the frequency distributions of the micro variables may be explicit variables of a macro model in addition to conventional economic variables. The second characteristic is that there is much more feedback or interdependent relationship among variables of a macro model. In micro models, partial analysis is used in which some variables, particularly market-determined variables, are taken as given, outside the model. It is generally assumed that an atomistic economic agent in a micro model does not have a feedback effect on markets.

National and International Models   Most applied models of the economy as a whole are built by using the national income and product accounts of a country. These macro models describe economic activity in the whole nation. In recent years, there has been more and more interest in modeling the world economy through tracing the flows of international trade and payments among countries. An international or supranational model brings together models of several countries or regional groupings of countries, put together in a consistent way to reflect intercountry or interregional trading relationships. For example, the project LINK model of world trade (Waelbroeck, 1976) combines macroeconomic models of some 20 countries and 5 regions that cover the whole world. Consistency in trade is imposed by making total world exports balance total world imports. International payments flows as well as international goods flows can be related to one another in a similarly consistent way, and supranational models of this type have also been constructed.

Supranational and Subnational Models   Macro models of a nation can be extended in two directions, either toward international economic relationships, as already described, or toward disaggregated regional economic relationships within a nation. Models of individual subregions of a nation have been constructed on a broad scale. These consist of models of states, metropolitan areas, or regional groupings of states. For the most part, individual regional models have been constructed that are open with respect to the nation; that is, national aggregates, determined as output from a national macro model, serve as input into a local regional model. If the region is large enough or strategic enough, it can feed back on national performance, and the two models (regional and national) can be solved together in an iterative fashion.

A fresh approach to regional model building is now taking place, in which national totals are built from the regional components. Lack of adequate data has made regional modeling more difficult to develop than national modeling, but this deficiency is gradually being overcome, and regional systems are being put together into a total national design. It is unlikely, however, that regional modeling will displace national modeling. It is more likely that the two approaches will remain complementary, with complete regional systems serving mainly to distribute national aggregates among local components.

Static and Dynamic Models   If a model is not specific about relative dating of its interrelated parts, it is static. A dynamic model, by contrast, interrelates magnitudes at different dates, or it interrelates levels, rates of change, and historical accumulations. A dynamic model shows how the economy evolves through time, both in its short-run patterns of the business cycle and in its long-run patterns of growth or decline.

Forecasting models, planning models, and policy simulation models are generally dynamic. They indicate time trajectories for the economy. A well-known static model has, however, been the input-output, or interindustry, model. This model shows how final demand in the economy requires or entices output from all the various industrial sectors through the workings of the matrix of technical coefficients. It also shows how prices of goods from different industrial origins get combined into prices for final goods purchased by households, businesses, governments, and foreigners. The fundamental equations of input-output analysis are written as

$$(I - A)X = F$$

where I = identity matrix
A = technical input-output coefficient matrix
X = column vector of industry outputs
F = column vector of final demands by sector

This model is static (everything is dated at the same time point). It is not stochastic, but it is generally numerical, and it is open. If it is tied to a macroeconometric model of the economy as a whole, to determine the components of F and prices by industrial sectors, then it can be used to allocate industry output levels and prices of final products. Various dynamic and stochastic extensions have actually been made, and the system is being used on both a regional and a supranational level. In a dynamic input-output model, there is a second matrix whose coefficients relate capital stocks to output levels or capital investment to changes in output, and the addition of the associated matrix expression to the fundamental equation makes the system dynamic.

Mainstream and Monetarist Models   The mainstream macro model of a national economy builds up the national product accounts by explaining first the main components of total expenditure. These are consumer, business, government, and net foreign expenditures, often by detailed types. It also explains the main components of national income such as wages, interest, rent, dividends, retained corporate earnings, income from self-employment, and transfer payments. There will be groups of equations to explain prices, wage rates, employment, productivity, labor force, unemployment, money markets, and credits markets. As already indicated, a complete input-output sector with interindustry flows of intermediate goods is also integrated into the largest of such national models.

The mainstream model pays a great deal of attention not only to total demand in the economy but also to the technical conditions of supply. At the present time, there is high interest in modeling more detail from the supply side in the form of the energy system, the agricultural system, the regulatory mechanism, labor-force participation, environmental conditions, and the incentive aspects of the tax transfer system.

Doctrinaire models of the financial system, known as monetarist models, create alternative types of structure in which the supply of monetary aggregates determines overall activity and price levels, which are then split into components through equations that are much like those of the mainstream models. The flow-of-funds accounts have been developed to the point at which they are combined with national income and input-output accounting systems to enlarge the mainstream model in a direction toward paying more attention to financial markets.

Use of Economic Models

Economic models are used in many ways: to work out theoretical implications of economic analysis, to test economic theories, to make economic forecasts, to plan economic development, to examine alternative economic policies, to simulate alternative scenarios for the economy, and to replay economic history. Much theoretical analysis of economic models is carried out by examining the mathematical properties of solutions to equation systems, both static and dynamic. The long-run or steady-state implications of a solution to a model are used to establish or test long-run properties of economic theory. Such long-run properties might be stability of key ratios, such as savings-income ratio, capital-output ratio, or wage–national income ratio. Also certain key balances should hold for the long run, balances between real interest rate and real growth rate and between international receipts and payments.

Numerical economic models are generally solved by electronic computation as simulations over time, either historical or future projections. Economic forecasting is the best known and most frequent of such applications of models. Historical values of lagged variables (the initial conditions) and future values of exogenous (external) variables are assembled as model inputs. Also tax coefficients and technological parameters are estimated or given values. The model with these inputs is fed into electronic computers, and the solutions of the model over future time constitute the forecast. The procedure is not automatic, in that much judgment of the forecaster usually goes into adjusting the model so that it approximates the observed levels of the economy at the initial stages immediately preceding the forecast. The adjusted model is then extrapolated over the forecast horizon.

Alternative forecasts based on different assumptions about economic policy (taxes, public spending, monetary policy, international trade policy, regulation of industry) or external environmental conditions are often generated. These show the estimated policy impacts over time. In longer-run projections, scenario inputs about economic behavior, policy variables, or changes in external conditions are then compared with a reference simulation. The reference simulation is not necessarily a strict forecast but a model solution that has widely accepted long-run or steady-state characteristics. These scenario investigations may be wanted by policymakers, long-range planners, and private-sector executives. Scholars examine such long-run scenarios for explaining or describing ideas about economic development. Such scenarios can be computed on a forward (prospective) basis or on a historical (retrospective) basis. In one case, models are used to examine what might be, and in the other, to examine what might have been.

References

Klein, L. R., *An Introduction to Econometrics,* Prentice-Hall, Englewood Cliffs, N.J., 1962; Klein, L. R. (ed.), *Comparative Performance of US Econometric Models,* Oxford University Press, New York, 1991; Klein, L. R., and R. M. Young, *An Introduction to Econometric Forecasting and Forecasting Models,* Heath, Lexington, Mass., 1980; Miller, Ronald E., Karen R. Polenske, and Adam Z. Rose (eds.), *Frontiers of Input-Output Analysis,* Oxford University Press, New York, 1989; Waelbroeck, J., *The Models of Project LINK,* North-Holland, Amsterdam, 1976.

(*See also* Econometrics; Economic forecasting methods; Economic forecasts; Statistical methods in economics and business, an overview)

Lawrence R. Klein

Economic planning

Economic planning is the process of consciously and systematically organizing economic and technical information into an internally consistent conceptual framework within the context of economic and noneconomic constraints toward the realization of a prescribed goal. The methods available to implement these plans are as varied as the countries themselves in which the techniques of planning have been introduced.

Some form of economic planning is used in every country of the world. The extent to which the methods of planning—organization, implementation, and impact—differ depends on the political, cultural, social, technological, and institutional profile of the individual countries.

Definition of Planning

According to Jan Tinbergen (1968), "planning should be seen as a manifestation of the ever-growing tendency consciously to organize human activity. In this process there is a continuous search for efficiency in its broadest sense." The planning process is predicted on the realization of a feasible goal or set of goals. Goals may include the maximization of profit for a business enterprise, full employment at relatively stable prices, or, more generally, the desirable economic and social development of a country. With such goals delineated, an economic plan—the blueprint of the economy—is a particularly useful tool to bring these predetermined goals into fruition, since a plan, as W. Arthur Lewis (1968) remarked, "organizes consistent thinking, helps to clarify what we expect, reveals its inconsistencies, and therefore . . . improve(s) the process of making decisions." A plan should not be rigidly adhered to since unforeseen developments and newly acquired information will modify both the stated goals and the methods of achieving them. A plan, as Wassily Leontief (1977) has said, "is not a forecast. The whole idea of planning assumes the possibility of choice between alternative feasible scenarios."

Theory of Planning

In establishing goals for either a business enterprise or a national economy, those responsible for achieving these goals would necessarily concern themselves with phenomena which, directly or indirectly, hasten or impede their realization. For example, a corporate planner for the domestic steel industry, in addition to requiring information on the availability of raw materials for steel and on the projected economic climate for the domestic economy, would no doubt require information regarding such matters as the projected level of world demand for steel, possible changes in pollution abatement standards, or perhaps even new techniques in the production of aluminum. Each of these will, even in the short term, affect the price of steel, the level of steel output, and, consequently, profits.

On the other hand, those vested with the responsibility of monitoring and coordinating the activities of a national economy would naturally concern themselves with all economic, social, political, and technological considerations that might, however indirectly, affect the performance and development of the economy and consequently the realization of the desired goals.

A prerequisite for developing a plan—either on a small scale, say, for a private firm, or on the scale of a national economy—is a body of facts. These facts consist of information available to the firm or nation about the stock of resources—labor, capital, and natural resources—that can be drawn upon during the course of the plan, about the structural or technical relationships that govern the way in which the economic variables interact with each other, and about the social and institutional restrictions imposed on the firm or the economy.

Since the activities of a firm, not to say of a national economy, are affected by both direct and indirect influences, some method must be developed to identify and describe these factors and to incorporate them into one internally consistent theoretical framework. A model is a mathematical representation of the structural relationships that link the producing and consuming sectors of the economy. The model should be capable of incorporating the technical or structural relationships that exist among the various sectors, the predetermined feasible goals as well as the factual data regarding the availability of factors of production and natural resources, and the social and institutional setting. The model should be sufficiently well specified in terms of its complexity to simulate closely the actual course of the economy. It should also possess the flexibility of incorporating adjustments in the light of political, social, technological, or institutional changes and the availability of new information governing the structural interrelationships of the economy, the factors of production, and the feasibility of achieving the prescribed goals. In this internally consistent, general equilibrium framework, both the direct and indirect effects of changes can be systematically tracked and measured in quantitative terms.

Planning and Economic Policy

The two main methodological planning tools currently employed by both developed and developing nations for the purpose of policy analysis are econometric models and input-output analysis. The former, pioneered by Tinbergen, Ragnar Frisch, and Lawrence Klein, is structured around Keynesian macroeconomic aggregates such as the consumption function, the investment function, a money and labor market, variants on the aggregate production function, and a government and foreign sector. The relationships linking the different variables are estimated by well-known statistical techniques such as regression analysis and hypothesis testing. Since fiscal and monetary policy are the two main instruments available to policymakers to coordinate the economy in the short run, econometric models are heavily weighted toward influencing the demand side of the economy. For example, if tax rates are reduced, by how much will expenditures on durables increase? Or on the other hand, if the dollar depreciates against foreign currencies, by how much will imports of manufactured goods decrease? If the Federal Reserve Board increases the supply of money, how will residential construction be affected? Since econometric models have the characteristic of internal consistency, both the direct and indirect effects of any single policy measure on the various markets and variables of the system can be quantitively assessed.

Input-output analysis, developed by Wassily Leontief in the 1930s, describes the structural profile of the economy by representing the various sectors of the economy in terms of their input requirements, i.e., raw materials and labor and capital, per unit of their respective output. By integrating all the producing sectors into one comprehensive, internally consistent framework, it is possible to estimate, in quantitative terms, the direct and indirect requirements that must be produced for any specified bill of demand, that is, level and composition of consumption, investment, and government expenditures and foreign trade.

Since traditional input-output models assume the final demand component as given rather than attempting to explain its level and composition, the main focus of this methodological framework is centered on the production and distribution sides of the economy, or more simply, on the supply side. As a result, the input-output technique is a particularly suitable tool for answering the following policy questions: For a given state of technology, what is the structure of industrial outputs that must be produced and the amounts of primary factors of production that must be provided in order to satisfy any given bill of final demand or any change in that bill of goods? How will the structure of production be affected by changes in technology or by the changing tastes of consumers? Because of the increasing lead time required to install new industrial capacity in the capital-intensive sectors, what level of current investment will be consistent with the projected future levels of final demand? The general equilibrium format of input-output analysis provides detailed and systematic answers, in an internally consistent way, to questions or sets of questions posed from the point of view of policymaking.

Not unexpectedly, the most refined and up-to-date economic modeling combines the use of econometrics with input-output analysis. The estimation of the demand side of the economy using the econometric approach, concomitant with the description of the supply side using the detailed sectorial approach of input-output analysis, has led to unparalleled success in coordinating the short-term management of the developed economies and in providing signals and insights for government planners in the developing nations.

The Scope, Range, and Impact of Economic Planning

Events that transpired over the 1980s in Eastern Europe and the Soviet Union discredited and inevitably are leading to the abandonment of highly centralized economic planning, the bedrock of communist thinking on economic matters. As these countries begin the arduous task of rebuilding their economies along market-oriented principles—with private ownership of economic assets, currency convertibility, and free movement of goods, capital, and people across borders—planning methods in these countries will begin to resemble those of the OECD countries.

China, too, at least until 1988, introduced a set of economic reforms that reduced the role played by central planners in agriculture and industry and opened the economy to the outside world. It is expected that continued prospects of improved living standards through enhanced integration with the world economy will further erode the position of central planning in the Chinese economy of the 1990s.

In the United States, medium-term economic planning is typically initiated at a decentralized level, by the individual firm or corporation. Both econometric models and input-output analysis are progressively being used for investment planning and sales management. Short-term management and coordination of the U.S. economy at large is under the general supervision of the President's Council of Economic Advisers, the Federal Reserve Board, and the Departments of Commerce and Treasury.

In some Western European countries, particularly in the countries of Scandinavia, both long-term and short-term planning efforts are usually vested in government ministries where continuous discussions among perennial adversaries, such as employees and employers, are negotiated within the framework of the existing economic models. In others, for example, France, the planning effort is "indicative." The role of the planners is to disseminate information to the various agents in the economy in order to lend consistency to the decisions made in the different sectors of the economy.

Economic planning in some of the successful Asian countries such as Japan, and more recently South Korea and Taiwan, is manifested by "industrial policy": selectively providing cheap credit, tax preferences, and trade protection to sectors of the economy that have been targeted by government planners as potentially competitive in the world economy. However, recent events in these countries in conjunction with international pressures from their major trading partners are likely to lead to less government intervention in allocating capital and protecting trade, leading to more reliance on market forces.

Development planning, the main focus of planning activities in the developing countries, involves the very rudimentary stage of coordination and management. Much of these efforts are concentrated on laying the foundation for achieving the general goal of increasing per capita incomes. These efforts include establishing a set of social and economic statistics and providing the appropriate economic infrastructure, road networks, power facilities, educational institutions, etc., toward the desired goal of industrialization.

With the preceding definition of economic planning, it would not be difficult to impute a significant part of the increase in per capita income over the past 40 years, particularly in the developed countries and the Northeast Asian developing countries, to the process of planning. Advances in the availability, processing, and storage of both economic and noneconomic information, in conjunction with a better understanding of the mutual interrelationships of the economy within the wider framework of political, social, institutional, and technological considerations, have made economic planning, in one form or another, an indispensable tool for policymakers in all nations.

References

Brada, J. C., E. A. Hewitt, and T. A. Wolf (eds.), *Economic Adjustment and Reform in Eastern Europe and the Soviet Union,* Duke University Press, Durham, N.C., 1988; Chenary, H. B., and T. N. Srinivasan (eds.), *Handbook of Development Economics,* North-Holland, Amsterdam, 1988; Klein, L. R., "The Supply Side," *American Economic Review,* vol. 68, no. 1, March 1978, pp. 1–8; Kornai, J., *The Road to a Free Economy: Shifting from a Socialist System (the Example of Hungary),* Norton, New York, 1990; Leontief, W., and H. Stein, *The Economic System in an Age of Discontinuity: Long-Range Planning or Market Reliance?* The Charles C. Moskowitz Memorial Lecture, College of Business Administration, New York University Press, New York, 1976; Leontief, W., with A. Carter and P. Petrie, *The Future of the World Economy,* A United Nations Study, Oxford University Press, New York, 1977; Lewis, W. A., "Economic Planning, Developmental Planning," in David L. Sills (ed.), *International Encyclopedia of the Social Sciences,* vol. 12, Crowell Collier and Macmillan, New York, 1968, pp. 118–125; Peterson, W. (ed.), *Advances in Input-Output Analysis (Technology, Planning and Development),* Oxford University Press, New York, 1991; Ranis, G., and T. P. Schultz (eds.), *The State of Development Economics,* Blackwell, Oxford, 1988; Taylor, L. (ed.), *Socially Relevant Policy Analysis: Structuralist Computable General Equilibrium Models for the Developing World,* MIT Press, Cambridge, Mass., 1990; Tinbergen, J., "Economic Planning, Western Europe," in David L. Sills (ed.), *International Encyclopedia of the Social Sciences,* vol. 12, Crowell Collier and Macmillan, New York, 1968, pp. 102–109; World Bank, *World Development Report 1991: The Challenge of Development,* Oxford University Press, New York, 1991.

(*See also* Econometrics; Economic forecasting methods; Economic forecasts; Economic models; Input-output analysis; Statistical methods in economics and business, an overview)

Ira Sohn

Economic rent

Economic rent is the payment made (or attributed) to a productive resource beyond what is necessary to get that resource to perform its function. Most commonly, rent is thought of as compensation "for the use of the original and indestructible powers of the soil," meaning the putting into production of a piece of available unimproved land that could be used for growing a crop or supporting a building even if it earned nothing as a result. This payment might be considered superfluous because it plays no role in "coaxing" the resource (e.g., the piece of unimproved land) into production. However, the payment is necessary in order to assure the renter who offers the highest payment that the resource will indeed be available to him or her and not to someone else. Thus, rent results from buyers' competing demands that bid up the resource's price even when the price rise does nothing to increase the supply of the resource in question.

The theory of rent is generally associated with David Ricardo, the British stockbroker, economic analyst, and legislator of the early nineteenth century who discussed the phenomenon in his book *Principles of Political Economy and Taxation.* Adam Smith's treatment of the issue was varied: sometimes he considered rent to be one of the factors helping to determine the price of a commodity; other times he saw rent as being determined by the price that a farmer could charge for a product. Ricardo clarified the matter by showing how a particular parcel of unimproved land might yield its owner a rental income if several potential users bid for it and were willing to pay rent because their only alternative was to farm on other, less productive land. (In this connection, improvements such as fertilizer applied to the land, or a building upon it, or a road for better access count as capital investments that do not give rise to payment of rent.)

One measure of rent is the difference in output between an acre of unimproved top-quality land and an acre of unimproved second-quality land that a farmer might have to cultivate because no more top-quality land is available. When all available top-quality land is in production, its owners can begin to charge their tenants rent up to the difference between the value of its output (per acre) and the value of output (per acre) of the next-best available land. If the landowners miscalculate and demand rent exceeding this difference, farmers will prefer to move to the second-quality land that is less productive but costs no rent, at least until it, too, is fully utilized and the next-best alternative is third-quality land. When only third-rate land is available, the owners of second-rate land can begin to charge rent, and the owners of prime-quality land can raise their rent, and so on.

An important aspect of rent is that it is the result of high demand and high price for land (in the aggregate), and that it does not itself push up the price of land or of farm products. As Ricardo stated, "Corn is not high because rent is paid, but a rent is paid because corn is high; and it has been justly observed that no reduction would take place in the price of corn although landlords should forego the whole of their rent. Such a measure would only enable some farmers to live like gentlemen."

An individual farmer might consider rent to be a cost that must be paid if the farmer wants to farm on better-than-marginal land; if the rent is not paid, someone else would bid the land. But farmers as a group cannot cite rent as a cost of production: rent arises only when their collective demand for land of a given quality exceeds the supply.

The same principle also pertains to some nonagricultural applications. For example, famous movie actors and professional athletes command very high salaries when competing studios or teams bid high for their services because their appearance assures large ticket sales. Yet the supply of such talent is strictly limited and cannot be increased; less-well-known substitutes simply do not command as much attention or bring in as much revenue. This fact gives the individual leading stars extraordinary power to demand high salaries, regardless of the fact that they do not now appear any more often than they did when they were less well known. However, in these and other corresponding cases, and contrary to the example of land, an initial wage or compensation is a cost of production: the top stars or athletes must first be enticed away from their prior occupations to become available to the film or professional sports industries. The salaries that must be offered in order to attract them to the industry in the first place are a cost that the industry must bear. Only the sum that is paid to them in excess of this amount—and it is often substantial—can be thought of as economic rent.

Other similar examples can be cited, especially where natural limitations, administrative regulations, or monopoly elements frustrate any expansion of supply.

References

Blaug, Mark, *Economic Theory in Retrospect,* 3d ed., Cambridge University Press, Cambridge, 1978; Krueger, A. O., "The Political Economy of the Rent-Seeking Society," *American Economic Review,* vol. 64, no. 3, June 1974, pp. 291–303; Lackman, C. L., "The Classical Base of Modern Rent Theory," *American Journal of Economics and Sociology,* vol. 35, no. 3, July 1976, pp. 187–300; Ricardo, David, *On the Principles of Political Economy and Taxation,* in Piero Sraffa (ed.), *Ricardo's Works and Correspondence,* vol. I, Cambridge University Press, Cambridge, 1951.

G. H. Mattersdorff

Economic systems analysis (*see* Comparative economic systems, an overview)

Economic theory of interest (*see* Interest, economic theory of)

Economic theory of profits (*see* Profits in economic theory)

Economics

No brief description can offer clear guidance to the content and character of economics—but numerous writers have attempted just that. An especially useless, though once popular, example is: "Economics is what economists do." Similarly, if somewhat less uselessly, a notable economist of the last century (Alfred Marshall) called economics "a study of mankind in the ordinary business of life." Another notable (Lionel Robbins, in the 1930s) described economics as "the science of choice among scarce means to accomplish unlimited ends." (This "definition" has considerable currency still, though no one seems to know just what choices, if any, it might exclude from consideration!) During much of modern history, especially in the nineteenth century, economics was called simply "the science of wealth." Less seriously, George Bernard Shaw was credited in the early 1900s with the witticism that "economics is the science whose practitioners, even if all were laid end to end, would not reach agreement."

We may make better progress by comparing economics with other subjects. Like every other discipline that attempts to explain observed facts (e.g., physics, astronomy, meteorology), economics comprises a vast collection of descriptive material organized around a central core of theoretical principles. The manner in which theoretical principles are formulated and used in applications varies greatly from one science to another. Like psychology, economics draws much of its theoretical core from intuition, casual observation, and "common knowledge about human nature." Like astronomy, economics is largely nonexperimental. Like meteorology (also largely nonexperimental), economics is relatively inexact, as is weather forecasting. Like particle physics and molecular biology, economics deals with an extraordinary array of closely interrelated phenomena (as do sociology and social psychology). Like such disciplines as art, fantasy writing, mathematics, metaphysics, cosmology, and the like, economics attracts different people for different reasons: "One person's meat is another person's poison." Though all disciplines differ, all are remarkably similar in one respect: all are meant to convey an interesting, persuasive (possibly entertaining), and intellectually satisfying story about selected aspects of experience. As Einstein once put it: "Science [one might add art] is the attempt to make the chaotic diversity of our sense-experience correspond to a logically uniform system of thought."

The scope of economics is indicated by the facts with which it deals. These consist mainly of data on output, income, employment, expenditure, interest rates, prices and related magnitudes associated with individual activities of production, consumption, transportation, and trade. Microeconomics deals with economic phenomena looked at "in the small"; macroeconomics with much the same phenomena looked at "in the large." Needless to say, economics deals directly with only a tiny fraction of the whole spectrum of human behavior, and so the range of problems considered by economists is relatively narrow. Contrary to popular opinion, economics does not normally include such things as personal finance, ways to start a small business, etc.; in relation to everyday life, the economist is more like an astronomer than a weatherforecaster, more like a physical chemist than a pharmacist, more like a professor of hydrodynamics than a plumber.

In principle, of course, almost any conceivable problem, from marriage, suicide, capital punishment, and religious observance to tooth brushing, drug abuse, extramarital affairs, and mall shopping, might serve (and, in the case of each of these examples, has served) as grist for some economist's mill. There is, after all, no clear division between "economic" and "noneconomic" phenomena. In practice, however, economists have generally found it expedient to leave the physical and life sciences to those groups that first claimed them, though not always (thus, economists have in recent years invaded territory once claimed exclusively by political scientists and sociologists, not to mention territories claimed by physical anthropologists, experimental psychologists, and paleontologists).

The Development of Economics

Economics, like every other intellectual discipline, has its roots in early Greece and Rome; but economics was first considered as a (minor) branch of domestic science (home economics) dealing with such matters as the management of slaves and the allocation of manure among alternative agricultural uses. In the revival of learning that followed the Middle Ages, economics emerged in a new guise as a branch of moral philosophy concerned with such issues as the ethics of loan interest and the "justness" of market-determined wages and prices. By the beginning of the eighteenth century, the subject had lost most of its theological overtones and had taken shape as an academic discipline, largely as a branch of political theory dealing with problems of government intervention in economic affairs. Then in 1776 the Scottish moral philosopher Adam Smith published the first edition of his monumental *Inquiry into the Nature and Causes of the Wealth of Nations,* and economics soon became an independent science.

The Vision of Adam Smith

Smith lived in an age when the right of rulers to impose arbitrary and oppressive restrictions on the political and economic liberties of their subjects was coming under strong attack throughout the civilized world. As other men of that time were arguing that democracy could and should replace autocracy in the sphere of politics, so Adam Smith argued that laissez-faire could and should replace government direction and regulation in economics. The "should" was so mixed with the "could" portion of Smith's analysis that much of his book seemed almost as much a political tract as a work of science. What gave the book lasting significance was the cogent case Smith made for believing that the economic activities of individuals would be more effectively coordinated through the indirect and impersonal action of natural forces of self-interest and competition than through the direct and frequently ill-conceived actions of government authorities. In effect, Smith opened minds to the existence of a "grand design" in economic affairs similar to that which Newton had earlier shown to exist in the realm of physical phenomena. The impact of Smith's ideas upon his contemporaries was widespread and immediate. As one modern sage observed: "Before Adam Smith there had been much economic discussion; with him we reach the stage of discussing economics."

That Smith's vision of the economy should ever have been considered original might seem strange to modern minds, but that would be because we now see economic phenomena in the light of his conception. As two leading scholars recently remarked, "The immediate 'common sense' answer to the question, 'What will an economy motivated by greed and controlled by a large number of different agents look like?' is probably: There will be chaos." That is certainly the answer that would have been given by most of Smith's contemporaries—before they read his book. The greatness of Smith's accomplishment lies precisely in the fact that he, unlike his predecessors, was able to think away extraneous complications and so perceive an order in economic affairs that common sense did not reveal.

It is one thing, of course, to say that Smith's conception of economic phenomena is original, another to suggest that it corresponds to contemporary experience. According to Smith, society in its economic aspect is a vast concourse of people held together by the desire of each to exchange goods and services with others. Each person is concerned directly only to further his own self-interest, but in pursuing that aim each "is led by an invisible hand" to promote the interests of others. Forbidden by law and social custom to acquire the property of other people by force, fraud, or stealth, each person attempts to maximize his own gains from trade by specializing in the production of goods and services for which he has a comparative advantage, trading part of his produce for the produce of others on the best terms he can obtain. As a consequence, the "natural forces" of market competition—the result of each person attempting to "buy cheap and sell dear"—come into play to establish equality between demand and supply for each commodity at rates of exchange (prices) that reflect supplies forthcoming from relatively efficient producers and demands forthcoming from relatively eager consumers. Common sense to the contrary notwithstanding, the economic system (so Smith and later writers argued) is an essentially self-regulating mechanism that, like the human body, tends naturally toward a state of equilibrium (homeostasis) if left to itself.

The Challenge of Lord John Maynard Keynes

Smith's version of the economic system as a naturally self-organizing and self-adjusting "social mechanism"—known latterly as classical or neoclassical economic doctrine (or sometimes, more shortly and perhaps satirically, as orthodox or conventional wisdom)—was never confirmed by factual evidence, as Newton's laws of motion were; all the same, classical doctrine dominated economic thinking and national economic policy in all advanced economies for the next 150 years, and it plays a prominent role in many countries (particularly the United States) to this day.

Whether right or wrong, classical theory was first seriously challenged by the great English statesman and economist Lord John Maynard Keynes, who claimed to see in the Great Depression of the 1930s evidence that the economic system was not self-adjusting, and whose followers argued that without continued government intervention the economic system would typically operate at levels of activity substantially lower than required to achieve full employment of labor and other resources. Exactly what Keynes said, or what he meant, or what he really meant, has been hotly disputed among economists for more than 50 years, conveying to many noneconomists the notion that economists as a group are uniquely quarrelsome and doubtfully competent. There is no merit in this notion. What is true, as the great English economist Joan Robinson once observed, is that "in a subject where there is no agreed procedure for knocking out error, doctrine has long life."

Perhaps time and further study will some day reveal whether the classical or the Keynesian conception of economic life accords more closely with experience. Meanwhile, the great worry is that, in the absence of professional competence to make valid diagnoses, we will treat cases of economic toothache as cases of lockjaw and kill our patient; or, no less seriously, we will leave apparently minor economic lumps untreated and so, through inaction, fail to cure problems that turn out to be terminal. On a brighter note, we may recall Lord Keynes's wistful observation: "If economists could someday manage to get themselves thought of as humble, competent people, on a level with dentists, that would be splendid!" Perhaps that time will one day come. If it does, and if economists are then able accurately to diagnose and prescribe cures for economic ills, they will have little reason to feel humble.

Professional Journals

Professional journals typically address a specialized audience, but four (three American, one British) are of more general use:

1. The *American Economic Review* has for more than a century published in its May issue a collection of papers by distinguished economists (the proceedings of its annual convention). These papers offer readable, self-contained accounts of problems of contemporary concern.

2. The *Journal of Economic Literature* (like the *American Economic Review,* a publication of the American Economic Association) publishes reviews of

almost all worthwhile books, abstracts of articles appearing in major professional journals, and, in each issue, one or two survey papers on topics of general interest.

3. The *Southern Economic Journal* (published by the Southern Economic Association) offers a sterling collection of book reviews in each of its quarterly issues.

4. *The Economic Journal,* published by the Royal Economic Society, reviews numerous books of current interest, lists recent publications in other countries, and provides useful short summaries of many of them. Attention should also be drawn to the centennial edition of *The Economic Journal* (January 1991), which contains short articles by 22 world-class economists, each of whom offers a personal view of the probable future of economics "In the Next Hundred Years."

Robert W. Clower

Economics of discrimination (*see* Discrimination economics)

Economies of scale

Economies of scale exist in the production of a specific product if the average cost of production and distribution is generally lower for larger-scale producers than for smaller-scale producers. Given the state of technology in an industry, a systematic relationship will exist between the size or scale of plants or firms operating in that industry and the lowest attainable level of average cost. With size or scale measured by the designed rate of output of the production facilities employed by the plant or firm, increases in the scale of production normally make possible reductions in average cost, at least to a certain size called the minimum optimal scale.

At Plant and Firm Level

Economies of scale can arise at both the plant level and the firm level. A plant is usually defined as a set of production facilities at a single location. Increasing the scale of the plant often generates economies of scale by facilitating greater specialization in the use of labor resources, a source of efficiency first described by Adam Smith in 1776 in the *Wealth of Nations.* In larger plants, more effective use may also be made of managerial talent and certain types of large-scale equipment, spreading the costs of these "indivisible" resources over a larger volume of output.

As plant size is expanded, eventually all opportunities for economies of scale are exhausted, and minimum optimal scale is reached. Still larger plant sizes may also be optimally efficient, there typically being a range of optimal plant scales. Eventually, however, diseconomies of scale may set in, as increasing plant size beyond some point is associated with rising average cost. Such diseconomies may arise from several factors, including rising transportation costs as more and more output is shipped from a single location to more and more distant markets, the increasing costs of overcoming worker preferences for smaller-scale organizations, and the increasing difficulties of managing larger-scale plants.

An individual firm can, and frequently does, operate more than one plant. In some industries, further economies of scale, beyond those obtainable through the operation of a single plant of minimum optimal scale, may result from multiplant operations. Such economies may arise from more effective use of managerial talent, economies associated with large-scale marketing and distribution, or lower prices of purchased inputs. When significant multiplant economies exist, minimum optimal firm size will exceed minimum optimal plant size. Firm sizes larger than minimum optimal scale may be optimally efficient also, at least to a point at which the increasing difficulties of managing and coordinating a large-scale enterprise may lead to the onset of diseconomies of scale.

Economies of Scope

One important complication to the foregoing discussion is the concept of "economies of scope." A plant will often produce more than one product—sometimes many. Under these circumstances, the average cost of producing a particular product, say product X, may depend not only on the rate of output of product X, but also on the rates of output of the other products. Production synergies may exist such that the average cost of producing product X is lower when it is produced in conjunction with other products than when it is produced alone. In some such cases, minimum optimal scale may be somewhat larger than would appear to be the case if the cost-output relationship for product X were examined in isolation. Economies of scope, while a common source of production economies at the plant level, may also extend to the multiplant operations of the firm, particularly marketing and distribution.

Effect of Cumulative Volume

A second complication concerns the effect of cumulative production volume on average cost. While the concept of economies of scale is usually defined as a static relationship between average cost and the designed rate of output, there is often a dynamic aspect to economies of scale as well. Commencing with the introduction of a new product, average cost may fall for a time as the cumulative volume of production increases over time, both for technical reasons and as the result of learning. Thus, average cost will be a function of both the current rate of output and the cumulative volume of output. In some cases, this latter relationship may be important enough to provide a critical cost advantage to early entrants into a market.

Scale Economies and Industry Structure

The importance of economies of scale varies widely from industry to industry. In some industries, technological conditions will yield economies of scale extending over a wide range of output size, and only very large firms can be optimally efficient. In other industries, economies of scale can be fully exploited at relatively small scales. In any industry, the relationship between the minimum optimal firm size and the size of the market served by the industry is potentially a key determinant of the competitive structure of the industry and its degree of seller concentration. In some industries this relationship will be such that the market demand can absorb the output of a large number of efficiently sized producers, and an industry structure characterized by many competing sellers and relatively low concentration is possible. In other industries, market demand will be sufficient to absorb the output of only a few efficiently sized producers, and the market will tend to be oligopolistic with relatively high concentration, particularly if there is a significant cost disadvantage inherent in operating at suboptimal scales. At the extreme, economies of scale may be so extensive (or the market may be so small) that there is room for only one efficiently sized producer in the market, a condition generally referred to as "natural monopoly."

Empirical Evidence

The actual incidence of economies of scale in specific industries and throughout the economy generally is an empirical question of great importance in the making of public policies toward industry, particularly in the areas of antitrust and regulation. Unfortunately, there are many pitfalls in this area of empirical research, and detailed estimates of the extent of economies of scale have been developed for relatively few industries in the United States, Great Britain, and a few other countries, primarily in the manufacturing sector.

The empirical evidence to date, which varies widely in quality, would support several tentative generalizations for the United States. In most U.S. manufacturing industries, minimum optimal plant scales are small relative to the national market, and real multiplant economies appear to be limited. Thus, high national concentration is rarely a technological imperative. However, in some industries the markets are regional rather than national in scope, and scale economies are large enough to dictate moderate-to-high concentration on a regional basis. And in a few industries, scale economies may explain high concentration on a national basis.

In general, concentration in the U.S. manufacturing sector appears to be much higher than would be expected on the basis of efficiency considerations alone. Therefore, the explanation for high concentration, where it exists, must often be found elsewhere.

References

Bain, Joe S., *Barriers to New Competition,* Harvard University Press, Cambridge, Mass., 1956; Robinson, E. A. G., *The Structure of Competitive Industry,* University of Chicago Press, Chicago, 1958, 1st ed., 1931; Scherer, F. M., and Ross, David, *Industrial Market Structure and Economic Performance,* 3d ed., Houghton Mifflin, Boston, 1990; Shepherd, William G., *The Economics of Industrial Organization,* 2d ed., Prentice-Hall, Englewood Cliffs, N.J., 1985.

(*See also* Advertising, economic aspects; Competition; Concentration of industry; Diminishing returns law; Integration; Mergers, takeovers, and corporate restructuring)

Brian C. Brush

Elasticity

Elasticity is generally the ratio of the relative change in a dependent variable in response to the relative change in an independent variable. Although relative changes in the variables can be expressed in different ways, arc elasticity is frequently used to measure the relative changes in the independent and the dependent variables. For price elasticity of demand, arc elasticity is an average elasticity measured between two different points on a demand curve. After noting arc elasticity as a statistical measurement technique, simple percentage changes will be used here. One formula for arc elasticity that applies to price elasticity of demand is

$$E_p = \frac{Q_1 - Q_2}{Q_1 + Q_2} \div \frac{P_1 - P_2}{P_1 + P_2}$$

Price Elasticity of Demand

Price elasticity of demand must always have been implicit in the minds of buyers and sellers. But the name itself and the exact definition are due to Alfred Marshall (*Principles of Economics,* 1890).

The coefficient of price elasticity of demand is defined as

$$E_p = \frac{\text{percentage change in quantity}}{\text{percentage change in price}}$$

where quantity is a function of price and where other variables (tastes, incomes, and the prices of related goods) are held constant. The coefficient of price elasticity is E_p, whose sign is negative owing to the inverse relation between quantity and price. Because it is a pure number, the coefficient makes it possible to compare the price elasticities of different products and services.

Discussion of price elasticities usually centers on the absolute values of the coefficients, their negative signs usually ignored. The coefficients can range in value from zero to infinity. Where the coefficient is zero, demand is said to be perfectly inelastic. The demand curve is a vertical line, which means that, no matter what the price, buyers would purchase the same quantity of the commodity. An example is a unique lifesaving drug. When the coefficient lies between zero and unity, demand is said to be inelastic.

A rise in price where demand is inelastic causes buyers to spend more on the smaller quantity, and thus sellers receive more. This follows from the definition of price elasticity—a price rise with an inelastic demand means that the percentage change in quantity is less than the percentage change in price, and therefore price multiplied by quantity increases. Empirical studies usually find that the demands for farm products are inelastic. The federal government's efforts to raise farm prices for the benefit of farmers have been predicated on the inelastic demands for farm products.

When the coefficient is equal to 1, demand has unitary elasticity. An occasional empirical result, unit elasticity is often an assumption in applied theoretical work. When the coefficient is greater than unity, demand is said to be elastic. When demand is elastic, a price reduction means that buyers spend more and that sellers receive more; a price increase means that buyers spend less.

A coefficient of infinity does not apply to products bought in markets by many thousands of buyers, but it does indeed have meaning for the demand for a seller's product as seen by that seller. For example, demand is infinitely elastic for the output of any one wheat farmer, who could sell all the farm's output at the prevailing price but who could sell nothing at a higher price.

Commodities with price-elastic demands are those with several close substitutes, with many uses, and with large positions in buyers' budgets. Time provides buyers with an opportunity to find substitutes, and over time demand tends to become less inelastic and also more elastic. Price inelasticity characterizes commodities without close substitutes and, above all, commodities on which buyers spend small fractions of their budgets.

Price elasticity plays a prominent role in monopolized markets because elasticity affects marginal revenue, where marginal revenue is

$$MR = P - P/E$$

When demand is very elastic, marginal revenue becomes closer to the price of the product. This means that a small decrease in price will increase sales and total revenue sharply. The airlines industry is wise about this relationship and sets the lowest price in the submarket with the most elastic demand.

Income Elasticity of Demand

Changes in quantities bought can also come from changes in buyers' incomes. When demand is a function of incomes, prices and other variables being held constant, elasticity is income elasticity of demand. It is defined as

$$E_Y = \frac{\text{percentage change in quantity}}{\text{percentage change in price}}$$

where E_Y is the coefficient of income elasticity. The sign of E_Y usually is positive, which is to say that quantities purchased go up and down with incomes. When E_Y is greater than 1, it is high. Products and services with low income elasticities are those occupying small positions in consumers' budgets. One way to define a necessity is to so name any good with a very low income elasticity. Such a definition is free of value judgments. Products with high income elasticities are those whose purchase takes large parts of consumers' budgets. These include expensive durable goods. Thus, luxuries have high income elasticities of demand. Negative income elasticities apply to so-called inferior goods. For them, increases in income cause declines in quantities bought. An inferior good is defined as any good with an inverse relation between changes in income and changes in quantities bought.

Generally, for all consumption goods there is a weighted-average income elasticity that, almost by definition, is equal to 1. Holding prices constant, that means that if there is a given percentage increase in income, the consumption of some goods will rise by more than the change in income; and the consumption of some goods by less. Because the increase in income is spent, on average, consumption will increase by about the same proportion as income.

Cross Elasticity of Demand

Cross elasticity of demand concerns the relations between the quantities bought of one commodity and the prices of another. The demand for commodity A is a function of the price of commodity B. Held equal are tastes, incomes, and commodity A's price. Cross elasticity is defined as

$$E_{AB} = \frac{\text{percentage change in quantity of A}}{\text{percentage change in price of B}}$$

When the sign of the coefficient E_{AB} is positive, A and B are substitutes. Thus, for example, a rise in the price of beef causes an increase in the purchase of chicken. The size of the coefficient shows how close A and B are as substitutes. Sometimes, in antitrust work, a monopolized product is defined as one whose cross elasticities with its substitutes are low. Cross elasticity is also used to express the competitiveness faced by a firm or firms, showing how the sales of firm C are affected by changes in the price charged by its rival, firm D. A negative coefficient signifies that A and B are complements. Complements play a relatively minor role in economic relationships.

Elasticity of Supply and of Substitution

Elasticity of supply is defined as

$$E_s = \frac{\text{percentage change in quantity supplied}}{\text{percentage change in price}}$$

It is therefore symmetrical with price elasticity of demand. The coefficient is usually positive, showing larger quantities are sold at higher prices.

A complex concept, the elasticity of substitution is a property of production functions. It is a measure of the ease or difficulty of substituting capital for labor in response to a change in the ratio of prices of labor and capital. In some production functions, the elasticity of substitution is assumed to be unity; many empirical studies have also shown values close to unity. This means that a given percentage increase in the ratio of the price of labor to the price of capital causes an equiproportional increase in the capital-labor ratio. The elasticity of substitution is also important in the analysis of the shares of labor and capital in national income.

Elasticity of Price Expectations

The elasticity of price expectations is a concept proposed by J. R. Hicks in 1939. The elasticity is defined as a percentage change in expected future prices divided by the percentage change in current prices. The coefficient can be positive or negative. If it is positive and greater than unity, the elasticity of price expectation is high, meaning that buyers and sellers, seeing current prices go up, will then expect future price to go up by even more. When the buyers and sellers act on this belief, they cause the very price increases they foresee. A high elasticity of price expectations is destabilizing. In contrast, a low elasticity means that increases in current prices are believed to cause smaller relative changes in expected future prices. If the coefficient is zero or negative, current price increases are regarded as merely temporary.

Multiple Use of Elasticity Concepts

Frequently two or more elasticity concepts can be used concurrently. For example, if overuse of a national park can be avoided by the imposition of a surcharge, the size of that surcharge will depend on the responsiveness of users. To prevent overuse, the surcharge would be high when users have low price elasticities of demand, high income elasticities of demand, and low cross elasticities. Also, monetary policies might not be successful in reversing business cycles, either expansion or contraction. This could happen when the price elasticities of business investment demands are low and are coupled with high positive coefficients of elasticity of price expectations.

References

Brown, Gardner, "Pricing Seasonal Recreation Services," *Western Economic Journal,* vol. 9, no. 2, June 1971, pp. 218–225; Hirshleifer, Jack, *Price Theory and Applications,* Prentice-Hall, Englewood Cliffs, N.J., 1988, chap. 5; Marshall, A., *Principles of Economics,* 9th ed., C. W. Guilleband (ed.), Macmillan, New York, 1961; Stigler, George, *The Theory of Price,* 3d ed., Crowell-Collier and Macmillan, New York, 1966, pp. 331–333; Watson, Donald S., and Mary A. Holman, *Price Theory and Its Users,* 4th ed., Houghton Mifflin, Boston, 1977, chaps. 3, 4.

(*See also* Competition; Consumer theory; Demand; Isoquant; Monopoly and oligopoly; Production function; Supply)

Mary A. Holman

Employment and unemployment

The modern-day concepts of employment and unemployment seem quite intuitive and, hence, would appear to be easily definable in terms universally understandable and acceptable to the economist and layperson alike. Most persons agree that if an individual is working—that is, engaged in some sort of physical or mental activity for which he or she is being remunerated—then that person should be classified as employed. And while there is clearly less of an instinctive feel for the meaning of unemployment, many persons, when asked to explain the concept, quite logically respond that it is simply the inverse of employment—*not* working. Yet, further reflection quickly shows that these definitions are substantially incomplete, not only with respect to a conceptual understanding of employment and unemployment, but, more importantly, in terms of the specific process of measuring the number of persons who fall into the two categories.

To illustrate, look at employment. How much work should a person do before he or she is considered employed—an hour, a day, a week, longer? Should a person who works 1 hour per week be considered just as employed as one who works 40? What about those who work in a family business but do not get a paycheck? And among those who are not working, how about persons who do not want a job, such as retired persons or those who do not want to work because they are staying home taking care of children—should they be viewed as unemployed? What about those who want a job but are not actually looking for work? How should persons on strike be classified, or those on layoff? Should persons be receiving unemployment insurance benefits in order to be considered unemployed? More broadly, should the concepts of employment and unemployment be universally applied, or should they vary according to unique social, cultural, or economic characteristics in any given country? These are but a few of the questions that social scientists have grappled with over the past 60 years or so in pinning down the circumstances that determine whether a person is employed, unemployed, or neither. In fact, few other economic concepts have generated as much controversy and interest in terms of their measurement and definition as employment and unemployment.

Early Concepts and Methods

Before the industrial revolution, the majority of the world's population toiled out of necessity in the production of food and little else, and so there was relatively little unemployment (as we know it), except for the normal seasonal slumps in farm work between the planting and harvesting periods and the sporadic displacement of labor occasioned by crop failures or other systemic shocks such as wars or plagues. Because of the substantial homogeneity of the labor force and the relatively stable pattern in economic activity (and also, of course, because of society's limited degree of economic/statistical sophistication), there was little demand for information on labor resources and their usage.

Indications of an emerging manufacturing sector in many countries around the beginning of the nineteenth century, however, ignited interest in obtaining information on the changing work force. Early data were limited mostly to the occupational characteristics of the population, as determined through national censuses. These data were reported in terms of the number of persons who usually earned money in a given trade; such persons were typically referred to as the "gainfully occupied" or "gainful workers." While useful for tracking long-term sectoral shifts in the economy and for making rough approximations of labor supply, the data could not be used to measure actual employment and unemployment levels, primarily because they did not indicate whether a person was currently working. This deficiency was not a major problem, though, so long as unemployment remained at relatively low levels.

As the process of industrialization intensified toward the end of the nineteenth century and on into the twentieth, it became clear that the shift from an agrarian economy to one based on manufacturing brought with it a wide range of new social and economic problems, not the least of which was sharply increased levels of both cyclical and structural unemployment. These fluctuations in the demand for labor stimulated interest in the development of new data sources for monitoring labor-market conditions over the business cycle. The earliest figures emerged in Europe, where administrative records from trade unions, employment exchanges, and, somewhat later, unemployment insurance systems (the first national system was inaugurated in Great Britain in 1911) were widely used to estimate unemployment. However, these statistics suffered from a number of limitations, most notably that of incomplete coverage. Trade union data obviously reflected joblessness among only those workers who were union members, and many unemployed persons did not register with employment offices for jobs or qualify or apply for unemployment insurance benefits.

Another approach, used more in the United States than in Europe (in part because of the relative shortage of administrative statistics in the United States), involved the indirect estimation of unemployment from the declines, or "shrinkages," in employment during cyclical contractions, but this technique also had its problems. The United States, for example, had initiated a monthly survey of business establishments in selected manufacturing industries in 1915, whereby employment was measured by the number of persons appearing on the payroll records of firms. While such surveys were reasonably timely and accurate barometers of changes in labor demand, it was recognized that they could provide only a rough estimate of the number of persons who lost jobs and certainly produced no information on the total stock of the unemployed at any given time. In addition to scope limitations, a big problem was that the establishment surveys could not identify persons who did not have any attachment to the firm, either currently or in the past. In particular, there was no way to account for those individuals who were looking for their first job.

Development of the Activity Concept

The most successful efforts to define and measure employment and unemployment on a systematic basis originated in the United States during the Great Depression, as a direct result of the unprecedented rise in unemployment during the period. As economic conditions deteriorated rapidly following the stock market crash in 1929, the need for more accurate and timely information on the number and characteristics of the unemployed intensified. Attempts at estimation were made as part of the decennial population census conducted in 1930, but unemployment was rising so fast that these figures were quickly rendered obsolete. Since the U.S. government had no mechanism in place for the regular collection of national unemployment statistics, much of the intelligence on unemployment during the Depression was based on data from numerous uncoordinated surveys of unemployment conducted by state and local governments and various estimates made by private organizations. Unfortunately, continued lack of agreement about how unemployment should be defined and measured led to substantial controversy over the true dimensions of the crisis.

Part of the problem with early surveys was the widespread reliance on the old "gainful-worker" concept as the basis for determining the size of the work force. Even though gainful workers were, by 1930, asked whether or not they were currently working, persons looking for their first job, who could not be reported as having gainful occupations in the first place, were still excluded from the unemployment counts. This limitation proved quite serious during the Depression, when many family members who had not previously worked entered the job market to make up for the income lost when the primary breadwinner was out of work. Hence, there was a valid concern that estimates of unemployment derived from the gainful-worker data were potentially much too low.

Another more general problem was that the criteria being used for determining one's attachment to the work force and interest in finding a job were often considered to be too subjective. For example, persons not working but expressing a "willingness to work" and "ability to work" often qualified as being unemployed. Critics countered that this did not constitute an adequate test of one's desire for and attempts to find a job, with the result that estimates of unemployment under this conceptual framework were too high.

These and other limitations plagued virtually all attempts at measuring unemployment during the worst years of the Depression. However, dissatisfaction with the concepts in use did spawn considerable research and experimentation with new concepts and survey designs, culminating, toward the end of the 1930s, with the development of a monthly national sample survey of households for determining the employment status of the population. This survey was formally instituted in March 1940 by the Work Projects Administration (WPA) under the rubric Monthly Report of Unemployment. The Census Bureau (which took over responsibility for the survey in 1942 when the WPA was dissolved) later renamed it the Current Population Survey (or the better-known acronym, the CPS), as it is known today.

Many notable features of this new labor-force survey distinguished it from previous attempts to measure the unemployed. Foremost was the adoption of an activity concept for determining a person's employment status. With this approach, persons were classified as either employed, unemployed, or out of the labor force based on what they were actually doing during a given week. In principle, if people reported themselves as working for pay during the week (as little as one hour), they were deemed employed. If they were not working but actively seeking a job, they were considered unemployed. All others were considered not in the labor force.

This method was found to be far superior to existing techniques for evaluating labor-force utilization. It facilitated a classification of all persons in the population based on their current labor-market status and eliminated the necessity for making value judgments concerning an individual's interest in finding work. In addition to providing better information on unemployment, it also produced the first regular comprehensive estimates of the number of employed persons in the nation, as well as an unprecedented look at the nature and extent of their work activity, such as their industry and occupational affiliation, class of worker (whether they worked for an employer, were self-employed, or worked without pay in a family business), the number of hours worked, and numerous other characteristics. Moreover, the survey provided data on the demographic characteristics of the employed and unemployed that heretofore were unavailable. Combining the demographic data with the data on unemployment, analysts got not only a better picture of the supply of labor but also a more complete measure of the demand for labor, thereby allowing a determination of the degree to which labor resources were underutilized.

The development of the activity approach to measuring employment and unemployment was rather revolutionary in the field of labor statistics. Just as revolutionary was the sample-based method for collecting the data. Before the 1930s, probability sampling had not been used to collect labor-market statistics (or, for that matter, most other types of economic data). But the need for timely and reliable information on the extent of unemployment during the Depression led to considerable research into the efficacy of probability sampling for collecting data on unemployment, including extensive experimentation with small surveys. By the end of the decade, the state of the art had progressed far enough to support the design of a national sample survey. Even though there was considerable initial skepticism about whether a sample survey of the population would provide reliable data, it was quickly concluded that the data collected through carefully designed samples were actually superior in quality (not to mention frequency!) to the information gathered through population censuses, owing to the advantages of using trained enumerators and carefully structured questionnaires.

Since the activity concept was introduced, only minor refinements of the basic employment and unemployment definitions have been made in the United States. From the start, however, not everyone was satisfied with the criteria used for classifying persons, and concerns regarding the accuracy and relevancy of the data led to four major reviews—in 1948, 1954–1955, 1961–1962, and 1978–1979, the latter two by presidentially appointed commissions—and nearly continuous scrutiny of the data from both within and outside the U.S. government. Most of the criticism has centered on the concept of unemployment, and this has led to a tightening of the definition over the years.

The most substantive series of revisions to the unemployment concept occurred in 1967, when recommendations from the President's Committee to Appraise Employment and Unemployment Statistics (assembled in 1961–1962 and commonly known as the Gordon Committee, after its chairman, Robert A. Gordon) were incorporated. (The 1963–1966 period was devoted to research on and testing of alternative methods for incorporating the various recommendations.) First, an availability test was added to make sure that a person classified as unemployed was currently available to take a job. This change was made because of the concern that some persons, particularly students, might be trying to line up work starting at some future date; because the raison d'être for the activity approach was to measure current labor-market conditions, it was felt that the possibility of including a person's interest in a future job diluted the pertinence of the figures.

Second, specific questions on job-seeking methods were added to the survey to ensure that persons reporting that they were looking for work were actively searching for a job, and a 4-week time period was established as the appropriate interval within which the search for work must have taken place. Previously, respondents did not have to describe what they had done to look for a job, nor did they need to indicate when they had looked ("last week" was presumed), and it was felt that this ambiguity also undermined the precision of the unemployment estimates.

Finally, the Gordon Committee recommended that information on persons who wanted jobs but were not actively seeking them, termed "discouraged workers," be collected on a regular basis. The measure finally adopted identified discouraged persons as those who want a job "now" but are not looking for work because they think they cannot find any.

There have been several other comparatively minor revisions to the definitions, but the present (1992) U.S. definitions of employment and unemployment, as presented next, are remarkably close to those first introduced more than 50 years earlier.

To be classified as employed, *a person must have, during the survey reference week, done any work at all as a paid employee, worked in their own business, profession, or on their own farm, or worked 15 hours or more as an unpaid worker in a family enterprise. Persons who were not working but had jobs or businesses from which they were temporarily absent because of illness, bad weather, vacation, labor-management disputes, or personal reasons, are also counted as employed.*

Unemployed *persons include those who were not employed during the reference week and were available for work (except for temporary illness), and had made specific efforts to find employment some time during the prior 4 weeks. Persons on layoff who expect to be recalled to their job, or those waiting to report to a job within 30 days, need not be looking for work to be classified as unemployed.*

The labor force *is the sum of all employed and unemployed persons—that is, those who have a job and those who are actively seeking a job. Persons not classified as employed or unemployed are considered* not in the labor force.

In 1994, several changes will be introduced into the CPS which will improve the identification and ease of measurement of employment and unemployment but will not alter the underlying concepts. One small exception will be that persons volunteering that they're awaiting a job (within 30 days) must also indicate recent job search in order to be classified as unemployed. This is essentially a cosmetic change—one that will limit the nonsearch acceptability to persons who report themselves to be on layoff and anticipating recall—as, in fact, very few persons actually volunteer that they are expecting to report to some future job.

In addition, the measurement of discouraged workers will be modified by incorporating recommendations made originally by the National Commission on Employment and Unemployment Statistics (the Levitan Commission) in 1979 and studied extensively during the 1980s. At present (again, in 1992), all persons who indicate that they want a job but aren't looking for work because they believe their search would be in vain are classified as discouraged workers. Under the new definition, only those persons who currently desire a job (though not currently seeking work), are available to take one, and have looked for a job sometime in the prior year will be classified as discouraged workers. By requiring some evidence of search activity, it is anticipated that the new concept will exclude many persons for whom discouragement is more a state of mind than a measurable response to poor job-market conditions.

Even though the original employment and unemployment concepts have remained largely intact as the official measures, disagreements continue to arise, particularly during recessions, concerning the inclusiveness of the unemployment definition. This is due, in part, to the tendency among many observers to interpret joblessness as a measure of hardship. Many believe that unemployment should encompass a wider range of labor-market difficulties than those embodied in the official definition, such as persons who are visibly underemployed (working part time involuntarily, but still classified as employed), as well as discouraged workers. At the same time, it has been argued that the current concept of unemployment includes some workers who don't have a bona fide "need" for a job, e.g., many young workers, for whom the condition of joblessness does not necessarily entail financial burdens. In response to these criticisms, a series of alternative definitions incorporating differing assumptions about who should be considered unemployed—running the gamut from the very narrow to the broad—were introduced by the U.S. Bureau of Labor Statistics (BLS) in the mid-1970s, and these have been published regularly since then. (BLS has had responsibility for interpreting and analyzing all labor-force data from the CPS since 1959.) Of course, these alternatives necessarily embrace differing normative judgments as to the labor-market circumstances that constitute hardship and thus are less suitable for the objective assessment of labor-resource utilization than the official definition of unemployment. Nevertheless, these measures are useful as ancillary yardsticks of labor-market performance.

Employment Statistics from the Establishment Survey

In addition to the employment figures available from the CPS, employment data continue to be obtained directly from employers, through the aforementioned establishment, or "payroll," survey, the monthly survey of business establishments first launched (for a few industries) in 1915. Now formally known as the Current Employment Statistics (CES) program, the survey has been greatly expanded over time, providing monthly estimates of nationwide employment for all industries except agriculture since 1939. Employment data from the establishment survey are conceptually different from those collected through the CPS, although this difference derives mainly from the nature of the survey and not from fundamental differences in the definition of employment. Most important, the figures are somewhat less comprehensive, since persons working outside of firms, such as the self-employed, private household workers, and persons working without pay in family enterprises, typically cannot be surveyed. Also, because people who hold more than one job may be counted each time they appear on a payroll record, the establishment survey technically measures the number of jobs, rather than the number of employed persons. The CES is generally perceived to produce more accurate and reliable data on employment changes than the CPS, owing to the substantially larger sample sizes afforded by the scalar economies in sampling (a single sampled firm may have thousands of employees) and to the fact that the data are taken from readily available employment records routinely maintained by most employers. In addition, whereas the household survey is uniquely suited to gathering information on the demographic characteristics of the employed, the payroll survey provides valuable industry detail on employment that cannot be reliably obtained from other sources.

Data Analysis and Use in Policymaking

As key barometers of aggregate economic activity, employment and unemployment statistics are instrumental in monitoring business-cycle conditions, and government policymakers have relied heavily on these data in order to develop and implement countercyclical economic policies and then to evaluate their effectiveness. In fact, the U.S. government is obligated, under the Employment Act of 1946, to pursue economic policies that "promote maximum employment, production, and purchasing power." These broad economic objectives were later reaffirmed in the Full Employment and Balanced Growth Act of 1978. Estimates of monthly employment growth, as measured through both the CPS and the CES, together with movements in unemployment and other cyclically sensitive labor-market indicators, figure importantly in making decisions about whether, and to what extent, monetary and fiscal policies should be pursued in order to maintain economic growth.

While the overall unemployment rate (the percentage of the labor force that is unemployed) is perhaps the best-known cyclical indicator, data on specific characteristics of the unemployed, such as their reason for looking for work, can shed considerably more light on changes in labor demand than can the overall unemployment rate alone. An increase in unemployment due to increases in the number of persons who have lost their jobs (job losers), for example, certainly suggests a declining demand for workers; however, increases in unemployment due to a growing number of new entrants or reentrants to the labor force, which might occur at the onset of an economic recovery, is not necessarily inconsistent with improving labor demand. (This can explain why the unemployment rate is sometimes described as a lagging indicator at recession troughs.) Similarly, information on the level of employment and hours of work in specific industries, available from the establishment survey, can be more informative in terms of assessing the health of the economy than the data on overall employment growth. Employment trends in the cyclically sensitive construction and manufacturing industries, for example, often serve as leading gauges of overall economic activity, as do changes in the number of hours worked in these industries.

Interest in monitoring the economy over the course of the business cycle is not limited to government policymakers. Participants in business and financial markets are also keenly interested in job-market data for clues about how well or how poorly the economy is operating, in order to develop both short- and long-run investment strategies and to anticipate policy changes on the part of the federal government. Of course, the public at large pays close attention to the labor-market figures, both for making personal financial decisions, such as when to make a major purchase or to change jobs, and for evaluating the performance of the political leadership.

Even in times of economic expansion, it is important to monitor labor-resource utilization in order to establish how efficiently and equitably the labor market is operating. To this end, employment and unemployment data are used extensively by government and private researchers to analyze how various population groups are faring in the economy and to evaluate longer-run economic trends in the structure and composition of the labor force. The wealth of demographic, socioeconomic, industrial, occupational, and geographical detail on employment and unemployment available through the household and establishment surveys, plus the long history of these surveys, provides researchers with copious data for undertaking such studies. In addition, these data can also be used in designing and administering various government-sponsored programs developed to assist those in need. For example, the federal Job Training Partnership Act (JTPA), which helps economically disadvantaged youth and adults by providing job training and other work-related skills, uses state and local-area unemployment rates (estimated using CPS data in conjunction with other data sources) to identify those areas of the country most in need of help because of a weak market for labor. Other programs use unemployment data to allocate funding for emergency food assistance and public works projects.

International Concepts

To promote the international comparability of statistics on employment and unemployment, the International Labour Office (ILO) established standardized definitions in 1954, at the Eighth International Conference of Labour Statisticians. These definitions were based largely on the concepts inaugurated in the United States more than a decade earlier, and as with the United States, there have been only minor revisions over the years. Even so, the ILO criteria for determining labor-force status are, in general, less rigid than the current U.S. concepts, reflecting the need to accommodate international variations in measurement techniques and differences in political and economic institutions, cultural and social customs, and so forth.

In terms of data-collection methods, the ILO does not actually recommend that employment and unemployment data be gathered through a labor-force survey like the CPS, nor does it stipulate how frequently the data should be collected. The reference period is defined as either one day or one week. The lack of specificity in these areas reflects, to a large degree, the fact that several European countries have historically relied on information from employment office registrations for their official monthly estimates of unemployment. (These countries also conduct labor-force surveys, but the figures obtained through these surveys do not usually represent "official" unemployment estimates. It should also be noted that, like the United States, many countries collect employment data through both household and establishment surveys.) As for actual concepts and definitions, the ILO definition of employment is quite similar to that used in the United States, except that unpaid family workers are included as employed regardless of the number of hours worked. The ILO criteria for determining unemployment, however, are somewhat less explicit, as there are no recommended tests for either job seeking or current availability. While most countries have attempted to comply with the ILO standards, the imprecise nature of some of the concepts, plus the fact that not all countries have followed every recommendation, has led to some dissimilarity in the employment and unemployment measures across countries. However, these differences are easily identified, and, in many cases, adjustments can be made which facilitate international comparisons.

References

Bregger, John E., "Unemployment Statistics and What They Mean," *Monthly Labor Review,* November 1971, pp. 22–29; Bregger, John E., "The Current Population Survey: A Historical View and BLS' Role," *Monthly Labor Review,* June 1984, pp. 8–14; Duncan, Joseph W., and William C. Shelton, *Revolution in United States Government Statistics, 1926–1976,* U.S. Department of Commerce, Office of Federal Statistical Policy and Standards, 1978; Goldberg, Joseph P., and William T. Moye, *The First Hundred Years of the Bureau of Labor Statistics,* U.S. Department of Labor, 1979; International Labour Organization, *Statistics of Labour Force, Employment, Unemployment, and Underemployment,* report prepared for the Thirteenth International Conference of Labour Statisticians, October 18–29, 1982, International Labour Office, Geneva, 1982; Morton, J. E., *On the Evolution of Manpower Statistics,* W. E. Upjohn Institute for Employment Research, Kalamazoo, Mich., 1969; National Commission on Employment and Unemployment Statistics, *Counting the Labor Force,* especially appendix volumes I–III, 1979; President's Committee to Appraise Employment and Unemployment Statistics, *Measuring Employment and Unemployment,* 1962; Social Science Research Council, *Labor Force Definition and Measurement,* Bulletin 56, Social Science Research Council, New York, 1947; U.S. Department of Labor, Bureau of Labor Statistics, *International Comparisons of Unemployment,*

Bulletin 1979, 1978; U.S. Department of Labor, Bureau of Labor Statistics, *BLS Handbook of Methods,* Bulletin 2285, 1988.

(*See also* Bureau of Labor Statistics; Labor force; Phillips curve; Statistical methods in economics and business, an overview)

Steven E. Haugen and John E. Bregger

Energy costs

Energy functions as an intermediate good in producing other goods and services. Energy costs, therefore, are the outlays for the energy used in producing these other goods and services. For example, consumers purchase electricity, natural gas, and a host of petroleum products. But it is the heat, light, cooling, and transportation produced by the energy that are the products desired, not the energy itself.

In addition to the direct use of energy to produce other goods and services, substantial amounts are used in producing, converting, and transporting energy supplies. For example, the production of electricity from primary energy forms (especially coal, but also large amounts of petroleum and natural gas) accounted for 36 percent of all U.S. energy consumption in 1990, measured in heat units, while the final energy delivered in the form of electricity amounted to only 11 percent. So energy costs are incurred at all levels, from the primary products of mine, farm, and forest to household production.

Energy and Economic Activity

Historians and others have pointed to the close relationship between energy use and economic development. The industrial revolution of the eighteenth and nineteenth centuries may be described in terms of an enormous increase in energy consumption, first in the manufacturing of metals and textiles, later in transportation and chemicals production. A similar, earlier revolution in production techniques occurred in the neolithic period, when the discovery of agriculture and the domestication of animals, leading to large-scale crop production, meant the conversion of solar energy for human use. Thus, a great increase in living standards, paralleling that of the industrial revolution, took place in the neolithic period. Today, we can observe a strong, though far from perfect, correlation between energy consumption per capita and real income per capita across nations. The less-developed nations consume far less energy per capita than the wealthier nations.

Until the late 1950s, the United States was a net exporter of energy. But low-cost petroleum, mainly from the Middle East, won an increasing share of the U.S. market so that, by 1977, net energy imports represented 24 percent of all energy consumption; the percentage subsequently fell and now stands at 17 percent. Concern over energy costs was heightened by the Arab oil embargo of 1973–1974 that reduced the flow of petroleum imports, and by the sharp increases in oil prices that followed the actions of the OPEC (Organization of Petroleum Exporting Countries) cartel.

The Arab embargo created great concern over possible economic disruption from use of the "oil weapon." The 1973–1975 recession, which to that time was the worst since World War II, is attributable in large part to the embargo and accompanying oil price hikes. World oil prices, which had been rising since 1970, quadrupled in 1973 and rose several times through 1981; they broke sharply thereafter and fell until 1986; since then, they have fluctuated at a lower level, with the exception of a brief price "spike" following the invasion of Kuwait. These abrupt price movements have served to disrupt the operations of individual firms and have caused the path of the aggregate economy to be erratic.

Responding to variations in domestic prices and in U.S. production, net imports of energy (which consist primarily of petroleum) have also fluctuated widely during the 1973–1990 period.

Domestic wholesale energy prices, though partially controlled until 1981, rose substantially from 1973 through 1981; they then fell until 1988. In real terms, that is, relative to a general price index, wholesale energy prices were lower in 1990 than in any year since 1974.

Energy Conservation

A major method of dealing with energy costs, supported intermittently by the federal government, is the promotion of energy conservation. (Another method is, of course, the expansion of energy production.) Energy conservation has led to controversy in both popular and technical discussion. The basic question is whether or not energy use can be constrained to a lower rate of growth in the future than in the past without serious consequences for the economy. That is, does energy conservation mean penury or merely adjustment? Proponents of the penury response have pointed to the extensive disruptions of the economy that have been associated with energy problems in 1973–1975 (the Arab oil embargo), 1979–1981 (the Iranian revolution), and 1990 (the Gulf war). Those who maintain that only adjustment is needed point to nations that use much less energy than the United States (such as Japan) and also have made major reductions in energy use during the same periods, yet have experienced healthy economic growth.

Energy Efficiency

A closely related aspect of energy costs is concerned with the efficiency of energy use. Many students of energy problems maintain that the United States is an energy waster, consuming large amounts of energy unnecessarily. In this connection, comparisons are made with other nations which have similar levels of income per capita. The United States and Canada generally fare poorly in such comparisons. Other analysts, however, point out that energy prices are generally lower in the United States and Canada than in other industrialized nations, both before and after the developments of the 1970s and 1980s, partly because of differential government policies and partly because of natural-resource endowments; U.S. and Canadian energy consumption patterns, it is argued, are therefore largely the result of relatively low energy prices.

Over the entire period for which we have reliable data, energy consumption (in heat units) per dollar of gross national product (in constant dollars) has fallen steadily. This pattern has continued since the embargo, but at an accelerated rate. From 1973 to 1990, energy consumption per dollar of real gross national product fell 28 percent. This development coincided with higher relative energy prices. Further, the recent pattern has been in the form of reductions in the relative importance of goods that use large amounts of energy in their production. That is, conservation of energy is taking place, in the short run, in the form of changes in product mix away from energy-intensive products.

Alternative Energy Sources

There has been an increased interest in exotic (that is, unconventional) energy sources since energy problems burst upon the world in the early 1970s. The U.S. Department of Energy and its predecessors, as well as private institutions, have subsidized and otherwise encouraged the development of alternative sources since the mid-1970s. Thus far, the results have had little commercial impact. Today electricity generated from wood, waste, and wind and from geothermal, photovoltaic, and solar thermal energy account for only a small fraction of the total.

Some boost to alternative motor fuels has been provided by the U.S. Environmental Protection Agency. Under the requirements of the Clean Air Act, cities with serious air pollution caused by motor fuels must use cleaner forms of fuel, such as ethanol or methanol. This has spurred the use of these crop-derived fuels, which would probably not otherwise be in extensive use because of their higher prices and technical difficulties.

References

Cipolla, Carlo M., *The Economic History of World Population,* Penguin, New York, 1978; Energy Information Administration, *Monthly Energy Review,* August 1991, U.S. Department of Energy; Myers, John G., and Leonard I. Nakamura, *Saving Energy in Manufacturing,* Ballinger, Cambridge, Mass., 1978; Richardson, Harry W., *Economic Aspects of the Energy Crisis,* Lexington Books, Lexington, Mass., 1975.

(*See also* Externalities)

John G. Myers

Environmental protection (*see* Economic incentives for environmental protection)

Escalator clause

An escalator clause is a provision of a contract that calls for the adjustment of the contract price or prices to reflect fully, or to some degree, changes in specific costs or in overall inflation. It is a specific application of the concept of indexation. The use of escalator clauses in contracts is predicated on expectations that the purchasing power of the dollar will change. Escalator clauses are generally more widely used when purchasing power is changing markedly and/or when the contract extends over a long period of time—particularly time periods beyond what might be viewed as a period in which future price changes may be known with some degree of certainty.

The types of contracts in which escalator clauses are most frequently found are social security and other government-financed retirement programs, long-term leases for both commercial and residential property, multiyear wage agreements, alimony agreements, and long-term procurement contracts.

The Index Used

The parties who elect to include escalator clauses in their contracts usually rely on one or more of several official U.S. government measures of prices and other costs. Government series are usually selected because of the impartiality with which they are compiled, ease of access, frequency of publication, absence of major revisions, and the likelihood that such indexes, without major alteration, will be published for a long time into the future.

The series actually selected usually bears some relationship to the price that is being escalated. If an escalation index were to be used to adjust a wage contract for future price inflation, then the consumer price index (CPI), representing changes in the purchasing power of the dollar with respect to things bought by consumers, would usually be the series used. The CPI may also be relevant for the escalation of alimony payments and retirement benefits, which, like wages, are used to purchase a bundle of consumer goods. For rents and other long-run procurement contracts, usually no single index is appropriate. Users frequently construct their own from various component price index series. For example, a landlord and commercial tenant may select for escalation of their long-term lease the CPI component for residential rent, the CPI for fuel oil and electricity, and a series on wages paid to individuals in the service industry (some of whom may service the commercial building). The three series would be added up using appropriate weights.

A company in a defense industry holding a long-term contract with the federal government for armaments may employ an escalator based on a weighted average of employment costs and the various materials, such as steel and nonferrous metals, used to produce the armaments. The index that comes closest to measuring pure hourly wage rate changes is the Bureau of Labor Statistics (BLS) employment cost index. It is available every 3 months in some detail. Separate indexes are provided for wages and for benefits. Series on the prices of commodities that manufacturers buy to transform into products produced under long-term contracts are usually obtained from the BLS producer price index (PPI), which contains monthly price indexes for some 3100 industrial commodities and some services.

Escalation Formulas

The contract may call for escalation in an exact step with the index used for escalation. For example, if the CPI rises 10 percent in the first year of a labor contract, wages may be increased by 10 percent. However, sometimes the increase in wages may be based on a formula that calls for translation into a given number of cents of wage increase per percentage points of change in the index being used for escalation. Under these circumstances, the percentage change in wages may not be equal to the percentage change in the price index used for escalation. And sometimes the formula may provide for an increase in wages equal to half the increase in prices or some other fraction. Finally, some contracts provide what are called caps, which limit the amount of escalation vis-à-vis the increase in prices. For example, a provision might be that wages will be raised by three-quarters of the percentage increase in prices up to a limit of 5 percent in any given year.

Importance to the Economy

There are various measures of the dollar volume of transactions in the U.S. economy that are subject to escalation. A recent study of users of the PPI for escalation found that contracts valued at more than \$100 billion were escalated by these indexes. Contracts covering at least 6 million unionized workers are escalated by the CPI.

Escalator clauses provide some kind of insurance that neither party to a contract will benefit unduly as a result of unforeseen inflation. Whether or not such clauses themselves contribute to inflation has been widely and inconclusively debated. It is clear, however, that their use has become increasingly pervasive over the last decade, and they are considered an important tool for use in adjusting for inflation.

References

Escalation and Producer Price Indexes: A Guide for Contracting Parties, Bureau of Labor Statistics, Report 570, September 1979; *Using the Consumer Price Index for Escalation,* Bureau of Labor Statistics, Report 732, October 1986.

(*See also* Consumer price index; Indexation; Inflation; Producer price index; Value of the dollar)

Joel Popkin

Estate and gift taxation (*see* Taxation, an overview)

Eurodollar market

The Eurodollar market is the market for U.S. dollar–denominated deposits placed under a regulatory regime different from the regulations applied to deposits used to execute transactions in the United States. Until 1981, this definition corresponded to U.S. dollar deposits in London, Frankfurt, Zurich, and other international financial centers such as Singapore, Hong Kong, Bahrain, and the Grand Cayman Islands. Since December 1981, Eurodollar deposits in the United States have been permitted in so-called international banking facilities (IBFs). These IBF deposits are subject to a lower regulatory burden than other dollar deposits in the United States, and so they compete effectively with Eurodollar deposits elsewhere. However, IBF deposits are only available to nonresidents, and they may not be used to conduct transactions within the United States.

Since its beginning in the late 1950s, the Eurodollar market has expanded to financial centers outside Europe and to currencies other than the U.S. dollar. Hence, the term "offshore currency market" is more appropriate to describe the market's location and its breadth of activity. At the same time, the array of financial products offered by the market has expanded. Eurocurrency deposits now extend to maturities of 5 years and longer, and lending vehicles range from direct bank-to-customer credits to multibillion dollar Eurocurrency syndications with complex financing terms.

The central idea underlying the rise of the Eurodollar market is "unbundling," that is, separating the exchange risk of one currency (the U.S. dollar) from its indigenous regulatory environment and combining it with the regulatory environment and political risk of another financial center (London, for example). This idea was again imitated with the Eurobond market, the Euro-commercial paper market, and the Euro-equity market. Derivative instruments, such as Eurodollar interest rate futures contracts, have also been developed to hedge interest rate risks associated with Eurocurrency depositing and lending.

The Eurodollar market and the broader offshore financial markets can usefully be thought of as parallel markets, offering a similar array of products to wholesale customers as they would find in domestic, or "onshore," markets. Two interesting economic issues are (1) how can the offshore and onshore markets coexist, and (2) what are the policy implications of having a parallel market seemingly outside the regulatory mechanisms that cover the onshore markets? We will discuss these topics after first reviewing the historical origins of the market and other descriptive information about the market.

Historical Origins

Several factors contributed to the early development of the Eurodollar market. In the late 1950s, following the Suez crisis, the British began to curtail the use of sterling to finance international transactions between third parties. To overcome this restriction, British merchant banks decided to use the U.S. dollar to conduct these transactions from accounts based in London. Since Bank of England regulations did not cover the U.S. dollar, banks were free to set competitive interest rates to attract deposits and offer external loans denominated in dollars.

At about the same time, the continuation of the cold war and East-West tensions made the Soviet Union (and other Eastern bloc countries) fearful of holding U.S. dollars in accounts in the United States. Instead, they shifted their dollar deposits to London and Paris, often with affiliates of state-owned Soviet banks. (The Paris bank *Banque Commerciale pour l'Europe du Nord* carried the cable address EUROBANK, which later became the generic name for institutions that accept offshore deposits.) American action to freeze Iranian deposits in 1979, Iraqi deposits in 1991, and deposits of certain alleged international criminals has validated the Soviet's fear.

A more important stimulus to the Eurocurrency market was the set of credit restrictions and capital controls imposed by the United States in response to an undesired buildup of dollars overseas (dollars that the United States had pledged to convert into gold at $35 per once). In 1963, the United States adopted the interest equalization tax, effectively an excise tax on American purchases of new or outstanding foreign securities. Rather than halt lending to foreigners, borrowing activity simply shifted offshore into the Euromarkets. In 1965, a voluntary foreign credit restraint program was adopted (that was made mandatory in 1968), aimed at reducing the transfer of funds overseas by American multinationals. In response, U.S. firms increased their financing directly in the Eurodollar market, providing further stimulus to the market's growth. All these U.S. policies were abolished in 1974.

Finally, in 1966 the Federal Reserve (via regulation Q) began limiting the amount of interest that commercial banks were allowed to pay on time deposits. With prime commercial paper rates higher than the regulation Q ceiling, large depositors shifted funds away from bank time deposits into nonbank financial assets and into Eurodollar deposits. By 1969, the interest differential favoring commercial paper over regulated bank deposits exceeded 2 percent. U.S. banks moved to establish offshore branches to fund themselves partly with cheaper Eurodollar deposits. In 1973, regulation Q ceilings were abolished for large deposits (greater than $100,000), but this left the door open for money-market mutual funds to earn higher Eurodollar returns by pooling funds from small investors.

Market Size and Composition

The data in Table 1 reveal the tremendous growth of the Eurocurrency market. The market has grown from essentially zero in the late 1950s to $6.4 trillion on a gross

TABLE 1   Dimensions of the Eurocurrency Deposit Market
(Billions of U.S. Dollars)

Year	Gross size	Net size	Eurodollars as % of gross
1970	110	65	81%
1975	485	255	78%
1980	1525	730	75%
1985	2846	1480	75%
1990*	6440	3445	48%[†]

* Break in data sources as described below.
[†] Based on liabilities in industrial reporting countries only.
SOURCE: For years 1970–1985, Morgan Guaranty Trust Co., *World Financial Markets,* various issues. For year 1990, Bank for International Settlements, *International Banking and Financial Market Developments,* Basel, Switzerland, 1992.

basis and $3.4 trillion on a net basis (netting out all offshore interbank deposits) at the end of 1990—slightly larger than the U.S. money supply as measured by M-2. By far the most important currency in the market is the U.S. dollar, although its market share has declined from the 75–80% range of the 1970s. The geographic reach of the market is now worldwide, but the dominant region remains Europe (with a 52 percent market share in 1990) and London (with 19 percent of the market in 1990) as the dominant offshore banking centers. Japan has substantially increased its market share (to 15 percent in 1990), coinciding with its capital-market liberalizations of the 1980s. The establishment of IBFs in 1981 helped the United States to attract offshore deposits from the Caribbean and elsewhere.

While deposit maturities extend out to 5 years, about 70 percent of the deposits have maturities less than 3 months and about 90 percent have maturities less than 1 year. Most of these deposits are issued on fixed-rate terms, but often longer maturities are issued as floating-rate notes or floating-rate certificates of deposit. The vast majority of deposits are for a fixed maturity, but some deposits are on "call," in which case funds would be delivered to the currency's home country in 2 working days.

Euromarket loans are much the same as those made in the domestic or onshore market. One difference is that borrowers in the Euromarket are typically large, well-known firms with high credit standing. As a result, less credit evaluation and documentation may be performed. Loan maturities range from short-term trade financing to 10-year commitments, the latter often referred to as medium-term Eurocredits. The pricing of any Euroloan longer than 6 months is typically structured on a rollover basis: at the start of each 3- or 6-month period, the interest rate is reset at a fixed amount greater than the current London interbank offered rate (LIBOR). Thus, a AAA-rated borrower might pay LIBOR plus ⅛ percent for a 6-month Euroloan and LIBOR plus ⅜ percent for a 5-year Euroloan. (In addition, there could be origination fees, commitment fees, and possibly syndication fees if this were a large loan.) The lending bank would gain some protection against interest rate changes, as LIBOR would be reset periodically. The borrower could hedge this risk, if he or she wished, using Eurodollar interest rate futures contracts.

Pricing of Offshore Deposits and Loans

For the offshore market to exist in tandem with the onshore market, two conditions must be met: first, there must be advantages for both depositors and borrowers to attract them to the offshore market, and second, there must be barriers or costs affecting some depositors and borrowers that prevent all banking activity from migrating offshore.

Onshore banks incur numerous costs in collecting deposits and servicing loans. The major categories of costs for U.S. banks are (1) non-interest-bearing reserves at the Federal Reserve, (2) FDIC insurance, (3) credit review, (4) asset-liability risk management, (5) taxes, and (6) administrative overhead. As a result, in June 1992 a U.S. bank might pay its marginal depositor R_D (say, 3.5 percent) and set a prime lending rate R_L (say, 6.5 percent), with the spread $(R_L - R_D)$ covering costs, risks, and profits. By comparison, offshore banks (1) earn interest on their voluntary level of reserves, (2) do not pay FDIC-like insurance, (3) deal primarily with known, high-quality credits, (4) price their loans on floating-rate terms to reduce interest rate risks, (5) often operate in tax havens or under other tax incentives, and (6) operate a wholesale business with lower overhead costs. Since their costs are lower, a Eurobank could earn profits by paying depositors R'_D (say, 4.0 percent) and setting its loans relative to LIBOR, R'_L (say, 4.25 percent).

Since depositors prefer higher deposit rates and borrowers prefer lower lending rates, what prevents all onshore transactions from migrating offshore? In this stylized model, American depositors bear the additional risks of exchange controls or taxes, and perhaps added inconvenience for U.S. dollar deposits in London or another Euromarket center. Institutional constraints may prohibit some depositors from placing deposits offshore. For borrowers, size and credit quality may act as a barrier to entry to the offshore market. Small firms and those with weaker credit ratings or without name recognition are more likely to have their loans indexed to the New York "prime" or some other onshore rate.

The pattern of interest rates noted above $(R_L > R'_L$ and $R'_D > R_D)$ can be altered when capital controls are present. For example, in the early 1970s, nonresident accounts in Germany were subject to non-interest-bearing reserve requirements, and depositors accepted lower Euro-DM deposit rates to avoid these costly controls. Similarly, when the onshore market is experiencing a "capital crunch"—interest rate controls or central bank guidelines leading to a shortage of funds—borrowers have been prepared to borrow at LIBOR even though it exceeds the quoted New York prime rate.

Policy Matters

As the Eurocurrency market developed rapidly and with relatively little regulation from national authorities, the impact of the market has at times been a source of concern. In the 1960s and 1970s, the primary concern was whether the relatively unconstrained lending activity in the Eurocurrency market led to a worldwide inflationary bias as well as a greater tendency toward exchange rate instability. By upsetting historical relationships between monetary aggregates and expenditure (i.e., velocity), the Eurocurrency market probably made the execution of policy more difficult for monetary authorities. However, as long as Euromarket conditions were linked to the onshore market, the standard policy tools were still able to affect monetary aggregates and short-term interest rates without direct control of the Euromarket.

After the collapse of the Herstatt Bank in 1974 and until the present, policy concern has shifted toward matters of supervision and prudential controls—in particular, the lack of a lender of last resort for offshore banks, the capital adequacy of offshore banking operations, and the adequate supervision of offshore loan portfolios. Under the auspices of the Bank for International Settlements (BIS), a committee was set up to address these supervisory and prudential concerns. The first statement from this committee, the Basle Concordat (1975), proclaimed that supervision of offshore banking establishments should be the joint responsibility of host and parent authorities. Supervision of liquidity would belong to host authorities, while supervision of solvency would be the responsibility of parent authorities. In 1980, the BIS announced an agreement requiring commercial banks to consolidate their worldwide accounts. This agreement enables bank examiners to regulate offshore and onshore operations on a consistent basis. The BIS capital adequacy guidelines for commercial banks that will be applied on a worldwide, consolidated basis are an important illustration of this concept.

As Kenneth Dam (1982, p. 322) remarked, "The notion that Eurocurrency banks operate beyond the reach of any government is patently incorrect." The challenge for regulators has been to bring the Euromarkets within a worldwide financial safety net without eliminating the dynamism and innovation that has characterized these markets since their inception.

References

Crockett, Andrew, "The Euro-Currency Market: An Attempt to Clarify Some Basic Issues," *IMF Staff Papers,* July 1976; Dam, Kenneth M., *The Rules of the Game,* University of Chicago Press, Chicago, 1982; Frydl, Edward, "The Debate over Regulating the Eurocurrency Markets," *Quarterly Review,* Federal Reserve Bank of New York, Winter 1979–1980; George, Abraham M., and Ian H. Giddy (eds.), *International Finance Handbook,* Wiley, New York, 1983, part 3; Klopstock, Fred H., "Eurodollar Market," in D. Greenwald (ed.), *The Encyclopedia of Economics,* McGraw-Hill, New York, 1981, pp. 346–349; Levich, Richard M., "The Euromarkets after 1992," in J. Dermine (ed.), *European Banking in the 1990s,* Blackwell, Oxford, pp. 373–399; Sarver, Eugene, *The Eurocurrency Market Handbook,* 2d ed., New York Institute of Finance, New York, 1990.

(*See also* Banking system; Business credit; Credit, an overview; Deposits; Interest rates; International economics, an overview; Money supply; Multinational corporation)

Richard M. Levich

European Community

The European Community (EC) has always had both economic and political goals. The earliest project, embodied in the treaty of Paris which established the European Coal and Steel Community in 1951, was intended to deal with the problems posed by Europe's growing steel surpluses and French dependence on imports of coal from West Germany against the background of the new Federal Republic's increasing economic and political strength. The preamble to the treaty emphasized political benefits still more than economic gains, however. The six signatory countries, Belgium, France, West Germany, Italy, Luxembourg, and the Netherlands, resolved to substitute for age-old rivalries the merging of their essential interests; to create, by establishing an economic community, the bases for a broader and deeper community among peoples long divided by bloody conflicts; and to lay the foundations for institutions that will give direction to a destiny henceforward shared. This relatively modest treaty was, in other words, intended to serve as the point of departure for a much more ambitious program, which, it was assumed, would gain momentum over the years.

The EC has remained a process rather than a finished entity. Its character is therefore best understood through its history, which has tended, as the original organizers hoped, to "create real solidarity" among its participants, and in doing so to change the political as well as the economic map of Europe.

This evolutionary process can be conveniently divided into three phases: 1950–1971, 1971–1986, and 1986–1992.

1950–1971: The Community of the Six

Between 1950 and 1971 the six Western European states referred to above concluded three major treaties: the treaty of Paris establishing the European Coal and Steel Community (1951) and two treaties signed in Rome in 1957, which created, respectively, the European Economic Community and Euratom. The European Economic Community and Euratom, established in Rome in 1957, were in practical terms grafted on to the original Community of Coal and Steel, a de facto position that was subsequently legalized in the merger treaty of 1967.

The strategic goal from the beginning was full political and economic union among the member states. The original Schuman Plan which launched the process on May 9, 1950, actually spoke of a European federation. The method chosen to arrive at this goal was, however, quite distinctive. It consisted essentially of two elements: the identification of a limited area of common concerns in which common policies could be developed and the establishment of four institutions that collectively exercised supranational authority within the areas defined by treaty. The idea was that the agenda of the EC would expand naturally, as mutual confidence grew and the reasonableness of developing common policies became evident.

This incremental approach to European union was dictated by both internal and external considerations. Internally, the architects of the original Community were well aware that an outright assault on national governments would be self-defeating. Neither Jean Monnet nor Robert Schuman had much sympathy with the more idealist federalists, and when, in 1953, a federalist move inspired originally by the Italian government to create a political union was killed at birth, those primarily responsible for launching the EC did not mourn its passing. There were also, however, external constraints on the development of an overambitious agenda. The EC was born in a period of undisputed American leadership of a Western bloc pitted against the Soviet superpower whose empire extended to the Community's own frontiers. Successive U.S. administrations supported European integration, but U.S. military supremacy and U.S. dominance within the international monetary system and the emerging international trade regime were more important facts of daily life than the rhetoric of U.S. Presidents in favor of a United States of Europe.

The EC's agenda and achievements in the first two decades were therefore essentially "low policy" in character. They were nevertheless impressive. The elimination of all quantitative restrictions on industrial goods traded among member countries, the achievement of a common agricultural policy, the establishment of a common market that provided for the free movement of goods and labor and a common external tariff, and the creation of a preferential regime for the former colonies of the member states were the most important in practical terms. The psychological and political impact of the EC successes was if anything even greater. Above-average economic growth in all the countries concerned confirmed the indispensability of the EC experiment to the governments of the original six and prompted members of the European Free Trade Area, established in 1960, and led by the United Kingdom, to conclude that they should either join the EC or adjust their economic policies to living with it as the dominant economic power in Europe. British applications to join in 1961 and 1967 were, however, rebuffed, largely because in the eyes of de Gaulle (and Adenauer) the British appeared likely to thwart progress toward political union.

As this latter point suggests, the leaders of the six still nursed hopes of economic and monetary union and political union, but internal political differences about how these objectives could be achieved and the external constraint of U.S. hegemony combined to undermine the various initiatives that were actually taken. De Gaulle, as French president, attempted in 1961 and 1962 to establish a political union, but his rejection of the supranational approach of the founding fathers and his obvious desire to consolidate French leadership provoked a negative response from his partners. Efforts by the European Commission and others in 1964 to launch a program for economic and monetary union were frustrated for quite opposite reasons.

The first two decades of the European Community were also important in terms of the development of EC institutions. The treaty of Paris had established four principal institutions: the High Authority, later renamed the European Commission in the treaty of Rome; the Council of Ministers; a Parliamentary Assembly; and a Court of Justice. The original hope of the architects of this treaty had been that the High Authority would increasingly acquire the attributes of a federal government. In reality, the institutional balance began to change rather rapidly in favor of the Council of Ministers, which was composed of one representative of each member state. Although many involved in the institutions, including in particular the first president of the European Commission, Walter Hallstein, clung to the original aspirations, the political system that actually developed was characterized principally by a partnership between the European Commission and the Council of Ministers. Using its exclusive right of initiative, the European Commission, when it functioned properly, exercised leadership by proposing policy and acting as the European conscience, but the Council of Ministers retained the final right to decide. Even the European Commission's executive powers, which it developed with particular effectiveness in external trade negotiations and in relation to the common agricultural policy, were dependent upon delegation by the Council of Ministers and required the cooperation of national administrations for their implementation. A practical consequence of this system was that the European Commission remained (and remains) a tiny body by comparison with the governments of member states.

The "government of Europe" was (and is) therefore best seen as a joint enterprise involving both the Commission and the Council. The supranational authority of this partnership was, however, maintained and consolidated, notably through a series of judgments by the European Court of Justice, some of whose members in this early phase modeled themselves on the Supreme Court in the United States. The most important principle established during these two decades was the primacy of Community law over national law. A Court of Justice ruling of 1964 provides the clearest statement of the doctrine:

By creating a Community of unlimited duration, having its own institutions, its own personality, its own legal capacity for representation on the international plane and more particularly, real power stemming from a limitation of sovereignty or a transfer of powers from the states to the Community, the member states have limited their sovereign rights, albeit within limited fields, and have thus created a body of law which binds both their individual citizens and themselves.

These positive developments in the integration process were, however, put under severe strain by opposition in national governments, and more particularly in France, to the "Brussels technocracy." The reaction was articulated most clearly by de Gaulle, but it is important to emphasize that the attitudes that he expressed were shared in some measure by leaders elsewhere, including Konrad Adenauer, the West German chancellor. It was, however, de Gaulle who carried his hostility furthest, provoking a year-long crisis in 1965–1966 during which the French government refused to participate in Council meetings. A "Luxembourg compromise" was eventually struck in 1966, at the cost, however, of the more extensive use of majority voting in the Council of Ministers envisaged in the treaty of Rome. As a result, the member-state governments retained separate veto rights on many of the most important items of EC business.

1971–1986: The Transformation of the Agenda and the Doubling of Membership

In the second phase of its development, the EC's original, rather modest, agenda was transformed and its membership doubled from six to twelve. The two developments are closely interrelated. Both, however, owed more to a series of external political and economic changes than to the gradual extension of the authority of the EC institutions originally envisaged. Of these external pressures, by far the most important were the collapse of the Bretton Woods system, the first oil shock, and other evidence that in a "post-American era," the world was a more dangerous place; the rise of Japan; and the increasing globalization of the international economy.

The initial impact of the breakdown of the international monetary system and the additional disorders caused by the rise in oil prices were almost catastrophic for the development of the EC. Intra-European exchange rates moved in all directions, and economic fundamentals, notably inflation rates, diverged dramatically. Nontariff barriers were erected within the EC as well as against non-EC partners, European growth rates slowed, and terms such as "Euro-sclerosis" and "Euro-pessimism" became part of the jargon of even academic commentators and analysts.

The response by EC leaders to this multilayered crisis was in many ways untidy and laborious. Between 1971 and 1986, however, the EC institutions and agenda were radically altered. The following developments were particularly important:

1. *The Enlargement of the Community.* The United Kingdom, Denmark, and Ireland join the Community in 1973, Greece in 1981, and Spain and Portugal at the beginning of 1986. The basic motivation in each case was political. France's veto on the United Kingdom was lifted partly because of pressure from its partners, but still more because of changes in the internal balance of power within the Community marked particularly by the increasing dominance of the West German economy and by the perceived end of U.S. hegemony which necessi-

tated a stronger and more autonomous Europe. In the case of the three Southern European countries, the primary concern was to consolidate democracy after the collapse of right-wing regimes.

Accommodation to the new members was not an easy process. The United Kingdom in particular caused numerous difficulties to the working of the system under both Labor and Conservative governments. The enlargements did, however, help significantly to advance two important systemic changes in the Community without which the gains of the third phase of the EC's development cannot be understood. The first concerned the role of the EC budget in European integration. Until the second half of the 1970s, it was widely assumed that if the EC was to advance toward an effective European union, it would have to develop a federal-level budget of significant proportions. The MacDougall Report of 1977 estimated that a minimum, "lightweight federal model" would require a budget of 7½ percent of GDP and 10 percent if defense was included. Prime Minister Thatcher's persistent efforts to reduce the United Kingdom's "net contributions" to the budget coupled with her insistence that public expenditure was a major source of economic malaise, helped to bring about a new and more modest consensus on the kind of budget that the EC really needed. These lower ambitions were reflected some years later when, in 1992, Commission proposals for a budget to sustain the Maastricht union amounting to 1.35 percent of GDP by the end of the decade were widely regarded as excessive. The second institutional change that was influenced by enlargement was the modification of the voting system to allow for more majority voting. There were other considerations (see below) that prompted this change in 1985–1986, but realization that a Community of 12 bound by a rule of unanimity would be paralyzed was a very important factor.

2. *The Increasing Politicization of the Community Institutions.* Three developments merit particular attention: the institutionalization of the European Council which brings together the heads of state and government at least twice a year and thereby ensures that high-policy matters can be discussed and improves the chances of implementation of decisions once taken; the introduction of a directly elected European Parliament instead of, as previously, a Parliamentary Assembly composed of members nominated by the national parliaments; and the appointment of more professional politicians to the European Commission. The European Commission in the 1950s had been dominated by professional civil servants and other nonpolitical figures. The European Commission of the 1980s was, by contrast, composed overwhelmingly of professional politicians. All developments can be seen as a response to the increasingly political nature of the problems with which EC leaders were faced both in the economy and in the international security system.

3. *Establishment of the European Monetary System (EMS).* The making of the EMS was the single most important development within the EC since its inception. It was a decision of the European Council, led by the West German chancellor and the French president, and imposed on an economic policy-making elite which was, notably in the Bundesbank, either openly hostile or very skeptical. The primary motivation was to defend Europe against the dam-

age of a depreciating dollar and the inadequacies of U.S. policy of which the dollar's fall was believed to be a symptom. The EMS had been preceded by ambitious plans for economic and monetary union before 1980 along lines articulated in the Werner Report of 1970 and by practical efforts at European collaboration in the Snake, an informal arrangement among nations for exchange rates to stick close together, within 2¼ percent of the parity rate. The EMS was, however, from the beginning quite distinctive. In the first place, it was backed by decision makers at the highest political level. Secondly, it was a Community institution, rather than an ad hoc grouping. As such, it extended the disciplines of European monetary integration to countries with weaker economies, such as Italy, where the lira was allowed to fluctuate within wider bands, and even to non-members, such as the U.K., whose economy was, even in the Thatcher years, subjected to skeptical surveillance by its Community partners, the majority of whom had accepted the exchange rate mechanism (ERM) disciplines. Thirdly, and most important, the practical consequences of maintaining a fixed exchange rate system quickly became apparent in the domestic politics of those states that participated fully. After a brief period (1979–1981) in which the system settled down, the devaluations of the Belgian franc and the French franc in 1982 and 1983 highlighted the domestic political sacrifices that the system required of members aspiring to keep up or catch up with West Germany. The political-economic crisis in France of 1982–1983 was particularly dramatic, posing President Mitterand with a stark choice between policies that were both nationalist and socialist and the European model, based both conceptually and operationally on West Germany. France's acceptance of the European imperatives prepared the way, politically, for French endorsement of wide-ranging internal economic liberalization through the Single Market program.

4. *The Single Market.* The initial response of the majority of European business-people directly affected by the global economic crisis of the 1970s was more often than not to seek protection from national governments. The ensuing internecine conflict in the EC, characterized principally by widespread resort to nontariff barriers, was soon perceived, however, as totally irrelevant in the light of the globalization of the international economy and, more specifically, of U.S. and Japanese competition. The correct strategy, it was widely believed, was the creation of a European Single Market that would provide European businesses with the kind of home market that their rivals had elsewhere. The European Commission, dominated in the early 1980s by one of its vice-presidents, Etienne Davignon, both encouraged and benefited from this emerging business consensus. Davignon built bridges to a business community which had by and large been ignored by the European Commission hitherto. The business community, too, organized itself at the European level. A European Round Table emerged under the leadership of the Volvo chief, Per Gyllenhamer, and even the moribund employers organization, UNICE, was reformed and revitalized. There were undoubtedly some among this coalition who wanted an active European "industrial policy," but the dominant note in the consensus was on internal liberalization and deregulation. The conversion of the French government to many if not all the elements in this new European political-business consensus following the crisis of 1982–1983 paved the way for the Delors-Cockfield Commission from 1985 onward.

5. *A Common Foreign and Security Policy.* The EC's attempts to formulate a common foreign policy through European political cooperation from the early 1970s onward were much less successful in many respects than the economic policy initiatives referred to thus far. They are nevertheless important as a reflection both of the fundamental nature of the changes in the international system and of the increasing politicization of the EC's agenda.

It is against this background that the EC's redefinition of its agenda and modification of its procedures in the Single European Act (1986) can be best appreciated. In general terms, the treaty confirmed the developments of the past 15 years. Both the European Council and the EMS were, for example, covered in its text. At the heart of the treaty was, however, a detailed program aimed at creating a Single Market by 1992. The 1992 project was intended to be the new motor of European integration. As the basic objectives of the program commanded the assent of all the major political players in the Community, the negotiators of the treaty were able to agree that in relation to this part of the EC's business at least, the insistence on unanimity in the Council of Ministers could be lifted. To an extent that perhaps few realized at the time, this extension of majority voting revolutionized the politics of the Community as a whole, enhancing the autonomy of the Council of Ministers as a group against individual members states and necessitating totally different political tactics by all the players as they sought allies to advance or protect their interests. The 1992 program quickly became identified with the new president of the Commission, Jacques Delors, and with Lord Cockfield, who had been sent by Mrs. Thatcher to Brussels expressly for this purpose. The success of the program can, however, only be understood against the background of the developments earlier in this second phase of the EC's evolution which have just been sketched out. The Single European Act legitimized reality as much as it changed it.

1986–1992: The Making of the
Maastricht Treaty

The extent to which the Single European Act and more particularly the 1992 program was to change the morale and image of the EC was masked by a lengthy ratification process that meant that the treaty did not come into force until the second half of 1987 and by the eruption of yet another dispute about the EC budget. Once this latter problem was resolved at a special meeting of the European Council in February 1988, however, the EC's fortunes seemed to rise exponentially as the credibility of the Single Market objective gained hold not only of policymakers but also of economic agents. By 1989 the debate about the Single Market had shifted from the feasibility of the legislative target which involved the passage of almost 300 directives by the end of 1992 to the implementation of the laws once passed. More important still, the Maastricht agenda had begun to take shape. Three aspects of this latter process merit attention:

1. At the Hanover meeting of the European Council in June 1988, members voted to establish the Delors Committee on Economic and Monetary Union. The Delors Committee, though chaired by the Commission president, was composed in the main of all the central bank governors of the EC. Despite hesitations and divisions, the Delors Committee was able by April 1989 to produce a

unanimous report that sketched out a three-stage plan for economic and monetary union. The program was endorsed in principle a few weeks later at the Madrid meeting of the European Council and brought a stage further at the European Council meeting in Strasbourg in December 1989 when a formal decision was taken to convene an intergovernmental conference on economic and monetary union.

2. The growing momentum of the Single Market program and other aspects of Community policy heightened the debate about the "democratic deficit" in 1988 and 1989 and, in the context of the parliamentary election of that year, prompted Chancellor Kohl to declare that by the time the next parliamentary elections were due in 1994, the Community should have significantly increased the powers of its Parliament. One of the central themes of the political union negotiations was therefore clearly posted at the highest level.

3. External reactions to the Community's success also left their mark. Members of the European Free Trade Area (EFTA) arguably perceived the importance of the 1992 program earlier than many inside the EC itself. Led by Austria, all six members of the EFTA carried out a major review of their relations with the EC in the course of 1987 and 1988. Their pressure for a more comprehensive agreement which would make them beneficiaries of the Single Market and assure them some influence over EC policymaking prompted Jacques Delors, the Commission president, to launch an initiative in January 1989 which eventually led to negotiations for a European Economic Area comprising both the EC and the EFTA countries. These solicitations from the EFTA, coinciding as they did with growing agitation about "fortress Europe" in the United States, Japan, and elsewhere, only underlined the external dimension of European integration and the power that its success already endowed on the EC. The EC leadership was at first surprised as much as gratified, and the first attempt to define a systematic EC external policy, a paper entitled "Europe, World Partner," which was adopted by the European Council at Rhodes in December 1988, was in many ways a rather crude, not to say naive, document. Its emergence indicated, however, that EC foreign policy, another major theme of the Maastricht process, was now firmly on the agenda.

Events in 1989 accelerated the movement toward intergovernmental renegotiation of the treaties. The Bush administration, for example, signaled through the President's Boston speech in May 1989 and by other means that the new administration would base its European policy henceforth on special relationships with Bonn and Brussels. Still more dramatically, when the crisis of communism led to the collapse of Central and Eastern European regimes in the latter half of the year, culminating in the fall of the Berlin Wall, it was to the Community that many in the newly liberated countries looked for assistance in their political and economic transition. Claims by the European Council at Strasbourg in December 1989 that the Community was "the cornerstone of the new European architecture and, in its will to openness, a mooring for a future European equilibrium" did not seem in any way farfetched. With German unification now not a dream but a fast-approaching reality, the emergence in the first few months of 1990 of a consensus that the intergovernmental conference on economic and monetary union should be linked with a conference on political union was scarcely surprising.

The Maastricht treaty, which was finally agreed upon at the meeting of the European Council in December 1991, was the most comprehensive redefinition of the European Community's aims in its 40-year history. Styled as a treaty of union, it broadened and deepened the powers of the Brussels institutions, regulated their relationships with one another and the member states, and tackled the problem of political accountability or democratic deficit.

The issue of the functions of the union was at the heart of the intergovernmental conference. Measured simply in quantitative terms, the results were impressive. The old article 3 of the treaty of Rome defined the activities of the Community in a series of subheadings that ran from A to K. The revised article extends from A to T. A qualitative judgment is, however, both more useful and still more impressive. The Maastricht treaty confers on the union important responsibilities in relation to all the major functions of a modern sovereign state. The following list illustrates this point:

1. The creation and management of a single currency

2. The coordination, supervision, and, where appropriate, enforcement of sound economic policies, particularly in budgetary matters

3. The establishment and safeguarding of a Single Market based on principles of free and fair competition

4. The maintenance of equity and, where necessary, the redistribution of wealth between richer and poorer regions

5. The preservation of law and order

6. The acknowledgment and development of the fundamental rights of individual citizens

7. The management of a common external policy covering all areas of foreign and security policy including the framing of a common defense policy that might in time lead to a common defense

The extent to which the union may or is likely to become involved in these areas of responsibility varies greatly. With the exception of the provisions regarding supplementary measures to consolidate the Single Market, by far the most concrete articles of the draft treaty concern the creation of a monetary union. The most important elements in the text involve

1. Progress toward a full monetary union among a majority of member states by the beginning of 1997 or a minority that satisfy certain criteria by 1999.

2. The establishment of criteria for entry into the monetary union designed to establish beyond doubt the commitment of the latter to price stability. Four are particularly important: the achievement of a high degree of price stability, indicated by a rate of inflation that is close to that of, at most, the three best-performing member states; the sustainability of the government financial position manifested in a current public-sector deficit of less than 3 percent of GDP and an accumulated public debt of less than 60 percent of GDP; the observance of the normal fluctuation margins provided for by the ERM for at least 2 years without devaluation; and the durability of convergence reflected in long-term interest rate levels.

3. The creation of a European central bank with statutes that guarantee its political independence.

These provisions accept in principle the possibility of a Europe of two or more speeds. It is vitally important in assessing the political significance of the Maastricht treaty, however, to emphasize that even member states that do not qualify for entry into the full monetary union will be associated with the management of the latter through membership in the Community institutions and will be subject to strict surveillance procedures designed to apply maximum pressure on them to conform to EC norms and therefore qualify for entry into the system. Furthermore, any state inside the EMU deemed by its partners to be pursuing economic policies incompatible with the stability of the union will be exposed to graduated sanctions culminating in financial penalties.

In institutional terms, the Maastricht treaty consolidates and refines the system that had already developed over the previous 40 years. The position of the Council of Ministers, the Committee of Permanent Representatives representing the member states, and the Secretariat of the Council of Ministers is reaffirmed and strengthened in striking manner vis-à-vis both individual member states and the European Commission. Among the most important provisions of the treaty as a whole are the affirmation of the existence of a single institutional framework responsible for all areas of Community policy and, within this framework, the primacy of the Brussels-based Committee of Permanent Representatives, serviced by the Council Secretariat. In this respect, the treaty can be seen as a significant step toward the centralization of authority within the Community, albeit through institutions that are staffed by the member states themselves. A categorization of the Community system as government by the member states, of the member states, for the member states is not unjustified. This does not mean that the Commission's role has been reduced. On the contrary, the Commission as a result of the treaty has a vital role in the surveillance procedures of the EMU and an official status in certain areas of Community business, including police and judicial affairs and foreign policy, where its standing was previously somewhat unclear.

Critics of the Maastricht treaty have fastened on the weakness of its measures to overcome the democratic deficit. These criticisms are, however, on closer inspection rather less relevant than they might otherwise seem. Given the complexity of a system in which the member states themselves are at the heart of the most important supranational institution, the Council of Ministers, enhanced powers for the European Parliament are only one of several appropriate responses to the problem of enhanced central power. It is therefore important to see the relatively modest improvements in the powers and responsibility of the European Parliament against the background of a series of provisions that are designed to strengthen political accountability in a more general sense. Of these the most celebrated is the enunciation of the principle of subsidiarity in article 3b, which states that the Community institutions should not do anything that cannot effectively be done at lower levels of government and, furthermore, provides those anxious about excessive centralization with the right to appeal where appropriate to the Court of Justice. Other decentralizing measures include the creation of a Committee of Regions which, though advisory in character, seems bound to acquire an increasingly prominent profile in the politics of the union.

Those responsible for drafting the Maastricht treaty acknowledged in the treaty itself that the evolutionary process initiated in the treaty of Paris was still not complete. They have therefore provided for a new intergovernmental conference no later than 1996 which will take up the unfinished business. The treaty of Maastricht nevertheless marks a major milestone in the transformation of the European Community from an association of states united for limited purposes to a union responsible, along with the member states themselves and, where appropriate, other lower instances of government, for all the principal functions of a modern state.

Although there were many differences among those who actually negotiated the treaty, the latter was agreed to in December 1991 by the governments of all the member states. Had the decision about its ratification been left in every state to the political elites represented in national parliaments, there seems little doubt that it would have been ratified without difficulty. The obligation of the Danish government, however, to submit the treaty to referendum and the subsequent, narrow, negative majority revealed and exacerbated a crisis of confidence throughout the Community between political elites and those whom they led.

The opposition to the Maastricht treaty in Denmark, France, and elsewhere was in many ways confused and deeply divided. In France, for example, many voted no because they wanted the Socialist government out, and still more, perhaps, because they wanted to stop the reform of the Common Agricultural Policy which a combination of internal budgetary constraints within the EC itself and international pressure particularly through the GATT negotiations necessitated and which had nothing whatsoever to do with the treaty. Even those who criticized the excessive power of the European Commission failed to observe that one of the more important features of the Maastricht treaty was precisely that it strengthened still further the authority of the Council of Ministers. The protests of 1992 are nevertheless profoundly significant for at least three reasons. In the first place, they confirmed how difficult the EC process is to understand or even explain. Secondly, through the knock-on effect—a combination of overevaluation of some of the weaker currencies of nations in the EC, the efforts to keep their interest rates high because of Germany's high interest rate policy, and the rigidity of the EC's fixed exchange rate system—on currency markets, they exposed both short- and medium-term flaws in Europe's progress toward an economic and monetary union. Thirdly, they underlined yet again a qualitative difference of outlook between the United Kingdom and its partners.

The knock-on effect on the European Monetary System is particularly important. Since 1987, the system had become for all intents and purposes a fixed exchange rate system in which adjustments against the central rate were no longer regarded as appropriate or for that reason probable. While confidence in the progress of European integration was high, this doctrine laid down from on high by central banks and ministers of finance prevailed. It was already clear, however, well before the political crisis of 1992 that the system had a number of weaknesses which in less optimistic times might be and in 1992 itself were brutally exposed.

The first was that some of the weaker currencies were quite clearly overvalued. Sterling in particular had been brought in, in 1990, to the ERM at a higher rate than the Bundesbank and many others regarded as appropriate. The lira's competitiveness declined more gradually but no less seriously. These weaknesses at the edges of the system were compounded by changes at the center. The costs of German unification and in particular the lax fiscal policy of the Bonn authorities forced the Bundesbank to maintain high interest rates, which made sense in German terms but not in European perspective. A third element was also important. Since the liberalization of capital movements within the Community, as a consequence of the Single Market program, the central banks were much more vulnerable than they had been hitherto to attacks on individual currencies. The subsequent "victories" over sterling and the lire, which were both forced to suspend their membership in the ERM, were against this background hardly surprising. Attacks on the French franc, however, which was not in any way overvalued, provoked a quite different kind of reaction.

Although, late in 1992, it is still impossible to see how precisely the story will work out, the paradoxical consequence of the crisis of confidence in the European Community's political system seems likely to be that an inner core of countries consisting of Germany, France, Benelux, possibly Denmark, and, after they have been admitted to the Community in 1995, most if not all the Nordic countries, Austria, and Switzerland will proceed faster than envisaged in the Maastricht treaty toward de facto monetary union. Given the robustness and maturity of the political structures that the Community has built up over the last 45 years, and the heavy dependence of the weaker economies on their links with the heartland of the European union, it is highly improbable that countries outside this inner core will choose simply to float. On the contrary, something more like the Maastricht arrangement which itself envisaged the possibility of a two- or three-speed Europe in the monetary field could be put in place alongside the development of the hard-core union. A question mark must remain over the U.K.'s participation, where the opposition has less to do with economics than with politics.

To sum up, the European Community has over 40 years acquired a more and more central place in policymaking in Western Europe. When the EFTA countries entered into negotiations with the EC about the European Economic Area, they were obliged to accept without modification almost 1500 pieces of detailed legislation which the EC had passed in the previous decades. Still more strikingly, when the West German government invoked the principle of state succession in its negotiation of German unification in 1990, it acknowledged that there were two successor states, the Federal Republic itself and the European Community. The Community is thus already a highly complex system of common laws and institutions with which national policymakers have to reckon in almost every conceivable situation. The journey forward is still, as Andrew Shonfield noted in a book published in 1973, in many ways a journey to an unknown destination. The signs are, however, that the speed of the travelers is increasing and that the destination is beginning to come more sharply into focus.

References

Gros, Daniel, and Niels Thygesen, *European Monetary Integration from the EMS to the EMU,* Longman, White Plains, New York, 1992; Hoffman, Stanley, and Robert Keohane (eds.), *The New European Community,* Westview Press, Boulder, 1991; Kapteyn, P. J. G., P. Verloren, and L. W. Gormley, *Introduction to the Laws of the European Communities,* Kluwer, Graham, and Trotman, U.K., 1990; Ludlow, Peter (ed.), *CEPS Annual Review of EC Affairs,* Brasseys, U.K., 1990, 1991, 1992; Ludlow, Peter, *The Making of the EMS,* Butterworths, U.K., 1992; Nugent, Neill, *The Government and Politics of the European Community,* Macmillan, U.K., 1989.

(*See also* Barriers to trade; Bretton Woods Conference; Economic blocs; Foreign exchange rates; General Agreement on Tariffs and Trade; International economics, an overview; Smithsonian Agreement)

Peter Ludlow

European Economic Community (*see* **European Community)**

Evolutionary Economics (*see* **Institutional economics)**

Exchange rates (*see* **Foreign exchange rates)**

Excise tax (*see* **Taxation, an overview)**

Expectations

It is a truism of economic thinking that what people do is influenced not only by events that have occurred in the past but also by expectations regarding events that have yet to occur. In its extreme form a truism has the homely characteristics of common sense. If one expected the world to end tomorrow, the relation between one's wealth, current income, and consumption would be dramatically different from what it would be if one expected the world to continue indefinitely. On a less drastic level, if one confidently expected prices to double over the next year, one's willingness to hold assets of various kinds would be different from what it would be if one expected prices to be at the same level a year hence. And if one were a 40-year-old parent with three children approaching college age, one's behavior would be very different from what it would be if one were a nonparent under identical circumstances.

While all economists recognize the crucial importance of expectations about future events in conditioning present behavior, economic analysis generally is not characterized by serious attempts to measure expectations, or to incorporate expectations into empirical work. Rather, most economic analysis tends to incorporate expectational notions into either theory or empirical work by formulations that focus on the stabilities inherent in economic life.

Adaptive Expectations

For example, a widely used method of incorporating expectational phenomena into economic thinking is to treat behavior as adaptive to the difference between expected and realized events. Phillip Cagan's classic analysis of hyperinflation is a good case in point (1956). The problem is to explain behavior under conditions where the rates of increase in prices are extreme. In Cagan's model, buyers expecting certain rates of price increase observed that actual rates of price increase were different, and revised their expectations (adapted to past error) by changing the next period's expectations by some proportion of the difference between last period's expected and actual outcomes. Thus, during a period of accelerating inflation, people would continually expect lower rates of price increase than are actually realized, since the adaptive behavior reflected in the model never quite catches up with actual events.

Cobweb Theory

An even earlier version of reaction to differences between expected and actual outcomes, which contained no provision for learning from past errors, is represented by the cobweb theory, devised to explain the relationship between agricultural prices and supply. In this expectational model, farmers had no basis for gauging next year's price except to assume it would be the same as this year's price. Production (planting) decisions for next year's supply were made on the basis of this year's price, extrapolated into next year as a forecast. Thus, if the current price were low because of abundant supply, farmers would restrict production because they expected next year's price to be equally low. But the resulting supply shortage would actually result in high rather than low prices next year. Thus, high prices would be observed next year, and when farmers extrapolated that year's high price to the following year, they would greatly expand production—again expecting the (high) price of that year to continue into the next year. The greatly augmented supply would therefore result in low prices, and so on. Depending on which assumptions are made about the responsiveness of supply and demand functions to price, this model indicates a situation of continually widening swings in both prices and production, with no tendency toward stable equilibrium.

In both the adaptive expectations and cobweb models, the role of expectations is handled by assumptions of extraordinary simplicity. The cobweb model assumes that nobody noticed that high prices one year would be followed by low prices the next year, and that there was no alternative to forecasting next year's price except by the assumption that it would be the same as this year's. Thus, in the cobweb theory, nobody learns from past experience. In the adaptive expectations theory, people learn from experience, but the nature of their learning is sharply circumscribed. For example, one would suppose that the reaction function between previous expectations and previous outcomes would depend on some of the serial properties of that difference. If people underguessed for several years in a row, one might expect them to adjust expectations by more than the difference between last year's expectation and last year's outcome, rather than by some fraction of the difference. More generally, one would like to suppose that the nature of the adaptation to past experience would itself be a variable rather than a constant.

Rational Expectations Theory

The most popular current theory dealing with expectational phenomena is known as the rational expectations theory. Here, it is argued that people make guesses about the future on the basis of the best information available to them at the time that a decision must be made. People are assumed to have enough information about the causes of future events, that is, to have a sufficiently good model of what determines the future, to behave in such a way that only genuinely new information will have an influence on either expectations or behavior. The model does not say that expectations are always accurate—indeed, forecasting errors are to be expected simply because forecasting models are not perfect. But the error embodied in such models is expected to have specific properties—not to be biased in terms of sign, and, of course, not to be predictable.

The proponents of rational expectations theory initially set out to explain why it was difficult to be consistently successful in certain kinds of speculative markets—securities, commodities, etc. In such markets, it may well be true that all existing information has been assimilated into decisions, that a sufficiently large number of people are continually concerned with improving forecasts of relevant variables so that only genuinely new information gives anyone an advantage, and, thus, that the spirit of rational expectations is indeed captured in market behavior. Attempts to extend the domain of rational expectations theory into problems of macroeconomic policy seem to be less successful, or at least are commonly judged to be so by many economists.

These models—adaptive expectations, the cobweb theory, and rational expectations—have a number of elements in common. They are concerned solely with expected values of relevant variables, that is, with the average or mean expectation, and are not concerned with the fact that expectations are in essence a probability distribution with dispersion (variance) as well as central tendency (mean). All infer the structure of expectations from observed errors in models where expectational phenomena are replaced by lagged values of nonexpectational phenomena. All point to the dubiousness of attempts to obtain direct measures of expectations, on the ground that true expectations are reflected by behavior and not by statements about the future obtained from economic actors. And all commonly, but not necessarily, focus on the expected or mean values of relevant variables, not on their dispersion; i.e., they tend to ignore the second or higher moments. Strictly speaking, the latter is not true of rational expectations models, since the information to be incorporated into expectations includes all moments of past distributions. Finally, a problem for all these types of models is that consumers may have to learn about the properties of the model; hence the formation of expectations is itself subject to a learning process.

Direct Measure of Expectational Phenomena

A body of research on expectational phenomena, which stands somewhat outside the mainstream of economics in the United States, takes issue with the propositions inherent in traditional expectational models. Its origins can probably be traced to the Swedish school of economics. An important feature of expectational analysis in this tradition is the importance given to uncertainty, or, alternatively, to the dispersion of expected values, in contrast to concentration on the mean or average expectation.

A given expectation associated with a small variance of possible outcomes will not necessarily lead to the same behavioral response as the same mean expectation associated with a large variance. In the first case, possible outcomes do not differ very much from the mean expected outcome, and the appropriate response may in effect ignore the variance. But when the variance of possible outcomes is large, different forces come into play which will often lead to different behavioral implications. For example, an entrepreneur facing an expected sales function with a given mean and a large dispersion will design a plant with greater flexibility than if faced with the same mean expected sales and less variance. And consumers, faced with a given mean expected income and a high variance, would be apt to take a more conservative stance than if faced with the same expectation but lower variance, simply because the cost of "surprises" is not symmetrical. The work by Albert Hart on business decision making and by F. Thomas Juster on consumer behavior explores this area more fully.

A related line of economic thinking, which has its roots more in psychological theory than economic theory, stresses a decision process that comes out of the interplay of past economic events, reactions to those events as forming persistent habits reflected in behavior, and modification of those persistent habits as a consequence of new information or new circumstances. This way of thinking about economic phenomena stresses not so much expectations—thought of as probability statements relating to future events—but rather a set of perceptions about the world that can be usefully described by terms such as attitudes, aspirations, and values.

For example, will a continued increase in real income lead to greater satisfaction with living standards, a feeling of satiation with consumer goods, and thus a higher rate of personal saving? In some theoretical formulations, that consequence would be expected. But writers such as George Katona (1951) point out that the realization of consumption goals is likely to lead to the formulation of more ambitious goals, while failure to reach goals may lead to a downward adjustment of goals rather than increased efforts to attain them.

An important difference between those who deal with expectations by implicit theorizing based on a structure of observed forecasting errors and those who deal empirically with expectations lies in the priorities given to measuring expectational phenomena and to the appropriate methods for empirical modeling of behavior. Implicit theorizing, whether it be adaptive expectations, cobweb theory, or rational expectations, infers the structure of expectations from the statistical properties of forecasting errors and places little priority on measuring expectational phenomena directly. Those who see expectations as coming from a complex structure dealing with the interplay of past events, probability distributions of expected outcomes, and perceptions of an attitudinal cast argue that there is no substitute for direct measurement of the expectations held by relevant economic actors like business executives and consumers.

On the side of appropriate models of behavior, theorists of the implicit expectations school, as well as many of those who argue for direct measurement of expectational phenomena, see behavioral relationships as sufficiently stable to warrant the use of time series data to gauge future events from the structure of past relationships. Theorists who focus on the way in which psychological perceptions act as a filter in determining the relationship of events, expectations, and aspirations to behavior are apt to believe that time series models will inevitably be misspecified, in that the future cannot be well forecast from knowledge of the particular structure existing in the past.

References

Cagan, Phillip, "The Monetary Dynamics of Hyperinflation," in Milton Friedman (ed.), *Studies in the Quantity Theory of Money,* University of Chicago Press, Chicago, 1956, pp. 25–117 [excerpts are reprinted as "The Theory of Hyperinflation," in R. J. Ball and Peter Doyle (eds.), *Inflation: Selected Readings, Penguin Modern Economics,* Penguin, Middlesex, 1969, pp. 117–135]; Ezekiel, Mordecai, "The Cobweb Theorem," *Quarterly Journal of Economics,* February 1938, pp. 255–280; Hart, Albert G., *Anticipations, Uncertainty, and Dynamic Planning,* Studies in Business Administration, vol. XI, no. 1, University of Chicago Press, Chicago, 1940; Juster, F. Thomas, and L. D. Taylor, "Towards a Theory of Saving Behavior," *American Economic Review,* vol. 65, no. 2, May 1975, pp. 203–209; Katona, George, *Psychological Analysis of Economic Behavior,* McGraw-Hill, New York, 1951; Lindahl, Erik R., *Studies in the Theory of Money and Capital,* Allen and Unwin, London, 1939; Lucas, Robert E., Jr., "Expectations and the Neutrality of Money," *Journal of Economic Theory,* vol. 4, no. 2, April 1972, pp. 103–124; Muth, John F., "Rational Expectations and the Theory of Price Movements," *Econometrica,* vol. 29, no. 3, July 1961, pp. 315–335; Sargent, Thomas S., and Neil Wallace, " 'Rational' Expectations, the Optimal Monetary Instrument and the Optimal Money Supply Rule," *Journal of Political Economy,* vol. 83, 1975, pp. 215–254.

(*See also* Cobweb theorem; Rational expectations)

F. Thomas Juster

Exports

Exports are, in the conduct of foreign trade, goods taken from one country into another country with the first country the exporter, the second the importer. The U.S. Bureau of the Census publishes monthly data on U.S. exports on two bases: seasonally adjusted and unadjusted.

In addition to monthly export statistics, the Balance of Payments Division of the U.S. Department of Commerce reports U.S. exports on a quarterly basis. These data are adjusted for various conceptual differences from the monthly series in order to make them comparable with other elements of the U.S. balance of payments. The main adjustments are for military sales, reconciliation with Canadian statistics, private gift parcels, and exports from the Virgin Islands.

In statements of the balance of payments and in national income accounts, the term "exports" is often used to mean total exports of services as well as goods. The main export services of the United States are military sales, tourist expenditures in the United States, transportation earnings of U.S. carriers, and earnings from U.S. investments abroad.

In the U.S. national income accounts the term "net exports" is applied to the overall balance of payments impact on the U.S. gross national product. Like the balance on goods and services, net exports is thus the difference between exports and imports of goods and services, but there are minor conceptual adjustments for exports between the balance of payments and national income definitions.

Importance of Exports

Between 1963 and 1989, the volume of world exports increased far more rapidly than world industrial production. Thus exports became more significant for economic growth and development in most countries. Models were developed showing "foreign trade multiplier" effects of exports on national income. Moreover, since 1971, exports are regarded as crucial to world economic balance. With the breakdown of the Bretton Woods system, exports came to be regarded as more critical than might have been indicated by their relatively small proportion of total U.S. gross national product—about 15.2 percent in 1990. With a floating dollar it was recognized that without rising exports the U.S. trade balance would deteriorate, the dollar would devalue, and prices of imports would rise and influence the overall U.S. price level.

Reasons for Poor Showing in Exports

However, widespread consciousness of the U.S. need to export has not resulted in sustained trade balance improvement. In fact, the U.S. trade merchandise balance (balance of payments basis), after improving to an $8.9 billion surplus in 1975, swung to a record $159.5 billion deficit in 1987.

One obstacle to U.S. exports in the 1980–1985 period was the overvaluation of the U.S. dollar usually attributed to higher U.S. interest rates to finance the U.S. fiscal deficit. But in the period 1985–1990, despite the declining dollar, exports failed to improve as much as had been expected. However, except over relatively long periods, the impact of currency depreciation on exports may be counterproductive because of the so-called J curve. The J curve arises because when a country devalues, the prices of its exports decline with respect to countries whose currencies have not devalued. The devaluing country expects to gain in export volume because its prices are lower.

But, immediately following a devaluation, export volume may not rise rapidly enough to offset the decline in export prices. Thus, the value of exports may decline in the short run.

Aside from the quantifiable effects of incomes and relative prices on exports, there are significant nonquantifiable influences. In spite of their growing importance, exports amount to a smaller percentage of the U.S. gross national product compared with other major countries where this percentage can be as high as 50 percent. Thus, U.S. manufacturers may emphasize exports in their overall business planning far less than would be done by some major U.S. competitors, notably Japan. And this lack of emphasis may be reflected in unaggressive marketing and product development not adapted to foreign markets.

Theories of the Export Market

On a more theoretical level, two theories have competed as explanations of exports in international trade. Comparative advantage theory implicitly assumes that technologies differ among countries so that each country specializes in the products that it can produce relatively more efficiently. However, since the 1950s, there has been widespread support for an alternative theory to explain exports. This is the Heckscher-Ohlin theory, which holds that technologies are approximately the same at least among developed countries. Without significant differences in technologies, international trade arises because countries tend to export those products that use their more abundant factors of production more intensively. For example, a country with an abundance of labor will tend to export cloth if that product uses labor intensively.

More recently, the Heckscher-Ohlin theory seems to be declining in popularity. With greater emphasis on high technology in products traded internationally, it appears unlikely that technologies are invariant between countries. Moreover, statistical evidence tends to favor comparative advantage. A study by G. D. A. MacDougall (1951) indicates that higher productivity leads to higher exports of a product, as might be expected from comparative advantage. On the other hand, a study by Wasily Leontief (1953) found that the United States, supposedly a capital-intensive country, tended to export less capital-intensive goods compared with its more capital-intensive imports, thus contradicting the Heckscher-Ohlin theory. More recently, similar results have been found in a worldwide study by Bowen, Leamer, and Sveikauskas (1987).

References

Bowen, Harry F., Edward E. Leamer, and Leo Sveikauskas, "Multicountry, Multifactor Tests of the Factor Abundance Theory," in *American Economic Review,* vol. 77, December 1987, pp. 791–809; Junz, H. B., and R. R. Rhomberg, "Price Competitiveness in Export Trade among Industrial Countries," *American Economic Review,* vol. 63, no. 2, May 1973, pp. 412–418; Kenan, Peter B., *A Model of the U.S. Balance of Payments,* Heath, Lexington, Mass., 1978; Leontief, W. W., "Domestic Production and Foreign Trade," *Proceedings of the American Philosophical Society,* vol. 97, 1953, reprinted in American Economic Association, *Readings in International Economics,* Irwin, Homewood, Ill., 1968; Lindert, Peter H., *International Economics,* 9th ed., Irwin, Homewood, Ill., 1991; MacDougall, G. D. A., "British and American Exports," *Economic Journal,* vol. 61, 1951, reprinted in American Economic Association, *Readings in International Economics,* Irwin, Homewood, Ill., 1968; Quinn, Melanie R., and James H. Sood, "Cutting through the Maze of Trade Data Classification," *Columbia Journal of World Business,* Fall 1978, pp. 54–71.

(*See also* Barriers to trade; Comparative advantage theory; Dumping; Foreign exchange rates; General Agreement on Tariffs and Trade; Imports; International economics, an overview; J curve; Protectionism)

James L. Burtle

Externalities

Externalities have been a part of economic theory since first discussed by Alfred Marshall, but since about 1960 the term has been expanded and employed more widely in economic analysis. An externality exists when an activity by one or more parties affects, for good or bad, another one or more parties who are not a part of, or are external to, the activity. Expressed another way, externalities result from a failure of private costs (or benefits) to equal social costs (or benefits), and economic inefficiency is the consequence.

Several common examples illustrate the problem. Steel production causes smoke, which damages the health and property of those who live near the plant. These nearby residents are external to decisions to produce steel but are damaged by that activity. Each of many fishermen who flock to a superior fishing site reduces the catch of all others there, imposing costs on them. External benefits arise when one homeowner keeps an attractive house and lot and adds to the pleasure of the neighbors.

If these external costs are ignored by the steel producers and the fishermen as they determine their costs and level of output, then steel and fish will be priced below their social cost of production and their output will be inefficiently high. Similarly, if the homeowner considers only his or her own pleasure, home maintenance will be assigned an artificially low value and will be below the socially optimum level.

Pecuniary and Technological Externalities

These examples typify the current emphasis on externalities. However, Marshall's original discussion of external diseconomies dealt with the firm purchasing a resource and thereby bidding up its price for all other users. Was the firm's true marginal cost of the resource only the market price paid by the firm, or should it include the increase in costs paid by all other users? Later analysis showed that the higher payments made by others represented economic rent to owners of the resource and that the market price paid for the resource was the price that would produce economic efficiency. A similar problem concerned external economies, which were shown to result from the lower prices of a decreasing-cost firm, supplying increasing amounts of some product to firms in another industry. However, no generally accepted proposal evolved for promoting Pareto optimality in this case.

The externalities described by Marshall were later classified as pecuniary, inasmuch as they produced changes in market prices of resources, which were taken into account by other buyers and sellers. The newer externalities, resulting from smoke, congestion, and well-kept lawns, were classified as technological, because they presumably affected the technical patterns of production and consumption by individuals. There was no price mechanism for dealing with these problems, and an extensive literature developed treating them as a form of market failure.

Ronald Coase's seminal article (1960) showed how technological externalities might be treated within accepted economic theory. He pointed out that negative externalities, such as smoke in the air, occur because people are using some asset—in this case, air quality—without paying for it. Were the asset owned and competitively priced, as Frank Knight earlier had suggested, a social optimum would obtain.

Coase also stressed the importance of transaction costs. While there might be social gain from less pollution, the cost of bringing parties together and effecting a trade for greater purity might exceed the gain. Many writers continue to consider such a case a market failure, but others have pointed out that transaction costs, like transportation costs, are real and must be considered if a social optimum is sought.

Perhaps Coase's most important contribution was to point out that externalities are reciprocal. When smoke from a mill bothers nearby residents, the mill imposes external costs on them. But if laws are enacted to reduce the output of smoke, the neighbors impose external costs on the mill. If natural forces of wind and gravity prevail, consumers of steel will gain at the expense of the neighbors who would like air of greater purity. If law allows the neighbors to prevail, they will gain cleaner air, at the expense of those who prefer more steel. Economists have recognized that the Pareto optimum level of pollution (or purity) is where the marginal benefit of additional purity is equal to the marginal cost of providing it, and this does not often call for complete elimination of pollution as we usually think of the term.

Policies to Deal with Externalities

Three broad policies have been advanced to deal with externalities.

1. Where transaction costs are high, government, it is argued, may instead regulate those affected by externalities to produce a Pareto optimum. There is strong empirical evidence, however, that these regulations often produce an equally inefficient, or worse, level of externalities by requiring levels of purity above the optimum and by requiring inefficient means for reducing pollution.

2. Taxes may be levied on those creating negative externalities and subsidies paid to those creating positive externalities. These sums are more accurately characterized as charges (instead of taxes) for the use of some asset, or payments (instead of subsidies) for providing the services of an asset. Again, there is the practical problem of determining how large the charges or payments should be and who should pay or be paid.

3. Where it is possible to designate the asset that two or more parties are seeking to use in mutually exclusive ways, property rights might be established and the owner would charge the users of the asset. This solution recognizes scarcity and treats the asset like other privately owned scarce resources.

Although most economists hold that externalities produce economic inefficiency and require one of the corrective measures just listed, others believe that many, if not most, technological externalities are Pareto-optimal, as are pecuniary externalities. They argue that a natural advantage, such as the location of a firm upstream, bestows rights akin to property rights, and residents downstream may pay upstream firms to reduce pollution if damages from pollution exceed the gains from using the environment to produce other goods. They also argue that transaction costs may explain the continued existence of externalities, and that such costs are real costs that must be considered. Indeed, they argue, if there were no transaction costs, there would be no externalities.

Many other problems may be analyzed as examples of externalities, spillovers, or neighborhood effects. Congestion, for example, occurs when too many parties try to use some asset, such as a highway. Because the price is below the optimum, each user imposes a cost on other users. Public goods and joint products may be considered forms of positive externalities in that when a good is produced to provide a service to one consumer, others may enjoy it at little or no cost. The problem of the free rider arises from other users seeking to benefit without paying. Even monopoly has been treated as an externality where the transaction costs of buyers bargaining for lower marginal prices exceed the gains they would realize.

References

Buchanan, James M., and W. C. Stubblebine, "Externality," *Economica,* vol. 29, November 1962, pp. 371–384; Coase, R. H., "The Problem of Social Cost," *Journal of Law and Economics,* vol. 3, October 1960, pp. 1–44; Dahlman, Carl J., "The Problem of Externality," *Journal of Law and Economics,* vol. 22, April 1979, pp. 141–162; Macaulay, Hugh, and Bruce Yandle, *Environmental Use and the Market,* Lexington Books, Lexington, Mass., 1977, pp. 39–42, 113–122; Mishan, E. J., "The Post-War Literature on Externalities: An Interpretative Essay," *Journal of Economic Literature,* vol. 9, March 1971, pp. 1–28.

(*See also* Economic rent; Energy costs; Government regulation of business; Marginal cost; Pollution abatement costs; Scarcity)

Hugh Macaulay

Factors of production

In the opening sentence of *The Wealth of Nations* (1776), Adam Smith remarks: "The annual labour of every nation is the fund which originally supplies it with all the necessaries and conveniences of life which it annually consumes. . . ." Thus, the "father" of modern economics recognized just one fundamental "factor" of production: labor—or, to use a more old-fashioned word, "work." Later writers introduced other broad composites such as "capital," "land," "entrepreneurship" (cf. Marshall, 1890, p. 400; 1920, p. 329)—not to mention a host of more contentious items ("organization," "knowledge," "Yankee ingenuity")—but in so doing seem mainly to have added terminology, not content, to Smith's original account of production processes.

As economics grew more "scientific" during the last half of the nineteenth century and beyond, "production" came to be defined more precisely as a ". . . physical coordination of productive services . . ." (Carlson, 1939, p. 2) and was conceived to be mathematically representable as a numerical time flow of output, say x, that could be expressed as an explicit function of a finite collection of scalar variables, say v_1, $v_2, \ldots v_n$). Each variable represented the numerical time flow of some objectively identifiable productive service (physical material or recognizable "force") or input, and it was assumed that we could write the production per unit of time of the quantity of output x as a function of the v's, viz, $x = f(V_1, v_2, \ldots v_n)$, thereby reducing to concise symbolic expression of process historically considered so difficult to characterize that most economists before 1870 regarded it as ineffable.

If the essentials of every productive process could be directly encapsulated as just indicated in a "flow-input, flow-output" production function, then as Paul Samuelson argued in his 1947 edition of *The Foundations of Economic Analysis* (p. 84), we would do well to avoid using the term "factor of production" in economic discussion because its meaning is woefully unclear (does it refer to a composite such as "labor" or "capital," or to ". . . any aspect of the environment which has any influence on production"?). Samuelson goes on to suggest that ". . . only 'inputs' be explicitly included in the production function, and that this term [i.e., the term 'input'] be confined to denote measurable quantitative economic goods or services."

There is good evidence from empirical research at the macro level (see Blanchard and Fisher, 1989, pp. 3–4) that the flow-input, flow-output representation of aggregate output as a function of a few variables denoting "measurable quantitative economic goods or services" is grossly inadequate for describing historical production experience. Is the problem that we can't clearly identify all relevant "measurable" inputs, that our measures of aggregate "input" and "output" are suspect, or just that production processes cannot be so simply represented? The answer is that we simply do not know. In addition, statistical studies of micro production processes raise difficult questions about the representability of production flows as functions of measurable input flows alone (cf. Alchian, 1959, pp. 23–24); again, we are unable to determine whether the problem lies in the difficulty of identifying all relevant inputs, in our inability accurately to measure usage of those inputs that are identified, or in the incorrect symbolic (functional) representation (econometric misspecification) of "production."

Probably the safest conclusion to be drawn from existing knowledge about real-world production processes is that we know little and understand less about most such activities, particularly when the output in question is a multidimensional service (e.g., university education, legal consulting, interior decorating). Perhaps there is something to be said for continuing to speak about "factors of production." That would be to return to an older and intellectually more modest tradition, a tradition of claims whose reach, especially by comparison with those of contemporary analysis, did not so evidently exceed their grasp.

When a TV commentator or talk show guest says, "We can't produce more without more and better factors of production," most people instinctively recognize that this assertion is possibly trite and obvious but is neither wrong nor silly; the assertion might even seem to be a prelude to more serious analysis, for it neither settles any question nor disclaims a need for further research. By contrast, the language of "input," "output," and "function" may seem simpler (in some sense) and more scientific (also in some sense), but it does not seem more informative than the traditional language.

Meanwhile, one will look in vain for the term "factor of production" in contemporary economics texts and treatises, but one will find frequent references to "inputs," "outputs," and (production) "functions." So the usage suggested by Paul Samuelson in 1947 has prevailed—jargon has won the day.

Apart from jargon, do modern economists (as distinct from production and marketing engineers) know anything about real-world production processes that was not known to Adam Smith in 1776? Perhaps we should reinstate the vague but curiosity-provoking phrase "factors of production" to refer to what Simon Newcomb (1886, p. 70ff.) elegantly described as "requisites in the mechanism of production." The term "input" could then be reserved for mathematical discussions.

References

Alchian, A. A., "Costs and Output," in M. Abramovitz et al. (eds.), *The Allocation of Economic Resources,* Stanford University Press, Stanford, 1959, pp. 23–40; Blanchard, O., and S. Fisher,

Lectures on Macroeconomics, MIT Press, Cambridge, Mass., 1989; Carlson, S., *A Study on the Pure Theory of Production,* Stockholm Economic Study No. 9, Stockholm University Press, 1939; Marshall, A., *Principles of Economics,* MacMillan, London, 1st ed., 1890; 8th ed., 1920; Newcomb, S. *Principles of Political Economy,* Harper, New York, 1886, pp. 70ff; Samuelson, P. A., *Foundations of Economic Analysis,* Harvard University, Cambridge, Mass., 1947; Smith, Adam, *An Inquiry into the Nature and Causes of the Wealth of Nations,* Random House, New York, Modern Library Edition, various dates.

Robert W. Clower

Family budgets

Family budgets are tools used (1) to describe the way in which an "average" family at any given income level actually spent its money; (2) to provide information, judged by a person or a group of people, about what commodities people need to attain different standards of living; and (3) to represent living standards, defined by scientists and experts based on appropriate scientific standards and translated into lists of foods, housing, clothing, and other goods and services in conjunction with actual buying practices of families.

Historical Highlights

The roots of budget studies can be traced to the 1830s, when LePlay initiated his series of family studies and collected data with E. Ducpetiaux. Utilizing these data, Engel formulated his famous law on the relationship between income and the proportion of income spent on food.

From 1870 to 1900, state bureaus of labor statistics made more than 100 family living studies. The most notable of these, directed by Henry Kemble Oliver and Carroll D. Wright in Massachusetts, set a pattern for both state and federal work in this area. In 1888, Congress instructed the U.S. Bureau of Labor Statistics to make analogous studies, which examined the relationship between income and expenditures.

Federal surveys in the twentieth century first included data on quantities of foods and then became increasingly comprehensive, including quantity data on clothing, furnishings, transportation, health, and other goods and services purchased. The first budgets in the United States were expressed in terms of quantities of goods and services to which prices were applied to determine the total budget cost. These were provided for in a 1907 act of Congress. Examples of early budgets include the cost of a "fair standard of living" in cotton-mill communities, the cost of budgets for specific industrial communities, a "minimum comfort budget" for railway employees, and budgets prepared by arbitration boards and commissions.

Changes and Developments in Federal Budgets

Budgets reflect the needs of different economic times. During the Depression of the 1930s an "emergency standard of living budget" was issued by the Works Progress Administration (WPA). In 1948, the City Worker's Family Budget, which measured the annual cost of a worker's family budget according to standards prevailing in 34 cities, was published by the Bureau of Labor Statistics. This budget was in response to a directive of the Labor and Federal Security Subcommittee of the House Appropriations Committee of the Seventy-ninth Congress. The budget for a "modest but adequate" living standard grew out of the need to measure place-to-place differences in cost of levels of living brought on by migration induced by war production and for appraisal of income tax exemptions. The Social Security Administration developed a budget for a retired couple at about the same time. Just over a decade later, both budgets were revised to include different lists of items, and their costs and were published for 20 large cities.

As interest in statistical methods and methodological improvements took place, family budget analyses became more sophisticated. Allen and Bowley's classic work on the variation of family expenditures in the mid-1930s was the first one to be based on preconceptions of modern mathematical theory of utility and exchange. Prais and Houthakker (1955, 1971), relying heavily on Allen and Bowley's 1935 work in family budget analysis, and Crockett and Friend (1960) derived income elasticities from a wide range of consumption data about two decades later. Later actual expenditure data from the 1960–1961 Survey of Consumer Expenditures, collected by the Bureau of Labor Statistics (BLS), were used. A quantity-income-elasticity technique was implemented to derive quantities of goods and services to represent a standard that met expressed social goals. This was for the 1966 City Worker's Family Budget and later budgets.

Spring 1967 standards-of-living budgets for an urban family of four people at three levels (lower, moderate, and higher) were estimated by the BLS for the urban United States, 39 metropolitan areas, and 4 nonmetropolitan regions. These budgets were updated periodically by the BLS, using the consumer price index, until autumn 1981, when the final report on family budgets was published. At that time the Federal Family Budget Program was eliminated in compliance with overall budget reduction.

Uses of Family Budgets

Family budget data have been used by legislators, program administrators, researchers, and educators for comparing families of different types, measuring changes in the level of living over time and in different areas, and evaluating the adequacy of family income. Specifically, these data have been used extensively in labor-management negotiations, in child support determinations, and in establishing eligibility for public housing or other welfare programs. Consumer educators and counselors have utilized the data with families and individuals for financial management comparisons of spending patterns, needs, and costs.

Family budget data, from consumer expenditure surveys, continue to provide a wealth of data to help improve the well-being of individuals and households. Researchers have provided and continue to contribute much valuable information on the relationship of income, household size, the family life cycle, and family type to family budgets. Other socioeconomic variables found related to expenditures have been education, occupation, and area of residence.

Advisory Committees

Committees of experts have been used to advise BLS staff in developing basic standards and measures to be used in their family budget projects. Technical committee members have been selected especially because of their background and reputation as authorities in studies of living costs.

References

Allen, R. G. D., and A. L. Bowley, *Family Expenditures: A Study of Its Variation*, P. S. King and Son, London, 1935; Brady, D. S., "Family Budgets: A Historical Survey," *Monthly Labor Review*, vol. 66, no. 2, February 1948, pp. 171–175; Bureau of Labor Statistics, *Autumn 1978 Urban Family Budgets and Comparative Indexes for Selected Urban Areas*, U.S. Department of Labor Bulletin No. 79-305, 1979; Bureau of Labor Statistics, "Final Report on Family Budgets: Cost Increases Slowed, Autumn 1981," *Monthly Labor Review*, vol. 105, no. 7, July 1982; Crockett, J., and I. Friend, "A Complete Set of Demand Relationships," in I. Friend and R. Jones, eds., *Proceedings of Conference on Consumption and Saving*, vol. 1, McGregor and Warner, Washington, D.C., 1960, pp. 1–92; Davis, J. S., "Standards and Content of Living," *American Economic Review*, vol. 35, no. 1, March 1945, pp. 1–15; Ferber, R., "Research on Household Behavior," *American Economic Review*, vol. 52, no. 1, March 1962, pp. 19–63; Groom, P., "A New City Worker's Family Budget," *Monthly Labor Review*, vol. 90, no. 11, November 1967, pp. 1–8; Kellogg, L. S., and D. S. Brady, "The City Worker's Family Budget," *Monthly Labor Review*, vol. 66, no. 2, February 1948, pp. 133–170; Prais, S. J., and M. S. Moutakker, *The Analysis of Family Budgets*, Cambridge University Press, Cambridge, 1955, 1971; Schultz, H., "Family Expenditure: A Study of Its Variation," *Journal of the American Statistical Association*, vol. 31, September 1936, pp. 613–617.

(*See also* Bureau of Labor Statistics; Cross-sectional analysis in business and economics; Standard of living)

Jeanne L. Hafstrom

Federal budget

Background

Before the Budget and Accounting Act of 1921, executive branch agencies prepared their own budgets, which were transmitted to the Congress through the Treasury without substantive review. The 1921 Act established the Bureau of the Budget in the Treasury, and it was moved to the new Executive Office of the President in 1939. That powerful agency, now called the Office of Management and Budget, prepares the budget for the entire government on behalf of the president who becomes directly involved in the decision-making process. The budget document issued on or before the first Monday in February each year comprises the President's recommendations to the Congress for the next fiscal year, which begins on October 1 of the same calendar year.

Budget Concepts

Through fiscal year 1968, the decision-making process in the Congress and executive branch focused on the administrative budget, which excluded the operations of government trust funds and some government enterprises. Because of the rapid growth in the relative importance of trust funds, especially those related to the financing of social security, a commission of outside experts recommended in the late 1960s that the emphasis be placed on the unified budget, which was adopted for fiscal 1969.

With a few minor exceptions, the unified budget includes all cash transactions of the government. The difference between cash outlays and receipts indicates the government's financing needs. For the most part, the deficit is financed by issuing Treasury securities, although gold sales, seignorage, and changes in cash balances are also recorded as deficit financing items. Receipts include tax revenues and most user fees, but when agencies engage in business-type activities, the proceeds from selling goods and services are defined as negative outlays that are netted against their other expenditures.

The unified budget originally recorded net direct lending as a cash outlay, and loan guarantees were not recorded until defaults resulted in expenditures. This created a strong bias in favor of subsidizing credit flows with guarantees because they had no immediate budget impact. The Budget Enforcement Act of 1990 corrected this flaw, and henceforth outlays will be defined to include the subsidy value of both direct loans and guarantees, thus putting guarantees and direct loans on an equal basis. The same act excluded the transactions of social security trust funds in computing the official deficit, but the focus of decision makers and the media has remained on the overall unified deficit.

The federal government's impact on the gross domestic product is recorded in the national income and product (NIA) budget. This budget differs from the unified budget in that real and financial asset sales and purchases are excluded from expenditure and revenue totals, corporate tax revenues are recorded on an accrual basis, defense expenditures are recorded when goods and services are delivered rather than when they are paid for, certain transactions are recorded on a gross rather than net basis, and government transactions in U.S. territories are excluded. The NIA deficit measures the impact of the federal government on national saving. However, the measure is flawed, because public investment is not differentiated from current expenditures in the NIA budget, and the depreciation of public assets is not recorded.

Budget Trends

As recorded in the unified budget, total federal outlays rose from 16.0 percent of GNP in 1950 to 23.2 percent in 1990 (see Table 1). The share of defense in GNP has varied up and down with world conditions, but since reaching a post–World War II peak of 14.4 percent during the Korean War in 1953, the overall trend has been downward. In 1990, defense's share of GNP was 5.5 percent. Net interest varied almost entirely between 1.0 and 1.5 percent of the GNP for the 30 years following 1950, but interest began to rise rapidly in the 1980s because of soaring deficits and high real interest rates. By 1990, net interest was 3.4 percent of the GNP.

Entitlements and other mandatory spending have, however, contributed most to the relative growth of the federal budget in the postwar period. This category rose from 5.4 percent of the GNP in 1962 to 10.1 percent in 1990, excluding the cost of deposit insurance. The two most important entitlements by far are social security and Medicare, which alone accounted for almost 56.6 percent of total entitlement and mandatory spending in 1990.

Nondefense discretionary spending grew faster than the GNP through most of the postwar period, reaching 5.3 percent of the GNP in 1980. Since that time, this category has been severely constrained, falling to 3.7 percent of the GNP by 1990. Indeed, with the exception of interest and defense, total spending grew more slowly than the GNP during the 1980s, falling from 15.1 percent in 1980 to 14.2 percent in 1990. Were it not for the high cost of resolving thrift and commercial bank deposit insurance claims in 1990, spending on items other than defense and interest would have fallen to 13.2 percent of GNP by 1990.

TABLE 1 Federal Budget, Receipts by Source and Outlays by Function, FY 1950–1990

	$ billions					Percentage of GNP				
	1950	1960	1970	1980	1990	1950	1960	1970	1980	1990
Receipts by source	$39.4	$92.5	$192.8	$517.1	$1031.3	14.8%	18.3%	19.5%	19.4%	19.1%
Individual income taxes	15.8	40.7	90.4	244.1	466.9	5.9	8.0	9.1	9.1	8.6
Corporation income taxes	10.4	21.5	32.8	64.6	93.5	3.9	4.2	3.3	2.4	1.7
Social insurance taxes	4.3	14.7	44.4	157.8	380.0	1.6	2.9	4.5	5.9	7.0
Excise taxes	7.6	11.7	15.7	24.3	35.3	2.8	2.3	1.6	0.9	0.7
Estate and gift taxes	0.7	1.6	3.6	6.4	11.5	0.3	0.3	0.4	0.2	0.2
Customs duties and fees	0.4	1.1	2.4	7.2	16.7	0.2	0.2	0.2	0.3	0.3
Miscellaneous receipts	0.3	1.2	3.4	12.7	27.3	0.1	0.2	0.3	0.5	0.5
Outlays by function	42.6	92.2	195.6	590.9	1251.7	16.0	18.2	19.8	22.1	23.2
National defense	13.7	48.1	81.7	134.0	299.3	5.1	9.5	8.3	5.0	5.5
International affairs	4.7	3.0	4.3	12.7	13.8	1.8	0.6	0.4	0.5	0.3
General science, space, and technology	0.1	0.6	4.5	5.8	14.4	0.0	0.1	0.5	0.2	0.3
Energy	0.3	0.5	1.0	10.2	2.4	0.1	0.1	0.1	0.4	0.0
Natural resources and environment	1.3	1.6	3.1	13.9	17.1	0.5	0.3	0.3	0.5	0.3
Agriculture	2.0	2.6	5.2	8.8	12.0	0.8	0.5	0.5	0.3	0.2
Commerce and housing credit	1.0	1.6	2.1	9.4	67.1	0.4	0.3	0.2	0.4	1.2
Transportation	1.0	4.1	7.0	21.3	29.5	0.4	0.8	0.7	0.8	0.5
Community and regional development	0.0	0.2	2.4	11.3	8.5	0.0	0.0	0.2	0.4	0.2
Education, training, employment, and social services	0.2	1.0	8.6	31.8	38.5	0.1	0.2	0.9	1.2	0.7
Health	0.3	0.8	5.9	23.2	57.7	0.1	0.2	0.6	0.9	1.1
Medicare	0.0	0.0	6.2	32.1	98.1	0.0	0.0	0.6	1.2	1.8
Income security	4.1	7.4	15.6	86.5	147.3	1.5	1.5	1.6	3.2	2.7
Social security	0.8	11.6	30.3	118.5	248.6	0.3	2.3	3.1	4.4	4.6
Veterans benefits and services	8.8	5.4	8.7	21.2	29.1	3.3	1.1	0.9	0.8	0.5
Administration of justice	0.2	0.4	1.0	4.6	10.0	0.1	0.1	0.1	0.2	0.2
General government	1.0	1.2	2.3	13.0	10.7	0.4	0.2	0.2	0.5	0.2
Net interest	4.8	6.9	14.4	52.5	184.2	1.8	1.4	1.5	2.0	3.4
Undistributed offsetting receipts	-1.8	-4.8	-8.6	-19.9	-36.6	-0.7	-1.0	-0.9	-0.7	-0.7

SOURCE   U.S. Office of Management and Budget, *Budget of the United States Government: Fiscal Year 1992*, U.S. Government Printing Office, Washington, D.C., 1991.

Two characteristics of federal spending are crucially important. First, very few programs constitute the bulk of the total. Four programs—defense, interest, social security, and Medicare—accounted for about two-thirds of total spending in 1990. Outlays on deposit insurance, which should start to fall rapidly in the mid-1990s, accounted for another 4.6 percent of spending in 1990.

Second, noninterest civilian spending is dominated by programs for the elderly. Benefits going to people over 65 accounted for almost one-half of such spending in 1991. Social security and Medicare account for most of this spending, but the elderly also receive civil service, military, and veterans pensions and account for a disproportionate share of Medicaid, food stamp, and housing subsidy outlays. However, social security and Medicare alone account for the bulk of the growth in noninterest civilian spending's share of GNP since just before World War II. More recently, the relative growth of these two programs has been even more dramatic. Between 1980 and 1990, the share of social security and Medicare in GNP rose by 0.8 percentage points, whereas the share of all other noninterest civilian programs fell 1.7 percentage points.

Because benefits for the elderly are so important, federal budget trends are crucially affected by the growth of the elderly population. That population will grow slowly in the late 1990s and the early twenty-first century because of low birth rates during the Great Depression. This group's population growth will accelerate rapidly after 2010, however, when the baby boom generation begins to retire.

The growth of social security and Medicare has profoundly affected the composition of revenues. Between 1950 and 1990, social insurance taxes have grown from 1.6 to 7.0 percent of GNP. The relative importance of individual income taxes grew from 5.9 to 9.1 percent of GNP between 1950 and 1970, but after growing rapidly for a brief period between 1978 and 1981, the share of individual income taxes fell to 8.6 percent of GNP by 1990. Corporate tax revenues have been on a pronounced downward trend relative to GNP since peaking during the Korean War at over 6 percent. By 1960, corporate tax revenues' share of GNP was 4.2 percent but then fell to a low of 1.1 percent of GNP in 1983 because of a recession. The Tax Reform Act of 1986 raised the corporate tax burden significantly, and its share of GNP was 1.7 percent in 1990. The relative importance of excise taxes has steadily fallen in the postwar period as periodic tax increases have failed to fully offset inflation's erosion of the real value of unit taxes on tobacco and alcohol. In 1950, excise receipts equalled 2.8 percent of GNP. By 1990, their ratio had fallen below 1 percent.

The total federal tax burden rose rapidly from 14.8 percent of GNP in 1950 to 19.5 percent in 1970. It has varied up and down since that time around a constant trend. In 1990, the overall tax burden of 19.1 percent was slightly below the 1970s level.

The combination of a constant tax burden over the last 20 years combined with a growing spending burden has, of course, resulted in a rapidly growing deficit. For almost all of U.S. history before World War II, budget deficits were a rarity except during wars and recessions. But budget surpluses occurred in only 3 years of the 1950s and in 2 years of the 1960s. The last budget surplus occurred in 1969. Nevertheless, the federal debt held by the public relative to GNP steadily fell from 114 percent at the end of 1946 to a postwar low of 24 percent in fiscal 1974. The ratio remained steady in the mid-1970s but then began a long, rapid rise. By the end of 1990, the debt had grown to 45 percent of GNP.

References

U.S. Office of Management and Budget, *The Budget of the United States Government,* published annually on a fiscal year basis.

(*See also* Debt and deficits; Federal budget process; Fiscal policy; Medicare program; Public capital; Social security)

Rudolph G. Penner

Federal budget process

Background

In parliamentary democracies, the formulation of budgets is an executive function. The United States is unusual in that its Constitution gives the Congress control over budget policy. The Constitution further states that "All bills for raising revenues shall originate in the House of Representatives."

Prior to 1865, the Ways and Means Committee of the House initiated both spending and tax bills, but the press of work after the Civil War induced the Congress to divide the work load between Ways and Means and a newly created Appropriations Committee. The latter is now divided into thirteen subcommittees, each responsible for initiating the appropriation bill that controls the direct spending activities of a particular set of agencies. The Senate Appropriations Committee, created in 1867, is organized in a similar manner.

Ways and Means and its Senate counterpart, the Finance Committee, remain responsible for tax legislation and for the laws controlling the most important entitlement programs, such as social security, Medicare, and Aid for Families with Dependent Children. Entitlement programs have grown to the point that the amount of noninterest spending controlled by Ways and Means is more than 70 percent of the total controlled by the Appropriations Committee, thus Ways and Means and Senate Finance have become the most influential committees of the Congress in formulating budget policy.

Some entitlements are, however, controlled by other committees. For example, agricultural subsidies and food stamps are controlled by the agriculture committees, and civil service pensions are controlled by the Post Office and Civil Service Committee in the House and the Governmental Affairs Committee in the Senate.

Before the Budget and Accounting Act of 1921, the executive branch had no overall budget process. Individual departments submitted budgets to the Congress through the Treasury, but there was no centralized review process. The Budget and Accounting Act established the Bureau of the Budget, which was originally within Treasury but was transferred to the Executive Office of the President in 1939. The Bureau of the Budget was renamed the Office of Management and Budget (OMB) in 1970. It reviews the budgets of all components of the government and assists presidents in formulating their budget recommendations to the Congress. The resulting budget for the following fiscal year, which begins October 1, is supposed to be issued on or before the first Monday in February each year.

Once the Congress completes its appropriations process for a fiscal year, OMB apportions spending authority to agencies on a periodic basis in order to smooth out spending over the year. Disbursements are recorded daily by the Treasury, and OMB issues a midyear report that updates the economic forecast and spending and revenue estimates. The comptroller general, through the General Accounting Office, audits agencies on behalf of the Congress. Auditing is done on a year-round basis.

The Executive Branch Budget Process

The internal process for formulating the President's budget varies somewhat from administration to administration, but it generally begins in the spring, when the director of OMB and staff review strategic budget issues. This stage ends in early summer, when OMB, acting for the President, transmits general policy directions and planning levels for spending to each department and agency. The agencies develop their budgets and make their requests to OMB, usually asking that their planned spending level be made more lenient. OMB staff hold adversary hearings with agency staff, and the results of the hearings together with other OMB staff analysis are presented to the OMB director in a series of meetings in the fall. The OMB director then makes recommendations to the President. Cabinet and agency heads have the right to appeal the President's decisions, but the OMB director attempts to minimize the burden on the President by negotiating with agency heads to settle most disputes without the need for a formal appeal to the president.

It is important to emphasize that this complex process results in nothing more than a set of recommendations to the Congress that it may either adopt or ignore. Presidents can veto appropriations bills that deviate significantly from their recommendations, but entitlement reform is more difficult. Unless the Congress acts, entitlement spending continues from year to year, and the President cannot veto inaction.

Presidents have occasionally refused to spend all the funds appropriated by the Congress, but the constitutional status of such impoundments was never settled, and most presidents use impoundments gingerly. However, after the election of 1972, President Nixon aggressively impounded civilian spending. The Congress was outraged, and the Nixon impoundments were challenged in court. Nixon was able to argue effectively that he had to use impoundments to limit total spending, because the Congress had no effective budget process. Spending and taxing decisions were made in a number of different committees, and no formal mechanism examined the results of their decisions on total spending, revenues, or the deficit.

Before the impoundment issue reached the Supreme Court, the Congress began the process of limiting the President's impoundment power legislatively. But the Congress felt the need to deflect Nixon's criticism by simultaneously creating a new congressional budget process.

The Congressional Budget and Impoundment Control Act of 1974

The new congressional budget process created budget committees in the House and Senate. These committees formulate budget resolutions in the spring of each year. The resolutions state targets for total spending, revenues, the deficit, and the public debt. They also suggest a functional breakdown for spending, but this breakdown is not binding. The resolution is a concurrent resolution, which means that it cannot be vetoed by the President.

The target for spending is allocated among committees, and the appropriations committees further allocate their totals among their 13 subcommittees. The Congress then proceeds to work on spending and tax legislation much as it did before the new process was established. An elaborate schedule is promulgated setting due dates for the passage of the resolutions, authorizations, and appropriations, but that schedule is seldom followed, and, often, a new fiscal year begins before final appropriations have been passed.

Originally, the process required that a second budget resolution be passed in mid-September. That resolution took account of economic and other changes since the first resolution. Reconciliation instructions could be passed at that time to force committees to adhere to their targets. Reconciliation instructions were not used to order significant savings in the early years of the new process. They were first used seriously during the Carter administration to order $8 billion in deficit reductions. The Reagan administration, however, utilized them more vigorously and very skillfully to enhance passage of its economic program in 1981. Instead of being used at the end of the budget process, they were used at the beginning to force certain changes in tax and entitlement laws. Since that time, the requirement for a second budget resolution has been eliminated, but reconciliation bills passed early in the budget process have become common and are often used to enforce budget agreements negotiated by the president and congressional leaders.

The new process also created the Congressional Budget Office (CBO) to provide the Congress with technical advice, so that the Congress had a nonpartisan source of information independent of OMB. The CBO provides an economic forecast which may be used by the budget committees. The CBO also provides estimates of the spending and revenue totals implied by a continuation of current policy for a 5-year period, and it tracks the activities of committees to see if they are deviating from their spending and revenue targets. In addition, the CBO performs program evaluations and provides 5-year cost estimates for every spending bill reported out of committee. The Joint Tax Committee provides analogous revenue estimates for proposed changes in tax law.

The CBO also evaluates the President's budget and reestimates its spending and revenue totals using CBO economic and technical assumptions. The director of the CBO is appointed for a 4-year term by the speaker of the House and the president pro tem of the Senate.

The Budget Act of 1974 stipulated two procedures through which a president can impound funds. The President was allowed to propose a deferral of spending, and, if neither the House nor the Senate passed a resolution releasing the funds, the deferral was allowed to proceed. The President was also allowed to propose a permanent cancellation of spending authority called a "rescission." If the House and the Senate do not act to approve a rescission within 45 days, the president must release the funds. The comptroller general has the responsibility of ensuring that all impoundment actions are reported to the Congress.

The president's deferral authority was altered when the Supreme Court ruled that one-house vetoes were not constitutional. Deferrals must now be endorsed by a law, and this makes them more difficult to obtain. The rescission power has been used periodically, but a large portion of rescission requests have been ignored by the Congress.

The effectiveness of the new congressional budget process was disappointing. Committees often violated their spending targets and had a tendency to adopt overly optimistic economic assumptions that had the effect of greatly understating the deficit problem. The legislative schedule promulgated by the new law was routinely violated, and the complexity of the process meant that the Congress was forced to spend a much greater portion of its time on budget matters.

Frustrations grew as it became apparent that the process was not capable of dealing with the large deficits created early in the Reagan administration. Consequently, the Congress, with the support of the administration, significantly amended the budget process in 1985.

The Balanced Budget and Emergency Deficit Control Act of 1985 and the Budget Enforcement Act of 1990

The budget legislation of 1985, better known as Gramm-Rudman-Hollings, stipulated strict deficit targets for 5 years culminating in a balanced budget for fiscal 1991. If the Congress did not attain the target legislatively, it was to be enforced by an across-the-board cut in spending known as a "sequester." Separate rules were created for defense and nondefense sequesters, and many welfare programs and social security were protected from automatic cuts. Special rules limited the cuts applied to programs such as Medicare and student loans.

The process initially depended on an average of the economic forecasts and other estimates of OMB and CBO, and the comptroller general used these estimates to administer the process. He also resolved any legal disputes arising between CBO and OMB. But the Supreme Court quickly ruled that the role of the comptroller general and the CBO was unconstitutional and that the Act had to be administered by the executive branch. After fiscal 1987, OMB was fully responsible for providing the economic forecasts and any other estimates that were required.

The new procedure had many flaws, but the most important was that it had to be based on the projected deficit which, in turn, was influenced significantly by OMB's economic forecast. This created a strong incentive to promulgate an overly optimistic economic forecast. That allowed the target to be met on paper, but when the forecast did not materialize, it made it very difficult to meet the next year's target. To meet the projected deficit target in any one year, the Congress also artificially shifted expenditures back into the previous fiscal year and to future years. The latter move also made it difficult to meet future targets, even on paper.

It proved impossible to meet the original target for fiscal 1988, and a new set of targets was promulgated in late 1987 with a balanced budget now promised for fiscal 1993. By early 1990, it again became apparent that the targets were impractical, and the budget process was again amended significantly after protracted negotiations between the President and congressional leaders.

The new process was more sensible than Gramm-Rudman-Hollings in that deficit targets were adjusted each year for changes that were out of the direct control of the Congress, namely changes in the economy and unexpected changes in the cost of entitlement programs and in the revenue yielded by existing tax laws. The new process focused on controlling the legislative actions of the Congress. Spending caps were stipulated for three categories of discretionary spending through fiscal 1993. The three categories were defense, international, and domestic spending. Any program expansion within a category had to be financed by a cut in some other program within the same category. Special pay-as-you-go rules were created for tax and entitlement policies. Any expansion of entitlements or any tax cut had to be financed by some other tax increase or entitlement cut.

If any of these rules were violated, a sequester was imposed only on the category that violated the rules. Thus the penalty for a violation was focused on the committee that was responsible rather than being diffused throughout the entire government as under Gramm-Rudman-Hollings. The new process also created complex new rules that make it much more difficult to avoid a sequester by artificially shifting spending backward and forward. A shift of spending to a previous fiscal year can provoke an immediate sequester. The pay-as-you-go rules must be satisfied for the budget year and for 5 years into the future.

The rules of the new process can be violated if the President and the Congress declare an emergency. This provision was used to finance the Gulf War. Because the President must agree that an emergency exists, the new process has given the President somewhat more influence in the budget process. The administration of the process by OMB has also given more power to the executive branch. OMB provides the economic forecast and the estimates and definitions necessary for enforcing the spending caps and the pay-as-you-go rules.

The Budget Enforcement Act also reformed the treatment of credit programs in the budget. Previously, the full amount of a direct loan was recorded as an outlay, and repayments were recorded as negative outlays. Loan guarantees had no budget implications until they defaulted. This created a strong bias toward using guarantees rather than direct loans. A credit budget was created to control credit programs of all types, but it was not very successful. The new process records the subsidy value of both direct loans and guarantees. Issuing agencies must obtain an appropriation to finance the subsidy value of credit programs, and the funds are deposited in a special fund to cover subsequent defaults.

Although the rules of the new process are sensible and would result in considerable deficit reduction if followed through the end of the agreement in fiscal 1995, they are also very complex and rigid. This makes it very difficult to respond to unanticipated events. In particular, the collapse of the Soviet Union made the spending caps for defense obsolete. Although Congress can cut defense below its cap, it cannot use the extra saving for anything other than deficit reduction. Many in the Congress and the administration would now like to use the extra saving to finance tax cuts or domestic spending increases.

The rules also make it difficult to respond to a recession. Under both Gramm-Rudman-Hollings and the newer process, the rules can be suspended by the Congress if either OMB or CBO forecast a recession or if the economy experiences two successive quarters of less than 1 percent growth. The Congress chose not to suspend the rules as the recession of 1990–1991 unfolded, but it became dissatisfied with the recovery which initially proceeded at a rate only slightly exceeding 1 percent.

As a result of these problems, the current budget process is unlikely to last through 1992. The new process is likely to be something similar and equally complex. Disciplining rules have to be complex, rigid, and somewhat arbitrary. Although budgeting might become more rational if it could be more flexible, the Congress is likely to feel the need for artificial discipline as long as the deficit remains a problem. It now appears as though that will be true for a very long time.

(*See also* Federal budget; Congressional Budget Office)

Rudolph G. Penner

Federal funds rate (*see* Federal Reserve policy; Monetary policy; Open-market operations)

Federal Reserve policy

A broad consensus among economists holds that Federal Reserve policy has a potent effect on economic activity in the short run. Policy adjustments alter the balance between the demand and supply of reserves available in the banking system and can be made by purchasing or selling securities in the open market, by varying the terms of borrowing from the Federal Reserve, and by changing reserve requirements. In general, changes in reserves more or less reliably alter various categories of deposits at financial institutions, which enter in the money supply and the total amount of depository credit. For the most part, variations in the quantities of reserves, money, and credit are promptly felt on the level of short-term interest rates, which in turn influence the exchange value of the dollar in world currency markets. Those short-term interest rates importantly determine long-term rates and financial wealth, which, along with the exchange value of the dollar, have significant consequences for private sector decisions on spending. Over time, though, real economic growth is determined by the expansion of the nation's productive capacity, a matter that is little influenced by monetary policy. However, Federal Reserve policy does have an important—indeed, most economists would argue, dominant— role in determining the rate of increase in the prices of goods and service over the long run.

In recent years, senior Federal Reserve policymakers often have identified the Federal Reserve's primary responsibility to be support of sustainable growth in real economic activity by providing a backdrop of a stable and predictable general price level. Such stability of prices would be accompanied by a moderate expansion in the stock of money in the long run. However, even accepting that long-run link, the influence of money on prices, is too unpredictable to be of much assistance in the short run. Instead, policy must be guided by other indicators as well, including financial market prices and measures of economic activity.

The original charter of the U.S. central bank, the Federal Reserve Act of 1913, spoke little to the economywide consequences of the institution, directing only that the Federal Reserve provide "a stable currency." Congressional intent was subsequently made plainer, and some measure of responsibility in attaining price stability and stabilizing real economic growth was placed on the Federal Reserve. Still, the legislated mandate of the Federal Reserve leaves policymakers much room for interpretation and the exercise of discretion in day-to-day operations.

The Instruments of Federal Reserve Policy

The Federal Reserve has four main instruments to make its intentions felt on economic activity, all of which first affect the banking system (defined to include commercial banks and thrift institutions). The reserves of depository institutions take the form of cash kept in their vaults and deposits held at their local Federal Reserve bank. Depository institutions hold these reserves to meet the unpredictable demands of their depositors for currency and to manage their clearing needs in processing transactions as well as to satisfy mandated reserve requirements. Those reserves can be owned outright by the depository institution or borrowed temporarily from other depository institutions or from its local Federal Reserve bank. Depositories with reserves greater than their own need routinely lend to institutions with deficient reserves by trading claims to reserve deposits. Market participants term those deposits "federal funds" and the rate on the loan of those interbank deposits the "federal funds rate." Depositories also can borrow from their local Federal Reserve bank through discount window loans, which are collateralized loans that are typically priced below the going market rate. However, banks are expected to exercise restraint in seeking such credit, in part by first turning to available market sources or funds.

In open-market operations, the operating arm of the Federal Reserve System alters the total level of reserve availability through the purchase or sale of government securities. When the Federal Reserve buys government securities, for example, it credits the selling bank with a deposit, thereby enlarging the stock of reserves for the banking system. Importantly, with an increased stock of reserve, depositories in the aggregate need to borrow fewer reserves to fulfill the needs of clearing and to satisfy reserve requirements. As a result, such an open-market operation is almost immediately reflected in a decline in the lending rate for overnight interbank deposits, the federal funds rate. Also, fewer reserves are borrowed from the discount window. Over time, banks use those added reserves, which do not bear interest, to generate income by making loans, creating new customer deposits in the process. Those deposits fall into one of the broad definitions of the monetary aggregates maintained and calculated by the Federal Reserve. Thus, an increase in reserves should reliably boost the stock of money.

Far less frequently than it conducts open-market operations, the Federal Reserve varies the discount rate, the rate charged depositories on collateralized loans from a Federal Reserve bank. From a policy perspective, the discount window is a passive tool. The Federal Reserve can make the terms of lending more or less attractive, but the effect on reserves depends on depositories' willingness to tap the discount window. As a result, the discount window cannot be used to manage the supply of reserves with any precision. A change in the discount rate, however, can be used at times to signal the firmness of the Federal Reserve's intentions, reinforcing actions that were or are planned to be taken via open-market operations.

More infrequently still, the Federal Reserve can alter reserve requirements on bank deposits. The Federal Reserve Act grants the central bank the authority to mandate minimum levels of reserves that a bank must hold to support various categories of deposits. That floor, expressed as a fraction of deposits in a specified category, is known as the "reserve requirement"; under current law the reserve requirement may be varied from 8 to 12 percent for transactions deposits and from 0 to 5 percent for certain nontransactions liabilities. A decrease in reserve requirements on transactions deposits, for instance, allows the same amount of reserves to support more deposits, thereby making bankers more willing to lend and to increase deposits. Lower reserve requirements also increase banks' lending margins, bolstering their willingness to lend.

Lastly, every public utterance of the chair of the Federal Reserve Board and other monetary policymakers is scrutinized by market participants attempting to define policy intentions from the public record. As a result, these officials have limited room to exercise "moral suasion" or to attempt to lead market participants and bankers to the desired end without explicit recourse to policy action. Publicized intentions, however, must be credibly attached to the possibility of action over time.

Other Policy Tools

The Federal Reserve on occasion has been given the authority to implement selective credit controls, with the last and brief episode occurring in 1980; that authority lapsed in 1982. Currently, the Board of Governors of the Federal Reserve System has direct control over a single category of credit, that used for the purchase of stocks and convertible bonds, in an authority initially granted to discourage what was viewed as excessive speculation in the equity market. The Board determines the maximum fraction of the purchase value of securities that can be financed, or the margin requirement for such purchases. Separate requirements are set for stocks and convertible bonds. Varied only infrequently, margin requirements have generally moved in a range between 50 and 80 percent.

The Channels of Federal Reserve Influence

An action to change reserves almost immediately influences the level of the federal funds rate. The current and the expected future levels of the federal funds rate, in turn, affect other short-term or money market rates, such as the yields on Treasury bills, commercial paper, and certificates of deposit. Longer maturity rates, which can be thought of as weighted averages of the current and expected future short-term rates, generally move less than do short-term rates. Nevertheless, changes in long-term rates, especially when sustained over time, profoundly influence the interest-sensitive sectors of the economy, including households' purchases of durable goods, home building, inventory accumulation, and business investment in plant and equipment.

As already discussed, an expansion of reserves, for example, exerts downward pressure on short-term and, to a lesser extent, long-term interest rates. Meanwhile, depository institutions, taking pains to turn those non-interest-earning reserves into income-producing assets, make loans and expand their deposit base. The money supply expands. With rates generally lower, the interest-sensitive part of spending stirs. As firms revise their investment decisions upward and home buyers encounter lower costs of home ownership, aggregate demand quickens, reinforcing itself through the multiplier expansion of income.

If economic policy in foreign countries is unchanged, a reduction in U.S. interest rates renders dollar assets less attractive, exerting downward pressure on the foreign exchange value of the dollar. A decline in the dollar's value in turn makes U.S. goods more attractive on world markets and foreign goods less attractive in the U.S. market, providing some stimulus to net exports. In addition to those direct effects on the economy, the reduction in interest rates also will tend to increase private wealth. The spur to spending from the trade sector and the increase in wealth should contribute to the pickup in economic activity.

Most analysts agree, however, that policy action cannot have a lasting effect on the pace of economic activity, which, in the long run, is dictated by the expansion of capacity that results from growth of productivity and the labor force. After the stimulative effect of an increase in reserve availability works its way through to higher income, the margin between aggregate spending and the economy's capacity to produce is reduced, leading over time to increases in prices. These price gains narrow the real effects of any policy action, and ultimately income must move in line with the economy's underlying productive capacity.

This causal chain linking monetary policy actions first to financial rates, next to real income, and finally to inflation is not immutable. Analysts differ as to the time each phase takes and the import each should be accorded. Indeed, many would argue that the length of each of those phases depends on the public's understanding of the policy actions—in particular, that the element of surprise may heighten the impact of a policy change. An easing, for instance, that was anticipated would have less impact on financial markets and income and would be translated more quickly into higher price than would an action that caught market participants unaware. However, frequent and unpredictable changes in the stance of monetary policy may confuse firms and households, increasing their uncertainty about the future. As a result of that uncertainty, investors may demand compensation in the form of a risk premium in interest rates, which could tend to depress investment and economic growth.

Indicators of Policy

Although the intermediate links are less predictable and their relative importance is certainly debated among economists, there is broad agreement that monetary policy ultimately has responsibility for the long-run rate of inflation. The historical record strongly suggests that changes in the general price level trace back in time to expansions in the money stock. However, this long-run association provides only limited help in determining policy over the short to intermediate horizon.

In principle, the lack of a single indicator summarizing the behavior of the economy need not be a problem. Policymakers, completely confident about the structure of the economy, could manipulate their policy instruments based on their accurate forecasting ability. In fact, no simple framework or complicated econometric model appears to capture the intricacies of the U.S. economy. In the absence of such a tool, Federal Reserve officials rely on intermediate indicators, such as various measures of the money stock and debt, to gauge the direction of the economy and the consequence of policy. Even in that regard, no single measure provides a complete reading on the economy; as a result, the monetary and credit aggregates are part, but only part, of that kit of indicators. The value of the information provided by various indicators has changed over time, and financial innovation has played havoc with the traditional relationships between money and economic activity, proving particularly troublesome in the mid-1970s and early 1980s, and a burgeoning of federal and private debt in the 1980s blotted out the century-long close correspondence between nonfinancial debt and gross domestic product.

At times, both Federal Reserve officials and market participants attempting to discern the future path of policy have turned to financial indicators. Such signals include the spread of long-term over short-term Treasury rates (the slope of the yield curve), the foreign exchange value of the dollar, and the prices of tradable commodities. These indicators, quoted almost continuously in financial markets, are more timely than many of the traditional financial and nonfinancial indicators. Further, since the return any of them provides will depend on future developments, their price movements may offer important signals as to investors' opinions on unfolding economic events, particularly with regard to the course of inflation. Commodity prices, for example, which are not as likely to be bound by formal or informal contracts as other goods or services, may respond in a more immediate and exaggerated fashion to aggregate demand pressures than do more inclusive general price indexes. Watchfulness to these indicators, however, has its drawbacks. The prices of specific commodities may be buffered by special factors that are uninformative about the overall economic scene, supply effects related to the Treasury's issuance of debt may twist the term structure, and foreign exchange markets may overreact at times to news. A policymaker reacting to that idiosyncratic variability will worsen, rather than smooth, the economic cycle. Presumably, by monitoring a wide array of indicators, the monetary policymaker can sift out the true nuggets of macroeconomic information.

International Considerations

At times, the foreign exchange value of the dollar serves as a direct objective of policy. In the floating-exchange-rate period since the collapse of the Bretton Woods agreement in 1973, the Federal Reserve, in close cooperation with the U.S. Treasury, has intermittently intervened in the foreign exchange market. By using foreign exchange reserves to buy dollars in the market or by selling dollars in the market to add to those reserves, foreign exchange operations seek to smooth the path of the dollar and to counter disorderly market conditions. Disorderly market conditions may be interpreted narrowly as short-run market disruptions or more broadly to encompass longer episodes when the value of the dollar appears out of line with economic fundamentals. The scale, scope, and frequency of these operations has varied considerably over the floating-exchange-rate period according to the U.S. administration's view of the efficacy of foreign exchange operations. Typically, the effects of foreign exchange operations on the reserves of depository institutions are offset by domestic open-market actions in a process known as sterilization.

The Policy Process

The main forums for formal deliberations on policy are the periodic meetings of the Federal Open Market Committee (FOMC). The FOMC is the steering group for policy, comprised of the 7 governors of the Board of the Federal Reserve System and 5 of the 12 presidents of the Reserve Banks, chosen on a rotating basis. (The president of the Federal Reserve Bank of New York is a permanent member.) The members of the FOMC, along with the nonvoting bank presidents, meet eight times a year to discuss policy and decide on operating instructions for the day-to-day conduct of policy. If necessary, the FOMC can delegate to the chair the authority to make intermeeting policy adjustments should conditions so warrant.

Twice a year, as mandated by the Full Employment and Balanced Growth Act of 1978, the Board of Governors of the Federal Reserve transmits to Congress reports reviewing the recent developments affecting economic trends and the objectives and plans of the FOMC with regard to the growth of the monetary and credit aggregates. The Board's chair presents testimony on the report. These plans for the aggregates are presented as targets or monitoring ranges for specific aggregates over the course of the calendar year. The reliance on rather wide target or monitoring ranges is a measure of the uncertainty attached to forecasting the economy.

References

Friedman, Milton, and Anna J. Schwartz, *A Monetary History of the United States, 1867–1960,* Princeton University Press, Princeton, N.J., 1963; Goodhart, Charles, *The Evolution of Central Banks,* MIT, Cambridge, Mass., 1988; Hallman, Jeffrey J., Richard D. Porter, and David H. Small,

"Is the Price Level Tied to the M2 Monetary Aggregate in the Long Run?," *American Economic Review,* vol. 81, no. 4, September 1991, pp. 841–858; Kohn, Donald L., "Monetary Policy in an Era of Change," *Federal Reserve Bulletin,* vol. 79, February 1989, pp. 53–57; Mauskopf, Eileen, "The Transmission Channels of Monetary Policy: How Have They Changed?" *Federal Reserve Bulletin,* vol. 76, December 1990, pp. 985–1008; Pauls, B. Dianne, "U.S. Exchange Policy: Bretton Woods to Present," *Federal Reserve Bulletin,* vol. 76, November 1990, pp. 891–908.

(*See also* Federal Reserve System; Inflation; Interest rates; Monetary policy; Money supply; Open market operations; Selective credit controls)

Vincent Reinhart

Federal Reserve System

The Federal Reserve System, our nation's central bank, was created by the Federal Reserve Act of 1913. Prior to the creation of the System, frequent financial panics arising from imbalances in the supply of money and credit had led to periodic episodes of bank failures, associated business bankruptcies, and general economic contractions. Following a particularly severe panic in 1907, several proposals were put forward for the creation of an institution designed to counter such financial disruptions. After considerable debate, the Federal Reserve System was established. Its original purposes were to provide an elastic currency—by accommodating temporary fluctuations in the demand for money and credit, to act as lender of last resort to commercial banks, and to improve the regulation and supervision of the banking system.

Over the years, it became clear that these original purposes were really part of broader national and financial objectives, including full employment, maximum sustainable economic growth, price stability, and reasonable balance in international transactions. Such objectives have been articulated by the Congress in several pieces of legislation, the most recent of which was the Full Employment and Balanced Growth Act of 1978. Among other things, this act calls upon the Federal Reserve to make public its objectives for money and credit as well as the relationships between these objectives and the economic goals of the administration and Congress. To enable the System to function more effectively in helping achieve the nation's economic goals, Congress also has amended the original Federal Reserve Act several times. The Depository Institutions Deregulation and Monetary Control Act of 1980, for example, was designed in part to enhance the System's ability to influence money and credit, which is the Federal Reserve's primary lever over economic activity and price trends.

The basic goal of monetary policy is to ensure that, over time, expansion of money and credit will be adequate for the long-run needs of a growing economy at reasonably stable prices. By fostering price stability—an environment in which inflation does not distort the decision-making processes of households and businesses—the Federal Reserve can lay the groundwork for maximum, sustainable economic growth over time. In the short to intermediate run, monetary policy also is conducted so as to combat cyclical economic fluctuations.

In addition to shaping monetary policy, the Federal Reserve also plays other, complementary roles designed to promote a sound and stable financial system. The System's role in bank supervision and regulation, for example, is intrinsic to its responsibility for the financial stability of the economy. In carrying out its mandate as a bank regulator, the Federal Reserve works with other agencies to promote a sound banking system, which is essential to the health of the economy and financial markets. The Fed plays a key part in the payments system as well, facilitating the smooth and reliable flow of funds upon which the economy rests by distributing currency and coin, clearing checks, and providing for electronic fund transfers. The System also administers a number of statutes designed to ensure that the public is well informed about its financial institutions and that credit is provided in a nondiscriminatory manner. Finally, as lender of last resort to the banking system, the Federal Reserve stands as a ready source of liquidity should crises or panics arise in financial markets.

By design, the Federal Reserve System enjoys a substantial degree of independence in its day-to-day decisions from the executive and legislative branches of government. Congress provided this independence in order to insulate the conduct of monetary policy from short-run political pressures. At the same time, however, all appointments to the Board that governs the Federal Reserve System are made by the President subject to the approval of the Senate, and, in accordance with the Full Employment and Balanced Growth Act of 1978, the System must report to the Congress twice a year on its monetary policies. In addition, the Federal Reserve is in frequent contact with other policymaking groups within the government, including the Treasury Department, the Council of Economic Advisers, the Office of Management and Budget, and several congressional committees. In view of these circumstances, and because the Federal Reserve works within the framework of the overall economic objectives established by the government, it is perhaps most accurate to characterize the System as "independent within government."

Structure and Organization

The organization of the Federal Reserve System reflects both the inherent complexities of central banking and the intent of the System's designers to ensure that it be both well-insulated from political influence and somewhat decentralized. The principal components of the System are the Board of Governors, the Federal Open Market Committee, and the Federal Reserve Banks. In 1990, the System employed over 25,000 people and incurred operating expenses of approximately $1.5 billion, of which nearly $200 million was accounted for by printing, issuing, and redeeming Federal Reserve notes.

The apex of the Federal Reserve's organization is the Board of Governors in Washington, D.C. The Board is an agency of the federal government consisting of seven members appointed by the President of the United States and confirmed by the Senate. Members' terms are for 14 years, and once a member has completed a full term, reappointment is not permitted. Terms are structured so that one expires every other year, providing for continuity of membership and also limiting the influence a particular President may have on the Board's composition. The President designates two members of the Board to act as its chair and vice chair, each for renewable terms of 4 years, also subject to Senate approval. Although the Board's responsibilities are many and varied, including regulation of various banking institutions, oversight of the operations of the 12 Federal Reserve banks, monitoring of the nation's payment system, and the implementation of federal laws pertaining to consumer credit, the Board's prime function is the formulation of monetary policy. The Board determines—within statutory limits—the percentages of various types of deposits that depository institutions must hold as reserves. The Board also reviews and approves the level of the discount rate—the rate of interest charged on loans that Federal Reserve banks make to depositories. Most important, the members of the Board constitute a majority of the Federal Open Market Committee (FOMC), which directs the conduct of the System's open-market operations and thereby the general course of monetary policy.

The membership of the FOMC includes, in addition to the 7 members of the Board of Governors, 5 of the 12 presidents of the Federal Reserve banks. The president of the Federal Reserve Bank of New York is a permanent member of the Committee, whereas the other Reserve Bank presidents serve 1-year terms on a rotating basis. By tradition, the Committee elects the chair of the Board of Governors as its chair and the president of the New York bank as its vice chair. The Committee meets approximately eight times a year in the Board's offices in Washington, although telephone consultations or other meetings may be held as necessary.

The FOMC is the most important policymaking body in the Federal Reserve System. It provides general direction for open-market operations, which are the most flexible and powerful tool of monetary policy. These operations, which involve the purchase and sale of government and federal agency securities in the domestic securities market, are carried out by the domestic trading desk of the Federal Reserve Bank of New York, under the auspices of the FOMC. By manipulating the cost and availability of bank reserves, open-market operations, together with discount window policy and reserve requirements, are designed to create overall monetary and credit conditions consistent with the nation's economic objectives. In addition to operations in the domestic securities markets, the FOMC also authorizes and directs operations in foreign exchange markets. Although foreign exchange policy is the statutory responsibility of the Treasury, most decisions are made jointly by the Treasury and the Federal Reserve, and the foreign exchange desk of the New York Fed actually handles the foreign currency transactions for both parties.

Other functions of the Federal Reserve System—including operation of the payments system, distribution of coin and currency, examination of certain types of banks, and fiscal agency functions for the Treasury—are implemented through a network of 12 Federal Reserve banks, which are located in Boston, New York, Philadelphia, Cleveland, Richmond, Atlanta, Chicago, St. Louis, Minneapolis, Kansas City, Dallas, and San Francisco. Branches of Federal Reserve banks have been established in 25 other cities. The Board of Governors in Washington provides general oversight and supervision for the operations of the regional Federal Reserve banks.

Federal Reserve banks operate under boards of nine directors, three of whom are appointed by the Board of Governors; the rest are elected by commercial banks that are members of the System. The directors of each Reserve bank select its president and first vice president, subject to the approval of the Board of Governors. They also oversee the operations of their bank, including the conditions under which loans are made to depository institutions and the rate of interest charged on these loans, also under the direct review and supervision of the Board of Governors.

Reserve banks collect a wide array of banking and financial data from depository institutions. These data are transmitted to the Board, where they are compiled and made available to the public in weekly and monthly statistical releases dealing with the monetary aggregates, interest rates, bank credit, and exchange rates. Data also are collected and published on industrial production and consumer and business finances. The research staffs at the Board and at the Reserve banks use this information, in conjunction with data collected by other public and private institutions, to assess the state of the economy and the relationships between the financial markets and economic activity. Staff members provide background for policy decisions of the Board and the FOMC by preparing detailed economic analyses and projections.

To provide additional assistance in conducting its complex and varied responsibilities, the System makes use of advisory and working committees. The Federal Reserve Act stipulates that a Federal Advisory Council, 12 private bankers elected by the Reserve banks, meet with the Board of Governors at least four times a year to proffer advice and policy recommendations on economic and banking developments. Other advisory groups include the Consumer Advisory Council and the Thrift Industry Advisory Council. The former group confers with the Board on consumer matters, and the latter organization, made up of representatives of savings banks, savings and loan associations, and credit unions, discusses developments in the thrift industry.

The Federal Reserve System derives its earnings primarily from interest on its holdings of securities acquired through open market operations and, to a lesser extent, from interest on its foreign currency assets, discount loans to depository institutions, capital gains on asset sales, and fees from services provided to depositories. In 1990, the total income of the Federal Reserve System amounted to about $25.5 billion. The Federal Reserve's income is allocated first to the payment of expenses and then to the statutory 6 percent dividend on Federal Reserve stock paid to institutions which are members of the System. Remaining earnings, which in 1990 totaled about $23.5 billion, are then paid into the U.S. Treasury. Since the Federal Reserve System was established, about 95 percent of the System's earnings have been paid into the Treasury. Even though the Federal Reserve turns over the bulk of its revenues to the Treasury, it keeps enough to cover its own expenses: By statute, the System is exempted from the congressional appropriations process.

Supervisory and Regulatory Responsibilities

Recognizing the importance of a sound banking system to the overall health of the economy and financial markets, the Federal Reserve Act cited as one of its purposes "to establish a more effective supervision of banking." Although the Federal Reserve System shares this responsibility with other federal agencies, the System is unique in its combination of monetary policy and regulatory roles. These two roles, moreover, are overlapping and reinforcing. The Federal Reserve brings to its decisions on supervisory and regulatory matters a wide perspective on the financial markets garnered from its monetary policy deliberations and an awareness of the general effects that actions affecting depository institutions may have on other sectors of the economy. Similarly, experience gained in the process of supervision and regulation enables monetary policy decisions to be grounded in a more knowledgeable assessment of how such decisions will interact with the depository system and financial markets more generally.

The Federal Reserve has primary supervisory authority over the domestic and international operations of all state-chartered banks that are members of the Federal Reserve System, all Edge Act and agreement corporations (domestic subsidiaries of U.S. banks licensed to do an international banking business), the U.S. activities of foreign banking organizations, and, perhaps most important, all bank holding companies. The Federal Reserve's supervisory authority over bank holding companies arises from the Bank Holding Company Act of 1956, as amended. Since most large commercial banks are owned by bank holding companies, this statutory authority accords the System supervisory responsibility for banking organizations that control the vast majority of deposits and assets in the U.S. banking system.

In examining an institution that falls under its supervisory purview, the Federal Reserve typically appraises the soundness of the institution's assets; evaluates its internal policies, operations, and management; analyzes certain key financial factors such as capital, earnings, and liquidity; reviews compliance with relevant banking laws and regulations; and makes an overall determination of the institution's solvency. In the case of bank holding companies, the System also examines any significant nonbank subsidiaries. If the Federal Reserve determines that the condition of an institution is not satisfactory, the System is responsible for requiring that organization to take steps to correct the situation. When the weakness of an institution reaches a critical level, the Federal Reserve, in conjunction with other government agencies, may play a significant role in designing a plan for financial and managerial assistance or, if the case warrants, for taking prompt and corrective action to liquidate the institution.

In the international arena, the Federal Reserve has statutory responsibilities with respect to the supervision and regulation of the international operations of U.S. member banks, Edge Act corporations, and bank holding companies. The Board of Governors has been given broad discretionary powers by the Congress to regulate the overseas activities of these institutions with the aim of allowing U.S. banks to be competitive with institutions of the host country. With regard to the U.S. operations of foreign banks, the International Banking Act of 1978 granted important supervisory and regulatory authority to the Federal Reserve as well as to other government agencies. Following rapid growth in the activities of foreign banks in the United States and a concomitant increase in their competitive impact upon domestic markets, this Act was designed to promote competitive equality by giving foreign banks operating in this country the same powers and subjecting them to the same restrictions and obligations that apply to domestically chartered institutions. The Federal Reserve's regulatory and supervisory authority was further expanded by the Foreign Bank Supervision Enhancement Act of 1991, which requires Federal Reserve approval to establish a branch, agency, commercial lending company, or representative office of a foreign bank in the United States and permits the termination of a license for a U.S. office under certain circumstances.

The Federal Reserve System also has statutory responsibility for the administration of several pieces of legislation designed to regulate bank structure, including the Bank Holding Company Act of 1956, as amended, the Bank Merger Act of 1960, as amended, and the Change in Bank Control Act of 1970. Under these acts, the acquisition of banks and closely related nonbanking activities by bank holding companies is subject to Board approval, as are mergers and other changes of control at state-chartered member banks and bank holding companies. In considering merger applications and applications by bank holding companies to acquire other institutions, the Board looks at the likely effects of the acquisition on bank competition, the convenience and needs for banking services of the communities affected, and the financial and managerial resources and prospects of the banking institutions involved. The Board's primary objectives are to promote the safety and soundness of the banking system, protect the public interest, and maintain a separation between banking and commerce. The Board does allow bank holding companies to engage in certain nonbank activities, however, if these activities are closely related to banking and can be shown to stimulate competition and to improve the financial services available to the public.

In recent years, the Federal Reserve System has been required by the Congress to implement a number of statutes designed to ensure that consumers have sufficient information and are treated fairly in credit and other financial transactions. The System is responsible for writing and implementing regulations to carry out many of these statutes and for the enforcement of these laws at state-chartered member banks. These laws include: the Truth-in-Lending Act, which requires financial institutions to disclose to the consumer the costs and terms of credit; the Equal Credit Opportunity Act, which prohibits discrimination in the granting of credit on the basis of sex, race, color, religion, etc.; the Electronic Funds Transfer Act, which provides a basic framework regarding the rights, liabilities, and responsibilities of consumers and financial institutions who use electronic transfer services; the Home Mortgage Disclosure Act, which requires depositories to disclose the geographic distribution of their mortgage-related lending so that the public can make informed decisions about whether institutions are meeting the housing credit needs of their communities; and, the Community Reinvestment Act, which encourages depositories to help meet the credit needs of their communities, particularly in neighborhoods of families with low or moderate income.

Federal Reserve Bank Services

The Federal Reserve banks, as the operating arms of the nation's central bank, provide a variety of services to depository institutions, the general public, and the U.S. government and its agencies. Many of these services relate to the nation's payments system, and others involve fiscal-agency functions, such as holding U.S. Treasury deposits and issuing, servicing, and redeeming U.S. government securities.

Since its inception, the Federal Reserve System has played an important role in the nation's payments mechanism, which is designed to move funds among financial institutions across the country. Indeed, a major reason for creating the Federal Reserve was to ensure that the nation had a safe and efficient means for transferring funds within the banking system. The System meets its payment system responsibilities by distributing currency and coin, processing checks for collection, operating electronic funds transfer networks, and providing for transfers of securities and coupon collection.

The Monetary Control Act of 1980 reaffirmed that Congress desired that the Federal Reserve participate actively in the payments system. The Act also extended Federal Reserve payment system services, as well as discount window privileges and reserve requirements, to all depository institutions. Previously, access to Fed services had been limited to member banks. In addition, the Act required the Federal Reserve to charge fees for many of these services, which had previously been available free of charge to member banks. These fees were required to be set in such a way as to recover the cost of providing the services, where the costs were to include not only the Federal Reserve's actual operating expenses but also estimates of the taxes and costs of capital the System would incur were it a private firm. By specifying that the Federal Reserve charge for services in this way, the Congress intended to encourage a more efficient and economic payments mechanism through explicit pricing and increased competition among public and private providers of payment services. The nation's payments mechanism has indeed become more efficient, largely through technological advances that have reduced the costs of check processing and electronic funds transfers.

One area of the payments system that the Federal Reserve handles single-handedly is the distribution of currency and coin. When the public needs to replenish its supply of cash, depository institutions order currency from their local Federal Reserve bank or branch, and the face value of that cash is then debited from the depository's reserve account at the Fed. When the public's need for cash diminishes, by contrast, depositories return the currency to the Reserve bank and have their accounts credited accordingly. Using sophisticated equipment to count cash, identify counterfeits, and destroy currency that is unfit for circulation, the Reserve banks paid out approximately $25 billion of net new currency and coin over 1990. With the proliferation of checks and electronic funds transfers, however, the use of currency as a payments vehicle has declined markedly since the creation of the Federal Reserve. In fact, currency and coin now account for only a very small proportion of all transfers of funds in the United States, and evidence suggests that a large fraction of Federal Reserve notes circulate outside of our country.

The Federal Reserve banks also collect and clear checks. When a depository institution receives checks drawn on other institutions, it may send them for collection to those institutions directly, or indirectly through a local clearinghouse, a correspondent institution, or a Federal Reserve office. In 1990, the Federal Reserve banks, together with their branches and several regional check processing centers, cleared approximately 18.5 billion checks with an average daily value of more than $50 billion. Although the Federal Reserve usually credits the reserve accounts of payee institutions on the day it receives the checks, it does not debit the accounts of payor institutions until it subsequently delivers the checks to those depositories. As a result, the same deposit may be on the books of two different institutions for several days, creating a phenomenon called "Federal Reserve float." Float has declined sharply since the 1970s, as the System has taken great strides to speed the movement of checks back to the payor institution. For the most part, this reduction in float has come at the expense of payor institutions through more prompt debiting of their Federal Reserve accounts. The System recovers the cost of the remaining float, as required by the Monetary Control Act, through fees to the payee institution. In response to the imposition of these fees, the use of private check-clearing arrangements has expanded.

Electronic fund transfer (EFT) systems have been evolving throughout the world in recent decades as a fast, secure, and less costly means of transferring money. The Federal Reserve System is directly involved in two types of EFT services: transfers of funds by wire and through automated clearinghouses (ACHs). Using Fedwire, which connects Federal Reserve offices, depositories, the Treasury, and other government agencies, banks can transfer large quantities of funds in and out of their Federal Reserve accounts, usually in a matter of minutes. Over 11,000 depository institutions used Fedwire in 1990 to effect more than 64 million transfers valued at nearly $200 trillion. Fedwire also handles book-entry security transfers, which enable holders of Treasury and government agency securities to exchange claims on these securities with other institutions throughout the country. This book-entry security system, begun in 1968, has grown rapidly in recent years, with nearly 11 million transfers valued at over $100 trillion conducted in 1990 alone.

The Federal Reserve also operates a number of ACHs, which provide clearing services to all depository institutions for electronically originated credits and debits.

Relative to paper checks, ACHs offer greater timeliness, increased convenience, and greater security. Many businesses and government agencies make their recurring payments for salaries, wages, interest, dividends, and the like through ACHs, with the proceeds credited directly to the payee's account at a depository without the prior issue of a paper check. Consumers also authorize their depository to make regular, recurring payments through ACHs for such obligations as mortgages or utility bills. In 1990, the Federal Reserve banks processed more than 1.3 billion ACH transactions valued at about $4.3 trillion; nearly 40 percent of these transactions were on behalf of the federal government.

As fiscal agents of the United States, the Federal Reserve banks function as the federal government's banker. They maintain the Treasury's checking accounts, clearing checks drawn against these accounts and processing funds transferred from these accounts through ACHs. They also monitor the tax receipts deposited in the special, interest-bearing tax and loan accounts maintained by the Treasury at over 12,000 depositories throughout the country, holding the collateral that those depositories pledge to support those deposits, and transferring funds out of those accounts and into the Treasury's accounts at the Fed whenever the Treasury wishes to make a payment. In addition, the Reserve Banks handle the operations involved in selling, servicing, and redeeming marketable Treasury debt as well as U.S. savings bonds. Finally, primarily through the Federal Reserve Bank of New York, the System also acts as fiscal agent for many foreign central banks and international organizations. Foreign official institutions channel a significant portion of their U.S. dollar receipts and payments through accounts maintained by the Federal Reserve Bank of New York. The New York Fed also holds assets, primarily U.S. Treasury securities and gold, in custody for these foreign institutions. The Bank imposes a fee on these institutions for most of its services.

All decisions related to the Federal Reserve banks' services are made independently of the System's functions in the areas of bank supervision and regulation and monetary policy. In essence, the System has erected an inviolable firewall between its role as a principal in the payments system and its monetary policy responsibilities, to ensure that it does not compete unfairly with private sector providers of services to depository institutions.

Brief History

Almost all nations have central banks, and among developed countries, the Federal Reserve is a relative newcomer. Prior to the creation of the Federal Reserve, there existed no central authority in the United States capable of exerting control over the supply of money and credit. Without an elastic currency and a lender of last resort, the U.S. economy was susceptible to periodic financial crises arising from imbalances in the supply of money that often resulted in severe economic contractions. An especially severe panic in 1907 made it patently clear that the lack of a central bank was a serious gap in the economic structure of the United States.

To remedy this deficiency, the Federal Reserve Act, drafted by Representative Carter Glass and Senator Robert Owen with the active participation of President Woodrow Wilson, was passed in 1913. It called for the creation of a system of regional Federal Reserve banks under the general supervision and direction of a Board of Governors in Washington. The original Board included the Treasury Secretary as well as the Comptroller of the Currency.

In the System's early years, monetary policy actions were limited primarily to making discount loans to member banks, largely at the discretion of the individual Reserve banks. After World War I, the Reserve banks began to engage in uncoordinated open-market purchases, designed primarily to increase their earnings. When it became clear that these open-market operations had a pronounced effect on bank reserves and deposits, some people in the System, particularly the president of the Federal Reserve Bank of New York, Benjamin Strong, argued for the coordinated, systemwide use of open-market operations as a counter-cyclical tool to influence reserve and credit conditions. Although the Open Market Investment Committee (OMIC) was created in 1923, it did not have exclusive power to approve the open-market operations of all Reserve banks, and many people in the System remained unconvinced of the need for, and utility of, coordinated open-market operations.

The absence of consensus concerning either the role or the power of the Federal Reserve to respond to cyclical forces, exacerbated by the untimely death of Benjamin Strong in 1928, proved to be a severe handicap to the System during the Great Depression. In fact, some have argued that the lack of sustained, aggressive open-market reserve infusions by the System during the early 1930s was largely responsible for the precipitous decline in the money supply which contributed to the disastrous contraction of economic activity.

To correct the shortcomings in the System's structure, several pieces of legislation, most notably the Banking Act of 1935, were adopted during the Depression. The basic thrust of these statutes was to consolidate the decision-making authority of the System. The Board of Governors was given authority to adjust reserve requirements of member banks and to supervise and oversee the granting of discount window credits by the Reserve banks. The Secretary of the Treasury and the Comptroller of the currency were removed from the Board and, most important, the Federal Open Market Committee was established as a statutory body to determine one systemwide, coordinated approach to open-market operations.

During World War II, monetary policy concerns took a back seat to the task of financing government expenditures. To help the Treasury finance its debt more cheaply, the Federal Reserve agreed to peg interest rates at low levels, essentially forfeiting an independent role for monetary policy. In 1951, the Federal Reserve and the Treasury reached an accord which enabled the System to resume an active and independent monetary policy. In the years since the accord, the Federal Reserve has sought to utilize monetary policy to combat short-run, cyclical economic fluctuations while putting in place the monetary and financial conditions necessary for maximum, sustainable economic growth over time.

References

Board of Governors of the Federal Reserve System, *The Federal Reserve System Purposes and Functions,* Washington, D.C., 1984; Board of Governors of the Federal Reserve System, *Seventy-Eighth Annual Report,* Washington, D.C., 1991; Meulendyke, Ann-Marie, *U.S. Monetary Policy and Financial Markets,* Federal Reserve Bank of New York, New York, 1989; Simpson, Thomas D., *Money, Banking and Economic Analysis,* 3d ed., Prentice-Hall, Englewood Cliffs, N.J., 1987.

(*See also* Banking system; Federal Reserve policy; Monetary policy; Open-market operations)

Joshua Feinman

Federal Trade Commission

The Federal Trade Commission (FTC) is a U.S. government agency created by the Federal Trade Commission Act of 1914, which lays down a general prohibition against use in commerce of unfair methods of competition and unfair or deceptive acts or practices. The Commission is headed by five commissioners, nominated by the President and confirmed by the Senate, each serving a 7-year term. The President names one commissioner to act as chair of the Commission. No more than three commissioners can be of the same political party.

The Federal Trade Commission attempts to ensure that the nation's markets operate competitively, that consumers have accurate information about the services and products they purchase, and that other federal agencies, state legislatures, and various other organizations receive economic analyses of potential actions. In recent years, for example, the FTC has provided extensive comments to the legislatures of about one-half the states concerning the competitive effects of proposed legislation. In addition, comments have been provided by the FTC to such groups as the American Bar Association, the National Association of Attorneys General, and to other federal agencies such as the Department of Agriculture, the Environmental Protection Agency, the Securities and Exchange Commission, and the U.S. Customs Service.

There are 10 offices of the FTC in major U.S. cities in addition to the Washington, D.C., head office. The Commission is divided into three bureaus: (1) the Bureau of Consumer Protection; (2) the Bureau of Competition; and (3) the Bureau of Economics. The Bureau of Consumer Protection is further divided into divisions of advertising practices, credit practices, marketing practices, service industry practices, and enforcement. The FTC conducts extensive economic and legal studies to assist it in deciding whether to bring enforcement action in a particular instance; the FTC also provides extensive economic research services to the Congress and to the executive branch of the U.S. government at their request.

Enforcement Actions

The FTC may begin its investigations in different ways, and it has different routes it may follow to remedy a problem. Most investigations are private in order to spare a company from unfavorable publicity should the investigation reveal no problem. If the FTC believes a violation of law occurred, it may attempt to obtain voluntary compliance by entering into a "consent order" with the company. A company agreeing to such an order need not admit any wrongdoing, but it agrees to stop the disputed practices outlined in the complaint. When the parties cannot agree on a consent order, the FTC may issue an administrative complaint. If an administrative complaint is issued, a proceeding is held before an administrative law judge similar to a court trial. Each party submits evidence, testimony is heard, witnesses are examined and cross-examined. If the administrative judge finds a law violation has occurred, a cease-and-desist order may be issued or other appropriate relief may be forthcoming. Decisions by administrative law judges may be appealed to the full Commission.

Final decisions issued by the Commission may be appealed to the U.S. Court of Appeals, with further appeal ultimately possible to the U.S. Supreme Court. If the FTC's position is upheld in court, its order becomes final, and the FTC may seek consumer redress in court if that seems indicated. Violations of the FTC's order in the future can be cured with injunctions or civil penalties.

In some circumstances, the FTC may go directly to court to seek an injunction, civil penalties, cease-and-desist orders, or other appropriate redress for injured consumers. Direct court action usually is taken in case of ongoing consumer fraud. Direct access to the courts allows the FTC to stop such frauds before a great number of consumers have been injured. The FTC also goes to court quickly when seeking injunctions against proposed mergers. The purpose is to prevent firms from commingling assets in such a way that it would be impossible to disentangle the firms. Often, mere announcement that the FTC plans to seek an injunction against a proposed merger is sufficient for the potential merging firms to change their plans.

The *Annual Reports* of the FTC contain a detailed listing of consent orders, administrative complaints, initial decisions, final decisions, injunctions, civil actions, and other actions taken. These *Annual Reports* provide a great deal of detailed information on specific companies involved in FTC actions, amounts of money recovered or saved through various actions, and FTC opinions on various state statutes proposed. Much of the information needed by the FTC to initiate investigations comes from consumer communications to the FTC. The Commission does not act to resolve individual problems, but if a significant number of consumers communicate with the Commission about a problem, an investigation is likely to be initiated. The Commission has a library open to the public at its head office with more than 1000 periodicals and more than 120,000 volumes dealing with legal, business, and economic matters.

References

U.S. Federal Trade Commission, *Annual Reports,* Washington, D.C., various years; U.S. Federal Trade Commission, *A Guide to The Federal Trade Commission,* Washington, D.C., 1991.

William J. Brown

Feedback (*see* Automation)

Financial distress

Parallel with the restructuring developments of the 1980s, a substantial body of literature has emerged on financial distress. Financial distress refers to some aspect of enterprise failure or insolvency. Flow basis insolvency can take two forms: A technical default occurs when a firm fails to meet one or more conditions of the financial agreements associated with its borrowing activities; technical insolvency occurs when cash flows are insufficient to meet debt service payments—interest and/or principal. Stock basis insolvency relates obligations to some definition or measure of assets. Accounting insolvency refers to a negative net worth. Legal insolvency relates obligations to the market value of a firm's assets. A firm is insolvent in an economic sense when the present value of expected cash flows is less than the present value of its obligations.

Voluntary Recontracting

When a firm experiences financial distress, the fundamental requirement is to identify and remedy the causes of its problems. This requires a review of and improvement in its strategies and operations. Reorganization and restructuring of management and control relationships in the firm may be necessary. In addition, financial readjustments may be required to keep the firm afloat while management and operating reorganizations are being carried out.

Two fundamental forms of recontracting are involved in financial readjustments. *Extension* is defined as a postponement of the date for the payment of interest or principal. *Composition* is a voluntary reduction or scaling down of creditors' claims on the debtor.

The procedures in a voluntary financial restructuring can avoid the complications of the legal processes. Initially a meeting is held between the debtor and creditors. A creditors' committee is usually appointed to negotiate with the debtor. After some meetings, a decision is made as to whether to continue with an informal "workout" procedure, to move to more formal legal recontracting, or to seek liquidation. If the negotiations remain informal, subsequent meetings are used to negotiate the recontracting.

Voluntary agreements often involve both extension of the date at which obligations must be paid as well as composition (reduction) of claims. In return, creditors receive some portion of equity ownership in the firm. This may even involve a shift from the previous control group to a new ownership control group. At a minimum, creditors will conduct closer monitoring and control of the firm in return for extension and/or composition.

Voluntary restructures, or workouts, have advantages and disadvantages. They are simpler than court-directed procedures. Lower legal investigative and accounting expenses are involved with greater flexibility in negotiations. Agreements can be reached more quickly, minimizing damage to the firm's reputation and its relationships with customers and suppliers. A major disadvantage of voluntary procedures is that agreement may be difficult to achieve with a large number of creditors or with creditors with divergent interests. Also, the debtor remains in control, which may result in the continued erosion of the firm's performance and assets. The use of court procedures confers some tax advantages which are lost under voluntary restructuring. When the debtor and creditors are able to work out recontracting terms in advance of initiating a Chapter 11 filing, the advantages of formal court procedures can be achieved through a "prepackaged bankruptcy." Delays and associated procedural costs are minimized at the same time that the legal and tax benefits of using the courts are obtained.

The Federal Bankruptcy Laws

Major bankruptcy statutes in the United States were enacted in 1898, 1938, and 1978. The 1978 act amended earlier bankruptcy laws whose provisions were regarded as inflexible and time consuming. The major parts of the 1978 act are Chapter 7 dealing with liquidation, Chapter 11 dealing with reorganization, and Chapter 13 for personal bankruptcies. Bankruptcy filings can be either voluntary or involuntary. The debtor remains in control unless the court specifies otherwise. An automatic stay is placed on interest and principal payments until completion of the reorganization. Interest accrues only on secured debt during the reorganization period.

Separate creditor committees may be created for different classes of creditors and owners. Financing after bankruptcy filing is given a priority status. The ability to obtain additional financing is often crucial in achieving a plan of reorganization. The 1978 act also permitted new uses for bankruptcy protection. It has been used as a means of negotiating new labor contracts (Continental and Eastern Airlines, Wilson Foods), consolidating liability suits (Manville and A. H. Robbins), and as a response to large damage awards (Texaco).

The Reorganization and Restructuring Processes

Two fundamental decisions need to be addressed by a firm in financial distress. The first is whether informal agreements can be reached with creditors. The second is whether the firm should be reorganized under bankruptcy proceedings or placed into liquidation. Both involve decisions as to how much creditors will realize under each alternative. For example, in the early stages of the financial distress of the Olympia & York companies in 1992, its owners, the Reichmann brothers, were of the opinion that creditors would perceive that more value would be preserved by avoiding formal reorganization proceedings. Hence the Reichmann brothers offered virtually no equity ownership compensation to O&Y's creditors in return for extending and scaling down its debts, and a voluntary restructuring of its debt could not be arranged with its creditors.

When the more formal legal procedures are employed, the traditional bases for evaluating a reorganization plan have been the standards of feasibility and fairness. The main tests of feasibility are that the firm can be successfully reorganized and restructured. The causes of financial difficulty must be uncovered and eliminated. If old management has been ineffective, new management talents must be brought in, obsolete inventories disposed of, and operations streamlined. Plant and equipment may need modernization. The operating activities of the firm, such as production, marketing, and administration, may need improvement. New products or markets may need to be developed to sustain earnings. Sometimes a merger is necessary to accomplish these requirements.

The basic doctrine of fairness states that claims must be recognized in the order of their legal priority. This is referred to as the "absolute priority doctrine" (APD). The legal priority of claims is set out in Chapter 5, Section 507, of the 1978 Bankruptcy Act:

1. Claims of secured creditors. If the unsecured creditors approve the plan as a class, the deficiency claims of secured creditors receive the same status as unsecured creditors.

2. Legal and other costs involved in the bankruptcy proceedings.

3. Expenses incurred after an involuntary procedure has begun but before a trustee is appointed.

4. Wages due workers earned within 3 months prior to the filing.

5. Claims for unpaid contributions to employee benefit plans to have been made within 6 months prior to the filing.

6. Unsecured claims for customer deposits, up to $900 per person.

7. Federal, state, and local taxes.

8. Unfunded pension plan liabilities up to 30 percent of the sum of common and preferred equity. The balance is a claim at the same level as general creditors.

9. General or unsecured creditors. Includes the deficiency claims of secured creditors and the amount remaining from item 8 above.

10. Preferred stockholders up to par value.

11. Common stockholders.

A decision must be made as to whether the value of the rehabilitated firm is greater or less than the liquidation value of its parts. Liquidation values depend on the degree of specialization of the firm's assets. The greater value of a firm after reorganization than in liquidation is often used to force creditors to compromise, even if the settlement is not viewed as fair.

The plan of reorganization will be evaluated by the bankruptcy court. A plan must provide proof of values for claims to be issued and assets to be retained or sold. Management may oppose liquidation even if it is the highest-valued strategy, because they may lose their jobs. Acceptance of a reorganization plan generally requires approval from all creditor classes. However, if the court views the plan as feasible and fair, it may "cram-down" a plan, following absolute priority. Shareholders have the right to vote, allowing them to hold up the approval process. They can use this right to extract valuable claims. Some classes of claimants may provide future financing as a basis for improving their position in bankruptcy versus absolute priority. An argument for protecting some junior claims is the large uncertainty associated with forecasts of the firm's future value.

Empirical studies find frequent departures from absolute priority. However, the magnitudes of the deviations are relatively small. Recoveries can be in cash, cash plus notes, notes and shares, or shares alone. Data show that on average secured bonds and bank debt suffer the smallest write-downs, even with deviations from absolute priority. Secured debt received 96 percent of its original claims, 84 percent in cash. Convertible bonds and common stock received the smallest proportional recovery, 33 and 19 percent, respectively, on average; only a fraction was received in cash. When a bargaining class makes an additional cash or equivalent investment, its bargaining status is elevated significantly.

Economic Issues Related to Financial Distress

A central issue is whether bankruptcy costs are substantial. If bankruptcy costs were insignificant, individual shareholder diversification could ignore firm-specific risks. The death and birth of firms would be relatively frictionless, and the organization values of firms could be ignored. Some writers have argued that bankruptcy costs must be insignificant because rational creditors (or a third party) would otherwise arrange private workouts where costs are minimal. However, asymmetric information and claimholder incentive conflicts may make private workouts difficult and potentially expensive. Court supervision during the bankruptcy process can ameliorate the holdout problem created by divergent creditor interests.

Costs of bankruptcy have been measured in a number of studies. Direct costs of bankruptcy include legal, accounting, advisory, and administrative fees. Direct costs of bankruptcy have been estimated as low as 1 to 2 percent up to 5 to 10 percent of the market value of the firm prior to bankruptcy filing.

Indirect costs of bankruptcy include: (1) The firm's lost right to make some decisions without legal approval; (2) financial distress may injure employees, customers, and suppliers; (3) management spends time working on the distress situation. Indirect costs can bring the total cost of bankruptcy up to 15 to 20 percent of the market value of the firm prior to filing. These do not include costs to other stakeholders. Suppliers lose their business to the distressed firm should it reduce or cease operations. Employees may become unemployed and may lose some pension benefits. Creditors suffer to the extent the values of their claims are reduced. Customers lose products. Managers and board members lose salaries and fees, as well as reputation.

A second major issue relates to the "underinvestment problem." Equity holders will sometimes forgo profitable investment opportunities because debt holders will be the major beneficiary. In the reorganization process, if debt holders reduce their claims, this will provide incentives to equity holders to undertake profitable opportunities.

Third, the postponement of the maturity date of the debt and the scaling-down process increase the cost of risky debt. The option to delay is an American option which, of course, increases in value with the extension of the maturity date. The required risk-adjusted interest rates increase from 50 to 255 basis points under alternative assumptions about the postponement of the maturity of debt, the proportion of costs saved paid to equity holders, the costs of bankruptcy as a proportion of the value of the firm, the original maturity of debt, and the time at which creditors buy out an option to remain in Chapter 11 (Franks and Torous, 1989).

Another economic issue is whether Chapter 11 gives too much power to managers in the reorganization process. The rights of the debtor management to remain in control of the firm and to propose the reorganization plan is said to give it too much power under the reorganization process to the disadvantage of the creditors. This issue remains under continued reassessment.

Liquidation and Assignment

Liquidation should occur when a firm is "worth more dead than alive." There are three types of liquidation: (1) In common-law assignment a debtor transfers the title of assets to a third party, which sells them, distributing the proceeds to the creditors. (2) In a statutory assignment a court appoints an assignee to liquidate assets and distribute the proceeds to creditors. All parties are notified of the assignment. (3) In an assignment plus settlement the creditors can agree beforehand that assignment represents a complete discharge of obligations. This is often handled by the adjustment bureau of a local credit managers' association.

Assignment saves time and expense relative to bankruptcy. The assignee may have more flexibility in disposing of assets than a bankruptcy trustee. Liquidation in bankruptcy has at least three advantages. It provides safeguards against fraud by the debtor during liquidation. It provides for an equitable distribution of the debtor's assets among the creditors. Insolvent debtors discharge their obligations and can begin a new enterprise.

Prediction and Returns

Formal models have been developed to predict financial distress in advance. Credit scoring is a method of estimating default probabilities. Altman (1968) pioneered the development of multiple discriminant analysis (MDA) to predict bankruptcy.

Stock prices also anticipate financial distress. Betker (1991) found that the average returns of all security holders are significantly negative for 2 years prior to default and positive (but not significant) during the following 4 years. He also found that security returns in the predefault period are negatively related to future write-downs and positively related to deviations from absolute priority. This is evidence that write-downs and deviations from absolute priority are partially anticipated.

References

Altman, Edward I., "Financial Ratios, Discriminant Analysis and the Prediction of Corporate Bankruptcy," *Journal of Finance*, vol. 23, September 1968, pp. 589–609; Altman, Edward I., "Bankruptcy and Reorganization," in Edward I. Altman (ed.) *Financial Handbook*, Wiley, New

York, 1981, section 35. Betker, Brian L., "An Analysis of the Returns to Stockholders and Bondholders in a Chapter 11 Reorganization," Jan. 18, 1991; Franks, Julian R., and Walter N. Torous, "An Empirical Investigation of U.S. Firms in Reorganization," *Journal of Finance,* vol. 44, 1989, pp. 747–779; Warner, J. B., "Bankruptcy Costs: Some Evidence," *Journal of Finance,* vol. 32, May 1977, pp. 337–347; Wruck, Karen Hopper, "Financial Distress, Reorganization, and Organizational Efficiency," *Journal of Financial Economics,* vol. 27, October 1990, pp. 419–444.

(*See also* Break-even analysis)

J. Fred Weston

Financial institutions

Financial institutions are of two types: (1) those providing financial intermediation, and (2) those providing direct financing. Both types of financial institutions aid in the process of moving funds from economic units with savings to economic units wishing to borrow funds so those units may spend more than they have available from their own resources. The assets of most (but not all) financial institutions are financial assets rather than physical assets such as machinery, plants, or transportation vehicles. Financial institutions are pivotal elements in the financial system of a nation.

Financial Intermediaries

Financial intermediaries hold as assets financial IOUs issued by borrowers and assets purchased in the money and capital markets. Intermediaries issue their own IOUs to customers. For example, customers of a commercial bank bring money to the bank and receive in return a promise by the bank to pay either to the depositor or to someone he or she designates all or part of the money originally deposited by the customer. The bank has received money and issued in return its IOU to the customer. Naturally, the bank invests the customer's money either in securities or in loans to borrowers (their IOUs to the bank). Commercial banks, savings and loan associations, mutual savings banks, and credit unions are called "deposit-type" financial intermediaries. Other types of financial intermediaries, such as insurance companies and pension funds, offer contracts to their retail customers rather than deposits and have come to be known as "contractual savings institutions."

The existence of financial intermediaries is of great value to the entire economy. Those with funds to invest benefit because the financial intermediaries offer services the customers want. For example, a person trying to save $25,000 to make a down payment on a house could accumulate the funds in a bank, savings and loan association, mutual savings bank, or credit union. The deposit account in the financial institution would pay interest, lessening the amount of money the depositor would need, and when the person wanted the money, it could be withdrawn immediately if it had been deposited in a demand deposit account. The depositor receives interest and high liquidity.

Similarly, borrowers from financial institutions benefit because they can go to a firm specializing in evaluating credit risks and in making loans. Because the institution makes many such loans, the cost per loan is low. The alternative to using financial institutions would be for savers to try to find a creditworthy person or firm that would borrow directly from the saver and pay the saver interest. The problem is that the borrower would want the money for a long time and could not repay whenever the saver wanted to use the money for making the down payment on a house. In other words, direct investment would lack liquidity for the saver, even if a satisfactory credit quality and interest rate could be negotiated.

Some of the more important financial intermediaries are (deposit-type) commercial banks, savings and loan associations, mutual savings banks, credit unions, (contractual) insurance companies, investment companies, finance companies, pension funds, real estate investment trusts, and leasing companies. Each type of business sells a specific financial service of benefit to the customer. Not all writers on financial markets agree as to exactly which types of businesses are financial intermediaries and which are other types of financial firms. Such firms as finance companies and investment companies (mutual funds) are the subject of some disagreement.

Investment companies (mutual funds) sell equity in the pool of securities the investment company manages, charging an investment fee for managing the securities. The securities issued by most investment companies are redeemable from the investment firm within approximately 1 week. The liquidity of such shares is therefore limited. However, some mutual funds provide checks depositors can write to redeem their shares plus wire transfer of funds within 1 day, offering as liquid an asset as a bank deposit. Such funds are primarily money-market mutual funds which invest in short-term securities whose prices do not change much, and they are highly liquid. The money-market mutual funds have grown to a size and stature in the financial system where they offer significant competition to deposit-type financial intermediaries. In sum, most mutual funds may be thought of as contractual financial intermediaries, although money-market mutual funds may be thought of as very similar to deposit-type financial institutions.

Other Financial Institutions

Some financial institutions provide services of a different type to their customers. Securities brokers and dealers, for example, facilitate direct investment from economic units with surplus funds to business firms wishing to obtain money by selling stock, bonds, or debentures. The securities dealers provide the service of obtaining the securities for their customers, but the dealers do not provide liquidity to investors, and the securities firms do not invest in the securities themselves (except to take inventory or speculative positions).

Investment banking firms are enormously important financial institutions which are not financial intermediaries. The investment banking firms do not issue their IOUs to the public in highly liquid form, although the firms may undertake both short- and long-term borrowing to finance themselves. Investment bankers assist firms in marketing their equity or debt securities by either (1) serving on a best-efforts basis, or (2) purchasing the securities from the issuing firm outright, then reselling them.

Mortgage bankers operate somewhat similarly to investment bankers. Using their own permanent financing plus any transitory financing needed, they acquire mortgages and subsequently resell them, usually in blocks of similar types of mortgages, to pension funds, savings and loan associations, and insurance companies. The U.S. government and some state governments operate agencies which finance certain types of activities for either individuals or businesses, using borrowing by the government entity to finance their activity. Those government agencies provide substantial amounts of financing, but because they do not provide liquid IOUs to those financing them and because they could not operate without the umbrella authority of the government which created them, they are not here classified as financial intermediaries. The Federal Home Loan Bank and the Federal National Mortgage Association have the largest amounts of loans outstanding among federal lending agencies.

Some loans are made by pawn firms, friends, relatives, and in other informal ways in our society, and they would also qualify as direct financial operations rather than as financial intermediaries. The total amount of such lending, including loans at illegally high rates of interest or for illegal purposes, is unknown. One type of financial institution holds largely physical assets, rather than financial assets, the safe deposit company. Such firms provide safe deposit facilities and often such ancillary services as escrow services to their customers.

References

Kidwell, David S., and Richard L. Peterson, *Financial Institutions, Markets, and Money,* 4th ed., Dryden, Hinsdale, Ill., 1990; Rose, Peter S., and Donald R. Fraser, *Financial Institutions,* 3d ed., Irwin, Homewood, Ill., 1988; Henning, Charles, William Pigott, and Robert H. Haney, *Financial Markets and the Economy,* Prentice-Hall, Englewood Cliffs, N.J., 1988.

(*See also* Banking system; Capital markets and money markets; Commercial banks: problems and solutions; Interest rates; Money markets; Mutual funds; Thrift institutions: problems and challenges)

William J. Brown

Financial instruments

Financial instruments are documents denominated in money usually indicating an obligation by one party to pay to another, but they may take any form. The familiar check is a negotiable financial instrument which may be transferred from one person to another by endorsement. The dollar bill is a financial instrument which may be transferred from one person to another without endorsement. For convenience of reference, financial instruments may be allocated to various categories, including capital markets, money markets, and financial transfers.

Capital Market Instruments

Securities with an original maturity of over 1 year are traded in the capital market. Stock certificates, bonds, debentures, certificates of deposit with maturities over 1 year, collateralized mortgage obligations, and beneficial interests in business trusts are all capital-market financial instruments. Most capital-market financial instruments are readily transferable from one owner to another, and there is a ready market for most such instruments. Stock certificates, for example, are endorsed on their back and sent to the transfer agent, who cancels the old stock certificate and issues a new stock certificate in the name of the new owner. Some securities exist only in book entry form without issuance of any certificate, some securities are registered with certificates issued, and some securities are in bearer form. Those in bearer form require no endorsement. Physically handing a bearer security from one owner to the new owner completes transfer.

Funds flowing through the capital market finance long-term investments, such as construction of roads, bridges, buildings, purchases of ownership positions in businesses, construction of apartments, and purchase of transportation equipment such as trucks and busses. Households, insurance companies, pension funds, savings and loan associations, mutual savings banks, and commercial banks are all large suppliers of funds to the capital markets. In dollar volume, mortgages on real property are the most important financial instrument traded in the capital markets, followed by common stocks, corporate and foreign bonds, U.S. Treasury notes and bonds, state and local government securities, and consumer installment debt.

Money-Market Instruments

Financial instruments in the money market have an original maturity of 1 year or less. Commercial paper (corporate IOUs), U.S. Treasury bills, negotiable certificates of deposit, banker's acceptances, and short-term debt of local governments are familiar types of financial instruments in the money market. In addition, banks trade among themselves reserves on deposit with the Federal Reserve System in what is known as the "Federal funds market."

There is a very large international market participated in by lenders and borrowers in Europe, Asia, the Middle East, and elsewhere on the globe comprising what is usually referred to as the "Eurocurrency" market. In that market, the world's major trading currencies are loaned and borrowed daily by both financial institutions, large corporations, and, to a lesser extent, by pension funds, mutual funds, and similar organizations. Some of these transactions have original maturities under 1 year; others have longer maturities and would be classed as capital-market transactions. (A "Eurocurrency" is a deposit in any currency other than the indigenous currency, e.g., a eurodollar deposit would be a dollar-denominated deposit in Switzerland.)

Trading in the money market, in contrast to capital-market transactions, primarily involves short-term liquidity adjustments of individual traders in the market. Banks with surplus reserves lend them to banks needing reserves for a day or two, corporations borrow or lend short-term funds, depending upon the seasonal state of their business, cities and states borrow in anticipation of taxes to be collected shortly, and financial and nonfinancial firms lend or borrow in international markets. To a very limited degree, some very aggressive borrowers may finance purchases of long-term assets with short-term loans which they renew frequently. That practice, however, is extremely risky because funds may not be available when the short-term loan matures, or the rate at which the loan can be renewed may be extremely high.

Trading in U.S. Treasury bills (maturities to 360 days), eurodollars, negotiable bank certificates of deposit, securities issued by federal agencies, and commercial paper dominate the money market. Significant, but lesser volumes of trading occur in banker's acceptances and in federal funds. Banker's acceptances are promises by a bank to pay a specified sum of money at a specific time. They normally arise from importing and exporting activities of the bank's commercial customers. The volume of federal funds fluctuates widely from period to period, depending upon the current state of monetary policy.

Another short-term (often overnight) financial market involves repurchase agreements to secure large loans, usually between major financial institutions in large cities. For example, U.S. government bond dealers in New York City and elsewhere often finance their large inventories with loans involving repurchase agreements. The borrower sells U.S. government securities to a lender for a very short time and at the time of sale enters into a contract to repurchase the securities at a specified price and time. With the sale and repurchase prices known, as well as the term of the loan, the difference represents the interest rate paid by the borrower. Since the loan is secured by U.S. government securities, it is very safe.

Financial Transfer Instruments

Some financial instruments do not involve lending or borrowing. Instead, they effect the transfer of funds from one economic entity to another. The check, drawn on a depository institution, is the most important of this type of financial instrument. Checks must be in writing and payable to a named entity or to bearer, be dated, be signed by their maker, be unconditional orders to pay a sum certain, contain the full promise, and be payable on demand or at a definite time. They are widely used by businesses and individuals to transfer funds. They have the disadvantage, however, that they must be physically transported to the paying institution for collection, involving high cost and considerable handling along the way.

Electronic transfers of funds are widely used by depository institutions and large entities through networks of automated clearing houses (ACHs). For example, some large payers of repetitive amounts, such as the Social Security Administration or insurance companies making pension payments to retirees, make those payments directly to the bank accounts of the recipients through electronic transfers. In addition, financial institutions can settle amounts owed to each other electronically, firms may wire funds to one another or to financial institutions. Depositors in depository institutions may make withdrawals, deposits, or transfers from one account to another from electronic teller machines, and depositors may also wire funds across the nation. Individual depositors have resisted, however, dramatic change to electronic banking, possibly because of concerns about banking privacy, or because they wish to utilize the "float" possible by issuing checks before the deposit has been made, knowing that the deposit will be made by the time the check arrives at their bank for collection.

References

Kidwell, David S., and Richard L. Peterson, *Financial Institutions, Markets, and Money* (4th ed.), Dryden, Hinsdale, Ill., 1990; Rose, Peter S., and Donald R. Fraser, *Financial Institutions* (3d ed.), Irwin, Homewood, Ill., 1988.

(*See also* Bond; Capital markets and money markets; Eurodollar market; Money markets; Stock)

William J. Brown

Firm theory

Economists use the word "firm" to denote the basic unit of organization which purchases the services of factors of production (workers, machines, etc.), undertakes their transformation into marketable goods and services, and sells these goods and services to final consumers or to other firms. As such, firms are one of the two types of elemental units that comprise the basic model of the microeconomy, the other being households, which are suppliers of factor services and buyers of firms' products. "Theory of the firm" denotes that body of theory which predicts how firms will behave under a variety of circumstances and how the predictable behavior of firms contributes to the overall behavior of a market economy.

The theory of the firm in perfect competition assumed a standardized form in the textbooks of neoclassical economics by the early twentieth century. In this theory, the firm is assumed to have available to it a given production technology (meaning a mapping from inputs to products), access to markets in which inputs can be purchased in unlimited quantities at market-clearing prices, and the ability to sell as much output as the firm is capable of producing at market-clearing prices. It is assumed that the firm determines the magnitudes of its input purchases, production, and sales by setting each variable at that level at which total profit—i.e., the difference between revenues and costs—is maximized. This problem is shown to have a unique solution in the short run when one or more factors of production present in fixed quantity—say, physical plant—cause the marginal cost of production to be eventually increasing. A unique solution consistent with a competitive industrial structure exists in the long run if the average production cost of each firm begins rising at an output level satisfying only a small part of market demand. The competitive profit-maximizing firm exhibits well-defined behaviors, some of which are quite general, e.g., the minimization of production cost for any given level of output. Some behaviors vary with assumptions about the technology, for example, its elasticities of factor substitution, homotheticity, and so on.

Extension of the model of perfect competition to the case of a firm having a monopoly in its product and/or factor market is straightforward. Extension to imperfectly competitive industrial structures, complicated by the potential indeterminacies arising from the interdependence of the choices and outcomes for the group of firms sharing a market, has helped to spawn the interest in game theory and strategic decision making which has been a lively part of economic theory, especially over the past two decades.

Although useful and almost universally accepted as a building block of microeconomic theory, the theory of the firm as just described has come to be regarded by many economists as insufficiently microanalytic for some purposes. Economists with an interest in elucidating the nature of the contractual structures and the relations between the various economic agents who interact under the rubric of business firms have pointed out that the theory of the firm does not explain why firms exist, why they maximize profits, or why long-run average costs are eventually increasing and that the theory assumes away problems of contractual compliance.

Why firms exist is a puzzle in the sense that the standard theory leaves unclear why the activities ascribed to firms are not undertaken by the agents involved, acting as a set of autonomous contractors. Why firms maximize profits is a puzzle insofar as entrepreneurs might pursue other goals, such as increasing their power over subordinates, and insofar as firms in monopoly positions might remain financially viable if they operated with positive but less-than-maximum profits. Increasing long-run average costs, often casually attributed to indivisibilities of management in standard theory, require more explicit microanalytic foundations. Contractual compliance is a problem, because self-interested workers for whom effort brings disutility at the margin could not be counted on to provide appropriate effort when their performance is too costly for employers to monitor. Hired managers might not maximize shareholders' returns for similar reasons.

A body of literature based on diverse methodological approaches has attempted to answer these and related questions. Ronald Coase and Oliver Williamson, the proponents of "transactions cost economics," have argued that the firm should be viewed as a governance structure and that its internal organization should be seen (at least in the most frequently encountered case) as hierarchical in nature. Hierarchy replaces the horizontal interactions of the market, in their views, when the costs of market contracting exceed those of hierarchical governance—for Coase, because the latter obviates the need for establishing prices of intermediate goods and services, for Williamson, because hierarchical governance controls postcontractual opportunism in the face of the transactional specificity of the assets. "Agency theorists" such as Michael Jensen and William Meckling have argued, to the contrary, that the firm is nothing more than a nexus of contracts between workers, managers, and capital suppliers and that the structure of these contracts and the choice between competing organizational forms is to be explained by the drive to minimize the costs of monitoring and bonding (a commitment device that serves as an alternative to it) when some actors are engaged as agents of others. The ideas of Marxian economists regarding the nature of the labor process and "the extraction of labor from labor power" have also contributed to the modern literature. Mathematical models of the relationships between principals and agents, and of such specific issues as the preference for internal over external hiring, the role of the firing threat in the disciplining of workers, and the relationship between earnings and marginal productivity over the course of a long-term employment relationship have been numerous but less easy to characterize as a group.

The theory of the firm has a number of spin-offs and extensions, such as the theory of the not-for-profit firm, the labor-managed firm, and the socialist firm. The more institutionally attuned literature described in the previous paragraph has been the principal meeting place of neoclassical economics with the field of organizational behavior, including work by sociologists, psychologists, and legal scholars. Although partly originating as a critique of standard theory, the new literature on the nature of firms shows signs of gaining broad acceptance from economists and of being absorbed into a broadened mainstream having room for multiple levels of modeling to deal with a multiplicity of theoretical and policy problems.

References

Coase, Ronald, "The Nature of the Firm," *Economica*, vol. 4, 1937, pp. 386–405; Jensen, Michael, and William Meckling, "Theory of the Firm: Managerial Behavior, Agency Costs, and Ownership Structure," *Journal of Financial Economics*, vol. 3, 1976, pp. 305–360; Milgrom, Paul, and John Roberts, *Economics, Organization and Management,* Prentice-Hall, Englewood Cliffs, N.J., 1992; Williamson, Oliver E., *The Economic Institutions of Capitalism: Firms, Markets, Relational Contracting,* Free Press, New York, 1985.

(*See also* Competition; Decision making in business, a behavioral approach; Monopoly and oligopoly; Production function)

Louis Putterman

Fiscal policy

Fiscal policy refers to the use of government tax and spending policies to achieve macroeconomic objectives. An outgrowth of Keynesian economics, fiscal policy has had a dramatic impact on economic and budget policymaking since World War II. Fiscal policy basically involves discretionary efforts to adjust federal tax and spending to stabilize fluctuations in aggregate demand. Since the 1970s, mounting empirical and theoretical criticisms have exposed many limitations of discretionary fiscal stabilization policy, and monetary policy has grown more important. Fiscal policy research has evolved toward the microfoundations of economic responses to fiscal changes, alternative measures of fiscal changes, the impact of expectations on those economic responses, and issues in deficit financing, including the interaction between monetary and fiscal policies and the long-run effects of mounting federal debt. Despite the well-documented flaws and limitations of traditional fiscal policy, it continues to carry significant weight among policymakers.

Up until the Depression, the primary guideline of budget policy was to keep the government budget balanced and small. In the 1930s, deficit-financed public works programs were explicitly designed to "prime the pump," but the Depression was considered extraordinary by policymakers and economists alike, and the earlier guidelines of fiscal policy remained intact. Beginning in the late 1930s, Keynesian macroeconomics took hold among mainstream economists, and discretionary fiscal policy as a positive initiative for recovery became acceptable. The ascendancy of fiscal policy was the basis for the Employment Act of 1946, which called for "the Federal Government to use all practical means . . . to promote maximum employment, production, and purchasing power." Early critics of discretionary fiscal policy recognized the positive contribution of automatic stabilizers in the budget to provide a countercyclical cushion to the economy but argued against active discretionary policy aimed at smoothing small variations in economic activity. Despite these criticisms, in ensuing decades, it became acceptable to use aggressive discretionary policy to stabilize relatively minor fluctuations in aggregate demand.

According to the early conventional Keynesian view, discretionary changes in the budget, either through spending or taxes, can alter aggregate demand and smooth fluctuations in nominal GNP. A spending increase or tax cut would increase disposable income and raise consumption and economic activity. Fiscal stimulus was presumed to shift out the IS curve in the IS-LM framework, with the resulting rise in interest rates having a dampening but not an offsetting impact on investment. The initial boost to aggregate demand generated subsequent increases in employment and spending: Fiscal multipliers measured the cumulative increase in national income relative to the original shift in the deficit. Initially, there was little distinction between the fiscal multipliers of changes in taxes or spending. Shifts in fiscal policy were presumed to affect economic outcomes by changing aggregate demand, not through allocative effects induced by changes in economic incentives generated by changes in taxes or spending. These changes were considered in a closed economy, with little regard to the feedback effects of international trade or finance. A discretionary shift toward fiscal restrictiveness through higher taxes or spending cutbacks was thought to have a symmetrical impact on aggregate demand and economic output. Whether fiscal stimulus would lift employment and real output or raise inflation depended on the amount of slack in the economy, reflected by the proximity of the economy to full employment.

Until the early 1970s, fiscal policy analysis and implementation focused heavily on what single measure of the budget best reflected the fiscal stance and the magnitude and time profile of the fiscal policy multipliers. Proponents of activist fiscal policy became increasingly bold about the ability of discretionary policies to manipulate aggregate demand. As an example of the influence of fiscal policy, in the 1962 *Eco-*

nomic Report of the President, the Council of Economic Advisers recommended—and the President proposed—that the President have the authority to change income tax rates within specified limits to help stabilize the economy (Bailey, 1962). The tax cuts of the Revenue Act of 1964 reflected the powerful influence of activist fiscal policy thought (Okun, 1970). Since then, a mounting number of refinements in the measurement of the fiscal stance, the growing controversies about the economic responses to a change in fiscal policy, and the general failures of discretionary policies to smooth economic fluctuations have revealed the many limitations of discretionary fiscal stabilization efforts. The mounting criticisms of the traditional fiscal policy framework have been conceptual as well as empirical in nature. These criticisms focus on these issues: (1) No single measure of the budget, however manipulated, reflects accurately the government's fiscal stance; (2) the timing and magnitude of the economic responses depend on a wide array of issues and assumptions that probably render traditional fiscal multiplier analysis inappropriate and misleading; and (3) the allocative effects of taxing and spending on economic performance is important—some would argue more important than the traditionally presumed fiscal policy impact on aggregate demand. In addition, the unprecedented deficit spending in the 1980s has raised concerns about the adverse impact of the rising federal debt on saving, investment, and long-run growth and has altered the fiscal debate accordingly.

As a result of these mounting challenges, the focus of budget policy has changed, and traditional fiscal policy is in widespread disarray. Whether discretionary fiscal policy is capable of smoothing short-run economic fluctuations independent of monetary policy is uncertain, and the merits of attempts to do so have been questioned, particularly relative to achieving long-run investment and growth objectives. Fiscal policy analysis has evolved more toward microeconomic foundations and allocative effects, with more reliance on general equilibrium models of open economies that incorporate international flows of goods and capital and encompass the difficult but important issues of expectations and intertemporal wealth considerations.

Measuring Fiscal Thrust

Early attempts to identify a single budgetary measure of fiscal stance recognized the aggregate budget (im)balance—deficit or surplus—as inadequate. These attempts incorporated the impact of economic conditions on taxes and spending flows and thereby failed to distinguish the impact of the budget on the economy from the impact of the economy on the budget. Certain tax and spending programs operate as *built-in stabilizers,* automatically providing a countercyclical cushion without legislative change. Recession generates increased spending for unemployment insurance benefits and various social service programs such as food stamps and suppresses income and social security tax revenues. These built-in stabilizers also exert fiscal drag on an economy growing faster than its long-run potential, as sustained strong economic growth shrinks certain outlays and raises tax revenues. The partial indexation of certain tax provisions for inflation has reduced the countercyclical impact of the built-in stabilizers, particularly as the economy overheats.

Early attempts to isolate the stance of discretionary fiscal policy from endogenously determined budgetary outcomes involved normalizing the tax and spending flows at what they would be under current law at *full employment.* A budget in surplus at full employment was considered "restrictive"; one in deficit, expansionary. The fiscal drag provided by the automatic stabilizers required discretionary fiscal policy to maintain full employment. Measuring the full employment surplus (deficit), which requires estimating full employment—a daunting task including calculating trends in productivity, capital, and labor—became a central analytical issue to fiscal policymaking.

The seeming inapplicability of full employment to short-term demand management led to the development of other benchmarks for measuring fiscal policy, including cyclically adjusted budgets and standardized budgets, measured in first difference and as a percentage of GNP. Despite these refinements, all these measures fail to convey the extent to which a fiscal stance is stimulative or contractionary. Criticisms of these traditional measures of fiscal thrust argue that such measures of the fiscal stance ignore inflation and broader measures of the government's budget stance, such as the stock of government liabilities; that the economic impacts of a discretionary change in fiscal policy depend on the mix of the change in taxes and spending and how the change in government debt is financed; and that private expectations about future macroeconomic policies significantly affect economic responses.

Inflation and Fiscal Policy

Variations in inflation may significantly affect the economic impact of fiscal policy through several avenues. Inflation affects tax revenues and federal outlays differently, thus altering the budget (im)balance. Progressive tax structures tend to raise revenues more than spending relative to GNP in response to inflation and to raise effective tax rates. Although some taxes are indexed to inflation, indexing is incomplete (e.g., depreciable assets), so higher inflation raises the cost of capital and discourages investment spending.

More important, a change in inflation affects the *real* value of government debt held by bondholders, altering their real wealth and consumption spending. More precisely, the impact on the real wealth of bondholders is affected by *expected* inflation (not current inflation), which may be affected by fiscal policy. The financial market response to a shift in fiscal policy may offset its intended thrust. A tax cut designed to stimulate output may be ineffective or counterproductive if it results in higher interest rates whose wealth impact on government bondholders results in significantly lower consumption or investment. The potentially negative impact on consumption of a rise in inflationary expectations presumably is higher when the outstanding publicly held debt is high relative to GNP. This impact occurs regardless of whether the deficit spending is financed with bonds or money.

Stocks versus Flows

Conventional fiscal analysis is based on budget deficits or surpluses, which are cash flow measures; many argue that these cash flow measures provide limited information about the economic and financial impacts of the budget, whereas broader measures of the stock of government debt or total liabilities may provide a more accurate assessment of fiscal policy effects. A change in taxes or spending generates a one-time change in the flows of spending, but these changes may be small relative to the economic effects of absorbing into private portfolios the change in the stocks of assets, government debt, or money stock, depending on how the change in fiscal policy is financed. Relative prices, the absolute price level, and the level of output continue to be affected until stocks of assets adjust fully to the change in government debt or money supply (Brunner, 1986). Similarly, the prices of financial assets (i.e., interest rates) reflect portfolio adjustments among stocks of assets, rather than simply changes in the cash flow budget.

Even broader measures of net government liabilities, including net social security liabilities, liabilities of government credit agencies and government guarantees, and government assets, affect income and consumption patterns well beyond the impact of cash flows. Government guarantees and credit subsidies clearly affect income and consumption decisions, but they are not counted in the federal budget until the funds are actually paid (Meltzer, 1991). Recent studies have derived estimates of government debt and net worth as the bases for reevaluation of the economic impact of fiscal policy (Eisner and Pieper, 1984; Eisner, 1986; and Bohn, 1992). This approach to fiscal policy analysis is just emerging in importance.

Aggregated Demand versus Allocative Effects

Early attempts to measure fiscal thrust based on the full employment budget determined that taxes and spending have different multipliers, which required an adjustment to standard Keynesian fiscal policy. Since then, significant advancements in understanding the role of monetary policy in smoothing fluctuations in aggregate demand and the issues about how deficit spending is financed have heightened the recognition that the economic impact of a discretionary change in fiscal policy is determined significantly—some would argue almost entirely—by the allocative effects generated by changes in specific tax and spending structures, rather than through changes in aggregate demand, as posited in standard Keynesian macroeconomic analysis.

Rather than treat the government sector as completely separate from the private economy, and fiscal policy as a separate tool that affects aggregate demand, it is important to recognize that the government's spending provides goods and services to the private sector, a portion of which may be substitutable for the private sector provision, and that the burden of the government's taxes may influence incentives to work, save, and invest. Thus, the government's budget policy allocates national resources and influences directly and indirectly both the mix of economic output and long-run economic growth.

The economic impact of a spending increase depends on the mix of government spending and whether any of that spending is a substitute for private consumption. Assuming no change in monetary policy—that is, no change in money supply—and assuming households disregard any futures tax implications of deficit spending, a rise in government consumption-oriented spending (i.e., transfer payments) will have a significantly smaller fiscal multiplier than government investment spending; government consumption-oriented spending will raise private consumption but crowd out private investment. Absent monetary accommodation, total national output would be little changed, but the share of consumption would rise, and the share of investment would fall. The rise in federal debt to finance consumption without adding to or reducing productive capacity would lower long-term economic growth. A rise in spending for investment-oriented activity would have a larger multiplier and would raise long-run growth if the marginal productivity of the government's investment spending exceeds the productivity of the private sector investment it crowds out.

Similarly, the economic impact of a change in taxes depends on the burden of the taxes, and the incentives or disincentives they create for work, saving, and investment. Insofar as certain tax changes may directly and significantly affect expected rates of return on investment, the allocative impacts of tax changes may be significant. Moreover, the financial market responses to discretionary fiscal changes also depend on the particular mix of spending and taxes and what they imply for expected rates of return on investment, productivity, and long-run economic growth, as well as the magnitude of the deficit. For example, the Tax Reform Act of 1986 had a significant impact on the level and mix of national output and rates of interest and exchange by changing relative prices and altering the costs of capital, even though, as proposed, it did not change projected deficits. Specifically, by eliminating the investment tax credit and accelerated depreciation instituted as part of the Economic Recovery Tax Act of 1981, the Tax Reform Act of 1986 lowered investment and generated a decline in interest rates and exchange rates. Standard Keynesian macroeconomic assessments that rely on changes in the deficit as a measure of fiscal impact on aggregate demand were not capable of capturing these economic and financial outcomes.

Issues in Deficit Financing and Expectations

The traditional fiscal policy assertion that a cut in taxes or increase in spending is stimulative is based on the assumption that a rise in government debt increases national wealth and that the debt service burden on government bonds does not influence consumption and investment. Although assessments of fiscal policy based on stocks rather than flows argued that the impact of debt finance on wealth was small (Brunner, 1986), Barro (1974) challenged the existence of a wealth impact for government debt and thereby argued the impotence of debt-financed fiscal stimulus. His resurrection of the Ricardian equivalence hypothesis argued that, in response to a rise in government debt, individuals will reduce consumption and raise saving in anticipation of higher future taxes. This hypothesis challenges the standard Keynesian assumption that individuals are deceived into believing that the increased stock of bonds as a result of debt-financed spending need not be repaid through higher taxes and constitutes a rise in net wealth. Barro extended the concept of rationality— that individuals are indifferent between bond- and tax-financed government spending—to superrationality in which individuals behave rationally across generations, adjusting their consumption and saving patterns in order to leave unchanged debt burdens on future generations.

Barro's Ricardian equivalence of tax- and debt-financed government spending denies the ability of discretionary fiscal policy to alter aggregate demand. His model is based on lump-sum taxes that do not alter relative prices or distort economic decisions. This affront to standard fiscal policy was met with sharp criticism, particularly its rigid assumptions about intergenerational rationality. Modifying some of the model's assumptions, including the introduction of bequest-constrained individuals, generates intergenerational wealth redistributions that partially invalidate the fiscal policy implications of Barro. However, empirical tests of Barro's Ricardian equivalence based on aggregate data that test the impact of government debt and deficits on interest rates, saving, and capital formation do not consistently refute Barro. Micro-based studies have more successfully refuted Ricardian equivalence.

In contrast to the technically difficult and unresolved issues arising from the challenge Barro's Ricardian equivalence poses for traditional fiscal policy, it is widely accepted that deficit spending financed by money rather than government debt is stimulative. Temporary reductions in interest rates associated with debt monetization accommodate an outward shift in nominal incomes and consumption without impinging on investment. Yet the effect of monetary stimulus on real economic variables is transitory; in the long run it can only raise inflation, which is inconsistent with sustainable economic expansion.

The Policy Mix Issue

With the rising importance of monetary policy as a stabilization tool, many traditional Keynesian economists have sought to adjust the mix of monetary and fiscal policies to manage aggregate demand and achieve a desired economic outcome. According to this approach, stimulative fiscal policy is to be accompanied by restrictive monetary policy and vice versa. Critics find unworkable inconsistencies in this policy mix approach, arguing that such attempts are generally counterproductive because monetary and fiscal policies are *not* substitutes in either their short- or long-run impacts. Fiscal policy alters the allocation of national resources between the public and private sectors and influences long-run potential output by altering incentives to consume, save, and invest but does not generate a *permanent* shift in aggregate demand. Moreover, the timing and magnitude of fiscal policy's short-run impact are uncertain. In contrast, monetary policy cannot raise real long-run output but may lower it by generating inflation.

Fiscal Policy and the Rising Government Debt

Since the early 1980s, the unprecedented budget deficits and sharply rising federal debt have recast the fiscal policy debate. Since 1975, the federal debt-to-GNP ratio has risen from 25 percent to 50 percent, its sharpest peacetime rise in U.S. history. Whereas the efficacy of fiscal policy as a means of smoothing fluctuations in aggregate demand has become uncertain, concerns about how the mounting debt will impinge on saving, investment, and growth have heightened. At issue is not just the level of deficits and how the mounting government debt may force the monetary authorities to monetize, but how the mix of spending and taxes affects current and future economic performance. Deficit spending for consumption-oriented transfer payments adds to the national debt and reduces the long-run capacity to grow, thereby redistributing wealth from future generations to the current one. Efforts to quantify these effects are scarce and unreliable. The disarray of fiscal policymaking and analysis since the early 1980s has reflected both the uncertainties about whether the earlier assumed short-run stabilization properties of fiscal policy work and an inability to reconcile short-run economic and political objectives with long-run concerns about the mounting debt.

References

Bailey, M. J., *National Income and the Price Level: A Study in Macroeconomics Theory,* McGraw-Hill, New York, 1962; Barro, R., "Are Government Bonds New Wealth?" *Journal of Political Economy,* vol. 82, 1974, pp. 1095–1117; Blinder, A. S., and R. N. Solow, "Analytical Foundations of Fiscal Policy," *The Economics of Public Finance,* Brookings, Washington, D.C., 1974; Bohn, H., "Budget Deficits and Government Accounting," Carnegie-Rochester Conference on Public Policy, 1992; Brunner, Karl, "Fiscal Policy in Macro Theory: A Survey and Evaluation," in R. W. Hafer (ed.), *The Monetary Versus Fiscal Debate,* Rowman & Allanheld, Lanham, Md., 1986; Eisner, R., *How Real Is the Federal Deficit?* MacMillan, New York, 1986; Eisner, R., and P. Pieper, "A New View of the Federal Debt and Budget Deficits," *American Economic Review,* vol. 74, 1984, pp. 11–29; Executive Office of the President, *Economic Report of the Pres-*

ident, February 1985; Meltzer, Allan, "Debt and Deficits: Some Measurement, Economic, and Political Issues," American Enterprise Institute, Annual Policy Conference, Washington, D.C., December 1991; Okun, A., "Achieving Sustained Prosperity" in A. Okun (ed.), *The Political Economy of Prosperity,* Brookings, Washington, D.C., 1970; Stein, Herbert, *The Fiscal Revolution in America,* University of Chicago Press, Chicago, 1969.

(*See also* Automatic stabilizers; Debt and deficits; Economic growth; Employment and unemployment; Federal budget; Federal Reserve policy; Incomes policy; Indexation; IS-LM model; Keynesian economics; Monetary policy; Multiplier; Taxation, an overview)

Mickey D. Levy

Fixed annuity (*see* Variable annuity)

Flexible manufacturing systems (*see* Automation)

Flow of funds

Flow of funds refers to a set of accounts that describe the sources and uses of saving in the economy. The accounts provide a means for analyzing financial flows between economic sectors (such as households, businesses, and government) and into and out of financial instruments (such as mortgages, corporate bonds, and bank loans).

Framework of Flow-of-Funds Accounts

Flow-of-funds accounts are an integral part of the economic accounts of a nation, and they are usually tied explicitly to the national income accounts. These latter accounts show receipts and outlays by sectors and by type of final product. The difference between receipts and outlays for each sector is a source of funds (saving). A second source of funds is borrowing. For each sector of the economy and for the economy as a whole, total saving must be equal to total investment, and, broadly speaking, investment takes two forms—purchases of tangible assets and net acquisition of financial assets. Thus, the flow-of-funds accounts are sometimes expressed as a system that provides the details underlying the following basic framework:

Sources of funds	Uses of funds
Saving (= receipts less outlays)	Purchases of tangible assets
Borrowing	Net acquisition of financial assets
Total =	Total

A second, equivalent framework for the flow-of-funds accounts is derived from the perspective of a balance sheet. A balance sheet for an economic sector shows the accumulated amount (or stock) of assets and liabilities at a moment in time, with assets less liabilities measuring the net worth of the sector. The flow-of-funds accounts show the changes (flows) of assets and liabilities over a specified period, highlighting flows of financial assets and liabilities. Under this framework, a generalized flow-of-funds statement for a sector would include the following broad elements:

1. Gross saving (from the national income accounts)
2. Gross investment
3. Investment in tangible assets (from the national income accounts)
4. Net investment in financial assets
5. Acquisition of financial assets *less* increase in financial liabilities
6. Borrowing
7. Change in other liabilities
8. Discrepancy

The heart of the flow-of-funds accounts is items 4 through 7, with added detail showing the types of financial assets and liabilities acquired by sector. The discrepancy (item 8) is the difference between measured gross saving and measured gross investment (item 1 less item 2). In theory, the discrepancy is equal to zero. In practice, however, the discrepancy for a specific sector may be significant relative to the size of gross saving or investment. The size of the discrepancy depends in part on the quality of the data available to measure the various flows. The absence of capital gains and losses as a source of funds in national income accounts also introduces a measurement problem, as investment for a sector no doubt reflects such gains and losses.

In addition to providing data on the financial flows of nonfinancial sectors of the economy, the flow-of-funds accounts in the United States and in a number of other nations provide considerable detail on the process of financial intermediation and on the significance of different types of financial instruments. Measurement of flows into and out of financial institutions such as banks, life insurance companies, and pension funds allows for analysis of their contribution to economic activity and for examination of changes in the relative importance of banks and other depository institutions, other types of financial institutions, and open-market financing.

In addition to statements of saving and investment by sector, information in the accounts can be grouped by type of financial instrument, indicating the sectors that raise funds by using a specific type of instrument and the sectors that offer funds through that type of instrument. For example, in the U.S. flow-of-funds accounts, tables show the amounts of mortgage credit provided by different financial institutions and from nonfinancial sectors. Tables also show the amount of such credit borrowed by each sector.

Flow-of-Funds Accounts in the United States

Work on flow of funds for the United States has a long history. A considerable effort after World War II, spirited by Professor Morris Copeland, led to the development of a set of accounts for the period 1939 to 1953 that was published by the Board of Governors of the Federal Reserve System in 1955. Work on the accounts at the Federal Reserve, most notably by Stephen Taylor in the 1960s and 1970s, has continued, and, at present, detailed tables for sectors and transactions are published for the latest quarter with a lag of about 6 weeks. In addition to the statements that show financial flows, companion statements provide data on financial assets and liabilities outstanding at the end of the quarter by sector and by instrument. The quarterly detail is available from 1952 forward. A separate publication, the *Balance Sheets for the U.S. Economy*, combines information on the value of tangible assets with the statements of financial assets and liabilities to derive domestic wealth and net worth by sectors of the economy. Data for the balance sheets are annual and begin in 1945.

TABLE 1   Sectors and Transaction Categories in the U.S. Flow-of-Funds Accounts

Sectors	Transactions
Households, personal trusts, and nonprofit organizations	Gold and official foreign exchange holdings
Nonfinancial business	Treasury currency and special drawing rights certificates
Farm	Life insurance reserves
Nonfarm noncorporate	Pension fund reserves
Nonfinancial corporate business	Net interbank claims
State and local governments	Checkable deposits and currency
U.S. government	Small time and savings deposits
Foreign	Large time deposits
Federally sponsored credit agencies	Money-market mutual fund shares
Federally related mortgage pools	Federal funds and security repurchase agreements
Banking system	U.S. deposits in foreign countries
Monetary authority	U.S. government securities
Commercial banking	Tax-exempt securities
U.S.-chartered commercial banks	Corporate and foreign bonds
Foreign banking offices	Mutual fund shares
Domestic affiliates of commercial banks (bank holding companies)	Corporate equities
Banks in U.S. possessions	Home mortgages
Savings and loan associations	Multifamily residential mortgages
Mutual savings banks	Commercial mortgages
Credit unions	Farm mortgages
Life insurance companies	Consumer credit
Private pension funds	Bank loans not elsewhere classified
State and local government employee retirement funds	Open-market paper
	Other loans
Other insurance companies	Security credit
Finance companies	Trade credit
Mutual funds	Taxes payable
Money-market mutual funds	Proprietors' equity in noncorporate business
Real estate investment trusts	Miscellaneous financial claims
Security brokers and dealers	
Issuers of securitized credit obligations	

Over time, the number of sector statements published has grown, in part to reflect the increasing complexity of the financial system. The private nonfinancial sectors include three business subsectors and the foreign sector, as well as households (see Table 1). The household sector includes data for individuals and for nonprofit institutions and personal trusts. (Work is currently under way to provide additional detail for these subsectors.) For the government, separate statements are shown for the federal sector and for state and local entities. For the state and local government sector, the data are divided into a general government sector and a sector for pension plans under state and local control. Such pension plans are considered a separate financial sector in the U.S. system of accounts. Financial sectors include statements for all major types of depository and nondepository institutions. In recent years, the growth of specialized financial instruments created by pooling financial assets such as mortgages, bank loans, or consumer credit receivables has led to a separate accounting of these instruments in a sector called "issuers of securitized credit obligations."

The number of financial instruments (often referred to as "transaction categories") detailed in the flow-of-funds accounts has also increased over the years. All major types of deposit categories are listed, along with other financial instruments that are used in measures of monetary aggregates. Mortgage credit is divided among loans for home, multifamily, commercial, and farm properties. In the markets for business credit, transactions in open-market paper, corporate bonds, equities, and mutual fund shares are listed along with several other types of instruments. Information on U.S. government securities and tax-exempt (municipal) debt instruments are provided also.

Uses of the Flow-of-Funds Accounts

Flow-of-funds accounts are widely used in the academic and business communities and in government. Historical data provide information on the evolution of the sources and uses of funds for sectors and on changes in financial market activity over the business cycle. The flow-of-funds data provide a comprehensive set of internally consistent information on a nation's financial system that can be used in much the same way that the national income accounts are used. Speeches and articles making use of statistical analysis of flow-of-funds data, either through econometric models or through other means, appear in a wide variety of publications.

Flow-of-funds analysis has been useful in formulating forecasts of overall economic activity. Both within government and outside, forecasts of national income and employment are now usually accompanied by at least some elements of flow-of-funds accounts, if not a full set of accounts. In a complete forecast of the economy, a flow-of-funds analysis provides a sense of the financial sources and uses of funds needed to carry out a projected level of nonfinancial activity. For example, the degree of borrowing required by the nonfinancial corporate sector may be analyzed in terms of the gap between its projected internal funds and anticipated outlays for capital goods and inventories. The size of this "financing gap" and how businesses meet it through equity markets, short- or long-term borrowing, or reductions in financial assets provide a view of anticipated financial market activities and ensuing pressures. The analysis in a flow-of-funds forecast describes also the degree of financial intermediation anticipated, or possible alternative paths to finance business, household, or government activity. As noted, the size of likely borrowings by sector can be deduced and used as a consistency check for the overall forecast.

Flow-of-funds analysis provides information on the changes in sector balance sheets, such as the substitution of debt for equity in the corporate sector in the 1980s and the subsequent reversals in the early 1990s. A forecast of balance sheet changes is useful in assessing the degree of financial stress on a sector and whether such stress is increasing or decreasing over a projection horizon. Finally, a flow-of-funds projection, like a forecast of national income and its components, is helpful in monitoring current developments in financial markets. Questions about the consistency of events with one's expectations provide a basis for assessing the stance of current policies.

A specific use of the flow-of-funds accounts by the U.S. monetary authority is to monitor domestic nonfinancial debt. In the late 1970s and early 1980s analysis by economists suggested that the relationship between borrowing and national income or between debt outstanding and national income was as stable as, or more stable than, that of money to national income. Indeed, figures from the flow-of-funds accounts showed that the ratio of debt to gross national product (GNP) had varied within a narrow band around 1.35 for most of the post–World War II period. The relatively constant ratio of debt to nominal GNP over the period prompted recommendations that the Federal Reserve adopt ranges for aggregate debt growth that would be consistent with desired growth in nominal spending. In 1983, the Federal Open Market Committee, the monetary policy arm of the Federal Reserve System, established for the first time a monitoring range for the growth of credit market debt of domestic nonfinancial sectors; this range is announced along with the annual target ranges for the monetary aggregates (M-1, M-2, and M-3). Over most of the 1980s, however, borrowing by both the federal government and nonfederal sectors was unusually strong, and the ratio of debt to GNP soared to nearly 1.9, implying that debt growth outpaced GNP growth by nearly 40 percent over this period. Analysis of this striking event in financial markets and of the subsequent flattening out of the ratio in the early 1990s has been facilitated by the detail and structure of the flow-of-funds accounts.

References

Board of Governors, Federal Reserve System, *Flow of Funds in the United States, 1939–1953,* December 1955; Board of Governors, Federal Reserve System, *Introduction to Flow of Funds Accounts, 1980;* Board of Governors, Federal Reserve System, *Balance Sheets of the U.S. Economy* (C.9), March 1992; Board of Governors, Federal Reserve System, *Flow of Funds Accounts, Seasonally Adjusted Flows, Fourth Quarter 1991* (Z.1 Flows), March 12, 1992; Board of Governors, Federal Reserve System, *Flow of Funds Accounts, Financial Assets and Liabilities, Fourth Quarter 1991* (Z.1 Outstandings), March 12, 1992; Friedman, Benjamin M., "Debt and Economic Activity in the United States," in Benjamin M. Friedman (ed.), *The Changing Roles of Debt and Equity in Financing U.S. Capital Formation,* University of Chicago Press, Chicago, 1982, pp. 91–110; U.S. Department of Commerce, Bureau of Economic Analysis, *An Introduction to National Economic Accounting,* Methodology Paper Series MP-1, 1985.

(*See also* Business credit; Capital markets and money markets; Consumer credit; Credit, an overview; Financial institutions; Financial instruments; Gross domestic product; Interest rates; Money markets; Mortgage credit)

Albert M. Teplin

Foreign direct investment

Foreign direct investment describes the acquisition of managerial control by a citizen, i.e., corporation, of a home nation over a corporation of some other host nation. Corporations that widely engage in foreign direct investment are called "multinational companies," "multinational enterprises," or "transnational corporations." The term "foreign direct investment" is something of a misnomer: When foreign direct investment takes place, investment in the economic sense may or may not occur. If, for example, a U.S. company acquires ownership of an ongoing British firm, foreign direct investment is deemed to have taken place; however, no net creation of productive capital, and hence no economic investment, has occurred. By contrast, if the same U.S. company creates de novo a subsidiary in Great Britain, building new plant and equipment, then both foreign direct investment and economic investment have taken place.

Foreign direct investment has been an important feature of the world economy throughout this century, but it became particularly prominent during the late 1950s and the 1960s, when large numbers of U.S.–based firms extended their operations internationally, and again during the 1980s, when large numbers of European and Japanese firms did likewise, including into the United States itself. (See Graham and Krugman, 1991.) By at least one measure, foreign direct investment now is of greater impact on world economic activity than is international trade: The combined sales of overseas subsidiaries of all international firms significantly exceeds the volume of trade (Julius, 1991).

Numerous economic analyses of foreign direct investment have begun with the assumption that real capital is exported from the home to the host nation, but this assumption is not necessarily true. Thus, foreign direct investment is not a special case of the international transfer problem, which has been a favorite subject of economists since John Maynard Keynes' early treatment of it (Keynes, 1924). Indeed, even when economic investment results from foreign direct investment, capital may not be transferred from the home nation to the host nation. Rather, the multinational corporation may acquire real capital from local (or third-nation) sources, financing this investment from local (or third-nation) sources. The multinational firm may thus act to intermediate host-nation savings into host-nation investment.

Exactly why foreign direct investment should take place at all has been the subject of considerable inquiry in recent years, the point having been made that in a world characterized by perfect markets for goods and factors of production, foreign direct investment would not occur. This argument suggests that imperfections in these markets must account for foreign direct investment, and theories based on imperfections in foreign exchange markets, financial markets, and markets for technology have been advanced.

Theories based on imperfections in financial markets derive from modern portfolio and capital asset pricing theories, which maintain that holding a diversified portfolio of financial securities rather than one or a few securities carries real benefits and that an internationally diversified portfolio is more beneficial than one containing securities of one nation only. Such theories assert that significant barriers to international portfolio diversification exist at the level of the individual investor and therefore that the multinational firm serves as a financial intermediary which enables investors to obtain the benefits of such diversification.

Most analysts however reject theories based on financial market imperfections in favor of ones based on real market imperfections. The pioneering work of this approach was the 1959 doctoral thesis of Stephen Hymer, published posthumously in 1976. Hymer noted that multinational firms tend to be larger in absolute size than most other firms and tend to operate in industries characterized by high seller concentration and high levels of investment in research and development. These findings have been confirmed by numerous researchers. Raymond Vernon (1971), for example, noted that the 187 international firms appearing on the *Fortune* 500 list were larger in terms of sales than the remaining 313, tended to spend more on research and development and advertising as a percentage of sales, and were concentrated in a relatively few industries. Hymer hypothesized that firms became international if they possessed intangible assets—either superior knowledge or technology (including superior management skills) or internal scale economies—that gave them real market advantages over local rivals.

Extensions of the Hymer hypothesis include that of Vernon (1966), who asserted that foreign markets for products embodying new or superior technologies would be served first via exportation from a home-nation firm and only later via local production in the host nation, after local rivals could generate substitutable products. This assertion is the basis of Vernon's "product life cycle" hypothesis of international trade and investment. Richard Caves (1971) and others have noted that the intangible assets of the multinational firm might include marketing and other managerial skills. F. T. Knickerbocker (1974) and Edward M. Graham (1978) have suggested that rivalry among major firms in oligopolistic industries may account for certain of their investment activities. Stephen Magee (1977) posited that in order to internalize the benefits arising from the development of a new technology, a private firm must hold a monopoly or quasi-monopoly over the commercial use of that technology. Because the patent system alone does not provide the innovating firm with sufficient market protection to enable it profitably to develop new technologies, the firm must extend its horizontal market power to ensure a captive market for new technologies, the extension including the penetration of foreign markets.

Buckley and Casson (1976) take a somewhat different tack from Hymer and his followers. Basing their reasoning on that of Coase (1934) and Williamson (1975), Buckley and Casson note that the critical issue is whether firms internalize activities within their organizations or use external contracting or arm's-length market transactions to achieve the same ends. Firms' decisions with respect to whether to internalize activities that span national borders thus determine whether foreign direct investment takes place. These decisions are likely to be based on relative efficiency considerations, that is, whether it is more economical to perform the activity internally or externally. Buckley and Casson thus put the theory of foreign direct investment into the context of the modern economic theory of the organization of the firm, a theory that has been developed considerably since Buckley and Casson's pioneering effort. See, for example, articles by Cantwell (1991), Dunning (1991) Ethier (1986), and Grossman and Hart (1986).

References

Buckley, Peter, J., and Mark C. Casson, *The Future of the Multinational Enterprise,* Macmillan, London, 1976; Cantwell, John, "A Survey of Theories of International Production," in C. R. Pitelis and R. Sugden (eds.), *The Nature of the Transnational Firm,* Routledge, London, 1991; Caves, Richard E., "International Corporations: The Industrial Economics of Foreign Investment," *Economica,* vol. 38, no. 149, 1971, pp. 1–27; Coase, Ronald H., "The Nature of the Firm," *Economica,* vol. 4 (new series), 1934, pp. 386–405; Dunning, John H., "The Eclectic Paradigm of International Production: A Personal Perspective", in C. R. Pitelis and R. Sugden (eds.), *The Nature of the Transnational Firm,* Routledge, London, 1991; Ethier, Wilfred J., "The Multinational Firm," *Quarterly Journal of Economics,* vol. 86, 1986, pp. 805–833; Graham, Edward M., "Transatlantic Investment by Multinational Firms: A Rivalistic Phenomenon?" *Journal of Post-Keynesian Economics,* vol. 1, no. 1, Fall 1978, pp. 82–99; Graham, Edward M., and Paul R. Krugman, *Foreign Direct Investment in the United States* (2d ed.), Institute for International Economics, Washington, D.C., 1991; Grossman, Sanford, and Oliver Hart, "The Costs and Benefits of Ownership: A Theory of Vertical and Lateral Integration," *Journal of Political Economy,* vol. 94, 1986, pp. 691–719; Hymer, Stephen H., *The International Operations of National Firms: A Study of Direct Foreign Investment,* M.I.T. Press, Cambridge, Mass., 1976; Johnson, Harry, G., "The Efficiency and Welfare Implications of the International Corporation," in C. P. Kindleberger (ed.), *The International Corporation,* M.I.T. Press, Cambridge, Mass., 1970; Julius, Dee Anne, *Global Companies and Public Policy: The Growing Challenge of Foreign Direct Investment,* The Royal Institute of International Affairs, London, 1991; Keynes, John Maynard, "Foreign Investment and the National Advantage," *The Nation and Athenaeum,* vol. 35, London,

1924; Kindleberger, Charles P., *American Business Abroad,* Yale University Press, New Haven, Conn., 1969; Knickerbocker, F. T., *Oligopolistic Reaction and Multinational Enterprise,* Harvard University Press, Cambridge, Mass., 1974; Magee, Stephen P., "Technology and the Appropriability Theory of the Multinational Enterprise," in J. N. Bhagwati (ed.), *The New International Economic Order: The North-South Debate,* M.I.T. Press, Cambridge, Mass., 1977; Vernon, Raymond, "International Investment and International Trade in the Product Cycle," *Quarterly Journal of Economics,* vol. 80, no. 2, May 1966, pp. 190–207; Vernon, Raymond, *Sovereignty at Bay,* Basic Books, New York, 1971; Williamson, Oliver E., *Markets and Hierarchies: Analysis and Antitrust Implications,* Free Press, New York, 1975.

(*See also* International economics, an overview; Monopoly and oligopoly; Multinational corporation)

Edward M. Graham

Foreign exchange management

Foreign exchange management is that branch of company financial management that arises when businesses carry out transactions and calculate profits and losses in foreign as well as domestic currencies. Foreign exchange management has become critical to most companies as international trade and investment have grown enormously since World War II. Moreover, exchange rates in relation to the dollar, which for most countries seldom changed in value between 1949 and 1971, have become more volatile since August 1971, when the United States stopped converting dollars into gold. With this greater volatility, most international companies are more vulnerable to losses on overseas operations. Two critical issues in dealing with this problem are (1) forecasts of exchange rates and (2) strategies for foreign exchange management given an exchange rate forecast.

Exchange Rate Forecasting

As exchange rate fluctuations have become a challenge to management, at least 20 consulting organizations in the United States alone have developed techniques for analyzing the foreign exchange market and are supplying forecasts of major exchange rates. Despite the wide range of foreign exchange forecasts, companies have tended to rely strongly on foreign exchange traders in the major banks for advice on the outlook for exchange rates. This advice has the advantage of reflecting the latest international money-market information that is likely to be available only to bank traders. Many foreign exchange traders would readily admit, however, that they have no special expertise in forecasting exchange rates beyond a short horizon, possibly 2 weeks. Thus, corporate money managers have tried to supplement advice from traders with longer-term forecasts extending ahead for at least a year.

Particularly in cases where exchange rates are fixed temporarily by action of central banks to support the foreign exchange market, a political approach has sometimes been advised for determining when and by how much an exchange rate is likely to change. It has been argued that if one knows enough about the background and monetary predilections of finance ministers, of directors of central banks, and sometimes of heads of governments, one can determine whether they will devalue or revalue the currency. Certainly political elements are an important ingredient in any evaluation of an exchange rate outlook. But the difficulties in a purely political approach should not be understated. High government officials are almost certain to be disingenuous in their statements on exchange rate policy. Even in cases where heads of government are determined to maintain a fixed exchange rate, this resolve may be vitiated by market forces. A country holding to a fixed exchange rate may face inescapable devaluation as it runs out of foreign exchange reserves or unavoidable revaluation as an avalanche of foreign currency enters the country, destabilizing its own money supply and price levels.

At the opposite extreme from the political approach to exchange rate forecasting are the efficient-market theorists and chartists who believe all foreseeable political and economic events have been discounted in current exchange rates. The efficient-market theorists believe that the discounting of future events has been carried to the point where no effective forecasting is possible and that foreign exchange management thus becomes of decidedly limited value. The chartists believe that any identifiable economic tendencies affecting an exchange rate have been discounted. Nevertheless, they hold that trends persist in the data relating to exchange rates and that effective forecasting depends on identifying trends and turning points. (Momentum and filter-rule analyses are forecasting approaches that are usually more mathematically rigorous than the chartist approach, but they are similar to charting in that political or economic variables have no explicit role in the forecast.) Because charts indicate basic trends in foreign exchange markets, charts may enable the forecaster to avoid wasting time in attempts to analyze random day-to-day events. But the bias of charts is to indicate that what is going up will continue to rise and vice versa. Thus, at an early stage in the development of exchange rate forecasting, as with longer-established areas of business forecasting, analysts began looking for lead indicators of exchange rate changes.

The most famous lead-indicator approach to exchange rate forecasting is called "purchasing power parity." This theory says that exchange rates tend to equalize world prices so that if prices in a country rise above world price levels, the exchange rate will tend to fall. Conversely, if price levels rise more slowly than in the rest of the world, the exchange rate will tend to rise. A variation of this theory is the use of money supplies instead of prices as the lead indicator. This approach is based on the theory that with a lag, prices tend to move in line with money supplies.

Purchasing power parity and money-supply data as lead indicators for exchange rate movements seem to be workable over long periods—5 years or more—but are less effective for the short run. For shorter periods, changes in a country's balance of payments—for example, the bulge in U.S. oil imports in 1977 to 1978—can adversely affect a country's exchange rate to a greater extent than would be indicated by purchasing power parity. Lead indicators based on a country's trade account are the reserves-imports ratio and the ratio of reserves to money supply. If the reserves-imports ratio declines to a low level—for example, if a country can finance only 2 or 3 months of imports out of its reserves—may mean that a country is dissipating reserves and may be forced to devalue. If the ratio of reserves to money supply rises to a level exceeding about 10 percent on an annualized basis, the country's reserve buildup, converted into local currency, may be creating such a rise in the money supply that the central bank will be forced to revalue to control inflationary pressures. (The use of either of these ratios as indicators implicitly assumes that there has been some control over the exchange rate by the central bank, which may be forced into action by too great an inflow or outflow of foreign exchange.)

Lead indicators, while sometimes useful, are often considered insufficient for an adequate exchange rate forecast. Some argue that the exchange rate outlook should be analyzed comprehensively in terms of all inflows and outflows of foreign exchange to and from a country instead of in terms of a lead indicator. This analysis should include inflows and outflows of foreign exchange for transportation, tourists, immigrant remittances, profit remittances, foreign aid, foreign investment, and all other important items in a country's balance of payments.

There is, however, a serious practical difficulty with comprehensive balance-of-payments analysis as a vehicle for exchange rate forecasting. This approach is simply too expensive to attempt to apply unless the foreign exchange manager has more resources than are usually available. Suppose currency forecasts are required for 10 countries. The balance of payments of each country involves 10 items, thus resulting in a total of 100 forecasts. And each of the balance of payments items may be as difficult to forecast as the exchange rate itself.

In view of both the inadequacy of single lead indicators for exchange rate forecasting and the complexity of balance-of-payments analysis, some attempts to forecast exchange rates have turned to computer-based econometric models, hoping to sort out the significant from the insignificant elements affecting exchange rates. Track records are not yet long enough to judge the success of these methods (or the claim of efficient-market theorists that sustained effective forecasting is not really possible). However, some differences among econometric forecasts are worth noting. It is convenient to classify these differences in line with four contrasting methods of exchange rate forecasting: (1) trade-weighted and bilateral forecasts, (2) partial and general equilibrium models, (3) general and unique specifications for forecasts, and (4) trade- and monetarist-oriented models.

Trade-Weighted and Bilateral Forecasts

Econometric models of exchange rate determination differ as to what type of exchange rate is being considered. The exchange rate ordinarily quoted in U.S. newspapers is, of course, the bilateral rate, e.g., 1.75 dm = $1. But this exchange rate with respect to the dollar is not the whole story for the deutsche mark because it also fluctuates in relation to the British pound, the French franc, and all other currencies. If, for example, the deutsche mark and pound both gain 10 percent against the dollar, the deutsche mark would not change in relation to the pound. This would be a different situation compared with the deutsche mark rising 10 percent against both the dollar and the pound. One way of expressing the overall change in the value of an exchange rate is to take a weighted average of all its percentage changes in relation to each other exchange rate. Weights are usually based on the relative amount of trade with each country.

Some forecasts of exchange rates begin by forecasting a trade-weighted exchange rate and then work backward to a bilateral rate. Other exchange rate forecasts go directly to bilateral exchange rates, usually in relation to the dollar. Bilateral exchange rates may miss important relationships to third countries of the currency being considered. Trade-weighted exchange rates, however, create special forecasting difficulties because each exchange rate depends on elements affecting every other exchange rate. More recently, it has become a widespread practice to adjust exchange rates for changes in the country's price level in order to obtain "real exchange rates." Suppose that an exchange rate depreciates by 10 percent and the price level rises by

10 percent. Then the real exchange rate would not change. One would expect this result from purchasing power parity. But in actual experience, real exchange rates as well as nominal exchange rates show strong volatility.

Equilibrium Models

General equilibrium models are complete systems for forecasting not simply exchange rates but most of the important macro variables in the world economy. The general equilibrium model might forecast GNP, the price level, and trade and interest rates, as well as exchange rates. Most of the variables affecting an exchange rate would be forecast in a general equilibrium model.

In a partial equilibrium model, however, only the exchange rate is forecast—usually in a single-equation model. Other variables in the equation are judgmentally forecast or are lagged variables for which past values are already known. Thus, partial equilibrium models have the disadvantage of possible guesswork involving the inputs into the model. And the output cannot be of better quality than the inputs. General equilibrium models, however, have the advantage that major variables in the model are forecast without guesswork. General equilibrium models are, however, expensive to construct. Moreover, a mistake easily identified in a partial equilibrium model may not be recognized readily in one of many equations of general equilibrium and, therefore, may vitiate the results of the whole model.

Specifications

When a number of exchange rates are forecast, one approach is to attempt a unique specification, i.e., to consider each country as a special case and to work with a series of experiments with a wide number of possibly relevant independent variables until an equation is found that fits past data and thus appears to provide a basis for a successful exchange rate forecast. The same process is repeated for each currency. Another approach is to use a general specification, deciding at the outset what independent variables are likely to be significant and then applying this general specification to all forecasts (though for each currency there will, of course, be differences in the estimated coefficients in the forecasting equations).

The use of unique specifications has the advantage that special characteristics peculiar to each currency are taken into account. All currencies are not forced into the same mold. However, without a general specification the danger is that simply by chance as a result of repeated trials an "explanation" will be found for past exchange rate movements for each country. These explanations built up without theory may not work into the future.

Trade and Monetary Theories

Finally, exchange rate forecasting methods differ with respect to the economic theory used as a basis for formulating models of exchange rate fluctuations. In an earlier period most standard exchange rate analysis focused mainly on the trade and current account balances with relatively little attention to capital accounts. More recently, however, this focus has been reversed in the so-called monetary theory of the balance of payments: Exchange rate adjustment is considered mainly a monetary process in which separate consideration of movements in trade and current accounts is not of crucial importance. Today, proponents of both theories are found in the competition among exchange rate forecasters. Some more eclectic forecasting groups combine elements of both theories. However, financial variables, notably interest rates, play a much more important role in foreign exchange rate forecasting today, compared with the 1970s, when there was much more emphasis on balance-of-payments data.

Accuracy of Exchange Rate Forecasts

Early attempts to forecast exchange rates were reasonably successful, but most foreign exchange rate forecasts failed in the early 1980s. In fact, in 1983, an influential paper by Meese and Rogoff suggested that models of exchange rate changes did no better than a random walk model. However, in 1990, that view was challenged by Engle and Hamilton, who showed that exchange movements followed a series of long waves rather than a random walk pattern. Another paper by Koedijk and Schotman (1990) developed a model that explained exchange rate movements better than a random walk. However, a really workable exchange rate forecasting method remains to be developed.

Foreign Exchange Management Strategies

Once a forecast of the exchange rate outlook is completed, the foreign exchange forecast must be applied to protect the company from foreign exchange losses. Potential foreign exchange losses depend on a company's exposure, that is, on its vulnerability to foreign exchange losses. Broadly, there are two kinds of exposure: commercial and translation. Commercial exposure arises when a company has an obligation to make or receive a payment in foreign currency, for example, on receipt of imported goods or for goods that the company has exported. In either case losses can arise. In the first case, with imports there would be losses from an appreciation in the exchange rate in relation to the dollar, thus raising the company's payment for its imported goods. In the second case, if there was a devaluation of the foreign currency, the company would lose on the payment for its exports. In some instances the company can avoid commercial losses by quoting prices in dollars, but this is not always acceptable to foreign customers or sources of supply. When billing in dollars is not possible, companies often use the forward foreign exchange market to avoid foreign exchange risk. This is a market in which currencies are sold forward at specific dates ahead. Forward rates may be higher or lower than current rates, commonly known as spot rates. In the language of foreign exchange trading, forward rates above spots rates are at a premium, and forward rates below spot rates are at a discount. Premiums and discounts in foreign exchange contracts are of major concern to the foreign exchange manager because they represent the cost of being covered against foreign exchange losses. The decision to hedge or not to hedge a foreign exchange exposure depends on the foreign exchange manager's assessment of whether the cost of a contract is worth the risk of losses from an exchange rate revaluation or devaluation.

Aside from the forward market, possibilities for hedging also arise, for the case of devaluation risk, in the borrowing of weak currencies with the possibility of repayment after a devaluation takes place. To head off a revaluation threat, the company may extend loans in the suspect currency. For larger multinational companies with subsidiaries operating in most countries and with a network of transactions among the subsidiaries, the exact hedging strategy may become complex, possibly even requiring the use of the computer as discussed by Lieberman (1978).

References

Baille, Richard T., and Patrick C. McMahon, "The Foreign Exchange Market, Theory and Econometric Evidence," Cambridge University Press, Cambridge, 1989; Eiteman, David K., and Arthur I. Stonehill, *Multinational Business Finance,* 5th ed., Addison-Wesley, Reading, Mass., 1989; Engle, Charles, and James Hamilton, "The Long Swings in Foreign Exchange Rates," *American Economic Review,* vol. 80, no. 4, September 1990, pp. 689–714; Frenkel, J. A., "Flexible Exchange Rates and the Role of News, Lessons of the 1970s," *Journal of Political Economy,* August 1981, pp. 665–675; George, Abraham M., *Foreign Exchange Management and the Multinational Corporation,* Praeger, New York, 1978; Jacque, Laurent L., *Management of Foreign Exchange Risk,* D. C. Heath, Lexington, Mass., 1978; Koedijk, Kees, and Peter Schotman, "How to Beat the Random Walk," *Journal of International Economics,* vol. 29, November 1990. Lieberman, Gail, "A Systems Approach to Foreign Exchange Risk Management," *Financial Executive,* Financial Executives Institute, New York, December 1978; Meese, R. A., and K. Rogoff, "Empirical Exchange Rate Models for the Seventies: Do They Fit out of Sample?" *Journal of International Economics,* vol. 14, January 1983, pp. 3–24; Mussa, M., "A Model of Foreign Exchange Rate Dynamics," *Journal of Political Economy,* February 1982, pp. 94–104; Riehl, Heinz, and Rita Rodriguez, "Foreign Exchange Markets," *A Guide to Foreign Currency Operations,* McGraw-Hill, New York, 1977; Rodriguez, Rita, and E. Eugene Carter, *International Financial Management,* 3d ed., Prentice-Hall, Englewood Cliffs, N.J., 1984; Shapiro, Alan C., *Multinational Financial Management,* Allyn and Bacon, Needham Hts., Mass., 1986.

(*See also* Foreign exchange rates; International economics, an overview)

James L. Burtle

Foreign exchange rates

Foreign exchange rates are market quotations of the prices of foreign currencies in terms of domestic currency, or equivalently, the reciprocal, foreign currency prices of the domestic currency. As such, they represent rates of exchange of one currency for another which are used for most of the myriad transactions crossing national boundaries, whether foreign trade, tourism, international investment, or short-term money flows between countries. These exchange rates may be set either by governments, as in the pegged exchange rate system, or by a combination of market forces and government policies, as in the floating exchange rate system.

Exchange rates may be quoted either for spot or immediate (i.e., 2-day) delivery of one currency against another, or for various forward delivery dates, such as 1 month, 3 months, and so on. The difference between spot and forward quotations generally reflects the difference between the costs of borrowing the two currencies for the relevant period.

Since each country has trade and investment relationships with a number of other countries, no single foreign exchange rate can adequately measure the purchasing power of the domestic currency over foreign currencies in general. The concept of effective exchange rate has been developed to measure the weighted average price of foreign currencies in terms of domestic currency. Various weighting schemes have been devised, including import weights to reflect purchasing power over imports, bilateral trade weights to reflect the importance of trade relations with individual foreign countries, global trade weights to reflect the importance of different currencies in world trade, and elasticity-weighted trade shares to reflect differing degrees of competitiveness of a country vis-à-vis different foreign countries. Further discussion of the exchange rate refers to the effective exchange rate concept.

Microeconomic Role

For an economy that is relatively open to foreign trade and investment, the exchange rate has important effects on relative prices. Changes in the price of foreign exchange affect the domestic price of imports, the profitability of producing import substitutes, the profitability of exports, and the domestic price of exportable goods. For large countries producing differentiated export products, such as manufactured goods over whose price they have significant influence, changes in the exchange rate frequently lead to changes in the terms of trade, the ratio of the price of exports to the price of imports. For a smaller country whose trade prices may be determined in world markets, changes in the exchange rate have significant effects on the prices of traded goods relative to the prices of goods which are not traded abroad because of high transportation costs or other barriers. By changing relative costs of production in different countries, changes in exchange rates significantly affect the profitability of investment in different countries. Since different groups of producers are likely to be involved in producing exportable goods, import substitutes, or nontraded goods, changes in the relative prices of these different types of commodities have major effects on the distribution of income among these groups and among consumers, as well as upon the allocation of resources among different sectors of the economy and among different countries.

Macroeconomic Role

The exchange rate is also important as a macroeconomic variable, influencing domestic inflation, unemployment, and the balance of payments. Changes in the price of foreign exchange affect domestic inflation both directly, through the prices of traded goods and their substitutes, and indirectly, through effects of the balance of payments via the income adjustment mechanism and the monetary adjustment mechanism. For example, if a change in the level of the exchange rate through its effect on relative prices generates a substantial surplus of exports over imports of goods and services, that surplus represents additional foreign demand for domestic goods and services over and above domestic demand for foreign goods and services. That foreign demand represents a source of income generation in the export sector which spills over in a Keynesian multiplier process to the rest of the economy, raising prices and production in both the export sector and elsewhere, depending on conditions of capacity utilization in the different sectors of the economy. If capacity is fully utilized, domestic prices and wages may be expected to rise in proportion to the exchange rate, eliminating the relative price effect on the balance of payments. This Keynesian income adjustment mechanism reaches equilibrium when the excess of domestic saving over domestic investment matches the net accumulation of foreign assets or net foreign investment represented by the export surplus. The same process works in reverse for a deficit in which imports of goods and services exceed exports.

The classical monetary adjustment mechanism operates under floating rates when private investment abroad (or foreign borrowing) is unable to finance the export surplus (or deficit) at given prices, incomes, interest rates, and exchange rates. If the surplus on current account payments for goods, services, and unilateral transfers exceeds private capital outflow or lending abroad at the current exchange rate, the monetary authorities may either change the pegged exchange rate or allow the price of foreign currencies to float downward. Monetary authorities may keep the exchange rate unchanged by selling domestic currency and buying foreign currency to hold up the price of foreign currency. In the latter case, the country's foreign exchange reserves rise along with its domestic money supply as the central bank creates additional money to pay for the foreign currency. The expansion in the domestic money supply will normally lead to a reduction in domestic interest rates and expansion in domestic spending, prices, and production. The resulting expansion will reduce the surplus in the balance of payments. This monetary adjustment process may be cut short by a monetary policy designed to prevent the rise in the money supply. This is called "sterilization" of the reserve movement.

Changes in foreign exchange rates—together with changes in domestic macroeconomic policy, direct controls over various components of the balance of payments, income adjustments, and monetary flows—represent the various possible mechanisms through which international payments imbalances are resolved. The process involves a mixture of adjustment policies, which seek to alter the existing surpluses and deficits, and financing, which seeks to provide both capital flows and monetary flows to enable their continuation.

Determinants

Various partial theories of exchange rate determination have been developed over the years which may in combination provide an adequate, if impure, explanation of the many factors affecting market-determined, or floating, exchange rates. The purchasing-power-parity, or monetary, theory observing that the exchange rate is the relative price of different currencies focuses on the relative purchasing power of the different currencies in terms of goods and services. The theory implies that exchange rates move to offset relative inflation rates in different countries, after allowing for shifts in the relative importance of traded and nontraded goods. (The qualification is required because the theory rests on equality of traded-goods prices, whereas the prices of nontraded goods can differ significantly between countries.) Most evidence suggests that the theory is correct only as a long-run approximation of reality, except under conditions of hyperinflation, since traded goods do not flow instantaneously from one market to another to equalize prices.

The interest rate–parity theory concentrates on capital flows and the factors determining the relationship between spot and forward exchange rates. Comparison of the return from short-term assets held in one currency with the return from assets in another currency covered against the risk of a change in the exchange rate shows that arbitrage will equate the domestic interest rate to the foreign interest rate plus the forward premium on the foreign currency.

The formula is

$$R_d = R_f + \frac{y - x}{x}$$

where R_d and R_f are the domestic and foreign short-term interest rates in percent per period, y is the forward price of foreign currency for delivery at the end of the period, x is the spot price, and $(y - x)/x$ is the forward premium on foreign currency, in percentage per period (Levich, 1985). The evidence suggests that this theory is usually valid except when capital controls, the risk of possible future capital controls, or other types of market uncertainty become important. Such factors are often significant in comparisons between domestic financial markets in different countries but are usually absent in comparisons between Eurocurrency-market interest rates.

The efficient-market theory postulates that the forward exchange rate is an unbiased predictor of the expected future spot exchange rate. Tests of this theory suggest that it may be valid in some average sense but that changes in exchange rates are not predicted very well by forward rates, indicating the presence of substantial risk in speculation on changes in exchange rates.

The asset-market theory of exchange rates integrates the various other theories into a complete intertemporal theory which can be cast in terms of flows in the balance of payments (Branson and Henderson, 1985). According to this approach, the exchange rate is determined in the short run by equality of supply and demand for assets denominated in different currencies. The demands for these assets depend upon the relative interest rates, forward premiums, and expectations of changes in exchange rates emphasized by the interest rate–parity and efficient-market theories. Changes in the supplies of these assets to private wealth holders in different countries depend on surpluses and deficits in the current account of the balance of payments, together with central bank intervention in the exchange markets. These surpluses and deficits, however, depend upon deviations of exchange rates from purchasing power parity in different countries as well as upon other factors such as changes in tastes and technologies and fluctuations in aggregate demand in different countries.

Historical Background

Elements of the basic theory of foreign exchange rates were developed by David Hume (1752), David Ricardo (1811), and earlier writers. Hume's analysis focused on the mechanism by which excessive money creation under the gold standard (or a pegged exchange rate) leads to domestic inflation, a balance of payments deficit, and an outflow of money. Ricardo, writing about the gold value of the pound sterling under the floating rate conditions prevailing during the Napoleonic Wars, emphasized the importance of excessive money creation and domestic inflation in determining the fall in the gold value of the pound. Cassel (1922) formulated the purchasing-power-parity doctrine in its modern form to help explain the movements of exchange rates in the period following World War I. The interest rate–parity theory was developed by Keynes (1923), and the modern asset-market and efficient-market theories are developments of recent writers such as Black (1973) and Dornbusch (1976).

Controversial Issues

Both the theory of foreign exchange rates and exchange rate policies have generated debate. Theoretical debates have frequently questioned the validity or the sufficiency of one or another of the theories. More frequently, practical economists and policy-oriented analysts have argued that exchange rates are determined by flows in the balance of payments, attributable to a myriad of causes, without recognizing the overall pattern of causation and influence suggested by the asset-market theory.

The efficiency of the forward exchange market is hotly debated, for efficiency together with interest rate parity implies that capital markets are essentially risk-free and that assets denominated in different currencies are perfect substitutes. Such a finding would imply that floating exchange rates could operate relatively free of central bank intervention to smooth out fluctuations in exchange rates.

The debate over pegged versus floating exchange rates involves a choice either for individual countries or for the international monetary system as a whole. The Bretton Woods system, established in 1944 on the basis of pegged rates among all countries, broke down in 1971 and was replaced with a mixed system of floating and pegging in 1973, formalized by the second amendment to the charter of the International Monetary Fund, effective in 1978. The proponents of pegged rates argue that pegging reduces the short-run variability of exchange rates and hence the riskiness of international trade and investment. At the same time the maintenance of a constant exchange rate requires that domestic inflation match foreign inflation to avoid excessive balance of payments surpluses or deficits, thus implying a certain discipline over and credibility for domestic monetary and fiscal policies.

The proponents of floating rates note that the failure of such discipline leads to occasional large changes in pegged exchange rates, changes which rectify departures from purchasing-power parity and introduce additional risk into foreign trade and investment as well as induce speculation against the central bank. However, these proponents argue that floating rates provide domestic economic policy with additional freedom by eliminating the Hume mechanism through which money flows into or out of the economy.

The critics of floating rates point out that large swings in nominal exchange rates since 1973 have not led to rapid adjustment of payments imbalances but have in many cases aggravated them, promoting increased pressure for protectionist policies in deficit countries and raising the short-run variability of exchange rates. Critics argue that the increased freedom for domestic policies has often been abused, reducing the credibility of monetary and fiscal authorities.

Policies to restrict exchange rate fluctuations to "target zones" have been proposed and agreed to in the 1987 Louvre Agreement among the United States, Germany, Japan, and other leading industrialized countries. Since 1979, members of the European Economic Community have restricted their exchange rates among each others' currencies within the European Monetary System, while allowing their currencies to float jointly against other currencies, such as the U.S. dollar and the Japanese yen.

References

Black, S. W., "International Money Markets and Flexible Exchange Rate," *Princeton Studies in International Finance,* no. 32, 1973; Branson, W. H., and D. W. Henderson, "The Specification and Influence of Asset Markets," in R. W. Jones and P. B. Kenen (eds.), *Handbook of International Economics,* vol. 2, North-Holland, Amsterdam, 1985; Cassel, G., *Money and Foreign Exchange after 1914,* Macmillan, London, 1922; Dornbusch, R., "Expectations and Exchange Rate Dynamics," *Journal of Political Economy,* vol. 84, December 1976, pp. 1161–1176; Hume, D., "Of the Balance of Trade," in *Political Discourses,* Fleming, Edinburgh, 1752, reprinted in E. Rotwein (ed.), *David Hume: Writings on Economics,* University of Wisconsin Press, Madison, 1955; Keynes, J. M., *A Tract on Monetary Reform,* Macmillan, London, 1923; Levich, R. M., "Empirical Studies of Exchange Rates: Price Behavior, Rate Determination, and Market Efficiency," in R. W. Jones and P. B. Kenen (eds.), *Handbook of International Economics,* vol. 2, North-Holland, Amsterdam, 1985; Officer, L. H., "The Purchasing-Power-Parity Theory of Exchange Rates: A Review Article," *IMF Staff Papers,* vol. 23, no. 1, March 1976, pp. 1–60; Ricardo, D., *The High Price of Bullion,* 4th ed., J. Murray, London, 1811.

(*See also* Balance of international payments; Balance of international trade; Exports; Imports; International economics, an overview; Liquidity, international; Value of the dollar)

Stanley W. Black

Forward contract (*see* Commodity exchange; Futures)

Free enterprise system (*see* Capitalism)

Free trade (*see* Barriers to trade)

Fringe benefits

The term "fringe benefits" is used synonymously with employee benefits. Although "fringes" are decorative outer edges, implying relative unimportance, estimates of fringe benefits for 1990 place costs to U.S. companies at $1,025.2 billion, an average of $12,402 per worker, or 38.4 percent of payroll. Comparable figures for 1975, 1955, and 1929 are $244.4 billion, $36.1 billion, and $1.5 billion, respectively. A definition as nonwage (nonsalary) benefits is common but involves a contradiction with payroll figures of the U.S. Department of Labor which include in wages and salaries pay for time not worked (although the worker is able to work) and pay for sick leave. Social insurance costs are included in fringe benefits. "Perquisites" is a term frequently applied to fringe benefits instituted for limited numbers of managerial employees; it is more rarely used to apply to all fringe benefits other than those mandated by social insurance laws. Some fringe benefits involve rights of employees, without requiring any monetary outlay.

Prior to the 1930s there was probably an upward trend in fringe benefits, though with many irregularities due to such factors as early diminution of payment in kind and a later increase and subsequent decline of company towns. In specific sectors of the economy, the railroad industry for example, an early relatively high level of fringe benefits was reached. Since the 1930s, government action and labor union pressure in negotiations have been dominant, sometimes interrelated, influences in the upward trend in value and in relative importance of fringe benefits. Employer initiative stemming from such reasons as personnel policy, social responsibility, competition, and personal gains of management from fringe benefits has also been important. Inflation has been a big factor in the rising cost of fringe benefits. During the 1980s, labor union pressure became less dominant.

In addition to federal and/or state legislation mandating Old Age, Survivors, Disability and Health Insurance (OASDHI), unemployment insurance, and worker's compensation, tax laws and rulings encourage employer expenditures for fringe benefits because of their classification as tax-deductible business expenses or investment tax credits. In addition, numerous state laws and some federal laws do not mandate fringe benefits but do determine some of their provisions if they are initiated. Examples of relevant federal legislation are the Taft-Hartley Act, the Employee Retirement Income Security Act (ERISA), the Equal Employment Opportunity Act, the Civil Rights Act of 1974, the Health Maintenance Organization (HMO) Act, the Age Discrimination in Employment Act, and the Older Workers Benefit Protection Act. Federal laws that free employee wages contributed for fringe benefits from taxation include section 403(b) of the Internal Revenue Code (for employees of government or nonprofit institutions) and ERISA, providing for individual retirement arrangements (IRAs). Along this same line, employees may use pretax income for child care and other benefits through flexible spending accounts.

Fringe Benefit Categories

Because the same fringe benefit may be used in different ways, clear-cut categorization is somewhat difficult. One group of fringe benefits includes pay for time a worker does not work though able to work. As a rule, these periods interrupt the normal work-time sequence, and the employee is expected to return to work. Examples are paid meal periods; paid rest or smoking breaks; vacations of an ordinary nature; individualized leave in connection with birthdays, elections, births, deaths, attendance at meetings, etc.; extended vacations; sabbatical leaves; and those parts of the guaranteed annual wage and call-in time that are not offset by wages for time worked. In those few industries having extended vacations, the practice has sometimes arisen of offering the choice of extra compensation instead of the extended vacation. Business interruption insurance may cover payroll.

Another category of fringe benefits includes pay or other benefits for time not worked because of physical condition (including pregnancy) or pay because of the existence of a specific physical condition. Examples are sick leave days, worker's compensation, short-term disability plans, long-term disability under OASDHI, long-term disability not under OASDHI, disability income and waiver-of-premium provisions of life insurance, disability income and pension accumulation provisions of pension plans, travel-accident insurance, and disability income provisions of unemployment compensation in a limited number of jurisdictions. Under schedule disabilities of worker's compensation laws, the dismemberment part of accidental death and dismemberment insurance, and similar provisions of travel accident policies, payment may be made to the employee, dependent on the incurrence of specific injuries but independent of actual work time lost. Frequently, offset provisions are included for the purpose of preventing duplication of benefits. Because of this, long-term disability income (not under OASDHI) is sometimes referred to as a "phantom" benefit. At times unused sick leave days may be taken in cash, either periodically or on separation from employment.

Unemployment compensation is provided for under federal and state laws. In addition, supplementary unemployment benefits (SUB) are established by firms in a minority of industries. The payment of such supplementary benefits is likely to depend on the status of funds that are established for this purpose. As already mentioned, the cash equivalent of unused sick leave may be available, as may accumulated vacation time, profit-sharing proceeds, deferred compensation, or an early pension. Termination or separation pay is another fringe benefit, and, where this is available, it is likely to vary with length of service. Often provision for payment of life and health insurance premiums is made for limited periods of unemployment. Placement services are sometimes established on an ad hoc basis, but this is mostly a fringe benefit of middle and upper management.

Health expense benefits almost invariably include surgical costs as well as a fairly complete range of other services utilized during hospitalization for limited periods (usually up to 1 year). Insurance of the employee's family is usual. Coverage may be extended to nursing homes. Otherwise, out-of-hospital medical expenses are included in major medical insurance, as is long-term hospitalization. HMOs, which under certain circumstances must be offered as alternatives to health insurance plans, stress preventive care. Otherwise, physical examinations are not likely to be covered, except under managerial perquisites. Some companies pay for health screening. Dental insurance may be an independent plan or may be included in major medical insurance. Prescription-drug coverage by itself is rare, as is vision care, although the former is frequently found in other health insurances. Medicare payments may be made for employees in the appropriate age category as well as for retirees.

Coverage of death benefits is found in OASDHI, life insurance, worker's compensation, accidental death and disability, travel accident insurance, and pension plans or other retirement arrangements.

Retirement benefits are generally approached through pension plans, and these cover most employees under OASDHI, with many coming under public and private plans in addition. Retirement benefits are also created through profit sharing, deferred compensation, stock bonus plans, employer contributions to IRAs, paid-up whole life insurance, savings plans, employee stock ownership plans (ESOPs), tax reduction act stock ownership plans (TRASOPs), stock-appreciation rights, and phantom stock and salary-continuation plans. The Simplified Employee Pension (SEP) allows wide variation in employer contributions. Life and health insurance may be continued for retirees.

Other fringe benefits include free or reduced-price meals; merchandise discounts; use of automobiles, airplanes, and yachts; club and professional society memberships; parking; educational expense support; professional society meeting expenses; low- or no-interest loans; airline and railroad passes; financial and tax counseling; child care centers; housing; and expense accounts. Prepaid legal expense and group automobile and homeowner's insurances have remained unimportant. Some fringe benefits are products of the times, examples being kidnap and ransom insurance and the provision of vans for transportation to work. Care for well and ill children and elderly relatives is in a developmental stage. There has been little enthusiasm for nursing home insurance. Some maternity and almost all paternity leave as well as computer-assisted work at home might be classified as "costless" fringe benefits.

Relatively great inflation in costs has made medical coverage a deeply troubled area of fringe benefits.

Fringe Benefits in Other Countries

Throughout the free world, fringe benefits follow various patterns. Fringe benefits are usually underdeveloped in underdeveloped countries. Social insurance laws may be somewhat disregarded, as in some countries in middle-belt Africa. There, as in underdeveloped countries elsewhere, the best fringe benefit systems are found in multinational companies. In many of the more highly industrialized countries, there is greater inflexibility in health and pension benefits than in the United States. Some examples of significant differences are very large separation pay (Mexico), lower retirement age for females than for males (Italy, Luxembourg), phased early retirement (Germany).

References

Greenough, William C., and Francis P. King, *Pension Plans and Public Policy,* Columbia University Press, New York, 1976; Mehr, Robert I., and Bob A. Hedges, *Risk Management: Concepts and Applications,* Irwin, Homewood, Ill., 1974; Leimberg, Stephan R., and John J. McFadden,

The Tools and Techniques of Employment Benefit and Retirement Planning, 2d ed., National Underwriter, Cincinnati, 1990; William M. Mercer Fraser Ltd., *International Benefit Guidelines 1991,* Leatherhead, Surrey, United Kingdom, 1991; U.S. Chamber of Commerce, *Employee Benefits,* Washington, D.C., 1991.

(*See also* Collective bargaining; Labor-management relations)

Theodore Bakerman

Futures

Futures refer to a futures contract which is a financial security created by an organized exchange for the purpose of buying or selling a commodity for future delivery.

Characteristics

There are basically three related ways to buy or sell a commodity: (1) the spot market, (2) the forward market, and (3) the futures market.

The first method is in the cash or spot market for immediate delivery. The price at which the exchange takes place is called the "cash" or "spot" price.

The second method is by entering a forward contract. A forward contract is an agreement made today between a buyer and seller of a commodity to exchange the commodity for cash at a predetermined future date (not today) at a price agreed upon today. The agreed-upon price is called the "forward" price.

The third method is by entering a futures contract. A futures contract is a financial security, issued by an organized exchange, to buy or sell a commodity at a predetermined future date (not today) at a price agreed upon today. The agreed-upon price is called the "futures" price. However, to guarantee that the buyers and sellers of the security will honor their future commitment, a system of margin requirements and daily settlements is implemented by the exchange. It is this daily settlement procedure which differentiates futures contracts from forward contracts and futures prices from forward prices.

Daily settlement is called "marking to market." Usually, when the buyer or seller of the futures contract opens a position, a margin account is also opened. A margin account is similar to a security deposit (usually cash or interest-bearing securities) held in the buyer or seller's name to guarantee that the terms of the futures contract are fulfilled. Marking to market occurs when the margin account's balance is adjusted at the end of each trading day. It is adjusted by the daily change in the futures price. For example, if the futures price increases on any particular day, the change in the futures price will be added to a buyer's margin account. Conversely, if the futures price falls, the change will be subtracted from a buyer's margin account. Daily settlement, in effect, pays out in cash the daily change in the value of the futures contract. The value of the futures contract, thus, returns to zero at the end of each trading day. If the margin account falls too low, additional margin will be requested. If the margin account's balance becomes too large, the surplus can be removed. Futures contracts only trade on organized exchanges.

Futures Exchanges and Futures Commodities Traded

Unlike forward contracts, which have been around for thousands of years, futures contracts are a more recent phenomenon. The first futures contracts were begun in

1848 with the opening of the Chicago Board of Trade. Since that time, trading in futures contracts has greatly increased.

Futures contracts are currently traded all over the world and against different types of commodities. In 1990 there were 11 exchanges in the United States alone and 39 exchanges in foreign countries. The three largest U.S. exchanges, in terms of volume of trade in 1990, were the Chicago Board of Trade, the Chicago Mercantile Exchange, and the New York Mercantile Exchange. The largest five foreign futures exchanges, in terms of volume of trade in 1990, were the London International Financial Futures Exchange (U.K.), Le Marché à Terme des Instruments Financiers (France), the Osaka Securities Exchange (Japan), the Tokyo Stock Exchange (Japan), and the Tokyo Commodity Exchange (Japan).

Futures contracts are written against over 50 different commodities. These commodities are divided into four types: (1) agricultural commodities and metals (e.g., corn, oats, wheat, crude oil, lumber, cotton, sugar, gold, silver, platinum), (2) interest-earning securities (e.g., U.S. Treasury bills, U.S. Treasury notes, U.S. Treasury bonds, eurodollar deposits, municipal bonds issued in the United States), (3) foreign currencies (e.g., British pound, Japanese yen), and (4) equity indexes (e.g., the Standard and Poor's 500, the New York Stock Exchange Index, the Japanese Nikkei index). Although the four types of commodities are exhaustive, the examples are not.

The commodity upon which a futures contract is written is necessarily standardized with respect to quality and quantity. Standardization facilitates increased volume. Futures contracts may require physical delivery of the commodity at the terminate date or require cash settlement. Furthermore, additional contractual requirements often are associated with traded futures in terms of price and position limits. These are imposed to reduce the likelihood of market manipulation.

The futures contracts traded and the exchanges upon which they trade are constantly evolving. Just 30 years ago, in fact, there were no contracts trading on interest-bearing securities, foreign currencies, or equity indices. In 1990, however, these three commodity types accounted for over 60 percent of all the contracts traded.

Uses

There are three major uses of futures contracts: (1) price discovery, (2) hedging, and (3) speculation. Price discovery is the use of futures prices to predict spot prices that will prevail in the future. These predictions are useful for production decisions involving the various commodities. The forecasting ability of futures prices differs significantly across the various commodities. Some futures prices provide good predictions, and others do not.

Hedging is the use of futures contracts to reduce the return variability of an investment portfolio or production process involving the cash commodity. This is, perhaps, the most important use of futures contracts. It is also the prime justification used for the approval of new commodity contracts by the Commodity Futures Trading Commission (CFTC). For example, consider an investment in the U.S. stock market by a mutual fund which has experienced an unusually good performance over the past year. To lock in these gains and to hedge possible adverse movements in the stock market, the mutual fund could short futures contracts on a stock index like the Standard and Poor's 500. As a second example, consider a farmer who is planting wheat for future harvesting when current cash prices are high. To lock in his high expected profits, he can sell wheat futures today for future delivery.

Speculation is the use of futures contracts to take an investment position and potentially profit from special information concerning the future spot price of a cash commodity. Futures markets are an efficient vehicle for speculation because of low transaction costs and high implicit leverage. The alternative to futures markets is taking a direct position in the cash commodity with storage.

Theory

It is possible under perfect market assumptions to determine the exact relationships among the spot price, forward price, and futures price. Consider an economy with frictionless trading in the spot commodity. That is, the spot commodity has no storage costs associated with it and it is possible to short sell the spot commodity with no restrictions imposed on the timing or quantity of the short sales. Furthermore, assume that the economy has traded sufficient assets to span all risks relevant to both the pricing of the spot commodity and the term structure of interest rates. This situation is called a "complete market."

We need some notation to describe these relationships. Let S_t be the spot commodity's price at time t where t is between 0 and T. Let F_t be the time t forward price for delivery of the spot commodity at time T. Let f_t be the time t futures price for delivery of the spot commodity at time T. Let B_t be the time t value of a money-market account starting with an initial investment of 1 dollar at time 0. Finally, let P_t be the time t value of a default-free zero coupon bond paying 1 dollar at time T for sure.

Under the above perfect market structure, it can be shown that there exists a simple method for calculating present values. The method involves the use of risk-adjusted probabilities, called "psuedo-" or "risk-neutral" probabilities. To calculate the present value of a future cash flow, simply take its expected value using the psuedo-probabilities, but only after discounting by the time value of money.

For example, letting $E(\cdot)$ be expectation with respect to the psuedo- or risk-neutral probabilities, the spot price can be written as its expected time T value, appropriately discounted, i.e.,

$$S_t = E[S_T(B_t/B_T)]$$

The quantity (B_t/B_T) corresponds to the interest earned on a money market account over the time period (t, T). As a second example, the zero-coupon bond's price is equal to the expected value of a dollar received at time T, i.e.,

$$P_t = E[1 \ (B_t/B_T)]$$

The first result available is the cost-of-carry relationship between the spot price and the forward price, and it is given by

$$F_t = S_t/P_t$$

The forward price is equal to the spot price, augmented by the interest earned by storing the spot commodity over the time period (t, T). Using the previous equations for the spot commodity's price and the zero-coupon's price, we can rewrite this cost-of-carry relationship as:

$$F_t = E[S_T \ (B_t/B_T)] \ / E(B_t/B_T)$$

This will be useful later on for comparison with the formula for futures prices.

Futures prices can be shown to equal the undiscounted expectation of the future spot price, i.e.,

$$f_t = E(S_T)$$

The reason for this is that, to a risk-neutral speculator, the futures price is an unbiased predictor of the future spot price.

The relationship between forward prices and futures prices can now be clarified. If interest rates are deterministic, then the forward price equals the spot price because (B_t/B_T) is nonstochastic, and it can be moved outside the expectations operator and cancelled. Otherwise, the futures price and the forward price differ. They differ because of the correlation between interest rate movements and the spot commodity's storage return.

It is possible to generalize these relationships to incorporate both more realistic market frictions and incomplete markets. Nonetheless, this simplest economy described above is enough to illustrate both the differences between these three prices and the fact that forward contracts are distinct from futures contracts.

References

Cox, John, Jonathan Ingersoll, and Steve Ross, "The Relationship between Forward Prices and Futures Prices," *Journal of Financial Economics,* vol. 9, no. 4, 1981, pp. 321–346; Edwards, Franklin, and Cindy Ma, *Futures and Options,* McGraw-Hill, New York, 1992; Fama, Eugene F., and Kenneth R. French, "Commodity Futures Prices: Some Evidence on Forecast Power, Premiums and the Theory of Storage," *Journal of Business,* vol. 60, no. 1, 1987, pp. 55–73; Kolb, Robert W., *Understanding Futures Markets* (3d ed.), Kolb, Miami, Florida, 1991; Jarrow, Robert, "The Pricing of Commodity Options with Stochastic Interest Rates," *Advances in Futures and Options Research,* vol. 2, 1987, pp. 19–46.

(*See also* Commodity exchange)

Robert Jarrow

Game theory, economic applications

Game theory is the mathematical analysis of principles of decision making in situations involving two or more players with (at least partly) conflicting interests. Its central problem was formulated by John von Neumann (1928) as follows: "n players S_1, $S_2, \ldots, S_n$ are playing a a given game of strategy, G. How must one of the participants play in order to achieve a most advantageous result?"

A game of strategy, said von Neumann, consists of a series of events each of which may have a finite number of distinct results; the results of some events are determined by chance and of others by the free decisions of the players; for each event it is known which player is to make the decision and how much the player knows about the results of the earlier events at the time the decision is made; when the outcome of all events is known, the payments the players $S_1, S_2, \ldots, S_n$ must make to each other are calculated according to a fixed rule. Von Neumann asserted that almost any event in daily life could be viewed as a game of strategy and that the principal concern of classical economics was as follows: "How is the absolutely selfish 'homo economicus' going to act under given external circumstances?"

Mathematicians and Game Theory

Von Neumann was a mathematical genius whose work has had a lasting impact on several fields of pure and applied mathematics and on quantum physics. His 1928 paper "On the Theory of Games of Strategy" was published in German in a mathematical journal and went virtually unnoticed by economists. His interest in doing a major work on game theory was kindled by the economist Oskar Morgenstern, who arrived in 1938 at Princeton University where von Neumann was a professor. The result of their collaboration was the classic *Theory of Games and Economic Behavior* (1944). Economic motivation is presented in Chapter 1 in a series of sections on the mathematical method in economics, the problem of rational behavior, the notion of utility, and the structure of game theory—solutions and standards of behavior. Four sections of Chapter 11 deal with the economic interpretation of general non-zero-sum games for cases of one, two, and three players and "the general market"; the rest of the book is heavily mathematical, and there is no attempt to relate the results to economics as distinct from other possible contexts.

Until the late 1950s the work of developing and extending game theory was done almost exclusively by mathematicians. Several of the concepts that proved to be of greatest importance for economists were the Nash bargaining equilibrium in 1950, the Shapley value in 1953, and the core by D. B. Gillies in 1953. In 1956 Harsanyi pointed out that a solution to the bargaining problem proposed by the economist Zeuthen in 1930 was mathematically equivalent to Nash's, and in 1959 Shubik demonstrated that the core of an n-person game was equivalent to the contract curve derived by the economist Edgeworth in 1881. Other economists noted that Nash's solution of the bargaining problem includes as a special case the duopoly model published by Cournot in 1838.

Economists and Game Theory

During the 1960s, an increasing number of economists became interested in reformulating problems of market structure and competition in game-theoretic terms, and by the late 1970s this was one of the most active and prestigious fields of economic research. As of 1979, nearly all publications in this tradition were directed toward clarifying economic theory; Telser (1978) was one of the few who tried to check game-theoretic models of oligopoly against market data.

The difficulties of applying game theory in real-life situations are suggested by Shubik's contrasting list of the major assumptions used (1) in game-theoretic models and (2) in behavioral models such as business management games that are intended to approximate the actual working environments of corporation executives:

Game Theory	Behavioral Theories
Rules of the game	Laws and customs of society
External symmetry	Personal detail
No social conditioning	Socialization assumed
No role playing	Role playing
Fixed, well-defined payoffs	Difficult to define and may change
Perfect intelligence	Limited intelligence
No learning	Learning
No coding problems	Coding problems
Primarily static	Primarily dynamic

SOURCE Martin Shubik, *Games for Society, Business and War: Towards a Theory of Gaming*, Elsevier, New York, 1975, p. 158.

Shubik saw game theory as "a useful bench mark and a fundamentally important methodological approach to the study of situations involving potential conflict" and devoted nearly half of his book to an elucidation of game theory even though his primary concerns were describing and improving behavioral games of the business management type. In real life, executives might use a game theory model with its well-defined rules and outcomes as a checklist for identifying those key aspects of a situation which depend on personalities, communication patterns, and loyalties specific to the situation.

In a similar spirit Johansen (1977) devoted about 40 pages of his practically oriented book on macroeconomic planning to a discussion of game theory. His conceptual model includes what he calls the Central Authority and a number of the larger noncentral decision makers whose preferences may be in conflict among themselves and with those of the Central Authority. These larger decision makers are keenly aware of the interdependencies involved and may be viewed as engaging in a sophisticated game of strategy; the situation cannot be resolved by using classical methods of maximization (e.g., by regarding the Central Authority as an autonomous decision maker selecting an optimal point on its own preference function). Johansen does not attempt to operationalize such a model but puts it forward for its conceptual value.

Core Theory

As of 1979, Telser had done more than anyone else to adapt the theory of the core of a game to economic applications. In his 1978 book, *Economic Theory and the Core,* he applied core theory to the analysis of externalities, public goods, and free riders; to specification of sufficient conditions for natural monopoly or natural monopsony; to certain problems in the theories of location and storage; and to empirical studies of storage and of price distributions. He also shows that the core is empty (i.e., no competitive equilibrium exists) for an industry in which all plants have identical U-shaped average cost curves and rising marginal costs—thus upsetting the familiar example of industry equilibrium that has appeared in most economics textbooks since 1930. In an earlier work Telser also applies core theory to the Cournot-Nash model of duopoly and to clarification of the conditions under which collusion can be expected to dominate competition in an industry (in the absence of legal restraints).

Harsanyi noted that the theory of games had not found extensive applications in the sciences of social behavior up to that time—mainly because the von Neumann and Morgenstern approach did not yield determinate solutions for two-person, non-zero-sum games or for n-person games. Harsanyi proposed a general theory of rational behavior in game situations which "by means of a few additional and more powerful rationality postulates" would provide determinate solutions for both of these game classes: "Only a theory providing determinate solutions can suggest reasonably specific empirically testable hypotheses about social behavior and can attempt to explain and to predict . . . the outcome of social interaction in various real-life social situations" (Harsanyi, 1977). Harsanyi reformulated many of the classificatory game theory models in such a way as to facilitate social science (including economic) applications.

The theory of the core on an n-person game as n becomes very large (in a certain sense, even infinite) has led to an impressive reformulation of general equilibrium theory. Aumann, Debreu, Vind, and Hildenbrand have been among the major contributors to this development. The core of a pure-exchange economy is the set of all allocations that do not exceed the sum of the endowments initially held by the n households participating in the economy and that cannot be improved upon by any coalition (set of households), including the coalition of all n households. Any allocation in the core is Pareto-efficient in the sense that there is no way of making every household better off. Aumann and Shapley (1974) make the assumption that the households form a continuum (i.e., the resources of each household constitute an infinitesimal piece of the entire economy) and show that, under the further assumption that utility may be transferred (i.e., side payments made) between households, there is a unique point in the core of the economy, and this point coincides with the Shapley value. They define the notion of competitive equilibrium for such an economy and show that this equilibrium yields a unique payoff (and, hence, a unique system of relative prices) which also coincides with the Shapley value and, therefore, with the unique core point.

References

Aumann, R. J., and L. S. Shapley, *Values of Non-atomic Games,* Princeton University Press, Princeton, 1974; Friedman, J. W., *Oligopoly and the Theory of Games,* North-Holland, Amsterdam, 1977; Harsanyi, John C., *Rational Behavior and Bargaining Equilibrium in Games and Social Situations,* Cambridge University Press, Cambridge, 1977, p. 4; Johansen, Leif, *Lectures on Macroeconomic Planning,* part 1: *General Aspects,* North-Holland, Amsterdam, 1977; Shubik, Martin, *Games for Society, Business and War: Towards a Theory of Gaming,* Elsevier, New York, 1975, p. 158; Telser, Lester G., *Economic Theory and the Core,* University of Chicago Press, Chicago, 1978; von Neumann, John, "Zur theorie der Gesellschaftssbiel," *Math. Annalen,* vol. 100, 1928, pp. 295–320; von Neumann, John, and Oskar Morgenstern, *Theory of Games and Economic Behavior,* 3d ed., Wiley, New York, 1953 (1st ed. originally published by Princeton University Press, Princeton, N.J., 1944).

(*See also* Competition; General equilibrium; Statistical methods in economics and business, an overview)

Ted K. Kaul and Karl A. Fox

General Agreement on Tariffs and Trade

Since the nineteenth century, the dominant view of most economists, at least those of the developed world, has been that an open, nondiscriminatory trading system among nations would maximize global economic welfare. It was not until 1947, however, that a major group of nations not linked by strong common cultural or imperial ties undertook to enter into a formal agreement to establish such a system. The agreement, the General Agreement on Tariffs and Trade (GATT), was initially signed by only 23 nations, but by 1992 this number had grown to more than 100. Seven multilateral tariff negotiations have been held since 1948, the results of which have been to extend the 1948 agreement, and an eighth "round" of negotiations is in progress at the time of this writing.

Three factors doubtlessly motivated nations to enter into the 1948 agreement. The first was the belief among many national leaders that the events leading to World War II were triggered by the Great Depression of the 1930s, which in turn was believed to have been prolonged and deepened by the very high tariffs enacted by virtually all the major trading nations during the early 1930s. Liberalization of the international economic system was widely perceived as a way to avoid recurrence of a similar calamity, and in this spirit a thorough reform of the international monetary system was undertaken during the 1940s as well as an effort to liberalize trade.

The second factor was the leadership role of the United States. The United States actually began the 1930s tariff escalation with the passage of the Smoot-Hawley Act of 1930, but in 1934 legislation was passed to enable the President to negotiate mutual reduction of tariffs on a bilateral basis. By the late 1930s, U.S. economic leaders became convinced that vastly reduced tariffs would be in the nation's best interest if these could be regulated multilaterally.

The third factor was the need to rebuild Europe following World War II. The belief of many European leaders was that an open international economic system was a prerequisite to this rebuilding.

In the years immediately following World War II, U.S. leaders saw the GATT as only one part of a more wide-ranging program to create an open international economy. This program was to have been embodied in an the International Trade Organization (ITO). Preparatory meetings for the creation of the ITO were held from the fall of 1946 through early 1948. As part of this work program, the GATT itself was drafted in Geneva, Switzerland, from April to October 1947 and was to have been part of the ITO charter. The charter itself was scheduled to be completed at the Havana Conference of 1948. By the time a draft charter was worked out, however, the spirit of international cooperation that had prevailed in the U.S. Congress during the immediate aftermath of World War II had waned, and by early 1950 it became clear that Congress would not accept the ITO. A somewhat more modest proposal for an Organization for Trade Cooperation was rejected by Congress in 1955, and thus the GATT became by default the central agreement.

Because it was seen originally as part of a wider-ranging agreement, the GATT came into effect on January 1, 1948, by means of a temporary "Protocol of Provisional Application," which established an administrative organization to implement the agreed-upon articles. Had the ITO come into being, this protocol would have expired and the administrative organization would have been absorbed into the secretariat of ITO. However, because this did not come to pass, the GATT administrative organization evolved into a permanent secretariat, now headquartered in Geneva, Switzerland.

The GATT as a Legal Entity

As a legal document, the GATT is not a single agreement but rather a series of agreements. Article I of the GATT contains the celebrated most favored nation (MFN) obligation under which each member nation must accord to other member nations' imports and exports treatment that is at least as favorable as that applied to the nation receiving the best access to its market.

Article II makes national obligations with regard to tariff schedules an integral part of the GATT and its treaty obligations. The general negotiations produced a series of agreements by participating nations—the European Community is represented as a single entity in the GATT—to limit tariffs on specific items to negotiated amounts, and the focus of most of the succeeding multilateral tariff negotiations has been on further tariff reductions.

Much of the remainder of the GATT is designed to prevent evasion of the tariff obligations of article II by the use of nontariff barriers. Article III outlines a national treatment obligation whereby member nations must not submit imports to more restrictive standards with respect to taxation or regulation than domestically produced goods. Article VII regulates customs valuation procedures, article VIII regulates import and export fees, article IX regulates required marks of origin, article X provides for transparency of trade regulations, and article XI, with exceptions, prohibits import quotas. Article XVI puts some restraint on export subsidies by governments.

As a step toward liberalization of international trade, the GATT was a major step forward, but even so it was riddled with exceptions. Principal exceptions are embodied in articles XII to XIV, allowing a nation to restrict imports under a balance-of-payments crisis; article XVIII provides special balance-of-payments safeguards applicable only to developing nations. Articles XX and XXI allow exceptions for purposes of implementing health and safety regulations and for national security, and article XIX (the escape clause article) allows temporary restraints on imports which cause serious or material injury to domestic producers. Article XXIV allows countries that participate in free trade areas or customs unions to deviate from article I with respect to trade from other member states. Article XXV allows signatory nations collectively, by a two-thirds majority, to grant waivers or exceptions to other obligations in exceptional circumstances.

Modifying Codes

Agreements reached in the "Tokyo round" of multilateral trade negotiations, concluded in Geneva in 1979, to a large degree focus on limiting or clarifying some of these exceptions and on eliminating nontariff barriers to trade. The agreements are embodied in a series of codes which modify or interpret the application of specific articles of the GATT. The codes cover:

1. Subsidies and countervailing measures, pertaining to articles VI, XVI, and XXIII, both limit the extent to which governments can subsidize exports and standardize procedures under which governments can impose countervailing duties (or other measures) on imports subsidized by exploring nations.

2. The antidumping code, pertaining to article VI, standardizes determination of dumping practices (exporting to a foreign market at a price below that charged in a domestic market) and establishes uniform remedies to be used by importing nations against firms found to be dumping and causing "material injury" to domestic producers.

3. Customs valuation, pertaining to article VII, defines standard procedures for valuing imports for customs duty purposes.

4. The government procurement code obligates a signatory government generally not to discriminate unreasonably against foreign sources of supply when procuring goods or services for its own use.

5. The technical-barriers-to-trade code forbids governments from using technical standards or certification requirements to discriminate unreasonably against imports of foreign-made goods.

6. Import licensing procedures simplify and standardize import licensing procedures.

7. The code for trade in civil aircraft virtually removes any tariff or nontariff barriers to international trade in civilian aircraft.

Two additional codes, the international dairy agreement and the bovine meat arrangement, attempt to ease trade restrictions pertaining to dairy and meat products.

New Issues

Whereas the Tokyo round focused on clarifying existing GATT provisions, the effort in the current "Uruguay round" seeks to expand the coverage of GATT rules to new areas such as services, direct investment, and intellectual property as well as to revisit "old" issues such as subsidies and countervailing measures, safeguards, antidumping, and the treatment of exceptions such as exist for the textiles and agriculture industries. The Uruguay round of negotiations began in late 1985, with a targeted completion by the end of 1990. As of the time of this writing (late July 1992), however, the negotiations had not been successfully concluded due to an impasse over differing U.S. and EC positions on agricultural reforms.

New issues include all the following:

A new general agreement on trade in services, which would establish new rules specifically to deal with services sectors that previously had not been subject to GATT law

An agreement on trade-related investment measures (TRIMs) that would limit the abilities of governments to impose certain types of performance requirements on the domestic operations of foreign-controlled firms that might have the effect of distorting international trade

An agreement on trade-related intellectual property (TRIPS) that would establish new rights and obligations of governments with respect to patents, copyrights, trademarks, trade secrets, and other matters pertaining to intellectual property

In addition, substantial institutional reform of the GATT process is sought under the Uruguay round. Reforms being contemplated would expedite the process for settlement of disputes and institute a new appeal procedure for panel rulings. Also, a regular trade policy review mechanism would be launched. An institutional framework would be created for administering the various new agreements concluded under the Tokyo and Uruguay rounds, the Multilateral Trade Organization (MTO). The MTO also would consolidate the dispute settlements provisions of the various new accords into one organizational entity. Individual nations would become members of the MTO, and to join a nation would be bound to accept the full terms of the GATT itself as well as the Uruguay round agreements and all Tokyo round codes except those on civil aircraft, government procurement, and meat and dairy arrangements.

Unfortunately, at the time of this writing, the widespread expectation was that the Uruguay round could fail. The major unresolved issues center around agriculture, where major disagreements exist between the United States and the European Community with respect to agricultural price and income supports and export subsidies.

References

Baldwin, Robert E., and J. David Richardson, *The Uruguay Round and Beyond: Problems and Prospects*, National Bureau of Economic Research, Cambridge, Mass., 1991; Brown, W. A., *The United States and Restoration of World Trade*, Brookings, Washington, D.C., 1950; Cline, William R., *The Future of World Trade in Textiles and Apparel*, Institute for International Economics, Washington, D.C., 1987; Curzon, Gerard, and Victoria Curzon, "The Management of Trade Relations in the GATT," in S. Shonfeld (ed.), *International Economic Relations in the Western World 1959–1971*, Oxford University Press, London, 1976; Dam, K., *The GATT: Law and International Economic Cooperation*, University of Chicago Press, Chicago, 1970; Diebold, William, "The End of the I.T.O.," *Essays in International Finance*, no. 16, Princeton University Press, Princeton, N.J., 1952; Evans, J. W., "The General Agreement on Tariffs and Trade," *International Organization*, University of Wisconsin Press, Madison, Wisc., January 1968; Feketekuty, Geza, *International Trade in Services: An Overview and Blueprint for Negotiations*, Ballinger, Cambridge, Mass., 1988; General Agreement on Tariffs and Trade, *Basic Instruments and Selected Documents*, Geneva, 1969, revised periodically; Hathaway, Dale E., *Agriculture and the GATT: Rewriting the Rules,* Policy Analysis in International Economics No. 20, Institute for International Economics, Washington, D.C., 1987; Hufbauer, G. C., and J. J. Schott, *Trading for Growth: The Next Round of Trade Negotiations,* Institute for International Economics, Washington, D.C., 1985; Jackson, J. H., *World Trade and the Law of GATT,* Bobbs-Merrill, Indianapolis, 1969; *Reforming World Agricultural Trade: A Policy Statement by 29 Professionals from 17 Countries,* Institute for International Economics, Washington, D.C., 1988; Rode, Reinhard, *GATT and Conflict Management: A Transatlantic Strategy for a Stronger Regime,* Westview, Boulder, Colo., 1990; Schott, Jeffrey (ed.), *Completing the Uruguay Round: A Results-Oriented Approach to the GATT Trade Negotiations,* Institute for International Economics, Washington, D.C., 1990; U.S. Senate Committee on Finance and U.S. House of Representatives Committee on Ways and Means, *Multilateral Trade Negotiations: International Codes Agreed to in Geneva, Switzerland, April 12, 1979,* 1979.

(*See also* Barriers to trade; Dumping; European Community; Exports; Imports; International economics, an overview; Protectionism)

Edward M. Graham

General equilibrium

General equilibrium analysis deals with the basic issues of economics: value, distribution, and welfare; however, it is the branch of economics that is the most technical and least accessible to the nonprofessional. Even a definition of general economic equilibrium is not easy to formulate. The concept of economic equilibrium suggests that market forces are in balance, whereas general equilibrium analysis is distinguished from partial economic equilibrium analysis by the requirement that the price of every good is free to vary and that all markets must clear. In partial equilibrium analysis the prices of several commodities are held fixed relative to one another, and spillovers between markets are largely ignored. General equilibrium analysis emphasizes relations among markets: A technological advance in the process of steel production typically not only changes the price of steel but, in general equilibrium, changes also wages in the steel industry, the price of aluminum, the demand for machines that make aluminum, the number of plants devoted to steel production, and so on.

Most general equilibrium theory refers to markets which have perfect competition and private ownership. Among the requirements of perfect competition is the assumption that consumers and firms act as if the amount that they buy or sell on each market does not affect the price in that market; private ownership means that all the land, labor, and capital in the economy is owned by consumers. Consider an economy in which there is perfect competition, private ownership, and a large number of consumers and firms. Equilibrium is described as follows: For every list of commodity prices, each firm has a production plan that maximizes profit among the plans that are technologically possible for the firm; similarly, each consumer has a consumption plan that is preferred among the plans that the consumer can afford given a certain level of wealth. The economic system (described by consumers, firms, and the distribution of ownership) is in equilibrium if firm plans and consumer plans are consistent. In the absence of equilibrium, either demand exceeds supply or supply exceeds demand on some markets, and prices must change to ration buyers or sellers. If demand exceeds supply in a market, there will be a tendency for prices to increase and ration buyers; similarly, if supply exceeds demand, prices will tend to fall. Equilibrium requires that the forces which bring about changes in prices are in balance; that is, equilibrium requires the equality between the demand and supply for each commodity.

History

Adam Smith's *The Wealth of Nations* (1776) is concerned with general equilibrium analysis. His insight that social equilibrium is determined by, yet different from, the action of individual agents is perhaps the single most distinctive characteristic of the general equilibrium point of view. Léon Walras, in his *Elements of Pure Economics* (1874) developed and studied an abstract model of general equilibrium that has most of the features of the general equilibrium models we study today, and F. Y. Edgeworth (1881) and V. Pareto (1909) provided the first rigorous formulations of the welfare notion that is now referred to as "Pareto efficiency." The fact that under rather general conditions equilibria are Pareto-efficient gives precise meaning to Smith's celebrated claim that individuals acting in their own self-interest unintentionally promote the social good.

Modern general equilibrium theory is a technical subject; however, its central themes remain at the heart of economic analysis. Abraham Wald (1936) was the first to prove a general theorem concerning the existence of equilibrium prices for an economy; his results were subsequently generalized by K. J. Arrow and G. Debreu (1954), L. W. McKenzie (1954), and Debreu (1959). Arrow (1951) used set theory to expose the precise relation between equilibrium and Pareto efficiency, and his formulation has been the basis for all subsequent analysis. More recently, the relation between competitive equilibrium and various game theory notions of equilibrium (in particular the core and Nash equilibrium) have been an important area of investigation. Shubik (1959), Scarf (1962), Debreu and Scarf (1963), Aumann (1964), and Hildenbrand (1974) studied the relation between the core and competitive equilibrium and generalized Edgeworth's analysis of the contract curve. Negishi (1961) generalized Cournot's partial equilibrium analysis of oligopoly (1938) to the case of general equilibrium and proved a theorem on the existence of an equilibrium with imperfect competition.

Equilibrium in an Edgeworth Box Economy

For exposition we begin with a highly simplified model in which the only consumers are Amy (A) and Bill (B) and there are two commodities. Suppose that there are X_1 units of the first good, X_2 units of the second, and that initially wealth is specified as follows: Amy is endowed with e_1^A units of the first good and Bill holds the rest ($e_1^B = X_1 - e_1^A$), Amy holds e_2^A units of the second good and Bill holds the rest ($e_2^B = X_2 - e_2^B$). The accompanying figure describes an Edgeworth box with horizontal dimension X_1 and vertical dimension X_2. Each point x in the box indicates an allocation of the total commodity amounts between Amy and Bill as follows: x_1^A and x_1^B represent the division of X_1; similarly x_2^A and x_2^B represent the division of X_2. Observe that the initial wealth point is an allocation of X_1 and X_2 and that it is indicated in the box. In the figure the preferences of consumers are summarized by the use of indifference curves. Amy's indifference curves are indicated by a solid line, and Bill's indifference curves are indicated by a dashed line. Amy improves her position by moving to an indifference curve that is above (and to the right of) the one she is on; Bill improves his position by moving to an indifference curve that is below (and to the left of) the one he is on.

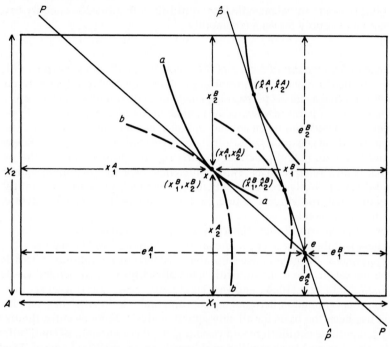

FIGURE 1

With the aid of the Edgeworth box diagram we can give a geometric representation of general equilibrium, at least for the case of two consumers and two commodities. First, we imagine that perfect competition prevails, so that each consumer believes that the amount being offered to buy or sell does not affect price. (Later, when we generalize the analysis to include many consumers, this assumption will appear more natural.) Now, consider the price list $(\hat{P}_1/\hat{P}_2)$. At these prices the sale of each unit of the first commodity will raise $\hat{P}_1$ dollars and allow the consumer to buy $\hat{P}_1/\hat{P}_2$ units of the second commodity. The collection of commodity pairs made possible by such purchases is indicated in the figure by the line $\hat{P}\hat{P}$. The most preferred bundle available to Amy is indicated by $(\hat{x}_1^A, \hat{x}_1^B)$. Similarly, at prices $(\hat{P}_1\hat{P}_2)$, the most preferred bundle available to Bill is $(\hat{x}_2^B, \hat{x}_2^B)$. The important point to note is that $\hat{x}_2^A + \hat{x}_1^B > X_2$, and $\hat{x}_1^A + \hat{x}_1^B < X_1$. The price list $(\hat{P}_1, \hat{P}_2)$ is not an equilibrium price list, since the independent actions of consumers do not balance. We might expect that the price of the second commodity will rise to ration the demand for that commodity. However, suppose that PP represents the commodity pairs that each consumer can attain via purchase and sales when the price list is (P_1, P_2). With these prices Amy and Bill have $(\hat{x}_1^A, \hat{x}_2^A)$ and $(\hat{x}_1^B, \hat{x}_2^B)$ as most preferred choices, and these choices balance the commodity supplies since $\hat{x}_1^A + \hat{x}_1^B = X_1$ and $\hat{x}_2^A + \hat{x}_2^B = X_2$. Observe that after each consumer executes the most preferred choice, the consumer is better off than he or she was at the initial endowment. Furthermore, the gains from trade are exhausted, since at the competitive allocation x, it is not possible to improve Amy's position without harming Bill. (Similarly it is not possible to improve Bill's position without harming Amy.) To see this, note that there are no points above the indifference curve *aa* that are also on (or southwest of) the indifference curve *bb*. Such an allocation is referred to as Pareto-efficient.

The discussion that follows is substantially more technical and is devoted to two of the major themes of general equilibrium analysis. First, under what general conditions is there always at least one equilibrium price for an economy? This question is addressed in the literature on the existence of competitive equilibrium. Second, are equilibria necessarily Pareto-efficient?

The Existence of Equilibrium Prices

It is known that the existence of equilibrium prices for an arbitrary economy is closely related to a classical result in mathematical analysis called the Brouwer fixed-point theorem. This theorem states that for every continuous function g defined on a convex, closed, and bounded subset of S of one-dimensional euclidean space and taking values in S, there exists a point $x \, \varepsilon \, S$ such that $g(x) = x$. However, for the case of just two commodities and pure exchange, the existence of equilibrium can be established by a completely elementary argument. Using the same notation as for the Edgeworth box case, we note that for each price list $P = (P_1, P_2)$, each consumer who prefers more to less makes a consumption plan $[x_1 \, (P), x_2 \, (P)]$ such that $P_1x_1(P) + P_2x_2(P) = P_1e_1 + P_2e_2$ income equals expenditure. If we index consumers by i, then for each i,

$$P_1x_1^i(P) + P_2x_2^i(P) = P_1e_1^i + P_2e_2^i$$

and summing over i, we conclude

$$P_1\sum_i \, [x_1^i \, (P) - e_1^i] + P_2\sum_i \, [x_2^i(P) - e_2^i] = 0$$

This equality is called Walras's law. Now fix the price of the second commodity at unity, so that P_1 indicates the price of commodity 1 relative to commodity 2, and assume that for a high enough price for commodity 1, say $\hat{P}_1$, every consumer chooses no more X_1 than held initially, and for a low enough price for commodity 1, say $\check{P}_1$, every consumer chooses at least as much X_1 as held initially. Since $x_1^i(\hat{P}_1, 1) \le e_1^i$ for all i and $x_1^i, (\check{P}_1, 1) \ge e_1^i$ for all i, we have

$$\Sigma \, x_1^i \, (\hat{P}_1, 1) \le \Sigma \, e_1^i \qquad \text{and} \qquad \Sigma \, x_1^i \, (\check{P}_1, 1) \ge \Sigma \, e_1^i$$

Provided that demand changes continuously with price, there will exist $\hat{P}_1 \ge \bar{P}_1 \ge \check{P}_1$ such that

$$\Sigma \, x_1^i \, (\bar{P}_1 , 1) = \Sigma \, e_1^i$$

that is, at $(\bar{P}_1, 1)$ demand is equal to supply in the market for commodity 1. But from Walras's law,

$$\bar{P}_1 \, [\Sigma \, x_1^i \, (\bar{P}_1 , 1) - \Sigma \, e_1^i] + 1[\Sigma \, x_2^j \, (\bar{P}_1 , 1) - \Sigma \, e_2^j] = 0$$

and so

$$\Sigma \, x_2^j(\bar{P}, 1) = \Sigma \, e_2^j$$

Thus, the price list $(\bar{P}_1, 1)$ leads to the equality of demand and supply in both markets.

One can establish the existence of equilibrium prices for economies with an arbitrary but finite number of commodities, say one, by confining attention to price vectors in

$$\mathcal{P} = \{P = (P_1, P_2, \cdots, P_l) : P_h \ge 0 \text{ for all } h \text{ and } \Sigma \, P_h = 1\}$$

and considering the function g from $\mathcal{P}$ to $\mathcal{P}$ defined by

$$(g(P))_h = P_h + \frac{(f(P))_h}{1 + \sum_k (f(P))_k} \quad h = 1, 2, \cdots, l$$

where $(y)_h$ denotes the hth coordinate of the vector y, and

$$(f(P))_h = \max\left[0, \sum_i (x_h^i(P) - e_h^i)\right]$$

If each consumer demand function x^1 is continuous on P, then the function g will be continuous. By the Brouwer fixed-point theorem, g must have at least one fixed point, and if $\bar{P}$ is a fixed point of g that is not on the boundary of $\mathcal{P}$, then $\bar{P}$ is an equilibrium price vector. The proof follows from Walras's law:

$$\sum_h P_h \left[\sum_i (x_h^i(P) - e_h^i)\right] = 0$$

The Pareto Efficiency of Competitive Equilibrium

Provided that there are no externalities in consumption or production, and provided that consumers prefer more of each commodity to less, every competitive equilibrium allocation is Pareto-efficient. This means that in a competitive equilibrium it is not possible to improve any welfare without making some other consumer worse off. The argument is somewhat simplified if there is a single firm, and it goes like this: In an equilibrium the firm and consumers are content with their plans, and supply equals demand. Let P be the equilibrium price list. Since each consumer chooses a most preferred consumption plan consistent with the value of his or her resource endowment and the income received from the firms, the consumer must be assigned a bundle with a higher value at price P in order to be better off. In fact, since each consumer prefers more of each commodity to less, if a consumer is to be kept at least as well off as in the competitive equilibrium, then he or she must be assigned a plan of value (at prices P) at least as great as the sum of the value of the resource endowment and the income received from the firm. If there are no externalities, then any distribution that makes one consumer better off and keeps every other consumer at least as well off must have a value at prices P that exceeds the total value of resource endowments plus the total of profits received from the firm. But since the resource endowment of the economy is fixed, this distribution can only be provided if the firm chooses a production plan that yields a greater profit at prices P than the original equilibrium plan. But such a plan is not possible because, in the equilibrium plan, the firm is at a profit maximum. Thus the resources of the economy cannot be used to make some consumer better off and keep every other consumer at least as well off.

References

Anderson, R., "An Elementary Core Equivalence Theorem," *Econometrica*, vol. 46, 1978, pp. 1483–1487; Arrow, K. J., "An Extension of the Basic Theorems of Classical Welfare Economics," in J. Neyman (ed.), *Proceedings of the Second Berkeley Symposium on Mathematical Statistics and Probability*, University of California Press, Berkeley, 1951, pp. 507–532; Arrow, K. J., "The Role of Securities in the Optimal Allocation of Risk-Bearing," *Review of Economic Studies*, vol. 31, 1963–1964, pp. 91–96, English translation of Arrow, 1953, reprinted in Arrow, 1970, pp. 121–133; Arrow, K. J., "Economic Equilibrium" in *International Encyclopedia of the Social Sciences*, vol. 4, Macmillan, Free Press, New York, 1968, pp. 376–386; Arrow, K. J., and Gerard Debreu, "Existence of an Equilibrium for a Competitive Economy," *Econometrica*, vol. 26, 1954, pp. 265–290; Arrow,

K. J., and F. H. Hahn, *General Competitive Analysis,* Holden Day, San Francisco, 1971; Aumann, R. J., "Markets with a Continuum of Traders," *Econometrica,* vol. 32, 1964, pp. 39–50; Aumann, R. J., "Existence of Competitive Equilibria in Markets with a Continuum of Traders, *Econometrica,* vol. 34, 1966, pp. 1–17; Bewley, T., "Existence of Equilibria in Economies with Infinitely Many Commodities," *Journal of Economic Theory,* vol. 4, 1972, pp. 514–540; Cournot, A. A., "Researches into the Mathematical Principles of the Theory of Wealth," Kelley, New York, 1960 (first published in French, 1938); Debreu, G., "The Coefficient of Resource Utilization," *Econometrica,* vol. 19, 1951, pp. 273–292; Debreu, G., "A Social Equilibrium Existence Theorem," *Proceedings of the National Academy of Sciences,* vol. 38, 1952, pp. 886–893; Debreu, G., *Theory of Value: An Axiomatic Analysis of Economic Equilibrium,* Wiley, New York, 1959; Debreu, G., "Economies with a Finite Set of Equilibria," *Econometrica,* vol. 38, 1970, pp. 387–392; Debreu, G., "Excess Demand Functions," *Journal of Mathematical Economics,* vol. 1, 1974, pp. 15–21; Debreu, G., and H. Scarf, "A Limit Theorem on the Core of an Economy," *International Economic Review,* vol. 4, 1963, pp. 235–246; Diamond, P., "The Role of a Stock Market in a General Equilibrium Model with Technological Uncertainty," *American Economic Review,* vol. 57, 1967, pp. 759–776; Duffie, D., and W. Shafer, "Equilibrium in Incomplete Markets, 1," *Journal of Mathematical Economics,* vol. 14, 1985, pp. 285–300; Edgeworth, F. Y., "Mathematical Psychics: An Essay on the Application of Mathematics to the Moral Sciences," Kelley, New York, 1953 (first published in 1881); Hart, O., "On the Optimality of Equilibrium When the Market Structure Is Incomplete," *Journal of Economic Theory,* vol. 11, no. 3, 1975, pp. 418–443; Hildenbrand, W., "On Economies with Many Agents," *Journal of Economic Theory,* vol. 2, 1970, pp. 161–188; Hildenbrand, W., "Core and Equilibria of a Large Economy," Princeton University Press, Princeton, N.J., 1974; Hildenbrand, W., and A. Kirman, "Introduction to Equilibrium Analysis," North-Holland, Amsterdam, 1976; Koopmans, T. C., "Three Essays on the State of Economic Science," McGraw-Hill, New York, 1957; Mas-Colell, A., "The Price Equilibrium Existence Problem in Topological Vector Lattices," *Econometrica,* vol. 54, 1986a, pp. 1039–1054; McKenzie, L. W., "On Equilibrium in Graham's Model of World Trade and Other Competitive Systems," *Econometrica,* vol. 22, 1954, pp. 147–161; Negishi, T., "On the Formation of Prices," *International Economic Review,* vol. 2, 1961, pp. 122–126; Pareto, V., "Manuel d'Economie Politique," Girard & Briere, Paris, 1909; Radner, R., "Existence of Equilibrium of Plan, Prices, and Price Expectations," *Econometrica,* vol. 40, no. 2, 1972, pp. 289–303; Radner, R., "Rational Expectations Equilibrium: Generic Existence and the Information Revealed by Prices," *Econometrica,* vol. 47, 1979, pp. 655–678; Samuelson, P. A., "An Exact Consumption-Loan Model of Interest with or without the Social Contrivance of Money," *Journal of Political Economy,* vol. 66, 1958, pp. 467–482; Scarf, H., "An Analysis of Markets with a Large Number of Participants," *Recent Advances in Game Theory,* Princeton University Press, Princeton, N.J., 1962; Shubik, M., "Edgeworth Market Games," in A. W. Tucker and R. D. Luce (eds.), *Contributions to the Theory of Games,* vol. IV, Princeton University Press, Princeton, N.J., 1959; Wald, A., "On Some Systems of Equations of Mathematical Economics," *Econometrica,* vol. 19, 1951, pp. 368–403 (first published in German in *Zeitschrift für Nationalökonomie,* vol. 7, 1936); Walras, L., "Elements of Pure Economics," William Jaffé trans., Allen & Unwin, London, 1954 (first published in France as "Eléments d'Economie Politique Pure," 1874–1877).

(*See also* Competition; Decision making in business: a behavioral approach; Demand; Distribution theory; Factors of production; Game theory, economic applications; Laissez faire; Microeconomics; Monopoly and oligopoly; Normative economics; Price theory; Supply; Welfare economics)

Hugo Sonnenschein

German historical school

The German historical school is so named because of its belief that only through detailed attention to historical development could economic analysis make real progress. The school thus came to criticize classical economic theory for its "cosmopolitanism" and its "perpetualism"—that is, for its claim that economics was founded on natural laws valid in all places at all times. This perspective led these economists to embrace empiricism and induction and to eschew abstraction and deduction. Their approach urged emphasis on the analysis of economic change and a focus on economic process rather than on presumed equilibrium states. Finally, they embraced interventionism, and although they did not all agree about what constituted correct policy, they appear to have agreed that economists *qua* economists had a role to play in its pursuit.

As is often true, this school was by no means without antecedents. Among many, the two mentioned most often are August Comte and Friedrich List. Adam Müller is also frequently mentioned.

The school was launched by the publication in 1843 of Wilhelm Roscher's *Grundriss zu Vorlesungen über die Staatswirthschaft nach geschichtlicher Methode* (*Outline of Lectures on Political Economy, following the Historical Method*). The period of its greatest influence is generally conceded to have ended in 1883 with the publication of Carl Menger's *Untersuchungen über die Methode der Sozialwissenschaften under der politischen Oekonomie insbesondere*. The movement continued to be extremely influential for many years thereafter, particularly in Germany, but it no longer went unchallenged.

Older versus Younger School

It is customary to break the German historical school into an "older" and a "younger" historical school (the older versus younger categorization appears to have begun with Charles Gide and Charles Rist). Where this is done, the undisputed major figures of the older German historical school are its founders, Wilhelm Roscher, Bruno Hildebrand, and Karl Knies. Joseph Schumpeter is one, however, who argues that this group did not constitute a true school because there was at least as much distinguishing them from each other as there was holding them together. Although his is perhaps a minority view, he concurs with the majority view that Gustav Schmoller, the leader of what is customarily referred to as the younger historical school, did indeed found a school. Lesser figures in the younger school include Lujo Brentano, Karl Bucher, Adolf Held, and George Friedrich Knapp. Schumpeter argues that there is a "youngest" German historical school with a claim to recognition as well, including Arthur Spiethoff, Werner Sombart, and Max Weber. Ultimately, the school influenced economic thought in a number of countries, with adherents (successors) in England, including John K. Ingram and Cliffe Leslie, and in the United States, the group known as the "American institutionalists."

The School's Emphasis

Roscher in his *Grundriss* established the school's historical emphasis and suggested a procedural approach to economics, all of which he ultimately elaborated in his *System der Volkswirtschaft*. Today it is generally the view that he promised more in the direction of reconstituting economic analysis than he was able to deliver.

Hildebrand's *Die Nationalökonomie der Gegenwart und Zukunft* (*Political Economy of the Present and Future*) represented a more decisive break with the classical tradition than did Roscher's work. His emphasis was on the need to recognize that economies are not static entities but evolving institutions.

Knies's major contribution was his *Die politsche Ökonomie vom Standpunkte der geschichtlichen Methode* (*Political Economy from the Standpoint of the Historical*

Method). He went further than the other two in denying the existence of natural laws in economics and is remembered for his espousal of the importance of statistics.

It was Gustav Schmoller who developed and crystallized the ideas of the older historical school. He argued that the older historical school had not gone far enough in denouncing the assumptions and methods of classical economics and had indeed at times slipped back into their ways, and he attempted to synthesize the argument of the historical school.

The work of Schmoller and his associates embroiled them in two controversies. Because of their espousal of social reform as a natural outgrowth of the historical approach, a journalist nicknamed them "Kathedersozialisten"—literally, socialists of the chair, or, more generally, academic or professorial socialists—academics who also taught socialism from the classroom. They chose to take it as a compliment and to brand their opposition reactionary.

Even more famous was the *Methodenstreit,* the controversy over method that began when Schmoller wrote an unfavorable review of Carl Menger's *Untersuchungen.* Menger was attacking the German historical school's rejection of the *weltanschauung* of classical economics. The issues were ultimately overdrawn on both sides but can be summarized as (1) empirically based induction versus abstract deduction, (2) emphasis on process or evolution versus acceptance of statistics in economic analysis, and (3) a broad multifaceted setting from which to pursue economics versus a narrowly defined economics with all the rest either held constant or defined out of consideration.

Influence of Historical School

Both Schumpeter and Wesley Clair Mitchell argue that by the time Schmoller had written his *Outline* at the turn of the century, he realized that he had gone too far, and they argue that denying the extremes of theory is a more modest, and thus preferable, departure from the mainstream than denying the need altogether for theory. Even though the *Methodenstreit* ultimately died out, it remains a direct antecedent of the institutionalist debate in the United States. It involved, therefore, issues that are still in contention.

Schumpeter regarded as a "myth" the idea that economics had ever passed through any period when it eschewed concern with history. He nonetheless concluded that at best the German historical school had made a positive contribution in directing the attention of economists to the need for grounding study of the emerging economy on the historical analysis of all the societal forces surrounding it.

As such, the German historical school influenced economics and economists in ways not always explicitly recognized. As noted already, they are linear antecedents of the American institutionalists (John R. Commons, Thorstein Veblen, Wesley Clair Mitchell, etc.). They had at least one other influence: The German historical school founded in 1872 the *Verein für Sozialpolitik* (*The Union for Social Politics*), a model for the group which established the American Economics Association in 1885.

References

Works by Major Members of the German Historical School

Hildebrand, Bruno, *Die Nationalökonomie der Gegenwart und Zukunft,* Literarisches Anstalt, Frankfurt-am-Main, 1848; Knies, Karl, *Die politsche Ökonomie vom geschichtlichen Methode,*

Braunschweig, 1853; Roscher, Wilhelm G. F., *Grundriss zu Vorlesungen über die Staatswirtschaft, nach geschichtlicher Methode,* Dietrich, Gottingen, Germany, 1843; Schmoller, Gustav F., *Grundriss der allgemeinen Volkswirthschaftslehre,* Duncker and Humbolt, Leipzig, vol. 1, 1900, vol. 2, 1904.

Works about the German Historical School

Dorfman, Joseph, in *Institutional Economics: Veblen, Commons and Mitchell Reconsidered,* University of California Press, Berkeley and Los Angeles, 1963; Gide, Charles, and Charles Rist, *A History of Economic Doctrines,* 7th ed., vol. 4, D. C. Heath, New York, 1947, chap. 1; Mitchell, Wesley Clair, *Types of Economic Theory,* vol. 2, Kelley, New York, 1969, chap. 19; Roll, Eric, *A History of Economic Thought,* 4th ed., Faber and Faber, London, 1973, chap. 7; Schumpeter, Joseph A., *History of Economic Analysis,* Oxford University Press, New York, 1954, chap. 4; Spiegel, Henry William, *The Growth of Economic Thought,* Prentice-Hall, Englewood Cliffs, N.J., 1971.

(*See also* Institutional economics)

Philip A. Klein

German unification: problems and prospects

On October 2, 1990 the German Democratic Republic (GDR) acceded to the Federal Republic of Germany (FRG). The result was the formation of one Germany with a land mass of 357,000 square kilometers and a population of 78.7 million. Thus, Germany has become the second largest country in Europe next to Russia. The basic questions are whether merging a socialist economy, the German Democratic Republic, into a capitalist economy, the Federal Republic of Germany, can be accomplished in the short run or long run without great difficulties, and, if a successful integration occurs, what will be the probable influences on the European Economic Community of which West Germany is a prominent member?

Short-Run Impacts of Unification

A close look at events leading up to the currency unification of July 1, 1990 and the subsequent political unification of October 2, 1990 reveals the following: The precursor of the above two momentous events was the signing by the two governments of the GEMSU Treaty (German Economic, Monetary and Social Union) in May 1990. The Treaty provided for monetary union by which the deutsche mark would become the only legal tender of the united Germanies, and the Deutsche Bundesbank would take charge of monetary policy. The Treaty also established that the GDR would adopt the institutions of the FRG. Among these private ownership, competition, market-determined prices, and the free movement of labor, capital, and services are emphasized. It must also be pointed out that private ownership and the privatization of the GDR economy are among the key objectives of the Treaty.

The political, expectational, and economic considerations which induced the quick unification of the two Germanies generated some immediate difficulties for the GDR. Contrary to early expectations, the miracle of the 1948 West German economy was not repeated by the experience of East Germany following the currency unification of July 1, 1990. In fact, the evidence suggests that the rate of currency conversion of the East German mark to the deutsche mark, i.e., one-to-one conversion rate for current payments, contributed toward a rise in production costs and an overvalued

East German output, inflated wages, and unemployment. (Financial assets and liabilities were converted into deutsche marks at a rate of M2:DM1 and financial assets of private households at M1.5:DM1). The cost explosion which followed the currency unification on top of the existing obsolete capacity and low productivity in East Germany adversely affected production and pushed unemployment up. It is estimated that 6 months after the monetary unification production fell by more than 20 percent and unemployment increased from 272,000 to 642,000. In addition, part-time unemployment went from 656,000 to 1,794,000. Because of the uncertainties concerning economic prospects in the East, more than 800,000 have moved to West Germany since November 1989. Many of these people are skilled workers. Interestingly, the favorable rate of currency conversion established for the East Germans and the substantial social transfers received by them were intended to stop this migration. In contrast, the West German economy experienced a boost following the unification. It is estimated that a stimulus to demand from East German purchases added about 1.5 percent to gross domestic product in 1990. This was accomplished without major inflationary pressures due to the existence of unused capacity in West Germany resulting from private investments and the inflow of East German labor.

Long-Run Problems and Prospects

Notwithstanding these immediate adverse economic effects of unification on East Germany, the major challenge is to arrest the short-run decline of the economy and at the same time to move as expeditiously as possible to the long-run rebuilding and transformation of East Germany.

These developments will undoubtedly be facilitated by the availability for adoption of the institutions of West Germany. Political stability, a sound social security system, and a system of well-functioning laws and regulations are among the institutions immediately accessible to East Germany. In addition, East Germany, following the currency unification, became the beneficiary of the macroeconomic stabilization policies of West Germany. Nevertheless, other institutional-economic changes and reforms are not going to be automatic. In this connection, much needed improvements in the levels of productivity and the privatization of the economy are going to take time.

For East Germany to develop into an internationally competitive producer it would need to raise its productivity. It is estimated that labor productivity in the GDR before the monetary unification of July 1, 1990 was about one-third of that in West Germany. This great disparity in East German productivity is attributed to the prevalence of obsolete capacity, lack of modern technology, deficient transportation and communications infrastructure, lack of incentives, and protected monopolies. In addition, it must be remembered that East Germany was under a communist rule and a centrally planned economy since the end of World War II. Because of that, the transformation of East Germany must take into account the following: (1) The GDR is not in harmony with that of the FRG in that it places more emphasis on agriculture, energy, mining, and manufacturing rather than services. (2) The GDR's labor has not been internationally competitive. About 70 percent of GDR exports were aimed at the less demanding markets of the so-called Eastern bloc. (3) A large percent of the GDR's capacity is relatively old. More than one-half is more than 10 years old and 21 percent is older than 20 years. (4) Public administration expertise in dealing with markets is lacking in GDR, and social overhead capital is deficient. The above characteristics of the GDR economy underscore the difficulties to be encountered in privatizing the economy of East Germany but also in raising its productivity levels. In regard to productivity, massive inflows of capital on a timely basis will be needed to prevent continued labor movements out of East Germany. An International Monetary Fund study estimates that to bring productivity levels in the East to about the levels of productivity in the West will require about 1,800 billion DM in 1990 prices in the next 10 years. Obviously this will not be a small undertaking, as capacity modernization has to start from scratch. In addition, financing the costs of unification will continue to be a major problem. During the first year since unification, costs amounted to $100 billion. Government transfers from West Germany to East Germany will be needed in the future to help build the social overhead capital in East Germany, to finance the deficits of GDR, to contribute to the social security system, and to assume the foreign debt of GRD. The source of funding these transfers will be another dilemma for West Germany. Exclusive reliance on internal borrowing may be destabilizing. Hence, the need to raise needed revenues via taxation will have to be given serious consideration.

Concerning privatization, private ownership is the focus of attention. Private ownership represents a basic condition to make decisions on economic grounds, to allocate capital efficiently, and to introduce structural change. The Unification Treaty mandates that confiscated property under communist rule must be given back to the original owners (restitution principle). If this is not possible, previous owners must be compensated (compensation principle). More than 1 million claimants have surfaced. In accordance with legislation passed by the GDR parliament, all state enterprises came under the ownership of the Trust Fund Institution (Treuhandanstalt) which was directed to restructure and privatize salvageable firms and to liquidate the others. The Trust was authorized to borrow in the capital markets in order to finance the restructuring of enterprises. However, this restructuring and sale of viable enterprises and the elimination of nonviable ones have experienced serious delays. The centralized nature of the Trust seems to have complicated matters. In addition, ambiguities concerning the restitution or compensation principles have contributed to these delays and have caused a great deal of ownership uncertainty. Lack of property titles in the GDR and preferences of claimants to sue in the courts rather than accept compensation have helped slow down the process of privatization. Uncertainty regarding the status of property rights has in turn discouraged private investment. It is clear that ownership uncertainty has to be eliminated if the process of privatization is to gain momentum. A substitution of the principle of restitution by financial compensation should be helpful. In this connection a new law in March 1991 has given preference to investment and job creation over restitution with financial compensation given to the original owners. Also, the creation of new enterprises is likely to be a promising means of bringing about the restructuring of the economy.

Thus, the long-run rebuilding of East Germany will depend on a number of measures aimed at the dual goals of privatizing and raising the productivity of the economy. These measures include the elimination of subsidization of noncompetitive firms, the privatization of state enterprises, the encouragement of private initiatives, the resolution of property right disputes, the deregulation of the economy, and the improvement of the investment climate. As mentioned before, the prospects for these developments to take place are enhanced by the following points: Monetary stabilization has been attained since July 1, 1990, the institutions of West Germany are available for adoption by the East, and the substantial savings of the West can be used to finance investments in the East.

German Unification and the European Economic Community

As German unification has unfolded, a number of concerns have been expressed among the European Economic Community (EEC) countries. Some of these concerns have to do with the possible costs of German unification on the EEC, and others are attitudinal.

One concern is that the problems associated with German unification will shift West Germany's attention away from the EEC and thus slow down progress toward European integration. In this connection, some fear a delay in the European monetary union because of the German monetary union. Others express concern that West German capital inflows in East Germany will compete with investments in the Mediterranean countries of the EEC. Non-EEC countries may also experience trade diversion.

The attitude of East Germans has also become subject to speculative concern. The view in this regard is that East Germans raised in the communist tradition may not feel "European" and thus will have a serious adjustment problem within the EEC framework, which is based on democracy, free markets, and European cooperation. But what perhaps has worried the Brussels leadership even more is that the enlarged Germany, in terms of size and economic power, will experience an increase in its influence. How Germany will use this expanded influence is not easy to say. However, it can be argued that as a key member of the EEC a strong Germany should help enhance the prestige of the EEC and might provide the impetus for a united Europe.

References

Kondassis, A. J., "The European Economic Community Thirty Years Later," *Journal of Applied Business Research,* Winter 1989–1990, pp 1–7; Mason, Paul, and Donogh McDonald, "The Macroeconomic Effects of German Unification," *Finance and Development,* International Monetary Fund, Washington, D.C., March 1991; Menke-Gluckert, Wanda, "Germany," *Europe,* Delegation of the Commission of the European Economic Community, March 1991, pp. 16–19; Siebert, Horst, *The Economic Integration of Germany,* Institute fur Weltwirtschaft, Kiel, Germany, September 1990; Siebert, Horst, Holger Schmeiding, and Peter Nunnenkamp, "The Transformation of a Socialist Economy," paper presented at the Seminar on Central and Eastern Europe: Roads to Growth, in Baden, Germany, April 15–18, 1991.

(*See also* European Community)

A. J. Kondonassis

Gini coefficient (*see* Lorenz curve)

Going private and leveraged buyouts

Going private refers to the transformation of a public corporation into a privately held firm. A leveraged buyout (LBO) is the acquisition, financed largely by borrowing, of the stock or assets of a hitherto public company by a small group of investors. The buying group may be sponsored by buyout specialists or by investment bankers. A variant of the LBO going-private transactions is the unit management buyout (MBO) in which a segment of the company is sold to members of management. Unit MBOs have represented more than 10 percent of total divestitures since 1981.

Characteristics of LBOs and MBOs

Firms have been going private for many decades—to avoid public disclosure of competitive information, to facilitate speed in the decision process, and (since the security acts of the early 1930s) to avoid the expense of reporting to the government. High leverage was also found, particularly in real estate investment firms. What was distinctive in the 1980s was the vast expansion in LBO activity. By 1981 LBO activity totaled $2 billion representing about 2½ percent of total merger and acquisition (M&A) activity. When M&A activity peaked in 1988 at $247 billion, LBO activity had grown to $61 billion representing about 25 percent of M&As. By 1990, when total M&As dropped to $108 billion, the LBO activity dropped to $4 billion for reasons to be discussed. LBOs-MBOs were often stimulated by the threat of a takeover, so in part they represented one form of defense against being acquired.

The LBOs and MBOs were initially financed with high debt ratios of about $9 of debt to $1 of equity. Many innovative forms of debt financing were employed. Between the top-level secured senior financing and the equity base, the many new forms of financing employed were referred to as "mezzanine" financing. The junior debt was often subordinated to the senior secured debt from banks. Because the coverages of cash flows to interest obligations were not much greater than 1, sometimes payment in kind (PIK) financing was employed in which interest was paid to creditors in the form of more of the same kinds of debt. Much of the high yield ("junk") debt was issued in connection with buyouts and takeovers.

LBOs and MBOs took place mostly in mature industries with predictable cash flows with little need for growth investments and low in R&D activity. By the end of the 1980s, about 40 percent of LBO and MBO assets had become publicly owned again. LBOs which remain privately owned have reduced debt levels, but they remain somewhat higher than prebuyout and median public company levels. Overall, the median life of a LBO or MBO is about 7 years. For LBOs-MBOs that go public again in a secondary initial public offering, the average life is about 3 years. Buyout sponsors and managers hold a median of 39 percent and a mean of 42 percent of post-LBO equity. After LBOs go public, insiders own a median of about 17 percent of the equity.

Operating Performance of LBOs-MBOs

On average, operating income net of industry adjustments is unchanged in the first 2 years and is 24 percent higher in the third year. Operating income in relation to both assets and sales is greater than industry changes by 20 percent. In the early LBOs-MBOs, the gains to the previous shareholders were 30 to 50 percent. The returns to LBO investors were 30 percent per year compounded.

Theories of Sources of Value Increase

Often a turnaround element was involved in the value increases. Either a strong management was in place, or experienced, able management was added to the organization. The initial high leverage reduced the equity segment of financing so that management, sponsors, and financing sources achieved a significant potential equity stake. Management also risked a significant proportion of its own wealth. Thus management incentives were aligned with owners with significantly enhanced risk and reward possibilities. Private ownership also increased the freedom of decision making by management.

The additional interest deductions from the increased debt is also a source of after-tax income increases. But since leverage is reduced over the life of the LBO and particularly for those that again go private, tax reductions cannot be the main motive. Nor can the size of the tax reductions account for the gains in income or value. Further, it is argued that the incremental gains to the U.S. Treasury more than offset its losses when the following incremental tax gains to the Treasury are considered: taxes on capital gains on sales by the shareholders who are bought out, taxes to the LBO as some assets are sold, taxes on LBO creditors' income, and taxes on the increased operating income of the LBO firms.

Resource Flows and Implications for Theory

The high returns that were earned during the first half of the 1980s attracted large volumes of funds. By 1988, there was enough LBO money around to finance an additional $250 to $300 billion of activity. Competition drove up prices. The early LBOs represented purchase prices of about 6 times cash flows. Later LBOs paid 20 to 30 times cash flows. Winning bids sometimes exceeded the second highest bid by as much as 50 to 75 percent. The turnaround opportunities were reduced in number. As a consequence, the LBOs of the second half of the 1980s earned much lower returns, and a higher proportion of them experienced financial distress.

Some writers argued that the LBOs represented a new form of business organization which solved the free cash flow problem faced by companies in low-growth industries by providing superior incentives. The lean staff organization of the sponsoring group was said to represent an economical method of monitoring business activity. Furthermore, it was argued that since there was a considerable degree of strip financing (financing sources held fractions of most forms of debt and equity), conflict of interest in corporate reorganizations would be minimized, and court intervention could be avoided, thereby achieving the "privatization of bankruptcy."

Others argued that the discipline of debt and concentrated ownership imposed costs of inflexibility to change. As equity stakes increase in values, managers bear an increasing amount of undiversified risk—reduced only by returning the company to public ownership. This view holds that buyouts represent "shock therapy" to the firms and, therefore, represent inherently transitory organizations. Well-conceived buyouts can create economic value. However, the increased values are cashed in by the participants most effectively by returning the organization to public ownership. In this sense, buyouts achieve organization improvements which can then be maintained in public companies with substantially reduced debt levels.

References

DeAngelo, Harry, and Linda DeAngelo, "Management Buyouts of Publicly Traded Corporations," chap. 6 in T. E. Copeland (ed.), *Modern Finance & Industrial Economics,* Basil Blackwell, New York, 1987, pp. 92–113; Jensen, M. C., "Agency Costs of Free Cash Flow, Corporate Finance, and Takeovers," AEA Papers and Proceedings, May 1986, pp. 323–329; Jensen, M. C., "Eclipse of the Public Corporation," *Harvard Business Review,* September–October 1989, pp. 61–75; Kaplan, Steven, "The Effects of Management Buyouts on Operating Performance and Value," *Journal of Financial Economics,* vol. 24, 1989, pp. 217–254; Kaplan, Steven, "The Staying Power of Leveraged Buyouts," *Journal of Financial Economics,* vol. 29, 1991, pp. 287–313; Muscarella, C. J., and M. R. Vetsuypens, "Efficiency and Organizational Structure: A Study of

Reverse LBOs," *Journal of Finance,* vol. 45, December 1990, pp. 1389–1413; Rappaport, Alfred, "The Staying Power of the Public Corporation," *Harvard Business Review,* January–February 1990, pp. 96–104; Smith, Abbie, "Capital Ownership Structure and Performance: The Case of Management Buyouts," *Journal of Financial Economics,* vol. 27, 1990, pp. 143–165.

[*See also* Junk (high-yield) bond market]

J. Fred Weston

Gold standard

In the decades before 1914, the gold standard was a type of monetary system with the following characteristics: The national monetary unit was defined in terms of a given quantity of gold; the central bank or treasury stood ready to buy and sell gold at the resulting fixed price in terms of the national currency; gold was freely coined and gold coin formed a significant part of the circulating medium; and gold could be freely exported and imported. The exchange rate between any two countries adhering to such arrangements was determined by the gold content of their respective monetary units and could vary from this parity only within a narrow band (the "gold points") reflecting the cost of shipping gold from the one country to the other. Private arbitrage shipments of gold, which became profitable when either of these limits was reached, prevented the band from being breached.

Gold-Exchange Standard

Arrangements of this kind—sometimes called the "gold-coin standard"—were not the only variant of the pre-1914 gold standard. A number of countries adopted or drifted into various forms of what has been called a "gold-exchange standard," in which the monetary authorities of the countries concerned held a substantial part or even the bulk of their reserves in the form of claims on currencies that were redeemable in gold, and they stood ready to buy or sell these currencies at fixed prices in terms of their own. Such official purchases or sales served to supplement, and in some cases virtually to substitute for, private gold arbitraging as a means of keeping exchange rates within narrow margins of parity. The holding of foreign exchange reserves enabled the authorities to economize on gold and to earn interest on these reserves without any significant risk of being unable to convert them into gold when needed. Gold coin tended to circulate to only a limited extent if at all in gold-exchange-standard countries, either because the authorities did not freely redeem their notes in gold or because of the public's preferences.

The overriding objective of economic policy under the pre-1914 gold standard was to maintain the redeemability (convertibility) of the national currency directly or indirectly into gold at the legal parity, i.e., to keep exchange rates fixed against other gold-standard currencies. Drains on a country's gold and/or foreign exchange reserves usually led to increases in central-bank discount rates or to other official actions designed to check the loss of reserves. Increased interest rates tended, in the short run, to stem the drain by attracting capital from abroad. In the longer run they did so, according to the traditional view, by improving the country's trade balance through their further effect on the money supply, prices, and economic activity. Although controversy still prevails as to exactly how the pre-1914 gold standard worked, the fact remains that from about 1880 to 1914 exchange rates among gold-standard countries remained fixed without support of payments or import controls, with virtually no countries forced off the gold standard once adopted, with a minimum of international cooperation, and with a relatively small stock of international reserves. However, this remarkable fixity of exchange rates may in some cases have been achieved at the cost of internal economic activity.

During World War I most countries suspended the redeemability of their currencies into gold (de facto or de jure), withdrew gold coins from circulation, and concentrated gold holdings in official reserves. The currencies of most belligerent countries did not, however, depreciate by much in terms of gold and the dollar because of official pegging operations supported by gold sales, foreign borrowing, liquidation of assets abroad, and imposition of some import and exchange controls. At the end of the war the United States was virtually the only country on a full gold standard.

Return to Gold

A dominant objective of economic policymakers after the war was to return to the gold standard at an early date. This was a laborious process that was not generally completed until 1927 because of the widespread economic dislocations that followed the war. In some cases the return to gold involved stabilization of the currency at the prewar parity, the most notable example being that of Great Britain in 1925. In other cases, such as that of France, Italy, and Belgium, currencies were repegged to gold at only a fraction of their prewar parities. In those countries where hyperinflation had occurred in the early postwar years, notably in Germany, the stabilization process necessitated the introduction of completely new currencies.

The international gold standard that was restored in the mid-1920s differed in several respects from that of the pre-1914 period. The gold-coin standard had virtually disappeared except in the United States, and gold holdings remained predominantly in official hands. Several countries, including Great Britain, adopted a so-called gold-bullion standard under which the currency was redeemable in gold but only in the form of bars of a minimum weight. This in effect made gold available only for purposes of settling international balances. The great majority of countries, partly in view of a prevailing belief in an actual or impending world shortage of gold, adopted varieties of the gold-exchange standard. The structure of exchange rates adopted seems to have been less appropriate to underlying price-cost levels and economic conditions than it was before 1914. For example, the British pound was believed to have been overvalued and the French franc undervalued. Finally, monetary authorities appear to have been less ready than before the war to gear their policies to the state of the balance of payments and to changes in their reserve holdings in view of their increased concern with internal economic stability.

The Breakdown of the Gold Standard

The restored international gold standard, which for the most part was a gold-exchange standard, broke down in 1930 to 1932 under the impact of the world depression, the virtual cessation of international lending, the massive liquidation by central banks of their foreign exchange holdings, and the large-scale flights of capital from individual countries. Great Britain abandoned the gold standard in September 1931, and the pound floated under official management until the outbreak of World War II. The United States suspended the gold standard in March 1933 at which time the redemption of dollars into gold and the export of gold were prohibited, and all gold coin and gold certificates were called in from circulation. On January 31, 1934, the United States returned to a modified gold standard, with the dollar price of gold being raised to $35 per fine ounce. At that repegged price the U.S. Treasury stood ready to buy and sell gold but only for legitimate monetary purposes, which in practice meant for international settlement. The prohibition on the holding of gold by private U.S. residents was continued. The currencies of the so-called gold bloc countries—France, Belgium, Switzerland, and the Netherlands—remained tied to gold at their existing parities until 1935 to 1936, when the currencies were devalued. Of those countries only Belgium continued thereafter to buy and sell gold at a fixed price until 1939.

The international monetary system set up at Bretton Woods, N.H., after World War II, which functioned until the early 1970s, had some similarities to gold-exchange-standard arrangements. The United States bought and sold gold at $35 per fine ounce in its dealings with foreign monetary authorities, and the latter bought and sold dollars against their own currencies at prices that remained fixed for considerable periods. But an essential difference was that countries were authorized under the Bretton Woods agreement to alter their exchange rates under specified circumstances, and from time to time many of them, including leading ones, did so. The fixity of exchange rates, a hallmark of the gold standard, could no longer be taken for granted. Since March 1973, currencies generally have been floating (including the dollar, no longer tied to gold), and even gold itself is no longer being used as an international means of settlement and is being phased out of the international monetary system. From time to time proposals have been made to reintroduce a "gold standard" in one form or another, but informed opinion has generally been firmly opposed to the restoration of a monetary role for gold.

References

Bloomfield, Arthur I, *Monetary Policy under the International Gold Standard: 1880–1914*, Federal Reserve Bank of New York, New York, 1959; Brown, William Adams, *The International Gold Standard Reinterpreted, 1914–1934*, 2 vols., National Bureau of Economic Research, New York, 1940; Cooper, Richard N., "The Gold Standard: Historical Facts and Future Prospects," "Brookings Papers" on Economic Activity I, 1952, in Michael D. Boraco and Anna I. Schwartz (eds.), *A Retrospective on the Classical Gold Standard, 1821–1931*, National Bureau of Economic Research, New York, 1984; McCloskey, Donald N., and J. Richard Zecker, "How the Gold Standard Worked, 1880–1913," in J. A. Frenkel and H. G. Johnson (eds.), *The Monetary Approach to the Balance of Payments*, University of Toronto Press, Toronto, 1976; Nurkse, Ragnar, *International Currency Experience*, League of Nations, Princeton, N.J., 1944.

(*See also* International economics, an overview; International Monetary Fund)

Arthur I. Bloomfield

Government regulation of business

Apart from public utility regulation, the concept of government regulation of business means the legal setting or maintenance of conditions required for a private enterprise system to function fairly, safely, and efficiently. Implementation of this concept usually involves creation of a public authority—a commission or agency—to establish rules of conduct for the businesses in a given industry or for all industry.

Recent years, especially during the Reagan administration (1981–1989), have seen some push for "deregulation," an attempt to lessen regulatory constraints on business enterprises. The push was extended into the Bush administration with its President's Council on Competitiveness, headed by Vice President Quayle. The Council has had some successes here and there in reducing the regulatory burden on business, but Congress has continued to promote new regulatory legislation including the Americans with Disabilities Act and amendments to the Clean Air and Civil Rights laws. As of this writing in April 1992, a moratorium on new federal regulations was in effect.

The Regulatory Agencies

Regulatory agencies have been largely introduced in three waves: pre–World War I, the 1930s, and the late 1960s to the 1990s. First of the regulatory commissions was the Interstate Commerce Commission (ICC), which was established in 1887 to supervise competition in the railroad industry. Regulation of pipelines, inland waterways, and trucking has since been added to the ICC's authority. Similarly, the Pure Food and Drug Act of 1906 created the forerunner agency to today's Food and Drug Administration; the Meat Inspection Act of 1907 provided for federal meat inspectors operating under the U.S. Department of Agriculture. And in 1914, Congress established the Federal Trade Commission (FTC) to prevent unfair competition and deceptive advertising.

The 1930s witnessed the birth of still other regulatory bodies, including the Federal Power Commission (FPC) in 1930, the Federal Deposit Insurance Corporation (FDIC) in 1933, the Securities and Exchange Commission (SEC) in 1934, the National Labor Relations Board (NLRB) in 1935, and the Civil Aeronautics Board (CAB) in 1938.

The 1960s to 1990s saw the birth of other regulatory agencies such as the Equal Employment Opportunity Commission (EEOC) in 1965, the Environmental Protection Agency (EPA) in 1970, the Occupational Safety and Health Administration (OSHA) also in 1970, the Consumer Product Safety Commission (CPSC) in 1972, and the Council on Wage and Price Stability (COWPS) in 1974. EPA staff growth has advanced significantly in the 1980s and 1990s, reaching 18,262 in December 1991.

Regulatory Reform and Costs

The rising economic impact of regulation has given rise to calls for regulatory reform and even deregulation. In 1978, Barry Bosworth of the Brookings Institution, then director of the Council on Wage and Price Stability, said in a memo that although proposed regulations might be beneficial, "they do imply a significant increase in the impact of regulation on the measured rate of price inflation." In a 1979 speech on regulatory reform, President Carter stated: "We must cut the inflationary costs which private industry bears as a result of government regulations." An ad hoc Federal Paperwork Commission during the 1970s counted 4,400 different federal forms in the federal inventory, outside of banking and tax forms. A 1978 law sponsored by Senator Edward M. Kennedy has brought about substantial deregulation of the airline industry and led to the extinction of the Civil Aeronautics Board in 1985.

Estimates of total regulatory costs, direct and indirect, vary widely. A 1979 White House report on regulatory reform noted estimates ranging from a high of $150 billion to a low of $25 billion. Murray L. Weidenbaum, director of Washington University's Center for the Study of American Business, held that regulatory costs for the U.S. economy in 1979 totaled $102.7 billion, the greatest proportion of which was in compliance costs to U.S. industry.

Pros and Cons

Proponents of regulation hold that industry cannot function in a legal vacuum. Private property rights have to be defined and provision made for redress against breaches of them. Proponents also hold that business competition is not self-regulating and, hence, requires antitrust statutes and other rules of fair play. They point to the pioneering work in the 1930s by economists Edward H. Chamberlin of Harvard University and Joan Robinson of Cambridge University who held that modern industrial competition is monopolistic or imperfect. Proponents argue that the state must proscribe monopolies, unfair competition, and the marketing of such things as dangerous drugs or unsafe playground equipment.

Proponents of deregulation concede that an orderly society and economy need proper rules and regulations for business behavior, including prohibition of fraud and force in business dealings. But they also argue that excessive regulation has added to inflationary pressures and has jeopardized U.S. competitiveness in world markets. They argue that in many instances regulatory agencies, however well-intentioned, have imposed costs on industry that surpass any benefits to society, including clean air and water. According to Yale Brozen (1979), for example, the initial $4 billion annual cost of auto-emission controls buys about $5 billion in antipollution benefits each year. But if the auto-emission standards planned for 1985 were to stay in effect, argued Brozen, society would then be getting only $6 billion in benefits for an annual outlay of $11 billion.

A frequently proposed type of law to meet the regulatory problem is the so-called sunset statute. Such a law provides for a periodic congressional review of regulatory bodies. Those not satisfying cost-benefit standards would then be closed down, probably in stages.

References

Brozen, Yale, "Regulatory Excess," paper for National Association of Manufacturers, Washington, D.C., March 29, 1979; Chamberlin, Edward H., *The Theory of Monopolistic Competition*, Harvard University Press, Cambridge, Mass., 1933; Clark, J. M., *Social Control of Business*, McGraw-Hill, New York, 1939; Miller, Roger Leroy, *The Economics of Public Issues*, 8th ed., Harper & Row, New York, 1990; Pegrum, Dudley F., *Public Regulation of Business*, Irwin, Homewood, Ill., 1959; Peterson, Mary Bennett, *The Regulated Consumer*, Green Hill, Ottawa, Ill., 1971; Robinson, Joan, *The Economics of Imperfect Competition*, Macmillan, New York, 1933.

(*See also* Cost-benefit analysis; Economic incentives for environmental protection; Pollution abatement costs; Externalities; Federal Trade Commission; Securities and Exchange Commission)

William H. Peterson

Grants economics

Grants economics identifies the size and traces the leverage of grant elements as they interface with exchange elements in different economic processes. A simple definition of a grant is an unmatched transaction where the net worth of one party—the grantor—diminishes while the net worth of the other party—the grantee—increases. Any transaction deviating from the norm of exchanging equal values contains certain grant elements. Beyond the clearly visible explicit grant—gift, aid, and unilateral transfer—exists a vast network of implicit grants in the private as well as public sectors of the economy. The visible explicit grants are only the tip of the iceberg, whereas the larger, amorphous bulk of implicit grants remains hidden and, therefore, often escapes attention.

It is a conventional view that goods, services, and factors of production move from one party to another at a matching price (quid pro quo). Yet there exists a broad assortment of subventions (subsidies, bounties, favoritism) on the one side and a broad assortment of tributes (underpayments, extortions, dispossessions) on the other side. However, because these cases do not fit the neat abstractions of dominant theories, they are usually relegated to gray areas (assumed away) and the analysis continues *ceteris paribus.* Unfortunately, by ignoring or downgrading production and distribution processes which do not fit the neoclassical pattern, one narrows the scope of economic policy analysis unnecessarily.

Since mixed-type transactions dominate, analysis must start with an identification of the exchange and grant elements. The measurement of an explicit grant is simple: the grant equivalent equals the market value. The size of implicit grants is more elusive, because such grants arise when the system of market prices is superseded. Thus, the grant elements embodied in trade protection will surface if one contrasts the world market price with the domestic price after the imposition of a tariff. Implicit grants accrue to the domestic producer and government at the expense of the domestic consumer and foreign producer. When the U.S. government purchased a bushel of wheat at $2.50 while the world market price stayed around $1.00, a grant equivalent of $1.50 was extended. Likewise, grant impact statements can be calculated about regulation Q in banking, the stipulation of routes-cum-fares for trucks. Monopoly power also creates implicit grants. Whether it is the stereotypic restraint of trade or restrictive admission into the ranks of labor unions, a common characteristic of all such practices is that the visible hand of powerful special interest groups preempts free-market solutions. Intrafirm subsidization is intriguing, particularly with multinational corporations. Other cases abound.

Studies utilizing the notion of grants economics have led to a variety of conceptual explorations as well as empirical works. In the field of finance, for example, loans are classified on a continuous scale, since they contain both a grant equivalent and an exchange equivalent. Generally, lower rates of interest, longer maturity times and moratorium periods, and higher market rates of discount (opportunity costs) will result in greater grant elements. The grant may be altered by certain trading stipulations supplementing these concessionary terms: for instance, reducing the grant for the recipient of foreign aid because of tying purchases in the donor country, or enhancing the grant for the homeowner in the United States because interest payments are deductible for income tax purposes. Grant ratio is the expression of the grant equivalent as a proportion of the face value of the loan ($g = GE/FV$). This ratio provides a standard for comparison as well as a base for deriving the sensitivity of the grant ratio with respect to contract terms and the trade-offs between them.

History of Grants Economics

The history of grant as an economic-social-political organizer is perhaps older than recorded history. Various unmatched transfers probably preceded exchange transactions as communities practiced reciprocal granting. As exchange became common, the terms of trade favored the stronger party, thereby transferring tribute to priests and kings and artists. Such was the dominant social characteristic through the feudal age. In modern times institutionalized transfers have provided a big push toward economic development, as illustrated by the enclosure movement in eighteenth-century England and collectivization in the twentieth-century Soviet Union. Nowadays, when traditional welfare roles—care for the poor, disabled, and elderly—are shifting from the family to the public sector, and as government undertakes to deliver an increasing bundle of public goods—education, health, recreation, transportation, research—the share of the grants economy grows.

The history of grant economics as a formalized concept began with the works of Kenneth Boulding, who subsequently formed, together with Martin Pfaff and Janos Horvath, the Association for the Study of the Grants Economy (ASGE) in 1968. The association is an instrument to explore a neglected area in economics and the social sciences. It holds conferences, organizes joint programs, and facilitates publications. Among the notable contributors are Abram Bergson, Evsey Domar, Wassily Leontief, Abba Lerner, James Morgan, Mancur Olson, Tibor Scitovsky, Robert Solo, Jan Tinbergen, William Vickrey, and Burton Weisbrod.

A Theory of Reciprocity

Much of the initial work in grants economics has dealt with the issues of the urbanized economy, and income distribution and redistribution as these affect efficiency and equity, the tax expenditure structure, externalities in the environment, and intrafamily and intergenerational granting. The international economy is a major field of inquiry. The inflation-unemployment dilemma is explained in part through institutional rigidities which generate implicit grants to those who restrain potential supply. A recurrent theme is that grants economics is a major instrument by which people hope to change the world for the better. In the macroeconomy a grant dollar tends to generate more production and income than an exchange dollar because the granting often stipulates complementary exchange transactions. As a network of policy instruments, the grants economy represents the heart of political economy, because routinely it is by pulling the levers of positive and negative subventions that the political system intervenes smoothly in the economic system.

On philosophical grounds, grants economics extends beyond neoclassical exchange economics, public choice, and radical economics in important respects, such as perceiving the motivation of economic actors and assessing the significance of distribution norms. Explaining individual behavior, institutional dynamics, and normative policies no longer requires regarding unselfishness as an aberration of rationality. Grant economics provides a theory of transfers by affirming the interdependence of utility functions among individuals that integrate into economic science such agents as love, altruism, hate, and fear. Thus, utility interdependence considers (1) the utility derived from the contemplation of another person's welfare and (2) the utility derived from giving because it conforms to the individual's norms. Hence benevolent behavior: the individual's increased utility due to more consumption is outweighed by the individual's decreased utility due to the perception of another's miserable state. This leads from the Pareto optimum to the Boulding optimum, bringing within the scope of economic analysis a human flair assumed away routinely in the name of value-free science. Now economics can tackle the axiom that whether life on earth is hell or heaven depends largely on the attitude of one human being toward others.

Grants economics has been accused of charting vague boundaries. But its boundaries are vague precisely because it is a link between all the disciplines of the social sciences. Providing a theory of reciprocity, it links economics, psychology, sociology, anthropology, and political science. Stretching over several disciplines, it points to the enormous economic importance of the family, an institution neglected in exchange economics. It is an important part of economics itself, where the grants structure profoundly affects the dynamics of the price system. Notwithstanding its versatility, the grants economy is subject to perverse effects. Just as the theory of market failures acknowledges that exchange economy cannot achieve certain types of economic ends, the pathologies of the grants economy call for diagnosis. It is a political irony that far from remedying all distortions brought about by the market process, regulations and subventions have often exacerbated these distortions. Indeed, grants economics could make a unique contribution to the regulatory reform through sorting out good grants from bad grants, i.e., those which achieve socially desirable goals from those with perverse effects.

Applied to specific cases (e.g., the export-import bank), grants economics has provided impact statements toward refinement in policymaking. It has been suggested that the U.S. Congress may require grant impact statements for every legislative and regulatory act, estimating who gains, who loses, and who stays unaffected. Likewise, the facilities of national account statistics might improve by including certain measures of grant elements.

References

Boulding, Kenneth E., *The Economy of Love and Fear: A Preface to Grants Economics*, Greenwood, Westport, Conn., 1976; Boulding, Kenneth E., Martin Pfaff, and Janos Horvath, "Grants Economics: A Simple Introduction," *The American Economist*, vol. 16, no. 1, 1972, pp. 19–35; Horvath, Janos, *Chinese Technology Transfer to the Third World: A Grants Economy Analysis*, Praeger, New York, 1976; Pfaff, Martin (ed.), *Grants and Exchange*, North-Holland, Amsterdam, 1976; Pfaff, Martin (ed.), *Association for the Study of the Grants Economy Tenth Anniversary Brochure*, INIFES, Augsburg-Leitershofen, 1978.

(*See also* Normative economics; Welfare economics)

Janos Horvath

Great Depression

The Great Depression of 1929–1941 was the longest and most severe period of economic depression in modern times. The beginning of the Depression is usually marked by the collapse of New York stock prices in October 1929. The economic stagnation that followed in the United States continued well into the mobilization effort that accompanied U.S. entry into World War II in late 1941. At its worst point in 1933, the U.S. economy had virtually ground to a halt. Gross national income (GNP) had fallen by almost one-half in the space of less than 3 years. Stock prices had fallen to 15 or 20 percent of their 1929 levels, and commodity prices had declined by about 25 percent, adding to the pessimism generated by the collapse of asset prices. One of the more obvious manifestations of that pessimism was the fact that in 1932 aggregate net investment in the U.S. economy was negative. The market for labor was equally bleak; one out of every four workers in the labor force was unable to find employment, and a substantial number of people could find only part-time work or had simply given up looking for work and were no longer even counted in the labor force. The crisis in the banking system was so serious that on March 6, 1933, newly inaugurated President Franklin Roosevelt declared a "bank holiday" to forestall a total collapse of the financial system in the United States.

The economic collapse of 1929–1933 was not the first time Americans encountered the specter of falling stock and commodity prices, bank failures, and unemployment. What set this economic downturn apart from previous economic crises was that recovery from the depths of this depression was excruciatingly slow. After a period of expansion from 1933 to 1936 that left the economic indicators well short of their 1929 levels, recovery was interrupted by a very severe downturn in 1937–1938. In late 1941—12 years after the stock market crash—more than 10 percent of the labor force was out of work, investment remained anemic, and GNP per capita had not yet returned to the 1929 level. The most protracted period of economic stagnation in U.S. history was not finally ended until the war effort of 1942–1945 finally mobilized the pool of idle labor and capital.

The U.S. economy was not alone in feeling the impact of this economic collapse. Throughout the industrialized world, prices and economic production plummeted, and unemployment rose to unprecedented heights. The impact of this worldwide depression, moreover, went far beyond the direct economic effects. In the United States the economic collapse prompted a major political realignment that eventually produced sweeping social and economic reforms that became known as the "New Deal." In Germany the economic crisis helped propel Adolf Hitler and the Nazi party to power. Elsewhere in Europe the changes were less profound, but the impact of a decade of economic stagnation and uncertainty left a legacy that remained etched in peoples' memories for the next three decades.

What caused this economic collapse? Fifty years after the Great Crash, there are still no unequivocal explanations for the severity and duration of the Great Depression. In part, this lack of consensus reflects the complexity of the historical event itself. However, the diversity of opinion also reflects differing views on economic theory and policy that emerged as "lessons" from the experience of the 1930s. Economic orthodoxy in 1929 was predicated on the proposition that market systems were self-correcting. Buttressing the natural tendency for economies to maintain employment and output was a system of international payments dictated by the rules of *gold standard* that had been the basis for international stability for the previous 100 years. Conventional wisdom ordained that, so long as monetary and fiscal authorities played by the "rules" of the gold standard, the severe "liquidation" of assets financial markets were experiencing in 1929–1930 would run its course and the system would right itself.

As the economic situation continued to worsen without signs of long-term recovery, some well-known economists began to question this orthodoxy. By the late 1930s, economists such as John Maynard Keynes in Great Britain and Alvin Hansen in the United States were espousing a new approach to economic policy that argued that the corrective tendencies in the marketplace were not strong enough to ensure full employment. These men urged governments to abandon reliance on the traditional notions that monetary institutions could "stabilize" markets and advocated that governments increase government outlays to boost aggregate spending in the economy. The "spending thesis," based in large measure on the arguments put forward in Keynes' book, *A General Theory of Interest, Employment and Prices,* represented one of the first major attempts to "explain" the events of the early 1930s by changing the way people viewed the "economic problem."

To Keynes and his followers, the economic collapse of the early 1930s stemmed from the *collapse of spending*—most notably the dramatic fall in *investment*. The economic stagnation which followed that collapse involved an interrelationship of investment, consumption, and income—combined with the pessimistic expectations—that discouraged aggregate spending and hindered recovery of both GNP and employment. The economy, instead of bouncing back to a full-employment equilibrium, remained mired in an underemployment equilibrium of aggregate demand and supply which only the "shock" of government spending could break. Monetary actions alone could not restore economic stability.

Not everyone agreed with this new *macroeconomic* approach. A vocal minority of economists argued that the root of the problem lay in the monetary collapse that occurred from 1929 to 1933. In 1929 there were roughly 25,000 banks in the United States; in 1933 there were only 14,000. The fall in the supply of money and credit associated with this banking collapse created powerful pressures for reduced economic activity. But was the bank collapse cause or effect? Might monetary authorities have stemmed the public's declining confidence in banks by meeting depositor's demands for cash? In 1963 economists Milton Friedman and Anna Schwartz published their *Monetary History of the United States,* which placed the blame for the banking collapse on inept monetary policy between 1930 and 1933. Apart from the recession of 1937 (also the fault of monetary mismanagement), the economic performance from 1933 to 1939 was simply a reflection of the disastrous depths to which the system had sunk as a consequence of the monetary collapse brought on by the ineptness of the Federal Reserve System (FRS) in 1929 to 1933. Had the FRS followed a sound monetary policy immediately after the stock collapse, the stagnation of the 1930s could have been avoided.

For three decades these two competing explanations dominated discussion of the "causes" of the Great Depression in the United States. There were some points of agreement in the debate. Both groups agreed that the impact of the stock market crash was profound. Both agreed that problems in the labor markets might have prolonged high unemployment. Finally, both sides gave very low marks to government economic policy over this period—though the nature of their criticisms differed. Keynesians complained that the government did not act quickly enough to implement spending programs. Monetarists chastised the passive role of the FRS in allowing the bank panic to proceed unabated from 1930 to 1933 and the FRS's stubborn resistance to a policy of monetary expansion through the mid-1930s, culminating with a disastrous decision to contract reserves in 1937.

For the most part, the debates between Keynesians and monetarists focused on issues of economic theory and policy rather than an interpretation of a historical event. Recent work by economic historians has called attention to a number of factors that remained largely submerged in the macroeconomic debates of Keynesians and monetarists. Structural aspects of the labor markets—particularly the evolution of personnel policies and labor relations in the United States that may have inhibited adjustments of employment and wages—made the economic system less able to respond to a catastrophic fall in aggregate demand. Sectoral shifts in the patterns of demand—most of which antedated the economic collapse of 1929—meant that some industries felt a much smaller stimuli for recovery than others. Continued stagnation of demand in industries that employed large numbers of industrial workers discouraged investment and stifled the expansion of jobs. Finally, the rapid growth of "consumer durables" and the accompanying rise in consumer debt in the 1920s may have contributed to the sluggish recovery of aggregate demand as households postponed consumption expenditures in order to pay off the accumulated consumer debt. These factors do not contradict the earlier debates; rather they suggest that the actual experience of the U.S. recovery was perhaps too complex to be captured by a simple economic model.

The theoretical debates, by focusing their analyses primarily on the U.S. experience, failed to put the Great Depression in a global perspective. They treated the worldwide depression as a phenomenon that was "exported" from the United States to the rest of the world via the international exchange mechanism. Economic historians who took a more global perspective of events in the 1920s and 1930s found that, far from being a passive receptor of the U.S. economic collapse, structural problems with the international economy played a major role in both the onset and the severity of the Depression in all the developed countries of the world. At the heart of this claim is an analysis of the economic dislocation caused by World War I, together with the rigidities of the *gold standard* that ruled international and domestic monetary policies throughout the 1920s and 1930s.

World War I created a massive dislocation in the international economy of the western world. Great Britain, the unquestioned international financial leader before the war, was strained to the point where it could not maintain that leadership after 1920. British efforts at maintaining the prewar value of the pound in the postwar era resulted in sluggish growth and high unemployment in Britain throughout the interwar period. Germany was faced in 1919 with a devastated economy and a burden of "reparation payments" exacted by the victorious Allies that posed enormous problems at home and distorted international capital markets for the next decade. Rather than addressing these difficulties, policymakers in the industrialized nations fought to retain a system of fixed exchange rates under the gold standard that favored countries which had excess reserves (such as the United States and France), while putting harsh penalties on those experiencing difficulties with international payments (such as Britain and Germany). Although countries losing gold had no choice but to implement monetary and fiscal policies that induced deflation, the recipients of gold inflows often elected to simply hoard the gold. The situation was further exacerbated by the unwillingness of any country—most notably the United States—to accept the responsibility of "lender of last resort" for the international capital market. Consequently, the collapse of international financial markets in 1929 to 1931 led to financial crises in virtually every major trading country. International commodity flows fell by a factor of three between 1929 and 1933. By 1933 the world economy had sunk down into the abyss of depression, and it would be two decades before the international system could return to "normal."

The events of the 1930s demonstrated the need for changes in both economic structure and the *regimes* governing economic policy. In the United States, those changes began with the economic reforms of the New Deal, a process that was to continue for the next 40 years. Throughout the industrial world, the experience of the economic catastrophe of the 1930s produced a major break with economic trends of the past. As important as the structural changes brought on by the Depression and World War II was the revolution in economic thinking that finally freed economic policy from the strictures of a regime of international and domestic finance that had governed policy options for the previous 100 years.

References

Bernstein, Michael A., *The Great Depression: Delayed Recovery and Economic Change in America, 1929–1939,* Cambridge University Press, Cambridge, Mass., 1987; Friedman, Milton, and Anna J. Schwartz, *The Great Contraction: 1929–33,* Princeton University Press, Princeton, N.J., 1965; Keynes, John Maynard, *The General Theory of Employment, Interest, and Money,* Harcourt Brace and World, 1936; Kindleberger, Charles P., *The World in Depression, 1929–1939,* rev. ed., Penguin, 1986; Temin, Peter, *Did Monetary Forces Cause the Great Depression?,* W. W. Norton, 1976; Temin, Peter, *Lessons from the Great Depression,* MIT Press, Cambridge, Mass., 1990.

(*See also* Business cycles; Chicago school; Federal Reserve policy; Fiscal policy; Gold standard; Keynesian economics; Monetary policy; Stock market crashes)

Roger L. Ransom

Gresham's law

Gresham's law is the empirical generalization that "good money drives out bad." Although it is named after Sir Thomas Gresham, an adviser to Queen Elizabeth I of England, who described it in 1588, the law by then was well known. It was stated by another English writer, Henry Holt, in 1551; by Nicholaus Copernicus in 1525; and by Nicholas Oresme, Bishop of Lisieux, in France around 1360. It was even known to ancient writers such as Aristophanes.

A good illustration of the principle underlying Gresham's law is found in recent U.S. experience. As late as the 1960s and early 1970s, silver dimes and quarters were circulating alongside their cupro-nickel equivalents. However, once the price of silver had risen to $1.29 per ounce, silver coins became worth more as silver than as coins: They were undervalued. The result was that whenever people found they had received silver coins, they held on to them, choosing instead to spend cupro-nickel coins or Federal Reserve notes. Silver coins disappeared from circulation. For the same reason, silver certificates, representing rights to silver dollars, rose in value relative to Federal Reserve notes and disappeared from circulation. Similarly, The "inferior" money (cupro-nickel coins and Federal Reserve notes) drove the "superior" money (silver coins and silver certificates) out of circulation.

Sir Thomas Gresham was concerned with a silver currency in which lighter-weight, worn, or clipped coins circulated freely, whereas full-weight coins were driven from circulation (they were hoarded, melted into bullion, or exported). Gresham's law was very important because it explained why it was very difficult, once the coinage had deteriorated, to raise the quality of the coinage by minting new coins. A vivid illustration was provided in 1696, when the English government instituted a policy of recoinage, buying worn silver coins and reminting them into full-weight coins. Not only was the supply of coins reduced, but the new coins that were issued did not circulate. The result was a shortage of money and a severe depression.

Gresham's law also explains why paper currency can drive metallic coins out of circulation, as happened with the continentals in the United States after 1778, the assignats in France during the revolution, and the greenbacks in the United States after 1861. Because paper currency was not as secure as metallic currency (people feared, often with good cause, that too much money would be printed and that it would lose its value), people chose to hoard metallic currency and to spend paper currency.

Gresham's law is also important in explaining the problems that occurred with bimetallism. A bimetallic system is one where a currency contains both gold and silver coins. In such a system the mint ratio (the ratio at which gold and silver are coined at the mint) is vital, because the metal which is overvalued at the mint will dominate, the undervalued metal disappearing into hoards and nonmonetary uses. Keeping the mint ratio equal to the ratio of market prices is an impossible task, because market prices fluctuate. In Britain, the recoinage of 1696 overvalued gold, with the result that, though the fact was not officially recognized until 1774, Britain moved on to a gold standard. In 1792, on the other hand, the United States set the mint ratio at 15:1, overvaluing silver, thus establishing a de facto silver standard. The change in the mint ratio to 16:1 in 1834, together with new gold discoveries which lowered the price of gold, reversed the situation, leading to a de facto gold standard. The discovery of the Comstock lode in Nevada in 1859, new processes for recovering silver from lower-grade ores, and political developments which greatly increased the supply of silver on world markets, reduced the price of silver relative to gold, sealing the fate of bimetallism.

As monetary systems have come to rely increasingly on purely token money, Gresham's law has become less relevant.

References

Backhouse, Roger, *Economists and the Economy,* Basil Blackwell, Boston, Mass. and Oxford, chap. 4, 1988, provides a concise account of monetary problems, including the English coinage crisis of 1696, and nineteenth-century bimetallism; Harrod, Charles P., *Economic Laws and Economic History,* Cambridge University Press, Cambridge, 1989, chap. 3, discusses these issues and argues that Gresham's law is of wider significance; Laidler, David, *The Golden Age of the Quantity Theory,* Philip Allan, Hemel Hempstead, 1990, provides a clear discussion of bimetallism and the debates surrounding it.

(*See also* Gold standard)

Roger E. Backhouse

Gross domestic product

A nation's output may be measured for an accounting period either by aggregating the market value of final products, the gross national product, or by summing the labor and property incomes earned in producing that output (plus certain nonfactor charges, e.g., indirect taxes, which affect market prices), gross domestic income. A third method which conceptually yields the same total, "value added," is obtained by deducting the value of purchased inputs and imports from the gross output of each industry, including government.

Gross domestic product (GDP) is an aggregation of expenditures for goods and services—outlays made for private consumption, business investment, and government. A fourth rest-of-the-world component, the excess of exports over imports (which may be negative) considers, respectively, that part of the national production that is sold abroad and deducts that part of foreign production which is sold domestically. Only "final" outlays enter into GDP in order to avoid double counting, since, for example, the value of flour in the intermediate production phase will be represented in the price of bread purchased by the final user.

Gross domestic income aggregates payments made to the factors of production—compensation of employees, corporate and proprietors' earnings, rent and interest—plus indirect taxes and some other minor items which affect selling prices. Conceptually equal to the sum of final expenditures, gross domestic income serves as a check on GDP estimates, with the difference between income and product reflected in the "statistical discrepancy"—typically small enough to inspire confidence, at the least, in the direction of change in the economy's growth, most of the time.

Gross national product (GNP), previously the commonly used national accounts aggregate in the United States, differs from GDP insofar as the latter excludes payment from abroad to domestic residents for labor and property services supplied there (so-called factor income) but includes payments to nonresidents for such services supplied domestically. A net of factor income is added to GDP to derive GNP. For countries which receive a large volume of nonresident labor and property income from abroad, as in the case of a large migrant labor force employed outside a country, GNP is a superior measure of general welfare. In the United States, net factor income from abroad is relatively small, so growth rates for the two output measures are very close, usually. The geographically bounded GDP is considered preferable for use in conjunction with national measures of production, employment, and productivity.

Because GDP is valued at market prices, "deflators" based on reported price indexes correct expenditures to secure measures of output expressed in constant dollar purchasing power. Although this process is very comprehensive and detailed, critics charge that the indexes in many cases make incomplete adjustment for improvements in value of a product or service—cases in point being computers, drugs, and medical services—and that benefits to consumers arising from shifts in the variety of goods are not measured at all. Finally, the absence of prices for output of nonmarket institutions such as government and nonprofit institutions constrains toward use of employment or other physical inputs as output measures, a procedure which fails to register productivity changes. Nevertheless, the GDP deflator is generally considered useful and broadly reliable as a measure of general price change for the overall economy—especially the fixed-weight variant, which is not affected by shifts in the composition of output, as is the more publicized GDP deflator.

Many types of market transactions are excluded from GDP—notably those deemed "intermediate" (as noted previously), transfer payments like social security, and all financial and nonfinancial transactions involving only an exchange of existing assets. However, some nonmarket goods and services, about one-tenth in total value, are added to GDP by imputation, since they correspond to market activities which are included in measuring output. Largest is the imputation of rental value on owner-occupied homes, since equivalent shelter is provided that renters otherwise enjoy by payment; other imputations are wages paid in kind, such as lodging to hotel employees or domestic servants, food and fuel consumed on farms, etc. Also, methods have been developed recently to reflect unreported activities in the so-called underground economy—moonlighting, working off the books, and bartering. However, due in part to estimation difficulties, the principle of imputation has not been extended to a number of unpaid activities, notably the services of homemakers and other household labor and the rental value of nonhousing durable goods.

The income and product accounts of the United States have been criticized on various conceptual and statistical bases, mainly directed at inconsistencies in the distinction between intermediate and final goods and services, definitions of income, consumption and investment, etc. For examples, costs of transportation to work are considered intermediate when paid by business, though final if paid by the employee; business security costs are classified intermediate, though final when the government hires police. Indeed, a large proportion of government outlays are said to be misrepresented as final rather than intermediate costs that facilitate business activity and, consequently, result in substantial double-counting of output. Perhaps more critical is the argument of understatement in investment by certain exclusions, which in the usual capital goods sense provide future incomes and output; these exclusions include outlays for research and development (R&D), computer software, intellectual property like film and recordings, and education and training. A few unofficial national accounts, developed by Robert Eisner, John W. Kendrick, and others, have included R&D and several like extensions of the investment account just noted. The contra argument is the high degree of uncertainty in estimating the rate of return of these outlays, the difficulty in identifying assets generated from R&D, a method for depreciating the "stock" of R&D, and the double counting that would arise from valuing both patents and R&D. A less controversial recommendation for expansion of the investment definition is to include nonmilitary government purchases of structures and equipment (since, e.g., automobile purchases in the private sector are considered a capital item).

Evaluation

The product and income statements lie within a more comprehensive and, in some countries, integrated System of National Accounts sponsored by the United Nations, which are linked on the one hand to input-output tables that track both the intermediate and final product flows by industry and, on the other, balance sheet asset and liability data which reveal the sources and uses of financing of economic activity. An unprecedented volume of information has been developed that not merely provides greater understanding of the sectoral structure and the significant magnitudes that contribute to economic activity but also enables quantifiable accounting-restrained sophisticated analysis of current and projected economic conditions, testing of economic hypotheses by econometric models (e.g., effect of monetary or fiscal policy on total GDP and employment) and a consistent framework for private and public planning related to spending, saving, investment, etc. Despite frailties of the estimates in many cases, difficulties of classification, and the several aforenoted and unnoted ambiguities, the use of these data has become standard internationally in private and public economic analyses.

The "numeraire" of the national accounts is in dollars or other currency, and consequently GDP should not be considered as a measure of general welfare. GDP includes market value purchases which may be worthless, harmful, and unethical. Outlays for cigarettes is a clear example, as is the less obvious "externality" costs of environmental pollution or depletion of natural resources that might be considered as offsets to GDP totals. In contrast, GDP excludes such clear benefits as unpaid volunteer social work, housewife services, the value of leisure, and good working conditions. The welfare aspect notwithstanding, the national accounts have proven indispensable to business and government decision making in the modern age.

History

Although the nineteenth century witnessed significant advances in the United States and abroad in the development of such national product and income concepts as value added, factor cost, and final expenditures, progress accelerated following the particular theoretical analysis of economic processes of consumption, saving, and investment provided by J. M. Keynes in 1936. The need for data on civilian and military output shares in U.S. mobilization efforts of World War II provided the inducement to build on work pursued at the National Bureau of Economic Research and the U.S. Department of Commerce in the 1920s and 1930s. In the post–World War II period, the UN Statistical Office developed a standard system of national accounts that was recommended for use by member nations. Estimates in simple or complex detail are now available for nearly all countries.

References

Carson, Carol, and Jeannette Honsa, "The United Nations System of National Accounts: An Introduction," *Survey of Current Business,* U.S. Department of Commerce, Bureau of Economic Analysis, June 1990; Kuznets, Simon, *National Income: A Summary of Findings,* National Bureau of Economic Research, Arno, New York, 1975; Ruggles, Richard, and Nancy D. Ruggles, *National Income Accounts and Income Analysis,* 2d ed., McGraw-Hill, New York, 1956; Young, Allen, and Helen Tice, "An Introduction to National Income Accounting," *Survey of Current Business,* U.S. Department of Commerce, Bureau of Economic Analysis, March 1985.

(*See also* Bureau of Economic Analysis; Economic forecasting methods; Economic forecasts; Flow of funds; Input-output analysis; National income accounting; Statistical methods in economics and business, an overview; System of National Accounts)

Herman I. Liebling

Growth accounting (*see* Economic growth)

Growth cycle (*see* Business cycles)

Guaranteed income (*see* Negative income tax)

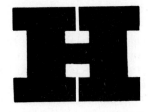

Health economics

This field of applied research and policy analysis divides into two rather distinct branches corresponding to the main issues and questions addressed. One branch concentrates on the *supply and demand in the markets for health-care services.* These markets are affected by institutional arrangements and public policies that are unusual, or at least extreme, when compared to other economic sectors. The second branch analyzes a broad range of environmental and behavioral *determinants of death rates, disability, or "health status"* of the population. Health services are only one set of influences on health status of the population. As in any other field of applied economics, researchers have sought to improve conceptual and quantitative understanding of behavior under existing conditions, leading to predictions of the likely effects of policy changes.

Markets for Health Care Services

One of the main challenges in this branch of research is to explain the rapid growth of real, age-adjusted health-care expenses. The health services sector of the U.S. economy now accounts for about 13 percent of GNP; the steady increase in this share has provoked continual public debate. After roughly three decades of intensive research, there is now some consensus among economists about the main causes of the "alarming" increases in health-care costs per unit of service and per capita. Authors point to all the following as important determinants of cost increases: invention of new technologies that improve outcomes of treatment, demand increases due to rising incomes and education levels, government-subsidized increases in the supply of physicians and hospital beds, and malpractice litigation that induces physicians to practice "defensive medicine." A most important causal and supporting factor is insurance that calls for the consumer to pay only a relatively small proportion of total charges directly at the time of service. Research on the adverse consequences of "overinsurance" can be traced back to Pauly (1968) and articles by M. Feldstein (1981). Effects of health insurance were demonstrated in a remarkable large social experiment, reported in Newhouse, et al. (1981).

Health-care markets and existing public policies are complex. These markets are replete with unusual economic features such as: (1) a major role for employer-provided health insurance; (2) an unusual predominance of not-for-profit organizations (hospitals) to produce services; (3) licensing of suppliers and many detailed regulations of entry into the market, as well as safety of operation, and prices; and (4) government financing of services directly (e.g., Medicare insurance coverage for elderly and disabled persons) or indirectly through tax subsidies.

These unusual features might serve as the response to rational concerns about market failure (especially because of uncertainty and vulnerability of the patient at a time of illness). Some of these features also serve to maintain a "safety net" for the well-being of the poorest citizens. However, some features may also reflect historical developments and rationales that are no longer compelling but have strong vested interests. For example, tax laws do not treat employer contributions to health insurance as employee income. This amounts to a large subsidy. This arrangement began with a political compromise in which the government chose to overlook fringe benefits of employment when enforcing wage and price controls during World War II. Now these arrangements to pool the risks and costs of health care are a source of inefficiency in the demands for services, inefficiencies in labor markets, and inequities related to life-cycle and household changes (see the survey article by Pauly, 1986).

During the 1970s, federal and state governments set up many regulatory programs to constrain the growth of health-care expenditures. Analysts later judged these efforts to be unsuccessful and to inhibit competition among health-care suppliers and insurance plans that might be beneficial. As examples of the research literature on this topic, see the edited volume, Olson (1981), and a longer monograph, Havighurst (1982). Federal and state policies in the 1980s aimed to encourage competition, e.g., through selective contracting with providers on a negotiated basis of price and utilization standards. An important area of current research is whether prices and quality of care are changing in response to competition among hospitals and physicians and whether there are adverse effects on distributional equity in the supply of health services. The evidence so far on results of enhanced competition in health services has not been very favorable (see P. Feldstein, 1988, chap. 12).

Determinants of Health Status

Some of the important issues raised in this branch of health economics are: (1) the proper valuation of lives saved or disabilities prevented by public health programs; (2) the effects on health status due to investments in traffic safety, control of addictive drugs, safety regulations, etc.; and (3) how and why the behavior of people to invest in their own health, or the health of their dependents, changes over time. Economists have applied a range of methodologies for cost-benefit analysis of programs that impact on health status. There is some controversy about whether and how to value the benefits of a health program on the basis of actual evidence of willingness to pay by individuals for reductions in risks of death or disability (for a discussion with practical illustrations, see Russell, 1986). Finally, some authors have focused on the likely variation among people in their rational choices of how much to invest in their own health status. An adequate evaluation of effects of public programs should consider indirect effects via changes in private decisions to invest in health status. For example, enforcement actions to reduce alcohol and tobacco consumption may have some of their effects diluted by increases in other risky behavior. By contrast, some general educational programs may have an augmented impact on health status later because high potential future earnings raise the productivity of health investments. For a discussion of demand for health and production of health see Grossman (1982).

References

Enthoven, A., *Health Plan,* Addison-Wesley, Reading, Mass., 1980; Feldstein, M. S., *Hospital Costs and Health Insurance,* Harvard University Press, Cambridge, Mass., 1981; Feldstein, P., *Health Care Economics* (3d ed.), John Wiley & Sons, 1988; Fuchs, V. R., *Who Shall Live? Health, Economics and Social Choice,* Basic Books, New York, 1974; Grossman, M., "Government and Health Outcomes," *American Economic Review,* vol. 72, May 1982, pp. 191–195; Havighurst, C., *Deregulating the Health Care Industry,* Ballinger, 1982; Newhouse, J. P., W. G. Manning, C. N. Morris, et al., "Some Interim Results from a Controlled Trial of Cost-Sharing in Health Insurance," *New England Journal of Medicine* vol. 305, 1981, pp. 1501–1507; Olson, M. (ed.), *A New Approach to the Economics of Health Care,* American Enterprise Institute, Washington, D.C., 1981; Pauly, M. V., "The Economics of Moral Hazard," *American Economic Review* vol. 58, 1968, pp. 531–537; Pauly, M. V., "Taxation, Health Insurance, and Market Failure," *Journal of Economic Literature,* vol. 24, 1986, pp. 629–675; Phelps, C., *Health Economics,* Harper Collins, New York, 1992; Russell, L. B., *Is Prevention Better Than Cure?* Brookings, Washington, D.C., 1986.

(*See also* Medicare program; Subsidies)

Bernard Friedman

Heckscher-Ohlin theory of exports in international trade (*see* International economics, an overview)

Hedging (*see* Commodity exchange; Futures)

Human capital

Human capital is the stock of economically productive human capabilities. These capabilities are formed or produced by combining innate abilities with investments in human beings. Examples of such investments include expenditures on education, on-the-job training, and health and nutrition. Such expenditures increase future productive capacity at the expense of current consumption. Since most capital stock deteriorates or depreciates with the passage of time, with intense use, or with lack of use, the stock of capital increases only when gross investment exceeds such depreciation (or, alternatively, if net investment is positive).

The amount of output of an economic entity depends upon the state of knowledge (or technology) for converting inputs into economic products, upon the efficiency with which such inputs are combined, and upon the service flows of such inputs. This abstraction is useful for considering the production of a nation, a farm, a firm, or a family. Before 1960 most economists focused on a triumvirate of primary inputs: human labor, natural resources, and the stock of physical capital (primarily plant and equipment). The production of other purchased inputs depended ultimately on this same trinity. Of course, it was realized that these primary factors varied in quality in the real world. Joseph Schumpeter, for example, in the early part of this century emphasized that some humans have unusual entrepreneurial qualities that result in their taking leadership positions by introducing economic innovations, applying better technology, opening up new markets, developing new products, making more efficient use of inputs, and locating new sources of inputs. Hypotheses were proposed that explained the difference in capabilities of humans with regard to entrepreneurship and other economic characteristics as due to familial and social conditions and to genetic endowments. But for many purposes qualitative differences among inputs, human or otherwise, simply were ignored. Even when qualitative differences were recognized, no theories were widely accepted that provided an economic structure for decisions related to investment in humans.

Human Capital School and Model

About 1960 Theodore Schultz, Gary Becker, and Jacob Mincer provided such a structure by introducing explicitly the notion that people invested in themselves to increase their stock of human capital. They emphasized the analogy between investment in physical capital and investment in human capital. Both involve forgoing current consumption to increase expected future production and earnings possibilities and, thereby, future consumption possibilities. For example, individuals may pay tuition and forgo current earnings while studying in college in part to increase their expected future earnings. Of course, there also may be other returns to education such as becoming a more knowledgeable or cultured person. But what the human capital school emphasizes is that purely economic returns relative to economic costs may be a major factor in determining such human capital investments.

The human capital model has had substantial impact on the economic profession, providing a more satisfactory framework for identifying the causes of macro, or national, growth. The model has permitted the incorporation of diversities of human capabilities into formal models that still are sufficiently simple to be manageable and has tied together investment in financial, physical, and human capital. The human capital model has improved the framework for analyzing the implications of private and social decisions relating to such areas as education, health, and nutrition, training programs, unemployment, income maintenance, family planning, the distribution of earnings, and women and youth labor-force participation and has spawned a large number of empirical efforts to measure the returns on various investments in humans, particularly in education. The model also has provoked broader theoretical and empirical considerations regarding the role of time in consumption and production, the role of family background in investments in humans, and the nature of intrafamilial consumption, production, and investment decisions.

Controversies

Despite such a major impact on economic thought—or perhaps because of that impact—a number of controversies about the human capital model currently exist on empirical and theoretical levels. One important issue revolves around the assumption that "perfect" information exists about alternatives both at a given point in time and in future periods. Users of the human capital model, for example, analyze fertility determinants under the assumption that choices are made on the basis of good knowledge concerning contraceptive options. Yet for some populations for which these models have been applied—particularly in the less-developed countries—there is considerable evidence that numerous individuals are not aware of modern contraceptive options. The estimations of the returns on education provide another example. Estimates are made under the assumption that individuals have a good estimate of the expected returns on the investment in terms of later earnings. But this implies that individuals deciding about going to college in the 1920s, to provide a specific illustration, had good expectations of the impact of the Great Depression, World War II, the postwar decolonialization, the electronic revolution, etc.

A second issue is related to whether individual or family preferences enter into human capital investment decisions. This is important because such preferences are not directly observable. Many authors assume that altruistic parents—those whose utility function includes each child's earnings, income, or consumption—distribute each child's human capital investment to help maximize this function. Unfortunately a solution to the most general altruistic model does not yield insight into the question of whether parents invest more or less resources in the more able child. Two more specific altruistic models with different treatments yield entirely different conclusions on how parents will behave on this issue. These models also differ as to how educational expenditures will vary with parent's income and how parents will divide up bequests and gifts to children.

A third issue is related to the empirical importance of the human capital model. In fact, observed variations in human capital investments such as education account for only a small part of variations in actual earnings among individuals. Moreover, recent studies suggest that the magnitude of such returns reported in many such studies may be biased upward because of a failure to allow for family background and related ability and motivation. The actual value of such returns, moreover, has important policy implications, since it indicates the extent to which human capital investments such as in education can be used to change the income distribution or to alleviate poverty.

A fourth issue is whether human capital investments, particularly in education or in training, actually increase productivity. An alternative explanation is that the attainment of such education is merely a means by which a capable individual signals his or her capabilities to potential employers.

References

Becker, Gary S., *Human Capital: A Theoretical and Empirical Analysis, with Special Reference to Education*, National Bureau of Economic Research General Series, no. 80, Columbia University Press, New York, 1964; Becker, Gary S., and N. Tomes, "Child Endowments and the Quantity and Quality of Children," *Journal of Political Economy*, vol. 84, no. 4, part 2, August 1976, pp. S143–S162; Behrman, Jere R., Z. Hrubec, Paul Taubman, and T. J. Wales, *Socioeconomic Success: A Study of the Effects of Genetic Endowments, Family Environment and Schooling*, Amsterdam: North-Holland, 1980; Behrman, Jere R., Robert A. Pollak, and Paul Taubman, "Parental Preferences and Provision for Progeny," *Journal of Political Economy*, vol. 90, no. 1, February 1982, pp. 52–73; Mincer, Jacob, "Investment in Human Capital and Personal Income Distribution," *Journal of Political Economy*, vol. 66, no. 4, August 1958, pp. 281–302; Schultz, Theodore W., "Education and Economic Growth," in N. B. Henry (ed.), *Social Forces Influencing American Education*, University of Chicago Press, Chicago, 1961.

(*See also* Economic growth; Productivity)

Jere R. Behrman and Paul Taubman

Implicit price deflator

The implicit price deflator is the price index that is usually associated with the gross national product (GNP) and its components. Such a deflator could, however, be constructed to deflate other economic time series.

The reason the price index for gross national product is called an implicit price deflator relates to the way in which it is constructed. Price indexes based on the Laspeyres formula are used to deflate in the greatest detail possible the various spending series that make up the gross national product. When these spending series are divided by the Laspeyres indexes, the result is a measure of spending in constant dollars. These constant-dollar spending series are then added up to form gross national product in constant dollars. When that total is divided into gross national product in current dollars, an implicit measure is obtained of the price index that will exactly reconcile the current and constant-dollar GNP figures. Since this index is implicitly derived as the quotient obtained by dividing the current-dollar figure by the constant-dollar figure, it is termed an implicit price index.

The formula for the implicit deflator is

$$\frac{\Sigma\, p_1 q_1}{\Sigma\, p_0 q_1}$$

where p_1 = price in the current period
q_1 = quantity in the current period
p_0 = price in the base period

It can be seen that multiplying the implicit price deflator times the Laspeyres index of output yields a measure that is the ratio of current-dollar GNP in the two time periods:

$$\frac{\Sigma p_1 q_1}{\Sigma p_0 q_0} \times \frac{\Sigma p_0 q_0}{\Sigma p_0 q_0} = \frac{\Sigma p_1 q_1}{\Sigma p_0 q_0}$$

The implicit price deflator, thus, is the only price measure that exactly reconciles a fixed-weight quantity index with a total value series. Comparison of the implicit price deflator with its base always yields a measure of pure price change for that time period based on current-period weights. In this respect, the implicit price deflator is a Paasche index, distinct from the other, more widely used measure of price change, a Laspeyres price index. The latter has base-period weights; the former, current-period weights.

The implicit price index, however, is not a fixed-weight index of prices for periods between the base and current period because its movements do not reflect price change alone. Indeed, they are a composite of changes in prices and changes in quantity when measured between periods other than the base period.

Problems and Alternatives

Because the implicit price deflator is not a measure of pure price change and is affected by changes in the composition of gross national product in constant dollars or by changes in the quantity weights, it has not been a totally satisfactory measure of pure price change for use and analysis of the gross national product. As a result, the Bureau of Economic Analysis (BEA), which is responsible for the estimation and publication of the national income and product accounts, has developed two other price series that more exactly approach measures of pure price change. One is a fixed-weight price index in which the deflators for the various components of gross national product are added up using base-period weights. Another measure developed by the BEA for analysis of prices associated with gross national product is the so-called Chain index, which is a base-period index, but one in which the base weights change from quarter to quarter. Thus, between any two quarters, it is a measure of pure price change. But for longer periods of time, changes in the Chain index reflect a mixture of price change and weight or quantity change.

The implicit deflator for gross national product has been available quarterly since 1946 from the Bureau of Economic Analysis. In addition, the BEA publishes annual estimates going back to 1929. Annual estimates before that have been developed by various scholars.

Reference

Department of Economics and Social Affairs, *Guidelines on Principles of a System of Price and Quantity Statistics,* Statistical Papers, ser. M, no. 59, United Nations, New York, 1977.

(*See also* Consumer price index; Cost of living; Gross domestic product; Index numbers; Statistical methods in economics and business, an overview)

Joel Popkin

Imports

Imports are defined as goods taken into one country from another country in the conduct of foreign trade, with the first country being the importer and the second country the exporter. In practice, imports are more complicated than this simple definition implies. One problem in analyzing U.S. import statistics is that they are valued on a customs basis excluding freight charges. In many other countries, however, imports are valued on a c.i.f. (cost, insurance, and freight) basis, including freight charges.

In addition to the monthly import data, reported by the U.S. Census Bureau, the Balance of Payments Division of the U.S. Department of Commerce also reports U.S. imports on a quarterly basis. These data are adjusted for various minor conceptual differences from the monthly series in order to make them comparable with other elements of the U.S. balance of payments.

Imports are subtracted from exports to obtain the "net exports" component of gross national product in the U.S. national accounts. But in this context the term "imports" may be confusing because it includes imports of services as well as imports of merchandise. In the broad definition, in addition to merchandise, imports include travel, transportation, military expenditures abroad, license and royalty payments, earnings on foreign investments in the United States, and other payments for services. However, payments of interest to foreign holders of U.S. government debt are included in the U.S. balance of payments but are excluded from net exports. In general, payments of interest on government securities are treated in the national accounts as transfer payments and are not included in GNP, which comprises only payments for goods and services.

Significance of Imports Growth

Since the early postwar years, imports have grown in significance to the U.S. economy. Between 1950 and 1989, U.S. imports grew from $9.1 billion to $493 billion from 3 percent to 9.25 percent of GNP. In the world economy the gain in the volume of imports was also sizable. The rapid growth in world imports is in marked contrast with the prewar decade when world trade stagnated as import restrictions were widely applied, often in retaliation to restrictions in other countries.

In the early postwar years, the growth of world trade seemed almost automatic, as incomes in most developed countries grew rapidly, technologies were transferred internationally, and tariff barriers were gradually broken down—in part because of more travel and better communication. World trade appeared to be able to solve its own problems with a minimum of interference from governments, all of which seemed to be its beneficiaries.

In the early 1970s, however, this image of world trade changed. The U.S. trade balance began to deteriorate, and in 1971 the United States moved into a trade deficit that was certainly a contribution to the devaluations of the dollar in December 1971 and February 1973. Moreover, in late 1973 U.S. imports received another shock in the more than fourfold rise in oil prices.

The surge in U.S. imports and the dollar devaluation brought into sharper focus two issues that were of minor importance in the 1950s and early 1960s. These were (1) unemployment attributed to competition from U.S. imports and (2) the impact of U.S. import prices on the U.S. price level generally.

Imports and Unemployment

In the earlier postwar period with rapid growth in the U.S. economy, there was less of a tendency for imports to displace employed workers. In the late 1960s, however, the overvaluation of the dollar made the United States less competitive and made U.S. employment more vulnerable to imports. As a result, the position of U.S. labor organizations switched from a view generally favorable to free trade to one favoring trade restrictions to prevent massive unemployment in industries competing with imports. A consciousness developed that there is a trade-off between unemployment arising from imports and the favorable effect of lower prices for consumers due to imports. In order to limit political pressures for controls on imports, the U.S. government has negotiated so-called orderly marketing agreements limiting imports from major exporting countries, particularly of consumer goods. On the other hand, the so-called Tokyo Round of trade negotiations was concluded in 1979 with significant reductions in tariffs and other trade restrictions. As of mid-1990, the so-called Uruguay Round of negotiations for further trade liberalization has not been completed mainly because of disagreements over trade restrictions in agriculture. In both Europe and North America, trade restrictions have been substantially reduced by area agreements in the European Community and the North American Free Trade Area. As of mid-1991, there were serious negotiations to include Mexico as well as the United States and Canada in the North American agreement.

Imports and the Price Level

The other aspect of U.S. imports that is now being reexamined is their effect on the U.S. price level. In the 1950s and early 1960s, U.S. imports tended to restrain U.S. inflation because prices of imports tended to be lower than prices of domestically produced goods. This effect was reversed after 1971 when depreciation of the U.S. dollar raised the price of imports. In the 1980–1985 period, however, the overvalued U.S. dollar made imports cheaper and contributed to lower U.S. inflation rates.

It is sometimes argued that devaluation does not have much effect on the U.S. price level because imports in 1978 were only about 8 percent of gross national product. This argument ignores, however, the fact that a much larger proportion of U.S. goods are internationally traded and, therefore, tend to move in line with the price of imports. Thus, if the U.S. dollar depreciates against the Japanese yen, the price of Japanese car imports may rise and exert an upward pull on the price of all U.S. autos. Moreover, with world tastes and production methods becoming more cosmopolitan, the percentage of goods with domestic prices affected by international trade is certainly rising.

Thus, imports have moved from a relatively passive part of the U.S. economy, mainly of interest to specialists, to a vital influence on the two key economic problems of employment and inflation.

References

Ahluwalia, Isher J., and Ernesto Hernandez-Cata, "An Econometric Model of U.S. Merchandise Imports under Fixed and Fluctuating Exchange Rates 1959–1973," *Staff Papers,* International Monetary Fund, Washington, D.C., November 1975; Deardorff, Alan, "Testing Trade Theories and Predicting Trade Flows," in Roland W. Jones and Peter B. Kenan (eds.), *Handbook of International Economics,* vol. 1, North-Holland, Amsterdam, 1984; Helpman, Elhanan, and Paul R. Krugman, *Market Structure and Foreign Trade,* MIT Press, Cambridge, Mass., 1985; Joy, James, and J. D. Stolen, "The Change in the U.S. Import Demand Function from the 1950s to the 1960s," *Review of Economics and Statistics,* vol. LVII, no. 1, February 1975, pp. 109–111; Khan, Mohsin S., and Knud Z. Ross, "Cyclical and Secular Income Elasticities of Demand for Imports," *Review of Economics and Statistics,* vol. LVII, no. 3, August 1975, pp. 357–361; Salvatore, Dominick, "A Model of Dumping and Protectionism in the United States," in *Weltwirtschaftliches Archiv Review of World Economics,* vol. 125, no. 4, 1989.

(See also Barriers to trade; Comparative advantage theory; Dumping; Exports; Foreign exchange rates; General Agreement on Tariffs and Trade; International economics, an overview; Protectionism)

James L. Burtle

Income

Income is most familiar to people as the amount of money received from participating in the labor market, that is, earnings from paid employment. Most would recognize that items such as interest payments on savings accounts or dividends from stocks also represent income. And it would be generally agreed that earnings from self-employment (e.g., the receipts of doctors and lawyers), less the expenses of doing business, represent income.

Economists attach a special significance to income payments that arise from current participation in the production process: these payments—whether they are wages and salaries associated with some number of hours worked; interest associated with the use of money; or dividends, rents, profits, etc.—are defined in such a way as to add up to the total income of society (i.e., to the national income). This total is then redistributed among the members of society by various voluntary and involuntary transfer and tax programs, which result in a new distribution of spendable or disposable income. Thus, social security payments are an important source of disposable income but are not part of production-related national income since recipients are not being paid for current participation in production.

Concepts

Among economists the most widely accepted analytical definition of income associated with the production process is that it represents the yield from wealth. Defining income in that way underlines the importance of relating the income concept to a corresponding wealth concept. The common sense of that idea is most easily established with reference to conventional financial assets. All would agree that the interest return on a $1000 savings account represents the income from that asset: that is, if an individual received a $60 annual payment from holding a $1000 savings account, that $60 represents income. Note that income has a clear time reference— the $60 is an annual rate of flow, while the asset that yields income—the savings account—does not, being a stock existing at a point in time.

But what about a slightly more complicated case, still within the realm of financial assets: what is the income of the owner of a share of common stock that sells at $100 and pays $5 annually in dividends? Certainly the $5 per share represents income and can be thought of as the dividend return from the shareholder's ownership of a part of the corporation. Over the course of any given time period such as a year, however, several other things might happen that could affect what we think of as the income from owning a share of stock: for example, the corporation typically earns more (after paying all expenses) than it actually pays out to the shareholders in dividends—that is, the corporation is likely to have retained earnings. And the price of the stock is likely to change, for any number of reasons.

Here, economists would probably say that the income of the shareholder is clearly different from the $5 per share paid on stock valued at $100 since the retention of earnings by the corporation presumably has made the corporation more valuable, hence likely to earn more in the future, hence likely to pay more dividends in the future, etc. A common view would be that the income of the shareholder consists of a proportionate share of the corporation's total earnings, not just the earnings paid out as dividends. Thus, undistributed profit per share might well be added to dividends per share to provide a more accurate measure of the income associated with ownership of stock.

Finally, what about a still more complex case—a self-employed business executive whose gross receipts are $100,000 per year and whose out-of-pocket expenses are $70,000 per year? Is the income from owning that business the remaining $30,000? If so, how would one characterize the asset that has yielded the $30,000 income?

Economists are apt to suggest that part of the $30,000 isn't really income at all, on the reasonable assumption that the true costs of conducting business are not represented in toto by the $70,000 out-of-pocket expenses, but should include depreciation of the company's assets as well. That is, the $30,000 differential between gross receipts and out-of-pocket expenses would be income only if the ability of the business to generate future income were to remain the same. But if the company's assets were depreciating because they were being used up in producing goods and services, some provision for replacing those assets would be needed, and that is commonly labeled depreciation.

As to the nature of the asset that has yielded the income of $30,000 (less depreciation allowance) from the business, most would say that the income comes from two sources: part represents a return on the capital assets invested in the business (equipment, inventories, working capital), and part represents a return on another kind of asset—the human skills of the business executive. It has become customary in recent decades to refer to the latter as the stock of human capital owned by the person who owns and manages the business.

It is now easier to see how one should view the wage and salary payments received by members of the population engaged in paid employment. These payments represent income, and they can be thought of as a return on knowledge, experience, and skills (i.e., on human capital assets). The difficulty with this idea may be seen by considering the income of medical interns or advanced graduate students: the former may be paid $10,000 to $15,000 a year during the 2 or 3 years they are polishing the skills of their trade, while the latter are likely to have an income of less than that while working as teaching or research assistants. Such people are apt to have about 20 years of formal schooling and can easily look forward to a future income of several times the amount paid while interning or teaching/assisting. Are the incomes of such people represented by what they are currently being paid?

Most economists would answer no to that question and argue that medical interns and teaching assistants are actually earning a much higher income than the nominal amount of money wages being paid to them because they are investing heavily in training designed to enhance future income. While there is usually no observable counterpart to the true income being earned by medical interns or teaching assistants, conceptually it would be represented by the amount that people with that level of training could earn if they were employed in a job that contained no training component, and hence no enhancement of skills and of future income.

Thus, the idea that only wage and salary payments are income does not hold up, unless the individuals receiving those wage and salary payments are in the situation of just maintaining their stock of skills at a steady state—neither adding to them nor allowing them to deteriorate. Otherwise, earnings may be higher or lower than actual income, when the latter is defined as the return on the human capital skills represented by ability, schooling, training, and experience.

Not all of wage income consists of direct payments. For example, health insurance paid for by an employer on behalf of an employee is clearly part of the employee's income—it simply constitutes services in kind in lieu of direct cash payments. Similarly, free or subsidized meals provided by employers, free or subsidized parking, payments into a pension fund, etc., all constitute part of employee income. The only issue that arises in these cases is one of quantification: since the employee may have no choice about the nature of the various benefits received in the form of free or subsidized goods and services, some fringe benefits may be worth less to the employee than they cost the employer. However, if the market for employment is sufficiently flexible, employees should be able to find employment opportunities that offer a set of fringe benefits that match their preference.

In a similar vein, owner-occupied housing, as well as personal automobiles and other durables, clearly yields income to their owners in the form of a flow of services. To understand that notion, one might consider the nature of income that takes the form of net receipts to the owner of a rental housing property or to the owner of an automobile leasing business—such receipts, after expenses, would represent income. Why should it matter whether the assets are owned by those who are in the business of providing such services or by those whose main occupation is something else but who happen to provide those services for themselves by virtue of ownership?

As in the discussion of fringe benefits, there is an empirical question of the appropriate measurement of income from such owned assets. Conventional practice in the United States is to impute income to homeowners by using valuations obtained from the rental value of comparable properties. At present, conventional U.S. practice does not make a similar imputation for automobiles or other durable assets owned by consumers.

Other questions do not have neat conceptual or empirical answers. For example, should tax payments be counted as part of the income of the taxpayer? Conventional practice in the United States is to treat income taxes and all social security taxes as part of employee income whether paid by employees or employers, but not to treat other taxes (e.g., sales taxes) in that way. Treating tax payments as part of income has some justification—people pay taxes and get in return certain services (national defense, public administration, subsidized schooling, etc.). While it is hard to argue that the distribution of such public services matches the distribution of tax payments, it is equally hard to think of any sensible alternative imputation to individuals or households of the services provided by government and paid for by taxes. One view is that taxes, and the public services provided by them, reflect the political preferences of the population as a whole and that people must typically get about as much services from government as they pay in taxes or else the tax-expenditure system would be changed to correspond to what people want.

How far should one stretch the concept of income to cover unpaid work of various sorts? The question is important, because over the last several decades many services formerly provided without compensation by household members for each other are now provided in the market by paid employees. And the reverse is also true—services formerly provided for pay in the market are now provided without pay by members of households for each other.

In the first category are activities such as child care and care of the elderly, which in earlier decades were almost exclusively provided within families or extended families, without compensation. Child care centers and institutional facilities for the elderly now abound in the United States, and the measure of earned income is affected in consequence. In the second category are activities such as domestic housework and entertainment. In earlier decades many millions of domestic workers were paid by households to cook, clean, etc., but in recent years the number of people employed in this activity has dwindled markedly. And in previous decades people were more likely than now to seek entertainment in movies, theaters, and similar establishments, whereas now television viewing in the home has significantly reduced the size of the paid entertainment market.

A little reflection suggests that the appropriate measurement of income flows associated with nonmarket activities is a complex problem, at both the analytical and the empirical levels. The most important factor to realize is that meaningful measures of income flows, and particularly of changes in income flows over time, depend crucially on the maintenance of consistency in the activities associated with the generation of income. For example, if the location of care for children and the elderly were to shift from within households to the market, the national income as conventionally measured would be much larger simply because of a transition in the location of activities. But the increase in income would be largely, if not entirely, illusory: it is not even clear that the quality of service provided to young and old would be better in commercial establishments than in households, although theoretically efficiency would be enhanced and thus fewer resources would be needed for the same product.

Income and Output

To an individual, income is a comparatively well-defined and easily understood concept, subject to the qualifications discussed previously. What may not be so easily recognized is that an appropriate definition of income has the property of making the total income of all members of society exactly equal to the total amount of output produced within that society. This identity between two different concepts—income and output—is achieved by defining one particular type of income flow as a residual that can be obtained only if one knows the amount of output.

To illustrate: The value of steel output is measured by the quantity of steel produced over some time period, multiplied by the average price of steel products. But all the contributors to this production process are paid income for their participation—workers in steel mills receive wages; suppliers of raw materials receive prices multiplied by quantities for their contribution; bondholders receive interest; stockholders receive dividends; owners of land on which steel facilities are located receive rent; etc. And there is a residual income receiver—the owners of the steel company—who receives the amount (positive or negative) that remains after all other payments, including dividends, have been made. This profits residual is simply the difference between the total value of steel output produced over some accounting period and the total amount of the income payments made to various factors of production. Since profits are also an income flow, it must, therefore, be definitionally true that the total value of steel output is equal to the total amount of income payments received by those involved in the steel industry.

One of the payments listed above does not represent income in the same sense as the others—the payments to suppliers of materials are not really income, but constitute receipts for the sale of goods from one firm to another. While that is true, exactly the same argument can be used to distribute the total value of materials purchased by the steel industry into payments to various inputs plus a profits residual. That is, suppliers of iron ore also pay wages to workers and managers, dividends to stockholders, interest to bondholders, etc., and they also would have a residual profit to balance the books, so to speak. Thus, all production of goods and services gives rise to an associated flow of income to participants in the production process, and that accounting identity gives rise to the double-entry-bookkeeping nature of our national income and product accounting system. Thus, economists speak interchangeably of the national income or the national product, knowing that the two are identically defined.

Real Income and Money Income

In an era when high inflation rates are commonplace, everyone is familiar with the difference between money income and real income. Money income reflects the nominal value of income flows to individuals, households, or society as a whole. Real income reflects the adjustment of these money-income flows to account for the fact that a given amount of money income will not buy as many goods and services in one period as in another because the average price of goods and services has changed (in the 1970s, for example, it rose significantly). Thus, real income is simply money income deflated by the appropriate price index. At the level of individuals, the money income of the person or household would be deflated by a price index reflecting the particular bundle of goods and services purchased by that person or household.

Put another way, the concept of real income represents command over resources—that is, the degree to which a given flow of money income is able to translate into a flow of consumable products such as food, clothing, utilities, housing services, vacations, haircuts, and insurance coverage. Hence we adjust the flow of money income in different periods of time by the degree to which a particular common bundle of consumable goods and services varies in price from one period to the next, i.e., by an overall index of price change. Another way to view the same phenomenon is to recognize that money-income flows are measured in nominal units (dollars, francs, pounds, etc.); the notion of real income takes account of the fact that the yardstick itself (dollars, francs, pounds, etc.) can shrink or grow depending on whether one can acquire more (or less) goods and services for any given amount of dollars, francs, pounds, etc. An important analytic concept associated with the difference between money income and real income is "money illusion"—the idea that consumers respond to money variables as if they were real variables. Thus consumers may increase spending when money income rises because they feel richer, even if prices have actually risen as much as income and they are not in fact richer.

References

Becker, Gary S., *Human Capital: A Theoretical and Empirical Analysis with Special Reference to Education,* National Bureau of Economic Research General Series, no. 80, Columbia University Press, New York, 1964; Jaszi, George, "The Conceptual Basis of the Accounts: A Reexamination," in Studies in Income and Wealth, vol. 22, *A Critique of the United States Income and Product Accounts,* National Bureau of Economic Research, Princeton University Press, Princeton, N.J., 1958, pp. 13–145; Juster, F. Thomas, "A Framework for the Measurement of Economic and Social Performance, Columbia University Press, New York, 1973, pp. 25–109; Kuznets,

Simon S., *National Income and Its Composition, 1919–1938,* vols. I, II, National Bureau of Economic Research General Series, no. 40, Arno, New York, 1941; Kuznets, Simon S., and Milton Friedman, *Income from Independent Professional Practice,* National Bureau of Economic Research General Series, no. 45, Arno, New York, 1954; Samuelson, P. A., "The Evaluation of 'Social Income' Capital Formation and Wealth," in F. A. Lutz and D. C. Hague (eds.), *The Theory of Capital: Proceedings of a Conference,* St. Martin's, New York, 1961; Schultz, T. W., "Investment in Human Capital," *American Economic Review,* vol. 51, no. 1, March 1961, pp. 1–17; U.S. Office of Business Economics, *National Income: A Supplement to the Survey of Current Business,* U.S. Department of Commerce, 1954.

(*See also* Gross domestic product; Income distribution; Money illusion; National income accounting)

F. Thomas Juster

Income distribution

What are the principles that determine how the annual output of goods and services is distributed among the population? Are these principles fair? Do they promote efficiency? What do they imply about how the degree of inequality will change in the course of economic growth or in response either to trade union or monopoly power or to different government policies? Will there be more or less poverty in the future? Many economists would say, along with David Ricardo, that distributional issues such as these are the central questions of all economics.

The process out of which the income distribution emerges is now dominated by the interaction between governments and markets. A government influences market allocations of material and human resources through its taxes (particularly corporate income taxes, property taxes, excise taxes, and capital gains and inheritance taxes), through its transfers (subsidies to selected industries and to education and health, as well as payments through the social security and welfare systems), and through its regulatory policies (particularly those of the Federal Reserve System, in the case of the United States). Once the market has allocated resources and established resource prices, indirect taxes having been taken into account, government taxes and transfers once again alter the income distribution (particularly through personal income taxes and transfers to those without marketable resources).

The Role of Markets

After nearly a century of intense debate, the main lines of what is now the orthodox distribution theory describing the role of markets were set down by Alfred Marshall near the close of the nineteenth century. Orthodox theory takes as its central question: What determines the prices at a point in time of each of the factors of production—labor, capital, entrepreneurship, and land. That is, what determines the wage rate, the interest rate, the profit rate, and the rental rate of land. The key contribution of Marshall and his contemporaries (particularly J. B. Clark) was to shift the question to prices in the present and away from shares in the future. Ricardo was intrigued by the question: What happens to the share of income going to landlords in the course of economic growth? Marx was interested primarily in the share of income decades in the future going to capital. Shifting the question away from shares brought income distribution under the general theory of price—i.e., the determination of the trading ratio at which supply and demand are equilibrated. Of course, once the price and equilibrium quantities determined by supply and demand are known, it is a small additional step to reckoning shares.

As orthodox economists see it, the key attribute that characterizes factor prices in equilibrium is that each factor is paid according to its contribution to the value of output. To see how this works, consider what would happen were this not the case. Employed workers whose productivity exceeded or could exceed their wage would find themselves being bid for and find their wages raised. Workers who did not produce what they cost would be fired. From such homely examples powerful implications follow. First, many would take the resulting distribution of income to be equitable—each is paid according to how diligently and effectively he or she contributes to meeting the desires of everyone else as expressed in the market. Furthermore, this distribution supports efficiency—each factor is bid into its highest and best use.

From the beginning, the idea that a market economy, capitalist or socialist, generates a fair but unequal income distribution has been controversial. Both critics and enthusiasts for markets have raised objections. Market advocates point to the impediments that make for less-than-perfect factor markets: trade unions, monopolistic resource sellers, monopsonistic buyers, race and sex discrimination, central bank control of interest rates, distortionary taxes on income from capital, and so on. Also, nearly all market advocates admit to the difficulties of calculating the productivity of a factor at the margin.

Nonbelievers come in many forms. The most outspoken critics have been followers of Joan Robinson and John Rawls.

The Robinsonians, or post Keynesians, start from the difficulty of calculating marginal products. Going further than the orthodox critics, they believe that the orthodox theory is not consistent. The theory is alleged to be wrong at its foundations. They contend that the outputs of factors of production working jointly cannot be partitioned among those separate factors, even analytically—that it cannot even be presumed that as more of one factor is added to, its productivity necessarily declines. In the market, these theorists continue, this ambiguity results in a conflict over shares among powerful coalitions (landlords, laborers, capitalists), with the bargaining power at the moment and the political skills of the contestants determining the outcome. In the hands of the post Keynesians, then, distribution theory returns to the determinants of shares. It is not surprising that they have redirected attention to Ricardo's work.

John Rawls and his followers have taken a different line of attack. Rawls simply rejects the ethical postulates of the orthodox view. Allocating the output of an economy to those who produce it in accordance to their contribution to output violates Rawls's view of justice—such rules of the game are simply not fair. It is not fair, he argues, that those born smarter or stronger then others should receive a larger share of output, even if they have contributed more to that output, unless it can be shown that such rules benefit those who are least productive. If such benefit cannot be so shown, and Rawls clearly doubts that it can, then other rules need to be devised. Devising alternative fair rules constitutes one frontier of the theory of income distribution.

The critics have been politically effective. No government now simply accepts the distribution of income as generated by markets. On the contrary, all governments now actively seek to affect income distribution.

The Role of Governments

Whether governments can alter the distribution of income in the long run has been debated by economists since John Stuart Mill. Around the turn of this century, V. Pareto was putting forth empirical support for his law—a law that held that inequality was roughly the same in all countries. Inequality, however, does differ from country to country, and governments do have some influence over inequality. While it is technically difficult for governments to significantly alter the distribution of incomes, the major obstacles appear to be political. In most developed countries, tax systems tend to be proportional, rather than progressive, for example, and that approach appears to be primarily a political decision. Similarly, transfer systems tend to benefit large segments of the population, not just the poor. If taxes were progressive and transfers were target-efficient, inequality would be less, but reducing inequality is not generally the most important economic objective of Western governments.

Economic Development and Income Distribution

Until recently, most studies concluded that inequality tended to remain the same in any one country over remarkably long periods. In the United States, for example, inequality appeared quite stable around its post–World War II level. Between 1970 and 1990, however, inequality, particularly wage inequality, rose significantly in the United States and other countries, prompting many economists to redirect their attention to what changes are likely to have produced this market outcome, and undermining the conventional belief in the long-term constancy of inequality within developed countries. A second piece of conventional wisdom now being reconsidered is Kuznets' hypothesis that inequality first rises and then falls as economic development progresses.

Another debate concerns the distribution of world income across countries and its trend. Some economists maintain that, given the nature of trade relations, the gap between rich and poor countries will tend to widen. Others believe that the incomes of the poorer countries will grow faster, causing the poorer countries to catch up to the richer. The debate has not been settled, and no unambiguous trend in international inequality has emerged from empirical studies of the post–World War II era.

References

Adelman, I., and S. Robinson, "Income Distribution and Development," in H. Chenery and T. N. Srinivasan (eds.), *Handbook of Development Economics,* North-Holland, Amsterdam, 1989; Atkinson, A. B., *The Economics of Inequality,* Clarendon, Oxford, 1975; Levy, F., and R. Murnane, "U.S. Earnings Levels and Earnings Inequality: A Review of Recent Trends and Proposed Explanations," in *Journal of Economic Literature* (forthcoming); Osberg, L. (ed.), *Economic Inequality and Poverty: International Perspectives,* Sharpe, Armonk, N.Y., 1991.

(*See also* Factors of production; Income; Negative income tax; Poverty; Social security; Taxation, an overview)

Eugene Smolensky

Incomes policy

An incomes policy is a policy aimed at reducing inflation by directly restraining the growth of nominal incomes. The term "incomes policy" includes a wide variety of specific policy actions through which governments may attempt to slow the growth of money wages and prices. In capitalist countries, such actions often rest on the belief that market power (particularly that of labor unions) is a significant source of upward wage and/or price pressure, although incomes policy may also be part of an effort to reduce inflationary expectations. In socialist countries, incomes policy may be used in an effort to keep money-wage increases within the targets set in an economic plan. Incomes policies have thus been used for various purposes, ranging from preventing the emergence of inflation to winding down an existing inflation. The policies can be comprehensive or selective in application, and they are generally viewed as a supplement rather than a substitute for fiscal and monetary restraint in countering inflation.

Types of Incomes Policies

Incomes policy can be quite informal, as when a public agency monitors and reports on wage and price decisions or when the President or some other political leader issues public appeals ("jawboning") for wage and price restraint. Since appeals to public opinion appear to have little influence on wage and price decisions, most incomes policies are more formal.

Most formal incomes policies include both a guideline for the behavior of wages, prices, and perhaps other incomes and a mechanism for enforcement of the policy. Some policies also include explicit exceptions to the general guideline to permit flexibility in allocating resources, to encourage productivity improvement, or to promote distributional objectives. Variations in one or another of these features account for the different types of incomes policy.

The most stringent policy guideline is a pay freeze—effectively a zero growth rate for wages, prices, and other incomes. When combined with fines, imprisonment, or other severe penalties for violating the guideline, such policies are referred to as "mandatory controls." Effective controls freeze relative wages and prices as well as the growth of nominal incomes. When relative wages and prices cannot adjust to reallocate resources in response to changing economic circumstances, shortages and surpluses emerge in various sectors, and the controls typically break down.

Concern with the tension of restraining nominal income growth while permitting allocational flexibility underlies the design of most of the less stringent approaches to incomes policy. Probably the most common formulation of voluntary wage-price guidelines permits nominal wages to grow at the trend rate of growth of economywide productivity. If both the wage rate and output per hour increase at the same rate, labor costs per unit of output remain constant. This arithmetic produced a zero-inflation guideline in early versions of this policy, which were developed to prevent outbreaks of inflation. When policies were introduced during periods of inflation, the wage guideline often permitted wage increases equal to productivity growth plus some fraction of past price inflation. The guidelines have sometimes varied for sectors with above- or below-average productivity growth to minimize allocational rigidities. In some instances, low-wage workers and workers who have produced notable productivity improvements have been partially exempted from the wage guideline. Enforcement mechanisms for productivity-based guidelines policies have included exhortation by government officials and the establishment of special review committees to evaluate wage and price decisions for compliance with policy guidelines.

A third type of incomes policy, the "social contract," involves multilateral negotiations between labor, management, government officials, and possibly other economic interest groups over the growth of incomes. The presence of the government reflects the fact that tax policies are an important influence on the growth of disposable incomes. In principle, governments could offer policy concessions to compensate labor for wage restraint. Other potential compensatory policies include wage indexation and legislation supporting the institutional position of unions. The social contract approach to incomes policy is most feasible in countries with centralized labor and management bargaining organizations.

A fourth type of incomes policy uses the tax system to give firms and workers incentives to moderate wage and price increases. Such tax-based incomes policies (TIPs) do not prohibit high wage or price increases but use the tax system to reward or penalize firms or workers according to their degree of compliance with incomes policy guidelines. A penalty TIP would impose a progressive tax surcharge on firms that had granted wage increases in excess of the guideline (Wallich and Weintraub, 1971). A reward TIP would provide progressive rebates to the firm for wage increases below the guideline. A policy could combine both features. Alternatively, a TIP policy could be applied to workers. In principle, TIP policies permit considerable allocational flexibility, since firms and workers can incur the tax and exceed the guideline if circumstances warrant. Western democracies have experimented very little with tax-based incomes policy, but TIPs have been used frequently in former Soviet bloc countries.

Prospects and Possibilities for Incomes Policy

Views on the prospective achievements of incomes policies are mixed. Proponents of incomes policy argue that it may reduce the amount of inflation associated with standard monetary-fiscal policies by stiffening the resistance of firms to excessive wage demands and by reducing inflationary expectations. If incomes policy has this effect, countries might slow inflation with less monetary and fiscal restraint and hence less unemployment. In addition, some incomes policies provide an alternative to the tax system for redistributing income. This latter objective has mainly been a goal in some European policies.

Economists are most skeptical of the value of mandatory controls on wages and prices. While such policies may temporarily restrain wage and price inflation, the rigid wage and price structures that result reduce the allocative efficiency of the economy and may build pressure for subsequent inflation. (The strongest case for such policies occurs during situations of extreme national emergency, as in wartime.) Most economists are equally skeptical that incomes policy can play a useful role in restraining inflation from excess demand, because business and labor are unlikely to be willing or able to cooperate when markets are tight.

Some economists also question whether incomes policies can be designed or implemented to achieve their objectives successfully. Designing an incomes policy involves choices regarding the policy's coverage, standards for income development, and compliance incentives. Coverage involves choices regarding what type of income and how much of the economy should be covered by policy rules. Comprehensive income coverage would require complicated rules governing the growth of wages, price, profits, rents, and interest income. Most incomes policies instead establish rules for the growth of nominal wages and prices, but the more limited the coverage of incomes, the greater the scope for allegations of policy-induced distributional inequities.

As the discussion of types of incomes policy indicates, there are many possible standards or rules for income growth. Very specific rules tend to lack flexibility and may cause distortions and inequities. Moreover, there is a danger that a specific guideline will be taken as a minimum rather than a maximum goal in collective bargaining and other income-determination processes. On the other hand, very broad rules may be difficult to apply to specific situations.

Many incomes policies may be weakened by an absence of compliance incentives. Unions contemplating compliance with the wage standards of an incomes policy face a "prisoners' dilemma" choice. If a union complies, its members will receive a small benefit in terms of reduced general inflation in return for the significant cost of accepting a lower wage increase. Everyone else in the economy will also get the benefit of lower inflation, even though they take no action to comply. In comparison with groups that do not comply, both the real wage and the relative wage of unions that comply with the standard will be lower. The incentives seem tilted against compliance, unless policies are designed with specific compliance rewards. Compliance problems can also make incomes policies costly to administer. The costs of government monitoring and enforcement agencies show up in the federal budget. Less visible are the compliance costs incurred in the private sector.

U.S. Experience

In the United States, mandatory controls have been employed in most wartime periods to facilitate the transfer of resources from civilian to war production. During World War I selective controls were imposed on prices and wages, although no formal statute was enacted. During World War II a comprehensive mandatory controls program was put into effect by the United States and other major nations. A wage and price freeze was followed by regulations on margins, prices, and wages. During the Korean conflict the United States initiated a general wage-price freeze, which was followed by mandatory controls on prices for selected items.

A voluntary incomes policy was introduced in 1962, when the Kennedy administration established "guideposts" for noninflationary wage and price behavior in an effort to slow the development of inflationary pressures during a peacetime economic expansion. This policy consisted of productivity-based standards for wage and price increases with no formal enforcement mechanism. This policy was abandoned in 1966 as the growth of demand increasingly produced many wage and price changes in excess of the standards.

The next general U.S. incomes policy was initiated in August 1971 by the Nixon administration. For the first time in peacetime the government initiated a policy of mandatory controls in the form of a 90-day freeze on all wages, prices, and profits. Several phases of less-stringent wage-price standards followed until April 1974. Econometric evidence suggests that wage and price increases may have been temporarily restrained in the early phases of the policy, only to catch up with their normal levels in later phases. Overall, the policy appears to have changed the timing but not the overall size of wage and price increases. This pattern of policy impact has also been observed in some incomes policies abroad.

The Carter administration initiated a voluntary anti-inflation program in 1977. Initially, the program consisted of public exhortation and budget recommendations.

When this effort failed to slow the pace of inflation, however, the program was formally strengthened in October 1978 with voluntary wage and price standards, regulatory reform, and changes in federal budgetary policy. The Carter administration also proposed a tax-based incomes policy known as "real-wage insurance." This policy would have provided workers who complied with the pay standard a tax credit if consumer price increases exceeded the government's policy target of 7 percent inflation. The intention was to reduce the risk of complying with pay standards. The proposal was not adopted by Congress because of its potential cost following the second round of OPEC oil price increases.

Foreign Experience

In comparison with the United States, foreign countries have experimented with a much wider variety of incomes policies during the post–World War II period. The types of policies adopted often reflect the structure of labor-market institutions. Countries with decentralized collective bargaining institutions have tended to adopt policies based on specific wage and price standards with formal review boards to monitor compliance. Countries with relatively centralized income-determination institutions, such as Austria, Australia, and Norway, have experimented with social contracts. A few countries, such as the United Kingdom, have tried both approaches. Former Socialist countries, such as Hungary and Poland, have been notable for their use of tax-based incomes policy.

During the 1960s, incomes policies were adopted in capitalist countries to prevent or retard the development of inflationary pressures as governments pursued full-employment growth policies. For the most part, the European incomes policy experiments of the 1960s were not regarded as successful in their efforts to produce long-term wage and price restraint. While econometric evaluations indicate that money-wage growth was at times restrained by 1 to 2 percentage points for 1 to 2 years, these periods were often followed by outbreaks of wildcat strikes and wage "explosions" in which wages increased more rapidly than would normally have been expected under prevailing economic conditions. The evaluations indicated that even less price restraint was achieved, so that the net effect of the policies may have been to reduce real wages.

During the 1970s, the combined effects of OPEC oil price increases and reduced profitability of industry in many European countries led governments to explicitly seek real-wage reductions through incomes policies. There was increased interest in the social contract approach to incomes policy during this period. Often the policies requested by unions as compensation for wage restraint conflicted with the broader objectives of incomes policies. Policies such as price controls and wage indexation tended to conflict with the need for lower real wages in Europe in the face of the oil price shocks, for example. By the end of the decade it was clear that under prevailing economic conditions, the social contract approach had been no more successful than the earlier approaches to incomes policy. Efforts by socialist bloc countries to use TIP policies to maintain income growth within plan targets also met with little success.

After some 40-odd years of postwar experience in countries with different ideological orientations and different labor-market institutional arrangements, it appears that the role for incomes policy is limited. Some varieties of policy may provide short-term wage and price restraint in situations where the economy is operating below capacity, but even then there is a danger of subsequent resurgence of wage and price pressures.

References

Adam, Jan, *Wage Control and Inflation in the Soviet Bloc Countries,* Macmillan, London, 1979; Flanagan, Robert J., David W. Soskice, and Lloyd Ulman, *Unionism, Economic Stabilization and Incomes Policies: European Experience,* Brookings, Washington, D.C., 1983; Okun, Arthur M., and George L. Perry (eds.), *Curing Chronic Inflation,* Brookings, Washington, D.C., 1978; Ulman, Lloyd, and Robert J. Flanagan, *Wage Restraint: A Study of Incomes Policies in Western Europe,* University of California Press, Berkeley, 1971; Wallich, Henry C., and Sidney Weintraub, "A Tax-Based Incomes Policy," *Journal of Economic Issues,* vol. 45, June 1971, pp. 1–19.

(*See also* Federal Reserve policy; Fiscal policy; Indexation; Inflation; Monetary policy)

Robert J. Flanagan

Increasing costs (*see* Diminishing returns law)

Increasing returns law (*see* Economies of scale)

Index numbers

Parenti (1940) and Kendall (1969) traced the historical origin of index numbers. C. Gini published in 1924 a seminal paper on index numbers that was the outcome of a long debate with Irving Fisher and Ragnar Frisch. Gini's 1924 article was followed by further studies published in 1931 and 1937 where he discussed the statistical and economic foundations of price indexes and made a pioneer contribution on utility functions considerations related to the construction of price indexes. Gini's contributions inspired new important developments by Frisch (1936) and by several contemporary scholars, among them Benedetti (1962), Konus (1958), and Diewert (1976, 1981).

Two different approaches can be distinguished in the study of index numbers: the statistical, which deals with their construction, and the purely economic, which deals with the theoretical foundations of the indexes.

An index number is a statistical measure of the percentage change observed in a single or composite variable. The comparisons may be chronological, geographical, or categorical. The majority of index numbers have been constructed to provide a dimensionless measure of the time path of economic phenomena such as prices, production, wages, imports, and exports. The price and production indexes, which are time series, have been in use longer than other indexes and are the best known.

Those with greatest influence on policymaking are the consumer price index (CPI); the producer price index (PPI), formerly the wholesale price index (WPI); and the implicit price deflator (IPD) for the gross national product.

The most familiar index is probably the consumer price index, which measures price changes of a constant market basket of goods and services over time. The constant basket is periodically revised to ensure that it is representative of the actual spending habits of the population to which it relates. The CPI is widely applied, and it serves various purposes. Because the CPI measures price changes at the final level of consumer demand, it is often used as an index of inflation and serves as an economic indicator to evaluate the success or failure of economic policies. A second use of the CPI is as a deflator of other economic series. A third use is as an escalator of various forms of income in order to maintain the purchasing power of the income recipients. In this use, the CPI is considered a cost-of-living index, although, technically, it is not a true cost-of-living index. In effect, it does not reflect the various substitutions that consumers tend to make in order to maintain their standard of living in the face of changing market conditions.

The PPI measures price changes of goods sold at the primary market level. The prices are basically those charged by manufacturers or wholesalers to retailers or to other distributors. Another important member of this family of price indexes is the IPD, which acquired relevance as an outcome of the development and implementation of the system of national accounts. Several types of the PPI can be obtained by performing an appropriate sectoral disaggregation of the IPD.

Another type of index of wide application in economics is that of the change in production over time. The index of industrial production is perhaps the best known, and it measures changes in the physical volume of output in manufacturing, mining, and utilities. The two major subgroups of manufacturers are durables and nondurables.

In international trade, in addition to the import and export price and volume indexes there is the terms of trade (TT). It purports to measure the relative change in the system of the goods being exported by a country with respect to the price system of the goods being imported. This index is used in the assessment of imported or exported inflation, and it was extensively discussed in the post–World War II debates between developing and developed nations.

Construction of an Index Number

Elementary Indexes   The first step in the construction of an index number is to define its purpose. The purpose of the index determines (1) the variable to be included, (2) the sources of the data, (3) the collection of the data, and (4) the formula for calculating the index.

If the index is intended to measure, say, price, production, or sales changes affecting a single variable, it can be directly defined and measured as the ratio of the observed prices, physical volumes of production, or dollar values of sales at the different periods of time. These ratios are called price relatives, quantity relatives, or value relatives and are elementary indexes. In general, the elementary index or relative of a single variable X at time t, with the base period 0, is $I_{t/0}(X) = X_t/X_0$. From the definition of a relative, the important property of circularity is deduced. This property means that the change in X can be measured between any two different dates and not only between the base and the current periods. Circularity implies both the time-reversal property, which means that if the order of the dates to be compared is changed, the new index is the reciprocal of the old index, and the linkage property, which means that the index $I_{t/0}(X)$ can be obtained by the successive multiplication of relatives that measure the change between two consecutive dates.

Composite Indexes   An index that measures the total change of a set of variables is called a composite index. The fundamental problem of a composite index is to find the appropriate formula to measure the average movement of the relatives. If the relatives are not scattered, the composite index is easy to measure and has a concrete meaning, whereas if the relatives are highly scattered, then no composite index provides a good representation. The most widely applied formulas for constructing a composite index were proposed by the German economists E. Laspeyres, in 1864, and H. Paasche, in 1874.

The Laspeyres composite index is a weighted arithmetic average of elementary indexes, where the weights are constant and they measure the relative importance of each component at the base period 0. That is,

$$L_{t/0}(X) = \sum_{i=1}^{n} w_{i0} I_{t/0}(X_i) \tag{1}$$

where X is the variable that results from the composition of n other variables, and X_i and w_{i0} are the weights given to the component variables at the base period 0. The sum of the weights w_{i0} is equal to 1.

The Paasche composite index is a weighted harmonic average of elementary indexes, where the weights are constant and they measure the relative importance of each component at the current period t. That is,

$$\frac{1}{P_{t/0}(X)} = \sum_{i=1}^{n} \frac{w_{it}}{I_{t/0}(X_i)} = \sum_{i=1}^{n} w_{it} I_{0/t}(X_i) \tag{2}$$

where $\sum_i w_{it} = 1$

In 1899, A. L. Bowley proposed to combine the Laspeyres and Paasche indexes to obtain a new index that I. Fisher (1927) called "ideal" because it fulfilled certain properties. The ideal index is the geometric mean of the Laspeyres and Paasche indexes. In symbols,

$$I_{t/0}(X) = \sqrt{L_{t/0}(X) P_{t/0}(X)} \tag{3}$$

If the set of weights w_{i0} and w_{it} are equal, then the Laspeyres index, which is an arithmetic average, is larger than the Paasche index, which is a harmonic average. The Laspeyres index will be smaller than the Paasche index if the relative weights w_i of the various components tend to decrease for those components with high elementary indexes and tend to increase for those components with low elementary indexes. None of the three indexes, Laspeyres, Paasche, or Fisher's ideal index, fulfills the circularity property. The ideal index, however, fulfills the time-reversal property discussed above.

Value and Price Indexes

The composite value index for a set of n commodities is, by definition,

$$I_{t/0} = \frac{\sum_{i=1}^{n} p_{it} q_{it}}{\sum_{i=1}^{n} p_{i0} q_{i0}} \tag{4}$$

The composite price indexes using the Laspeyres and Paasche formulas are, respectively,

$$L_{t/0}(P) = \frac{\sum_i p_{it} q_{i0}}{\sum_i p_{i0} q_{i0}} \tag{5}$$

$$P_{t/0}(P) = \frac{\sum_i p_{it}q_{i0}}{\sum_i p_{i0}q_{i0}} \tag{6}$$

Formulas (5) and (6) are related to (4) as follows: the two price indexes are equivalent to the total value index if the quantities of the latter are held constant. In the Laspeyres formula the constant quantities correspond to the base period 0; and in the Paasche formula, they correspond to the current period t. Similar kinds of equivalence are observed for quantity indexes where the prices are kept constant and the quantities vary.

The composite price indexes shown in (5) and (6) are constructed by computing aggregate values, and, as such, they show the relative change in the total value (total expenditure) of a given set of commodities that results from differences in prices between the current and the base periods. By introducing a simple transformation, formulas (5) and (6) can be equivalently expressed as weighted averages of price relatives, where the weights are value or expenditure weights; in effect,

$$\frac{L_{t/0}(P) = \sum_i p_{i0}q_{it}(p_{it}/p_{i0})}{\sum_i p_{i0}q_{i0}} \tag{7}$$

$$P_{t/0}(P) = \frac{\sum_i p_{it}q_{it}}{\sum_i p_{it}q_{it}(p_{i0}/p_{it})} \tag{8}$$

Price indexes constructed as weighted averages of elementary indexes are valuable for analyzing the impact of the price change of a single item or a subgroup of items on the global price movement.

The discrepancy between the Laspeyres and Paasche price indexes was calculated by the statistician L. V. Bortkiewicz in 1924. The formula for the discrepancy between the two price indexes is

$$P_{t/0}(P) - L_{t/0}(P) = \text{cov} \, \frac{I_{t/0}(p_i), I_{t/0}(q_i)}{L_{t/0}(Q)} \tag{9}$$

The discrepancy is the weighted covariance between the price and quantity relatives. The Paasche index is (1) smaller than the Laspeyres index if, on average, price and quantity vary in opposite directions; (2) greater than the Laspeyres index if, on average, price and quantity vary in the same direction; and (3) equal to the Laspeyres index if there is no correlation between price and quantity.

Constant-Utility Price Index

The constant-utility price index can be considered the true cost-of-living index but is still an abstract concept of economic theory. The elements involved cannot be obtained from only price and quantity data, and, thus, the index cannot be estimated in practice. The Laspeyres and Paasche indexes are used as rough approximations instead.

The constant-utility price index is a measure of the change in prices of a set of commodities that produce constant utility or satisfaction to an individual consumer assumed to be a utility maximizer. The members of the set do not need to be identical, but their utility to the consumer must always be the same. The constant-utility price index is, thus, strictly confined to an individual consumer with a fixed preference map. The preference map comprises two sets of intersecting functions—one made of convex indifference surfaces and the other made of Engel curves. The indifference surfaces correspond to a given level of utility, and points on a given surface show the various combinations of goods and services that provide constant utility or satisfaction to the consumer. The Engel curves cut across the indifference surfaces and show how purchases change as the consumer's income increases at constant market prices. The assumption is made that the consumer always balances his or her budget, given income and the market prices. For this the consumer chooses the quantities and set of commodities that maximize utility. The constant-utility price index is then the quotient of two budgets or expenditures at optimal level for different market prices but that give a constant utility.

References

Allen, R. G. D., *Index Numbers in Theory and Practice,* Aldine, Chicago, 1975; Benedetti, C., "Teorie e tecniche dei Numeri Indici," *Metron,* vol. 22, no. 1–2, 1962; Diewert, W. E., "Exact and Superlative Index Numbers," *Journal of Econometrics,* vol. 4, no. 2, 1976; Diewert, W. E., "The Economic Theory of Index Numbers: A Survey," in A. Deaton (ed.), *Essays in the Theory and Measurement of Consumer Behaviour,* Cambridge University Press, Cambridge, 1981; Eichorn, W., R. Henn, O. Opitz, and R. W. Shepard, *Theory and Applications of Economic Indices,* Physica-Verlag-Wursburg, West Germany, 1978; Fisher, F. W., and K. Shell, *The Economic Theory of Price Indices,* Academic Press, New York, 1972; Fisher, Irving, *The Making of Index Numbers,* Houghton Mifflin, Boston, 1927; Frisch, Ragnar, "Annual Survey of General Economic Theory: The Problem of Index Numbers," *Econometrica,* vol. 4, 1936, pp. 1–38; Gini, C., "Quelques Consideration au Sujet de la Construction des Nombres Indices des Prix et des Questions Analogues," *Metron,* vol. 4, no. 1, 1924; Gini, C., "On the Circular Test of Index Numbers," *Metron,* vol. 10, no. 1, 1931; Gini, C., "Methods of Eliminating the Influence of Several Groups of Factors," *Econometrica,* vol. 5, no. 1, 1937; Kendall, M. G., "The Early History of Index Numbers," *Review of the International Statistical Institute,* vol. 37, no. 1, 1969; Konus, A. A., "Consumer Price Indexes and Demand Functions," *Review of the International Statistical Institute,* vol. 26, no. 1-3, 1958; Parenti, G., "La Tecnica ed il Significato dei Primi Numeri Indici dei Prezzi," *Economia,* vol. 26, no. 5-6, 1940.

(*See also* Consumer price index; Economic forecasting methods; Implicit price deflator; Industrial production index; Inflation; Leading indicator approach to forecasting; Producer price index; Seasonal adjustment methods; Statistical methods in economics and business, an overview; Time series analysis)

Estela Bee Dagum and Camilo Dagum

Indexation

Indexation is the tying of deferred payments to the value of an index, usually a price index. Cost-of-living adjustment (COLA) clauses in labor contracts, the linkage of interest and/or principal payments to the price level (indexed bonds or bank deposits) and the automatic adjustment of tax brackets for inflation are important examples of indexation. Other forms of indexation include payments linked to the exchange rate or to the price of a particular commodity (for instance, gold or wheat).

Indexation makes it possible to use long-term contracts even when there is considerable uncertainty about the future price level, and, thus, the value of money. In practice, indexation has been most widespread in countries experiencing high rates of inflation [e.g., in Finland (until 1968), Israel, Brazil, and Argentina]; however, there are few nonsocialist countries where there is no indexation of any sort. Limited forms of wage indexation have been used in reforming formerly socialist economies, such as Poland. Braun (1976), H. Giersch (1974), and S. Page and S. Trollope (1974) provide details on the types and extent of indexation prevalent in the period up to the seventies, when relatively high inflation in the industrialized countries produced considerable interest in indexation. S. Fischer (1983) summarizes in tabular form the use of different forms of indexation in 40 countries.

Index clauses have been used for centuries. Willard Fisher (1913) traced them back as far as 1747, when the Massachusetts Colony specified that interest and principal, and later wage, payments were to be based on the value of an index of corn, beef, wool, and leather prices.

Indexation in Practice

Wages   Indexation of wages is common, though less so in the United States than elsewhere. The extent of indexation in formal contracts changes with the inflation rate: in the late seventies in the United States, about 60 percent of workers covered by major union contracts had escalator clauses, but such workers constituted only about 10 percent of the work force. In some countries, such as Israel and Belgium, coverage by index clauses applied to almost all workers. Escalator clauses do not typically increase wages 1 percent for each 1 percent increase in the price index. The adjustment may be partial or may have a cap, or upper bound. Adjustments to wages may be made at prespecified time intervals (monthly, quarterly, etc.) or when the price index has increased by some definite percentage since the base period (threshold agreements). Wage indexation tends to stabilize the real wage within the life of a contract; real-wage flexibility over longer periods need not be significantly affected by indexation, since real wages can be renegotiated at contract time.

Financial Instruments   Indexation of financial instruments is less widespread than wage indexation. More or less comprehensive capital-market indexation has been used in Israel, Brazil, and Finland in the postwar period. Linked instruments have included savings deposits, long-term government bonds, and mortgages. Bonds linked to the price of the firm's own output (e.g., third-class railway tickets) were issued in France and Israel in the 1950s. The United Kingdom since the late 1970s has issued long-term indexed bonds, after initially introducing indexation in the form of indexed savings bonds available in small quantities to wage earners and pensioners.

It is noteworthy that no indexed bonds have been issued by private firms in the most developed capital markets in recent times, despite high rates of inflation, considerable public and professional discussion, and continuing innovation in the capital markets. Commodity futures have some of the characteristics of an indexed bond, though commodity contracts are only short term. An attempt to introduce a futures contract tied to the consumer price index (CPI) was made in the United States in 1987, but it did not succeed. Reasons for the absence of privately issued index bonds remain unclear (Fischer, 1975, 1977a), though the small degree of price-level uncertainty in the short term must be partly responsible.

Social Security and Pensions   Social security payments and government pensions are indexed in many countries, including, since 1972, the United States. The linkage in the United States is to the consumer price index. Social security benefits are adjusted by legislative action. Private pensions are not generally indexed, in part because there is no financial instrument available to pension funds that will generate a safe real rate of return.

The Tax System   Indexation of tax brackets is widespread, including in Canada and the United States. Indexation of the taxation of capital and profits is more difficult, both administratively and politically (Aaron, 1976). The essential notion would be to tax real interest and real capital gains. Political difficulties would arise in applying the same principle to the deductions for interest payments, since mortgage borrowers would lose most of their interest deduction. A similar issue arises in the case of the corporate income tax, where the question is whether only real interest payments would be deductible or, equivalently, whether corporations would be required to treat capital gains resulting from the fall in the real value of outstanding bonds as income. In the case of depreciation allowances, indexation to the general price level would be simple.

A separate tax and indexation issue concerns the possible tax treatment of indexed bonds under the present U.S. tax system. The question is whether the indexed portion of any payment by a borrowing firm would be treated as interest, and therefore deductible from corporate income, or would be treated as a distribution of profits. The only circumstance in which such payments should be treated as a profit distribution is if the payment is closely linked to the firm's own performance.

Other   Indexation is used in life insurance contracts, in rental agreements, and in long-term construction and manufacturing contracts. In the latter cases, payments are usually tied to specific components of the producer price index, and an attempt is made to match the type of product or the costs of inputs for that product.

Theoretical Issues

Indexation has been supported by such distinguished economists as A. Marshall, S. Jevons, J.M. Keynes, M. Friedman, and J. Tobin. Their arguments have generally been based on the efficiency of indexation as a means of removing inflation risk from long-term contracts, or on the distributional equity of doing so.

The major theoretical issue in the case of wage indexation concerns its effects on the stability of the economy. Over the lifetime of the labor contract, indexed wages tend to be inflexible in real terms. Thus, any policies or adjustments relying on the flexibility of real wages will be hampered by wage indexation. Devaluation is the most important example (Fischer, 1988). In some cases, governments have sought and obtained the suspension of indexation at the time of a devaluation. Alternatively, as in Brazil in the late 1960s, wages can be indexed to expected inflation, though there is then, of course, a real issue about how the expected future inflation is to be agreed upon. Policies that do not require real-wage flexibility could be helped by indexation. Gray (1976) and Fischer (1977b) have shown that indexed wages tend to stabilize the economy in the face of nominal disturbances, defined as those that in the presence of fully flexible prices would affect only equilibrium absolute prices. Similarly, indexation exacerbates the effects of real disturbances, which require a change in the real wage as part of the economic adjustment to them.

In 1974, the most recent occasion on which there was full discussion of the merits of indexing, the argument was that wage indexation would permit a more rapid deceleration of inflation with less unemployment by making nominal wages more responsive to policy-induced reductions in the price level (Friedman, 1974). By the same token, inflation would accelerate more rapidly, with less real output effect, as a result of expansionary aggregate demand policy. Fellner (1974) argues that indexation is of little help in reducing the inflation rate, since the rate of price increase first has to be reduced in order to get the beneficial effects of the indexation.

Another important issue concerns the index to which wages and other contracts should be linked. Devaluation, and similarly the imposition of excise taxes to reduce aggregate demand, would be partly self-defeating if wages rose automatically in response to price increases resulting from such policy changes. Accordingly, the appropriate index to which to tie wages, from the viewpoint of the stability of the economy, would exclude imported goods and indirect taxes.

Other objections to wage indexation are based on the argument that indexation increases both the instability of the economy and the average rate of inflation by making more inflation necessary to achieve the same adjustment of real claims.

In the case of capital indexation, the major issues concern the effects of such indexation on total savings and on portfolio allocations. It has also been argued that indexation makes it possible to maintain the operation of the capital markets under inflationary conditions, and that stabilization policy could be improved by government issue of an indexed bond.

The effect of the availability of indexed instruments on total savings is theoretically and empirically indeterminate. The availability of a safe asset would be likely to reduce the extent of portfolio shifts to real assets such as housing and gold in the presence of uncertain inflation. Of course, if the rate of inflation were certain, nominal interest rate adjustment could completely compensate for inflation.

Governments are well placed to issue indexed bonds since their nominal revenues can be expected to increase with the price level. Private firms' willingness to issue indexed bonds would depend on the correlation of their earnings with the aggregate price level. Blinder (1977) has suggested that firms would be willing to tie interest payments to the price of their own outputs, and that a mutual fund of such bonds would provide a close approximation to an indexed bond. The willingness of firms to issue such bonds would depend on whether changes in their output prices are chiefly the result of demand or cost shifts, and on the tax treatment of such bonds.

In the absence of indexation, long-term lending and borrowing would tend to dry up as uncertainty about the inflation rate increased, and bond transactions would be concentrated at the short end of the maturity spectrum. It has often been suggested that the introduction of indexed bonds would adversely affect the equity markets, but there is no theoretical reason to think this. British experience since the government issued indexed long-term bonds provides no support for this argument. Tobin (1963) suggests that government issue of an indexed bond would make it easier for the monetary authority to affect the rate of investment by providing it with control over the supply of an asset which is a close substitute for capital. One benefit of the introduction of government indexed bonds would be that the real interest rate would become a known number rather than, as at present, one that has to be (imperfectly) estimated.

Policy Issues

The main policy issues are concerned with whether or not the government should issue indexed bonds and index the tax system. The policy issue for wage indexation is whether or not it should be encouraged, in part by the government's indexing the wages of its own employees. This depends on the primary source of disturbances to the economy.

The most common argument against government support for indexation is that indexation reduces the incentive to avoid inflation by making it easier to live with it. This argument can be supported in some game-theoretic models of inflation (Fischer and Summers, 1989).

Tax systems have been only partially indexed, notably through indexing of tax brackets. However, the more serious inflation-induced distortions in the tax system arise on the side of capital income, where there has been very little attempt at reform.

Indexation of U.S. savings bonds has received wide support from American economists. These now bear a floating interest rate, which makes them at least a partial inflation hedge. There is no obvious reason why the Treasury has not introduced price-indexed-linked savings bonds, as has been done in the United Kingdom. At the same time, it should be recognized that social security is equivalent to the provision of indexed bonds in limited quantities to American workers. Few of the objections to government issue of a marketable indexed bond, such as its adverse effects on the ability of corporations to raise funds, would apply to a small experimental issue.

A renewal of inflation at high rates would likely lead in the United States to the piecemeal introduction of indexation as inflation-induced distortions become more obvious and the prospect of their disappearance through the ending of inflation becomes less likely. But international experience shows that indexation arrangements are, at best, clumsy instruments for dealing with inflation.

References

Aaron, Henry J. (ed.), *Inflation and the Income Tax,* Brookings, Washington, D.C., 1976; Blinder, Alan S., "Indexing the Economy through Financial Intermediation," in Karl Brunner and Allan Meltzer (eds.), *Stabilization of the Domestic and International Economy,* Carnegie-Rochester Conference Series on Public Policy, vol. 5, North-Holland, Amsterdam, 1977; Braun, Anne R., "Indexation of Wages and Salaries in Developed Countries," *IMF Staff Papers,* International Monetary Fund, Washington, D.C., March 1976, pp. 226–271; Fellner, William, "The Controversial Issue of Comprehensive Indexation," in Herbert Giersch et al. (eds.), *Essays on Inflation and Indexation,* American Enterprise Institute, Washington, D.C., 1974; Fischer, Stanley, "The Demand for Index Bonds," *Journal of Political Economy,* June 1975, pp. 509–534; Fischer, Stanley, "On the Non-Existence of Privately Issued Index Bonds in the United States Capital Market," in E. Lundberg (ed.), *Inflation Theory and Anti-Inflation Policy,* Macmillan, New York, 1977a; Fischer, Stanley, "Wage Indexation and Macroeconomic Stability," in Karl Brunner and Allan Meltzer (eds.), *Stabilization of the Domestic and International Economy,* Carnegie-Rochester Conference Series on Public Policy, vol. 5, North-Holland, Amsterdam, 1977b; Fischer, Stanley, "Indexing and Inflation," *Journal of Monetary Economics,* November 1983, pp. 519–542; Fischer, Stanley, "Real Balances, the Exchange Rate, and Indexation: Real Variables in Disinflation," *Quarterly Journal of Economics,* February 1988, pp. 27–50; Fischer, Stanley, and Lawrence Summers, "Should Governments Learn to Live with Inflation?" *American Economics Review,* May 1989, pp. 382–387; Fisher, Irving, *Stabilizing the Dollar,* Macmillan, New York, 1920; Fisher, Willard, "The Tabular Standard in Massachusetts History," *Quarterly Journal of Economics,* May 1913, pp. 417–454; Friedman, Milton, "Monetary Correction," in Herbert Giersch et al. (eds.), *Essays on Inflation and Indexation,* American Enterprise Institute, Washington, D.C., 1974; Giersch, Herbert, "Index Clauses and the Fight against Inflation," in Herbert Giersch et al. (eds.), *Essays on Inflation and Indexation,* American Enterprise Institute,

Washington, D.C., 1974; Gray, JoAnna, "Wage Indexation: A Macroeconomic Approach," *Journal of Monetary Economics,* April 1976, pp. 221–235; Page, S. A. B., and Sandra Trollope, "An International Survey of Indexing and Its Effects," *National Institute Economic Review,* no. 70, 1974, pp. 46–60; Tobin, James, "An Essay on the Principles of Debt Management," in Commission on Money and Credit, *Fiscal and Debt Management Policies,* Prentice-Hall, Englewood Cliffs, N.J., 1963.

(*See also* Escalator clause; Incomes policy; Inflation)

Stanley Fischer

Indicator approach to forecasting (*see* Leading indicator approach to forecasting)

Indicator forecasting (*see* Economic forecasting methods)

Individual income taxation (*see* Taxation, an overview)

Industrial capacity (*see* Industrial production index)

Industrial concentration (*see* Concentration of industry)

Industrial operating rate (*see* Industrial production index)

Industrial production index

The industrial production index (IPI) is a monthly measure of real output in the manufacturing, mining, and electric and gas utilities industries. Whether for the total or each component, the quantity of current output is expressed as an index number, that is, as a percentage of that series' output in the comparison base period, 1987 at this writing. The National Bureau of Economic Research uses the IPI as an important coincident cyclical indicator; products and materials that fluctuate widely over the business cycle constitute most of industrial output.

The first estimate of output for a month is published around the fifteenth of the following month in the Federal Reserve statistical release, *Industrial Production and Capacity Utilization* G.17(419). The first estimate is preliminary and subject to revision in each of the subsequent 3 months as new source data become available. After the fourth month, indexes are not revised further until the time of an annual or benchmark revision. The average revision to the percentage change in the total monthly IPI, without regard to sign, from the first to the fourth estimates was 0.27 percentage point during the 1972–1988 period.

Structure: Industry and Market Groups

The total IPI is constructed from 250 individual series, each of which is classified into both (1) an industry group and (2) a market group. The industry structure follows the standard industrial classification (SIC) and covers mining, which includes major groups 10–14; manufacturing, groups 20–39; and electric and gas utilities, part of major group 49. Manufacturing industries produce about 85 percent of industrial output. Much of the basic information for the series and their weights has been collected in surveys of producers classified by industry. Data on industry output may be compared with input and capacity figures to provide insights into industrial productivity, supply conditions, and possible inflationary pressures. A few of the major industry groups have been published since 1919; most of the major groups previously mentioned have been published since 1947.

For purposes of economic analysis, the 250 individual series are classified by primary type of market use and recombined into market groups. The broadest market delineation is by stage of processing and distinguishes materials, which typically require further processing within manufacturing, from final and intermediate products. Final products mainly include durable and nondurable goods sold to consumers, as well as business equipment and defense and space equipment. Intermediate products are expected to become inputs in nonindustrial sectors, such as construction, agriculture, and services. Further disaggregation of the major market groups is shown in the monthly statistical release.

Monthly, Annual, and Benchmark Data

The underlying data used to estimate monthly changes in the real output of industry are obtained, to the extent possible, from basic statistical series that express output in physical quantities (steel in tons, automobiles in units, and so on). The movements in such physical product series indicate the monthly changes in production without regard to movements in prices. For many products, especially complex items like machinery and computers, meaningful monthly physical product data are not available. In such cases, change in monthly output is estimated on the basis of the monthly change observed in relevant inputs, usually production-worker hours or kilowatt-hours expended in the process of production.

In 1991, over 130 physical product series contributed nearly 40 percent of the value-added weight of the total industrial production index, while series estimated on the basis of production-worker hours and kilowatt-hours together contributed about 60 percent. The physical product data are obtained from various private trade associations and government agencies. Hours of production workers are collected in the monthly establishment survey conducted by the Bureau of Labor Statistics; this survey provides data for the pay period that includes the twelfth of the month. The kilowatt-hours data are collected in voluntary surveys conducted by the Federal Reserve District Banks from electric utilities and from manufacturing and mining establishments that generate electric power for their own use (cogenerators). The electric utilities report their sales, either by calendar month or by latest relevant reporting period, to industries usually classified by three-digit SIC codes.

Although the monthly output and input data provide a timely measure of cyclical movements independent of price movements, monthly physical product data may not cover the entire output of the industry that they represent; moreover, the relationship between input and output varies cyclically and over time. As a result, the monthly data are adjusted in annual and benchmark revisions to more comprehensive indexes of production. Some of these are developed from annual physical output data, such as reported by the Bureau of Mines and the Department of Energy, but most are derived from the deflation of the value of output reported by the Bureau of the

Census in the *Annual Survey of Manufacturers* and the quinquennial *Censuses of Manufactures and Minerals Industries.*

Weights, Aggregation, and Linking

The total IPI and its major groups are composed of individual indexes of production that are not all of equal economic significance. To avoid double counting, the weight of each series counts only the value added by the process of production that is being measured. This is particularly important because the IPI includes individual indexes that measure output at different stages of production—iron ore, raw steel, steel mill products, and trucks, for example. For most series, value added for industries comes from the *Censuses of Manufactures and Mineral Industries,* which measure value added as the value of production less the cost of purchased materials (but do not exclude purchased business services). The value-added weights for utility industries are based on factor income. Value-added weights for individual series can be expressed as proportions of total value by industry ($1397 billion in 1987, the latest base year). For a period (t) since 1987, aggregate indexes for groups, or the total IPI, are calculated by first multiplying each series index ($I_{t,i}$) in the group expressed as a percentage of output in 1987 by its corresponding 1987 proportional weight (W_i); then the weighted indexes are summed and divided by the sum of the weights (Σw_i) for the series in the group. Thus, each aggregate index in period t equals $\Sigma w_i I_{t,i} / \Sigma W_i$.

The total index covers the years since 1919, years that have encompassed prosperity and depression, war and peace, emergence and disappearance of industries, price stability and inflation. Change challenges the measurement of the physical volume of production. How, for instance, does one compare the volume of output in 1920 with that in 1980 when so many products have come into being since 1920 and so many old products are no longer made? New products lead to new series. Changes in the composition of output, unequal movements in items of output, and shifts in price relationships among items (such as occurred with the explosion of energy prices in the 1970s) change the proportions in the index. These developments force the selection of new weights. New weights and new series influence the movement of the aggregated total index as well as the movement of its major components.

The industrial production index is not compiled directly from a single set of weighted time series that extend continuously back to 1919. To keep the index for each period descriptive of that period, it is built in chronological segments, each with its own base year, weights, and series. The segments are then linked in a continuous time series. As a result, neither the weights nor the series used to estimate output in 1919 are much like those used in 1990. The first segment of the total index covers the 1919–1922 period; this segment combined 60 series based on physical products and on materials consumption. Indexes from 1923–1938 are based largely on 81 physical product and production-worker-hour series. Since then, the number of series grew; after 1972, about 250 physical product, production-worker-hour, and kilowatt-hour series have been combined with value-added weights that have been updated in 1972, 1977, 1982, and 1987. The resulting index can be described as a linked Laspeyres quantity index.

The linking of series typically joins one span of years' records to a later span, each of which contains indexes that have a different base and different weights. Typically, linking starts from the latest span and moves backward in time. Thus industrial production indexes for the post-1987 period expressed in terms of the 1987 base are linked to indexes for the 1982–1987 period on a 1982 base. Although the index is calculated in chronological segments, each with its own base year, each of the linked published production indexes is ultimately expressed as a percentage of its annual level in the reference base year, which since the 1990 revision is 1987.

Output, Capacity, and Utilization

In the Federal Reserve's monthly statistical release, estimates of industrial capacity and capacity utilization also are published. The capacity indexes are specifically designed to be used with the IPI and are expressed as percentages of output in the same base year as the IPI. The capacity indexes attempt to capture the concept of sustainable practical capacity, which is defined as the greatest level of output that a plant can maintain within the framework of a realistic work schedule, taking account of normal downtime, and assuming sufficient availability of inputs to operate the machinery and equipment in place. Capacity utilization for an industry is the ratio of the monthly, seasonally adjusted IPI for the industry to the index of capacity for that industry. The movements of the IPI largely determine the monthly and cyclical changes in utilization rates because the short-term changes of output are typically larger than those of the capacity estimates. Analysts use utilization rates in their consideration of price and investment developments.

Aside from the IPI, the most important data sources used to estimate the capacity indexes are (1) capacity utilization rates drawn from surveys, such as the Census Bureau's *Survey of Plant Capacity,* and (2) industry data on output and capacity expressed in physical quantities, such as tons, available from private industry sources, trade associations, and the Bureau of Mines. Econometric techniques are used to blend these data and to smooth erratic year-to-year changes in estimated capacity.

References

Armitage, K., and D. A. Tranum, "Industrial Production: 1989 Developments and Historical Revision," *Federal Reserve Bulletin,* vol. 76, April 1990, pp. 187–204; *Industrial Production—1986 Edition,* Board of Governors, Federal Reserve System, Washington, D.C., 1986; Raddock, R. D., "Recent Developments in Industrial Capacity and Utilization," *Federal Reserve Bulletin,* vol. 76, June 1990, pp. 412–435.

(*See also* Business cycles; Index numbers; Statistical methods in economics and business, an overview)

Carol Corrado and Richard Raddock

Industrial revolution

The term "industrial revolution," and the concept it represents, is mildly controversial. The French used the term *révolution industrielle* in the early nineteenth century to describe the process of mechanization of the cotton textile industry then in progress. Karl Marx used the term in *Das Capital,* but it was Arnold Toynbee's *Lectures on the Industrial Revolution in England* (1884) that firmly established the term in the lexicon of historians. According to Toynbee, the essence of the industrial revolution was the substitution of capitalist competition for the medieval regulations that had previously controlled the production and distribution of wealth. Toynbee wrote of an England on the "eve" of the industrial revolution in 1760, but he dated the transformation somewhat later, from the end of the eighteenth and beginning of the nine-teenth centuries. The term has subsequently been applied to the industrial transfor-mations of other countries (and sometimes to technological transformations in specific industries). The term is controversial to the extent that it implies a sudden change. The fruits of the first industrial revolution did not come rapidly. It was not until relatively late in the nineteenth century that industrialization led to substan-tially more rapid aggregate economic growth and to rising living standards for the average citizen. Although recent scholarship has emphasized the gradualness of the process, most historians remain comfortable with the term, because the transforma-tion was ultimately revolutionary. The nature (occupational structure and growth characteristics) of economies that have passed through an "industrial revolution" is radically different from those that have not.

Some definitions of the concept since the time of Toynbee have stressed organiza-tional transformation, an industrial revolution often associated with the adoption of the factory system. Many historians identify accelerating technological change, or the application of science and empirical knowledge to the production of commodities for the market, as the most salient features of the industrial revolution. This is associated with the invention and adoption of new and improved machinery, the discovery and adoption of new sources of power, transport innovations, the use of large-scale pro-duction, and increased division of labor. The enlargement of the typical unit of pro-duction means that the household is no longer the primary economic unit for productive purposes, and there is a need for a large pool of mobile labor resources. The share of the work force engaged in agriculture declines, and there is migration of labor from rural to urban areas.

An industrial revolution is often associated with increased capital accumulation. Savings and investment increase as a proportion of national income; innovative financial institutions arise to facilitate the mobilization of capital; and industrial profits, most of which are reinvested, increase. New social and occupational classes emerge and are defined by their relationship to or ownership of the means of pro-duction. In many cases, major demographic changes occur with the revolution. The birthrate increases, and as the revolution progresses, the death rate decreases. The result is rapid population growth, which provides both a source of labor and a mass market for the products of the expanding industries. As the industrial revolution matures, the rate of population growth declines, allowing for rising per capita living standards. Social and political institutions that are inimical to continued growth weaken or disappear and are replaced by institutions that foster or accept growth and development. The culmination of the process of industrialization is a rapid and sus-tained increase in the rate of growth of total and per capita output and incomes.

The First Industrial Revolution

The first industrial revolution began in England around the middle of the eighteenth century. It was not inevitable that an industrial revolution should occur first in Eng-land, but there were a number of preconditions that favored the process of industri-alization. These included a highly developed and productive agricultural sector (in which around 70 percent of the land had been enclosed by private agreement as early as 1700), an aggressive and sophisticated commercial class, a business environment relatively free from excessively burdensome government regulation, an adequate inland transportation system (turnpikes, improved rivers, and canals), an adequately financed and fiscally responsible government, and a class of entrepreneurs willing to take risks in the search for profits.

Many historians cite a wave of technical innovations that occurred around mid-century as signaling the advent of the industrial revolution. In the early stages of the process the most spectacular advances were made in the textile, iron, and power-machine industries. In the textile industry major breakthroughs in spinning and weaving occurred in what David Landes (1969) has called "a sequence of challenge and response." Kay's flying shuttle (1733) was meant to be used for wool but was not adopted until the 1760s when it was applied to cotton manufacture. It exacerbated an existing imbalance between weaving and spinning. The response came with Hargreaves's spinning jenny (1764), Arkwright's water frame (1769), and Crompton's mule (1779). By then the previous imbalance had been reversed. Cartwright's power loom (1789) followed, and eventually the entire production process was brought into the factory. These inventions and organizational changes increased output per unit of labor input on the order of 200-fold, increased the supply of cotton cloth tremendously, and substantially lowered its price. The cotton textile industry was the fastest-growing industry in England in the last half of the eighteenth century. Still, some historians believe that the role of cotton in the industrial revolution has been overemphasized. Much of the growth of the industry came at the expense of the older textile industries, especially wool, and forward and backward linkages to other industries may have been modest (the raw material was imported, water rather than coal was the main source of power, and it did not create a heavy demand for new transport facilities). The iron industry was different from the cotton textile industry in that it created a derived demand for domestic raw materials (iron ore and limestone, but especially coal). The major technological breakthroughs were in smelting with coke, developed by Abraham Darby of Coalbrookdale (invented in 1709 but not widely adopted until the price of charcoal rose in the 1750s), and the puddling process discovered by Henry Cort (1784). This led to an increase in the scale of the typical iron furnace and to a 30-fold increase in the output of iron between 1760 and 1800. Perhaps the most important of the inventions of the era was James Watt's steam engine (patented in 1769). By adding a separate condenser to the Newcomen atmospheric engine, Watt increased the efficiency of the engine by a factor of 4. This freed the engine from having to be located near a source of fuel and made it a potential source of mechanical power for all industries. The adoption of the steam engine gave an impetus to the coal industry, which in turn induced change in transportation technologies. Although innovations such as these were spectacular, they alone did not bring about the industrial revolution in England. Most of the technological change that occurred took place in small steps, often on the shop floor; the important consideration may be that technological change came to be accepted, expected, and gradually institutionalized.

The effects of the industrial revolution in England ultimately were profound and widespread. Growth involved an expansion of the flow of goods and services and a reduction in the amount of human effort needed to produce a unit of output. This should lead to a rise in the standard of living of the average member of society. Whereas there is no doubt that the long-term benefits in terms of material living standards have been substantial, there is considerable controversy regarding the immediate effects of the industrial revolution on the worker. A pessimistic school of thought derives from the writings of Karl Marx, Friedrich Engels, the Fabian socialists, Toynbee, and, more recently, E. J. Hobsbawm. The pessimists argue that although the industrial revolution brought about a tremendous increase in the output of goods and services, the ownership of these commodities was very unevenly spread; and the majority of society, the working poor, saw a marked deterioration in their standard of living for at least several generations. The industrial revolution ushered in a world of satanic mills, squalid cities, and social discontent. The optimists draw upon J. R. McCulloch, T. Tooke, J. H. Clapham, T. S. Ashton, and, more recently, R. M. Hartwell. They argue that although the revolution created hardship for some individuals (handloom weavers being an example), the majority of the working population bene-fited from falling finished goods prices, rising real wages, and increased employment opportunities. Unfortunately, the wage, income, and employment data of the time are too fragmentary to allow a definitive answer, and historians are still arguing the issue. What is clear is that after the middle of the nineteenth century the common worker fared much better than in the previous century: there was more regular employment for all members of the family, the composition of the labor force shifted toward more highly specialized, hence more highly skilled, occupations, and more and better con-sumer goods were available for purchase.

The Spread of the Industrial Revolution

The industrial revolution in England affected the course of all subsequent industrial transformations, although not all nations followed the same path to industrialization. The industrial revolution began earlier in some nations than in others, and the pace of industrialization has varied considerably. The first nations to benefit from the English experience were France, Belgium, Germany, and the United States.

France was something of an anomaly, industrializing without ever experiencing a sudden transformation. The demographic experience of France, with its low popula-tion growth rate, was not at all like that of most industrializing countries. France was in a particularly good position to emulate England, with a larger population (hence potentially larger labor pool and home market) than England, a traditional rival. France was also a relatively wealthy country, with a flourishing overseas trade, a sophisticated scientific community, and a government after 1815 that was willing to foster expansion of the manufacturing sector. France had disadvantages, however, including the severe political difficulties between 1790 and 1815, internal customs barriers, a rudimentary transportation sector, and inadequate coal resources. Each of these hampered the process of industrialization. Political considerations eventually played a large role in France's drive toward industrialization. By the 1830s, French government and financial officials, aware of increasing economic and military weak-ness relative to England, attempted to duplicate the innovations that had made Eng-land prosper. Between 1830 and 1914 France increased its per capita production to the level that existed in England and joined the industrialized world.

Germany (not politically unified until after the Franco-Prussian War of 1870–1871) had peculiar political disadvantages that delayed the process of indus-trialization, but with the establishment of the Zollverein (customs union) in 1833, the transformation of the German states began. Coal and pig iron production accelerated, the railroad was laid in the 1840s, and the textile industry was mechanized. Although the traditional industries played an important role in Germany's transfor-mation, developments in new industries, especially chemicals and electricity, enhanced Germany's process of industrialization. The rate of increase of production per capita approached and then surpassed that of England by the turn of the twentieth century.

The magnitude of the initial financial capital necessary for the industrial concerns of France and Germany in the 1840s to the 1890s was much larger than it had been for English firms decades earlier (many of which were financed through retained earnings). In order to be competitive, these concerns had to be larger than the optimal size of a generation earlier. This meant that the mobilization of capital was a serious bottleneck in these nations, but large financial institutions grew up to address these problems (the Kreditbanken and Crédit Mobilier), which made the experience of industrialization fundamentally different in France and Germany than it had been in England.

The United States joined the ranks of the industrialized nations about the same time as France and Germany. The peculiar nature of factor endowments in the United States had postponed industrialization until well into the nineteenth century. The relative dearth of labor and capital and the abundance of land and natural resources (including energy) determined the process. Industrialization came to the United States coincidentally with expansion to the West. The key phases of the process were the mechanization of textile production in the Northeast after 1815, the more far-reaching process of developing an infrastructure, especially the building of canals and railroads between 1825 and the 1850s, the development of the highly mechanized "American system" of manufacturing (resource-using and capital and skilled-labor saving), and the adoption of large-scale manufacturing in the late nineteenth century. By 1914 the United States was a major industrial power.

By the turn of the twentieth century, a number of countries, including Sweden, Norway, Denmark, Holland, Russia, Italy, Canada, Australia, and Japan (the only non-Western nation among the group), had begun the process of industrialization. Russia presents an interesting case. Still an agrarian country in the 1860s, with no railroads, no banks, and little manufacturing, Russia doubled industrial output by the 1880s, largely as a result of the aid of the Russian state. During the last decade of the nineteenth century, the growth of Russian industry outstripped that of nearly all other industrializing countries (although in terms of per capita income Russia was hampered by a primitive agricultural sector). More rapid growth was a common phenomenon for countries that came relatively late to industrialization. Continued technological progress in the developed countries laid the basis for a more rapid rise in productivity and output per capita in the latecomers, because the latecomers could immediately adopt the most advanced techniques. According to Alexander Gerschenkron, this was one of the "advantages" of backwardness.

From the standpoint of the 1990s, the world contains an array of nations at very different stages of industrial development and economic growth. As the nations that have passed through an industrial revolution continue to expand, the gap between the industrialized and nonindustrialized world continues to widen. The nonindustrialized nations contain the majority of the world's population. Nearly 70 percent of the people in the world live in countries in which per capita income is less than 10 percent of that of the industrialized world. Some nations have been more successful than others in responding to the challenge of the industrialized world. W. W. Rostow (1978) has argued that the beginnings of an industrial revolution can be seen in countries such as Brazil, Mexico, Argentina, China, Taiwan, and South Korea. Rates of growth in some of these countries (especially those in Asia) are currently higher than those in the industrialized countries, but the South American countries have started to fall behind again, and so the question remains whether or not these rates of growth can be maintained into the future. Whether or not the least-developed countries of the world can modernize and industrialize remains a serious concern to development economists.

References

Cameron, Rondo, "A New View of European Industrialization," *Economic History Review*, vol. 38, February 1985, pp. 1–23; Crafts, N. F. R., "Industrial Revolution in England and France: Some Thoughts on the Question, 'Why Was England First,' " *Economic History Review*, vol. 20, August 1977, pp. 429–441; Landes, David, *The Unbound Prometheus*, Cambridge University Press, Cambridge, 1969; Rostow, W. W., *The World Economy*, University of Texas Press, Austin, 1978.

(*See also* Innovation; Productivity; Stages theory of economic development; Technology)

William J. Hausman

Industrial robots (*see* Automation)

Inequality of income or wealth (*see* Lorenz curve)

Inflation

Inflation means generally rising money prices of goods and services. To understand what inflation is and is not, consider the above definition in detail:

Goods and Services. This refers not to stocks or bonds or other financial assets, but to the tangible and intangible commodities that economic agents produce and sell to one another. These are commodities to be consumed or held for future use: e.g., food, haircuts, shelter, houses, health care, schooling, cars, tractors, and machine tools.

Money Prices. This refers to amounts of money, dollars and cents in the United States, per commodity unit, e.g., per pound of butter, gallon of gasoline, haircut, bus trip, kilowatt-hour, or diesel engine. In contrast, imagine the barter prices at which one commodity trades for another: e.g., 3 gallons of gas for 1 hour of labor, 2 bus fares for 1 pound of butter, 1 haircut for 100 kilowatt-hours. From the money prices for any two commodities can be calculated their implicit barter price, their relative price in economists' language. Inflation does not refer to movements of relative prices, but to movements of absolute prices, i.e., money prices.

Rising. This does not mean "high." By some measures, money prices in the first quarter of 1991 were 52.6 percent higher than 10 years earlier. Thus, in the interim the annual average inflation rate was 4.2 percent. (If $100 deposited in 1981 earned this rate, compounded continuously, it would have become $152.57 after 10 years.) If by some miracle prices had ceased to rise and were the same at the beginning of 1992 as a year earlier, the inflation rate would have been zero for the year 1991. But a dollar would still have bought only 65.5 percent as much, and could have been obtained by selling only 65.5 percent as much, as in January 1981.

Generally.   Inflation refers to pervasive, widespread increases of money prices. A rising price for a single commodity, even beef or oil, is not per se inflation, any more than declining prices of pocket calendars or digital time pieces represent deflation.

Measurement of Inflation

To measure inflation over a month or a year or a decade, it is necessary to average the diverse changes in thousands of specific prices. This is not easy, and it is bound to be arbitrary. If prices all moved together in proportion, there would be no ambiguity about the direction and amount of change in the price level. But they do not; relative prices are always changing. In practice, statisticians, usually in government agencies, calculate price indexes. In these indexes commodities are weighted by their importance in consumer budgets, or in the gross national product (GNP), or in other aggregates. Indexes with weights differing in concept or in base data give different results.

Averaging and weighting are not the only problems. Products change in design and quality, for better or worse. A truck, a computer, a pair of skis, a subway ride—these are not the same as a year ago, let alone 10 years ago. Wholly new products are introduced; others vanish from the scene. According to the U.S. consumer price index, prices were 365 percent higher in 1978 than in 1940. But television was not available then at any price, and new 1940 Ford cars are not available now. The physician may do more or less for the patient in an hour than formerly, but statisticians cannot measure units of health and can only enter in the index the rise in the fee per visit.

Though the measurement of inflation is inevitably imprecise, the standard price index numbers capture the big changes. For example, the years 1974 to 1978, when the GNP price index increased an average 6.8 percent per year, were very different from 1965 to 1969, when it rose 1.8 percent per year.

Money and Inflation

Inflation is by definition a monetary phenomenon, a decline in the commodity value of the monetary unit of account, the dollar in the United States. Deflation, too, is monetary, a rise in the commodity value and commodity cost of a unit of money. (From 1929 to 1933, for example, prices fell at, on average, 6.7 percent per year.)

To understand inflation and deflation, therefore, it is necessary to review the role of money in economic life. An economy where goods and services are always bartered directly for each other would be spared inflation or deflation. Such an economy would also be terribly inefficient. Perhaps the village cobbler can trade shoes for the farmer's eggs, and even promise shoes tomorrow for eggs today. But imagine the difficulties if steel plants had to pay their workers in steel ingots, or else trade the ingots for eggs and shoes and other goods more to their employees' tastes. Without money, much time and effort would be spent seeking and executing mutually advantageous trades, and much capital would be tied up in inventories. To escape these inefficiencies the people of even primitive societies have agreed among themselves on a common trading commodity, a money.

The money of a society serves as a commonly accepted medium of exchange and as a unit of account and calculation. Goods and services can be traded for money rather than directly for other goods and services. The cobbler can sell shoes for money and use the money later to buy eggs, as well as leather, nails, and the services of an apprentice. The steel plant can sell ingots for money and pay employees in money, and the workers can find and buy what they individually want. Prices can be quoted and values calculated in units of money. Imagine the difficulty of keeping track of barter prices for all possible pairs of commodities.

These are money's functions. But what is money? It is whatever the society collectively fixes upon, by convention and tradition and in modern nations by law. The substances chosen have differed widely, including cattle, land, rocks, silver, gold, and engraved paper. Some, so-called fiat moneys, have had no value except that conveyed by their status as money. Others have been commodities with intrinsic value in consumption (such as cigarettes among prisoners of war) or production. Even commodity moneys have had, thanks to their monetary designation, more value in terms of other goods and services than they would have had on their own. Some things make more convenient moneys than others, but the vast advantages of money to the society are gained by agreeing on a common medium of exchange and account, whatever it is. In this respect, money is a social institution comparable to language. In both cases, the immense contribution to social cooperation and communication depends on the general currency of whatever medium is chosen.

Money is also a store of value, in which individuals can save and hold wealth for future use. Otherwise, it would be useless as a medium of exchange. The farmer parts with eggs for the cobbler's money only because the farmer expects the money will later be acceptable payment for shoes or seed or fence wire, tomorrow or next week or next year. Everyone who accepts fiat money—or commodity money such as cigarettes or silver in excess of consumption needs—is counting on its future acceptability to others.

But money is not, of course, the only store of value available to savers and wealth owners, or even the principal form of wealth. Even in primitive societies land, livestock, and other commodities are more important vehicles of wealth. This remains true in modern economies, where ultimate ownership of real properties is often indirect, expressed through a network of financial claims.

In a modern national economy, many assets and debts are denominated in the monetary unit of account. Some of these are media of exchange, but most are not. In the United States, for example, the basic physical manifestation of the dollar is the fiat issue of currency—paper bills and coin—by the federal government. The federal government also has outstanding obligations to pay specified amounts of these dollars, some on demand (notably the deposits of commercial banks in Federal Reserve Banks), some on stated future dates (Treasury bills, notes, and bonds). Currency and demand deposits do not bear interest; time obligations do. In addition, nonfederal debtors have issued an immense volume and variety of dollar-denominated obligations, some payable on demand, others at future dates. The debtors include banks, savings institutions, state and local governments, business firms, individuals (homeowners, car buyers, department store customers, students, etc.), and foreigners. Most of these IOUs bear interest, but demand obligations (e.g., bank checking accounts) generally do not.

In addition to currency itself, some promises to pay currency on demand are generally or frequently acceptable instruments of payment. These include not only checkable deposits in banks and savings institutions but also the obligations of credit card and traveler's check companies and of some mutual funds.

When inflation or deflation alters the value of the dollar, it affects the real values of all dollar-denominated obligations, whether private or public, whether demand or time, whether media of payment or not. For this reason, both the causes and consequences of changing values of the dollar qua unit of account extend far beyond government issues of basic dollar currency and beyond the dollar means of payment supplied by banks.

Throughout history, the value of monetary stores of value has been variable and unpredictable. Considering the nature of money, this is not surprising. The notion that price stability or predictability is natural and normal, while inflation and deflation are pathological aberrations, is an abstraction with little realistic foundation. People save for future consumption, for their old age, or for their children. But whatever form of wealth they accumulate, they can never be sure what value it will have when they or their heirs need it. Since they cannot store precisely the commodities they will want to consume, they are always dependent on what other people will be prepared to pay for their assets. This is true of land, houses, personal skills (human capital), machines and tools, and common stocks. It is certainly true of money, the value of which depends not on its intrinsic utility in consumption or production, but always on what others expect its value will be to them. Investors are always speculating about the relative values of goods and titles to them, on the one hand, and money and titles to money, on the other. Fluctuations in the value of money are costs societies have to pay for the efficiency that monetary institutions contribute in trade and division of labor. The problem is to keep the fluctuations from being so violent that they negate those positive contributions.

Anticipated and Unanticipated Inflation

In a hypothetical pure case of anticipated inflation everyone correctly foresees the future path of the money price of every commodity. In deciding how many dollars to borrow or lend, for how long, and at what interest rates, everyone can correctly calculate the depreciation of the dollar vis-à-vis the commodities consumed and produced. Lenders expecting more inflation demand more interest in compensation, and borrowers likewise are able and willing to pay it when they expect to repay their debts in depreciated currency. As Irving Fisher observed 70 years ago, in these circumstances market interest rates would adjust point for point of expected inflation, leaving unchanged all real interest rates (those implicit in the expected future amount of each commodity purchasable directly or indirectly by a unit of the commodity today). The path of the real economy—relative prices, physical quantities—would be independent of the rate of inflation anticipated. The inflation would make no difference and would do no one either harm or good.

This abstraction contains a valuable practical lesson. The more thoroughly adjusted an economy becomes to an ongoing inflation, the less consequential is the inflation.

However, there are a number of economic institutions that adjust slowly, if at all, to changes in actual and expected inflation rates. One crucial rigidity is the zero nominal interest rate on base money—currency and its equivalents. Legal or conventional interest limitations often apply to demand and savings deposits and to loans and mortgages, though these rate ceilings can be and have been changed at intervals. Their ceilings prevent the Fisher adjustment of nominal interest rates to expected inflation. With higher inflation, the real rate of return from holding currency becomes lower (more negative). As owners of wealth seek to substitute other assets of money, the reduction of real rates spreads to them. Since it modifies the structure and level of real rates of return, expected inflation is not neutral. One effect of higher expected inflation is to induce economies in cash management; holding periods are shorter, money turns over faster, more costs are incurred, and more resources are diverted in order to avoid losses on depreciating assets uncompensated by interest. Against these social costs are possible gains from greater capital formation. In some circumstances, it may not be possible to get real interest rates low enough to encourage a socially desirable degree of accumulation of productive capital unless the attractiveness of holding monetary assets is diminished by expectations of inflation.

Unanticipated inflation is different. People have made monetary commitments on the basis of price expectations that in the event turn out wrong. Examples of such commitments are loans of a few weeks, wage contracts of 1 to 3 years, life and retirement insurance contracts, 30-year mortgages, and long-term bonds and leases. The economy is always carrying heavy baggage of contracts made at various dates in the past, with various expectations about prices today and in the future. Deviations of inflation rates from past expectation will bring capital gains to some, capital losses to others. As every history student knows, unexpected inflation is good for debtors, who borrowed at low rates, and bad for their creditors. By the same token, farmer debtors revolted against the deflations of 1879 to 1896 and 1926 to 1933; it wasn't possible to pay off 6 percent loans when grain prices were steadily declining. Pensioners and civil servants enjoyed the deflations but suffered from wartime and postwar inflations.

Redistributions of this kind are painful disappointments and often cruel disasters for the losers. But several points should be remembered:

1. There are winners as well as losers. The nation as a whole does not lose except as its foreign debts become unexpectedly onerous or its foreign loans yield disappointing real returns.

2. Gains and losses occur whenever events fail to confirm the expectations held when contracts and commitments were made, not from inflation per se. The culprit could be deflation, or any deviation of actual prices up or down from previously expected paths. For example, in the 1970s many companies incurred debts at double-digit interest rates premised on the continuation of inflation at 8 to 12 percent per year. Many householders assumed mortgages at rates they expect to pay from inflation in their wages and in real estate values. Since inflation was dramatically curbed in the mid-1980s and early 1990s, these debtors are in trouble.

3. Inflation and deflation are by no means the sole sources of unexpected income redistributions. Most capital losses and gains are related to mistakes and surprises that afflict forecasts of relative prices and of real economic phenomena. Consider, for example, current or imminent retirees who in the 1960s and 1970s sought protection from inflation by investing in common stocks rather than fixed-dollar securities. Consider enterprises that built glass office buildings or bought gas-guzzling cars just as the Organization of Petroleum Exporting Countries (OPEC) was raising prices. Consider young people who committed themselves to teaching careers in the 1960s and 1970s and later found education to be a declining industry.

Inflation and the Quantity of Money

As media of exchange, currency circulates from hand to hand and checking balances from account to account. At any instant of time, however, every dollar of money in circulation is in someone's hands or someone's account. At the end of any business day, it is possible in principle, though not in practice, to account for the entire stock by a census of the amounts held by everybody. At the end of the next business day, the census would find quite a different distribution even though the total stock was virtually unchanged.

How big a stock does it take to handle the business of the nation? The answer clearly depends on, among other things, prices. If all prices were halved, would it not be possible to execute the same trades with a money stock half as large? If all prices were doubled, would it not take a circulating stock twice as large to make the same real transactions? Affirmative answers are plausible, and they are the kernel of an ancient and important doctrine. Although it is commonly known as the quantity theory of money, a more descriptive label is the quantity of money theory of prices.

The doctrine goes back at least to David Hume, and in its modern form of monetarism its leading protagonist is Milton Friedman. In its starkest form, the proposition is that prices are proportional to the quantity of money. Suppose, for example, the stock of money in dollars were doubled. Having more than needed to handle transactions at prevailing prices, households and businesses would try to get rid of excess money holdings by buying more goods and services. But the excess money would not be extinguished, merely transferred to other households and businesses, which would act in the same manner. In the process the money prices of goods and services would be bid up until they were high enough so that the stock of money would no longer be excessive. That occurs when prices have doubled. In summary, there is a certain amount of purchasing power that the society needs and wants to hold in the form of money. Whatever the nominal, or dollar, stock of money, prices will adjust until the purchasing power of this stock is the needed and desired amount. By extension, the quantity theory says that the rate of inflation depends on the rate of increase in the nominal money stock.

History provides at least some rough confirmations. As Hume observed, European inflation in the sixteenth and seventeenth centuries was associated with the discovery of gold in the New World and its importation and monetization. In the late nineteenth century, a gold shortage produced deflation in Europe and North America, reversed at the turn of the century when new technology and discovery flooded the world with South African gold. History is full of inflations resulting from undisciplined issues of fiat moneys, e.g., Continentals by the rebellious American colonies, Civil War greenbacks, German marks in the 1923 hyperinflation, the currencies of almost every Latin American country again and again.

Nevertheless, the quantity theory is an incomplete explanation of inflation in advanced capitalist democracies in the late twentieth century. The sources of inflation are more complex and diverse, and the cures less obvious and sure than the theory suggests.

A popular capsule explanation of inflation is "too much money chasing too few goods." Now money chasing, or "money on the wing" in the words of the English monetary economist D. H. Robertson, is not the same as what Robertson called "money at rest." The stock of money enumerated in the hypothetical census above is at rest in its holders' pockets, vaults, and accounts at the end of the business day. Money is chasing or on the wing when it circulates during the day, moving from one holder to another as goods are bought and sold and other transactions are consummated. Irving Fisher expressed the relationship of circulation to stock in the concept of velocity, or turnover—the average number of times a dollar is transferred within a period. (This can be measured for checking accounts by calculating the ratio of the aggregate dollar value of checks drawn to average balances in the accounts debited.) But the bulk of these transactions is not for purchases of the final goods and services counted in the GNP, whose prices are those relevant for inflation. A more restrictive concept, GNP velocity, tells the average number of times a dollar of money stock buys GNP goods and services during a year.

The Equation of Exchange

Fisher provided a framework for analysis, the equation of exchange. For the purpose at hand it can be written $MV = PQ = Y$, where M is the stock of money, V its GNP velocity per year, P the GNP price index, Q the real (constant-price) GNP per year, and Y the dollar GNP per year. The equation is actually an identity, since V can be estimated only by dividing GNP in dollars per year (PQ) by M. In this framework the quantity theory holds if V and Q are constants, independent of M and P. Then P must move proportionately to M. However, both theoretical reasoning and empirical evidence cast doubt on the two premises of the quantity theory, at least during short-run cyclical fluctuations in economic activity.

The equation of exchange may also be written in terms of year-to-year rates of growth; the following is a close approximation:

(% growth of M) + (% growth of V) = (% growth of P)

$$+ (\% \text{ growth of } Q) = (\% \text{ growth of dollar GNP}) \quad (1)$$

$$\frac{\Delta M}{M} + \frac{\Delta V}{V} = \frac{\Delta P}{P} + \frac{\Delta Q}{Q} = \frac{\Delta Y}{Y}$$

As an illustration of Equation (1), consider 1978 relative to 1977. Dollar GNP Y rose 12 percent from \$1900 billion to \$2128 billion. But the real volume of goods and services produced, Q, increased only 4.4 percent. The difference was the inflation rate, 7.6 percent. On the left-hand side of the equation, the money stock, as measured by M-1, grew 7.3 percent, from \$335 billion average in 1977 to \$360 billion in 1978. Velocity rose by 4 percent from 5.7 in 1977 to 5.9 in 1978.

If the changes in velocity $\Delta V/V$ and in real output $\Delta Q/Q$ are constants, independent of other terms in Equation (1), the inflation $\Delta P/P$ and money growth $\Delta P/P$ must vary together point for point. In this dynamic form, the quantity theory does not require that velocity V and output Q be unchanging—they may have nonzero trends and vary unsystematically around them. The trend of output Q is constrained by trends of labor force and productivity, which change slowly and gradually. In the United States since the Second World War, these trends have yielded average growth of real GNP of 3 to 4 percent per annum. As a result, the average inflation rate has been 3 or 4 points less than the average growth of Y, dollar spending on GNP. In cyclical short runs, there are considerable deviations from the trend; year-to-year values of $\Delta Q/Q$ vary from -2 to 8 percent. During business cycles, fluctuations in Y and in $\Delta Y/Y$ are generally registered in output Q and $\Delta Q/Q$, at least as much as in prices P and $\Delta P/P$.

Velocity V is not a mechanical property of money, but the outcome of the decisions and behaviors of millions of individuals. A way to interpret velocity is to notice that its reciprocal $1/V$ is roughly the average length of time an individual holds a dollar between transactions. (In this context the relevant measure of velocity refers to all transactions, not just to GNP purchases and sales. The figures given above imply holding times of 2½ days for the United States and ⅔ day for New York City.) But holding periods are economic decisions. In between necessary transactions, funds can be taken out of cash and placed in interest-bearing assets. The incentive is the interest earned. Against the interest gains must be set the inconveniences, costs, and risks of keeping cash balances low by making frequent conversions into and out of other assets. The incentive becomes relatively stronger when interest rates are high. The downward trend of velocity in recent decades of rising interest and inflation rates is an empirical confirmation, as are the procyclical movements of both velocity and interest rates. Inflation itself heightens the incentive to economize cash holdings and shorten holding periods, to acquire either real assets rising in price or financial assets with interest rates reflecting the inflation. Interest rates also reflect monetary policies. In business-cycle short runs, active restriction of monetary growth will, other things being equal, be associated with tight credit markets and high interest rates, and thus with high velocity of money. On these systematic effects are superimposed more volatile changes in liquidity preferences and expectations, as well as innovations in financial markets, institutions, and technology.

The following sections discuss some sources of inflation in the late twentieth century in industrial societies with democratic and capitalist institutions. Monetary factors are always important, though in some instances their role is accommodative rather than initiative. In any event, it is always necessary to ask why monetary expansion is occurring, given that modern governments and central banks have the capacity to prevent it. The answer may be that the government finds printing money and consequent inflation the expedient way of mobilizing resources for war or other government purposes. Or the answer may be that the government regards the economic consequences of severe anti-inflationary monetary policies, with their political and social by-products, as the greater evil.

Excess-Demand Inflation

In the classic inflation drama, government is the principal actor and villain. It needs more goods and a larger work force, typically for war. The economy is already operating close to its normal capacity. If government is to buy more, private citizens will have to buy less. Higher taxes are the straightforward way to achieve this shift, but government cannot or will not levy them. Instead, the sovereign simply prints the money needed, or at least enough new money so that the rest can be borrowed cheaply. New government demands accumulate in addition to diminished private demands, and the economy cannot supply both. In terms of the equation of exchange, the higher growth of dollar spending induces little extra GNP and spills into higher inflation. The government gets what it wants. The price rise squeezes out private citizens caught by surprise, especially those dependent on fixed-dollar incomes and assets. Thus, inflation earns its reputation as the cruelest tax.

The drama has played many times throughout history, in the United States as elsewhere. The most recent performance, subdued compared with most previous wartime inflations, accompanied the Vietnam war. In 1966 President Johnson, against his economists' advice, chose not to ask Congress for higher taxes to pay for his escalation of the conflict. By 1968, defense spending had increased more than 50 percent and had thrown the budget into a $12 billion deficit at a time when unemployment was well below the official 4 percent target. The economy was overheated for most of 4 years, and the inflation rose from 2 percent per year to 5 percent. Comparing 1968 with 1965, money-supply growth had accelerated from 4.7 to 8.1 percent, and GNP velocity increased from 4.1 to 4.5 percent.

Excess demand need not be so striking as in wartime, and it need not be government spending that initiates the acceleration of dollar GNP. A dollar chasing goods is a dollar, whoever the spender. A boom in business investment or housing construction or purchases of consumers' durable goods could outrun the economy's productive capacity. Worldwide private speculative stockpiling of materials was a significant inflationary factor in 1973, as it had been in 1950 at the outset of the Korean war. (Thereafter, President Truman kept Korean war procurement noninflationary by insisting on a stiff dose of taxation to pay for it.)

Easy monetary and credit policies may be the source of excess demand. Business investment, home building, purchases of cars and appliances, and inventory building may be overstimulated by opportunities to borrow at interest rates low relative to anticipated returns in dollars or in use. One symptom of such policies will be high rates of monetary growth $\Delta M/M$. The period 1972–1973 is a widely cited example. Monetary growth in 1972 was 9.1 percent. Dollar GNP rose 10.1 percent, real GNP 5.7 percent. The inflation rate accelerated in the following year to 6 percent, the highest year-over-year rate since 1948.

Inflation without Excess Demand: "Stagflation"

Excess demand is not the only inflation story. Simultaneous inflation and excess supply afflicted the world economy through much of the 1970s. The symptoms of excess supply are abnormally high unemployment of labor and underutilization of productive capacity. In the United States in 1975, for example, unemployment averaged 8.5 percent of the labor force, compared with an average of 5.4 percent over the previous 5 years. Industry was operating at 74 percent of capacity, compared with 83 percent on average from 1970 to 1974. Inflation, at 9.7 percent according to the GNP price index, could scarcely be attributed to contemporaneous excess demand.

The lesson of stagflation, and of earlier experience as well, is that inflation has a life of its own, in several senses.

1. Historical patterns of wage and price increase have a strong momentum during periods of excess supply. They respond slowly and erratically to economic circumstances reflected in monetary spending, unemployment, excess capacity, and GNP growth.

2. A modern economy appears to have an inflationary bias. Inflation rates rise more easily and more quickly in response to excess demand than they fall in response to excess supply.

3. Accidents may occur; events not connected with the state of the economy or with monetary and fiscal policies can change price levels as well as relative prices, and affect inflation rates at least temporarily. Recent examples are union wage push (1970–1971), world food shortages (1973), good harvests (1976), and, of course, OPEC (1973).

The inertial inflation continues because it is self-consistent and because it becomes habitual and expected. Workers, unionized or unorganized, look at the wage gains of their peers and seek to do as well or better. They seek to catch and overtake the cost of living too, and cost-of-living adjustment (COLA) clauses help. Employers pay the pattern wage increase in their labor markets and industries, knowing they will not jeopardize their competitive position by doing so. Industrial pricing is strongly cost-based. If hourly labor costs are rising 9 percent per year, and productivity is increasing 2 percent, the average industry will raise prices 7 percent, and this will be reflected in the workers' cost of living. The same real outcomes would occur if wage inflation were 4 percent and prices were rising 2 percent, as in the early 1960s. Only if dollar wage rates rise, on average, no faster than labor productivity, can there be stability in price levels. But a higher pattern, once built in, is very stubborn.

The pattern can change, for better or worse. Wage inflation is not wholly insensitive to economic conditions. Econometric estimates are that the difference between a 7 percent unemployment year and a 6 percent unemployment year is a quarter to half a percentage point of inflation. Even on the more optimistic estimate, it would take 6 years of the higher unemployment rate to wring 3 points from the inflation rate. It is this dismal calculus that leads the governments here and abroad to seek more direct solutions—wage and price controls or less drastic and less mandatory interventions in private wage bargains and price decisions.

The inflationary bias is that wages and prices respond faster to demand pressure than to excess supply. Expanding firms and industries in tight labor markets are ready to bid above pattern for the labor they need; their existing employees are delighted. But it's not so easy for employers in less prosperous industries and regions to pay less than the prevailing pattern. Queues of job seekers at the factory gate, willing to work for less than those inside, seldom force rapid wage reduction. Existing employees, even if not under union contract, have considerable collective power; wage patterns give way only when the financial plight of the employer is a credible threat to their jobs. Minimum wages and unemployment insurance benefits limit downward movements of wages. Similarly, industrial firms raise prices when demand for their products is strong but are reluctant to compete by price-cutting when demand is slack.

Inflexibility and inflationary bias appear to be developments of our twentieth-century amalgam of industrial capitalism and social democracy. In nineteenth-century Britain and the United States, prices and money wages moved freely down and up. Periods of deflation were not prosperities, especially for farmers in debt, but output growth continued. As late as 1919, a sharp postwar inflation of commodity prices in the United States pulled money wages up; but both promptly fell just as sharply, and the setback to output and employment was small and short-lived. In the 1920s and 1930s, however, deflation of wages and nonagricultural prices occurred very slowly in both countries in spite of prolonged mass unemployment and idle capacity. The deflations that did occur did not seem to ameliorate the situation.

These observations led John Maynard Keynes to challenge the orthodox economic view that flexibility of wages and prices would restore full-employment equilibrium after monetary or nonmonetary disturbances. His challenge is still relevant, though it may be a pattern of inflationary increase of wages and prices, not just their level, that resists competitive pressure.

The modern economy does not behave like a world of atomistic competition among small shops, farms, and unorganized workers. True, there is still a "flex-price" sector as well as a "fix-price" sector. Not all sellers can set their own prices. In agriculture and mineral extraction, in which there are numerous producers of identical commodities, prices are determined in impersonal auction markets. But the flexible price sector has declined relative to the economy. In any case, farmers and other competitive producers have obtained government-supported price floors, making their prices, too, less flexible down than up.

In these circumstances large increases in individual prices become sources of inflation for the whole economy. Food prices rise because of bad weather. Oil prices rise because of OPEC. Hospital prices rise because of medicare. Such events require changes of relative prices: scarcer goods naturally become more expensive. In a world of flexible prices, this could happen without inflating economywide price indexes. Dollar prices of other goods would fall enough to balance the increases in food, energy, and medical care. In our world, that does not happen. Instead, as in the years 1973–1974 and 1978–1979, large upward adjustments of prices of important commodities bring double-digit inflation.

The Unemployment-Inflation Trade-Off

In a strikingly empirical study published in 1958, A. W. Phillips showed that in the United Kingdom from 1861 to 1957 unemployment among trade union members was negatively correlated with rates of increase in money wages. The relationship was curvilinear: the rate of wage inflation appeared to be much more sensitive to variation in the unemployment rate when unemployment was low than when it was high. This shape embodies the asymmetries that lead to inflationary bias. Phillips curves fit for other countries and to modern statisticians told the same story. Moreover, a Phillips curve relationship appeared to describe price inflation as well as wage inflation, as could be expected if prices are essentially marked-up labor costs.

Macroeconomic theorists warmly embraced the Phillips curve for several reasons. Keynesian economics contained no theory of inflation except for an economy operating at full employment with excess demand. According to the model of Keynes' *General Theory,* there should be no continuing inflation when the economy is operating below its full-employment capacity. For that situation, which he regarded as usual in peacetime, Keynes provided a theory of the price level (it would move upward as employment and output increased) but not a theory of inflation (the price level should be stable or may be declining if employment and output are stable). But there were plenty of cases, especially after the Second World War, when inflation kept going although employment and other measures of utilization were stable or declining. The concept of full employment itself was troublesome in peacetime. Did the occurrence of inflation mean the economy was fully employed, even though employment did not look full according to unemployment rates and other statistics? The Phillips curve appeared to solve, or to finesse, these problems by making the inflation rate, rather than the price level, an increasing function of employment and capacity utilization, and by making fullness of employment a matter of degree rather than a yes-or-no condition.

Elevated from an empirical scatter diagram to a functional macroeconomic relationship, the Phillips curve also implied that monetary and fiscal policymakers faced a usable trade-off, by which lower unemployment rates could be obtained at the cost of higher inflation rates and vice versa. Whether any government explicitly made policy on this basis is doubtful, but the notion of trade-off certainly has been indirectly influential.

In 1967 and 1968, Edmund Phelps and Milton Friedman independently raised serious theoretical questions about the Phillips curve and the reliability of the Phillips trade-off as a basis for policy. They argued that rational workers, unions, and firms will take account of inflation and expected inflation in setting wages and prices, so that only deviations from the expected trend will be related to unemployment rates. Thus, the eventual inflation effects of a reduction in unemployment would be much greater than the initial impact. Events after 1966—inflation rates increasing while unemployment rates were low but stable—supported these arguments.

According to Phelps and Friedman, there is in principle only one unemployment rate—Friedman's natural rate—at which wages and prices will continue on their anticipated path, whatever inflation rate that may imply. (Thus, full employment reappears in new guise, but with considerable residual mystery about why it involves so much unemployment.) If unemployment is held by policy below the natural rate, inflation will be ever accelerating. Symmetrically, if unemployment is held above the natural rate, inflation will decelerate and eventually there will be ever-faster deflation. The latter implication may seem empirically doubtful, but the theory does not exclude the possibility that downward adjustments are slower than upward adjustments.

A common synthesis is to combine a short-run Phillips curve with the natural rate. Even though there may be no long-run trade-off, the short-run relationship tells how hard or easy it is to diminish the prevailing inertial inflation by running the economy for a time with unemployment higher than natural. Once this has been done, once price expectations have been revised downward or eliminated, the economy can return to the natural rate without re-igniting the previous inflation.

But how can policymakers know what the natural rate is? The new classical macroeconomists, Robert Lucas, Thomas Sargent, and others, say they cannot and should not try. These theorists take the old Phelps-Friedman argument a long step farther. They regard the economy—labor markets included—as always in equilibrium, with neither excess supply nor excess demand. Prices and wages adjust to clear markets, subject to the expectations that the actors form with the information they have. In this sense, the economy is always at its natural rate, but this rate itself varies. Future policies are an important dimension of economic expectations. So the predictability or capriciousness of policymakers is crucial for the stability or volatility of the economy. The recommendation is that the makers of monetary policy simply announce and stick to noninflationary rates of monetary growth. Workers and employers will expect zero inflation and behave accordingly. The economy will then gravitate quickly to its correct-information natural rate of unemployment. To put it another way, whatever rate it moves to will be that natural rate.

Monetary Accommodation

Inertial inflation and increases in important specific prices confront central banks and governments with cruelly difficult choices. Shall they accommodate these price movements or not? That is, shall they permit a growth of monetary spending Y sufficient to sustain normal increases of output and employment at rising prices? If they do so, they are doing nothing to arrest the inflation itself, and indeed they are in a sense ratifying the behavior and the institutions that bias the economy toward inflation. (With accommodation, incidentally, $\Delta M/M$ and $\Delta P/P$ may be positively correlated, as quantity theory suggests, but the causation runs in reverse, from prices to money stock.) If they do not accommodate, then as in 1974 to 1975 they will depress output and employment, while the counterinflationary effects are uncertain and slow at best.

The makers of monetary and fiscal policy in democracies are always seeking politically acceptable compromises. Their natural bent is to lean against the evil wind of the day, to fight inflation when it is the most vivid popular complaint, and to combat recession and unemployment when they become the uppermost concerns. Business cycles due to stop-go alternation of policies are the result. Some economic observers believe that a resolute irreversible commitment of nonaccommodation would melt the rock of inertial inflation much faster than previous experience under countercyclical and semiaccommodative policies would suggest. Others believe that nonaccommodative policies will eliminate inflation only at great and prolonged cost in lost output and employment, and quite possibly not at all. They are reconciled either to living with inflation, possibly accelerating inflation, or to limiting wage and price increases directly by more or less formal controls.

Inflation as Symptom

Inflation is, as already emphasized, a monetary phenomenon. But inflation may also be the symptom of some real economic, social, and political difficulties. The monetary authorities may choose accommodation in the belief that inflation is one of the less-painful manifestations of the underlying disease.

It is an economic burden on a society to fight a war, and usually to lose one. Inflation is probably not the most orderly or just way to distribute the burden. But doing it differently would not avoid the basic social cost, the diversion or loss of productive resources. After the First World War, the victorious Allies imposed punitive reparations on the German people. The German government mistakenly tried to pay the victors by printing marks and selling them in the foreign exchange markets for the francs and pounds it was required to deliver. As the mark depreciated in the exchange markets, the German government had to print more and more, and the result was the most famous hyperinflation of history. As disastrous as the inflation was, the original burden on the German economy, which had to be shouldered one way or another, was still the reparations. In the 1970s the OPEC cartel inflicted a heavy social loss on oil-importing countries, whose residents had to work harder and longer to import a barrel of oil. This is the true and unavoidable cost. The OPEC price boosts also inflated U.S. price indexes, but that is a symptom rather than the cause of losses of real income. Even if sufficient wage reductions were absorbed to keep the price indexes from rising, U.S. citizens still would be losing to OPEC.

A more disquieting possibility is that inflation is the symptom of deep-rooted social and economic contradiction and conflict, between major economic groups persistently claiming pieces of pie that together exceed the whole pie. Inflation is the way that their claims, so far as they are expressed in nominal terms, are temporarily reconciled. But it will continue and indeed accelerate so long as the basic conflicts of real claims and real power continue.

There are a number of possible scenarios of conflict inflation in the 1970s. A common story is that a combination of misfortunes—OPEC, long-run energy shortage, environmental dangers and costs—has sharply lowered the paths of potential output, real wages, and real returns on capital investment. But it has not lowered the standards of real-income progress to which employed workers are accustomed, or the profit rates that managers and shareowners expect. The relative price shocks of the mid-1970s are the source of serious and lasting conflict, not simply of a temporary bulge of inflation statistics.

References

Cambridge Economic Handbook, originally published by Cambridge University Press, Cambridge, 1922; Fisher, Irving, *The Purchasing Power of Money,* rev. ed., Macmillan, New York, 1926; Friedman, Milton, "The Role of Monetary Policy," *American Economic Review,* vol. 58, no. 1, March 1968, pp. 1–17; Friedman, Milton, and Anna Schwartz, *A Monetary History of the United States,* National Bureau of Economic Research, Princeton University Press, Princeton, N.J., 1963; Hume, David, "Of Money," in T. H. Green and T. H. Grose (eds.), *Essays, Moral, Political, and Literary,* vol. I, 1977, Longman, New York, 1912; Keynes, John Maynard, *The General Theory of Employment, Interest, and Money,* Macmillan, London, 1936; Lucas, Robert, and Thomas Sargent, "After Keynesian Macroeconomics," *After the Phillips Curve,* Federal Reserve Bank of Boston Conference Series, no. 19, Federal Reserve Bank of Boston, Boston, 1978, pp. 49–83; Phelps, Edmund S., "Phillips Curves, Inflation Expectations, and Optimal Employment over Time," *Economica,* vol. 34, August 1967, pp. 254–281; Phillips, A. W., "The Relation between Unemployment and the Rate of Change of Money Wage Rates in the United Kingdom, 1861–1957," *Economica,* vol. 25, November 1958, pp. 283–299; Robertson, Dennis A., *Money,* 4th ed., University of Chicago Press, Chicago, 1959.

(*See also* Consumer price index; Deposits; Employment and unemployment; Federal Reserve policy; Fiscal policy; Incomes policy; Index numbers; Interest rates; Keynesian economics; Labor unions; Monetary policy; Money illusion; Money supply; Neoclassical economics; Phillips curve; Price theory; Quantity theory of money; Stagflation; Value of the dollar; Velocity of circulation of money)

James Tobin

Infrastructure

Infrastructure refers to those economic activities that enhance, directly or indirectly, output levels or efficiency in production. Essential elements are systems of transportation, power generators, communication and banking, educational and health facilities, and a well-ordered government and political structure.

The term "infrastructure" was introduced in the early 1950s by the North Atlantic Treaty Organization (NATO) in its studies on war mobilization. Studies of infrastructure have since become part of the literature on economic development. Economists differentiate infrastructure from the more traditional uses of private capital accumulation for plant and equipment. However, once established, infrastructure is viewed as facilitating increases in private investment. It thus represents a necessary, although not sufficient, condition for development.

Development economists sometimes use the term "social overhead capital" as a synonym for infrastructure. Social overhead capital, or economic investment whose output provides services for more than one industry, is further divided into economic overhead capital and social capital. Economic overhead capital refers to the necessary capital accumulation for roads, power transmission systems, telecommunications, etc.; social capital is investment in such services as education, health, police, fire, etc.

A common feature of economic infrastructure is its high initial fixed cost and its relatively low variables costs of operation. As its benefits accrue to numerous diverse groups, its value is often difficult to measure precisely. With high fixed and declining marginal costs, and with the difficulties of pricing and capturing its pecuniary reward, the infrastructure does not conform to normal market investment analysis. Thus, infrastructure development financed by private capital tends to be regulated by government agencies. Frequently, even in some developed countries, government financing has been relied on to create the infrastructure. In fact, most economists believe as did Prebisch in 1949 that it is the role of governments to guide and facilitate the correct pattern of investment through infrastructure creation. This mixture of private and public financing—although usually with public control in either case—is in part responsible for the broad definition of infrastructure.

While there is diversity in views of the infrastructure concept, there is unanimity in views of its necessity. For economic development infrastructure is viewed as providing the outputs and services necessary to generate higher levels of national output by linking and subsidizing its diverse users.

Problems of Size, Timing, and Pricing

The necessity of a growing infrastructure has been argued from both the demand and supply perspective. From either point of view infrastructure generates incentives for further private investment. Both forms also base this argument on infrastructure's externalities and its large capital requirement.

As an example, it is often argued that development is slowed owing to the limited size of local markets. If disparate small markets can be linked through investments in transportation and communication networks, the extended market will provide incentives for further private industrial investment and output. Since no group of investors can either carry out or reap the full advantages of the extensive infrastructure project, it is left to the government.

On the supply side, infrastructure development can reduce costs in two ways. By charging only incremental costs, infrastructure investment can subsidize existing industries and their customers and generate incentives for new firms. An example of this form of externalities is power generation.

Social capital can also generate private externalities. For example, the establishment of an educational system not only adds to the general welfare of a nation but also reduces the expense burden of an industry to train its own work force.

The debate about infrastructure centers not on its role, but rather on its timing in a nation's development. As large power plants and even road networks in less-developed nations often operate with excess capacity, critics argue that smaller, privately operated investments would have chosen plants of a more appropriate size. Furthermore, there is a concern that too fast an increase in public outlays on public infrastructure creation detracts from capital accumulation and contributes to inflationary pressures.

The pricing of infrastructure's output has also come under question. Frequently, pricing policies based on marginal-cost pricing generate revenues far below both economic costs and what is needed to finance investment and operating and maintenance expenditures (resulting in the subsidization advantage). As taxes make up the revenue shortfall, it is not clear, under welfare economics, whether the disincentive and resource reallocation effects of taxation offset the projects' subsidization benefits. Lastly, social capital investments may be too extensive and premature, generalizing negative externalities. For example, an extensive array of social services available in the major cities of low-income nations has attracted the uneducated and unskilled to urban areas. The resulting overcrowding and substandard housing conditions have posed additional development problems.

Owing to the ownership and general welfare implications of infrastructure investment, economists of the socialist nations have become interested in the subject. However, infrastructure's definition and problems of size, timing, and pricing appear to be no less real to this group than to the more market-oriented development economists. Consequently, infrastructure services in most nations generate poor financial returns and absorb much public finance, when in fact they are capable of earning appreciable surpluses.

References

Anderson, Dennis, "Infrastructure Pricing Policies and the Public Revenue in African Countries," *World Development,* vol. 17, no. 4, 1990, pp. 525–542; Churchill, Anthony, *Road User Charges in Central America,* World Bank Staff Occasional Papers, no. 15, Johns Hopkins University Press, Baltimore, Md., 1972; Fiedorowick, K., "Planning of the Economic Infrastructure," *Eastern European Economics,* vol. 16, no. 1, Fall 1977, pp. 48–73; Hagen, Everett E., *The Economics of Development,* rev. ed., Irwin, Homewood, Ill., 1975; Hirschman, Albert O., *The Strategy of Economic Development,* Yale University Press, New Haven, Conn., 1958; Kindleberger, Charles P., and Bruce Herrick, *Economic Development,* 3d ed., McGraw-Hill, New York, 1977; Prebisch, R., "The Economic Development of Latin America and Its Principal Problems," *Economic Bulletin for Latin America,* vol. 7, no. 1, February 1962, first published in 1949.

(*See also* Stages theory of economic development)

Rexford A. Ahene and Bernard S. Katz

Innovation

Innovation is a pragmatic concept. It refers to the infusion of something new into real-world processes; hence, it excludes abstractions such as new theories or concepts. Innovations may come about as a result of such new theories or concepts, as a result of new inventions, or simply as a result of new ways of implementing previously known principles. The concept is value-free, but under the assumption of rationality, innovations are commonly taken to be oriented toward progress and, therefore, an improvement, at least in the innovator's own evaluation.

In economics, innovation means one of three things:

1. The implementation of changes in production, i.e., changes in the production function

2. The introduction of new types of commodities in the market, i.e., the appearance of new supply functions

3. Procedural changes introduced into markets or the economy as a whole, i.e., social reform

Of these, the first is the most important and can also be translated to apply to the process of consumption via the technology of the consumption concept.

In economics, innovation is not necessarily viewed as wholly beneficial, primarily because of frequent inherent conflicts between the interests of the innovator and those of the market or society as a whole. For example, the introduction of a new piece of improved machinery may upgrade productivity, but it may also bring about technological unemployment (at least in the short run), and, in addition, may cause environmental damage.

The concept of innovation is not among the most commonly found subjects in the history of economic thought, particularly, prior to the 1950s and 1960s; but where it does appear, it tends to occupy a place of fundamental importance. The one name in the history of economic thought most closely associated with the analysis of innovation belongs to the Austrian, later American, economist Joseph A. Schumpeter. In his theories of economic development, business cycles, and, more generally, the course of and the outlook for the capitalist process, the concept of innovation assumes a position of central importance.

In brief, Schumpeter starts his analysis by postulating a static economy, characterized by a given, undisturbed circular flow of economic activity. From time to time, the circular flow is disrupted by an innovation, undertaken by a profit-seeking entrepreneur. Successful innovations will then be imitated by others until the innovation becomes absorbed into a new circular-flow pattern. This, according to Schumpeter, is the essence of economic development. It also leads to cyclical fluctuations in economic activity.

In his outlook, however, Schumpeter predicted the demise of capitalism partly because he foresaw the disappearance of investment opportunities, caused in no small measure by anticipated decline in the innovative entrepreneurial spirit. Socialism would then ensue, according to Schumpeter. Clearly, worldwide events of the 1980s and 1990s, culminating in the collapse of the Soviet Union, do not bear out Schumpeter on this point.

In his analysis of the capitalism-to-socialism process, Schumpeter incorporated a number of concepts advanced earlier by Karl Marx, particularly on subjects of innovation and technology, but Schumpeter was no Marxist. He foresaw the demise of capitalism, but he did not advocate it.

After the death of Schumpeter in 1950, the subject of innovation, along with more general aspects of technological change and research and development, moved into the limelight in the economics profession. This surge of interest is attributable to the *Sputnik*-inspired international space race and to important defense-related innovations made during the period. The literature of the late 1950s and early 1960s was predominantly empirical in character, but it produced at least two important conceptual propositions, one in contradiction to Schumpeter, the other focusing on a phenomenon neglected by Schumpeter.

The first of these propositions challenged Schumpeter's assertion that innovators tend to be large, monopolistic firms. Findings of the 1950s and the 1960s have shown that considerable innovative activity can be attributed to firms not meeting these criteria. The second proposition was more important. In Schumpeter's treatment, the knowledge foundation of innovation was not a factor. What mattered was entrepreneurship, and given the presence of entrepreneurship, there was no dearth of new know-how or of inventions required for the innovation process.

During the 1950s and the 1960s when economists first recognized the economic importance of research and development, innovation became a link in the newly postulated chain of progress: research and development—invention—innovation—economic growth and development. In other words, innovation and the inventions required for progress were taken out of the conceptual class of freely available or spontaneously forthcoming amenities and were incorporated into the class of regular, planned economic activity. Inasmuch as basic research constitutes an important part of the gamut of progress, and inasmuch as governmental promotion of basic research is a prerequisite, a link between government patronage and innovation was established, a link that would have appeared alien to Schumpeter.

Other questions concerning innovation during the 1950s, 1960s, and 1970s centered on the link between innovation and the profit incentive: on the character of capital-saving, laborsaving, and neutral innovation; on the diffusion of innovation in industry; and on the relationship between innovation and economic growth, on both the micro and the macro scale. Empirical measures of innovation consist of direct counts (of named innovations) and counts of patents, licenses, and copyrights.

During the decade of the 1980s, mainstream economists continued to pay close attention to the link between research and development and innovation, and in these deliberations, many emerged with a sense of frustration over the inability of the neoclassical route to accommodate the dynamics of innovation and began to seek answers along evolutionary or "neo-Schumpeterian" lines.

The essence of this approach is a deemphasis of purely theoretical optimization and equilibrium schemes in favor of an examination of paths of technological progress and innovation, under different patterns of organizational behavior in differing structures of business. This approach relies heavily on empirical inputs obtained by econometric investigation and the use of mathematical methods (e.g., Markov chains) that are usually not found in mainstream neoclassical analysis.

References

Mansfield, Edwin, *The Economics of Technological Change,* Norton, New York, 1968; Nelson, Richard R., Merton J. Peck, and Edward D. Kalachek, *Technology, Economic Growth and Public Policy,* Brookings, Washington, D.C., 1967; Nelson, Richard R., and Sidney G. Winter, *An Evolutionary Theory of Economic Change,* Belknap Press, Cambridge, Mass., 1982; Schumpeter, Joseph A., *Business Cycles,* McGraw-Hill, New York, 1939; Schumpeter, Joseph A., *Capitalism, Socialism, and Democracy,* Harper, New York, 1950.

(*See also* Economic growth; Research and development; Technology)

Theodore Suranyi-Unger, Jr.

Input-output analysis

Input-output analysis is the study of the exchanges of goods and services among industries. It describes the inputs necessary to produce the outputs of the various sectors of the economy. To study questions such as how reductions in defense spending would affect employment in various industries, or how oil price increases influence other prices, or what widespread use of electric automobiles would do to other industries, one combines the empirical data of the input-output table with basic mathematical methods.

Input-Output Accounting

Input-output analysis usually begins from an intersectorial flow table showing who bought how much of each industry's products in a particular year. A hypothetical intersectorial flow is shown in Table 1. The economy is divided into a number of producing sectors, listed down the left side of the table. In the simple example shown here, only four sectors are distinguished. (In practice, published tables range from about 30 to over 400 sectors, with tables having 40 to 100 sectors being the most common.)

Across the top of the table are listed these same sectors, but they are listed as purchasers. The cells of the table then show the sales from the seller sector on the left to the buyer sector at the top. Thus, in the table, agriculture sold $76 billion of products to industry. The sale from one producing sector to another is called an intermediate flow. Further to the right, beyond the first double line, are the sales to final demands—personal consumption, investment, exports, and government. Imports appear as a negative column. Thus, although the $76 billion shown for purchases of industry from agriculture includes imported products, the sum across the "Agriculture" row will—because of the negative entry in the import column—give exactly the domestic production of agriculture.

Below the first double line in Table 1 appear the factor payments by industry. Only three have been shown: labor income (wages, salaries, and supplements), capital income (profits, interest, and depreciation), and indirect taxes (property, excise, and sales taxes), but actual tables often show much more detail.

The sum of the "Total" row, $1221 billion, is also the sum of the "Final demand" column and is the gross national product (GNP). The entries in the "Total" row under the "Intermediate sales" columns show the gross outputs of the sectors; the entries under the "GNP components" columns show the values for the components in the product side of the usual, aggregate national income and products account (NIPA). The entries in the "Total" column show, in the rows for producing industries, the gross outputs of these industries (matching exactly the outputs shown in the "Total" row), while in the value-added rows, the total factor payments appear, as in the income side of the NIPA. Thus, the input-output table may be viewed as an expansion of the NIPA, and is, in fact, a valuable tool in establishing accurate NIPA.

Within this general framework, there are numerous variations. Some of the most important include the following matters:

Sectors.   Sectors may be defined by commodity, by establishment, or by company groupings.

Pricing.   Flows may be priced in producer prices or in purchaser prices. The meaning of the entries in the "Trade and transportation" row depends on the pricing used. In producer price tables, they show margins on the goods received by the sector named at the top; in purchaser price tables, they show the margins on goods shipped by that sector.

Imports.   Sometimes imports are completely separated from domestic output, and two tables are given. Often imports are shown as a positive row instead of as a negative column, but this practice causes problems in working with the tables.

Basic Mathematics of Input-Output

An input-output flow table of this sort may be used to answer many questions about how changes in one part of the economy will affect other parts; it may also be used in economic forecasting to achieve consistency between forecasts of final demands and forecasts of industry outputs and factor incomes, or consistency among forecasts of various industries. For these uses, one needs to define the input-output coefficient,

$$a_{ij} = x_{ij}/q_j$$

where x_{ij} = flow from industry i to industry j
q_j = output of industry j

TABLE 1 Illustrative Input-Output Table (Billions of dollars)

Buyers / Sellers	Intermediate sales				Total inter-mediate	GNP components						Final demand	Total
	Agri-culture	Industry	Trade and trans-portation	Services		Personal consumption	Fixed invest-ment	Change in inventory	Exports	Imports	Govern-ment		
1. Agriculture	—	76	—	4	80	20	0	-3	10	-8	1	20	100
2. Industry	8	150	30	45	233	313	110	12	50	-48	30	467	700
3. Trade and transportation	1	15	3	5	24	249	10	—	2	-5	20	276	300
4. Services	2	50	10	20	82	276	5	—	30	-33	40	318	400
5. Total intermediate (= 1 + 2 + 3 + 4)	11	291	43	74		858	125	9	92	-94	91	1081	
6. Labor income	66	260	170	200	—	—	—	—	—	—	140	140	
7. Capital income	20	130	70	106									
8. Indirect taxes	3	19	17	20									
9. Total value added (6 + 7 + 8)	89	409	257	326	1081	—	—	—	—	—	140	140	1221
10. Total (5 + 9)	100	700	300	400	—	858	125	9	92	-94	231	1221	1221

The requirement that the output of sector i should be equal to the sum of intermediate plus final demands (f_i) for this sector may be written

$$q_i = \sum_j a_{ij} + f_i$$

There is one such equation for each sector. The equations can be solved with changed values of the f's or a_{ij}'s to study the effects of these changes on the outputs of all industries. In matrix form, these equations may be written

$$q = Aq + f$$

or

$$q = (I - A)^{-1}f$$

The matrix A is often called the direct-requirements matrix, and $(I - A)^{-1}$ is then called the total-requirements matrix because the element of it in the ith column shows how much sector i will be required to produce in order for sector j to deliver one unit of output to final demand.

Input-output relations also apply to prices, for the value of one unit of output of a good is the sum of material costs and value added per unit of product; thus

$$p_j = \sum_i a_{ij}p_i + v_j$$

where p_j is the price of product j and v_j is the value added per unit of output of this product. By thinking of p and v as row vectors, these equations may be written

$$p = pA + v$$

or

$$p = v(I - A)^{-1}$$

where $(I - A)^{-1}$ is the same total-requirements matrix that appeared above.

History of Input-Output Tables

Input-output was introduced by Wassily W. Leontief in 1936. A large, 450-sector table was undertaken to describe the United States in the year 1947, but the work was never published in full detail. An 82-sector table for 1958, prepared by the Department of Commerce and published in 1965, launched the regular preparation of input-output tables as part of the NIPA in the United States. Tables with 360 to 450 sectors have been published for 1963, 1967, 1972, 1977, and 1982, each with a lag of 6 to 9 years between the reference year of the table and its publication date. Annual tables with under 90 sectors, and based on only a partial reconciliation with the national accounts, have been published for a number of years.

Other countries began preparing tables regularly during the 1960s. Annual tables are available for France, Norway, Germany, the Netherlands, and the United Kingdom, with as little as 2 years between the reference year and the publication date. Tables have been made for over 120 countries, including all the major developed countries, most socialist countries, and many less-developed countries. Tables have also been made for a number of states and cities.

Applications

A typical early application of input-output analysis was to change a part of the final demand vector—for example, by replacing a portion of defense spending by an equal volume of foreign aid or consumption expenditure—and to calculate the consequent changes in the output and employment in various industries. The price equations were used, first in Israel and then in several socialist countries, to calculate factor-cost prices. A uniform rate of return was assigned to capital in all industries, and all subsidies were eliminated (in the calculations). Foreign currency for importing was assumed to be "made" by exports, and the corresponding value of the foreign currency in terms of the factor-cost prices was calculated. Such prices could be used to obtain better measures of true social costs of various projects than could be derived from actual selling prices.

Since the 1960s, input-output analysis has played an increasing role in econometric forecasting models where it connects the product side of the model with the income side. That is, it connects the expenditures on final demand categories, such as consumption or investment by product bought with labor and capital income, in the industries that contributed to making the products. Models using input-output analysis in this way are now operating in several developed economies, and efforts are being made to link them together.

In the late 1970s much interest centered on making the input-output coefficients sensitive to prices. The question of price-induced substitution among energy sources has generated particularly lively debate. Many other applications are described in the proceedings of the International Conferences on Input-Output Techniques, which have taken place about once every 4 years since the early 1950s.

In the 1980s, input-output tables have been frequently used in the form of social accounting matrices in static computable general equilibrium (CGE) models. They continue to be central to dynamic multisectoral macroeconomic models which extend CGE modeling to include relations over time.

In 1989, the International Input-Output Association, founded shortly before, began the publication of *Economic Systems Research,* a journal devoted to research involving input-output methods.

References

Brody, A., and A. P. Carter (eds.), *Input-Output Techniques,* North-Holland, Amsterdam, 1972; Leontief, Wassily W., *The Structure of American Economy,* 1st ed. (1919–1929), Harvard University Press, Cambridge, Mass., 1941; 2d ed. (1919–1939), Oxford University Press, New York, 1951; Polenske, K. R., and J. V. Skolka (eds.), *Advances in Input-Output Analysis,* Ballinger, Cambridge, Mass., 1976.

(*See also* Economic forecasting methods; Economic models; Economic planning; Macroeconomics; Microeconomics; National income accounting; Statistical methods in economics and business, an overview)

Clopper Almon, Jr.

Institutional economics

"Institutional economics" is the term most commonly used to denote the school in American economic thought associated with Thorstein Veblen, John R. Commons, and Wesley Clair Mitchell. The name has served to underline the emphasis that this group placed on looking at the economic decision-making process against the entire cultural and social context within which it operates. It has often been described as a movement of dissent against the assumptions and perspective of classical and neoclassical economic theory. In this it reflects its antecedents in the German historical school, most particularly Gustav Schmoller, as well as the utopian socialists and others. Contemporary institutionalists argue that institutionalism is more than mere dissent.

The essence of institutionalism lies in a view of economics as evolving entities that both shape and express the emergent choices of society concerning the uses to which resources shall be put. The view of this interactive process by which societal values are formed and through which resource decisions are made is institutionalism's most distinctive feature, and it is what ultimately distinguishes it from other schools of economic thought. Institutionalism stresses process and evolution rather than statics or equilibrium. The natural condition for participants in economic decision making is conflict rather than harmony. Moreover, institutionalists believe that political economy subsumes markets and prices but transcends exclusive focus on them because the real focus must be on analysis of the process by which modern societies express emerging societal values as they are reflected in the entire resource-allocation process. As such, institutionalists believe that the emphasis must be on how values are formed, not on how prices are formed, and on how the valuational system changes through time. Therefore, institutionalists are concerned with economic progress and ideas of progress, how they are formed and change, rather than merely on economic growth. Because these questions involve the entire institutional structure of society over time, the name "institutionalism" has stuck, although evolutionary economics is perhaps more appropriate. It also explains why institutionalists have had perhaps their greatest impact in the field of development economics.

The Three Founders

Veblen devoted himself to critical examination of the American capitalist system and bequeathed to institutionalism his concern with the cultural milieu within which economic decisions are made. He began with a distinction between industrial values and pecuniary values, which in one form or another is found in the thinking of most institutionalists. The industrial values derive preeminently from the technological process, and nowhere did this process make itself more prominent than through the impact of industrialization on successive capitalist economies. It was this aspect of evolving economies which most interested Commons. He focused on the impact of industrialization on economies previously analyzed preeminently by classical economists through the assumptions of Smithian competitive economics. He argued that the inherent conflict in society, expressing itself in labor-management disputes in the industrializing United States during the last quarter of the nineteenth century and the first quarter of the twentieth century, required a new perspective in economic theory, one that Commons called the economics of collective action. A larger role for the public sector was an inevitable concomitance.

Mitchell looked at these same emergent phenomena and concluded that a primary requirement of economic analysis was for a far more profound knowledge of the facts of economic development than economic theorists had previously demanded. His use of statistics in economic analysis led to the founding of the National Bureau of Economic Research and permanently influenced the character of economic research in the United States. His main concern was with the instability evidenced by evolving economies and led to his path-breaking work in business-cycle measurement and analysis.

Neoinstitutionalists

In the wake of the three founders there were a number of economists who qualified as institutional economists. Prominent among them were Richard Ely, J. M. Clark, Rexford Guy Tugwell, and Gardiner Means. Other institutionalists included Walton Hamilton, Robert F. Hoxie, Selig Perlman, A. B. Wolfe, Morris Copeland, and Edwin F. Witte. In 1972 Allan Gruchy suggested the term "neoinstitutionalists" for the second generation of institutionalists, a term he applied to John Kenneth Galbraith, Clarence Ayers, Gunnar Myrdal, and Gerhard Colm. If this group represents the most prominent of institutionalists who wrote in the post–World War II years, they were followed by a number of economists whose work has appeared over the past quarter century in the Association for Evolutionary Economics' *Journal of Economic Issues,* which is dedicated to both clarifying and advancing institutionalists' views.

Present Influence of Institutionalism

There is disagreement about the present influence of institutionalism. There are those who regard institutionalism as essentially the dissent expressed by the founding trio, and, as such, a movement that is dead. Paul Samuelson has taken this view, arguing that institutionalism "withered away" 40 years ago. On the other hand, one could argue that many institutionalist views and concerns have found their way into mainstream economic thinking. Current interest in economic development invariably focuses on the institutional structure within which economic decisions are made in precisely the manner that institutionalists have always insisted is essential to economic analysis. Current concern with the quality of life, with the costs of growth to the environment, and with the ultimate direction in which economic activity is thrusting the modern world reflects the interest in economic progress, which has long been an institutionalist hallmark, rather than in mere growth.

One of the more important developments of recent years has been the burgeoning of interest among Europeans in institutionalism and the institutionalist approach. There is now a fairly large number who believe that American institutionalism has much to offer as an approach to studying European economic conditions as well. They have founded a new association, the European Association for Evolutionary Political Economy (EAEPE). Organized in the late 1980s, the association now holds annual meetings which have drawn large numbers of economists from both Western and Eastern Europe. The EAEPE has close ties to the Association for Evolutionary Political Economy, and its members are also publishing very prolifically.

References

Breit, William, and William Culbertson, Jr. (eds.), *Science and Ceremony: The Institutional Economics of C. E. Ayres,* University of Texas Press, Austin, 1976; Commons, John R., *Institutional Economics: Its Place in Political Economy,* 2 vols., University of Wisconsin Press, Madison, 1959; Dopfer, Kurt, "Elemente einer Evolutionsokonomik: Prozess, Struktur, und Phasenubergange," *Studien zur Evolutorischen Okonomik* I. Neue Folge, Bd. 195/I, pp. 19–47; Dorfman, Joseph, et al., *Institutional Econo ʾics: Veblen, Commons and Mitchell Reconsidered,* University of California Press, Berkeley, 1963; Gruchy, Allan G., *Contemporary Economic Thought,* Macmillan, New York, 1972; Gruchy, Allan G., *The Reconstruction of Economics, An Analysis of the Fundamentals of Institutional Economics,* Greenwood Press, New York, 1987; Mitchell, Wesley Clair, *Business Cycles, The Problems and Its Setting,* National Bureau of Economic Research, New York, 1927; Stadler, Markus, *Institutionalismus Heute,* Campus Verlag, Frankfurt, 1983; Tool, Marc (ed.), *Evolutionary Economics,* 2 vols., Sharpe, Armonk, N.Y., 1988; Tool, Marc, and Warren J. Samuels (eds.), *The Methodology of Economic Thought,* 2d ed., Transaction

Publications, New Brunswick, N.J., 1989; Veblen, Thorstein, *The Theory of the Leisure Class: An Economic Study of Institutions,* rev. ed., New American Library, New York, 1953.

(*See also* Economics; German historical school; Neoclassical economics)

Philip A. Klein

Integration

Firms may grow through horizontal integration or vertical integration. In instances of horizontal integration, the firm increases its production capability of a specific product. For example, when Alcoa built new aluminum reduction plants, it engaged in horizontal integration. Vertical integration occurs when a firm expands into the industry of one of its suppliers or one of its customers. For example, when Ford began producing its own spark plugs, it had vertically integrated. Similarly, when a newspaper distributes directly to home subscribers rather than through independent carriers, it has engaged in vertical integration. Integration—whether horizontal or vertical—can occur through internal expansion or through merger.

Horizontal Integration

The primary motivation for horizontal integration is greater profit. There are two basic ways that increased size can enhance profit: (1) greater efficiency, which reduces cost, and (2) greater market power. Clearly, the former is socially preferable to the latter.

Scale economies can emerge in any of three ways:

1. Product-specific economies that accompany increases in the production of a particular good
2. Plant-specific economies that stem from increases in the total output of a particular plant
3. Multiplant economies flowing from the operation of multiple plants

These economies lead to higher profits through cost savings associated with lower unit production costs, volume discounts on inputs, financial ability to hire more sophisticated management, development of a more efficient sales force, better promotional efforts, and reduced distribution costs.

When large size appears to be associated with market power, the antitrust authorities can intervene in two ways. Internal expansion can be attacked through section 2 of the Sherman Act, which condemns any person who monopolizes, attempts to monopolize, or conspires to monopolize any part of interstate commerce. Horizontal mergers can be challenged under section 7 of the Clayton Act, which forbids mergers that may substantially lessen competition or tend to create a monopoly.

The Alcoa case provides a good example of how internal expansion may be challenged. Between 1912 and 1940, Alcoa was the sole producer of virgin aluminum ingot in the United States in spite of the fact that it had no patent protection. After determining that Alcoa did indeed enjoy monopoly status, the Supreme Court turned to the question of whether Alcoa was guilty of illegally monopolizing the aluminum industry. The Court found that Alcoa's monopoly was not inevitable; it was not thrust upon it. The Court noted that Alcoa developed new uses for aluminum and encouraged demand to expand. As demand expanded, Alcoa expanded its production facilities. Between 1912 and 1934, Alcoa increased its production capacity by 800 percent while there was no new entry. The Court found Alcoa guilty.

Firms can also expand by merging with other firms in the industry. These efforts can be challenged under section 7 of the Clayton Act, which is preventive in nature. It is designed to stop any tendency for market structure to evolve toward monopoly. The judicial interpretation of section 7 can be traced to a series of Supreme Court decisions handed down in the 1960s. These decisions signaled an extremely harsh environment for horizontal mergers. The Supreme Court appeared to find whatever was necessary in order to rule against the merging firms. In some cases (e.g., *U.S. v. Continental Can Co.*, 1964), the Court broadened the product market definition so the two firms would be horizontal competitors. In other cases [e.g., *U.S. v. Aluminum Co. of America (Rome Cable)*, 1964], substitute products were eliminated to raise the market shares of the merging firms. The Court's standards for demonstrating probable anticompetitive effects were not very demanding. In some cases (*U.S. v. Von's Grocery Co., 1966*), slight increases in concentration in highly competitive markets were condemned. In summarizing his view of the Court's analysis of merger decisions, Justice Potter Stewart was moved to complain that "the sole consistency that I can find is that in litigation under §7, the Government always wins."

In 1984, the Department of Justice (DOJ) issued merger guidelines to provide signals of its intention to pursue horizontal mergers. The message of the guidelines was that the precedents of the 1960s would not be employed in reaching administrative decisions on which mergers to challenge. These guidelines set out reasonable standards for defining relevant geographic and product markets. In evaluating the industry structure, the DOJ guidelines use the Herfindahl-Hirschman index (HHI), which is calculated by summing the squared market shares of the firms in the industry. The spectrum of values that the HHI can assume is divided into three regions:

1. *Unconcentrated.* If the postmerger HHI is below 1000, the industry is characterized as unconcentrated and mergers will not be challenged absent extraordinary circumstances.

2. *Moderately Concentrated.* If the postmerger HHI falls between 1000 and 1800, the industry is deemed to be moderately concentrated. A challenge is unlikely unless the merger produced a change in the HHI of 100 points or more.

3. *Highly Concentrated.* If the postmerger HHI exceeds 1800, the industry is highly concentrated. If the change in the HHI was 50 points or more, that merger is apt to be challenged.

Thus, one can see that mergers are likely to be challenged only where concentration is quite high. Moreover, in analyzing potential anticompetitive effects, DOJ would consider other factors such as changing market conditions, ease of entry, the ability of fringe firms to expand production, special buyer characteristics, and considerations of efficiency.

Vertical Integration

As a product moves from being a collection of raw materials to being a finished good in the hands of a consumer, many distinct production and distribution functions are performed. Basic raw materials must be extracted and transported. Intermediate products that are employed as inputs in the later stages of production must be fabricated from these raw materials, and these must also be transported. Finally, the various intermediate inputs must be combined or assembled into a final good that must then be distributed and sold to the ultimate consumer. In principle, each of these myriad functions could be performed by a separate specialized firm. In that event, the output of each firm is sold in market transactions. Alternatively, a single firm could perform each function and simply transfer the outputs internally.

A firm is said to be vertically integrated if that firm transfers internally from one department to another a commodity that could be sold in the market without major adaption. From this definition, it follows that virtually all firms are vertically integrated to some degree. Most firms carry out some function or manufacture some tool or part that could, "without major adaption," be purchased from another firm. Moreover, no firm is totally vertically integrated since all firms purchase some inputs or services that they could, in principle, manufacture or provide themselves.

As with horizontal integration, the primary motivation for vertical integration is a quest for higher profits. In many instances, these higher profits flow from greater efficiency and should be applauded. There is a great deal of controversy regarding the circumstances under which vertical integration can increase profits through an increase in market power. When DOJ suspects that a vertical merger unduly enhances market power, it can challenge the merger under section 7 of the Clayton Act.

Specific motivation for vertical integration can usefully be categorized into three groups: (1) that which involves government actions, (2) that which may arise even if intermediate and final product markets are competitive, and (3) that which is spawned by monopoly power at one or more of the stages of production.

Differential taxation, price controls, and profit regulation are examples of government actions that may provide incentives for vertical integration. Competition can provide fertile ground for vertical integration to achieve efficiencies in assuring sources of supply, in reducing transaction costs, and in exploiting technological interdependencies. When monopoly power exists at some stage of the production and distribution process, there is concern that vertical integration can be used to increase existing market power of the firm or to lever the firm into a second market. For the most part, these fears are unfounded, but they persist nonetheless.

Vertical integration is thought to have several potential anticompetitive consequences. First, vertical integration in an industry might leave no independents and thereby require new entrants to enter at two or more stages of production. This is thought to raise entry barriers. Second, vertically integrated firms can squeeze independents by raising supply prices and/or reducing final goods prices. Third, vertically integrated firms can foreclose markets to their independent rivals. This was the rationale for the adverse rulings in *U.S. v. E. I. du Pont de Nemours & Co.* (1957) and *Brown Shoe Co. v. U.S.* (1962).

The DOJ merger guidelines express concern with vertical mergers that (1) create competitively objectionable barriers to entry, (2) facilitate horizontal collusion, or (3) permit the evasion of rate regulation. The focus of the guidelines is on how a vertical merger may influence horizontal competition in some market. For the most part, a vertical merger will not be challenged unless the HHI in the acquired firm's market exceeds 1800.

References

Blair, Roger D., and David L. Kaserman, *Law and Economics of Vertical Integration and Control*, Academic Press, New York, 1983; Blair, Roger D., and David L. Kaserman, *Antitrust Economics*, Irwin, Homewood, Ill., 1985; Bork, Robert, "Vertical Integration and the Sherman Act: The Legal History of an Economic Misconception," *University of Chicago Law Review*, vol. 22, Autumn 1954, pp. 157–201; Coase, Ronald, "The Nature of the Firm," *Economica*, vol. 4, November 1937, pp. 386–405; Scherer, F. M., and David Ross, *Industrial Market Structure and Economic Performance*, Houghton Mifflin, Boston, 1990.

(*See also* Concentration of industry; Conglomerate; Mergers, takeovers, and restructuring)

Roger D. Blair

Interest, economic theory of

The concept of interest embraces theories of time preference, marginal productivity, liquidity preference, and loanable funds. However, these apparently diverse views of interest can be grouped into two broad classes: real and monetary. Real theories of interest are long-run theories in which interest is the return for real abstinence and the yield on real capital. Monetary theories of interest are short-run theories in which the monetary (also called the nominal) rate of interest is the cost of borrowing money and selling securities, and the yield on lending money and purchasing securities. Expressed differently, the real rate of interest is determined by the demand for and supply of real savings, whereas the monetary rate of interest is determined by the demand for and supply of money (or, alternatively, the demand for and supply of securities). The modern link between real and monetary theories of interest is that the monetary rate of interest should approximately equal the real rate plus (or minus) the expected rate of inflation (or deflation).

Real Theories of Interest

Real theories of interest have a long doctrinal history, first appearing in the writings of Richard Cantillon and David Hume in the eighteenth century. But they were developed principally by Eugen von Böhm-Bawerk and Knut Wicksell in the nineteenth century and by Irving Fisher in the early twentieth century. Real theories held sway until the Keynesian revolution of the mid-1930s. They were then overshadowed by monetary theories, as monetary authorities manipulated their national money stocks and nominal interest rates as part of an effort to stabilize employment at high levels. More recently, real theories have provided the base for contemporary theory as the high inflation rates of the 1970s and the reemergence of neoclassical monetary economics resulted in empirical studies of the impact of money and inflation on interest.

The two parts to real theories of interest are the act of saving and the use of saving. The act of saving includes both abstinence from consumption and the release of real resources for use in the production of new plant and equipment. Interest is a reward for the act of saving and the provision of real capital. Theoretically, there is some interest rate that is just equal to the rate at which each saver is willing to substitute future for current consumption. Generally, the higher the rate of interest, the greater the saving and the willingness to sacrifice present consumption.

Just as savers have a choice of consuming present or future goods, producers have a choice of producing present or future consumable goods. When producers divert current resources from the production of present to future goods, new real capital is added to their resources, with a resultant net gain in their ability to produce future consumables. The ratio of this net gain to the new capital that generated it is called the yield on capital (or, alternatively, the marginal product of capital). Given diminishing returns, and other things remaining the same, the greater the amount of real capital, the lower its yield. Firms must compare this yield from new capital with the interest cost of obtaining the funds needed to acquire the real resources devoted to producing the new capital. Since the yield on capital decreases as more capital is acquired, it follows that the amount of capital demanded can only expand as the interest cost of funds decreases.

The real rate of interest is set when the yield on capital is just equal to the rate at which the saver abstains and substitutes future for current consumption. This real rate is ultimately determined by the time preferences of individuals for present and future goods and by underlying real productivity forces such as technology, the availability of raw material resources, and the stock of capital. Productivity forces change slowly over time, and thus the real rate of interest also changes slowly.

Monetary Theories of Interest

Monetary theories of interest, like real theories, have a long doctrinal history dating from the mercantilists and John Locke in the seventeenth century, who regarded interest as the "price of the hire of money." Early nineteenth-century classical economists and the neoclassical economists of the late nineteenth and early twentieth centuries held principally to real theories of interest, but recognized that money-stock changes may have a temporary effect upon market interest rates. They reasoned that in high-employment economies, an increase in the stock of money would temporarily depress market rates below the real rate of interest and, given the relatively fixed rate of production, the price level would rise, leading to a decrease in the real supply of money and thereby causing the market rate to return to the original real level.

As noted earlier, high-unemployment levels of the 1930s and expansive monetary policies of the post–World War II period caused most economists to utilize monetary theories of interest. J. M. Keynes (1936) developed the principal monetary theory, the liquidity preference approach. The logic of this theory was that an expansive monetary policy would cause the market rate of interest to decrease and, if the demand for goods were responsive to interest rate variation, the demand for investment goods would rise. In turn, firms, given their excess capacity, would increase production and hire more workers with little price change. Given continued monetary expansion and excess productive capacity, the market rate could be below the long-run real rate of interest for extended periods. This view works best for depressed economies with little or no inflation.

Contemporary Interest Theory

The extended inflation of the 1970s and the subsequent period of declining but above-normal real rates of interest during the 1980s and early 1990s caused economists to reassess their theory of interest. They built upon the neoclassical analysis developed by Irving Fisher (1930). Leading proponents of the new view were Friedman [see Gordon's *Milton Friedman's Monetary Framework* (1974)] and Eugene

F. Fama (1975). Extensive empirical research was conducted by William E. Gibson (1972), Fama (1975), Levi and Makin (1979), Hamilton (1985), Huizinga and Mishkin (1986), and Behzad Diba and Oh (1991). The contemporary view argues that the nominal (market) rate of interest is equal to the real rate plus the expected inflation rate.

The new theory presents the following model. Assume a high-employment economy in a dynamic equilibrium where the nominal and real rates of interest are equal. The growth rate of money is just equal to the long-run real growth rate of output, and prices are constant. Now postulate an increase in the growth rate of money. Initially the market rate of interest will decline, investment demand will expand, and incomes will rise. Individual firms will at first believe that the rise in demand is unique to them; they will use their resources more intensively and bring some idle resources into production. As demand, incomes, and production increase, the demand for money will rise and the market rate of interest will begin to increase. Additionally, prices and wages will also rise, thereby reducing the real stock of money, causing the nominal interest rate to rise still further and the rate of production to return to its original growth rate. Unlike the neoclassical model, the contemporary model assumes that the nominal interest rate will not stop rising once it returns to its original level. It will stop rising only if the growth rate of money is reduced to its original level and prices stop rising. So long as the growth rate of money is greater than the growth rate of output, there is excess demand for goods, and people will expect inflation to be maintained. Savers will insist on receiving a nominal interest rate on savings at least equal to the real rate plus the expected inflation rate, so that there is no deterioration in their real return. Borrowers similarly will be willing to pay the real rate plus the rate of inflation since they know that the higher prices will enable them to pay a nominal rate above the real rate. Thus, the contemporary theory of interest unites the real and monetary theories with a price expectation effect.

A Problem for Modern Theory

One problem confronting the empirical verification of modern theory is that expected rates of inflation cannot be observed and measured directly. Only information about past and current inflation rates is available. This makes it difficult for lenders and borrowers to estimate the expected real rate of interest on borrowed funds. Current economists avoid this issue by utilizing rational expectations models. According to these models, people may make forecasting errors, but they learn from them. This view enables forecasters to estimate expected real interest rates from current and past observations of actual inflation and realized nominal interest rates. Of course, if people do make systematic errors, then empirical verification of contemporary theory becomes difficult. Even so, the general nature of the relationships discussed in the theory of interest provides a useful, if not precise, description of the process whereby the real interest rate, the nominal interest rate, inflation, and monetary policy are connected.

References

Diba, Behzad, and Seonghwan Oh, "Money, Output, and the Expected Real Interest Rate," *Review of Economics and Statistics,* vol. 73, no. 1, February 1991, pp. 10–17; Fama, Eugene F., "Short-Term Interest Rates as Predictors of Inflation," *American Economic Review,* vol. 65, no. 3, June 1975, pp. 269–282; Fisher, Irving, *The Theory of Interest,* Macmillan, New York, 1930, reprinted by Kelley, New York, 1965; Gibson, William E., "Interest Rates and Inflationary Expectations: New Evidence," *American Economic Review,* vol. 62, no. 5, December 1972, pp. 854–865; Gordon, Robert J. (ed.), *Milton Friedman's Monetary Framework,* University of

Chicago Press, Chicago, 1974; Hamilton, James D., "Uncovering Financial Market Expectations of Inflation," *Journal of Political Economy,* vol. 93, no. 6, December 1985, pp. 231–274; Huizinga, John, and Frederic S. Mishkin, "Monetary Policy Regime Shifts and the Unusual Behavior of Real Interest Rates," *Carnegie-Rochester Series on Public Policy,* vol. 24, Spring 1986, pp. 231–274; Keynes, John M., *The General Theory of Employment, Interest, and Money,* Harcourt Brace Jovanovich, New York, 1936; Levi, Maurice D., and John H. Makin, "Fisher, Phillips, Friedman and the Measured Impact of Inflation on Interest," *Journal of Finance,* vol. 34, no. 1, March 1979, pp. 35–53.

(*See also* Classical school; Expectations; Interest rates; Keynesian economics; Mercantilism)

John J. Klein

Interest rates

Interest is the price paid for the use of money over time. It is usually expressed as a rate charged or earned per period, hence interest rate. In turn, interest rates are typically expressed as a percentage of a principal (initial amount) borrowed or loaned. Thus, in the formulation

$$S = P(1 + it)$$

a sum S (such as \$110) will result from a principal P (\$100) if the interest rate i is 10 percent (0.10) for one time period t.

There are innumerable refinements and practical applications of interest calculations, the most important of which is compound interest (meaning interest on interest). In the formula

$$S = P(1 + i)^n$$

S is the sum to which a principal P will accumulate at interest rate i if the interest is compounded for n periods. This equation, which is usually solved using logarithms, shows that any given principal and interest rate will result in larger sums the more frequent and prolonged the compounding is.

This formula is the foundation of virtually all calculations involving the mathematics of finance. Thus, it is helpful in personal finance if one seeks to determine the true interest rate one has to pay on a discount loan (where the loan value at maturity is the principal and one receives only a discounted sum, the proceeds, at the outset); or if one obtains an installment loan, requiring periodic repayments, but where the interest rate is stated as a percentage of the original principal.

The formula is also basic to present-value calculations in which one seeks to determine, for example, which price (principal) should be paid for a series of future payments (e.g., a pension or annuity). Similarly, the formula is needed to calculate periodic payments such as one makes in repaying (amortizing) a mortgage loan within a given period at a stated interest rate.

The most important application of the basic interest formula is asset pricing, an application of present-value calculation. The market prices of interest-bearing securities and interest rates themselves are directly and inversely correlated, as shown in the formula

$$PV = \frac{1}{(1 + i)^n}$$

where *PV* stands for present value, *i* for the interest rate, and *n* for the relevant period.

Assume a security has been sold at a par value of 100 and bears a prevailing interest rate of 4 percent per annum. Assume further that the general interest rate level subsequently rises to 8 percent. Then, the security initially traded at 100 will inevitably decline in price at below par. (In order to determine by how much, the simple formula must be expanded to allow for periodicity of interest and capital repayments.)

This is so, of course, not because of the mere existence of mathematical equivalencies of the prices of securities at a single defined interest rate, but rather because supply and demand force interest-paying securities of similar characteristics into line with each other. Thus, a potential investor in long-term bonds of a given company who could obtain 8 percent on a new issue of that company may actually prefer to purchase a seasoned (outstanding) bond of that company. However, if the coupon rate (the originally stated interest rate) of the outstanding bond is indeed only 4 percent, its price must be adjusted so that the yield (the actual interest rate) becomes a close equivalent of the current rate before the investor will seriously consider buying the seasoned bond. The process of forcing asset prices and yields into line with changing market forces is known as portfolio adjustment.

History of Interest Rates

Interest has been a subject of intense study and dispute virtually throughout recorded economic history. In the Roman era and in the early phase of industrialization during the eighteenth century, interest was viewed objectively as one among many prices. For much of the Middle Ages and throughout the history of the Islamic world, however, interest has in effect been a term of opprobrium. A charge for the use of money was often considered unjust per se and hence to be forbidden by law. Thus, official interest rate regulations are as old and traditional as interest itself.

The United States began as a capital-poor country with abundant investment opportunities. Hence, high interest rates for imported European capital were readily acceptable. By the 1830s, however, a pronounced split between the Eastern (lending) and the Western frontier (borrowing) interests began to develop, partly because the beginnings of central banking in the United States (especially the Second Bank of the United States) were interpreted by borrowers as inimical to easy money. The hostility to lenders and to interest reached a peak in the 1870s with the Populist movement. Many state usury laws, fixing maximum permitted rates of interest on a variety of transactions, date from this period. More generally, government influence upon, if not outright control of, interest rates has been considered a legitimate governmental function in the United States.

With the establishment of the Federal Reserve System in 1913 a federal influence upon money and capital markets became more systematic and accepted. The Federal Reserve itself and most economists, however, largely neglected the potential influence of interest rates on aggregate economic activity. During the Great Depression of the 1930s, the ineffectiveness of even very low interest rates in stimulating borrower demand led to a downgrading of interest rate studies.

During World War II and the early postwar period, short-term interest rates were held rigidly stable by Federal Reserve action—first as a part of price controls, later to help prevent a much-feared postwar depression. This spell was broken with the March 1951 Accord between the U.S. Treasury and the Federal Reserve under which short-term interest rates once again became flexible. (The U.S. government in effect conceded that the inflationary consequences of the Korean war were being aggravated by the public's ability to convert interest-bearing securities into cash—monetization of debt—at Federal Reserve–guaranteed prices.)

This Accord may be said to mark the beginning of recent interest rate history and theory. The Federal Reserve became expert at manipulating the federal funds and Treasury bill rates for monetary policy purposes. A variety of new fixed-yield instruments developed in the financial markets, as pockets of potential investor and borrower attraction were explored. Theoreticians were busy updating and refining interest rate theories with the firm conviction that interest rates were indeed a vital determinant of aggregate economic performance. Meanwhile, the general interest rate level showed a modest updrift in 1951 to 1965 under the influence mainly of the gradual absorption of excess liquidity from World War II and the early postwar years.

Since the mid-1960s and into the early to mid-1980s, interest rates were dominated by the influence of rising (and eventually large-scale) inflation. The general interest rate level rose to historic peaks in 1981–1982, with the banks' prime rate well above 20 percent. Rates subsided in the late 1980s and early 1990s, but the aftermath of inflation continued to cast a shadow on the potential for lower rates.

New interest rate–denominated securities proliferated, partly because of the pervasive internationalization of financial markets and partly because of the increased sophistication of market participants and the active search for market niches through refined versions of derivative securities.

Interest rate policy also became increasingly global during the 1980s. National policies—laws and regulations as well as monetary policy—became subject to rather unpredictable influences as financial flows across national frontiers multiplied manifold. In addition, the interrelation of interest and quantity of money—i.e., cost versus availability—again became an acute theoretical and policy question.

Liquidity, Risk, and Term Structure of Interest Rates

In highly developed financial markets, hundreds of interest rates are quoted (and the corresponding securities traded) at any one time. In terms of their respective yields, the most important characteristics of such trading instruments are their relative liquidity and risk. Liquidity refers to the breadth of a security's market. Roughly, the larger the trading volume per trading period relative to the total outstanding, the more liquid the security. However, the amount of price change induced by marginal shifts in supply and demand is another relevant and not necessarily coincident measure of liquidity. Risk, of course, refers to the degree of uncertainty attached to the borrower's compliance with all terms and conditions of the security, most importantly, timely payment of interest and repayment of principal.

Liquidity and risk are closely, although by no means perfectly, correlated with the maturity of a security. Financial markets make major distinctions between short-term securities (usually up to 1 year in original maturity), medium-term or intermediate securities (usually 1 to 5 years in original maturity, but frequently up to 10 years), and long-term securities (with original maturity of up to 25 years, or longer).

Yield Curves

Interest rates for securities of comparable quality usually rise (slope upward) along a yield curve as the maturity lengthens, reflecting lesser liquidity and greater risk for the longer maturities. Thus, short-term interest rates on corporate securities (prime commercial paper, 4 to 6 months) have been below long-term rates (AAA corporate bonds) far more frequently and for longer periods than the opposite case, although occasional instances of higher short-term rates than long-term rates have occurred.

An upward-sloping yield curve is often equated with a normal-term structure of interest rates. An inverted yield curve (short rates above long rates) calls for special explanations beyond liquidity and risk. One explanation for such occurrences during the 1970s and the 1980s is the impact of sudden and severe Federal Reserve restraint on the availability of short-term credit at the peak of an economic boom. The demand for such credit is far less elastic than short-term borrowing. In addition, it is expected that short-term rates will again fall below long-term rates so that a succession of short-term borrowings will eventually average less in cost than a single long-term borrowing at the time of the "credit crunch."

Variety of Interest Rates

The federal funds rate is the shortest of all broadly based rates. It is the rate for one-day trades among commercial banks of reserve balances at Federal Reserve Banks. The rate is highly sensitive to Federal Reserve operations aimed at lowering or raising the general level of short-term rates. Treasury bill rates (short-term borrowing of the U.S. Treasury) and large certificate of deposit rates (short-term borrowing by banks) as well as commercial paper rates (corporate indebtedness) are sensitive to the federal funds rate. There are also close links between U.S. short-term rates and those in foreign money centers, especially Eurodollars (offshore balances denominated in U.S. dollars).

Among long-term rates the most frequently quoted key rate is the 30-year U.S. Treasury bond. Mortgage rates (loans secured by real estate) fall into two main classes—residential and commercial. In the wake of extensive U.S. government efforts to make residential mortgages more liquid (i.e., give mortgages some of the characteristics of "uniform merchandise" as are U.S. government securities), mortgage rates have averaged close to corporate bond rates since the 1970s, while they were typically above bond rates in earlier decades.

Corporate long-term rates, on the other hand, have undergone a process of increased diversification during the 1980s. As rising average corporate indebtedness led to downgrading of ever-larger parts of the corporate universe, the category of high-yield bonds grew in importance. These are below-investment-grade instruments, also known as "junk bonds." Such bonds typically yielded from 5 to 10 percentage points above long-term governments at issue (and perhaps 20 to 25 points more in cases where eventual restructuring or outright delinquency occurred).

Interest futures are a development of the late 1970s when the Chicago Board of Trade began to permit trading in Treasury bills for delivery as much as 18 months ahead, followed by forward trading in government-backed mortgage packages. By buying Treasury bills forward, it is possible to assure oneself of an interest rate certain on funds not received until a later date. A speculator can, of course, attempt to make a profit by outguessing the course of interest rates. (For example, let us say one contracted to buy Treasury bills at a future date at a price yielding 8 percent. If the price of the bills rose at any time up to and including the delivery date to a yield of, say, 7 percent, one could profitably sell that contract.) More extensive futures trading (including options on futures) was developed in the 1980s. Such "derivatives" came to be heavily traded.

Interest Rate Theory and Forecasting

The rationale for the level of and changes in interest rates has been a scholarly subject for roughly two centuries. With the development of large-scale computer models of the economy and of econometric examination of interrelationships between numerous variables, it has become possible to attempt structured interest rate forecasting.

Interest rate theorizing begins by declaring one particular interest rate (or the general interest rate level) to be the dependent variable on the left-hand side of an equation (or series of equations), followed by a search for that set of explanatory variables on the right-hand side of the equation(s) that logically and functionally best explains the dependent variable by accepted statistical standards.

As in all analytical economic reasoning, two divergent tendencies compete in the mind of the interest rate theorist. The first tendency is to be comprehensive with respect to both interest rates and their explanation. This correctly assumes that everything depends on everything else. This tendency would lead one to a dynamic general equilibrium model in which the entire spectrum of interest rates would be endogenous—i.e., it would help to explain and be explained by the evolution of and changes in the entire economy. The other tendency is to focus on one interest rate or set of rates (i.e., first long rates and then short rates, or vice versa) and to settle for explanatory variables that are simply assumed to be independent of interest rates. This occurs either because the theorist is struck by the need to explain an unusual phenomenon in a particular segment of the money and capital markets or simply because partial equilibrium analysis is a more achievable goal. The approaches overlap, especially in the case of interest rates, because of the undeniable interrelationship of all rates.

The real-rate-plus-inflation theory of long-term interest rates, formulated by Irving Fisher in the early twentieth century, is an illustration of partial equilibrium analysis. Fisher broke down observed bond rates into a real component—a reward to the answer for consumption forgone—and an inflation component, which would compensate the investor for the expected depreciation in the purchasing power of currency of principal repayments and of interest during the term of the bond. Drawing on nineteenth-century predecessors, Fisher held that the real rate was fairly constant: it depends on the combination of the capital stock (on the demand side) and on savings habits (on the supply side). The inflation component, however, was highly variable, depending on actual inflation experience.

Renewed attention has been paid to Fisher's theory along with mounting inflation and rising interest rates since the late 1960s. The theory has proved sturdy under extensive empirical testing and has an intuitively convincing logical foundation. One serious weakness is that inflationary expectations are not easily measured directly. (A distributed lag or a more simple averaging of past actual inflation experience, used by Fisher and others, is only a substitute for actual expectations.) Yet the theory is the most satisfactory explanation for the strong, general upward trend of interest rates in the late 1970s, and their subsequent decline (with the inflation rate) in the mid-1980s. Also, it has become clear that short-term rates as well as long-term rates react to inflation. However, short-term rates have wider swings than long-term rates and rise less predictably with inflation.

The liquidity preference theory of interest, formulated by John Maynard Keynes, focuses heavily on short-term interest rates. (Striving for generality, Keynes added a "marginal efficiency of capital" theory of long-term rates, but apart from exploring and emphasizing investment incentives—the demand side of the real interest rate—the explanation does not vary much from Fisher's theory and earlier theories.) Keynes held that the public's liquidity preference (the demand for money or near-cash equivalents) would vary inversely with interest rates at any particular time, but that liquidity preference would shift with general economic conditions. On the supply side of the determinants of short-term rates, Keynes referred to banking policy (roughly equivalent in today's terms to monetary policy, central bank policy, or, in the United States, Federal Reserve policy).

In a famous example of applied interest rate theory which reflects the experience of the Great Depression, Keynes postulated a "liquidity trap"—a condition in which no realistically possible additional supply of funds could drive interest rates down sufficiently to stimulate additional credit demand. (Note that liquidity here refers to the general economy, not to the liquidity of a particular security as previously discussed.) Hence, Keynes downgraded the role of interest rates and of money in the business cycle, which was his main focus.

The loanable funds theory of interest rates, the origin of which is usually associated with the Swedish economist Knut Wicksell, is self-explanatory—one seeks to identify the proximate causes of interest rate variations by analyzing the supply and demand of credit. Wicksell was searching for a natural rate of interest (a concept that bears a resemblance to Fisher's real rate), around which market rates would fluctuate according to a cyclical demand and supply factor.

An important modern-day offspring of this theory is flow-of-funds analysis. This exercise originated at the Board of Governors of the Federal Reserve System during the late 1940s to early 1950s when it was felt that financial flows could and should be fitted into a comprehensive and internally consistent framework as a supplement to the (conceptually similar) national income and product accounts. Flow-of-funds analysis is hardly an interest rate theory per se since an ex post identity of the supply and demand of funds amounts to accounting rather than analysis. In practice, however, flow-of-funds exercises have been attempted increasingly on an ex ante basis.

In reconciling credit supplies and demands, interest rate predictions are a fall-out—quite typically including reasoned opinions about relative interest rates (short term versus long term, bonds versus mortgages, etc.), over and above a general interest rate forecast. One key element of the iterative process required to produce ex ante equality between supplies and demand is to judge how much total credit and liquidity the central bank will permit or encourage. Thus, there is a clear link with monetary theory and policy.

Recent theorizing about interest rates has aimed at synthesizing older thoughts in the light of modern institutional circumstances and enhanced measurement capabilities. According to one leading study by Martin Feldstein and Otto Eckstein (1970), the fundamental determinants of the long-term corporate bond rate are liquidity, debt, inflation, and expectations. Liquidity (used again in its general sense) refers to monetary policy—how much liquidity does the Federal Reserve inject into the economy? Debt refers to the amount of government debt the market is being asked to absorb relative to corporate demands. Inflation represents the discount on future purchasing power of principal and interest and is estimated on the basis of the experience of recent years. Expectations, finally, refers to the customary continuity of the financial markets—interest rates of immediately preceding periods influence those of the current period.

It is worthy of special note that the relative explanatory power of each preceding theory (that of Keynes, that of Fisher, and flow-of-funds analysis) can now be tested. Thus, for 1954 to 1969 the Feldstein-Eckstein formula suggests that liquidity was the most important explanatory factor in the rise of long-term rates over that period. Inflation was rapidly gaining in relative importance toward the end of that period and was crucial in the decades of the 1970s and 1980s.

Interest rate forecasting remains in a fairly primitive state despite immense statistical work. The key problem is that for any very short period ahead extraneous factors can upset the average past relationships which are the basis of all forecasting equations. In addition, for longer periods ahead the coefficients of the independent variables may change substantially, depending on actual experience with these explanatory variables in the meantime—i.e., the accuracy of the interest rate forecast depends on a correct forecast of the independent variables that determine the predicted result for the dependent variable. For example, any forecast of short-term interest rates depends on a current appraisal of the likely course of monetary policy (liquidity), which is known not to be mathematically predictable. (For the same reason, the information content of interest rate futures is dubious.) Yet monetary policy functions within reliably known parameters—toward real economic growth, against inflation and disorderly financial markets. Hence, the forecaster is driven back to an attempt to integrate interest rates with a full-fledged model of the economy as a whole, which complicates the statistical task and multiplies the potential errors.

References

Feldstein, Martin S., and Otto Eckstein, "The Fundamental Determinants of the Interest Rate," *Review of Economics and Statistics,* vol. 52, November 1970, pp. 363–375; Homer, Sidney, *A History of Interest Rates,* 2d ed., Rutgers University Press, New Brunswick, N.J., 1977; Kaufman, Henry, *Interest Rates, the Markets, and the New Financial World,* Times Books, New York, 1986; Kohn, Donald L., "Policy Targets and Operating Procedures in the 1990s," *Monetary Policy Issues in the 1990s,* Symposium, Federal Reserve Bank of Kansas City, 1989; Levi, Maurice D., and John H. Makin, "Fisher, Phillips, Friedman and the Measured Impact of Inflation on Interest," *Journal of Finance,* vol. 34, no. 1, March 1979, pp. 35–53.

(*See also* Business credit; Consumer credit; Credit, an overview; Debt; Disintermediation; Interest, economic theory of; Keynesian economics; Mortgage credit; Yield curve)

Francis H. Schott

Interindustry analysis (*see* Input-output analysis)

International Bank for Reconstruction and Development (*see* World Bank)

International economics, an overview

International economics adds an essential global dimension to traditional domestic economic analysis concerning how individuals, families, and organizations balance their expanding needs and wants against the limited resources available to satisfy them.

The peoples of the nations of the world continually seek to supplement and maximize their welfare by a wide variety of interactions and exchanges across boundaries. Differences in aspirations; human, natural, and capital resources; technology; culture; social and political systems; and other factors are always apparent and lay the foundation for mutually advantageous economic relationships and conflicts.

With modern communications, the world is increasingly better informed on what is occurring beyond political borders. This fact alone is a powerful irresistible force for greater internationalization in the years ahead. Now riding on this tide is a wave of democracy and market orientation.

How Nations Are Classified

Nations have been long classified into groups that indicate their economic strengths and weaknesses as well as their stage of development.

Industrial or developed nations are those that have achieved substantial manufacturing and service capability in addition to advanced techniques in agriculture and raw material extraction.

Developing nations are usually those whose production sector is dominated by agriculture and mineral resources and are in the process of building up or modernizing industrial capacity. Typically, these sectors not only serve home markets but also produce for exports. The objective is to try to earn funds from selling abroad in order to have buying power available for future purchases of foreign goods and services. Also, the aim can be to reduce dependence upon foreigners, i.e., to pursue import substitution policies. To achieve a reasonable balance between international payments and revenues is a constant challenge.

Much attention in international economic and political affairs understandably focuses on the welfare gap between the developed and developing nations. Comparisons are frequently made among countries using such measures of economic progress and competitive strength as cultivated land area, population, per capita income and wealth, unit labor costs, prices, external debt, and monetary reserves.

For several decades the leading Western, free (noncommunist) industrial nations have been referred to as the First World. The Second World has encompassed the socialist-communist nations. But more and more, these Second World nations and states are being included as developing countries as they adopt more market-oriented democratic principles. The Third World has covered developing countries. There is some reference to the resource-poor nations in the Third World group as the Fourth World.

Most of the trade of the world occurs between the industrialized countries. The remaining nations strive to strengthen their economies by trade, barter, aid, and concessions from the major developed nations. The petroleum-rich countries, particularly the Organization of Petroleum Exporting Countries (OPEC), control much of the world's immediately available energy resources which the industrial nations need in order to keep their economies functioning.

The emerging countries with resources and expanding industrial capability, e.g., Singapore, South Korea, Hong Kong, and Taiwan, are more and more called the new industrial countries (NICs or "Tigers"). Thailand, Malaysia, Mexico, and Chile are moving toward the same status.

The generalization is often made that most of the richer nations are located in the Northern Hemisphere and the poorer nations in the Southern Hemisphere. This has given rise to the expression "North/South" in reference to many international problems, confrontations, and dialogues. East/West has also been used to describe similar problem relations among nations, but with diminishing intensity as political and economic tensions have eased between communist and capitalist countries.

International Economic Theory

International economic theorists have developed three important theoretical conclusions:

1. The theory of comparative advantage states that mutually advantageous trade will always be possible because trade patterns will be based on relative prices rather than absolute prices. That is, no one country can have a comparative advantage in all commodities. As initially formulated, the theory of comparative advantage is based on labor-cost differentials. Later researchers have shown that both supply and demand factors play a role in determining the relative prices of commodities that form the basis for mutually advantageous exchange.

2. The Heckscher-Ohlin theory states that a country will tend to export the commodity that uses relatively more of the factor of production that is relatively most abundant in that country. The theory assumes that countries have different quantities of the various factors of production such as land, labor, and capital, but have identical production functions.

3. The factor-price equalization theory states that under absolutely free international trade, not only the prices of the traded products but also the prices of the factors of production (inputs) such as land, labor, and capital will be equalized among countries.

Official International Organizations

Many official international bodies have been formed through the years to facilitate trade and to solve pressing problems, for example: (1) to provide a means for discussing and addressing grievances among nations, e.g., the United Nations; (2) to formulate rules and procedures for commercial and other interactions between countries, e.g., the Organization for Economic Cooperation and Development (OECD), United Nations Commission for Trade and Development (UNCTAD), European Economic Community (EEC); (3) to supervise and monitor global monetary and related affairs, e.g., the International Monetary Fund (IMF); (4) to assist in planning and financing development projects, e.g., the International Bank for Reconstruction and Development (World Bank); and (5) to offer direct aid, e.g., as offered by various regional development banks around the world.

In addition, important unofficial or quasi-official organizations have emerged to supplement global discussions, particularly with private-sector perspective and participation, e.g., the International Chamber of Commerce, Pacific Economic Cooperation Conference (PECC), and Trilateral Commission.

Few nations are willing to give up much of their sovereignty and accede to direction in their economic affairs from the outside, unless they see offsetting gains or have no other choice. The poorer nations generally look to international organizations for direct assistance and also tend to seek redistribution of global wealth and technology from the economically stronger nations.

Efforts to achieve more global coordination in economic and related policies among major nations are slowly progressing.

Ideological differences among nations are always evident in economic policies and actions and affect participation in world organizations and agreements. Basic disagreements have been most evident in the extent to which market forces are encouraged and permitted to operate. The socialist-communist nations for decades isolated themselves from global economic markets and sought to control their domestic markets by regulatory edict. Eventually this approach failed, and market forces have been allowed to function, but not without serious transitional adjustments. The Western industrial nations vary in the permitted freedom of markets, but the degree of freedom is now substantially greater and deeper rooted.

Developing nations with natural resources or commodities to sell usually strive for international agreements—sometimes in the form of cartels such as OPEC—which aim to moderate price fluctuations (mainly on the down side) and ensure steadily increasing demand and revenues for their goods. Because price stabilization is difficult to achieve in the real dynamic markets of the world, is very expensive in recessionary periods, and is inflationary, many developed countries are reluctant to join in rigid commodity agreements.

Population in many respects determines and foreshadows the world's and each nation's needs and demands for goods, services, and jobs. The more than 5 billion people already living on the earth and the prevailing excess rate of births over deaths indicate that international economic and related questions merit high-priority attention throughout the world if future tensions and conflicts are to be minimized. For developing nations—in particular, for those with large and growing populations—the problem of unemployment poses a constant threat to social and political stability. Massive migration toward lands of greater opportunity may well be a major worldwide phenomenon in the future.

Yet shortages of skilled and experienced workers are appearing as technology accelerates and requires more and better trained persons. Accordingly, a brain drain from one nation to another often occurs as high-caliber specialists are attracted away from their home country.

Many nations achieve recognized comparative advantages, i.e., relative superiority in cost, quality, and service for certain goods, which can benefit many or all nations if such advantages are widely made available. Such advantages, however, can be lost to other competing nations over time. When this happens, or where no comparative advantage exists, demands on domestic governments frequently arise for protection against job losses and sales and profit reductions from foreign-made goods and services. "Dumping" occurs when one nation's products are sold in another's market below cost or the prices that prevail at home.

Protectionism and Free Trade

Protectionism takes many forms. Tariffs or taxes are levied on imports, and nontariff rules, in the form of quotas, quality and labeling standards, and a myriad of other restrictions, tend to keep foreign nations' goods and services out of domestic markets. Subsidies to domestic firms similarly disadvantage foreign competitors although foreign consumers get cheaper goods as a result.

The absence of protectionism is termed free trade, wherein goods and services flow across international boundaries on the primary basis of comparative advantage. Free trade is commonly under attack from protectionists.

The United States and most other countries offer in their laws certain trade preferences favoring some nation's goods and services for economic, political, and social reasons. The best-known U.S. preference is the so-called most-favored nation status. Any nation so qualified by the U.S. Congress is permitted to pay only the lowest level of U.S. tariffs. Nonqualifying nations face stiffer barriers against their goods when they seek to export into the U.S. market. Some element of international prestige is associated with the most-favored nation title.

Tariff and nontariff barriers are the subject of continuing global debate and confrontation. National leaders have constituents who fear foreign inroads into their markets and/or demand special terms and conditions favoring their products over others. Periodically, the principal nations join in detailed and lengthy multilateral negotiations to reduce trade barriers. These are mainly under the aegis of the General Agreement on Tariffs and Trade (GATT). The overriding objective is to try to keep trade as free and open as possible so as to encourage greater world growth, employment, income, and investment. History records many instances where growing protectionism has led to international trade wars and eventually has caused political wars among belligerents.

When multilateral talks falter, bilateral agreements escalate between individual nations. Moreover, when global negotiations stall, there is a strong tendency for groups of nations with common geography and interests to form economic blocs, e.g., the European Economic Community, North American Free Trade Agreement (U.S., Canada, and Mexico), Association of Southeastern Nations, etc. The future role of the United States in global affairs is changing because this nation—despite its superpower status—cannot alone police the world or dominate developments as in the past. Hence, global progress will depend more and more on alliances and "shared leadership."

Few nations can survive for long in economic isolation from the rest of the world simply because political/geographical boundaries do not coincide with the natural resources, skills, and other essentials for the betterment of human welfare. Moreover, in matters of the environment, energy, and water, each nation has an impact on its neighbors and potentially more and more of the world.

World trade and financial flows reflect sharp variances in needs and advantages among individual countries. At any given time some nations will show surpluses in trade and payments balances, while others will experience corresponding deficits.

Balance of trade refers to the relationship of imports to exports of goods and services. Balance of payments is a more comprehensive measure that is defined variously to include financial investment flows of different maturities and purposes. Official or government-to-government payments and receipts also influence importantly changes in economic relationships among countries.

Aggregate surpluses and deficits must balance for the world as a whole. Chronic surpluses or deficits in any single country or region will cause economic and political repercussions and tensions. Surpluses often must be invested outside the nation, while deficits constitute international accounts payable which must be paid from reserves or financed by loans, financial aid from international bodies, or foreign government grants.

Actual measures of economic and financial flows between nations and across the world tend to be weak, with large annual "errors and omissions"; yet these data form the basis for major policy decisions with far-reaching consequences for war or peace.

Foreign Investment and Transnational Corporations

Investment in one country by individuals and organizations from another is an important aspect of international economics. In fact, trade and investment are closely related if not inseparable.

Investment may be for portfolio (i.e., in the form of securities) or direct capital (i.e., productive facilities). Colonialism and imperialism have often been described in terms of powerful nations exploiting the human and natural resources of weaker, less-developed countries. While some exploitation charges still remain, most developing as well as developed nations now substantially control the types, scopes, and ownership terms of investments made by foreigners. Improved living standards, especially in developing nations, are highly dependent upon foreign and domestic investment, trade, and technology.

In present times most foreign investors become active only after political agreements have been made between their own government and that of the nation in which investments are planned.

Much global private investment is made by transnational corporations (TNCs), also widely referred to as multinational corporations (MNCs). Technical distinctions in classifying such global corporations are sometimes made to reflect whether multinational investments and operations are made exclusively by an executive group from one nation or by a combination of different national investment leaders, or by varying degrees of joint public and private ownership. Clearly, these transnational organizations play a major role in world trade and investments because of their demonstrated management skills, technology, financial resources, and related advantages.

MNCs are now a relentless force of internationalism. They blend research, manufacturing, and distribution on a global scale to extract ideas and procedures from national markets and weave them into worldwide goods and services. Moreover, MNC officials become more knowledgeable of cultures and have rising incentives to promote peace.

MNCs, nevertheless, must frequently confront governmental and other critics who contend that such far-flung companies are able to minimize or avoid national regulation by virtue of their ability to shift new (and at times old) investments from one country to another. Some governments have adopted exacting rules that MNCs must follow in their countries, the most common of which requires a majority or significant minority of domestic as opposed to foreign ownership. Specific "national content" minimum standards are often required in goods produced by foreign-owned or -controlled companies.

Developing nations in particular face some dilemma in formulating policies covering investments by foreigners. They usually have an urgent need for foreign investment assistance, but domestic political considerations can dictate severe tax and other laws, including nationalization, which discourage new foreign investment. Many developing nations have been successful, however, in providing attractive tax and other incentives to foreign investors for sufficient time periods to ensure a satisfactory return on the original investment.

Crucial dimensions of foreign investments include intellectual property and technology transfer, not only at the outset of an investment but also subsequently to ensure that the facilities remain competitive. The question of whether or not such technology transfer is a matter of international right of developing countries, and what price, if any, is to be paid for it, is a source of intensive international debate.

Taxes clearly have an appreciable impact on international flows of funds, trade, and investment. Tax treaties exist between many, but by no means all, nations. Accordingly, the final payment or return to an international seller or investor can be sharply affected by the nature and level of taxes, the extent to which reciprocal tax offsets are permitted between nations, and the prospect for changes in taxes.

International Banking and Financial System

London, New York, Frankfurt, Tokyo, Singapore, Hong Kong, and many other global cities constitute important financial centers which, linked by almost instant communications, enable nations and the overall world economy to function around the clock to serve people.

The global money system continues to be dominated by the U.S. dollar. The German mark, Japanese yen, and Swiss franc are also key currencies. A number of other money units play important roles in specific regional markets. The European currency unit (ECU) is gaining recognition. The physical transfer of actual paper money, coins, gold and silver bullion, and traveler's checks among nations is small compared with the massive volume of credit, deposits, foreign exchange, and investment funds moving daily across boundaries.

Each national currency necessarily has a value for international exchange purposes. A host of developments, including economic and political news and confidence, will influence the value of a currency. Through time, economic performance, reserves, and the relative rate of inflation seem to be among the most important determinants of value.

Economic theory can again provide some perspective. The purchasing power parity theory on exchange rate determination states that changes in exchange rates will tend to reflect the changes in the relative price levels in the different countries. That is, a rise in the price level of a country will tend to be offset by a fall of the exchange rate so that the price of the country's export and import commodities will remain the same in world markets. The theory is supported by much empirical evidence in the long run, but has not proved to be a highly reliable guide for short-term fluctuations.

An elaborate global system of foreign exchange trading provides the mechanism by which individual currency values are continually determined for transaction purposes. Ordinarily, governments will intervene through purchases or sales in foreign exchange markets to seek to stabilize the value of their currency. Collective intervention is also undertaken from time to time by major nations, especially the Group of Seven (G-7): the United States, the United Kingdom, Germany, France, Canada, Japan, and Italy.

A fixed exchange policy prevails when a currency is linked to some monetary standard and its value remains unchanged within narrow limits except for a major shift in underlying conditions. Whenever a change in value is made, it occurs by official government action and may be either a devaluation, i.e., loss in value, or a revaluation, i.e., gain in value.

A floating exchange policy means in principle that the value of a currency will fluctuate with changing market conditions. A "free" float indicates little or no government intervention, while a "dirty" float describes the situation in which significant government intervention occurs from time to time but considerable variation in the value of the currency nevertheless persists. A "crawling peg" refers to a system of fairly regular or automatic adjustments in the exchange rate of a country.

A translation gain or loss occurs from currency-value changes being applied to accounting statements of assets and liabilities of business firms.

International Reserves and Monetary Supervision

The financial reserves of each nation are a measure of strength used by international leaders and investors in judging risks. "Hard" currencies are usually in strong demand and backed by substantial reserves and general economic strength, while "soft" currencies lack these attributes. Capital resources are more and more accepted as the fundamental indicator of economic and financial power of financial and commercial organizations. Capital stringencies loom as a persistent problem in the years ahead.

Major international lenders and investors as well as official institutions use various types of risk measures to evaluate the economic and financial strength of the countries of the world. Transfer risk concerns the prospect for being able to repatriate collected funds from the borrowing country. Credit risk pertains to the ability of the borrower to fulfill the repayment terms of the original loan agreement.

Financial reserves usually include U.S. dollars, other key currencies, special drawing rights (SDRs) issued by the IMF, and gold. In recent years the official IMF policy has been to deemphasize gold as too inflexible a reserve for dynamic global monetary and economic purposes, but the use of gold persists. SDRs are based on a basket of currencies and are made available to IMF members by allocation from time to time to provide additional liquidity for the international monetary system. SDRs, however, are restricted to government-to-government use.

The IMF offers financial assistance to member nations who confront balance of payments difficulties. Its economic and currency surveillance and conditions vary directly with the progress and prospects for improved economic and financial stability of the country applying for support.

The central, or government policy-level, banks—e.g., the Federal Reserve in the United States, the Deutsche Bundesbank in Germany, the Bank of Japan, and the Bank of England—are primarily responsible for the overall direction and function of domestic monetary policy and operations, and supervise related international activities as well. The central banks of the leading Western nations generally work closely to improve the global monetary system, and to conduct varying degrees of coordinated currency-support actions in times of severe market fluctuations.

The IMF serves in many respects as a lender of last resort to central banks.

The former socialist-communist nations are becoming more involved in world trade and finance in order to achieve their economic growth and welfare goals.

Fundamental changes are taking place in the global financial system. This is because of excess institutional capacity, heavy private and governmental debt problems, inadequate capital at a time when regulatory capital requirements are increasing, technology, speculation, deregulation, privatization, statutory revisions altering competition, entry of former communist nations into world markets and international economic and financial organizations, and a host of other developments.

Personal Involvement in International Economics

Many individuals become directly involved in international economics as tourists and students abroad. They quickly learn differences in cultures, currencies, prices, economic standards, laws, and many other matters. Most important, they sense differences in relative values of the goods and services available. Such experiences reinforce the need for ongoing firsthand exchanges which are essential to improve human relations and welfare on a global scale.

The widely acknowledged growing interdependence of nations virtually assures that international economics will continue to receive increasing attention in all countries. The greatest challenge facing the peoples of the world is to keep the global economic, social, financial, and political systems operative through all periods of growth, recession, inflation, currency fluctuations, shortages, and surpluses.

References

Bank for International Settlements, *59th Annual Report*, Basle, June 12, 1989; Business Roundtable, *American Excellence in a World Economy*, Business Roundtable, New York, 1987; Kahn, Herman, *World Economic Development*, Westview Press, Boulder, Colo., 1979; Kahn, Herman, *The Coming Boom*, Simon & Schuster, New York, 1982; Kaufman, Henry, *Interest Rates, the Markets, and the New Financial World*, Times Books, New York, 1986; Krueger, Anne O, "Prospects for Liberalizing the International Trading System," Working Paper 2409, National Bureau of Economic Research, Cambridge, Mass., October 1987; Leveson, Irving, *American Challenges—Business and Government in the World of the 1990s*, Praeger, Westport, Conn., 1991; World Bank, *World Development Report*, Washington, D.C., annually.

(*See also* Balance of international payments; Balance of international trade; Barriers to trade; Bretton Woods Conference; Cartel; Comparative advantage theory; Dumping; Eurodollar market; European Community; Exports; Foreign direct investment; Foreign exchange rates; General Agreement on Tariffs and Trade; Infrastructure; International investment position; International Monetary Fund; Liquidity international; Multinational corporation; Organization for Economic Cooperation and Development; Protectionism; Smithsonian Agreement; Special drawing rights; Stages theory of economic development; Subsidies; Technology; Value of the dollar; World Bank)

Walter E. Hoadley

International investment position

The international investment position of a country is usually defined as the difference between values of (1) the assets held abroad by its residents and (2) the liabilities of domestic residents to foreign residents and of foreign investments in the equities of domestic enterprises or in domestic property.

The compilations of the international investment position of a country are frequently assumed to be comparable, and to have functions similar, to balance sheets of business enterprises. There are important differences, however.

The balance sheets of private enterprises may be used by current or prospective lenders to, or investors in, these enterprises to evaluate the risks associated with these investments and with the receipts of incomes derived from them.

The potential use of the compilations of the international investment position of a country for these purposes is very limited, however, because the assets and liabilities reported in these compilations are not linked in the same manner as in the balance sheets of private enterprises and thus do not assist foreign investors in evaluating the risk associated with specific investments. The compilations may, however, help foreign investors to evaluate risks that affect the receipt of their claims in the currency they expect. The compilations show assets in international trading currencies and other international reserves held by the monetary authorities and banks of the country, which may be compared with the country's liabilities. Such comparisons indicate the foreign exchange resources of the monetary authorities and banks that would be available to convert the payments of outstanding liabilities by domestic residents in the domestic currency into the currency required by foreign creditors. There is always a question, however, whether other uses of these assets for other purposes have higher priorities.

The balance sheet of private enterprises also serves the purpose of measuring the equity of their owners. The compilation of the international investment position does not measure the wealth of residents of a country, although it is sometimes assumed to do so. The international investment position is usually only a small part of the aggregate wealth, most of which consists of the assets held by domestic residents within their country.

A major problem in the compilations of the international investment position, as well as the national balance sheet, is the method used in the valuation of its assets, both those located abroad and those within its territory, and of the assets held by foreign residents in the country including all claims against domestic residents. In the compilations of balance sheets for private enterprises the use of acquisition prices based on bookkeeping records is preferred over market values, which have to be estimated. In periods of rising prices this reduces the valuation of assets below their market value and has an equal effect on the valuation of the owners' equity.

A Rising Negative Balance in U.S. International Investment Position

In the United States, the Bureau of Economic Analysis (BEA) has published for many years compilations of the international investment position. Most of the data used in these compilations are based on reports by U.S. financial and nonfinancial enterprises and government agencies, which are based on their financial records and thus represent book values. Only for domestic holdings of foreign long-term securities and for foreign holdings of domestic long-term securities are market values estimated. These compilations showed a peak of net assets in 1981 and a declining trend thereafter, with foreign assets in the United States overtaking U.S. assets abroad in 1985 and this negative balance continuing to rise in subsequent years. This declining trend in the international investment position, as measured in these compilations, reflected mainly the cumulative effects of the rise in capital inflows relative to capital outflows reported in the compilations of the balance on international transactions.

Perhaps concerned with the repercussions of the statistics showing the rising negative balance in the U.S. international investment position, several economists developed alternative measures of the investment position that substantially raised the values of the assets and thus derived a large positive net position. The changes were obtained mainly by revaluing U.S. direct investments abroad and official gold holdings from book to estimated market values.

In 1991, the BEA, after an intensive study, produced two estimates of the values of U.S. direct investments abroad and of foreign direct investments in the United States. One estimate included a revaluation of the equity of U.S. direct investments in foreign affiliates and of foreign investments in U.S. affiliates by revaluing tangible assets and land from historic acquisition to current prices, and also by revaluating the officially held gold stock to current prices. The second estimate included an attempt to revalue the equity in direct investments to market values.

The new estimates by the Department of Commerce show that the net international investment position at the end of 1990 based on the first of these valuation concepts was negative by $440 billion, and the net position based on the second concept was negative by about $290 billion. Although these negative figures are smaller than those based on book values, the descending trends are nearly parallel.

Both of the new series are subject to estimating difficulties. Data used to indicate changes in prices for equipment and structures purchased by the foreign affiliates of U.S. corporations may not be quite adequate. Market price estimates for equities held by U.S. corporations in their foreign affiliates, based on general stock market prices in the countries where the affiliates are located, do not necessarily reflect potential effects of differences in management of U.S.-owned and foreign-owned firms on the market values of their equities, nor do they reflect the industrial distribution of the affiliates. Furthermore, the position based on market price is subject to changes in stock market prices, and thus is not a stable indicator of the country's international investment position.

The current cost valuation estimates are intended to be consistent with the valuation principles used in measuring the aggregate net assets, or wealth, held by domestic residents. Thus they would facilitate an analysis of the levels and changes of the international investments in the broader frame of the aggregate national investment position.

References

Eisner, Robert, and Paul J. Pieper, "The World's Greatest Debtor Nation?" in *The North American Review of Economics and Finance,* vol. 1, no. 1, JAI Press, Greenwich, Conn., 1990; Landefeld, J. Steven, and Ann M. Lawson, "Valuation of the U.S. Net International Investment Position," in *Survey of Current Business,* U.S. Department of Commerce, Bureau of Economic Analysis, May 1991; Scholl, Russell B., "The International Investment Position of the United States in 1990," in *Survey of Current Business,* June 1991; Ulan, Michael, and William G. Dewald, "The U.S. Net International Investment Position: Misstated and Misunderstood," in James A. Dorn and William A. Niskanen (eds.), *Dollars, Deficits, and Trade,* Kluwer Academic Publishers, Norwell, Mass., for the Cato Institute, 1989.

(*See also* Foreign direct investment)

Walther Lederer

International Monetary Fund

The purpose of the International Monetary Fund (IMF) is to promote international monetary cooperation through a permanent institution that provides the machinery for consultation and collaboration on international monetary problems. Specifically, the function of the IMF is to facilitate the expansion and balanced growth of international trade, to promote orderly and stable foreign currency exchange markets, and to contribute to balance of payments adjustment. To further these objectives, the IMF monitors members' macroeconomic policies, makes financial resources available to them in times of balance of payments difficulties, and provides them with technical assistance in a number of areas.

Much of the IMF's work is centered on annual consultations with each member country to ensure that its national policies in the area of economic growth, price stability, financial conditions, and exchange rates take into account their consequences for the world economy and avoid unfair exchange policies. To ensure compliance with these basic tenets, the Fund is empowered to exercise firm surveillance over the exchange rate policies of member countries.

History

The IMF's charter, embodied in the Articles of Agreement, was agreed upon at the International Monetary and Financial Conference held at Bretton Woods, New Hampshire, in July 1944. In December 1945 the required number of countries had ratified the agreements, and in March 1946 the first meeting of the Board of Governors was held. The IMF commenced operations on March 1, 1947, at its headquarters in Washington, D.C.

Other milestones in the history of the IMF include:

May 1948, first drawing of foreign exchange by a member country

January 1962, adoption of the general agreements to borrow (GAB), which constituted an important supplement to the IMF's financial resources

February 1963, establishment of the compensatory financing facility, designed to assist countries that experience a temporary shortfall in export earnings

June 1969, inception of the buffer stock financing facility, which can be used to finance commodity stockpiles

July 1969, adoption of the first amendment to the Articles of Agreement, providing for the allocation of special drawing rights (SDRs) to member countries, with the first allocation of SDRs made on January 1, 1970

September 1974, implementation of the extended fund facility, which provides medium-term assistance to member countries seeking to overcome structural balance of payments problems

April 1975, establishment of an oil facility to help oil-importing countries finance the increase in petroleum prices

February 1976, establishment of the Trust Fund, funded by revenues from gold sales, to aid developing countries with low-interest assistance

August 1977, establishment of the supplementary financing facility to make additional resources available to member countries requiring balance of payments financing in larger amounts and for longer periods

April 1978, adoption of the second amendment to the articles providing for liberalized exchange arrangements, the legalization of floating exchange rates, steps designed to eliminate the role of gold in the international monetary system, and enunciation of the goal to make the SDR the central international monetary reserve asset

March 1986, establishment of a structural adjustment facility to provide balance of payments assistance to qualifying members in support of macroeconomic and structural adjustment programs

December 1987, the establishment of the Enhanced Structural Adjustment Trust to provide loans on concessional terms to eligible members to support programs to strengthen substantially and in a sustainable manner their balance of payment position

August 1988, expansion of the compensatory financing facility to include a contingency financing element under which additional financing may be provided to support adjustment programs that might be thrown off track by adverse exogenous developments

Structure

As of December 1991 the IMF was composed of 156 member countries; in addition, a number of republics of the former U.S.S.R. are in the process of joining the organization. Each member is represented by a governor on the IMF's Board of Governors, most of whom are ministers of finance, presidents of the country's central bank, or persons of similar rank. Virtually all day-to-day policy decisions are delegated to the Executive Board, which is made up of 22 representatives of the member countries. The Executive Board is presided over by the managing director, elected for a 5-year term, who is also chief of staff of the IMF.

Each member has a quota which is based on a complex formula that takes account of the country's size and its general importance in world trade and finance. The quota determines the amount of financial resources the member has to make available to the IMF (subscription) and its access to the Fund's facilities, its entitlement to SDR allocations, as well as its voting power. Part of each member's subscription is paid in reserve assets, and the remainder in the member's own currency.

Operations

IMF member countries may utilize the Fund's resources if they find themselves in balance of payments difficulties. Drawings normally will be in the context of policy measures—an adjustment program—intended to correct the balance of payments position and are linked to progress under that program. Technically, use of the Fund's resources takes the form of a member using its own currency to purchase other currencies (or SDRs) held by the IMF. Drawings on the Fund's resources that do not exceed 25 percent of the member's quota normally require that the member make a reasonable effort to overcome its balance of payments problem. Purchases beyond that amount—i.e., drawings in the so-called upper credit tranches—usually are made in the context of an adjustment program. Repayments to the IMF are normally to be made within 3 to 5 years, but under the extended facility the country may have up to 10 years to repay the financing provided by the Fund.

References

de Vries, M. G., *The International Monetary Fund, 1966–1971: The System under Stress;* vol. I, International Monetary Fund, Washington, D.C., 1976; de Vries, M. G., *The International Monetary Fund, 1972–1978: Cooperation under Trial,* vols. I, II, International Monetary Fund, Washington, D.C., 1985; *Financial Organization and Operations of the IMF,* Pamphlet no. 45, 2d ed., International Monetary Fund, Washington, D.C., 1991; Horsefield, T. K., *The International Monetary Fund, 1945–1965: Twenty Years of Cooperation,* vols. I, II, International Monetary Fund, Washington, D.C., 1976.

(*See also* Bretton Woods Conference; Foreign exchange rates; Gold standard; Less-developed country debt; Smithsonian Agreement; Special drawing rights)

H. Robert Heller and Günter Wittich

International payments balance (*see* Balance of international payments)

International trade balance (*see* Balance of international trade)

Investment function

An investment function is the relation between the acquisition of capital and a set of explanatory variables. Capital is defined as buildings, equipment and inventories, and sometimes intangibles, such as knowledge and technique, which are both outputs of the productive process and inputs to future production.

In private-enterprise economies such as the United States, investment is characterized as gross private domestic investment, that is, residential housing construction and business acquisition of new industrial plants, of machinery and equipment, and of additional inventory. Most work on estimating investment functions in recent years has been on a disaggregative rather than an aggregative basis. Thus, estimates of investment functions have been made separately for plant or structures, for equipment, for inventory investment, and for residential housing construction; or for various sectors of the economy, such as manufacturing, utilities, railroads, and commerce. There have also been attempts to estimate investment functions for individual firms.

In the classical economic tradition and in its Marxian branch there is the notion that business profits are entirely or partly accumulated as capital investment. Thus, investment becomes a function of profits. The more profits there are, the more investment there is.

Since capital accumulation appeared to contribute to greater productivity and economic growth, this view of the investment function seemed to many an appropriate justification both for having a profits system and for having a large share of national income going to profits.

To Marx, the profits-investment relation held the seeds of serious contradiction. As profits and the competitive striving for growth and lower costs brought on more capital accumulation or investment, the economy became periodically and increasingly plagued by crises of excessive capital and a falling rate of profit and underconsumption which left insufficient demand for products of additional capital.

Keynes' Ideas

These ideas about profits and investment were developed by John Maynard Keynes in *The General Theory of Employment, Interest and Money* (1936). Keynes emphasized that, whatever the contribution of investment to economic growth, investment was an essential component of the total effective demand which determined the rate of output and, hence, of employment in the economy. And to Keynes, there was no assurance that the total aggregate effective demand coming from consumption and investment would be sufficient to stimulate enough production to use all of the labor services that would be supplied at full employment. Hence, an insufficiency of investment demand, as well as of consumption demand, was viewed in the Keynesian system as a prime cause of both cyclical and chronic underemployment. The investment function projected by Keynes, borrowing from the American economist Irving Fisher, made investment depend upon its marginal efficiency or gross profitability. This depended upon the expected returns from investment and its cost or supply price. And the profitability or marginal efficiency in turn must be related to the financial cost of investment or the rate of interest. Thus, firms would invest in additional plant, equipment, or inventories only as long as the rate of return on each unit of investment exceeded the rate of interest, or only as long as the present discounted value of expected future returns, that is, the demand price of capital goods, exceeded or was at least equal to the supply price or cost.

A direct application of this formulation is to be found in James Tobin's "Q model" of investment. Tobin's Q is the ratio of an index of the value of capital taken from stock market quotations, presumed to be a measure of demand price or the value of expected future returns from capital, to an index of the replacement cost of capital, taken to be a measure of the supply price. To the extent that the ratio is greater than 1, firms will find it most advantageous to construct new capital, that is, invest. To the extent that the ratio is less than 1, purchase of existing firms to acquire existing capital would be cheaper than constructing new capital, and investment would not be indicated.

The Q model has the great virtue of offering a market measure of otherwise unobservable expected profits in the form of their present value. It has presented great difficulties in empirical application, however, due to problems relating to tax considerations, distinctions between the valuation of firms and the prices of the few shares traded at any one time, and the fact that the stock market valuations reflect much more than the physical capital that would be included in the traditional measures of investment.

Development of Investment Functions

It is important to note the essential difference between indicating that investment depends upon profits and asserting that investment depends upon its expected profitability. That investment is determined by and may be explained by profits has simple and long-standing appeal. Yet this view may be considered a negation of the rational underpinning of the profit system in the United States. If enterprises repeatedly reinvest their profits without regard to the investment's profitability, the conditions for optimal, long-run utilization of resources are defied. Profits earned in the past should not automatically be reinvested. Presumably they are not if a profit system is functioning efficiently.

Acceptance of the notion that investment depends upon its expected profitability opens the way to systematic construction of investment functions, but leaves open serious problems in their specific estimation. A key word here is "expected." Expected profitability relates to expected returns or expected cost savings, which in turn will depend upon how additional capital will contribute to output: the role of capital in the production function. Expected profitability will also depend upon current and expected prices of capital goods and other possible inputs to production.

And it will depend upon the demand for the product of capital: quantities; prices; and slopes, or elasticities, of demand curves.

Since investment is the acquisition of additional capital, and the amount or rate of investment is the rate of speed at which additional capital is acquired, or, in mathematical terms, the derivative of capital with respect to time, investment will also depend upon the capacity in the capital goods industries and the relative costs of acquiring capital more or less rapidly. Both because the expectations that determine investment may be formed gradually and because the costs of investing all at once—building a new factory in an hour—are prohibitive, responses of investment to its determinants are distributed over time.

In principle, the past is irrelevant and the only current data relevant to investment decisions are the amounts and capabilities of the already existing capital stock and the prices of capital goods and their associated current financial costs. In practice, we use a variety of past and present proxy variables for the generally absent information for the essential expectations of the future.

Investment may be viewed as the acquisition of capital for replacement, including modernization, and for expansion. The rate of investment will then depend upon the rate at which existing capital is replaced and the expectation of increases in future demand. It will also depend upon the desired capital-output or capital-labor ratios, which will in turn relate to technological factors (that is, the production function) and relative prices of capital and labor.

A meaningful price of capital would involve the initial cost or supply price of the capital goods being purchased, the expected rate of depreciation or wearing out or replacement requirements of the capital to be acquired, the interest or financial cost of the funds invested in the capital, and any expected capital loss due to changing prices of capital goods. These elements, along with relevant tax parameters, have been incorporated by Dale W. Jorgenson (1963) into a "rental price of capital," which plays a key role in a neoclassical investment function widely estimated in recent years. The lower the rental price of capital, the greater the capital stock that firms would find optimal or would desire in order to produce any given rate of output or to increase output by any given amount. The greater the expected output, the greater will be the demand for capital; moveover, the greater the increases in expected output, the greater will be investment.

This leads finally to a general formulation of an investment function in which the rate of investment (1) depends upon past changes in demand, sales, or output, which presumably generate changed expectations of future demand, sales, and output, and (2) also depends upon past changes in the rental price of capital, which generate changes in the desired and effected capital-output ratio. We thus have a distributed-lag function in which investment is related positively to past, current, and, to the extent they are known, expected future changes in sales or output and changes in the rental price of capital.

Controversy Continues

Many empirical or econometric studies attempted to estimate some or all of the parameters of investment functions in these terms. Results have varied, and controversy continues as to the relative importance of different variables as well as to the lags in response.

There has been fairly widespread agreement that changes in demand are critically related to investment. In accordance with sophisticated modern versions of the acceleration principle, the rate of investment is found to depend upon the acceleration of the rate of output or general demand. Thus, past growth in sales or output generates investment. Faster growth generates more investment; slower growth a decline in investment. Empirical studies confirm clearly that investment is related to past changes in sales or output. The lags in response can be substantial, however, with some investment related to changes in sales of the previous few quarters but significant amounts related to changes of the previous year or two or even, in some studies, to changes dating as far back as 7 years. And since it is ultimately expected future demand that is important, the lags or the relative magnitude of effects due to past changes apparently depends upon the varying relation between past changes and expectations of the future.

In Jorgenson's original neoclassical formulation, the rental price of capital was assumed to have a powerful effect (stemming from certain stipulations about the production function, perfect competition, and, implicitly, expectations). On the basis of this assumption, particularly powerful effects were predicted for changes in tax parameters, such as accelerated depreciation for tax purposes and the investment tax credit, as well as changes in interest rates that might be induced by monetary policies.

Considerable further work (by Eisner and others) has cast doubt on the magnitude of such substitution effects induced by changes in the rental price of capital and the monetary and tax policies that would bring them about. These relate in part to the fact that reductions in the price of capital will bring on more investment only as existing capital gradually requires replacement. And numerical estimates have raised doubt about the underlying elasticity of substitution of capital and, hence, of the response of investment to changes in the price of capital, at least in the short run.

Application of the acceleration principle, relating investment to changes in the rate of output and to the pressure of demand on capacity, has been complicated by the implication of notions of permanent income for investment. This suggests that changes in demand which are deemed essentially transitory will have little or no effect upon investment, and only to the extent that such changes are viewed as permanent will investment be affected.

While investment functions discussed here have most direct relevance to investment by business firms, similar considerations may be present for all economic units, including households, nonprofit institutions, and governments, to the extent that they are attempting to decide upon optimal rates of investment in all kinds of capital. Ultimately, investment is viewed as a function of its expected profitability or contributions to value and net worth, dependent in turn upon expected or projected demand or output; relative prices of capital and other inputs; rates of discount, or future expected returns, which are likely to be increased by higher perceptions of risk; and costs of adjustment and of obtaining information.

References

Ackley, Gardner, *Macroeconomics: Theory and Policy,* Macmillan, New York, 1978, especially pp. 607–667; Chirinko, Robert S., and Robert Eisner, "Tax Policy and Investment in Major U.S., Macroeconomic Econometric Models," *Journal of Public Economics,* vol. 20, no. 2, 1983, pp. 139–166; Eisner, Robert, "Econometric Studies of Investment Behavior: A Comment," *Economic Inquiry,* Journal of the Western Economic Association, March 1974, pp. 91–104; Eisner, Robert, and R. H. Strotz, "Determinants of Business Investment," in Commission on Money and Credit,

Impacts of Monetary Policy, Prentice-Hall, Englewood Cliffs, N.J., 1964, pp. 59–223; Jorgenson, D. W., "Capital Theory and Investment Behavior," *American Economic Review,* vol. 53, no. 2, May 1963, pp. 247–259, reprinted in L. R. Klein and R. A. Gordon (eds.), *Readings in Business Cycles,* Irwin, Homewood, Ill., 1965, pp. 366–378; Keynes, John Maynard, *The General Theory of Employment, Interest and Money,* Harcourt Brace Jovanovich, New York, 1936, especially pp. 135–164; Tobin, James, and William Brainard, "Asset Markets and the Cost of Capital," in Bela Belassa and Richard Nelson (eds.), *Economic Progress, Private Values and Public Policy: Essays in Honor of William Fellner,* North-Holland, Amsterdam, 1977.

(*See also* Business investment in new plants and equipment; Capital formation)

Robert Eisner

IS-LM model

The *IS-LM* model is a standard representation of the Keynesian system in a form that is particularly suitable for comparative static analysis. Two curves (the *IS* and *LM* curves) are obtained whose intersection determines the equilibrium income and interest rate in the economy. The apparatus is particularly useful as a means of examining the effects of changes in underlying conditions which shift one or the other of the curves, but not both.

The *IS* curve is the graph of the equation that defines all combinations of income and interest rate for which the goods market is in equilibrium. This equation is obtained by substitution of the goods-market equations to obtain a single equation in income and interest rate, taking as given certain conditions such as the levels of government expenditures, taxes, the capital stock, and the state of expectations. Similarly, the money demand and supply equations are solved to obtain a single equation in income and the interest rate, graphed as the *LM* curve, in which certain conditions such as the nominal quantity of money or base money and the price level are taken as given. The equilibrium income and interest rate are determined by the intersection of the (normally) downward-sloping *IS* curve and (normally) upward-sloping *LM* curve. This equilibrium is the only combination of income and the interest rate for which the goods market and the money market can be simultaneously in equilibrium.

A change in the underlying conditions will shift the *IS* or *LM* curve, or both, and so change the equilibrium combination of income and the interest rate. Standard results, for example, are that an increase in government expenditures (or any other factor that increases aggregate expenditures at the original equilibrium income and interest rate) will shift the *IS* curve to the right and, therefore, increase both income and the interest rate. Also, an increase in the nominal supply of money (or any other factor that would create an excess of supply of money at the original equilibrium income and interest rate) will shift the *LM* curve to the right and so increase income but reduce interest rates. Just as with supply and demand analysis, ambiguity may arise when a problem implies simultaneous shifts in both curves.

The *IS-LM* model was first proposed by John Hicks (1937) as an exposition of the central argument of John Maynard Keynes' *General Theory* (1936). It was widely popularized by Alvin Hansen (1953) and refined by Don Patinkin (1956). In the 1960s and at least early 1970s, it was the standard tool of most macroeconomic analysis. A lengthy presentation can be found in T. F. Dernburg and D. M. McDougall (1976), and a compact presentation can be found in M. R. Darby (1979).

In recent years, the *IS-LM* model has lost much of its dominance as a tool of macroeconomic analysis. In part, this reflects the increased importance of problems and conditions which involve simultaneous shifts in both the *IS* and *LM* curves. More significant has been new interest in dynamic problems of how the economy adjusts over time to a change in underlying conditions. The *IS-LM* model can be used in a sequential short-period analysis which takes account of shifts in the *IS* and *LM* curves due to changes in capital stock, expectations, price level, and money supply, but such analysis is awkward and confusing compared with explicit dynamic macroeconomic models. Nonetheless, the *IS-LM* model remains an important tool for the analysis of problems involving the impact effect of changes in underlying conditions in the goods market.

References

Darby, Michael R., *Intermediate Macroeconomics,* McGraw-Hill, New York, 1979; Dernburg, Thomas F., and Duncan M. McDougall, *Macroeconomics,* 5th ed., McGraw-Hill, New York, 1976; Hansen, Alvin H., *A Guide to Keynes,* McGraw-Hill, New York, 1953; Hicks, John R., "Mr. Keynes and the 'Classics': A Suggested Interpretation," *Econometrica,* vol. 5, April 1937, pp. 147–159; Keynes, John Maynard, *The General Theory of Employment, Interest, and Money,* Macmillan, London, 1936; Patinkin, Don, *Money, Interest and Prices,* Harper & Row, New York, 1956.

(*See also* Keynesian economics; Static analysis)

Michael R. Darby

Isoquant

An isoquant is the locus of all labor-capital quantities that generate a particular output level.

Let production be governed by the one-output, two-output production function

$$q = f(L, K)$$

where q is quantity of output, and L and K are respective quantities of labor and capital input. This function is assumed to be continuous with continuous first- and second-order partial derivatives. Let $q = 100$. The implicit form for the corresponding isoquant is $f(L, K) = 100$.

Families of Isoquants

Three curves from a family of isoquants are pictured in the accompanying figure, in which labor and capital are measured on the axes. Each isoquant has a label specifying the output level to which it corresponds. Since each point in the labor-capital diagram corresponds to some output, each point lies on some isoquant. Since labor and capital increments normally result in output increments, isoquants farther from the origin correspond to higher output levels. Isoquants normally are negatively sloped as pictured in the figure on page 585, since an increment in the quantity of one input with output constant normally implies a decrement in the quantity of the other.

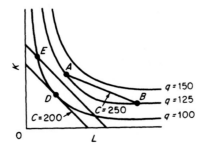

The Rate of Technical Substitution

The slope of an isoquant gives the rate at which one input may be substituted for the other while output is maintained at a constant level. This rate of technical substitution (RTS) is sometimes called the marginal rate of substitution. Differentiating totally the production function gives

$$dq = f_L \, dL + f_K \, dK$$

where f_L and f_K are the partial derivatives of the production function and are called the marginal products of labor and capital, respectively; and dq, dL, and dK are differentials (i.e., changes for the output and input quantities). Let $dq = 0$ to reflect the constant output along an isoquant so that

$$\text{RTS} = -\frac{dK}{dL} = \frac{f_L}{f_K}$$

By this definition the RTS is the negative of the slope of an isoquant and is measured by the ratio of the marginal products of the inputs. It is positive and the isoquant negatively sloped as long as the marginal products of the inputs are positive.

The RTS, which gives quantity of capital per unit of labor, normally is assumed to decrease as the quantity of labor increases relative to the quantity of capital, i.e., as one moves from left to right along an isoquant. A decreasing RTS, which means that $-d^2K/dL^2$ and $d^2K/dL^2 > 0$, corresponds to isoquants with the convex shape pictured in the figure. Consider the line segment connecting points A and B, both of which are on the isoquant for $q = 125$. Convexity means that all points on that line segment between A and B are on isoquants with $q > 125$.

Cost Minimization

The production cost, denoted by C, corresponding to a point in the figure is given by $C = wL + rK$, where w and r are fixed unit prices for labor and capital, respectively. An isocost line is the locus of all input combinations with a specified cost level. The straight lines in the figure above with levels $C = 200$ and $C = 250$ provide examples. If the firm desires to produce 100 units of output, it can produce at any point on the appropriate isoquant. Point E entails a production cost of 250, but is not efficient because other points on the isoquant have lower cost. Point D gives the minimum cost (200) for the production of 100 units. No point on the isoquant lies on a lower isocost line.

The minimum cost of producing an output quantity under usual assumptions is given by a tangency, such as D, between an isoquant and an isocost line. A cost function gives minimum production cost as a function of output, and can be constructed from the locus of the minimum-cost tangency points corresponding to different output levels.

Homogeneous Production Functions

A production function is homogeneous of degree k if

$$qt^k = f(tL, tK)$$

The first-order partial derivatives for a function homogeneous of degree k are homogeneous of degree $k - 1$. Consequently,

$$\text{RTS} = \frac{f_L(L, K)}{f_K(L, K)} = \frac{t^{k-1}f_L(tL, tK)}{t^{k-1}f_K(tL, tK)} = \frac{f_L(tL, tK)}{f_K(tL, tK)}$$

The RTS is unchanged if the quantities of labor and capital are unchanged by the same proportion. This means that one isoquant is sufficient to represent the entire family of isoquants. Other isoquants in the family can be obtained by integration since their slopes (i.e., their RTSs) are known at each point.

Production functions for which the RTS depends only upon the labor-capital ratio are called homothetic. This class includes all homogeneous production functions as well as some production functions that are not homogeneous.

The Elasticity of Substitution

As one moves from left to right along a convex isoquant, both the RTS and capital-labor ratio decline. The elasticity of substitution is denoted by

$$\sigma = \frac{d \ln (K/L)}{d \ln (f_L/f_K)}) = \frac{d (K/L)}{d (f_L/f_K)} \frac{f_L/f_K}{K/L}$$

where ln denotes the natural logarithm. If the capital-labor ratio declines proportionately more than the RTS, σ is greater than 1. If it declines proportionately less than the RTS, σ is less than 1. If they decline in the same proportion, σ equals 1. The degree of substitution between the inputs increases as σ increases.

In general, the elasticity of substitution varies as one moves along a given isoquant. A production function with a constant elasticity of substitution (CES) is given by

$$q = A[\alpha L^{-p} + (1 - \alpha)K^{-p}]^{-k/p} \quad \text{for} \quad \begin{matrix} A > 0 \\ < \alpha < 1 \end{matrix}$$

where $p = (1 - \sigma)/\sigma$ reflects the constant elasticity of substitution.

The CES production function is homogeneous and of degree k. As σ approaches zero the isoquants approach right angles with no substitution possible. As σ approaches ∞, the isoquants approach straight lines (similar to the isocost lines), with perfect substitution possible.

References

Frisch, Ragnar, *Theory of Production*, Rand-McNally, Chicago, 1965; Henderson, James M., and Richard E. Quandt, *Microeconomic Theory: A Mathematical Approach*, 3d ed., McGraw-Hill, New York, 1980, chaps. 4, 5; Hirschleifer, Jack, *Price Theory and Applications*, 4th ed., Prentice-Hall, Englewood Cliffs, N.J., 1988; Varian, Hal R., *Microeconomic Analysis*, 3d ed., Norton, New York, 1991.

(*See also* Elasticity; Production function)

James M. Henderson

J curve

The reaction of the balance of payments to exchange rate changes is hardly ever smooth and stable. Economists coined the term "J curve" to describe one plausible roller-coaster ride that the balance of payments might take in response to a devaluation of a fixed exchange rate or depreciation of a floating currency. Since depreciation is prescribed as the cure for a balance of payments deficit, one would hope for at least a positive effect. But rather than adjusting steadily, the balance often is observed to move in a negative direction before later improving, tracing out a letter "J" when graphed. This period of disappointment is not, of course, a comfortable prospect for policymakers, who grow impatient as their prescription seems to be making the disease worse, perhaps over a lengthy period of adjustment.

Some Recent History

In a most memorable recent episode, the dollar nearly doubled in value between the late 1970s and early 1985. The U.S. balance of payments deficit (on current account) rose to an unprecedented $122 billion in 1985. In March of 1985, the dollar began a rapid descent which took it down by about half in just about 3 years. The U.S. deficit disappointed commentators, however, by worsening to over $160 billion in 1987. Frightening conclusions that "the laws of economics have been repealed" or "exchange rates just do not seem to matter anymore" were common in the press.

Even some in the international economics profession were caught up in the pessimism. While rejecting suggestions that "the U.S. cannot compete at any price," these experts reacted with more sophisticated explanations. "Pricing to market" is a phrase invented to describe the tendency of foreign producers to cut profits and hold prices down in order to maintain their newly won share of the U.S. market. "Hysteresis," the difficulty of regaining a market once lost, has also been cited to explain the apparent stubbornness of the U.S. deficit.

587

Others, by contrast, simply invoked the J curve and urged patience, in the face of critical comments about the "J" having become an "L." When it finally occurred, the trade balance's turn was a powerful one, confirming the J curve, but still leaving room for future research on the importance of such factors as pricing to market and hysteresis.

Stability and Trade Adjustment

Balance of payments adjustment is largely determined by elasticities of demand. At the extreme, U.S. demand for German and Japanese automobiles could be completely unresponsive to changes in price. A halving of the dollar's value would simply raise the dollar price of imported cars, tending to worsen the U.S. balance of payments. Unless foreign demand for U.S. goods were to respond with sufficient speed and force, the U.S. balance would indeed worsen. Such a perverse change is even more likely when the balance of payments starts from a large deficit: export growth would have to be very powerful to overcome this (possibly temporary) tendency of imports in dollars to expand.

This state of affairs could, in principle, be permanent, meaning that the world is truly unstable. That is, the natural adjustments of exchange rates would exacerbate the very same imbalances that caused them. The so-called Marshall-Lerner condition is a formal way of describing the simple condition for stability. It holds that if the sum of a country's domestic elasticity of demand for imports and the foreign demand elasticity (for the country's exports) exceeds 1, the foreign exchange equilibrium is stable. A more sophisticated general equilibrium analysis takes into account the effects of exchange rate adjustments on real incomes and also on the supply side of both the domestic and foreign economies. But the Marshall-Lerner condition is generally thought to capture the essence of the story.

Even if it begins from an unstable equilibrium, the exchange rate once disturbed will adjust sufficiently to reach a new stable equilibrium. But a stable equilibrium could be at a far different exchange rate from the previous one. The possibility of unstable equilibriums may be more than an intellectual curiosity. The potential for this type of foreign exchange market instability in certain cases is now being taken seriously by many observers.

Elasticities of Demand in the Short and Long Run

Much more widely accepted as realistic is the possibility that demand is quite inelastic over short periods, so that exchange rate fluctuations temporarily move the balance of payments perversely. Later, as demand adjusts to higher prices, the expected direction of movement reasserts itself. That is, we observe a J curve.

The length of the downward section of the "J" is determined by the size and speed of adjustment in demand and also by the initial degree of payments imbalance. Furthermore, a more recent literature on the "pass-through" effect, a close relative of the pricing-to-market phenomenon, focuses on the adjustment of prices to exchange rate changes. Incomplete or sluggish adjustment of prices obviously affects the observed balance of payments adjustment.

Some Evidence

Based on empirical studies of import and export demand across many countries in many periods of time, the Marshall-Lerner condition seems virtually certain to hold in the long run. At the same time, short-run elasticities of demand are found to generally be only about half the size of long-run elasticities. The evidence implies that J curves should characterize the behavior of the balance of payments in most cases.

Not surprisingly, therefore, most large-scale models generate J-curve responses to exchange rate changes. In the DRI/McGraw-Hill model of the U.S. economy, for example, a dollar depreciation is predicted to cause the balance of payments to deteriorate temporarily. In fact, with everything else equal, it does not even regain its previous level for over one year; thereafter, a significant improvement is expected.

With lags this long, uncertainty and pessimism about balance of payments adjustments are understandable. Still, the overreaction of policymakers and market participants while on the downside of the J curve has costs which better knowledge could avoid.

References

Branson, William H., "The Trade Effects of the 1971 Currency Realignments," Brookings Papers on Economic Activity, 1972, pp. 15–69; Goldstein, Morris, and Mohsin S. Khan, "Income and Price Effects in Foreign Trade," in Ronald W. Jones and Peter B. Kenen (eds.), *Handbook of International Economics,* vol. II, North-Holland, Amsterdam, 1985, chap. 20; Haberler, Gottfried, "The Market for Foreign Exchange and the Stability of the Balance of Payments: A Theoretical Analysis," *Kyklos,* vol. 3, 1949, pp. 193–218; Helliwell, John F., and Tim Padner, "Empirical Studies of Macroeconomic Interdependence," in Ronald W. Jones and Peter B. Kenen (eds.), *Handbook of International Economics,* vol. II, North-Holland, Amsterdam, 1985, chap. 21; Marshall, Alfred, *The Pure Theory of Foreign Trade,* London School of Economic and Political Science, London, 1930.

(*See also* Balance of international payments; Foreign exchange rates; Value of the dollar)

David G. Hartman

Joint Economic Committee of Congress

Since 1946, the Joint Economic Committee (JEC) has served as one of the main conduits through which the economics profession conveys ideas and recommendations to Congress on economic conditions and economic policies.

The JEC consists of 20 members of Congress equally divided between the House of Representatives and the Senate. Each house's delegation consists of six members from the majority party in that house and four members from the minority party. The committee elects a chair and vice chair who serve for two years, with a member of the Senate chairing during even-numbered Congresses and a member of the House during odd-numbered Congresses. The committee members are assisted by a professional staff of about 25, most of whom have advanced degrees in economics or related fields.

An Advisory Service to Congress

The JEC (originally called the Joint Committee on Economic Report) was established by the Employment Act of 1946 (79th Cong., Pub. L. 304, 60 Stat. 23), which set broad economic goals for government policies and specific responsibilities for the JEC: "(1) to make a continuing study of matters relating to the Economic Report [of the President]; (2) to study means of coordinating programs in order to further the policy of this Act; and (3) as a guide to the several committees of Congress dealing with legislation relating to the Economic Report, not later than March 1 of each year . . . to file a report . . . containing its findings and recommendations, . . . and from time to time to make such other reports and recommendations . . . as it deems advisable." Each spring, the committee issues its annual report, with its recommendations for economic policy.

The Employment Act intended that the JEC should function as an economic advisory service to the Congress, paralleling the executive branch role of the Council of Economic Advisers, which was also created by the Employment Act. The JEC differs from other congressional committees in that it does not consider or report legislation, does not oversee programs, may not authorize or appropriate money, and has no regulatory authority. Nonetheless, the JEC serves a unique role in the Congress by having the freedom to examine the government's entire range of economic policies, macro and micro, and to focus on their long-term consequences, whereas other committees have more limited jurisdictions and must follow agendas that are frequently set by legislative deadlines.

Impact on Policy

Although there were no congressional precedents for the Joint Economic Committee, the model for the JEC was the Temporary National Economic Committee (1938–1941), whose chairman, Senator Joseph O'Mahoney of Wyoming, also chaired the JEC. The JEC in its early years conducted major hearings and issued reports covering such areas as monetary and fiscal policies, inflation, employment and unemployment, federal subsidy programs, and the quality of federal economic statistics, to name only a few. The JEC pioneered the process of issuing compendiums of papers on the topics of upcoming hearings and also pioneered the use of panels of expert witnesses, thus encouraging a divergence of views and creating a platform for new ideas on public policy.

Over the years, the JEC has frequently explored areas of policy significance long before they became the subject of widespread concern. In 1949, an examination of low-income families identified problems of economic opportunity and income distribution that led, in the 1960s, to the War on Poverty. The JEC's examination of the federal budget process and the current services budget concept contributed to enactment of the Budget Act of 1974, which established the congressional budget process. A major 1985 study entitled "Hard Choices: A Report on the Increasing Gap between America's Infrastructure Needs and Our Ability to Pay for Them" provided an early examination of our deteriorating infrastructure and the cost of repairing it. The JEC's large-scale investigation of the economy in 1959 and 1960 under the title "Study of Employment, Growth, and Price Levels" has frequently been cited as the basis for much of the economic program for the Kennedy administration. The JEC has held hearings and published papers on a wide variety of other economic issues as well; the committee published almost 1600 hearing records, studies, and reports during its first 45 years.

The JEC serves as an important source of information on the economy to the Congress and the public. Since 1971, the JEC has held regular monthly hearings on the employment and unemployment situation, during which committee members question the commissioner of labor statistics on current labor-market conditions. Each year, the JEC has examined CIA analysts on the economies of the Soviet Union and China and, on a rotating 3-year cycle, publishes major compendiums of papers on the economies of the Soviet Union, China, and the Eastern European countries.

Reflecting the breakup of the Soviet Union at the end of 1991, JEC volumes now focus on the new Commonwealth economies. Throughout its existence, the JEC has documented the benefits of high-quality federal statistics; each month the JEC publishes *Economic Indicators,* a compilation of the most recent economic data issued by federal statistical agencies.

Some observers of the JEC believe its major contribution has been to educate both the Congress and the public concerning economic issues and policies. In turn, some observe that the committee has in fact educated many economists and given them both motivation and opportunity to work on major policy issues in the public sector.

The Future of the Joint Economic Committee

On occasion, efforts to consolidate and simplify House and Senate committee structures have included recommendations to eliminate the JEC and allocate its responsibilities to other committees. The congressional budget structure erected in the 1970s, including the massive Congressional Budget Office (CBO), has led some to argue that the JEC is redundant and no longer serves a useful role that can't be filled equally well by other committees or by the CBO. Questions about the committee's usefulness have also been raised at times when economic policy issues were the subject of acrimonious partisan debate, as occurred during much of the 1980s, when the JEC frequently expressed concerns about government economic policies.

Nonetheless, it is widely accepted that the JEC serves a function in the Congress that other committees would find hard to fill. With no legislative jurisdiction or existing programs to defend, the JEC is in the unique position of being able to bring a fresh and independent viewpoint to the consideration of economic policy issues. It can offer integrated solutions to problems and make policy recommendations that cut across the jurisdictions of other committees. With freedom from legislative deadlines, it can place primary importance on the long-run consequences of economic policies. With no legislative jurisdiction, the JEC has little power of its own. The committee's successes and influence have been due to the quality of its economic analyses and recommendations and the respect of the Congress for its members.

(*See also* Congressional Budget Office; Council of Economic Advisers)

William R. Buechner

Joint venture

A business venture is an undertaking involving some element of risk or uncertainty of outcome. A joint venture is such an undertaking conducted by two or more partners who share the risks. The partners may be individuals, corporations, governments, or some combination of these three.

Although almost any joint-stock corporation fits this description, the term "joint venture" is usually limited to certain special cases as illustrated by the following examples:

1. Two large international oil companies jointly form a subsidiary to explore for oil in a region where the chances of finding commercial deposits are less than certain.

2. A multinational firm establishes a subsidiary with local partners in a developing nation to manufacture and sell in that market. The market is protected by the government so that only firms with some local ownership may sell in it.

3. A firm currently operating in a market wishes to exploit a technology held by a second firm. The second firm wishes to participate in this market, but faces substantial barriers to entry (e.g., the need to set up a costly distribution network). These two firms agree to form a jointly held subsidiary to appropriate mutually rents from the market using the first firm's access to the market and the second firm's technology.

4. As a special case of the previous example, a large manufacturing firm based in a Western nation forms a joint venture with a state-owned enterprise in the Peoples' Republic of China. The Western firm seeks to sell within China but is unable to do so unless in partnership with the state-owned firm, while the state-owned firm seeks the Western firm's managerial expertise.

5. Two firms wish to develop a new technology but face uncertain costs of development and prospects for success. They agree to proceed by creating a joint research and development subsidiary.

In all these cases, the immediate owners of the joint venture are firms not otherwise linked by way of common ownership, control, or strategy. Such joint ventures can be viewed as a subset of "strategic alliances," i.e., cooperation agreements between independent firms.

All these examples involve some element of imperfect competition. In examples 2 and 4 this imperfect competition results from governmental action, so these joint ventures are efforts to overcome governmental obstacles to doing business and/or to exploit governmentally created and controlled monopolies.

Example 1, typical of numerous arrangements in the natural-resource industries, and sometimes example 5 are typically justified by participating firms as being necessary to diffuse risk. Modern portfolio theory holds, however, that joint ventures among established firms are unnecessary for reasons of risk spreading at the level of the firm, given that individual shareholders can minimize risk via portfolio diversification. But an exception is the case where the individual firm faces the substantial probability of bankruptcy. Such joint ventures are interpreted by some economists as devices for mutual appropriation of rents by firms operating in oligopolistic industries, where any risk that is reduced by the venture is that of one firm taking any unilateral action that would threaten the rent.

Joint ventures may be economically justified if the partner firms possess complementary capabilities. Such might be the case in example 5, for instance, if the two firms each possessed specialized research personnel not possessed by the other. Complementarities can also be present in examples 2 and 4, but in each of these cases they have more to do with political than with economic considerations.

References

Chenais, François, "Technical Cooperation Agreements among Firms," *STI Review*, vol. 4, 1988, pp. 51–119; Friedmann, W. G., and G. Kalanoff (eds.), *Joint International Business Ventures*, Columbia University Press, New York, 1961; Hilton, D. H. W. van, *Joint Ventures*, Kluwer, Deventor, The Netherlands, 1968; Hladic, K. J., *International Joint Ventures*, Lexington Books, Lexington, Mass., 1985; Ordover, J., and R. Willig, "Antitrust for High-Technology Industries:

Assessing Research Joint Ventures and Mergers," *Journal of Law and Economics,* vol. 28, 1985, pp. 311–333; Pogue, G. A., and K. Lall, "Corporate Finance: An Overview," in Stewart C. Myers (ed.), *Modern Developments in Financial Management,* Praeger, New York, 1976, see also article by J. S. R. Shad in same volume; Scherer, F. M., "Research and Development Resource Allocation under Rivalry," *Quarterly Journal of Economics,* vol. 81, no. 3, August 1967, pp. 359–394; Stopford, J. M., and L. T. Wells, *Managing the Multinational Enterprise,* Basic Books, New York, 1972, chaps. 9, 10; Tirole, Jean, *The Theory of Industrial Organization,* MIT Press, Cambridge, Mass., 1989; Vernon, Raymond, "Foreign Enterprise and Developing Nations in the Raw Materials Industries," *American Economic Review,* vol. 60, no. 2, May 1970, pp. 122–126.

(*See also* Competition; Monopoly and oligopoly)

Edward M. Graham

Judgmental forecasting (*see* Economic forecasting methods)

Juglar cycle

Clément Juglar, a French physician who lived from 1819 to 1905, gave up the practice of medicine in favor of the study of statistics and economics in his late twenties. His interest in cycles was spurred by a study he had done in which he had found cyclical behavior in birth, death, and marriage rates in France. His ground-breaking work in business cycles, published in 1860, is credited with being the first to observe that business activity followed a cyclical pattern. Before Juglar the concern of economists was with the explanation of the crisis, that point in time when the economy turned downward, each such historical episode having its own cause or set of causes such as wars, droughts, gold outflows, credit stringencies, and so on. Juglar's contention was that the crisis (panic) was simply the natural reaction to the excesses developed during the expansion period. The contraction phase is then a period of adjustment where the previous maladjustments are corrected. Juglar referred to the contraction period as the liquidation phase in which the excess or redundant capital was eliminated through depreciation or obsolesence and business failures. However, he found the primary cause of the cycle to be the alternating periods of rising and falling prices which affect exports and imports, the balance of payments, and gold flows. When the liquidation period has run its course, the economy is prepared for the prosperity phase to commence. Thus, in Juglar's framework the business cycle is made up of three elements: prosperity, crisis, and liquidation, and each must follow the other in that order.

In recognition of the importance of Juglar's contributions to the analysis of business cycles, Professor Joseph A. Schumpeter named the intermediate-length cycle the Juglar cycle. The Juglar cycle, which averages about 9 years in length, is also variously referred to as the fixed-investment cycle, the major cycle, the normal wave, and, during the nineteenth and early twentieth century, the business cycle or the trade cycle. In the Schumpeterian schema, three classes of business cycles proceed at the same time: the Kondratieff cycle with an average length of 54 years, the Juglar cycle which oscillates about the Kondratieff, and the Kitchin cycle of 40 months' duration which in turn oscillates about the Juglar. According to Schumpeter's analysis of his data, there were six Juglar cycles to one Kondratieff, and three Kitchins to every Juglar. (In more recent times the Kuznets cycle has been added to the list.) Whenever all three cycles were in the same phase, that phase was exceptionally intense. This was one of the explanations of the intensity of the Great Depression of the 1930s. While a number of economists still find this approach to be of some value, probably due to the dominance of the National Bureau of Economic Research in the study of business cycles, it has fallen out of favor. The NBER asserts that during any given time period, only one cycle is in progress.

Business-Cycle Theories

Generic theories of the business cycle, that is, those that are not specific to particular time spans or to specific industries, are most readily related to the Juglar cycle. These theories have been classified in a number of ways, but the classification that has been most widely accepted is that proposed by Gottfried Haberler in his *Prosperity and Depression* (3d ed., 1941). Each of the theories presented here focuses on different features of economic systems capable of generating business cycles. None of them individually is able to explain every historical episode, but if one takes an eclectic approach, incorporating aspects of all of them, one probably has the tools needed to understand what goes on during business fluctuations.

Purely Monetary Theory

Any theory of business cycles must in some fashion include the role of money in the economic system. In some theories money plays a dominant role, and in others money plays only a supporting role. As the name implies, the purely monetary theory argues that variations in the supply of money, or in its velocity of circulation, are necessary conditions for changes in the monetary value of the nation's output. Ralph G. Hawtrey is accepted as the foremost exponent of this theory. According to him, expansions begin when traders, i.e., basically inventory holders, are encouraged to borrow from the banks by lower interest rates. If banks have excess reserves, this borrowing results in an increase in the money stock, which allows for additional spending without a corresponding reduction of spending in other sectors. As long as the money expansion continues, the growth in incomes and spending will continue. However, at some point the banks' excess reserves will be depleted and interest rates will rise in order to reduce bank loans, which in turn will lead to reductions in the money supply. Thus, the crisis is precipitated, and the contraction phase sets in with a declining supply of money and with reductions in incomes and spending. During the contraction, excess reserves build up, preparing the system for a new expansion. In Hawtrey's version of the purely monetary cycle, the gold standard and gold flows played crucial roles. Of course, with the abandonment of the historical gold standard, the theory has had to be altered considerably, but contemporary monetarists still maintain money as the central element in their theory of the business cycle.

Underconsumption Theories

The most influential of the early underconsumption theorists was the British economist John A. Hobson (1858–1940), whose most prominent predecessors were Malthus (1766–1834) and Lord Lauderdale (1759–1839). Significant aspects of the underconsumption theory are found in many later economists' theories, including those of John Maynard Keynes and Alvin Hansen. Underconsumption is synonymous with oversaving, which means that the underconsumptionists believe that saving is, at least sometimes, excessive relative to the need for investment. It also means that consumption can be too small to utilize the total productive capacity of the economic system, and thus precipitate unemployment and lower incomes, and less production than the economy is capable of producing.

According to underconsumption theories, households do not increase their spending on consumption at as rapid a rate as their incomes rise during the upswing of the business cycle. And this causes difficulties: During this phase the capital stock is growing and improving, making greater output of consumer goods and services possible; but even though income is growing at the same rate as is output, the demand for consumption is growing at a slower rate. This leaves unused productive capacity and therefore a decline in investment demand at the very time that saving is increasing. This all means that consumption plus investment demand is less than the amount that producers are able and willing to produce, and a crisis and contraction are in the offing.

Explanations of this circumstance vary with the writers. Hobson said it was because consumption skills are less well developed than production skills. It takes time for people to learn how to improve their standard of living when their incomes increase. On the other hand, producers are very skilled at developing and introducing new ways to produce more and better goods. In contemporary language, the interpretation is that the production lag is shorter than the consumption lag. Most underconsumptionists also believe that the distribution of income is another serious contributor to the problem. During business expansions, wage-income growth lags behind property-income growth, and since workers consume a larger proportion of their income than do profit, interest, and rent recipients, their argument is that consumption will not rise as fast as national income.

Nonmonetary Overinvestment Theory

It is generally agreed that the most outstanding feature of business cycles is the variability of investment spending over the span of the cycle. The term "overinvestment" refers to the observed tendency of investment to increase to the point where the capital stock is excessive relative to the demand for the output it is capable of producing. The nonmonetary version of the theory considers the role of money to be a passive one, a necessary but not a sufficient condition. Indeed, some of its earliest proponents did not even count it as a necessary condition. In this theory, the expansion in business activity begins when a surge in investment demand occurs, and follows a period of depression during which the capital stock has deteriorated in value, the availability of liquid capital has accumulated, interest rates are at low levels, and costs generally have fallen. At the beginning of the upturn, the cost of capital goods is relatively low; and since interest rates are also low, it can be a time when it is profitable to invest in plant and equipment. When investment spending increases, the incomes of those involved in producing the capital also increase, generating an increase in the demand for consumer goods as well. While the expansion is in progress, the competition for resources drives all prices up. Two critically important developments are taking place: (1) the stock of capital goods is growing, and (2) the supply of funds available for investment, which grows in the early stage of the expansion from the large profits earned, at the later stage becomes exhausted. This causes interest rates to rise, making further investment unattractive. At the same time, the larger stock of capital as it comes on line is capable of producing larger quantities of consumer goods, but the demand for consumption will be insufficient since incomes will fall when investment declines. At this point producers will discover that they have overinvested. A business contraction ensues, and continues until the need for investment again develops and the supply of loanable funds grows to a point where interest rates fall. The economy is then prepared for an upturn.

Monetary Overinvestment Theory

The real aspects of the business cycle, as already outlined as the nonmonetary overinvestment school, provoke very little criticism by those we refer to as monetary overinvestment theorists. The main argument between the two groups revolves around the issue of how much importance to attach to the monetary side. Most closely associated with the name of F. A. von Hayek, the monetary overinvestment theory stresses the distinction between the natural rate of interest and the market rate. The natural, or equilibrium, rate is the rate that would prevail when the amount of voluntary saving by households is equal to the amount of investment planned by business units. The market rate is the rate of interest set by market forces. On the supply side the primary market force is primarily saving, but it can also include increases in the money stock and "dishoarding" of funds (an increase in the velocity of money). On the demand side the main market force is investment, but it can also include "hoarding" (a decrease in velocity). Equality of the natural and the market rate of interest is an equilibrium condition that implies a constant level of national income and hence no business cycle.

However, the equilibrium can be disturbed by an increase in the money stock precipitated by a number of events such as increases in bank reserves by central bank purchases in the open market, lowering of required or desired reserves, or decreases in the discount rate (bank rate). If one of these actions occurs, banks would have more reserves than they wish to have and would increase their holdings of loans and investments, thereby increasing the supply of money and at the same time lowering the market rate of interest. While this process is going on, the market rate will be below the natural rate. This initiates the upturn and the expansion phase of the cycle because the lower market rate induces business firms to increase the rate of investment spending. On the other hand, there is less incentive for households to save, which means that there is greater incentive to spend on consumption. Since both consumption and investment demands have increased, without a corresponding increase in output to satisfy those demands, the price level increases. Hayek and others in this group assume that since it is businesses that are causing the money stock to grow by their borrowing, resources will flow into the production of investment goods and away from the production of consumer goods. This is referred to as "forced saving" since consumers are forced to consume less in real terms than they wished to do, because of the inflation. The expansion can continue in this way as long as the expansion in the money stock continues, but when the banks run out of excess reserves, as they must without further injections by the central bank, they will be compelled to raise the market rate of interest, decrease the volume of loans and investments, and thus stop the money-supply growth. The contraction period now begins: business firms find it difficult to fund their expansion plans, unemployment increases, and incomes and prices fall. Overinvestment has happened.

Psychological Theory

While all business-cycle theories incorporate psychological aspects of human behavior, those theories that emphasize this element are called psychological theories. Much of the underlying economic analysis is the same as or similar to other more purely economic explanations. Since virtually all economic decision making involves the future, and since the future is fraught with uncertainty, optimism and pessimism may play an important role. Since the business community is closely interrelated, waves of optimism or pessimism may pervade that community and exaggerate the economic swings. A. C. Pigou and John Maynard Keynes, in particular, laid heavy stress on psychological factors in their analyses of business fluctuations. Contemporary attempts to treat uncertainty in a rigorous way include the theory of adaptive expectations and the theory of rational expectations.

Modern Business-Cycle Theories

The business-cycle theories summarized here provided later economists with a basic understanding of the dynamics of the macroeconomy. It was left for the current generation of economists to put these insights into a rigorous format such that what were essentially speculations could be subjected to both mathematical and empirical tests. Recent work on the major, or Juglar, cycles has taken on a decidedly mathematical direction. Since cycles can occur only where the adjustment of economic activity to change takes time, most of the modern theories are based on time lags. The lags are in the time required to adjust production to changes in demand, or in the time required for consumption or investment activity to react to changes in incomes, prices, interest rates, and other relevant variables. The acceleration principle, where one variable (consumption, for example) is a function of the rate of change rather than the absolute level of another variable (income, for example), is at the heart of many of these mathematical models. The old arguments continue between those who believe that the cycle is basically a monetary phenomenon and those who put their faith in the real business-cycle analysis.

References

Clark, John J., and Morris Cohen (eds.), *Business Fluctuations, Growth and Economic Stabilization, A Reader,* Random House, New York, 1963; Haberler, Gottfried, *Prosperity and Depression,* 3d ed., League of Nations, Geneva, 1941; Hall, Thomas E., *Business Cycles: The Nature and Causes of Economic Fluctuations,* Praeger, New York, 1990; Hansen, Alvin, *Business Cycles and National Income,* Norton, New York, 1964; Juglar, Clément, *A Brief History of Panics,* 3d ed., D. W. Thom (trans.), Putnam's, New York, 1916; Niehans, Jurg, *A History of Economic Theory, Classic Contributions, 1720–1980,* Johns Hopkins University Press, Baltimore, Md., 1990; Schumpeter, Joseph A., *Business Cycles,* vol. I, McGraw-Hill, New York, 1939; Tinbergen, Jan, and J. J. Polak, *The Dynamics of Business Cycles,* University of Chicago Press, Chicago, 1950; Valentine, Lloyd M., and Dennis F. Ellis, *Business Cycles and Forecasting,* 8th ed., South-Western, Cincinnati, Ohio, 1991.

(*See also* Acceleration principle; Business cycles; Kitchin cycle; Kondratieff cycle; Kuznets cycle)

Lloyd M. Valentine

Junk (high-yield) bond market

One of the most important developments in corporate finance in the late 1970s and throughout the 1980s has been the reemergence of publicly owned and traded low-rated corporate debt. Originally offered to the public in the early 1900s to help finance some of our emerging growth industries, these high-yield/high-risk bonds virtually disappeared after the rash of bond defaults during the Depression. In

1978–1988, however, the junk bond market catapulted from an insignificant element in the corporate fixed-income market to one of the fastest-growing and most controversial types of financing mechanisms. The term "junk" emanates from the dominant type of low-rated, speculative bond issues outstanding prior to 1977 when the "market" consisted almost exclusively of original-issue investment-grade bonds that fell from their lofty status to a higher-default-risk, speculative-grade level. These so-called fallen angels amounted to about $8.5 billion in 1977. At the middle of 1991, fallen angels still made up over 20 percent of the $210 billion publicly owned junk bond market.

High-yield bonds are straight (nonconvertible) debt issues that are rated by the independent rating agencies, e.g., Moody's and Standard & Poor's, as noninvestment-grade (double B, single B, and triple C) and typically sell at 3 to 5 percent yield spreads over comparable maturity T bonds. At the start of 1990, however, these high-risk obligations were selling at an all-time record yield spread of about 7.5 percent over Treasuries, reflecting the market's heightened risk perception. Indeed, at that time the high-yield public debt market was at a critical juncture in its evolution and the outlook beyond 1990 was clouded, perhaps even vulnerable to collapse. As of this writing in mid-1991, the market has rebounded and investors were requiring, on average, a 6 percent premium over U.S. Treasury bonds in order to invest in high-yield bonds.

In addition to fallen angels, the market is composed of issuers who, beginning in 1977, began to go directly to the public to raise capital for growth purposes. Early users of junk bonds were energy-related firms, cable TV companies, airlines, and assorted other industrial companies. This type of financing is a form of securitization of what heretofore was the sole province of private placements financed by banks and insurance companies. The emerging growth company rationale coupled with relatively high returns to early investors helped legitimize the sector. On the underwriting side, most investment banks ignored junk bonds until 1983–1984, when their merits and profit potential became more evident.

Synonymous with the market's growth was the emergence of the investment banking firm Drexel Burnham Lambert and its junk bond wizard, Michael Milken. Drexel established a potent link of issuers and investors and, along with the market's growth, rode the wave of new financing and the consequent surge in secondary trading to become one of the most powerful investment banks in the late 1980s. The incredible rise in power of this firm was followed by an equally dramatic fall resulting first in a government civil indictment and huge fine for various misdealings and finally the firm's total collapse and bankruptcy in February 1990.

By far, the most important and controversial aspect of junk bond financing was its role in the corporate restructuring movement from 1985 to 1989. High-leverage transactions and acquisitions, such as leveraged buyouts (LBOs, which involve a publicly owned firm that is purchased and then becomes a private company when its common shares are retired and no longer available to be bought and sold in the public market) and leveraged recapitalizations (debt-for-equity swaps), transformed the face of corporate America, leading to a heated debate on the economic and social consequences of firms being transformed from public to private enterprises with debt-equity ratios of at least 6:1. These transactions involved increasingly large companies, and the multibillion dollar takeover became fairly common, finally capped by the huge $25 billion RJR Nabisco LBO in 1989. LBOs were typically financed with about 60 percent senior bank debt, about 25 to 30 percent subordinated public debt (junk bonds), and 10 to 15 percent equity. The junk bond segment is sometimes referred to as mezzanine debt, i.e., having a priority in case of liquidation between the balcony senior debt and the basement equity.

As these restructurings flourished, resulting in huge fees to advisers and underwriters and premiums of 40 to 100 percent to the old shareholders that were bought out, the system led to excesses in both the prices paid and the amount of leverage used. As long as the market was willing to buy these new debt offerings and the risk-return trade-off appeared to be favorable, the growth in junk bonds and restructuring continued. In the period 1986–1989, between $25 billion and $35 billion per year was raised by publicly issued, straight high-yield debt, and about 70 percent of these funds went to restructurings. From 1978 to 1988, investors in junk bonds received an average return spread of about 2.5 percent per year greater than they would have earned from T bonds after adjusting for losses from defaults. Default rates averaged between 2 and 3 percent per year depending upon how they were measured.

The bottom fell out of the market in the last 6 months of 1989 and for the entire following year due to a number of factors including a marked increase in defaults, government regulation against S&Ls holding junk bonds, fears of higher interest rates and a recession, and, finally, the growing realization of the leverage excesses of certain ill-conceived restructurings.

One measure of those excesses is the resulting defaults on many of these poorly planned issues. A traditional indicator of defaults is the annual default rate which compares the dollar amount of default in a 12-month period to the amount outstanding that could default. The default rate in 1989 jumped to 4 percent involving more than $8 billion of debt and skyrocketed in 1990 to 10.1 percent on more than $18 billion of defaults. The pendulum of growth and returns swung dramatically in the opposite direction as junk bond prices plummeted, yields skyrocketed, and new issues dried up. The leverage boom of the 1980s was over.

While the amounts and rate of default continued to escalate in the first half of 1991, investors in junk bonds saw their fortunes rebound. This irony of excellent returns in the face of growing defaults is explained by the excessively low prices on most bonds at the end of 1990 and the improving economic outlook combined with lower interest rates in 1991.

Will the junk bond market survive? Yes, it probably will, but the growth will almost certainly be slowed dramatically and the new offerings will revert to more soundly financed capital structures. Indeed, the pendulum will swing back toward equity financing, at least for many of the firms that already have a large amount of debt on their balance sheets. Restructurings will also continue, with the mezzanine debt increasingly being of the private placement (not publicly traded) variety.

(*See also* Bond; Bond rating agencies; Capital markets and money markets; Money markets)

Edward I. Altman

Keynesian economics

Keynesian economics is a body of economic theory and related policy associated with the English economist John Maynard Keynes. Keynes wrote many books, but the phrase "Keynesian economics" refers especially to *The General Theory of Employment, Interest and Money* (1936). The ideas and analytical techniques of the *General Theory* stimulated what was called the new economics and more generally the Keynesian revolution. Keynes challenged the fundamental tenets of classical and neoclassical economics stemming from Adam Smith, David Ricardo, John Stuart Mill, Alfred Marshall, and A. C. Pigou. Classical and neoclassical economists hold that a private enterprise economy based on a market system is normally in equilibrium only at full employment. If it departs temporarily from full employment, forces are set in motion to restore equilibrium at full employment. Classical and neoclassical economics allow for voluntary unemployment, by the idle rich and the lazy poor, and for frictional unemployment arising from circumstances such as changing jobs, but it does not allow for involuntary unemployment by those wage earners willing and able to work and actively seeking employment. This self-adjusting system was associated with a policy of laissez faire in a general way.

In contrast, Keynes' general theory of employment postulates that a capitalist economy may be in equilibrium at less than full employment and that the classical/neoclassical economics is a special case in this more general theory. Moreover, Keynes called the characteristics of the classical/neoclassical special case misleading and its teaching disastrous if applied to the real world. Keynes did not accept the automatic, self-adjusting nature of capitalism and believed that under laissez faire chronic, large-scale unemployment is likely to occur. In this sense, his general theory repudiates the theoretical foundations of laissez faire capitalism. He recommended positive fiscal and monetary policies as a means to alleviate unemployment.

Theory of Effective Demand

Keynesian economics is primarily a theory of effective demand, the volume of which is determined by two factors, the propensity to consume and the inducement to invest. The propensity to consume expresses a functional relation between amounts of consumption at varying levels of national income. As income changes, consumption changes in the same direction but by less than the change in income. If national income increases, for example, consumption will increase but by less than the increase in income. The ratio of the increment in consumption to the increment in income is called the marginal propensity to consume and is one of the central concepts in Keynes' theory.

The inducement of business executives to invest is determined by their expectations concerning probable future profits on capital assets, on the one hand, and the rate of interest at which they can borrow for investment, on the other hand. The functional relation between the expected rates of profit and the amounts of current investment is called the schedule of the marginal efficiency of capital, or, more simply, the investment demand schedule. Investment in any period is carried to the point at which the marginal efficiency of capital expressed as a rate of discount on expected future earnings is equal to the rate of interest. Current investment in durable capital assets is the focal point of Keynes' analysis, and because expectations about the return on long-term investments are highly uncertain, investment in durable capital assets is subject to sudden and wide fluctuations. Confidence in expectations is precarious because knowledge about the future is highly uncertain.

Among the complex relations that determine national income and employment, investment is the strategic factor. Low levels of investment are associated with low levels of employment, and fluctuations in investment are associated with wide fluctuations in employment and national income. If investment does not increase, employment cannot increase, given the propensity to consume. There is nothing automatic about increases in investment as there is about increases in consumption (as income rises).

In Keynes' theory of effective demand, investment is strategic because it disburses purchasing power that will be spent for consumer goods without adding to the volume of consumer goods currently coming into the market. The amount of consumer goods a business finds profitable to produce depends on the amount of investment goods being produced. The demand for consumer goods derives from two sources: from the incomes of those employed in producing consumer goods and from the incomes of those employed in producing investment goods.

For example, if a national output of 100 consists of 80 in consumption goods and 20 in investment goods, the 80 in demand needed to clear the 80 in consumption output is 64 + 16: 64 is four-fifths of the income of 80 received by those producing consumer goods; 16 is four-fifths of 20 received by those producing investment goods. The ratio of income derived from the consumer sector to income derived from the investment sector is 4:1 (80:20). This ratio remains constant within a relatively small range of fluctuations in income. So if investment falls by 1, from 20 to 19, consumption will fall by 4, from 80 to 76. Total effective demand is now 76 + 19 = 95. A reduction of 1 in investment has resulted in a fall of 4 in consumption and a total fall of 5 in income. If investment were to rise by 1, from 20 to 21, consumption would rise by 4, from 80 to 84, and income from 100 to 105. This relation is called the investment multiplier, which in this example is 5. It expresses the quantitative relation between changes in income resulting from changes in investment.

Keynes' theory emphasizes demand rather than supply. Current investment is not important in the theory of effective demand because presumably it adds to future productive capacity. Investment is primarily important as a means of disbursing purchasing power into the economy. Any activity that disburses income without simultaneously bringing consumption goods to the market can perform the function of investment as a component of effective demand. For example, government expenditures paid out of loans affect the demand for consumer goods in the same way as private investment.

Compensatory Fiscal Policy

Compensatory fiscal policy is the program most closely associated with Keynesian economics. If the amount of effective demand generated by the private sector is insufficient for full employment, the deficiency can be compensated for by increased expenditure in the public sector. In order for public expenditure to have its desired effect, to increase employment and national income, it must be financed in a manner that will not reduce private spending. Public expenditure paid for out of taxation is not desirable for this purpose because it will reduce disposable (aftertax) income and, hence, will reduce private consumption. Consequently, the increase in public spending should be in the form of loan expenditures. Moreover, expenditure by loans from banks is preferable to loans from private individuals because borrowing from banks is less likely to reduce existing spending in the private sector. The resulting deficit in the governmental budget is necessary in order to avoid substituting public for private spending.

In Keynesian policy, governmental deficits are desirable only when spending in the private sector is insufficient to generate demand for the desired level of employment. If demand in the private sector is brisk, there is no need for government deficits, and government spending should be paid for entirely out of current taxes.

Keynesian Influence on the U.S. Economy

Keynesian economics had some influence on the New Deal of Franklin D. Roosevelt. Although Roosevelt criticized President Hoover for failing to balance the federal budget, by his second term (1937–1941) Roosevelt embraced deficit spending as a necessary condition for prosperity. After several years of economic expansion from 1933 to 1937, the American economy went into a tailspin early in 1937 just as the cash budget came into balance for the first time since 1929. At the urging of Federal Reserve Board Chairman Marriner Eccles, Roosevelt recommended the resumption of large loan expenditures designed to increase aggregate demand for goods and services. Eccles, a Utah banker, independently had arrived at Keynesian principles of loan expenditures as a means to prosperity from deep depression. Eccles and other Keynesians recommended that the federal budget should be balanced only at a high level of national income. Attempts to balance the budget at low levels of national income would only make the depression worse. They gave priority to a balanced economy over a balanced budget.

Keynes showed the versatility of his general theory of effective demand by applying to wartime inflation the same framework of analysis he had worked out primarily as a guide to escape from peacetime depression. Wartime inflation arises primarily from excessive demand, whereas peacetime depression is caused primarily by deficient demand. Pointing out that taxation and voluntary saving would be insufficient to prevent inflation during World War II, Keynes devised an anti-inflationary plan under which additional, nontax deductions would be made from incomes during the war and some payments would be deferred until after the war. This was a plan for involuntary or forced saving during wartime. The purpose of the extra wartime withholding of income was to reduce the demand for consumption at a time when only limited supplies of consumption goods were available. While Keynes did not oppose all direct price controls and administrative rationing in wartime, his plan had the advantage of giving maximum freedom of choice to consumers in spending their incomes left over after taxes and deferred compensation. Repayment after the war would have the advantage of offsetting a deficiency of demand in the postwar period, which was anticipated by Keynes and others.

In the United States under the Employment Act of 1946, macroeconomic policies of a Keynesian type became the chief instrument for maintaining and stimulating high-level employment. During the 1950s, when filling war-induced backlogs of demand provided a buoyant economy, automatic stabilizers such as progressive taxation and unemployment compensation were sufficient to limit economic downturns to mild recessions. Under progressive income tax rates personal disposable income does not fall as rapidly as national income and helps to offset the decline in the aggregate demand in a downturn. With unemployment compensation, workers who lose their jobs continue to receive income for a substantial period while they are unemployed, and this blunts the fall in demand that would otherwise occur.

Although built-in stabilizers moderate business recessions, they also weaken economic recoveries. Beginning in the 1960s, fiscal drag and full-employment surplus were Keynesian-type concepts used to analyze and explain fiscal policy. Progressive income taxes act as a brake, or a fiscal drag, on economic expansion and may prevent full recovery. The longest unbroken economic expansion in American history occurred between 1961 and 1968, for a period of more than 100 months. In order to sustain the expansion and avoid a possible break in it arising from fiscal drag, major reductions were made in income tax rates in 1964 when the economy was still operating far short of full employment. The amount of purchasing power extracted from the economy by a large budgetary surplus that would exist at full employment might abort the realization of full employment. Discretionary fiscal policy in the form of the big tax cut of 1964 helped to prolong the expansion to a record length. Keynesian economics achieved its greatest influence during the Kennedy-Johnson administrations. During that period members of the President's Council of Economic Advisers were Keynesians almost without exception.

Criticism of Keynesian Economics

During the 1970s Keynesian economics came under increasing criticism because of "stagflation," the simultaneous existence of stagnation (high unemployment) and persistent inflation. The coexistence of recession and inflation presented an apparent dilemma in terms of remedies along Keynesian lines. If demand were stimulated in order to reduce unemployment, inflation would accelerate; and if demand were deliberately constricted to combat inflation, unemployment would rise.

During his first term as President, Richard Nixon tried without success to curb inflation by deliberately inducing a mild recession. During the election year 1972 the Nixon administration imposed mandatory price and wage controls as an antiinflationary policy. Shortly after the election these controls were relaxed and prices spurted upward. The U.S. consumer price index reached the double-digit level for only the second time after World War II during the recession year 1974. A substantial part of this inflation resulted from the quadrupling of oil prices by the Organization of Petroleum Exporting Countries (OPEC) and a sharp rise in world grain prices. In the midst of this inflation came the great recession of 1974 to 1975, the worst economic decline in the American economy since the Great Depression of the 1930s. Although inflation slowed down in 1976, it began to rise again in 1977 and continued at high levels throughout the remainder of the 1970s. In 1979 the consumer price index rose 13.3 percent while unemployment hovered around 6 percent.

Keynesian theory and policy are designed to deal with inflation caused by excess general demand but not with inflation resulting from increases in individual commodities such as petroleum and food. Untangling cost-push inflation from generaldemand inflation is not easily accomplished. Thus, Keynesian economics did not seem to provide satisfactory answers to the perplexing problems of the inflation-ridden, semistagnant 1970s.

A frequent criticism of Keynesian economics is that its application to policy has led to inflation. Observations on this important criticism are limited to three points:

1. Increases in effective demand may at first increase employment, but beyond a critical point they will lead to a sharp rise in prices. The critical point is known as the full-employment rate of unemployment. It was fixed at 4 percent by President Johnson's Council of Economic Advisers. The appropriate rate will vary with circumstances, but if set too low it will contribute to inflationary wage and price increases.

2. If Keynesian policies are credited with eliminating major depressions in the post–World War II period, they may be blamed for contributing to inflation in the sense that in pre-Keynesian times depressions were a market-oriented form of price control. For example, between 1929 and 1933 commodity prices fell by approximately 20 percent in the United States. Secular inflation may be part of the price paid for eliminating major depressions.

3. The flexibility required for successful fiscal policy may not be politically feasible, or may work with such long political lags as to render otherwise sound fiscal policy ineffectual. Presumably, to increase tax rates is politically more difficult than to lower tax rates, and to decrease governmental expenditures is politically more difficult than to raise them. These political conditions impart an inflationary bias to fiscal policies of a Keynesian type, although this might seems as much a weakness of political democracy as of Keynesian economics.

The monetarist school became the chief critics of Keynesian fiscal policies. Monetarist policy requires only a steady and modest increase in the quantity of money. Little else is needed by way of government intervention into the private economy. Monetarists asserted that fiscal policy cannot influence the rate of output or employment except in a negative way. They favored major cutbacks in government expenditures and called for a balanced budget. Keynesians viewed monetary policy as a necessary complement to fiscal policy. When employment expands in response to fiscal expansionary measures or for other reasons, an increase in the money supply is needed to finance the additional transactions demand.

The Keynesian framework provides a mechanism for testing the conditions under which purely monetary policy might be effective. An increase in the quantity of money would need to lower the rate of interest by a sufficient amount to stimulate an increase in investment. Whether an increase in the quantity of money would have little or much effect on the rate of interest depends on the shape of the liquidity-preference curve. Keynes felt that beyond a certain point, increases in the quantity of money would not have much effect on the rate of interest because the demand for money becomes highly elastic at low levels of interest. If, however, the rate of interest could be lowered by increasing the quantity of money, its effect depends in turn on the shape of the invest-ment demand schedule. If this schedule in inelastic, that is, relatively unresponsive to changes in the rate of interest, then monetary policy would not have much effect on investment and employment. On the other hand, if the investment demand schedule is elastic, relatively small changes in the rate of interest would increase investment by rel-atively large amounts. If investment can be increased through monetary policy, the effect on income depends on the size of the investment multiplier. During the Great Depression when Keynes wrote the *General Theory,* he felt that monetary policy would have little effect either on the interest rate directly or on investment and employment indirectly. A main reason for this pessimism about monetary policy was that any changes in the rate of interest would be insignificant in relation to wide fluctuations in the marginal efficiency of capital.

Keynes was more hopeful about monetary policy in economic conditions other than a deep depression. During his early career he had championed monetary policy, but in later years he believed that monetary policy remained important primarily as a complement to fiscal policy.

A leading criticism at a purely theoretical level is that Keynes failed to demon-strate that the economic system can be in equilibrium at less than full employment. If Keynes' theory is dependent on special assumptions such as inflexible wages and prices, it may be viewed as a special and not as a general theory. A. C. Pigou and oth-ers argued that if wages and prices are completely flexible in a downward direction, the real value of certain types of existing wealth will increase with a fall in the price level, and this in turn will increase consumption demand and hence reduce unem-ployment. Pigou acknowledged that this wealth effect has no practical significance for policy because wages and prices cannot be made perfectly flexible. Keynes' answer to Pigou's purely theoretical point was that in a monetary economy, such as Keynes was analyzing, the assumptions of complete flexibility of wages and prices is not consistent with the essential properties of money, as discussed by Keynes in Chapter 17 of *General Theory.* It is the properties of money, in a monetary economy, that cause wages and prices to be sticky. If wages and prices happen to be inflexible because of institutional reasons such as strong labor unions and minimum-wage laws, that is incidental and does not have any bearing on Keynes' basic theory.

Keynesian economics originated as a response to a deeply felt need at a time when traditional economics, resting on the premise that the economy tends always toward full employment, had very little to offer by way of explaining the Great Depression. Keynes' seminal ideas made him the most influential economist of the twentieth cen-tury in both economic theory and economic policy. With passing decades, Keynesian economics required modifications in order to remain relevant to changing economic and historical conditions.

References

Hicks, John R., *The Crisis in Keynesian Economics,* Blackwell, Oxford, 1974; Keynes, John Maynard, *The General Theory of Employment, Interest and Money,* Harcourt Brace Jovanovich, New York, 1936; Morgan, Brian, *Monetarists and Keynesians,* Wiley, New York, 1978; Wonnacott, Paul, *Macroeconomics,* Irwin, Homewood, Ill., 1974.

(*See also* Automatic stabilizers; Business cycles; Capitalism; Classical school; Consumption function; Economics; Employment and unemployment; Expectations; Fiscal policy; General equilibrium; Inflation; Interest rates; Investment function; Laissez faire; Macroeconomics; Marshallian economics; Multiplier; Neoclassical economics; Post Keynesian economics; Real balance effect theory)

Dudley Dillard

Keynes effect (*see* Real balance effect theory)

Kitchin cycle

Joseph Kitchin, a British statistician and economist, developed the notion that business fluctuations could be divided into two categories: major cycles and minor cycles. Writing in 1923, he described major cycles as "so-called trade cycles, which are merely aggregates usually of two, and less seldom of three minor cycles," and minor cycles as "averaging three and one third years (40 months in length)." In recognition of Kitchin's work on minor cycles, Joseph A. Schumpeter (1939) named the 40-month cycle the Kitchin cycle, which then became an element in Schumpeter's three-cycle schema of the Kondratieff cycle (54-year average duration), the Juglar cycle (9- to 10-year average duration), and the Kitchin cycle (40-month average duration). Other names for the short cycles are inventory cycles, minor cycles, and American cycles.

The data Kitchin used were of commodity prices, bank clearings, and interest rates in Great Britain and in the United States from 1890 to 1922. While the length of the cycles over that span of time varied somewhat, the dispersion was surprisingly small. W. L. Crum (1923) published his study with much the same results in the same issue of the *Review of Economics and Statistics.*

Kitchin's contribution was almost entirely statistical, as he offered very little in the way of theoretical explanation of the observed phenomenon, stating simply: "These minor cycles are apparently the result of a rythmical movement due to psychological causes, though, through prices of vegetable foods, they may be influenced by excess or deficiency in crops which fall out of tune with normal cycles."

Since Kitchin's time, the 40-month cycle has gained considerable credence because most of the post–World War II business cycles have been of that approximate duration. It must be said that the statistical methodology used by Kitchin was, by today's standards, extremely crude. Furthermore, the data available to him were seriously limited. The National Bureau of Economic Research and the Department of Commerce's Bureau of Economic Analysis as well as a host of other private and governmental agencies have constructed hundreds of significant economic time series with which to measure and evaluate the phases of business cycles. Consequently, the level of sophistication in business-cycle research has improved markedly since Kitchin's work was published.

Explanations of Kitchin Cycles

While many factors contribute to the explanation of business cycles, and while each historical cycle contains its own peculiar features, modern theorists place great stress on inventory investment as the major explanation of minor cycles. Examination of the empirical evidence of the postwar cycles lends strong support for this emphasis. Moses Abramowitz (1948), in particular, has conducted a highly detailed study of the behavior of inventories in the prewar period and concluded that inventory variations conformed well with the cyclical phases in general economic activity. It is also clear that in the postwar period inventory buildup characterized the expansion phases, and inventory liquidation took place during every recession. In the 1953–1954 recession, the decrease in inventories accounted for about 50 percent of the decline in GNP; and in the 1949, 1960–1961, 1967, 1969–1970, and 1974–1975 recessions, the inventory reduction was as great as or greater than the decrease in GNP. According to Abramowitz's prewar study and according to Carl Dauten's postwar analysis, fluctuations in inventory lag behind general business activity by several months.

In order to understand the significance of inventory behavior to general economic conditions, it is necessary to relate inventories to sales and to production. Short-run, such as weekly, fluctuations in sales can be met by merchants or manufacturers by the opposite or inverse movement of inventories without changing the rate of production. For example, if sales increase in one week and in that week production remains the same, inventories would fall by the amount of the sales increase. By the same token, a decline in sales would result in an increase in inventory. Thus, inventories can change, either because of a change in sales which could be anticipated or unanticipated or because of a change in the production rate which is usually, but not always, a conscious decision of the firm's management.

When the demand for goods and services increases in a more or less continuous fashion, as would be the case when the business cycle begins its expansion phase, firms will find their inventories being depleted and will react to this by increasing output or increasing orders from their suppliers. They might also raise prices in order to slow down unit sales. The important aspect of the increased production generated by the increased sales is that production will increase by a larger percentage than the increase in sales. The reason for this magnification is that output will have to increase to replenish the loss of inventories, but firms will also wish to increase the absolute level of inventories in order to be able to service the larger volume of current sales. This is an example of the acceleration principle applied to inventories. The increased output will be further accentuated when managers take the growth in sales to be indicative of even greater growth in the near future, or when inflation is anticipated, or when higher interest rates are expected in the near future.

Once inventories have reached the level desired by the firms involved, the only need for production of goods is to meet current demand, which means that output will be less than it had been, since production to increase the level of inventory is no longer needed. Even a decrease in the rate of increase in final demand can precipitate a reduction in the output of the commodities, and a decrease in demand will generate a magnified reduction in output, bringing on what is referred to as an inventory recession. The downswing will continue until the redundant inventory has been eliminated, at which point any increase in primary demand can set off the recovery phase as just described.

Many economists are of the opinion that this scenario will be seriously ameliorated or even eliminated as more firms begin utilizing modern computer-assisted models of inventory control and the Japanese-favored "just-in-time" inventory management technique. It also may be of some significance that service industries where inventories tend to be small or even nonexistent have grown relative to manufacturing and other producers.

Investment in fixed capital also varies with business fluctuations in about as convincing fashion as do inventories, which indeed is Schumpeter's explanation of the Kitchin cycle when the innovations involved have a short gestation period. The other series that exhibit close conformity with the business cycle are consumer durables.

References

Abramowitz, Moses, *The Role of Inventories in Business Cycles,* occasional paper 26, National Bureau of Economic Research, New York, 1948; Crum, W. L., "Cycles of Rates on Commercial Paper," *Review of Economics and Statistics,* vol. 5, no. 1, January 1923, pp. 17–27; Kitchin, Joseph, "Cycles and Trends in Economic Factors," *Review of Economics and Statistics,* vol. 5, no. 1, January 1923, pp. 10–16; Metzler, Lloyd A., "The Nature and Stability of Inventory Cycles," *Review of Economics and Statistics,* vol. 23, no. 3, August 1941, pp. 113–129; Schumpeter, Joseph A., *Business Cycles,* vol. 1, McGraw-Hill, New York, 1939; Valentine, Lloyd M., and Dennis F. Ellis, *Business Cycles and Forecasting,* 8th ed., South-Western, Cincinnati, Ohio, 1991.

(*See also* Business cycles; Business inventory; Juglar cycle; Kondratieff cycle; Kuznets cycle; Stock-flow analysis)

Lloyd M. Valentine

Kondratieff cycle

The longest business cycle found in economic experience is called the Kondratieff cycle. The name was assigned by Joseph A. Schumpeter in his two-volume study, *Business Cycles* (1939), in recognition of the contributions of the Russian economist Nikolai D. Kondratieff. Kondratieff himself referred to the cycles as "long waves." He wrote, "The wavelike fluctuations are processes of alternating disturbances of the equilibrium of the capitalistic system; they are increasing or decreasing deviations from the equilibrium levels." Kondratieff was not the first to discover long waves. In particular, two Dutch Marxist economists, Van Gelderen and De Wolff, preceded him, as did the Russian Marxist A. I. Helphand (known as Parvus). Indeed, European economists have over the years shown much more interest in the Kondratieff cycle than have the Americans.

The Statistical Evidence

Kondratieff analyzed a number of economic time series for France, England, the United States, Germany, and the world. In most of these series he concluded that a long cycle was evident. On the other hand, in a few series, namely French cotton consumption, U.S. wool and sugar production, and several others, the long-wave pattern was not established. Statistical analysis of the data led Kondratieff to conclude that there existed a general cycle with an average duration of approximately 54 years.

Establishing historical dates for the various phases of cycles is a major preoccupation of business-cycle analysts. Kondratieff contented himself with interval estimates of the turning points, that is, the period of time when a business expansion ended and a contraction set in, and again when the contraction turned into an expansion phase. He produced the following table:

Wave	Duration
First long wave	1. The rise lasted from the end of the 1780s or the beginning of the 1790s until 1810–1817.
	2. The decline lasted from 1810–1817 until 1844–1851.
Second long wave	1. The rise lasted from 1844–1851 until 1870–1875.
	2. The decline lasted from 1870–1875 until 1890–1896.
Third long wave	1. The rise lasted from 1890–1896 until 1915–1920.
	2. The decline probably begins in the years 1914–1920.

These cycles of general economic activity showed what Kondratieff felt was a high degree of parallelism in the capitalistic economies of Europe and in the United States with the exception of such unusual events as the American Civil War and the Napoleonic Wars. This correspondence in behavior was true of price-level indexes in the different countries, in interest rate series, in wages, in foreign trade, and in production and consumption data. Soviet economists were highly critical of Kondratieff's assertion of the existence of the long wave. Most of the criticisms they offered were legitimate professional questions about the data used, the statistical techniques employed, and the theoretical bases, and would have been accepted by Western scholars. However, the intensity of the arguments seems to have been mainly politically motivated since, as George Garvy (1943) pointed out, one of the implications of Kondratieff's analysis was that the long waves were a part of the continuous evolution of capitalistic economies, and that the downswing starting in 1914–1920 would in time be followed by another turning point and an economic expansion. This was contradictory to the Soviet dogma at that time that capitalism was approaching the stage of its final disintegration. Kondratieff had been director of the Moscow Business Conditions Institute and a highly respected economist and government official. But he was discharged from his position and in 1930 was arrested and accused of being the head of the illegal Peasants Labor Party. The remainder of his life was spent in the Gulag, where it is said that he was tortured to such a degree that he went insane and died. His work has been entirely ignored by Soviet economists.

Explanations of the Evidence on the Kondratieff Cycle

Kondratieff was careful not to claim to have discovered the causes of the long waves, though he did say, "We are also of the opinion that the long waves arise out of causes which are inherent in the essence of the capitalistic economy." He does, nevertheless, observe certain empirical characteristics of the cycles he studied which point toward theoretical explanations developed by other economists.

1. He noted that the long waves and the shorter cycles were interrelated in some way since during the expansion phase of the long waves, the periods of prosperity in the intermediate cycles (Juglar or 10-year average cycles) were longer and depression periods shorter; and during the contraction phase of the long cycle, depressions were longer and prosperities shorter.

   Schumpeter extended this analysis to form his basic three-cycle schema in which six Juglar cycles were contained in each Kondratieff cycle, and three Kitchin cycles revolved around each Juglar.

2. Kondratieff agreed with Karl Marx's analysis of one of the causes of business cycles. That was the idea that reinvestment in fixed capital goods occurred in a periodic rhythm. Given a period of growth in production and installation of buildings, machinery, and so on, a business-cycle expansion would be under way; and when investment slowed down, a recession or depression would begin. As the downswing was taking place, this capital would deteriorate over time and would need to be replaced. The period during which the capital was being replaced would constitute the new expansion.

3. Agriculture suffers most severely during the depression phase of the long waves. Kondratieff's findings are in line with those of most other investigators. W. S. Jevons and H. L. Moore, in particular, made agricultural cycles the basis of their business-cycle theories.

4. Important inventions or discoveries are made during the downswing of the long waves, but their application and introduction into the economic system occur in the early stages of the upswing. Kondratieff denied that scientific or technical discoveries were random or accidental events. They happen in large part because of the pressure of necessity generated by the hard times of the depression when the need to find cost-cutting techniques, new products, new markets, or new raw material sources becomes intense. However, the discoveries, inventions, or new ways of producing things will not be applied until conditions are right—when interest rates, wages, material costs, etc., are low and when the existing capital stock has been depreciated or inventory stock depleted. These conditions arise when the depression has gone on for some time, and so the stage is set for recovery.

   Schumpeter made the important distinction between inventions or discoveries and innovations (the application or introduction of the inventions or discoveries) the heart of his explanation of business cycles. Cycles of different lengths were the result of innovations requiring different lengths of time for their absorption into the economy. According to Schumpeter's historical analysis, the first Kondratieff wave was associated with a group of important innovations of the industrial revolution, specifically canals and road building, cotton textiles, coal and iron development and mining, and the steam engine, which played an important role in all the other developments. The second long wave was produced by railroad construction and steel. The third wave took place during the years of the exploitation of the opportunities in the electric power, automobile, and chemical industries.

5. Wars and revolutions take place during expansion phases of the long waves, according to Kondratieff, "They originate from real, especially economic, cir-

cumstances." Marxist economists stress the interrelationship between wars and revolutions and economic conditions.

6. The opening up of new countries and the development of lagging economies seemed to Kondratieff to take place mainly during periods when the needs of the advanced economies for new sources of raw materials and new markets for their output were greatest, that is, during expansion periods.

7. The discovery of gold, increased production of gold in old mines, and the resulting increase in gold and money stock also occur mainly in the early stages of economic expansion. These are not random events but are caused by a favorable economic climate—when the general price level is low and, therefore, the value of gold high; when costs of production of gold (mainly wages) are low; and when banks and bank borrowers have the incentive to expand the supply of currency and demand deposits.

Evaluation

The hypothesis of the existence of the Kondratieff cycle has not fared particularly well in the judgment of many economists. The criticisms are mainly statistical. First, 2½ cycles are not enough to establish such a hypothesis. Furthermore, students who have used different techniques of trend and short-run cycle elimination do not find the same pattern that Kondratieff found. Another point often made is that the only strong support of Kondratieff's position is found in the price-level series and in interest rates, whereas the real series such as production and consumption data seem not to exhibit the long-wave conformity.

However, the behavior of economies in the 1970s and 1980s seems to have inspired renewed academic interest in long waves, a large number of books and articles having been published since 1973 on the subject. Professor Jacob J. van Duijn (1983), a Dutch economist, utilizing more sophisticated statistical techniques than those available to Kondratieff, concludes that long waves do exist empirically in real production as well as in value series. He stresses that the long wave is a worldwide phenomenon, though individual economies are affected in different ways. In his extension of Kondratieff's analysis, van Duijn dates the upper turning point at 1929, where Kondratieff had it at 1914–1920. Further, van Duijn adds a fourth cycle whose lower turning point is 1948 and upper turning point is 1973. Much of the long-wave research in the United States is being done at the MIT System Dynamics Group by, among others, J. W. Forrester and John D. Sterman. Using simulation models, they too conclude that long waves exist in real-world economies. One of their most significant contributions is to make plausible arguments concerning the length of various time lags sufficient to produce cycles of the duration of Kondratieff waves.

References

Daniels, Guy, *The Long Wave Cycle* (a translation of Kondratieff), Richardson and Snyder, New York, 1984; Garvy, George, "Kondratieff's Theory of Long Cycles," *Review of Economic Statistics,* vol. 25, no. 6, November 1943, pp. 203–220, reprinted in Alvin Hansen and Richard V. Clemence (eds.), *Readings in Business Cycles and National Income,* Norton, New York, 1953, pp. 438–466; Kondratieff, Nicolai D., "The Long Waves in Economic Life," *Review of Economic Statistics,* vol. 17, no. 6, November 1935, pp. 105–115, reprinted in *Readings in Business Cycle Theory,* American Economic Association, Blakiston, Philadelphia, 1944, pp. 20–42; Schumpeter, Joseph A., *Business Cycles,* 2 vols., McGraw-Hill, New York, 1939; Valentine, Lloyd M., and Dennis F. Ellis, *Business Cycles and Forecasting,* 8th ed., South-Western, Cincinnati, Ohio, 1991. van Duijn, Jacob J., *The Long Wave in Economic Life,* Allen and Unwin, London, 1983.

(*See also* Business cycles; Juglar cycle; Kitchin cycle; Kuznets cycle)

Lloyd M. Valentine

Kuznets cycle

The term "Kuznets cycle" is customarily used to denote secular swings in economic growth rates exhibiting a duration of approximately 15 to 20 or more years. The cycle is named for Simon S. Kuznets, who made extensive studies, particularly of American economic development, and found evidence of such long swings in many economic activities, but most particularly in the building construction industry. In his early work Kuznets dated long swings for the period prior to World War I. Generally, he dated peaks in 1873, 1892, and 1913, and troughs in 1878 and 1896, although there was some variation from one measure of economic activity to another. In addition to studying building construction, Kuznets analyzed population changes, capital formation, income, gross national product (GNP), and other factors.

Cycles in Growth Rates

The distinctive feature of Kuznets cycles is that they are cycles in growth rates rather than in the absolute expansion and contraction of the level of activity. The name was first attributed to this phenomenon by W. Arthur Lewis and P. J. O'Leary (1955). Kuznets was not, of course, alone in his interest in growth rate fluctuations. Others included most notably Arthur F. Burns, Moses Abramowitz, Brinley Thomas, and A. F. Cairncross.

Lewis and O'Leary summarize a great deal of statistical evidence covering a number of countries in addition to the United States. They conclude that there is evidence supporting the notion of long swings in economic activity, notably in the United States, Germany, and France, where they date three such cycles prior to the First World War, and in the United Kingdom, where they find evidence of a fourth, although in series other than production.

Even though the Kuznets cycle is primarily associated with the U.S. construction industry, it is by no means confined either to that measure of economic activity or to the United States, but is regarded as a phenomenon visible in growth rates in most major industrial economies in the 40 years before World War I. Kuznets and others have also argued that these growth rate swings can be found for the 1920s and 1930s, with Kuznets placing a later peak in 1921 and a trough in 1931. The latter statistics are based on his analysis of both total and per capita income.

Cause of Long Swings

The question of what the cause or causes of long swings might be is unclear. Kuznets (1930) concluded, "While the causes of such fluctuations in the rate of secular growth are still obscure and their recurrence not too widely known, sufficient study has been made to affirm their existence." His emphasis on the high visibility of long swings in building construction has led others, notably Brinley Thomas (1973), to argue that demographic factors, including particularly immigration waves to the United States, are undoubtedly central in explaining the long swings. Thomas argues that building cycles in Britain and the United States were inversely related in the 70 years before World War I, and that the explanation for them in both countries lies in immigration waves. Building in the United States increased after a wave of immigrants arrived; building in Britain would fall after a wave of emigration. Thomas broadened his argument ultimately to relate long swings to what he termed "population-sensitive capital formation." Whether long swings can or cannot be adequately explained by demographic factors is still debatable, even for the pre–World War I period. Lewis and O'Leary (1955) conclude for roughly the same period analyzed by Thomas that the United States, Britain, Germany, and France were "remarkably independent of each other."

Is the Kuznets Cycle a Valid Concept?

Whether or not long swings, assuming their existence is granted for the earlier period, continue in the post–World War II period is again a debatable proposition. The Kuznets technique for examining instability by looking at deviations from the trend has been adapted to what are called growth cycles today—short cycles in growth rates visible in many market-oriented economies. Moses Abramowitz (1956) has argued that even though much of his own work supports the notion of long swings for the earlier period (i.e., 1840–1914), it cannot remain a valid concept in the post–World War I world because there have been historical and institutional changes that preclude its reemergence. Thomas is not so sure that the Kuznets cycle is dead, but argues that certain forces that affected Kuznets cycles earlier clearly either are radically changed or have disappeared. These include immigration waves to the United States, an increase in governmental knowledge about the appropriate application of stabilization policies to avoid severe depressions, and an increase in the absolute and relative size of all levels of government.

Finally, a remaining anomaly is that while Kuznets cycles have always been called "long swings," the term was never meant to apply to the longest recurring pattern economists have considered—the 40- to 60-year cycle typically called the Kondratieff cycle. R. A. Gordon (1961) was, therefore, more accurate when he called Kuznets cycles "intermediate swings." Whether or not the 16- to 22-year growth rate cycle remains a viable concept, economists are increasingly finding that examining cyclical activity in trend-adjusted forms is a rich field for promising research.

References

Abramowitz, Moses, *Resources and Output Trends in the United States since 1870,* occasional paper 52, National Bureau of Economic Research, New York, 1956; Gordon, R. A., *Business Fluctuations,* 2d ed., Harper & Row, New York, 1961; Kuznets, Simon S., *Secular Movements in Production and Prices,* Houghton Mifflin, Boston, 1930; Lewis, W. A., and P. J. O'Leary, "Secular Swings in Production and Trade, 1870–1913," *The Manchester School of Economics and Social Studies,* vol. 23, May 1955, pp. 113–152; Thomas, Brinley, *Migration and Economic Growth,* 2d ed., Cambridge University Press, Cambridge, 1973.

(*See also* Business cycles; Juglar cycle; Kitchin cycle; Kondratieff cycle)

Philip A. Klein

Labor force

The labor force is a measure of marketable, productive human resources. The labor force represents the economically active portion of the population. In the aggregate, it can be expected to expand continuously over time in step with population growth, but this growth can be quite variable, changing in response to all types of economic, social, and even psychological events.

Changes in the labor force and its components are used as measures of overall economic performance, assisting in the determination of the mix of monetary and fiscal policies used in response to changing economic trends. Macroeconomists consider the labor force as one input into aggregate production. If, in the short run, the size of the population is considered fixed, then the amount of *labor supplied* fixes limits on the amounts of goods and services the economy can produce.

Information on changes in the size and composition of the labor-force participation can be used in planning for economic growth. With an understanding of the factors which influence labor-force participation, projections can be made about the size of the labor force in the future and thus the need for jobs.

Definitional Issues in Measuring the Labor Force

In 1970, the United Nations and the International Labour Office formally recommended that a "labor force" approach be taken in all population censuses. This approach is based on the division of the population into two groups: the economically active population and the noneconomically active.

An economic activity is defined as an occupation or endeavor in which the person who performs a service or does work receives compensation and assists in the production of marketable goods and services. The main category of work excluded under this definition is domestic consumption—work around the home which is not undertaken for pay. Other endeavors outside the scope of the market include volunteer activity and attending school. There is no intention of including only "desirable" work or passing any sort of qualitative judgment on the value of nonmarket work. If a family hires someone to do the clothes washing, housecleaning, and other chores formerly performed by family members, those very same activities would then constitute labor-force activity.

Formally, the economically active population is defined by the United Nations as: "All persons of either sex who furnish the supply of labor for the production of goods and services during the time reference chosen for the investigation."

In most uses of the "labor-force" concept, persons are either in or out of the labor force by definition. The determination is made on the basis of their recent activity, so the definition must be based on a particular reference period that clearly frames the meaning of the word "recent." One's availability for work or work status is tested as of a particular point in time.

The present standard has been widely adopted for use in most economically oriented statistical surveys of populations. The labor-force concept replaced the "gainful-worker" concept used in most surveys through the 1930s.

There are many variations in definitions that greatly affect international comparisons of the labor force. The choice of the reference period used will obviously affect labor-force counts. Whether a day, week, month, or year is chosen will affect the counts of persons performing some activity. Clearly, the longer the period, the higher the counts of employed and unemployed. If a comparatively short period is used, specificity will be enhanced, but it will also subject the measure to occasional statistical "noise" due to weather-related or other special circumstances. However, some respondents have difficulty recalling events. Research has shown that using longer reporting periods covering extended periods has produced inconsistent results when compared to concurrent interviews describing much shorter periods.

The amount of work or search effort needed to qualify for inclusion in the labor force is also critical. In the United States and most other countries, one hour of paid work in the reference *week* classifies an individual as "employed" and therefore in the labor force. Unemployed persons must have searched in the last 4 weeks and be currently available for work.

One of the most difficult groups to classify is unpaid family workers. Persons working on family farms are clearly contributing to a marketable product, but they often receive no direct payment in the traditional form of wages. It is very difficult to separate persons performing casual or routine household maintenance from those persons actually contributing to marketable goods and services.

Another measurement problem involves nonactive statuses, for both employed and some unemployed persons. Persons with jobs but not working at them during the survey period must be accounted for. The classic case is the person who took a week off with pay and has "gone fishing." But persons who miss work due to bad weather conditions or because they are out on strike and are not paid for such absences also must be dealt with. In most countries, including the United States, these workers are counted as employed and thus in the labor force. Persons laid off from jobs, without pay, and expecting recall may not be looking for work, the activity criterion for unemployment; they are counted as unemployed and, again, are in the labor force.

Other factors affecting the measurement of the labor force are the *age levels* used. In the United States, the labor force is limited to those over 16 years of age; there is no upper age limit. Some countries such as Sweden and Malaysia employ upper limits as well.

Cultural expectations will also affect the labor-force counts. For example, in countries where cultural constraints discourage women from labor-force activities, women's participation in the labor force is lower. In particular, Middle Eastern and Latin American countries have very low rates of women's labor-force participation. Conversely, countries with liberal attitudes in this regard have higher degrees of female—and overall—participation.

Labor-Force Measures

The most frequently used measures of labor-force activity are the age-sex specific *participation rates.* These rates are defined as the labor-force members of a particular age-sex group divided by the total population of that same age-sex group. For example, the labor-force participation rate for women ages 25 to 34 in the United States in 1991 averaged 73.3 percent: 15,782,000 women ages 25 to 34 in the labor force divided by 21,536,000—the civilian noninstitutional population of women of that age group.

In the aggregate, participation rates follow a pattern. In general, more developed countries have higher overall labor-force participation rates. Developing countries typically have younger age structures, with associated lower participation of the youngest members as well as the greater likelihood that women are home taking care of their children rather than participating in the labor force.

Trends in Labor-Force Participation

In most of the world's countries, the most consistent change in the labor force has been the very sharp increases in women's labor-force participation. In the United States, for example, the participation rate of women in the prime childbearing ages has nearly doubled in the span of 25 years (1965 to 1990). More than half of mothers with children under 1 year of age now work in the United States.

Participation Rates of Men   For men, the pattern of participation appears similar in almost every country in the world. Across most countries, nearly all prime-aged males (those 25 to 54) are in the labor force, regardless of the level of development. At younger ages, participation rates depend on the length of formal schooling before entry into the full-time labor force. The rates also differ across countries for older men, depending on the usual patterns of retirement. The participation rate for all men has fallen somewhat in the post–World War II years, as the population of younger persons has risen relatively and as participation among workers of retirement ages has fallen dramatically, with the advent of extensive pension and social security plans.

Participation Rates of Women   The participation rates of women vary widely across different age levels and across different societies. Women's participation rates are related to the life cycle of marriage and family. In many societies, only single or divorced women work for income; marriage is cause for withdrawal from the labor force, widowhood cause for reentry. In other societies, women work after marriage until they have children.

For example, in some countries with cottage or home industries where many women can work at home, women's participation rates are fairly close to men's rates throughout the life cycle. Many African countries exhibit rising participation rates for women beyond the childbearing ages.

Probably the most common pattern of participation for women is one in which the female labor force is mostly comprised of single or young married women without children, with most women dropping out when they become mothers. This pattern was typical in the United States and other Western countries for many years. In the United States, a double-peaked configuration of participation rates was observed, in which women entered the labor force at younger ages, exited from it in the peak childbearing years, and returned sometime after their children reached school age. In recent years, however, this dip in the age profile of participation rates has disappeared, as young women with children have maintained relatively high rates of labor-force participation throughout their children's preschool years. In other words, women's *pattern* of labor-force participation now largely mirrors that of men.

Issues in Labor-Force Participation

Since most males are typically in the labor force during their middle years, historically, most of the interest in studies of labor force participation has centered on persons in the so-called secondary labor force: youth, elderly persons, and, depending on the specific country and period of time, women. To analyze these people's participation, economists have begun to set their study within a broader framework. Since most people live as members of households, rather than alone, the decision to work is best viewed as a *household* rather than individual choice.

Economists have studied the decision to work in the context of the income or resources of the household and the opportunities in the form of market wages facing the individuals in the household. It is generally assumed that an increase in income, with no other changes, will cause the household to work less. Increased income allows the household to "purchase" more nonmarket, leisure time. For example, in the face of an inheritance, typical decisions that might be made by the family would be that a son or daughter should stay in school longer, a grandparent retire earlier, or a working wife devote full time to homemaking.

A change in the wage rate facing a household member is more complicated. For the same number of hours of work, income is higher. With increased income, the family may be able to hire domestic help to assist with some chores. However, a rising wage also causes a *substitution effect* for those already working. Because wages are higher, work is more attractive, and the family will act to rearrange activities to allow for greater work due to the change in relative prices. Thus, the net effect of rising wages is not known a priori. The questions surrounding these effects have provided the fuel for considerable research on a number of topical areas.

Fertility   The birth of a child increases the amount of household work. This work is usually performed by the mother, some other family member, or someone hired to care for the child. Whether women with infants leave the labor force depends on how the family values these alternative arrangements for child care.

Almost without exception, a strong negative relationship is observed between fertility and women's labor-force participation. A major question is: Which way does causation run? If fertility is a function of labor-force activity, then a country faced with overpopulation would be well advised to encourage women's work in their development strategy. However, if work is timed around fertility, it would make little difference in a development policy. Female labor away from home seems to lower fertility, whereas work which can be carried on at home has less effect. Children on a farm can help with work.

The importance of career interruption is also significant. If a woman is involved in a series of pregnancies, spaced at randomly timed intervals, she may be hampered in certain types of "career" jobs and training by some employers who cannot or will not rearrange work schedules. This has resulted, some argue, in job and training discrimination against women. In the past, women have chosen occupations where such interruptions are not critical, such as secretarial work, teaching, or nursing. However, these occupations tend to be lower paid, which reduced the "costs" of having a child. Today's women in the labor force have much more occupational diversity and greater earnings opportunities than in decades past.

The costs of child care affect women's labor-force participation. In the past, when the industry mix was dominated by manufacturing, jobs were less specialized. Generations of families might all work for the same employer, leading to an extended family network in a small geographic area. This network would help provide a source of inexpensive child care alternatives, as families combined their time and resources. Costs of child care alternatives are especially important for single-parent households and nontraditional families.

Similarly, the cost of domestic service or help affects participation. As women have moved into more professional jobs in recent years, their earnings potential in many cases far exceeded the costs of domestic service.

All in all, the relationship between women's labor-force participation and fertility is still unresolved. Although fertility and participation are obviously negatively related, the strength of the impact as well as the causality is still open to question.

Unemployment   Unemployment is one component of the labor force, so it might seem that its relationship to the labor force would be straightforward. However, higher unemployment acts as a drag on labor-force growth. Persons outside the labor force might delay their decision to enter, and persons already in the labor force in an unemployed status might be more inclined to drop out altogether.

This effect, known as the *discouraged worker hypothesis,* is that, as unemployment rises, participation falls (and vice versa during periods of expansion). People are less likely to look for work if they believe that their search efforts will be futile. An alternative hypothesis, known as the *additional worker hypothesis,* states just the opposite: As unemployment rises, participation rises. After unemployment has been high for a longer time, individuals in the household will enter in search of jobs to make up for the loss of income by the primary earner.

In recent times, researchers have usually found that the discouraged worker effect dominates the additional worker effect. The "additional worker" is likely to be a low-income, or "secondary" earner, whereas a discouraged worker could also be the primary earner. The existence of an additional worker effect also depends on a source of secondary workers. In today's labor force, many married women are already working, and thus fewer are available to join the labor force in response to changing conditions. The additional worker effect, if it occurs at all, only appears after the unemployment rate has been high for a long period.

Dynamics   The labor-force concept measures one's status at a point in time. It does not reveal one's work history or document the timing of changes in status. For example, with most available measures, we often cannot tell whether a "retired" person left his or her career job last month or 10 years ago. If an individual leaves a job after many years and then finds a part-time job to keep busy, that person's labor-force status will be recorded simply as "employed," even though a major change has occurred. Similarly, we can identify "job losers," but we do not know exactly when they lost their jobs.

The distinction between the present activity and the recent past is particularly important in discussing the concept of discouraged workers. Although there is a consensus that workers who have become discouraged about their job prospects and have given up searching should be identified, how to distinguish these persons within the total out-of-labor-force group is not always clear. The classification of discouraged workers—especially whether they should be counted among the unemployed—has long been a topic of debate.

Retirement   The general trend in the participation rates of older workers has been sharply downward. For example, for men over the age of 65, participation rates in the United States fell from levels above 45 percent in 1948 to about 15 percent in 1991. The participation rate of men 55 to 64 years of age dropped from about 90 percent to about 65 percent in the same period.

Participation rates for older workers are related to a number of factors, including their health status, their financial security, and the age composition of the overall population. It is believed that the social security retirement systems in most developed countries have helped to provide a better standard of living for many older workers. Coupled with private pensions, these systems provide a means of support for older persons, who are therefore better able to leave their jobs. In addition, the demand for older workers to remain in the labor force is a function of population composition. As the post–World War II "baby-boom" generation entered the labor force in the 1960s and 1970s, the growth of the size of the labor force was sufficient to meet the rising demand for labor. However, in the 1980s and 1990s the so-called baby-bust era, labor shortages for entry-level and lower-skilled service jobs were observed. Many of these positions were filled by older workers who returned to part-time work to supplement their retirement incomes. In addition, the pressure for older workers either to retire or to remain on their jobs is affected by the supply of potential replacements available to employers.

Future Developments

Two of the most important trends in the labor force in the past are likely to continue and even grow in importance in the coming years. In most developed countries, the biggest single development in the postwar era has been the large-scale entry of women into the labor force. Their entry is an unfinished revolution, whose final effects will not be known for many years. This restructuring of the workplace has had far-reaching impacts, affecting not only work but also the family. How individuals value and use time has changed as the two-earner family has become the norm rather than the exception. As more married couple families work, time at home with the family has been reduced, leaving many couples searching for new ways to increase their time at home.

Work arrangements that provide individuals with greater flexibility, such as part-time work, flextime, home-based businesses, and flexible workplaces are being offered by some leading edge establishments to help retain their valuable human resources. These changes modify the traditional employer-employee relationship, extending beyond such basic items as benefits, vacations, and pensions.

The other significant labor-force development to watch in the near future is the aging of the work force and the shifts in demographic composition. The large cohort of individuals born between the middle 1940s and the middle 1960s will begin to reach retirement age early in the twenty-first century. As they do, the population of prime age working adults will be relatively much smaller than it was in the past. Early retirement and leisure options available to older workers in the past may be reduced, as establishments and governments attempt to cope with the labor shortage and the demographic imbalance. The supply of young workers available to fill entry-level and low-skill jobs will drop, leaving labor-intensive, service-oriented economies with a possible labor shortfall. Filling the gap with incremental changes in the pay and benefits is a likely scenario for businesses, one which will generate its own ripple of labor-force effects.

References

Cain, Glen, "Labor Force Concepts and Definitions in View of their Purposes," in National Commission on Employment and Unemployment Statistics, *Counting the Labor Force,* Washington, D.C., 1979; National Commission on Employment and Unemployment Statistics, *Counting the Labor Force,* Washington, D.C., 1979; President's Committee to Appraise Employment and Unemployment Statistics, *Measuring Employment and Unemployment,* Washington, D.C., 1962; Shack-Marquez, Janice, "Issues in Labor Supply," *Federal Reserve Bulletin,* June 1991, pp. 375–387; Standing, Guy, *Labor Force Participation and Development,* Geneva, International Labour Office, 1978; United Nations, *Principles and Recommendations for the 1970 Population Censuses,* Statistical Papers, Series M, No. 44, 1967, pp. 61–63.

(*See also* Demographics and economics; Employment and unemployment)

Francis W. Horvath and John E. Bregger

Labor-intensive industry (*see* Capital-intensive industry)

Labor-management relations

Often the term labor-management relations is used interchangeably with the terms "labor relations" or "industrial relations," which are regarded as synonymous by practitioners and scholars alike. The field of labor-management relations is relatively new, having more or less developed in the 1930s during the Great Depression. The labor-management relations function developed as a result of the legitimation of the trade union as a social institution during the New Deal era of President Franklin D. Roosevelt. The growth of trade unionism and labor relations during the period 1930 to 1945 is directly related to labor laws which were designed to balance the relative bargaining powers of employers and employee representatives engaged in collective bargaining of labor agreements.

The first significant federal labor law was the Railway Labor Act of 1926, which applies only to the railway and airline industry. Then in 1932, the Federal Anti-Injunction Act, commonly referred to as the Norris-LaGuardia Act after its congressional sponsors, was passed to restrict severely the use of court injunctions in labor disputes now broadly defined beyond the immediate employer-employee relationship. But the real landmark legislative act in the field of labor-management relations is the National Labor Relations Act passed in 1935, commonly called the Wagner Act after the late Senator Robert Wagner of New York. These federal labor laws, girded by the judiciary, played an important part in the legitimation and growth of trade unions and collective bargaining in the United States. Accompanying this growth naturally was the development of the field of labor-management relations.

Although, theoretically, trade unionism and collective bargaining are not necessarily required for the field of labor-management relations, prior to the origin of strong labor unions there was little activity in the field of labor-management relations, which needed the important ingredient of strong employee representatives standing in a complementary relationship with management to evolve into a legitimate field of practice and study. It is generally recognized that trade unionism and collective bargaining are the cornerstones and modus operandi of labor relations in the United States.

Labor-management relations is an important field in search of a theoretical construct. According to John T. Dunlop of Harvard University, a former secretary of Labor, in a landmark treatise on industrial relations systems (1958), "Facts have outrun ideas. Integrating theory has lagged behind expanding experience. The many worlds of industrial relations have been changing more rapidly than the ideas to interpret, to explain, and to relate to them."

There is little debate regarding the conclusion that the great number of facts arising from the real-world practice of labor-management relations has more or less overwhelmed scholars in the field, somehow preventing the development of a neat body of theoretical principles to form a common body of knowledge to assist in the study and development of the field. Scholarship in the field emanates from a variety of disciplinary backgrounds which in itself inhibits a common body of principles. Among these disciplines are economics, industrial sociology, management, psychology, labor law, history, group dynamics, game theory, and social psychology. Although each of these disciplines has made significant contributions to the study of labor-management relations, no single individual is capable of mastering all these disciplines as they apply to the field. Thus, developing an integrated theoretical construct embracing the various social and behavioral sciences involved is difficult due to the complexity of the field. Notwithstanding this current situation, countless scholars from many fields of study are engaged in working toward the goal of finding common threads which make up the field of labor-management relations; from these common threads will ultimately come the theoretical underpinnings that are currently lacking.

Three Contexts

The day-to-day workings of the industrial relations system are carried out by what Dunlop calls "actors" to refer to participants or parties to industrial relations activity. There are three sets of actors: (1) managers and their hierarchial superiors; (2) workers and trade union representatives; and (3) regulatory rule makers representing some form of government. An understanding of the behaviors of the three sets of actors, and, therefore, the industrial relations system, requires a recognition of what Dunlop refers to as the three contexts: (1) the market context; (2) the context of technology at the workplace; and (3) the context of power relations of the enveloping society, as reflected in the workplace.

The market context is fundamental to the understanding of an efficient pricing and allocation system of the work force in the various private and public sectors to meet the demands of consumers and citizens. It is the market context which dictates the broad parameters within which the actors must devise acceptable work rules and compensation packages. The relative value of the services or products in the market-place influences the nature of technology in providing a particular service or product by establishing, at a given time, the feasibility of various levels of capital investment. And it is this capital investment which determines the productivity, and, hence, the value of workers performing the services. In other words, the relative worth of labor producing a given product or service ultimately depends on the value placed upon that product or service by those who demand such products or services in the marketplace. Obviously, if the workplace technology is such to render labor highly productive and efficient, one should expect high rates of pay and generous fringe benefits.

Over time these contexts are dynamic and change with improvements in ways of doing things, such as new discoveries or inventions of better and more efficient methods of production. Ordinarily, the more capital-intensive the method of production, the more productive will be the labor producing a given product. Thus, labor receives higher rewards in modern capital-intensive industries compared with early nineteenth-century handicraft industries because output per worker-hour, or labor productivity, is higher under modern conditions compared with the more primitive labor-intensive methods of production of the preindustrial era.

The third context, that of power relations, is critically important because it is in large part the result of the dynamic interactive forces involving the three actors. The actors interact with the goal of establishing substantive rules to govern their relationship in the day-to-day operations. It is the third actors, the regulatory rule makers in the legislative, judicial, and executive branches of government, who establish the legal environment that governs the behaviors of the other two actors: employers and employee representatives. The rule makers protect the interests and equities of all concerned, not the least of which is the public interest, by providing rules for peaceful pursuit of industrial relations activities and resolutions of disputes between employers and employees. The goal is to avoid or minimize job actions such as work stoppages or employee lockouts which could jeopardize the peace and tranquility of the public.

Labor-Management Relations in the Public Sector

In the United States the principal laws which govern labor-management relations are the Railway Labor Act of 1926, the National Labor Relations Act of 1935 (amended by the Labor-Management Relations Act of 1947), and the Labor-Management Reporting and Disclosure Act of 1959. These are laws enacted by the federal government to regulate employer-employee relations in industries involved in interstate commerce over which the U.S. Constitution provides jurisdictional authority and regulatory responsibility to the federal government. In January 1962, President John F. Kennedy issued Executive Order (EO) No. 10988, which for the first time granted collective bargaining rights to federal employees and which has significantly altered the nature of labor-management relations in federal employment. President Richard M. Nixon reaffirmed the basic principles of EO 10988 in the superseding Executive Order No.

11491, issued on October 29, 1969, and that was subsequently amended in May 1975 by EO 11836, promulgated by President Gerald Ford.

The above executive orders, or presidential actions, accompanied by parallel counterpart legislative and executive actions on the part of state and local governmental authorities, have significantly influenced the nature of labor-management relations in the public sector. Labor-management activity in the public sector is no longer set apart from the mainstream of labor relations in the United States as a separate and distinct segment with totally different rules and regulations. Indeed, there are certain nominal differences governing labor-management relations in the public sector (e.g., the denial of the right to strike or the prohibition of compulsory union membership in the federal sector), but the overall characteristics of public-sector labor relations in the United States are essentially identical with those in the private sector. Although there is no market context in the strictest use of that term in the public sector, the various levels of government are empowered to go into the marketplace for worker and other required resources to provide services demanded by citizens. Government must compete in the marketplace with private bidders for these resources. Thus, government or public employers are affected by market forces which establish the underlying conditions for the setting of wages, benefits, and other conditions of employment. Labor relations activity in the public sector is subject to essentially the same market and technological forces found in the private sector. These forces ensure efficient utilization of scarce resources in providing public services.

The United States versus Western Europe

Labor relations in the public sector in the United States differ significantly from their counterpart in Western European countries fundamentally because labor relations and the institution of collective bargaining are so vastly different in other parts of the world compared with the United States. Contrasted with labor unions in the United States, trade unionism and political parties are closely allied in many European countries. Windmuller (1974) states:

> *For almost a century now, the relationship between trade unions and political parties has been an integral element of the political systems of Western European countries. . . . Virtually all trade unions and their confederations pursue some of their key objectives through long-established links with political parties, and most political parties take into account the claims of trade unions when formulating their programs and objectives, even if they lack formal links to unions. There is hardly any alternative. . . . Therefore, political parties aspiring or clinging to power can no more afford to disregard the vital concerns of major trade union groups than trade unions can afford to abstain from participation in the political process.*[1]

This is not to suggest that labor organizations are not politically active in the United States. But there is no alliance between organized labor and the political parties in the United States, a situation which is quite different from the links which prevail between labor and labor parties in Europe and other parts of the world. Broadly speaking, however, labor relations systems abroad and in the United States are comparable in that mechanisms are put into place to govern the relationships between employers and employees and union-management groups.

---

[1]Reprinted by permission of *Industrial and Labor Relations Review.*

Decisions have to be made regarding substantive issues in the employer-employee relationship regardless of the nature of the employer, public or private, and irrespective of the country of domicile. Although day-to-day labor-management relations are more governed by a collective bargaining agreement in the United States compared with Western Europe, processes must be devised to determine such things as rates of pay, eligibility conditions for benefits, and individual job rights or security; and systems are developed to resolve individual and collective employer-employee differences. These mechanisms and/or processes are inherent in virtually all labor relations systems. Some are perhaps more formal (i.e., legislative) than others, but nevertheless subsystems (procedures or conventions) are devised to establish a network of rules to assist in the making of unavoidable decisions in the workplace.

The Labor Agreement

In the United States, the labor relations function has developed as a result of the evolution of the labor union as a social institution and the acceptance of collective bargaining as the principal modus operandi in labor relations. Free collective bargaining, resulting in a written labor agreement or contract, is the cornerstone of labor relations policy. Long an axiom in organized labor circles is the motto, "No contract, no work!" Hence, the contract or labor agreement is a vital part of labor-management relations, since it constitutes the essence of the agreed-upon rights and privileges, duties, and responsibilities of the parties to the agreement. That is, the labor agreement is the governing document which sets forth the respective interests of employers and employees in substantive provisions in accordance with the prevailing system of jurisprudence. Collective bargaining, however, is more than negotiating a labor agreement. Contract negotiations are but a part of the collective bargaining process. It is the day-to-day administration of the terms and conditions of the labor agreement, which the late Walter Reuther referred to as the "living document," that concerns the bulk of the activities of labor relations practitioners. The labor relations system in the United States, in both private and public sectors, is centered around the labor agreement, which governs the relationship between parties. Beyond the determination of wages, benefits, and other conditions of employment, the labor agreement provides for the preservation of individual and union security, management prerogatives, and a host of other concerns.

Perhaps the most important provision of the labor agreement is that which establishes the steps of the formal grievance procedure to adjudicate employee complaints pertaining to managerial actions which allegedly violate the labor agreement. This system of due process provides for the resolution of employee grievances in a fair and equitable manner. If a particular grievance cannot be resolved between the employer and employee representatives at increasingly higher levels of authority, the matter is then heard by a third-party neutral labor arbitrator for final dispensation. This system of private arbitration is unique to the United States and reflects the U.S. system of jurisprudence. The parties to an unresolved dispute mutually determine who the neutral arbitrator shall be to conduct a formal hearing to adjudicate the matter, and the arbitrator's decision is final and binding on the parties. This unique characteristic of the labor relations system in the United States, labor arbitration conducted by private citizens, is a milestone in the movement toward industrial harmony that originated from practices developed during World War II to avoid work stoppages. The system of private labor arbitration and the practice of reducing to a written labor agreement the results of negotiating terms and conditions of employment between employers and representatives of their employees are landmark contributions to labor-management relations in the United States.

Labor-management relations systems are dynamic and evolve within the three contextual influences indicated. Although predicting future developments in labor-management relations precisely may be difficult, if not impossible, Dunlop's theoretical construct allows for analysis of the major currents and influences of a given industrial relations system.

References

Beal, E. F., E. D. Wickershap, and P. K. Kienast, *The Practice of Collective Bargaining*, 5th ed., Irwin, Homewood, Ill., 1976; Brent, Alan E., and T. Zane Reaves, *Collective Bargaining in the Public Sector*, Benjamin/Cummings, Menlo Park, Calif., 1978; Dunlop, John T., *Industrial Relations Systems*, Holt, Rinehart and Winston, New York, 1958, p. vi; Nesbitt, Murray B., *Labor Relations in the Federal Government Service*, The Bureau of National Affairs, Washington, D.C., 1976; Sloane, Arthur R., and Fred Witney, *Labor Relations*, 7th ed., Prentice-Hall, Englewood Cliffs, N.J., 1991; Spero, Sterling D., *Government as Employer*, Southern Illinois University Press, Carbondale, Ill., 1988; Windmuller, John P. (ed.), "European Labor and Politics: A Symposium," *Industrial and Labor Relations Review*, vol. 28, no. 1, October 1974, p. 3; Windmuller, John P. (ed.), "European Labor and Politics: A Symposium," *Industrial and Labor Relations Review*, vol. 28, no. 2, January 1976; Windmuller, John P., *Collective Bargaining in Industrialized Market Economics: A Reappraisal*, International Labor Organization, Geneva, 1982.

(*See also* Collective bargaining; Government regulation of business; Labor unions)

Sam Barone

Labor Statistics Bureau (*see* Bureau of Labor Statistics)

Labor theory of value

The labor theory of value is a doctrine developed by the English classical economists, chiefly Adam Smith, David Ricardo, and John Stuart Mill; this doctrine had older roots in the seventeenth-century political philosophy of John Locke and before that in the Greek and Roman ideas of market exchange. The doctrine was subsequently adopted by Karl Marx, who gave it the notoriety that it has since acquired.

Three Distinct Theories

The labor theory of value is in fact three distinct theories: it is a theory of relative prices, that is, an explanation of how the exchange ratios between goods are determined in a regime where independent producers compete with each other to maximize their own advantage—the labor theory of relative value; it is a theory of welfare economics, that is, a statement to the effect that an individual or a society is better off as a result of an economic change—the labor theory of absolute value; finally, it is, in its Marxist version, a theory of the nature of profit as a type of income, asserting in effect that profit is unpaid labor appropriated by capitalists as a consequence of the institution of private property—the labor theory of surplus value. In Smith, the labor theory of relative value is relegated to precapitalist times, and Smith focuses instead on the labor theory of absolute value. In Ricardo, it is the labor theory of relative value that is in the foreground, but there is also a labor theory of absolute value, different from and opposed to that of Smith. In Marx, we have all three versions; in particular, the labor theory of surplus value is turned into a special case of the labor theory of relative value.

Outside the Marxist camp, the labor theory of value in any of its meanings disappeared from economics around 1870. But the experience of central economic planning in the Soviet Union, which was said to be based on material balances and calculations of the labor requirements of production, and the emergence of Leontief's technique of input-output analysis, revived interest in the discredited labor theory of value. Modern mathematical economists have rigorously developed the implications of nonsubstitution theorems in which relative prices are entirely determined by labor inputs independent of the pattern of final demand; in short, they have worked out the necessary and sufficient conditions to render the labor theory of relative value a true explanation of prices. The object of this exercise, however, is to explore fully the analytical properties of certain economic models.

No one any longer believes that the labor theory of relative value throws much light on actual pricing problems, and even the Soviet planners never made any serious use of the theory. As a species of welfare economics, the labor theory of absolute value is nowadays regarded as a method of making gross comparisons of welfare, as when Soviet living standards are compared with U.S. ones by asking how many hours of work would be required in each of the two countries to buy specific articles of consumption at going wages and prices. Such comparisons assume that the disutility of labor, the irksomeness of an hour of physical effort, is the same in the two countries, an assumption which Smith defended in the *Wealth of Nations.*

Marxian Interpretation

The validity of the labor theory of surplus value remains a matter of controversy even among Marxist economists: the structure of Marx's argument involves a gross manipulation of arithmetic averages and totals—the so-called transformation problem—that fails to carry conviction. These technical difficulties are sometimes evaded by the argument that Marx meant only to express the ethical doctrine that property income ought to accrue to workers and not to capitalists. The labor theory of surplus value, according to this interpretation, is a theory of natural rights rather than a positive theory of profits. But Marx clearly believed that he had demonstrated that total output, and hence the proportion retained as profits, is entirely created either by living labor or by "dead" labor invested in machines. The more the complexities of this theory are understood, the more difficult it is to give credence to the theory.

Misinterpretations and Confusion

One of the features that makes the labor theory of value so difficult to understand is that its advocates consistently misunderstood the intentions of their predecessors: Ricardo misinterpreted Smith's meaning, and Marx in turn misinterpreted Ricardo's meaning. Ricardo was convinced that Smith tried to formulate a labor theory of relative value and that he became confused between the concept of the labor "commanded" by a commodity and the labor "embodied" in a commodity. The labor-commanded theory cannot possibly be a theory of relative value, and to suggest that Smith could have confused such different phenomena as the labor price and the labor cost of a commodity is simply absurd. Smith did not try to formulate a labor theory of relative value but rather a labor theory of absolute value.

Ricardo was the first economist in the history of economic thought to insist on the labor theory of relative value: He believed that commodities exchange in ratios that are approximately equal to the ratios of labor required to produce them. Ricardo was aware that these ratios are only approximately equal because commodities cannot exchange exactly in proportion to relative labor costs when they are produced in time periods of unequal length, or with machines of unequal durability, or simply with different ratios of fixed to working capital. Marx recognized that the labor theory of relative value can never account completely for the relative prices of reproducible commodities, not to mention the prices of nonreproducible commodities. Marx dealt with the problem posed by Ricardo by focusing attention on a "typical" commodity produced by a ratio of capital to labor that is an average for the economy as a whole, and both his theory of relative prices and his theory of profits is true only of this typical commodity.

What is really extraordinary is that neither Ricardo nor Marx, nor even Ricardo's and Marx's numerous followers, ever raised the question of whether it is always possible to calculate the numbers of labor-hours "embodied" in the production of commodities. The notion was that the living labor was directly observable and that the "dead" labor invested in machines was in principle observable by examining the machine tools industry, so that every component input into the production of a commodity could be reduced to labor invested in the past at some earlier stage of production. No doubt, this series of past investments of labor was very long and probably infinite because there never was a time when the first tool was created by bare hands; however, an infinite sum of dwindling quantities can add up to a finite number, so this difficulty is not itself fatal. However, all this is true only if production structures are linearly sequential, that is, if raw materials feed into a later processing stage, being processed in turn with the aid of labor and machines into a finished product. Thus, to give a single example, raw cotton is carded and spun into gray yarn and then the gray yarn is woven into gray cloth, which is then dyed into cloth salable to consumers. But suppose instead that production is sequential but circular, that is, iron ore is mined and smelted into steel which is then used to make steel machines, which in turn makes final consumer goods but is also used to make mine-drilling equipment to extract iron ore. If we now attempt to calculate the labor embodied in a product made with one of these steel machines, we will find ourselves adding live labor to dead labor ad infinitum. It is impossible to arrive at a finite sum of labor inputs applied in the past when the production process is circular, and, unfortunately, modern interindustry analysis has shown that circular production processes are in fact more typical of modern industry than linear production processes.

This is a fatal objection to the labor theory of value to which there is simply no answer. Be that as it may, it is a striking fact that such brilliant thinkers as Adam Smith, David Ricardo, John Stuart Mill, and Karl Marx writing about the labor theory of value over a period of almost 100 years never once asked themselves how one actually calculates the total amount of labor required to produce a commodity.

References

Blaug, M., *Economic Theory in Retrospect,* 4th ed., Cambridge University Press, New York, 1985, chaps. 2, 4, 6, 7; Gordon, D. F., "Value, Labor Theory of," in D. L. Sills (ed.), *International Encyclopaedia of the Social Sciences,* vol. 16, Free Press, New York, 1968, pp. 279–283.

(*See also* Classical school; Normative economics; Welfare economics)

Mark Blaug

Labor unions

Labor unions are organizations of employees established to bargain with employers concerning wages, hours, and conditions of employment. Unions are democratic institutions whose central purpose is improving the economic conditions of their members.

Categories, Importance, and Functions

Workers are organized in unions on either an industrial, craft, or professional basis. In an industrial union workers of an employer generally will be affiliated with similar locals of other employers in a like industry, thus forming a national union. The craft or professional group will have representatives of various employers in a local union which is similarly affiliated with like workers in a national union.

In the United States there are 110 unions and associations with 16.7 million members. As we all know, the number of union members has declined from nearly 23 million in the late 1970s. Nevertheless, in 1990 the number of union members accounted for 16 percent of the total labor force and 20 percent of nonsupervisory wage and salary employees in nonfarm establishments.

There is a general confederation of unions called the American Federation of Labor-Congress of Industrial Organizations or, more commonly, the AFL-CIO. Ninety national and international unions affiliated with the AFL-CIO. The AFL-CIO deals primarily with issues of public policy, international relations with foreign trade unions, and coordination of activities between unions in support of their common goals and objectives.

National and local unions engage in direct collective bargaining activities with specific employers concerning the detailed contracts that set forth wages and conditions of employment. Contracts may cover numerous employers in an industry nationwide, such as the United Mine Workers' contracts with many coal companies. Some contracts may be with one employer nationwide, such as the United Auto Workers' contract with General Motors. Some contracts may cover just one plant or group of plants or stores of a multiplant corporation, such as United Food and Commercial Workers' contract with Safeway stores in Washington, D.C. Electricians may have one contract with all electrical contractors in an area. More than one union may have contracts with a single employer with each contract representing certain crafts, as is frequently the case in the railroad industry or the printing industry. Some public employees may be organized on a craft or professional basis, such as fire fighters or teachers; others may be organized on an overall industrial basis, such as the American Federation of State, County, and Municipal Employees, or the American Federation of Government Employees.

At the state and local levels, AFL-CIO state and local central bodies also exist to deal with common state and local concerns. Such state and local AFL-CIO bodies represent the local unions in local or state public policy matters.

Generally, it is believed that unions tend to raise the wages of their members. Studies by Ashenfelder (1978) and Lewis (1986) indicate that unions tend to lead to a 10 percent differential in favor of such workers. However, some economists dispute the ability of unions to raise the wages of workers above general market equilibrium levels.

There is general agreement, however, that unions bring a system of jurisprudence to the workplace that provides a means of governing on-the-job relationships, resolving individual grievances, and providing due process in disciplinary and discharge cases. The union contract restricts the employer's ability to take unilateral personnel actions. The contract generally ensures equal treatment of all workers according to the specific provisions of the contract. (See Freeman and Medoff, 1984.)

Collective Bargaining

Unions achieve their wage and working conditions improvements through bargaining collectively with employers. When the collective bargaining process does not result in a mutually agreed contract, workers may strike to try to enforce their demands concerning wage and conditions of employment. Major strikes provide frequent headlines in the newspapers; however, on the average, strikes occur in fewer than 3 percent of all negotiations, and 97 percent of the negotiations lead to settlements without disruption of working relationships. In very few instances, employers may lock out employees in a negotiating dispute. Most contracts contain a no-strike provision for the term of the contract, with unresolved differences as to contract interpretation being adjudicated by private arbitrators.

The basic rights of the employee to organize into unions and to engage in collective bargaining are guaranteed in the Labor-Management Relations Act. That law gives the National Labor Relations Board authority to conduct secret-ballot elections to determine workers' desires regarding unionization and provides a mechanism for certifying unions selected by a majority. That law also obligates employers and unions to bargain collectively in good faith and provides help to the parties in bargaining through the mediative efforts of the Federal Mediation and Conciliation Service. The internal democratic structure and financial responsibility of unions are spelled out in the Labor-Management Reporting and Disclosure Act.

Legislation similar to the Labor-Management Relations Act exists for employees in the railroad and airline industries under the Railroad Labor Act. Special legislation or executive orders govern federal and postal labor relations, and separate state laws govern union recognition or collective bargaining for state and local government employees.

History

Unions trace their history to the earliest days of the nation. Unions of carpenters and shoemakers were organized shortly after the Revolution. Initially, the courts and the laws tried to restrict the rights of workers to form and join unions. However, in spite of repeated prosecution, unions grew and expanded in the nineteenth century. The organization of unions was plagued by strong employer opposition, and many strikes were the result of employer refusal to recognize or bargain with unions.

The first national unions were founded in the 1850s representing workers in the printing industry (International Typographical Workers Union), the machinists (International Association of Machinists), and molders (International Molders and Allied Workers Union). Many unions use the title "international" in their name, indicating their representation of workers in the United States and Canada. They usually do not represent workers in other countries.

The American Federation of Labor (AFL) traces its history to 1881—at the founding convention a number of existing national unions joined in a confederation of national unions. Earlier confederations had failed to flourish for any prolonged period, but the AFL was the turning point in continuity for a labor federation in the United States. In 1937 the Congress of Industrial Organizations (CIO) split off from the AFL, and the CIO was founded as a separate organization. Its special emphasis was to organize workers on an industrial basis. The two separate union federations merged to form the AFL-CIO in 1955.

Unions exist in most democratic societies as a basis for providing workers with a means of representation and with a voice in determining their wages and working conditions. These free unions have formed various international confederations such as the International Confederation of Free Trade Union and the International Confederation of Christian Trade Union. In Soviet societies, unions were established to provide a framework for encouraging worker productivity. Marxist theory had postulated that unions were to become a fulcrum for the overthrow of the bourgeois state. However, Marxist theory never held that unions could actually negotiate with employers concerning wages and working conditions. Some of the unions in Western society trace their antecedents to medieval guilds, and unions are considered an important economic and political element in most Western societies.

Since the 1930s, when Congress enacted a number of basic labor laws, unions have played an important role in labor relations in the United States. The Norris-LaFollette Act of 1932, made employer antiunion actions illegal, such as the blacklisting of union workers or the requirement that workers pledge not to join a union (yellow-dog contracts). The Wagner Act of 1935 set up the machinery for certifying unions as bargaining agents for workers and set forth a national policy that encouraged collective bargaining as a means of giving workers a voice in their work environment. Furthermore, during the 1970s and 1980s union efforts resulted in collective bargaining laws at the state level which impact on public employees.

References

Ashenfelder, Orley, "Union Relative Wage Effects: New Evidence and a Survey of Their Implications for Wage Inflation," in Richard Stone and William Peterson (eds.), *Econometric Contributions to Public Policy*, Macmillan, London, 1978, pp. 31–63; Bok, Derek C., and John T. Dunlop, *Labor and the American Community*, Simon & Schuster, New York, 1970; Brooks, Thomas R., *Toil and Trouble: A History of American Labor*, rev. ed., Dell, New York, 1972; Freeman, Richard B., and James L. Medoff, *What do Unions do?*, Basic Books, New York, 1984; Kochan, Thomas A., Harry C. Katz, and Robert B. McKersie, *The Transformation of American Industrial Relations*, Basic Books, New York, 1986; Lewis, H. Gregg, *Union Relative Wage Effects: A Survey*, University of Chicago Press, Chicago, 1986.

(*See also* Collective bargaining; Labor-management relations)

Rudy Oswald

Laissez faire

The French expression, *"laissez faire, laissez passer,"* means, "Let events go ahead and happen as they might." To pursue a policy of laissez faire means that the government chooses not to intervene and instead allows ordinary market forces to work themselves out. The term is attributed to a legendary conversation between a merchant and the French Minister of Finance Colbert. Colbert, a supporter of mercantilist remedies for business problems, asked the merchant what the state might do to help the business community, whereupon the merchant replied, *"Laissez-nous faire!"*

Nonintervention and Free Trade

The term is still used to refer to the policy of nonintervention. Writing in *Newsweek* (13 August 1979), Paul Samuelson described a "hard-boiled consistent advocate of laissez faire" as one who, when asked whether the state should subsidize companies that have fallen on bad times, would reply, "let the losers bite the dust. Ours is a profit-and-loss system. If they can't shape up to the market, let them go through the wringers of bankruptcy. The system will be better off for it. Liquidations and closedowns are the healthy catharsis of an effective economic system." And the weeding and pruning that occurs in the market has been hailed by many economists such as Alfred Marshall, Herbert Spencer, Armen Alchian, Richard Nelson, Jack Hirshleifer, and Sidney G. Winter as a process analogous to natural selection in nature. This process makes organizations and institutions better adapted to the needs of the community.

Historians sometimes use the term "laissez faire" to describe the economic policy of removing tariffs and other barriers to international trade. But this connection between free trade and laissez faire is somewhat misleading. Most supporters of free international trade did not consider themselves laissez faire economists. The leading members of the classical school largely supported free international trade but went out of their way to explain why the noninterference principle or laissez faire rule was not without exceptions. Even John Bright, the most hardboiled of the Manchester school of free trade liberals, was a supporter of the child labor laws that restricted employment among children. John Stuart Mill (*Principles of Political Economy*, 1848) summed up the attitude of the classical school when he wrote that "laissez faire, in short, should be the general practice: every departure from it, unless required by some great good, is a certain evil." Historically, nearly every economist of authority had a rather detailed list of great goods for which departures from the laissez faire principle were permissible. Political items on the agenda for state reform included public sanitation; public education; antitrust legislation; public utility regulation; construction of bridges, harbors, and roads; demand management; national defense; central banking; and the creation of a patent reward system.

In the history of economic thought there have been few thinkers who have considered themselves pure laissez faire economists. It was only among the early French liberal economists of the first part of the nineteenth century that something of a reverence for the widespread application of the laissez faire principle flourished. The Paris group, which consisted of Jean Baptiste Say, Charles Comte, Gustav Molinari, Charles Dunoyer, and Frederick Bastiat, recognized that economic activity is founded on voluntary exchange and that voluntary exchange benefits both contracting parties. Political activity requires taxes, and taxes are obtained by involuntary exchange. Therefore, it seemed to follow that the way to promote a harmony of interests in society (and increase in social welfare) was to minimize if not eliminate the role of the state in economic life and encourage private provision of all goods and services. In the United States, French liberal thinking had some impact on the private property anarchist movement that still flourishes among libertarian economists in the United States and England of which the leading American authorities are Murray N. Rothbard and David Friedman. In Europe, French liberal thought influenced the writings of some members of the Austrian school of economics, especially Ludwig von Mises (*Human Action,* 1949).

A Paradox

The paradox of the laissez faire position is that what exists in the real world at any moment is the outcome of laws and rules founded on numerous earlier state interventions. The existing distribution of property rights titles is the consequence of all that has happened before. Either this existing distribution is just or unjust. If it is unjust, then political action may be needed to remedy it. And so we have the laissez faire economist advocating coercion to rectify previous coercions. Exactly who is to administer the new round of coercions? A revolutionary tribunal? If the distribution is declared just, then the laissez faire economist becomes the friend of reactionary interests in society and a political conservative. It appears that we must distinguish between laissez faire as an attitude or general rule and laissez faire as a consistent social philosophy. In its former form it has many proponents; in its latter form it is accepted by only a handful of thinkers.

References

Francis, Mark, "Herbert Spencer and the Myth of Laissez-Faire," *Journal of the History of Ideas,* vol. 39, April/June 1978, pp. 317–328; Friedman, David, *The Machinery of Freedom: Guide to Radical Capitalism,* 2d. ed., Open Court, La Salle, Ill., 1989; Kittrell, Edward R., "Laissez Faire in English Classical Economics," *Journal of the History of Ideas,* vol. 27, October/December 1966, pp. 610–620; Liggio, Leonard P., "Charles Dunoyer and French Classical Liberalism," *Journal of Libertarian Studies,* vol. 1, Summer 1977, pp. 153–178; Moss, Laurence S., "Private Property Anarchism: An American Variant," in G. Tullock (ed.), *Further Exploration in the Theory of Anarchy,* University Publications, Blackburg, Va., 1974; Nelson, Richard R., and Sidney G. Winter, *An Evolutionary Theory of Economic Change,* Harvard University, Cambridge, Mass., 1982; Rothbard, Murray N., *Power and Market,* Institute for Humane Studies, Menlo Park, Calif., 1970; Samuelson, Paul A., "Judging Corporate Handouts," *Newsweek,* August 13, 1979, p. 58.

(*See also* Austrian economics; Barriers to trade; Classical school; Manchester school)

Laurence S. Moss

Law of diminishing returns (*see* Diminishing returns law)

Leading indicator approach to forecasting

The economic system can be viewed as thousands of economic processes that we call "indicators." Some of these processes reach highs (peaks) and lows (troughs) before the general economy reaches them and are thus called "leading" indicators. Those that represent the general economy are called "coinciding" indicators, because their timing at peaks and troughs of the business cycle tends to coincide with the timing of the general economy. There are also "lagging" indicators, whose timing at peaks and troughs tends to be later than that of the general economy. These three timing phases—leading, coinciding, and lagging—are incorporated into what has long been known as the indicator approach to economic analysis and forecasting.

Leading Indicators

Leading indicators decline before the general economy at peaks; they recover sooner at troughs. The Commerce Department's Bureau of Economic Analysis (BEA) each month publishes 300 economic indicators in its monthly *Survey of Current Business.* Of these, 65 indicators are classified as leading the general economy during the business cycle. On average, their lead time before peaks is about a year and about 5 months before troughs.

In addition to publishing 65 indicators that lead the economy, the BEA also publishes the so-called leading indicator composite that is made up of 11 leading indicators. It is a popular index for sensing the state of the general economy for the next several months. The 11 indicators are: housing permits, liquid assets, money supply, stock market, average workweek, sensitive prices, business formation, layoff rate, plant and equipment orders, inventories, vendor performance, and new consumer orders. The average postwar prerecession lead for the 11 as a composite is 11 months, and the 11 individual lead times range from 6 to 12 months (standard deviation: 2.12 months). These 11 leaders by no means peak and trough at the same time. Rather, they spread across a wide timing spectrum of their own. (Note that those leading indicators used at troughs are not necessarily the same as those used for peaks.)

Recent Revisions

The leading indicators are reevaluated and updated every few years. They developed a serious weakness during the 1974–1975 recession, when researchers discovered that indicators that included inflation actually kept the composite index rising, even after the recession began. In effect, they prevented the composite from leading the recession. This problem, however, was overcome by including only deflated indicators among the 11 leaders in the major revision that followed the 1974–1975 recession. The leading indicator composite prior to the revision had an average lead before recessions of about 5 months. The newly revised composite adopted by the BEA in 1976 had a lead time of 10 months—twice as long as the earlier inflated composite. Such a dramatic change in lead time is significant. If government policymakers initiate an economic policy that impacts on the coinciding indicators 6 to 12 months later, it is desirable to test the impact of the policies on the leading indicators before they impact on the coinciders. Needless to say, a leading indicator with a 10-month lead time would be better for this purpose than one with only a 5-month lead.

Policy versus Traditional Indicators

If there is cause and effect in the economic system, then it would follow that various economic processes peak and trough at different times. In the early postwar years, the indicator approach was criticized for not being causal. It was regarded by some as an "omen" system. These criticisms have subsided partly because the leading indicators used today include many that are considered causal. These are generally indicators that are closely related to federal government policies, which most economists regard as being causal in nature. One sequence goes like this: The Fed initiates a policy to lower interest rates. This action immediately affects the number of new houses started: cause and effect. The rates also trigger later leading indicators to peak or trough, these in turn signaling that the government policies are or are not working. So, in effect, there are today two types of leading indicators—those that are policy-related and those that are of the more traditional kind. The policy indicators tend to have longer leads than do the latter.

The policy-related leading indicators tend to lead the general economy by the longest time—1 to 2 years at peaks—and emanate from both monetary and fiscal policy. These indicators include such things as money supply, interest rates, and taxes. Other long leaders are closely affected by these, such as housing starts, housing permits, liquid assets and new businesses—all indicators that are critically dependent on federal government economic policies.

Leading indicators with a medium length of lead—6 to 12 months at peaks—are much more likely to correspond to the behavior of factory operations than to government policy. These relate to orders, profits, and employment. These have been called "smokestack" indicators and serve the very valuable purpose of confirming whether the longer-lead policy indicators are working.

The shortest leads—1 to 6 months—are highly influenced by things like inventories. Although inventories represent sensitive leading characteristics, they pose serious problems as leading indicators. For one thing, inventory statistics are not easy for the reporting company to report correctly. In addition, they have a serious problem of being reported late. These problems cause inventories to lose their already rather short leads. Although they are important leading indicators, it is difficult to benefit from their leads, given their dual defects of lateness and shortness of lead.

Indicator Approach versus Econometric Approach

The indicator approach is often contrasted with the econometric approach in analyzing and forecasting the macroeconomy. Actually, the two approaches are quite compatible. The timing considerations that are so important to the indicator approach are equally important in econometrics, but they are treated differently. In econometrics, timing differences are handled by means of regression lags. For example, it is no surprise that housing starts are a leading indicator of furniture sales. We cannot put furniture into the foundation of a house under construction. It is several months before a new house is sufficiently completed to begin moving in the furniture. Consequently, it is logical to conclude that an important part of furniture sales is a function of new houses for which construction began several months prior to sale of the furniture. One of the great contributions of econometrics is the ease with which it can incorporate lead or lag timing relationships within the model through its principal tool—regression. Still, econometrics is weak in graphic portrayal. Graphics, however, is one of the special advantages of the indicator approach. Indeed, since so many users of both the econometric and the indicator approaches are required to justify their forecasts by both visual and verbal methods, the indicator approach represents a solid addition to econometrics.

One of the most serious challenges to indicator economics is the fact that the leading indicators have reasonably stable mean lead times but suffer badly with respect to their standard deviations around their means. This statistical defect forces indicator economists to use large numbers of leading indicators since one or even several leaders are simply not statistically reliable. The *Survey of Current Business's* (SCB's) 65 leading indicators published every month help economists avoid concentrating on too few views of economic performance. The 65 indicators also enable economists to segment economic performance by process. These performance sectors include employment, production, consumption, capital investment, inventories, prices, costs, profits, money and credit—a sufficient number of processes to allow considerable research and monitoring into special areas of the economy.

Five-Phase Timing Model

One of the more interesting aspects of the indicator approach—again made possible by the large number of indicators available to the public through the BEA—is to expand the system from the traditional three-phase to a five-phase timing model. In the newer five-phase system, the customary three timing phases—leading, coinciding, and lagging indicators—are included as the middle of the system. But there is a new beginning and a new ending that more closely parallel a total beginning-to-end economic structure. The new beginning is a sector reserved for federal government policy and related indicators. These are considered to be first-cause indicators, which are followed by the leaders, coinciders, and laggers. At the end of the system are the final-effect indicators—prices. This system, beginning with the causal policies and ending with prices, conforms well to modern economic theory. It is well-documented that monetary policy impacts on production 6 to 12 months after being initiated. It is also well-documented that policy tends to impact on prices (final effects) 18 to 24 months after initiation. The five-phase indicator system conforms closely to this economic reality.

References

Center for International Business Cycle Research, Graduate School of Business, papers and reports, Columbia University, New York; McLaughlin, Robert L., "A New Five-Phase Economic Forecasting System," *Business Economics,* National Association of Business Economists, Cleveland, September 1975; U.S. Department of Commerce, *Survey of Current Business,* published monthly.

(*See also* Econometrics; Economic forecasting methods; Economic models; Statistical methods in economics and business, an overview.)

Robert L. McLaughlin

Less-developed country debt

Less-developed country debt, or LDC debt, has become a quite dynamic topic with the convulsive changes in Eastern Europe and the breaking away of the republics of the old Soviet Union. Just a few years ago, the LDCs were commonly understood to encompass the poorer Third World countries—with the Soviet Union and Eastern Europe a "Second World" below the industrial economies of the United States, Canada, Western Europe, Japan, and Australia-New Zealand. Not only have the boundaries of nation states changed since the fall of the Berlin Wall in 1989, but now the world is more neatly divided into just two groups—the industrial countries and the "developing" economies. The International Monetary Fund, probably the leading arbiter of country classifications, divides the world into two groups: 23 industrial countries and 138 developing countries of varying income levels. The developing countries include the traditional "LDC" economies in Africa, Asia, the Middle East, Latin America, and the Caribbean and now also some countries of Southern Europe, Eastern Europe, and the new states of the old Soviet Union. For the sake of convenience, these 138 developing economies can be referred to as the LDCs in this survey.

LDC debt is understood to mean the external indebtedness, both public and private, of the developing countries. As of 1991, the total external debt of the developing countries was almost $1.5 trillion. About $1.3 trillion of the debt was of long-term maturity of over 1 year, and the balance was short-term. By types of creditors, commercial banks were the largest lenders, holding $608 billion of the nearly $1.5 trillion; other private lenders were owed $288 billion; and official lenders—the IMF, World Bank, regional development banks, governments—held $597 billion of the debt.

The greatest public attention of LDC debt has focused on the Latin American countries, as the de facto defaults of many of these countries in 1982 almost precipitated a world financial crisis. Reflecting this, the countries of Latin America and the Caribbean are the largest borrowers among developing countries, with about 32 percent of the total external debt. The Asian countries (obviously excluding Japan) are the second largest debtors with 25 percent of the obligations, followed by the African countries with 16 percent. Eastern Europe and the old Soviet Union owe about 11 percent of the debt, and the smaller developing countries of Europe and the Middle East owe the balance of 16 percent.

The best understanding of the LDC debt can be gained in terms of analyzing historical cycles of expansion and retreat of lending. Some analysts contend that external debt exhibits regular cycles of rise and fall and rise, starting especially with the borrowings of the newly independent Latin American republics early in the nineteenth century in London. Focusing just on the Latin American debt, the cycles have been boom in the 1820s; defaults in the 1830s; another revival in the 1870s; and then a panic in London in 1890 as problems with Argentine loans almost brought down the venerable Barings investment bank save for the intervention of the Bank of England.

Following World War I, another frenzy of Latin American borrowings took place in the United States via the investment banking arms of U.S. banks. Most of these 1920s bond issues were in default in the 1930s. The banks returned to Latin American lending in the early 1970s, impelled in part by the recycling of the OPEC balance-of-payments surpluses. U.S. banks were joined by Canadian, European, and Japanese banks in making direct loans to Latin American governments and to private companies during the 1970s, and total long-term Latin American debt rose sixfold from $28 billion in 1970 to $172 billion by 1980. But a bad stew of deteriorating world conditions—recession, rising interest rates, falling commodity prices—made a large part of the Latin American debt buildup hard to service as banks found it difficult to justify roll-over finance and new lending. Thus, the early part of the 1980s in Latin America was an era of reschedulings of debt as maturities were extended while "concerted" or involuntary lending took place for liquidity purposes under the auspices of the International Monetary Fund.

While the Latin American economies became mired in debt-servicing problems and stunted economic growth in the 1980s, the more dynamic and export-oriented East Asian economies adjusted successfully to a world of constrained finance and escaped (except for the Philippines) the LDC debt crisis sparked in Latin America. Because of these different experiences, a distinct tiering has developed of countries with debt-servicing problems and those without—Brazil and South Korea, for example, serving as polar opposites among the LDCs in this differentiation.

For Latin America, a second phase in their debt crisis was attempted in 1985 with U.S. Secretary of the Treasury James Baker's plan for growth accompanied by economic reforms and increased lending by the World Bank and the commercial banks. This program was partially successful, but as the commercial banks began to develop methods for reducing their debt through swaps for equity and other investment vehicles, the solution to the Latin American debt problem came to be seen more in terms of reducing the debt "overhang"—a stock of debt too large to be serviced. Finance Minister Kiichi Miyazawa of Japan (who became prime minister in 1991) proposed a plan in 1988 to convert bank loans into long-term bonds, with debtor country guarantees to be deposited with the IMF. Part of this idea was incorporated in the March 1989 proposal of U.S. Treasury Secretary Nicholas Brady for official support of voluntary debt reductions by commercial banks in exchange for bonds, with guarantees provided from IMF and World bank disbursements to countries undertaking economic reforms.

The Brady Plan finally broke the logjam of excessive LDC debt, and by 1991 five countries—Mexico, Venezuela, the Philippines, Costa Rica, Uruguay—had completed agreements for a one-quarter reduction, or $20 billion, of their commercial bank debt plus associated debt service reductions. Other countries—notably Chile and Argentina—reduced bank debt through swaps for equity, especially through privatization of state enterprises. For most of these countries, the resolution of the debt problem with the banks seemed to be the key for renewed investor confidence, faster economic growth, and the shift to their direct access of market financings in the terms of international bonds and equity markets, with a much smaller reliance on commercial bank debt.

Although the bank debt of the LDC countries received most of the public's attention as well as the concern of industrial country governments, the debt owed to official institutions was resolved by other means. This took the form of "Paris Club" reschedulings by the leading creditor governments, at facilities offered by the Bank of France in Paris. Although the bank debt predominated for the Latin American countries, the problem of the government-to-government debt was concentrated mainly in the poorer sub-Sahara African countries and in Eastern Europe and the Soviet Union. Because of these countries' lower income levels, creditor country governments have increasingly offered to unilaterally cancel part of the debts of such countries. For example, Paris Club creditors have agreed to forgive debts of Poland and Egypt by 50 percent. Larger reductions, sometimes full cancellation, have been offered to low-income sub-Sahara African countries. By 1990, cancellation of official debt amounted to almost $6 billion, most of it to the sub-Sahara countries.

For Eastern Europe and the Soviet Union, much different arrangements for handling their external debt problems have been initiated. Poland has accepted the write-down of its debt, but Hungary has refused to consider any concessions for fear of losing its creditworthiness. For the old Soviet Union, quite extraordinary debt arrangements have been made because of difficulties in determining who is, or are, the ultimate obligor(s) of debt undertaken by the central government of the former Soviet Union. With a total convertible currency debt estimated at between $57 billion and $71 billion (excluding arrears), the principal on the Soviet obligations was deferred for the year 1992, with interest being paid, in anticipation of more permanent arrangements with creditors. But practical difficulties had to be resolved as to the division of the foreign exchange payments to be assumed by the newly independent components of the Commonwealth of Independent States.

The topic of external debt of the LDCs has spawned an enormous literature, centering on causes of the Latin American debt crisis of 1982–1989 and continuing with many ideas for solutions that were proposed along the way before general acceptance of officially sponsored debt reduction was finally carried out in 1990. Excessive lending by the banks have been seen by some analysts as the cause; others have pointed to excessive country borrowings to finance ill-advised projects; still other economists have cited the demise of the fixed exchange rate system and the ensuing volatilities of currencies and interest rates. No single cause can explain the boom and bust of the external debt cycle—the factors are many and interdependent. But there does seem to be general agreement that the worst of the LDC debt crisis has passed and that as of 1991–1992 most of the Latin American countries, notably Mexico, Venezuela, and Chile, had made a successful transition to obtain bond and equity financing from the international capital markets, joining the more successful Asian and European developing countries. The sub-Sahara African countries face a longer road to resolve the debts still owed to creditor governments and eventually to gain access to the commercial credit markets.

As to the outlook for another generalized LDC debt crisis, most observers agree that the commercial banks are not likely to resume large-scale balance-of-payments loans. The banks will likely confine themselves to more secure trade and project finance. The main channels for the external financing of the LDCs will likely center on the private international credit markets along with foreign direct investment and credits from governments and official multilateral lenders.

References

Dawson, Frank G., *The First Latin American Debt Crisis, The City of London and the 1822–25 Loan Bubble,* Yale, New Haven, Conn., 1990; Devlin, Robert, *Debt and Crisis in Latin America,* Princeton, Princeton, N.J., 1989; Holley, H. A., *Developing Country Debt, The Role of the Commercial Banks,* The Royal Institute of International Affairs, 1987; International Monetary Fund, *World Economic Outlook,* Washington, D.C., October 1991; Sachs, Jeffrey D., *Developing Country Debt and Economic Performance,* vols. 1–4, National Bureau of Economic Research, 1989; World Bank, *World Debt Tables, 1991–1992, External Debt of Developing Countries,* vol. 1, *Analysis and Summary Tables.*

(*See also* Commercial banks: problems and solutions; International Monetary Fund; World Bank)

A. Blake Friscia

Leveraged buyouts (*see* Going private and leveraged buyouts)

Liberalism

In the seventeenth century, liberalism emerged as the radical philosophy that attacked authoritarianism and paternalism in the political sphere by defending the rights of the individual against the commands of monarchs and other rulers. The seventeenth-century philosopher John Locke questioned claims to political authority based on birth, social status, privilege, and divine right. Political authority either derived from the consent of the governed or else was illegitimate. Later in the eighteenth century, liberals added the notion of the "rule of law," the idea that government in its legislative capacity had to enact general rules that apply to all citizens equally. The substitution of the rule of people for the rule of law created a capricious, uncertain, and sometimes cruel community life. This early variety of liberalism—often termed "classical liberalism"—stimulated the development of the social sciences by insisting that what holds society together and promotes a bustling and orderly commercial economy is the mutual interplay of the passions and interests of ordinary citizens in the market.

A basic principle of liberal thought is that individuals are the best and most accurate judges of their own interests and can be relied upon to pursue those interests with great dedication and creativity. The mighty arm of the state with its web of regulations and bureaucratic agents often does more harm than good when trying to substitute administrative methods of organization for impersonal market processes that spring out of self-interested individual action.

The philosopher and American revolutionary, Thomas Paine, capsulized the radical side of classical liberalism when he wrote that "society is created by our wants, government by our wickedness."

Classical Liberalism

Classical liberals are not anarchists and at the very least recommend a minimal state: a state that protects lives, defines property rights, and enforces private contracts. A great many classical liberals (such as Adam Smith and the later classical school of economists) went somewhat further and requested that the state build and maintain certain public works (bridges, canals, highways, harbors, recreational parks, and so on), maintain standing armies, provide basic education, promote invention and innovation, and intervene in the market on a limited scale for specific humane purposes such as the enactment and enforcement of child labor laws.

Generally, the classical liberal believes in the general rule of laissez faire and wants to preserve self-regulating market processes as much as possible. The classical liberal is confident that with the enactment of strict constitutional safeguards and the elimination of monopoly and the never-ending varieties of special-interest legislation, peace and material progress are within the reach of all societies and all social classes. The leading works of classical liberalism include Adam Smith's *Wealth of Nations* (1776), Herbert Spencer's *The Man versus the State* (1892), Friedrich A. Hayek's *Constitution of Liberty* (1960), Ludwig von Mises's *Liberalism: A Socio-Economic Exposition* (1962), and Milton Friedman's *Capitalism and Freedom* (1962).

Reform Liberalism

By the end of the nineteenth century, this brand of liberalism—antiauthoritarian in its politics and promarket in its economics—lost ground. A new style of liberalism competed with classical liberalism and became the dominant form by the first half of this century. Stemming from the work of Jeremy Bentham (*The Principles of Morals and Legislation*, 1848), John Stuart Mill (*Principles of Political Economy with Some Social Applications*, 1848), T. H. Green (*Lectures on the Principles of Political Obligation*, 1895), Alfred Marshall (*Principles of Economics*, 1890), John Dewey (*Liberalism and Social Action*, 1935), and John Maynard Keynes (*Essays in Persuasion*, 1931), reform liberalism continued to speak of individual freedom and liberty but (paradoxically) advocated an expansion of the state in the marketplace. Whereas the classical liberals defined freedom negatively to mean the absence of coercion or force in human relationships, the reform liberal spoke instead of "positive freedom." More specifically, individuals are free when they start out on an equal footing in the marketplace. Reform liberals support progressive taxation, taxes on inheritance, capital gains (windfall) taxes, state-supported higher education, compulsory public health projects, and a variety of leveling measures to promote a special notion of distributive justice in the marketplace. In the area of macroeconomic policy, reform liberals advocate demand-management policies to keep the economy out of recession and are willing to regulate industries if the allocation of resources can be improved. The idea is to spread the means of social advancement more evenly in the marketplace regardless of birth, social status, privilege, and inherited family income.

Unlike the early group of classical liberals, reform liberals do not believe that individuals enter into society with certain natural rights such as the right to life and to personal property. Rather, they follow Jeremy Bentham and argue that private property, individual liberty, and open markets are justified because they are expedient; that is, socially desirable institutions promote the "greatest good for the greatest number." According to Bentham, the greatest good can often be enhanced by social experimentation backed up by the sanction of law even when this necessitates violating order, traditions, and norms. Most shocking to classical liberals, the reform liberal is not overly concerned with the dangers of a powerful state turning into tyranny. The reform liberal is confident that, as long as democratic forms of government are maintained, the political system will attract and select reasonable leaders to manage power in a humane and responsible manner.

Despite its inherent vagueness and reliance on intuitive feeling for how much intervention is to be permitted and for what the limits of that intervention are, there can be no denying the enormous impact reform liberalism has had on Western democracies over the last 100 years. Unfortunately, reform liberalism has often drifted toward the older socialist program of nationalizing industry. Policies that began promising quick results with a few controls for limited purposes have ended up requiring more and more controls until (in some cases) nationalization of the industry became imperative, and governments kept technologically out-of-date industries alive rather than allow unemployment to happen. Policies designed to secure equality of results may stifle private economic incentives and initiatives, and this is what has forced economies as diverse as England and Sweden to rely more and more on state subsidies and frequent devaluations in the external value of their currencies.

This trend toward escalation of government control of the economy was predicted by the older classical liberals such as Ludwig von Mises (*Socialism*, 1951) and Friedrich A. Hayek (*The Road to Serfdom*, 1944).

Reform liberalism merges into socialism when it utilizes the state and its coercive machinery to impose a national plan on the alleged chaos of the marketplace. When reform liberalism becomes socialism as it did in the writings of G. B. Shaw, Beatrice and Sidney Webb, and other Fabian writers at the turn of the century, a doctrinal position emerges that is diametrically opposed to that of classical liberalism. The idea of limiting the state and encouraging decentralized markets for the means of production is abandoned completely.

The use of the term "liberalism" to refer to these fundamentally different policy models is apt to confuse students of intellectual history. Both liberalisms share the same fundamental goal of promoting individual self-development; they differ only on the means to be employed. This difference, however, remains a major one and is the source of many rich controversies in political and social philosophy.

References

Freden, Michael, "J. A. Hobson as a New Liberal Theorist: Some Aspects of His Social Thought until 1914," *Journal of the History of Ideas,* vol. 34, July–September 1973, pp. 421–442; Friedman, M., and Rose D. Friedman, *Capitalism and Freedom,* University of Chicago, Chicago, 1962; Galbraith, John Kenneth, *Economics and the Public Purpose,* Houghton Mifflin, Boston, 1973; Hayek, Friedrich A., *Law, Legislation and Liberty,* 3 vols., University of Chicago Press, Chicago, 1973; Keynes, Milo (ed.), *Essays on John Maynard Keynes,* Cambridge University Press, Cambridge, 1975; Mises, Ludwig von, *Liberalism: A Socio-Economic Exposition,* 1962; Nozick, Robert, *Anarchy, State and Utopia,* Basic Books, New York, 1974; Rawls, John, *A Theory of Justice,* Harvard University Press, Cambridge, Mass., 1971; Wolff, Robert Paul, *Understanding Rawls: A Reconstruction and Critique of "A Theory of Justice,"* Princeton University Press, Princeton, N.J., 1977.

(*See also,* Classical liberalism, Laissez faire)

Laurence S. Moss

Linear programming

Mathematical programming is the development and solution of a class of mathematical models in which the value of an "objective" function of many variables is optimized (maximized or minimized) subject to a set of "constraint" functions that limit the feasible values of those variables. Linear programming is an important special case where the objective and the constraint functions are all linear.

"Programming" as used above refers to planning or scheduling the activities of an organization and not to programming in the sense of preparing instructions for a computer. The term is appropriate because many planning and scheduling problems can be formulated as mathematical programs. For example, linear programming has been employed in business in a tremendous variety of ways, ranging from the selection of ingredients appropriate to producing the cheapest cattle feed of a given nutritional value to the determination of profitable sites for plant locations. The military has also used linear programming in a variety of ways, including planning ammunition plant production schedules and selecting bombing targets.

Besides producing an optimal program, solutions to mathematical problems implicitly include "shadow prices" for each constraint. These prices represent the marginal increase in the value of the objective function with respect to the relaxation of each constraint. This provides decision makers with guidance as to which constraints are the most important and thus which they should most intensively manage.

History

Francois Quesnay, a French economist, attempted in his *Tableau economique* (1758)—a crude example of a linear programming model—to interrelate the role of the landlord, the artisan, and the peasant. It was not until 1823 that Jean Baptiste Joseph Fourier, a French mathematician, appeared to see the potential of linear programming and developed an elimination algorithm for solving systems of linear inequalities. Until the late 1930s little further interest was shown in linear programming. Then in 1939 Leonid Kantorovich, a Russian mathematician, published a description of how he had formulated some industrial scheduling problems as linear programs.

Allied governments assembled the first operations research teams during World War II, and interest in mathematical programming intensified. However, the lack of efficient algorithms for solving linear programs and computers for executing those algorithms stymied the use of linear programming.

G. B. Dantzig developed the Simplex algorithm for solving linear programs in 1947, and, with the first electronic computers becoming available, linear programming became a useful tool. Industrial use became common in the 1950s, and use continued to expand in the 1960s and 1970s as more computer power became available and as researchers developed special techniques for solving certain classes of very large problems.

The 1980s were a decade of marked advancement in the field. Researchers had long been aware that the Simplex algorithm could be very inefficient on poorly behaved large problems, and many researchers had speculated that other algorithms might perform better. In 1979 L. G. Khachiyan, a Soviet mathematician, proved that more efficient algorithms could exist. In 1984, N. Karmarkar published and demonstrated such an algorithm. Active research on these "interior-point" algorithms continues today.

References

Baumol, W. J., *Economic Theory and Operations Analysis,* Prentice-Hall, Englewood Cliffs, N.J., 1961; Dantzig, G. B., *Linear Programming and Extensions,* Princeton University Press, Princeton, 1963; Dorfman, R., P. Samuelson, and R. Solow, *Linear Programming and Economic Analysis,* McGraw-Hill, New York, 1958; Ford, L., and D. R. Fulkerson, *Flows in Networks,* Princeton University Press, Princeton, 1962; Hadley, G., *Linear Programming,* Iowa State University Press, Ames, Iowa, 1962; Schrijver, A., *Theory of Linear and Integer Programming,* Wiley, New York, 1986.

(*See also* Economic models; Game theory, economic applications; Input-output analysis; Operations research; Physiocrats; Simulation in business and economics)

Brian E. Leverich

Liquidity, corporate

Corporate liquidity is a measure of a firm's ability to meet its maturing cash obligations. Liquidity is important to management because of (1) a significant risk-return trade-off, (2) the terms and conditions of additional financing, and (3) the risks of insolvency and bankruptcy cost. The risk-return trade-off arises because the investment in current assets may yield less than the firm's cost of funds. In addition, short-term debt may be less costly than long-term debt or equity funds, which push the firm toward use of short-term debt.

But if liquidity pressures develop in that a firm has difficulty meeting its maturing obligations, new financing may be available only under very unfavorable loan agreement restrictions and at relatively high interest costs. In the extreme, the insolvency of the firm may lead to bankruptcy and liquidation. The result may be relatively large drains due to bankruptcy costs. Bankruptcy costs may be high because of the need to liquidate assets under pressure at distress prices below their economic values. In addition, the administrative costs of bankruptcy, which include fees to lawyers, trustees, referees, receivers, liquidators, etc., average 20 percent of the book value of assets. Thus because of bankruptcy costs, liquidity management can affect the value of the firm.

Corporate Liquidity Measures

Although most assets have a degree of liquidity, the most liquid of assets are cash and marketable securities. Corporate liquidity measures reflect the amounts of these two types of assets held by firms. Liquidity is a measure of the ability to convert these liquid assets into money values. Two dimensions are involved: (1) the time necessary to convert an asset into money and (2) the risk of a difference or loss between the asset's stated value and the amount of money realized for the asset.

Variations in the liquidity positions of firms arise in part because all types of current assets move closely with changes in sales levels. When sales rise for seasonal, cyclical, or competitive reasons, the need for transactions cash, receivables, and inventories will rise (and conversely). If sales rise and then decline, short-term financing is appropriate. If sales have a strong growth component, the current assets should be financed more with longer-term financing sources. Thus, effective sales forecasting is essential for managing associated current asset movements and their financing.

A number of measures of exposure have been developed to evaluate a firm's liquidity position as it reacts to different money-market conditions. Some key liquidity ratios and reference levels are listed in the accompanying table:

Ratios	Reference levels
1. Current assets to current liabilities	1.75–2.00 times
2. Cash plus marketable securities to current liabilities	25 percent
3. Cash plus marketable securities to net revenues	5 percent
4. Current liabilities to net revenues	18–20 percent
5. Net income plus depreciation to the change in gross total assets	1–1.1 times
6. Short-term, interest-bearing debt to long-term debt	25 percent
7. Stockholders' equity to total assets	50–55 percent

Although these ratios may in practice fluctuate from the given reference levels in response to changes in money- and capital-market conditions, wide disparities are to be avoided. If the ratios deteriorate greatly, the risks of insolvency are increased. If the ratios are too strong, some losses in potential returns are incurred.

For Major Liquidity Management Policies

Corporate liquidity management is employed to maximize revenues while holding risks of insolvency to desired levels. Major liquidity management policies include:

(1) effective cash mobilization, (2) cash flow forecasting, (3) identification of needs for protective liquidity, and (4) productive use of liquid assets.

Cash mobilization aims at the reduction of funds tied up in the process of receiving and collecting checks and in the routines of the transfer of bank balances to the points where they will be most useful. In the management of cash the firm seeks to accelerate collections and to handle disbursements so that maximum cash is available. Collections can be accelerated by means of concentration banking, a lockbox system, and the use of telegraphic transfers. Disbursements can be handled to give maximum transfer flexibility and optimal timing of payments.

In recent years, electronic payments and electronic data interchange have improved the technology of cash mobilization. FEDWIRE is the wire transfer system operated by the Federal Reserve System. About 80 percent of dollar amount of transactions use these wire transfers for the same day of settlement. This represents only about 11 percent of the number of transactions, indicating that it is cost-efficient only for large dollar amounts. The automated clearinghouse (ACH) system is used for electronic transfers for next-day settlement for smaller transactions. The increased use of computer-related systems is moving the economy toward electronic data interchange (EDI), which can transmit business information electronically in computer-processable format. The key requirement for the further development of EDI is widely accepted data format and communications standards. Various trade associations have been active in seeking to develop the requisite national standards. Wide implementation of EDI would cause modification of traditional practices in areas such as credit terms based on paper/mail/manual processing. EDI would also help improve forecasts of the timing of cash flows.

Given the total level of liquid assets, composed of cash and marketable securities, the firm must determine the optimal division between these two assets. The optimal level of cash is the greater of (1) the compensating balance requirement of the firm's commercial bank and (2) the optimal level of cash determined by an appropriate cash inventory model. The cash balance models show that cash depends upon the predictability of future cash flows, the volatility of future cash flows, the fixed cost of security transactions, and the carrying costs of holding cash—the interest income on marketable securities.

A final area of liquidity management involves an aggressive approach to the most productive use of money assets. This approach represents an analysis of the alternative marketable securities in which the firm can invest. These securities can be evaluated in relation to their (1) default risk, (2) marketability, (3) maturity, and (4) taxability. Taking the cash flow pattern of the firm into account, a marketable securities portfolio can be formulated and modified over time consistent with the key characteristics of the securities employed. The categories of investments likely to be included in the marketable securities portfolio include: Treasury securities, government agency securities, bankers' acceptances, commercial paper, repurchase agreements, and certificates of deposit.

International Dimensions of Liquidity Management

With the globalization of financial markets, liquidity management has increasingly utilized international financial instruments and international financing. The international financial instruments are the foreign counterparts of domestic categories of investments.

International financing has reflected expanded activities and new forms. International banking services have grown in size and variety. Much international banking activity takes place offshore in activities generally referred to as the Euromarkets, consisting of Eurocurrency deposits, Eurocommercial paper, and Eurobonds. Eurocurrency deposits are bank deposits denominated in any foreign currency, not just those of European countries; they account for 86 percent of the foreign-owned deposits of banks. Eurocommercial paper is a short-term debt instrument issued and sold outside the country of the currency in which it is denominated. Eurobonds are the long-term debt counterpart. The international banks make unsecured Eurodollar loans with maturities on the shorter end. Interest rates on Eurodollar loans are tied to the London Interbank Offer Rate (LIBOR)—the rate at which banks lend Eurodollars to one another. Floating rate notes are medium-term securities carrying a floating rate of interest reset at regular intervals such as quarterly or half-yearly in relation to some reference rate, usually LIBOR.

Another innovation is the development of note issuance facilities (NIFs). An individual NIF is a line of credit or revolving facility that enables a borrower to issue a series of "Euronotes" over the medium term. The market for NIFs is a type of Eurocommercial paper market which is a mechanism for high-grade borrowers to raise funds cheaply.

References

Hill, Ned C., and William L. Sartoris, *Short-Term Financial Management,* Macmillan Publishing, New York, 1992; Pavel, Christine, and John N. McElravey, "Globalization in the Financial Services Industry," *Economic Perspectives,* Federal Reserve Bank of Chicago, May–June 1990, pp. 3–18; Searby, Frederick W., "Cash Management: Helping Meet the Capital Crisis," in J. Fred Weston and Maurice Goudzwaard (eds.), *The Treasurer's Handbook,* Dow Jones-Irwin, Homewood, Ill., 1976, chap. 20; Weston, J. Fred, and T. E. Copeland, *Managerial Finance,* 9th ed., Dryden Press, 1992, chaps. 18–20.

(*See also* Business credit; Eurodollar market; Financial distress)

J. Fred Weston

Liquidity, international

International liquidity comprises the financial assets that governments, or usually their central banks, hold as reserves to meet international contingencies. The term may be used to refer to the reserves of an individual country or to the sum of reserves of all countries.

The financial assets that make up international liquidity include gold, foreign currencies (of which the dollar is the most widely held reserve currency), and claims on the International Monetary Fund that may be used unconditionally. The International Monetary Fund publishes monthly data on the amount and composition of countries' reserves and, less frequently, data on the currency composition of their foreign exchange reserves.

At present the subject of international liquidity receives much less attention than in past decades for two reasons: First, when most countries had exchange rates that were fixed except for rare depreciations or appreciations, changes in their balance-of-payments positions tended to be reflected in changes in their international reserves. Countries in deficit lost reserves, and countries in surplus gained reserves as they sold or bought foreign exchange as a means of maintaining their established exchange rates. Today, many countries have floating exchange rates and are not required to buy or sell foreign exchange in response to every upward or downward pressure in their foreign exchange markets. Second, private capital has become much more mobile in the past two decades as countries have abandoned controls on such capital movements, as new financial instruments have developed, and as the information and computer revolutions have increased global access to news. As a result, flows of private funds now finance a larger fraction of international payments imbalances, leaving less to be financed by shifts in official reserves.

Countries in the European Community that are members of the exchange-rate mechanism of the European Monetary System do strive to maintain fixed exchange rates among their own currencies. They are expected to keep their currencies within ±2¼ percent of each other, and this requires their central banks to intervene more in foreign exchange markets than countries with floating exchange rates. Except for Germany, these countries do not publish information about the extent of their central banks' interventions in exchange markets.

Among the components of international liquidity, gold is much less focused on than in the past. Although countries still hold gold in their reserves, they rarely buy or sell it. Gold may now be regarded as part of the national patrimony, like the National Gallery or the Louvre. It no longer has international monetary significance.

The reserves of members of the International Monetary Fund include about $28 billion of special drawing rights (SDRs), which were first created in 1970 as a supplement to traditional forms of reserves. In recent years, no additional allocations of SDRs have been made.

Among foreign exchange reserves, the dollar continues to be the most important reserve currency. But there has for many years been a growing tendency for some other currencies to be held as reserves. In particular, the German mark now comprises about one-fifth of the official foreign exchange holdings of all countries, and the share of the dollar is more than one-half. The Japanese yen accounts for about one-tenth of foreign exchange.

References

International Monetary Fund, *Annual Report, 1991,* Washington, D.C., pp. 77–83; Solomon, Robert, *The International Monetary System, 1945–1981,* Harper & Row, New York, 1982; Ungerer, Horst, et al., *The European Monetary System: Developments and Prospects,* Occasional Paper 73, International Monetary Fund, 1990.

(*See also* Balance of international payments; Balance of international trade; Bretton Woods Conference; European Community; Foreign exchange rates; International economics, an overview; International Monetary Fund; Smithsonian Agreement; Special drawing rights)

Robert Solomon

Liquidity preference (*see* Interest rates; Yield curve)

Location theory

Location theory is a set of propositions that yields a systematic exposition and explanation of the spatial organization of economic activities including both business firms and households. Traces of location theory may be found in the writings of many classical economists, including Smith, Ricardo, and Mill, and interest in plant location theory may be attributed to three Germans: Launhardt, von Thünen, and Weber. They (particularly Launhardt and Weber) set the stage for what is today called the "least-cost theory of plant location." Their analytical framework was essentially that of pure competition, as all buyers were assumed to be located at a given market center, with prices of goods fixed and the demand for each product unlimited relative to any seller's supply. The location choice involved production factor substitutions as sellers searched for the site offering lowest delivered cost to the market.

Proponents of the Least-Cost Theory

The many writers who followed Weber asserted that manufacturing locations were determined by the desire to locate at least-cost sites. Some, such as Palander, Schneider, and Hoover, were also interested in the size of the firm's market area and, thus, in a sense, concerned with variable demands over space. The majority, however, disregarded the locational effects of varying demands over the landscape. Thus Preodöhl was interested solely in developing a substitution cost analysis. Cassel, Krzyzanowski, Engländer, and Isard also were interested in this. Ritschl inquired into the changing patterns of costs and locations over time. Linke and other students of Weber stressed labor and agglomerative differentials in explaining and measuring industrial displacements from transport centers. Holmes and others (E. Hedlund, D. C. Hague, and P. K. Newman) evaluated industrial orientations to materials, labor, market, etc.; Dechesnes was similarly inclined.

The Demand (Locational Interdependence) Approach

The von Thünen approach applies to agricultural locations, and that of Launhardt and Weber applies to certain manufacturing locations. But the increasing awareness during the early post–World War II years of the limits to their cost-only framework stimulated an opposite view of plant location.

Under the influence of Fetter, Hotelling, Lerner and Singer, Smithies, Chamberlin, and other writers, interest centered on locational interdependence. This conception disregarded cost, since the costs of procuring and processing raw materials were assumed to be equal at all locations, and explained the location of firms as the endeavor to control the largest market space, in effect, the seller becomes a locational monopolist. Among other factors, locational interdependence requires appraisal of the shape (character) of the demand curve and the influence on site selection of entrepreneurial conjectures about rival firms' location policies. These considerations determine the degree of intraindustry dispersion over the landscape and the extent to which locational monopolies could arise and led directly to the generalization given by the maximum-profit theory of plant location.

The Theory of the Maximum-Profit Plant Location

August Lösch reached the core of the "location" problem when he noted that to seek the location of lowest cost is as wrong as looking for the site offering greatest sales. He conceived initially of a homogeneous landscape in which a monopolistic producer sells over a circular market area. This conception led him ultimately (under a Chamberlinean perspective) to depict a spatial competitor whose long-run trading area is reduced in size to that of a zero profit hexagon. This polygon minimizes total distances from its center to all points in the market area, whereas the hexagonal network fills the entire landscape. Within given industries, total effective demand is therefore maximized. W. A. Lewis, in generalizing his own picture of the ideal size and number of firms, recognized the hexagon as the market area that yields stable equilibrium.

Lösch recognized that different industries would possess different-size hexagons which in turn would generate different interindustry concentrations. But differential intraindustry costs would arise as a result of different agglomerations. Although he therefore recognized variability of costs and demand at alternative sites over the now-heterogeneous landscape, he failed to combine an analysis of intraindustry cost *and* demand differentials in one model. At the same instant, he disregarded the conjectural variations of entrepreneurs and the impact of cost differentials thereon. The fact that extraordinary concentrations of homogeneous (intraindustry) business units could therefore result was ignored as he confined his frame of reference to an "ideal," not actual, landscape.

Large and Small Firms

When costs vary widely among locations, large firms tend to concentrate, ceteris paribus, in the particular city or district which is least in cost relative to the whole market area (Florence, 1962). Only the foolhardy dare chance a movement away from the center of a market area if doubt exists as to the probability of symmetrical locations. The location of the smaller firm is, according to this reasoning, somewhat more flexible. For example, small plants disperse relatively more than large firms and frequently locate in less industrialized areas (Greenhut, 1956, chap. 3).

Price Systems

Different price systems generate different locations. The upshot is that within certain well-defined limits of pricing, any plant locator tends to visualize different-size market areas over the economic landscape. When pricing and location are competitive, cost and demand are codeterminers of location (Thisse, 1975).

Spatial Microeconomics

Location theory in recent years has gone well beyond the century and a half described above. One extension, not discussed here, was based on the writings of W. Isard and called "regional science." The strictly location economics extension to be discussed here is called spatial microeconomics. This offshoot centers on the question of whether classical price theory, based on time only, is relevant to a space economy. Suffice it to say for present purposes that the reality of costs of distances signify that any advanced theory of the firm must not only accept the idea of a lowest long-run average cost (LRAC) curve but cope with alternative LRAC curves based on uneconomic and economic locations besides uneconomic and economic sizes and shapes of the trading areas of firms. Most emphatically, the theory of the firm in economic space must focus on oligopoly and behavioral uncertainty (Ohta, 1988). This notion of economic space generated interest in game theoretics structure by Thisse (1975), by Beckmann (1986), and by Gabszewicz (1992). But would long-run profits apply to the space economy?

If profits are excessive compared to the behavioral uncertainty applicable to a given oligopolistic activity, a windfall exists. But if there is a windfall, the free entry of heterogeneous-size firms over the landscape will reduce price and profits. A set of locations and market area shapes and sizes results in profits that are perfectly commensurate with the industry's uncertainty. A mapping is thus obtained from the concept in pure competition theory of differential rents for differences in abilities and risks to the space economy's concept of differential profits for different industry levels of behavioral uncertainties (Greenhut, Norman, and Hung, 1987, chap. 19).

Relevance of Location Theory

Although von Thünen's theory centered primarily on agricultural produce and its transport to a central market (the concentric ring idea), his analysis is used today in evaluating the allocation of activities within urban centers. And whereas Weber took each plant location as a single point, his analysis underlies the operations research work used by multiplant manufacturers in determining location choice. In corresponding form, Hotelling's insights into agglomeration combined with the maximum-profit theory of location explains the coexistence of small- and large-scale operations in the same industry. Perhaps most critically, the required evaluations of oligopoly locations and related utility-disutility conjectures apply to nonspatial issues, e.g., product differentiation, medicine, even the CAPM model of finance theory (Greenhut and Greenhut, 1991), and, in a global context, the waves of direct foreign investments (locations) designed to avoid high transport costs and other barriers (MacLeod, Norman, and Thisse, 1987).

References

Beckman, M. J., and J. F. Thisse, "The Location of Production Activities," in E. S. Mills and P. Nijkamp (eds.), *Handbook of Regional and Urban Economics,* vol. 1, North Holland, Amsterdam, 1986; Cassel, G., *Theoretische Nationalökonomie,* 3d ed., W. Schall, Leipzig, 1923, pp. 83–96; Chamberlin, E. H., *The Theory of Monopolistic Competition,* 5th ed., Harvard University Press, Cambridge, Mass., 1946, appendix C; Dechesnes, L., *La Localization des Diverses Productions,* Les Editions Comptables, Commerciales et Financières, Brûxelles, 1945; Engländer, O., "Kritisches und Positives zu einer allgemeinen reinen Lehre vom Standort," *Zeitschrift für Volkswirtschaft und Sozialpolitik,* vol. 5, 1927, pp. 435–505; Fetter, F., "The Economic Law of Market Areas," *Quarterly Journal of Economics,* vol. 38, 1924, pp. 520–529; Florence, P. S., *Investment Location and Size of Plant,* National Institute of Economic and Social Research, Study VII, Cambridge University Press, London, 1938; Florence, P. S., *Post-War Investment, Location, and Size of Plant,* Cambridge University Press, London, 1962; Gabszewicz, J. J., and J. F. Thisse, "Location," in R. Aumann and S. Hart (eds.), *Handbook of Game Theory and Economic Applications,* North Holland, Amsterdam, 1992; Greenhut, John, and M. L. Greenhut, "A Theory of Inflationary Impacts on Stock Prices," WEA Convention, July 1991; Greenhut, M. L., *Plant Location in Theory and in Practice,* University of North Carolina Press, Chapel Hill, 1956, Greenwood Press, Westport, Conn., 1982, 4th printing; Greenhut, M. L., G. Norman, and C. S. Hung, *The Economics of Imperfect Competition,* Cambridge University Press, London, 1987; Hague, D. C., and P. K. Newman, *Costs in Alternative Locations: The Clothing Industry,* National Institute of Economic and Social Research, Cambridge University Press, London, 1952; Hedlund, E., *The Transportation Economics of the Soybean Processing Industry,* University of Illinois Press, Urbana, 1952; Holmes, W., *Die Lederindustrie (Erzeugende und Verarbeitende),* Tübingen, n.p., 1913; Hoover, E. M., *Location Theory and the Shoe and Leather Industry,* Harvard University Press, Cambridge, Mass., 1937; Hoover, E. M., *Location of Economic Activity,* McGraw-Hill, New York, 1948, chap. 4; Hotelling, H., "Stability in Competition," *Economic Journal,* vol. 39, 1929, pp. 41–57; Isard, W., "Distance Inputs and the Space Economy: Part I: The Conceptual Framework," *Quarterly Journal of Economics,* vol. 65, 1951, pp. 181–198; Isard, W., *Methods of Regional Analysis,* MIT Press, Cambridge, Mass.,

1960; Krzyzanowski, W., "Review of the Literature of the Location of Industries," *Journal of Political Economics,* vol. 35, 1927, pp. 278–291; Launhardt, W., *Mathematische Begründung der Volkswirtschaftslehre,* B.G. Teubner, Leipzig, 1885; Lerner, A. P., and H. W. Singer, "Some Notes on Duopoly and Spatial Competition," *Journal of Political Economy,* vol. 45, 1937, pp. 445–486; Lewis, W. A., "Competition in Retail Trade," *Economica,* vol. 12, 1945, pp. 202–234; Linke, A., *Plant Location,* McGraw-Hill, New York, 1930; Lösch, A., *Die Räumliche Ordnung der Wirtschaft,* Gustav Fischer, Jena; 1944; MacLeod, W. B., G. Norman, and J. Thisse, "Competition, Tacit Collusion and Free Entry," *Economic Journal,* vol. 97, 1987, pp. 189–198; Ohta, H., *Spatial Price Theory of Imperfect Competition,* Texas A&M University Press, College Station, 1988; Palander, T., *Beiträge zur Standortstheorie,* Alqvist and Wiksell Boktryckeri, Uppsala, 1935; Predöhl, A., "Das Standorsproblem in der Wirtschaftstheorie," *Welt Wirtschaftliches Archiv,* vol. 5, 1925, pp. 294–321; Predöhl, A., "Zur Frage einer allgemeinen Standortstheorie," *Zeitschrfit für Volkswirtschaft und Sozialpolitik,* vol. 5, 1927, pp. 756–763; Ritschl, H., "Reine und Historische Dynamik des Standortes der Erzeugungszweige," *Schmollers Jahrbuch für Gestzgebund,* vol. 51, 1927, pp. 813–870; Schneider, E., "Bemerkungen zu einer Theorie der Raumwirtschaft," *Econometrica,* vol. 3, 1935, pp. 79–101; Smithies, A. F., "Optimum Location in Spatial Competition," *Journal of Political Economy,* vol. 49, 1941, pp. 423–439; Thisse, J. F., Contribution à la théorie microéconomique spatiale, Ph.D. dissertation, University of Liege, Belgium, 1975; Von Thünen, J. H., *Der Isolierte Staat in Beziehung auf Landwirtschaftslehre und Nationalökonomie,* 3d ed., Schumacher Zarchlin, Berlin, 1875; Weber, A., *Theory of Location,* trans. by C. J. Friedrich, University of Chicago Press, Chicago, 1928.

(*See also* Regional economics; Urban economics)

Melvin L. Greenhut

Long-run forecasts (*see* Economic forecasts)

Long-term interest rates (*see* Interest rates)

Lorenz curve

The Lorenz curve is a graphic device which presents a vivid picture of the extent of inequality in the size distribution of wealth or income and its components. (Occasionally, the curve is used to represent other distributions as well.) The curve (see the figure on page 652) consists of a unit square, a diagonal to that square, and at least one true curve which passes through the endpoints of the diagonal. The horizontal axis represents the cumulative share of population units and runs from 0 to 100 percent. The vertical axis represents cumulative shares of income (or wealth) and likewise ranges from 0 to 100 percent. Perfect equality is represented by the diagonal. At point z, for example, 30 percent of the population receives 30 percent of income. The closer the curved line is to the diagonal, the smaller is the degree of inequality.

Gini Coefficient

One summary measure of the degree of inequality is the ratio of the shaded area in the figure to the entire area under the diagonal ($A/A + B$). This measure is called the "Gini coefficient" (or concentration ratio) after its inventor, the Italian statistician and demographer Corrodo Gini. For developed countries the Gini coefficient of earned pretax income tends to be around 0.4.

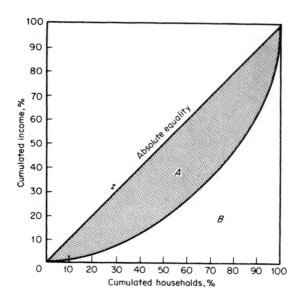

The Gini coefficient has been much criticized. Trying to capture a whole curve with one number can, of course, be misleading. The Gini coefficient has been faulted for being insensitive and difficult to calculate accurately. It has also been character-ized as devoid of normative content. Should two Lorenz curves cross, for example, one cannot say which of the underlying distributions is the more equal without fur-ther defining inequality, and comparing their Gini coefficients may be misleading. Moreover, even when Lorenz curves do not cross and hence a comparison of Gini coefficients does tell which distribution is more equal, one cannot say precisely *how much* more equal; that is, the Gini coefficient is not a cardinal measure of inequal-ity. A third defect of the Gini, in the eyes of many, is that it is less sensitive to changes in the tails of a distribution than to changes in the middle. Such shortcom-ings limit the Gini coefficient's usefulness in analyzing changes in inequality and its components.

The shortcomings of the Gini coefficient (and of other common inequality mea-sures) have led some theorists to construct alternative measures by specifying at the outset properties seen as desirable (such as cardinality or the ability to unambiguously rank all distributions) and then imposing the conditions needed to guarantee them. Although these alternative measures do extend the range of potential conclusions that can be drawn, they come at the cost of added (and perhaps debatable) statements about the nature of inequality. Any cardinal measure, for example, must satisfy, among other conditions, the "strong principle of transfers," which holds that the change in inequality resulting from a transfer between two individuals depends only on the individuals' income shares (and not on their ranks in the income distribution, as with the Gini coefficient). A more general drawback of these measures is that many of the necessary conditions have little intuitive appeal. None of the newer measures show much sign of supplanting the Gini coefficient as the most widely used sum-mary statistic for describing inequality. The Gini's continued popularity no doubt derives largely from the vivid representation given to it by the Lorenz curve.

Wilford King's Work

The Lorenz curve is named after its American inventor (there are coincident European inventors), Max Otto Lorenz. Lorenz spent all his professional life as a government statistician unconcerned with distributional issues. It fell to Wilford King, who apparently worked with Lorenz at the University of Wisconsin, to promote use of the diagram. One oddity in this history is that Lorenz drew his curve with income on the horizontal axis and recipients on the vertical. It was not until 1921 that King (in collaboration with Wesley Clair Mitchell and others) drew what he already referred to as the well-known Lorenz curve in the way that it is now customarily drawn. Between 1905 and 1921, the curve was drawn by King and others in every conceivable variant.

Widespread familiarity with the curve was deferred until the publication of textbooks that first appeared after World War II. Prewar texts (including one coauthored by Lorenz) devoted little space to income or wealth inequality among persons and none to the Lorenz curve. Until the war there simply were not enough current data to make a chapter on inequality, or presentation of the Lorenz curve, interesting.

References

Cowell, F. A., *Measuring Inequality: Techniques for the Social Sciences,* John Wiley, New York, 1977; Jenkins, S., "The Measurement of Income Inequality," in L. Osberg,(ed.), *Economic Inequality and Poverty: International Perspectives,* M. E. Sharpe, Armonk, N.Y., 1991; Lorenz, Max O., "Methods of Measuring the Concentration of Wealth," *Journal of the American Statistical Association,* vol. 9, no. 70, June 1905, pp. 209–219; Mitchell, Wesley Clair, Wilford I. King, Frederick R. Macauley, and Oswald W. Knauth, *Income in the United States: Its Amount and Distribution, 1909–1919,* Harcourt, Brace, New York, 1921; Sen, A. K., *On Economic Inequality,* Norton, New York, 1973, chap. 2.

(*See also* Income distribution; Poverty)

Eugene Smolensky

Macroeconomics

The word macroeconomics means economics in the large. The macroeconomist's concerns are with such global magnitudes as total production, total employment, the rate of change of overall prices, the rate of economic growth, and so on. The questions asked by the macroeconomist are in terms of broad aggregates—what determines the spending of all consumers as opposed to the microeconomic question of how the spending decisions of individual households are made; what determines the capital spending of all firms combined as opposed to the decision to build a new factory by a single firm; what determines total unemployment in the economy as opposed to why there have been layoffs in a specific industry. Macroeconomists measure overall economic activity; analyze the determinants of such activity by the use of macroeconomic theory; forecast future economic activity; and attempt to formulate policy responses designed to reconcile forecasts with target values of production, employment, and prices.

An important task of macroeconomics is to develop ways of aggregating the values of the economic activities of individuals and firms into meaningful totals. To this end such concepts as gross domestic product (GDP), national income, personal income, and personal disposable income have been developed. The addition of apples to oranges is accomplished by valuing each commodity by its market price.

Macroeconomic analysis attempts to explain how the magnitudes of the principal macroeconomic variables are determined and how they interact. And through the development of theories of the business cycle and economic growth, macroeconomics helps to explain the dynamics of how these aggregates move over time.

Macroeconics and Policy Issues

Macroeconomics is concerned with such major policy issues as the attainment and maintenance of full employment and price stability. Considerable effort must first be expended to determine what goals are feasible. Experience teaches that it would not be possible to eliminate inflation entirely without inducing a major recession combined with high unemployment. Similarly, an overambitious employment target would produce labor shortages and wage inflation. During the 1960s it was believed that unemployment could be reduced to 4 percent of the labor force without causing inflation. More recent experience suggests that reduction of unemployment to 5.5 percent of the labor force is about as well as we can do. During the 1950s and 1960s output per worker-hour (labor productivity) grew at a rate of about 3 percent a year. Added to labor-force growth adjusted for a trend toward shorter hours, this implied growth of potential output of about 4 percent a year. But productivity growth slumped after 1968 and more so after 1973, so that potential output now grows much more slowly. Finally, during the early 1960s a 4 percent rate of price inflation would have been regarded as intolerable. Today, after the rapid inflation of the 1970s, a 4 percent inflation rate is generally considered quite acceptable.

Tools of Macroeconomic Policy

The principal tools of macroeconomic policy are monetary policy and fiscal policy. Monetary policy in the United States is under the control of the Board of Governors of the Federal Reserve System. The Federal Reserve controls the supply of money and credit in a number of ways. The most important Federal Reserve instrument stems from its authority to purchase and sell government securities in the so-called open market. Credit tightening, for example, may be accomplished by an open-market sale. The purchasers of the government securities transmit money balances to the Federal Reserve, thereby reducing the nation's money supply. This, in turn, reduces bank lending power and drives up the cost of borrowing. The hoped-for outcome is less borrowing and spending by the private sector of the economy. The Federal Reserve is also empowered to lend funds to its member banks. It may raise or lower the interest rate (the rediscount rate) at which it lends the funds, thereby discouraging or encouraging bank borrowing.

The other principal tool of macroeconomic policy is fiscal policy. This means the use of the federal budget to add or subtract purchasing power from the economy. To stimulate the economy, government expenditures may be raised directly or taxes may be reduced, thereby enabling individuals and firms to increase their spending. The opposite set of policies could be employed if aggregate demand is excessive, because higher taxes and less government spending would reduce total spending and help slow inflation.

The principal vehicle of fiscal policy is the federal budget. The annual budget plan is developed by the administration and submitted for review by the congressional budget committees. Changes in the tax code must be legislated by the Congress, and the tax system is administered by the Internal Revenue Service under the general supervision of the secretary of the Treasury.

Beginning in 1983, the economy experienced mammoth budget deficits that, in five of the next eight years, exceeded $200 billion. These huge deficits make it very difficult to use fiscal policy as a tool of economic stabilization inasmuch as tax cuts to stimulate the economy would further add to the size of the deficit. Some macroeconomists bemoan the virtual loss of fiscal policy as a stabilization tool, and others, usually described as monetarists, welcome it because they have never believed in the efficacy of fiscal policy as a stabilization tool. A third group believes that the policies, in order to be effective, should be carefully coordinated. For example, during a recession it would be appropriate to reduce taxes. However, this implies that the Treasury must engage in added borrowing. As a result, bond prices will decline and interest rates will rise, thereby discouraging private borrowing and expenditure. If the tax cut were accompanied by open-market purchases by the Federal Reserve, this expansionary monetary policy could prevent the rise in interest rates.

A Coherent Macroeconomic Plan

A coherent macroeconomic plan for the economy should have the following ingredients. First, those responsible for fiscal and monetary policy should agree on a set of reasonable quantitative targets and objectives for the coming year. The second need is for a detailed and careful quarterly forecast of economic activity, based on the assumption that policy will remain unchanged. This is called a "base-line forecast." The third need is to compare the forecast with the targets and to agree on the magnitude and mix of the policy changes that would be required to alter the forecast so that its outcome coincides with the established targets.

Although the Budget Act of 1974 envisioned such an approach to macroeconomic planning, the very rapid inflation of the 1970s, the acute recessions of 1981–1982 as well as the recession that began in 1989, the development of enormous trade and budget deficits, all suggest that macroeconomic problems are a long way from being solved. Some of this failure represents a failure of economic analysis; some is due to failures in economic education; and a large part is due to the fact that economic policy decisions are frequently dominated by political and ideological considerations.

Changing Concerns of Macroeconomic Policy

During the deeply depressed 1930s, the primary concern of macroeconomics was the restoration of full employment. During the 1950s, policy was primarily concerned with the control of inflation. This then gave way in the early 1960s to renewed emphasis on high employment and rapid economic growth. Primary emphasis focused on demand management policies inasmuch as it was thought that these policies could contribute importantly to all these goals.

During the 1970s, the United States, as well as other industrial economies, experienced a new and puzzling phenomenon called "stagflation," variously defined as a situation in which both unemployment and inflation were simultaneously too high or both were rising at the same time. Stagflation created a nasty dilemma for macroeconomic policy. Monetary fiscal policies designed to lower unemployment by raising spending were likely to generate more inflation, and policies designed to lower inflation by reducing spending were likely to add to unemployment.

The world food shortages of the early 1970s and especially the rapidly rising energy costs suggested that the supply side of the economy was in need of attention as well as the demand side. Indeed, it became quite clear that supply restrictions were playing a major role in generating and perpetuating stagflation. For example, when the Organization of Petroleum Exporting Countries (OPEC) raised the price of oil in 1974, and again in 1979, these price increases raised the price level in the U.S. economy. Because consumers had to spend a larger fraction of their incomes on energy, the amount of income that consumers had left to spend on other things was sharply reduced. Production and employment, therefore, fell at a time when prices were rising.

Another major upheaval in macroeconomic thought and the approach to policy has been necessitated by the switch, in 1973, from a system of fixed international rates of currency exchange to exchange rates determined by market forces. This switch has proved especially significant because of the development of enormous foreign exchange markets in which hundreds of billions of dollars in national currencies are exchanged on a daily basis. Only a small fraction of these currency transactions is needed to finance trade; the remainder finances capital transactions, many of a very short-term nature. Such short-term capital movements have demonstrated a strong sensitivity to interest-rate differentials between countries.

Much of traditional macroeconomic analysis has been rendered obsolete by these developments. For example, when the Federal Reserve embarked on a more restrictive monetary policy in late 1979, interest rates rose in the United States, thereby attracting foreign capital in search of higher returns. The resulting capital inflow raised the demand for the dollar, thereby appreciating its international value. As a result, imports became cheaper for Americans, and exports became more difficult to sell. The effect of the resulting trade deficit was deflationary due to stagnation of export trade and the substitution of foreign-produced goods in place of domestic output. Indeed, the deflationary effect was far greater than anticipated. Although inflation dropped sharply, the economy suffered its worst recession since the Great Depression of the 1930s.

Similarly, the subsequent fiscal policies of the Reagan administration, combining tax reduction with increases in defense spending, converted a $38 billion 1979 federal budget deficit into a $222 billion deficit in 1985. Standard macroeconomic theory would have predicted massive inflationary effects from these expansionary fiscal policies. However, inflation did not materialize because the expansionary effects of the fiscal policies were largely transmitted to other countries. Because the rising budget deficit pushed up interest rates, the capital inflows accelerated, the dollar continued to appreciate, and the trade deficit continued to worsen. Since this meant that Americans were now consuming large volumes of foreign-produced goods and services rather than domestically produced goods and services, the expansionary thrust of the fiscal policies was, to a large extent, felt elsewhere.

These developments once again highlight the need for policy coordination, not only between domestic monetary fiscal tools but also—because domestic policies are likely to have significant effects on other countries—between the policies of the major industrial countries.

References

Dernburg, T. F., *Macroeconomics*, 7th ed., McGraw-Hill, New York, 1985; Dernburg, T. F., *Global Macroeconomics*, Harper and Row, New York, 1989.

(*See also* Dynamic macroeconomic models; Economics; Microeconomics)

Thomas F. Dernburg

Malthusian theory of population

Thomas Robert Malthus was best known as a demographer, but like many of his contemporaries he studied and wrote in several fields. He was a clergyman, demographer, economist, and a professor of history and political economy in the East-India College, Hertfordshire.

The basic concept of his social theory is that population tends to increase more rapidly than the food supply. Population tends to increase geometrically, whereas food—the means of subsistence—tends to increase only arithmetically according to the most widely recognized formulation. "The ultimate check to population," Malthus wrote (1817a), "appears then to be a want of food arising necessarily from the different ratios according to which population and food increase. But this ultimate check is never the immediate check, except in cases of actual famine."

The immediate checks were classified, according to Malthus under two general headings—"the preventive, and the positive checks." The former consist of conscious and deliberate limitations on sexual activity either by late marriage or by abstinence. Few people, Malthus felt, would follow such preventive checks. Voluntary—premeditated—birth control was immoral and a vice, which, with all the other vices, was not to be tolerated.

The positive checks are those which really check population growth, i.e., disasters of one form or another—war, pestilence, famine, etc.—and vice. In the 1817 edition, exactly half of the total pages in the four volumes are devoted to discussion of these positive checks.

Malthus summarized his beliefs as follows: "The tendency in population fully to keep pace with the means of subsistence must in general prevent the increase of these means from having a great and permanent effect in improving the condition of the poor" (1817b). Further, he stated, "Natural and moral evil seems to be the instruments employed by the Deity . . . if we multiply too fast, we die miserably of poverty and contagious diseases" (1817c).

Petty's Earlier Analysis

Why was such a pessimistic outlook accepted by so many in his time? Many of his contemporaries, including William Godwin, held contrary opinions, but Malthus outshouted them all. Further, Malthus said little that William Petty had not written about 150 years earlier, yet Petty is unknown outside the academic field.

Analysis of the historical situation in England around 1800, in comparison with the situation at the time of Petty around 1650, provides clues regarding Malthus's excellent public relations. To begin, Malthus's theories were accepted so wholeheartedly because they fitted in with what the country's leaders wanted to hear, namely, that it is impossible for the masses to improve their level of living. Any efforts to improve their lives—by increasing wages, for example—would simply result in their having more children and thus continuing to live as poorly as ever. What Malthus and so many of the political leaders failed to understand clearly was that the industrial revolution was already underway and that science and technology would increase production—both food and nonfood—so greatly as to be able to support a much larger population at a much higher level of living. Some other writers at that time recognized the growth of industry and its implication, but such recognition meant that wages could be increased and the plight of the poor alleviated. This thought was not welcomed by England's leaders.

Petty had written about the multiplication of humanity—*Mankind and Political Arithmetic*—in the middle of the seventeenth century. At that time the world seemed to be empty of people. The vast Western Hemisphere was still unpopulated by Europeans (the Native American population was disregarded), and even Great Britain was still not fully populated. Hence, Petty could only speculate about population growth and calculated that it might take 2000 years to fully populate the world. Nobody worried about what might happen 2000 years hence.

By the time Malthus wrote, however, far more data on population growth were available. The U.S. Census of 1790 together with earlier colonial censuses indicated that the Western Hemisphere was filling rapidly. The English Census of 1801 showed that population was increasing more rapidly than had been thought. Petty's "2000 years hence" had already arrived, or shortly would. And, if a lowered birthrate via voluntary birth control was inadmissable, then Malthus had to be correct, in the opinion of England's rulers.

Changing Times: Changing Views of Population

One problem with the Malthusian theory of population is that its proponents based their beliefs on a very few and rather poor quality statistics from a few European countries which were entering what had been termed the "Industrial Revolution."

Birth control, in one form or another, has been known for many millennia. *Coitus interruptus* is mentioned in the Old Testament (Genesis 38). But in ancient times and among primitive people today, birth control was not much used because the death rate was so very high that a very high birthrate was needed to sustain the population. Malthus's positive checks may have explained population growth in the primitive and/or economically underdeveloped countries, but these positive checks had little relevancy for modern industrialized and economically developed populations.

Hence, when large-scale economic growth became evident in a few European countries and the United States in the eighteenth and nineteenth centuries, it was thought that the means of subsistence were more than able to keep up with population growth. The positive checks were now deemed irrelevant. During these few "glorious" decades population grew slowly in Europe and rapidly in North America. What was happening in the rest of the world was largely unknown and thought to be irrelevant.

One of the by-products of economic growth was the acceptance of birth control in the more economically developed parts of the world. With the positive checks no longer operative, birth control became permissible in the more developed countries.

One product of colonialism was that the European powers had to suppress the positive checks, or they, the Europeans, must leave the colonies. An example close to home is the effort made by the United States to eradicate yellow fever when we were building the Panama Canal. Eradicate the fever or forget the Canal. So population gradually began increasing in the eighteenth and nineteenth centuries in some of those countries where the positive checks had ruled for millennia.

Following World War II the industrialized countries of Europe "discovered" the poor and economically underdeveloped countries. In the twentieth century, due to the efforts of the League of Nations and the United Nations, reasonable statistics on the population growth rate became available. Population growth in the underdeveloped countries was bounding ahead at double the rate of that in the more developed countries. Malthus's positive checks were no longer viable checks.

	Average Annual Growth of World Population				
	1920–1937	1950–1960	1960–1970	1970–1980	1980–1990
Total	1.1%	1.8%	1.8%	1.8%	1.7%
More-developed countries	NA	1.3	1.1	0.8	0.6
Less-developed countries	NA	1.9	2.2	2.2	2.1

SOURCES: U.S. Census Bureau, *Statistical Abstract,* and United Nations, *Population Year Book.*

Now the more developed countries urge the adoption of birth control in the less developed countries; they have to choose between birth control and continuing to support "remittance" countries.

Can birth control win over the positive checks? Perhaps the twenty-first century will provide an answer. We believe "Yes" if nations act rationally.

References

Malthus, Thomas R., *An Essay on Population,* J. Johnson, London, 1798, Murray, London, 1817:(a) Book I, chap. 2, p. 17, (b) Book III, chap. 13, p. 11, (c) Book IV, chap. 1, p. 65.

(*See also* Industrial revolution; Zero population growth)

A. J. Jaffe

Manchester school

The English classical economists were free traders, which in the circumstances of their times meant that they were unalterably opposed to the British system of agricultural protection enshrined in the so-called corn laws. Throughout the period of the industrial revolution in the first half of the nineteenth century, there were annual motions in Parliament in favor of free trade and a more or less continuous agitation against the corn laws. The free trade movement took on new force, however, with the formation of the Anti-Corn Law League in 1838, under the leadership of Richard Cobden and John Bright, two self-educated Manchester businessmen who pioneered the use of the mass rally as an instrument of political persuasion. As a result of their efforts, aided by a severe harvest failure in Great Britain and the imminent threat of a famine in Ireland, the corn laws were at last repealed by the Tory government in 1846.

In the protracted parliamentary debate that led up to repeal, Disraeli, the opposition Whig leader, spoke contemptuously of the movement for repeal as the Manchester school, referring no doubt to the fact that the campaign against the corn laws had its center among the cotton manufacturers in and around Manchester. The label stuck and was soon applied as a term of abuse not only to free traders but to all followers of the laissez faire principle of government. For Cobden and Bright, the unilateral repeal of the corn laws was only a first step toward a worldwide system of free trade, which would eventually banish colonies, diplomatic jockeying, and wars, ushering in a new era of international peace. Such aspirations were linked in their minds with a hostility to factory legislation and trade unionism at home because they thought that least government is always best government. It was this compound of interconnected ideas that came to be described by the term Manchester school, and the label was then employed indiscriminately to caricature the ideas of the English school of classical political economy. Thus, it was enough for any nineteenth-century German protectionist and interventionist to refer to "Smithianismus" and "Manchesterertum" to convey to their readers a whole series of repugnant ideas made up of free trade, laissez faire, anti-imperialism, pacifism, and political individualism.

The case for free trade, however, as stated by Smith, Ricardo, and John Stuart Mill, was hedged by a number of qualifications which called for gradual and partial repeal of the corn laws rather than the total and immediate abandonment of agricultural protection advocated by Cobden and Bright. The leading British economists of the 1830s and 1840s held themselves aloof from the popular debate on free trade and indeed disavowed the vulgar propaganda of the Anti-Corn Law League. And although the agitation for repeal drew on the general free trade position of the classical economists, the campaign which finally secured the repeal of the corn laws in 1846 based itself, more often than not, on arguments directly contrary to the spirit and even the letter of the works of Smith and Ricardo.

Moreover, in the great controversies of the time regarding the legitimate role of government, the English classical economists generally adopted a pragmatic attitude toward government intervention, which allowed frequent exceptions to the general rule of laissez faire. They sanctioned public control over the issue of money; they endorsed factory legislation, albeit haltingly; and they supported state assistance for emigration. Despite individual differences over such questions as state aid to paupers, the legal rights of trade unions, and public control of elementary education, none of the classical economists can be characterized as die-hard enemies of all forms of state intervention. In short, there never was a Manchester school of economists, although there certainly was a Manchester school of business executives and politicians.

References

Blaug, M., *Ricardian Economics,* Greenwood, Westport, Conn., 1973, chap. 10; Grampp, W. D., *The Manchester School of Economics,* Stanford University Press, Stanford, 1960; O'Brien, D. P., *The Classical Economists,* Clarendon, Oxford, 1975, chap. 10.

(*See also* Classical school; Laissez faire)

Mark Blaug

Market segmentation hypothesis (*see* Yield curve)

Marketing channels (*see* Channels of marketing)

Marginal cost

Marginal cost is the increment in total cost incurred by a producer as the result of a unit increase in quantity produced. This concept is used in the theory of the firm in conjunction with marginal revenue to help determine the profit-maximizing level of output; it is used in welfare economics to evaluate the consequences of the market structures of reality and their deviation from the standard of perfect competition. Recently, it has been used to judge the conduct of firms with market power in relation to antitrust statutes, the Sherman Act in particular. Marginal cost has also been used as a measuring criterion in identifying predatory pricing behavior.

Profit Maximization and Efficiency

Economic profit is the difference between total revenue and total cost, but profit maximization is accomplished on a unit-by-unit basis, considering increments in revenue (marginal revenue) and in cost (marginal cost) incurred with each unit produced. Clearly if $MC < MR$, the firm can increase its profits by expanding output, since by so doing it obtains more in additional revenue than the added cost of the incremental output. Similarly, a profit-maximizing firm has an incentive to reduce its output if marginal cost exceeds marginal revenue ($MC > MR$). By doing so, it is saving in total cost more than it loses in revenue. Thus, the firm can maximize profit only if it selects an output level at which $MC = MR$.

Marginal cost can be used to judge whether an output level is socially optimal. For convenience, let us use q^* to denote the profit-maximizing level of output, let p^* be the maximum price at which q^* can be sold, let MC^* be the marginal cost of producing a small increment of output if the firm is already producing q^*, and let there be no other resource costs of production outside those incurred by the firm. If p^* exceeds MC^*, then productive social resources are wasted. The reason is that MC^* is the social cost of attracting from other uses the additional resources needed to produce a contemplated increment in output, while p^* reflects consumers' willingness to pay for that added output. Therefore, if p^* is greater than MC^*, a cost-benefit test shows at once that society would be better off if resources were diverted from other uses into the production of the commodity in question. The reverse is true if p^* is less than MC^*. Thus, marginal cost plays a key role in testing whether the economy's resources are allocated efficiently.

Algebraic and Geometric Analysis of Marginal Cost

For a firm that produces only one product—the fictitious single-product firm—the geometry and mathematics of various costs is particularly simple. Let q_0 be the initial level of output and TC_0 the associated total cost. Let q_1 denote some higher level of output and TC_1 the associated total cost. We can then define the increments $\Delta TC = TC_1 - TC_0$ and $\Delta q = q_1 - q_0$. Forming the ratio $\Delta TC/\Delta q$ we obtain an (approximate) measure of the marginal cost. (The smaller we make the increment in output Δq, the smaller is the degree of imprecision.)

To evaluate the marginal cost properly at a point such as q_0, calculus techniques are needed. Specifically, the marginal cost of q_0 is the derivative of the total cost function evaluated at that point, $\Delta TC/\Delta q$ at q_0.

Figure 1 illustrates the mathematical analysis. On the horizontal axis we plot total output per unit of time and on the vertical axis the total cost. It follows from the diagram that when the increase in output becomes very small, the ratio $\Delta TC/\Delta q$ becomes approximately equal to the ratio $B'B/\Delta q$, which is the slope of the tangent to the total cost curve at point q_0. The slope of that tangent is the true marginal cost at q_0.

For a single-product firm we can easily illustrate the relationships between the marginal cost and the average cost AC, which is equal to the total cost divided by the

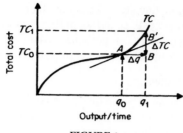

FIGURE 1

associated level of output; that is, $AC = TC/q$. As indicated in Figure 2, $MC = AC$ at that level of output, denoted by q_0, at which the average cost curve reaches its lowest point. This geometric relationship can be summarized compactly by the formula $MC = AC(1 + e)$, where $e = (\Delta AC/\Delta q)(a/AC)$ is the (approximate) elasticity of the average cost curve. We see that if AC is constant, as it will be if there are constant returns to scale, MC will equal AC; if AC is rising so that $\Delta AC/\Delta q$ is positive, MC will be higher than AC. Other cases can be worked out using similar reasoning. The degree of economies of scale at a given output level q_0 is equivalent to AC/MC at q_0. Returns to scale are increasing where $AC/MC > 1$, constant where $AC/MC = 1$, and decreasing where $AC/MC < 1$.

For a multiproduct firm the above analysis does not hold because of the presence of common costs—costs that cannot be allocated on any rational criterion among the various products. For example, there is no rule that correctly allocates the costs of the railroad track among various types of freight carried by the railroad. Consequently, one cannot form the expression $AC = TC/q$ for each type of freight. However, it is possible to use the concept of ray average cost in order to calculate the average cost of producing a bundle of commodities.

Fortunately, at least in theory, it is possible to calculate the marginal costs for each separate type of freight, and this is the main piece of information needed for optimal decisions relating to multicommodity production. Determining the marginal cost of one particular kind of output in a multiproduct firm involves multivariate differential calculus. Consider a cost function $TC = TC(q_1, \ldots, q_N)$ for a firm that produces N products. In this case, the marginal cost of output i is defined as the partial derivative of the total cost function TC with respect to q_i (i.e., holding all other output levels constant).

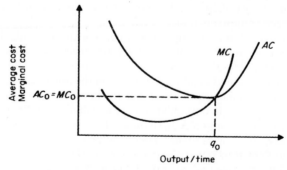

FIGURE 2

It is important, in the multiproduct case, to distinguish marginal cost from incremental cost. Incremental cost, in the notation used above, would be equivalent to $TC(q_1, \ldots, q_N) - TC(q_1, \ldots, q_{i-1}, q_{i+1}, \ldots, q_N)$. That is, the incremental cost is the difference between the total cost of producing all outputs and the total cost of producing all outputs except output i. This incremental cost may or may not include some fixed costs necessary to the production of output i only.

Short-Run versus Long-Run Marginal Cost

The marginal cost of producing additional output depends critically on whether the entrepreneur anticipates that the additional demand that elicits this output will persist for a long or only for a short period. If the latter, it is perhaps best to expand production using overtime labor and employing the existing capital stock more intensively. But if the rise in demand is expected to endure, the entrepreneur may decide to purchase additional capital equipment and employ more full-time labor.

In general, it is less costly to produce additional output when the quantities of all inputs—labor, capital, land, etc.—can be properly adjusted to new demand conditions. Consequently, the long-run marginal cost (LRMC), with all inputs fully adjusted to additional outputs must be lower than the short-run marginal cost (SRMC), which is calculated for the case where some input quantities are fixed by earlier decisions. Similarly, if output is contracted, the marginal saving in cost from reducing output by one unit is larger when all inputs can be orderly released than it is when some inputs are fixed at their old levels. Figure 3 illustrates those relations on the assumption that the firm initially expects to produce indefinitely q_0 units of output per unit of time and where q_1 and q_2 are some other possible level of output which may or may not prevail for a long period. The arrows from A to B indicate that over time the marginal cost will fall toward its long-run value equal to MC_1. This process of adjustment will be the faster the more certain is the entrepreneur that q_1 will be sold for a long period of time. It will be also the faster the cheaper it is to adjust the necessary inputs quickly to their most desired levels.

Marginal Cost and Industry Structure and Behavior

Marginal-cost pricing is essential to economic efficiency, as discussed above. It has been thought, however, that only in perfect competition would unregulated profit-maximizing firms produce where $p = MC$. Monopolies, oligopolies, and monopolistic competitors would all produce at lower output levels than competitive industries facing the same costs. Here, with $p > MC$, unexploited gains from trade would exist

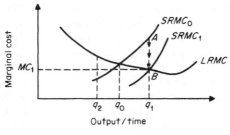

FIGURE 3

because of the lack of competition. Recent work in contestable market theory has identified free entry and exit as the crucial issue, demonstrating that with as few as two firms, a "sustainable industry configuration" requires $p = MC$ for all outputs.

Declining marginal costs are a sufficient but not necessary condition for natural monopoly. This is so because declining marginal costs imply declining average costs, and declining average costs imply subadditivity of the cost function, which is the criterion for natural monopoly. A cost function is subadditive if it is cheaper to produce an output level q at one firm than it is to break up production over several smaller firms.

Declining marginal costs pose a welfare problem. Profitable operation of a natural monopoly requires that price at least cover average costs. But economic efficiency requires that price equal marginal cost. Since marginal cost is less than average cost in this case, efficient production will generate negative profit: $p = MC < AC$. In such a situation, "second-best" pricing designed to maximize efficiency while holding the firm to zero profits results in the Ramsey rule $p = AC > MC$.

Social and Private Marginal Cost

It is entirely possible that, from the standpoint of society, the cost of adding one more unit of output will not correspond to the cost incurred by the entrepreneur. This divergence between social and private marginal cost may occur for various reasons. Perhaps the most important is the presence of external benefits or costs. For example, when one whose occupation is fishing decides to spend more time catching more fish, then labor must increase and more fuel must be used for the boat. This constitutes private marginal cost. However, disregarded is the fact that such decisions as depleting the stock of fish affect others who fish, who now must spend more time— and additional resources—to catch the same quantity of fish as they did before. This additional expenditure must be added to private marginal cost in order to calculate social marginal cost, which includes all of society including the producers.

Even in perfectly competitive markets, if external costs exist (i.e., if social marginal cost exceeds private marginal cost), the equilibrium level of output Q^* will be above the optimal level Q^0. On every unit of output between Q^0 and Q^*, the marginal benefit received by consumers will be greater than the private marginal cost but less than the social marginal cost. Thus, each of these units will reduce total welfare.

The opposite case arises when a farmer spends additional resources on pest control and thereby reduces the number of pests in the field of neighboring farmers who now can use smaller quantities of resources to keep pests at their previous level. The preceding analysis explains in part why the government taxes firms emitting pollutants and subsidizes such activities as research and development. Calculation of optimal taxes and subsidies requires knowledge of the amount of the external cost (i.e., of the difference between social and private marginal cost).

A discrepancy between social and private marginal costs can also arise because some of the productive inputs purchased by firms are not sold at prices equal to their marginal costs. For example, if steel were monopolized so that the price of steel exceeded its marginal cost, users of steel would be induced to economize on the use of steel and to use other inputs to a greater degree than they otherwise would. This socially unwarranted substitution is induced by a difference between private above social marginal cost. It also explains in part why there are incentives for vertical mergers.

Estimation of Marginal Cost

Two basic methods are used to estimate marginal cost empirically. The first is to look at historical cost data and relate annual changes in costs to annual changes in outputs. In doing this, special care must be taken to separate out all those influences such as inflation that can cause costs to change even when there is no change in quantities produced. Indeed, it can be said that for this reason raw accounting data cannot yield correct estimates of marginal cost. In practice, statistical estimation of marginal cost requires careful, sophisticated techniques.

The second basic method is engineering analysis. This entails the design of the best production arrangement for two different levels of output. The cost difference, when divided by the change in output, yields an estimate of marginal cost. For a large firm this procedure may involve complex and large-scale computer simulation. The disadvantage of engineering estimates is that they are based on hypothetical situations, whereas historical estimates are based firmly on actual experience. This disadvantage becomes an advantage if technological progress, for example, is rapid, so that the past becomes a poor indicator of future costs. It is also clear that the marginal cost of a new product line cannot be estimated directly from historical data.

References

Baumol, William J., *Economic Theory and Operations Research,* 4th ed., Prentice-Hall, Englewood Cliffs, N.J., 1977; Baumol, William J., John C. Panzar, and Robert D. Willig, *Contestable Markets and the Theory of Industry Structure,* 3d ed., Harcourt Brace Jovanovich, New York, 1988; Machlup, Fritz, *The Economics of Sellers' Competition,* Johns Hopkins Press, Baltimore, 1952.

(*See also* Competition; Contestable markets; Firm theory; Marginal revenue; Microeconomics; Normative economics; Subsidies; Welfare economics)

Janusz A. Ordover

Marginal revenue

Marginal revenue is the (positive or negative) increment in total revenue obtained by a seller (firm, group, cartel) through a unit increase in the quantity sold. This concept is used chiefly in the theory of the firm for the determination of the output and selling price at which profit is maximized, that is, the quantity for which the excess of marginal revenue over marginal cost is zero, or, in the case of incomplete divisibility, above zero by the smallest possible amount.

The concept is much older than its name. The concept was used in mathematical form by Augustin Cournot in 1838. Around 1930 almost a dozen economists developed it simultaneously in verbal, geometric, and algebraic analyses. The clearest expositions, including the term marginal revenue, were by Joan Robinson and Edward H. Chamberlin.

Algebraic Argument

It is customary to use infinitesimal calculus (differential coefficients) and point elasticities of demand. Since quantities of product are not always perfectly divisible and prices must be varied by finite magnitudes, it is preferable to calculate with first differences and arc elasticities of demand.

Denoting the higher price as p_1 and the smaller quantity saleable at that price as q_1; and the lower price as p_2 and the larger quantity saleable as q_2, marginal revenue will be the difference between $p_2 q_2$ and $p_1 q_1$, or the same as the difference between the (positive) sales gain $p_2(q_2 - q_1)$, and the (negative) price loss, $q_1(p_2 - p_1)$. Thus, $MR = p_2(q_2 - q_1) - q_1(p_1 - p_2)$ [or plus $q_1(p_2 - p_1)$, which is negative because $p_2 < p_1$]. If arc elasticity of demand is written as $[(q_2 - q_1)/q_1]/[(p_2 - p_1)/p_2]$, or $p_2(q_2 - q_1)/q_1(p_2 - p_1)$, one recognizes that it is equal to the ratio of the sales gain to the price loss.

Conforming with the original definition of marginal revenue as the revenue change resulting from an increase in quantity by just one unit, and thus making $q_2 - q_1 = 1$, the above expressions become even simpler. Marginal revenue, expressed as the excess of the sales gain over the price loss, becomes $p_2 + q_1(p_2 - p_1)$. Arc elasticity of demand becomes $p_2/q_2(p_2 - p_1)$. Hence,

$$MR = p_2 + p_2(1/v) \qquad \text{or} \qquad MR = p_2(1 + 1/v)$$

which of course is less than p_2, since v is negative.

Using differential calculus, $MR = dTR/dQ$. For a firm selling more than one product, the marginal revenue from selling another unit of product i is the partial derivative of the multivariable function TR.

Geometric Representation

The usual geometric representation is through continuous curves, analogous to infinitesimally small variations in price and quantity and to point elasticities. Thus, if DD' is the demand curve, its point elasticity at R, that is at price OP (= QR) and quantity OQ (= PR), is equal to the ratio OP/PY, where Y is the intercept of the tangent through R with the ordinate. Marginal revenue for quantity OQ can be found by deducting a stretch equal to PY from the price or average revenue, QR.

Thus, we obtain QS as marginal revenue corresponding to the average revenue QR (Figure 1). If we constructed the complete marginal revenue curve, it would satisfy the condition that for each point the area bordered by the curve and the two axes (the integral of the marginal revenues of all additional units of the quantity sold) would be equal to the rectangle inscribed between the demand curve and the axes (average revenue times quantity).

It is more instructive to draw stepped curves, corresponding to finite differences of price and quantity, and arc elasticities between consecutive points. In Figure 2, marginal revenue is shown for the sixth and the sixteenth units. The price losses

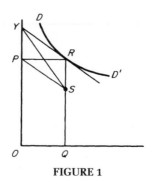

FIGURE 1

being deducted from the sales gains, marginal revenue is represented by the light-shaded lower parts of these gains.

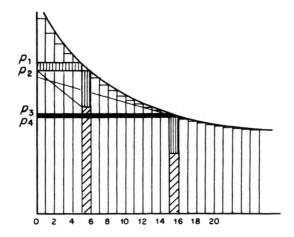

Total sales	Sales gain	Price loss	Marginal revenue
$5p_1$			
$6p_2$	$1p_2$	$5(p_1 - p_2)$	$p_2 - 5(p_1 - p_2)$
$15p_3$			
$16p_4$	$1p_4$	$15(p_3 - p_4)$	$p_4 - 15(p_3 - p_4)$

FIGURE 2

The geometric relationship between elasticity of demand and marginal revenue is most clearly seen in the sets of graphs combined in Figure 3. In order to show larger areas, we make the quantity change in larger lumps. Elasticity of demand is represented by the ratio of the sales gain to the price loss, marginal revenue by the difference between sales gain and price loss.

Marginal, Average, and Total Revenue

The four concepts of total revenue (TR), price or average revenue (AR), marginal revenue (MR), and price elasticity of demand (v), are logically interrelated.

With infinitely elastic demand ($v = INF$), TR increases proportionately with q, the quantity sold. Along such a horizontal demand curve, $p = AR = TR/q$ is constant as q increases. In this case, $p = MR$. When applied to an individual firm's demand curve, this defines pure (or perfect) competition, implying the seller's belief that larger quantities of output could be sold at an unchanged price. Since profit maximization requires that $MR = MC$, profit maximization results in economically efficient production: $P = MC$.

Where demand is elastic ($v > 1$ in absolute value), any percentage increase in q will exceed the corresponding percentage decrease in p along the demand curve. In this situation, as q increases, TR increases (though less than proportionately), and MR declines even faster than price and is definitely below the price (provided that price

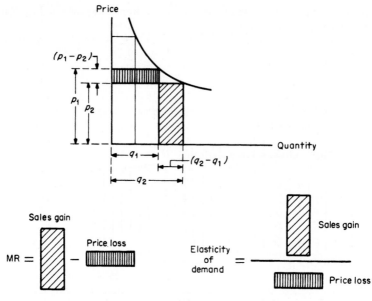

FIGURE 3

discrimination is excluded). With unit-elastic demand ($v = 1$), TR remains constant because q increases at the same proportion as p is reduced; the demand curve showing AR ($= p$) in that range has the shape of a rectangular hyperbola, and $MR = 0$ (which is obvious, with TR constant). In a range of $v < 1$, demand is inelastic, TR declines when q increases, AR declines even faster, and MR is negative.

In sum, positive marginal revenue is associated with elastic demand, zero marginal revenue with unit-elastic demand, and negative marginal revenue with inelastic demand. Along a straight-line demand curve going from the price axis to the quantity axis, demand will become more elastic as price rises (and quantity falls) and more elastic as price falls (and quantity rises). The corresponding marginal revenue curve to a straight-line demand curve begins at the same point on the vertical (price) axis and falls at twice the rate of the demand curve, so that marginal revenue becomes zero (demand becomes unit-elastic) at the midpoint of the curve.

Without subsidies or other special incentives, no unregulated profit-maximizing firm would ever set its price so low or offer so large a quantity for sale, that marginal revenue is negative. Since profit maximization requires $MR = MC$, whenever production cost is positive, MR must be positive at the profit-maximizing output.

The above argument, however, does not mean that demand will never be inelastic in an industry. In maximizing profit, the firm is considering its own marginal revenue and thus its own firm's demand curve. Every perfectly competitive firm faces by definition perfectly elastic demand, but the output of the entire industry may be such that market demand is inelastic in the relevant range. It is true, however, that where the firm and industry demand curves are identical (i.e., in the case of a monopolist), profit maximization precludes output high enough or price low enough for inelastic demand.

Theoretical and Practical Uses

The theory of the firm as a part of the theory of prices and allocations deals with imaginary decision makers. Marginal revenue in this theory is calculated or constructed from average revenue, which in turn is calculated from total revenue. Since in reality firms can rarely know total revenues or, still less, average revenues to be obtained for different quantities of particular products, one might think that it would be hopeless for them to calculate marginal revenues, yet, in actual practice things are quite different: Incremental revenues and incremental costs are much easier to take into account than totals or averages. A decision maker in reality does not draw curves or calculate averages, either of recorded data of the past or of expected data of the future. As decision makers consider accepting or rejecting particular orders or making adjustments in production plans, they think exclusively in terms of what incremental revenues and incremental costs are likely to be involved. The practically important question is always what difference would it make to the firm's net revenue if this or that change were made. This incremental thinking corresponds to the marginal calculus which the theorist applies to the abstract hypothetical decisions of the imaginary firms in the constructed models.

References

Chamberlin, Edward Hastings, *The Theory of Monopolistic Competition,* 5th ed., Harvard University Press, Cambridge, Mass., 1933, 1946; Cournot, Augustin, *Researches into the Mathematical Principles of the Theory of Wealth,* Paris, 1838, Macmillan, New York, 1897, 1927; Machlup, Fritz, *The Economics of Sellers' Competition,* Johns Hopkins Press, Baltimore, 1952; Robinson, Joan, *The Economics of Imperfect Competition,* Macmillan, London, 1933.

(*See also* Elasticity; Firm theory; Marginal cost; Microeconomics)

Fritz Machlup and
Janusz A. Ordover

Marshall-Lerner condition (*see* J Curve)

Marketing research and business economics

Philip Kotler defines marketing as "a social and managerial process by which individuals and groups obtain what they need and want through creating and exchanging products and values with others." Marketing research is used to assess the market's response to the firm's marketing inputs which include promotional activities such as price discounting, placement of in-store displays, multimedia advertising, and couponing; expanding distribution; and product development and enhancement. The goal of marketing research is to assist the firm in determining the most effective, i.e., most profitable, mix of marketing inputs given knowledge of the marketplace.

As a formal scientific discipline marketing research began in the early twentieth century with most analyses being based on survey data. In the 1930s, the A. C. Nielsen Company began collecting in-store data using manual audits. Today, with the advent of scanning technology, the amount of timely data available from stores and household panels has grown exponentially. Coincident with this data explosion, the data delivery systems and the techniques used to analyze the data have become increasingly sophisticated. Marketing research is an integral part of organizations in both the consumer durable and nondurable goods sectors, and in recent years the use of marketing principles has become increasing prevalent among nonprofit and government sectors.

Marketing research is interdisciplinary requiring the knowledge of economists, operations researchers, psychologists, and statisticians. For the economist, the economic theory of consumer behavior and the theory of the firm provide basic building blocks. Marketing research can be viewed as an operational or tactical activity and as a strategic activity. Although both activities require knowledge of the workings of the marketplace at both the macroeconomic and microeconomic levels, tactical analyses focus on monitoring a product's performance and testing the effectiveness of marketing programs relative to competitors. Strategic research involves selecting and prioritizing marketing opportunities.

In order to understand the marketplace, the researcher must define the market in terms of both the geographic unit and the product class and collect data. Data on consumer purchases permit an analyst to determine what was sold and how particular brands performed relative to each other. In addition to sales and price information, causal data assist the analyst in understanding the reason that sales took place. Examples of causal data are newspaper advertising which indicates the extent of retailer advertising support, display activity, and coupon ads. Another important source of information for understanding the source of sales is television advertising. Measuring the effects of television advertising is relatively difficult owing to the dynamic effects such advertising has on consumer behavior, however.

Once the data are collected, the analyst may choose to evaluate the information by simply looking at the raw series together over time or compute straightforward measures such as market share in order to arrive at a qualitative assessment of market activity. Statistical models might be estimated in order to address issues such as temporary price reduction effectiveness, the extent of cannibalization due to promotional activity, i.e., the extent to which sales of one specific product decline as a result of promoting another similar product produced by the same manufacturer, the competitive effects of promotions, differences between markets, competitive pricing points, and long-term price elasticities.

Forecasting is an activity likely to be undertaken by a business economist working in a marketing research department. Conventionally, business economists have been responsible for producing forecasts for the macroeconomic environment or for activity within industry groups. More recently, forecasting movements in mature product categories, in segments within categories, and in brands has increased in importance.

Forecasting the success or failure of new product introductions is also important. New product introductions require a considerable amount of a firm's resources, and failure to read the marketplace correctly and early in the development process can lead to costly errors. The development of a new brand begins with the identification of new market opportunities. Consumer survey research directed at identifying the market response to the brand concept and elements of the marketing mix, e.g., pricing, is typically conducted. On the basis of the survey a firm may decide to continue with the development plans for the brand, revise current plans in response to the survey results and retest, or cancel development plans completely. Comparisons may also be made between attitudes toward the new concepts and existing products.

Given a decision to proceed with the product introduction, data collected on consumer attitudes and/or actual behavior from selected test markets may be modeled in order to predict response variables such as market share and sales under different circumstances.

One of the most recent developments in marketing research is the application of systematic and scientific marketing research methods internationally. It is true that most marketing research focuses on national rather than international issues. The relative importance of multinational research is increasing and will continue to expand as economic unions grow in importance (e.g., the Single European Act, the Canada-U.S. Free Trade Agreement, and the proposal for a North American Free Trade Agreement).

International research refers to research conducted outside of the country where the sponsoring firm's headquarters is located. International research may involve analyses of a single market outside the country in which the organization is headquartered for the purpose of extending the distribution of an existing product or introducing a new one. The research effort may involve a comparison of the marketing effort for particular categories and brands across two or more markets. The research may be tactical or it may be strategic. For example, from the operational standpoint, a firm may want to monitor sales and promotional activities for it's own products and those of competitors. On the strategic side, the estimation of relatively sophisticated sales response models may provide valuable insight into differences between markets and help identify best demonstrated practices.

International market research introduces problems in addition to those found in domestic research. There are the obvious problems posed by differences in language, culture, economic environment, and geography. There are also more subtle differences such as those in legal restrictions on permissible types of promotional activities, distribution channels, and the availability of information. Further, the lack of comparability of data across borders is likely to place limitations on research. A product sold in one country may also be sold in another under the same or a different brand name. There may also be slight differences in the brand from one country to the next, e.g., flavoring. Finally, because of differences in consumer behavior and attitudes, definitions of product categories may vary between countries.

Effective market research requires the integration of data from many sources including governments, manufacturers, retailers, and consumers. Technology continues to advance making available more data of higher quality and better information delivery systems. The role of the business economist in marketing research is changing from that of only providing macroeconomic analyses and industry studies to that of developing ways for utilizing and analyzing the data most effectively in order to increase knowledge of the marketplace.

References

Dudley, J. W., *1992—Strategies for the Single Market,* Kogan Page Ltd., London, 1989; Kotler, P., *Marketing Management,* 6th ed., Prentice-Hall, Englewood Cliffs, N.J., 1988; Worcester, R. M. and J. Downham, (eds.), *Consumer Market Research Handbook,* 3d ed., Elsevier Science Publishers B.V., Amsterdam, 1986.

(*See also* Advertising, economic aspects; Anticipation surveys, business; Anticipation surveys, consumer; Consumer theory; Consumption function; Firm theory; Sampling in economics)

Phillip A. Cartwright

Marshallian economics

Marshallian economics takes its name from Alfred Marshall, who was professor of economics at Cambridge University in England from 1884 to 1908 and who is generally regarded as the founder of the Cambridge school of economics. The term "neoclassical" is often used to describe Marshall's economics. His famous *Principles of Economics,* first published in 1890 and running to its eighth edition by 1920, is sometimes regarded as the *locus classicus* of neoclassical economics and is also usually regarded as one of the greatest works ever written in the field of economics.

A Method of Analysis

In recent years there has been a revival of interest in, and growing sympathy with, Marshall's method of analysis, as compared with general equilibrium analysis. Marshallian economics is not just a set of theories or hypotheses to explain the working of a capitalist, market system: it is much more a method of analysis or a framework within which to operate.

As Marshall realized and continually emphasized, an economic system is one of perpetual change and evolution. Businesses are born, grow, and decay; demand and supply conditions for commodities alter; population changes affect labor supply as do migration movements, education, and changing social mores. In other words, economic systems are complex structures of interrelated factors, all of which are subject to change. This is what makes economics such a difficult subject and often makes those studying it despair of achieving any rigorous, useful results. How should such complexities be handled? Simplification is clearly necessary—this, after all, is the essential ingredient of scientific inquiry—but oversimplification must be avoided.

Two simplifications are the hallmark of Marshallian economics and remain part of the tool kit of contemporary economics. One concerns the breakdown of complex interrelationships, the other the handling of time. Marshallian economics is often referred to as partial equilibrium analysis and is sometimes contrasted unfavorably with general equilibrium theory. What does this contrast imply? Let us consider the demand for a commodity. It is possible to conceive of the demand for, say, beefsteak depending on all relative prices in the system, because ultimately all commodities compete for limited consumer income—this would be part of the general equilibrium approach. This assumption implies that all markets are interrelated; Marshall accepted that this might be an appropriate theoretical specification but went on to argue that in realistic, empirical terms the demand for beefsteak, for example, would be dominated by one or two variables—the price of beefsteak compared with the prices of other meats and consumer income. Thus, an increase in the demand for beefsteak was assumed to have its major impact in the market for beefsteak and closely related markets (lamb, pork, chicken) so that the analysis is only partial. It does not consider all the possible interrelations; it focuses on the important ones. Second, Marshallian economics takes these major influences on demand one by one, ceteris paribus; that is, we look at the effect of a fall in the price of beefsteak given initially the price of lamb, pork, and chicken and given consumer income. Allowance for changes in some of these initial conditions is then made.

Time, of course, is a continuous variable—it does not stop and start but goes on and on inexorably. To make it amenable to inquiry, Marshall artificially broke time down into a series of planning periods, which were associated with the degree of fixity of the factors under control. Let us take an example used by Marshall: Suppose that there is a sudden, unexpected increase in the demand for fish. Marshall considered the supply response in three planning stages. In the immediate—or market—period, price will simply rise as the extra demand at the quayside faces an unchanged catch—notice that Marshall assumed that prices adjust instantaneously to clear the market. If the increased demand continues, more trawlers will put to sea or fish more frequently, extra deck hands will be signed on, etc., so that in the short period (or partial adaptation period) the supply of fish to the market will respond to the price increase signal, although at rising marginal and average cost.

If the rise in demand is now regarded as permanent by the fishing industry, increase in fleet size will occur, accompanied, via a rise in relative earnings, by a rise in the labor force. Thus, supply will permanently adjust by full adaptation to the change. In this case, it is possible that the increase in output may occur without any rise in average or marginal cost. Indeed there could even be a decline.

This analysis of time leads us into the central aspect of the theoretical structure of Marshallian economics. This is what Marshall called the "theory of value," or what is now called the "theory of relative price determination." The basic argument is that relative prices and changes in them are determined by the demand and supply conditions in different markets and the changes in these conditions. These are the so-called laws of supply and demand so often referred to in economic discussions. As was implicit in our fishing example, it is clear that the shorter the planning horizon over which a change in underlying conditions is allowed to have effect, the greater will be the influence of demand conditions.

Thus, returning to our fish market example, we see that in the very short period with a given stock or catch it is the strength of demand that determines price. As we move into the partial adaptation period, supply factors also play their part in price determination, and in the full adaptation period (or long period) supply factors come to dominate price formation.

We have then a vision of an economic system in which changing demand and supply conditions in the various commodity, factor, and financial markets are continuously altering the set of relative prices.

As relative prices alter, decision makers—business executives, householders, suppliers of labor—adjust their behavior accordingly. What principles do they use in making these adjustments to their market behavior? In answering this question we arrive at another central theoretical idea of Marshallian economics—the principle of substitution. It works as follows; decision makers—business executives, householders, workers—are assumed to be individual welfare maximizers; that is, they take actions in response to changing economic circumstances that will, in their subjective judgment, maximize the interests of the unit that they represent. Of what does this welfare consist? For business units it is long-run expected profits; for household and suppliers of labor it is expected utility.

Any change in relative prices will make existing plans nonoptimal and hence will encourage substitution. A business executive, faced with a rise in the relative cost of a factor of production will attempt to lower the proportion of that factor being used. A household will respond to a rise in the price of potatoes by buying more rice or pasta and fewer potatoes. Suppliers of labor will respond to a rise in overtime hourly rates by adjusting the division of their time between work and leisure.

The central importance of the principle of substitution is clear; it is the mechanism by which an economy adjusts to changes in the underlying economic structure, and the signalling system for this mechanism to operate is the system of relative prices. Notice that adjustment in the Marshallian system depends crucially on the existence of price flexibility. But in some markets we have price stickiness where prices do not respond instantaneously to clear markets. This is especially true of the labor market, and much recent work in Keynesian economics has centered on this point.

The monetary and macroeconomic aspects of Marshallian economics are often portrayed in a somewhat stereotyped manner as a belief in the twin assumptions of full employment and the quantity theory of money. This does less than justice to Marshall's actual contribution. Perhaps his foremost work here is the analysis of the demand for money as a stable function of real income or wealth. This is the prototype of important later work associated especially with Milton Friedman.

References

Blaug, M., *Economic Theory in Retrospect,* 4th ed., Cambridge University Press, Cambridge, 1985, chaps. 9, 10, 15; Marshall, A., *Principles of Economics,* 9th ed., edited by C. W. Guillebaud, Macmillan, New York, 1961.

(*See also* Cambridge school; Chicago school; Consumers' surplus; Demand; General equilibrium; Marginal cost; Marginal revenue; Neoclassical economics; Normative economics; Quantity theory of money; Welfare economics)

                                                                Bernard A. Corry

Marxism

Marxism is a unified social science, representing a particular viewpoint of the combined disciplines of philosophy, history, economics, sociology, and political science. Marxists believe that the non-Marxist disciplines are each too narrow and do not recognize many of the most important problems that lie within several disciplines at once. Moreover, society is viewed as one unified organism, having political, economic, and other aspects. Marxism originated with Karl Marx, who drew on three sources: (1) German philosophy, especially Kant and Hegel; (2) British classical economics, especially Adam Smith and David Ricardo; and (3) French revolutionary thought. Marxism was the official dogma in the Soviet Union, and continues to be in China and Cuba. These regimes are now in crisis, but Marxism is being rejuvenated in a nondogmatic form by many social scientists around the world.

Marxist Philosophy of Science of Economics

First, Marxist philosophy is materialist, devoid of all religious superstition, and it embraces science as a problem solver, based on facts of experience. Yet materialism is not simple empiricism, for Marxists believe that every so-called fact is only found, interpreted, and integrated within some theoretical and ethical framework—there is no such thing as a fact aside from theory and value judgments. Second, it is determinist in that science can discover regularities of natural and social behavior, which determine what will happen in any given situation. Marxism thus rejects the doctrine of free will, though it also rejects any notion that history is predetermined by God or any other force above human beings. Third, it is humanist, in the sense that nothing is higher than humanity, and all decisions should be made on the basis of the needs of the majority of humanity, recognizing that the majority of humanity is the oppressed working class. Fourth, it is dialectic, in the sense that it instructs the social scientist to ask questions (1) about conflicts within society, (2) among opposed groups interrelated with all other groups, and (3) as to the form of change, both gradually within a society and by possible revolution from one social form to another. These dialectical methods of approach are only questions to be asked; they are not dogmas or answers of any sort.

The Interaction of Economics and Ideas

The historical approach of Marxism is also materialist in that it does not accept any notion of ideas arising in a vacuum. All ideas emerge from some social environment. Marxism calls the entire range of ideas plus the entire range of social and political institutions (including law, government, and the family) a social superstructure. This superstructure is determined by the economic base of society, which includes technology, material capital, and human relations among classes in the productive process. Marxism is completely opposed to economic determinism. Economic determinism sees that the superstructure is determined by the economic base, but it denies that the base is also determined by the superstructure. Marxism insists that the superstructure of ideas and sociopolitical institutions fully determines the economic base. Revolutions occur, for example, in the form of new ideas and new political institutions brought about through sociopolitical strife—and these new political institutions help create or support new economic institutions. However, revolutions occur only when fixed human relationships among classes in production conflict with the rapidly widening possibilities presented by new technological forces of production. For example, a slave-owning society cannot take advantage of advanced industrial technology and will resist the spread of industry. When this occurred in the United States, it led—through ideological, theological, social, and political conflict—to the revolution known as the Civil War, which ended slavery.

In sociology, Marxism explains the form of sexual and family relations as well as the form of racial relations as parts of the superstructure determined by, but reacting upon, the economic base. For example, a slave society will have very different racial and gender relations from a capitalist society, each being appropriate to and supportive of its economic base. In political science, Marxism explains the behavior of government on the basis of the needs of society and the needs of the ruling class of society. The Egyptian government under the pharaohs arose partly to control the Nile and partly because of the need for armed forces (and priests and ideology) to support slavery. Of course, a particular form of government, like particular forms of racial and gender relations, then act upon and determine the economic base.

Capitalism and Poverty

Early primitive peoples had classless societies, according to Marxist anthropology. Since then, societies have been divided into a ruling class (which rules and exploits) and a working class (slaves, serfs, or free workers). Under capitalism, the value of every commodity is determined by the labor time in it. But the worker is paid only an equivalent of the value of the goods necessary to his or her average consumption. The difference produced by the worker above the value of the wage is the surplus value, which is the source of all profits, rent, and interest. The system causes poverty not only by paying low wages but by the periodic economic depressions and unemployment which are characteristic of capitalism and only capitalism. According to radical economists, capitalism is also the basic cause of imperialist attempts to dominate and exploit other countries.

Marxists see a future of classless, strifeless society. In its early stages of socialism, there is cooperative or collective ownership, but there are still differential wages according to work done. In the latter stage of communism, there will be collective ownership and collective use according to need.

References

Marx, Karl, *Das Capital,* 3 vols., International Publishers, New York, vol. 1, 1867; Mehring, Franz, *Karl Marx: The Story of His Life,* University of Michigan Press, Ann Arbor, Mich., 1962; Sherman, Howard J., *Foundations of Radical Political Economy,* M. E. Sharpe, Armonk, N.Y., 1989, Sweezy, Paul, *Theory of Capitalist Development,* Monthly Review Press, New York, 1958.

(*See also* Capitalism; Communism; Comparative economic systems, an overview; Labor theory of value; Socialism)

Howard J. Sherman

Mass production (*see* Economics of scale)

Measures of money (*see* Federal Reserve policy; Monetary policy; Open-market operations)

Medicare program

Medicare is a national health insurance program for most citizens over age 65 and certain disabled persons. The program was initiated for the elderly in 1966, under Title XVIII of the Social Security Act. Amendments in 1974 extended coverage to those persons who receive cash benefits under the Social Security program for disability. In addition, coverage was extended to most people who need renal dialysis or a kidney transplant as a result of chronic kidney disease, regardless of age. Since then, legislative acts continue to modify the program with regard to eligibility for benefits, the types and amounts of services covered, regulation and payment of suppliers of service, and cost sharing by beneficiaries. Each of these aspects of the program can strongly affect the economic impact of the program and is perennially the subject of public debate.

The program is administered by the Health Care Financing Administration in the Department of Health and Human Services. Most operational work in managing claims and benefit payments is contracted out to regional intermediaries who are typically themselves private health care insurers.

Eligibility and Financing

Medicare consists of two parts, administered separately: (1) insurance for hospital stays and skilled nursing care (Part A); and (2) supplementary medical benefits (Part B). Part A coverage requires no subscription fees or premium payments by eligible persons. Payments to suppliers for services under Part A are made from a trust fund whose revenues derive from a payroll tax on employers and workers. Clearly, the design of Part A is that of social insurance with involuntary enrollment, forced saving through the payroll tax, and avoidance of "free riders" on public charity by those who might have opted out of voluntary programs. Unlike an insurance plan purchased in the marketplace, Medicare has some potential progressivity, since premiums paid through the payroll tax are related to income. However, medical care use after age 65 is affected by longevity, regional availability of services, and demands, all of which may be related to income and thereby may lead to more benefits per dollar of contribution for high-income enrollees—a regressive effect. Even though the program originated with the widespread conviction that private markets for retirement and disability insurance had failed, adversely affecting people of any income level, some authors have argued for introducing means testing of benefit payments to achieve a more progressive net impact.

Part B coverage of physician and related professional services is voluntary. Eligible persons who elect insurance coverage under Part B pay a monthly premium. There is also significant cost sharing for these services. Remaining financial obligations of the government to pay for services under Part B are met by general revenues. More than 95 percent of all eligible persons enroll for this coverage.

In 1991, approximately 30.3 million aged and 3.3 million disabled persons were covered by Medicare. About 7 million persons received some benefits under Part A, and about 26 million persons received benefits under Part B.

Types and Amounts of Services Covered

Total Medicare benefit payments in 1987 were $82 billion, of which $72 billion were for services to the elderly. About 65 percent of payments went to hospitals, and 28 percent went directly to physicians and related suppliers of professional services. Only a small amount went for nursing homes and other personal health care such as prescription drugs taken at home. Seen another way, the Medicare share of all health care expenses for services to the elderly was 70 percent for hospital care, and 61 percent for physician services. However, of $60 billion spent by or for the elderly for nursing home care and other personal health products and services such as drugs and eyeglasses, Medicare paid only a tiny proportion (less than 10 percent).

Proposals for increased coverage of long-term care have been debated in Congress and in appointed commissions. Although there is substantial demand for such insurance in some segments of the population, the effective demand to pay for this coverage, by people young enough and healthy enough to pool risks without a high degree of self-selection, appears to be insufficient for a market solution. Cost estimates for public insurance coverage of long-term care are quite high, and the effects of "moral hazard" (i.e., demand response) could be large. Public coverage would be fraught with difficulty in carefully specifying when a person would qualify for services.

Regulation of Hospitals and Physicians

A major feature of the program has been free choice by the beneficiary among all licensed suppliers of service. Claims are subject to review by peer review organizations composed of health care professionals outside government. When treatments are found to be inappropriate or the quality of care is poor, payment may be denied and/or further disciplinary action may be taken. Private insurers have begun to contract selectively with hospitals and physicians on the basis of price and demonstrated quality, partly in order to benefit from scale economies, in particular, treatments. This type of selective contracting may be attractive for Medicare and its beneficiaries as well as part of general change in policy to promote more competition in health care.

Formulas for Payment to Hospitals and Physicians

Since Medicare payments represent a substantial fraction of the income of most hospitals, surgical specialists, and some other physician specialists, Medicare does not fit the model of a "price-taker"; policymakers recognize that Medicare rules have a large impact on the economic behavior in supply of health care. Until 1982, hospitals were "reimbursed" for their allowable expenses on the basis of reasonable cost, determined by a detailed system for reporting and auditing of actual hospital expenses at the end of the fiscal year. Since there were no criteria for measuring actual expenses against some standard "efficient" level, the system was widely criticized for promoting unwarranted increases in costs for services and new technologies of little extra benefit. In addition, planning agencies to constrain the growth and investment by the hospital industry appeared to be ineffective.

In 1983, a system of prospective pricing of inpatient stays was enacted, eventually covering most hospitals and inpatient stays. Prospective prices for each of about 500 diagnostic-related groups are essentially set by averaging baseline costs within those groups, allowing for geographic variation in labor costs, annual updates for general inflation, and a limited number of special features of hospitals and communities. In the earlier years of prospective pricing there was clear evidence of reduced costs and more efficient treatment. However, costs per case have continued to rise more rapidly than is explainable by input prices or productivity. There appears to be substantial excess capacity among hospitals and reduced net revenue margins. Consolidation in the industry has proceeded quite slowly.

Physicians have been reimbursed on the basis of "usual and customary" charges, but these are limited by "prevailing rate" screens originally set at the 75th percentile of charges for each procedure in a particular geographic area. The prevailing rate limits are updated annually using indexes of input cost, modified by policy decisions to limit charges when the volume of services grows faster than a specified target rate. Physicians, unlike hospitals, are permitted to bill patients for the balance of their charges that Medicare will not allow for payment. Beginning with 1992, a new fee schedule for physician services has been implemented that attempts to base relative charges on relative resource costs. The new schedule has substantially reduced the allowed payments for many surgical procedures and raised the payments for office consultations.

Cost Sharing by Beneficiaries

Although the cost-sharing provisions of Medicare are somewhat complex, in essence the patient is required to pay a deductible per inpatient stay ($628 in 1991) and some coinsurance for days 60 to 90 of a benefit period which may overlap calendar years. There is an additional lifetime reserve of 60 days. Only a very small percentage of beneficiaries ever exhaust the limits on days of coverage. Still, the question of improving "catastrophic" coverage is quite lively in view of its importance in the theory of insurance and the progress made by private insurers in offering catastrophic coverage to the majority of enrollees in group plans.

Skilled nursing facility care after hospitalization is covered for up to 100 days, with coinsurance after the 20th day. Home health visits on an intermittent basis for skilled nursing services are covered after hospitalization. In practice, this benefit covers a very small percentage of the use of home health care services purchased by the elderly and disabled. Physician bills are covered up to the "allowable charge" maximum, subject to an annual deductible ($100 in 1991) and 20 percent coinsurance. One-half or more of the doctors in some specialties will charge patients directly for amounts greater than the allowable limit.

There is a thriving market in supplemental insurance, known as "medigap" policies. Nearly two-thirds of the elderly either have such supplementary coverage through their employer or by individual purchase. Individual insurance policies are regulated by state agencies, subject to some federal oversight. Primarily, the medigap policies pick up the Medicare deductibles and coinsurance. Therefore, they tend to defeat any cost-containment goals of the Medicare cost sharing and can increase Medicare expenses.

In some geographic areas, Medicare enrollees now have an option to enroll in a health maintenance organization that receives a fixed rate per enrollee, depending on some personal characteristics. The enrollee will find most regular cost sharing eliminated, a greatly reduced burden of filing for claims, and perhaps some additional coverage of services matched by additional monthly enrollment charges. These organizations are believed to control total expense better than the mainstream fee-for-service practice of medical care. The supply and use of this type of option is growing slowly, and there are concerns about improving the accuracy of pricing the rates per person for Medicare and policing the quality of care.

In the late 1980s, Congress enacted a "catastrophic" program to reduce cost sharing for some Medicare expenses by people with large expenses and to improve coverage of skilled nursing care and prescription drugs. It was hoped that the additional coverage, in addition to its value as insurance, would reduce the demand for medigap plans. However, there was no major increase in coverage for long-term care of a custodial rather than recuperative nature. This program included a new involuntary premium charge to the elderly. After widespread negative reaction by the elderly themselves, this program was rescinded. There is continuing debate on improving the insurance protection under Medicare, but future changes are likely to be: (1) better coordinated with the regulation and perhaps taxation of medigap plans; and (2) more attentive to willingness of the public to pay higher premiums—voluntary or involuntary, or payroll taxes.

References

Davis, K., and D. Rowland, *Medicare Policy,* Johns Hopkins University Press, Baltimore, 1986; Pauly, M. *Medical Care at Public Expense,* Praeger, New York, 1971; U.S. Congressional Budget Office, *Restructuring Health Insurance for Medicare Enrollees,* Washington, D.C., June 1991; U.S. House of Representatives, Committee on Ways and Means, *Overview of Entitlement Programs,* WMCP:102-9, Government Printing Office, Washington, D.C., 1991; U.S. Prospective Payment Assessment Commission, *Medicare Prospective Payment and the American Health Care System, Report to the Congress,* Washington, D.C., June 1991 (annual since 1985).

(*See also* Health economics; Social security)

Bernard Friedman

Medium-run forecasts (*see* Economic forecasts)

Mercantilism

Mercantilism was an economic policy pursued by almost all the trading nations in the late sixteenth, seventeenth, and early eighteenth centuries, which aimed at increasing a nation's wealth and power by encouraging the export of goods in return for gold. Mercantilists played down the role of agriculture and stressed the importance of manufacturing and service industries.

Mercantilists deemed commercialization and industrialization as key objectives. They developed the balance-of-payments concept primarily because they considered it in the national interest to overbalance imports with exports and thus to acquire "treasure" (precious metals). Thomas Mun, a director of the East India Trading Company and one of the best-known seventeenth-century English mercantilist authors, explained the significance of the balance of payments in *England's Treasure by Foreign Trade*.

The Mercantilist Program

As part of the mercantilist program, individual governments promoted large investments in export industries; built high tariff walls to restrict imports, which could be produced domestically; restricted exports of domestic raw materials, which could be used by the domestic industry; interfered with the emigration of skilled workers; encouraged immigration of skilled workers; and, in several cases, prohibited sales of precious metals to foreigners.

Since one country's gold gain almost always resulted in a gold loss to one of its trading partners, not all nations could succeed at the same time. This resulted in sharpened trade rivalries. When successful, mercantilist policies generally resulted in full employment of a country's resources and led to rapid economic growth.

Mercantilism, Cameralism, and Colbertism

In England, the mercantilist writers were largely merchants, and their writings were usually in the form of pamphlets. The German-Austrian brand of mercantilism, called "cameralism," was different because the writers, for the most part, were government advisers, public administrators, and teachers, and their treatises were in book form. They stressed domestic industrialization rather than commercial expansion. Their aim was to foster home industry and a self-sufficient economy. The German-Austrian cameralists, such as von Hornigk, argued for the protection and subsidization of specific industries and suggested that the aim of infant industry protection and subsidization was to bridge an initial period for industries that later would be profitable without further protection.

The French type of mercantilism (Colbertism) was more rigorous than the English brand and was administered with the aid of a trained civil service staff under Jean Baptiste Colbert. France used strict government control and regulations to bring about national economic unification and industrial growth; as one of the more rigorously mercantilistic nations, it did not fare too well.

The physiocrats, who came along later in the eighteenth century, held significantly different views from the mercantilists. They believed that the major element in economic prosperity was the productivity of land and that a natural order was far more important than legislative and administrative decisions.

Classical economists of the late eighteenth century indicated that mercantilist policies resulted in inflation and a low level of consumption. Moreover, Adam Smith, the founder of the classical school, accused mercantilists of not being able to distinguish between wealth and what they called treasure, pointing out that the accumulation of treasure is merely instrumental to the acquisition of wealth (consumable and usable goods).

Mercantilists exist today, the best example being the Japanese, who emphasize exports of manufactured goods and continue to make laws which limit imports.

References

Blaug, Mark, *The Early Mercantilists: Thomas Mun, Edward Misselden, Gerard De Malynes,* Pioneers in Economics Series, vol. 4, Gower, England, 1991; Galbraith, John Kenneth, *Economic Perspective,* Houghton Mifflin, Boston, 1983, pp. 38–45; Fellner, William, *Modern Economic Analysis,* McGraw-Hill, New York, 1960; Heckscher, Eli, *Mercantilism,* Macmillan, New York, 1955; Mun, Thomas, *England's Treasure by Foreign Trade,* Doubleday, Garden City, N.Y., 1953; Smith, Adam, *The Wealth of Nations,* Random House, New York, 1937.

(*See also* Balance of international payments; Balance of international trade; Classical school; Physiocrats)

Douglas Greenwald

Mergers, takeovers, and corporate restructuring

The takeover and restructuring activities that began in the late 1970s represented a complex new economic development. To provide perspective, the earlier merger movements are reviewed. The first was at the turn of the century, when horizontal mergers between firms in the same industry resulted in high concentration in many industries. It can be argued that the effects of the early mergers on the industrial structure of the United States have been overstated for the following reasons:

1. Industries were typically not atomistic before the merger movement—concentration was already substantial.

2. The merger activity represented the transformation of regional firms into national firms implemented by the completion of the transcontinental railroad system in the late 1800s.

3. Concentration also developed in industries where firms disappeared by bankruptcy rather than merger.

4. High concentration developed in other developed countries in which merger activity was not important until after World War I.

Merger Activity in the 1920s

The second major movement during the 1920s represented vertical integration—merging firms in the same industry but in different stages of operation, mining, manufacturing, or distribution. A reason suggested is that the development of national advertising, promotion, and selling media stimulated firms to integrate vertically to achieve economies of scale in rounding out their product lines for efficient distribution systems.

During the period 1940 to 1947, some 2500 firms were absorbed in mergers. However, the initiative usually came from the acquired firm which was typically small. Concentration was little affected. Tax considerations appeared to play a role in the mergers.

The Celler-Kefauver Act of 1950 amended the Clayton Act of 1914 to close the asset purchase loophole and granted additional power to make illegal those mergers that had a tendency to increase concentration. The relative importance of horizontal and vertical mergers thereafter declined in relation to conglomerate mergers, or mergers of unrelated firms. The conglomerate merger movement peaked in 1968 and 1969 when the total amount involved in large mergers for the two years combined was $56 billion. A more threatening antitrust climate toward conglomerate mergers and change in accounting treatment as well as tax treatment of mergers resulted in a substantial decline in conglomerate mergers by 1970.

The Takeovers and Restructuring of the 1980s

Although the merger activity of the 1980s fits into the broad pattern of historical movements, it has new characteristics and impacts. It was larger in dollar terms, but the peak in numbers at 3336 in 1986 was below the 6107 in 1969. The peaks in dollars were 44 billion in 1968 and 247 billion in 1988, dropping to 69 billion by 1991. Mergers represented less than 2 percent of total corporate assets in both years. Mergers were 7 percent of the market value of equities in 1988 compared with 4 percent in 1968 and under 3 percent in the intervening years. During the 1970s mergers were generally below 2 percent of GNP as was the case for the 1926 to 1930 period. Merger activity in relation to gross national product was about 5 percent in 1968 and 1988. Mergers at the turn of the century represented about 13 percent of GNP, dwarfing all subsequent merger movements.

Potential explanations for the restructuring activities of the 1980s include the following: (1) increased international competition; (2) changing technologies—increased competition between industries; (3) changing manufacturing methods—economies of scale to flexible manufacturing systems and economies of scope; (4) oil shocks causing repeated adjustments in mix of production input factors; (5) changed management of human resources—hierarchy to participative management; (6) fluctuating exchange rates—changing prices of buying and selling goods and companies; (7) changed antitrust policy—due to increased competition reflecting the above factors plus reactions to other changes in government policies; (8) deregulation accelerating in the 1970s in airlines, banking, the S&L industry, other financial services, broadcasting, cable, communications, transportation, oil, and gas—these industries accounted for almost one-half of all M&A activities during the 1980s; (9) innovations in financial services—deregulation stimulated new entry, excess capacity pressures on profit margins, innovative products, speculative investments; and (10) a 10-year period of economic stability and growth which encouraged the use of higher debt ratios, increased leverage.

Forms of Restructuring and Their Results

Table 1 provides an overview of the many forms of restructuring activities (M&As) and their returns. Most achieve positive returns—some quite large. The few negative returns are small.

TABLE 1   Forms of Restructuring and Their Financial Results

Forms of restructuring	Event returns (%)
Expansion	
Merger studies	
Acquired firms	20
Acquiring firms	2 to 3
Tender offer studies	
Acquired firms	35
Acquiring firms	+2 to –2
Joint ventures	
Absolute	2.5
Scaled by investment	23
Sell-offs	
Spin-offs	2 to 4
Divestitures	
Sellers	0.5 to 1
Buyers	0.34
Equity carve-outs	2
Changes in ownership structure	
Leverage and ownership adjustments by exchange offers	
Debt for equity	14
Preferred for equity	8
Leverage and ownership adjustments by share repurchases	16
Going private	20
Leveraged buyouts	40 to 50
Leveraged cashouts	20 to 30
Employee stock ownership plans (ESOPs)	–4 to +4
Takeover defenses	–4 to +4

Mergers and Takeovers   On average the gains to target firms in mergers are about 20 percent and about 35 percent in tender offers. Bidding firms had only normal returns in the earlier years, but with government regulations and sophisticated merger defenses in the 1980s they have experienced negative returns. The combined net gains to bidders and targets have averaged 7 percent to 8 percent over the last two decades.

The premiums and gains stem from a number of factors: (1) Tax benefits account for a fraction of the gains. (2) Some gains come from efficiency increases resulting from turnaround improvements. (3) Some price gains take place because the takeover or restructuring activity signals that future performance will improve. (4) Some wealth redistribution from bondholders to shareholders occurs, but it represents only a small fraction of the premium. In some cases "give ups" by workers may also be involved. (5) The winning bidder often pays too much.

Joint Ventures   Joint ventures are new enterprises owned by two or more participants. They are typically formed for special purposes for a limited duration. Each participant expects to gain from the activity but also must make a contribution. When scaled to the size of investments, joint ventures achieve a 23 percent return.

Spin-offs   In a spin-off the parent distributes shares on a pro rata basis to its existing shareholders, creating a new legal entity. A spin-off represents a form of dividend to existing shareholders. Studies of spin-offs find positive gains to the parent of 3 percent to 5 percent.

Divestitures   A divestiture involves the sale of a portion of the firm to an outside third party. Event studies of divestitures have found significant positive abnormal two-day announcement returns of between 2 percent to 3 percent for selling firm shareholders, higher when the percentage of the firm sold is larger.

Equity Carve-outs   In an equity carve-out the parent sells a portion of the firm via an equity offering to outsiders. A new legal entity is created. Equity carve-outs on average are associated with positive abnormal returns of 2 percent. This is in contrast to findings of negative returns of about 2 percent when parent companies publicly offer additional shares of their own stock.

The reasons for the positive returns in spin-offs and in equity carve-outs relate to management incentives. Homogeneous organization units may be managed more effectively and be evaluated more accurately by financial analysts. In addition, managers may receive incentives and rewards more closely related to actual performance when their segment's results are not obscured in consolidated financial reports. For divestitures the gains result from the shift of resources to higher valued uses.

Changes in Ownership Structure

Share Repurchases   The corporation buys back some fraction (on average 20 percent) of its outstanding shares of common stock resulting in significant positive abnormal returns to shareholders of about 13 percent. A number of hypotheses have been advanced to explain the gains. Tax effects appear to be a partial explanation. Increased leverage may account for some of the shareholder wealth increase. Repurchases may signal increases in future cash flows.

Exchange offers usually involve the exchange of debt or preferred stock for common stock. The theories related to positive returns from exchange offers are similar to those for share repurchase: (1) the exchange offers increases leverage, (2) the exchange implies an increase in future cash flows, and (3) the exchange implies that the common stock is undervalued by the market.

Going Private and Leveraged Buyouts   "Going private" refers to the transformation of a public corporation into a privately held firm as discussed in another entry.

ESOPs and MLPs   An employee stock ownership plan (ESOP) is a type of stock bonus plan which invests primarily in the securities of the sponsoring employer firm. By 1990 over 10,000 ESOPs had been established embracing about 12 million employees. Successive legislative enactments provided tax advantages to ESOPs. Payments by corporations to the ESOP to meet both its interest and principal payments to the lender are fully deductible. From the standpoint of the lender, one-half of the interest received is excluded from taxable income. In closely held corporations a chief executive can sell a substantial proportion of stock to the ESOP, maintain control of the company, and obtain various tax subsidies as well. ESOPs have also been increasingly used as a takeover defense.

Defensive Restructuring   One form is a scorched earth policy which is by a corporation incurring large debt and selling off parts of the company, using the newly acquired funds to declare a large dividend to existing shareholders. A second involves selling off the crown jewels, that is, disposing of those segments of the business in which the bidder is most interested. A third is to dilute the bidder's voting percentage by issuing substantial new equity. A fourth is share repurchase without management sale. A fifth is to issue new securities to parties friendly to management, including the creation or expansion of an ESOP, allied with or controlled by management. A sixth form of defensive restructuring is to create barriers specific to the bidder. For example, antitrust suits may be filed against the bidder, or the firm may purchase assets that will create antitrust issues for the bidder.

Poison Pills   Poison pills are warrants issued to existing shareholders giving them the right to purchase surviving firm securities at very low prices in the event of a merger. The effect of poison pills is to severely dilute share values after a takeover. These risks may cause bidders to make offers conditional on the withdrawal of the poison pill. The poison pill gives incumbent management considerable bargaining power since it can also set aside the warrants if, for example, later bidders offer higher prices and other inducements.

Poison Puts   A third type of merger defense was stimulated by the decline in bond values as a result of the RJR-Nabisco leveraged buyout in December 1988. It permits the bondholders to put (sell) the bonds to the issuer corporation or its successor at par or at par plus some premium.

Antitakeover Amendments   Fair price provisions provide that all shareholders must receive a uniform, "fair" price—aimed as a defense against coercive two-tier offers. Supermajority amendments require two-thirds or more shareholder approval for a change of control. A staggered or classified board of directors may be used to delay the effective transfer of control. Another type of charter amendment is reincorporation in a state with laws more protective against takeovers.

Golden Parachutes   Golden parachutes are separation provisions in an employment contract that provide for payments to managers under a change-of-control clause. The rationale is to help reduce the conflict of interest between shareholders and managers. Although the dollar amounts are large, the cost in most cases is less than 1 percent of the total takeover value. Recent changes in tax laws have limited tax deductions to the corporation for golden parachute payments and have imposed penalties upon the recipient. A theoretical argument for golden parachutes is that they motivate managers to make firm-specific investments of their human capital and to take a longer-term view in seeking to enhance values for shareholders.

Are Mergers Successful?

The most rigorous of empirical studies of merger success are those performed in financial economics. These use a market model to test for performance that differs from the risk-return trade-offs set by general market relationships. The data are consistent with the finding that the acquired firms have not been performing up to their potential or that the performance of the acquired firms has been improved. The shareholders of acquiring firms do not gain and probably lose on average. This result is consistent with a competitive market in acquisitions of companies, which causes potential gains for acquiring firms to be competed away into premiums or gains to the shareholders of acquired firms.

The restructuring activities of the 1980s were driven by the globalization of markets, technological and financial innovations, deregulation, tax changes, fluctuating exchange rates, other changes in environments, and modified antitrust policies which recognized the new competitive realities. At least a dozen theoretical explanations have been invoked, most are efficiency enhancing. Mergers, tender offers, joint ventures, sell-offs, LBOs, security repurchases and exchanges all show net gains. Takeover defenses sometimes help shareholders, sometimes entrench management. Excesses, overbidding, and other mistakes have also occurred.

References

Beckenstein, Alan R., "Merger Activity and Merger Theories: An Empirical Investigation," *Antitrust Bulletin*, Spring 1979, pp. 105–128; Bradley, Michael, Anand Desai, and E. Han Kim, "Synergistic Gains from Corporate Acquisitions and Their Division between the Stockholders of Target and Acquiring Firms," *Journal of Financial Economics*, vol. 21, 1988, pp. 3–40; Ellert, James C., "Mergers, Antitrust Law Enforcement and Stockholder Returns," *Journal of Finance*, vol. 31, May 1976, pp. 715–732; Gershon, Mandelker, "Risk and Return: The Case of Merging Firms," *Journal of Financial Economics*, vol. 1, 1974, pp. 303–335; Jensen, Michael, "Agency Costs of Free Cash Flow, Corporate Finance and Takeovers," *American Economic Review*, vol. 76, 1986, pp. 323–339; Morck, Randall, Andrei Shleifer, and Robert W. Vishny, "Characteristics of Hostile and Friendly Takeover Targets," in A. Auerbach (ed.), *Corporate Takeovers: Causes and Consequences*, University of Chicago Press, Chicago, 1988; Weston, J. Fred, *The Role of Mergers in the Growth of Large Firms*, University of California Press, Berkeley, 1953; Weston, J. Fred, Kwang S. Chung, and Susan E. Hoag, "Mergers, Restructuring, and Corporate Control," Prentice-Hall, Englewood Cliffs, N.J., 1990.

(*See also* Concentration of industry; Conglomerates; Integration)

J. Fred Weston

Microeconomics

The word "micro" means small, and microeconomics means economics in the small. The optimizing behavior of individual units such as households and firms provides the foundation for microeconomics. Microeconomists may investigate individual markets or even the economy as a whole, but their analyses are derived from the aggregation of the behavior of individual units. Microeconomic theory is used extensively in many areas of applied economics. For example, it is used in industrial organization, labor economics, international trade, cost-benefit analysis, and many other economic subfields. The tools and analyses of microeconomics provide a common ground, and even a language, for economists interested in a wide range of problems.

At one time there was a sharp distinction in both methodology and subject matter between microeconomics and macroeconomics, i.e., economics in the large. The macroeconomist focuses upon topics such as total output, total employment and unemployment, the level and rate of change of the price level, and the rate of overall economic growth. The methodological distinction became somewhat blurred during the 1970s as more and more macroeconomic analyses were built upon microeconomic foundations. Nonetheless, major distinctions remain between the two major branches of economics. For example, the microeconomist is interested in the determination of individual prices and relative prices (i.e., exchange ratios between goods), whereas the macroeconomist is interested more in the general price level and its change over time.

Optimization plays a key role in microeconomics. The consumer is assumed to maximize utility or satisfaction subject to the constraints imposed by income or income earning power. The producer is assumed to maximize profit or minimize cost subject to the technological constraints under which the firm operates. Optimization of social welfare sometimes is the criterion for the determination of public policy. Opportunity cost is an important concept in microeconomics. Many courses of action are valued in terms of what is sacrificed so that they might be undertaken. For example, the opportunity cost of a public project is the value of the additional goods that the private sector would have produced with the resources used for the public project.

Theory of the Consumer

The individual consumer or household is assumed to possess a utility function which specifies the satisfaction which is gained from the consumption of alternative bundles of goods. The consumer's income or income-earning power determines which bundles are available to the consumer. The consumer then selects a bundle that gives the highest possible level of utility. With few exceptions, the consumer is treated as a price taker—that is, the consumer is free to choose whatever quantities income allows but has no influence over prevailing market prices. In order to maximize utility the consumer purchases goods so that the subjective rate of substitution for each pair of goods as indicated by the consumer's utility function equals the objective rate of substitution given by the ratio of their market prices. This basic utility-maximization analysis has been modified and expanded in many different ways.

Theory of the Producer

The individual producer or firm is assumed to possess a production function, which specifies the quantity of output produced as a function of the quantities of the inputs used in production. The producer's revenue equals the quantity of output produced and sold times its price, and the cost to the producer equals the sum of the quantities of inputs purchased and used times their prices. Profit is the difference between revenue and cost. The producer is assumed to maximize profits subject to the technology given by the production function. Profit maximization requires that the producer use each factor to a point at which its marginal contribution to revenue equals its marginal contribution to cost. Under pure competition, the producer is a price taker who may sell at the going market price whatever has been produced. Under monopoly (one seller) the producer recognizes that price declines as sales are expanded, and under monopsony (one buyer) the producer recognizes that the price paid for an input increases as purchases are increased.

A producer's cost function gives production cost as a function of output level on the assumption that the producer combines inputs to minimize production cost. Profit maximization using revenue and cost functions requires that the producer equate the decrement in revenue from producing one less unit (called marginal revenue) to the corresponding decrement in cost (called marginal cost). Under pure competition, marginal revenue equals price. Consequently, the producer equates marginal cost of production to the going market price.

Price Determination in One Market

Microeconomic theory is sometimes called "price theory," since price determination occupies a major position. Consider first price determination for a single consumers' good in a market for which all buyers and sellers are price takers. Consumers are the buyers, and producers are the sellers. A demand function for each consumer expresses quantity purchased as a function of commodity prices and income. These are constructed from the conditions for utility maximization subject to income constraints. An aggregate demand function is obtained by summing the demand functions for all the individual consumers. It gives the aggregate quantity of the good under consideration that will be purchased at each possible set of prices and income.

A supply function for an individual producer expresses quantity produced and supplied as a function of output and input prices. These are constructed from the conditions for profit maximization. An aggregate supply function is obtained by summing the supply functions of all the individual producers.

Assume now that the prices for all goods and inputs and inputs other than the one under investigation are at predetermined levels. The price of that good is the only variable determining its aggregate demand and supply. An equilibrium price is one at which quantity demanded equals quantity supplied. The market is said to be cleared. In graphic analyses a downward-sloping demand curve and upward-sloping supply curve are plotted in a price-quantity diagram. Equilibrium price and quantity are given by their intersection. The supply and demand analysis is easily extended to producers' goods markets in which producers are both buyers and sellers, and to labor markets in which consumers are sellers and producers are buyers.

General Equilibrium

The determination of equilibrium for a single market is designated as partial equilibrium because the prices in all other markets are held at predetermined levels. If one is interested in the price system as a whole, there is no assurance that consistent results will be achieved through the determination of equilibrium prices taking one market at a time. Prices and quantities for all goods are determined simultaneously in a general equilibrium, sometimes called "multimarket equilibrium," analysis.

General equilibrium is often determined by solving a system of simultaneous equations, one for each market, with market prices as variables. Relative prices, i.e., exchange ratios between goods, are determined in a general equilibrium analysis. It is common to set the price of some legal commodity (cash crop) equal to 1. Let the price of a bushel of wheat equal 1. Now, the price of a barrel of oil, for example, is expressed in terms of the number of bushels of wheat for which a barrel will exchange. Money prices are normally within the domain of the macroeconomist.

Welfare Economics

The object of welfare economics is the evaluation of alternative allocations of economic resources. Positive microeconomics shows how resources would be allocated if underlying assumptions were realized; normative, or welfare, economics asks how resources should be allocated. The tools of microeconomics are used extensively in welfare economics. For example, a social optimum may require that the price of each good equal its social marginal cost. In some analyses the conditions for social optimum are determined by maximizing the utility of one person assuming that the utility level of all other members of society are at predetermined levels.

References

Henderson, James J., and Richard E. Quandt, *Microeconomic Theory: A Mathematical Approach,* 3d ed., McGraw-Hill, New York, 1980; Hirschleifer, Jack, *Price Theory and Applica-*

tions, 4th ed., Prentice-Hall, Englewood Cliffs, N.J., 1988; Mansfield, Edwin, *Microeconomics: Theory and Applications,* 7th ed., Norton, New York, 1991; Varian, Hal R., *Microeconomic Analysis,* 3d ed., Norton, New York, 1991.

(*See also* Competition; Consumer theory; General equilibrium; Macroeconomics; Marginal cost; Marginal revenue; Normative economics; Opportunity cost; Price theory; Production function; Utility; Welfare economics)

James M. Henderson

Models, economic (*see* Economic models)

Monetarism (*see* Monetary policy)

Monetarist theory (*see* Chicago school)

Monetary overinvestment theory (*see* Juglar cycle)

Monetary policy

Commercial banks have a unique power. They can literally create money. This function is accomplished through extending loans and making investments. To do so, banks need reserves which are provided primarily by the central bank, the banker's banker. The essence of monetary policy is to control the release of reserves in a manner which stimulates bank lending and investing in support of consumer and business spending, as well as government outlays in order to foster economic growth without contributing to inflationary pressures. Consequently, monetary policy has the capacity to exert an enormous impact on the level of employment, the volume of output, and the rate of inflation and serves as a major policy tool for influencing economic activity.

Basically, two conditions are required for banks to create money. One is the widespread acceptance of what might be called "bank money." At one time, bank money consisted largely, if not exclusively, of paper currency. However, in time, banks were restricted in issuing their own currency and were able to maintain their money-creation role through the introduction and then the widespread adoption of the use of checks (demand deposits) as a means of payment. The other necessary condition is the ability of banks to function either by operating experience or by regulatory requirement with reserve balances being maintained at only a fraction of their deposit liabilities; that is, under a fractional reserve system. (If banks held reserves equal to 100 percent of their deposit liabilities, banks could not create money, and they would serve solely as intermediaries between depositors and borrowers.)

The Discount Rate

The instrument of monetary policy at the time the Federal Reserve System was established by Congress in 1913 (and until changes were introduced or legislated in later years) was the discount rate, the rate charged banks for borrowing reserves from their

Reserve banks. (The System consists of the Board of Governors in Washington and 12 regional Reserve banks.) Fundamentally, the discount window was open to satisfy all the banks' seasonal demands for reserves. However, the rate was (and still is) changed for cyclical purposes. A rise in the discount rate is intended to discourage bank borrowing at the window and, thus, restrain credit expansion. Conversely, a decline is intended to make reserves more readily available and, presumably with a resultant drop in the cost of borrowing, to increase the demand for bank credit. (This instrument today is generally ineffective as a policy tool unless "window" borrowings become unusually large. Then, the Federal Reserve can exert pressure on banks to moderate any excessive extension of credit. However, at all times, changes in the discount rate serve as signals to the credit and securities market of shifts in monetary policy.)

From the beginning, the board of directors of each Reserve bank has been required to set periodically the discount rate for their individual Reserve bank subject to the review and determination of the Federal Reserve's Board of Governors. The Board of Governors' role, in turn, entails mainly this review process and the coordination in general of Federal Reserve activities.

In time, the Reserve banks began to coordinate their monetary policies on an informal basis. This cooperative effort grew out of the Reserve banks' accidental discovery of a new instrument of monetary policy—open-market operations. The Reserve System covers its operating expenses primarily through earnings generated from the loans it makes to banks and on its investments in securities. It does not receive any appropriations from Congress. (In fact, for some years now, the Federal Reserve has been transferring to the Treasury nearly all its accumulated earnings surplus.) In its very early years, however, most of the Federal Reserve's income came from interest earned on loans to banks. During the recession of the early twenties, bank needs for reserves ebbed as loans and deposits fell off. With the resulting decline in borrowing at the discount window, the Reserve banks' earnings contracted. To generate replacement income, the individual Reserve banks began to purchase government securities. It soon became apparent that such purchases were self-defeating. They began to realize that these operations created reserves which, in turn, enabled banks to repay their discount-window borrowings. Moreover, since the market for government securities was, and still is, concentrated in New York City, the New York Reserve Bank (the major bank in the System) bore the brunt of the decline in discount-window borrowings. In these circumstances, largely at the urging of the New York Reserve Bank, the Reserve banks began to coordinate their open-market operations on an informal basis.

Open-Market Operations

The Federal Reserve soon recognized that its open-market operations are a powerful policy tool to influence the availability of reserves and, in turn, bank credit activities. Unlike the discount window through which it had to rely on changes in the discount rate to influence the demand for reserves, the Federal Reserve was now aware that it could actively intervene to affect reserve availability. Open-market purchases add to reserves and stimulate bank credit and deposit creation; open-market sales reduce reserves outstanding and tend to restrict bank credit and deposit creation.

Through this new policy instrument, the Reserve banks moved toward becoming a more unified system. At first, with no legislative requirement or guidance, the individual Reserve banks were still free to ignore the open-market policy recommendations of the majority. The Banking Act of 1935 centralized the Federal Reserve's authority in the seven-member Board of Governors and provided for a uniform monetary policy with each Reserve bank required to participate in the System's open-market operations. More specifically, the Act established the Federal Open Market Committee (FOMC), which was given the basic responsibility for determining monetary policy for the entire System.

In further recognition of monetary policy's potential, the Banking Act of 1935 authorized the Federal Reserve to vary bank reserve requirements—the percentage of a bank's deposit liabilities which must be held in an eligible reserve balance. Initially such funds were considered to be a source of liquidity in the event of a cash squeeze, say, from heavy deposit withdrawals. Eventually, it became apparent that owing to the penalties which would be incurred if a bank's reserve balances were drawn below its required reserves, these funds would not be used unless the bank was ready to close its doors permanently. As part of this recognition, it was perceived that in view of the large volume of deposits outstanding, a small fractional change in the reserve-requirement percentage could have a substantial impact on the ability of banks to expand reserves. (With a 10 percent reserve requirement, for example, banks can extend loans and investments—deposits—10 times the available free reserves, whereas a 25 percent reserve requirement reduces the expansion potential to a factor of 4.) Accordingly, the Act gave the Federal Reserve the authority to vary reserve requirements within a prescribed range. Moreover, as part of the shift to concentrate authority in Washington, the Board was given sole responsibility for setting reserve requirements.

With these changes, the roles of the Reserve banks' boards of directors were effectively neutralized. These boards do not have any influence on monetary policy. They do retain an advisory position with respect to establishing the discount rate. However, with the Board of Governors' authority to review and to approve each Reserve bank's discount rate, the power to effect rate changes lies essentially with the seven board members in Washington. Furthermore, the Reserve banks boards of directors are not privy to any of the policy decisions of the FOMC or the Board of Governors until they are released to the general public.

An Independent Agency

The Federal Reserve System occupies a special position within the federal government. Congress has established the Federal Reserve as an independent agency. Neither the President nor the Congress has a direct control over or influence on monetary policy. Their only involvement, other than through the laws enacted to govern the Federal Reserve, is indirectly through the appointment and approval of the Board of Governors' members. This does not mean that the central bank can insulate itself from the national government and completely ignore the policies being pursued by the administration in power. For policy to succeed, there has to be a spirit of cooperation between the two. The Federal Reserve's particular niche, or responsibilities, has been best described as follows: "It is independent within, but not independent from the federal government."

The FOMC

The FOMC is by far the most important body within the Federal Reserve System with regard to setting monetary policy. It convenes now 10 times a year to review economic, credit, and monetary developments and to determine the policy which is best suited to achieve its basic objectives. At the conclusion of each meeting, a directive is issued to the individual responsible for executing the FOMC's policy, the manager of the System Open Market Account, who is located at the New York Reserve Bank. These directives instruct the manager with regard to the open-market policies which should be followed until the next meeting is held. In effect, the directive guides the manager in determining the amount of reserves which should be released (or absorbed) through purchases (or sales) of government securities.

Target Rate for Federal Funds Rate

An important element in the directive is the target range specified for the federal funds rate. Federal funds represent reserve deposits held at the Reserve banks or potential claims on such balances. These balances typically are purchased by banks short of reserves and are sold mainly by banks with an excess of such funds. However, the amount of bank reserves outstanding is subject to wide fluctuations through payment flows and currency movements over which the Federal Reserve has no control. The federal funds rate quickly reflects the impact of such changes on reserve availability and generally provides the FOMC manager with a good indication of the need to add or to drain reserves in order to keep the federal funds rate within the target range specified in the directive. If reserves are short, banks will bid up the federal funds rate, and, to keep the rate on target, the manager purchases government securities to provide the needed reserves. Conversely, if reserves are plentiful, the federal funds rate tends to decline, and, in this situation, the manager sells government securities to absorb the amount of reserves needed to restore the rate to the target level.

The targeting of the federal funds rate is an initial objective of monetary policy, and it serves two purposes. One is to act as a signaling device for the FOMC manager for offsetting the seasonal flows in bank reserves which are not controllable by the Federal Reserve. These flows frequently can cumulate, within a period as short as a few days or a week, to an amount which represents a substantial portion of the total reserves outstanding. Moreover, these flows tend to be completely reversed at an early date. It is generally agreed that the Federal Reserve (particularly through open-market operations) should offset these swings. Otherwise, for example, at such times as Christmas when there is a large seasonal drain of reserves, owing to the increased demand for currency during the holiday season, there would be extreme tightness in the money markets. (In fact, one of the objectives in establishing the Federal Reserve was to eliminate the seasonal money squeezes which were a frequent problem prior to 1913.) However, it is most difficult to predict with satisfactory accuracy changes in the supply of or need for reserves. The seasonal influences on reserve availability are not stable. Also, such random factors as computer failures, inclement weather, and labor strikes can interrupt payment flows and affect reserves outstanding. With the bidding or offering of federal funds changing quickly in response to these flows, the manager is provided with a sensitive barometer for measuring the need to take appropriate offsetting action. The great bulk of the Federal Reserve's open-market operations is attributable to this objective—to counteract the disruptive seasonal reserve flows.

Bank Credit and Money Supply

The other function served by the FOMC's federal funds target is to create money-market conditions which are considered to be conducive to achieving what might be called the Federal Reserve's intermediate monetary policy objectives—the behavior of bank credit and the money supply. The federal funds rate is the key rate in the money market. It has an important influence on the cost of funds to banks and other borrowers in the money market and, in turn, tends to affect rate levels in much of the credit and securities market. For example, in increasing its target level for the funds rate and eventually tightening bank reserve positions sufficiently to maintain this new, higher funds rate target, the Federal Reserve can depress monetary growth in two ways. The higher funds rate level, in stimulating increases in other short-term interest rates, causes the public to manage money balances which earn no or relatively low rates of interest more tightly relative to spending needs. At the same time, the eventual curtailment of bank reserve growth by the Federal Reserve to maintain its higher funds rate target serves to limit the banking system's ability to expand credit and deposits.

The links between changes in money-market conditions (which the Federal Reserve can control very closely) and changes in bank credit and money supply (upon which the Federal Reserve has only an indirect effect), however, are somewhat loose. Many factors beyond those under the Federal Reserve's direct control influence the public's willingness to borrow and to hold cash balances. Frustrations in being able to achieve satisfactory control over bank credit and the money supply has led the Federal Reserve to change its operating targets over time.

Prior to the mid-sixties, the directives typically instructed the FOMC manager in a general (nonquantitative) way with regard to the degree of reserve expansion and the tone of the money market. As criticism developed that this tactic was not successful in achieving adequate control over bank credit and the money supply and that the Federal Reserve was not paying adequate attention in the policy directives to its intermediate goals, the FOMC in 1966 adopted the so-called proviso clause. (The critics, however, failed to recognize or consider that the FOMC at each meeting did review bank-credit and money-supply developments and that the behavior of these aggregates influenced the FOMC's decisions.) This clause required the manager to make appropriate adjustments in the money-market targets whenever bank-credit growth deviated significantly from acceptable rates. However, no explicit target rates of growth were specified.

A more significant change was made in the meeting held on February 15, 1972. At that session, the FOMC decided that "it was desirable to increase somewhat the relative emphasis placed on reserves while continuing to take appropriate account of money market conditions. Committee members believed that doing so would enhance their ability to achieve desired intermediate monetary objectives." For the first time, the FOMC adopted a quantitative goal. At that time, the target measure used was a reserve aggregate RPD (reserves against private deposits). In early 1974, the FOMC added the behavior of the narrow and broadly defined money supply (M-1 and M-2) to the directive. Over time, these aggregates began to receive greater attention in the committee's deliberations and greater emphasis in the directive itself. (In March 1976 RPD was dropped). Moreover, in March 1975, Congress passed Concurrent Resolution 133, which stated that the Federal Reserve should "maintain longrun potential to increase production." In November 1977, the substance of this resolution was added to the Federal Reserve Act. In turn, this provision was superseded by the requirements of the Full Employment and Balanced Growth Act of 1976 (the Humphrey-Hawkins Act).

The most rigorous attempt to use a quantitative measure as an intermediate target for open-market operations began in October 1979 in reaction to the unacceptably high rates of inflation which occurred in the 1970s. The FOMC now began to target reserve measures calculated to be consistent with desired 3-month growth rates of M-1. By late 1982, it became apparent that the linkage between M-1 and economic activity was not very stable. In response, the FOMC shifted to using discount window borrowings as the target for open-market operations. This target has only a very vague relationship to the Federal Reserve's desired rates of growth in the monetary aggregates. Despite this change in operating technique, the FOMC, as required by the Humphrey-Hawkins Act, twice a year (in February and in July) reports to Congress the target range for the monetary aggregates and for bank credit over a 1-year period which it believes will further its desired economic objectives. (Initially, goals were set for M-1, M-2, and M-3, but now ranges are specified only for the last two aggregates.) The FOMC meets at eight other times in the year and at each of the ten meetings, it now prescribes the borrowing target which it believes will help foster the 1-year growth rates in the monetary aggregates given to Congress. At these sessions, the FOMC also prescribes a federal funds target which it believes is consistent with its many policy objectives.

Federal Reserve Policy Shortcomings

The Federal Reserve has had some difficulties achieving its ultimate policy objective—a steady, sustainable rate of economic growth with low rates of inflation and unemployment. Wide swings in output and employment have occurred on occasion. Moreover, the underlying rate of inflation, at times, has been most unsatisfactory. Furthermore there is little reason to be confident that periodic sharp upward price movements can be avoided in the future.

Monetary policy has shortcomings for a number of reasons. One, there is the problem of defining and measuring money. Two, there is the question of whether the Federal Reserve can control satisfactorily the growth of credit and money. Three, there are a number of nonmonetary influences which complicate the Federal Reserve's decision-making processes or have an independent important influence on economic developments.

Defining and Measuring Money

For some time there has been a problem pertaining to devising an appropriate definition of money. Initially, there were difficulties with regard to choosing among the common measures of money—M-1, M-2, and M-3—as to which aggregate should be targeted or should serve as a policy guide. Now, particularly with the advent of monetary deregulation in the early 1980s, there are the added questions concerning the treatment of such balances as NOW and money-market accounts, RPs and Eurodollars, as well as other forms of near moneys. On top of these conundrums, there exists a huge latent money supply. This latter phenomenon, by itself, serves to demonstrate how futile it is to arrive at a satisfactory composite of money which could serve as an approximate target for Federal Reserve policy actions.

The latent money supply represents funds which can be acquired with virtually no delay. They are as readily available for spending as an actual balance in a checking account. Obtaining a measure of these funds, as will be explained shortly, would be much more troublesome than trying to decide which of the accepted measures of money is the most meaningful, because there is no rigorous or reliable method for counting these balances.

The latent money supply consists of claims on spendable funds and does not appear as a liability on any bank's or other financial intermediary's ledger. The most prominent of such claims are bank loan commitments. A bank can ill afford to refuse to honor them, particularly when the customers have been paying a fee to receive the commitments. Only if the commitment holder is on the verge of bankruptcy is it conceivable that the commitment would not be honored. The loan commitments are huge and can be activated (converted into a deposit) immediately merely by the drawing of a check or, at most, providing a day or so notice that the line is being drawn on.

Similar to the loan commitments are the lines of credit extended to consumers and business firms as well. Banks, in most circumstances, actively offer overdraft privileges to creditworthy potential borrowers. Here, merely drawing a check puts "money in the bank." And then there are the ubiquitous credit cards. In effect, credit cards today in many instances are better than "money in the bank." At many establishments credit cards are readily acceptable, whereas personal checks are not.

The inherent problem in obtaining a useful measure of outstanding loan commitments and credit lines is that business firms typically have commitments and lines far in excess of their actual credit needs. The maintenance of excess commitments serves as a form of insurance. Particularly, if firms expect credit availability to tighten, they will acquire more commitments then they conceivably could use.

With regard to individuals, interpreting the relevance of any data on their credit lines is probably even more difficult. The typical consumer has an array of credit cards. Surely the sum of the credit lines extended to individuals must overstate their potential use by a massive amount.

No deep analysis is needed to demonstrate that the latent money supply could be used to trigger an explosion of business and consumer spending. Thus to arrive at a meaningful measure of money to serve as a guide to the Federal Reserve as to whether its policy is appropriate in the face of anticipated economic developments, these potential balances should be included. And yet, for the reasons just mentioned, this is not possible. In effect, what is needed to overcome this hurdle is a reading of the confidence indexes more specifically, the spending plans of the business community and consumers and, in turn, the extent to which they intend or will need to draw on their huge latent money balances. The futility of getting this information should be self-evident. These circumstances should make it readily apparent that the Federal Reserve officials have enormous problems in formulating an appropriate monetary aggregate target.

Controlling the Money Supply and Bank Credit

Not only are there these conceptual problems, but there are as well adequate grounds to question whether the Federal Reserve can control satisfactorily the growth of money and its equivalence, bank credit. It is an article of faith for many analysts, particularly monetarists, that money is a direct function of the supply of reserves. In other words, monetarists believe that changes in the money supply are a direct result of the Federal Reserve's manipulation of the reserve base. This causality may be true in the long run, and then, perhaps only at the point where the economy is on the verge of a credit crunch. However, in actual practice, the relationship between the supply of and demand for bank credit (and, in turn, money) and changes in reserves is much less direct. Banks today are almost continuously offering loans aggressively. Such policies typically are not stopped by Federal Reserve efforts to hold back on the release of reserves. It is most unusual for a bank to shackle its loan officers merely because the Federal Reserve is reducing reserve availability. Perhaps loan officers may be cautioned to be more selective because of concern over increased credit risks but, on the whole, there generally is still an open door for the creditworthy borrower. Also, as mentioned above, there are the huge loan commitments and established credit lines. These cannot be reduced readily with each change in Federal Reserve policy, although changes in loan costs can and do influence the demand for bank accommodations.

There have been important exceptions to the bank behavior just noted. Prior to the start in 1978 of the phasing out of Regulation 2, which set ceilings on the rates banks could pay on certain deposits, banks, at times, would be compelled to become restrained in extending credit. This development occurred whenever market interest rates rose above the regulation Q ceilings and there was a loss of funds to competing institutions so that banks were pinched for resources to make loans. Also the credit controls instituted during the Nixon and Carter administrations inhibited banks' ability to extend credit. And then, the establishment of stringent capital requirements in the late 1980s and early 1990s in the face of huge loan losses, particularly on loans to foreign governments and to real estate borrowers, contributed to a sharp contraction in the banks' willingness as well as their ability to lend.

Banks have been behaving in the aforementioned nonresponsive way especially since the introduction of liability management. They recognize that, at a price, they can raise all the funds needed to support their loan activities in, for example, the CD and Eurodollar markets and through money-market funds. As a last resort, there is always the Federal Reserve's discount window. Banks cannot use the window as a permanent source of funds. Nevertheless, for the banking system, as a whole, the window always seems to be open to meet increases in the banking system's required reserves which the Federal Reserve is not willing to accommodate through its open-market operations.

One would think that such bank "free-wheeling" lending policies would be deterred by concerns that the rate charged on a business loan may turn out to be too low because the cost of borrowed funds may soon rise. Such fears were an important influence once. Now, however, with business loans typically made with a floating rate, tied generally to the prime rate, such concerns are not a factor for these credits. With regard to consumer loans, the spread has typically been wide enough to protect the lender against most increases in the cost of funds.

Bank investment decisions seem to be more responsive to shifts in Federal Reserve policies than do the banks' loan activities. However, such behavior stems largely from banks now being more active participants in the securities markets rather than responding passively to an actual or even anticipated tightening or easing in the availability of reserves. In other words, in making portfolio decisions, banks make no attempt to gauge the availability of reserves, per se. Their primary focus is on the current and expected future cost of carrying securities. Although, of course, expectations regarding the future course of monetary policy and thus reserves availability should influence their interest rate forecasts. In any event, as a matter of course, they expect the managers of their money positions to be able to raise all the funds needed to support their investment decisions as is the case with regard to their loan activities.

A well-managed bank today monitors the outlook for interest rates very closely and will try to move its investment portfolio before there is an overt Federal Reserve policy change. Banks want to minimize potential capital losses or conversely to maximize potential capital gains. Apart from these considerations, banks tend to hold a considerable amount of securities on a spread basis—the difference between their cost of money and the interest earned on the investment. As long as funds are available at a favorable rate, their investment decisions will be insulated from considerations regarding the immediate availability of reserves.

Nonmonetary Influence

To make good policy decisions, the Federal Reserve needs reliable data on the economic outlook and particularly where the economy is currently with respect to the phase of the business cycle. Needless to say, economic forecasting is far from being an exact science. The dynamic changes in the business world and consumer behavior make it most difficult to develop confident models for projecting economic growth and price movements. Policy decisions, per force, must be based on fallible judgmental decisions. Moreover, much of the actual data released by the Federal Government are not too reliable. Typically most of the data are subject to sizable revisions. In these circumstances, the Federal Reserve cannot move boldly ahead to alter an established policy. It has to be cautious and temperate in its moves. But then, too often, the Federal Reserve tends to be falling behind rather than being ahead in the policy actions called for in the developing economic circumstances.

The Federal Reserve is not alone in having the potential for having an important influence on economic developments. There is, of course, fiscal policy. Government budgeting operations have the capacity to override as well as to reinforce actions taken by the Federal Reserve.

Also, monetary policy can be frustrated by the problems created by cartels, such as OPEC, supply shortages (stemming particularly in agriculture from droughts), and government programs such as Medicare and Medicaid where the authorities have so much difficulty controlling costs. These problems are beyond the Federal Reserve's capacity to ameliorate. Surely, the Federal Reserve cannot influence the weather, and the other problems have to be corrected through structural changes.

The Positive Side of Federal Reserve Policy

The earlier observations may seem to suggest that the Federal Reserve has no control over the growth of money and credit. This is essentially true over the short run. In time, however, albeit perhaps belatedly, there is a positive reaction to monetary policy. An expansion of credit and deposits subject to reserve requirements, which is disturbing to the Federal Reserve, will create a need for reserves in excess of the Federal Reserve's willingness to meet. At this point, the lines at the Federal Reserve banks' discount windows begin to increase. As such borrowings rise, and especially as they are prolonged, monetary policy becomes increasingly effective. However, the positive response generally does not come as indicated earlier, through banks closing up shop and refusing to make loans. Rather the positive effects come largely through the borrowers beginning to stay away or having increasing difficulties qualifying for a loan. Also, banks in these circumstances are not going to be avid purchasers of government securities. There is the increased scarcity of reserves. Also, banks have to be concerned about the decline in the value of such assets which results from the rise in interest rates.

It might also be noted that despite everything that has been said earlier, the Federal Reserve has sufficient policy clout to cut off completely any growth in the money supply and bank credit that is contributing to disturbing inflationary pressures. The fact that, as a rule, the Federal Reserve does not do so reflects, apart from not having perfect information regarding the economy, a difficult dilemma that faces the monetary authorities. There is an obvious concern that a too severe or too precipitous shut off in the supply of reserves would lead to a serious rise in unemployment and a disastrous decline in economic activity—that is, the cure would be worse than the disease. Also as the economy approaches the peak of a business cycle, the Federal Reserve seems to become increasingly concerned as to how far it can increase pressure on bank reserves and the availability of bank credit without precipitating a severe money panic, and an accompanying severe financial distortion. Consequently, it seems to be willing to accept some instability and inflation in order to avoid the huge social costs which would result from rising unemployment and declining business profits and investment.

Conclusion

Despite the Federal Reserve's limitations to "fine-tune" the economy, there is much to be said in support of its role in fostering the nation's well-being. In no way can a steep or even a moderate rate of inflation be stopped if monetary policy allows bank-credit and money-supply growth to fully accommodate price excesses. By the same token, monetary policy alone cannot effectively dampen inflationary excesses. As noted earlier, many nonmonetary factors embedded in the economic structure contribute heavily to the behavior of prices. For this reason, the fight against inflation requires, along with a tight monetary policy, restraint through the federal government's fiscal operations sufficient to help curtail excessive demand pressures on the economy. Further, an effective anti-inflation policy requires longer-term efforts at breaking rigidities and imperfections on the supply side, including productivity—enhancing measures and moves to combat monopolistic pricing practices.

References

Board of Governors, Federal Reserve System, *Open Market Policies and Operating Procedures—Staff Studies,* 1971; Board of Governors, Federal Reserve System, *The Federal Reserve System, Purposes and Functions,* 6th ed., 1974; Federal Reserve Bank of New York, *Monetary Aggregates and Monetary Policy,* New York, 1974; Friedman, Milton, and Anna Schwartz, *A Monetary History of the United States,* Princeton University Press, Princeton, N.J., 1963; Meek, Paul, *U.S. Monetary Policy and Financial Markets,* Federal Reserve Bank of New York, New York, 1982; Meulendyke, Anna Marie, *U.S. Monetary Policy and Financial Markets,* Federal Reserve Bank of New York, New York, 1989.

(*See also* Chicago school; Federal Reserve policy; Federal Reserve System; Economic forecasting methods; Inflation; Interest rates; Money supply; Open-market operations; Velocity of circulation of money)

Irving M. Auerbach

Monetary theories of interest (*see* Interest, economic theory of)

Money illusion

The term money illusion is used in two distinct ways in the literature, first, as a common sense description of the frequently observed ". . . failure [of individuals] to perceive that the dollar, or any other unit of money [e.g., the Italian lira, the French franc, the German mark, etc.], expands or shrinks in value [with the passage of time]" (Fisher, 1928, p. 4), and *second,* to describe a technical property of hypothetical demand and supply functions, namely lack of "zero-degree homogenity" in all money-denominated variables (Howitt & Patinkin, 1980, p. 820). Absence of money illusion in the second sense requires that quantities of "real" goods and services bought or sold by a person *not* be affected by a change in the unit of account [thus, figuring all prices, financial assets and liabilities, income, etc., not in U.S. dollars but rather in terms of imaginary units such as "Martian pebbles," or a reformed currency such as the "new" French franc (equal to 100 "old" French francs), etc., should, in theory, mislead no one as to the size or significance of any "real" transaction].

In actual experience, almost everyone, at one time or another, displays some hint of money illusion in the first sense. At the end of the 1980s, for example, most people were horrified by the sheer numerical magnitude of the U.S. national debt, which ran into the trillions of dollars; some were also impressed that the U.S. national income in a single year was more than twice as many trillions of dollars as the U.S. national debt. Both numbers were huge, and both probably will become much larger in the next century; but neither number is cause for emotional vibration. (Would we, or should we, feel poorer or richer if our unit of account were the Italian lira, of which, as this essay was being written, about 1300 were required to purchase one U.S. dollar at a local bank.)

Why do so many people seem to exhibit the common-sense kind of money illusion? Probably because we live in a world dominated by money figures, and we can't help becoming accustomed to certain current money magnitudes as "large" or "small" in the here and now; so unless current money prices change substantially and often (as has happened in many countries during severe inflations), we easily overlook or "forget" that such words as "large" and "small" have no absolute meaning. One billion is always a large number *relative* to the number ten, but 2.5 billion molecules of water, despite their numerosity, don't make a good-sized rain drop.

Perhaps the earliest and clearest recognition of the common-sense kind of money illusion is found in David Hume's 1752 essay "Of Money" (pp. 37–38). There, in a scant two pages, Hume not only describes and illustrates the common-sense notion of money illusion but also offers a perceptive analysis of the short-run tradeoff between unemployment and inflation that is now commonly known as the "Phillips curve" (cf. Friedman, 1968).

Does anyone suffer from money illusion in the second sense? It is hard to say anything definite about that, because the second kind of money illusion refers to a mathematical property of relations that have no real-world counterpart. Don Patinkin (1956, pp. 23–24) puts the proposition in a contrapositive fashion, perhaps in an attempt to make the money illusion concept more "operational." Thus, he describes a person as suffering from money illusion" . . . if his excess-demand functions do *not* depend solely on relative prices, real income, and real balances [so] an individual free of money illusion will definitely be affected by [an equal proportionate change in money prices *alone*]." But this procedure is no help in identifying the presence or absence of "zero-degree homogenity," because a person may be free of money illusion in the second (technical) sense yet suffer from (and behave in accordance with) money illusion in the first sense; the existence of money illusion is too slippery to be identified on the basis of observed behavior.

The second kind of money illusion came into prominence some 50 years ago when Wassily Leontief (1947) argued that a fundamental difference between Keynes and earlier economists lay in the fact that Keynes ascribed "money illusion" in the second sense to wage earners, whereas earlier economists did not. But Keynes might well have had nothing more in mind than money illusion in the first sense when he said (as he *did* say, in *The General Theory*, 1936, p. 8): ". . . it may be the case that within a certain range the demand of labor is for a minimum money-wage and not for a minimum real wage." Keynes's famous teacher, Alfred Marshall, earlier made a similar remark (*Money Credit & Commerce*, 1924, p. 19): ". . . employees, not altogether unreasonably, fear that when nominal wages are once let down they will not be easily raised. So they are inclined to stop work rather than accept a nominal reduction even though it would not be a real one." Here we have to deal with behavior that is neither obviously irrational nor necessarily based on illusion; and surely no one would, on this basis, attribute to Marshall what many otherwise thoughtful and competent theorists have attributed to Keynes: the assumption that worker supply functions do *not* possess the "zero-degree homogenity" property.

The two concepts of money illusion identified here, although logically distinct, are factually indistinguishable; hence, it would probably be desirable to reserve the term "money illusion," which should probably be confined for the first (common sense) meaning, as in Hume and Fisher. Money illusion in the sense of the "zero-degree homogenity property" would then go the way of the dodo bird: become extinct. Zero-degree homogenity is a perfectly definite concept, and so may be used unambiguously in theoretical discourse; but to speak of "money illusion" when one merely refers to the absence of the zero-degree homogenity property from hypothetical functions that no other person can objectively inspect is to invite needless confusion and misunderstanding.

References

Fisher, I., *The Money Illusion*, Adelphi, New York, 1928; Friedman, M., "The Role of Monetary Policy," *American Economic Review*, vol. 58, March 1968, pp. 1–17; Howitt, P., and D. Patinkin, "Utility Function Transformations and Money Illusion: Comment," *American Economic Review*, vol. 70., Sept. 1980, pp. 819–822; Hume, David, 1752, as reprinted in E. Rotwein, *David Hume*Writings on Economics*, University of Wisconsin, Madison, 1955; Keynes, J. M., *The General Theory of Employment Interest and Money*, Harcourt Brace, New York, 1936; Leontief, W., "Postulates: Keynes' *General Theory* and the Classicists," chap. 19 (pp. 232–242) of Harris, S., *The New Economics*, Alfred Knopf, New York, 1947; Marshall, A., *Money, Credit and Commerce*, MacMillan, London, 1924; Patinkin, D., *Money, Interest and Prices*, Row Peterson, New York, 1956.

(*See also* Inflation; Value of the dollar)

Robert W. Clower

Money-market fund (*see* Mutual funds)

Money markets

The money market consists of a set of institutions and arrangements through which the supply of and demand for short-term funds are brought together. It is a market for usually standardized, short-term financial assets which are close substitutes for money;

they are often referred to as "near money." Financial assets maturing in one year or less customarily are considered short-term, and money-market instruments are close substitutes for money because they are financial assets with minimum maturity and credit, or default, risk. Maturity risk is minimal, since the short-term nature of money-market instruments limits the volatility of their prices as interest rates change. Thus, money-market instruments are subject to far less maturity risk than are long-term securities such as government bonds and corporate bonds, which are traded in the capital market. Credit, or default, risk of money-market instruments is also minimal since the principal desire of investors in money-market paper is to acquire financial assets which quickly can be converted into cash without the risk of undue losses. Consequently, only prime-quality borrowers such as government and government agencies, large commercial banks and other financial institutions, and highest-rated nonfinancial corporations have ready access to the money market as a source of funds.

The major money markets in the world have no central trading place similar to the stock and commodity exchanges, and there is no official central clearing agency. Yet money markets are centered in major cities such as New York, London, Tokyo, Chicago, and San Francisco where most of the dealers, who buy securities for their own position and sell from their inventories, are located and where the final reconciliation of transactions takes place. The dealers, who form the nucleus of the money market, are constantly in touch with each other and with major borrowers and investors throughout the world. They engage in arbitrage to take advantage of temporary and small price differentials, and this serves to keep prices of the different money-market instruments virtually uniform among the various dealers; and since dealers themselves must finance their positions, or inventories, of financial assets, they are constantly looking for excess money balances at the lowest possible interest cost to them. Thus, they help to even out interest rate differentials for similar securities among various geographical areas. Through the borrowing and lending of temporarily idle cash balances by both financial and nonfinancial, domestic and foreign entities, the money market is the locus of marginal adjustments between the demand for and supply of funds throughout the nation and among the world's major financial markets. In this sense, the money market is both a national and international market; it is not only a low-risk but also a high-information financial market.

Major Participants

Among the principal participants in the money market, in addition to the dealers, are the large commercial banks, sometimes referred to as the money-market banks; the U.S. government and several federal agencies; the Federal Reserve System; and large nonfinancial corporations. The banks are both lenders and borrowers. They are lenders to the market, holding part of their reserves in short-term securities which can be sold quickly for cash and with little risk of capital loss; they are also borrowers in the market, selling short-term notes such as negotiable time certificates of deposits (CDs) and, through their bank holding companies, commercial paper to raise additional funds for lending. A number of banks are large-scale dealers in money-market instruments and are principal participants in the highly specialized submarket known as the federal-funds market.

Central banks in most industrialized countries, as well as in some developing countries, are heavily engaged in the money market, both on behalf of the government and in their capacity of conducting monetary policy. For example, the Federal

Reserve System, the Bank of Canada, and the Bank of England are large holders of short-term government securities and are responsible for maintaining orderly money-market conditions in which funds flow smoothly without major upset in interest rates. In order to accomplish this, and to pursue specific monetary policy goals, the Federal Reserve and other central banks conduct open-market operations through the money market, buying and selling short-term government securities, such as Treasury bills, and engaging in repurchase agreements and matched sale-purchase transactions (also called "reverse purchase" agreements through which the Federal Reserve sells securities to dealers and simultaneously makes a commitment to repurchase the securities at a future date) with primary dealers in government securities. In addition, the Federal Reserve makes huge transactions in the money market on behalf of foreign monetary authorities and international financial institutions, such as the International Monetary Fund (IMF).

The U.S. government is a major user of money-market funds. In recent years, about 35 percent of U.S. Treasury marketable debt outstanding has had an average maturity of less than one year. A large proportion of this debt is maturing every week and has to be refinanced through Treasury bills, notes, and bonds. The weekly auctions of Treasury bills establish key money-market interest rates that are closely followed by all participants and observers of financial markets and are used as benchmark rates for a wide variety of financial instruments.

Nonfinancial corporations use the money market as a source of short-term finance by issuing commercial paper (see below); and they invest temporarily excess cash in short-term debt securities with low credit risk. In some money markets (New York, London, Tokyo), foreign governments, central banks, and nonofficial foreign entities are significant net lenders. For example, the U.S. money market is a reserve center (and the U.S. dollar is a reserve currency) in which foreigners hold their external reserves and working balances in the form of short-term financial assets such as U.S. Treasury bills, bankers' acceptances, negotiable time certificates of deposits, and commercial paper. To them, as well as to other investors in the money market, low risk and high liquidity are of prime importance. At the same time, they earn some income on their surplus funds.

Types of Money-Market Paper

Most major financial markets are dominated by transactions in government obligations. In the United States, about one-third of U.S. Treasury marketable debt are securities with maturities of less than one year. In mid-1991 U.S. Treasury marketable public debt outstanding was close to $2.3 trillion. Most of these securities are Treasury bills with maturities of 3 months, 6 months and 52 weeks, issued in denominations of $10,000 and up. Three-month and six-month bills are auctioned weekly and are sold at a discount (i.e., they are zero-coupon securities sold at a dollar price less than their redemption value at maturity). The 52-week bills are usually auctioned every 4 weeks. Cash management bills are issued at irregular intervals with maturities from a few days to nine months. Spot transactions in Treasury bills by the primary dealers in U.S. government securities (about 40 commercial banks and investment firms) totalled more than $30 billion *per day* in 1991. Future and forward transactions added another $10 billion to the daily turnover. This transaction volume in short Treasury securities far exceeds the volume of turnover in any other segment of the money market, making the market for short-term government obligations more efficient than any other financial market in the United States.

However, the growth of many private money-market instruments has surpassed even that of short-term government obligations since the 1980s. Among the important private instruments actively traded in the U.S. money market are negotiable time certificates of deposits (CDs) issued by banks and thrift institutions in denominations of $100,000 or more, with typical maturities ranging from 60 to 120 days. The issuing banks compete for corporate and other funds with Treasury bills and other types of short-term money-market paper, and interest rates are closely related to other money-market rates. Banks also issue variable-rate CDs with interest rates adjusted every 30, 90, or 180 days, and the benchmark rate may be a composite CD rate published by the New York Federal Reserve Bank or the prime rate or the London interbank rate (LIBOR). The daily trading volume in CDs issued by U.S. domestic banks was in excess of $3 billion in 1991.

Eurodollar CDs and Yankee CDs have gained prominence since the 1980s. Eurodollar CDs are dollar-denominated certificates of deposit which are issued by foreign branches of large U.S. commercial banks and foreign banks, mainly located in London, as well as the largest Japanese banks. Yankee CDs are dollar-denominated short-term notes issued by foreign banks domiciled in the United States, including Japanese, Canadian, British, German, and Dutch banks.

Other money-market instruments are commercial paper and bankers' acceptances. Commercial paper, with maturities typically ranging from 30 days to 9 months, is issued by more than 2000 rated (by Moody's Investors Service, Standard & Poor's) nonfinancial corporations, including utilities, bank holding companies, finance and insurance companies, and a number of foreign corporations and foreign government agencies. This kind of borrowing is used to finance seasonal working capital requirements, currency swaps, and bridge financing for acquisitions. Commercial paper is generally backed by bank lines of credit and is issued either through dealers or directly by the borrowing entities. Major investment banks make an active secondary market in commercial paper which is bought and sold on a discount basis and is considered highly liquid. The volume of commercial paper outstanding has grown from $100 billion in the early 1980s to more than $550 billion in mid-1991, of which about $200 billion was sold through dealers and the remainder was directly placed paper.

Bankers' acceptances are used to finance domestic and international transactions. They are bills of exchange which have been accepted by a bank and, thus, are irrevocable primary obligations of the accepting bank. The market for bankers's acceptances is the oldest segment of the New York money market. During nearly 100 years of usage in the United States, there has been no known principal loss on bankers' acceptances. They have original maturities of 180 days or less; they are acceptable for discount and purchase by the Federal Reserve System, which is also a major participant in the secondary market on behalf of foreign central banks and monetary authorities. The volume of bankers' acceptances was about $50 billion in mid-1991, half of which was used to finance U.S. exports and imports.

Other money-market instruments include short-term tax-exempt notes issued by states, municipalities, and other public agencies, either in anticipation of tax revenue or as interim financing prior to a bond sale. A number of U.S. government–sponsored agencies issue short-term paper in the form of discount notes or floating-rate notes. For example, the Federal National Mortgage Association (Fannie Mae) issues short-term notes with maturities tailored to investors' needs up to 360 days, and there is an active secondary market for these notes maintained by a number of investment and commercial banks which distribute the notes. The Student Loan Marketing Association (Sallie Mae) has for many years issued short-term, unsecured discount notes; in addition, it is now issuing short-term floating rate notes on a regular basis with weekly adjustment of the interest rate, using as a benchmark the 91-day Treasury bill rate.

Other segments of the money market include trading in federal funds or bank excess reserves which are borrowed, usually for one day only, by banks faced with temporary reserve deficiency. The federal funds market rate is one of the most closely watched money-market interest rates. Brokers' loans, or loans made by banks to brokers and dealers for purchasing and carrying securities, are an established part of the money market. More recently, a number of money-market futures and options have become standard money-market instruments. Interest rate futures contracts on three-month U.S. Treasury bills were introduced in the mid-1970s and are actively traded on the Chicago Mercantile Exchange (CME). Other interest rate products, including three-month Eurodollar time deposit futures, have been introduced since then and are used by investors to hedge against changes in interest rates. The CME also offers trading in standardized options on Treasury bills and Eurodollar time deposit futures contracts.

The U.S. money market is still centered in New York, the domicile of the major participants, but it is becoming more diffused with technological advances in communication. It is by far the largest market as measured by volume of turnover, variety of dollar-denominated instruments actively traded, and number of participants, with increasing participation of foreign banks and brokers. The markets in the standard short-term instruments, such as Treasury bills, commercial paper, and negotiable time certificates of deposits, are extremely efficient; their transaction costs are low and small price and yield changes bring forth a large volume of orders to buy and sell. The wide range of money-market instruments with different risk-return characteristics facilitates quick and low-cost adjustment by lenders to changes in their liquid-asset preferences and by borrowers to changes in their short-term debt preferences.

References

Board of Governors, Federal Reserve System, *Federal Reserve Bulletin* (published monthly); The First Boston Corporation, *Handbook of U.S. Government and Federal Agency Securities,* 35th ed., Probus Publishing Company, Chicago, Ill., 1992; Livingston, Miles, *Money and Capital Markets: Financial Instruments and Their Uses,* Prentice-Hall, Englewood Cliffs, N.J., 1990; Rose, Peter S., *Money and Capital Markets,* 3d ed., Business Publications, Inc., Plano, Tex., 1989; Stigum, Marcia, *The Money Market,* 3rd ed., Dow Jones-Irwin, Homewood, Ill., 1990.

(*See also* Capital markets and money markets; Federal Reserve System; Financial institutions; Financial instruments; Flow of funds; Interest rates)

Holger Engberg

Money supply

Money is essential to the operation of any economy, as a medium of exchange and as a store of value, or temporary abode of purchasing power. In primitive economies, some widely used and generally acceptable commodity, such as salt, tobacco, furs, feathers, shells, copper, iron, gold, or silver, emerged by common practice as a convenient medium of exchange, thus permitting greater specialization in production and trade than would have been possible in a pure barter system. In modern economies, money, or the money supply, is some combination of coin issued by governments, paper currency or notes issued by governments or banks, and bank deposits (Humphrey, 1988).

The crucial role of the money supply in the economy makes the following issues important to households, businesses, and government policymakers: (1) effects of changes in the money supply, such as price inflation, recessions, and fluctuations in interest rates and exchange rates; (2) monetary policy, or how money supply should be made to behave; (3) how the money supply is created and controlled; and (4) what should be included in the definition of the money supply used for monetary policy and as a variable in private and public economic forecasting. In 1992, ideas on all these issues were changing rapidly because of new findings in monetary research, worldwide inflation, disinflation, economic instability, unstable foreign exchange rates, and technological innovations in financial institutions and markets.

Effects of Changes in Money Supply

Experience and research in many countries after the mid-1960s greatly increased emphasis on the role of changes in money supply in explanations of inflation and economic instability and in public policies designed to counter them. This increased emphasis on behavior of the money supply was, in part, a revival of a classical tradition in monetary theory that was widely accepted before the Great Depression caused it to be virtually eclipsed by the income-expenditure theory of John Maynard Keynes. New scientific tools, such as econometrics and computers, and the availability of greatly improved monetary and economic data added many new elements in an emerging consensus on effects of money-supply changes.

Major long-run changes in inflation rates do not occur without major changes in growth rates of the money supply in the same direction. The great worldwide price explosion of 1974 to 1980 was preceded by very large increases in growth rates of the money supplies of all the major industrial countries extending over almost a decade. The reduction of inflation to much lower rates in all major countries, by 1992, was preceded by reductions in money-supply growth rates which began in 1979. Although it is generally agreed that real shocks, such as crop failures or restrictions on oil supplies, can increase inflation rates for periods of a year or more, the underlying trend rate of inflation is now attributed by many economists to the trend rate of growth of the money supply.

Many economists also believe that sudden decelerations in the growth rate of the money supply can cause business recessions. Although there is disagreement on the channels of transmission through which money-supply changes influence incomes, output, employment, and prices, both Keynesian and monetarist economists agree that a sudden, large reduction in the growth rate of the money supply of a country will result in reductions in the growth rates of total spending and real output, or a recession, within a year. In August 1991, for example, the Federal Reserve Bank of St. Louis reported that the recessions which began in the United States, Canada, France, Switzerland, and the United Kingdom in 1990 followed a substantial slowing of money-supply growth in each country (Federal Reserve Bank of St. Louis, 1991). The widespread dismay in financial markets and in the U.S. government, from President Bush on down, over slow growth in M-2 in 1991 is evidence that recognition of money-supply effects in business fluctuations is by no means confined to monetarist economists (Wessel, 1991).

Recognition of the effects of money-supply changes on inflation and economic activity during the 1960s and 1970s also greatly changed the general view of how money supply influences interest rates. Although Irving Fisher demonstrated as early as 1896 that inflation expectations were the principal determinant of changes in market interest rates (nominal rates), most economists and people in financial markets before the mid-1960s believed that a government or central bank could reduce interest rates by increasing the money supply or could raise interest rates by reducing the money supply. By 1992, however, economists and market practitioners alike generally agreed that the so-called liquidity effect of an increase in money growth on interest rates is likely to be offset by effects of changes in income and inflation expectations in the opposite direction later on. The painful experience of investors with inflation after the mid-1960s convinced many that an increase in the growth rate of the money supply will mean higher interest rates in the future, as Fisher would have predicted, rather than lower interest rates. This understanding of how inflation expectations affect interest rates, however, did not deter politicians in both major parties from beseeching the Federal Reserve to reduce interest rates with easier policies in 1991.

Experience and research since the mid-1960s also demonstrated that the effects of money-supply changes are not restricted to the country in which they occur. When money growth rates and inflation began to accelerate in the United States in the early 1960s, this country had increasing balance-of-payments deficits. Central banks and governments of other countries were obliged by the Bretton Woods Agreement to buy up dollars flowing out of the United States, in order to keep their exchange rates within agreed parity limits. By issuing more of their own currencies in exchange for dollars, these countries increased their domestic money supplies and, in effect, imported inflation from the United States.

Under the floating-rate system, or managed float, which replaced the Bretton Woods adjustable-parity system in 1973, international effects of changes in growth rates of money supply appear principally, but not entirely, in exchange rate changes. When a country such as the United States increases the rate of growth of its money supply in relation to rates of growth of money supplies of other countries, the exchange rate of its currency in terms of other currencies will tend to fall, in response to actual or expected changes in relative inflation rates. The resulting changes in exchange rates impose internal adjustment costs on the other countries, by changing the relative prices and rates of production of domestic and internationally traded goods and services. These costs can be substantial in countries such as Germany, Japan, and Switzerland, in which a large part of gross national product enters into international trade. Therefore, money-supply changes originating in a large country transmit inflationary or recessionary impulses to other countries through a fixed-exchange-rate system or impose other significant costs through changing exchange rates in a floating-rate system.

Monetary Policy

The question of whether growth of the money supply should be governed by rules or by monetary authorities exercising discretionary powers has been debated probably since it was first discovered that money does not manage itself. Use of a commodity standard such as the gold standard to determine the money supply automatically was finally discontinued in the 1960s and probably will never be resumed. An alternative procedure would be to make a government-controlled money behave as though it were a commodity-based money, that is, to grow at a steady rate. Clark Warburton, Milton Friedman, and others long advocated that idea as the most effective way to achieve a reasonable degree of stability in economic activity and the price level. Believers in monetary rules are afraid that long-run price-stability goals will be sacrificed for short-run income stabilization, unless the monetary authority is required to achieve prescribed values of some nominal variable that it can control, such as the monetary base or some other monetary aggregate (Judd and Motley, 1991; Warburton, 1953).

Discretionary use of money-supply changes to offset changes in inflation rates, and thus to combat business cycles, was advocated by Irving Fisher and other monetary economists before the Great Depression. After the rise of income-expenditure theories in the 1930s, changes in growth rates of the money supply were not believed to have more than minor, slow effects on economic activity. However, policymakers after World War II attempted to supplement fiscal policies with changes in money-supply growth rates as contracyclical instruments and in pursuit of full employment. These policies proved to have an inflationary bias.

By 1980, recognition of the disturbing and often perverse effects of discretionary changes in growth rates of the money supply on economic activity, inflation rates, interest rates, and exchange rates led more economists and even some policymakers to advocate reducing the variability of money-supply growth rates. They argued that attempts to counteract business cycles with discretionary changes in money growth rates did more harm than good. Although no monetary authority in the world has specifically renounced its discretionary powers over rates of monetary expansion, some have begun to behave almost as if they had, by announcing target money growth rates in advance. Japan, Germany, and Switzerland, in particular, have reduced inflation by gradual reductions in money growth. Although they did not call their actions rules, their actual policies have been similar to what believers in monetary rules would have prescribed (Meltzer, 1991).

Rational expectations theory, which developed in the 1970s, provided an impressive rationale for the use of a steady money growth rule rather than discretionary changes in money growth rates (Federal Reserve Bank of Minneapolis, 1977). Economists of this school argue that workers and managers of business firms learn to anticipate changes in fiscal and monetary policies. If they believe, for example, that a restrictive monetary policy intended to combat inflation will be followed by an expansionary policy, they will not reduce rates of increase in wages and prices. This explains the persistence of high inflation rates during recessions—stagflation—that developed after the mid-1960s in Europe and North America.

Control of the Money Supply

The money supply is jointly determined by decisions of the government or central bank, commercial banks, and the public. The government and central bank control the supply of monetary base, or high-powered money, which consists of paper currency and coin issued by the government and liabilities of the central bank to commercial banks. The money supply held by the public is some multiple of the monetary base so that an increase in the monetary base provided by the government and the central bank will cause the money supply to increase by more than the increase in the base. In 1991, in the United States, for example, a $1 increase in monetary base (St. Louis Federal Reserve Bank definition) would result in an increase of about \$2.55 in narrowly defined money supply, M-1 (see Walter, 1989, for definitions). It is clear, therefore, that a purchase or sale of government securities by the Federal Reserve for any reason has a multiplied effect on money supply, through its effect on the monetary base.

The multiplier determining the size of the money supply per unit of monetary base is not constant. Decisions of the banks regarding the quantity of reserves they want to hold in the form of currency or in deposits at the central bank, in relation to their deposits, and decisions of the public regarding the shares of their money holdings they want to keep in currency and in bank deposits change the multiplier and, thus, change the quantity of money supply associated with any given quantity of monetary base. Although such a change in the multiplier can produce unanticipated changes in the money supply over short periods, a substantial body of research indicates that these changes can be predicted well enough to be offset by changes in the monetary base. Therefore, the monetary authorities should be able to keep growth of the money supply within a tolerable range of error around a desired growth path, if they ever decide to try.

In actual practice, except for a brief period in the late 1970s and early 1980s, growth of the money supply in most countries is essentially an incidental result of central bank actions in pursuit of other objectives, such as to stabilize interest rates or foreign exchange rates or to facilitate the financing of government budget deficits. By 1980, however, the central banks and governments of many countries, including the United States, the United Kingdom, West Germany, Italy, Japan, Spain, and Switzerland, were attempting to achieve more precise control over their money supplies through reducing emphasis on operations designed to stabilize interest rates or exchange rates and increasing emphasis on direct control of the monetary base or other monetary aggregates. On October 6, 1979, for example, the Federal Reserve System of the United States announced that it had changed open-market operating procedures to place more emphasis on controlling bank reserves directly in order to provide more assurance of attaining basic money-supply objectives.

Following the 1979 change in procedures, the Federal Open Market Committee explicitly targeted reserve measures estimated to be consistent with desired three-month growth rates of M-1. This was a radical break from all earlier procedures, which had generally used interest rates or money-market conditions as targets for open-market operations. In late 1982, however, the Federal Reserve returned essentially to interest rate and money-market-conditions targeting. It explained its return to its old procedures on the grounds that the relationships between M-1 and economic activity had deteriorated so much as to make M-1 an unreliable policy objective (Meulendyke, 1988, 1989). After the 1982 shift away from money-supply targeting, the range of variation in month-to-month growth rates of monetary base, M-1, and M-2 increased, and fluctuations in money-market interest rates narrowed.

How Money Supply Should Be Defined

The final issue of concern in considering the nature and behavior of the money supply is the one of how money should be defined and measured for conducting monetary policy and for analytical purposes. Interest in this problem has increased greatly in recent years as innovations in financial markets and in governmental regulation of financial institutions have increased the number and variety of financial assets available to households and business firms for possible use as money or substitutes for money. Some economists fear that failure to make adequate allowance for new forms of money or money substitutes in conventional measures of the money supply could impair the effectiveness of monetary policy. The U.S. Federal Reserve System frequently responds to this concern with new definitions of the monetary aggregates it publishes (Tatom, 1990; Walter, 1989).

The lack of any general agreement among economists and policymakers on criteria for deciding what should be included in the money supply makes the problem of defining and measuring the money supply difficult. At one extreme are those economists who emphasize the transactions function of money. They generally prefer a narrow definition which includes currency in the hands of the public and those deposits at banks that are actively used for carrying out transactions. Disagreements within this group generally concern questions of whether a particular liability of a bank or other financial institution is used in transactions.

At the other extreme are economists who emphasize liquidity, or the ease with which a particular financial asset can be converted into something which can be used for making payments. They prefer a broader definition which includes time deposits at a wide variety of financial institutions, shares in money-market mutual funds, and other financial assets. They are afraid that the supplies of some of these items might increase when the monetary authorities attempt to restrict growth of more narrowly defined aggregates and, thus, might frustrate achievement of the policy objectives.

Another criterion on which economists and policymakers differ is the closeness of the relationship between a particular monetary aggregate and the ultimate objectives of policy, such as national income and prices. Economists who emphasize this criterion would not rely on a priori characteristics of money in deciding on a definition of money. They would instead use empirical testing of the various proposed measures to find the ones which would yield the most reliable predictions of incomes and prices when used as a policy instrument or forecasting tool.

The degree of controllability by the central bank or government is another major issue in the selection of a money-supply definition. Some economists argue that the proper monetary aggregate for policy purposes would be the one that can be most reliably predicted from changes in variables under direct central bank control, such as a central bank's own portfolio of assets or monetary base. They would settle the issue by empirical testing. This would permit the monetary authorities to set monetary policy targets in terms of variables over which they have the greatest degree of control (Laidler, 1990).

Conclusions

The disagreements among economists and policymakers regarding effects of money-supply changes, monetary policy, how the money supply should be controlled, and the proper definition of the money supply should not be viewed as evidence that efforts to control the money supply are futile. The money supply is too important to be left uncontrolled. The debates are instead essential contributions to improvement in society's prospects for achieving stability in the purchasing power of money, higher long-run rates of growth in real income and employment, and more stable international exchange rates.

References

Bank of England, "Monetary Base Control," *Bank of England Quarterly Bulletin,* vol. 19, no. 2, June 1979, pp. 149–159; Federal Reserve Bank of Minneapolis, "Rational Expectations—Fresh

Ideas That Challenge Some Established Views on Policy Making," *1977 Annual Report,* Minneapolis, Minn., pp. 1–13; Federal Reserve Bank of St. Louis, "International Economic Conditions," August 1991, St. Louis, p. 1; Friedman, Milton, and Anna J. Schwartz, *Monetary Statistics of the United States: Estimates, Sources, Methods,* National Bureau of Economic Research, Columbia University Press, New York, 1970, part 1, pp. 89–197; Hetzel, Robert L., "The Monetary Responsibilities of a Central Bank," *Economic Review,* Federal Reserve Bank of Richmond, September/October 1988, pp. 19–31; Humphrey, Thomas M., "Rival Notions of Money," *Economic Review,* Federal Reserve Bank of Richmond, September/October 1988, pp. 3–9; Judd, John P., and Brian Motley, "Nominal Feedback Rules for Monetary Policy," *Economic Review,* Federal Reserve Bank of San Francisco, Summer 1991, no. 3, pp. 3–17; Laidler, David W. E., *Taking Money Seriously and Other Essays,* M.I.T., Cambridge, Mass., 1990; Meltzer, Allan H., "Is Monetarism Dead?," *National Review,* Nov. 4, 1991, pp. 30–32; Meulendyke, Ann-Marie, "A Review of Federal Reserve Policy Targets and Operating Guides in Recent Decades," *Quarterly Review,* Federal Reserve Bank of New York, Autumn 1988, pp. 6–17; Meulendyke, Ann-Marie, *U.S. Monetary Policy and Financial Markets,* Federal Reserve Bank of New York, New York, 1989; Tatom, John A., "The Effects of Financial Innovations on Checkable Deposits, M1 and M2," *Review,* Federal Reserve Bank of St. Louis, July/August 1990, pp. 37–57; Walter, John R., "Monetary Aggregates: A User's Guide," *Economic Review,* Federal Reserve Bank of Richmond, January/February 1989, pp. 20–28, Warburton, Clark, "Rules and Implements for Monetary Policy," *Journal of Finance,* vol. 8, no. 1, March 1953, pp. 1–21; Wessel, David, "The Outlook: Money-Supply Puzzle Is Troubling the Fed," *The Wall Street Journal,* Oct. 7, 1991.

(*See also* Bretton Woods Conference; Deposits; Federal Reserve policy; Federal Reserve System; Foreign exchange rates; Inflation; Interest rates; Monetary policy; Open-market operations; Smithsonian Agreement)

A. James Meigs

Monopoly and oligopoly

Monopoly is a market structure with only a single seller of a commodity or service dealing with a large number of buyers. When a single seller faces a single buyer, that situation is known as bilateral monopoly.

The most important features of market structure are those which influence the nature of competition and price determination. The key element in this segment of market organization is the degree of seller concentration, or the number and size distributions of the sellers. There is monopoly when there is only one seller in an industry, and there is competition when there are many sellers in an industry. In cases of an intermediate number of sellers, that is, something between monopoly and competition, there can be two sellers (duopoly), a few sellers (oligopoly), or many sellers (atomistic competition). Today the term monopoly is usually extended to include any group of firms which act together to fix prices or levels of production. Complete control of all output is not necessary to exercise monopoly power. Any combination of firms which controls at least 80 percent of an industry's production can dictate the prices of the remaining 20 percent.

Monopoly versus Competition

Pure monopoly is a theoretical market structure where there is only one seller of a commodity or service, where entry into the industry is closed to potential competitors, and where the seller has complete control over the quantity of goods offered for sale and the price at which goods are sold. Pure monopoly is one of two limiting cases used in the analysis of market structure. The other is pure competition, a situation in which there are many sellers who can influence neither the total quantity of a commodity or service offered for sale nor its selling price. Hence, monopoly is the exact antithesis of competition. It is generally agreed that neither of these two limiting cases is to be found among existing market structures.

The monopolist establishes market position by ability to control absolutely the supply of a product or service offered for sale and the related ability to set price. Theoretically, profit maximization is the primary objective, and it is often possible to achieve this by restricting output and the quantity of goods offered for sale. Levels of output are held below the quantity that would be produced in a competitive situation. Hence, monopoly is of interest to economic policymakers because it may impede the most efficient possible allocation of a nation's economic resources.

Monopolies held by individuals or organizations may begin by the granting of a patent or a copyright, by the possession of a superior skill or talent, or by the ownership of strategic capital. The huge capital investment necessary to organize a firm in some industries raises an almost insurmountable barrier to entry in these monopolistic fields and, thus, provides established corporations in these industries with potential monopoly power.

The use of such monopoly power may lead to the development of substitute products, to an attempt at entry into monopolistic fields by new firms (if profits are high enough), or to public prosecution or regulation. The antitrust policy of the federal government has prevented the domination of an industry by one firm or even a few firms. Moreover, with the growth of international trade and investment, it is no longer possible to determine whether an effective monopoly exists by studying market shares. The recent competitive pressures from Japanese sellers of autos and electronic products have resulted in more competition and less monopoly power on the part of U.S. manufacturers. Thus, the trend during the last 40 years or so in the United States has been away from monopolies in many industries and toward oligopolies.

Oligopolies

An oligopoly exists when a few sellers of a commodity or service deal with a large number of buyers. When a few sellers face a few buyers, that situation is known as bilateral oligopoly. In the case of oligopoly a small number of companies supply the major portion of an industry's output. In effect the industry is composed of a few large firms which account for a significant share of the total production. Thus, the actions of the individual firms have an appreciable effect on their competitors.

However, it does not follow as a consequence of the presence of relatively few firms in an industry that competition is absent. Although there are few firms in an industry, they may still act independently, and the outcome of their actions is consistent with competition. With few firms in an industry, each takes into account the likely repercussions of its actions. For example, each seller knows that if he or she lowers prices, the few competitors will immediately follow suit and lower their prices, leaving the seller with roughly the same share of the total market but lower profits. However, the seller may be reluctant to raise prices because competitors might not follow this lead. One feature of markets with few sellers is that prices are often stable, except during periods of very rapid inflation. Also, prices of oligopolistic industries generally fluctuate less widely than in more competitive industries.

Other Monopolies

Aside from private monopolies, there are public monopolies. One example of a public monopoly in the United States is the nonprofit postal service. There is also the "natural" monopoly, which exists when it is more efficient, technically, to have a single seller.

Although the precise definition of monopoly—a market structure with only a single seller of a commodity or service—cannot be applied directly to a labor union because a union is not a seller of services, labor unions have monopolistic characteristics. For example, when a union concludes a wage settlement which sets wage rates at a level higher than that acceptable to unorganized workers, the union clearly contributes to monopolistic wage results. In effect, the price of labor (wages) is set without regard to the available supply of labor.

References

Edwards, Corwin D., *Maintaining Competition,* McGraw-Hill, New York, 1949; Hamburg, Daniel, *Principles of a Growing Economy,* Norton, New York, 1961, pp. 518–557; Kahn, Alfred E., *The Economics of Legislation: Principles and Institutions,* MIT Press, Cambridge, Mass., 1988; Robinson, Joan, *Economics of Imperfect Competition,* St. Martin's, London, 1969; Samuelson, Paul A., and William D. Nordhaus, *Economics,* 14th ed., McGraw-Hill, New York, 1992, chap. 11.

(*See also* Competition; Price theory)

Douglas Greenwald

Mortgage credit

Mortgage lending is a major activity of today's financial markets. In 1990, the $3.6 trillion in outstanding mortgage debt comprised almost half of the total debt of the nonfinancial sectors of the U.S. economy. As such, total mortgage debt was almost four times larger than corporate debt and almost five times greater than consumer debt, municipal debt, or the value of bank loans. Virtually two-thirds of all household liabilities were mortgages.

The mortgage loan is a debt instrument pledging real property to ensure the performance of the contract. Although mortgages are used to finance the acquisition of land and the construction or purchase of commercial structures, the single most important use of mortgage debt is home financing. Home mortgage debt represents almost 70 percent of total mortgage debt.

Mortgage Types

The mortgage contract most often associated with home finance is the fixed-rate, level-pay mortgage. The terms of this type of mortgage include the amount borrowed, the interest rate, the term to maturity, the payment frequency, origination fees, and any prepayment options. These conditions determine a fixed periodic payment, part of which is interest and the remainder of which reduces the principal of the loan. Although the overall payment remains unchanged, the amount allocated to interest shrinks throughout the life of the contract, and the amount representing the reduction of principal grows. In this way the loan is completely extinguished, or amortised, over the life of the contract.

Traditionally, the most common maturity was 30 years, and the most often used payment period was monthly. More recently, 15-year mortgages have become more common, as have biweekly payment periods. These options cause the mortgage to amortise more quickly, thus reducing the overall interest payments. Moreover, the smaller, more frequent biweekly payments may also fit more easily into the home-buyer's budget.

During the 1970s and 1980s, high and volatile interest rates, together with rapidly rising home prices, triggered a number of innovations to the traditional mortgage contract. Some of these changes were designed to make it easier for the borrower to cope with higher monthly payments, and others were aimed at helping lenders address the interest rate risk associated with fixed-rate lending.

The simplest of these innovations was the graduated payment mortgage (GPM). This type of loan contrasts with the traditional fixed-rate loan in that mortgage payments are reduced during the early years and then increased over the remaining life of the contract according to a predetermined schedule. The lower initial monthly payments were designed to accommodate younger, perhaps first-time, home buyers who might have trouble qualifying for a loan at their current salary but whose incomes were expected to grow. Because the reduced early payments allow for less principal reduction, GPMs amortize more slowly than a comparable fixed-rate loan. In some cases, the early payments are insufficient to cover even the interest costs, and the shortfall is added to the loan balance. In such cases, the loan is said to experience negative amortization.

The adjustable-rate mortgage (ARM) was one of the most important innovations in the history of mortgage finance. Long a staple of home financing in Canada, the concept of a variable interest rate and monthly payment was not adopted in the United States until the 1970s. By allowing the interest rate and monthly payment to adjust to current market conditions, these loans can be beneficial to both borrower and lender. This type of loan helps financial institutions manage interest rate risk, thus stabilizing the flow of mortgage credit. The loan can benefit borrowers because it is generally tied to a short-term interest rate, and thus it often carries a lower interest rate and monthly payment than its long-term fixed-rate counterpart.

The terms of an ARM contract differ from those of a fixed-rate mortgage. In addition to the loan amount and term to maturity, the ARM contract generally specifies an initial rate, index, margin, payment frequency, repricing frequency, annual and life-of-loan interest rate or payment caps, loan points or fees, prepayment conditions, and conditions governing negative amortization.

Within any repricing period, ARMs act just like a fixed-rate loan. That is, the payment is fixed, and part of the payment is interest and the remainder reduces the principal. At each repricing date, a new rate and payment are determined based on the margin and any movement in the index. The new payment is calculated so as to fully amortize the loan over the remaining life of the contract. If payment or interest rate limits prevent the rate or payment from adjusting fully, the shortfall (negative amortization) may be added into the remaining principal.

The basic mortgage contract has been adapted in a number of other ways to address specific problems. Pledged account mortgages (PAMs) and builder buydowns were developed to reduce the monthly payment and make it easier for an individual to qualify for a loan. Shared appreciation mortgages (SAMs) provide a lower interest rate in exchange for a proportion of the property appreciation. Reverse annuity mortgages

(RAMs) are structured to provide the mortgagor with a monthly cash inflow for the life of the loan at which time the property conveys to the lender. This allows individuals to receive a cashflow without forfeiting the use of the property in the interim.

Sources of Mortgage Credit

The flow of mortgage credit is facilitated by the operation of two markets, primary and secondary. The primary market is comprised of those institutions that originate and/or hold mortgage loans, primarily thrift institutions, commercial banks, and insurance companies. These institutions raise funds by offering savings deposits and collecting insurance premiums. They then funnel the proceeds through to the mortgage market. Although thrift institutions historically dominated the mortgage origination market, commercial banks and mortgage bankers currently originate more mortgage loans.

In 1990, mortgage companies originated over 35 percent of all one- to four-family mortgages, commercial banks had about 33 percent of the market, and thrift institutions originated about 30 percent of the home loans. Thrift institutions nevertheless remain major holders of mortgage loans. At the end of 1990, thrift institutions held about 28 percent of all home loans, and commercial banks held about 15 percent. The biggest single holder of home mortgage loans are the mortgage pools, which hold over 35 percent. These institutions are actually part of the secondary market.

The secondary market includes institutions that buy and pool mortgage loans and repackage the cash flows, thus creating securities that are more appealing to a broader class of investors. In this way they tap nontraditional sources of funds. The secondary market is dominated by government or government-sponsored agencies such as the Government National Mortgage Association (Ginnie Mae), the Federal National Mortgage Association (Fannie Mae), and the Federal Home Loan Mortgage Corporation (Freddie Mac).

At its inception, the major tool of the secondary market was the mortgage-backed security (MBS). Mortgages were collected into pools, and then securities were issued granting the holder a pro rata share in the interest and principle payments, including prepayments, made to the pool. These early MBSs were more liquid than the underlying mortgage loans and had a different risk profile owing to the diversification and overcollateralization of the pools. They also spread the risk of prepayments across the entire pool. A principal drawback of these early pass-through securities was that they continued until the last mortgage was repaid and thus had an uncertain maturity.

In order to rectify this problem, the collateralized mortgage obligation (CMO) was developed. This instrument provided a share in a pool of mortgages but differed from the MBS in that it established subclasses, or tranches, of debtholders. Although interest payments to the pool were distributed to all shareholders, all principal payments were directed first to a single tranche until that tranche was retired and then went to successive tranches. In this way the CMO created a series of debt instruments that had more specific maturities and behaved more like a bond.

Although CMOs were an improvement over the simple pass-through, they suffered from certain tax considerations that made them cumbersome to issue. These problems were addressed in the 1986 Tax Act with the creation of the real estate mortgage investment conduit (REMIC), which was essentially a CMO without the problematic tax aspects.

The ability to reconfigure the cash flow of a mortgage reached its zenith with the development of interest-only (IO) and principal-only (PO) stripped securities. These securities provide returns that are highly sensitive to changes in the interest rates or prepayment conditions and thus provide investors with a way to hedge against changes in market conditions.

Government Influence in the Mortgage Markets

Because of the political and social importance attached to home ownership, the government has sought to influence the flow of mortgage credit in many ways. On a very broad level, the government's monetary and fiscal policy affect the level of interest rates and determine the background for real estate finance. In a much more direct way, the deductibility of mortgage interest and the provision of direct guarantees through the Veteran's Administration and Federal Housing Administration are intended to foster home ownership.

The government has provided indirect support to the mortgage market through the provision of deposit insurance and the establishment of the Federal Home Loan Bank System. Although the primary purpose of deposit insurance is protection of the payments mechanism, deposit insurance helps stabilize the flow of funds to depository institutions and underpins the supply of mortgage credit. The FHLB system is a government-sponsored entity that was created in the 1930s to facilitate the flow of mortgage credit by making long-term advances to depository institutions.

The government was also instrumental in the development of the secondary market. Ginnie Mae was established in 1968 as a government agency backed by the "full faith and credit of the U.S. government" to pool government-guaranteed VA and FHA mortgages and issue mortgage-backed securities. In 1970, Freddie Mac was founded as a government-sponsored enterprise to provide similar services for conventional mortgages. The secondary market was enhanced further in the early 1980s when Fannie Mae began its pass-through program operating in both the conventional and government-guaranteed market.

References

Fabozzi, Frank J. (ed.), *Mortgage Backed Securities New Strategies, Applications and Research,* Probus Publishing Company, Chicago, 1987; Fabozzi, Frank J. (ed.), *The Handbook of Mortgage-Backed Securities,* Probus Publishing Company, Chicago, 1988; Lederman, Jess (ed.), *Mortgage Banking: A Handbook of Strategies, Trends and Opportunities,* Probus Publishing Company, Chicago, 1989.

(*See also* Business credit; Consumer credit; Credit, an overview; Real estate investment trusts; Selective credit controls; Thrift institutions: problems and challenges)

Martin A. Regalia

Multinational corporation

The definition of a multinational corporation (MNC), or alternatively, multinational enterprise or transnational corporation, has long been subject to debate (see, e.g., Aharoni, 1971). Some consensus seems to exist that a multinational firm is one which exercises managerial control over operations in more than one national market. Exactly what constitutes managerial control, however, is an issue over which there also is debate, involving political and legal as well as economic issues. There would be little argument that a corporation headquartered in one nation holds managerial control over foreign branch operations or wholly owned (or even majority-owned) subsidiaries. It is, however, argued that effective managerial control can be exercised by the corporation over subsidiaries in which it has but a minority interest, or even over foreign firms in which it holds no equity but operates via a management contract or some other contractual device. The U.S. Department of Commerce, for example, defines a firm in the United States to be under foreign control if 10 percent or more of its equity is held by a foreign investor.

If one assumes that the issue of managerial control can be resolved, the above definition of a multinational corporation would include any firm which controlled operation in a nation other than that which constituted the firm's principal market, even if these operations were very small relative to its domestic operations. Most scholars, however, consider a multinational corporation to be a large firm for which nondomestic operations account for some significant portion of total firm revenues. In a study published in 1971, for example, Raymond Vernon used multiple criteria to distinguish between the multinational and nonmultinational of the 500 largest U.S. industrial firms. Of these firms, 187 were deemed to be multinational on the basis of the criteria, and these had substantially greater average sales and numbers of employees than the nonmultinational remainder. More recent studies suggest that the worldwide total of firms which are multinational by similar criteria is on the order of about 1000 (United Nations Centre for Transnational Corporations, 1992).

Why Do Firms Become Multinational?

To a large extent, theories about why firms become multinational parallel theories of foreign direct investment. Foreign direct investment is the recorded capital movement resulting from an investor (usually a firm) in one nation acquiring control of a firm in some other nation via acquisition or establishment. (Increases in retained earnings in the acquired or established firm, under balance-of-payments accounting, typically are also counted as foreign direct investment flows.)

Of a number of approaches to the theory of foreign direct investment, those that pertain to the organizational theory of the firm are probably most relevant to explaining the multinational firm per se. (The pioneering work in this regard is Buckley and Casson 1976. See also Ethier 1986.) This theory holds that economic activities can be organized either as markets, where economic "agents"—buyers and sellers of the factors of production and intermediate products—are independent, or as hierarchies, where at least some activities are bound together in an organization under common ownership and control. The extent of the firm's boundaries are determined by the transactions costs of market organization versus hierarchical organization; the greater the economies of "internalizing" economic activities within an organization, the larger the span of the organization. When economies of "internalization" of international activities are significant relative to use of market mechanisms (e.g., licensing or export), the firm will become multinational. The reader should consult Casson (1976) and Cantwell (1991) for more detailed accounts of the organization theory of the multinational corporation.

Social Welfare Consequences

The social welfare consequences of the multinational corporation are the subject of ongoing debate. At the time of this publication, the tide worldwide is running very much in these corporations' favor, that is, most analysis comes out praising these firms as enhancing welfare in the nations in which they operate. [For a summary, see United Nations Centre for Transnational Corporations (1992).] Analysts have not always been so sanguine, however. The reader might wish to consult Gilpin (1974), Goldfinger (1974), Musgrave (1975), and United Nations Economic and Social Council (1978) for contrary views.

References

Aharoni, Yair, "On the Definition of Multinational Corporations," *Quarterly Review of Economics and Business,* vol. 11, no. 3, Autumn 1971, pp. 27–38; Buckley, Peter J., and Mark C. Casson, *The Future of the Multinational Enterprise,* MacMillan, London, 1976; Cantwell, John, "A Survey of Theories of International Production," in Christos N. Pitelis and Roger Sugden (eds.), *The Nature of the Transnational Firm,* Routledge, London, 1991; Casson, Mark C., *The Firm and the Market,* Basil Blackwell, Oxford, 1976, and The MIT Press, Cambridge, Mass., 1976; Ethier, William J., "The Multinational Firm," *The Quarterly Journal of Economics,* vol. 101, no. 4, 1986, pp. 805–833; Gilpin, Robert, *U.S. Power and the Multinational Corporation,* Basic Books, New York, 1974; Goldfinger, Nathan, "A Labor View of Foreign Investment and Trade Issues," in R. E. Baldwin and J. D. Richardson (eds.), *International Trade and Finance,* Little, Brown, Boston, 1974; Musgrave, Peggy B., *Direct Investment Abroad and the Multinationals: Effects on the United States Economy,* U.S. Senate Subcommittee on Foreign Relations, Washington, D.C., 1975; United Nations Centre for Transnational Corporations (UNCTC), *World Investment Report 1992,* New York, 1992; United Nations Economic and Social Council, Commission on Transnational Corporations, *Transnational Corporations in World Development: A Re-examination,* New York, 1978; Vernon, Raymond, *Sovereignty at Bay,* Basic Books, New York, 1971.

(*See also* Foreign direct investment; Integration)

Edward M. Graham

Multiplier

The multiplier deals with the magnified impact, or chain reaction, on income of increases in public spending or private capital investment. R. F. Kahn (1931) pointed out, in his pioneering study, that the case for public works as a recovery measure usually includes reference to the "beneficial repercussions that will result from the expenditure of the newly-employed men's wages." The nature and extent of these repercussions had not, however, been analyzed at that time.

The Multiplier in Practice

Kahn showed that the successive spendings would most likely form a converging series and that the size of the ultimate expansion would depend on the leakages which occur at each round of spending. If, for example, people spend two-thirds of any addition to their incomes on home-produced consumer goods—the rest being saved or otherwise immobilized—the total increase in income from additional x dollars spent on public works would be

$$x = \frac{2}{3x} = \frac{2}{3} \cdot \frac{2}{3x} \cdots$$

This is, of course, a geometric series the sum of which is $x/(1 - 2/3)$.

J. M. Clark (1934) realized independently that the successive spendings out of an increase in income would form a converging series with a finite sum, but he did not develop this insight into a full-fledged theory of the multiplier. J. M. Keynes (1936), however, employed the multiplier as a key element in his *General Theory*.

Three Offsets to the Multiplier

For the multiplier to take effect, the initial increase in spending must be net. There are three possible types of offset to increased public works (or other) spending. First, if the government raises taxes, the increased spending of those employed on the public works will be offset, to a greater or lesser extent, by the decreased spending of the taxpayers. The amount of the offset, Kahn noted, "would depend on the extent to which the increased taxes are paid at the expense of consumption rather than of saving." Later development of this point led to the balanced-budget multiplier theorem in accordance with which an equal increase in spending and in taxes will increase income by exactly the amount of the increased spending. This holds only if the tax increase is designed in such a way as to yield an amount of additional revenue at the new higher level of income equal to the increased government expenditure. Otherwise, the multiplier will not be equal to 1.

If, instead of raising taxes, the government borrows the money, there may be an unfavorable impact on private investment. As incomes expand, consumers and business concerns will normally want to increase their money holdings. Unless the economy is in a state of extreme liquidity, this will raise interest rates, thus crowding out some private investment. The banking system can obviate this danger by increasing the money supply by the appropriate amount. It should be noted that even in a continuing program of government spending and borrowing, the quantity of money would not go on increasing indefinitely. Once the demand for increased money holdings created by the higher level of income had been satisfied, the government could finance its spending by borrowing the increased saving generated by the larger income without exerting upward pressure on interest rates.

The third type of offset is less direct. Specific businesses might find their interests adversely affected or business in general might suffer a loss of confidence. Repercussions of either type might be favorable as well as unfavorable.

Impact on Money versus Real Income

Finally, the multiplier might operate to increase money income but not, or not to the same extent, real income. What happens will depend on the elasticity of supply and the behavior of wages as employment increases. In the 1930s discussion of the multiplier was usually based on the assumption that the large amount of unemployment and excess capacity would ensure an elastic supply and that unemployed workers would be willing to accept jobs at constant or slightly reduced real wages.

References

Ackley, Gardner, *Macroeconomics: Theory and Policy,* Macmillan, New York, 1978; Clark, J. M., *Strategic Factors in Business Cycles,* National Bureau of Economic Research, New York, 1934; Kahn, R. F., "The Relation of Home Investment to Unemployment," *Economic Journal,* vol. 41, June 1931, pp. 173–198; Keynes, J. M., *The General Theory of Money, Interest and Employment,* Harcourt Brace Jovanovich, New York, 1936.

(*See also* Keynesian economics)

Alan Sweezy

Mutual funds

A mutual fund is one type of a broad set of savings vehicles known as investment companies. The business of these companies is to invest in securities such as stocks, bonds, and short-term money instruments.

A mutual fund is an open-end investment company, which means that investors who want to own shares in it buy those shares directly from the company, thereby adding to its assets. Those investors who no longer want to participate may redeem their shares from the company, thereby withdrawing assets. (Some investment companies, known as closed-end funds, do not continuously offer new shares or redeem shares when investors no longer want to own them; they trade in the equity market, as the shares of any corporation are traded.) All new shares are purchased, and outstanding shares are redeemed, at the fund's net asset value per share on the date of the transaction. Net asset value is the difference between the total assets and any liabilities owing, divided by the number of shares outstanding. Many funds add a sales charge or load to the purchase price, most of which goes to a salesperson; the stockholders of many funds also pay for the costs of advertising and marketing the fund.

Size and History

Investment companies originated in Europe in the nineteenth century and were well established in the United States by 1900. The industry has had two recent periods of accelerated growth. From 1960 to 1970, the number of funds increased from 160 to 360, the shareholder count went from 5 million to nearly 11 million, and assets expanded from $17 billion to almost $50 billion. In 1970, mutual funds held over 6 percent of the total market value of shares listed on the New York Stock Exchange, up from less than 2 percent in 1950.

Growth slowed during the early 1970s and then went into reverse. Net redemptions were heavy after 1972 and drained more than $6 billion from fund assets from 1973 to 1978.

The 1980s witnessed another great surge in mutual fund ownership and growth. Mutual fund ownership is now widely distributed. Sixteen percent of households with incomes below $25,000 own mutual funds, and this percentage rises to 55 percent among households with incomes above $75,000.

The most significant innovation since the 1960s has been the money-market fund, which enabled small investors, formerly restricted to savings accounts with interest ceilings, to enjoy the higher rates then available on a wide variety of unrestricted money-market instruments. As most of these funds include check-writing privileges, they have become a useful substitute for, or complement to, regular checking accounts. From a small beginning during the 1970s, money-market mutual funds reached $200 billion in assets by 1982, equal to total commercial bank demand deposits; money-market mutual funds then grew to about $500 billion by 1990, exceeding demand deposits by $200 billion. The number of money-market fund accounts rose from 500,000 accounts in 61 funds in 1978 to 21.6 million accounts in 508 funds by 1990.

But the growth of mutual funds other than money-market funds has also been spectacular. Assets rose tenfold during the 1980s and exceeded $600 billion by 1991, even as individual investors were liquidating nearly a trillion dollars of their direct holdings in common stocks. Three hundred billion dollars came into mutual funds just during the three years from 1985 to 1987; net inflow during 1990 came to $51 billion. Some 2400 new funds made their appearance during the decade, with as many as 477 in 1987 alone. The number of shareholder accounts swelled from 8 million in 1980 to 40 million in 1990. About 75 percent of these accounts are owned by individuals, with the remainder held by businesses, fiduciaries, and other institutional investors. Two-thirds of the funds involve sales charges paid to salespersons, and one-third are no-load funds sold primarily through advertising.

The growth pattern of the mutual fund industry in the 1980s reflects the more conservative attitude of individual investors that followed widespread disillusionment with equities during the 1970s. Although equity funds grew from $41 billion in 1980 to $246 billion in 1990, bond and so-called income funds have swelled over the same period from only $17 billion in less than 200 funds to $325 billion in 1235 funds.

Advantages and Disadvantages

By pooling the savings of a large number of investors, investment companies permit each shareholder to enjoy broad diversification and economies of scale that bring down the cost of professional management, transaction costs, and custodian fees. Government regulations protect the investor through full disclosure of fund assets, performance records, operating expenses, management personnel, and investment objectives. A majority of the board of directors must be unaffiliated with the group managing the assets and have the responsibility of hiring and firing managers.

Mutual funds can serve both broad and highly specialized investment objectives. Some funds aim to protect capital, while others offer aggressive high-risk investing. The variety of funds is striking. There are funds that invest in options and futures, in international securities of all kinds, government-guaranteed mortgages, commodities, particular industries such as energy or new technology, and companies that are emerging from bankruptcy. Index funds that buy and hold broad representations of the market, both domestic and foreign, without active trading or efforts to pick the winners, have been able to demonstrate superior performance in many cases and offer lower fees and transaction costs; their popularity, as a result, is increasing steadily.

Criticism of the mutual fund industry comes from two directions: (1) As the fee managers receive is directly related to the size of the fund's assets, managers may pursue practices that may be adverse to the best interests of the shareholders; and (2) the performance record does not justify the costs paid by the stockholder in management fees and brokerage commissions.

Concerns about conflicts of interest persist. Do managers strive for short-term performance and take high risks to get publicity and appear to be the "hot" fund of the year, just to attract new money at the expense of the shareholders' best interests? Do bond fund managers try to attract new investors by reaching for high yield at the expense of quality and safety? Are transactions more frequent than they should be in order to repay brokers who recommend a fund's shares? Are some funds so broadly diversified that they can offer nothing better than average performance—reduced by operating costs and management fees?

These allegations in many cases are overstatements or unfair. An increasingly sophisticated shareholder community receives protection from the combined impact of government regulation, supervision by unaffiliated directors, the risk of lawsuits for failures of fiduciary responsibility, and the mere threat of large-scale redemptions by disgruntled shareholders.

There is a more meaningful criticism. A long string of careful studies has questioned the ability of most actively managed mutual funds to outperform passive index funds that buy and hold broad representations of the market as a whole, such as the Standard & Poor's 500 stock composite and similar indexes for the bond market and for markets in foreign countries. These and other studies also confirm that past performance is an unreliable guide to what an investment manager may achieve in the future. Although some funds will always outperform the market indexes in any one year, and a few will outperform over a period of years, the data suggest that even the most skilled investor will have little chance, other than pure luck, of identifying these funds in advance.

But there is another side to this argument. Most small investors, operating on their own, have great difficulty in achieving adequate diversification and incur relatively high transactions costs. It is also fair to ask whether they would have both the time and the experience to do as well as professional managers in an increasingly institutionalized market, especially in the more exotic and specialized areas such as government-guaranteed mortgages and international securities that are available through mutual fund investing. Professionally managed funds may not "beat the market" with any consistency, but they may still "beat the individual investor" at the same game. Most individual investors agree, as the explosive growth of the mutual fund makes clear.

References

Bogle, John C., "Selecting Mutual Funds," *Journal of Portfolio Management,* vol. 18, no. 2, Winter 1992, pp. 94–100; Grinblatt, Mark, and Sheridan Titman, "Mutual Fund Performance: An Analysis of Quarterly Portfolio Holdings," *Journal of Business,* vol. 62, no. 3, 1989, pp. 393–416; Heidi Fiske Associates, *The Environment for the Investment Company Industry in the 1990s,* The Investment Company Institute, Washington, D.C., 1990; Investment Company Institute, *Mutual Fund Fact Book,* Published annually in Washington, D.C.; Jensen, Michael J., "The Performance of Mutual Funds in the Period 1945–64," *Journal of Finance,* May 1968, pp. 389–416; Treynor, Jack L., "How to Rate Management of Mutual Funds," *Harvard Business Review,* January–February 1965, pp. 63–75.

(*See also* Closed-end investment companies; Financial institutions)

Peter L. Bernstein

National Bureau of Economic Research

The National Bureau of Economic Research (NBER) is a private, nonprofit, nonpartisan research organization dedicated to improving the understanding of the U.S. economy. With offices in Cambridge, Massachusetts; New York City; and Palo Alto, California; and working arrangements with top economists at universities across the country, the NBER undertakes scientific studies, based on empirical observation, on varied topics of economic interest.

The NBER makes no policy recommendations; instead, it seeks to make objective analyses available to those who are in a position to make policy decisions. In order to ensure its independence and objectivity, the NBER is governed by a board of directors which represents many diverse interests: business, universities, labor, and certain professional organizations (including the American Economic Association, the Committee for Economic Development, and the American Statistical Association). All official NBER publications must be approved by the board.

Major Areas of Research

The research of the NBER falls into several major areas: economic fluctuations; business taxation and finance; financial markets and monetary economics; labor markets; and international trade, finance, and investment. Additional programs and special projects deal with private pensions and social insurance, historical development of the American economy, health and family economics, law and economics, and productivity and technological change. Within these broad categories, specific topics of particular relevance are explored. Studies, made at the end of the 1980s, included an analysis of international saving, the changing economy of Eastern Europe, a comparison of health care costs in the United States and Canada, and an analysis of labor markets in Europe and the United States.

The NBER was organized in 1920 in response to a growing demand within the government and the academic sector for objective determination of the facts bearing upon economic problems and their impartial interpretation. The founding economists included N. I. Stone, Edwin Gay, John Commons, and Wesley Mitchell.

The Bureau's original executive committee chose national income and its distribution as the first NBER research topic—the second topic was business cycles. Within the next few years, a Planning Conference was established, out of which came ideas for the Conference on Research in Income and Wealth and the Universities-National Bureau Committee.

The Conference on Income and Wealth was organized in 1936 by the NBER in cooperation with universities, government agencies, and other research institutions. With the aim of improving the conceptual base of governmental economic statistics, the group reports on methodology, data, and research findings in income and wealth, consumption, saving, and other related areas.

The Universities-National Bureau Committee was originally established so that academic economists and their NBER counterparts could confer periodically on topics of common interest. Conference topics during the latter part of the 1970s included youth unemployment, social security, taxation and fiscal policy, rational expectations and monetary policy, and international macroeconomics.

Over the last 70 years, the NBER has been a pioneer in the development of widely used measures of national income, capital formation, business cycles, and business and economic indicators. Perhaps the Bureau is best known for its business-cycle research: when the U.S. Department of Commerce began publishing its *Business Conditions Digest* in 1961, it acquired its historical data from the NBER. The Bureau continues to assist the government in its analysis of economic fluctuations.

NBER research has also made fundamental contributions to the development of economics as an empirical science. Simon Kuznets won the 1971 Nobel Prize for his NBER work on national income accounting, capital accumulation, and economic growth. In 1976, Milton Friedman was awarded the Nobel Prize for work done at the Bureau on monetary economics and household consumption behavior.

(*See also* Business cycles; National income accounting)

Martin Feldstein

National income accounting

The national income accounts provide information about the operation of the economic system in terms of specific activities such as production, consumption, and capital formation; they show the transactions taking place between enterprises, households, government, and the rest of the world. A simplified example of a set of national income accounts for the United States for the years 1988–1990 is given in Tables 1 through 5.

National Income and Product Account

Table 1 shows the national income and product account for the United States. On the right-hand side of the account, the disposition of the gross output of the economy (gross national product) is shown in terms of the purchases made for private consumption (consumer expenditures), public consumption (government expenditures), and capital formation (gross domestic investment), and the net sales made abroad (exports less imports).

TABLE 1   U.S. National Income and Product Account (Billions of dollars)

	1988	1989	1990		1988	1989	1990
N1 Payments to individuals (P6)	3707	3993	4212	N5 Personal consumption expenditures (P3)	3238	3450	3657
Wages and salaries	2431	2573	2705	Durable goods	458	475	480
Other labor income	226	242	258	Nondurable goods	1060	1130	1194
Proprietor income	354	379	403	Services	1721	1846	1983
Rental income	16	8	7	N6 Government purchases of goods			
Interest	548	643	680	and services (G1)	963	1026	1098
Dividends	102	114	124	Federal	380	400	424
Business transfers	30	32	35	National defense	297	301	314
N2 Payments to government (G7)	912	963	1013	Nondefense	83	99	110
Corporate profits tax	136	135	132	State and local	582	626	674
Indirect taxes	389	414	440				
Employer social insurance	249	264	281	N7 Gross private domestic investment (S1)	741	771	741
Interest	116	119	125	Fixed	721	743	746
Dividends	8	9	10	Nonresidential	488	512	524
Surplus of government enterprises	14	22	25	Structures	140	146	147
				Producers' durables	348	366	377
N3 Retained income (S3)	606	607	609	Residential structures	233	231	222
Undistributed profits	71	49	39	Change in inventories	26	28	−5
Capital consumption allowances	514	554	576				
Inventory and capital consumption				N8 Exports (F1)	552	626	673
adjustments	21	4	−6	Merchandise	324	370	398
N4 Less: Adjustments	352	363	369	Services	228	256	275
Subsidies (G3)	31	29	28	N9 Less: Imports (F2)	626	672	704
Government interest (G4)	199	215	231	Merchandise	450	481	503
Consumer interest (P4)	94	102	108	Services	176	191	201
Statistical discrepancy (S6)	28	17	2				
Gross national income	4874	5201	5465	Gross national product	4874	5201	5465

NOTE: Detail may not add to totals due to rounding.
SOURCE: *Survey of Current Business*, vol. 70, no. 7, July 1990, and vol. 71, no. 7, July 1991.

The left-hand side of the account shows how the funds that are generated by productive activity in the economy are distributed to individuals for their role in the production process and to governments for taxes or other payments, or are retained by producers. The compensation of employees includes the wages, salaries, and fringe benefits paid by employers. Proprietor income includes the income of the self-employed and the net income of unincorporated business. Payments of property income such as rental income, dividends, and interest include not only payments made to individuals but also payments made to nonprofit institutions such as churches and charitable and educational institutions. The tax payments made to government include direct taxes, such as the corporate tax, and indirect taxes, such as sales, excise, and property taxes and customs duties. The government may also receive property income either from interest or from the surpluses generated by government enterprises.

Not all the gross income that is generated by productive activity is paid out by producers, however; some is retained as undistributed profits. In addition to undistributed profits, producers charge depreciation to allow for the using up of their capital goods, and these funds are retained for replacement of capital goods. The reported undistributed profits and depreciation may in periods of rising prices reflect the effect of price changes since businesses use original costs rather than replacement costs in their bookkeeping. For this reason, the national income accounts include inventory and capital consumption adjustments to correct the overstatement of profits arising from price changes.

Finally, some additional adjustment items are required to bring the left-hand side of the national income and product account into balance with the right-hand side, for certain types of payments are made to producers which provide them with income that they in turn distribute to individuals or to government or retain, but that are not considered to be part of the gross national product and so are not included on the right-hand side of the account. These include subsidies and government and consumer debt interest. If the government pays a subsidy to a producer, this will not appear as a sale of a good or service on the right-hand side of the account, but it will provide the producer with income that can be distributed or retained. The total of the left-hand side of the national income and product account will exceed the total of the right-hand side by the amount of the subsidy, and introducing the subsidy as an adjustment will bring the two sides of the account into balance.

Similarly, it is generally agreed by national accountants that government interest and consumer interest do not constitute productive activity, and they should be treated like subsidies. Even after all the conceptual adjustments are made, however, one should not expect the two sides of the accounts to show an exact statistical balance since the estimates for various items are based on different and often conflicting statistical sources. For this reason, a statistical discrepancy item is introduced to bring the two sides of the account into balance.

Personal Income Account

Table 2 shows the personal income account, which provides information about the income received by individuals and nonprofit organizations, and its use. The payments from producers are shown on the right-hand side of the personal income account; they correspond exactly to the same set of transactions as shown on the left-hand side of the national income and product account in Table 1. In addition to these

TABLE 2 U.S. Personal Income Account (Billions of dollars)

	1988	1989	1990
P1 Personal tax and nontax payments (G8)	592	659	699
Federal	415	464	493
Income taxes	406	453	479
Estate and gift taxes	8	9	12
Nontaxes	2	2	2
State and local	177	195	207
Income taxes	90	102	106
Other taxes	15	15	17
Nontaxes	72	78	84
P2 Personal consumption expenditures (N5)	3238	3450	3657
Durable goods	458	475	480
Nondurable goods	1060	1130	1194
Services	1721	1846	1983
P3 Transfers to abroad (F4)	2	1	1
P4 Interest paid by consumers (N4)	94	102	108
P5 Personal saving (S4)	146	172	180
Personal outlays and saving	4071	4384	4645

	1988	1989	1990
P6 Payments from producers (N1)	3707	3993	4212
Wages and salaries	2431	2573	2705
Other labor income	226	242	258
Proprietor income	354	379	403
Rental income	16	8	7
Interest	548	643	680
Dividends	102	114	124
Business transfers	30	32	35
P7 Transfer payments from government (G2)	557	605	660
Federal	426	459	497
Social insurance benefits	373	402	435
Veteran benefits	15	15	16
Other	38	42	46
State and local	132	146	163
Social insurance benefits	43	50	51
Direct relief	82	91	103
Other	7	5	9
P8 Less: Employee social insurance contributions (G9)	194	213	226
Personal income	4071	4384	4645

payments by producers, however, individuals and nonprofit institutions may receive transfer payments made by the government. These include social security benefits, veterans' pensions, welfare relief, and grants made to nonprofit institutions. Total personal income is thus the sum of the income received from producers and transfer payments received from the government.

The disposition of personal income is shown on the left-hand side of the account broken down into (1) payments to the government, (2) consumer expenditures, (3) transfers to abroad, (4) interest paid by consumers, and (5) personal saving. The payments made to government include all the taxes that individuals pay such as income taxes, social security taxes, estate and gift taxes, and other tax and nontax payments such as motor vehicle licenses, fees, and fines.

Consumer expenditures are identical to the consumer expenditure item appearing on the right-hand side of the national income and product account; this item includes the expenditures of nonprofit institutions as well as those of individuals. Transfers abroad represent the net transfers that individuals and nonprofit institutions make to the rest of the world; this would include remittances, gifts, and private relief. Interest paid by consumers is not considered to be a purchase of a service, but corresponds to the same item shown as an adjustment in the left-hand side of the national income and product account. Finally, personal saving is residually determined as the difference between personal income and the total of personal outlays. It represents the amount of personal income which is not spent.

Government account

The government account (Table 3) presents the consolidated receipts and outlays of federal, state, and local government. On the right-hand side of the account, the payments received from producers and individuals are shown; these are, of course, the same items as are shown on the left-hand side of the national income and product account and the personal income account. In similar manner, most of the items appearing as outlays of government on the right-hand side of the government account appear as receipts by producers and individuals. As already noted, government interest and subsidies appear as adjustments in the national income and product account since they are not considered to be payments for services. Government may also make payments abroad, including both interest and transfer payments. Finally the government surplus, like personal savings, is determined residually and is the difference between government receipts and outlays. When outlays exceed receipts, the surplus will be negative, indicating that the government is running a deficit.

Foreign Trade Account

The foreign trade account (Table 4) shows the current account transactions between the various sectors of the U.S. economy and the rest of the world. The sales of goods and services by U.S. producers to the rest of the world are shown on the left-hand side of the account as exports. The right-hand side of the account shows the payments to abroad to purchase imports and the payments abroad made by government and individuals. Net foreign investment in this account is residually determined as the difference between total receipts from abroad and total payments made to abroad.

Gross Saving and Investment Account

Finally, the gross saving and investment account (Table 5) shows gross domestic investment and net foreign investment on the left-hand side of the account, and all

TABLE 3 U.S. Government Account (Billions of dollars)

	1988	1989	1990		1988	1989	1990
G1 Government purchases of goods and services (N6)	963	1028	1098	Government outlays and surplus	1698	1835	1938
Federal	380	400	424				
National defense	297	301	314	G7 Payments from producers (N2)	912	963	1013
Nondefense	83	99	110	Corporate profits tax	136	135	132
State and local	582	626	674	Indirect taxes	389	414	440
				Employer social insurance	249	264	281
G2 Transfer payments to individuals (P7)	557	605	660	Interest	116	119	125
Federal	426	459	497	Dividends	8	9	10
Social insurance benefits	373	402	435	Surplus of government enterprises	14	22	25
Veteran benefits	15	15	16				
Other	38	42	46	G8 Personal tax and nontax payments (P1)	592	659	699
State and local	132	146	143	Federal	415	464	493
Social insurance benefits	43	50	51	Income taxes	406	458	479
Direct relief	82	91	103	Estate and gift taxes	8	9	12
Other	7	5	9	Nontaxes	2	2	2
				State and local	177	195	207
G3 Subsidies paid (N4)	31	29	28	Income taxes	90	102	106
				Other taxes	15	15	17
G4 Government interest paid (N4)	199	215	231	Nontaxes	72	78	84
G5 Payments to abroad (F3)	43	49	54	G9 Employee social insurance contributions (P8)	194	213	226
Interest	30	36	39				
Transfers	13	13	15				
G6 Surplus (S5)	-95	-88	-131				
Federal	-142	-134	-166				
State and local	47	46	35	Government receipts	1698	1835	1938

TABLE 4   U.S. Foreign Trade Account (Billions of dollars)

	1988	1989	1990
F1 Exports (N8)	552	626	673
Merchandise	324	370	398
Services	228	256	275
Total receipts from abroad	552	626	673

	1988	1989	1990
F2 Imports (N9)	626	672	704
Merchandise	450	481	503
Services	176	191	201
F3 Payments to abroad by government (G5)	43	49	54
Interest	30	36	39
Transfers	13	13	15
F4 Net transfers to abroad by individuals (P3)	2	1	1
F5 Net foreign investment (S2)	–119	–96	–86
Total payments to abroad and net foreign investment	552	626	673

TABLE 5   U.S. Gross Saving and Investment Account (Billions of dollars)

	1988	1989	1990
S1 Gross private domestic investment (N7)	747	771	741
Fixed	721	743	746
Nonresidential	488	512	524
Structures	140	146	147
Producers' durables	348	366	377
Residential structures	233	231	222
Change in inventories	26	28	–5
S2 Net foreign investment (F5)	–119	–96	–86
Gross investment	628	675	655

	1988	1989	1990
S3 Retained income (N3)	606	607	609
Undistributed profits	71	49	39
Capital consumption allowances	514	554	576
Inventory and capital consumption adjustments	21	4	–6
S4 Personal saving (P5)	146	172	180
S5 Government surplus (G6)	–95	–88	–131
Federal	–142	–134	–166
State and local	47	46	35
S6 Statistical discrepancy (N4)	–28	–17	–2
Gross saving and discrepancy	628	674	656

the saving items (i.e., retained income, personal saving, and government surplus) and the statistical discrepancy on the right-hand side. The system of accounts is fully articulated in that transactions appear in two different accounts, and every account is balanced either by a residual saving entry or by a statistical discrepancy.

The national income accounts record the transactions that take place in the economy and thus reflect the current prices that exist in any given period. As a consequence, the year-to-year change will be the result of both the price and the quantity changes. In order to measure the real change in output occurring over time, the current-price transactions data are deflated to yield constant-price data. Generally speaking, it is the final sales of the gross national product (right-hand side of Table 1) which are most often shown in constant dollars.

History

National income accounting has been an evolutionary development resulting from early attempts to measure the income of the nation by such men as William Petty and Gregory King in the late seventeenth century. The worldwide development of national income measurement has been chronicled by Paul Studenski. In the United States, the National Bureau of Economic Research pioneered the estimation of national income in the 1920s and 1930s under the leadership of Wesley Clair Mitchell, Simon Kuznets, and other scholars. Since the mid-1930s, the Department of Commerce has published statistics on national income, and since 1947, full sets of national income accounts have been presented annually. The United Nations published an annual *Yearbook of National Accounts Statistics,* containing data for over 100 countries.

Uses and Limitations

Almost all countries of the world currently prepare some form of national income accounts on their economies. Centrally planned economies prepare estimates of net material product, which differs from national income because it excludes the value of nonmaterial services such as public administration and defense, personal and professional services, and similar activities. Where foreign transactions are important, as in many European countries, gross domestic product (GDP) is more frequently used than GNP because, unlike the GNP, the GDP excludes output produced abroad to which residents have a claim.

These national accounts are used as the basis for countries' fiscal and monetary policy and provide information on the rate of growth, the degree of inflation, and the interrelations among households, government, and foreign trade. The national income accounts have become as important to countries as business accounts have become to enterprises.

It is sometimes argued that national income statistics are misleading and deficient since they do not adequately measure the welfare of a nation. On the one hand, it is pointed out that such things as environmental pollution, the effects of crime, and other disamenities are not deducted from output. On the other hand, nonmarket activities, increases in leisure, advances in medical knowledge, and the introduction of superior products are not included in the measurement of output. These arguments are, of course, valid and point out the limitations of national income accounting statistics. These statistics should not be used to measure welfare, a use for which they are not intended. Nevertheless, they have been found to be very useful in providing valuable information about the operation of the economic system.

References

Carson, Carol, "The History of the National Income and Product Accounts," *Review of Income and Wealth,* ser. 21, June 1975; Eisner, Robert, *The Total Incomes System of Accounts,* University of Chicago, Chicago, 1989; Kendrick, John, *Economic Accounts and Their Uses,* McGraw-Hill, New York, 1972; Ruggles, Richard, and Nancy D. Ruggles, "Integrated Economic Accounts for the United States, 1946–1980," *Survey of Current Business,* vol. 62, no. 5, 1982; United Nations, *Yearbook of National Accounts Statistics,* annually; U.S. Department of Commerce, "The National Income and Product Accounts of the United States," *Survey of Current Business,* July issue, annually.

(*See also* Gross domestic product; System of national accounts)

Richard Ruggles and Nancy D. Ruggles

Nationalization of industry

In 1992, a working definition of "nationalization of industry" might be "the opposite of privatization." As little as a few years ago, national, or public, ownership of enterprises engaged in commercial activity was widespread throughout many nations of the world. Within the formerly communist nations, virtually all ownership of the means of production of course was vested in the state. But among the democracies of Western Europe, the state typically owned significant business activity. Indeed, most enterprises engaged in public utilities and transportation in these nations still are state-owned, and publicly owned firms participate actively in other sectors. Among developing nations, that the government should own and control enterprises engaged in the production of exportable natural resources was an act of faith during the 1970s (Seidman, 1975). Even in the private-market-oriented United States, state-owned enterprises operate public utilities in some areas of the nation, including most mass transit services. And although in the United States many private firms operate in the utilities sectors, these sectors tend to be heavily regulated by the state.

State ownership or regulation of natural monopolies has been justified as a means to prevent private firms from engaging in monopolistic pricing or other socially non-desirable modes of behavior. However, growing evidence during the 1970s and 1980s suggested that state-owned monopolies very often exercise their monopoly power as abusively as do private-owned ones. Furthermore, state-owned firms whose monopoly position is accomplished via the fiat of the state very often turn into inefficient and poorly run bureaucracies.

Extensive nationalization of nonnatural monopoly industries in industrial nations has often resulted from the actions of a political movement that ascribes economic benefit to public ownership of the means of production. In Great Britain, for example, the Labor Party during the 1960s and 1970s adhered to a philosophy of democratic socialism, and sought nationalization of certain industries under this program on the belief that this would increase economic efficiency and improve the distribution of income (Robson, 1960). In the early 1980s, after the Socialist Party came to power in France, a number of large French firms were nationalized partly on the basis of a belief that these firms were accumulating huge hidden profits that could be tapped in order to finance new social programs. This belief was quickly shown to be wrong; most of the newly nationalized firms, rather than contributing to the public purse, instead proved to be a drain upon it. In communist countries, of course, private ownership of business enterprises has been viewed as the root of all social and economic evil, and thus public ownership has been all-pervasive.

Noneconomic Considerations

The rationale for nationalization of industry, however, is not always based on economic considerations. Italy has a long record, for example, of rescuing bankrupt private firms by placing them under state ownership and control. This occurred even under the fascist government of the 1930s. Firms thus nationalized have included many for which, arguably, liquidation would have been an economically more sound alternative. In Italy (and elsewhere), publicly owned but economically unviable enterprises can be sustained only by subsidization, which raises serious questions pertaining to economic efficiency.

In a number of developing nations, many nationalization efforts during the 1970s and early 1980s were specifically targeted toward foreign-owned firms. Although such nationalization might be justified on economic grounds, expropriation of foreign firms often represents a political response by a government to nationalistic or xenophobic sentiments within a nation. This is especially likely to be the case where foreign firms play a major or dominant role in the economy of the nation (Moran, 1973). Efforts to establish associations between the socioeconomic characteristics of a nation and the propensity of the nation to expropriate targeted foreign firms (as opposed to broad efforts to nationalize whole industries or sectors irrespective of ownership) have largely been inconclusive (Kobrin, 1979). This underscores the noneconomic nature of many expropriatory actions. Some evidence exists to suggest, however, that expropriation is more likely to take place in industries characterized by mature technologies than in younger industries (Kobrin, 1980). At any rate, following the emergence of the Third World debt crisis in the early 1980s, the nationalizations stopped, and by the early 1990s many of those nations that had led the charge against multinational firms during the 1970s were actively seeking foreign direct investment.

It should be noted that nationalistic sentiments with respect to foreign-owned firms can be as strong in advanced industrialized nations as in developing ones. For example, in Canada sentiments against U.S. ownership of much of Canadian industry were rampant in the late 1970s, even though it is not at all clear that the economic performance of U.S.-owned firms in Canada was anything but positive.

Economic Efficiency

The presence of nationalized firms in mixed economies such as those of some Western European nations raises a number of issues pertaining to economic efficiency. Under neoclassical economic thinking, efficiency is maximized if numerous enterprises openly compete for sales of output and procurement of factor inputs in unregulated markets (unregulated here implies both no state regulation and no collusion among enterprises or sellers of factor inputs) and if each enterprise strives to maximize profits. In a state-owned enterprise, however, individual managers may feel less bound to maximize profit than would managers in a private firm, especially if the state-owned enterprise receives a government subsidy or is subject to evaluation of performance by national authorities on criteria other than economic ones. Such a relaxation on the part of managers doubtlessly would reduce efficiency, particularly in cases where the firm was subject to little or no competition.

Defenders of state ownership of industry maintain, however, that nationalized firms can confer upon the community external benefits that private firms would not take into account and that justify behavior other than profit maximization. It is not difficult to conceive of such externalities (abatement of pollution, for example), but it is difficult to quantify a trade-off between these and the efficiency losses that might result from non-profit-maximizing behavior. The case probably can be made that where such externalities exist, the firm should be compensated for the cost of bearing them but otherwise ought to strive to maximize profits (see papers by Arrow and Raiffa in Vernon and Aharoni, 1980).

Even if it were to be determined that the state-owned enterprise should strive to maximize profits and not be the recipient of direct government subsidies, some shielding from the competitive rigors of the market is nonetheless likely to ensue from the mere fact of state ownership. This is especially true in capital markets. In these markets, it is likely to be perceived that the creditworthiness of the nationalized firm is implicitly guaranteed by the state. Thus, the riskiness of the state-owned firm would be perceived by the market as less than that of an otherwise identical private firm, which would reduce capital costs to the former firm. The resulting implicit subsidy would result in some distortion in the allocation of resources. It is possible also that state-owned firms may pay higher-than-market wages or grant extraordinary employment security to employees, although this is certainly not always the case. Despite this possibility, Wiseman (1963) suggests that there is little evidence in British experience to suppose that relations between labor and employer were better in state-owned enterprises than in privately owned ones.

Whatever the trade-offs between loss of economic efficiency and external gains that might ensue from nationalization of industry, it is clear that in the 1980s public sentiment in many nations turned away from advocacy of public ownership. In Great Britain and Sweden, for example, social democratic parties were voted out of office in 1979 and replaced by conservative governments committed to denationalization of industry. Following nationalizations in the early 1980s, the French socialist government was talking about privatization in the late 1980s, although little of this actually occurred. Numerous developing countries however actually have privatized formerly state-owned enterprises, and, of course, in the late 1980s, communism collapsed in the nations of Eastern Europe and the former Soviet Union.

References

Coase, R. H., "The Problem of Social Cost," *Journal of Law and Economics,* vol. 3, 1960, pp. 1–4; Friedmann, Wolfgang (ed.), *Public and Private Enterprise in Mixed Economies,* Columbia University Press, New York, 1974; Gunnerman, Jon P., *The Nation-State and Transnational Corporations in Conflict with Special Reference to Latin America,* Praeger, New York, 1975; Hanson, Albert H. (ed.), *Nationalization: A Book of Readings,* Macmillan, London, 1963; Kobrin, Stephen J., "Political Factors Underlying the Propensity to Expropriate Foreign Enterprises," MIT Sloan School of Management, Cambridge, Mass., 1979, mimeograph; Kobrin, Stephen J., "Foreign Enterprise and Forced Divestment in LDC's," *International Organization,* vol. 34, 1980, pp. 65–88; Moran, Theodore H., "Transnational Strategies of Protection and Defense by Multinational Corporations: Spreading the Risk and Raising the Cost for Nationalization in National Resources," *International Organization,* vol. 27, 1973, pp. 273–288; Moran, Theodore H., *Multinational Corporations and the Politics of Dependence: Copper in Chile,* Princeton University Press, Princeton, N.J., 1979; Robson, William A., *Nationalized Industry and Public Ownership,* University of Toronto Press, Toronto, 1960; Seidman, Ann (ed.), *Natural Resources and National Welfare: The Case of Copper,* Praeger, New York, 1975; Shepard, William G., "Cross Subsidiary and Allocation in Public Firms," *Oxford Economic Papers,* New Series, vol. 16, 1964, pp. 132–160; Vernon, Raymond, and Yair Aharoni (eds.), *State-Owned Enterprise in the Western Economies,* St. Martin's, New York, 1980;

Weekly, J. K., "Expropriation of U.S. Multinational Investments," *MSU Business Topics,* vol. 25, 1977, pp. 27–36; Wiseman, Jack, "Guidelines for Public Enterprise: A British Experiment," *Southern Economic Journal,* vol. 30, 1963, pp. 39–48.

(*See also* Communism; Marxism; Multinational corporation; Socialism)

Edward M. Graham

Negative income tax

The negative income tax is a program for a guaranteed minimum income that has received considerable attention from economists in the United States in the last two decades. It would operate through the federal income tax system and would provide income maintenance payments based solely on low income, in contrast to existing programs that use such criteria as age or family composition, sometimes in combination with need, in the determination of eligibility.

The three essential characteristics that may vary among negative income tax proposals are (1) the amount of the income guarantee, which varies with family size; (2) the rate at which existing family income is reduced (or taxed) when it exceeds zero; and (3) the break-even level of income at which eligibility for a grant disappears. Proponents generally favor taxing existing income at a rate less than 100 percent, in order to preserve incentives to work. In fact, with a tax rate of less than 100 percent, the family always benefits from more earnings, as the accompanying table (illustrating a negative income tax with a guarantee of $5000 a year for a family of four and a tax rate of 50 percent) indicates:

Earnings	Grant	Total family income
0	$5,000	$5,000
$2,000	4,000	6,000
4,000	3,000	7,000
6,000	2,000	8,000
8,000	1,000	9,000
10,000	0	10,000

With a 50 percent tax rate, the break-even point will always be twice the guaranteed income. Thus, such a plan designed to eliminate the poverty gap—that is, the extent to which the family's income falls below the federally determined poverty line—would be very costly. With a poverty line of $6700 for a nonfarm family of four (in 1979), the break-even point would be $13,400 and would bring almost half of all families into the program. Partly for this reason, and partly because of concern over work incentives, most serious proposals have advocated a guaranteed income below the poverty line, or in some cases a higher tax rate.

History

Rhys Williams (1943) of Great Britain is credited with having first proposed a guaranteed minimum income, with a plan of the social dividend type—differing from the negative income tax in providing for a standard government allowance for all families, and then taxing preallowance income so that the tax would be less than the allowance for poor families and more than the allowance for nonpoor families. The first proposal to receive much attention in the United States was made by Milton Friedman (1962), who called for a negative income tax that would replace all existing income maintenance programs, including social security. Although support for the negative income tax grew among economists in the 1960s, the majority favored replacing existing public assistance programs, but not social insurance, by the negative income tax.

In January 1968, the President appointed a Commission on Income Maintenance Programs to study income maintenance policies. However, by the time the Commission issued its report (in the fall of 1969) calling for a "universal income supplement" plan of a negative income tax type, a new President had been elected and had sent a proposal for a family assistance program to Congress. The proposal, calling for a federally guaranteed minimum income for families with children, and for the aged, disabled, and blind, passed the House but was defeated in the Senate Finance Committee. Congress did, however, enact the Supplementary Security Income Program, providing a guaranteed minimum income for the aged, disabled, and blind, in 1972, and also provided for a modest tax credit for low earners in 1974. Not until 1988 was a major revision of Aid to Families with Dependent Children (AFDC) enacted, with emphasis on requiring states to provide training and job programs, but with the amount of welfare payments left to the states.

Pros and Cons

Proponents of a negative income tax argue that existing income maintenance programs fail to reach many poor people. Moreover, the major existing public assistance program, AFDC, is administered in a punitive manner in many states and has other serious weaknesses as follows:

1. The financial burden is inequitable, falling heavily on large cities with high welfare recipient rates.

2. AFDC fails to help the working poor and may encourage family splitting because, with certain exceptions, aid is available only if one parent is incapacitated or absent from the home.

3. Earnings are taxed too heavily, resulting in disincentives to work.

4. Wide variations in payment levels among states are alleged to induce poor families to migrate to states with comparatively high payments.

Opponents object to expanding the scope and cost of welfare payments. Some economists are skeptical on the grounds that (1) family splitting might be encouraged, (2) income tax provisions would have to be extensively revised to provide for a smooth transition between negative and positive tax payments, and (3) the combination of cash payments plus food stamps plus housing subsidies would seriously impair work incentives unless all but cash payments were abolished. There are other, more technical objections as well.

Meanwhile, the negative income tax has been the subject of the most extensive social science experiments ever conducted, under federal financing but carried out by nonpublic research groups. The earlier experiments (in New Jersey and elsewhere) focused primarily on the impact on work incentives and indicated a very slight tendency for work effort to be reduced as a result of income maintenance. Later experiments in Seattle and Denver showed more significant negative effects on work incentives, along with a greater tendency for couples in the experimental group than for those in the control group to split up (Spiegelman and Yaeger, 1979).

The negative income tax has received less attention abroad than in this country, probably because all other industrial countries have family allowance systems, most of which operate somewhat like social dividend plans except that payments are made only on behalf of children. In Great Britain, however, the Conservative government proposed a credit income tax plan in 1972.

The prospect of adoption of a negative income tax in the near future in the United States appears most unfavorable for several reasons: (1) the high cost of a program with a significant income guarantee in the face of a severe budget deficit, and (2) the somewhat unfavorable results of the experiment, especially in a Seattle and Denver. The issues involved will, however, continue to be of interest to economists for both their welfare and macroeconomic implications. Meanwhile, the social experiments have provided a wealth of data illuminating theories of economic motivation.

References

Friedman, Milton, *Capitalism and Freedom,* University of Chicago Press, Chicago, 1962; Masters, Stanley, and Irwin Garfinkel, *Estimating the Labor Supply Effects of Income-Maintenance Alternatives,* Academic Press, New York, 1977; Report of the President's Commission on Income Maintenance Programs, *Poverty amid Plenty,* 1969; Spiegelman, Robert G., and K. W. Yaeger, *An Overview of the Seattle and Denver Income Maintenance Experiments,* Stanford Research Institute, Menlo Park, Calif., 1979, unpublished paper; Williams, Rhys, *Something to Look Forward to,* MacDonald, London, 1943.

(*See also* Poverty; Social security)

Margaret S. Gordon

Neighborhood effects (*see* Externalities)

Neoclassical economics

The most remarkable feature of neoclassical economics is that it reduces many broad categories of market phenomena to considerations of individual choice and, in this way, suggests that the science of economics can be firmly grounded on the basic individual act of subjectively choosing among alternatives.

Neoclassical economics began with the so-called marginalist revolution in value theory that emerged toward the end of the nineteenth century. Strictly speaking, neoclassical economics is not a school of thought (in the sense of a well-defined group of economists following a single great master) but more a loose amalgam of subschools of thought, each revolving around such acknowledged masters as Alfred Marshall in England, Léon Walras in France, and Carl Menger in Austria. What these subschools have in common is the importance they attach to explaining the coordinating features of market processes in terms of plans and subjective evaluations carried out by individuals in the market subject to the constraints of technological knowledge, social custom and practice, and scarcity of resources.

The Subschools

In England, Marshall's appointment to the chair of political economy at Cambridge University in 1885 marked the start of the Cambridge school—a variant of neoclassical economics that stressed continuity with the past achievements of the classical school, especially the economics of David Ricardo and John Stuart Mill. In 1890 Marshall published his *Principles of Economics,* which demonstrated how the forces that determine the normal prices of commodities can be explained by means of supply and demand in the context of firms struggling to survive within industries. Marshall's disciples included A. C. Pigou, D. H. Robertson, Ralph Hawtrey, and to some extent the controversial John Maynard Keynes. (During the 1930s, Keynes turned against his old master by explaining how subjective evaluations can lead to discoordinating market processes and the unemployment of labor and disuse of capital.)

In France, Walras founded the general equilibrium school with the publication of his *Elements of Pure Economics* (1874). This school would eventually take root in Lausanne, Switzerland, through the contributions of Vilfredo Pareto, especially in his *Cours d'économie politique* (1896–1897). Some of Walras's teaching reached England by way of A. L. Bowley's *Mathematical Groundwork of Economics* (1924). Like Marshall, Walras and his followers were concerned with a supply and demand account of market pricing, but Walras went somewhat beyond Marshall and investigated the mathematical conditions under which all markets could be in equilibrium simultaneously.

In Austria, Carl Menger founded the Austrian school with the publication of his *Principles of Economics* (1871). Subsequent professors at the University of Vienna, such as Friedrich von Wieser, Eugen von Böhm-Bawerk, and later Ludwig von Mises and Friedrich A. von Hayek, focused on the essential problems of economic organization by starting with Menger's insights about the importance of economizing action in shaping economic institutions in the market. Among Austrians, the important task of economic reasoning is to disaggregate economic phenomena so that the events can be made intelligible in terms of basic market forces of supply and demand operating through the decisions of individuals.

Demand versus Supply

The basic theme of marginalist economics, as emphasized by William Stanley Jevons in his *Theory of Political Economy* (1871), is that an individual's estimation of worth of any object or service depends on the least most important use that would go unsatisfied should that individual have to give up that unit. Jevons, Marshall, and Walras each recognized the link between the amount of supply in an individual's possession and the intensity of the subjective benefit experienced, but it was the Austrian school, and later the economists at the London School of Economics during the 1930s, who carefully developed the full implications of the idea that every choice necessarily involves a forgone opportunity. From this the neoclassical school defined rationality in the market as involving a constant comparison and substitutions of bundles of commodities (and services) until one (affordable) bundle is found where the satisfaction received from the marginal dollar spent on all lines of expenditure is equal. A rise in price encourages substitution away from the more expensive commodity in favor of its alternatives. The principle of substitution (as defined by Marshall) implies that at higher prices the rate of individual demand never increases—called the first law of demand. The second law of demand is simply that the substitution effect is greater the longer the time the market has to adjust. The notion of substitution is potentially one of the most radical of all ideas in the social sciences and has been used to criticize much of current social thought based on the misleading notion that national "needs" exist in some fixed unalterable form.

On the supply side of the market, producers are viewed as constantly trying to discover ways of substituting one bundle of resources for another in an effort to find the cheapest way of producing any amount of supply and thereby to survive in the market. Marshall developed the model of firms and industries in which unexpected shifts in demand caused firms to adjust their output gradually, first in the short run by exploiting their capacity more intensively and second in the long run by altering their capacity altogether. As time went by, Marshall hypothesized, firms become more pliable in both their size and organization, and the character of equilibrium between supply and demand becomes more firmly grounded. Marshall also allowed for learning and discovery of new forms of economic organization to encourage economies of scale. The first law of supply is that the increase in quantity will be greater the greater the increase in price; and the second law of supply is that for any given price rise, the increase in the quantity supplied will be greater the longer the time the market is permitted to adjust.

Marginal Productivity and Economic Efficiency

Neoclassical economists estimate the worth of one resource when used in conjunction with several others by looking at the marginal productivity. A resource's marginal productivity is found by varying that factor's amount, holding other factors constant, and observing what happens to output. The more output is diminished by the removal of one unit of a factor, the greater is that factor's marginal product. It remained for Phillip Wicksteed to show in 1898 that, in the absence of economies or diseconomies of scale, when each factor is paid the equivalent of its marginal product, the joint product of all the factors will be paid out without anything left over. Later neoclassical writers such as Paul Douglas in the 1920s and Robert Solow in the 1960s used this theory of factor pricing to measure the contributions of labor, capital, and innovation to the growth of American per capita income. Douglas's startling finding (*Theory of Wages,* 1934)—that the relative share of the national dividend received by the workers has remained fairly constant over time—served as a serious blow to the then-popular Marxist claim that as capitalism developed, the working class got a smaller share of a growing pie.

Neoclassical economics bases a great deal of its policy analysis on a particular notion of economic efficiency. If it can be shown that policy A achieves a certain objective with fewer scarce resources than policy B, then policy A is preferred to policy B and it is described as more efficient. When comparing the combined value of resources, one must compare the opportunity costs incurred by the resource owners themselves in making marginal units of supply available—what is termed marginal cost—with the value provided to the consumers when the resources are applied in their present applications. By assuming that market prices are (rough) indexes of value and, therefore, an acceptable basis for policy analysis, neoclassical economists evaluate programs in terms of their measured costs and benefits. Policies generating greater benefits than costs are said to be economically efficient.

In the 1940s neoclassical policy analysis reached a plateau with the articulation of the compensation principle derived from a pattern of reasoning first expressed by Pareto. The claim is made that particular forms of government intervention are justified if those who gain wealth by the intervention gain at least enough to compensate the losers of wealth, even if no actual attempt to compensate is made. By this criterion many politically popular government policies cannot be justified. Tariffs and other barriers to free international trade, for example, impose more harm on buyers than the limited benefits they convey to local suppliers. But the losers are spread out and diffused, while the gainers are few in number and lobby for trade barriers on foreign products. So these uneconomic policies remain politically popular.

Criticism of Neoclassical Economics

In the 1970s neoclassical economics came under attack for a variety of reasons. Reform liberals contend that the aforementioned efficiency criterion ignores considerations of equity because market prices already imply a particular underlying distribution of wealth which the neoclassical writers take as a given. A complete policy analysis must start with an analysis of who ought to own wealth and for what purposes. Another group of critics, the neo-Ricardian school, claims that neoclassical economics has betrayed the mission of the older classical school because of the neoclassical school's insistence on the supply and demand model. According to Piero Sraffa and his disciples, relative demand or utility plays virtually no role in defining relative commodity prices in long-run equilibrium and, therefore, plays little part in determining the social distribution of wealth. Here the technological conditions that surround the production of certain types of goods, especially those consumed by the working class, affect the distribution of income, and, therefore, the task of economic theory is to explain how surplus value is extracted from the working class and used by others. According to the Sraffa group, neoclassical economics represents an aberration from the more profound analysis allegedly offered by David Ricardo and further developed by Karl Marx. The Sraffa–neo-Ricardian school is quite content to do away with individual valuation in the marketplace and concentrate instead on the objective or technological conditions of long-run equilibrium. The attempt is to show that the distribution of income after some basic subsistence allotment to the workers is politically determined and therefore plays no part in the reproduction of annual output within the framework of capitalist social institutions.

Among neoclassical writers, the modern Austrian school adherents such as Israel Kirzner, Murray N. Rothbard, and Ludwig Lachmann are less concerned with the details of equilibrium positions such as described at length in Paul Samuelson's *Foundations of Economic Analysis* (1948) and more concerned with the process by which markets adjust or fail to adjust to change. Modern Austrians challenge attempts to measure opportunity costs by claiming that it is illegitimate to assume that market prices are equilibrium prices. They therefore reject the methodological basis of cost-benefit analysis.

In summary, the neoclassical school offers a remarkably diverse body of concepts to explain the operation of the market in terms of the twin forces of supply and demand. In terms of its admittedly limited concept of economic efficiency (estimated in econometric studies by assuming that market prices are indexes of costs and benefits), neoclassical economics offers a basis for criticizing the most wasteful of government policies by showing that less expensive alternatives exist.

References

Becker, Gary S., *Economic Theory,* Knopf, Chicago, 1971; Buchanan, James, *Cost and Choice,* Markham, Chicago, 1969; Dobb, Maurice, *Theories of Value and Distribution since Adam Smith: Ideology and Economic Theory,* Cambridge University Press, Cambridge, 1973; Ferguson, C. E., *The Neoclassical Theory of Production and Distribution,* Cambridge University Press, Cambridge, 1971; Gomes, L., *Neoclassical International Economics,* St. Martin's, New York, 1990; Moss, Laurence S., and John M. Virgo (eds.), "Carl Menger and Austrian Economics," *Atlantic Economic Journal,* vol. 6, no. 3, September 1978, pp. 1–69; Tullberg, R. W., *Alfred Marshall in Retrospect,* Elgar, U. K., 1990.

(*See also* Austrian economics; Cambridge school; Classical school; Cost-benefit analysis; Demand; Marshallian economics; Opportunity cost, Supply; Utility)

Laurence S. Moss

Neoinstitutionalists (*see* Institutional economics)

Net investment (*see* Capital formation)

New industrial state

The new industrial state, as this term has come into use, describes the now-accomplished transition from the dominant entrepreneurial firm of classical literature to the large and highly organized corporate enterprise of the modern economy. By common calculation, about 60 percent of all industrial activity is now in the hands of fewer than a thousand great firms. In these firms, individual motivation has given way to that of a highly organized complex of technicians, other specialists, and the guiding officers who constitute the management. To them has been given the designation the "technostructure."

The motivation of the technostructure turns on its search for stability and a controlled market environment. Planning and control, in some measure, replace spontaneous initiative. The technostructure has a central and indispensable role in much modern technological development, commanding as it does an extensive range of specialized talent.

Involved here is a sharp conflict between established economic theory and the reality of the modern technocratic enterprise. Market control is essential for corporate planning. Present is also what has been called the approved contradiction. Established theory assumes profit maximization by the owners of the enterprise—this, indeed, is still basic in all economic instruction and formal theory. If true, however, this means that the technostructure, in common parlance the management, possessing the power in the enterprise, nonetheless forgos maximization for itself to accomplish it on behalf of the owners or stockholders, these latter being effectively powerless and largely unknown. Or does it? Recent experience suggests a strong disposition by management to maximize returns for itself. And corporate raiding in pursuit of these returns and leveraged buyouts in their defense affirm the point. So also does everyday comment on creative compensation and perquisites. In modern capitalism, profit maximization or some of it is not for the owners of capital but for the heads of the technostructure who hold the decisive power.

The concept of the industrial state embraces other aspects of an economy that comprises large corporate entities. These include the companionate relation of the great business firm to the state and its support to the defense establishment and military expenditure. The tendency to bureaucratic sclerosis in the large corporate enterprise is also a central fact of the industrial state, as is the proliferation of layers of management. Proof of the latter lies in the way they are "shed" in circumstances of economic distress. In contrast with the power-dominant and strongly acquisitive entrepreneur of an earlier period, the trade union is seen to have a declining role in the industrial state.

In recent times and with the end of the cold war, a question arises as to the military support to the technostructure and vice versa. On this the jury is still out: the more general association of industrial, bureaucratic, and political power remains strong.

A more recent manifestation of this association is the support that Japan and, in lesser measure, Germany accord their civilian industrial complex in the form of research, financial, and infrastructure investment—and also, in the case of Japan, some direct and indirect trade protection. In the higher development of the industrial state the relationship between government and industry is increasingly close.

Reference

Galbraith, John K., *The New Industrial State,* 4th ed., Houghton Mifflin, Boston, 1985.

John Kenneth Galbraith

Nonmonetary overinvestment theory (*see* Juglar cycle)

Normative economics

In economics, as in all social sciences, a clear line has been drawn between the positive and the normative, that is, between the study of how things are in fact and how they ought to be. Positive economics is independent of any value judgment, while normative economics concerns itself with how our economic lives ought to be arranged; what goods and services ought to be produced; how the production of such goods and services should be organized, and by whom; how ownership of productive factors such as land, labor, capital, or material inputs should be distributed; and how income and, therefore, the consumption of goods and services should be distributed among members of the larger society including other nations of the world as well as unborn future generations. In other words, normative economics looks at the utilization of resources, their organization into productive activities, and the distribution of their benefits among people presently existing and yet to be born, and asks, "Are some arrangements better than others?" and "Is there a best arrangement?" In order to approach such questions, criteria are needed for what is good or best. Such criteria depend on the political, philosophical, and theological perspective of the appraiser. Within the mainstream of the Western liberal tradition a few principles of appraisal have acquired near-universal allegiance as being helpful, though not necessarily decisive, for judgment of an economic system.

Three Principles of Appraisal

The first of these principles is that an economy is to be judged by the outcomes it produces, that is, specifically by the bundles of goods and services (of all types privately or publicly produced and privately or publicly consumed) it effectively assigns to individuals at the various times throughout their lives. (A contrasting view might be that outcomes are not the primary object to be appraised, but rather that the processes of transition from one state to another are primary.) Thus, modern economists would ask, "Is this particular assignment of goods and services good; can it be improved upon within the resource limitations available?"

The second basic principle is that for appraising the assignment of goods to people, the individual is the only judge of how the goods and services affect the individual's well-being—the so-called doctrine of consumer sovereignty. (The principle has limits; it would seem to break down if applied to children and the senile, and many believe the effects of some activities on the welfares of some people should be ignored. For example, even though person A is offended by person B's private religious practices, the effect should be ignored.)

The third principle of normative economics is that judgments of the overall or social goodness of economic outcomes depend solely on the corresponding set of individual evaluations of individual welfares and not, for example, on an organic concept of society or the state.

The Pareto Criterion

Given that economic states of the world are to be appraised on the basis of individuals' self-evaluations of their own outcome positions and on nothing else, a widely accepted criterion for judging alternative states is the so-called Pareto-improvement criterion. This criterion proposes that one situation (call it X) is Pareto-preferred or superior to another (call it Y) if no one is worse off at X than at Y and if at least one person is better off at X than at Y. If both X and Y were economically feasible states, then the Pareto-improvement criterion would judge that the configuration of resources, production, and distribution of goods at X was superior to that at Y.

In the accompanying figure the curve PP indicates the limit on economically feasible welfare outcomes between two individuals. All points to the northeast of X are Pareto-superior to X, including point S, point T, and all points in between them on the PP curve. Point W is Pareto-superior to X but economically infeasible. The Pareto criterion will judge any point below the PP curve to be inferior to some point or points on the curve; similarly, it will judge any point on the curve to be superior to some points beneath it. It will not, however, compare points on the curve—S versus T, for instance—nor will it compare any points such as X and R or X and V. In short, the Pareto criterion does not imply any judgments of the desirability of absolute redistribution (relative distribution possibly, since A at point Y might be said to be much better off relative to B than at point X).

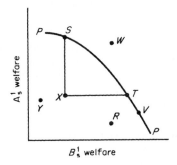

The Pareto criterion, however, is incomplete in two respects. First, it does not allow comparisons between social states when one or more persons gain at the expense of others; and second, it does not identify the best, or optimal, social state among those available (the entire curve *PP* in the figure). In order to allow for the first shortcoming, many believe that a criterion of potential Pareto improvement is satisfactory. This roughly is the criterion that one state *V* is preferable to another *X* if the people who benefit from the change could compensate the people who lose from the change so that all groups would end up as net beneficiaries. The potential Pareto criterion is implicit in all benefit-cost analysis, but it is not universally accepted because (aside from some technical difficulties associated with it) it requires only the potential for compensation, not actual compensation. Thus, the potential Pareto criterion could recommend a move from *X* to *V*, even though *A* would be utterly impoverished, simply because *B* could more than compensate *A* for that loss.

The Best Social Welfare Function

At best, even if the potential Pareto criterion is accepted, our norms for evaluating alternative economic states would be incomplete. We still would have no basis for judging movements along the curve *PP* where some people gain, others lose, and no compensation could redistribute gains so that all benefit. Within the realm of individualistic normative criteria several formulas for weighting or counting individual welfares so as to arrive at a social welfare function have been proposed. Among these are the Benthamite-utilitarian function and those attributed to Bergson, Nash, Arrow, and Rawls. All attempt to identify the best alternative social state out of a given environment, e.g., the best of the set contained by *PP* in the diagram.

Thus, modern normative economics has become concerned with how different axioms and assumptions lead to different rules for choice of outcomes. Three examples may elucidate the character of the logical connections which preoccupy modern normative economics. As a first example, Nash (1950) proposed that social welfare is best represented as the product of individual utilities. His proposal depends crucially on the assumption that the welfare level of each person in a completely autarkic, noncooperative economy is highly relevant to the division of welfare when individuals cooperate. As a second case, Arrow's (1970) concept of a social welfare function crucially involves the assumption that no possible set of circumstances should produce a dictator (i.e., an individual whose preferences govern social choice irrespective of others' preferences). And lastly, there is Rawls's (1971) notion that the best economic organization and distribution of goods is that which would be unanimously endorsed by a society of individuals if a vote were taken before anyone knew what his or her place in the economic order would be.

References

Arrow, Kenneth J., *Social Choice and Individual Values*, 2d ed., Yale University Press, New Haven, Conn., 1970; Boulding, Kenneth E., "Welfare Economics," in Bernard F. Haley (ed.), *Survey of Contemporary Economic Theory*, vol. II, Irwin, Homewood, Ill., 1952; Nash, J. F., "The Bargaining Problem," *Econometrica*, vol. xviii, no. 2, 1950, pp. 155–162; Pigou, Arthur C., *The Economics of Welfare*, Macmillan, New York, 1932; Rawls, John, *Theory of Justice*, Harvard University Press, Cambridge, Mass., 1971.

(*See also* Capitalism; Communism; Comparative economic systems, an overview; Marxism; Socialism; Utility; Welfare economics)

Martin C. McGuire

North American Free Trade Area (*see* Economic blocs)

Open-end investment company (*see* Mutual funds)

Open-market operations

In the U.S. economy of the post–World War II decades, open-market operations have been the chief instrument of Federal Reserve monetary policy. The term "open-market operations" refers to central bank purchases and sales of government securities in the national money market for the immediate purpose of affecting the availability and cost of bank reserves, but with the broader aim of affecting the availability and cost of money and credit in the economy.

Complementing open-market operations in the United States are two other major instruments of policy: the discount mechanism and reserve requirements. Of the three, open-market operations are the most flexible. Lending through the discount window—originally conceived as the heart of Federal Reserve policy—is at the initiative of the banks, making it difficult for the System to gauge the precise amount of reserve provision associated with any given discount rate. There does tend to be some rough association, though, of greater pressures on reserve availability with greater recourse to the discount window. Compared with open-market operations, changes in reserve requirements are a blunt instrument, for even small adjustments can have large effects on reserve needs. The level of reserve requirements, interacting with interest rates, affects profitability of depository institutions since holdings of required reserves represent nonearning assets. Reserve-requirement changes have not been frequent. They have been used to influence the banks' asset-liability structure as well as to affect the policy climate.

Open-market operations have been able to serve as the cornerstone of central bank policy in the United States because of the existence of a broad and active market in U.S. government securities. Trading volume on outstanding government debt is very large, and Federal Reserve operations typically represent only a small fraction of total transactions. Consequently, the market permits the Federal Reserve to operate readily on a substantial scale without causing wide changes in market prices, a feature that contributed to open-market operations having become the favored tool of policy in the United States.

A number of other countries have begun making use of open-market operations in recent years. In some instances they have taken steps to encourage the creation of an active market for government securities to facilitate the conduct of open-market operations. The instrument that is purchased or sold is not always a government security. Some central banks buy short-term private debt. Others sell their own debt into the market. Thus, open-market operations are not unique to the U.S. economy, although their use in the United States has a longer history and is more highly developed than in most other countries.

The Federal Open Market Committee

Federal Reserve open-market operations are carried out in the United States by the trading desk at the Federal Reserve Bank of New York, under the policy guidance of the Federal Open Market Committee (FOMC). The Committee is composed of the seven members of the Board of Governors of the Federal Reserve System and five of the twelve regional Reserve Bank presidents. (However, all twelve presidents participate in the FOMC meetings, which are usually held eight times a year in Washington, D.C.) The head of the Board of Governors also chairs the FOMC. The New York Reserve Bank president is always a voting member of the Committee and traditionally serves as its vice chair, while the other four voting Reserve Bank presidents are drawn on a rotating basis, for one-year terms, from among the other eleven Reserve Bank presidents.

Open-market operations are directed by the Manager for Domestic Operations of the System Open Market Account, a senior officer of the New York Reserve Bank. Operations are conducted mainly in U.S. Treasury securities, and to a lesser degree in the securities of federally sponsored agencies (such as the Federal Home Loan Banks). Central bank purchases of securities add to bank reserves, thus accommodating or encouraging the expansion of money and credit, while sales of securities extinguish bank reserves and inhibit the growth of money and credit.

The Federal Reserve conducts its operations with primary dealers in government securities (about 40 in 1991). Many dealers are part of diversified financial firms, while others are subsidiaries of major bank holding companies. A number are U.S. subsidiaries of foreign financial institutions. Transactions with dealers are conducted on a competitive, best-price basis through a process called a "go around" in which all the dealers with which the desk trades are contacted. The Federal Reserve also conducts operations directly with official foreign accounts—institutions that arrange investment activities through the Federal Reserve. Such purchases or sales are undertaken when the transactions meet the reserve objectives of the Federal Reserve as well as the investment needs of the foreign account.

The form of operations depends on the duration and size of needs to add or absorb reserves. Relatively permanent reserve needs, consistent with growth of money and credit in an expanding economy, may be met through outright Federal Reserve purchases of government securities of varying maturity—from bills maturing within a year to notes and bonds of as much as 30 years' maturity. The Federal Reserve holds the full range of Treasury securities. Outright sales are less frequent than purchases since the long-term trend of Federal Reserve holdings has been upward. Typically, the Federal Reserve exchanges its maturing holdings for a like amount of newly offered securities, the only way it is permitted to buy securities direct from the issuer. On occasion the Federal Reserve may also redeem some of its maturing security holdings. Redemptions of maturing securities, like sales, absorb reserves.

When the perceived need for reserves is very large, temporary, or uncertain in duration, the Federal Reserve may purchase securities under a repurchase agreement—buying the securities for delivery the day the trade is arranged and committing to sell the same securities back to the dealer 1 to 15 days later at the original price plus interest. If there is a need to drain reserves on a temporary basis, especially if the need is large, the trading desk may arrange matched sale-purchase transactions, in which the System sells securities on the day the trade is arranged and commits to repurchase them at a later date—usually 1 to 7 days later.

Temporary needs to add or absorb reserves result from technical factors that affect the supply of reserves—e.g., the size of the cash balance the U.S. Treasury holds at the Federal Reserve, the volume of Federal Reserve float, or the amount of currency in circulation—and from seasonal variation in the demand for money and credit. The bulk of open-market operations on a day-to-day basis is undertaken to offset the impact of these factors on the availability of reserves.

Monetary Policy Objectives

The theory and conduct of Federal Reserve open-market operations have evolved over time in response to changes in the economy and in economic and public opinion. The Federal Reserve resumed its pursuit of an active monetary policy after the Treasury-Federal Reserve Accord of 1951. Initially, policymakers gave little explicit attention to money and credit growth as such. Open-market policy during the 1950s and early 1960s was directed at ease or restraint, as deemed appropriate in the prevailing economic circumstances. Under a policy of ease, the Federal Reserve bought government securities vigorously, thus providing the banking system with relatively ample reserve availability in order to stimulate the economy by reducing interest rates and inducing banks to invest and lend more readily. At other times, there was a policy of restraint, designed to curtail the availability of reserves through slowing down central bank purchases, or even making net sales of securities, thus tending to raise interest rates and induce banks to curtail the availability of credit to their customers.

Beginning in the mid-1960s, increasing emphasis was placed on growth of money and bank credit. At first, this emphasis was expressed through proviso clauses directing the manager to alter somewhat the thrust of contemplated operations during the month between FOMC meetings if bank credit did not appear to be growing as expected. By the early 1970s, the proviso clause had given way to Committee directives calling for moderate, faster, or slower growth in money and bank credit, with side constraints placing limits on changes in the federal funds rate. The federal funds rate is the overnight interest rate on interbank transactions in reserve balances held at the Federal Reserve; this rate became in practice the immediate focus of Federal Reserve open-market operations. It has been the key rate affecting other short-term rates and to lesser degree other interest rates in the economy.

Starting in 1972, the FOMC began to use quantitative growth targets for key measures of money (monetary aggregates) and bank credit. Initially these targets extended two quarters ahead; in 1975 they were extended four quarters ahead. Then the Humphrey-Hawkins legislation of 1978 formalized the targeting period to a calendar year. At the same time, the FOMC typically specified tolerance ranges for growth in monetary aggregates for a 2-month period ending with the month following the Committee's meeting; achievement of growth within these ranges was deemed to be consistent with the Committee's longer-term growth objectives. As the month between FOMC meetings proceeded, the trading desk was expected to modify its federal funds objective in response to incoming information on the monetary aggregates, raising the funds rate within its allowable range if 2-month growth in the aggregates was coming in toward the high side of the 2-month ranges, and lowering the funds rate if monetary growth was running low in relation to the 2-month ranges. The tolerance bands for the federal funds rate established between 1972 and 1979 ranged from ¼ to 1½ percentage points, with the rate sought immediately after the meeting usually in the middle of the range.

The desk could encourage a higher or lower federal funds rate by providing either fewer or more reserves than the banking system desired to meet requirements and provide a cushion for clearing needs or other purposes. When the desk added or drained reserves with the funds rate at a level where it previously would not have conducted an open-market operation, participants in the federal funds market quickly concluded that a policy shift had occurred and adapted their reserve management strategies accordingly.

Through the 1970s, these procedures became increasingly well established. Growing market sensitivity to movements in the federal funds rate encouraged a pattern of cautious rate adjustments. Money growth tended to overshoot the targets more often than not, and the small incremental adjustments to the funds rate often lagged behind what, in retrospect, seemed to be needed.

Reserve Targeting Approach to Open-Market Operations

In October 1979, in order to provide greater assurance of achieving its monetary growth objectives and make a forceful commitment to fighting inflation, the FOMC modified its approach to open-market operations. Emphasis was placed on supplying the volume of reserves estimated to achieve the desired monetary growth (focusing primarily on a narrow measure, M-1), while much greater latitude was permitted in the federal funds rate. Reserves were adjusted to achieve desired growth paths for total reserves and nonborrowed reserves (total reserves less borrowings from the Federal Reserve discount window).

In the event that the banking system's demand for total reserves exceeded the nonborrowed reserves provided, the banks would have to borrow additional reserves at the discount window. Because access was limited as to amount and frequency, banks sought to bid reserves away from other banks in the federal funds market, until the funds rate rose to the point where some banks would decide to use the discount window. Excessive borrowing could also encourage the Federal Reserve to increase the discount rate. The higher rates and concerns about future access to the window that developed when there was excessive monetary growth would in time encourage banks to adjust their policies for asset and liability management, leading in turn to slower growth in money and credit. Correspondingly, unduly weak growth in money and credit and a policy of supplying the nonborrowed reserves consistent with desired growth in aggregates would lead to a decline in borrowing from the Federal Reserve. This would mean a more abundant and less costly availability of bank reserves that would be expected to encourage credit formation and stimulate money growth.

The same types of open-market transactions continued in use after 1979, but the guidelines for market entry changed. Outright purchases and sales of Treasury securities addressed secular or seasonal reserve needs that extended over several weeks. Temporary transactions were used to make short-term adjustments to bring reserves onto the weekly path. Entry times were standardized to late morning for temporary transactions and early afternoon for outright transactions, rather than being tied to intraday movements in the funds rate.

The reserve targeting approach, with refinements, was followed until the autumn of 1982. It helped give the Federal Reserve the room it needed to let interest rates rise, and it helped achieve slower average rates of increase for both money and prices. But it also permitted volatility in money and interest rates that came to be viewed as excessive. Meantime, the behavior of M-1 was shifting as a result of interest rate deregulation and the creation of new types of money substitutes. It was becoming a less reliable guide to policy actions. Accordingly, the approach to policy shifted again in late 1982.

Emphasis on Borrowed Reserves and the Federal Funds Rate

During most of the 1980s, the FOMC focused on a variety of economic and financial indicators for determining its policy stance, especially since the monetary aggregates continued to be affected by institutional changes and had to be interpreted cautiously. It continued to set targets for reserve measures and to follow the basic approaches to temporary and longer-term reserve adjustments introduced in 1979. The measure that took center stage was borrowed reserves. The approach depended upon the banks' reluctance to borrow that derived from rationing of access to the discount window.

Adjustments to the objective for borrowing were made when the FOMC interpreted the various economic and financial indicators to be calling for more or less reserve restraint. Generally, an increase in borrowing would be associated with a rise in the federal funds rate and a fall in borrowing with a decline. The association was not precise, however, because other factors besides the cost of funds could change banks' willingness to borrow.

Until the stock market crash in October 1987, the FOMC was generally willing to accept much of the variability in the funds rate that emerged in the pursuit of the borrowing objectives. However, the worries about the health of the economy and the financial system that followed the crash and developing strains in the banking system seemed to increase banks' reluctance to borrow, and this has made the relationship between borrowing and the federal funds rate less dependable. Consequently, while continuing to set borrowing targets, the Federal Reserve has become more sensitive again to the behavior of the funds rate. Much of the time, estimates of reserve needs associated with the borrowing objective and the behavior of the federal funds rate give consistent indications of the appropriate open-market operations. But when they are in conflict, the desk gives considerable weight to the behavior of the funds rate so as to avoid giving a misleading impression about the thrust of policy.

References

Black, Robert P., "Reflections on the Strategy of Monetary Policy," Federal Reserve Bank of Richmond *Economic Review,* July/August 1990, pp. 3–7; Greenspan, Alan, "1992 Monetary Policy

Objectives," Federal Reserve Board, February 19, 1992; Heller, H. Robert, "Implementing U.S. Monetary Policy," *Federal Reserve Bulletin,* vol. 74, no. 7, July 1988, pp. 419–429; Madigan, Brian F., and Warren T. Trepeta, "Implementation of Monetary Policy," in *Changes in Money Market Instruments and Procedures: Objectives and Implications,* Bank of International Settlements, March 1986; Meek, Paul, *Open Market Operations,* Federal Reserve Bank of New York, 1985; Meulendyke, Ann-Marie, *U.S. Monetary Policy and Financial Markets,* Federal Reserve Bank of New York, 1990; Meulendyke, Ann-Marie, "A Review of Federal Reserve Policy Targets and Operating Guides in Recent Decades," *Intermediate Targets and Indicators for Monetary Policy: A Critical Survey,* Federal Reserve Bank of New York, July 1990; "Monetary Policy and Open Market Operations during 1991," Federal Reserve Bank of New York *Quarterly Review,* Spring 1992, forthcoming; Mote, Larry R., "Looking Back: The Use of Interest Rates in Monetary Policy," Federal Reserve Bank of Chicago *Economic Perspectives,* vol. 12, no. 1, January/February 1988, pp. 15–29; Partlan, John C., Kausar Hamdani and Kathleen M. Camilli, "Reserves Forecasting for Open Market Operations," Federal Reserve Bank of New York *Quarterly Review,* Spring 1986, pp. 19–33.

(*See also* Banking system; Credit, an overview; Federal Reserve policy; Federal Reserve System; Interest rates; Monetary policy; Money supply)

Peter D. Sternlight and Ann-Marie Meulendyke

Operating rate, industrial (*see* Industrial production index)

Operations research

Operations research (OR) has both a general and a more specific technical meaning. The historical and more general definition is that OR is the application of scientific analysis to the decision-making process, with problems typically arising in the areas of military planning, industrial management, economic analysis, and the determination of public policy. In a narrower technical sense, OR refers to a number of mathematical modeling techniques, including optimization and simulation methods, which find frequent application in the study of rational decision making.

History

Although operations research first appeared as an organized discipline during World War II, earlier researchers pioneered the field with their work. In the late 1800s, the time and motion studies of Frederick Taylor introduced scientific analysis into factory management. The Danish mathematician A. K. Erlang studied the problems of congestion in telephone networks in his 1909 publication, *The Theory of Probability and Telephone Conversations.* This work initiated the use of "queueing models," which have had applications to a far broader range of problems. In the same era, F. W. Lanchester brought the tools of mathematical analysis to bear upon problems of military science, demonstrating the principle of concentration, or *n*-square law, and establishing other relationships that have had a profound influence on the conduct of modern wars.

During World War II, civilian scientists in several Allied countries worked in groups that were ultimately to become the first operations research teams. These individuals applied scientific analysis to the study of military planning and policy. After the conclusion of the war and as the world emerged into the nuclear era, defense planners observed that they would need scientific programming techniques to coordinate rapidly the energies of an entire nation in the event of any future war.

Under the auspices of the U.S. Air Force, in June 1947 a team of economists and mathematicians called Project SCOOP (Scientific Computation of Optimal Programs) began intensive work on modeling the military forces and the civilian economy. During this period G. B. Dantzig developed the simplex method for computing optimal solutions to linear programs.

By 1950, linear programming and the other tools of operations research had begun to make their way into industrial applications. Their use accelerated as business executives became aware of their potential and as the growing capabilities of electronic data processing made large-scale mathematical modeling feasible. W. Cooper, A. Charnes, and others used linear programming techniques to solve problems of petroleum refinery scheduling, achieving the first major success of OR in business. Fruitful applications in the food processing, iron and steel, transportation, and power-generation industries followed quickly. By the end of the decade, OR applications in the private sector had grown too numerous and too diverse to catalog.

During the 1960s, operations research matured into a recognized and independent discipline: OR departments and degree programs became common in major universities, and most of the larger corporations included at least one OR team within their organizations. Continuing research resulted in new and productive applications for government and industry.

The field grew further in the 1970s, with researchers addressing many issues in energy and economic policy following the onset of the energy crisis. While most of the basic categories of operations research models were well established, workers in the field continued to refine and extend those tools.

The advent of microcomputers in 1980s and the general explosion in available computing power led to some new areas of focus. Operations researchers studied techniques for embedding models in decision support systems (DSSs), and they also explored applications of widely available microcomputer software (such as spreadsheets) to OR modeling. Operations researchers also imported and used various techniques developed by other disciplines, for example, expert system technology developed by the artificial intelligence community.

General Methodology

There is a basic methodology routinely employed in OR studies. The first step is the formulation of the problem. The OR analyst studies the problem at hand and attempts to identify the overall objectives of the system and any constraints that limit the range of possible actions.

The next step is the construction of a mathematical model of the system under study. The analyst models the intrinsic structure of the problem with mathematical relationships and, when an optimization model is being developed, represents the objectives explicitly in a function of the model's variables and parameters. The analyst almost always must simplify and approximate the practical problem to obtain a computationally tractable model.

Following the construction of the model, the OR analyst must derive a solution. While algorithms exist for the solution of many of the most commonly used models, an analyst can often significantly reduce the amount of computational effort required by exploiting any special structure present in the problem. Also, analysts occasionally encounter problems for which no efficient solution techniques are available. (The technical vernacular for these problems is "NP-complete.") However, the analyst can use heuristic algorithms for many of these problems and often obtain good or, in some cases, even optimal solutions.

Once the OR analyst has obtained a solution, he or she must review and test it. One simple, but revealing, technique is to vary the inputs to the model and observe whether the changes in the solution seem plausible. This test will frequently uncover errors or omissions in the initial formulation. When applicable, a more systematic approach is the use of a retrospective test. The analyst uses historical data to reconstruct the past and then determines how well the model would have performed if it had been employed at that time.

Frequently, the solution the OR analyst obtained from the tested model will be used in an environment where the input data are not precisely known. In this case the analyst conducts a sensitivity analysis to identify the range of input parameter values over which the given solution remains valid. This type of analysis will frequently identify parameters that the analyst should estimate with particular care, and in some extreme circumstances can lead the analyst to select a solution that is slightly suboptimal but robust in its response to variations in the parameters. Also, when the solution is to be applied repeatedly, the analyst can use sensitivity analysis to determine acceptable ranges over which parameters may be allowed to vary before the analyst must use the model to determine a different solution for the new conditions.

General Classification of OR Models

The standard texts in this field categorize the most frequently used models by their structures and areas of application into several categories.

1. *Mathematical Programming.*   Programming in this context means planning or scheduling, not the preparation of instructions for a computer. A mathematical program comprises an objective function that is to be maximized or minimized over values of decision variables that satisfy a set of auxiliary constraint inequalities. Linear programs have objective functions and constraints that are linear in an algebraic sense. There are algorithms that can solve certain kinds of linear programs with special structures even when they have very large numbers of variables and constraints. Nonlinear programs have algebraic nonlinearities in their objectives or constraints. Computationally, the presence of such nonlinearities generally makes the solution of problems of even moderate size difficult except in a few special cases. Integer programs are those in which some or all of the decision variables must have only integer values. Most integer programs fall into the category of hard (NP-complete) problems for which no efficient algorithm is available, and hence OR analysts must resort to heuristic methods that do not guarantee optimality.

2. *Game Theory.*   OR analysts model many competitive and cooperative situations abstractly as games. An analyst specifies a game by identifying a set of players, a set of actions that are available to each player, and a set of rewards or payoffs determined by the actions that the players choose to take.

3. *Inventory Theory.*   Analysts model a wide range of problems abstractly in terms of the acquisition, storage, and disposal of stock. Models in this field are

grouped by the standard texts into those that deal with deterministic demands and those that deal with stochastic (probabilistic) demands, and those in which there are convex costs (diseconomies of scale) and those in which there are concave costs (economies of scale).

4. *Reliability Theory.* Because component failures tend to occur at random times, these models are principally statistical in nature. The standard texts subdivide these models into those that, given a set of data, seek to estimate a parameter (such as the mean or variance) of the distribution of a component's life, those that estimate the life of a system given the reliabilities of the system's components, and those optimization models that treat policies for the repair and replacement of components.

5. *Queueing Theory.* As their name indicates, queueing theoretical models are applicable to situations in which customers periodically arrive at a configuration of servers, where they wait in line until they have access to a server for some length of time. The theory generally assumes customers to arrive for service at random times and also assumes the service time they require is randomly distributed. OR analysts can model queues in a bank or at a gas station in this manner, as they also can model demands upon a telephone network or a central processing unit in a time-sharing computer system.

6. *Dynamic Programming.* Models in this category are useful in selecting optimal sequences of decisions over time, where the reward obtained at any given time generally depends upon past decisions and the operation of some chance mechanism. These models are useful, for example, in analyzing situations in which it might be desirable to incur temporary losses in view of possible long-run gains.

7. *Simulation.* Simulation models are fundamentally different from the models within the preceding classes because simulations are primarily useful for comparing proposed courses of action rather than constructing a particular optimal solution. Because the model invokes no optimization procedure, analysts can build simulation models with a very detailed structure. However, there is no guarantee that even the best of the proposed courses of action will approximate the actual optimal solution to within any degree of accuracy. For example, in assigning 1000 people to 1000 jobs, a comprehensive simulation certain to find the best matching is impractical because it would require even the most advanced computers millions of years to examine each possible combination.

Probable Future of Operations Research

As technology advances and the issues and choices faced by individual and institutional decision makers become more complex, operations research and its allied disciplines will have a continuing and increasingly important role in the analysis of problems and the determination of the optimal solutions. Advances in mathematical techniques and the common availability of high-performance computer work stations are enabling OR to fulfill that expanded role.

References

Churchman, C. West, et al., *Introduction to Operations Research,* Wiley, New York, 1957; Dantzig, George B., *Linear Programming and Extensions,* Princeton University Press, Princeton, N.J., 1963; Hillier, F. S., and G. J. Lieberman, *Introduction to Operations Research,* 5th ed.,

Holden-Day, San Francisco, 1990; *International Abstracts in Operations Research,* 1961; Wagner, H., *Principles of Operations Research,* 2d ed., Prentice-Hall, Englewood Cliffs, N.J., 1975.

(*See also* Business inventory; Game theory, economic applications; Linear programming; Simulation in business and economics; Stock-flow analysis)

Brian E. Leverich

Opportunity cost

The concept of opportunity cost was introduced by the neoclassicists of the nineteenth century. Opportunity costs also are called user costs or alternative costs. The opportunity cost of producing a good or service (or of otherwise satisfying some economic want) is the real economic cost associated with the production process. Opportunity costs consider what must be forgone in real terms to produce a unit of output of a good or service.

For example, the opportunity cost of using labor, raw materials, and other resources to produce a unit of product X is the number of units of the next-best alternative product that must be sacrificed to produce that unit of X. Thus, the real economic cost to society of producing some product, such as a ship, is the value of the other items that cannot be produced with the same resources, such as additional automobiles and appliances, because of the steel and other resources that have been used up in the construction of the ship.

Opportunity costs are an important concept because the supply of factors of production is limited in any economy. Given a limited supply, it is important that resources be used in a manner that produces the maximum amount of output that is consistent with consumers' desires, as measured by their willingness to pay for various goods and services.

The best use of any resource is the use that offers the highest return, given a level of risk. Thus, the opportunity cost of an investment in Delta Airlines bonds that promises to yield 10 percent per annum is not the rate of return that could be earned investing a similar amount in TWA bonds, because these investments do not have equal risk. The high degree of competition that prevails in well-developed capital markets, such as those in the United States, most of Western Europe, and Japan, virtually assures that financial instruments, such as bonds and common stock, will be priced to reflect their true opportunity cost.

In many cases, the measurement of the opportunity cost of using real resources, such as labor, machinery, buildings, or raw materials, is simple and closely parallels accounting definitions of cost. For example, most items that a firm purchases have an opportunity cost equal to the actual cost of the item. Thus, if a firm buys 100 gallons of fuel oil for $110, the firm must forgo its claims to whatever else the $110 will buy. In the case of rented or hired factors, such as rented buildings or labor services, the opportunity cost normally is equal to the dollar cost of the rental, considering all explicit costs, such as retirement benefits and other benefits that normally are paid in addition to wages.

There are, however, instances where these explicit costs may not fully measure the economic opportunity cost of the resource being used. When commodities are rationed and their prices are fixed, such as occurs in centrally planned economies like the former Soviet Union, a firm or an individual may place a value on a resource that is higher than its established price. In normal circumstances, however, market-determined prices of input factors provide a good estimate for the opportunity cost of an input.

Illustrations

The following two examples illustrate the opportunity cost concept. First, consider a farmer who has decided to plant oats this year. The farmer expects to be able to sell the crop for $60,000. The land also could be used to grow soybeans, which the farmer could sell for $70,000. The opportunity cost of growing oats to the exclusion of soybeans is the difference between the value of the oat crop and the value of the soybean crop, or $10,000. Using the opportunity cost concept, the farmer should employ his resources in the manner that achieves the maximum return, in this case growing soybeans.

The opportunity cost of capital supplied by the owners of a firm is the rate of return those funds could have earned in the next-best alternative investment of equal risk. Consider the case of a consultant who earns $100,000 per year working for Anderson Consulting. The consultant decides to take her accumulated life savings of $500,000 and open a new independent consulting firm, structured as a sole proprietorship. The owner/consultant's compensation from this new venture will be the accounting profits recorded by the firm. The new firm shows accounting net profits of $95,000 per year. However, no real profits have been earned because the opportunity cost of the consultant's time was $100,000 per year and the opportunity cost of the money invested in the firm is equal to the return that could be earned on a venture of equal risk. Assuming a conservative measure of this capital cost to be 15 percent, or $75,000 per year, the new firm actually had economic losses of $80,000 per year, rather than the reported profits of $95,000.

References

McGuigan, James R., and R. Charles Moyer, *Managerial Economics,* 6th ed., West, St. Paul, Minn., 1993; Pindyck, Robert S., and Daniel L. Rubinfeld, *Microeconomics,* Macmillan, New York, 1989.

(*see also* Neoclassical economics)

R. Charles Moyer

Options

A European-type put (call) option is a security that offers the right to sell (buy) a specified quantity of a particular financial or real asset at a specified price, the exercise price, on a specified date, the expiration date. An American-type option allows its owner to exercise the option on or before the expiration date. If an option is not exercised on or before that date, it is said to expire and becomes worthless.

Options are derivative securities, as are forwards, futures, and swap contracts. Forward contracts are very close economic substitutes for futures. Swap contracts are essentially equivalent to a portfolio of long and short positions in forward contracts of various maturities on two different underlying assets. However, options and forward contracts are fundamentally different securities. Both provide for the purchase (or sale) of the underlying asset at a future date. But a long position in a forward contract requires an unconditional purchase of the asset at the forward price. In contrast, the owner of a call option can choose whether or not to purchase the asset at the exercise price. Similarly, a short position in a forward contract requires an unconditional sale of the asset, whereas the put-option owner has the choice of selling the asset at the exercise price. Hence, forward contracts can have negative values, but option contracts cannot.

Risk-Management Activities

The main function served by derivative securities (including options) within the financial system is risk management. All risk-management activities can be decomposed into combinations of three pure methods of managing risk. These three basic categories, the three functional dimensions of risk management, are:

1. Reducing the risk by selling the source of it. In general, adjusting a portfolio by moving from risky assets to a riskless asset to reduce risk can be done either in the spot cash market or in a futures or forward market. Futures, forwards, and swaps permit efficient implementation of this dimension of the risk-management function.

2. Reducing the risk of diversification. Diversification consists of simultaneously pooling and subdividing risks. While it does not eliminate risk in the aggregate, diversification redistributes that risk so as to reduce the risk faced by each person. Futures, forwards, and swap contracts on stock and bond market indexes facilitate implementation of this fundamental dimension of risk management by greatly improving transaction efficiency in both cost and speed.

3. Reducing the risk by buying insurance against losses. Insurance permits the owner of an asset to retain the economic benefits of ownership, while eliminating the uncertainty of possible losses. Of course, this retention of the "upside" while deleting the "downside" of asset ownership is not free. The fee or premium paid for insurance substitutes a sure loss for the possibility of a larger loss. In general, the owner of any asset can eliminate the downside risk of loss and retain the upside benefit of ownership by the purchase of a put option. As will be shown, the purchase of a call option together with riskless debt is economically equivalent to owning the asset and insuring its value against loss. Thus, whether put or call, the option is a fundamental security that serves the central risk-management function of providing insurance to its owner.

To derive this structural relation between put and calls, note that options are exercised only if to do so adds to value. Thus, at expiration, the value of a put option is given by max $[0, E - V]$ and the value of a call option is given by max $[0, V - E]$, where E denotes the exercise price of the option and V denotes the price of the underlying asset. Consider an investment strategy that combines a call option and U.S. Treasury bills with a total principal amount of E and a maturity date the same as the option's expiration date. At expiration, the combined value of the portfolio is given by max $[0, V - E] + E = $ max $[E, V]$. Next, consider an alternative strategy that combines the underlying asset and a put option. At expiration, the combined portfolio value is given by $V + $ max $[0, E - V] = $ max $[E, V]$. Because the payoff patterns to the two strategies are identical, they are economically equivalent.

If there are no taxes and transaction costs and if the underlying asset pays no dividends during the life of the options, then European-type call and put prices at time t, $C(t)$, and $P(t)$, respectively, must satisfy

$$C(t) = V(t) - Ee^{-r(T-1)} + P(t) \tag{1}$$

where r is the riskless interest rate and T is the common expiration date of the options. This price relation is called the put-call parity theorem.

The classic portfolio-selection theory of Harry Markowitz and James Tobin holds that the investor should control his or her risk exposure first by forming a well-diversified portfolio of all the risky assets and then, if necessary to adjust the risk further, by allocating his or her wealth between this diversified risky portfolio and the riskless asset. Hence, their theory covers the first two functional dimensions of risk management. It does not, however, explicitly take account of the opportunity structure provided by the third dimension: insurance. Given the basic role of options in implementing this method of risk management, it is perhaps not surprising that option-pricing analysis, together with intertemporal portfolio theory, is an important tool in the development of the theory of financial intermediation and insurance. It has proved particularly useful in the areas of risk-sharing and risk-pooling product identification, product implementation and pricing, and risk management and control for an intermediary's entire portfolio.

Expansion of the Use of Options and Option Analysis

The first organized exchange for trading options on common stocks was the Chicago Board Options Exchange (CBOE), which was created in 1973. However, options on commodity futures were traded on the Chicago Board of Trade in the 1920s, only to be banned by Congress in the 1930s. Bachelier (1900) describes and provides references on the institutional terms of over-the-counter options on government bonds and shares that were traded in Europe during the late nineteenth century. Joseph de la Vega's (1688) book describing the workings of the Amsterdam stock exchange indicates that options and securities similar to modern financial futures contracts dominated trading activities in this leading financial center of the seventeenth-century Western world. Bernstein (1992) reports that Aristotle's anecdote about Thales in Book I of *Politics* is the first recorded mention of a financial option.

The initial success of the CBOE was followed by an extraordinary global expansion in markets throughout the late 1970s and the 1980s to include options on fixed-income securities, currencies, stock and bond indexes, a variety of commodities, and even swap contracts. This expansion was not, however, the principal reason that option-pricing theory became one of the cornerstones of financial economic theory during that same period. Instead, this central role for options analysis derives from the fact that optionlike structures pervade virtually every part of the field. Black and Scholes (1973) and Merton (1974) provide an early example: shares of stock in a firm financed in part by debt have a payoff structure that is equivalent to a call option on the firm's assets where the exercise price is the face value of the debt and the expiration date is the maturity date of the debt. Option-pricing theory can thus be used to price levered equity and, therefore, corporate debt with default risk.

Identification of similar isomorphic relations between options and other financial instruments has led to pricing models for seniority; call provisions and sinking fund arrangements on debt; bonds convertible into stock, commodities, or different currencies; floor and ceiling arrangements on interest rates; stock and debt warrants; and rights and standby agreements. In short, option-pricing theory provides a unified theory for the pricing of corporate liabilities.

The option-pricing methodology has been applied to the evaluation of noncorporate financial arrangements including government loan guarantees, pension fund insurance, and deposit insurance. It has also been used to evaluate a variety of employee compensation packages including stock options, guaranteed wage floors, and even tenure for university faculty.

Among the more recent extensions of option analysis is its application in the evaluation of operating or "real" options in the capital budgeting decision problem. For example, a production facility that can use various inputs and produce various outputs provides the firm with operating options that it would not have with a specialized facility that uses a fixed set of inputs and produces a single type of output. Option-pricing theory provides the means of valuing those production options for comparison with the larger initial cost or lower operating efficiency of the more flexible facility. Similarly, the choice among technologies with various mixes of fixed and variable costs can be treated as evaluating the various options to change production levels, including abandonment of the project. Research and development projects can be evaluated by viewing them as options to enter new markets, expand market share, or reduce production costs.

As these examples suggest, option analysis is especially well suited to the task of evaluating the "flexibility" components of projects. These, corporate strategists often claim, are precisely the components whose values are not properly measured by traditional capital budgeting techniques. Hence, option-pricing theory holds forth the promise of providing quantitative assessments for capital budgeting projects that heretofore were largely evaluated qualitatively. Smith (1976, 1979), Mason and Merton (1985), Merton (1989, 1992), and Pindyck (1991) provide detailed discussions of those wide-ranging developments in option analysis along with extensive bibliographies.

Option-Pricing Theory

The lineage of modern option-pricing theory began in 1900 with the Sorbornne thesis, "Theory of Speculation," by the French mathematician Louis Bachelier. The work is rather remarkable because, in analyzing the problem of option pricing, Bachelier derives much of the mathematics of probability diffusions—this, 5 years before Einstein's famous discovery of the mathematical theory of Brownian motion. Although, from today's perspective, the economics and mathematics of Bachelier's work are flawed, the connection of this research with the subsequent path of attempts to describe an equilibrium theory of option pricing is unmistakable.

It was not, however, until nearly 75 years later, with the publication of the seminal Black and Scholes article (1973), that the field reached a sense of closure on the subject and the explosion in research on option-pricing applications began. Bernstein (1992) provides a brief history of the development of the Black-Scholes option-pricing model.

As with Bachelier and later researchers, Black and Scholes assume that the dynamics for the price of the asset underlying the option can be described by a diffusion process with a continuous sample path. The breakthrough nature of the Black-Scholes analysis derives from their fundamental insight that a dynamic trading strategy in the underlying asset and a default-free bond can be used to hedge against the risk of either a long or short position in the option. Having derived such a strategy, Black and

Scholes determine the equilibrium option price from the equilibrium condition that portfolios with no systematic risk must have the same return as a default-free bond.

Using the mathematics of Itô stochastic integrals, Merton (1973, 1977, 1992) formally proves that with continuous trading, the Black-Scholes dynamic portfolio strategy will hedge all the risk of an option position held until exercise or expiration, and therefore that the Black-Scholes option price is necessary to rule out arbitrage.

Along the lines of the derivation for general contingent-claims pricing in Merton (1977, 1992), a sketch of the arbitrage proof for the Black-Scholes price of a European call option on a non-dividend-paying stock in a constant interest rate environment is as follows.

Assume that the dynamics of the stock price, $V(t)$, can be described by a diffusion process with a stochastic differential-equation representation given by

$$dV = \alpha V dt + \sigma V dz \qquad (2)$$

where α is the instantaneous expected rate of return on the stock; σ^2 is the instantaneous variance per unit time of the return, which is a function of V and t; and dz is a standard Wiener process. Let $F[V,t]$ satisfy the linear partial differential equation

$$0 = \tfrac{1}{2}\,\sigma^2 V^2 F_{11} + rVF_1 - rF + F_2 \qquad (3)$$

where subscripts denote partial derivatives and r is the interest rate. Let F be such that it satisfies the boundary conditions

$$F/V \le 1 \qquad F(0,t) = 0 \qquad F[V,T] = \max[0, V - E] \qquad (4)$$

Note from (4) that the value of F on these boundaries is identical to the payoff structure on a European call option with exercise price E and expiration date T. From standard mathematics, the solution to (3) and (4) exists, is unique, and is nonnegative everywhere.

Consider the continuous-time portfolio strategy which allocates the fraction $w(t) \equiv F_1[V,t]V(t)/P(t)$ to the stock and $1 - w(t)$ to the bond, where $P(t)$ is the value of the portfolio at time t. Other than the initial investment in the portfolio, $P(0)$, there are no contributions or withdrawals from the portfolio until it is liquidated at $t = T$.

The prescription for the portfolio strategy for each time t depends only on the first derivative of the solution to (3) – (4) and the current values of the stock and the portfolio. It follows from the prescribed allocation $w(t)$ that the dynamics for the value of the portfolio can be written as

$$\begin{aligned} dP &= w(t)P\, dV/V + [1 - w(t)]rP\, dt \\ &= F_1 dV + r[P - F_1 V]dt \end{aligned} \qquad (5)$$

As a solution to (3), F is, by construction, twice-continuously differentiable. Hence, it is valid to apply Itô's lemma to express the stochastic process for F as

$$dF = [\tfrac{1}{2}\,\sigma^2 V^2 F_{11} + \alpha V F_1 + F_2]dt + F_1 \sigma V\, dz \qquad (6)$$

where F is evaluated at $V = V(t)$ at each point in time t. But F satisfies (3). Hence, we can rewrite (6) as

$$dF = F_1 dV + r[F - F_1 V]dt \qquad (7)$$

Define $Q(t)$ to be the difference between the value of the portfolio and the value of the function $F[V,t]$ evaluated at $V = V(t)$. From (5) and (7), we have $dQ = rQ\, dt$, which is a nonstochastic differential equation with solution $Q(t) = Q(0)\exp[rt]$ and $Q(0) = P(0) - F[V(0), 0]$. Hence, if the initial investment in the portfolio is chosen so that $P(0) = F[V(0),0]$, then $Q(t) \equiv 0$, and $P(t) = F[V(t), t]$ for all t. For the prescribed portfolio strategy to be feasible, the value of the portfolio must never be negative. As already noted, $F[V,t]$ is nonnegative for all V and t. Therefore, $P(t)\{=F[V(t), t]\} \geq 0$ for all t, and the strategy is feasible.

Thus, we have constructed a dynamic portfolio strategy in the stock and a default-free bond that exactly replicates the payoff structure of a call option on the stock. The solution of (2) and (3) for F and its first derivative F_1 provides the "blueprint" for that construction. The standard no-arbitrage condition for equilibrium prices holds that two securities with identical payoff structures must have the same price. It follows, therefore, that the equilibrium price of the call option at time t must equal the value of the payoff-replicating portfolio, $F[V(t), t]$.

In the special case where σ^2 is a constant, the solution to (3) and (4) is given by

$$F[V,t] = V\phi(x_1) - Ee^{-r(T-t)}\phi(x_2) \tag{8}$$

where $\phi(y)$ is the cumulative normal density function and $x_1 \equiv [\log(V/E) + \sigma^2(T-t)/2 + r(T-t)]/\sigma\sqrt{T-t}$ and $x_2 \equiv x_1 - \sigma\sqrt{T-t}$. Equation (8) is called the Black-Scholes option-pricing formula because this is the case solved in their 1973 paper.

The extraordinary impact of option-pricing theory on financial economic research and practice can in large part be explained by three critical elements: (1) the assumptions for its valid application are relatively weak; (2) the variables and parameters required as inputs are either directly observable or relatively easy to estimate, and there is computational ease in solving for the price; and (3) the methodology in adapting it to the pricing of other options and optionlike securities is of a general nature.

Although framed in an arbitrage type of analysis, the derivation does not depend on the existence of an option on the stock. Hence, the replicating trading strategy and price function provide the means and the cost for an investor to create synthetically an option when such an option is not available as a traded security. The findings that the equilibrium option price is a twice-continuously differentiable function of the stock price and that its dynamics follow an Itô process are derived results, not assumptions.

The striking feature of the price function given by (3) and (4) is not the variables and parameters that are needed for determining the option price, but instead those not needed. Specifically, determination of the option price and the replicating portfolio strategy does not require estimates of either the expected return on the stock, α, or investor risk preferences and endowments. In contrast to most equilibrium models, the pricing of the option does not depend on price and joint distributional information for all available securities. The only such information required is about the underlying stock and default-free bond. Indeed, the only variable or parameter required in the pricing function that is not directly observable is the variance rate function σ^2. This observation has stimulated a considerable research effort on variance rate estimation in both the academic and practicing financial communities.

With some notable exceptions, such as in (8), Equations (3) and (4) cannot be solved analytically for a closed-form solution. However, powerful computational methods have been developed to provide high-speed numerical solutions of those equations for both the option price and its first derivative (cf. Geske and Shastri, 1985).

As in the original Black and Scholes article, the derivation here focuses on the pricing of a European call option on a non-dividend-paying stock. The methodology is, however, easily adapted to allow for the American feature of early exercise and to adjust for dividends on the stock (cf. Merton, 1973, 1992). Moreover, the methodology can also be applied to the pricing of other securities with payoff structures contingent on the price of the underlying stock. Consider, for example, the determination of the equilibrium price for a European put option with exercise price E and expiration date T. Suppose that in the original derivation the boundary conditions specified for F in (4) are changed to match the payoff structure of the put option on those boundaries. That is, we now require that F satisfy $F \le E$; $F[0,t] = E \exp[-r(T - t)]$; $F[V,T] = \max[0, E - V]$. Once F and its derivative are specified, the development of the replicating portfolio proceeds in identical fashion to show that $P(t) = F[V(t), t]$. With the revised boundary conditions, the portfolio payoff structure will match that of the put option at exercise or expiration. Thus, $F[V(t), t]$ is the equilibrium put-option price. Given the pricing formula for the call option, one could, as an alternative, solve directly for the put price by using the put-call parity theorem in (1). As shown in Merton (1977, 1992), the same procedure can be used to determine the equilibrium price for a security with a general contingent payoff structure, $G[V(T)]$, by changing the boundary conditions in (4) so that $F[V,T] = G[V]$. A particularly important application of this procedure is in the determination of pure state-contingent prices.

Let $\pi[V,t; E,T]$ denote the solution of (3) subject to the boundary conditions

$$\pi/V \le 1 \qquad \pi[0,t; E,T] = 0 \qquad \pi[V,T; E,T] = \delta(E - V)$$

where $\delta(x)$ is the Dirac delta function with the properties that

$$\delta(x) = 0 \qquad \text{for } x \ne 0$$

and $\delta(0)$ is infinite in such a way that

$$\int_a^b \delta(x)\, dx = 1 \qquad \text{for } a < 0 < b$$

By inspection of this payoff structure, it is evident that this security is the natural generalization of the Arrow-Debreau pure state-contingent securities to an environment where there is a continuum of states defined by the price of the stock and time. That is, loosely, $\pi[V,t; E,T]dE$ is the price of a security that pays \$1 if $V(T) = E$ at time T and \$0, otherwise.

As is well known from the Green's function method of solving differential equations, the solution to Equation (3) subject to the boundary condition $F[V,T] = G[V]$ can be written as

$$F[V,t] = \int_0^\infty G[E]\pi[V,t; E,T]dE \qquad (9)$$

Thus, just as with the standard Arrow-Debreau model, once the set of all pure state-contingent prices, (π), are derived, the equilibrium price of any contingent payoff structure can be determined by mere summation or quadrature.

To underscore the central importance of call-option pricing in the general theory of contingent-claims pricing, consider a portfolio containing long and short positions in call options with the same expiration date T where each "unit" contains a long position in an option with exercise price $E - \varepsilon$, a long position in an option with exercise price

$E + \varepsilon$, and a short position in two options with exercise price E. If one takes a position in $1/\varepsilon^2$ units of this portfolio, the payoff structure at time T with $V(t) = V$ is given by

$$\{\max[0, V + \varepsilon - E] - 2\max[0, V - E] + \max[0, V - \varepsilon - E]\}/\varepsilon^2 \tag{10}$$

The limit of (10) as $\varepsilon - 0$ is $\delta(E - V)$, which is the payoff structure to a pure state-contingent security. If $F[V,t; E,T]$ is the solution to (3) and (4), then it follows from (10) that

$$\pi[V,t; E,T] = \lim_{\varepsilon \to 0} \{F[V,t; E - \varepsilon, T] - 2F[V,t;E,T] + F[V,t; E + \varepsilon, T]\}/\varepsilon^2$$

$$= \frac{\delta^2 F[V,t; E,T]}{\delta E^2} \tag{11}$$

Hence, once the call-option-pricing function has been determined, the pure state-contingent prices can be derived from (11). See, for example, Banz and Miller (1978), Breeden and Litzenberger (1978), and Ross (1976).

For additional references on option-pricing theory and application along these lines, see the excellent books by Cox and Rubinstein (1985) and Hull (1989). See also the Cox and Huang (1989) survey article on the martingale approach to option pricing.

References

Bachelier, L., *Theorie de la Speculation,* Gauthier-Villars, Paris, 1990 [English translation in P. Cootney (ed.), *The Random Character of Stock Market Prices,* rev. ed., MIT Press, Cambridge, Mass., 1967, pp. 17–78]; Banz, R. W., and M. H. Miller, "Prices for State-Contingent Claims; Some Estimates and Applications," *Journal of Business,* vol. 51, October 1978, pp. 653–672; Bernstein, P. L., *Capital Ideas: The Improbable Origins of Modern Wall Street,* Free Press, New York, 1992; Black, F., and M. Scholes, "The Pricing of Options and Corporate Liabilities," *Journal of Political Economy,* vol. 81, May–June 1973, pp. 637–659; Breeden, D. T., and R. Litzenberger, "Prices of State-Contingent Claims Implicit in Option Prices," *Journal of Business,* vol. 51, October 1978, pp. 621–651; Cox, J., and C. Huang, "Option Pricing Theory and Its Applications," in S. Bhattacharya and G. Constantinides (eds.), *Frontiers of Modern Financial Theory: Theory of Valuation,* Rowman & Littlefield, Totowa, N.J., 1989, pp. 272–288; Cox, J., and M. Rubinstein, *Options Markets,* Prentice-Hall, Englewood Cliffs, N.J., 1985; de la Vega, J. P., "Confusion de Confusiones," 1688, English translation by H. Kallenbenz, *The Kress Library Series of Publications,* no. 13, Kress Library of Business and Economics, Cambridge, Mass., 1957; Geske, R., and K. Shastri, "Valuation by Approximation: A Comparison of Alternative Option Valuation Techniques," *Journal of Financial and Quantitative Analysis,* vol. 20, March 1985, pp. 45–72; Hull, J., *Options, Futures and Other Derivative Securities,* Prentice-Hall, Englewood Cliffs, N.J., 1989; Mason, S., and R. C. Merton, "The Role of Contingent Claims Analysis in Corporate Finance," in E. I. Altman and M. G. Subrahmanyan (eds.), *Recent Advances in Corporate Finance,* Irwin, Homewood, Ill., 1985, pp. 7–54; Merton, R. C., "Theory of Rational Option Pricing," *Bell Journal of Economics and Management Science,* vol. 4, Spring 1973, pp. 141–183; Merton, R. C., "On the Pricing of Corporate Debt: The Risk Structure of Interest Rates," *Journal of Finance,* vol. 29, May 1974, pp. 449–470; Merton, R. C., "On the Pricing of Contingent Claims and The Modigliani-Miller Theorem," *Journal of Financial Economics,* vol. 5, November 1977, pp. 241–250; Merton, R. C., "On the Application of the Continuous-Time Theory of Finance to Financial Intermediation and Insurance," *Geneva Papers on Risk and Insurance,* vol. 14, July 1989, pp. 225–262; Merton, R. C., *Continuous-Time Finance,* rev. ed., Basil Blackwell, Oxford, 1992; Pindyck, R. S., "Irreversibility, Uncertainty, and Investment," *Journal of Economic Literature,* vol. 29, September 1991, pp. 1110–1152; Ross, S. A., "Options and Efficiency," *Quarterly Journal of Economics,* vol. 90, February 1976, pp. 75–89; Smith, C. W., "Option Pricing: A Review," *Journal of Financial Economics,* vol. 3, no. 1/2, January–March 1976, pp. 3–51; Smith, C. W., "Applications of Option Pricing Analysis," in J. L. Bicksler (ed.), *Handbook of Financial Economics,* North-Holland, Amsterdam, 1979, pp. 79–121.

(*See also* Arbitrage; Capital budgeting; Commodity exchange; Futures)

Robert C. Merton

Organization for Economic Cooperation and Development

The Organization for Economic Cooperation and Development (OECD) is an intergovernmental organization of 24 industrialized nations whose hallmarks are pluralist democracy, respect for human rights, and market economy. Its basic purpose is twofold: (1) to contribute through cooperative efforts to economic growth, employment, financial stability, and a rising living standard in member countries; and (2) to promote economic development of all nations and trade among them by assisting countries in their efforts to achieve these goals.

History

The OECD was formed on December 14, 1960, as a successor organization to the Organization for European Economic Cooperation (OEEC), whose main purpose was to coordinate the post–World War II economic recovery of Europe and to administer aid provided by the United States through the Marshall Plan. The OECD commenced operations on September 30, 1961, at its headquarters in Paris. In addition to the 18 European members of the OEEC, the United States and Canada were among the original member countries. Since then, Australia, Finland, Japan, and New Zealand have joined the Organization, bringing the total to 24 member countries.

Structure

The Organization is composed of over 200 committees and working parties, which cover virtually all the activities of modern government, other than defense and sport. The topics covered include economic policy, development assistance, public management, trade, international consumer affairs, tourism, sea transport, labor force, social policy, education, environment, science, industry, agriculture, and other areas of concern. Meetings of committees and working parties are attended by expert delegates from member-country capitals, and in some cases from a few selected nonmember countries also, most notably Mexico.

The Organization also carries out a policy assistance program administered by its newly created Center for Co-Operation with European Economies in Transition; and with three of these countries—the Czech and Slovak Federal Republic, Hungary, and Poland—it carries out a special Partners in Transition program. A dialogue on selected topics of common interest is also carried out with six Dynamic Asian Economies (DAEs)—Hong Kong, Korea, Malaysia, Singapore, Taiwan, and Thailand.

The various committees and working parties of the OECD are served by an international Secretariat, which is headed by the secretary-general, who is assisted by three deputy secretaries-general and an assistant secretary-general. In turn, the Secretariat is composed of various directorates that are organized along functional lines.

The Organization is governed by its Council, which meets fortnightly at the level of permanent representatives (ambassadors) of the 24 member countries. These meetings are presided over by the secretary-general of the OECD, who is appointed by the Council for a 5-year term. The Council also meets at the ministerial level, generally once a year, and the chair rotates among the member countries. An Executive Committee assists the Council in its work.

Several semiautonomous agencies also operate within the OECD framework. Among the most important are the International Energy Agency, created in 1974 to assist in the implementation of energy policies; the Nuclear Energy Agency, established in 1958 to promote the use of nuclear power for peaceful purposes; the Development Center, which has responsibilities in areas of research, liaison, information exchange, and expert assistance related to development problems; the Road Research Program; and the Center for Educational Research and Innovation.

Operations

The OECD performs a wide variety of functions and tasks. Among them are the collection and dissemination of statistical information on the member countries, the conduct of basic research and policy studies, and formal policy actions taken by the Council.

The Secretariat maintains extensive data banks and publishes relevant statistical information on the member countries. It also engages in regular economic forecasting exercises and publishes its findings. Frequently, groups of experts are called upon to provide further advice and assistance.

On a more formal level, the OECD Council may adopt decisions which are binding upon member countries, or recommendations for their voluntary consideration and possible implementation.

In sum, the OECD serves as an international clearinghouse for a wide variety of governmental activities that have to be coordinated in today's interdependent world.

Reference

OECD: History, Aims, Structure, Organization for Economic Cooperation and Development, Paris, 1971.

(*See also* International economics, an overview)

John Llewellyn

Pareto-improvement criterion (*see* Normative economics)

Payroll taxation (*see* Taxation, an overview)

Peace economics

Peace economics is a newly emerging field of study. It is generally concerned with (1) resolution, management, or reduction of conflict in the economic sphere, or among behaving units in their economic activity; (2) the use of economic measures and policy to cope with and control conflicts whether economic or not; and (3) the impact of conflict on the economic behavior and welfare of firms, consumers, organizations, government, and society. Central to the field are analyses of conflicts among nations, regions, and other communities of the world; measures to control (deescalate) arms races and achieve reduction in military expenditures and weaponry; and programs and policies to utilize resources thus released for more constructive purposes.

Economic Theories and Econometric Applications Help to Achieve Goals

To achieve its goals, peace economics must cover understanding of the behavior of individuals and groups of individuals ranging from the local community up to the nation, alliances of nations, and international organizations such as the United Nations and GATT. It draws upon utility, production, public choice, and welfare theories—theories at both the micro and macro level, involving both practical and general equilibrium/disequilibrium frameworks. It embodies game-theoretic, strategic, and other reaction-interaction analyses among parties, wherein hostility and friendliness, and cooperation and defection, are involved. Behaving units are taken to engage in appropriative (e.g., military ventures) as well as productive activities, with war often viewed as a rational, purposeful choice of decision makers. During the cold war era, much investigation was devoted to models of deterrence and attack capability, the inherent propensity for certain types of weaponry to lead to escalation of arms races, the need for the development of nonthreatening weapon systems, and procedures for qualitative arms control. With the demise of the cold war and the relaxation of controls on developing nations by the former Soviet Union and the United States, concern has arisen with the emergence of arms races among developing nations and their acquisition of nuclear weapons.

At the empirical and applied level, a number of econometric, computable general equilibrium and other studies have examined the impact, particularly at the national level, of military expenditures on inflation, unemployment, budget deficits, trade and balance of payments, and the general problem of allocation of resources between military and peacetime (social welfare) programs. Along with these have been analyses of the effect of political conflict upon trade and of trade upon the hostility of nations. Numerous input-output investigations have examined the impact of increases and cutbacks of military expenditures on output and employment by economic sectors at national, regional, and local levels. Closely associated with these have been studies concerned with conversion of defense-oriented activities to peacetime operations— with the retraining of workers employed in such activities, the retooling of plant and equipment and restructuring of industry, the reorientation of management to a competitive market economy, and the identification of desirable and effective offset programs. A most recent development is the incorporation of arms-race models and political variables in econometric, input-output, and potentially computable general equilibrium models of the world economy.

Another major line of inquiry relates to the impact of arms expenditures on the level of investment in the civilian economy. In particular, is there a negative impact and a consequent slowdown in the growth of the national economy? Economic warfare studies stem from such considerations. Further, are military research and development expenditures at the expense of civilian expenditures, and is the resulting increase in industry and overall national productivity significantly less, even though the spillover effects of the former may be major? With regard to developing countries, a hotly debated thesis is that arms production is job-creating, develops a market for the product of domestic firms, and stimulates the acquisition of labor skills and entrepreneurship, all of which spark and foster industrialization.

Other specific topics with which peace economics is concerned are guerrilla warfare, terrorism, and revolution as means to achieve ends; the expected utility of war, the effectiveness of economic sanctions, boycotts, and embargoes; alliance behavior and burden sharing; the properties of particular games like prisoner's dilemma, hawk-dove, and chicken; particular arms-race models (e.g., the pre–World War I British-German dreadnought race); case studies of the effects of military expenditures in a given nation (e.g., India); the nature and scope of international arms trade; organizational politics models involving resource allocation; lobbying efforts, particularly of the military-industrial complex; the effectiveness of arms expenditures as a counter-cyclical force; the probabilistic and nonprobabilistic models of war initiation, maintenance, and termination; the pollution aspects of military operations; the benefits and costs for each participant in a violent outbreak; and the economics of an international police force. Peace economics is distinct from defense economics, which has been primarily concerned with the efficient operation of a defense establishment (e.g., the U.S.

Department of Defense), its budgeting process and weapons procurement, and missile war simulations to evaluate deterrence and attack capabilities of different weapon systems and their cost-efficiency.

Another major concern of peace economics is with conflict management procedures (CMPs). Such procedures (e.g., veto incremax, max the min in rank improvement, and determination of priorities) involve extensions of Cournot/Edgeworth frameworks, oligopoly theory, game theory, coalition analysis, programming methods, and other economic tools.

As with those in many other areas of social science, law, and other professions, peace economists have explored possibilities for institutional change, particularly that which could influence the operation of key economic forces in the national and world systems—e.g., foreign aid and the financial support of development projects that can significantly affect internal unrest and the hostility a nation levels at its neighbors and others.

Leading figures in the field have been Jan Tinbergen, Wassily Leontief, and Kenneth Boulding, all of pre–World War I vintage. Since the early 1980s, the Peace Science Society (International) has been organizing *conflict and peace economics* sessions jointly with the American Economics Association at the latter's annual convention; and recently ECAAR (Economists Against the Arms Race) has focused the interest of many outstanding economists, including a number of Nobel laureates, on critical peace issues.

References

Boulding, Kenneth E., *Conflict and Defense,* Harper & Row, New York, 1962; Isard, Walter, *Arms Races, Arms Control and Conflict Analysis: Contributions from Peace Science and Peace Economies,* Cambridge University Press, New York, 1988; Leontief, Wassily, and Faye Duchin, *Military Spending: Facts and Figures, Worldwide Implications and Future Outlook,* Oxford University Press, New York, 1983; Tinbergen, Jan, and Dietrich Fischer, *Warfare and Welfare; Integrating Security Policy into Socio-Economic Policy,* St. Martin's Press, New York, 1987; for worldwide statistics on military expenditures, arms trade, and related elements, see Stockholm International Peace Research Institute, *Yearbook of World Armaments and Disarmaments,* Oxford University Press, New York, annually.

Walter Isard

Pension funds

A pension fund is a plan established and maintained by an employer to provide for systematic benefit payments to employees after their retirement. Thus, pension fund assets are actually a pool of capital set aside for the purpose of meeting future liability payments. Pension funds are an important factor in income distribution and in the saving and investment function. They currently account for a significant share of personal savings, and they are clearly one of the largest sources of investment capital.

Daniel M. Holland (1966) said, "A pension plan has fiscal counterparts that may be compared roughly to a bath tub with its drain and faucets both open. The faucets represent fund inflows—that is, contributions by employers and by employees—and fund earnings; the drain represents fund out-flows (i.e., benefit payments)."

Pension funds represent the largest and fastest-growing segment of institutional capital. According to the Federal Reserve Board, pension fund reserves held by the household sector at the end of 1991 totaled $3.71 trillion compared with $997 billion at the end of 1981, $278 billion at the end of 1971, and $104 billion at the end of 1961.

Private Pension Funds

About 75 million people in the United States have pension plans, less than 50 million in the private sector. Until 1974 private pension plans were quite diverse, but federal legislation in the late 1970s has resulted in plans with similar general features.

There are two major types of private pension funds, the noninsured and the insured. Under insured pension plans, pension obligations are funded by premium payments made by the sponsoring company to a life insurance company. In turn, the life insurance company guarantees that it will make specified annuity payments in the future. Life insurance companies attempt to maximize their return on investment of the premiums, but various state laws governing life insurance company activities constrain their investment latitude. During the late 1960s and the 1970s, pension plans that allow life insurance companies greater investment latitude were developed and they grew rapidly in the 1980s. These so-called deposit administration plans are similar in nature to the noninsured type of pension plan, but they are managed by life insurance companies. For smaller companies and for programs in which relatively few employees are covered, conventional insured plans tend to predominate.

In the case of noninsured pension plans, company contributions are generally paid into a trust fund at a bank or a trust company. The trustee holds and invests the accumulated funds. In turn, the trustee makes benefit payments to the plan's participants based on the specific provisions of the program.

The importance of pension funds to the economy, the size of the asset commitments, the number of employees covered by the plans, and the cost to stockholders of providing pension benefits make' it essential that investment of pension fund assets be managed by highly competent professionals.

A trustee may be given either wide investment latitude or limited latitude in investing the assets, with fixed maximum percentages of assets to go for common stocks, for a specific industry or company, for foreign securities, or for private placements. The trustee may need approval of a designated cotrustee before investments can be made, or the trustee may act solely as a custodial agent and invest only at the direction of the company.

Over the years, the use of conventional insured plans has declined relative to the noninsured plans because the latter permits use of different investment manager relationships as well as imposes fewer portfolio restraints. In effect, the burden of meeting benefit obligations has shifted from the life insurance company to the sponsoring company.

With the United States entering an era when fewer and fewer young workers will be forced to support a growing population of retired workers, actuaries and other pension experts indicate that enormous stresses are building up in pay-as-you-go social security and pension funds for workers in the private sector.

Current Problems of Private Pension Plans

Underfunding   The majority of U.S. firms' pension plans are well funded in investments, but when a company fails and has an underfunded pension plan its employees suffer. In 1992, the Pension Benefit Guarantee Corporation (PBGC) estimated that about 5 million workers and retirees were included in underfunded plans.

Some individuals who count on pensions from their employers may lose a significant amount of money that they believe is due them. In 1992, PBGC guaranteed only the first $28,227 a year of a pension. Those retirees whose pensions are higher than that might see them reduced. For those employees who took early retirement, the guarantee may be as low as $12,000 per year.

Need for Indexing   Very few pension plans—actually less than one-third of firms' plans—take care of the inflation that occurs after a worker retires. However, retirees need protection from a drop in the real value of their pensions. Their pensions, like Social Security, should be indexed to the consumer price index, even though inflation protection is not cheap.

Other Problems   Although it is now illegal, some companies continue to fire employees just before they would be eligible for retirement benefits. Some financially distressed companies cut back their annual contributions to their employees' future pensions. In other instances, companies are promising employees improved future pensions without increasing payments to the pension funds.

State and Local Government Pension Plans

These plans generally are established and maintained under complex laws which dictate, in large part, the administrative and investment policy. Most public pension plans require considerable employee contributions as well as employer contributions.

Public pension funds have traditionally invested in bonds—tax exempt but low yielding—issued by the sponsoring government agency. The trustees of these plans are usually elected or appointed public officials, not professional fund managers. Moreover, they are limited in their investment decisions because of state laws regulating the handling of public funds. Since public pension plans are public, they are open to examination by political partisans. Obviously, this situation is not conducive to aggressive investment management. It has been suggested that, from an actuarial viewpoint, many state and local pension plans are technically bankrupt.

History

Before World War II, pension plans were largely limited to the public sector and executives in private industry. In 1946, the United Mine Workers and the coal industry settled for a $100-per-month pension benefit to be paid in addition to social security payments. In 1949, a steel industry fact-finding commission strongly endorsed a pension welfare benefit program as opposed to direct wage increases at that time. In that same year the United Auto Workers and Ford negotiated a $100-per-month noncontributory (by employees) plan. Since then, noncontributory pension plans have grown significantly.

Favorable tax regulation has provided significant employer incentive for establishment and maintenance of employee pension plans. Company contributions are considered tax exempt from federal corporate income tax liability. In addition, pension fund investment earnings—both income and capital gains—are also exempt from federal corporate income tax liability.

In 1974, Congress passed the Employees' Retirement Income Security Act (ERISA), which provided protection for the pensions of workers in private industry. The act was aimed at safeguarding the pension rights of more than 23 million workers covered by private pension plans at that time.

Minimum funding standards required pension managers to put aside enough funds to ensure payments of workers' pensions. Also, rules were established determining proper management of pension funds. American companies have to prudently invest pension money in diversified instruments, for the most part stocks and bonds.

All employees 25 years old or older and with 1 year of work experience in the company must be enrolled in the plan. However, the employer could select one of three alternative investing formulas that would guarantee an employee at least part of the pension whether or not the employee continued working for the same company until retirement.

The federally run PBGC was also established. Its function is to protect workers' benefits in the event that their companies go bankrupt. Employees are also allowed to transfer pension fund credits from one employer to another.

Another important innovation of ERISA was the provision permitting an individual not covered by a company pension plan to establish his or her own retirement plan that would qualify for special tax treatment.

References

Bodie, Zvi, et al., eds., *Financial Aspects of the U.S. Pension System,* National Bureau of Economic Research Project Report, University of Chicago, Chicago, 1984; Holland, Daniel M., *Private Pension Funds,* occasional paper no. 97, National Bureau of Economic Research, Columbia University Press, New York, 1966; Murray, Roger F., *Economic Aspects of Pensions: A Summary Report,* National Bureau of Economic Research, New York, 1968; Tucker, Richard J., *State and Local Pension Funds,* Securities Industry Association, Washington, D.C., 1972.

(*See also* Financial institutions; Financial instruments; Saving)

Douglas Greenwald and
Edward G. Mayers

Perestroika

Perestroika means different things to different people. The interpretations have in common an association with the years of leadership of Mikhail S. Gorbachev (1985–1991), first as general secretary of the Communist Party, the most powerful office in the Soviet Union, and subsequently as President of the U.S.S.R. (from October 1988). The presidency was previously an appointed ceremonial office, but it now gained greater weight thanks to indirect elections as Gorbachev sought to impart democratic and popular authority to his reforms and as he found the party increasingly obstructive (see article "Decline of the Soviet Economy," pp. 259–262, for background). The present article examines Gorbachev's vision and achievements and the more radical calls for change by commercial interests, administrators, and academics impatient for reform which culminated in the complete political breakup of the Soviet Union.

Gorbachev's Perestroika

Many Western observers construe perestroika as a process of replacing all earlier organizational and behavioral rules of the socialist Soviet economy by the organization, economic behavior, and property rights that are supposed to characterize capitalist economies. They measure Gorbachev's success against this standard. But Gorbachev himself intended no such radical transformation when first using the term in an address before the Communist Party Central Committee in June 1985 (". . . the Central Committee isn't thinking only about accelerating the rate of growth of the economy. What we're talking about is a new quality of growth, a shift to intensive development . . . a structural re-shaping [*strukturnaya perestroika*] of the economy, use of effective forms of management, organization, and worker incentives, and a more complete solution of social problems").

Gorbachev's invocation of perestroika, a word traditionally used in a wide variety of senses including refinishing or renovation, reorientation of attitude or philosophical position, and tuning of musical instruments, rather than *zamenenie* or *peremenenie*, words which carry a much more decisive meaning of substitution or replacement, or prevrashchenie with its sense of converting or turning into, confirms the view that Gorbachev intended improvements within the existing social framework rather than a complete escape from the past into a capitalist system. Apart from inclusion of higher consumption levels and greater political freedom as part of his vision for this improved life, Gorbachev had no idée fixe about how the economy should proceed, relying instead on an evolving pragmatic adoption of solutions that would conduce to the two main goals. He recognized the striking achievements of Soviet experience to the mid-1970s—its high rates of economic growth, universal education and literacy, social mobility, comparatively equal income distribution, and great improvements in life expectancy—as well as its more recent shortcomings, including bureaucratic corruption, fragmentation of investment, and self-serving behavior of ministries. Even when talking in terms of "radical economic reform" by mid-1988 in a speech to the 27th Party Congress, it was within the context of continued existence of the socialist system, albeit modified to encourage private activity and also a stricter market discipline within state-owned enterprises.

Decisions and Policies

Gorbachev's first major moves after assuming office were directed at reduction of international tensions through arms reduction and a unilateral moratorium on nuclear testing. Though undramatic in direct terms of economic reform, these moves had profound economic implications, constituting as they did a recognition of the incompatibility of continued high military expenditure (estimated roughly at 15 to 20 percent of GNP) and increases in private consumption from the then-current levels of around 40 to 45 percent of GNP. Indeed, even 20 years earlier the unsustainability of these two goals was recognized by Khrushchev, who himself resolved to undertake military reduction. Deemphasis of the military sector explains Gorbachev's efforts to end Soviet involvement in Afghanistan (finally completed in February 1989); his decision not to intervene in the abandonment of socialist principles by the Warsaw Pact nations of Eastern Europe and the breakdown of Comecon (Council for Mutual Economic Assistance), the intrabloc trading union; and his signing of several treaties with the United States. Other policies that he stressed from the start promoted frank and public discussion—summed up by him and others in the word "glasnost" (openness)—not theretofore known, which in turn led to changes in the political structure, release of political prisoners, and easier emigration.

His 6 years in office saw a host of new procedures and legislation which would affect fundamentally the organization and operation of the economy. One subtle change introduced without fanfare in 1988 was the addition of Western-style gross national product to the Soviet macroeconomic measures traditionally relied on. Since GNP includes the services sector, this move helped to legitimate work performed in this sector which provides a good opening for small business, especially sole (or family) proprietorships and cooperatives.

Among changes with more direct economic importance was the July 1987 law on the socialist enterprise, which dictated strict adherence to the principles of profitability (*khozraschet*) and self-financing (*samofinansirovanie*) through either bank loans or retained profits. State subsidies would no longer be permitted. Market relations were to take place in direct foreign trade participation and interenterprise transactions, subject, of course, to fulfilment of now-reduced official state orders. Equally important was the June 1988 law on cooperatives which, inter alia, permitted joint ventures with foreign investors and allowed the hiring of labor, previously forbidden. Price reform and adjustments were also recognized as desirable to permit the market itself to induce socially desirable decisions, with concern for lower-income groups mitigating the impacts of price change impacts.

Other important economic changes include laws on ownership; new agricultural organizational forms, including long-term leaseholds; conversion of the existing state bank (*Gosbank*) from its traditional enterprise supervisory and control activities to those of a proper central bank with fractional reserve banking and provision for a commercial banking sector; introduction of new personal and enterprise taxes as well as sales taxes which had a value-added structure; and clearly defined rules for cost accounting, which would be necessary to determine profits. The conception and drafting of these laws depended, of course, on economic expertise far beyond the personal capacities of Gorbachev himself, but they were all consistent with his goals. Some details, such as the 70-30 republic-federal split of the sales tax revenue, were added to the law itself by presidential decree, demonstrating his continuing and assiduous concern.

Obstacles to Gorbachev's Program

Frictions and impediments to Gorbachev's program arose in four principal sources:

1. Party bureaucrats whose jobs were threatened opposed even mild change, as did many citizens in and out of the party whose lifetime beliefs were now being denied.

2. Entrenched bureaucrats seeking ground-floor entry to a radically transformed privately owned economy pushed for faster dispersal of state property than Gorbachev had envisaged.

3. Separatist aspirations intensified within the 15 individual Soviet republics, most successfully realized by the three Baltic republics, but pushed by most of the others with force sufficient to destroy the existing political order, replacing it with the Commonwealth of Independent States (*Sodruzhestvo nezavisimykh gosudarstv—SNG*) at the end of 1991. But even before this reconstitution, proponents of separatism opposed reforms which were not viewed as going far enough in the dispersal of economic power, held up transmission of funds to the central budget, and contributed to the climate of uncertainty in industrial hierarchical relationships.

4. The budget deficit was accelerating, and the accompanying macroeconomic concern increasingly focused on money-supply growth and inflation as the overriding problem of the economy. The appropriate cure involved taking monetary and fiscal measures: confiscating rubles to reduce the money supply and removing subsidies (through price rises) to lower the expenditure side of the budget. Price increases would have the additional advantage of stimulating production, it was thought. As these proposals were increasingly bruited, and as inflation, though still mild, officially reached 7 to 10 percent levels, consumers strove to convert money by hoarding physical commodities; and workers, especially in agriculture, resorted increasingly to subsistence production and barter, generating shortages of consumer goods.

In early 1991, consumer prices were raised by as much as 250 percent, but the government withdrew the increases in the face of strong public opposition. Moreover, the focus on subsidy reduction through price increases to eliminate the deficit was not in keeping with socioeconomic constraints, elementary macroeconomic considerations, and the realities of the budget in the first place. While food products were heavily subsidized (nearly 90 billion rubles in 1989), food was still not cheap for perhaps one-third of the total population, so that the sharp increases would immiserize a large social group if wages were not immediately indexed to compensate, which would raise prices straightaway, and if pensioners—about one-seventh of the total population—were not given budgetary assistance, which would reintroduce a deficit.

Overlooked by many decision makers was the possibility of reducing the deficit by raising budget revenues, especially through higher enterprise taxes. During the 1980s prices in industry were already being raised in connection with input cost review and a shift to a greater use of negotiated prices. One effect of these price increases was a total national increase in profits of 52 percent between 1985 and 1989. But because taxes were not raised accordingly, the funds remaining in enterprise hands soared, with the portion going to the enterprises' economic stimulation funds (ESP) rising from 16 to 49 percent. The ESP is used for worker incentive awards, social consumption (e.g., housing), and new technology. Between 1985 and 1989 the total increase in the annual volume going to this fund rose by 80.2 billion rubles, which almost exactly equaled the total budget deficit in the latter year. Although it appears that a large part of this fund was directed into self-financed investment (which grew from 3.1 to 51 percent of total state enterprise investment between 1986 and 1989), it apparently did little to stimulate production. This accumulation was pointed to with alarm in the 500-Day Plan but appears to have drawn little attention elsewhere in macroeconomic debate. The new tax law (July 1990) did regularize and standardize profits taxes (some of which were previously termed "contributions out of free remainder of profits" and some "deductions from profits"), but at the time of this writing it is too early to ascertain its financial impact.

One of the main voices for radical reform was Boris Yeltsin, President of the Russian Republic and a long-time adversary of Gorbachev. His economic advisers' views included full-scale and rapid conversion to a market economy through dispersal of state property, although it never was clear that this could be done in a way to avoid the inherent unfairness in entrenched bureaucrats. Foreign participation was encouraged, but there has been little inflow of foreign capital either to participate in existing enterprises or to start new business. Prices would be set wholly in terms of market conditions, although with no consideration of the restricted supply of goods. Doing this in early 1992 resulted in an increase of over 300% in consumer prices and set off protests by consumer groups and politicians, including Russian Vice-President Rutskoi. Frictions and competition among the individual states over division of assets, acquisition of goods at differentiated prices, the general breakdown of supply, and monitoring of foreign food contributions all contribute to the uncertain future of the SNG as of early 1992.

References

Ekonomicheskaya gazeta (The Economic Gazette, with name change since 1990 to Ekonomika i zhizn'—Economics and Life) Moscow, contains most of the laws cited here; Gorbachev, M. S., Perestroika i novoe myshlenie dlya nashei strany i dlya vsego mira (Perestroika and New Thinking for Our Country and the Whole World), Moscow, Polit. Literat. Pubs., 1987, published in English by Harper & Row, 1987; Izbrannnye rechi i stat'i (Selected Speeches and Articles), Moscow, Political Pubs., 1985; Selected Speeches and Articles, Progress Pubs., Moscow, 1987 (expanded version of Russian language edition); Gorbachev/Yeltsin Working Group, Transition to the Market, Part I (The Concept and Program) & Part II (Draft of Legal Acts), ["The Five-Hundred Day Plan"], Moscow, Sept. 1990; Narodnoe khozyaistvo SSSR (National Economy of the USSR—statistical yearbook), Moscow, various years.

Alan Abouchar

Permanent income hypothesis

The permanent income hypothesis relates total consumption to the income flow that would be obtained if current human and nonhuman wealth were converted to a real (constant-dollar) perpetuity. This income stream is termed "permanent income." It is applied both to individual households and to the aggregate economy. In its strictest form, consumption is hypothesized to be a constant fraction of permanent income. Thus consumption with respect to permanent income or wealth is 1.

The permanent income hypothesis differs sharply from the earlier Keynesian absolute income hypothesis of the consumption function, which related consumption to current measured income. The permanent income and life-cycle hypotheses of the consumption function are equivalent in their full theoretical formulations, but in practice differ in the particular empirical approximations used for statistical estimation and testing.

The permanent income hypothesis has been the principal means by which macroeconomists have reconciled low marginal propensities to spend current income with a secularly constant and high average propensity to spend income. The marginal propensity to consume (MPC) is the ratio of the change in consumption to the change in current income. The average propensity to consume (APC) is the ratio of consumption to current income. Early Keynesian economists had explained consumption as a linear function of current income. When this function was estimated using the 1930s data, a MPC of about 0.7 was obtained. Compared with the observed APC of 0.9, this suggested that the ratio of consumption to income would fall as income rose over time. The secular stagnation thesis asserted that investment opportunities would be insufficient to fill the growing gap between income and consumption, so that a steadily deepening depression would occur unless there was offsetting growth in government expenditure. When the post–World War II data became available, it was soon obvious that in fact consumption rose just about in proportion to income.

Friedman's Early Work

Milton Friedman (1957) showed that the concept of permanent income, which he had developed previously (Friedman and Kuznets, 1945) to explain household consumption, also could explain aggregate consumption. Friedman first applied the microeconomic analysis of Irving Fisher and John Hicks to observe that pure consumption of service flows (not expenditures) is related to a household's wealth, the real interest rate, and other factors which can be neglected when averaging over all households. For the type of utility functions that imply the observed constant secular average propensity to consume, pure consumption will equal the product of real wealth and a function of the real interest rate. Finally, if the real interest rate on perpetuities is a constant, as in the neoclassical growth model, pure consumption equals a constant times permanent income. Short-run fluctuations of current income around permanent income will affect pure consumption only in proportion to the small change that they induce in wealth and permanent income. Over time, pure consumption will grow in proportion to permanent income. Thus, we observe a small MPC defined for current income and a high, secularly constant APC.

The permanent income hypothesis thus gave the theoretical basis for rejecting the secular stagnation thesis, a concept already suffering by comparison with the facts. In addition, the low estimated marginal propensities to spend current income implied smaller values for Keynesian multipliers than previously supposed, so that the economy's apparent stability was enhanced.

Recent Empirical Work

Empirical work following Friedman's lead initially met with mixed success as summarized by Thomas Mayer (1972). Conflicting estimates of the effect of current income on permanent income and hence consumption were reported. Michael Darby (1974) showed that the conflicting estimates could be reconciled by noting that Friedman's permanent income hypothesis referred to pure consumption and not to consumer expenditures. Indeed, under Friedman's hypothesis, fluctuations in current income around permanent income should affect expenditures on durable and semidurable goods over and above the effect on consumption. A statistical bias was introduced which varied according to whether the analyst used data closer to pure consumption or consumer expenditures and to whether annual or quarterly observations were used. Darby also showed that a particular estimator of permanent income proposed by Friedman is the one implied by the permanent income hypothesis.

Empirical work aimed at explaining consumer expenditures (such as Darby, 1977–1978) has found both permanent and transitory (current minus permanent) income important, as well as other factors that influence household investment in durable and semidurable consumer goods such as automobiles, refrigerators, and clothing. Friedman's earlier implications for the secular stagnation hypothesis and Keynesian multipliers ultimately have proved correct.

Almost simultaneously Hall (1978) turned the permanent income hypothesis around by arguing that current consumption is proportional to current permanent income, and so changes in consumption can occur only if there are changes in permanent income. Leaving aside planned changes in permanent income and consumption due to planned saving, Hall emphasized that variability in consumption growth must reflect unexpected changes in wealth over the period of concern. This "rational expectations" version of the permanent income hypothesis eliminated the difficult problem of estimation of permanent income—or, alternatively, total human and non-human wealth. This simplicity is a powerful argument for Hall's approach. Empirical work in the area over the next decade attempted to implement this rational expectations approach, but the strict implications of the model repeatedly failed to be confirmed. It appears that this failure may be explained by the empirical intractability of finding an empirical measure of pure consumption devoid of elements of household investment in durable and semidurable goods. Thus, economists must ultimately either solve this problem or else continue to use estimates of permanent income or total wealth to explain consumption and consumer expenditures.

References

Darby, Michael R., "The Permanent Income Theory of Consumption—A Restatement," *Quarterly Journal of Economics,* vol. 88, May 1974, pp. 228–250; Darby, Michael R., "The Consumer Expenditure Function," *Explorations in Economic Research,* vol. 4, National Bureau of Economic Research, New York, Winter–Spring 1977–1978, pp. 645–674; Friedman, Milton, *A Theory of the Consumption Function,* Princeton University Press, Princeton, N.J., 1957; Friedman, Milton, and Simon Kuznets, *Income from Independent Professional Practice,* National Bureau of Economic Research, New York, 1945; Hall, Robert E., "Stochastic Implications of the Life Cycle–Permanent Income Hypothesis: Theory and Evidence," *Journal of Political Economy,* vol. 86, April 1978; Mayer, Thomas, *Permanent Income, Wealth, and Consumption,* University of California Press, Los Angeles, 1972.

(*See also* Chicago school; Consumer theory; Consumption function; Income; Rational expectations; Wealth)

Michael R. Darby

Personal income taxation (*see* Taxation, an overview)

Phillips curve

Phillips curve analysis poses the economic issues of the existence and stability of an inverse relationship between unemployment and inflation in the United States (and other advanced capitalistic countries) and, if this should be validated, the choice by policymakers of a socially acceptable combination between the two parameters.

In the traditional classical view, price and wage flexibility effectively maintains the economy at, or close to, a full-employment potential gross domestic product. Indeed, this assumption was "synthesized" into latter-day Keynesian thought—the high unemployment of the 1930s was ascribed precisely to maladjustments in these markets due to the stickiness in money-wage levels not contemplated in the older theory. Since downward stickiness was the problem, policy measures that generated some degree of inflation could validate employment-raising wage levels; and so a menu of inflation and unemployment rates appeared to be presented to policymakers in the 1960s, who could then decide what the trade-off might be.

While Irving Fisher in a mostly forgotten 1928 work had made an early contribution to the relationship between prices and unemployment, the modern debate was initiated in a study by A. W. Phillips (1958) showing a stable, nonlinear inverse relationship between the change in the wage rate and the unemployment rate during 1861 to 1957 in the United Kingdom. This was subsequently extended and refined in 1960 by Richard G. Lipsey, who independently also found a stable negative relationship between wage inflation and the demand for labor (as well as making an allowance for frictional unemployment); and by Bent Hansen, who described frictional unemployment as a feature of a labor market with incomplete information by job seekers of job vacancies in order to explain how wage inflation could vary with the same unemployment rate. The transformation to a trade-off between price (rather than wage) inflation and unemployment rates was made later in several ways by other economists, frequently by means of an assumption of constant markup pricing on unit labor costs by firms, resulting in an inflation rate that registers the differential between the change in money wages and the change in labor productivity.

Keynesian Theory

Keynesian theory had viewed inflation as a condition arising only when demand was in excess of full-employment output (while, in the monetarist approach, the impact of increased demand via money-supply growth could result in higher prices much sooner). Implicitly, Keynesian theory assumed that prices would be inflexible downward if circumstances of high unemployment and large supplies prevailed, and would be stable and in equilibrium at the point of full employment. (Graphically, this would be represented by the mirror-image L-shaped graph, with price change on the ordinate and real gross national product, GNP, on the abscissa of a set of axes.)

This perspective of the onset of inflation beginning at full employment appeared increasingly at odds with actual price and unemployment developments in the 1950s and 1960s. While it was rare that the general level of prices declined significantly when unemployment was high in this period, prices of many commodities whose raw materials costs are large (raw industrial products, agricultural products, etc.) or which are subject to import competition were sensitive to demand changes. As demand and employment eased, inflation rates sometimes were reversed or, more frequently, slowed. Moreover, it was argued that product and factor markets need not be in the presumed equilibrium state at full employment—indeed, this might be rare and perhaps unrealizable in the real world since it would express an unusual situation of balance in supply and demand in all markets. Long before that point, premature inflation would ensue because production bottlenecks would have been registered in some sectors. This would be particularly evident in labor markets, where immobilities in supply among regions and occupations, lack of information of job vacancies, union or racial discrimination, etc., generate shortages of skilled workers long before full employment is reached. Finally, the market power of labor unions and big business might more easily be exerted during periods of rising demand (which provide a cost-push inflation explanation of the trade-off between inflation and unemployment rates).

The emergence of inflation long before full employment was reached appeared clearly evident in the data for the 1950s and 1960s in the major industrialized countries. Accordingly, a policy dilemma was posed to the authorities, who were confronted by probable inflation if stimulative macroeconomic measures were used to reduce unemployment. On a graph where price change is marked on the ordinate and the unemployment rate on the abscissa, the policy choice in the 1960s for the United States resembled a round L. On such a graph, an inflation rate of 3½ percent was related to a so-called full-employment unemployment rate of 4 percent.

However, the terms of trade-off, to the advantage of inflation, appeared to worsen at the turn of the decade. Moreover, the apparent stability of the Phillips curve was shattered by data for the 1970s when inflation and unemployment rates increased simultaneously—the former doubling in the United States, Germany, and Japan during 1970 to 1974 relative to 1965 to 1969. Supporters of Phillips curve analyses argued that this represented merely a worsening of the trade-off—a rightward shift of the curve. This shift was ascribed to a changed composition of the labor force toward greater representation of women and teenagers (who are employed at jobs at less-than-average productivity and are more frequently unemployed), more aggressive union behavior, sharply rising energy costs, and greater disincentives to work resulting from government income maintenance programs. The range of choices remained, but the cost of inflation was higher at given unemployment rates. Another view in support of an underlying Phillips curve was that the data of the 1970s did not fit into the curve only because of special externally influenced factors such as the oil and agricultural supply shortages and devaluation of the dollar.

Monetarist Analysis

In contrast, the very existence of a stable Phillips curve in the long run was questioned by Milton Friedman, Edmond Phelps, and others in the late 1960s and 1970s. Ideologically connected with the classical analysis that real wages determine the demand for and supply of labor, Friedman (1966) and Phelps (1972) assign a critical role to anticipated and unanticipated rates of inflation. At a given anticipated rate of inflation, unemployment will cling to a so-called natural or equilibrium rate. The latter rate is considered equivalent to sustainable full employment, after allowance for frictional and structural involuntary unemployment plus voluntary unemployment (that induced by unemployment compensation, welfare payments, two-income households, etc.). This rate has been judged to be in the range of 5½ to 6½ percent in the late 1970s, in contrast with 4 to 5 percent assumed as full employment in U.S. government reports and others.

The natural rate of unemployment in a state of equilibrium emerges whenever inflation is completely anticipated. Under that condition, contractual arrangements presumably will have been adjusted to the inflation rate, relative prices in product and factor markets would remain unchanged, and output would remain unaffected. However, should prices rise at an unanticipated rate, say, because of excess stimulation through expansionary monetary or fiscal policy, this will become evident sooner to employers than to workers, whose wages in any event tend to change more slowly owing to contractual arrangements and other immobilities. Employment increases because real wages have declined, temporarily unbeknown to the workers. It is this misperception by workers that draws them into employment and reduces unemployment below the natural rate. Conversely, when money wages decline, the misperception of a decline in real wages leads workers to leave jobs and seek others that pay more—in the process raising unemployment above the natural rate. In this sense, a short-term Phillips curve does provide a trade-off between inflation and a lowered unemployment rate.

The long-run results are different. As misperceptions concerning unanticipated inflation are dissipated, workers will require higher money wages to restore their previous real income, which reduces profits, lowers employment, and raises unemployment to the natural rate. But while the real economy has reverted to its natural level, its output is sold at high prices. Indeed, in the so-called accelerationist view, only additional bouts of inflation—always containing some element of temporary misperception of the inflation rate—would succeed in keeping unemployment below the natural rate. Accordingly, stimulative macroeconomic policy by the authorities in the long run would remain a no-win game because workers' real wages eventually adjust to inflation. Over time, the Phillips curve is vertical—when it is "expectations-augmented."

In the Friedman-Phelps view, adaptive expectations represent the time interval of lessening misperceptions between the expected and the actual inflation rates and provide the basis for the accelerationist theory. (The latter may be conceived graphically as a layered series of negatively sloped, short-run Phillips curves, depicting successively higher and worse trade-offs as long as excess demand prevails, and a vertical, long-run curve positioned at the natural unemployment rate.)

Rational Expectations and the New Classicism

In the new rational expectations approach, past rates of inflation that affect adaptive expectations represent only part of the information necessary to make a more or less accurate inflation prediction. Because of spreading sophistication and knowledge of the economic system, in a model sense, economic agents may now make decisions rationally, eliminating any gap between actual and expected inflation. Since the role of money growth in creating inflation is well understood by rationally acting economic agents, there are no lags or surprises concerning actual and anticipated rates of inflation, and bargains are made accordingly; therefore, no impact on real economic variables results from shifts in economic policy. While the adaptive model implies that lags may influence the course of the real economy for a short period of time, the rational expectations approach concedes such changes in neither the short nor the long run, except through a random mechanism, making economic policy essentially useless. It was possible to describe the business cycle by an equation that says four-fifths of the deviation from trend GNP depends on its value in the previous year and the remainder by a random component (unusual, unanticipated fiscal and monetary change and other random developments like wars or oil shortages).

Still, there were significant departures of actual- from full-employment potential GNP not so easily dismissed. Robert Lucas and Thomas Sargent, identified as new classicists, attribute such departures to imperfect information in firms concerning price developments in the economy. Mistakenly thinking in a period of generally rising prices that demand for their products alone is increasing, the firms produce more and raise GNP above potential. Eventually, disappointment sets in and cutbacks are made. In this view, changes in government stabilization policies lead to confusion and errors in price expectations and instability in the economy. However, empirical findings by Frederick Mishkin and others do not find "price surprises" significantly correlated with GNP fluctuations. Moreover, the information-based models in rational expectations continue to assume price and wage flexibility in the short run (with some exceptions), a strong voluntary component in being unemployed, and belief in market equilibrium—conditions that many economists, particularly "liberal" Keynesians, allege do not correspond with the stickiness in these markets observable in the real world. The major difference in the two approaches thus becomes one of whether policy is effective or not—the classicists thinking not, the Keynesian activists remaining hopeful.

Other major issues of difference between so-called liberal Keynesian and conservative monetarist analyses center on the magnitude of the natural rate of unemployment and the costs of departure from it. With respect to the natural rate, changes in the demography of the labor force due to higher proportions of women and youths and expanded income maintenance programs appear to have raised the noninflationary unemployment rate to the neighborhood of 6 percent—and even higher rates are conceivable in view of supply-side or external influences such as rising costs of energy and raw materials and the declining value of the dollar in recent years. Efforts to lower unemployment rates by stimulative demand policies appear to have commanded an increasingly heavier inflation cost, to have embedded expectations of accelerating inflation into market processes, and to be self-defeating in the long run. As part of a disinflation program, conservatives propose micro measures which improve the functioning of labor markets by reducing the mismatch of job vacancies and the unemployed, facilitating competition in product and labor markets, lessening disincentives to work and to invest, etc. On the macro level, a sufficiently long cooling-off period in the economy is considered necessary to break inflationary expectations. By contrast, liberals dispute significant disinflation effects of high unemployment, citing studies that show flat trade-offs when unemployment rises above the natural rate, deploring the social costs of unemployment, and recommending government price and wage controls in demand management of inflation. In the early 1990s, some rational expectationists were discouraged by the costly 1980–1982 disinflation, while liberals became uncomfortable by the danger of fiscal activism during a period of already high budget deficits.

References

Fisher, Irving, *The Money Illusion*, Adelphi, New York, 1928; Friedman, Milton, "The Role of Monetary Policy," *American Economic Review*, vol. 56, no. 1, March 1966, pp. 1–17; Lipsey, Richard G., "The Relation between Unemployment and the Rate of Change of Money Wage Rates in the United Kingdom, 1862–1957, A Further Analysis," *Economica*, vol. 27, February 1960, pp. 1–31; Lucas, Robert, Jr., "Some International Evidence on Output—Inflation Trade-Offs," *American Economic Review*, vol. 63, 1973, pp. 326–334; Okun, Arthur, "Efficient Disinflationary Policies," *American Economic Review*, vol. 68, no. 2, May 1978, pp. 348–352; Phelps, Edmund S., *Inflation Policy and Unemployment Theory: The Cost Benefit Approach to Monetary Planning*, Norton, New York, 1972; Phillips, A. W., "Relationships between Unemployment and the Rate of Change in Money Wage Rates in the United Kingdom, 1862–1957," *Economica*, vol. 25, November 1958, pp. 283–299; Sargent, Thomas J., and Neil Walbee, "Rational Expectations, the Optimal Monetary Instrument and the Optimal Money Supply Rate," *Journal of Political Economy*, vol. 83, 1975, pp. 214–254.

(*See also* Chicago school; Employment and unemployment; Federal Reserve policy; Fiscal policy; Incomes policy; Inflation; Keynesian economics; Labor force; Monetary policy; Money illusion; Post-Keynesian economics; Rational expectations; Rigid prices)

Herman I. Liebling

Pigou effect (*see* Real balance effect theory)

Planning, economic (*see* Economic planning)

Physiocrats

The physiocrats were a group of *economistes* (as they were called in French, the first ones to bear that label) who reacted against the views of the mercantilists and asserted instead that productivity of land is the major force behind economic prosperity. The group was headed by François Quesnay, physician to King Louis XV and Mme. Pompadour, who took a short but intense interest in economic doctrine. The physiocrats' thinking exerted a powerful influence on leading citizens like Robert Turgot, who was Louis XVI's minister of finance; Pierre Samuel du Pont de Nemours, the French industrialist who later came to the United States; and, on the other side of the English Channel, Adam Smith, the well-known professor of moral philosophy at Glasgow College in Scotland.

Fundamental to physiocratic doctrine is a strong belief in a natural order transcending legislative and administrative decisions, a conviction that ran exactly counter to mercantilist views prevalent throughout Europe earlier in the eighteenth century. The mercantilists had played down the role of agriculture and had stressed the contribution of processing, manufacturing, and service industries in raising the value of a nation's exports. They had, through a system of taxes, tariffs, and direct controls, taken steps to discourage and even limit imports. And they had glorified the resulting accumulation of precious metals as the hallmark of a nation's prosperity and power.

Physiocrats, by contrast, considered these policies damaging to the public interest. They believed that only the agricultural sector produces new wealth—the so-called *produit net* that is left over after all of a farmer's costs have been met. This *produit net* could be claimed by landlords as rent and be spent by them in the economy at large. Or it could be taxed by the government—at least in part—without affecting farmers' incentives to produce as much and as efficiently as possible. The physiocrats were single taxers; they proposed dismantling the complex system of taxes and regulations that the mercantilists had installed in an effort to regulate the economy and channel it toward export industry and commerce. According to the physiocrats, this effort not only placed too heavy a burden on agriculture but also interfered with the self-serving incentive of individual businesses to maximize their own profits and, in the process, buttress the collective welfare of the nation. In their view, expanding the network of trade required commercial cooperation rather than exploitation, especially with respect to agriculture. "*Laissez faire, laissez passer,*" a slogan much used by the physiocrats, signifies their antiregulation, antitariff philosophy.

Hoping to document agriculture's contribution, Quesnay devised the famous *Tableau Economique,* which attempted to trace specifically the flow of production and wealth through a nation's economy. Though not clear in many ways, it was much admired at the time of publication. Even today, it is lauded as the first schematic presentation of how goods and payments move in a circular flow, or how national income and output interact and balance out. From another point of view, the *Tableau* can be pictured as a rudimentary input-output table that attempts to show how the productive class (i.e., the agricultural sector) supplies other producers (the physiocrats called the other producers "sterile"), permits them to subsist and to make capital investments, and thus supports the economy as a whole.

Adam Smith, who visited France repeatedly in order to learn more from his friend Quesnay, later wrote that physiocracy represents a reaction to the excesses of mercantilism. The doctrine retains some support to this day, especially in farm communities, among environmentalists, and in resource-oriented economies. But its single-minded emphasis on primary production as the only source of income and wealth has reduced its status to that of a curiosity in the history of economic analysis.

References

Blaug, Mark, *Economic Theory in Retrospect,* 3d ed., Cambridge University Press, Cambridge, 1978; Fellner, William, *Modern Economic Analysis,* McGraw-Hill, New York, 1960, pp. 40–48.

(*See also* Input-output analysis; Laissez faire; Mercantilism)

G. H. Mattersdorf

Pollution abatement costs

Ideally, pollution abatement costs should refer to the true opportunity costs of a policy or strategy intended to reduce the level of pollution, where the term "opportunity costs" refers to what society foregos in material and psychic benefit when resources are redirected to support the policy. So defined, pollution abatement *costs* differ from pollution abatement *expenditures.* Indeed, many pollution abatement strategies are possible without the need for any expenditure of funds. These strategies, nevertheless, have opportunity costs to the extent that, in the long run, they lower the level of production, reduce employment opportunities, or lead to the elimination or degradation of certain pollution-causing goods previously demanded by the consumer.

Breaking Down Pollution-Control Costs

It is often important to distinguish between pollution-control costs engendered by policy and pollution-control costs that have other origins such as "goodwill" or profitability. Complete discharge of valuable raw materials is clearly not in the interest of the profit-maximizing firm. Neither is it in the firm's interest to eliminate completely the discharge of raw materials since the costs of control will eventually exceed the value of recovered raw materials. Generally there is an ideal profit-maximizing level of control somewhere between these two extremes. If one is interested in assessing the costs of governmental pollution-control policy, it should be recognized that this policy is usually not necessary to force a rational polluter to eliminate that amount of discharge that would be eliminated in any event in the interests of profitability. Therefore, the costs associated with this amount of discharge should not be considered as costs of pollution-control policy. Only the unprofitable control costs engendered by the policy should be so considered.

Unfortunately, given the standard accounting practices used by firms, in practice it is extremely difficult to separate out the unprofitable control costs from the profitable costs. Often engineering analysis and good judgment must be intelligently integrated with the available cost data. The task is further complicated because the data often represent expenditure information and not cost information. Expenditure data differ from cost data in that they are influenced by the firm's institutional setting. For example, two firms with the identical control costs may generate different expenditure data depending on such factors as whether certain inputs necessary for control, such as land, are already owned by the firm or whether they must be purchased or rented.

Identifying the truly incremental costs of pollution-control policy is also complicated by severe joint-cost problems. While many pollution problems can be attacked at the point where residuals are discharged to the environment (so-called end-of-pipe controls), often it is cheaper to reduce residuals through either process changes, input changes, product-mix changes, or a combination of these strategies in addition to end-of-pipe controls. Thus, facing pollution restrictions, a firm might decide to discontinue the production of one of its products and to produce the remaining products with a different technique requiring new investment and annual outlays for materials. Since capital replacement and material purchases are an ordinary occurrence, it would be a mistake to attribute all these outlays to the pollution-control strategy. However, estimating the portion of the outlays exclusively engendered by the control strategy requires a complex analytical effort.

Most current pollution-control cost estimates are extremely short run in that they implicitly assume that the polluter faces fixed demands. The longer-run implications of product substitution, declines in investments, effects on innovation, and managerial efficiency (in both the public and private sectors), which conceivably could result from costly environmental regulatory programs, are usually not reflected in the cost figures. However, recent analyses of the effects of regulation on productivity and a growing concern about the administrative burden, on the private sector, of a large number of regulations are stimulating researchers to broaden their concepts of environmental costs to include the longer-run and indirect implications of policy.

References

Cremeans, John E., and Frank W. Seagal, "National Expenditures for Pollution Abatement and Control, 1972," *Survey of Current Business,* vol. 55, no. 2, February 1975; Hanke, Steve H., and Ivors Gutmanis, "Estimates of Industrial Waterborne Residuals Control Costs: A Review of Concepts, Methodology, and Empirical Results," in Henry M. Peskin and Eugene P. Seskin (eds.), *Cost Benefit Analysis and Water Pollution Policy,* Urban Institute, Washington, D.C., 1975; Kopp, Raymond J., and Michael Hazilla, "The Social Cost of Environmental Quality Regulations: A General Equilibrium Analysis," *Journal of Political Economy,* vol. 98, no. 4, August 1990; U.S. Environmental Protection Agency, *Environmental Investments: The Costs of a Clean Environment,* EPA 230-12-90-084, December 1990.

(*See also* Economic incentives for environmental protection; Externalities; Government regulation)

Henry M. Peskin

Population theory (*see* Malthusian theory of population)

Portfolio management theories

The main reason for saving and investing is to provide for future needs. Parents with children put away a little money each month and invest it with the hope that they will have enough funds to pay for their children's college education. Others save and invest for retirement, and still others save and invest to buy something down the road—like a new home. Intermediaries often do the actual saving and investing on behalf of their beneficiaries. For example, a corporation sets up a pension plan to provide for its employees' retirement income. As another example, a donor wants to achieve a philanthropic goal and gives a foundation money to invest to achieve this purpose.

Thus, investing is not an end in itself, but rather a means to obtain some goal. With this notion in mind, portfolio theory has developed in order to allow an investor to invest in the most efficient way to achieve the objective. Exactly how an investor should structure a portfolio depends upon the investor's current circumstances and goals.

In 1952, Harry Markowitz set forth a mathematical model that showed how an investor should optimally combine assets into a portfolio so as to obtain the greatest expected rate of return for any given level of risk. As subsequent researchers discovered, the Markowitz model made some underlying assumptions about the behavior of investors and the structure of asset returns that put some limitations on its applicability. However, these limitations are not significant for many investment situations. But even where the limitations could be significant, Markowitz's model contained the essential insights for the development of more general portfolio theories. For his contribution, Markowitz received the Nobel Prize in economics.

Before Markowitz

In 1934, Benjamin Graham and David Dodd published their classic book *Security Analysis,* which epitomized through its many revisions the investment process before the intellectual acceptance and understanding of Markowitz's portfolio theory. The focus of Graham and Dodd, as well as many investors of their time, was on the individual security. Their advice was to examine the fundamentals of a company to determine the intrinsic value, which even in their own words they called an "elusive concept."

Graham and Dodd believed that the intrinsic value of a security was a function of the "earning power" of a company and that the current price of a security could be greater or less than this intrinsic value. The process of forming a portfolio involved ferreting out those securities whose current market prices were below their intrinsic values. Since they believed that the price of an undervalued security would ultimately return to the intrinsic value of that security, a portfolio of such securities would necessarily be a good portfolio.

In this pre-Markowitz view, a prudent investor would evaluate the suitability of an investment according to its own characteristics. If each investment in a portfolio was suitable for an investor, then the overall portfolio would also be suitable. This view that the evaluation of each asset on its own merits is central to the investment process became associated with the "prudent-man" rule. As the common law developed, a trustee who invested in highly speculative securities might well face a lawsuit for recovery of losses if one of the securities became valueless even though the entire portfolio turned in impressive gains. The way in which security returns interact within a portfolio—the underlying fundamental insight of modern portfolio theory—had no bearing on prudent investing.

Markowitz's Insight

As a graduate student at the University of Chicago, Markowitz concluded what may appear obvious today, that the attribute of a portfolio that should be of most interest to an investor is the total return on the portfolio, not the returns of the individual securities except insofar as they contribute to the total return of the portfolio itself.

Markowitz then noted that a portfolio's total return is uncertain, so that buying a portfolio of risky assets is equivalent to buying a lottery ticket, or more precisely a probability distributions of returns. There are many ways to describe the characteristics of a probability distribution, and Markowitz chose two statistics: the expected return and the uncertainty of obtaining the expected return as measured by the standard deviation of the total return.

(The expected return has a precise statistical definition, which does not correspond to the common definition of "expected" as "considered likely or certain." To take an example, consider a lottery that returns either *plus* 20 percent or *minus* 10 percent, each equally likely as determined by the flip of a coin. The expected return is defined as the sum of each possible outcome weighted by the probability of obtaining that outcome, and in this case is the sum of 20 percent multiplied by the 50 percent chance of obtaining this first return and minus 10 percent multiplied by the 50 percent chance of obtaining this second return, or an expected return of 5 percent. Thus, this lottery will never yield its expected return, always producing a return 15 percent greater than expected or 15 percent less than expected. A good way of conceptualizing the expected return statistic is to think of it as the center of the possible outcomes with actual outcomes falling to either side of it and sometimes by large amounts. In turn, the standard deviation is a statistical measure of how far away actual returns can be from the expected return, with increasing values indicating greater dispersion of outcomes.)

Again, something that may appear obvious today but that has profound implications for investing was Markowitz's observation that any sensible investor would choose from all portfolios with the same level of risk, as measured by standard deviation, that portfolio with the greatest expected return. Similarly, any sensible investor would choose from all portfolios with the same expected return that portfolio with the smallest standard deviation. Markowitz then developed the mathematical algorithm to determine the set of portfolios satisfying these two conditions, which he dubbed "the efficient set of portfolios." The least-risky portfolio in this efficient set will have the smallest expected return. As risk increases, the expected return of the efficient portfolios will increase. Any sensible investor will weigh the increase in expected return against the increase in risk to settle on an actual portfolio to hold.

This new view of evaluating a portfolio in terms of its risk and expected return is totally at variance with the old prudent-man rule. When Markowitz examined the formula for the standard deviation of return, he discovered that the risk of a portfolio depended in large part upon how the returns of individual securities interacted among themselves and not very much upon the volatility of the return of any individual asset. As an extreme example, consider two highly volatile assets with the property that when one asset realizes a return less than expected, the other asset realizes a return greater than expected. The return on a portfolio of these two assets could be very predictable, with the better-than-expected return of one of the assets always offsetting the worse-than-expected return of the other asset—even though the investor has no idea in advance which asset will be the disappointing one.

In contrast to the old prudent-man rule, which said that each asset had to be evaluated individually, Markowitz's approach would permit the inclusion in a portfolio of such individually volatile securities as junk bonds, futures, exotic derivatives, and options. Some would interpret the prudent-man rule as precluding these types of assets, and certainly a trustee who excluded these types of assets would be more assured of conforming to the prudent-man rule. In 1974, the passage of ERISA (Employee Income Security Retirement Act) finally stated that, at least for private pension funds, the return on the total portfolio is what matters and thereby overrode the central premise of the prudent-man rule. Still, many personal, state, and municipal trusts are subject to the old prudent-man rule.

Sharpe's Contribution

To employ Markowitz's algorithm to determine the efficient set required an inordinate number of statistical estimates for any reasonable-size problem. The interaction of the returns of every conceivable pair of assets had to be ascertained. With 1000 assets, there are 499,500 distinct pairs, and each of these pairs would need to be examined—an impossible task. Markowitz proposed a method for simplifying this task, but it was William Sharpe, another Nobel laureate, who provided the economic theory that made Markowitz's insight a practical way of investing money.

Sharpe assumed that there was a rate at which investors could borrow or lend, like the rate on Treasury bills, and that all investors held the same view of the probabilistic characteristics of individual assets, known in the jargon as "homogeneous expectations." Another way to state this last assumption is that no investor believes his or her expectations are better than other investors' and therefore is willing to accept the market expectations implicit in the current prices. Exploiting these two assumptions, Sharpe showed that every investor would hold the market portfolio consisting of all risky assets weighted according to their market weights in conjunction with a position in the risk-free asset. Those investors who wanted less risk than the market portfolio would put a portion of their money into the market portfolio and then cushion the risk with a position in the risk-free asset. Those investors who wanted more risk would buy the market portfolio on margin, which means borrowing to finance further investment in the market portfolio.

Sharpe also developed the capital asset pricing model (CAPM) that related the expected return of an individual asset to a portfolio measure of risk for that asset, known by the Greek letter beta, or β. Some assets will on average have greater returns than the market when the market is up and greater losses when the market is down, while other assets will on average have smaller returns when the market is up and smaller losses when the market is down. Those securities whose returns on average mirror market returns have a β of 1. Those securities whose returns on average amplify the returns of the market have a β greater than 1, while those securities whose returns on average attenuate the returns of the market have a β less than 1. A security whose returns on average reverse those of the market has a negative β. (Few equities have negative βs, but some derivative assets do have such negative βs and serve to reduce the risk of a portfolio.) According to the CAPM, the expected return of an individual asset monotonically increases with its β.

Some Complications

The essence of Markowitz's theory is that the return on the entire portfolio is all that matters and the actual assets in the portfolio are inconsequential except as each asset helps to determine the overall return on the portfolio. For many investment situations, this proposition is perfectly adequate. However, there are times when what is in the portfolio does make a difference. As an illustration, consider an investor who currently lives in Pennsylvania but wants to retire to Marco Island in Florida. To hedge against fluctuations in the value of homes on Marco Island, the investor might rationally decide to invest in a house there today even though that might not be the home that the investor ultimately wants. If Marco Island real estate values increase, the value of that house will increase. If the real estate values fall, the value of that house will decrease. But whatever happens, the investor at retirement will be able to trade that house in for a comparable home in that area.

Better yet for this investor would be to buy a share in a diversified portfolio of homes in the Marco Island area—thus diversifying away the specific vagaries of sections of the Marco Island real estate market. If such an option were available, the investor would now be faced with spreading his or her money over three types of assets: the market portfolio of risky assets, a portfolio of Marco Island real estate, and a risk-free asset.

Today, many investors determine the general types of risks to which they want to expose their money, construct well-diversified portfolios that are exposed to each of these types of risks, and then determine an optimal allocation over these portfolios. Other types of risks might include international equity risk and interest rate risk.

Conclusion

Modern portfolio theory recognizes that the overriding consideration in investing is the returns on the overall portfolio—not the returns on the individual assets, contrary to the earlier prudent-man rule. The implication is that an investor will decide on a limited number of well-diversified portfolios and allocate money among these portfolios so as to satisfy optimally his or her goals.

References

Blume, Marshall E., "On the Assessment of Risk," *Journal of Finance,* vol. 26, 1971, pp. 1–10; Blume, Marshall E., and Jeremy J. Siegel with a Foreword by Paul A. Samuelson, "The Theory of Security Pricing and Market Structure," *Journal of Financial Markets, Institutions and Instruments,* vol. 1, August 1992; Graham, Benjamin, and David L. Dodd, *Security Analysis: Principles and Technique,* McGraw-Hill, New York, 1934; Markowitz, Harry, "Portfolio Selection," *Journal of Finance,* vol. 7, 1952, pp. 77–91; Markowitz, Harry, *Portfolio Selection: Efficient Diversification of Investments,* Wiley, New York, 1959; Merton, Robert, "An Intertemporal Capital Asset Pricing Model," *Econometrica,* vol. 41, 1973, pp. 867–887; Sharpe, William, "Capital Asset Prices: A Theory of Market Equilibrium under Conditions of Risk," *Journal of Finance,* vol. 19, 1964, pp. 425–442.

(*See also* Arbitrage; Asset pricing models; Random walk hypotheses; Risk premium an investment)

Marshall E. Blume

Post Keynesian economics

Keynes (1936, p.v) addressing *The General Theory of Employment, Interest and Money* chiefly to his "fellow economists," insisted that:

> The postulates of the classical theory are applicable to a special case only and not to the general case. . . . Moreover, the characteristics of the special case assumed by the classical theory happen not to be those of the economic society in which we actually live, with the result that its teaching is misleading and disastrous if we attempt to apply it to the facts of experience.

Keynes (1936) believed that he could logically demonstrate why "Say's Law . . . is not the true law relating the aggregate demand and supply functions" (p. 26) when we model an economy possessing real-world characteristics; and until we get our theory to accurately mirror and apply to the "facts of experience," there is little hope of getting our policies right.

Keynes (1936) compared those economists whose theoretical logic was grounded in Say's law to euclidean geometers living in a noneuclidean world,

> who discovering that in experience straight lines apparently parallel often meet, rebuke the lines for not keeping straight—as the only remedy for the unfortunate collisions which are taking place. Yet, in truth, there is no remedy except to throw over the axiom of parallels and to work out a non-Euclidean geometry. Something similar is required today in economics. (p. 36)

To throw over an axiom is to reject what the faithful believe are "universal truths." The Keynesian revolution in economic theory was therefore truly a revolt. It aimed at rejecting some fundamental axioms of orthodox theory to provide a general logical foundation for a model that was not tied to Say's law but instead was closely related to the real world in which we happen to live. Unfortunately, since Keynes, mainstream macrotheorists, seduced by a technical methodology that promised precision and unique results at the expense of applicability and accuracy, have reintroduced more sophisticated forms of the very axioms Keynes rejected almost a half-century ago. Consequently the Keynesian revolution was almost immediately shunted onto a wrong track as more obtuse versions of the axioms underlying a Say's law world became the keystone of modern mainstream theory. Monetarists, new classical economists, neoclassical synthesis (or old) Keynesians, and new Keynesians have all reconstructed their brand of macrotheory on the foundations of those "universal truths" that Keynes struggled to overthrow.

Post Keynesian economics attempts to revive Keynes' revolutionary analysis. Post Keynesians create a model of an entrepreneurial economy that does not rely on the restrictive axioms that are the logical foundations of the aforementioned orthodox schools of economic thought. The major axioms rejected by the post Keynesians are (1) the gross substitution axiom, (2) the money-is-neutral axiom, and (3) the orthodox presumption of an ergodic economic system. (Axiom 3 is usually embodied in the rational expectations hypothesis and the ordering axiom of the subjective probability foundation of expected utility theory.)

The characteristics of the real world which Keynes believed could be modeled only by overthrowing these three axioms are:

1. Money matters in the long and short run; i.e., money is not neutral. Money affects real decision making. Despite Milton Friedman's use of the motto "money matters," he remains faithful to the neutral-money axiom and does not permit money to affect the long-run outcome of his system (Friedman, 1974).

2. The economic system is moving through calendar time from an irrevocable past to an uncertain future. In Keynes' conception of uncertainty, decision-making agents "know" that past economic evidence is not a reliable basis for calculating the probability of future economic outcomes. (See Davidson, 1982–1983). Keynes (1937) wrote: "The sense in which I am using the term [uncertainty] is that . . . there is no scientific basis on which to form any calculable probability whatever. We simply don't know." This sense of uncertainty violates the orthodox presumption of an ergodic economic system. An ergodic system means that the future can be reliably predicted through probability distributions.

3. In a world where the future cannot be predicted on any scientific basis using either subjective or objective probability analysis, humans have developed the institution of forward contracts in money terms as a means of efficiently organizing time-consuming production and exchange processes. (See Davidson, 1980). The money-wage contract is the most ubiquitous of these efficiency-oriented contracts. Modern production economies are organized on a money-wage contract-based system.

4. Involuntary unemployment, rather than full employment, is a common outcome in a laissez faire market-oriented, monetary production economy where the gross substitution axiom is not applicable to savers' choices between liquid and nonliquid assets.

The Gross Substitution Axiom

The gross substitution axiom is the backbone of orthodox economics. It is the assumption that any good is a substitute for any other good. This axiom means that if the demand for good x goes up, its price will rise, inducing demand to spill over to the now relatively cheaper substitute good y. For an economist to deny this "universal truth" is revolutionary heresy. As in the days of the Inquisition, the modern-day College of Cardinals of mainstream economics destroys all nonbelievers—if not by burning them at the stake, then by banishing them from the mainstream professional journals. Yet Keynes' *General Theory* analysis, which rests on "The Essential Properties of Interest and Money" (1936, chap. 17) propagates this heresy.

The essential properties that Keynes associated with money (and all other liquid assets, i.e., assets readily resalable for money in a well-organized market) are:

1. Their elasticity of production is (approximately) zero; i.e., these assets are not readily reproducible by the employment of labor by private-sector entrepreneurs.

2. The elasticity of substitution between money (liquid assets) and producible goods (goods possessing high elasticities of production) is (approximately) zero. In other words, the gross substitution axiom does not apply regarding the substitutability between money and producible goods.

The first essential property, a zero elasticity of production, can be translated as meaning that money does not grow on trees. If money grew on trees (i.e., if money had a high elasticity of production), then workers without current employment could always be hired to harvest the money trees, as long as the marginal utility of money exceeded the marginal disutility of reaching up to pluck the fruit of the money trees. If money and other liquid assets are nonproducible, and if people buy less out of current income to save more in the form of nonproducible liquid assets, then there will be a reduction in demand for workers to produce producible goods, while this increase in liquidity demand does not increase the demand for workers to harvest liquidity trees.

Any increase in demand by savers for nonproducible assets will increase their price. If the gross substitution axiom was applicable, rising prices of nonproducibles would induce savers to substitute reproducible durables for nonproducibles in their wealth holdings. Consequently, nonproducibles would not be the ultimate resting places for savings (Davidson, 1972, 1977, 1980). Demand would spill over into producible goods markets and restore employment opportunities. The gross substitution axiom therefore assures the restoration of Say's law and denies the logical possibility of involuntary unemployment. If the gross substitution axiom is rejected as not being universally applicable, then increased aggregate savings without concomitant increased autonomous spending will cause involuntary unemployment. A change in relative market prices between nonproducible assets and producible goods cannot cure unemployment unless gross substitution is presumed applicable.

To overthrow the axiom of gross substitution in an intertemporal context is truly heretical. It changes the entire perspective on what is meant by "rational" or "optimal" savings, on why people save or what they save. Hicks (1979) noted that all Keynes needed to say was that income was divided between current consumption and a vague provision for the uncertain future. Hicks added the mathematical assumption that "planned expenditures at specified different dates in the future have independent utilities [and are gross substitutes] . . . this assumption I find quite unacceptable. . . . the normal condition is that there is strong complementarity between them [consumption plans in successive periods]" (pp. 76–77). Indeed Danziger, Vander Gaag, Smolensky, and Taussig (1982–1983) have shown that the facts regarding consumption and saving behavior by the elderly are incompatible with the notion of intertemporal gross substitution of consumption plans. Yet this presumption underlies both life-cycle models and overlapping-generation models currently so popular in mainstream macroeconomic theory.

In the absence of the axiom of gross substitution, income effects (e.g., the Keynesian multiplier) predominate and can swamp any hypothetical neoclassical substitution effects. Consequently, relative price changes through a flexible pricing mechanism will not be the cure-all snake-oil medicine usually recommended by many neoclassical doctors for the unfortunate economic maladies that are occurring in the real world.

The Neutrality-of-Money Axiom

The neutrality-of-money axiom implies that money is a veil, so that all economic decisions are made on the basis of real phenomena and relative prices alone. Money does not matter. It cannot affect employment and real-output outcomes. To reject this neutrality axiom does not require assuming that agents suffer from a money illusion (see Keynes, 1937, vol. 13, p. 411). It merely means that money can matter in both the short run and the long run, or as Keynes (1937) put it:

> The theory which I desiderate would deal . . . with an economy in which money plays a part of its own and affects motives and decisions, and is, in short, one of the operative factors in the situation, so that the course of events cannot be predicted in either the long period or in the short, without a knowledge of the behavior of money between the first state and the last. And it is this which we ought to mean when we speak of a monetary economy. (vol. 13, pp. 108–109)

Can anything be more revolutionary? In this passage from an article entitled "The Monetary Theory of Production" (and I emphasize the word "monetary"), Keynes specifically rejects the neutrality axiom. Once we admit that money is a real phenomenon, that money matters, then orthodox economic analysis collapses and it is no longer possible to prove that a general clearing of all markets is an inevitable outcome of a freely flexible price system. Arrow and Hahn (1971) have demonstrated (pp. 356–357) that:

The terms in which contracts are made matter. In particular, if money is the goods in terms of which contracts are made, then the prices of goods in terms of money are of special significance. This is not the case if we consider an economy without a past or future. . . . If a serious monetary theory comes to be written, the fact that contracts are made in terms of money will be of considerable importance. (pp. 356–357)

Moreover Arrow and Hahn (1971, p. 361) demonstrate that if contracts are made in terms of money (so that money affects real decisions) in an economy moving along in calendar time with a past and a future, then all existence theorems are jeopardized. The existence of money contracts—a characteristic of the world in which Keynes lived and in which we still do—implies that there need never exist, in the long run or the short run, any rational expectations equilibrium or general equilibrium market-clearing price vector.

The Ergodic Presumption

Most neoclassical and new classical economists suffer from the pervasive form of envy that we may call the "economist's disease"; that is, these economists want to be considered as first-class scientists dealing with a "hard science" rather than be seen as "second-class" citizens of the scientific community dealing with the non-precise "social" and "political" sciences. These economists, mistaking precision (rather than accuracy) as the hallmark of "true" science, prefer to be precise rather than accurate.

Precision conveys the meaning of "sharpness to minute detail." Accuracy, on the other hand, means "care to obtain conformity with fact or truth." For example, if you phone the plumber to come fix an emergency breakdown in your plumbing system and he responds by indicating he will be there in exactly 12 minutes, he is being precise, but not exercising care to obtain conformity with fact or truth. If he says he will be there before the day is over, he is being accurate, if not necessarily precise.

Most economists, unfortunately, prefer to be precisely wrong rather than roughly right or accurate. The presumption of an ergodic economic system permits economists to act as if they were dealing with a hard science where data are homogeneous with respect to time. In an ergodic world, observations of a time series realization (i.e., historical data) are useful information regarding the probability distribution of the stochastic process that generated that realization. The same observations also provide information about the probability distribution over a universe of realizations that exist at any point in time such as today, and the data are also useful information regarding the future probability distribution of events. Hence by scientifically studying the past as generated by an ergodic situation, present and future events can be forecasted in terms of statistical probabilities. (Compare Davidson, 1982–1983.) In the absence of an ergodic system, there is no scientific basis for calculating the probability of future outcomes.

Keynes (1936, chap. 16) rejected this view that past information from economic time series realizations provides reliable, useful data that permit stochastic predictions of the economic future. In a world with important nonergodic circumstances—our economic world—liquidity matters, money is never neutral, and neither Say's law nor Walras's law is relevant. In such a world, Keynes' revolutionary logical analysis is relevant.

Mainstream economic theory has not followed Keynes' revolutionary logical analysis to develop what Arrow and Hahn have called a "serious monetary theory" in which contracts are made in terms of money in an economy moving from an irrevocable past to an uncertain, nonergodic future. Post Keynesian economics has taken on the task of providing a serious monetary theory following the analytical leads provided by Keynes.

References

Arrow, K. J., and F. H. Hahn, *General Competitive Analysis,* Holden-Day, San Francisco, 1971; Danziger, S., J. Vander Gaag, E. Smolensky, and M. K. Taussig, "The Life Cycle Hypothesis and Consumption Behavior of the Elderly," *Journal of Post Keynesian Economics,* vol. 5, 1982–1983; Davidson, P., *Money and the Real World,* Macmillan, London, 1972; Davidson, P., "Money and General Equilibrium," *Economie Appliquee,* vol. 30, 1977; Davidson, P., "The Dual Nature of the Keynesian Revolution," *Journal of Post Keynesian Economics,* vol. 2, 1980; Davidson, P., "Rational Expectations: A Fallacious Foundation for Studying Crucial Decision Making Processes," *Journal of Post Keynesian Economics,* vol. 5, 1982–1983; Friedman, M., "A Theoretical Framework for Monetary Analysis," in R. J. Gordon (ed.), *Milton Friedman's Monetary Framework: A Debate with His Critics,* University of Chicago Press, Chicago, 1974; Hicks, J. R., *Causality in Economics,* Basic Books, New York, 1979; Keynes, J. M., *The General Theory of Employment, Interest and Money,* Harcourt, New York, 1936; Keynes, J. M., "The General Theory," *Quarterly Journal of Economics,* 1937; reprinted in D. Moggridge (ed.), *The Collected Writings of John Maynard Keynes,* Macmillan, London, 1973.

(*See also* Cambridge school; Expectations; Income distribution; *IS-LM* model; Keynesian economics; Laissez faire; Macroeconomics; Neoclassical economics)

Paul Davidson

Poverty

Poverty was largely ignored by both the academic and policy communities before the mid-1960s. Having survived the Great Depression and having experienced a substantial growth in real incomes, Americans tended to think that affluence was widely shared. Most social legislation during and after the Depression assumed that poverty would be limited to a small group of people with little attachment to the labor force—retired, disabled, and widowed persons. These people would be cared for by the income support system established by the Social Security Act of 1935.

In 1962 Michael Harrington wrote *The Other America,* describing conditions of severe material deprivation in Appalachia. His book brought wide public attention to poverty. Beginning about the same time, the growing resistance of urban blacks to de jure discrimination gained wide media coverage. The combination of these factors led Presidents Kennedy and Johnson to treat poverty as a public policy problem. In 1964, Johnson declared "war" on poverty.

In order to fight this war, policymakers needed to know the size of the poverty problem. Defining the scope of poverty proved to be difficult. While there was wide agreement that a family was poor if its income fell below some poverty threshold, there was much less agreement over where to set the threshold. After much discussion, a poverty line was defined in terms of the Department of Agriculture's minimum food budget. The cost of the minimum food budget necessary to sustain a family during temporary emergencies was multiplied by three to reflect the assumption that food constituted one-third of the total budget. These poverty lines, which vary by family size and farm-nonfarm residence, became the basis for tabulating poverty statistics.

Both liberals and conservatives criticized these poverty thresholds. Liberals argued that the poverty lines were unrealistically low since the food budget used by the Department of Agriculture was never meant to sustain people over long periods of time. Conservatives argued that the thresholds were too high, since many people in underdeveloped countries who would not classify themselves as poor survived on much lower incomes.

These poverty lines, which are still used for counting the poor for official government purposes, are adjusted only for increases in the cost of living. Therefore, during periods of economic growth the difference between the poverty lines and real median income increases. For this reason the official poverty lines are said to reflect an absolute definition of poverty—the same minimal food basket is used in every year. A relative definition of poverty would set the poverty lines as a percentage of the incomes of other families, for example, at one-half of median family income. These poverty lines would then increase with both inflation and economic growth.

Trends in Poverty

In 1965 there were 33 million poor families by the official definition. They made up 17.3 percent of the U.S. population. While most of the poor were white (67 percent) and most were nonfarm residents (87 percent), the incidence of poverty was higher among blacks (47 percent) and farm dwellers (34 percent).

The substantial economic growth of the 1960s and early 1970s was accompanied by a decline in poverty. By 1973 the incidence of poverty had reached 11.1 percent. This period of growth was followed by a period of retrenchment in social programs and a reduction in economic growth. Between 1973 and 1979 median family income grew by only 3.7 percent and poverty rates actually rose, from 11.1 percent in 1973 to 11.7 percent in 1979.

This increase in poverty during a period in which the median family was making small gains reflected the growing inequality of income in the United States. To use the popular analogy, the tide was rising, if only slowly, but all boats were not being lifted by the rising tide.

With the onset of the 1982 recession, median incomes dropped and poverty rates rose rapidly. By 1983 poverty rates had reached 15.2 percent, a level higher than at anytime since 1965. Almost two decades of progress against poverty were wiped out in three years. The ensuing recovery turned out to offer relatively little relief. While real median family income regained its previous peak by 1985, poverty rates fell only to 14.0 percent by 1985, well above the historical low of 11.1 percent reached in 1973. The rest of the 1980s saw continued growth in median family income and slow decline in poverty rates. By 1989 poverty reached 12.8 percent, which was no lower than the 1968 poverty rate. The lack of substantial progress against poverty, in spite of average family income reaching all-time highs, further demonstrated that rising inequality of income could largely offset the effects of economic growth.

The 1970s and 1980s were also periods of rapid changes in the demographic composition of the poor. While persons in female-headed households only constituted 26.5 percent of persons in poor families in 1965, they made up 48.5 percent of the poor by 1989. This increase in the "feminization" of poverty partially accounts for the rise in poverty rates. Meanwhile the elderly made up an increasingly small proportion of the poor.

Not only did poverty fail to come down for many groups, but poverty also became more geographically concentrated, especially for urban blacks. As a result of residential desegregation, nonpoor blacks were able to move out of urban ghettos. The result was an increasingly isolated "urban underclass."

Public Policy toward Poverty

Under the Johnson administration, the Office of Economic Opportunity (OEO) was established to coordinate and administer a variety of programs to eliminate the root causes of poverty. Education, training, and increased participation in local decision making became the cornerstones of that effort. The assumptions behind the programs launched during this period were that if people had skills, they could earn their way out of poverty, and that if they had access to political power, public institutions would work in their behalf. It was thought that these micropolicies, accompanied by expansionary monetary and fiscal policy, would eliminate material deprivation in short order.

Initially the decline in absolute poverty during the 1960s and early 1970s was attributed to economic growth trickling down to the poor in the form of higher earnings. This view was undermined by evidence that much of the reduction in poverty during the late 1960s was the result of increases in government transfers. The high poverty rates that remained after the substantial economic growth of the 1980s further weakened the link between growth and poverty reduction.

This led to microeconomic policies to try to reduce poverty. These policies can be broadly divided into supply- and demand-side policies.

Supply-Side Policies

The recognition of the key role played by rapidly increasing transfers in the 1960s and early 1970s led to important shifts in public policy. Several major welfare reform proposals were developed by the Nixon, Ford, and Carter administrations. The general thrust of these early reforms was to "make work pay." It was believed that a reorganized welfare system would eliminate many of the perverse work disincentives in the existing programs.

Economists recognized that there are two sources of work disincentives in any transfer program. First, the recipient may use the transfer payment to buy leisure by working less. The work disincentive from this source varies directly with the size of the transfer. Another source of work disincentive is caused by varying the benefits according to the amount of other income available to the recipient. Under most programs, benefits are reduced as a welfare recipient earns more income. The work disincentive from this source varies directly with the rate at which benefits are reduced as earnings increase (the benefit reduction rate).

Policy analysts pointed out that work disincentives in existing programs could be reduced by offering lower payments or reducing the benefit reduction rate. The latter solution, however, has the consequence of letting people with fairly high earnings continue to receive transfer payments. There is an inherent conflict between providing work incentives, giving adequate payments to recipients, and targeting the program to low-income people. While different administrations made different choices among these goals, all viewed work incentives as central to their programs.

This "carrot" approach to welfare reform, proposed by Presidents as different as Nixon and Carter, focused on increasing work incentives. The carrot of incentives was largely replaced by the stick of work requirements during the Reagan and Bush administrations. Rather than trying to induce people into the market by "making work pay," the new reforms focused on requiring certain recipients to work in the market in order not to lose their welfare benefits.

Demand-Side Policies

The second thrust of public policy was to institute programs aimed at increasing the demand by employers for low-income people. Tax credits for businesses that hired welfare mothers met with limited success. While employers were reimbursed for up to half the wages paid subsidized workers, firms were reluctant to hire workers who were eligible for the subsidy for fear that these subsidies signaled that these workers were less productive.

The second method of increasing demand was to make welfare recipients more attractive to private employers by providing training. This approach was politically more popular than direct public service employment, since the latter would increase the size of the public sector. The hope that small amounts of training would lead to large increases in private employment was quickly dashed. Research showed that cost-effective training programs required large expenditures to counter the substantial problems faced by welfare recipients. Small investments, such as teaching welfare recipients how to apply for jobs, had little or no effect on their future employment.

While there is still wide disagreement over what should be done to reduce poverty, there is now a wide consensus that simple cures do not exist. The poverty population is simply too diverse to be affected by a single policy. For example, economic growth can reduce poverty among families with an underemployed adult, but growth will do little to help families already working full time or to help single-parent families with child care responsibilities. Roughly two-thirds of all poor household heads are not expected to work—disabled, aged, women with children. For these people economic growth and work incentives are not an issue. Neither are they important for the 11 percent of the poor who already work full time. Training may help the latter group, while yet other programs are necessary for those not expected to work.

The result of the increased recognition of the diversity of the poverty population has been a shift away from simple solutions, such as the negative income tax. Policies that are tailored to the circumstances of different groups have gained increasing support.

References

Danziger, Sheldon, and Daniel Weinberg, *Fighting Poverty,* Harvard University Press, Cambridge, Mass., 1986; Wilson, William J., *The Truly Disadvantaged,* University of Chicago Press, Chicago, 1987.

(*See also* Negative income tax)

Peter T. Gottschalk

Price-earnings ratio

The price-earnings ratio is the relationship between the current market price of a corporation's common stock and that company's per-share earnings. The ratio indicates how much investors are willing to pay for $1 of earnings in a given corporation.

As published in the stock market columns of major newspapers, it is computed by dividing the latest annual earnings per share into the closing price of the stock on the last day the market was open. For instance, suppose XYZ Corporation's latest income statement showed annual earnings of $4 per share. If the price of XYZ's common stock closed at $40 a share yesterday, its price-earnings ratio would be 10:1.

Evaluation of Stocks and Bonds

Securities analysts and others interested in determining the intrinsic value of a common stock have found the price-earnings ratio a useful tool. Evaluating other kinds of securities is relatively easy compared with evaluating common stock. For example, to determine the value of a bond, the analyst calculates the present value of the interest receipts and the principal, discounted at the appropriate interest rate—that is, the rate that accounts for the degree of risk involved. If bond A is riskier than bond B, a higher rate would be used for bond A, and therefore its present value would be lower. In other words, bond B is worth more than bond A. When evaluating a preferred stock, the analyst expects the dividend to be paid indefinitely and, thus, treats it as a perpetual annuity, whose present value is found by dividing the amount of the annuity (annual dividend, in the case of preferred stock) by the appropriate interest rate.

Although the same method—discounting future receipts—would also apply to the evaluation of common stocks, two serious difficulties complicate the procedure. First, while the analyst knows what the dollar receipts will be for bonds and preferred stocks, he or she does not know with certainty what they will be for common stocks. Consequently the analyst must forecast future earnings, dividends, and stock prices— clearly not an easy task. Second, unlike the fixed receipts expected on bonds and preferred stocks, investors anticipate that a common stock's earnings, dividends, and price are expected to grow, obviating the use of present value of annuity formulas.

In order to overcome these difficulties and determine a common stock's value, academicians set up various models based on different growth rate assumptions, while practicing securities analysts use the price-earnings ratio. Analysts estimate the earnings per share for the coming year and apply the appropriate price-earnings multiple to find the stock's value. An example should make this clear: When evaluating ABC Corporation's common stock, an analyst first forecasts that earnings per share will be $5 next year. Then the analyst determines current price-earnings ratios for companies with similar growth prospects and risk to those of ABC Corporation. If these ratios are around 10:1, the analyst then applies a 10-times multiple to ABC's earnings per share (10×5) and estimates the stock's value at $50 per share. If there are any special circumstances that apply to ABC Corporation, the analyst modifies the price-earnings multiple to account for them.

Use of Price-Earnings Multiples

The use of price-earnings multiples allows those evaluating common stocks to take into consideration companies with different growth prospects and varying degrees of risk. The greater the growth rate expected, other things remaining equal, the higher the price-earnings multiple used; the riskier the company, other things remaining equal, the lower the multiple applied.

At any given time, the stock market shows a wide range of price-earnings ratios, reflecting the disparate growth potentials of different industries and the companies within them. And as the projected growth rate of a company changes, or its risk increases or decreases, investors will respond by changing the price-earnings multiple they apply to earnings. Aside from the shifting fortunes of individual companies, the general level of price-earnings ratios changes dramatically over time, mirroring investors' overall views of common stocks as an investment. For example, from the end of World War II until 1952, the price-earnings ratio of the Standard & Poor's 500 stock index remained below 10:1. During the rest of the 1950s, the price-earnings ratio climbed and from 1958 until 1972; it never fell below 15:1, reflecting the strong economy during that period. The decade from 1973 to 1982 saw the price-earnings ratio below 10:1 in most of the years. Since then, it has increased, reaching levels around 20:1 in 1991. The key influences are economic, financial, and political changes; and how these factors affect investors' attitudes determines the overall level of price-earnings ratios.

Reference

Cohen, Jerome B., Edward D. Zinbarg, and Arthur Zeikel, *Investment Analysis and Portfolio Analysis,* 5th ed., Irwin, 1987.

(*See also* Bond; Stock; Stock exchange; Stock price averages and indexes)

Henry C. F. Arnold

Price measurement

Among the many economic statistics, prices are one of the most difficult to measure. There are six major issues that pervasively affect the ability to measure price levels and price changes.

Quality Change

The first issue concerns the problem that arises when the quality of an item being priced changes. Quality change has two aspects: definition and measurement. There are several approaches to defining quality change. One, based on neoclassical theory, is that it is equal to the long-run marginal cost (equals marginal revenue) of making the change. The second is the change in the product's ability to produce satisfaction if it is a consumer's good, and to produce output if it is a producer's good. A third method of defining quality change for a producer's good is a change in its ability to produce net revenue. The second and third definitions may be consistent with the first. The appropriate definition of quality change ultimately adopted in price measurement frequently depends on the uses to which the price data are being put.

The second aspect of accounting for quality change is how to make the adjustment. A frequently used method is to link in the new quality item for the old one. This requires that price observations on both qualities be collected for an overlapping time period. Its use assumes that the existing market price differential between the old and new qualities measures the quality difference. The second method is the so-called direct-comparison method. Here the items are compared and if deemed to be similar enough, the change is regarded simply as a price change and no adjustment for quality is made. A third method, if the concept is appropriate, is to obtain from sellers estimates of the cost of making the changes associated with the quality change. These resulting figures are then used to account for the difference between the price of the old and new quality in the same time period. If, for example, those costs do not fully account for an increase in price, then only part of the observed price difference is due to quality change. The remainder is treated as a price change.

Because of the limitations resulting from the assumptions underlying the use of linking or direct comparison and the lack of cost data, growing reliance is being placed on regression analysis. Regressions are used to quantify the impact on price of various characteristics of an item that reflect its quality. For example, speed and size of memory are two such characteristics used to calculate price indexes for computers. Those indexes had previously not been calculated because of the rapid and complex model changes that occur for such equipment.

New Products

Related to quality change is the issue of dealing with new products. It may in fact be quite difficult to establish the difference between a new product and a change in the quality of an existing product. For example, television sets and antibiotics were new products when first marketed. One problem associated with new products is to determine what product they replace or to determine, if they have not fully replaced an existing product, what share of the market basket represented by an index the new product has taken. Such determination is related to solving the most difficult problem with respect to products—when to begin to price them for official price measures. Frequently, new products appear on the market at a very high price, but as they gain acceptance and are mass-produced, the price falls. Meanwhile, the importance of the new product in terms of total purchases by either consumers or producers has increased.

Transaction Prices

A third issue pertaining to price measurement is that of collecting the actual prices at which transactions take place and not list prices. Frequently, items are sold at standard discounts, and, depending upon business conditions, those discounts may change. Such changes may go undetected when price data are collected. It is usually assumed that producer price indexes (PPIs) suffer from this problem more than consumer price indexes (CPIs).

Pricing of Infrequently Purchased, Custom-Made Goods

A fourth problem is how to price infrequently purchased, custom-made goods. Ships and aircraft are ready examples. In such cases, the usual practice was to represent the price of such items by a weighted average of the cost of the materials and labor used to produce them, both adjusted for changes in productivity. Since the 1970s there has been a growing tendency to use a variety of more direct methods of pricing.

Contract versus Spot Prices

The fifth issue relates to whether contract or spot prices are appropriate. Frequently, this decision depends on the use to which the price data are to be put. For example, if the prices are to be compiled into an index for use as a deflator of output (to estimate constant-dollar output), a weighted average of the two kinds of prices should be used, since some output is sold under contract and some at the spot price. If the prices are being used in an index designed to be an early-warning indicator of inflation, the spot price may be more appropriate.

Related to this problem is that of whether the price obtained should relate to orders or shipments. Again, the considerations are similar. Prices of orders, which would include prices at which new contracts are entered into, would be a better gauge of current price change than prices of shipments, which may include goods being delivered at prices previously agreed to.

Methods of Measuring Price Levels and Price Changes

A sixth issue relates to the two methods used to measure prices and price changes. The first and more widely used is the so-called specification basis for pricing. This requires the drawing up of a precise description of the item to be priced and an endeavor to price the same item each time period. Specification pricing is viewed as an important vehicle for recognizing, if not measuring, quality change and in signaling the appearance of new products in markets.

However, pricing by tightly drawn specification may present some difficulties. Producers or distributors may not carry the precise specification of the item that is selected, or if they do, they may not have it in stock each time prices are collected for the index. This has led some statistical agencies responsible for publishing price indexes to use a looser specification which increases the frequency with which a price may be found for the item. This means that different specifications of the same item may be priced in different stores. Use of a looser specification does not eliminate the need to collect prices for exactly the same thing for two consecutive time periods. It merely eliminates the need to collect prices for exactly the same thing in every single outlet. This approach is feasible for price indexes like the CPI, the purpose of which is not to measure the level of prices but rather their rate of change. To measure the level of prices would require one precise specification for each item.

The other method employed to measure prices is the so-called unit-value approach, in which total shipments or orders are divided by some quantity indicator. This method is most frequently used in area where products are homogeneous. For example, a measure of the prices charged by refineries for gasoline may be derived by dividing the total value of shipments of refineries by the total number of barrels shipped. The method works best when the product is uniform. It is useful in detecting changes in actual transactions prices since, if both shipments and barrels can be properly measured, discounts that might otherwise go unreported will be reflected in the dollar shipment figure.

On the other hand, unit values are plagued with the so-called product-mix problem. If a refinery ships two grades of gasoline, if the mix of its shipments changes between those two grades in a particular time period, and if the price of each grade is different, the resulting price measure can be different from that of the preceding period without any change of prices having taken place.

Other Problems

Obviously, there are other problems encountered in price measurement. One is how to treat seasonal items which disappear from markets at certain times or are extremely scarce. The treatment of taxes and the government services they purchase and of prices for assets and insurance are other problems. Most of these problems are ones that must be solved at the conceptual level before measurement problems can be addressed.

The problems associated with the measurement of prices over time also pertain to price measurement across space. The problem of quality change through time is analogous to not being able to find the same product for pricing in two different places either because it is in short supply in one of the two or because consumers do not demand it. Thus, if one were trying to compare clothing prices in two different locations of the United States, a problem would arise in trying to price winter coats in both Boston and Miami.

References

National Bureau of Economic Research, *The Price Statistics of the Federal Government: Review, Appraisal and Recommendations,* NBER General Series, no. 13, Washington, D.C., 1961; Ruggles, Richard, *The Wholesale Price Index: Review and Evaluation,* Council on Wage and Price Stability Report, June 1977; Triplett, Jack E., "The Measurement of Inflation: A Survey of Research on the Accuracy of Price Indexes," in Paul H. Earl (ed.), *Analysis of Inflation,* Lexington Books, Lexington, Mass., 1975.

(*See also* Consumer price index; Index numbers; Producer price index)

Joel Popkin

Price theory

Price theory, or microeconomic theory, is concerned with how the price system handles the problem of allocating scarce resources in market economies. Price theory deals with how relative prices are determined, not with how the general price level is determined. The latter task requires a separate theory such as the quantity theory of the demand for money.

Price theory can be divided into five subcategories: (1) the theory of demand and consumer behavior, (2) the theory of the business firm, (3) the theory of market organization, (4) the theory of distribution, and (5) the theory of general equilibrium and welfare economics.

Theory of Demand and Consumer Behavior

In the standard modern approach to demand theory, the consumer's preferences are represented by a utility function defined as a function of the quantities of the goods and services that constitute the individual's consumption bundle. The major theoretical value of the utility function lies in the information it provides about the individual's willingness to trade one good for another in the consumption bundle, which is measured by what is called the marginal rate of substitution. The marginal rate of substitution of X for Y is the amount of good Y that would have to be added to the individual's consumption bundle to exactly compensate for the utility lost by the removal of one unit of X from the consumption bundle.

The simplest form of the theory of demand assumes that the consumer has a given income and faces a given set of prices of goods and services. The consumer then chooses a consumption bundle so as to maximize utility subject to the constraint that the total expenditure on the goods and services purchased does not exceed income. The consumer's decision may be stated as a formal mathematical problem. Let $x_1, \ldots, x_n$ represent the quantities of goods 1 to n; let $p_1, \ldots, p_n$ represent the prices of these n goods; and let M represent income. The consumer's utility function is $U(x_1, \ldots, x_n)$. The consumer's choice of a consumption bundle is given by the solution of

$$\max_{x_1, \ldots, x_n} U(x_1, \ldots, x_n) \tag{1}$$

subject to

$$M \geq p_1 x_1 + p_2 x_2 + \cdots + p_n x_n \tag{2}$$

where Equation (2) is the income or budget constraint and where the quantities $x_1, x_2, \ldots, x_n$ are understood to be nonnegative. [In this formulation, M is often treated as money income (dollars) and price is measured as dollars per unit of the good. Note, however, that the only purpose served by money in this model is as a unit of account. Actually, any commodity can be used as the unit of account or *numéraire*.]

The solution to this constrained maximization problem depends on the values of $p_1, \ldots, p_n$ and M. As prices and income are varied, the utility-maximizing quantities of the goods will change. The relationship between the quantity demanded of a good and prices and income is known as a demand function. Given some fairly weak conditions on the utility function, it can be shown that the demand function will exhibit an inverse relationship between the quantity demanded of a good and the price of a good when prices of other goods and income are held constant. That is, as the price of a good increases, the quantity demanded of that good will decrease. This inverse relationship between the quantity demanded of a good and its price is known as the law of demand. The market demand curve is obtained by aggregating the demand curves of the individuals in the market.

There are several extensions of this basic model. One important extension makes income endogenous by treating leisure time as a good and allowing the individual to sell time at a given market wage rate. Another extension is to introduce multiple time periods along with interest rates so that investment, savings, and life-cycle consumption patterns may be analyzed. The model has also been modified to deal with consumer choice in the presence of risk, thereby allowing extensions to capital theory, the demand for insurance, inventory planning, and other stochastic models.

Theory of the Business Firm

In standard microeconomic theory, the firm is modeled as an economic unit that employs inputs such as capital and labor and uses these inputs to produce a good or service that is sold to consumers or, in some cases, to other producers. The technological process by which the firm transforms inputs into outputs is represented analytically by a production function.

One production function that is used widely in both theoretical and empirical work has the form

$$Q = AK^\alpha L^\beta$$

where Q is output, K is the capital input, and L is the labor input. The parameters α, β, and A are technologically determined. This functional form is usually referred to as a Cobb-Douglas or long-linear production function.

The production function typically allows for the substitution of inputs so that there are many input combinations that will produce a given output. In the simplest

case, the firm faces a given set of prices for the inputs and a given production function and then chooses that combination of inputs which produces the desired output
at the lowest total cost. The problem is analytically similar to the consumer maximization problem discussed previously. Indeed, the mathematical dual of the problem faced by the firm is to maximize output for a given level of cost just as the
consumer maximizes utility for a given budget. The critical difference is that the
firm's desired level of output is not determined until output price is considered.

Thus, for a given output and given input prices, it is possible to determine the
input combination which produces that output at lowest total cost. The resulting
association between output and the cost of producing that output is called the total-
cost function. For each level of output the total-cost function shows what the cost of
producing that output will be when the inputs are chosen in an optimal manner.

In order to go from the theory of cost to the theory of supply, some additional
assumptions are needed. If the firm chooses output levels to maximize profit and if
the firm is a price taker in the output market, then the amount the firm will supply at
any given output price can be determined using the total-cost function. The resulting
association between output price and the quantity supplied by the firm is known as
the supply schedule (sometimes called supply curve or supply function) for the firm.
In the simplest case, the industry supply schedule can be determined by simply
adding the quantities supplied by the firms in the industry for each output price. This
simple means of deriving the industry supply schedule is complicated by two considerations: (1) the presence of externalities and (2) the entry of firms into and exit of
firms from the industry.

Externalities arise when the combined activities of all firms in the industry affect
input prices or technology. If the industry uses a specialized input, it is possible that
the price of that input will be bid up as firms try to purchase more of it. Thus, from
the viewpoint of any individual firm, total cost is affected by both its level of output
and the industry level of output. In this case, the industry supply schedule cannot be
found by a simple horizontal addition of the supply schedules of the firms in the
industry because these firms' supply schedules shift as industry output changes.
Similarly, there may be external effects that change the production functions of the
individual firms.

Entry and exit of firms will also affect the industry supply schedule. The effect of
entry and exit of firms on the output of the industry is often analyzed by distinguishing between short-run and long-run industry supply schedules. The short-run supply
schedules refer to the output decisions of existing firms, while the long-run supply
schedules allow for changes in supply because firms have entered or left the industry. This distinction between short-run and long-run supply is also used to account
for the fact that during short time intervals it is not feasible for the firm to fully adjust
its inputs.

Theory of Market Organization

In both the theory of the firm and the theory of demand, price is treated as exogenously given to the economic agents involved. By linking these two sides of the market, both price and quantity can be determined endogenously. The mechanism for
doing this is usually described in terms of supply and demand curves such as those
shown in the accompanying figure. The curve labeled *DD* in the figure is the demand
curve from the theory of consumer behavior. The supply curve, labeled *SS*, comes
from the theory of the firm. Even though the previous analysis treats price as the

independent variable, it is conventional in economics to represent price on the vertical axis in graphs of demand and supply curves.

The *DD* and *SS* curves represent aggregates across consumers and firms, respectively. The equilibrium price is the price at which *DD* and *SS* intersect. It is denoted by $\bar{P}$ in this figure. This is the market-clearing price in that at this price, the quantity supplied is equal to the quantity demanded. At prices above $\bar{P}$, the quantity supplied exceeds demand—there is a glut which tends to drive prices down. At prices below $\bar{P}$, the quantity demanded exceeds the quantity supplied—there is a shortage which tends to drive prices up. When price is equal to $\bar{P}$, quantity supplied equals quantity demanded and the market is cleared. Supply and demand analysis is a powerful tool for analyzing the effects of taxes, changes in income and wages, crop failures, and other phenomena relating to the quantity produced and sold of a good and the price at which this exchange takes place.

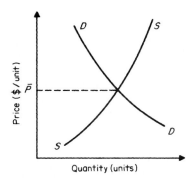

This model of supply and demand is generally associated with perfect competition, which assumes that the buyers and sellers act as price takers, that the good is homogeneous across sellers, that there are no government regulations or other artificial prohibitions that prevent exit from and entry to the industry, and that both sellers and buyers have complete information about price and other relevant variables. There are other forms of market organization in which the sellers or buyers may act as price makers. This is true of pure monopoly where there is only one seller. The single seller directly faces the market demand curve and explicitly recognizes that an increase in output will result in a decrease in price and vice versa.

Theory of Distribution

In addition to the question of what is produced and sold, economists are interested in knowing what determines the prices and income of the factors of production such as capital and labor. The answer is usually developed in terms of the theory of marginal productivity. The marginal product of a productive factor is the additional output that is produced if one more unit of the factor is employed, while holding the employment of all other factors constant. According to the law of diminishing returns, or more precisely the law of variable proportions, the marginal product of a factor ultimately declines as more of the factor is used. If the firm is assumed to maximize profit and is a price taker in both the input market and the output market, then in equilibrium the quantity employed of a productive factor will be such that marginal product multiplied by output price will equal the price of the factor. By using this kind of analysis, including extensions to the case of several inputs, a factor demand function can be derived. Aggregating these factor demand functions across firms with appropriate adjustment for external effects leads to a market demand function for the productive factor. This factor demand function can be combined with a factor supply function to determine the price and quantity employed of the productive factor.

This theory is a simple comparative static theory. In the case of long-lived productive factors such as capital, it is sometimes more appropriate to develop a dynamic model that explicitly takes into account the intertemporal nature of the capital accumulation or investment decision.

Other extensions of the theory of distribution involve analysis of noncompetitive markets for inputs and outputs.

Theory of General Equilibrium and Welfare Economics

Many problems in price theory are analyzed using partial equilibrium techniques. In other words, the analysis typically concentrates on a single market and ignores the interactions between the market being studied and other markets. This often proves to be a fruitful approach, and economists have used partial equilibrium analysis in the study of a wide variety of practical and theoretical problems. Nonetheless, it is sometimes important to broaden the scope of the analysis in order to understand how equilibrium is achieved in all markets simultaneously. General equilibrium analysis deals with this question. General equilibrium analysis embodies many of the techniques of partial equilibrium analysis but introduces new concepts to deal with the interdependencies among the markets.

Much of price theory is descriptive or positive, but many economists are interested in price theory as a normative device for evaluating economic efficiency and welfare. The welfare criterion most often used for normative evaluations is that of Pareto optimality. If an economic equilibrium has the property that no reallocation of resources can make one or more of the economic agents better off without making one or more other agents worse off, then that equilibrium is said to be Pareto-optimal. Pareto optimality uses the utility functions of the individual economic agents as the yardstick for the terms "better off" and "worse off." Thus, all agents would benefit (or at least not lose) by moving from a non-Pareto-optimal equilibrium to one that is Pareto-optimal. The conditions of Pareto optimality are achieved by a competitive equilibrium but may be violated by the presence of monopoly, taxes, pollution, and other externalities that drive a wedge between private and social costs, or between private and social benefits. The effects of these externalities may be partially or fully self-canceling when they are present simultaneously.

Historical Development of Price Theory

These five categories constitute what is known as neoclassical price theory and are the result of about 200 years of intellectual evolution. Although scholars have been concerned with the issues of economic organization from the time of Aristotle, the modern theory of price began to emerge as a system of scientific principles only with the work of François Quesnay and Adam Smith. Major contributors to the development of modern price theory include the nineteenth-century writers Thomas Malthus, David Ricardo, Jean Baptiste Say, Nassau William Senior, and John Stuart Mill. The early development of utility theory, which played a major role in the unification of price theory, can be found in the work of Hermann Heinrich Gossen, Carl Menger, and Léon Walras. Further development of utility theory and of general equilibrium theory occurred in the latter nineteenth and early twentieth centuries in the work of Walras, Vilfredo Pareto, Francis Ysidro Edgeworth, Eugeny Slutsky, Knut Wicksell, and Irving Fisher. The neoclassical partial equilibrium theory that synthesized much of the earlier work was one of the important accomplishments of Alfred Marshall.

Although the general structure of price theory has changed little in the last 60 years, there have been numerous refinements and extensions of this basic framework. Beginning with the work of Henry L. Moore, economists undertook statistical and empirical measurement of such phenomena as demand and supply schedules. The interest in empirical research grew rapidly, especially after the appearance of high-speed digital computers in the 1950s, and by the 1960s had developed to the point where special statistical and econometric techniques had been devised for dealing with propositions and hypotheses from the theory of price.

The number of important theoretical contributions during the past half-century is too large to consider in detail. However, brief mention of some of this work helps convey a general picture of how economic theory has been developing. The *Foundations of Economic Analysis,* by Paul Samuelson (1948), and the *Theory of Value,* by Gerard Debreu (1959), together provide a comprehensive mathematical statement of the formal structure of price theory. Debreu and Arrow (1961) also showed how state-preference analysis could be used to extend price theory and general equilibrium theory to situations involving risk. The work of George Stigler (1968) opened important new frontiers in industrial organization, the economics of information, and the positive theory of government regulation. Gary Becker (1976) has shown how the principles of price theory extend to many areas such as discrimination, marriage, and criminal behavior that traditionally have not been thought of as part of the domain of economic analysis. Finally, there has been a growing body of research that treats principles of price theory as the basis of all economic theory, including the macroeconomic issues of inflation, unemployment, and the business cycle (Phelps et al., 1970).

The ingenious application of many of the ideas and principles of price theory has had great practical consequences in recent years in areas such as corporation finance, law, and government regulation of business and economic activity. While a large number of individuals have contributed to these developments, three researchers should be mentioned for the path-breaking nature of their work: George Stigler (1961, 1965), whose work in regulatory economics and the economics of information was recognized with the award of the Nobel Prize in economics in 1982; Merton Miller (1977; Miller and Modigliani, 1958, 1961), who won the Nobel Prize in 1990 for his pioneering work on dividend policy, corporate capital structure, and the cost of capital and business investment decisions; and Ronald Coase (1937, 1960), who became a Nobel laureate in 1991 in recognition for his writings on the nature of the firm and the relation of social cost and the legal system in market economies. The insights of these three individuals have opened major areas of scholarly research and have had a great impact on the thinking and actions of practitioners and policymakers.

References

Becker, Gary S., *Economic Theory,* Knopf, New York, 1971; Becker, Gary S., *The Economic Approach to Human Behavior,* University of Chicago Press, Chicago, 1976; Coase, Ronald H., "The Nature of the Firm," *Economica,* vol. 4, 1937, pp. 386–405; Coase, Ronald H., "The Problem of Social Cost," *Journal of Law and Economics,* vol. 4, October 1960, pp. 1–44; Debreu, Gerard, *Theory of Value,* Yale University Press, New Haven, Conn., 1959; Debreu, Gerard, and Kenneth Arrow, "The Role of Securities in the Optimal Allocation of Risk Bearing," *Review of Economic Studies,* vol. 51, April 1961, pp. 91–96; Friedman, Milton, *Price Theory,* Aldine, Chicago, 1976; Gould, John P., and Edward P. Lazear, *Microeconomic Theory,* 6th ed., Irwin, Homewood, Ill., 1989; Miller, Merton H., "Debt and Taxes," *Journal of Finance,* May 1977; Miller, Merton H., and Franco Modigliani, "The Cost of Capital, Corporation Finance, and the Theory of Investment," *American Economic Review,* vol. 48, October 1958, pp. 261–297; Miller, Merton H., and Franco Modigliani, "Dividend Policy, Growth and the Valuation of Shares," *Journal of Business,* vol. 34, October 1961, pp. 411–432; Neumann, John von, and Oskar Morgenstern, *Theory of Games and Economic Behavior,* 3d ed., Princeton University Press, Princeton, N.J., 1953, reprinted by Wiley, New York, 1964; Phelps, E., et al., *Microeconomic Foundations of Employment and Inflation Theory,* Norton, New York, 1970; Samuelson, Paul, *Foundations of Economic Analysis,* Harvard University Press, Cambridge, Mass., 1948; Stigler, George J., "The Development of Utility Theory," *Journal of Political Economy,* vol. 58, August and October 1950, pp. 307–327, 373–396; Stigler, George J., "The Economics of Information," *Journal of Political Economy,* June 1961; Stigler, George J., "The Economist and the State," *American Economic Review,* March 1965; Stigler, George J., *The Organization of Industry,* Irwin, Homewood, Ill., 1968; Stigler, George J., *The Theory of Price,* 4th ed., Macmillan, New York, 1987.

(*See also* Competition; Consumer theory; Demand; Diminishing returns law; Elasticity; Firm theory; General equilibrium; Microeconomics; Monopoly and oligopoly; Normative economics; Supply; Utility; Welfare economics)

John P. Gould

Prime rate (see Business credit)

Producer price index

Producer price index is the generic name applied to indexes of prices charged by producers. As such, they exclude excise taxes, freight insurance, and other costs involved in transferring commodities to purchasers. The term producer price index is in juxtaposition to an index of purchaser prices such as the consumer price index. In the United States the producer price index (PPI) and its component indexes cover manufacturing, mining, electric and gas utilities, agriculture and some service-sector industries. The indexes are being expanded to include all sectors of the economy. The Bureau of Labor Statistics (BLS), which compiles the PPI, also compiles somewhat similar indexes for items that constitute U.S. foreign merchandise trade.

History

The PPI is the oldest price series published by the U.S. government. It first appeared in 1902 with back data provided to 1890. At its inception, the PPI, which until 1978 was called the wholesale price index (WPI), included detailed price series for about 250 commodities produced in the agricultural, mining, and manufacturing sectors of the economy. The number of individual series has grown steadily over the years and in 1991 totaled about 3100.

The indexes are calculated using the Laspeyres formula. Most indexes are published monthly, and selected series are seasonally adjusted.

The various component indexes are added together to form several major aggregate indexes. Until 1978, all the items for which price series existed were added up into an aggregate of all commodities for the WPI. Two major subcomponents were (1) farm products and processed foods and feeds and (2) industrial commodities. The latter subcomponent represented about 75 percent of the total.

It became increasingly clear that the aggregation of all the commodities to a single total produced an index that was not as useful as it could be. The problem was that the industrial commodities component, for example, contained the price of iron ore, the price of steel, and the price of cars, each weighted by total shipments of those commodities. If the price of iron ore rose and triggered an increase in the price of steel and the price of autos, the addition of those three increases amounted to an overstatement of the rise in producer prices if, for example, one wanted to compare it with the behavior of consumer prices. In the late 1960s, work began at the BLS on the development and analysis of prices in the so-called stage-of-process index structure. The WPI was aggregated into separate indexes for crude, intermediate, and finished goods. The relationships among those three components and of the components with the consumer price index became the subject of analysis, and models were built encompassing these indexes. By studying prices by stage of process, the analyst was able to detect early warnings of inflation at early stages of production, which might in turn be passed on to final users such as consumers.

Although stage-of-process indexes had been calculated from the WPI since the turn of the century (the BLS reports that such calculations were made at the request of students of price indexes), the use of these indexes was not widely understood. As a result, they were not part of the major components of the WPI which received wide publication. In 1978 the BLS renamed the wholesale price index the producer price index and began to emphasize three major components of that index: finished goods; intermediate materials, supplies, and components; and crude materials for further processing. These three indexes are now the most widely analyzed components of the producer price index.

Prior to the renaming of the index as the producer price index and the emphasis on disaggregation by stage of process, another need developed for producer prices. Analysts were interested in studying the behavior of constant-dollar output by industry. One way of doing so was to calculate the value of output in current dollars and to deflate that series by an appropriate index. But industries and products are not necessarily synonymous. Some industries produce as secondary products commodities that are primary products in other industries, and the value of production for an industry could include both its primary production and that part of its production which was largely produced in another industry. Therefore, the deflation of such value aggregates requires that special indexes be developed that take into account the composition of primary and secondary products in the value of an industry's output. Such series, referred to as industry-sector price indexes, first appeared in 1963.

The PPI is a system of indexes capable of configuration into an infinite number of combinations depending on the purpose of analysis. The old wholesale price index and its industrial commodities aggregate, the stage-of-process indexes, and the industry-sector price indexes provide three examples of the diversity with which aggregates can be formed from a basic set of producer prices.

Calculation of the Indexes

The component indexes of the PPI are added together using value-of-shipments weights from the various industrial censuses. Since December 1986 weights are based on 1982 data. Producer prices in the manufacturing sector are weighted by shipments collected in the quinquennial Census of Manufactures. Similarly, mining, agricultural, and other censuses are used to develop weights for those index components.

The stage-of-process index structure requires that those weights be further refined. For example, formerly the price of refined petroleum products would be weighted for the industrial commodities component of the wholesale price index by the total value of shipments of petroleum products. In the stage-of-process framework, that weight must be split depending on the uses to which refined petroleum products are put. Such products going to chemical manufacturers for further manufacture would be classified in the stage-of-process index for intermediate materials, supplies, and components. Most gasoline going to final users would be classified in the finished goods index. The process of splitting shipment weights by stage of process is usually accomplished through the use of an input-output table.

The industry-sector price indexes provide yet another example of how value of shipment weights must be modified. The value of the output of steel mill products may not be all produced in the steel industry. On the other hand, some steel mills may produce some products, such as chemicals, that are produced primarily in another industry. Therefore, the value of the weight represented by total shipments of steel mill products must be distributed between the steel industry, which produces such products as primary products, and other industries, which may produce them as secondary products. While the value-of-shipments weights used currently in the PPI are generally those of 1982, the allocation of those weights for the stage-of-process components is based on the 1972 input-output table.

The reference base is currently 1982 = 100 for all series that existed in that year. The selection of a reference base is arbitrary. Any time period can be selected to equal 100 without affecting the rate of change of the index except by 0.1 percent from time to time due to rounding. Traditionally, however, the reference base of U.S. government statistics is changed about once every 10 years.

Problems

Many of the problems of price measurement apply to producer price indexes. There is always the problem of making appropriate adjustment for quality change. Tightly developed specifications are used to collect prices for the index in order to facilitate the adjustment of such prices for quality change.

The problem of obtaining true transaction prices is one that is assumed to affect the producer price index more than other indexes. The reason is that in the United States most prices for consumer commodities are fixed and indicated by a price tag. In the manufacturing and other sectors of the economy, prices may have a greater tendency to be negotiable even though list prices are published. A major study of this problem in the PPI was carried out in the 1960s. It offered no conclusive evidence that systematic error owing to the list-transaction price problem was introduced into the larger aggregates of the index.

Another problem of price measurement that arises in connection with discussion and interpretation of the PPI is whether the prices collected should be of new orders or of shipments. For purposes of measuring industry output in constant dollars, the shipment price is usually the one desired. On the other hand, for analyzing and forecasting inflation, the order price is a more desirable one to obtain. The current producer price index is based on shipment prices.

References

Early, John F., "Improving the Measurement of Producer Price Change," *Monthly Labor Review,* April 1978, pp. 7–18; U.S. Department of Labor, "Producer Prices," *Handbook of Methods,* Bureau of Labor Statistics Bulletin 2285, April 1988.

(*See also* Consumer price index; Escalator clause; Implicit price deflator; Index numbers; Price measurement)

Joel Popkin

Production function

Let n inputs be utilized in a production process which yields m output. The engineer describes the production process in terms of variables such as pressure, density, and horsepower. The economist describes the production process in terms of a production function through which the quantities of outputs produced are functionally dependent upon the quantities of inputs used. The economist's production function incorporates the engineering technology; however, its inputs and outputs usually are quantities that are bought and sold in the marketplace. It also incorporates a degree of optimization. Given values for all the inputs and values for all but one output, the production function specifies the maximum attainable value for the remaining output. Similarly, given values for all the outputs and all but one input, it specifies the minimum permissible value for the remaining input.

Most production functions are defined for a single output. The number of inputs depends upon the purpose for which the production function is used and the level of aggregation employed. Economywide production functions relate a nation's total output to its aggregate labor and capital inputs. On an establishment level a specific output, such as motorcycles, may be related to an array of inputs such as handlebars, tires, wheels, leather, etc., as well as direct labor and capital inputs.

Some Properties of Production Functions

A wide variety of mathematical formats are used for production functions. These include continuous functions, discontinuous functions, and systems of functions with rules explaining which is applicable for particular circumstances. Most of the major properties of production functions can be illustrated by the following one-output, two-input function:

$$q = f(L, K)$$

which is continuous with continuous first- and second-order partial derivatives, and where q denotes the quantity of output secured, and L and K denote the respective quantities of labor and capital used. The function is limited to nonnegative output and input levels. In some cases the input domain may exclude some nonnegative values.

The average product of labor is q/L, and, similarly, the average product of capital is q/K. The marginal product of labor is the rate at which the quantity of output increases per unit increase in the input of labor, with the input of capital unchanged as given by the partial derivative of L with respect to q: $\partial q/\partial L \equiv f_L$ for short. A possible graph for the average and marginal products of labor is shown in the accompanying figure. These shapes are often assumed by economists, although many other shapes are possible. The positions of the curves depend upon the value of the fixed quantity of capital.

The marginal and average products of labor first increase and then decline as the quantity of labor is expanded relative to the fixed quantity of capital for the case shown in the figure. The value of f_L eventually becomes zero and may even become negative. Similar curves may be constructed for f_K and q/K, assuming a variable quantity of capital and a fixed quantity of labor. An isoquant gives the loci of all input values which yield a fixed output level.

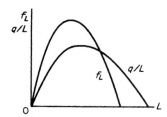

Returns to Scale and Homogeneous Production Functions

Let both inputs increase (or decrease) by the same proportionate amount. For convenience, limit attention to input increases. The production function exhibits decreasing returns to scale if output increases by a smaller proportion. There are constant returns to scale if output increases by the same proportion, and increasing returns to scale if it changes by a greater proportion. In general, a particular production function may exhibit decreasing, constant, and increasing returns to scale depending upon the initial labor and capital quantities and their proportionate change.

A production function is homogeneous of degree k if

$$qt^k = f(tL, tk)$$

for nonnegative values of t. If input quantities are changed by the proportion t, output is changed by the proportion t^k for all input values with the domain of the production function. If $k = 1$, there are constant returns to scale, with output changing by the same proportion as the inputs. Such production functions are said to be linearly homogeneous. Thus, if $k < 1$ ($k > 1$), there are decreasing (increasing) returns to scale throughout

Assume that a production function is homogeneous of degree 1, and let $t = 1/L$ so that

$$q/L = f(1, K/L) = F(K/L)$$

In this form, output per worker is expressed as a function of the capital-labor ratio. This form of production function is used in most economic growth models.

The Cobb-Douglas production function is given by

$$q = AL^\alpha K^{1-\alpha}$$

where $A > 0$ and $0 < \alpha < 1$. It is homogeneous of degree 1, and is used extensively in both theoretical and empirical analyses. The parameter α is the share of total output going to labor if labor is paid the value of its marginal product. Similarly, $1 - \alpha$ is capital's share. The constant-elasticity-of-substitution production function provides a generalization of the Cobb-Douglas function.

Multiple Outputs

A production function with two outputs and two inputs may be written in implicit form as

$$F(q_1, q_2, L, K) = 0$$

where q_1 and q_2 are the quantities of two outputs. This function gives maximum-output (maximum-input) levels when the other three arguments are at fixed levels. It is assumed to be continuous with continuous first- and second-order partial derivatives. Its properties are similar to those of the one-output functions if one of the outputs is held constant.

Consider a situation in which the quantities of labor and capital are given, and it is desired to consider the trade-offs between the two outputs. A transformation function (or transformation curve) is constructed by selecting a level for one of the outputs and determining the maximum level for the other from the production function. Given the definition of the production function, the same result is achieved regardless of which of the outputs is assumed to be fixed. The rate of product substitution (i.e., the slope of a transformation curve) is given by

$$-\partial q_2/\partial q_1 = \frac{\partial F/\partial q_1}{\partial F/\partial q_2}$$

The preceding minus sign transforms the rate into a positive number since $\partial q_2/\partial q_1$ is inherently negative (i.e., an increase in the level of one output reduces the maximum attainable level for the other).

A transformation curve also can be constructed from distinct production functions for the two outputs. In this case an explicit optimization procedure is used to maximize one of the output levels, given fixed values for the other output, labor, and capital.

Linear Production Functions

Linear, sometimes called fixed-coefficient, production functions are frequently used. It is assumed that α_L and α_K units of labor and capital, respectively, are required to produce 1 unit of output. The linear production function is given by

$$q = \min(L/\alpha_L, K/\alpha_K)$$

Direct substitution between the two factors is not possible. Each of the factors may be limiting. However, substitution between labor and capital is sometimes achieved by allowing the simultaneous use of several distinct linear processes for the production of a particular good.

References

Frisch, Ragnar, *Theory of Production,* Rand-McNally, Chicago, 1965; Henderson, James M., and Richard E. Quandt, *Microeconomic Theory: A Mathematical Approach,* 3d ed., McGraw-Hill, New York, 1980, chaps 4, 5; Hirschleifer, Jack, *Price Theory and Applications,* 4th ed., Prentice-Hall, Englewood Cliffs, N.J., 1988; Varian, Hal R., *Microeconomic Analysis,* 3d ed., Norton, New York, 1991.

(*See also* Firm theory; Isoquant)

James M. Henderson

Productivity

Productivity denotes the relationship between output and one or all associated inputs, in real terms. In neoclassical economics, the concepts of marginal and average productivity are an important part of value and distribution theory under the assumption of static equilibrium conditions. In dynamic economic analysis, the concepts and measures of average and total productivity ratios, which reflect the impacts of cost-reducing technological and organizational changes, are an important variable helping to explain changes in economic aggregates and structure, and in costs and prices.

Static Productivity Concepts

Marginal productivity of the factors of production is an important theoretical concept. It refers to the increase in output associated with a given increase in a factor input, if the quantity of other inputs and technology are held constant. It is hypothesized that beyond some point (the optimal combination of inputs), the marginal productivity of a factor declines—i.e., output increases less than proportionately to the input. Conversely, marginal costs (input cost per incremental unit of output) rise as marginal productivity falls since productivity and unit costs are the opposite sides of the same coin.

The average total unit-cost curve of the firm can also be interpreted as the inverse of a total productivity curve (output per unit of all inputs, or real-cost elements). Unit costs decline as output rises up to the point of the most efficient rate of utilization of a fixed plant; thereafter they rise—so total productivity rises up to that point, then falls.

There is also a long-run productivity concept in neoclassical theory, associated with Alfred Marshall's notions of increasing, constant, and diminishing returns in different industries. If output increases faster than inputs (including overhead factors) as the scale of production increases, the increasing return (decreasing unit cost) reflects the operation of economies of scale, not technological innovation since static conditions of constant technological knowledge are still assumed. Diminishing returns presumably characterize extractive industries as increasing output necessitates resort to poorer land or to more intensive use of existing land. In other industries, productivity and unit-costs remain essentially flat as the scale of operations and number of plants increase.

Finally, there is the notion of the production function. Under static conditions, a given volume of output can be produced with different combinations of the factors, as depicted by a production isoquant. The actual combination of inputs depends on their relative prices, which determine the least-cost combination.

In comparative statics, if cost-reducing technological change is assumed, this is depicted by shifts of productivity curves upward, downward shifts of marginal and unit-cost curves, and a shift to the left of production isoquants. Actually, the notions of average and marginal productivity under hypothetical static assumptions are difficult, if not impossible, to implement statistically. This is not true of productivity concepts under more realistic dynamic conditions.

Dynamic Productivity Concepts

In contrast to the static concepts, there is a family of average productivity ratios relating output to one or more inputs over time which reflect the effects of cost-reducing innovations in the ways and means of production and other dynamic forces. The precise meaning of the average productivity ratios depends on the concepts and methods used to measure outputs and inputs, discussed subsequently. Productivity can be measured for the business economy, industries, firms, and organizational units for which separate records are kept.

The ratios of output to individual inputs, or classes of inputs, are called partial productivity ratios. The most common of these is the familiar output-per-labor-hour measure, which is particularly important since labor is the dominant cost of production in the economy, and the major part of value added in most industries. The partial productivity measures reflect factor substitutions as well as changes in productive efficiency. Thus, output-labor ratios reflect increases in capital and other nonhuman inputs per labor-hours, as well as cost-reducing technological innovations.

Only if output is related to all associated inputs is the net saving in real costs per unit of output measured, and thus the increase in productive efficiency. Such measures are called total productivity ratios. When gross output is measured, the associated inputs not only are the factors of production—human (labor) and nonhuman (human-made capital goods and land or other natural resources)—but also include the purchased intermediate products—the materials, supplies, energy, and other services consumed in the production process. A variant of the total productivity measure is total factor productivity, in which net output of the intermediate product purchases is measured, and the resulting real value added is related to the factor inputs above. Since the sum of value added by industry equals national product, total factor productivity estimates by industry have the advantage of consistency with national measures. But since managements of firms are interested in the least-cost combination of all inputs, and in conserving over time in the use of intermediate goods and services as well as of factor services, total productivity measures are of interest for establishments, companies, and industries. At the national level, the total and total factor productivity measures are identical, for in consolidating production accounts of all industries, interindustry sales and purchases of intermediate products wash out, and the value of the final products that compose gross national product (GNP) equals the gross factor costs of production, plus indirect business taxes less subsidies since GNP is measured at market prices.

It is clear that the concept of productivity is rooted in the notion of the production function, that the volume of output depends on the volume of inputs used in production and on the state of the art (technology). As technology advances, reflected in shifts in the production function as discussed previously, more outputs can be produced with the same inputs. To use the simple Cobb-Douglas production function, devised in the mid-1920s:

$$Q = Ak^{\alpha}L^{\beta}$$

In this formulation, A is the technology scalar that constrains the amount of output Q that can be obtained from given quantities of labor L and capital K. The exponents α and β relate to the marginal products of the factors, or, if index numbers are used to fit the function, the percentage shares of gross income. If the production function is linear and homogeneous, of degree 1, there are no scale economies and α and β sum to 1.0. If cost-reducing technological changes occur through time, this is reflected in shifts in the scalar A. The rate of change in the scalar could be measured by a time trend $(1 + r)_t$ in the place of A. Or, more flexibly, the period-to-period rates of change in the productivity scalar can be computed as the difference between the rates of change in output and a weighted average of the rates of change in the inputs:

$$\Delta A/A \equiv \Delta Q/Q - \alpha\Delta K/K - \beta\Delta L/L$$

This is why total factor productivity has sometimes been called a residual—that part of the change in output that cannot be explained by the change in input.

Another way to measure the productivity scalar is as the ratio of output to a weighted average of inputs, as discussed at the outset:

$$\frac{Q}{K^\alpha L^\beta}$$

As a practical matter, total input has been measured as an arithmetic rather than a geometric mean of the component inputs. The difference is small unless the rates of change of the inputs differ substantially. Also, instead of the weights coming from the exponents of a statistically fitted production function, factor shares in national income are used.

Since the Cobb-Douglas function was formulated, various other types of production functions have been developed. But the type of function assumed as background for total productivity measures affects chiefly the system of weights, and it has been demonstrated that weighting differences have relatively little impact on the movement of productivity, at least over intermediate time periods.

Measurement

Gross output is measured as a weighted quantity aggregate

$$\sum_{i=1}^{n} Q_x P_0$$

with units of each of the n goods and services produced in the given period x weighted by base-period prices P_0, or unit costs. Actually, for production and productivity analysis, in contrast to welfare analysis, unit-factor-cost weights are preferable to market prices in measuring relative resource costs since they are not distorted by indirect business taxes less subsidies. But as a practical matter, market prices are generally used as weights or as deflators of current values. Instead of directly weighting quantities, one ideally can obtain the same results by deflation of values by Paasche-type price indexes. This method is preferred if value and price data are more plentiful than detailed quantity data. The same methodology is used to estimate intermediate inputs as to estimate outputs, whether the real intermediate costs are deducted from gross output to obtain real value added or are treated as an input. After all, the intermediate inputs are the outputs of the supplying industries. Special problems of measuring output, particularly adjustments for quality change, are not discussed here, but it should be noted that they may impart some downward bias to estimates of real product and productivity.

Labor input is frequently measured merely as the sum of hours worked. When data on hours paid for rather than worked are used, there is an upward bias to the extent that paid leave has risen. Some investigators (Denison, 1974) adjust labor input for the impact of increased education per worker on earnings and for other qualitative factors. Others have weighted labor-hours by industry, occupation, sex, and educational attainment. The quality-adjusted hours have risen significantly faster in the United States and many other countries than have unweighted hours. If unweighted hours are used as input, then the increase in labor quality may be viewed as part of the explanation for the increase in the residual.

Similarly, nonhuman factor input may be measured in terms of the total real stocks of capital (plant, equipment, inventories, and land) multiplied by the base-period average rate of return. Or the real stocks may be measured by industry and weighted by the base-period rate of return in each. In the latter case, relative shifts of capital to industries with higher rates of compensation mean that weighted capital input rises faster than the aggregate. If the aggregate is used in the denominator of the ratio, then interindustry shifts in capital become part of the explanation of productivity change.

Most specialists think the real gross stocks of depreciable capital goods are a better measure of output-producing capacity than the net stocks, which reflect the decline in value of fixed capital goods as they age. Some adjust the real stocks and inputs for changes in rates of utilization of capacity; others do not on the grounds that in an economy based on private property, capital carries a charge regardless of rates of utilization. If capital input is not so adjusted, changes in rates of utilization are a factor helping to explain cyclical changes in the productivity ratio.

Real input costs are added to obtain total input to be divided into the real value of output. If index numbers of the inputs are used, each is weighted by its base-period proportion of costs to obtain index numbers of total input. The quotients of index numbers of output and of inputs yield index numbers of productivity.

Causal Forces

The meaning of productivity changes (or differences) has been analyzed by a priori reasoning; by regression analyses relating differences in rates of productivity growth to differences in levels and/or rates of change of causal forces; and, at the aggregate level, by growth accounting studies, pioneered by Edward F. Denison.

When productivity is measured in terms of output per labor-hour, increases in non-labor inputs per hour contribute to productivity gains, as noted previously. If the rate of change in the capital-labor ratio is weighted by the share of capital in factor cost, the resulting rate of substitution of capital for labor exactly explains the difference between the rates of change in labor productivity and in total factor productivity.

Denison's estimates show that more than half of the growth in total factor productivity in the United States since 1948 has been due to advances in technological knowledge as applied in production. A major part of these advances in the modern era stems from formal research and development programs. But there is still a significant amount of informal development of cost-reducing innovations and practices. Also, the rate of diffusion of innovations affects the pace of productivity advance. In part, this reflects the rate of investment in new plant and equipment which embody the latest technology.

If labor input is measured in terms of undifferentiated hours worked, then the effect of increased education and training per worker helps explain productivity growth. So, too, do other factors affecting the quality of labor, such as the average health status of workers and the conditions in the workplace. Changes in the ratio of actual to potential efficiency of workers can be important and reflect the skill of management in motivating workers to perform well. Shifts in the age-sex mix also affect productivity if there is a net shift toward groups with higher or lower average compensation and value added per hour. In the United States in the late 1960s, for example, the rise in youthful entrants into the labor force with less average pay and experience had a significant negative effect on productivity growth. Beyond some point, a declining average quality of land and mineral reserves also has a negative effect on productivity.

As labor and capital move from industries with lower rates of remuneration to higher-pay industries, this raises productivity if the factor inputs are not weighted on an industry basis. This factor is related to the degree of mobility of resources.

The rate of growth of demand and output itself affects productivity with respect to opportunities for economies of scale. The degree of cyclicality of demand also influences productivity—a relatively stable growth rate is more favorable than fluctuating demand. If growth is measured between years of different rates of utilization of capacity, this, too, will affect the rate unless adjusted for it.

Finally, if the productivity measure is confined to the business economy, the net impact of government may be important. Some governmental activities foster business; others, such as regulation, may increase real costs without increasing business output as measured. It is claimed that environmental, health, and safety regulations have had a negative impact on productivity in the United States during the past decade.

Behind the proximate determinants of productivity change stand the basic values, attitudes, and institutional forms and practices of a society. These generally change only slowly, and in any event affect productivity through the more immediate causes just discussed.

Economic Impacts

Growth of real income per capita is the product of increases in factor input per capita and of total factor productivity. In the United States since 1919 there has been no increase of input per capita—as declining hours worked per capita have offset rising real capital per capita—so all of the 2.3 percent a year average annual rate of growth of real income per capita has been due to increasing total factor productivity.

Productivity growth has also offset rising factor prices with respect to unit costs. Thus, from 1948 to 1966 in the United States, average hourly labor compensation and the price of capital together rose at an average annual rate of almost 5 percent, but productivity was rising by nearly 3 percent a year; consequently, unit costs and prices were going up by only around 2 percent a year, on average. After 1966, productivity growth decelerated and factor price increases accelerated so that inflation of unit costs and the general price level accelerated even more—until the disinflation of the 1980s.

On an industry basis, relative changes in productivity and in prices are negatively correlated in the long run. That is, average factor prices show much the same rate of increase in most industries so that industries with the largest productivity gains show the smallest increases in unit costs and prices, and vice versa. To the degree that demand is price-elastic, and if price elasticities are not outweighed by income elasticities working in the opposite direction (or in extractive and service industries), relative changes in prices and in demand (output) are also negatively correlated. Therefore, relative changes in productivity and in output are positively correlated. This correlation is reinforced by scale economies. It is strong enough that there is not a significant degree of correlation between relative changes in productivity and in employment. In this sense, there is no technological unemployment, although there is obviously some temporary displacement of workers in particular occupations, industries, and localities.

Industries with relative increases in productivity and relative price declines also tend to fare better in international markets—unless their counterparts abroad are doing relatively even better. International differences in general productivity movements are only one factor influencing relative changes in price levels and currency values, however. Relative factor price movements can, and often do, counteract the effects of favorable relative productivity changes in comparative price-level movements, and vice versa. The purchasing power of currencies depends not only on relative prices but also on the impact of financial flows on the supply of and demand for currencies. But it can be said that nations with relative productivity gains will be increasing their real consumption per capita, not only of domestic products but of imported goods as well.

References

Denison, Edward F., *Accounting for United States Economic Growth, 1948–1969*, Brookings, Washington, D.C., 1974; Kendrick, John W., *Understanding Productivity, An Introduction to the Dynamics of Productivity Change*, Johns Hopkins Press, Baltimore, Md., 1977; Kendrick, John W., and Beatrice Vaccara (eds.), *New Developments in Productivity Measurement and Analysis, Studies in Income and Wealth*, vol. 44, University of Chicago Press, Chicago, for the National Bureau of Economic Research, 1980; Nadiri, M. I., "Some Approaches to the Theory and Measurement of Total Factor Productivity: A Survey," *Journal of Economic Literature*, vol. 8, no. 4, December 1970, pp. 1137–1177; *Measuring Productivity: Trends and Comparisons from the First International Productivity Symposium*, Unipub, New York, 1984.

(*See also* Economic forecasting methods; Economic forecasts; Economic growth; Employment and unemployment; Human capital; Index numbers; Innovation; Neoclassical economics; Production function; Research and development; Technology)

John W. Kendrick

Profits in economic theory

Profits are generally defined as the excess of total revenues of an enterprise over its total costs. On the revenue side, there are questions about both the quality and the nature of the revenues and their timing. Revenues are not synonymous with cash payments. Goods and services sold are contributions to revenues at the time of sale, even if payment is not current. Sales of assets or other portfolio switches, such as the sale of securities for cash, do not in themselves constitute revenues. Even the excess of proceeds over cost in the sale of capital assets is generally considered capital gains rather than profits for accounting and tax purposes.

Costs present even more formidable problems. They do not include the purchases of assets. While omitting many cash expenditures, costs also include a number of accounting charges that do not involve out-of-pocket payments. The most important of these encompass depreciation or estimates of the exhaustion of values of existing capital.

Various Views

Profits in economic theory have been variously seen as the return to ownership or capital and the return to the entrepreneur. Where ownership and entrepreneurship coincide, as in a simple single proprietorship in which the owner's own capital is used to run the firm, this notion perhaps has some meaning. Most modern firms, however, are not of that sort. Capital is extensively borrowed, and most owners of equity have little to do with plant management or entrepreneurship. In practice, separate returns to ownership, management, and entrepreneurship are nevertheless difficult to identify.

Where capital is partly owned and partly borrowed, accounting conventions denote a return to borrowed capital as interest while including the return to the owned capital as profit. Where owners work in managing their firms, the value of their labor or managerial services is usually included in profit, except to the extent that owners formally pay themselves salaries.

Where capital and labor markets are perfect and where there is freedom of entry for new firms, the return to capital in equilibrium would be the market rate of interest adjusted for risk, and the return for labor performed by managers would similarly be the opportunity cost of their services elsewhere, perhaps again adjusted for risk. On the presumption that risk aversion is dominant and on the further assumption that owning a firm is relatively risky, the risk adjustment might make the income of owner-managers somewhat higher than what they would earn as employees and as lenders of their capital. To the extent that owner-managers prefer the independence that goes with entrepreneurship, however, they may actually continue in situations where their earnings are less than they could receive otherwise.

Under the conditions stated above, however, there is no further residual (other than the possible risk premiums) which would create profit in equilibrium, for even monopoly profit would be wiped out with free entry of competitors, reducing the industry to a situation of monopolistic competition with no profit beyond the return necessary to prevent capital from being withdrawn. Since entrepreneurship has no cost, new entrepreneurial talent embodied in new firms would enter an industry with profits, until the increased supply of product lowered prices (or pushed up costs) to the point where there were no profits. Profits thus become a transitory phenomenon of change or adjustment.

Profits: The Key Element in Innovation

Thus, as emphasized by Joseph Schumpeter, profits become the key element in innovation in a dynamic, changing economy. Profit seekers are driven to bring forth new processes and products. These profits from innovation are earned only at the introduction of the innovation, for after awhile others copy the changes and compete away the profits. Profits then are the lure that keeps the economy seeking new and more efficient ways of meeting real and potential human wants.

All this applies when there is freedom of entry. Entrepreneurship itself, however is not homogeneous and in infinite supply. Some individuals or firms may possess or acquire through experience unique talents of organization which cannot be competed away by new firms led by new entrepreneurs because there are no new entrepreneurs with comparable talents. Further, combinations of costly information, imperfect capital markets, and risk aversion may make it difficult if not impossible for new firms to enter into successful competition with established industrial giants such as General Motors, General Electric, IBM, and AT&T. This difficulty may be compounded by economies of scale, in production or in marketing, which leave room for only one or two very large, really successful firms in an industry. In these situations there will be profits over and above the normal return to originally invested capital. If owners cannot exercise sufficient control to appropriate all this extra return, some of it may well be distributed among management in the form of exceptionally high salaries and bonuses. Some may also be distributed to workers in higher wages.

Government frequently becomes the source of monopoly profits by offering contracts, franchises, and licenses to firms without seeking adequate competitive bidding. Along with this role of government may go regulations that interfere with entry and thus favor businesses already in the industry, as in the case of airlines, trucking firms, and taxicab companies.

Aside from these circumstances, profits in a competitive economy are the carrot that leads participants to the most efficient market solutions, occasionally requiring correction for externalities, that is, costs of market activities, such as pollution, which are not borne by the direct participants in the activity. Profits, then, are ever to be strived for, but never long enjoyed.

References

Kierstead, B. S., "Profit," in David L. Sills (ed.), *International Encyclopedia of the Social Sciences,* vol. 12, Collier and Macmillan, New York, 1968, pp. 547–552; Knight, Frank H., *Risk, Uncertainty and Profit,* London School of Economics and Political Science Series of Reprints of Scarce Tracts in Economic and Political Science, no. 16, London, 1921, 1933; Robinson, Joan, *The Economics of Imperfect Competition,* St. Martin's, New York, 1933, 1961; Schumpeter, Joseph A., *The Theory of Economic Development: An Inquiry into Profits, Capital, Credit, Interest and the Business Cycle,* Harvard University Press, Cambridge, Mass., 1939.

(*See also* Capitalism; Innovation; Profits measurement; Return on investment; Risk premium on investment)

Robert Eisner

Profits measurement

Profits are normally defined as the residual left after revenues are used to pay for the factors of production. More simply, profits are revenues minus costs. As usual, when this is used to define measurements, the results are seldom as simple as the concepts.

In normal use there are a few concepts that are commonly used to measure profits and make comparisons over time or across different firms or economic situations. These include profits reported by public companies to their shareholders, often called financially reported earnings; profits reported on corporate income tax returns; profits data reported in analyses of the stock market, such as earnings per share for widely followed stock market indexes; and profits measures included in the national income and product accounts (NIPA) used to tabulate gross domestic product (GDP). All these profit measurements have their own definitions. Different measures are used for different kinds of analyses. These measures are defined below.

Financially Reported Profits

When most people think of a company's profits, they are referring to the "bottom line" shown on the firm's income statement. This figure is computed in accordance with accounting principles prescribed by the Securities and Exchange Commission (SEC), the Financial Accounting Standards Board (FASB), and similar groups. While companies outside the United States follow their own national accounting principles, most industrialized nations have defined accounting systems for use by public companies.

The accounting principles define what kinds of expenditures are costs, what types of purchases can be treated as capital investment, and how depreciation should be calculated. However, merely because two different companies both use U.S. generally accepted accounting principles (GAAP) does not mean that their accounting treatments are the same. First, there are often differences among industries on how different expenses or taxes are treated or how revenues are recognized. Second, there are numerous situations where an individual company can elect a particular type of accounting treatment or can even alter its accounting procedures on occasion.

One example is inventory valuation. When goods are sold from inventory, they can be valued on either a first-in first-out (FIFO) basis or a last-in last-out (LIFO) basis. As a result, any analysis of a company must consider the particular definitions used for revenues, expenses, and profits. Care must also be taken to adjust for any significant changes in accounting done over time or any differences between otherwise comparable companies. Not all accounting adjustments or changes are initiated by a company's management. At times the FASB may order a change in accounting procedures that results in substantial changes to a company's reported profits. A recent example is making provisions for financing retirees' medical benefits.

Financially reported profits for public companies are made available annually and quarterly. The quarterly reports are less comprehensive but do show profits data for the quarter. Reporting is required by SEC regulations, which specify the timing and the information that must be included. These data are compiled by the SEC and are available to the public, and to financial analysts, through the SEC and various private firms. Standard & Poor's Compustat Services compiles these reports and makes the data available in as-reported and standardized formats which restate accounting data according to procedures established by Compustat. These data, which cover all industrial companies making filings with the SEC, are comparable across firms.

Profits Based on Income Tax Returns

In the United States, most firms maintain two sets of accounts. The first set is for financial reporting, as discussed above. The second set is calculated in accordance with the U.S. Internal Revenue Code and related regulations and is reported on income tax returns. In most cases, profits reported to the Internal Revenue Service (IRS) differ from profits reported to shareholders. The tax code may allow depreciation charges to be accelerated or permit shorter lives for certain kinds of assets. In other cases, the treatment of various expenses or the accounting for acquisitions may be different for tax purposes than for financial reporting. In most cases, profits reported on tax returns are less than profits reported to shareholders. The lower tax-return profits tend to lower income taxes as well.

While all companies are required to comply with IRS regulations, one should not assume that the tax-return profits reported by two different companies are always comparable or measured on the same basis. With tax-return profits, as with financially reported profits, there may be variations from firm to firm or over time.

Stock Market Analyses

One of the most common uses of profit measures is investment analysis of public companies. Analysts often seek benchmarks to measure profits and profitability against. A common question about almost any proposed stock investment is the company's "p-e," or price-earnings ratio. This is its price divided by its earnings per share (EPS). The EPS is the aftertax financially reported profit divided by the number of shares outstanding.

A company's stock price may be high or low because of the number of shares outstanding. After all, when a stock splits, its price drops because of the change in shares outstanding while the company's total market value remains the same. Provided that there are no significant differences between two companies' accounting, their p-e ratio should give some idea of their relative value in the stock market. A firm with a high p-e ratio is one where the stock market expects strong earnings or sees unusually good protection against declines and failures.

What figure represents a high p-e ratio depends on the overall figures for the stock market. To gauge this, a profit measure that relates to the stock market or the overall economy, rather than a single company, is used. The two most common measures are earnings per share for the Standard & Poor's 500 stock index and the profit measures included in the national income and product accounts.

S&P 500 Earnings per Share   The S&P 500 is an index of 500 stocks traded on the New York and American Stock Exchanges and on the NASDAQ National Market System. The index is calculated as the total market value (or market capitalization) of the companies in the index divided by a scale factor called the index divisor. The scale factor sets the index value to 10 for the base period of 1941 to 1943. The divisor is adjusted when the composition of the index changes.

Earnings, dividends, and related profit or financial measures are calculated for the overall index and used as a guide to the condition of the stock market and the economy. Earnings per share are defined as the total earnings of all companies in the index divided by the divisor. Earnings are based on financial profits as reported in SEC filings and compiled by Standard and Poor's Compustat. The earnings figures are based on primary earnings from continuing operations. Extraordinary gains and losses are excluded from the total. Total earnings for the 500 companies are divided by the divisor to yield earnings per share. The divisor acts as the number of shares outstanding for the index, and the calculation is similar to calculating earnings per share for a single company. While common usage is to quote the S&P 500 index in dollars, strictly speaking it is measured in index points. In the same way, the earnings-per-share measure is strictly index points per nominal share, not dollars per share. Earnings per share are not seasonally adjusted. As a result, earnings are often reported as the sum of the most recent four quarters. These are called "trailing four-quarter earnings."

The p-e ratio is sometimes inverted (to the earnings-price ratio) and quoted as a percentage to make it comparable to an interest rate. A similar measure that is also used to gauge profit rates is the dividend yield. This is the dividend per share divided by the stock index value.

Earnings per share and related statistics are compiled for the overall index and for about 85 industry groups within the overall index. Annual and quarterly data are published by Standard and Poor's Corporation and are commonly used to develop industry benchmarks.

NIPA Profits   Profits reported as part of the GDP data are the other set of composite figures commonly used in economic analysis. The national income and product accounts are the measures used to derive GDP and GNP. GDP can be derived from the "incomes" side or the product side; profits are part of the incomes side. Within the NIPA there are three key profits measures—profits before tax, profits after tax, and profits from continuing production. The last, a before-tax concept, is also called economic profits. Data reported in the NIPA, unlike almost all other profit concepts, are seasonally adjusted. Moreover, the data are typically reported at annual rates, not quarterly rates.

Profits before tax are profits as reported on corporate income tax returns. As discussed above, these figures can be based on a variety of depreciation, inventory accounting, and other assumptions. To make these profit figures consistent with the data in the NIPA, adjustments are made to put all figures on a current-cost inventory basis (essentially LIFO) and to remove the effects of accelerated depreciation. The inventory valuation adjustment (IVA) is added to profits before tax, and this new figure is published for the overall economy and for selected nonfinancial industries.

A second adjustment is the capital consumption adjustment (CCAdj). This converts depreciation to "true" service lives and a straight-line basis from accelerated depreciation figures normally reported in tax returns. The resulting figure is economic profits.

At the same time, corporate income taxes are deducted from the profits-before-taxes figure taken from the income tax return to yield aftertax profits. While the government does not report economic profits on an aftertax basis, many analysts deduct corporate tax payments from economic profits to derive this measure. It is usually thought of as being similar in concept to financially reported profits.

The profits figures in the NIPA do not cover individual firms. Rather they cover three broad aggregates—financial companies, nonfinancial companies, and the rest of the world. Financial companies include the profits of the Federal Reserve System which are returned to the U.S. Treasury annually. The "rest of the world" aggregate represents earnings of U.S.-owned operations outside the United States.

Because the NIPA profits are part of the overall accounting system, other special adjustments are possible. In particular, profits data report, which is included in the GDP press releases, includes a table showing the gross domestic product of nonfinancial business, payments to various factors, profits taxes, and profits. These figures are used, in turn, to derive data on current-dollar cost and profit per unit of constant-dollar gross domestic product. The latter figures provide details on profit margins and payments. For 1991, economic profits—profits before tax with inventory valuation adjustment and capital consumption adjustment—totaled $205.4 billion and accounted for 6.7 percent of U.S. gross domestic product, while after tax profits of $120.6 billion accounted for 3.9 percent of GDP of nonfinancial business.

References

Mennis, Edward A., *How the Economy Works,* New York Institute of Finance, New York, 1991; *Standard & Poor's Analysts Handbook,* Standard & Poor's Corporation, New York, 1991; U.S. Department of Commerce, *Corporate Profits: Profits before Tax, Profits Tax Liability and Dividends,* Methodology Papers, U.S. National Income and Product Accounts, May 1985, NTIS PB85-245397; U.S. Department of Commerce, Bureau of Economic Analysis, *Gross Domestic Product and Corporate Profits Press Release,* BEA 92-10, published monthly; U.S. Department of Commerce, *Survey of Current Business,* published monthly, various issues.

(*See also* Capitalism; Price-earnings ratio; Profits in economic theory)

David M. Blitzer

Program trading (*see* Arbitrage)

Property taxation (*see* Taxation, an overview)

Protectionism

Protectionism, in the context of international trade, is a term used to describe any movement by a government to alter the flows of such trade. Narrowly interpreted, the term refers to policies to tax or otherwise to limit imports. Taken broadly, the term also encompasses such measures as any direct subsidy or tax on the production of traded goods, multiple exchange rates, and, indeed, any other governmental intervention affecting trade flows (Corden, 1971, chap. 1).

According to classical international trade theory, any such intervention reduces global economic welfare, a conclusion that has remained a tenet of virtually all orthodox theory since it was first articulated early in the nineteenth century by David Ricardo. According to classical theory, international trade, freely conducted among nations without governmental intervention, allows regional producers to specialize in the production of goods and services in which the region possesses comparative advantage. The resulting international specialization assures optimal use of the world's finite resources. A key assumption behind this conclusion is that the structure of industries supplying goods is that of "perfect competition," i.e., that the number of producers is very large, so that each producer acts as a price taker in the relevant market.

Are There Benefits from Protectionist Policies?

Economists recognize, however, that under some circumstances individual nations might benefit from protectionism. One long-recognized case is embodied in the optimal-tariff argument, which states that in the absence of retaliation by its trading partners, a nation can gain advantage by imposing a limited tariff on imports. But because world efficiency would be reduced, the optimal-tariff nation's gain would be exceeded by losses accruing to its trading partners. A second, and controversial, long-articulated case is that of infant industries. Some economists, especially those advocating developing nations' interests, argue that in order to create competitive firms in new industries, governments must temporarily protect these firms from international competition. The protection is to be afforded only for as long as it takes the firm to learn the technologies and management skills required to compete.

During the past 10 years or so, a number of new ideas have emerged where protectionism, broadly defined, can work to an individual nation's advantage. These ideas, somewhat loosely collectively termed "strategic trade policy," are all based on the existence of imperfect (monopolistic or oligopolistic) competition. Where imperfect competition exists, government intervention in the form of subsidies to domestic producers or protection from imports can have the effect of shifting producers' rents from foreigners to domestic residents. In such cases, there can be benefits to the domestic economy; benefits to the world economy are ambiguous. As with the optimal-tariff argument, strategic trade policies work only in the absence of retaliation by foreign governments. A highly readable exposition of the new literature is Helpman and Krugman (1989); a very useful survey is Richardson (1990).

Why nations often actually choose to pursue protectionist policies is perhaps better explained by political reasons than economic ones. The opening of an economy to external trade necessitates certain adjustments. Industries in which the economy enjoys comparative advantage can be expected to expand, while industries at a comparative disadvantage must contract and release resources for the expanding industries. Frictional costs of adjustment may cause laborers and holders of capital in the contracting industries to resist the change and, if these constituencies exert political influence, force the nation to adopt protectionist policies. The factor-price equalization theorem of neoclassical trade theory posits that as adjustment occurs, factors of production that are employed intensively in the expanding industries will gain in share of national income at the expense of factors of production employed intensively in contracting industries. (This theorem assumes, of course, that factors are at least partially substitutable and that different industries have different factor intensities.) If this theorem is correct and if the losing factor of production represents a political constituency, further political pressure for protectionist policies may arise.

Because freer trade leads to a net gain for an economy (except possibly in cases under which optimal tariffs, infant industry, or strategic trade policy arguments might apply), a strong argument for avoiding protectionism can be made on economic grounds. Although some constituencies may experience a welfare loss as a result of freer trade, the losses are more than offset by other constituencies' gains. Arguably, it is therefore preferable that a nation's government require gaining constituencies to compensate the losers for their losses than it is for the nation to adopt protectionist policies.

References

Balassa, Bela, et al., *The Structure of Protection in Developing Countries,* Johns Hopkins Press, Baltimore, Md., 1971; Baldwin, Robert, "The Case against Infant Industry Protection," *Journal of Political Economy,* vol. 77, May 1969, pp. 295–305; Corden, W. M., *The Theory of Protection,* Oxford University Press, London, 1971; Ellis, H. S., and L. A. Metzler, *Readings in the Theory of International Trade,* Irwin, Homewood, Ill., 1950; Helpman, E., and P. R. Krugman, *Trade Policy and Market Structure,* MIT Press, Cambridge, Mass., 1989; Johnson, H. G., *Aspects of the Theory of Tariffs,* Allen & Unwin, London, 1971; Krugman, Paul R., *Rethinking International Trade,* MIT Press, Cambridge, Mass., 1991; Krugman, Paul R., "Is Free Trade Passé?" *Journal of Economic Perspectives,* vol. 1, no. 1, 1987, pp. 31–144; Lerner, Abba, "The Diagrammatical Representation of Demand Conditions in International Trade," *Economica,* no. 3, August 1934, pp. 319–334; Marshall, Alfred, *The Pure Theory of Foreign Trade,* London School of Economics and Political Science, London, 1930; Metzler, L. A., "Tariffs, the Terms of Trade, and the Distribution of National Income," *Journal of Political Economy,* vol. 57, no. 1, 1949, pp. 1–29; Myint, H., "The Gains from International Trade and the Backward Countries," *Review of Economic Studies,* vol. 22, no. 58, 1954–1955, pp. 129–142; Ohlin, Bertil, *Interregional and International Trade,* Harvard University Press, Cambridge, Mass., 1933; Ricardo, David, *On the Principles of Political Economy and Taxation,* London, 1817; Richardson, J. David, "The Political Economy of Strategic Trade Policy," *International Organization,* vol. 44., no. 1, 1990, pp. 107–135; Samuelson, P. A., "International Trade and the Equalisation of Factor Prices," *Economic Journal,* vol. 58, 1948, pp. 163–184; Spencer, B., and J. Brander, "International R&D Rivalry and Industrial Strategy," *Review of Economic Studies,* vol. 50, 1983, pp. 707–722.

(*See also* Barriers to trade; Exports; Imports; International economics, an overview)

Edward M. Graham

Psychology theory (*see* Juglar cycle)

Public capital

The public capital stock can be literally defined as those categories of capital goods which are owned by the government sector. On neoclassical grounds, the fundamental rationale for government ownership of a portion of the national capital stock is that certain types of capital provide services that are in the nature of public goods. Typically, such a good is characterized by a high (in the extreme, infinite) cost of excluding any particular individual from its consumption and a low (in the extreme, zero) cost of supplying it to an additional individual. Under such conditions, individual firms would fail to provide a socially optimal level of the good either because the ability to capture the returns to production is lacking or because efficiency dictates too low a price to cover costs of production.

The service flow from defense capital—national security—clearly conforms to the economic definition of public goods. In practice, however, the service flow from various categories of the public capital stock may have varying degrees of private good characteristics. It is clearly feasible, at quite low cost, to exclude individuals from driving on interstate highways. Nevertheless, if the highway is uncongested, such exclusion would be inefficient and government provision is rationalized. Only if the highway were congested, so that use by additional drivers imposed costs on current drivers in the form of additional delay, would there be the potential for private, efficient provision.

In the United States, the public capital stock is composed of streets and highways, buildings (schools, hospitals, and other buildings such as general office buildings, police and fire stations, and courthouses), sewer systems, water-supply facilities, other structures (such as electric and gas facilities owned by the government), and equipment. As of the end of 1990, the stock of public capital totaled $4.7 trillion, an amount one-half as large as the nonresidential fixed private capital stock of $9.4 trillion. The military capital stock (primarily equipment although inclusive of military barracks and other structures) is $0.9 trillion, so that the nonmilitary public capital stock equals $3.8 trillion, an amount 40 percent as large as the private capital stock.

Public Capital and Quality of Life

It is convenient to follow Hansen (1965) and distinguish between two categories of (nonmilitary) public capital: social overhead capital (SOC) and economic overhead capital (EOC). SOC is pointed toward directly improving the quality of life by providing social services; EOC lays out a basic foundation for private economic activity. Of course, a particular category of public capital may perform dual roles; a highway may allow vacationers better access to public parks (SOC) and simultaneously improve the distribution of goods and services (EOC).

Table 1 indicates some of the more important linkages between social overhead capital and quality of life. For instance, municipal waste facilities may improve health through reduced viral infection, improve aesthetics by limiting odors and litter, and allow for an increase in economic opportunities—thereby increasing the quality of life of unemployed individuals.

While large, the public capital stock has been shrinking relative to the private capital stock for the past two decades, a result of a depressed level of public capital accumulation in recent years. The growth rate of the nonmilitary public capital stock

TABLE 1 Infrastructure and Quality of Life

Infrastructure investment	Attributes of human habitat					
	Health	Safety	Recreation	Aesthetics	Economic opportunity	Leisure
Transportation						
Highways	Increased air quality	Reduced accidents	Increased access		Increased employment Increased access	Increased discretionary time
Mass transit	Increased air quality	Reduced accidents	Increased access		Increased employment Increased access	Increased discretionary time
Airport		Reduced accidents	Increased access		Increased employment	Increased discretionary time
Waste Management						
Municipal waste facilities	Reduced viral infection, etc.			Reduced odors, litter, and turbidity	Increased employment	
Solid-waste facilities	Reduced toxicity			Reduced odor	Increased employment	
Law Enforcement						
Police stations, courts, prisons	Reduced drug use	Reduced crime			Increased employment	
Fire Stations		Reduced risk				
Hospitals	Increased access				Increased employment	

equaled 4.3 percent per year during the 1960s, 2.0 percent during the 1970s, and 1.4 percent during the 1980s. There are many reasons for this shift in public investment trends. The construction of the interstate highway system caused a spurt of road construction. The need to educate the baby-boom generation induced an increase in school construction during the 1960s. And, in general, an increase in transfer payments beginning in the middle of the 1960s crimped public investment spending.

As a result, at the beginning of the 1990s there is widespread concern about whether the existing stock of SOC can adequately support quality-of-life requirements and improvements in the ways traced out on Table 1. Apprehension appears to be greatest in the areas of the environment and transportation. For instance, in 1978, approximately 20,000 municipal landfills were operating in the United States; by 1986, fewer than 6000. And the Council on Environmental Quality forecasts that by 1993 about 2000 of the remaining landfills will be at capacity and others will be closed as new environmental standards take effect. Our transportation network is being subjected to an escalating degree of congestion. The Federal Highway Administration forecasts that vehicle-hours of traffic delays on urban highways will grow from 722 million hours in 1985 to 3869 million hours by 2005—an increase of 436 percent.

Public Capital and Economic Performance

Besides the direct contribution of public capital to the consumption of goods and leisure, we may follow Meade (1952) and postulate that the public capital stock acts as an uncompensated factor in the neoclassical production function

$$y = f(l,k,g)$$

where y = output of goods and services, l = private labor input, k = private capital, and g = public capital. The returns from the public capital stock are earned as rents to either private labor or private capital, driving a wedge between factor rewards (wages and the return to private capital) and the respective factor productivities.

Various recent studies have attempted to estimate the contribution of public capital to private production. In general, these studies have found that (1) the contribution of public capital to private production is positive with output elasticities that range from 0.03 at the municipal level (Eberts, 1986), to 0.15 at the state level (Munnell, 1990), to 0.40 at the national level (Aschauer, 1989a); (2) the assumption of constant returns to scale across private *and* public inputs is appropriate (Aschauer, 1989a; Munnell, 1990); and (3) the rents to public capital flow evenly (on a percentage basis) to labor and private capital (Aschauer, 1989a; Munnell, 1990).

A conservative reading of the empirical evidence leads to the conclusion that in the United States the rate of return, or marginal product, of public capital is in the same range as that of private capital. With this information, it is possible to employ a growth accounting framework to assess the contribution of public capital accumulation to productivity growth in the United States over recent decades. Such a calculation yields the result that approximately 10 percent of the slowdown in productivity growth during the 1970s and 1980s can be attributed to the reduced pace of public capital accumulation in recent years. Other research (Aschauer, 1989b) indicates that public capital accumulation helps explain why postwar productivity growth has been relatively low in the United States when compared with that of Japan, Germany, and other industrialized economies.

These considerations have led to increased attention to the role of public capital in national economic growth. While it is generally agreed that public capital should be considered to have a substantive influence on private production, more research needs to be devoted to ascertaining the exact magnitude of effect. Other topics for future research include the impact of public capital on the demands for private factors of production, the effect of public capital investment on different industries, and the role of public investment in promoting regional economic development.

References

Aschauer, David A., "Is Public Expenditure Productive?" *Journal of Monetary Economics,* vol. 23, no. 2, March 1989a, pp. 177–200; Aschauer, David A., "Public Investment and Productivity Growth in the Group of Seven," *Economic Perspectives,* vol. 13, no. 5, September/October 1989b, pp. 17–25; Aschauer, David A., "Infrastructure: America's Third Deficit," *Challenge,* vol. 34, no. 2, March/April 1991, pp. 39–45; Eberts, Randall W., "Estimating the Contribution of Urban Public Infrastructure to Regional Growth," *Working Paper 8610,* Federal Reserve Bank of Cleveland, December 1986; Hansen, Niles M., "Unbalanced Growth and Regional Development," *Western Economic Journal,* vol. 4, Fall 1965, pp. 3–14; Meade, James E., "External Economies and Diseconomies in a Competitive Situation," *Economic Journal,* vol. 62, March 1952, pp. 54–67; Munnell, Alicia H., "Why Has Productivity Growth Declined? Productivity and Private Investment," *New England Economic Review,* January/February 1990, pp. 3–22; U.S. Department of Commerce, Bureau of Economic Analysis, *Fixed Reproducible Tangible Wealth in the United States,* 1925–1985, Washington, D.C., 1987.

(*See also* Infrastructure; Productivity; Wealth)

David A. Aschauer

Purchasing power of the dollar (*see* Value of the dollar)

Purely monetary theory (*see* Juglar cycle)

Quantity theory of money

The quantity theory of money might more properly be called a family of theories which explain relationships among money, prices, and incomes. These theories assign a primary causal role to changes in money supply in explaining changes in national incomes and prices. Quantity theories, developed as early as the sixteenth century, explained changes in a nation's price level by changes in the stock of money. Today, quantity theory refers to the theory of the demand for money, as developed in a synthesis of classical and Keynesian views by Milton Friedman and others. Modern quantity theory is used to help explain fluctuations in business activity, interest rates, exchange rates, as well as inflation.

Early History

The quantity theory has an extremely long history. One of its earliest formal statements came in 1568, when Jean Bodin demonstrated by careful observation and analysis that the flood of gold and silver from the New World was the principal cause of the price revolution in Europe—the great inflation that followed the discovery of America. Although John Locke made one of the earliest clear formulations of the quantity theory in 1691, numerous English mercantilists preceded him by from 40 to 90 years in expressing simple versions of quantity theories to explain changes in the purchasing power of money in terms of goods and commodities.

David Hume added the idea that an increase in the quantity of money would stimulate an increase in economic activity and trade in the interval between the money-supply increase and the time when it would be fully reflected in the resulting rise in prices. He argued that prices of different goods are affected in turn and that the "diligence of every individual" would be quickened before the increase in quantity of money increased wages of labor.

Adam Smith, David Ricardo, John Stuart Mill, and other classical economists explained changes in the general level of prices by changes in the quantity of money and its velocity of circulation. In general, they argued that an increase in the money supply—gold, silver, and bank notes—would be followed by a proportional rise in prices.

From the 1930s to the Mid-1960s

The quantity theory fell into disrepute during the Great Depression. Because the monetary authorities had failed to stem the Depression, theorists widely believed that money does not matter. In Keynesian theory—which almost completely displaced the quantity theory for a time—money and monetary policy were important only as they were able to influence a narrow range of interest rates. After the early 1950s, however, a reformulated and improved quantity theory of money won many new adherents among professional economists, policymakers, and the general public in the United States and other countries.

One of the main reasons for the revival of the quantity theory was the experience with inflation following World War II. Countries that tried to hold interest rates down by increasing growth of their money supplies suffered inflation. Countries that curbed money growth succeeded in reducing inflation. The revival was supported by an explosion of economic research in universities and government agencies into the causes of inflation and recessions, especially after the advent of computers reduced the cost of doing large-scale econometrics work. Efforts of economists in banks and other businesses to improve their ability to forecast business activity, inflation rates, interest rates, securities prices, and foreign exchange rates also did much to increase the emphasis on money in explanations of economic and financial developments.

Portfolio Adjustments in the Quantity Theory

The key reformulation of the quantity theory was Milton Friedman's "The Quantity Theory of Money—A Restatement," which he published in 1956. The central point in his restatement is that the quantity theory is not a theory of output, money income, or prices but is a theory of the demand for money. He treated money as an asset or capital good, so that the demand for it is a problem in capital theory.

Quantity theories such as those of Irving Fisher in the 1920s emphasized the demand for money as a medium of exchange in transactions (Fisher, 1922). Today's quantity theory is more general. Money is treated as one asset in a whole portfolio ranging from land and other real assets through equities and other securities. In this view, money-supply changes influence output, employment, and prices through a portfolio-adjustment process. The modern quantity theory thus draws on some of the monetary theories of John Maynard Keynes.

The key assertion of modern quantity theory is that people want to hold some command over real purchasing power in the form of money. How much money they want to hold depends in a stable way upon what their income is, what other assets they have, interest rates, and how much they expect prices of goods and services to change. The public, however, cannot change the total amount of nominal money, or number of dollars, pounds, marks, francs, rupees, or yen existing in the economy at a given time. The size of the nominal money stock is determined by the banks and the monetary authorities in most countries today. In earlier times, the discovery and depletion of gold and silver mines and changes in international trade balances caused large changes in national money stocks.

If the money stock grows faster than the amount people want to hold, they individually try to hold down their balances to their desired levels in two main ways: (1) They adjust their balance sheets by purchasing assets or paying off debts, or (2) they use current flows of income and expenditures to add to assets or to reduce indebtedness. Because one person's expenditure is another's receipt, individuals' attempts to adjust their cash balances put other people out of adjustment, causing repercussions throughout the economy. These attempts at adjustment increase the flows of expenditures and income and tend to raise the price level. The adjustments will continue until the real value—purchasing power—of the existing nominal money stock is again equal to what people want to hold. If the money stock does not grow as fast as the demand for it, individuals trying to build up balances tend to reduce flows of expenditures and income and thus put downward pressure on prices. In this way, quantity theorists believe, changes in money supply influence incomes and prices in both directions.

Portfolio adjustments take time. In the United States, the full effects of a change in money-growth rates on inflation may appear two or more years after an acceleration or deceleration in money growth. Effects on real incomes appear with lags of six to nine months.

Key Issues and Disputes

The quantity theory, in numerous versions, is being tested by an enormous volume of empirical research and intellectual debate in the United States and other countries. One key research issue is the stability of the demand for money. If the demand for money were proved to be highly unstable or volatile or if it were a simple function of interest rates alone, as some theories have asserted, changes in the supply of money would not have a predictable influence on income, employment, and prices. Keynesian theory, for example, implies that people are willing to vary the amounts of money they are willing to hold by large amounts in response to small changes in interest rates and that the velocity of circulation is, therefore, highly unstable. If this were true, changes in money supply would have little effect on spending. Nevertheless, tests over a great variety of circumstances and for many countries indicate that the demand for money does have the stability and other properties required for predicting effects of changes in money supply. The predictions of short-run effects of money-supply changes on some important variables such as interest rates and business activity, however, are not precise enough to justify confidence in the monetary authorities' efforts to fine-tune economies through discretionary changes in money supply. The dynamics of the process are not well enough understood for that.

The other key issue in dispute is the question of whether the supply of money and the demand for money are independent. A long-standing criticism of the quantity theory is that the quantity of money supplied responds passively to changes in the demand for it. The critics argue that the observed correlations between changes in money supply and changes in income reflect the influence of income on money supply rather than the influence of money supply on income (Tobin, 1969). There are some effects of income changes on money supply because of the influence of business conditions on the operations of central banks and other monetary authorities. In mild business cycles, a tendency of central banks to accommodate changes in credit demands—usually in attempting to stabilize interest rates—makes it difficult to determine whether changes in money supply initiate the changes in business activity or if the changes in business activity affect the money supply. Nevertheless, there is much evidence that the direction of influence is primarily, though not exclusively, from money to income and prices.

Much of the evidence in support of independence of money supply and money demand is historical. For example, the massive work of Milton Friedman and Anna J. Schwartz (1963) and a companion study by Phillip C. Cagan (1965) demonstrated that money supply was determined independently of money demand, because the money supply of the United States has been controlled by a wide variety of institutional arrangements and forces, many of which could not conceivably have been much influenced by the state of the demand for money. These studies also demonstrated the powerful influence of money-supply changes on U.S. economic history by relating them to all the business cycles that have been identified by the National Bureau of Economic Research over the period 1867–1960.

Financial innovations and worldwide changes in the regulation of financial markets during the 1970s and 1980s have not invalidated the quantity theory. Although there are many theoretical and empirical issues still to be settled, the quantity theory of money is especially relevant to understanding and combating one of the most critical problems of the world today, inflation (Hallman, Porter, and Small, 1991). As Anna J. Schwartz says in a review of monetary experience since she and Milton Friedman published their monumental *Monetary History,* "The United States and the rest of the world have undoubtedly changed in many ways during the past two decades, but there is no convincing evidence that these changes have weakened the lagged effects of monetary actions on both economic activity and prices or have significantly disturbed the length of the lags (Schwartz, 1990)."

References

Auerbach, Robert D., *Money, Banking and Financial Markets,* 2d ed., Macmillan New York, 1985, pp. 330–357; Cagan, Phillip, *Determinants and Effects of Changes in the Stock of Money, 1875–1960,* National Bureau of Economic Research, Columbia University Press, New York, 1965; Fisher, Irving, *The Purchasing Power of Money,* 2d rev. ed., Macmillan, New York, 1922; reprinted in *Reprints of Economic Classics,* Kelley, New York, 1963; Friedman, Milton, "The Quantity Theory of Money—A Restatement," in Milton Friedman (ed.), *Studies in the Quantity Theory of Money,* University of Chicago Press, Chicago, 1956; Friedman, Milton, and Anna J. Schwartz, *A Monetary History of the United States, 1867–1960,* National Bureau of Economic Research, Princeton University Press, Princeton, N.J., 1963; Gordon, Robert J. (ed.), *Milton Friedman's Monetary Framework: A Debate with His Critics,* University of Chicago Press, Chicago, 1974; Hallman, Jeffrey J., Richard D. Porter, and David H. Small, "Is the Price Level Tied to the M2 Monetary Aggregate in the Long Run?" *The American Economic Review;* vol. 81, no. 4, September 1991; Hetzel, Robert L., and Yash P. Mehra, "The Behavior of Money Demand in the 1980s," *Journal of Money, Credit, and Banking,* vol. 21, no. 4, November 1989, pp. 455–463; Keynes, John Maynard, *A Treatise on Money,* vol. 1, Macmillan, New York, 1930, chap. 14; Laidler, David, "The Legacy of the Monetarist Controversy," *Federal Reserve Bank of St. Louis Review;* vol. 72, no. 2, March/April 1990, pp. 49–64; Pigou, A. C., "The Value of Money," *Quarterly Journal of Economics,* November 1917, pp. 38–65, reprinted in Lutz, F. A., and L. W. Mints (eds.), *Readings in Monetary Theory,* Irwin, Homewood, Ill., 1951; Schwartz, Anna J. "Monetarism and Monetary Policy," Paper prepared for Southern Economic Association Annual Meeting, November 20, 1990; Tobin, James, "A General Equilibrium Approach to Monetary Theory," *Journal of Money, Credit and Banking,* February 1969, pp. 476–509.

(*See also* Business cycles; Chicago school; Federal Reserve policy; Inflation; Keynesian economics; Monetary policy; Money supply; Post Keynesian economics; Real balance effect theory; Velocity of circulation of money)

A. James Meigs

Radcliffe report (*see* Banking school)

Radical economics[1]

In the 1960s there were three powerful protest movements in the United States. The Civil Rights movement protested racist discrimination. The women's movement protested sexist discrimination. The peace movement protested the unpopular war in Vietnam. These three movements needed and created a theoretical approach that would explain the problems and justify their protests. Radical groups formed in each of the academic social sciences. The radical economists formed the Union for Radical Political Economics and published the *Review of Radical Political Economics,* which has successfully continued publishing to the present.

Radical political economy was influenced by Institutionalism and by post Keynesianism, but its deepest roots lie in the tradition begun by Karl Marx. Radicals are indebted to Marx for inspiration, for the questions they ask, and for the methods they use, but few accept all his analyses. Radical economists stress the need for everyone to think independently, so they will not blindly follow Marx or anyone else. The intellectual strength and staying power of radical economics have been confirmed by a steady growth in scholarly publications by radical economists and by increasing recognition of radical economics as a legitimate area of study and research at major U.S. universities (Sherman, 1987; Sawyer, 1989).

"Political economy" is a term first used to describe the writings of the classical British economists (Smith, Ricardo, et al.) whose work—like that of Marx—drew

---

[1]This article draws heavily on an article on the same subject by Thomas Weiskopf in the first edition of this encyclopedia.

upon and combined many of the disciplines into which the social sciences were subsequently divided. Political economists reject the compartmentalization of academic disciplines in general; they seek in particular to integrate into economic analysis the kinds of variables and relations that have largely become the intellectual property of sociologists and political scientists. A major concern of political economy is the analysis of power—the sources of political and economic power and the ways in which different kinds of power interact with political and economic life.

Radical World View

Radical political economy unites the interdisciplinary orientation of political economy with a set of intellectual premises stemming from a radical world view. This world view begins with a vision of a radically new social order that is both egalitarian and liberating: People are free to develop their full potential as human beings without being dominated by others. Distant as such a prospect may seem from the perspective of the contemporary real world, radicals are optimistic about the possibility of ultimately achieving it. This optimism derives from the perception that human behavior and socioeconomic institutions are not based on inalterable aspects of human nature and inevitable technological imperatives but instead are significantly influenced by the socioeconomic environment—an environment that is itself continually evolving and amenable to fundamental change over time.

According to the radical world view, any given socioeconomic environment can best be characterized by its particular structure of socioeconomic classes. In virtually all past and present societies this structure has been highly unequal, with dominant classes utilizing their superior power in an effort to maintain a social order in which their interests tend to prevail in conflict with the interests of subordinated classes. But such circumstances are inherently unstable; changes in the socioeconomic environment will eventually arise out of the struggle between classes, whose power relations change with the historical development of each society. From this general analytical perspective, radicals draw the inference that it is not enough to curb the excesses of existing socioeconomic environments in order to achieve significant progress toward a more humane social order; rather, it is essential to bring about fundamental changes in those environments. This conclusion leads to the radical political commitment to support movements of subordinated classes that challenge the structural foundations of unequal social orders and the dominant classes that sustain them.

Key Premises of Radical Political Economy

Radical political economy is differentiated from contemporary mainstream economics in several ways: First, economic behavior cannot adequately be analyzed in terms of universal human propensities and formal optimizing models; instead, the influence of historically specific socioeconomic institutions on people's behavior patterns must be brought into the analysis. Second, economic processes should not be modeled mainly in terms of marginal changes from unchanging basic structures and tendencies toward equilibrium. Instead, economists must analyze historical evolution in the shape of class conflicts, driven by the fact that rigid class structures have held back technological change.

Third, radicals do not believe in religious or supernatural explanations but believe that any event or process can be adequately explained by normal scientific research.

Fourth, the radical approach is relational in that it asks what are all the interactions between each apparently isolated problem and the whole matrix of society. Fifth, radicals recognize that the good of human beings is the highest ethical standard; they recognize that every significant statement in the social sciences is a combination of facts and ethical values; radical values reflect the needs of the oppressed and exploited groups. Sixth, radical political economists orient their scientific inquiry to the needs of political movements for fundamental social change. This orientation influences the choice of topics for study, the kinds of questions asked, the manner in which knowledge is communicated, and the people to whom it is communicated.

Much of the literature in radical political economy is therefore concerned with such issues as the sources of inequality in the distribution of income, wealth, power, and control; mechanisms of class conflict in both microeconomic and macroeconomic settings; tendencies toward crises within contemporary class societies; and transitions from one kind of socioeconomic system to another. The most important contributions of radical political economy have been in the following areas:

1. Price and value theory, with defense, critique, and modification of Marx's labor theory of value
2. Theories and facts of the labor movement, labor segmentation, and discrimination against minorities and women
3. Theories and facts of economic crises and business cycles
4. Theories and facts of economic concentration and industrial organization
5. Theories and facts on the symbiosis between government and big business, the government fiscal crisis, and monetary policy
6. Theories and facts on imperialism by the advanced capitalist countries and obstacles to development in the underdeveloped countries
7. Theories and facts on the comparison of different economic systems

Effect of Soviet Collapse

Although the Soviet Union claimed to be socialist, most radicals have long viewed the Soviet Union as an inefficient dictatorship, antithetical to both democracy and socialism. Its demise may open the door for an upsurge of democratic socialism in the world. Moreover, the nature of the Soviet collapse is seen as evidence of the correctness of radical analysis. The Soviet Union did not die merely because of misdeeds of Stalin or of some wrong psychological attitudes. The Soviet regime fell through class conflict. This conflict was caused by the constraints that the stagnant class relations of production (including a petrified bureaucracy and the entrenched privileges of Communist Party leaders) put on the improvement of the forces of production, especially holding back urgently needed improvements in technology. No marginal analysis could comprehend such a revolutionary change. Radical political economy considers that it has the best tools to comprehend such changes.

References

Sawyer, Malcolm, *Challenge of Radical Political Economy*, Barnes and Noble, Sarage, Md., 1989; Sherman, Howard, *Foundations of Radical Political Economy*, M. E. Sharpe, Armonk, N.Y., 1987; Weiskopf, Thomas, "Radical Economics," in D. Greenwald, ed., *Encyclopedia of Economics*, McGraw-Hill, New York, 1982.

(*See also* Capitalism; Communism; Comparative economic systems, an overview; Labor theory of value; Marxism; Socialism)

Howard J. Sherman

Random walk hypothesis

The random walk hypothesis originated in the 1960s. It states that successive stock price changes are identically distributed, independent random variables. If this is so, past security price movements cannot be used to forecast future prices. Hence, trading on new public information cannot earn profits in excess of what would be earned using a buy-and-hold policy.

If the random walk hypothesis holds for stocks traded in a particular capital market, this is a sufficient condition for that market to be called weakly efficient. Extensive tests for this type of efficiency by means of serial correlation and run tests were first undertaken by E. F. Fama (1965b), using 30 Dow Jones industrial stocks. In general, the tests supported the hypothesis.

Study of non–U.S. capital markets has been made by Dryden (1970) using prices on 15 stocks traded on the London Stock Exchange. Praetz (1969) tested Australian stocks, and Conrad and Juttner (1973) German stocks. C. W. J. Granger (1972) provides a full bibliography of these so-called weak-form tests. Not all these tests in less active markets supported the random walk hypothesis because there was substantial serial correlation in regression residuals.

As Granger indicates, there are many ways to express the random walk hypothesis. Those tested include:

1. The RRW, or raw random walk model
$$P_t = E(P_{t+1} | P_{t-j}, j \geq 0)$$
   in which the sequence P_t is a martingale

2. The LRW, or log random walk model, which is a submartingale

3. The CRW, or capital return random walk, which is also a submartingale, where $a(T)$ is the expected or normal wealth ratio over T time units:
$$W(T)C_t = E(C_{t+T}^+ | P_{t-j}, j \geq 0)$$

where P_t = the price of security at time t, preferably dividend-adjusted
        C_t = capital returns, preferably including dividends at time t
   $W(T)$ = expected or normal wealth ratio over T
      T = time unit
     $W(T) > 1$

The vertical line and the term following it mean "given security prices at times less than j such that j is greater than or equal to zero."

Most investigators choose the LRW model because variability in price change depends to some extent on price level. For example, more absolute variability is likely in higher-priced stocks. This problem is eliminated when differences between log prices are used. Also, log P_t minus log P_{t-1} is the yield with continuous compounding from holding the stock over one period (less the yield attributable to dividends), so that the LRW model has some of the attractive attributes of the CRW model.

Generally, first serial correlation coefficients approaching zero are taken to indicate a lack of dependence between successive stock market prices, but this conclusion depends on the conjecture that log stock price differences are normally distributed. Yet Fama, Dryden, and others have all found fairly large deviations from normality in stock price-change (and stock return) distributions in the direction of leptokurtosis— too many observations near the mean of distributions and too-fat tails.

This may have led Fama (1965*a*) to generalize the Sharpe-Lintner asset pricing model to markets where returns may have stable, nonnormal Paretian distributions, but in doing so he was forced to assume that distributions of random variables in the asset pricing model are symmetric, with three parameters instead of two, as compared with the Sharpe-Lintner model. Thus, a characteristic exponent was added to the mean (or expected) return and standard deviation of prices (or returns) in the portfolio selection process.

These objections have significance because stable and unstable Paretian distributions form a large class to which the normal distribution belongs, but all other members of that class have infinite variance. Hence, if stock return or stock price distributions are of this class, it is not possible to calculate correct standard errors. Moreover, variance enters into the denominator for the serial correlation coefficient, so that tests using this variable as a measure of randomness have little value.

In general, investigators have acknowledged this difficulty but have upheld the use of least squares when large samples are involved. Indeed, under these conditions, according to Granger (1972), "the infinite variance property is remarkably unrobust, so that the more one becomes familiar with the statistical properties of random variables with infinite variance, the more relaxed one becomes about using standard techniques."

However, using more limited samples, Jennergren and Korsvold (1974) showed that serial correlation coefficients for Swedish stocks with lag 1 were generally much larger than serial correlation coefficients for Norwegian stocks, whereas serial correlation for more actively traded West German stocks, according to Conrad and Juttner (1973), were substantially higher. Given the difference in size and activity in these markets, relative serial correlation coefficients did not support Granger's (1972) contention that inactive stocks in smaller markets might very well violate random walk.

However, nonparametric runs tests involving changes in signs, not magnitudes, showed mean absolute standardized variables for differencing at interval 1 that upheld Granger's supposition, with the amount of indicated dependence between changes increasing as the size of markets and trading activity declined. Runs tests were also used by Fama (1965*b*) to support the random walk hypothesis as early as 1965, and they are useful because they bypass some of the distribution problems involved in using least squares.

One reason, advanced by Jennergren and Korsvold, for the poor performance of serial correlation coefficients in determining the randomness of the returns of relatively inactive issues may have general applicability. They surmise that gaps in the series mean that the time series selected comes from different populations because the number of trading days between transaction days changes from issue to issue. Moreover, this increases variance and decreases mean absolute serial correlations for less frequently traded stocks because variance enters the formula for calculating serial correlation coefficients in the denominator. One might also observe that, even in more active markets, many issues trade very little on most days, so that price changes are insignificant. However, in other periods, owing to news about these or related issues, there may be major price changes. If these periods of major price change vary from stock to stock, it might also be argued that the meaningful data in their time series come from different populations.

Spectral analysis can also test the randomness of stock price returns and stock prices. If the random walk hypothesis is correct, the spectrum of the error series should be completely flat. Granger and Morgenstern (1963), as well as Cootner (1964), present many estimates that support random walk using spectral analysis.

Challenging random walk in terms of weak-form tests of market efficiency, Alexander (1961) used various filter rules, claiming returns well in excess of buy-and-hold, but Fama and Blume found his results to be biased by the assumption that stocks could be bought at the lows plus some assumed percent and sold at the highs minus the same percent—executions that could not have been made in actual markets. Bias was also introduced by the use of stock price indexes, which do not reflect dividends. Fama and Blume (1966) therefore used individual Dow-Jones industrial stocks, assuming they were bought or sold on the opening of the day selected by the filter rule. With execution problems eliminated as a possible source of bias, they showed that (when brokerage fees were included) most of the filters used by Alexander failed to produce returns in excess of buy-and-hold.

Nevertheless, filter sizes of 5, 1, and 1.5 percent produced average returns per security on long positions that were greater-than-average returns for buy-and-hold, indicating some positive persistence in small stock price movements. There was also evidence of negative dependence in intermediate-sized stock price movements (for filter sizes greater than 1.5 percent and less than 12 percent), so that average losses on short positions were greater than average returns from buy-and-hold.

The positive dependence that resulted from the use of small filters, according to Fama and Blume, could be used to outperform buy-and-hold by 2.5 percent if floor traders (who would pay no commission on the numerous transactions that would result) used only long positions and if no funds were idle. However, clearinghouse fees, operational expenses, and the cost of some idle funds would wipe out this advantage, especially if getting in and out at the times selected by the filters required orders to be placed with specialists.

Some caveats to this conclusion: Nothing prevents specialists from engaging in this sort of trading themselves, using excess funds that might otherwise be idle. Hence, specialists' fees might be avoided. Also, if trades using small filters were restricted to overnight transactions in volatile, high-priced issues, operational costs might be minimized. However, if this supposition is correct, we encounter a central argument in support of random walk, namely, that if excess returns from this operation were possible, other specialists would be likely after a short period to enter this market so that these excess-return opportunities would be extinguished.

The other technique that Fama and Blume found promising involved the use of large filters (perhaps 5 percent), executing short signals in reverse. In that case, any indicated large negative results from intermediate-sized price changes on short positions would become positive. However, this operation would be especially vulnerable to the "idle funds" constraint, since such opportunities are relatively infrequent.

In the same vein, James (1963) as well as Van Horne and Parker (1967), found that trading rules based upon moving averages of past prices do not yield profits greater than buy-and-hold, although Levy (1967) claimed that "the theory of random walk has been refuted" on the basis of results from relative strength or portfolio upgrading rules. But Jensen (1972) showed that Levy's claims were overstated. Jensen and Bennington (1970) further deflated Levy's results by suggesting that even the remaining excess was due to "a subtle form of selection bias, namely that, given enough computer time, it should be possible to come up with a trading rule that works for a particular group of random numbers." But the same rule should not work on another set of random numbers. They therefore replicated Levy's results on a different body of data and showed them to be spurious.

In general, the random walk hypothesis provides "an extremely good approximation to whatever may be the truth," according to Granger. He adds, however, that "it is only an 'average' kind of law, and may not hold true for all securities at all times." One should add that only relatively simple, linear relationships have been investigated. Thus, chartists, stock market technicians, and security analysts, who were first thought to be threatened, have survived perhaps because only relatively primitive forecasting devices have been proscribed by the advocates of the theory.

On the other side of the fence, in 1972 Granger outlined a random walk theory with reflecting barriers, i.e., the open buy-and-sell orders of specialists' books, a theory which is remarkably like chartism. Granger concluded that the correlation between adjacent price changes is negative, since some time is spent "bouncing off reflecting barriers," and he talked of their being reduced in thickness and thus weakened, which chartists will recognize as penetration of a resistance or support area. Since open orders are often placed at particular levels on specialists' books to protect trading profits and at other levels to initiate trades after breakouts above resistance—generally in areas of heavy previous volume—it is clear that Granger is close to accepting a primitive form of chartism as an appropriate model for transaction prices in markets that permit the buildup of open orders.

So-called semistrong tests of market efficiency are concerned with the speed of price change in response to new information such as stock splits, quarterly earnings reports, and the like. Fama, Fisher, Jensen, and Roll (1969) showed that, since stock splits were often associated with above-market-average earnings and dividend increases, the market used split announcements to "revaluate the stream of expected income from shares." Further, price changes as a result of split announcements were shown to be completed by the end of the split month, although there was substantial evidence that most of the reaction took place immediately after announcements. Finally, the evidence indicated that the market reacted only to the dividend implications of splits, since, if dividend increases were not forthcoming, stock prices returned to the market-adjusted presplit level.

The authors also showed that the cross-sectional average residuals were positive for at least 30 months prior to splits, so that earnings improvements probably presaged split rumors and finally split announcements, but the high degree of persistence which this implies, which would also imply dependence in stock prices, was shown to be the result of averaging. There was no serial correlation between regression residuals of individual securities. Thus, if each stock was bought after its split announcement, no excess profits in excess of buy-and-hold would have been earned, since individual stocks would have already reflected the "good news."

Little empirical work has been done on strong-form tests of market efficiency, which are concerned with whether all available price information, both public and private, is reflected in stock prices. But tests of results of mutual funds managers using average returns from funds support the conclusion that, as a group, fund managers are not able to outperform randomly selected portfolios. Thus, if these individuals, or other market professionals, had had access to privileged information or had had a special ability to interpret public or private information, either commission and clearance costs plus other expenses or an inability to act promptly would probably have prevented these advantages from making themselves felt.

According to Granger, however, there is limited evidence that corporate officers and other insiders, as well as specialists on stock exchanges, are able to use the information that is available to them to generate excess profits. If they have been able to do so, these returns have not been substantial enough to cause serial correlation of errors in tests of the various random walk models using data from the large markets of the United States, but such returns would help to explain the presence of substantial serial correlation in smaller and less well-regulated markets in other countries.

Many of the workers who have developed ingenious ways to test the random walk or efficient-market hypothesis have also been active in a related field, namely, the development of capital asset pricing models that (in the early models) equate market portfolio returns with a risk-free rate, sometimes given exogenously, plus a risk premium determined by the covariance of individual stock and stock market returns—the so-called mean-variance capital pricing models.

The general equilibrium models of Sharpe (1964), Lintner (1965), and Mossin (1966) for determining prices of capital assets under conditions of uncertainty evolved directly from the models of Markowitz (1959) and Tobin (1958) of the one-period investor as an expected one-period utility maximizer, which were in turn based on the expected-utility model of von Neumann and Morgenstern in *Theory of Games and Economic Behavior* (1953).

The literature of capital asset pricing models is extensive and beyond the scope of this article. However, according to Jensen, "the models show promise of being of great help in addressing many important practical issues," including (among others) "valuation theory and the determination of the cost of capital."

An extensive literature challenges the random walk hypothesis, especially in the strong form that supports the capital asset pricing model (CAPM), much of it objecting to the theory's assumptions. For example, it has been shown that one consequence of the violation of the CAPM assumption that all investors are same-period, one-period utility maximizers would be that multiperiod investment horizons would take the market-clearing portfolio off the efficient frontier.

Many observers have also objected to the use of stock exchange data in proofs of the CAPM, since, in theory, the CAPM consists of all capital assets, including foreign stocks and bonds, all real estate, tax hedges, art and collectors items, and so forth. Moreover, the correct market value of these other assets must be determined in order to calculate their proper percentage representation in the market portfolio, but this has not been attempted. However, if these less-liquid assets were included, the inefficiency of the market portfolio would probably increase substantially.

Other objections to the random walk hypothesis in its strong form include the fact that there is a spread between borrowing and lending rates that is not accounted for in most of the CAPM literature. Also, many institutional investors are barred from borrowing and tend to prefer high-yield issues for tax reasons compared with individual investors who prefer capital gains for the same reasons, which appears to violate the assumption of homogeneous expectations for market participants.

This fact suggests that there is not one but a linear combination of several efficient portfolios that are nonadjacent corner solutions of the quadratic program used to calculate expected returns. If this is true, the linear combination of these portfolios will not constitute another efficient portfolio. Finally, many observers, including random walk proponents, have objected to the risk-free rate, since this rate is not risk-free if it does not fully reflect inflation.

References

Alexander, S. S., "Price Movements in Speculative Markets—Trends or Random Walks," *Industrial Management Review*, vol. 2, 1961, pp. 7–26; Conrad, K., and D. J. Juttner, "Recent Behavior of Stock Market Prices in West Germany and the Random Walk Hypothesis," *Kyklos*, vol. 26, 1973, pp. 576–599; Cootner, P. H. (ed.), *The Random Character of Stock Market Prices*, MIT Press, Cambridge, Mass., 1964; Dryden, M. H., "A Statistical Study of U.K. Share Prices," *Journal of Political Economy*, vol. 17, 1970, pp. 369–389; Fama, E. F., "Portfolio Analysis in a Stable Paretian Market," *Management Science*, vol. 11, January 1965a, pp. 404–419; Fama, E. F., "The Behavior of Stock Market Prices," *Journal of Business*, vol. 38, 1965b, pp. 34–105; Fama, E. F., and Marshall E. Blume, "Filter Rules and Stock Market Trading Profits," *Journal of Business*, vol. 39, no. 1, part II, January 1966, pp. 226–241; Fama, E. F., Laurence Fisher, Michael C. Jensen, and Richard Roll, "The Adjustment of Stock Prices to New Information," *International Economic Review*, vol. 10, no. 1, February 1969, pp. 1–21; Granger, C. W. J., "A Survey of Empirical Studies of Capital Markets," in G. Szego and K. Shell (eds.), *Mathematical Methods in Investment and Finance*, North-Holland, Amsterdam, 1972; Granger, C. W. J., and D. Morgenstern, "Spectral Analysis of New York Stock Market Prices," *Kyklos*, vol. 16, 1963, pp. 1–27; James, F. E., Jr., "Monthly Moving Averages—an Effective Investment Tool," *Journal of Finance*, March 1963, pp. 29–40; Jennergren, L. Peter, and Paul E. Korsvold, "The Non Random Character of Norwegian and Swedish Stock Market Prices," *Swedish Journal of Economics*, vol. 76, no. 2, June 1974, pp. 171–185; Jensen, Michael C., *Studies in the Theory of Capital Markets*, Praeger, New York, 1972; Jensen, Michael C., and George A. Bennington, "Random Walks and Technical Theories: Some Additional Evidence," *Journal of Finance*, vol. 25, no. 2, 1970, pp. 469–482; Levy, Robert A., "Random Walks: Reality or Myth," *Financial Analysts Journal*, vol. 23, no. 6, November–December 1967, pp. 69–77; Lintner, John, "The Valuation of Risk Assets and the Selection of Risky Investments in Stock Portfolios and Capital Budgets," *Review of Economics and Statistics*, vol. 47, February 1965, pp. 13–37; Markowitz, Harry, *Portfolio Selection: Efficient Diversification of Investments*, Wiley, New York, 1959; Mossin, Jan, "Equilibrium in a Capital Market Asset," *Econometrica*, vol. 34, October 1966, pp. 768–783; Praetz, P. D., "Australian Share Prices and the Random Walk Hypothesis," *Australian Journal of Statistics*, vol. 11, 1969, pp. 123–139; Sharpe, William F., "Capital Asset Prices: A Theory of Market Equilibrium under Risk," *Journal of Finance*, vol. 19, September 1964, pp. 425–442; Tobin, James, "Liquidity Preference as Behavior toward Risk," *Review of Economic Studies*, vol. 25, February 1958, pp. 65–68; Van Horne, J. C., and G. G. C. Parker, "The Random Walk Theory: An Empirical Test," *Financial Analysts Journal*, November–December 1967, pp. 87–92

(*See also* Asset pricing models; Economic forecasting methods; Economic forecasts; Portfolio management theories; Statistical methods in economics and business, an overview)

Arnold X. Moskowitz

Rational expectations

Economists recognize that in many circumstances people are influenced not only by actual events both past and present but also by expectations of future events. In making purchases in the stock market, a person's decision depends not only on the current price but also on that person's expectation of the future price of the stock in question. In purchasing a house, a person is concerned not only with the current price but with the resale value, the future price, about which one must form an expectation. A firm making an investment decision—should it build a new factory—wants to know the cost of building the factory and wants to know the profits that it will earn in the future from operating the factory. These future profits are unknown, but the firm can form an expectation of these future profits in order to guide its investment decision.

In all these examples, an economic decision maker is concerned with forecasting an event which is not currently known by the decision maker. In these situations, we say that economic behavior depends on expectations, and we require a way to model the formation of these expectations.

Static and Adaptive Expectations

The importance of expectations has led economists to try many alternative approaches to explaining expectations. An early method was to assume static expectations—that the expectation of a variable was fixed and unchanging. For instance, the expectation that the price of a stock would always return to some constant level, regardless of the actual price level this period, would be a static expectation. A more recent and at one time widely used approach was adaptive expectations, in which the expectation of a variable is adjusted depending on how well the last-known value and the forecast of that value agreed. If the forecast and actual value differed, the expectation of future values would be adjusted. Thus, adaptive expectations had decision makers changing their forecasts when past forecasts were shown to be inaccurate.

A key feature of adaptive expectations is that it is backward looking—it compares last-known values of a variable to forecasts of that variable in order to compute the current forecast. Only past forecast errors will lead to revisions in adaptive expectations of future variables.

The above theories of expectation formation suffer from the problem that they allow individuals forming expectations to be systematically fooled by certain types of changes in the behavior of the variable being forecast. In the static expectation model, any permanent change in the level of a variable—such as a permanent increase in the price of a stock, or a permanent increase in the price of housing—would lead to ongoing mistakes in forecasting the variable in question, because static expectations do not adjust. What about adaptive expectations? The adaptive expectations hypothesis has an individual adjusting his or her forecast to past forecasting errors—differences between the last-known value and the forecast of the last-known value. This can eventually lead to correct forecasting after a permanent shock, but it causes a long series of forecast errors during the period in which expectations adjust to the new permanent level of a variable. Moreover, adaptive expectations can lead to ongoing errors if a variable's rate of growth is increasing over time. Such would occur when forecasting price levels during periods of gradually rising inflation. Finally, the backward-looking nature of adaptive expectations means that adaptive expectations do not adjust even to predictable changes in the behavior of economic variables unless these changes first cause a discrepancy between past forecasts and actual values.

Rational Expectations Hypothesis

To address these concerns, John Muth proposed the "rational expectations" hypothesis in 1961. This hypothesis states that "expectations, since they are informed predictions of future events, are essentially the same as the prediction of the relevant economic theory" (p. 316). At its most basic level the rational expectations hypothesis states that expectations are formed on the basis of all available information relevant to the behavior of the variable being forecast. These expectations are formed so as to eliminate systematic sources of forecast error. Thus, the available information is used to generate a forecast that accords with what economic theory would predict from that same information. There should be no predictable, systematic errors in forecasting, although there may be—and almost certainly will be—unpredictable, nonsystematic forecast errors.

As an example of rational expectations, suppose an investor were considering purchasing shares of stock in a major corporation. She or he will want to know the current price but also will want to form an expectation of the future price. When the investor wakes up at 7 a.m. and turns on a morning news show, a story suggests that the corporation has suffered a tremendous unexpected loss in one of its operations, and revenue forecasts have been revised downward drastically. How does our investor now forecast future profits and hence the future price of the stock? Adaptive expectations suggests that the investor will compare the actual price during trading that day to his or her previous forecast, and if there is a discrepancy the investor will revise the forecast of tomorrow's price. Rational expectations says the investor will reduce her or his forecast immediately, since the investor knows that the present value of future profits determines the price of the stock, and future profits have declined. Hence, rational expectations makes use of economic theory to form and change forecasts in response to new information.

What are some properties of rational expectations? To accord with the rational expectation hypothesis, expectations must exhibit several properties. The first is that they must be unbiased, so that *on average* the expectation is equal to the true value. For example, an expectation of the price of a stock is unbiased if, on average, the expectation is correct. This does not mean that the expectation is ever precisely correct, just that errors in forecasting the true value average out to zero. Second, expectations must be efficient, in that they incorporate all known information, past and present, that actually influences the true value. For instance, suppose a 1 percent increase in the unemployment rate this week makes the price of a stock decline by 2 percent next week. In this case, if I observe a 1 percent increase in the unemployment rate, I should lower my expectation of next week's stock price by 2 percent. Third, the error I make in forming my forecast or expectation of a variable should be unpredictable at the time I make my forecast. Thus, I shouldn't make a forecast that I know will contain an error. If my forecast of stock prices is always low by 5 percent, then I should raise my forecast by 5 percent so that I am no longer making such a *predictable* error. Note, however, that *unpredictable* errors are not precluded. Finally, forecasts should be consistent. If in May I forecast the price of a stock in June, and if in April I had also forecast the price of the stock in June, then the change in my forecast from April to May should only be due to new information available to me in May but not in April.

A good source for more detail on the properties of rational expectations forecasts is the book by Steven Sheffrin (1983). Notice that most of these conditions are fairly intuitive. Your forecasts or expectations should on average be the same as the variable you are trying to forecast. Your errors should not be predictable. Changes in your forecast should only occur because you have received new information. The idea of rational expectations has gained tremendous support in part due to the commonsense nature of these conditions.

Critiques and Rejoinders

However, there are critiques of the rational expectations hypothesis. Part of the opposition seems to arise due to the policy implications of rational expectations. In macroeconomics, the rational expectations hypothesis was initially advanced within a group of models that have come to be known as "new classical models." These models included rational expectations as a key feature but also included the idea of a natural rate of output on the aggregate supply side of the model. Output would deviate from the natural rate only if the actual price level deviated from the forecasted price level. These features in an otherwise Keynesian model led to the conclusion that there is no room for systematic policy to effectively change output. In such a model output only differs from the natural rate when price expectations differ from actual prices. In order to permanently increase output, policy would have to lead people to forecast a price level below the actual price level on an ongoing basis. If price expectations were adaptive, this could be done with a policy of gradually accelerating inflation. The backward-looking nature of adaptive expectations would then cause the actual price level to exceed the adaptive expectation of the price level on a continuing basis. However, with rational expectations this cannot occur, since any policy that attempts to *systematically* raise actual prices above expected prices will be counteracted by adjustments in the expected price level. Hence forecasters will not be systematically fooled, and hence systematic policy cannot raise the level of output above the natural rate.

Such a strong *policy ineffectiveness* result was first demonstrated by Lucas (1973). Sargent and Wallace (1975) made this point most clearly in an otherwise Keynesian model of the economy. Fischer (1977) and Taylor (1980) provide rejoinders to demonstrate that even with rational expectations, labor contracts which preset the nominal wage might provide a way for policy to be effective. In these models, policy is effective because wage rates do not adjust to policy actions within the contract period. There are many other potential sources of policy effectiveness within versions of these models, and McCallum (1980) provides a useful survey. He points out sources of policy effectiveness ranging from price stickiness to real balance effects. In addition, the policy effectiveness question can be expanded to ask how alternative policies affect rational expectations and the informational content of market prices. Bradley and Jansen (1988) examine this issue, as well as the influence of informational differences on output. Finally, there is a related literature in models of the type introduced by Barro (1980). Noticeably absent in all of this discussion of policy effectiveness is any debate over the assumption of rational expectations. Instead, the debate centers on features of the model other than rational expectations. This illustrates that the rational expectations hypothesis has replaced adaptive expectations as the main working hypothesis in macroeconomic modeling.

Perhaps the main surviving criticism of the rational expectations hypothesis involves the claim that it makes extreme assumptions about the ability of individuals to collect and process information. According to this view, the requirement that forecasters use the relevant economic theory is too strong, since the average individual in the economy cannot possibly be sophisticated enough to know and use the types of models employed by economists to study various markets in the economy, and even economists sometimes disagree on the correct model to use in various situations. The rejoinder to this attack is that individuals do not have to actually make such calculations, just as consumers do not have to actually calculate ratios of marginal utility and price in order to choose among goods. Indeed, Muth recognized this point in his original work on the subject, where he writes: "[the hypothesis] . . . does not assert that the scratch work of entrepreneurs resembles the system of equations in any way" (p. 317).

What about the issue of choosing the relevant economic model? This is an important question and the subject of much ongoing research. James Bullard (1991) provides a useful survey. A general conclusion that seems appropriate based on a number of alternative learning processes studied to date is that learning processes, if they converge at all, tend to converge to rational expectations. In this way rational expectations may provide a good benchmark for the final result of a learning process.

References

Barro, Robert J., "A Capital Market in an Equilibrium Business Cycle Model," *Econometrica,* vol. 48, 1980, pp. 1393–1417; Bradley, Michael D., and Dennis W. Jansen, "Informational Implications of Money, Interest Rate, and Price Rules," *Economic Inquiry,* vol. 26, 1988, pp. 437–448; Bullard, James B., "Learning, Rational Expectations, and Policy: A Summary of Recent Research," *Federal Reserve Bank of St. Louis Review,* vol. 73, 1991, pp. 50–60; Fischer, Stanley, "Long-Term Contracts, Rational Expectations, and the Optimal Money Supply Rule," *Journal of Political Economy,* vol. 85, 1977, pp. 191–206; Lucas, Robert, Jr., "Some International Evidence on Output-Inflation Trade-offs," *American Economic Review,* vol. 63, 1973, pp. 326–334; McCallum, Bennett T., "Rational Expectations and Macroeconomic Stabilization Policy," *Journal of Money, Credit, and Banking,* vol. 12, 1980, pp. 716–746; Muth, John F., "Rational Expectations and the Theory of Price Movements," *Econometrica,* vol. 29, 1961, pp. 315–335; Sargent, Thomas J., and Neil Wallace, " 'Rational' Expectations, the Optimal Monetary Instrument, and the Optimal Money Supply Rule," *Journal of Political Economy,* vol. 83, 1975, pp. 214–254; Sheffrin, Steven M., *Rational Expectations,* Cambridge University Press, Cambridge, 1983; Taylor, John B., "Aggregate Dynamics and Staggered Contracts," *Journal of Political Economy,* vol. 88, 1980, pp. 1–23.

(*See also* Economic forecasting methods; Economic models; Expectations; Futures; Inflation; Keynesian economics; Macroeconomics; Options; Phillips curve; Post Keynesian economics)

Dennis W. Jansen

Real balance effect theory

The direct effect of changes in real money holdings upon the demand for goods and services is known as the real balance effect. Changes in real cash balances take place when changes in the quantity of money and/or in the price level occur. An increase (decrease) in real money holdings is presumed to increase (decrease) aggregate demand.

Accordingly, people are assumed to maintain a proportional relationship among the alternative forms in which they hold their wealth. When a change in the supply of one form of wealth occurs, people attempt to regain their former distribution of wealth holdings. Thus, the real balance effect theoretically is but one of many possible types of wealth effects.

How the Real Balance Effect Operates

Assume that, at a given price level, an increase in the nominal stock of money (M) occurs. People now have more real money (M/P) relative to their other wealth holdings than formerly. They have an excess supply of money balances and seek to divest themselves of a portion of their increased money holdings by increasing their demand for real goods and services. Additionally, they increase their demand for various financial assets, although most analysts confine the scope of the increase in demand to goods and services. Decreases in the nominal stock of money will have opposite results.

The real balance effect also operates when the price level changes. For example, a decrease in the price level (P), at any given nominal stock of money (M), will again increase the real stock of money (M/P) and disturb the optimal-wealth portfolio of individuals. There will again be an increase in real aggregate demand. Increases in the price level have opposite results.

Historical Background

The logic of the real balance effect is straightforward. Real balance effect theory preceded and then became part of the revival of the quantity theory of money initiated by Milton Friedman and culminating in the monetarist movement of the 1970s. First developed by A. C. Pigou (1943) and originally known as the Pigou effect, the real balance effect was later elaborated by Don Patinkin (1951, 1965) and used to resolve numerous theoretical problems important in classical and Keynesian monetary economics. Among the issues resolved were (1) the classical dichotomy, (2) the neutrality of money, (3) the unitary elasticity of demand-for-money curve, and (4) the possibility of simultaneous less-than-full employment and downward price flexibility.

Four Theoretical Issues Resolved
by the Real Balance Effect

First, according to the classical dichotomy, the monetary sector of the economy determines the general price level, whereas the demand for and supply of goods and services determine relative prices. Hence, the price level has no effect on the demand for and supply of individual goods and services. The real balance effect denies the existence of this dichotomy, since any change in real balance will affect the demand for and supply of goods and services. Although this dichotomization of the real and monetary sectors was apparently settled by Patinkin's refinement of the real balance effect, some economists such as J. Niehans (1978) have denied that the dichotomy even existed in the classical literature except as an example of lack of clarity.

Second, closely connected with the issue of the classical dichotomy is the question of whether the stock of money is neutral in its real effects on the economy. Given a classical model producing at full employment, an increase in the nominal stock of money (M) creates an excess demand for goods and services through a positive real balance effect. By degrees the individual prices of various commodities must rise, and, accordingly, so must the general price level (P). The increase in the price level decreases the volume of real-money balances (M/P), which in turn generates a decrease in the demand for goods and services (a negative real balance effect). Ultimately, the price level rises in proportion to the initial increase in nominal money balances, and people have the same level of real money holdings with which they started. Thus, money has been neutral, the final behavior of people is unchanged, and the price level is higher.

Third, classical economists had argued that the demand for money balances (*M*) changes in proportion to the price level (*P*), that is, that the demand for money has unitary elasticity with respect to prices. The real balance effect demonstrated that this only follows when the stock of money (*M*) is changed. Were the stock of money unchanged and the price level increased, the amount of money demanded would increase by relatively less than the price level increase. Were people to increase their demand for money (*M*) in proportion to the rise in prices (*P*), they would sell off part of their holdings of goods. Were they successful in this effort, they would have fewer real goods and the same amount of real money balances (*M/P*) as they had prior to the price level change. Hence, their proportions of real money and goods would be disturbed. From this it follows that the increase in the demand for money must be less than in proportion to the price level increase.

And fourth, it had been argued by Keynesian economists that the attainment of full employment is impossible even if prices are flexible downward. The reasoning behind this view is that money affects the demand for goods and employment only through its prior effect on the interest rate. According to the Keynes effect, a decrease in the price level would increase the real stock of money and force interest rates down. If the demand for goods were insensitive to interest, a decrease in the price level would not stimulate the demand for goods and services. Even if aggregate demand responded to the interest rate, however, a decrease in the price level could still be ineffectual should there be some low interest rate (the liquidity-trap interest rate) at which people would no longer be willing to lend to borrowers. The real balance effect mechanism, however, transmits price level changes directly to changes in aggregate demand rather than indirectly through interest rate changes.

An Unresolved Issue

The real balance effect was developed as a theoretical construct. As such it has gained wide acceptance and use among monetary economists. Only one major theoretical issue appears to be unresolved, the nature of the monetary assets through which the real balance effect operates. Most economists feel that the real balance effect operates only through changes in the amount of currency issued by governments. They reject the idea that it works through the principal component of the money stock, i.e., checking deposit accounts. They reason that checking deposit money is created when debt is created and that a drop in the price level, for example, increases both real checking deposit holdings and real outstanding debt. Any increase in aggregate demand coming from the rise in real money holdings would be offset by a decrease in aggregate demand coming from the rise in real debt. A few economists (B. Pesek and T. Saving, 1967) have argued that net worth is increased in the creation of checking deposits and that deposit money should be included among the assets causing the real balance effect.

The Real Balance Effect Evaluated

How relevant is the real balance effect to the real world of economic policy? When real balances change as a result of nominal money-stock (*M*) changes, at any given price level, there is an abundance of empirical evidence that changes in the money stock and aggregate demand are positively related. However, most economists agree that the real balance effect associated with price level change is difficult to measure and that this real balance effect is likely to be offset in the real world by the effects arising from changing price expectations. For example, as prices rise, an anticipation of still further price rises will lead to increased spending rather than to the decreased spending called for by decreasing real balances. Similarly, as prices fall, adverse expectations concerning the future of the economy will lead to less spending rather than to the increased spending called for by increasing real balances. The changes in real balances associated with price change will have economic significance only when people expect future prices to remain about the same as current ones. That expectation is an explicit assumption of the theory. Although this was a legitimate theoretical assumption and was empirically relevant for the 1960s, it did not apply to the inflation of the 1970s and early 1980s. Nor did a decreased rate of inflation in the recessions of 1981–1982 and 1990–1992 have a positive impact on aggregate demand. Most economists now include price expectation effects in their models of the macroeconomic process. This is not to denigrate the significance of the real balance effect, since most contemporary macroeconomic models now include wealth effect variables.

The crux of the issue is as follows: Changes in the quantity of money have interest rate, real balance, and price expectation effects. The combination of these effects means that increases (decreases) in the growth rate of the money stock will in the short run increase (decrease) the growth of output, employment, and prices, but will in the long run only increase (decrease) the growth rate of prices.

References

Friedman, Milton (ed.), *Studies in the Quantity Theory of Money,* University of Chicago Press, Chicago, 1956; Gordon, Robert J. (ed.), *Milton Friedman's Monetary Framework: A Debate with His Critics,* University of Chicago Press, Chicago, 1974; Klein, John J., *Money and the Economy,* 6th ed., Harcourt Brace Jovanovich, New York, 1986; McCallum, Bennett T., *Monetary Economics: Theory and Policy,* Macmillan, New York, 1989, pp. 120–122; Niehans, Jurg, *The Theory of Money,* Johns Hopkins Press, Baltimore, 1978; Patinkin, Don, "Price Flexibility and Full Employment," in F. A. Lutz and Lloyd Mints (eds.), *Readings in Monetary Theory,* Irwin, Homewood, Ill., 1951; Patinkin, Don, *Money, Interest, and Prices,* 2d ed., Harper & Row, New York, 1965; Pesek, Boris P., and Thomas R. Saving, *Money, Wealth, and Economic Theory,* Macmillan, New York, 1967; Pigou, A. C., "The Classical Stationary State," *Economic Journal,* vol. 53, 1943, pp. 343–351.

(*See also* Interest, economic theory; Interest rates; Keynesian economics; Money supply; Quantity theory of money; Wealth)

John J. Klein

Real bills doctrine (*see* Banking school)

Real business cycles

Real business cycles can be defined as aggregate fluctuations whose impulses are real shocks. These shocks typically are factors that affect people's constraints or technology sets. Technology shocks are an important example. So are public finance shocks, such as changes in tax rates, including taxes on real liquidity services. Monetary misperceptions are an example of shocks excluded by this definition, as are taste shocks.

Ever since the pioneering works in growth theory in the 1950s and 1960s, starting with Solow (1956) and others, model environments used to address questions in the area of growth, and recently more and more in business-cycle theory as well, have used as a building block a specification of the relation between inputs in the production of goods and services and the corresponding outputs. In its most basic form, the aggregate production function can be stated as

$$y_t = f(k_t, n_t, z_t)$$

where y_t is aggregate output in period t, k_t is the aggregate capital stock at the beginning of period t, the labor input is n_t, and z_t represents the state of the technology which, for many purposes, has been assumed to be exogenous. A typical functional form is

$$f(k_t, n_t, z_t) = z_t n_t^\theta k_t^{1-\theta}$$

where θ is a parameter between zero and one. With this notation, then, an example of real business cycles are cycles set in motion by fluctuations in z_t. Clearly, a change in z_t changes the marginal products of the two inputs. If the shocks to z_t typically are long-lasting, with associated effects on expected future productivity of capital, the influence on investment behavior can be particularly powerful. Primarily due to the corresponding wealth changes, consumption behavior will be affected as well. The consumption path will be much smoother, however, than the investment path. Model environments indicate that such technological shocks along with their propagation over time through consumption, investment, labor input, and other economic decisions give rise to cycles in aggregate activity which look quantitatively quite similar to the actual business cycles of the postwar U.S. economy. For example, in the models as in the data, both consumption and investment are highly procyclical, with investment relatively much more volatile. In terms of the behavior of the labor input, however, the wealth effect points in a countercyclical direction. A question addressed in the literature is whether offsetting substitution effects reasonably can be large enough to make hours of work as procyclical and as volatile as they are in the data, or whether other factors, such as labor indivisibilities, or perhaps problems in measuring the labor input, are at the heart of this issue.

In another pioneering article, Solow (1957) proposes a simple method for measuring technological change as the residual after accounting for the contribution to output from the two inputs. Although the focus then was on the contribution to long-term growth, more recently a similar approach has been used to measure the cyclical volatility of z_t. The idea can be seen by taking logarithms on both sides of the resource constraint, using the above functional form, and rearranging

$$\log z_t = \log y_t - \theta \log n_t - (1 - \theta) \log k_t.$$

In economies with this production function, the parameter θ can be calibrated to equal the average labor share of GNP. Thus, with time series for the three aggregates on the right side of this equation, a time series for the technology variable z can be computed and its statistical properties analyzed. Prescott (1986) models the process for z as a first-order auto-regressive process

$$\log z_{t+1} = \rho \log z_t + \varepsilon_{t+1}$$

where the ε's are random shocks with positive mean. Using quarterly postwar U.S. data since the Korean War, he finds that ρ must be close to 1 and that the standard deviation of ε is about 0.75 percent. Allowing for variable capital utilization changed the estimate very little.

Most people accept the idea that there is variation in the rate at which the technology improves. It also seems reasonable that factors will play a role for the aggregate relation between aggregate output on the one hand and capital and labor inputs on the other that have little to do with technological advance in a narrow sense of the term as referring mainly to research and development. Some have wondered, however, how reasonable it is to think that z could drop enough to give rise to declines in output of magnitudes seen in major recessions. First, one can note that if the trend of z displays growth at an average rate of 2 percent per year, say, then even a few quarters of about zero change in z theoretically would be associated with a drop in real GNP, due mainly to the large reduction in investment expenditures. Second, it is easy to think of examples of changes that can be translated into actual drops in z. From the point of view of the domestic economy, a substantial rise in the oil price means that a larger amount of domestic resources will be sent abroad in exchange for the more expensive raw material. New regulations may affect the relation between inputs and outputs in such a way as to translate into a lower z, as may legal constraints affecting the nature of contracting between firms and workers.

In order to evaluate the role of real shocks for fluctuations, real business-cycle theory was developed. The estimate of the fraction of actual business cycles accounted for by technology shocks of the magnitudes measured by Prescott (1986), say, depends on the features of the model economy that in essence provide the propagation mechanisms for these shocks. Thus, real business cycle theory is the application of general equilibrium theory to the quantitative analysis of aggregate fluctuations. The model environments used are intertemporal and describe explicitly the optimizing decisions of the people inhabiting those environments. Early applications were Kydland and Prescott (1982), who focused on the role of aggregate technology shocks, and Long and Plosser (1983), who studied the role of sectoral technology shocks. Subsequently, the theory's use has broadened to include the study of the roles of a variety of factors.

The foundation for real business-cycle theory is the neoclassical growth model. Thus, a description of aggregate production is a central component of any real business-cycle theory. A typical model environment includes, in addition to a description of the business sector, an explicit statement of the preferences of the members of the household sector. Of particular importance for business-cycle theory is the implied ability and willingness to substitute intertemporally. Some questions dictate adding a government sector, others a foreign sector.

This model framework goes beyond the standard growth model by admitting an important role for nonmarket time in households' preferences, in some models also in household production, thus giving rise to cyclical variability in hours of work. With explicit functional forms for the utility and production functions, with the stochastic process for the z's specified, with laws of motion for state variables such as capital and inventory stocks, and with values assigned to all the parameters, such an economy can be simulated with the help of a computer. Most of the parameter values can be calibrated to growth facts that change little from one cycle to the next, or to panel data. The resulting time series share many of the key properties of aggregate time series for actual market economies, suggesting that a considerable fraction [about two-thirds by some estimates; see Kydland and Prescott (1991)] of the output variation in postwar U.S. business cycles can be attributed to technological shocks.

A model economy with only technology shocks as an impulse naturally displays some deviations or anomalies relative to the facts. Given the implied shifts in marginal products, a property of the theory is a high positive correlation between labor input and productivity, although this same correlation is close to zero in the data. This value is consistent, however, with the finding that a fraction in the neighborhood of two-thirds of the cycle is accounted for by such shocks. Any other source accounting for the remainder would imply movements along given marginal product curves and therefore a tendency toward negative correlation between labor input and productivity. A combination of both leads to the prediction of a correlation near zero.

Another deviation, at least in early real business-cycle models, is that the labor input fluctuates substantially less than do hours of work in the data. Partly for reasons of tractability, these economies assumed that all the labor-input variation is in the form of changes in hours per worker. Hansen (1985) went to the opposite extreme and assumed that hours per person are indivisible. As a consequence, his model economy displayed substantially greater labor-input volatility. In actual economies, there is of course variation along both margins. This is also a property of the model environment used in Kydland and Prescott (1991) as a basis for their estimate of the role of technology shocks for the cycle.

It is likely that measured aggregate hours, which give equal weight to workers of very different skills, overstates the labor-input volatility. The extent of this measurement problem depends on how much more volatile the hours of the lower-skilled workers are relative to those of the higher-skilled.

References

Hansen, Gary D., "Indivisible Labor and the Business Cycle," *Journal of Monetary Economics,* vol. 16, 1985, pp. 309–327; Kydland, Finn E., and Edward C. Prescott, "Time to Build and Aggregate Fluctuations," *Econometrica,* vol. 50, 1982, pp. 1345–1370; Kydland, Finn E., and Edward C. Prescott, "Hours and Employment Variation in Business Cycle Theory," *Economic Theory,* vol. 1, 1991, pp. 63–81; Long, John B., and Charles I. Plosser, "Real Business Cycles," *Journal of Political Economy,* vol. 91, 1983, pp. 39–69; Prescott, Edward C., "Theory Ahead of Business Cycle Measurement," *Carnegie-Rochester Conference Series on Public Policy,* vol. 25, 1986, pp. 11–44; Solow, Robert M., "A Contribution to the Theory of Economic Growth," *Quarterly Journal of Economics,* vol. 70, 1956, pp. 65–94; Solow, Robert M., "Technical Change and the Aggregate Production Function," *Review of Economics and Statistics,* vol. 39, 1957, pp. 312–320.

(*See also* Business cycles; Consumption function; Economic forecasts; Economic models; Investment function; Production function; Productivity; Technology; Time series analysis)

Finn E. Kydland

Real estate investment trusts

Real estate investment trusts (REITs) function like a closed-end investment company. The two principal types of REITs are equity REITs and mortgage REITs. Equity REITs invest largely in commercial real estate and manage these investment holdings for income and long-term profit. Mortgage REITs typically invest in construction and development loans and long-term commercial mortgages. Provided certain tests are met (e.g., an ownership test, an income test, an asset test, and a distribution test), REITs are not taxed on distributed taxable income. Such tests are intended to ensure that REITs are passive investment vehicles.

Major Characteristics

REITs provide several advantages to all types of investors, including:

1. Relatively low per share prices
2. Continuous pricing of the shares in the secondary market
3. Increased liquidity when compared to other forms of real estate ownership
4. Professional management with shared costs
5. Majority of earnings paid out to shareholders (high dividend payout rates)
6. Optimal diversification into real asset markets
7. Elimination of the typical corporate "double taxation" providing the REIT remains qualified for such purposes
8. Securities and Exchange Commission (SEC) and state-level reporting, auditing, and filing procedures similar to other publicly traded shares

Equity REITs also provide investors with an opportunity to invest funds either in a diversified portfolio or in a single building (i.e., a single-purpose trust). Equity REITs may be structured as a finite-life or non-finite-life REIT. A finite-life REIT is a self-liquidating REIT with a predetermined liquidation date. Equity REITs can also be classified as cash-out REITs or development REITs. Cash-out REITs acquire property interests in existing properties, whereas development REITs specialize in the construction and development of real estate.

One of the major drawbacks with REITs is the belief that REIT shares trade like stocks and not like real estate. In a 1991 study conducted by Wilshire Associates, Inc., it appears that, over the period 1978 through mid-1991, REIT performance more closely followed equity securities than real estate values. This result may partially be due to the fact that the real estate index for this study, the Russell-NCREIF Index, uses appraisal estimates rather than market transactions to construct the index.

Comparing REIT shares with stocks, the REIT shares trade less frequently than do shares of major corporations. This may lead to imperfect pricing in the marketplace, since information regarding the REIT may not be completely priced into the security at all times. There is also the potential problem of adverse agency relationships between the REIT's management and its shareholders.

History

REITs came into existence in the early 1960s when the U.S. Congress provided unincorporated business trusts the same nontax treatment that mutual funds had enjoyed since the 1930s—no business-level taxes are levied provided that virtually all income was paid to investors in the form of dividend income. In 1976, the U.S. Congress allowed corporations to qualify as REITs providing that they conduct themselves in conformity with REIT provisions of the Tax Code. Since then, most REITs are formed as corporations (as opposed to business trusts) due to the much simpler securities and business laws that exist for corporations. Business trusts are not as universally accepted as corporations in other jurisdictions. For example, a REIT formed as a business trust in Massachusetts must create a subsidiary business trust or corporation to operate in Texas, since Texas does not recognize other states' business trusts. In addition, shareholders of business trusts may be held financially liable beyond their equity ownership. This is not the case with corporate ownership, where a shareholder is financially liable to the corporation up to an amount equal to his or her equity stake in the corporation.

By the late 1960s, mortgage REITs had shown to be better performers than their equity counterparts. During the early 1970s as interest rates starting rising to all-time highs, mortgage-lending institutions became less able to supply real estate investment capital, allowing mortgage REITs to absorb the excess demand for funds. However, as interest rates fell, the mortgage REITs began to suffer a long-short squeeze due to the short-term nature of their assets and the long-term nature of their liabilities. By 1974 when the prime rate hit double digits, the shakeout period for mortgage REITs occurred, and primary emphasis was now placed on the ownership and long-term development of income-producing real estate and only a small emphasis on construction and development financing.

Between 1975 and 1987, equity REITs experienced steady appreciation in value, as measured by the National Association of Real Estate Investment Trusts (NAREIT). Over this period the competitive environment for REITs had changed. Due to changes in the tax treatment of real estate income (primarily the Tax Reform Act of 1986) and the dramatic decreases in interest rates in the mid-1980s, REITs became more attractive forms of real estate investment than limited partnership units and tax-free funds. In addition, the focus of REITs has changed dramatically, with their structures developing the following dimensions:

1. One hundred percent specified acquisitions versus blind pooling
2. Purchasing existing properties versus developing properties
3. Finite life versus open-ended
4. Use of leveraged versus unleveraged purchases
5. Single property type funds versus multipurpose funds

These are some of the reasons for the rapid growth in equity REITs from the mid-1970s to the late 1980s.

Recent Developments

Since the period of steady appreciation in REITs from 1974 to 1987, the REIT industry has experienced a recession, with the NAREIT Index falling from a high of 117.88 in February 1987 to a low of 56.20 in October 1990, a decline in value of 52.32 percent. However, interest rates have since fallen, and the real estate market appears to be firming up. As of December 1991 the NAREIT Index has since risen to 72.33, a partial recouping of the major loss in value that was experienced in the late 1980s. The liquidity of REITs relative to other forms of real estate investment will remain a major influence that investors perceive as beneficial, and older, more seasoned REITs will be able to capitalize on any sustainable rising real estate market conditions that occur in the future. An additional point of reference is necessary. Even though the NAREIT Index has had severe valuation swings in the 1980s and early 1990s, the annualized dividend yield for REITs has remained fairly constant at about 10 percent.

As of December 1991, there were 209 tax-qualified REITs (135 of these REITs trade on major stock exchanges) with assets valued at $45.9 billion (an increase of 3.38 percent from 1990). Of this total asset value, 38 mortgage REITs comprise 51.1 percent, 122 equity REITs comprise 38.3 percent, and 33 hybrid REITs comprise 10.6 percent. During the year 1991, 35 offerings were completed; the NAREIT Index rose 23.60 percent to 72.33 with dividend yields averaging 9.19 percent, resulting in a total return (with dividends reinvested quarterly) averaging 35.22 percent.

REITs in Other Countries

American REITs differ from British land trusts in that the British land trusts revalue their holdings every year, whereas the U.S. REITs are valued at historical cost minus depreciation. In addition, British land trusts are allowed to focus on frequent trading and speculation and on direct operation of a realty business. Canadian REITs are not directly comparable, since the government imposes the requirement that a certain proportion of the REIT's assets be held in home mortgages. Japanese real estate stocks are unlike U.S. REITs in that the real estate stocks pay a very low dividend. Also there are five Japanese real estate stocks traded on the Tokyo Stock Exchange which have a market capitalization of nearly $34 billion, which is approximately 75 percent of the entire U.S. REIT market.

References

Alex, Brown & Sons, Inc., *Real Estate Stocks Monitor*, Second Quarter 1990, Baltimore, Md., July 1990; National Association of Real Estate Investment Trusts, *REIT Sourcebook: A Complete Guide to the Modern Real Estate Investment Trust Industry*, National Association of Real Estate Investment Trusts, Washington, D.C., 1992; Nicholson, John, in *Encyclopedia of Economics*, McGraw-Hill, New York, 1981; Torres, Michael, *Institutional Investment in Real Estate Securities*, The REIT Report, vol. 11, no. 4, Fall 1991, pp. 1, 3–5; Wurtzebach, Charles, and Mike Miles, *Modern Real Estate*, 4th ed., Wiley, New York, 1991; Zisler, Randall, *The Goldman Sachs Real Estate Report*, New York, October 1985.

(*See also* Interest rates; Mortgage credit)

Thomas W. Hamilton and James D. Shilling

Real theories of interest (*see* Interest, economic theory of)

Reform liberalism (*see* Liberalism)

Regional economics

In macroeconomics we study the performance of the national economy. In regional economics we study the performance of a "piece" of the national economy, that piece being defined geographically in a way that makes sense from a scientific perspective and/or a political perspective.

The scientific perspective would lead us to select "pieces" and treat them as regions in terms of their internal homogeneity, their distinctiveness as compared to other parts of the country, and the dominance of intraregional transactions as compared to interregional transactions.

But these "ideal" criteria might lead us to define regions in a way which would not conform to political boundaries. That would handicap us in two ways: We might lack the data with which to conduct our regional analyses, and we might not have the "client" who is interested in the results of our analyses.

So, in practice, we find regional economics dealing with cities, counties, metropolitan areas, states, and multistate regions. The benefits in terms of available data and client interest generally exceed the loss in scientific "rigor."

The variables of interest with respect to the chosen region of study typically are similar to those employed by macroeconomists: the industrial structure or composition of the regional economy, its level of output and employment, its rate of growth, the level of productivity, total and per capita income, and the rate of unemployment.

The region is an "open" economy in the sense that capital, labor, and commodities move freely across its borders. It is "closed" only in the limited sense that it is bounded by subnational political boundaries.

Theories and Models

In the simplest of formulations, a region is viewed as a place with an economic base which is comprised of enterprises which locate in this place to serve markets both inside and outside the region. The region's comparative advantage in a particular industry may derive from its unique resource endowments, its good access to markets and raw materials, or the availability of labor and other inputs on favorable terms.

All the employment in the region associated with the region's comparative advantages of this kind comprise the so-called basic sector. But total regional employment will be larger because of the "multiplier," another concept borrowed from macroeconomics, which captures the added activity and employment generated by the demands of the basic industries and their workers for goods and services which must be produced locally.

In this framework, whether a regional economy grows or declines over time depends crucially on the fortunes of the basic industries, whose fortunes, in turn, depend on the level of external demand for the output of those industries, the continuing competitiveness of that region as a location for such industries, and the value of the multiplier.

Missing from such a model of a region are the factors which operate on the supply side to affect both the region's competitive posture and the value of the multiplier in the course of growth and development. In the last 25 years much effort has been expended to develop more sophisticated regional models, some for specific regions, others for the country as a whole broken down by regions, which do explicitly incorporate supply issues. Cost factors such as wage levels and housing prices are introduced and dealt with endogenously within the model.

Regional Economics and Public Policy

Aside from its intrinsic scientific interest, regional economics is pursued for its relatively rich policy yield. It has potential value to many private and public decision makers within a region. Investments in physical capital—whether private or public—

which support the production and the provision of goods and services to the region's households and enterprises must necessarily be informed by estimates of current and future levels of demand within the region.

Thus, state and local governments, financial institutions, and public utilities have been prominently involved in the production and consumption of regional analyses and forecasts. The fiscal capacity of state and local governments, particularly with the decline of federal support in recent years, is closely linked to the performance of the economy within these jurisdictions.

Policymakers are also concerned with the impact of state and local expenditures, taxes, and regulations on the competitive posture of their basic industries.

Regional economics also informs national policy. The federal government invests heavily in infrastructure which is region-specific: transportation, waste treatment, water supply, recreation, postal services. In this role, the federal government takes its place alongside state and local governments as a consumer of regional economics. The increasing emphasis on geographic detail in the decennial census and the regional focus in the Bureau of Economic Analysis reflect the federal government's interest in regional data and the government's role as a producer as well as a consumer of regional economic analysis.

Regional economics is at the heart of federal policies and programs aimed at stimulating private investment in regions which are economically anemic. In the decade or so after 1965, such policies and programs were pursued by the Economic Development Administration (EDA) of the U.S. Department of Commerce and the Appalachian Regional Commission (ARC), a federal/state organization created by Congress to address the serious economic problems of that multistate region.

Both EDA and ARC have provided significant support for research on the central questions of regional economics. with EDA emphasizing basic research and ARC, applied research.

Relation to Other Disciplines

Of all the subfields in economics, regional economics has probably had the most intimate contact with other disciplines. Geographers, of course, have been concerned for a long time with the economic map of the world and of specific countries. In earlier years, they tended to stress pure description. In recent years, they have become much more analytical, and they compete with economists for the attention of other researchers and policymakers.

Sociologists, particularly demographers, have also interacted heavily with economists in the study of regions on such issues as migration and population forecasting. When the dynamics of regional growth are considered, there is natural contact with historians. When the focus is on the interplay between the regional economy and the public sector, political scientists often get involved.

The most significant reflection of the interdisciplinary nature of regional economics is the Regional Science Association, created in 1954 by Walter Isard, one of the pioneers in the field. The Regional Science Association meetings and publications serve as a forum for researchers in all the relevant disciplines, as well as for planners and policymakers. A worldwide network of regional science organizations and journals has developed during the last 35 years so that scholars working on regional issues in their respective countries have many opportunities to be in contact with each other.

Great impetus to the development of the field was also provided in the 1950s at Resources for the Future, a nonprofit research institute in Washington now heavily committed to energy and environmental issues.

References

Hoover, Edgar M., *An Introduction to Regional Economics,* 2d ed., Knopf, New York, 1975; Kain, John F., and John R. Meyer (eds.), *Essays in Regional Economics,* Harvard University Press, Cambridge, Mass., 1971.

(*See also* Location theory; Macroeconomics; Urban economics)

Benjamin Chinitz

Rent (*see* Economic rent)

Regression analysis in business and economics

Regression analysis is a method of estimating functional relationships between two or more variables. Economic theory is largely concerned with such relations (production functions, demand functions, supply functions, consumption functions, and the like). Marginal product, marginal revenue, marginal cost, marginal propensity to consume, and similar concepts are defined as the slopes or derivatives of those functions at specified points. When economists in the early 1900s first attempted to estimate the demand functions of economic theory from market data on prices and consumption of farm products, regression analysis presented itself as the most logical and appropriate tool.

The most influential of these economists, Henry L. Moore (1917), set out in 1908 to develop "the statistical complement of pure economics," and by 1917 he was convinced that multiple regression analysis was both necessary and sufficient for this task:

> *No matter how complex the functional relations between the variables, it can derive "empirical laws" which, by successive approximations, will describe the real relations with increasing accuracy. . . . When the method of multiple correlation [we would now say regression] is thus applied to economic data it invests the findings of deductive economics with "the reality and life of fact"; it is the Statistical Complement of Deductive Economics (p. 173).*

In his last book, Moore (1929) proposed an implementation of the general equilibrium model of Walras. Its principal elements were to be comprehensive sets of empirical demand, supply, and production functions estimated by multiple regression techniques. Thus, Moore viewed the range of applications of regression analysis in economics as conterminous with the economy itself.

Simple Linear Regression

As a statistical technique, regression analysis is used in many disciplines and is generally associated with the method of least squares. The technique may best be illustrated for the case of simple linear regression.

Suppose Y is a variable that is functionally dependent on another variable X and that the relationship is believed to be linear. Given a set of n observations, each consisting of a pair of values Y_i and X_i, where $i = 1, 2, \ldots, n$, we wish to determine the parameters a and b of a straight line, $Y = a + bX$, which best expresses the assumed relationship.

We approach the problem by graphing the n observations with the values Y_i measured on the vertical axis and the corresponding values X_i on the horizontal. The resulting set of n points (dots) is called a scatter diagram. If all the points appear to lie exactly on a straight line, we can simply draw a line through them with a ruler and extend it until it intersects the Y axis. At this point, $X = O$ and $Y = a$. The slope b can be calculated from the relationship $b = (Y - a)/X$; thus, if we choose $X = 10$ and find that the corresponding value of Y on the straight line is $a + 7$, then $b = 7/10$, or 0.7. If the value of the intercept a is 20, the equation of the line is $Y = 20 + 0.7X$.

In general, the points of the scatter diagram will not lie exactly on a straight line, and it is customary to estimate the parameters a and b by the method of least squares. We postulate that

$$Y_i = a + bX_i + u_i \qquad i = 1, 2, \ldots, n$$

where u_i is random error with an expected value of zero. The expected value of Y_i is presumed to be an exact linear function of X_i, namely, $Y_i = a + bX_i$, and the error term $u_i = Y_i - Y_i$ expresses itself as a deviation of Y_i above or below this function. The method of least squares requires that the sum of the squared deviations be minimized.

The resulting regression line passes through the point of means at which

$$Y = \bar{Y} = \sum_{i=1}^{n} \frac{Y_i}{n} \text{ and } X = \bar{X} = \sum_{i=1}^{n} \frac{X_i}{n}$$

The sum of the squared deviations of the Y_i from their mean, namely,

$$\sum_{i=1}^{n} (Y_i - \bar{Y})^2$$

is smaller than the sum of squared deviations of the Y_i from any other point. The regression line partitions the sum of squares

$$\sum_{i=1}^{n} (Y_i - \bar{Y})^2$$

into two additive components; one of these,

$$\sum_{i=1}^{n} (\bar{Y}_i - \bar{Y})^2$$

is regarded as "explained" by the regression relationship, and the other,

$$\sum_{i=1}^{n} (Y_i - \hat{Y}_i)^2 = \sum_{i=1}^{n} u_i^2$$

as "unexplained."

To simplify notation, we may write deviations from the means as

$$y_i = Y_i - \bar{Y} \quad \text{and} \quad x_i = X_i - \bar{Y}.$$

Then the slope b of the regression line can be computed from the formula

$$b = \frac{\displaystyle\sum_{i=1}^{n} y_i x_i}{\displaystyle\sum_{i=1}^{n} x_i^2}$$

and the intercept a from the formula

$$a = \overline{Y} - b\overline{X}$$

The proportion of the sum of squares

$$\sum_{i=1}^{n} Y_i^2$$

explained by the regression relationship may be written as

$$r^2 = \frac{\left(\sum\limits_{i=1}^{n} y_i x_i\right)^2}{\sum\limits_{i=1}^{n} y_i^2 \sum\limits_{i=1}^{n} x_i^2}$$

where r^2 is called the coefficient of determination of y by x, or simply the squared correlation coefficient.

Multiple Regression

Many economic relationships involve more than two variables; for example, the quantity of meat (Q) demanded by consumers is a function of its retail price (P) and of consumer income (Y). This function could be linear in either arithmetic or logarithmic form, or it could be nonlinear (curvilinear) in various ways. When three or more variables are involved, the least-squares estimate of a function is called a multiple regression equation.

Moore had no special interest in agriculture, but he found that the most promising data available for his attempts to estimate empirical demand and supply functions were time series of prices, consumption, and production of farm products. His successes were followed up in the early 1920s by a group of young economists in the newly established U.S. Bureau of Agricultural Economics and in some of the agricultural colleges. Most notable of these economists were Mordecai Ezekiel, Frederick V. Waugh, Holbrook Working, Louis H. Bean, and Elmer J. Working. Moore's one direct disciple, Henry Schultz, also made impressive contributions from his vantage point at the University of Chicago. In their hands, the estimation of statistical demand functions using multiple regression techniques reached a high level of sophistication by the end of the 1920s. Their technical and empirical achievements are summarized in Ezekiel's *Methods of Correlation Analysis* (1930).

Some problems frequently encountered in regression analysis as applied to economic time series, including high intercorrelation among the independent variables and autocorrelation in the residuals, were clarified during the 1930s by Ragnar Frisch, Tjalling C. Koopmans, and Herman Wold. Paul H. Douglas began his work on production functions in the late 1920s, and Joel Dean made many regression estimates of statistical cost functions from 1937 on. Jan Tinbergen used multiple regression techniques (supplemented by the "bunch map analysis" methods of Frisch and Koopmans) to estimate his 45-equation model of the U.S. economy published in 1939. Henry Schultz's monumental work, *The Theory and Measurement of Demand* (1938), combined major presentations of economic theory and multiple regression techniques with detailed empirical studies of the demands for farm and food products.

During the 1920s and 1930s there were many arguments about the place of regression analysis in economics and business which now seem rather pointless. Few U.S.

economists active in those decades had much training in mathematics; many had studied economics as a verbal, historical, institutional, or descriptive subject, and most of those who had been exposed to a course in business or economic statistics had not advanced beyond "cookbook" recipes for fitting a least-squares trend to a time series. In this environment, some young economists who learned the techniques of freehand graphic curvilinear regression or of linear multiple regression analyses made extravagant claims and ridiculous mistakes. Thus, in 1934 Ragnar Frisch asserted that "a substantial part of the regression and correlation analyses which have been made on economic data in recent years is nonsense" because of the combined (and unrecognized) effect of random errors in and high intercorrelation among the explanatory variables. Chance correlations were sometimes mistaken for cause-and-effect relations, regression lines were extrapolated far beyond the range of the supporting data, and forecasts made on the implicit assumption of unchanging economic structures went awry when the structures did in fact change. It should be stressed that few such mistakes were made by the leading figures in the development of statistical demand analysis.

Currently, the place of regression analysis in economics and business may be summarized as follows: Functional relations between economic variables may be technological (e.g., steel is an input in the production of automobiles); institutional (e.g., receipts from the personal income tax are a function of personal income and the schedule of tax rates); or behavioral (e.g., the quantity of beef demanded by consumers is a function of its retail price and their disposable income). Economists who take pains to stay informed about the technological, institutional, or behavioral factors relevant to a particular functional relationship and about the sources, magnitudes, and natures of the errors that may be present in each variable can obtain useful knowledge by fitting a regression equation which approximates the function during the period to which the data refer. In doing so, they may obtain sufficient insight to adjust their regression coefficients when technology, tax schedules, or behavior change over time; thus, they can continue to make useful estimates or forecasts despite changes in structure.

References

Ezekiel, Mordecai, *Methods of Correlation Analysis,* 1st and 2d eds., Wiley, New York, 1930 and 1941; Ezekiel, Mordecai, and Karl A. Fox, *Methods of Correlation and Regression Analysis: Linear and Curvilinear,* 3d ed., Wiley, New York, 1959; Fox, Karl A., *Intermediate Economic Statistics,* vol. I: *An Integration of Economic Theory and Statistical Methods,* 2d ed., Krieger, Huntington, N.Y. 1980, reprint of *Intermediate Economic Statistics,* Wiley, New York, 1968; Fox, Karl A., and Tej K. Kaul, *Intermediate Economic Statistics,* vol. II: *A Guide to Recent Developments and Literature,* 1968–1978, Krieger, Huntington, N.Y., 1980; Frisch, Ragnar, *Statistical Confluence Analysis by Means of Complete Regression Systems,* Universitet, DET Okonomiske Institutt, Oslow, 1934; Moore, Henry L. *Forecasting the Yield and Price of Cotton,* Macmillan, New York, 1917; Moore, Henry L., *Synthetic Economics,* Macmillan, New York, 1929; Schultz, Henry, *The Theory and Measurement of Demand,* University of Chicago Press, Chicago, 1938; Seber, G. A. F., *Linear Regression Analysis,* Wiley, New York, 1977.

(*See also* Economic forecasting methods; Seasonal adjustment methods; Statistical methods in economics and business, an overview)

Tej K. Kaul and Karl A. Fox

Research and development

Commonly abbreviated as R&D and used in the singular, research and development encompasses all systematic or organized endeavors aimed at the creation or furtherance of knowledge. The various types of activities within the R&D entity have been classified in a number of different and not always consistent ways, but the best known and the most widely used breakdown of R&D is basic research, applied research, and development.

Basic research, also called "scientific" or "fundamental research," pertains to phenomena and relationships found in nature, including human nature, taken in an individual or collective context. Hence, the objective of basic research is to expand knowledge in the sciences, both natural and social.

Applied research, sometimes called "technological" or "engineering research," has as its objective the formulation of concepts and methods and the invention of devices and techniques that can be used as inputs into some human-originated process, product, or event. Hence, applied research is more likely to be mission-oriented, i.e., to have predefined goals and objectives, than is basic research.

Development is the process of perfecting a new kind of product or activity that does not require or no longer requires the creation of new basic or applied knowledge. Development precedes the routine or mass introduction of new products or activities. Unforeseen problems and flaws are corrected during the development process, and, in some classifications, pilot and prototype production is considered as the final stage of development.

In addition to this tripartition based on the substance of R&D, there are other types of classifications based on institutional or functional criteria. Hence, the literature has numerous references to industrial, academic, and defense R&D, or to offensive versus defensive R&D.

As indicated, the R&D entity, or at least many of its components, pertain to social, as well as to natural or technological, phenomena. R&D components can also be interpreted to apply to management, the arts, or the humanities, but in most cases, the interest of economists in R&D is directed toward physical, chemical, biological, technological, or engineering endeavors. The potential of such endeavors can lead to the invention of new products and processes and to innovations in the process of production and consumption.

R&D and Economics

The integration of R&D into the conceptual structure of economics exemplifies a curious epoch in the history of economic thought. During that epoch, a set of new concepts were incorporated into an established philosophical and theoretical framework that was not fully prepared to accommodate those new concepts. Accordingly, modifications were in order, and the modifications, whenever deemed necessary, were applied to the R&D concept rather than to existing economic theory. As will be seen, some gaps and anomalies still remain in the economic interpretation of research and development.

Economists began to take serious and extensive interest in R&D shortly after World War II. This burst of interest is commonly attributed to three main causes: the devastation of the European scientific infrastructure during the war; the Sputnik-inspired international space race of the 1950s and 1960s; and a series of hot and cold wars during the same period. By the early 1970s, the momentum provided by the three causes was lost, and the actual performance of R&D ebbed, as did much of the interest of economists in the subject. There are many examples in the history of economic thought where interest in a given subject is closely linked to the coming and passing of current events. However, the case of R&D in the history of economic thought is noteworthy because of its acuteness as well as its brevity.

Nevertheless, the subject of R&D has come to occupy an important position in contemporary economics, particularly with regard to questions that relate to technological change, productivity, economic growth, and economic development. The surge of interest in the subject originated in the United States, but by the early 1960s, the international literature had become richly infused with economic treatments of research and development.

With a few notable exceptions, economists have accepted the conventional classification of R&D activities as basic research, applied research, and development and have made this tripartition the basis for the analysis of the incentives to undertake R&D. The incentive, of course, depends on an economic evaluation of expected returns from undertakings in comparison with alternative employment opportunities of R&D resources. The accuracy with which returns from R&D can be predicted is widely agreed to be the highest in the case of development; it is believed to be lower for applied research; the lowest, if it exists at all, is for basic research. Hence, the incentive of profit-motivated private enterprise to undertake R&D is commonly ranked in the same order. Both this ordering and historical performance put major responsibility for undertaking basic research in the hands of the federal government, as well as academic and nonprofit institutions. In addition, the federal government assumes responsibility for a considerable volume of applied research and development, aimed at the provision of social or collectively consumed goods, such as national defense, health, and environmental protection.

Within the conceptual framework of economics, R&D is commonly viewed as an investment, that is, the outlay of resources for the acquisition of some form of capital. The definition of invested resources and of the resulting capital, however, depends on whether the topic at hand is closer to the philosophical-theoretical or the empirical and policy-oriented end of the gamut of economic inquiry. At the philosophical-theoretical end, inputs into the R&D process are expressed as human creativity and intellectual effort, both direct and embodied in R&D plant and equipment. The output of R&D viewed in the same context is knowledge. Such abstractions are not useful in quantitative investigations, much less in policy-oriented empirical ones. Rather than attempting to mold the established edifice of economic theory and method to accommodate these abstractions, perhaps in a manner in which the abstractions of utility and welfare are accommodated, economists have decided to abandon the concepts of creativity, intellect, and knowledge and have adopted representative or surrogate concepts instead.

Accordingly, at the input end of the R&D process, the resources are represented by R&D expenditures, the employment of R&D personnel, and the use of plant and equipment. On the output side, the capital produced by R&D is taken to be represented by, or embodied in, increased productivity, new types of production processes, new kinds of goods and services, and more generally, economic growth and development, on both the macro and micro levels. In addition, the output of R&D activity is represented by patent, publication, and literature citation counts.

By the end of the 1980s, the subject had become standard fare in both micro and macroeconomic writings and textbooks, after economists had enough time to look inside the "black box" to see to what extent R&D and its results were intra- or extra-market phenomena. Their findings then made it possible to model the R&D process by means of "R&D production functions," "learning functions," "innovation possibility frontiers," and similar sophisticated devices. The main inquiries were focused on such subjects as the intra- and the interfirm diffusion of knowledge; further diffusion of that knowledge to industries, sectors, and the world; the pursuit of R&D under differing competitive conditions; and, of course, the possibility of constructing improved optimization and equilibrium schemes.

In spite of the impressive strides in those endeavors, many economists were left with the conclusion that optimization and equilibrium-oriented neoclassical theory is not capable of accommodating the dynamics of the R&D phenomenon. Some such skeptics then abandoned the time-honored neoclassical path and chose divergent approaches. These approaches are best described in connection with the subject of innovation. It is noteworthy that a surprisingly large portion of the R&D literature is backed up by credible empirical verification.

Allocation of Resources for R&D

The extent to which progress in the conceptual treatment of R&D has facilitated the allocation of resources to the activity remains an open question. In private business, R&D allocation decisions are still made to a large extent on a project-by-project basis, by the use of ad hoc criteria, by the extrapolation of past magnitudes, or by rules of thumb. In the government, the allocation of R&D resources remains largely a political process in the hands of the legislative and executive branches.

References

National Science Foundation, *Science Indicators,* National Science Board, Washington, D.C., published biannually; Nelson, Richard R. (ed.), *The Rate and Direction of Inventive Activity: Economic and Social Factors,* National Bureau of Economic Research, Princeton University Press, Princeton, N.J., 1962; Rosenberg, Nathan, *Technology and Economics,* Cambridge University Press, Cambridge, Mass., 1962; Stoneman, Paul, *The Economic Analysis of Technological Change,* Oxford University Press, Oxford, 1987; Subcommittee on Domestic and International Scientific Planning and Analysis of the Committee on Science and Technology, *Selected Readings on Research and Development Expenditures and the National Economy,* U.S. House of Representatives, 94th Cong., 2d Sess., April 1976, serial Z; Subcommittee on Science, Research, and Development of the Committee on Science and Astronautics, *Selected Reading on Science, Technology, and the Economic,* U.S. House of Representatives. 92d Cong., 1st Sess., October 1971, serial E.

(*See also* Economic growth; Innovation; Productivity; Technology)

Theodore Suranyi-Unger, Jr.

Restraint of trade

The term restraint of trade refers to those forms of business behavior that are prohibited by section 1 of the Sherman Act of 1890: "Every contract, combination in the form of trust or otherwise, or conspiracy in restraint of trade or commerce among the several states, or with foreign nations, is declared to be illegal." This proscription contains a general, albeit vague, principle that private efforts to eliminate competition are prohibited. In contrast to current legislation that carefully defines its terms, the Sherman Act contains no definition of what constitutes a restraint of trade because in the late 1800s, that term did not have a commonly understood meaning. Restraint of trade acquired its current meaning through a series of judicial decisions that constitute the body of antitrust law.

Public Policy Concern

There has been much debate about the historical purposes of the Sherman Act. This debate surfaces from time to time, and the question remains open, but there is no doubt that the economic foundation for our present concern with restraints of trade resides in the possibility of social welfare losses. Profit maximization by a monopolist causes a misallocation of resources that yields social welfare losses. The hostility toward restraints of trade flows from our concern that cooperation among putative competitors can result in price and output decisions that approximate those of a monopolist.

Since the public policy concern is with collusive monopoly, it is clear that not all restraints of trade are objectionable. For example, an employment contract restrains trade by preventing another employer from hiring a specific worker. For another example, when a business is sold, the sales agreement often includes a noncompete clause preventing the seller from opening a clone of the business that was just sold. Ex ante this benefits the seller as it permits the full capitalization of the business's going concern value. Ex post it protects the buyer from an erosion of that going concern value. Such restraints are ancillary to a legitimate business transaction. They promote economic activity and are generally desirable. Accordingly, they have been deemed "reasonable," and, therefore, they are not illegal.

Unreasonable restraints, which do violate the law, are those that inhibit, suppress, or destroy competition. In principle, such restraints can approximate the monopoly results and thereby diminish social welfare. Analytically, one can distinguish horizontal and vertical restraints.

Horizontal Restraints

From the very beginning, the Supreme Court has held that price fixing is precisely the kind of restraint of trade that the Sherman Act was designed to prevent. There have been a few stumbles along the way, but the central thrust of the case law has been to make price fixing a per se violation of section 1 of the Sherman Act. This can be traced quite clearly to the Supreme Court's opinion in the 1927 case of *United States v. Trenton Potteries Company:*

> *The aim and result of every price-fixing agreement, if effective, is the elimination of one form of competition. The power to fix prices, whether reasonably exercised or not, involves power to control the market and to fix arbitrary and unreasonable prices. The reasonable price fixed today may through economic and business changes become the unreasonable price of tomorrow. Once established, it may be maintained unchanged because of the absence of competition secured by the agreement for a price reasonable when fixed. Agreements which create such potential power may well be held to be in themselves unreasonable or unlawful restraints, without the necessity of minute inquiry whether a particular price is reasonable or unreasonable as fixed. . . .*

This view was reiterated, clarified, and extended by the Supreme Court in its 1940 opinion in *United States v. Socony-Vacuum Oil Company:*

Under the Sherman Act a combination formed for the purpose and with the effect of raising, depressing, fixing, pegging or stabilizing the price of a commodity in interstate or foreign commerce is illegal per se.

This remains the rule of law to the present.

There is, of course, more than one way to skin a cat, and those intent on finding a way to emulate monopoly pricing have explored plenty of alternatives. As these schemes surface, their equivalence to price fixing is determined, and the business practice in question is outlawed. Bid rigging is an obvious close cousin to price fixing and has been condemned (*United States v. Addyston Pipe & Steel Co.,* 1898). A similar fate awaited customer allocation schemes (*United States v. Addyston Pipe & Steel,* 1898), market division or territorial allocation, (*United States v. Topco Associates, Inc.,* 1972), boycotts or concerted refusals to deal (*United States v. General Motors Corp.,* 1966), minimum fee schedules for professional services (*Goldfarb v. Virginia State Bar,* 1975), information exchanges influencing price (*United States v. Container Corporation of America,* 1969) withdrawal of interest-free credit (*Catalano, Inc. v. Target Sales, Inc.,* 1980), among others.

Vertical Restraints

Usually, vertical restraints are imposed by a supplier upon its customers. There is considerable disagreement on the competitive significance of vertical restraints even among economists. As a result, the judicial decisions in this area have caused some dispute. These restraints take many price and nonprice forms.

Resale Price Maintenance   In a resale price maintenance case, the supplier sells its product on the condition that the buyer not resell the product below a specified price. This prevents discount houses from cutting the resale price below the minimum price selected by the manufacturer. Reasoning that vertical price fixing was analogous to horizontal agreements on price, the Supreme Court ruled that it was illegal per se in *Dr. Miles Medical Co. v. John D. Park & Sons* (1911). Although the court has had opportunities to overrule *Dr. Miles,* it has declined to do so.

Maximum Resale Price Fixing   This practice limits the reseller's freedom to raise price above that specified by the supplier. Invariably, maximum resale price fixing occurs when the supplier is trying to prevent the reseller from exercising monopoly power. Nonetheless, the Supreme Court ruled that this practice is illegal per se in *Albrecht v. Herald Co.* (1968).

Territorial and Customer Restrictions   In many instances, suppliers restrain resellers from going outside specified territories or from selling to certain classes of customers. For example, Schwinn prohibited its authorized dealers from reselling bicycles to other retailers—in particular, discount houses. Following a 10-year period during which such restraints were illegal per se, the Supreme Court decided in *Continental T.V. v. GTE Sylvania* (1977) that this kind of vertical restraint should be evaluated according to the rule of reason. This means that the courts must weigh the procompetitive and anticompetitive consequences to determine whether on balance the restraint is unreasonable.

Tying Arrangements   When a seller conditions the sale of good A (the tying good) on the buyer's agreement to buy good B (the tied good), we have an example of a tying arrangement. If a tying arrangement exists, the seller has market power in the tying good market, and a not insubstantial volume of commerce is affected in the tied good market, then the tying arrangement is illegal per se. These criteria evolved through many Supreme Court decisions, but the latest word was offered in *Jefferson Parish Hospital District No. 2 v. Hyde* (1984).

Exclusive Dealing   In an exclusive dealing arrangement, a supplier will sell to a reseller on the condition that the reseller buy all of its requirements from the supplier. For some reason, the Supreme Court has always been able to identify the presence of some procompetitive justifications for exclusive dealing. Accordingly, these arrangements have never borne the per se label. The two most important decisions involving exclusive dealing are *Standard Oil Co. v. United States* (1949) and *Tampa Electric Co. v. Nashville Coal Co.* (1961).

Our economic understanding of various vertical restraints continues to develop over time. Along with it, the antitrust treatment of these restraints evolves as well. Eventually, the law and economics of vertical restraints ought to converge.

References

Areeda, Phillip, and Louis Kaplow, *Antitrust Analysis,* 4th ed., Little, Brown, Boston, 1988; Blair, Roger D., and David L. Kaserman, *Antitrust Economics,* Irwin, Homewood, Ill., 1985; Bork, Robert, *The Antitrust Paradox,* Basic Books, New York, 1978; Hovenkamp, Herbert, *Economics and Federal Antitrust Law,* West Publishing, St. Paul, Minn., 1985.

(*See also* Antitrust policy; Competition; Government regulation of business; Mergers, takeovers, and corporate restructuring)

Roger D. Blair

Return on investment

Return on investment (ROI) is a measure of the yield or return on invested capital, as in an existing business, or of the expected return on prospective investments, as in consideration of proposed plant or equipment purchases.

Return on invested capital (sometimes called "ROE" for return on equity) is usually a measure of the relative profitability of a firm or industry. A useful measure for analytical or comparative purposes, it is to be distinguished from perhaps the most popular measure of profitability, the sales margin, which is the percentage of each sales dollar represented by profit.

Two Principal Measurements of ROI

The two principal measurements of ROI are ratios of net profit to net worth and of net profit to total assets. The ROI ratio of net profit to net worth is commonly expressed as a percentage and shows the rate of return on equity capital, i.e., the original investment plus reinvested earnings. The percentage is derived by dividing net worth into net profit. The resulting percentage is an indication of the yield on the stockholders' accumulated investment

$$\text{ROI for net worth} = \frac{\text{net profit (after taxes)}}{\text{net worth}}$$

For example,

$$\frac{\$1,400,000}{\$10,000,000} = 14\%$$

The ROI ratio of net profit to total assets is also expressed as a percentage and is derived from dividing net profit by total investment, i.e., all assets. This percentage reveals the earning capability of the entire capital stock involved in the enterprise. The percentage can then be used to compare other potential investments open to management apart from further investment in the enterprise.

$$\text{ROI for total assets} = \frac{\text{net profit (after taxes)}}{\text{total assets}}$$

For example,

$$\frac{\$14,000,000}{\$200,000,000} = 7\%$$

Both ROI examples above enable management to get a better perspective on the profitability of the enterprise, especially in comparison with industry standards and the current cost of capital—e.g., interest rates.

Commonly, industrial firms attain their return on invested capital through high sales margins and low turnover, whereas retail firms make their ROI through low sales margins on high turnover. In broad industry numbers, the return on invested capital for industrial firms can be found in the *Quarterly Financial Report for Manufacturing Corporations,* published by the Federal Trade Commission.

Three Methods of Weighing Relative Profitability

ROI calculations on new investments are ways to plan fixed-asset expenditures, usually of large magnitude. They provide, in other words, methods of weighing the relative profitability of possible purchases of new plant or equipment against alternative investment opportunities over a span of years. Three methods of weighing this profitability are payback, average rate of return, and discounted cash flow.

The popular payback method offers a means of determining the number of years of net attributable income required to recover a given investment. Payback calculations are simple to figure and easy to comprehend and show the length of time of exposure to risk, including obsolescence. But the method is an indirect ROI. It does not tell of income generated beyond the payback time span, nor does it consider how income is acquired, i.e., the general pattern of cash throw-off over time. The accompanying table illustrates all three methods. It assumes the cost of Project X and Project Y to be $45,000 each and the estimated life of each project to be 8 years.

In the example, Project X would pay off in 1¾ years, and Project Y would pay off in 4½; but in the fourth, fifth, sixth, seventh, and eighth years, Project Y would still be generating cash, and Project X would not.

The relative profitability of each project is ignored by the payback method of ROI calculation; however, the average-rate-of-return method takes into account this profitability. Average cash flow under Project Y is $10,000, whereas under Project X it is only $7500. By dividing the original investment of $45,000 into each of these figures, we find that the ROI, under the average-rate-of-return method, is 22.2 percent for Project Y and 16.7 percent for Project X. The average-rate-of-return method has the advantage of simplicity.

Payback on Projects X and Y

Year	Production gains before expenses		Expenses including depreciation* and taxes		Cash flow	
	X	Y	X	Y	X	Y
1	$70,000	$50,000	$40,000	$40,000	$30,000	$10,000
2	60,000	50,000	40,000	40,000	20,000	10,000
3	50,000	50,000	40,000	40,000	10,000	10,000
4	40,000	50,000	40,000	40,000	0	10,000
5	40,000	50,000	40,000	40,000	0	10,000
6	40,000	50,000	40,000	40,000	0	10,000
7	40,000	50,000	40,000	40,000	0	10,000
8	40,000	50,000	40,000	40,000	0	10,000

* Depreciation is treated differently under discounted cash flow.

The discounted-cash-flow ROI method not only considers the cost of capital funds over the life of the project but also allows for the differences in time during which the investments generate cash, which itself yields income. Thus, Project X generates $60,000 in 3 years, during which time Project Y generates only $30,000. Allowing for these and the other income differences over the 8-year investment life, the ROI under the discounted-cash-flow method comes to 19.5 percent for Project X and 14.9 percent for Project Y.

References

Bierman, Harold, Jr., *Implementing Capital Budgeting Techniques,* rev. ed., Harper Business Publications, New York, 1988; Horngren, Charles T., *Cost Accounting: A Managerial Emphasis,* 4th ed., Prentice-Hall, Englewood Cliffs, N.J., 1977, especially pp. 375–423; Solomon, Ezra, *The Theory of Financial Management,* Columbia University Press, New York, 1963, especially pp. 120–137; Terborgh, George, *Business Investment Policy,* Machinery and Allied Products Institute, Washington, D.C., 1958; Weston, J. Fred, and Eugene F. Brigham, *Managerial Finance,* 6th ed., Dryden Press, Hinsdale, Ill., 1978, especially pp. 40–44, 283–340.

(*See also* Profits measurement; Risk premium on investment)

William H. Peterson

Ricardian equivalent (*see* Debt and deficits; Fiscal policy)

Right-to-work laws

Right-to-work laws are state laws which mandate that neither membership nor non-membership in a labor union may be made a condition of new or continued employment. Such laws exist expressly in 21 states (Alabama, Arizona, Arkansas, Florida, Georgia, Idaho, Iowa, Kansas, Louisiana, Mississippi, Nebraska, Nevada, North Carolina, North Dakota, South Carolina, South Dakota, Tennessee, Texas, Utah, Virginia, and Wyoming) plus American Samoa and cover private-sector employment subject to a key federal statute, the National Labor Relations Act of 1935 (NLRA). More than 30 states offer right-to-work protection to at least some segment of their public employees. Finally, all federal (including postal) employees are protected by right-to-work legislative or executive order provisions.

The subject of considerable controversy in recent years, right-to-work laws have the practical effect of making illegal any closed shop, union shop, agency shop, or maintenance-of-membership clauses in union contracts. Indeed, where right-to-work protection exists, no person can be required as a condition of employment to join, assist, or support financially a labor organization.

History

Right-to-work laws are expressly provided for in section 14(b) of the Taft-Hartley amendments (1947) to NLRA. Earlier, however, the National Industrial Recovery Act of 1933 (declared unconstitutional on other grounds in 1935) provided protections against compulsory unionism in section 7(a), and the Railway Labor Act of 1926 was amended in 1934 to provide similar guarantees (amended later in 1951 to permit the union shop). The first state to provide express right-to-work protection was Florida in its 1944 constitutional amendments, thus preceding the passage of Taft-Hartley's section 14(b) by some 3 years; the most recent state to pass such protective measures was Idaho by statute in 1986.

Right-to-work political controversy occurred in 1965 when a concerted effort was made, with the active backing of President Lyndon Johnson, to repeal Taft-Hartley's section 14(b). The effort failed, as have similar though less active attempts in later years. On the state level, right-to-work provisions have been enacted in a variety of ways (public referendum, statute, petition, constitutional amendment, etc.). In only two cases has existing right-to-work protection in the private sector been removed (Indiana in 1965; Louisiana in 1956, but reenacted in broader form in 1976).

Union Benefit and Free-Rider Notions

Closely related to the right-to-work issue as a phenomenon having economic implications are the concepts of union benefit and free rider. Proponents of compulsory unionism (in a sense, the antithetical position to right-to-work) argue that since unions supposedly benefit all whom they represent and since they must by law (with very few, limited exceptions) represent all employees in a bargaining unit (duty of fair representation) for which they are the certified agent, it follows that nonmember employees are free riders. Such employees enjoy the claimed benefits of union representation on terms and conditions of employment but, being nonmembers, pay none of the costs that the union incurs in representing them. Other arguments for compulsory unionism include the assertion that having all employees in the union brings stability to the work force, reduces the incidence of strikes (particularly unauthorized, or wildcat strikes), enables the union to moderate its demands, furnishes members with psychic income, permits a grievance procedure, and provides the union with a steadier financial base.

Arguments for Right-to-Work Laws

Opponents of compulsory unionism (i.e., those who favor right-to-work laws) argue contrarily that stability is won at the expense of allegedly unchecked union discipline which interferes with the civil rights (e.g., the right not to join) of coerced members, that a union which doesn't need to perform services for employees as a means of convincing them that membership is a benefit may not be a responsible or responsive union, that strikes of all kinds appear not to have been reduced where compulsory unionism exists, and, generally, that too little factual evidence exists to support all the union proponents' claims. Most pertinently, right-to-work advocates have begun in recent years to challenge the fundamental factual basis of the union-benefit, free-rider argument by analyzing the employees' net returns attributable to union representation. Scholarly research, on the whole, had tended either to support these challenges or to erode the more extreme claims of economic harm allegedly stemming from right-to-work laws. Clearly, a considerable amount of research still needs to be done before these arguments can be sorted out by the thoughtful analyst or policymaker.

The right-to-work controversy is almost solely limited to the United States and Great Britain. The phrase may also be found in British political debates, where it is solely a slogan of the radical left (particular of Trotskyist factions), referring to an alleged responsibility of the government to provide employment to citizens.

References

Bennett, James T., and Manuel H. Johnson, "Free Riders in U.S. Labour Unions: Artifice or Affliction?" *British Journal of Industrial Relations,* vol. 27, no. 2, July 1979, pp. 158–172; Haggard, Thomas R., *Compulsory Unionism, the NLRB, and the Courts: A Legal Analysis of Union Security Agreements,* Labor Relations and Public Policy Series Report 15, Wharton School, Philadelphia, 1977; Hanslowe, Kurt, L., et al., *Union Security in Public Employment: Of Free Riding and Free Association,* Institute of Public Employment Monograph 8, New York State School of Industrial and Labor Relations, New York, 1978. Reid, Joseph D., Jr., and Roger L. Faith, "Right to Work and Union Compensation Structure," *Journal of Labor Research,* vol. 8, Spring 1987, pp. 111–130; Sultan, Paul, *Right to Work Laws: A Study in Conflict,* Institute of Industrial Relations Monograph 2, University of California, Los Angeles, 1958.

(*See also* Labor unions)

William H. Peterson

Rigid prices

Rigidity or *stickiness* are words used to characterize the seeming insensitivity of price movements to changes in aggregate demand. Two kinds of price movements evoke the terms *rigid* or *sticky.* One is when there is a lag in the responsiveness of the level of prices to changes in demand. The other is when the response, regardless of its timing, is not symmetrical with respect to the direction in which demand changes—for example, if prices are less flexible when the demand change is downward than when it is upward. Rigidity can be reflected in nominal price movements or in the behavior of markups over costs. In either case, the more rigid the price, the greater the effect on output of changes in demand.

Most analyses of price behavior support the conclusion that price stickiness has increased since the end of World War II (Zarnowitz, 1989). This is particularly evident when producer prices are analyzed. Prior to World War II, they both rose and fell. Since 1946, declines have been rare. Consumer prices have always fluctuated less than producer prices. As the post–World War II period lengthened, it even became increasingly difficult to observe periods when the rate of consumer price inflation slowed as output fell.

Administered Prices

As a result of those developments, neither Keynesian nor monetarist economic models have been particularly helpful in predicting inflation over a period two or so years ahead (Okun, 1981). Thus, such macro theories seem incomplete, and many hypotheses have been advanced to explain why prices are sticky. The earliest one of significance was developed by Gardiner C. Means and called "administered pricing" (1935). He defined the term as the process by which prices are set and held constant for a series of transactions over a period of time. It was initially demonstrated empirically by constructing a frequency distribution of price index components according to the number of months for which each was unchanged. This produced a bimodal distribution with peaks at about 1 and 10 months. The components were then grouped into two composite indexes depending on whether they were closer to one mode or the other. The composite for the price indexes that changed frequently was much more volatile than for the other, suggesting it was more responsive to demand changes. Means found that during the mid-1950s the price index for markets dominated by prices that change less frequently stayed well above the other, implying a longer-term upward bias of price levels in industries that changed prices less frequently. These results of infrequent price change were characterized as administered pricing.

Some thought the behavior of Means's index for prices that changed infrequently was a reflection of errors in measuring prices. In particular, it was thought to reflect the failure of businesses to report the prices at which actual transactions took place. George Stigler undertook to collect and compile prices he obtained from buyers on the view that they would report the actual price at which the transaction took place (Stigler and Kindahl, 1970). His view was that the seller, by contract, the typical reporter of price data to government agencies, would report the price from its published list rather than reveal the extent to which discounts were being given. Stigler did find evidence of greater downward flexibility of prices collected from buyers than from sellers. However, he characterized his results as inconclusive with respect to whether prices cleared markets.

Source of Price Rigidity

So the notion that certain prices were sticky—less responsive to demand change than expected—continued to prevail. Thus, research was undertaken to determine the source of price rigidity. One hypothesis advanced was that it reflected the concentration of firms in an industry. It had long been recognized that the price level would be higher if markets were less competitive. But the hypothesis required that the rate of change of prices could be affected by industry concentration. There was evidence that price-unit cost ratios behaved countercyclically in some industries (Popkin, 1977). Subsequently, other researchers have shown that those industries in which margins moved countercyclically tended to be concentrated industries (Domowitz, Hubbard, and Petersen, 1986).

But another line of reasoning to support rigid prices had already emerged that did not depend on the presence of concentration. An early formulation of this hypothesis was that prices were set by trial and error, using formulas, and that errors in the formulas were not quickly apparent. In one variant, firms were thought to set prices as a markup over unit costs. The markup was set to achieve some target rate of return on investment. This view often relied on the assumption that the marginal cost curve was fairly flat over the range relevant to meeting most incoming demand, so standard or average unit costs could be measured and then marked up (see Eckstein, 1964).

Another important category of explanations for sticky prices relates to the cost of making price changes. Producers may wish to wait until they are certain that any changes in supply-demand conditions are not transitory. When such shifts are short-lived, an immediate price response may be too costly.

Regardless of the hypothesis selected to support the notion of sticky prices, most include the notion that prices (and wages) adjust only with a lag to changes in demand and costs. Thus, prices would continue to rise in the early stages of a recession because producers were still adjusting them to reflect recent increases in materials prices and wages. Research also suggests that prices adjust more slowly than wages. Thus, the ratio of wages to prices, on average, tends to be procyclical (see Blanchard, 1987).

A number of possible reasons have been put forth to explain the lag in price adjustment. In a survey (conducted by Blinder, 1991), firms were asked to evaluate the importance of 12 factors that could explain price rigidity. Several of the reasons cited most often would give rise to a lag in the adjustment process. The reason cited most frequently was that the speed and service with which orders are filled are viewed as part of the price charged. When demand is rising, delivery lags lengthen and services diminish; price may not change.

Another reason for the lag may be contracts that are fixed in nominal terms or implicit contracts that produce the same result. Especially for goods made to order, there may be two observable prices, one at which new orders are being accepted and one at which previous orders are being shipped. The BLS producer price indexes are based on prices at which shipments of previous orders are made.

Thus, a number of reasons for price rigidity do not suggest the administered pricing views of Means. These reasons may be consistent with competitive behavior. Nonprice factors, such as those discussed above, may play an important role in clearing competitive markets. Sometimes these nonprice factors are directly observable. For example, if the price is below equilibrium, suppliers may initially meet the excess demand by selling from inventories or by letting delivery lags lengthen by permitting unfilled orders to rise. (For a framework reflecting this process, see Popkin, 1977.)

Price rigidity that does, however, connote market imperfections is almost always present when it can be shown that there is real price rigidity as opposed to nominal price rigidity. Real rigidity is not merely the reflection of temporary adjustment lags. It occurs when, for example, markups—the ratio of price to unit labor costs—change autonomously. Such a change could occur if the number of sellers in a market diminished such that competition was reduced. A change in the ratio of wages to prices—real wages—is another example of real rigidity. Real wages might rise in response to increased union bargaining power, for example. Conversely, markups and real wages would be expected to fall in response to deregulation or to a decline in the number and size of unions.

References

Blanchard, O. J., "Aggregate and Individual Price Adjustment," *The Brookings Papers on Economic Activity*, vol. 1, The Brookings Institution, Washington, D.C., 1987, pp. 57–122; Blinder, A. S., "Price Stickiness in Theory and Practice: Why are Prices Sticky? Preliminary Results from an Interview Study," *The American Economic Review*, vol. 81, May 1991, pp. 89–96; Domowitz, I., R. G. Hubbard, and B. C. Petersen, "Business Cycles and the Relationship between Concentration and Price-Cost Margins," *Rand Journal of Economics,* vol. 17, no. 1, Spring 1986, pp. 1–17; Eckstein, O., "A Theory of the Wage-Price Process in Modern Industry," *The Review of Economic Studies,* vol. 31, October 1964, pp. 269–271; Means, G. C., "Industrial Prices and Their Relative Inflexibility," U.S. Senate Document 13, 74th Congress, 1st Session, Washington, D.C., 1935; Okun, A., *Prices and Quantities: A Macroeconomic Analysis,* The Brookings Institution, Washington, D.C., 1981; Popkin, J., "An Integrated Model of Final and Intermediate Demand by Stage of Process: A Progress Report," *The American Economic Review,* vol. 67, no. 1, February 1977, pp. 141–147; Stigler, G., and J. Kindahl, *The Behavior of Industrial Prices,* NBER General Series, no. 90, Columbia University Press, New York, 1970; Zarnowitz, V., "Cost and Price Movements in Business Cycle Theories and Experience: Hypotheses of Sticky Wages and Prices," NBER Working Paper Series, no. 3131, October 1989.

(*See also* Competition, Concentration of industry; Consumer price index; Demand; Inflation; Labor unions; Marginal cost; Monopoly and oligopoly; Price theory; Producer price index)

Joel Popkin

Risk premium on investment

The risk premium on investment is the incremental return required to compensate investors in projects or securities with uncertain outcomes. In percentage terms, the risk premium is the difference between the rate of return expected for a given investment and a specified risk-free rate of return. The risk-adjusted rate of return on investment is the sum of the risk-free rate plus the risk premium.

Measurement of the risk premium has great practical importance for evaluating investment decisions in a world subject to random disturbances. Business executives and economists need a simple and accurate technique to quantify the risk premium. Such a technique must be grounded in sound economic principles to avoid a serious misallocation of capital.

Theorists and Risk Premium on Investment

The connection between risk and return on investment has been mentioned by classical economists from Adam Smith on. The primary emphasis of interest rate theorists such as Böhm-Bawerk and Fisher was the determination of an equilibrium rate of return in an environment of perfect foresight. The analytic techniques of net present value and internal rate of return were developed in this classical framework.

Several economic theorists emphasized the importance of uncertainty in economic behavior. Frank Knight recognized the significance of random events in determining realized rates of return. Keynes stressed the role of expectations in selecting the level of investment. However, these economic theorists did not offer a model of a systematic relationship between risk and return.

Capital Asset Pricing Model

During the 1960s, research into the behavior of securities prices led to the formulation of the Sharpe-Lintner capital asset pricing model. This theory uses the relative variation in expected return of an investment as the measure of risk. Investors expect greater returns from riskier investment projects, whose results vary more than the capital market as a whole. Equilibrium among investors determines the risk premium associated with a given risk level. The capital markets reflect this equilibrium in the prices set for securities, the claims to the cash flows generated by the investments.

If the theoretical assumption of this model can be accepted and if values can be assigned to a risk-free return and the market price of risk, then the risk premium can be expressed as proportional to the expected rate of return on a market index:

$$E(R_i) - R_f = \beta_i \, [E(R_m) - R_f]$$

where $E(R_i)$ and $E(R_m)$ are the expected rates of return on investment i and the market index, respectively; R_f is the risk-free rate of return; and β_i, the measure of relative riskiness of investment i, is estimated statistically using historical data on securities prices. Actual returns on a market index, such as the Standard and Poor's 500 Index, are used for calculations rather than the expected returns, $E(R_m)$.

Importance of Risk Premium on Investment

The risk premium on investment is important in both theoretical and applied economics. In the theory of the firm, the risk premium refines the economist's understanding of optimal investment decisions. In macroeconomic theory, the connection is made between increased uncertainty from shocks to the economic system and the aggregate levels of capital formation. On the applied side, the risk premium potentially offers an improved rule for the investment decision as well as an explanation for the different rates of return observed in various industries. In economic regulation, the risk premium has direct application in rate setting cases.

Advantages and Disadvantages

Expression of the risk premium in terms of the capital asset pricing model has several advantages. The theory integrates the firm's evaluation of investment projects with the securities markets' valuation of the claims to the cash generated by these projects. A numerical value for the risk premium can be estimated. Finally, the theory is buttressed by the empirical research on the capital asset pricing model.

Difficulties are found with this precise formulation of the risk premium. The capital asset pricing model specifies a normal distribution of returns with constant parameters. Cash flows from a specific project may not conform to this model, and business conditions clearly change at different points in time. Expected returns are conditional on the information set at the point in time, and the information available to business managers is generally asymmetric from that known to outside investors and measured in the β_i. Movements in the risk-free rate of return result from volatility in inflation rates. Several problems hamper the calculation of β_i. There are problems in statistical estimation, since there is evidence that securities returns deviate from the normal distribution. Choice of an appropriate proxy for the project's cash flows may be difficult. Controversy surrounds the choice of a sufficiently comprehensive market index.

Alternative approaches to measuring the risk premium have been suggested. A more generalized model, the arbitrage pricing theory, has expected returns to be proportional to several variables. This model is used in securities analysis but has been more difficult to apply in project evaluation. Cash flows could be adjusted to their certainty equivalent value and discounted at the risk-free rate. In practice the calculation of certainty equivalents and choice of an appropriate risk-free rate has operational difficulties. More elaborate models based on the pricing of stock options present similar computational problems.

The concept of risk premium on investment is widely used in economics and is similarly defined in non-English dictionaries of economics.

References

Cohn, Richard A., and Franco, Modigliani, "Inflation and Corporate Financial Management," in Edward I. Altmann, and Marti G. Subrahmanyam (eds.), *Recent Advances in Corporate Finance,* Irwin, Homewood, Ill., 1983, pp. 341–370; Fama, Eugene F., "Risk-Adjusted Discount Rates and Capital Budgeting under Uncertainty," *Journal of Financial Economics,* vol. 5, no. 1, August 1977, pp. 3–24; Hirschleifer, Jack, *Investment, Interest, and Capital,* Prentice-Hall, Englewood Cliffs, N.J., 1970; Knight, Frank H. *Risk, Uncertainty and Profit,* Houghton Mifflin, Boston, 1921; Knight, Frank H., "Interest," in Edwin R. A. Seligman, and Alvin S. Johnson (eds.), *Encyclopedia of the Social Sciences,* vol. 7, Macmillan, New York, 1932, pp. 131–144; Knight, Frank H. "Profit," in Seligman and Johnson, ibid, vol. 12, pp. 480–486; Knight, Frank H., "Risk," in Seligman and Johnson, ibid., vol. 13, pp. 392–394; Mason, Scott P., and Robert C. Merton, "The Role of Contingent Claims Analysis in Corporate Finance," in Altmann and Subrahmanyam (eds.), *Recent Advances in Corporate Finance,* Irwin, Homewood, Ill., 1983, pp. 7–54; Ross, Stephen A., "A Simple Approach to the Valuation of Risky Streams, *Journal of Business,* vol. 52, no. 3, July 1978, pp. 453–475; Seitz, Neil E., *Capital Budgeting and Long-Term Financing Decisions,* Dryden, Hinsdale, Ill., 1990.

(*See also* Asset pricing models; Return on investment; Venture capital)

Joseph B. Starshak

Robots, industrial (*see* Automation)

Sampling in economics

Most of the applied quantitative research done in business economics is based upon sample information. The objective of the research is to learn about specific attributes of a population such as the mean or variance. Although in theory it might be possible to take a census or obtain information on the random variable of interest from every population member, this is likely to be prohibitively expensive. For this reason, sample statistics such as the sample means and sample variances are used to estimate population parameters, test hypotheses about the parameters, and make decisions. Even in cases where a complete census is taken such as the decennial census of population in the United States, there may be inaccuracies such as undercounts due to the under representation of certain groups. When census figures are thought to be in error, survey work will often be done to estimate the extent of the error.

In business economics, information such as the average income of a population living in a geographic area or the expectations for sales and profitability over a specified time horizon within a particular industrial group is frequently of interest. Survey research is a convenient, cost-effective way to gather information on a broad range of topics such as economic activity, consumer awareness with respect to new product concepts and introductions, and expectations of future economic activity, e.g., sales, profits, and investments. In addition to the survey research published by the Bureau of the Census, well-known economic surveys in the United States are the consumer confidence surveys published by The Conference Board and the University of Michigan Survey Research Center, the Business Expectations Survey published by The Dun and Bradstreet Corporation, and the surveys of employment and prices conducted by the Bureau of Labor Statistics.

Prior to data collection, the researcher must address four issues. First, it is necessary to have a clear idea as to the type of information required and to determine whether the members of the population are known. Second, it is important to decide who from the population should be selected. This decision is often difficult as the sampling units can be defined in many different ways, e.g., age, sex, income level, age and sex. Third, how the sample should be selected and how many members of the population to select must be decided in order to yield conclusions that are considered reliable. Fourth, the method of contact must be determined.

Assuming the information required is defined and is known to be collectible, the decision concerning the appropriate way to select the sample will in large part be determined by the business issue under consideration and the resources provided to the researcher. The most common procedures for sample selection are simple random sampling, stratified random sampling, cluster sampling, and two-phase sampling. Nonprobabilistic methods such as quota sampling may also be used in some instances, and these methods may produce accurate estimates. Because the sample is generally not random, it may not be possible to determine the statistical reliability of the estimates, however. For this reason, nonprobabilistic approaches are not discussed below.

A simple random-sampling procedure is one in which every possible sample of a given number of objects is equally likely to be chosen. Although the concept of drawing a simple random sample might be appealing, it may be the case that characteristics of population members have a significant relationship to the topic of interest or subgroups of the population are of interest, and it is possible that simple random sampling could yield a sample overrepresenting some groups and underrepresenting others. In such cases, it is preferable to stratify the sample by breaking the population into unique subgroups and taking a random sample from each subgroup.

A different approach is more likely to be used when a survey is to be taken over a large geographic area such as a regional market. It may be the case that the researcher does not have a list of the population or that the population members are widely dispersed over the geographic unit. If the area can be divided into smaller groups or clusters, it will be relatively cost-effective to take a simple random sample of clusters and take a census in each of the sample clusters.

In some instances two-phased sampling is appropriate. This procedure involves conducting an initial study involving a small proportion of the population members. Although the two-phased approach may take more time, it does have the advantage of identifying both questions that need revision as well as extensions to the survey. Furthermore, the statistical information collected from the initial study may provide useful information for designing the second phase of the survey.

In choosing a sample size a number of factors are relevant. Although large sample sizes are known to yield more reliable results than small samples, the size of the sample is likely to be constrained by the costs incurred by collecting large samples. The researcher must weigh the trade-offs between cost in terms of time and money, accuracy, and overall credibility of the study.

The three most commonly used methods of contact are telephone, mail, and interview. Whereas telephone interviews are a convenient way to gather information over a short period, they must be very brief and impersonal. Further, the sample is limited to persons having telephones. Mail questionnaires have the advantage of reaching a broad audience and avoiding any bias that might be introduced by a person conducting the interview. The primary disadvantages are that the response rate may be low, and responses may take a long time to receive. The third method of contacting, interviews, may be done on a one-on-one basis or undertaken with a group of respondents. The primary impediment to interviews is the reluctance on the part of potential participants to spend time.

Once the data are collected, the researcher must tabulate the data, analyze frequency distributions, and decide which measures of central tendency and dispersion are most appropriate for answering the questions under study. In some cases, more advanced statistical techniques may be used to build explanatory models of the most important variables. When analyzing the data, it is important to keep in mind that there are possible sources of error. Perhaps the most obvious source of error is due to the random-sampling variation that occurs when the number of units measured is less than the population. Error may also occur due to failure to measure some of the units in the sample. This may be due to oversight, failure to locate some of the units, or nonresponse. There may be measurement error due to insufficient information on the part of the respondent or response bias. Finally, errors may occur due to mistakes in editing, recording, and tabulating the outcomes.

References

Cochran, W. G., *Sampling Techniques,*Wiley, New York, 1977; Williams, B., *A Sampler on Sampling*, Wiley, New York, 1978.

(*See also* Computers in economics; Data banks; Marketing research and business economics; Statistical methods in economics and business, an overview)

Phillip A. Cartwright

Satisficing*

The verb to satisfice, with its origins in Northumbria, means to attain or accept a satisfactory solution to a problem. A satisfactory solution meets the needs of the situation and achieves the aspirations of the solver or decision maker. Satisficing may be contrasted with optimizing, which is finding the best solution, one that maximizes the utility realizable from the situation.

Satisficing and Optimizing

Consider the problem of selecting a menu of foods that will meet all nutritional requirements for calories, minerals, and vitamins at a minimum cost. This optimal diet problem is usually formulated and solved using linear programming.

Now modify the problem by removing the cost minimization criterion, replacing it with the constraint that the cost must not exceed a certain amount. The solution to this modified, satisficing, problem, if it exists (its existence is not guaranteed), is quite different from the solution to the optimization problem. In general, if a solution to the satisficing problem exists, that solution will not be unique. There will be many points in the feasible set.

None of these solutions is best, since "best" has not been defined. However, the amount of time and computation required to find one or more satisfactory solutions

*Permission granted by MacMillan to include this new article on "Satisficing" since a different article on this subject by the same author appeared in the new *Palgraves*.

will generally be far less than the time and computation to find the solution of the optimization problem. And satisficing solutions can be found for many problems where the optimum simply cannot be discovered with present or prospective computers.

Computational Costs

In selecting decision procedures, computational cost and feasibility are crucial. Finding the sharpest needle in a haystack (in which the distribution of needles of varying sharpness is random) is entirely different computationally from finding a needle sharp enough to sew with. The time required to find the sharpest needle varies with the size of the haystack; the time required to find a satisfactory needle is independent of the size of the stack, depending only on the density of needles in it. If we model the world as an infinite haystack, as it surely is, the latter problem is solvable, the former is not.

Economic theory generally poses decision problems as though the alternatives of choice and the consequences (or probability distribution of consequences) following from each alternative were given in advance, requiring no computation to find them. These conditions are seldom met in the real world, where the costs of searching for and evaluating alternatives may be very large and where alternatives must be sought sequentially and without exhaustion. Under these circumstances, satisficing criteria provide a stop rule to terminate search. As soon as a satisfactory alternative is found, it can be accepted.

It has sometimes been suggested that satisficing searches can always be converted into searches for an optimum by taking the computational cost of search into account. According to this view, the search should be continued until the expected marginal cost of finding and evaluating the next alternative exceeds the expected marginal gain of that alternative over the best previously discovered.

This conversion of a satisficing search into a search for an optimum may sometimes be advantageous, but advantageous or not, it complicates the computational problem, often to the point of infeasibility. In optimal search, the decision maker must evaluate not only given alternatives but also the expected cost of finding new ones and their expected value if found. Only for relatively routine and repetitive choices can these quantities be estimated at all realistically.

Moreover, casting decision making in the form of optimal search implies that the decision maker has an automatic generator of new alternatives and omits entirely the whole design process that enables human beings (or computers) to plan novel courses of action. Discovering, inventing, and designing new alternatives is a major occupation in all organizations and is the core of those activities we call "entrepreneurial."

Another common proposal for preserving optimization is to replace the real-world choice problem, for which optimization is computationally infeasible, with a simplified approximation which admits the explicit computation of the "optimum." To distinguish this procedure from true optimization, we may call it "pseudo-optimization." For example, in the game of chess, the optimum strategy is to consider all possible sequences of moves, by self and opponent, assign the values 1, 0, and −1, to the outcomes according to whether they win, draw, or lose, and minimax backward, choosing the best move for each side, propagating these values back to the present position.

The approximation used in most computer chess programs is to search to a specified depth (far short of the end of the game), assign to each terminal position a value derived from an estimated evaluation function, and use these approximate values to minimax backward. There is no theoretical reason that such an approximation should choose better moves than a satisficing procedure that looks explicitly for a "good enough" move, halting its search when it finds one. In fact, pseudo-optimization is simply a particular form of satisficing. The closer the approximation to the uncomputable reality, the better pseudo-optimization is likely to choose.

Only a chess program that can carry out enormous computations (calculating 50 million continuations of the game, say) will play a high-quality game using pseudo-optimization. Even then, it will be beaten by strong human players who, as is known from experiments, compute only about one hundred continuations. But regardless of the amount of computation, the chess-playing programs are only very approximate optimizers (whence their defeatability). In short, they are satisficers, and equally so are the human grand masters who can still defeat the best programs.

Bounded Rationality

Turning from normative to positive considerations, the empirical evidence is overwhelming that people—consumers, employees, businesspeople—typically satisfice rather than optimize. The reason, summed up in the phrase "bounded rationality," is that their computational means are far too limited to permit them to generate all alternatives (or even to calculate the optimal search rule) and to estimate a probability distribution of outcomes for each alternative.

Moreover, empirical evidence shows that people do not usually have consistent utility functions defined over all alternatives. In fact, they normally have great difficulty in comparing alternatives that differ along incommensurable dimensions. One house is larger than another, but is more expensive; the larger house requires a longer commuting trip than the other, but is in a pleasanter neighborhood. And so on. These incommensurabilities can be resolved if the decision maker selects a satisfactory level along each of the dimensions and searches for an alternative that meets all these constraints. Observation has shown that this is what people commonly do.

The important question for economics is not whether people are optimizers— clearly they are not—but what computational techniques they use to reach satisfactory solutions to the problems of choice that face them. As we have just seen, replacing real-world problems by approximations whose optimal solutions are within the computational means available, that is pseudo-optimizing, is one way of satisficing. It is not the only one, and in fact it is rarely used by people in complex situations involving important qualitative considerations.

Setting Aspiration Levels

As a substitute for an infeasible optimum search procedure, people commonly terminate search when the best solution found thus far meets all the constraints they have set. As suggested above, these constraints can be interpreted as levels of aspiration. Human aspirations, in turn, are commonly based on expectations resting on past experience or on comparisons with the attainments of other individuals.

People tend to aspire for a future that is a little better than the present. Comparing themselves with others who are similar and in similar circumstances, they also aspire to outcomes as good as or a little better than the outcomes for those others. When aspirations are reached, especially if they are reached easily, they attend to adjust upward. When outcomes fall short of aspirations, the aspirations tend to adjust downward.

The gradual adaptation of aspirations to reality might be regarded as a variant on the search theory that was rejected earlier. However, adaptation of aspirations differs fundamentally from pseudo-optimization in that it makes no pretense of forming its expectations in any optimal way. Hence, unlike optimal search theory, a model of adaptive aspirations makes no excessive demands on the decision maker's computational capabilities.

Search Heuristics

Many human decisions are made in vast search spaces, where even satisfactory outcomes are scattered quite sparsely. With limited computational resources, success in solving problems and making satisfactory choices requires that the search be carried out very selectively. Selectivity is accomplished by drawing upon knowledge of the structure of the search space and of the relation of the points in that space that have been reached to possible solutions.

For example, finding a feasible solution in a space that is defined by constraints in the form of linear inequalities (as in linear programming) can be a rather simple hillclimbing exercise. Measures of how close the present situation is to meeting particular constraints can be used to steer the search in promising directions.

In most practical domains the rules of thumb, often called heuristics, that guide search provide no guarantees of correctness. Computer programs have been written, for example, that, when given empirical data, search for laws that fit the data. There is no guarantee that such laws exist or that the heuristics used to guide the search will actually find them. Nevertheless, in practice, programs of this kind have been quite successful.

One powerful heuristic, widely used, is means-ends analysis. The problem solver compares the present situation with a desired situation, notices which conditions for satisficing are unmet, then takes an action that experience shows is likely to satisfy at least one of these unsatisfied conditions. Another very general procedure, divide-and-conquer, separates the problem into subproblems and tries to find satisfactory solutions for each of these. A general heuristic for economic decision making is "Buy cheap and sell dear." Of course to apply it, the actor must know the proper meanings, for the given situation, of "cheap" and "dear."

Focus of Attention

Simplifying choice by attending to only a few of the most important aspects of the real-world situation is a universal aspect of human decision making. One might regard focusing attention as the most fundamental of all heuristics for choice. It was referred to earlier as "approximation," but the latter term understates its centrality and the vast distance that separates reality from human representations of it.

In explaining human choice, it is generally far more important to specify correctly what variables the decision makers are attending to than to make precise estimates of the optimal values of those variables. For example, public choice theory often postulates that people vote for candidates and measures that best advance their economic interests. A much more plausible postulate is that people vote for candidates and measures that *they perceive* as advancing their economic interests. The choices of a voter whose focus of attention is on inflation may be very different from those of a voter focusing on unemployment, or the foreign trade balance, or the level of savings.

People have reasons for what they do, reasons that can be usually be expressed in terms of a few salient variables. The focal variables are not fixed once and for all but change with shifts in focus of attention, shifts that are heavily influenced by social processes. Once the focal variables have been determined in a given situation, the exact procedure used to pseudo-optimize or satisfice is likely to have only second-order effects upon choice.

Implications for Economics

Since the theory of the firm and microeconomics in general are concerned with the decisions of economic actors, they need at their foundations a realistic theory of decision making processes. Research in cognitive psychology, in marketing, and to some extent in other areas of business economics has identified bounded rationality as a prominent and constraining feature of human decision making and has shown the central role of satisficing mechanisms in choice processes. Hence, microeconomic theory needs to be reformulated in terms of these concepts and its pseudo-optimization assumptions replaced by more realistic ones.

The need to bring satisficing into macroeconomics becomes most obvious when we direct attention away from static analysis, where formal theory has been most successful, toward economic dynamics. Understanding such medium-term phenomena as the business cycle, inflation, and unemployment calls for understanding human-bounded rationality. Understanding economic development and growth requires an understanding of the aspiration levels and satisficing heuristics of entrepreneurs and investors, who play a central role in the long-term dynamics of the economy.

Empirical Tests

Optimization theory is, at least at first appearance, a strong theory. Once its assumptions have been accepted, a great number of inferences can be drawn from them. All sorts of assertions can be made about the world without going out into the world to test whether they are empirically true. Modern equilibrium theory is a monument to the power of the utility maximization axioms when they are combined with the assumption of perfect competition.

In apparent contrast, satisficing theory has weaker implications. Before conclusions can be drawn from it, satisfaction levels must be specified along many dimensions, and the mechanisms for adjustment of aspiration levels defined, including the magnitudes of the adjustment parameters. For application to economic affairs, satisficing theory must be augmented by a great deal of empirical research to estimate the system parameters.

But the contrast in the requirements of the two approaches is more apparent than real. The conclusions that microeconomists, using optimization techniques, draw about the operation of firms, and the conclusions macroeconomists draw about employment or taxation, are extremely sensitive to the particulars of the models of reality that are postulated. The boundary conditions are not inferred from the theory but are exogenous, driving the theory. The soundness of the conclusions that can be drawn depends wholly on the empirical validity of the postulates of the model.

Satisficing models of economic phenomena, like optimizing models, gain their validity and their power of predicting and explaining economic phenomena from the empirical correctness of their basic postulates. This would seem obvious if it had not been denied so frequently in tracts on methodology in economics. Empirical research aimed at discovering sound postulates is critical to the progress of satisficing theory, and thereby to the future of economics.

References

Hogarth, R. M., *Judgment and Choice: the Psychology of Decision,* Wiley, New York, 1980; Radner, R., "Satisficing," *Journal of Mathematical Economics,* vol. 2, 1975, pp. 253–262; Simon, H. A., "A Behavioral Model of Rational Choice," *Quarterly Journal of Economics,* vol. 69, 1955, pp. 99–118, reprinted in Simon, 1982, chap. 7.2; Simon, H. A., *Models of Bounded Rationality,* M.I.T. Press, Cambridge, Mass., 1982; Simon, H. A., "Rational Choice and the Structure of the Environment," *Psychological Preview,* vol. 63, 1956, pp. 129–138, reprinted in Simon, 1982, chap. 7.3; Stigler, G. J., "The Economics of Information," *Journal of Political Economy,* vol. 69, 1967, pp. 213–225; Winter, S. G., "Satisficing, Selection and the Innovating Remnant," *Quarterly Journal of Economics,* vol. 85, 1971, pp. 237–261.

(*See also* Decision making in business: a behavioral approach; Second best)

Herbert A. Simon

Saving

All current income is divided between consumption and saving. Saving is the process of withholding current income for future use and reflects resources freed for investment in tangible and financial assets. When current outlays exceed current income, dissaving occurs. Over any time period, the major sectors of the economy—households, business, and government—may be saving or dissaving. Individuals save when their personal income exceeds their personal outlays, including taxes. In a similar way business saving is the difference between receipts and outlays, including any dividends paid out. Thus, business saving is equal to retained earnings. Government surpluses are a form of saving; deficits are a form of dissaving. In national income accounting, gross saving includes allowances for depreciation of tangible assets. Also, in an accounting sense, in any period saving equals investment. The channels through which gross saving flows into gross investment, including financial intermediation, are traced in the flow-of-funds accounts (FFA). Because saving is the primary source of funds for investment, it is the critical component for enhancing productivity and growth, the means by which a nation raises its standard of living. As a result, the understanding of saving behavior has been important for the study of a wide variety of topics in economics, including growth of the economy, tax analysis, and economic development.

The table below, from the National Income and Product Accounts (NIPA), shows the major categories of saving in the United States. Depreciation allowances are the largest component; they represent the funds needed to maintain the current capital stock, including the housing stock and business plant and equipment. Government saving is subject to a variety of political and economic considerations. Changes in tax rates, budget programs, and the state of the economy determine the size of federal, state, and local government surpluses (or deficits). Theories of saving have focused mostly on the determinants of personal saving, which is both a sizable component of the total and an essential element in understanding macroeconomic developments.

Components of U.S. Gross Saving, 1991
(billions of dollars)

Total	708
Private	902
Personal	200
Undistributed corporate profits	76
Depreciation allowances	626
Government	−136
Federal	−166
State and local	30
Memo: Gross domestic product	5,678

SOURCE: U.S. Department of Commerce, Bureau of Economic Analysis, *Survey of Current Business,* Washington, D.C., July 1992, p. 76.

Personal Saving

The most frequently used measure of personal saving is that provided in the NIPA. It is the difference between aftertax personal income and personal outlays. The latter are primarily composed of personal consumption expenditures and interest payments. Other measures of saving are available. A commonly cited alternative is provided in the flow-of-funds accounts (FFA). That measure of saving is compiled from the sum of investment in tangible and financial assets less the increase in financial liabilities (such as consumer and mortgage debt). The flow-of-funds measure differs from the NIPA measure in a number of ways, the most important being the treatment of outlays on consumer durables (net of depreciation) as a form of saving (investment). In the NIPA such spending is consumption only. As a result, personal saving in the FFA is higher than that in the NIPA.

From the NIPA, the personal saving rate—personal saving divided by disposable personal income—has varied widely since 1929. It was negative during the Great Depression in the early 1930s and as high as 25 percent during World War II, when consumption opportunities were limited. Since World War II the saving rate has averaged around 6½ percent, with little indication of any long-run trend. However, as shown on the chart below, the rate averaged about 7½ percent in the 1970s before drifting down over the 1980s in an irregular fashion. The peak in the 1980s was about 9½ percent at the end of the recession in 1981, and the low was 3½ percent in late 1989. In 1990 and 1991, the saving rate was somewhat higher—5 to 5½ percent. Nonetheless, persistently low saving rates over the past decade have been a concern of policymakers because they imply reduced funds for capital investment.

A number of factors have been shown to affect the saving rate over recent decades. The deceleration of inflation is believed to have damped saving rates as have increases in household net worth owing to the rise in the stock market and real estate values. Changes in the composition of income toward transfers and away from wages and salaries also may explain some of the decline of the personal saving rate in the 1980s relative to the 1970s. Finally, demographic effects may have changed the average saving rate. The proportion of heads of households over 65, for example, rose from 18 percent in 1960 to 21 percent in 1991. Because older households are expected to save less than younger households, this change may have had a depressing effect on the saving rate.

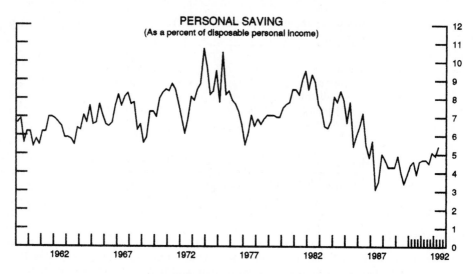

PERSONAL SAVING
(As a percent of disposable personal income)

The factors that influence personal saving are summarized in the life-cycle and permanent-income theories—the standard framework for analysis of saving and consumption. These theories assume that households consider both current and expected future income in their decisions about saving. The value of asset holdings are also important. The theories consider the fact that financial markets allow households to borrow against future income in order to alter the path of their consumption. It is assumed by both theories that households prefer to consume more rather than less but that they also prefer to smooth their consumption over their lifetime. The implications of the theories are that personal saving should be high when income is temporarily high and low when income is temporarily low, as households will keep consumption levels fairly even over relatively short periods, despite fluctuations in income. The theory also implies that saving by very young and very old will be low, while that for middle-age groups will be higher. Increases in wealth holdings reduce the saving, according to the theories.

References

Ando, Albert, and Franco Modigliani, "The 'Life Cycle' Hypothesis of Saving: Aggregate Implications and Tests," *American Economic Review,* vol. 53, March 1963, pp. 55–84; "Economic Statistics: Measuring Economic Performance," *Economic Report of the President Together with the Annual Report of the Council of Economic Advisers,* chap. 7 (715GPO: 1992), pp. 239–290; Friedman, Milton, *A Theory of the Consumption Function,* Princeton University Press for National Bureau of Economic Research, Princeton, N.J., 1957; Kennickell, Arthur B., "Demographics and Household Savings," Finance and Economics Discussion Series 123, Board of Governors of the Federal Reserve System, Division of Research and Statistics, Washington, D.C., 1990; Lipsey, Robert E., and Helen Stone Tice (eds.), *The Measurement of Saving, Investment and Wealth, Studies in Income and Wealth,* vol. 52, National Bureau of Economic Research, University of Chicago Press, Chicago, 1989; Wilcox, David W., "Household Spending and Saving: Measurement, Trends, and Analysis," *Federal Reserve Bulletin,* Board of Governors of the Federal Reserve System, Division of Research and Statistics, Washington, D.C., January 1991.

(*See also* Chicago school; Classical school; Consumer theory; Consumption function; Flow of funds; Income; Keynesian economics; National income accounting; Permanent income hypothesis)

Albert M. Teplin

Say's law of markets

The most popular definition of Say's law of markets is Keynes's concise dictum: Supply creates its own demand. J. Maynard Keynes interpreted the classicists, i.e., pre-1930s orthodox economists, and Jean Baptiste Say in particular, as stating that production (supply) generates income which will be used completely and instantaneously to purchase (demand) commodities, so supply creates its own demand at all times. Say's law holds in a barter economy where commodities are traded for commodities, but such is not the case in a monetary economy.

Production does indeed generate an exactly equal quantity of income. Current national income and product accounts utilize this identity. However, in a monetary economy income need not be spent completely and instantaneously on commodities. Individuals may prefer to hoard their income temporarily or expend it on financial assets. When this is the case, current supply exceeds the demand for commodities, and a general glut occurs. Firms respond by curtailing production, and incomes fall. If Keynes's version of Say's law held, however, recessions would never occur, since demand would always be sufficient to justify full-employment output, which is in the self-interest of firms to produce because full-employment output is also the profit-maximizing level of output. As technical progress and other factors cause output to increase over time, the economy would adjust automatically to its potential without need of government intervention. Economies unfortunately do not always produce maximum potential output. The existence of recessions is sufficient evidence to invalidate Say's law, as defined by Keynes. Government spending is the Keynesian remedy for recessions.

The law of markets is only a 4-page chapter in the first edition of Say's *Traité d'économie politique,* published in 1803. After being translated from the French, the book became one of the most popular economics texts in England and the United States largely because it was easier reading than Adam Smith's *Wealth of Nations.* However, the expository skills which served Say well as a popularizer of Smith were unsuited to the precise and clear expression of complex theory in a relatively new discipline like economics, where even the distinction between supply and demand as schedules versus quantities was not understood. Say spent more than a decade attempting to clarify and explain his law of markets without much success. In large part Keynes was merely echoing charges levied earlier by Malthus and other so-called unorthodox nineteenth-century economists. On the basis of some of Say's writings, the Malthus-Keynes version of the law of markets is not an unreasonable interpretation. However, by the fifth and final edition of the *Traité* published in 1826, an expanded chapter on markets contains several sentences indicating that supply necessarily creates its own demand only in the long run. Moreover, the Malthus-Keynes version clearly misinterprets the law as expressed by many of Say's supporters, most notably J. S. Mill (1844). Mill viewed his statement of the law as only an improvement on Say's exposition, without changing in any way Say's thought. By 1850 the debate over Say's law died from exhaustion without resolve, with the majority siding with Say and Mill.

When Keynes rekindled the debate approximately a century later, the weight of his international reputation, combined with the advantage of firing the first salvo, quickly convinced most economists, unfamiliar with the original sources, of the validity of Keynes's interpretation. Many current elementary textbooks still accept the Malthus-Keynes version of Say's law, thereby placing Say in a lower circle of economists. Keynes's interpretation did not go unchallenged for long, however. Joseph Schumpeter, the universally respected historian of economic analysis, strongly defended Say against the Malthus-Keynes criticism, and most advanced books now side with Schumpeter. The renewed emphasis on supply-side economics has further elevated Say.

The Mill-Schumpeter alternative version of Say's law states that demand was and will remain insatiable, so demand cannot explain the growth of output over time. Growth is due to increasing productive capacity. Insatiable demands are not always manifested; recessions do occur temporarily. Ultimately, however, the insatiable demands are revealed, and increasing production, however large, will be justified. If secular stagnation occurs, it is due to supply constraints. Developing countries can ignore demand and concentrate on transportation, education, and other supply-oriented policies. Workers in general need not be afraid of being permanently displaced by more productive machines. The machines will generate a profit which ultimately will be spent and lead to a rehiring of workers. Say's law also implies that recessions are not cured by restricting imports, which are income to foreigners and sustain our exports. Supply-reducing and make-work policies are to be avoided. Although this may seem obvious, import quotas, soil banks, and featherbedding are but three policies indicating ignorance of Say's law.

References

Keynes, J. M., *The General Theory of Employment, Interest and Money,* Harcourt Brace Jovanovich, New York, 1936, chaps. 2, 3; Mill, J. S., *Essays on Some Unsettled Questions of Political Economy,* Parker, London, 1844, essay 2; Mongiovi, G., "Notes on Say's Law, Classical Economics, and the Theory of Effective Demand," in *Contributions to Political Economy,* vol. 9, 1990, pp. 69–82; Say, J. B., *Treatise on Political Economy* (Eng. trans.), Grigg R. Elliott, Philadelphia, 1834, chap. 15; Schumpeter, J. A., *History of Economic Analysis,* Oxford University Press, New York, 1954, pp. 615–625; Sowell, T., *Say's Law: A Historical Analysis,* Princeton University Press, Princeton, N.J., 1972.

(*See also* Classical school; Supply-side economics)

Paul A. Meyer

Scarcity

In ordinary speech, the word *scarcity* is used to mean "rarity," "dearth," "famine," and the like. But in economics the word refers to the relationship between availability and desirability of a commodity. A commodity may be economically scarce even though units of it are extremely abundant, as are fast foods (hamburger sandwiches, fried chicken pieces, etc.) in the United States. Like all commodities that command positive money prices in modern societies, fast foods are economically scarce in the sense that there are always vastly more claimants for fast foods than could be satisfied if such foods were freely available at zero prices to all who wanted them.

Since a commodity is "any desirable good or service," economic scarcity might be said to follow almost by definition from the basic assumption that every individual has unlimited wants for commodities. The notion of scarcity, as conceived by economists, is, indeed, little more than a common-sense way to characterize societies in which the wants of individuals are vast relative to the resources available to satisfy them, i.e., societies in which virtually everyone, even the rich, would like "more." Scarcity thus appears to be an inherent condition of all societies, animal as well as human, about which we have historical knowledge. Such is, indeed, the central message of Darwin's classic account of "the struggle for survival"; Darwin's original ideas occurred to him, in fact, from reading the 1798 *Essay on Population* by the economist T. R. Malthus.

Economic scarcity entails not merely a limitation of commodities relative to wants but also a necessity to *ration* available commodities among potential claimants; hence, scarcity leads to competition among individuals for a share of available (but relatively limited) commodities—to a literal "struggle for survival" in cases where available commodities are required for continued biological existence. But it bears noting explicitly that the word *scarcity*, as used here, is *not* synonymous with "shortage." Crude oil, of which many billions of barrels are available in known reserves and of which many billions more are known to be dicoverable, is scarce because we want (and have a use for) vastly more crude oil than can be provided at zero prices. At current prices, however, there is no shortage of crude oil; one can acquire any desired quantity on short notice by paying the going market price.

As long as scarcity exists, some kind of rationing device is inevitable, because, without rationing, there simply aren't enough commodities to go around among all who want them. As for the nature of the rationing device, it may take any of countless different forms. Available supplies may be allocated among potential claimants according to relative wealth, strength, beauty, slyness, military power, initiative (first come, first served), patience (last to leave a long line), and so forth. When any kind of rationing occurs, it is natural to refer to the rationing process as "competition." So scarcity may be said to imply competition of one kind or another, although in some cases—as when space on particular stretches of city street is "rationed" by traffic lights, for example—the rationing process may seem so impersonal and so peaceful that it will be called not "competition" (which sounds aggressive and hectic) but "coordination." In this, as in many other instances, particular forms of "coordination," when examined closely, will be found to represent disguised forms of nonprice competition—effective ways of allocating limited resources among contending parties without the process ending up as a "war of all against all."

References

Heyne, Paul, *The Economic Way of Thinking*, 1st through 6th eds., Science Research Associates, Chicago, chap. 4.

(*See also* Distribution theory; Malthusian theory of population)

Robert W. Clower

Seasonal adjustment methods

The estimation of seasonal variations has always been a complex problem because seasonality varies and is not directly observable. Changes in economic phenomena result from many forces and, therefore, do not follow a set path with mathematical rigidity. The statistician's task has been to find methods that allow for constantly changing conditions. Estimations of the seasonal variations are currently mainly based on univariate time series models. The basic assumption for this approach is that the observed time series can be decomposed into a systematic part that is a well-determined function of time and into a random part that obeys a probability law. The random element is assumed to be identically distributed with constant mean, constant variance, and zero autocorrelation. A survey of developments in seasonal adjustment is given by Pierce (1980).

The majority of the methods for seasonal adjustment of economic time series fall into two broad categories. The first derives from general regression and linear estimation theory; the second depends mainly on the application of moving averages or linear smoothing filters. A very few exceptions do not fall into this broad classification, including probably the best known, the SABL (seasonal adjustment Bell Laboratories) method developed by Cleveland, Dunn, and Terpenning (1978). SABL uses a combination of moving averages and medians.

The optimality of the various seasonal adjustment methods depends on the fulfillment of the assumptions upon which each method relies. Because there is no unique model applicable to all time series in all situations, no method of estimation should be used uncritically as the one giving unique optimal solution. This, however, does not preclude a larger scope of applications for some methods than for others.

Regression Methods

The use of regression methods is not new. In the late 1930s, several statisticians proposed to fit polynomials by the least-squares method to estimate the seasonal variations. The regression methods assume that the systematic part of a time series can be approximated closely by simple functions of time over the entire span of the series. In general, two types of functions of time are considered. One is a polynomial of fairly low degree that fulfills the assumption that the economic phenomenon moves slowly, smoothly, and progressively through time (trend). The other is a linear combination of sines and cosines of different frequencies representing oscillations, strictly periodic or not, that also affect the total variation of the series (cycle and seasonals).

These functions are estimated by least-squares methods. For efficient estimates, the random component must be independent; otherwise, an appropriate version of generalized least squares must be applied. For certain regression functions, such as fixed periodic functions, polynomial time trends, and interaction of the two, ordinary least-squares estimates are asymptotically efficient if the random part is second-order stationary, that is, the mean and variance are constant and the covariance is a function only of the time lag. Therefore, if differences are taken to ensure stationarity, ordinary least squares are generally adequate. If the relationship among the components is multiplicative, the standard procedure is to take logarithms, and then differences, in order to transform the generating mechanism of the series into an additive form with a stationary random term.

The most common model specified for the decomposition of an economic time series by regression methods assumes a stable or linearly moving seasonality and a trend cycle represented by a polynomial of a relatively low degree. Unless the parameters are assumed to vary within the time span of the series, these models lack flexibility and imply a deterministic behavior of the components. For these reasons, regression methods have seldom been applied for time series decomposition; rather they have been applied to estimate seasonality in econometric models by inserting dummy variables that capture the seasonal variations of the related variables.

Linear Smoothing Techniques

The seasonal adjustment of economic time series with linear smoothing filters, or moving averages, was known in the early 1920s but seldom applied. One of the main reasons for this fact was that the best-known seasonal annihilator, the centered 12-month moving average, was found to be a poor trend-cycle estimator.

The majority of the seasonal adjustment methods today officially adopted by statistical agencies are based in linear smoothing procedures. These methods assume that systematic components of a time series do not fluctuate greatly in any small interval of time but still cannot be well approximated by simple functions of time over the entire range of the series. The assumptions are made for subintervals. They are of a local character, whereas those of regression methods concern the entire interval. Methods based on linear smoothing techniques can adequately estimate seasonal variations, trends, and cycles that change in a stochastic manner, that is, as new observations enter into the series, the level and/or the slope of the systematic components change adaptively.

The simplest method of smoothing data is to take a moving weighted average of the data and center the results. The weights are moved one position to the right of the observed data to obtain successive smoothed values. The weights can be obtained by fitting polynomials or by summation formulas developed by actuaries. In the first case, the weights are functions of the length of the moving average, say, $2m + 1$, and of the degree of the polynomial to be fitted, say $p < 2m + 1$.

However, the basic principle of the summation formulas is the combination of operations of differencing and summation in such a manner that when differencing above a certain order is neglected, these formulas will reproduce the functions operated on. Most of the methods based on moving averages or linear smoothing filters are descriptive *nonparametric* procedures in the sense that they lack explicit models for each unobserved component.

In most recent years, however, several attempts have been made to develop *model-based* methods where univariate statistical models are explicitly assumed for each component. The explicit models mainly belong to the Gaussian ARIMA (autoregressive integrated moving average) type (Box and Jenkins, 1970) or some variants from it. Two procedures have been followed for the development of model-based seasonal adjustment methods. In the first, each of the unobserved components, trend, cycle, seasonality, and irregulars is assumed to follow a Gaussian stochastic process, and in the other procedure, the observed data are assumed to follow an ARIMA model, and from it similar types of models are deduced for each component. Engle (1978) called the first approach "structural," given its similarity to the problem of identification of structures consistent with a given reduced form in econometric models. The second approach is referred to as the "reduced form," again, given its analogy to that which is observable or identifiable from the data in econometrics. The first structural models were based on simple regression models where each component was assumed to follow a deterministic function of time. Extension of simple regression models to stationary and nonstationary stochastic processes were made by Hannan (1967), Hannan, Terrell and Tuckwell (1970), Grether and Nerlove (1970), Pagan (1973, 1975), Engle (1978), Akaike (1980), Schlicht (1981), Kitagawa and Gersch (1984), Harvey (1984), Burridge and Wallis (1984), Durbin (1984), and Maravall (1985).

The two more notable examples of the reduced-form approach for seasonal adjust-ment are the model-based ARIMA methods developed by Burman (1980) and Hillmer and Tiao (1982).

Structural and reduced-form model-based seasonal adjustment methods have sel-dom been used by statistical agencies or for practical purposes. Most statistical agen-cies apply the Census method II X-11 variant developed by Shiskin, Young, and Musgrave (1967) or the X-11-ARIMA method developed by Dagum (1980). The basic assumptions of these two methods are implicit in the kind of moving averages they use for the decomposition. These moving averages first detrend the data and then remove the seasonal variations. For central observations (approximately all the val-ues of the series except those corresponding to the first and last three years), both methods make the assumption that the trend cycle follows a cubic within the span of one or two years depending on the amount of irregular variations, and that the seasonal variations, for each month separately, can be well approximated by a straight line over the span of seven years. These assumptions are adequate for a large class of economic time series. For current observations, however, the X-11 moving averages approximate well only a straight line for the trend cycle and a constant for the seasonals. However, the X-11-ARIMA uses a flexible combination of weights that adapts to the series in question. These weights capture the most recent movements of the series. The weights result from the combination of the extrapolation of ARIMA models that fit and extrapolate well with the fixed smoothing filters of the X-11 method.

The properties of the combined linear filters applied to obtain a seasonal estimate have been analyzed by Wallis (1974 and 1982) and Young (1968) for the X-11 variant and by Dagum (1983) for the X-11-ARIMA. It is inherent to all linear smoothing pro-cedures that the end observations cannot be smoothed with the same set of symmet-ric filters as applied to central observations. Because of this, the estimates for recent observations must be revised as more data are incorporated into the series. The pat-terns of revisions introduced by the various combined filters have been extensively studied by Dagum (1982 and 1987).

References

Akaike, H., "Seasonal Adjustment by Bayesian Modelling," *Journal of Time Series Analysis,* vol. 1, 1980, pp. 1–13; Box, G. E. P., and G. M. Jenkins, *Time Series Analysis: Forecasting and Con-trol,* Holden-Day, San Francisco, 1970; Burman, J. P., "Seasonal Adjustment by Signal Extrac-tion," *Journal of the Royal Statistical Society,* ser. A, vol. 143, 1980, pp. 321–337; Burridge P., and K. F. Wallis, "Unobserved-Components Models for Seasonal Adjustment Filters," *Journal of Business and Economic Statistics,* vol. 2, no. 4, 1984, pp. 350–359; Cleveland, W. S., D. M. Dunn, and F. Terpenning, "Graphical Analysis of Seasonality and Nonlinear Seasonal Adjust-ment," in A. Zellner (ed.), *Seasonal Analysis of Economic Time Series,* U.S. Government Print-ing Office, 1978, pp. 201–231; Dagum, E. B., *The X-11-ARIMA Seasonal Adjustment Method,* Statistics Canada Catalogue no. 12-564E, Ottawa, 1980; Dagum, E. B., "The Effects of Asymmet-ric Filters on Seasonal Factors Revisions," *Journal of the American Statistical Association,* vol. 77, 1982, pp. 732–738; Dagum, E. B., "Spectral Properties of the Concurrent and Forecasting Linear Filters of the X11ARIMA Method," *Canadian Journal of Statistics,* vol. 11, 1983, pp. 73–90; Dagum, E. B., "Monthly versus Annual Revisions of Concurrent Seasonally Adjusted Series," in I. B. MacNeill and G. J. Umphrey (eds.), *Time Series and Econometric Modelling,* Kluwer, Dordrecht, 1987, pp. 131–146; Durbin, J., "Present Position and Potential Develop-ments. Some Personal Views in Time Series Analysis," *Journal of the Royal Statistical Society,* ser. A, 1984, pp. 161–173; Engle, R. F., "Estimating Structural Models of Seasonality," *Seasonal Analysis of Economic Time Series,* in A. Zellner (ed.), U.S. Government Printing Office, 1978, pp. 281–297; Grether, D. M., and M. Nerlove, "Some Properties of 'Optimal' Seasonal Adjustment," *Econometrica,* vol. 38, 1970, pp. 682–703; Hannan, E., "Measuring of a Wandering Signal and Noise," *Journal of Applied Probability,* vol. 4, 1967, pp. 90–102; Hannan, E., R. D. Terell, and N. Tuckwell, "The Seasonal Adjustment of Economic Time Series," *International Economic Review,* vol. 11, 1970, pp. 24–52; Harvey, A. C., "A Unified View of Statistical Forecasting Procedures," *Journal of Forecasting,* vol. 3, no. 3, 1984, pp. 245–275; Hillmer, S. C., and G. Tiao, "An ARIMA Model-Based Approach to Seasonal Adjustment," *Journal of the American Statistical Association,* vol. 77, 1982, pp. 63–70; Kitagawa, G., and W. Gersch, "A Smoothness Prior-State Space Modeling of Time Series with Trend and Seasonality," *Journal of the American Statistical Association,* vol. 79, 1984, pp. 378–389; Maravall, A., "On Structural Time Series Models and the Characterization of Components," *Journal of Business and Economic Statistics,* vol. 3, no. 4, 1985, pp. 350–355; Pagan, A., "Efficient Estimation of Models with Composite Disturbance Terms," *Journal of Econometrics,* vol. 1, 1973, pp. 329–340; Pagan, A., "A Note on the Extraction of Components from Time Series," *Econometrica,* vol. 43, 1975, pp. 163–168; Pierce, D., "A Survey of Recent Developments in Seasonal Adjustment," *American Statistician,* vol. 34, 1980, pp. 125–134; Schlicht, E., "A Seasonal Adjustment Principle and a Seasonal Adjustment Method Derived from this Principle," *Journal of American Statistical Association,* vol. 76, 1981, pp. 374–378; Shiskin, J., A. H. Young, and J. C. Musgrave, "The X-11 Variant of the Census Method II Seasonal Adjustment Program," Technical Paper 15, U.S. Bureau of the Census, Washington, D.C., 1967; Wallis, K. F., "Seasonal Adjustment and Relations between Variables," *Journal of the American Statistical Association,* vol. 69, 1974, pp. 18–31; Wallis, K. F., "Seasonal Adjustment and Revision of Current Data: Linear Filters for the X-11 Method," *Journal of the Royal Statistical Society,* ser. A, vol. 145, 1982, pp. 74–85; Young, A. H., "Linear Approximations to the Census and B.L.S. Seasonal Adjustment Methods," *Journal of the American Statistical Association,* vol. 63, 1968, pp. 445–457.

(*See also* Index numbers; Regression analysis in business and economics; Seasonal variations in economic time series; Secular trend; Statistical methods in economics and business, an overview; Time series analysis)

Estela Bee Dagum

Seasonal variations in economic time series

A great deal of information on economic activity occurs in the form of time series where observations are dependent and the nature of this dependence is of interest in itself. The time series are generally compiled for consecutive and equal periods, such as weeks, months, quarters, or years.

Traditionally, four types of movements have been distinguished in the analysis of economic time series, namely, (1) the trend, (2) the cycle, (3) the seasonal variations, and (4) the irregular fluctuations. The feasibility of the decomposition is basic for time series analysis, the study of the cycle and economic growth and the study of seasonality. The four components are not directly observable, and, therefore, assumptions must be made on their behavioral pattern.

The trend corresponds to a variation persisting over a long period. The trend tends to be associated with the structural causes of the phenomenon in question. In some cases, the trend shows a steady growth; in others, it may move downward as well as upward.

The cycle is a quasi-periodic oscillation characterized by alternating periods of expansion and contraction. It is generally associated with the current state of the economy and referred to as the "business cycle." It lasts from 3 to 4 years on average. For much analytical work, the trend and the cycle are combined because for series covering relatively short periods, the trend loses importance.

The seasonal variations represent the effect of the climatic and institutional events that repeat more or less regularly each year. They affect the evolution of economic time series recorded only for periods of less than a year.

The irregular fluctuations represent unforeseeable movements related to events of all kinds. They have a stable random appearance, but, in some cases, extreme values may be present. These extreme values, or outliers, have identifiable causes, such as strikes or unseasonal weather, and, therefore, can be distinguished from the much smaller irregular variations.

A large class of flows and stocks series related to production, shipments, sales, and inventories are also affected by other types of variations such as trading-day or calendar effects. Trading-day variations represent the "within-month" fluctuations due to the number of times a particular day or days of the week occur in a calendar month. These variations are systematic and may strongly influence month-to-month comparisons.

Nature of Seasonal Variations

There is no important economic series which shows only trend, or only seasonal variations, or only irregulars. These components are interrelated, and, for most economic series, they influence one another. Among these components, the influence of the seasonal fluctuations in human activity has long been recognized. The organization of society, the means of production and communication, the habits of consumption, and other social and religious events have been strongly conditioned by both climatic and conventional seasons. The seasonal variations in agriculture and construction, the high pre-Easter and pre-Christmas retail sales are well known. There are three main characteristics of seasonality: (1) The phenomenon repeats each year with certain regularity, but it may evolve; (2) seasonality can be estimated and separated from the other factors that affect the total variations of the series; and (3) seasonality is caused mainly by noneconomic forces, exogenous to the economic system.

It is generally accepted that there are four causes of seasonality in economic time series, namely, the calendar, timing decisions, weather, and expectations. Although the causes of seasonality are generally exogenous to the economic system, human intervention can modify their extent and nature. For example, seasonal variations in the automobile industry are affected by manufacturers' decisions regarding the extent of model changeover each year.

Changes in the seasonal patterns of a given series can be due to several reasons. A decline in the importance of the primary sector in the gross national product modifies seasonal patterns in the economy as a whole, as does a change in the geographical distribution of industry in a country extending over several climatic zones. Changes in technology alter the importance of climatic factors. For most economic time series, an evolving seasonality is more the rule than the exception. This is particularly true for long series of 20 years or more. The assumptions of stable seasonality, that is, of seasonality that repeats exactly every year, is good for a few series only. Depending on the main causes of seasonality, the seasonal variations can change slowly or rapidly, gradually or abruptly, and in a deterministic manner or in a stochastic manner.

Various models have been proposed for gradual changes in seasonal variations whether of a stochastic or of a deterministic type. These models have been grouped into two main categories—models that assume that the generating process of seasonal variations varies in amplitude only and those that assume that the generating process varies in both amplitude and phase. The assumption that seasonality changes gradually, slowly, and in a stochastic manner is perhaps the most widely applied today.

A second characteristic of seasonality is that the phenomenon can be separated from the other forces—trend, cycle, and irregulars—that influence the movement of the series and that it can be estimated adequately. The seasonal variations are distinguished from trend by their oscillating character, from the cycle by being confined within the limits of an annual period, and from the irregulars by being systematic.

Finally, the third characteristic, i.e., that the main causes of seasonality are exogenous to the economic system, is one of the main reasons for the removal of seasonality from the observed series to produce a seasonally adjusted series. The adjusted series thus reflects only variations in the trend, the cycle, and the irregulars. The removal of the seasonal variations from a time series, however, does not indicate how the series would have moved had there been no seasonal variations; rather, it shows more clearly the trend cycle abstracted from seasonality.

Seasonally Adjusted Data and Economic Analysis

The information given by seasonally adjusted series plays an important role in the analysis of current economic conditions, particularly in determining the stage of the cycle at which the economy stands. Such knowledge is useful in forecasting subsequent cyclical movements and provides the basis for decision making to alter the level of economic activity. It is particularly important around turning points because, for example, failure to recognize a downturn in the business cycle may lead to the adoption of policies to curb expansion when, in fact, a recession is under way.

In the absence of seasonally adjusted data, analysts who wish to get a picture of the economic situation undistorted by exogenous variables related to seasonal variations may make comparisons with the same month of the year before. Such comparisons however, show only what has happened a year after, not what was happening during the year and not what is happening currently. To evaluate the current state of the economy, the analyst should be able to measure cyclical changes for each month over less than a one-year span, for example, to compare May with April or May with February (three-month span).

Decision making based on unadjusted data can lead to wrong policies, especially if the series is strongly affected by seasonal variations. The average absolute monthly percentage change in seasonal variation can be much greater than the corresponding changes in the irregular or trend cycle. Several studies of selected economic indicators for the United States show that the absolute average month-to-month percentage change in the seasonal component runs between three and seven times the absolute average percentage change in the trend cycle or in the irregulars over the same time spans.

The measurement of seasonality is also very useful for short-term decision making. The knowledge of the seasonal pattern of economic activities facilitates planning for the utilization of economic resources during periods of peak loads and inactivity. This knowledge can also be applied for better integration of economic activities characterized by opposite seasonal patterns. Resources which formerly served only one purpose can serve additional purposes and thus reduce the burden imposed by seasonality on the whole economy.

References

Dagum, Estela Bee, "The Estimation of Changing Seasonal Variations in Economic Time Series," in K. Namboodiri (ed.), *Survey Sampling and Measurement,* Academic Press, New York, 1978, pp. 217–228; Kendall, Maurice G., and A. Stuart, *The Advanced Theory of Statistics,* vol. 3, Hafner, New York, 1966; Zellner, Arnold (ed.), *Seasonal Analysis of Economic Time Series,* U.S. Bureau of the Census, Washington, D.C., 1978.

(*See also* Seasonal adjustment methods; Secular trend)

Estela Bee Dagum

Second best

An economic policy or policy outcome is described as "second best" when it is desired to emphasize both that it is the best available under the circumstances and that a "first best" exists that is preferable but not feasible in the present case because of important structural or other strongly embedded constraints. It is emphatically not meant to imply that the policy is second *class* or simply inferior because of poor planning or execution.

All economic behavior is constrained, and so is a first-best policy or outcome— constrained by resource availability, technology, institutions, and so on. What makes for a second-best situation is the existence of additional constraints which *could* be removed but not by the policymaker, who must accept them as given. The term second best is used to draw attention to the additional constraints imposed on the policymaker, to make a point. Almost all actual economic policy is second best in the sense being used here, but the context does not generally call for the point to be made or the term to be used.

It is well known, for example, that a redistribution considered desirable on, say, moral grounds can be efficiently attained by "lump-sum" taxation (taxes specific to each individual which are totally independent of that individual's behavior). This is the first-best solution. However, for political or even informational reasons, such taxation may not be possible, and the term second best is widely used in the public finance literature to mean the unavailability of lump-sum taxes. In their absence, any one of many income tax schedules could redistribute income while satisfying the political or other constraints but with a loss of efficiency due to individuals substituting untaxed leisure for taxed work. The second-best solution would be that tax schedule which provides the best mix of redistribution and efficiency according to some appropriate criterion.

To give another example, the economy satisfies the condition for efficiency in the mix of goods it produces if price equals marginal cost in all industries. But suppose we have one sector of the economy for which this is true, another sector dominated by monopoly practices (in which price is above marginal cost), and a third sector under public control. What is the optimal pricing policy for the public sector? Should it adopt marginal cost pricing? The first-best solution in this case is to eliminate the monopoly pricing practices, then set the public sector prices at marginal cost. But if the monopoly is entrenched, perhaps for political reasons, the second-best public sector policy is designed to give the best output mix for the economy subject to the persistence of the monopoly. In general, this will not be marginal cost pricing.

There were scattered observations in the literature of neoclassical economics prior to the 1950s that some distortionary policies, considered undesirable in general, might nevertheless be appropriate in particular circumstances. The examples included countervailing monopolies, customs unions with tariffs, and nonuniform indirect taxes. Lipsey and Lancaster (1956) showed that such examples were special cases of a general theory of the second best which could be paraphrased as follows:

> *Even when universal satisfaction of the traditional marginal conditions for Pareto efficiency (price ratios equal marginal rates of substitution equal marginal rates of transformation) gives a first-best solution, the second-best solution may require that they not be satisfied in some sectors if they cannot be satisfied in all.*

Note that the original Lipsey-Lancaster paper had a precautionary purpose—to warn against the blanket piecemeal application of policy rules generally accepted as desirable to situations in which they could not be applied universally. This is sometimes referred to as "negative" second-best theory, even though the arguments were established by outlining positive solutions to second-best problems. The term "positive" second-best theory is sometimes used (especially in the literature on optimal taxation) to emphasize attempts to compute second-best solutions.

Working through the logic of a simple second-best problem is the best way to illustrate the reasoning involved and the conceptual and practical problems of implementation. Consider the second of the examples given above, that of the three-sector economy with entrenched monopoly. If only the competitive and monopoly sectors were operating, the monopoly good would be relatively overpriced (and the competitive good underpriced) relative to resource costs. Ignoring the distributive effects of monopoly profit (which can be taxed away), the economy is inefficient because there is too much of the (relatively) cheap competitive good and too little of the expensive monopoly good, as compared with the optimal mix that would result from universal marginal cost prices.

Now consider the public sector, and suppose its output is a substitute for both the competitive and monopoly goods. If the public sector output is priced at marginal cost, then, like the competitive sector initially, it will be too cheap relative to the monopoly good, and there will be too much of the competitive and public sector output relative to the monopoly sector. If priced at the same markup over marginal cost as the monopoly good, there will be too little relative to the competitive good. To find the appropriate policy, we must optimize our welfare criterion subject to all the usual constraints of technology and resources plus the additional constraint that monopolistic behavior will rule in one sector. In general, the solution will be that the public sector should price above marginal cost but not as far above as the monopoly.

The implementation problem is that the optimal choice of the public sector markup over marginal cost in the range between zero and the monopoly level depends on the exact demand and cost relationships between the sectors. Generic descriptive policies such as "price at marginal cost" or "leave it to the competitive market" may hold for first-best solutions in simple economies but not for second best. However, note that similar difficulties of implementation arise in first-best policies for real-world economies with important externalities and/or significant scale economies in production or consumption, in which generic rules also fail.

Typically, the additional constraints that make an optimizing problem second best rather than first best involve behavioral relationships, themselves generally resulting from optimization within limited subsets of the economy. In optimal income tax problems, for example, individuals are assumed to make a preferred labor-leisure choice subject to the tax schedule, and the schedule must be optimally chosen subject to this. Although the technical difficulties of solving such problems are considerable, strategic feedback can be ignored, since any individual has negligible weight. Collusion among individuals with similar incomes can change this, of course, and then a different approach is required.

In some important contexts, strategic behavior cannot be ignored. For illustrative purposes, the monopoly in the three-sector problem is assumed to adopt a mechanical pricing rule (a fixed percentage above marginal cost, for example), based on appropriate behavior in the absence of intervention. Any realistic analysis of such a case would, however, consider the monopolist's ability to affect the outcome by a change in behavior, and the sophisticated second-best solution would require a game-theoretic approach in which both the monopolist and the policymaker take each other's potential reactions into account.

Sometimes it is possible to achieve first-best results with what are apparently second-best policies. If the monopolist in the above example adheres to a fixed percentage markup over marginal cost whatever the policymaker does, and if all income is spent, the first-best result can be achieved by setting the public sector price the same percentage above marginal cost as the monopolist and imposing a sales tax of that same percentage on the competitive sector, provided monopoly profit is taxed away and all the revenues are returned to consumers in appropriate shares. It is also possible for the economic structure to be such that second-best policy is simply a limited application of the first-best, as for example when the deviant sector is separable in both production and consumption from the other sectors.

The first best is usually taken to be well defined in the sense that there is agreement on which constraints considered are taken to be irremovable and unchangeable (mainly resources, technology, and tastes). But there is enormous variety in the kinds of additional constraints that make the problem one of second best and thus in the policies that may be called second best. There are even layers of such solutions when constraints are added on top of those in the second-best case. Occasionally a policy or outcome may be called "third best" or "nth best" to emphasize the load of additional constraints being carried. Generally, however, second best is used quite broadly to cover all that is not first best.

References

Davis, O. A., and A. B. Whinston, "Piecemeal Policy in the Theory of Second Best," *Review of Economic Studies,* vol. 34, 1967, pp. 323–331; Diamond, P. A., and J. A. Mirrlees, "Optimal Taxation and Public Production," *American Economic Review,* vol. 61, 1971, pp. 8–27, 261–278; Dixit, A. K., "Welfare Effects of Tax and Price Changes," *Journal of Public Economics,* vol. 4, 1975, pp. 103–123; Faith, R., and E. Thompson, "A Paradox in the Theory of Second Best," *Economic Inquiry,* vol. 19, 1981, pp. 235–244; Guesnerie, R., "Production of the Public Sector and Taxation in a Simple Second Best Model," *Journal of Economic Theory,* vol. 10, 1975, pp. 127–156; Hagan, K. P., "Optimal Pricing in Public Firms in an Imperfect Market Economy," *Scandinavian Journal of Economics,* vol. 81, 1979, pp. 475–493; Lipsey, R. G., and K. J. Lancaster, "The General Theory of Second Best," *Review of Economic Studies,* vol. 24, 1956, pp. 11–32; Negishi, T., "The Perceived Demand Curve in the Theory of Second Best," *Review of Economic Studies,* vol. 34, 1967, pp. 315–321.

(*See also* Satisficing)

Kelvin J. Lancaster

Secular trend

The concept of secular trend has been used in economics to represent smooth variations over a long period of years. The causes of this movement are mainly attributed to the growth of the population, technological progress, capital accumulation, and new ways of organization. For the majority of economic time series, the evolution of the trend tends to be smooth, gradual, and either stochastic or deterministic in character. There are cases, however, where the evolution abruptly changes its level and/or its slope. When this happens, the economic time series is said to have a structural change, that is, a new structural composition. To this type of phenomenon belongs what René Thom calls a "catastrophe." Structural changes do not always manifest themselves in an abrupt manner. The higher the aggregation level of the phenomenon that the series represents, the more difficult it is for a structural change to produce sudden breaks in the trend. For example, the substitution of old firms by new ones that utilize a more advanced state of technology rarely will show abrupt changes at the industry aggregate level. However, a technological change affecting the mode of production of a firm will introduce discontinuity in its trend. The longer the period for which an economic series is recorded, the higher is the probability of structural changes affecting the period's trend.

The measurement of the secular trend is based on the assumption that (1) the process has structural stability and (2) the data are homogeneous through time. The trend is not an isolated movement. Its presence in economic phenomena is affected by other movements that contribute to the total variation of the observations. The other best-known types of movements are (1) the cycle, (2) the seasonal variations, and (3) the irregulars. The cycle is a movement of quasi-periodic appearance related to the fluctuations of the economic activity, alternately increasing and decreasing. The cycle takes the graphical form of a function that rotates around the trend. The seasonal variations represent the effect of climatic and institutional events that repeat with certain regularity over a year. The irregulars represent unforeseeable events of all kinds, and generally the irregulars have a stable random appearance, although some extreme values may be present. These components of the trend are not directly observable, and assumptions must be made as to their behavioral pattern.

Methods of Trend Estimation

The estimation of the secular trend has always posed a serious problem to statisticians. The problem is not one of mathematical or analytical complexity but of conceptual complexity. This problem exists because the trend is not a directly observable variable, and its definition as a smooth, broad movement of an economic phenomenon over a long term is statistically vague. The concept of "long" in this connection is relative, and what is measured as trend for a given span might well be part of a long cycle once the series is significantly extended. To avoid this problem of complexity, statisticians have resorted to two simple solutions: One consists of estimating trend and cyclical fluctuations together, calling this combined movement the *trend cycle;* the other consists of defining the trend in terms of the series length, denoting it as the longest movement, periodic or not.

The simplest model assumed for an economic time series is the regression or error model, where the series is assumed to be composed of a smooth deterministic trend and an independent random component (Anderson, 1971). The most common representation of the trend is by means of functions of time, whether polynomials of low degree or of transcendental functions. Polynomial trend equations take the form

$$Y_t = a + bt + ct^2 + dt^3 + \ldots + ht^n \tag{1}$$

The straight line is the particular case where only a and b are different from zero. In such a case, the trend has a constant slope; it changes by a constant amount per unit of time. When the term ct^2 is added, the trend follows a curve where c measures the rate of change in the slope at the origin. If the polynomial trend is a cubic, i.e., d is not zero, the curve changes direction twice.

The variate-difference method has been used primarily to examine the degree of the polynomial of best fit, a point reached when the sum of squares of the residuals does not change significantly for higher differences. This method provides a kind of lower limit of the degree of the polynomial which will represent the trend. Polynomial deterministic trends are generally used for series of up to 30 years, but for larger spans other functions seem to be more appropriate. Three of the most widely applied functions called "growth curves," are the modified exponential, the Gompertz curve, and the logistic.

The modified exponential trend is written as follows:

$$Y_t = a + bc^t \tag{2}$$

where a is real
$\quad b \neq 0$
$\quad c > 0$
$\quad c \neq 1$

This function is a modification of the exponential function $Y = bc^t$ to which a constant has been added. For this type of function, the proportionate rate of increase or decrease of the trend is constant.

$$Y_t = ab^c c^t \tag{3}$$

where $a > 0$
$\quad b > 0$
$\quad c > 0$
$\quad b \neq 1$
$\quad c \neq 1$

and its log transformation becomes

$$\log Y_t = \log a + c^t(\log b) \tag{4}$$

where $c > 0$
$\quad c \neq 1$

and the logistic function is

$$Y_t = \frac{1}{a + bc^t} \tag{5}$$

where $c > 0$
$\quad c \neq 1$

These two types of functions have basically the same shape—an elongated S that indicates the pattern of growth. They are also called saturation curves because the growth converges with a finite upper limit.

The functions (1) through (5) are generally fitted to the observed series by least-squares procedures. If the trend is a smooth function of time but still cannot be well approximated by simple functions over the whole range of the series, then linear smoothing techniques can be applied. Smoothing a time series provides a representation of the trend at a given point in time by a weighted average of the observed values over that point. The weighted average of the random elements will generally be a small value, and, hence, the weighted average of the observed data will estimate the trend well. The weighted average is applied in a moving manner to obtain successive smoothed values. The longer the span of the average, the smoother is the fitted curve.

Another kind of model that can be postulated for trend estimation is a stochastic process. This model implies that the random disturbances are autocorrelated and that time affects both the systematic and nonsystematic part of the process. Trends subject to stochastic changes in level and/or slope can be approximated by stochastic processes models. The autoregressive integrated moving averages (ARIMA) processes have been intensively studied, and their application to concrete cases has increased significantly in recent years (Box and Jenkins, 1970). The ARIMA processes seem to be appropriate for trend estimation over a relatively short period.

Two simple models for trend estimation are the IMA (0,1,1) and the IMA (0,2,2), which take the form, respectively,

$$y_t = y_{t-1} + a_t - \theta a_{t-1} \tag{6}$$

where $\mid \theta \mid < 1$

or equivalently

$$(1 - B)\, y_t = (1 - \theta B)\, a_t$$

where $By_t = y_{t-1}$

and

$$y_t = 2y_{t-1} - y_{t-2} + a_t - \theta_t a_{t-1} - \theta_2 a_{t-2}$$

for

$$\theta_2 + \theta_1 < 1 \tag{7}$$
$$\theta_2 - \theta_1 < 1$$
$$1 < \theta_2 < 1$$

An equivalent representation of (7) is

$$(1 - B)^2 y_t = (1 - \theta_1 B - \theta_2 B^2) a_t$$

The a_t is a purely random process which may be regarded as a series of random shocks that drives the trend. The ARIMA models allow for the inclusion of a deterministic polynomial trend of any degree d.

For a crude approximation, θ can be interpreted as the extent to which the residuals incorporate themselves in the subsequent history of the trend. As θ approaches 1 in equation (6), the maximum impact of the residuals on the subsequent evolution of the series is approached.

For $\theta = 1$, model (6) reduces to a type of random walk model which has been mainly used for financial data such as stock market prices (Granger and Morgenstern, 1970). In such models, as time increases, the random variables tend to oscillate about their mean value with an ever-increasing amplitude. The use of random walk models in business and economic series has received considerable attention during recent years to modelize trend behavior and/or seasonal variations (see, for example Nelson and Plosser, 1982; Harvey, 1985; Dagum and Quenneville, 1991).

Economists and statisticians are also often interested in the "short"-term trend of socioeconomic time series. The short-term trend generally includes business cycle fluctuations and is referred to as "trend cycle." Most seasonal adjustment methods such as Census method II X-11 variant (Shiskin, Young, and Musgrave, 1967) and X-11-ARIMA (Dagum, 1980) estimate stochastic trends using linear filters applied to the observations. Studies on the properties of these trend-cycle estimators have been made by Young (1968) and Dagum and Laniel (1987). Other important studies on stochastic trend estimators have been made by Burman (1980), Cleveland and Tiao (1976), Kenny and Durbin (1982), and Pierce (1975).

References

Anderson, T. W., *The Statistical Analysis of Time Series,* Wiley, New York, 1971; Box, G. E. P., and G. H. Jenkins, *Time Series Analysis: Forecasting and Control,* Holden-Day, San Francisco, 1970; Burman, J. P., "Seasonal Adjustment by Signal Extraction," *Journal of the Royal Statistical Society,* ser. A, vol. 143, 1980, pp. 321–337; Cleveland, W. P., and G. C. Tiao, "Decomposition of Seasonal Time Series: A Model for the Census X11 Program," *Journal of the American Statistical Association,* vol. 71, 1976, pp. 581–587; Dagum, E. B., *The X11ARIMA Seasonal Adjustment Method,* Catalogue no. 12-564. Statistics Canada, Ottawa, 1980; Dagum, E. G., and N. J. D. Laniel, "Revisions of Trend-cycle Estimators of Moving Averages Seasonal Adjustment Methods," *Journal of Business and Economic Statistics,* vol. 5, 1987, pp. 177–189; Dagum, E. B., and B. Quenneville, "Dynamic Linear Models for Time Series Components," *Journal of Econometrics* annual issue, vol. 53, 1991, pp. 333–351; Granger, C. W. J., and O. C. Morgenstern, *Predictability of Stock Market Prices,* D. C. Heath, Lexington, Mass., 1970; Harvey, W. G., "Trends and Cycles in Macroeconomic Time Series," *Journal of Business and Economic Statistics,* vol. 3, 1985, pp. 216–227; Kenny, P. B., and J. Durbin, "Local Trend Estimation and Seasonal Adjustment of Economic and Social Time Series," *Journal of Royal Statistical Society,* ser. A, vol. 145, 1982, pp. 1–41; Nelson, C. R., and C. J. Plosser, "Trends and Random Walks in Macroeconomic Time Series: Some Evidences and Implications," *Journal of Monetary Economics,* vol. 10, 1982, pp. 139–162; Pierce, D. A., "On Trend and Autocorrelation," *Communication Statistics,* vol. 4, 1975, pp. 163–175; Shiskin, J., A. H. Young, and J. C. Musgrave, *The X11 Variant Census Method II Seasonal Adjustment Program,* Technical Paper no. 15, U.S. Bureau of the Census, Washington, D.C., 1967; Young, A. H., "Linear Approximations of the Census and BLS Seasonal Adjustment Methods," *Journal of the American Statistical Association,* vol. 63, 1968, pp. 445–471.

(*See also* Index numbers; Random walk hypothesis; Regression analysis in business and economics; Seasonal adjustment methods; Seasonal variations in economic time series; Statistical methods in economics and business, an overview; Time series analysis)

Camilo Dagum and Estela Bee Dagum

Securities and Exchange Commission

The Securities and Exchange Commission (SEC) is an independent, federal administrative agency that regulates the securities industry. Composed of five members appointed by the President, the SEC was created by the Securities Exchange Act of 1934 to administer and enforce federal securities laws, which were designed to provide investors with adequate information about public offerings of stocks and bonds and to protect them from the malpractice of securities brokers and dealers.

After stock prices plummeted in the wake of the October 1929 crash (from 1929 to mid-1932, the Dow-Jones industrial average dropped almost 90 percent), Congress undertook a massive investigation of the securities markets. Led by Ferdinand Pecora, the Senate Committee on Banking and Currency compiled thousands of pages of testimony that showed the existence of many abuses in the securities industry. For example, pooling operations had manipulated the prices of more than 100 New York Stock Exchange–listed stocks, and corporate insiders had profited by using information not available to stockholders and the general public.

These abuses seriously eroded investor confidence, hindering the capital investment vital to economic growth. Their revelation led Congress to enact several laws fashioned to restore the public's faith in the nation's financial markets. The first law passed—the Securities Act of 1933—requires full disclosure of all pertinent information pertaining to a public offering of securities. The purpose is to provide potential investors with a firm foundation on which they may realistically judge the value of the stocks or bonds being offered. With the exception of state, local, and federal government securities and offerings under $1.5 million (which must comply with the SEC's Regulation A), the act requires issuers of securities in interstate commerce or through the mails to file with the SEC a registration statement, which contains all the relevant information. In addition, a prospectus including this information must be delivered to investors. Until the registration is in effect (which means that the SEC has not raised any objections but *does not* imply approval of the issue by that agency), selling the securities is unlawful. Violation of the law subjects the persons responsible to criminal as well as civil penalties.

The Securities Exchange Act of 1934 grants to the SEC broad regulatory powers aimed at promoting fair trading practices and protecting investors from fraud, manipulation, and other abuses. National securities exchanges (nine of them, at the end of 1989) must register with the SEC and adopt rules governing the conduct of their members that conform with SEC regulations concerning investor protection. Brokers and dealers engaged in the over-the-counter securities market also have to register with the SEC, which monitors their activities. Specific trading activities, such as short sales, stabilization transactions, and options trading on national securities exchanges are also regulated. Violators of federal securities laws are subject to SEC discipline, which includes revocation of registration, expulsion from national securities exchanges, and criminal prosecution.

Corporations, whose stock is listed on a national securities exchange, or which have assets of $1 million or more and at least 500 shareholders, or which have issued securities under the Securities Act of 1933, must periodically report financial and other corporate information to the SEC. These companies must comply with SEC rules when soliciting proxies and other authorizations from holders of registered securities. Disclosures of the holdings and transactions by directors, officers, and holders of more than 10 percent of the equity securities of the companies must be made monthly to the SEC.

The Public Utility Holding Company Act of 1935 empowers the SEC to regulate electric and gas utility holding companies in order to limit them to single coordinated systems. Furthermore, the act calls for the simplification of the corporate and capital structures of these companies. This law reflects Congress's reaction to the concentration of economic power that resulted from extensive pyramiding within utility holding companies. The Investment Company Act of 1940 requires mutual funds and other investment companies to register with the SEC, which regulates their activities to protect investors. Under the Investment Advisors Act of 1940, persons who counsel others about security transactions, for compensation, have to register with the SEC. The act authorizes the SEC to issue rules prohibiting fraudulent or deceitful acts. The SEC also administers the Securities Acts Amendments of 1975, which direct it to facilitate the establishment of a National Market System. Finally, the SEC participates as an adviser in corporate reorganizations (Federal Bankruptcy Act of 1978) and helps safeguard the interests of bond purchasers (Trust Indenture Act of 1939).

Along with its regulatory responsibilities, the SEC also collects, compiles, and publishes various financial and economic data, including weekly reports on New York and American Stock Exchange trading and monthly reports on insider trading.

References

Seligman, Joel, *The Transformation of Wall Street: A History of the Securities and Exchange Commission and Modern Corporate Finance,* Houghton Mifflin, Boston, 1982; *United States Government Manual 4991/92,* Office of the Federal Register, National Archives and Records Administration, Washington, D.C., July 1, 1991.

(*See also* Bond; Government regulation of business; Stock; Stock exchange)

Henry C. F. Arnold

Selective credit controls

As commonly understood, selective credit controls are restraints imposed directly on the extension of defined forms or categories of credit. In a broader view, selective credit controls can include, in addition to the foregoing, interest rate controls, limits on the amount of credit that may be extended either to individual borrowers or by individual lending institutions, differential taxes imposed on borrowers, and subsidies available to specified classes of lenders.

Selective Credit Controls in the United States

Following the narrower of these concepts, experience with selective credit control in the United States began when the Federal Reserve System was authorized, under the Securities Exchange Act of 1934, to regulate credit used in buying or holding securities. Regulation was imposed initially on equity shares and on convertible bonds traded on national stock exchanges but was subsequently broadened to cover securities traded off the exchanges. The control method is for the Federal Reserve to determine the maximum loan value of a specified group of securities, stated as a percentage of market value. Where, for example, the loan value is set at 60 percent, the purchaser or holder is required to have a margin, or equity, in the security serving as collateral for the loan of not less than 40 percent of market value.

In the control of stock market credit, the purpose is to prevent conditions such as the ones that led to the 1929–1931 stock market collapse that preceded enactment of the 1934 legislation. Margin purchases of stock had been widespread in the late 1920s, with brokers borrowing heavily from commercial banks to extend credit to their customers. When declines in stock prices provoked demands for additional margin that many customers could not supply, forced sales of stocks to forestall credit losses by brokers intensified market disorder. Supporting the case for controls, it was also believed that the use of credit in stock market transactions tended to drain it from the nonfinancial side of the economy.

In administering the regulation of stock market credit, the Federal Reserve Board varies loan values not only with stock market conditions and the volume of credit being used in security purchases but with an eye also to general economic and financial conditions. If deemed to be appropriate, loan values may be raised when credit is eased and lowered when it is tightened.

The second use of selective credit controls was authorized in August 1941, four months before the bombing of Pearl Harbor, when President Roosevelt issued an executive order under The Trading with the Enemy Act of 1917 on the authority of which the Federal Reserve Board put into effect a rule (regulation W) placing restraints on the extension of credit for the purchase of a designated list of consumer durable goods (automobiles, appliances, furniture, etc.). The regulation was designed to reduce consumption demand for goods utilizing materials and labor believed to be needed more urgently in defense industries and applied to all types of lenders. It was also hoped that it would moderate the increase of prices of scarce resources, supplementing the anti-inflationary effects of taxes and voluntary savings, and that it would help create a backlog of consumer demand that would be useful in the postdefense period.

Regulation W was first applied only to installment-type credit, whether granted as a cash loan or in association with a sales contract, but the regulation was extended later (May 1942) to charge account credit and single-payment loans. Restraints consisted of a minimum down-payment requirement and a maximum repayment period (maturity) and were tightened twice in 1942, ultimately raising the former to 33⅓ percent for virtually all listed articles and lowering the latter to 12 months. Restraints were subsequently relaxed—in some cases by discontinuing altogether the listing of a commodity, in other cases by relaxing restraints in stages—and were abandoned entirely in June 1949.

Employing similar methods, regulation W was reinstated in September 1950, incident to prosecution of the war in Korea, under authority of the Defense Production Act of 1950. Again, the major purpose was to facilitate the transfer of resources from civilian to defense use. Restraints continued until May 1952, when authority expired in keeping with the Defense Production Act Amendments of 1952.

During the Korean conflict, and under the same authority as permitted reimposition of regulation W, the Federal Reserve Board also issued regulation X (October 1950), limiting the use of credit in purchasing homes and in financing home improvements. In this case also, the major purpose was to conserve scarce materials for defense purposes and moderate increases in their prices. As in regulation W, restraint was applied by setting minimum down-payment requirements and maximum repayment periods. Regulation X was discontinued in 1952 when authority for its use lapsed.

A sharp increase in 1955–1956 in the amount of installment credit extended to consumers, accompanied by a marked liberalizing of contract terms, revived concern that the use of credit would have an unduly expansionary effect on the economy, cause inflation to accelerate, and possibly lead to a troublesome decline in credit quality. There was initially an interest in the reimposition of selective controls, but pressure for this receded when lending to consumers stabilized in the latter half of 1956. President Eisenhower's response to the episode was to ask the Federal Reserve Board to evaluate the arguments pro and con for standby authority to impose selective controls. Based on its study (published in 1957), the Board recommended against a grant of standby authority.

The matter lapsed, then, until 1969, when the Credit Control Act of 1969 was passed, with far wider scope than anything previously contemplated. Designed specifically to control inflation generated by excessive credit extension, the 1969 law authorized the president to regulate all the terms on which credit is extended, including interest rates, and extended the authority to all forms of credit.

The powers granted in the 1969 law lay unused for a considerable time but were invoked by President Carter in 1980 (March 14), supplemented in that effort by a "voluntary credit restraint program," a program of "marginal requirements on managed liabilities," and restraints on money-market mutual funds, as "a basic part of the fight on inflation." The whole group of controls was abandoned, however, before 1980 was over, when it became clear that the problem to be coped with was recession not inflation and that the controls may have had a hand in producing the downturn. On December 8, 1980, President Carter signed a bill that ended presidential credit control authority as of July 1, 1981, but he made no secret of his belief that it should be continued. A subsequent effort to restore the authority died in Congress.

Although the 1980 legislation ended selective credit control authority of the conventional type, at least for the time being, it did not end the interest of the Federal Reserve System in consumer credit. On the contrary, the System has been increasingly involved, utilizing a broad-based Consumer Advisory Council in this connection, in monitoring, and in various respects regulating, the extension of credit to consumers by banks and other financial and nonfinancial agencies. Its object in this activity, however, and the object of the law underlying it, is not to influence the volume of credit extended or the contract terms being employed (down payment, maturity, interest rates, etc.) but to ensure that correct and intelligible information on these terms is available to the borrower and that no discrimination is practiced in access to credit with respect to race, gender, location of residence, and other essentially personal characteristics of the borrower.

Pro and Con on Selective Controls

Although experience with selective credit controls has shown that they are difficult to administer effectively and equitably, the difficulties encountered in that regard have not been so great as to render the idea of controls clearly impractical, leaving room for divergent views on their merits. Critics emphasize the difficulty of administering selective controls fairly and equitably and maintain that their effectiveness in emergency situations is typically due as much to shortages of materials as to the tightening of credit terms. They also assert that the inflation-restraining effects of selective controls are small, considering the narrow range of credit affected, and are better achieved by the methods of conventional monetary policy. Proponents, however, view selective credit controls as a way of achieving needed allocations of credit, as well as exerting limitation on its aggregate volume, and maintain that there is less upward pressure on interest rates when selective credit controls are used than would result from exclusive reliance on the aggregative, indirect approach of monetary policy.

But the debate over selective credit control commonly concerns questions of far wider scope than those involved in regulations W and X, running to the question of the "management" of the economy by government. On one side of the argument are those who have confidence in the ability of government to perform that function constructively and equitably, and who have an urge to move in that direction. On the other side are those who prefer the less interventionist forms of economic control.

References

Board of Governors of the Federal Reserve System, *Consumer Installment Credit*, vol. 1, pt. 1, 1957, chaps. 4, 6; *Payments in the Financial Services Industry of the 1980s,* Conference Proceedings, Federal Reserve Bank of Atlanta, Quorum Books, Greenwood Press, Westport, Conn., 1984; Schreft, Stacey L., *Credit Controls, 1980,* Federal Reserve Bank of Richmond, Economic Review, November–December 1990; *Studies in Selective Credit Policies,* Federal Reserve Bank of Philadelphia, August 1975; Young, Ralph A., *Instruments of Monetary Policy in the United States,* International Monetary Fund, Washington, D.C., 1973.

(*See also* Business credit; Consumer credit; Credit, an overview; Federal Reserve policy; Federal Reserve System; Monetary policy; Mortgage credit)

Raymond J. Saulnier

Short-run forecasts (*see* Economic forecasts; U.S. business obsession with short-run performance)

Short-term interest rates (*see* Interest rates)

Simulations in economics and business

Simulations refer to data generated by the use of a computer which resemble or simulate results of an experiment. In natural and biological sciences, the experimenter would use the actual physical setup or observe the behavior of actual living organisms to generate experimental data. In economics and business, often the experimenter is not in a position to use the actual economy or parts thereof or the actual business enterprise and its environment (customers, markets, managers, workers, etc.) to perform an experiment. Economists instead create the experimental situation in a computer and generate data which are believed to have characteristics similar to data obtained from an actual experiment. The word simulation refers to the act of generating data in such a manner. This brief essay describes the use of simulations in economics and in business.

In econometrics, which is "the art and science of using statistical methods for the measurement of economic relations" (see Chow, 1983, p. 1), simulations are used to generate artificial economic data from an econometric model which is a set of equations describing an economy or parts thereof. In the model-building stage, simulations can also be used to generate possible estimates of the parameters of a model, the parameters being numbers characterizing an economic relation such as the slope and the intercept of a linear equation relating consumption expenditure and income. Statistical formulas are used to compute estimates of the parameters of a model from economic data. For example, if quarterly data on consumption expenditure and income are available from 1953 to 1992 and if one wishes to estimate an equation explaining consumption expenditure as a linear function of income, one might choose to estimate the slope and the intercept by the method of least squares which minimizes the sum of squares of the deviations of observed consumption expenditure from the linear function of income. More complicated statistical formulas are required to estimate the parameters of a system of equations explaining many variables describing an economy (see Chow, 1983).

To decide on which formulas to choose, one can use statistical theory based on the theory of probability. One can also use simulations especially when mathematical derivations based on the theory of probability become difficult. To do so, one specifies a system of equations or some other mathematical model describing the economy. The model incorporates random components capturing the influences of factors too numerous to measure individually. Using random numbers for the random components and assuming the values of the parameters of the model to be known, one generates from the computer artificial economic data. Using a specified set of statistical formulas, the experimenter can obtain a set of estimates of the model parameters for each set of artificial data generated. Repeating the experiment many times yields many sets of estimates. These estimates can be compared with the "true" values of the parameters which the experimenter has artificially created at the beginning of the experiment, thus helping in evaluating the properties of the statistical formulas. The term *stochastic simulations* is used when random numbers are used in generating the data from the computer. In statistical estimation theory, stochastic simulations are used in more ingenious ways than suggested in the above description. Interested readers may refer to the works of McFadden (1989) and Pakes and Pollard (1989) on the method of moments and of Geweke (1989) on Bayesian method for estimating parameters.

Once an econometric model is estimated using actual economic data, its dynamic properties can be studied by mathematical analysis or simulations. Dynamic properties include cylical properties such as degrees of variations and trends of individual economic variables and lead-lag relations among them. These and other properties help to describe business cycles. An early study using stochastic simulations to generate cyclical properties from an econometric model for comparison with observed properties of U.S. business cycles is Adelman and Adelman (1959). A good exposition of simulations of econometric models is Pindyck and Rubinfeld (1981, chaps. 12–14). Simulation methods are used to study cyclical properties of econometric models by varying the nature of policy variables subject to government control such as money supply and government expenditures. The objective of such studies is the evaluation and design of government economic policies. This subject is studied in Chow (1975). However, caution should be exercised to ensure that the econometric model remains essentially unchanged when government policies change, as pointed out by Lucas (1976). Research in the 1980s and early 1990s has been devoted to finding econometric models which are stable under changes in government policy, models that can properly forecast the reactions of economic agents to government policies. Besides econometrics, the study of optimization and other techniques in economic theory also use simulation methods. Interested readers may refer to Judd (1992) for a study of numerical methods in economics.

In business, simulations can be used in a variety of ways to simulate a business environment in order to study the responses of the actors. The actors can be two or more business firms in a duopoly or oligopoly situation. To study the behavior of the firms, a mathematical model is used depicting the environment facing each firm which includes (1) its demand function, which may have prices, product qualities, and advertising expenditures of the competitors as variables, (2) its production function showing outputs as functions of inputs, and (3) relevant market information such as the wage rates and input prices. The player representing the management of each firm would receive data for each period from the computer concerning its own firm, the market, the past actions of its competitors. The player would be asked to respond by deciding on variables such as price, output, and advertising expenditures of that firm. Such business games, often played by business school students, can serve as a teaching device and can be used to generate experimental data which may describe the way firms actually behave. In making business decisions, managers or marketing executives may use computer models to simulate the environment they are facing, including the possible responses of the consumers and of their competitors so that the managers can choose the best options available.

References

Adelman, Irma, and F. L. Adelman, "The Dynamic Properties of the Klein-Goldberger Model," *Econometrica,* vol. 27, 1959, pp. 596–625; Chow, Gregory C., *Analysis and Control of Dynamic Economic Systems,* Wiley, New York, 1975; Chow, Gregory C., *Econometrics,* McGraw-Hill, New York, 1983; Geweke, John, "Bayesian Inference in Econometric Models Using Monte Carlo Integration," *Econometrica,* vol. 57, 1989, pp. 1317–1340; Judd, Kenneth L., "Numerical Methods in Economics," Stanford University, Hoover Institution, mimeo, 1992; Lucas, Robert, Jr., "Econometric Policy Evaluation: A Critique," in Karl Brunner and A. H. Meltzer (eds.), *The Phillips Curve and Labor Markets,* North-Holland, Amsterdam, 1976, pp. 19–46; McFadden, Daniel, "A Method of Simulated Moments for Estimation of Discrete Response Models Without Numerical Integration," *Econometrica,* vol. 57, 1989, pp. 995–1026; Pakes, Ariel, and David Pollard, "Simulation and the Asymptotics of Optimization Estimators," *Econometrica,* vol. 57, 1989, pp. 1027–1058; Pindyck, Robert S., and D. L. Rubinfeld, *Econometric Models and Economic Forecasts,* McGraw-Hill, New York, 1981.

(*See also* Computers in economics; Cross-sectional analysis in business and economics; Data banks; Dynamic analysis; Dynamic macroeconomic models; Econometrics; Economic models; Economic forecasting methods; Game theory, economic applications; Linear programming; Time series analysis)

Gregory C. Chow

Simultaneous equations in business and economics

Simultaneous-equation estimation is a family of statistical techniques which proceeds from the assumption that the disturbances in different equations of an economic model are, or are likely to be, correlated with one another. This contrasts with the assumption almost universally made in economics prior to 1944 that the disturbances in different equations of a model were statistically independent (uncorrelated). Under this earlier assumption, each equation could be estimated separately by ordinary least squares—a single-equation technique.

Trygve Haavelmo's article "The Probability Approach in Econometrics" (1944) showed no evidence that he had heard of the 30 years of cumulative experience in applied econometric research prior to 1944 (much of it in the United States). Haavelmo was a student of Ragnar Frisch, the first Nobel Prize winner in Economics and one of the pioneers in econometrics. Haavelmo, an econometrician, was a resident associate at the Cowles Commission, first located at the University of Chicago and later at Yale. He also received the Nobel Prize in Economics. Following publication of the 1944 article, there should have been passionate scholarly discussion and careful testing of its merits as a guide to applied econometric research. This did not occur because the scholarly community had been badly disrupted in Germany since 1933, in Austria since 1938, and in the whole of Europe since 1939. Some economists who might have moderated the discussion were in German-occupied countries, and others were working to capacity in war-related activities.

In order to concentrate on the implications of correlated disturbances in equations, Haavelmo and his equally brilliant associates neglected important problems that had long been recognized by applied econometricians:

1. At any given time, some of the variables that theoretically belong in a model may not yet have been measured.

2. Some of the variables measured are subject to substantial errors.

3. High intercorrelation among the independent variables in models fitted to economic time series is more nearly the rule than the exception.

Among the problems that were emphasized by Haavelmo and his colleagues, who apparently were unaware that the problems had been dealt with earlier by others, were:

1. The "identification problem" in the case of Marshallian simultaneous demand-and-supply curves. This problem was formulated and solved explicitly by Marcel Lenoir in 1913 and E. J. Working in 1927, and it was well understood by Mordecai Ezekiel and Holbrook Working in the mid-1920s.

2. The identification problem in the general case including both lagged and non-lagged variables. Moore in 1914 was seeking a causal explanation of business cycles in the following sequence: (a) cycles in rainfall in the U.S. Midwest cause, (b) cycles in crop production, which cause (c) cycles in crop prices, which might cause (d) cycles in other sectors of the economy. Thus, rainfall (an exogenous variable) during the spring and summer determines the size of the crop harvested in the fall and sold during the fall and winter; hence, crop production is a predetermined variable in the demand functions for crops: $P_t = f(Q_t)$. In 1917, Moore also fitted a supply function for cotton in the form $Q_t = f(P_t - 1)$.

Moore contrasted his dynamic approach (which included lagged variables and a strong interest in prediction) with the static, simultaneous approach of Alfred Marshall. Moore's recursive supply-and-demand equations embodied a dynamic mechanism which later became known as the "cobweb model." This mechanism was recognized independently and separately by Schultz, Ricci, and Tinbergen in 1930, and discussed in detail by Ezekiel in 1938. The cobweb model is an example of what Herman Wold later called a causal chain in which each equation can be estimated separately and without bias by least squares.

The identification problem was also solved and applied to more complicated models, some in economics and some in genetics, by Sewall Wright in 1921, 1925, and 1934.

Details of Haavelmo's Approach

The accompanying equations illustrate some elements of Haavelmo's simultaneous-equations approach in terms of the Marshallian demand-and-supply curves. Since P and Q are always synchronous in this model, the subscript t can be dropped.

Suppose we have a set of price-quantity observations which we believe to have been generated by the following model:

$$\text{Demand:} \quad Q = a + bP + u \tag{1}$$
$$\text{Supply:} \quad Q = \alpha + \beta P + v \tag{2}$$

where u and v are regarded as random disturbances. From a statistical point of view we have no basis for distinguishing between these two equations since both contain the same variables and both have random disturbances. It can be shown that the least-squares regression of Q upon P is, in an indefinitely large sample,

$$B = \frac{b\sigma_v^2 - (b + \beta)\sigma_{uv} + \beta\sigma_v^2}{\sigma_v^2 - 2\sigma_{uv} + \sigma_v^2} \tag{3}$$

where $\sigma_{uv} = r_{uv}\sigma_u\sigma_v$. If the demand curve has not shifted (i.e., if $\sigma_u = 0$), $B = b$; if the supply curve has not shifted (i.e., if $\sigma_v = 0$), $B = \beta$. In general, B does not equal either of the structural coefficients, and neither of them is identifiable. If equations (1) and (2) constitute the true and complete model, there is, in general, no way by which b and β can be estimated from the data.

The situation is different if each equation includes a different predetermined variable (i.e., a variable which is statistically independent of u and v), say Y and Z, in the demand and supply functions, respectively:

$$\text{Demand:} \quad Q = a + bP + cY + u \tag{4}$$
$$\text{Supply:} \quad Q = \alpha + \beta P + \gamma Z + v \tag{5}$$

where u and v again are random disturbances; Q and P are now referred to as endogenous variables which are assumed to be correlated with u and v. Writing all four variables in lowercase letters as deviations from their respective means, we can express q and p as functions of the predetermined variables and the disturbances and obtain the reduced form of the model as follows:

$$p = \left(\frac{c}{b-\beta}\right)y + \left(\frac{\gamma}{b-\beta}\right)z + \frac{y-u}{b-\beta} \tag{6}$$

$$q = \left(\frac{c\beta}{b-\beta}\right)y + \left(\frac{\gamma b}{b-\beta}\right)z + \frac{bv-\beta u}{b-\beta} \tag{7}$$

The coefficients of the reduced-form equations may be estimated by least squares. The structural coefficient β can be estimated as the ratio of the coefficients of y in equations (6) and (7); b can be estimated as the ratio of the coefficients of z. Knowing β and b, we can readily derive c and γ from the coefficients of equation (6); a and α can be estimated from the other coefficients since the (sample) means of Q, P, Y, and Z are known. The model consisting of equations (4) and (5) is just identified (i.e., our information is sufficient to make a unique estimate of each structural parameter).

In other models it may be possible to identify some of the structural equations but not others. The necessary and sufficient conditions for identifiability of a given equation in a set of m simultaneous linear equations can be summed up in three propositions:

1. At least $m - 1$ of the total number of variables in the system (counting lagged endogenous variables as separate variables) must be absent from the given equation.

2. Each of the other $m - 1$ equations in the system must contain at least one variable which does not appear in the given equation.

3. The matrix formed of the coefficients in the other $m - 1$ equations of variables absent from the given equation must be of rank $m - 1$ (i.e., the matrix must contain at least one set of $m - 1$ columns and $m - 1$ rows which form a nonzero determinant).

The Haavelmo Bias

Haavelmo's approach was brilliantly conceived, but it rested on an untested assumption that nearly all econometric models were of the synchronous type, in which each equation contained two or more endogenous variables, the disturbances in different equations were correlated, and least-squares estimates of the structural coefficients were badly biased. If this assumption were true, it raised the possibility that nearly all results hitherto obtained by single-equation (least-squares) methods were invalid because they had ignored what Herman Wold referred to as the "Haavelmo bias." As of 1945 this possibility was particularly alarming to Wold, for in that year he had nearly finished the statistical side of an investigation of consumer expenditures, all the numerical results of which might be subject to the Haavelmo bias.

Wold immediately undertook a critical examination of the traditional single-equation method and its logical foundations. Wold's conclusion (stated in a paper presented at a 1947 meeting of the Econometrics Society and published in 1949) was that the traditional method was free from Haavelmo bias when applied to a certain general class of models which was "wide enough to cover most, if not all, dynamic models used in econometric research up to 1940." Wold cited Jan Tinbergen's pioneer 1939 work in applying model sequence analysis or process analysis to statistical data in his 45-equation model of the U.S. economy during 1919 to 1932 and stated that "it is precisely this type of the systems, properly specified, which goes free from the Haavelmo bias." In his later work, Wold repeatedly and forcefully emphasized the importance of causal chain, or recursive, models in econometrics; the cobweb model is the earliest (and perhaps the simplest) representative of the type.

Wold's position was viewed as the correct one by most econometricians who had done serious work with data prior to 1944. Few or none of them adopted Haavelmo's approach. A younger group accepted Haavelmo's assumption of correlated disturbances at least provisionally and developed several additional techniques (two-stage least squares, instrumental variables, principal components, and others) for handling the first stage of estimation represented by the reduced-form equations (6) and (7). As experience in applying such methods to data accumulated, it turned out that the estimates in many cases were so close to those obtained by least squares that the differences were not statistically (or economically) significant. It also turned out that the simultaneous methods were more sensitive than were ordinary least squares to high intercorrelation among predetermined variables and that specification errors in one equation could substantially affect the estimated coefficients of others. By the mid-1970s, applied econometricians felt free to use ordinary least squares or one of the simultaneous-equation methods depending upon the characteristics of particular equations and subgroups of equations in a complete model.

Koopmans (1945), who helped extend, explain, and popularize Haavelmo's approach, stated that errors in variables were disregarded in order to concentrate on the central problem of disturbances in equations. The computing instructions for applying Haavelmo's concepts to data embodied the assumption that all variables were measured without error, and these instructions were carried forward uncritically into a number of textbooks. As a result, several cohorts of graduate students were trained in the belief (sincerely held by instructors who had done no empirical research) that errors in variables were of no consequence. Only in the 1970s did econometricians trained in this tradition begin to recognize the need for dealing explicitly with errors in variables.

References

Christ, Carl F., *Econometric Models and Methods*, Wiley, New York, 1966; Ezekiel, Mordecai, "The Cobweb Theorem," *Quarterly Journal of Economics*, vol. 52, 1938, pp. 255–280; Fox, Karl A., and Tej K. Kaul, *Intermediate Economic Statistics*, vol. II: *A Guide to Recent Developments and Literature, 1968–1978*, Krieger, Huntington, N.Y., 1980; Haavelmo, Trygve, "The Probability Approach in Econometrics," *Econometrica*, vol. 12 (supp.), 1944, pp. 1–118; Koopmans, Tjalling C., "Statistical Estimation of Simultaneous Economic Relations," *Journal of the American Statistical Association,* vol. 40, 1945, pp. 448–466; Lenoir, Marcel, *Etudes sur la Formation et le Mouvement des Prix,* Giard and Brière, Paris, 1913; Moore, Henry L., *Economic Cycles: Their Law and Cause,* Macmillan, New York, 1917; Tinbergen, Jan, "Statistical Testing of Business Cycle Theories," vol. II: *Business Cycles in the United States of America, 1919–1932,* League of Nations, Economic Intelligence Service, Geneva, 1939; Wold, H. O., "Statistical Estimation of Economic Relationships," *Econometrica,* vol. 17 (supp.), 1949, pp. 1–21 (see also "Errata," *Econometrica,* vol. 19, 1951, p. 227); Working, E. J., "What Do Statistical Demand Curves Show?" *Quarterly Journal of Economics,* vol. 41, 1927, pp. 212–235; Wright, Sewall, "The Method of Path Coefficients," *Annals of Mathematical Statistics,* vol. 5, Institute of Mathematical Statistics, Hayward, Calif., 1934, pp. 161–215.

(*See also* Cobweb theorem; Econometrics; Economic models; Regression analysis in business and economics; Statistical methods in economics and business, an overview)

Tej K. Kaul and Karl A. Fox

Small business

A small business can be defined as an enterprise managed and operated by an individual or group of individuals who directly bear the risks and reap the rewards of their efforts. The owners make the major decisions affecting the enterprise, including production, human resources, marketing, and financing.

The term *entrepreneur* is often used interchangeably with *small businessperson,* although there is an important distinction between them. Not all small-business owners are entrepreneurs, and not all entrepreneurs operate small businesses.

The number of small businesses in the United States has increased 54 percent since 1980. As of 1989, there were approximately 20.1 million nonfarm businesses, of which 99 percent are considered small by the U.S. Small Business Administration (SBA). About half of the 20 million businesses operate full-time; the rest part-time.

Historically, small businesses have always added a more than proportional share of new jobs relative to their employment share. The small-business share of net new jobs increases most rapidly during the recovery stage of a business cycle and during the earlier parts of the expansion phase of the cycle. As the economy approaches full employment during the later stages of an expansion, larger firms tend to produce a larger share of jobs.

Small businesses employ 50 percent of the private work force, contribute 44 percent of all sales in the country, and are responsible for 38 percent of the gross national product. Currently, an estimated 4.6 million businesses are owned and operated by women, up from 2.6 million in 1982. The growth rate of the receipts of women-owned businesses was three times that of men-owned businesses for the period from 1977 to 1987. Black-owned businesses increased 27.6 percent from 1982 to 1987, from 308,260 to 424,165.

The U.S. Small Business Administration has industry-specific definitions for small business, utilizing maximum sizes based on gross receipts and employment levels. In the retailing sector, a business is considered small if sales do not exceed $2 to $7.5 million, with the limit varying based on the specific type of business. In the services sector, the range is $2 to $8 million. In wholesaling, the range is $9.5 to $22 million. In manufacturing, employment size is the defining element, with a business considered small if it employs fewer than 250 to 1500 employees, depending on the industry.

The high failure rate of small firms has been widely reported, with figures ranging from 6 to 8 out of 10 new businesses failing within the first few years of operation. These failures can largely be attributed to poor planning, weak management, and under-capitalization. Despite these daunting statistics, the lure of owning one's own business has remained strong, and new business incorporations have continued to increase.

References

Bunzel, John, II, *The American Small Businessman,* Arno, New York, 1962; Carosso, Vincent P., and Stuart Bruchey, *The Survival of Small Business,* Arno, New York, 1979; Carson, Deane, *The Vital Majority: Small Business in the American Economy,* U.S. Government Printing Office, Washington, D.C., 1973; Hollander, Edward D., *The Future of Small Business,* Praeger, New York, 1967; Hollingworth, A. Thomas, and Herbert H. Hand, *A Guide to Small Business Management,* Saunders, Philadelphia, 1979; Phillips, Joseph D., *Little Business in the American Economy,* University of Illinois Press, Urbana, Ill., 1958; U.S. Chamber of Commerce, *Small Business Its Role and Its Problems,* Washington, D.C., 1962; U.S. Small Business Administration, *The State of Small Business: A Report of the President, Transmitted to the Congress,* U.S. Government Printing Office, Washington, D.C., 1990.

Bernard H. Tenenbaum and Ronald W. Dickey

Smithsonian Agreement

The Smithsonian Agreement of 1971 represented a stage in the transition of the international monetary system from the fixed exchange rate, dollar-denominated pattern of Bretton Woods to the current system of a managed float.

Under the Bretton Woods Agreement of 1944, all member nations stated their currency values in terms of gold, with only the United States pledged to convertibility. With this unique status, the dollar became an international standard of value and the universally accepted asset for international payments. Aside from occasional devaluations of foreign currencies, the system worked quite effectively for a quarter of a century.

Bretton Woods System Severely Tested

Problems with the system developed as the U.S. balance-of-payments surplus of the early 1960s was eroded not only by the appreciation of the dollar as other currencies were devalued but also in reaction to the inflation caused by the Vietnam War. The persistent balance deficit in the second half of the decade was the direct cause of the decline in the gold stock and the deterioration of the reserve position of the United States.

As a result, by the early 1970s the Bretton Woods Agreement became increasingly unworkable as central banks struggled to maintain stable exchange rates and provide liquidity to finance growing world trade. In the spring and summer of 1971 the principles of the Bretton Woods system were severely tested as increasing offers of dollars for deutsche marks forced Germany to move temporarily to a floating exchange rate. At the same time, the Japanese central bank absorbed billions of dollars in an attempt to maintain the yen-dollar parity. As it faced greater pressures to exchange its money liabilities for its gold assets, the United States had to decide upon a course of action to fight the dollar outflow. Among the choices were curtailing U.S. foreign investment, cutting back its military presence, losing gold, or raising gold's price—a devaluation of the dollar.

In a dramatic move on August 15, 1971, the United States chose to suspend its currency convertibility, thus "closing the gold window." The dollar was now officially inconvertible into gold. The move signalled the U.S. conviction of a need for realignment of exchange rates. In addition, the United States imposed a punitive 10 percent surcharge on its imports. On the surface the measure was defended on the grounds that other countries experiencing balance-of-payments deficits had chosen the same policy in the 1960s. Effectively, however, the measure was employed as a bargaining tool in the quest for realignment.

After the announcement, and for the next 4 months, financial centers and international exchange markets were confused. With an undefined value of the dollar, which was the standard of the international currency system, nations sought to protect their currencies' international value in different ways. West Germany and the Netherlands allowed their currencies to float. Both England and Japan defended their currencies so as to maintain preexisting gold and dollar parity. France, in turn, established a two-tier system, a fixed-dollar rate for commercial transactions and a floating rate for all other money exchanges.

Details of the Agreement

The diversity of national concerns kept the European Economic Community nations from unifying on a position with respect to the dollar. Meetings under International Monetary Fund auspices, as well as conferences of the Group of Ten (composed of the financial ministers of the industrialized nations of the free world), were unable to resolve national differences. Finally, agreement on the exchange rate impasse was essentially reached in mid-December, as President Nixon and President Pompidou met to discuss the realignment of currency values.

These summit talks were quickly followed by a meeting of the Group of Ten in Washington, D.C., at the Smithsonian Institution on December 17 and 18, 1971. This conference managed to rescue the Bretton Woods arrangement through a devaluation of the dollar and a revaluation of various other currencies. With its gold definition changed from $35 to $38 per ounce of gold, the dollar declined by 8.55 percent from its initial Bretton Woods parity. (The United States also removed its arbitrarily imposed 10 percent import surcharge.)

With the dollar devaluation came changes by some of the other Group of Ten nations. With respect to the dollar all currencies rose by varying percentages: in Belgium, by 11.57; Italy, 7.54; Germany, 13.58; Japan, 16.88; the Netherlands, 11.57; and Sweden, 7.49. The French franc and the British pound maintained their gold parities, thus rising to the dollar by 8.55 percent. The Canadian dollar, which had been floating, retained its status. Since the Smithsonian Agreement only embraced the Group of Ten, other nations shortly followed exchange rate strategies that were in their own best interests, aligning themselves with other major currencies. All nations had the option of establishing new parity values or choosing a temporary, or central, rate.

In addition to the restructuring of currency values, the Smithsonian Agreement amended the Bretton Woods band specifications. Originally currencies were permitted to move 1 percentage point above or below their par value, and rates were kept within the band primarily through the buying and selling of a nation's own currency with U.S. dollars. The Smithsonian Agreement widened the band about parity to 2.25

percentage points in the belief that a wider margin of fluctuation would reduce speculative attacks on currencies as well as permit a nation greater flexibility and more time in executing domestic policies to stabilize its currency's external value.

The Agreement Replaced

The new arrangement stabilized the foreign exchange markets for a short time, causing capital outflows from the United States to diminish significantly, but temporarily. The mounting U.S. trade deficit, however, gave rise to new rumors of devaluation, bringing about the floatation of the pound by mid-1972. The speculations grew stronger as the United States approached a $10 billion balance-of-payment deficit in 1973. To reduce their exposure to dollars, banks and multinational corporations elected to convert their dollar holdings into other currencies, causing a massive flow of the dollar to European money markets and forcing the German and Japanese central banks to absorb enormous amounts of the U.S. currency in defense of its value.

A second devaluation of the dollar, which raised the price of gold to $42.22 an ounce in February 1973, stopped neither the speculation nor the flow of the dollar to Europe. It did, however, produce massive confusion which in turn brought about a suspension of transactions in all foreign exchange markets. When the markets were reopened in March, the currencies of the Western world were no longer fixed against gold.

The float was intended as a temporary measure, to be removed once order had been restored in foreign exchange markets. However, in the face of continued speculation and devaluation of the dollar, and the unwillingness of the European central banks to undertake further massive and expensive foreign exchange interventions, it became a permanent arrangement.

The Smithsonian Agreement was developed to address the problem of dollar glut ensuing from the persistent U.S. balance-of-payments deficit. However, the Agreement failed to address the problem and after only a few years was replaced in 1973 by a system of managed floating which was legalized at a conference in Kingston, Jamaica, in January 1976. Despite its ultimate failure, the Smithsonian Agreement clearly showed that international agreements are only as good as their strongest link. The United States, without prior consultation with its trading partners, forced major revisions in the international payments network. The Agreement also pointed to the inability of the Bretton Woods arrangement to adjust to changing trade patterns. The international economic environment of the 1970s was not to be governed by the economic relations existing in the 1940s.

References

Eckes, Alfred E., Jr., *A Search for Solvency: Bretton Woods and the International Monetary System, 1941–1971,* University of Texas Press, Austin, 1975; Moffitt, Michael, *The World's Money: International Banking from Bretton Woods to the Brink of Insolvency,* Simon and Schuster, New York, 1983; Solomon, Robert, *The International Monetary System, 1945–1976,* Harper & Row, New York, 1977; Williamson, John, *The Failure of World Monetary Reform, 1971–74,* New York University Press, New York, 1977.

(*See also* Balance of international payments; Balance of international trade; Barriers to trade; Bretton Woods Conference; Foreign exchange rates; International economics, an overview; International Monetary Fund; Liquidity, international; Value of the dollar)

Bernard S. Katz and Shiva Sayeg

Social contract (*see* Incomes policy)

Social dividend (*see* Negative income tax)

Social overhead capital (*see* Infrastructure)

Social security

Since its founding in 1935, the social security system has attained a greatly expanded role in income maintenance for the elderly and the disabled. In 1990, some 95 percent of jobs were covered; almost 40 million persons received benefits (while the work force numbered 125 million and the population some 250 million); and about two-thirds of Americans over 65 relied on social security for more than half their income. Indeed, improved social security payments are the main reason for a lower percentage of poverty among the elderly than in the general population. However, a rising proportion of elderly and the consequent large and rising financial requirements of the Social Security Trust Funds have caused much questioning of the ultimate viability of the system and of its value for presently young workers.

Historical Highlights

For the first 40 years of the system its history is one of gradual and significant expansion of coverage, benefits, and contributions. Since the late 1970s, however, future benefit promises have leveled off and in some cases been curbed while contribution requirements continue to rise amidst growing attention to costs.

The original 1935 legislation, aimed at retiring workers, was first expanded in 1939 with the addition of dependent and survivor benefits (and became known as old-age and survivor insurance—OASI). With the addition of disability insurance in 1956 the acronym changed to OASDI, and this group of benefits (mainly retirement pay) has continued to be the core of social security. (It should however be noted that disability insurance has a trust fund and contribution rate distinct from retirement and survivor financing.) A further large expansion took place with the addition of Medicare in 1965—i.e., compulsory hospitalization insurance (HI), or part A of Medicare, along with optional doctors' bill insurance (part B of Medicare). The medical benefits again have a separate trust fund and contribution rate but are, in effect, an extension of the social security safety net for the elderly.

The first major one of numerous liberalizations of retirement and survivor coverage occurred in 1950 when benefit levels were raised, the wage base was increased, and a new schedule of gradually increasing tax rates was adopted. Large groups of workers not previously covered were also included. Following further changes in the 1960s, including the introduction of an actuarially discounted early retirement benefit (at age 62), a truly massive expansion occurred in 1972. A 20 percent increase in benefits was accompanied by a provision for future automatic cost-of-living adjustments to benefits and the wage base for contributions.

By the late 1970s, the likelihood of future financial problems for the system surfaced. A technical flaw in the law was raising "replacement rates" (the ratio of retirement benefits to preretirement earnings) beyond the original intent of the legislators. Correction of this flaw in 1977 set a precedent in terms of curbing future potential benefits and was accompanied by a further rise in contribution rates. Nevertheless, the slow growth of real wages in the late 1970s and early 1980s plus high inflation put pressure on Social Security finances. Simultaneously, the virtual certainty of the rise in the beneficiary population relative to the (contributing) working population became a concern. By the first decade of the twenty-first century the post–World War II baby boom (roughly 1945–1965) would translate into an unusually large number of retirements.

After an intense political struggle, the recommendations of a National Commission on Social Security (headed by Alan Greenspan, a past chairman of the President's Council of Economic Advisers and future chairman of the Federal Reserve) were adopted in 1983. The financial outlook for the system was improved sharply by raising contribution rates, by subjecting to income taxes a portion of the benefits of upper-income recipients, and by extending the basic retirement age in gradual increments (so as to reach 67 early in the next century).

These changes, combined with the economic growth of the mid- and late 1980s, generated surpluses in the OASDI Trust Funds in the late 1980s and early 1990s, pushing any possible exhaustion of these Funds into the second or third decade of the twenty-first century. The rapid rise of medical costs, however, necessitated in the 1990s a rise in the wage base relevant to HI contributions well beyond the requirements of OASDI. Even so, HI was headed for acute financial pressures by the turn of the century, and the optional doctors' bill insurance (Part B of Medicare) could be kept feasible only by substantial annual premium increases, thus cutting into the adequacy of retirement and survivor allowances.

Recent Status

The secretary of Health and Human Services has responsibility for social security, which is administered by a commissioner. The trustees of the funds (the secretaries of Health and Human Services, of Treasury and of Labor, plus two public members) prepare annual reports and recommendations to Congress, supplemented with a thorough review by an Advisory Council every four years. The adequacy of the funds is subject to various tests which resemble, but are not identical with, standard actuarial examinations. Typically, a range of economic and demographic assumptions are arrayed by degree of optimism and pessimism. Each scenario yields future financial-result projections expressed as a balance of future payrolls, positive or negative. As noted, the OASDI funds have generally been held sound for decades ahead since the 1983 amendments, but concern over Medicare continues to be voiced regularly.

Social security projections are indeed highly sensitive to economic and demographic assumptions. As regards economic factors, financial forecasts improve with larger real GNP (or GDP) growth as well as with a larger labor force and real wage gains and with lower inflation and unemployment. As regards demographics, positive factors include high fertility and net immigration as well as high mortality.

As noted, the average social security benefit rose rapidly relative to current wages until the mid-1980s (in fact, at about double the wage rate between 1950 and 1983). With the average replacement ratio now stabilized at roughly 40 percent, it is important to point out that actual replacement rates range from a high of roughly 55 percent for low-pay workers to a minimum of about 27 percent for workers who always earned the maximum amount subject to social security taxes. This is the (intended) consequence of the computation of the primary insurance amount (PIA), which gives heavier weight to the first few hundred dollars of average insured monthly earnings (AIME) during one's working years than to additional earnings.

The PIA itself stood in 1991 at around $12,300 for retirees having worked at the maximum subject to tax. The PIA was 50 percent higher for couples unless the lower-earning spouse had acquired benefits exceeding 50 percent of those applicable to the higher-earning spouse. The PIA is subject to reduction for postretirement earnings above a modest sum (less than $10,000 in 1991) until age 70 when full benefits become available regardless of outside earnings.

Meanwhile, the contribution rate for the 1990s had risen to 15.3 percent of covered earnings for the self-employed and to half that percentage each for the employer and the employed where such a relationship exists. Of the 15.3 percent, 11.2 percent went to OASDI, 1.2 percent to DI, and 2.9 percent to HI. Covered OASDI earnings were up to $53,400 in 1991—more than double the median income of full-time workers—and covered HI earnings up to $125,000, meaning that well over 90 percent of all wage earners had to pay hospital insurance contributions on all their earnings.

Problems and Issues

Despite major achievements in improving the status of the elderly over the past half-century, malaise pervades public attitudes and a portion of professional opinion with respect to the future of social security. In the case of the public, doubts regarding the ability of the government to deliver on social security promises are the crux of the matter. In the case of professionals, questioning centers on the feasibility of inducing the working population to give up enough of its purchasing power to sustain the consumption of a much-enlarged older portion of the population. Underlying the concerns of both groups are (1) the known demographic trends; (2) low real-wage gains, reflecting low productivity and capital formation; and (3) the already-heavy burden of social security taxes and the disproportionate rise in health costs so crucial to the aged.

The ratio of workers to beneficiaries stood at about 3 to 1 in the early 1990s. It is almost certain to decline to 2 to 1 by 2020. (The retirement of the post–World War II baby boomers begins around 2010.) The decline in the relative number of working people will be reinforced by low population growth (related to low fertility) since about 1970 plus the likely peaking of labor-force participation rates as practical limits to multiple-earner families are reached. Calculations of needed net immigration to offset these factors suggest that the required figures are politically unattainable (and possibly economically counterproductive when the social service requirements of immigrants are taken into account, along with their social security contributions).

An increase in real wages raises social security receipts without a corresponding rise in benefits, which after retirement are indexed only to inflation and not to real-wage gains. Real wages in turn reflect productivity, which is influenced by education, technology, and capital formation (i.e., the amount of capital per worker). The 1984–1990 experience under the 1983 reforms of social security shows that the positive experience of the trust funds should have been even better had historical real-wage advances prevailed. Thus, macroeconomic performance is a crucial ingredient in the future burden of social security on the then-active population. Naturally, a better result is possible in the late twentieth century and beyond, but the early 1990s are not reassuring.

Finally, social security taxes are probably near the upper limit of political tolerance, so that "the easy way" of raising required contributions when trust fund developments so indicate may not be available. Social security contributions exceed personal income tax obligations for perhaps a quarter of all wage earners. They have risen from 30 percent of federal revenues to almost 40 percent in the 1975–1990 period. The net impact of social security by income groups is uncertain. The regressivity of a uniform contribution rate and an upper limit to the wage base subject to tax may be offset by the skewing of benefits toward the lower end of preretirement earners and by the taxability of benefits at the upper end. Nevertheless, the perception of a disproportionate impact on low and medium wage earners persists. The need to raise Medicare contributions and premiums constantly is of course related to the general medical-cost rise problem but influences public attitudes toward social security.

Unfortunately, the net accumulations in the trust funds during the late 1980s (and possibly most of the 1990s) have coincided with heavy federal deficits on balance of all other accounts. Unlike private pension fund growth, which funnels savings into capital formation, social security net inflows have financed the (heavily consumption-oriented) general outlays of the federal government. These facts have rendered moot a longstanding controversy as to the effect of social security on savings. Any positive effect of social security per se has been swamped by massive total-government dissaving (although it is true that the government's impact might have been even worse without social security surpluses).

Against this background, the argument for "privatizing" workers' provision for retirement has gained ground. Savings accumulations under such existing plans as individual retirement accounts (IRAs) and employment-related accounts (401k plans) have been positive. Could they be extended? However desirable, pursuing any such proposal must consider government requirements for alternative financing, the explicit and implicit benefit promises made to current workers, and the difficulties of forcing provision for one's retirement into everyone's personal plans without blanket taxation.

In practice, it is likely that social security will be kept intact into the indefinite future by a combination of tightening up on benefits, by controlling medical costs, and by raising contribution rates and Medicare premiums further. It is true that such a forecast partially justifies the apprehensions of young workers. The rate of return (through benefits) of one's social security contributions, which was extremely favorable for the first five decades of the system, is almost certain to decline.

Public policy aimed at improved real growth is desirable for many reasons. In the case of social security better growth would ease the enlarged burden on the young and/or the diminution of benefits for the old that present trends portend for the next century.

References

Carlson, Keith M. "The Future of Social Security: An Update," *Federal Reserve Bank of St. Louis Review,* vol. 73, no. 1, January–February 1991, pp. 33–49; Council of Economic Advisers, "Economic Status of the Elderly," *Economic Report of the President 1985,* Washington, D.C., 1985, pp. 150–186; Myers, Robert J., *Social Security,* 3d ed., Irwin, Homewood, Ill., 1985; U.S. Department of Health and Human Services, Social Security Administration, "Actuarial Status of the OASI and DI Trust Funds," *Social Security Bulletin,* vol. 54, no. 6, June 1991, pp. 2–11, and "Social Security Programs in the United States," *Social Security Bulletin,* vol. 54, no. 9, September 1991, pp. 2–19. (The Social Security Administration provides free simplified handbooks on Social Security and Medicare benefits at social security offices throughout the United States.)

(*See also* Medicare program; Negative income tax)

Francis H. Schott

Socialism

Socialism has three different aspects: it refers to (1) a set of ideas or ideologies, (2) a set of political parties, and (3) a group of economic systems. The concept of socialism is both the criticism of capitalism and the idea of an alternative society. Socialist ideology has been mainly devoted to the criticism of capitalism. It holds that capitalism is primarily responsible for poverty, the exploitation of workers, pollution of the environment, unemployment and inflation, racial and sexual discrimination, and imperialist domination of other countries—which is the basic cause of war. Socialism, however, is described as producing a society of cooperation and collective ownership, in which there is a high degree of equality, no discrimination, no poverty, no exploitation, and no war.

Varieties of Socialist Ideology

The most widespread form of socialism is Marxism. Marxist socialism has been the official dogma of over one-third of the world, but those governments are now mostly collapsing. Marxism claims to be scientific in that it has a highly developed philosophy, economics, and historical view as well as a political program. Within Marxist ideologies, there are again many varieties, including the Soviet and Chinese views, as well as many independent Marxist views held by assorted scholars. Marxists view socialism as a stage in human social development that normally comes after a stage in economic evolution when capitalism has proved itself inadequate for human needs.

In addition to Marxism, there are many other views of socialism. In the early and mid-nineteenth century, the most popular view of socialism was that of a utopian colony of like-thinking and cooperative individuals with no use for money and with completely democratic decision making on all issues. Throughout Western Europe there is a form of socialist ideology which labels as socialism any large amount of welfare reform within capitalism. In Western Europe, both the Socialist and the Communist parties agree that socialism must be democratic in its political forms.

The term socialism also applies to various political parties. From a few hundred adherents in the 1840s, Socialist and Communist parties have become a powerful force in most countries. Karl Marx founded an International Workingmen's Association, lasting from 1864 to 1876, which included a number of small parties and many trade unions. A Second International was formed in 1889, which has united many social democratic parties from that time to the present.

The social democratic parties, mostly in Western Europe, advocate a limited amount of nationalization of industry; high welfare payments for unemployment, health care, and other purposes; and continued private capitalist ownership as the dominant economic form. They assume political democracy and very gradual changes. The Soviet Communist party for many years advocated complete public ownership of all industry, central planning of all economic activities, and one-party political control—but that has now greatly changed, with the official line of the party now a type of market socialism. There is also a vaguely defined socialism advocated by the leading political parties in much of Africa.

Finally, the term socialism includes various kinds of noncapitalist economic systems. In Scandinavia, England, Germany, and France, socialism has brought cradle-to-the-grave welfare schemes plus a small amount of public ownership. In the Soviet Union and Eastern Europe, socialism meant an entirely new economic system. All industry was owned by the government and run by government managers. Half of agriculture was government-owned; the other half was owned collectively by large groups of farmers (though with strong government direction). Economic planners designated objectives for the whole economy, stating how much of every commodity was to be produced, what its price should be, where labor was to be allocated, and where capital and materials were to be allocated. These plans were legislated and had to be followed by every manager. Wages were paid according to the amount of work done, its degree of difficulty or skill, favorable or unfavorable geography (such as the Arctic in the Soviet Union), and so forth. Managers received several times the salary of ordinary workers. Consumers could buy any commodity for which they had money. But it was illegal to own a factory or to produce anything for private profit by employing other people. This system has now been abolished in Eastern Europe and is changing rapidly in the Soviet Union.

China followed the Soviet Union in government ownership and in one-party political control. The Chinese, however, had a much smaller spread of income, so that a manager received only two or three times the average wage, whereas a Soviet manager received eight or nine times the average wage. The Chinese also insisted that most managers and intellectuals do some manual labor at times. China is slowly changing its economic system.

References

Cole, G. D. H., *A History of Socialist Thought,* 6 vols., Macmillan, New York, 1953–1959; Dobb, Maurice, *Welfare, Economics and the Economics of Socialism,* Cambridge University Press, Cambridge, 1970; Zimbaist, A., H. Sherman, and S. Brown, *Comparing Economic Systems,* 2d ed., Harcourt Brace Jovanovich, San Diego, 1988.

(*See also* Capitalism; Communism; Comparative economic systems, an overview; Decline of the Soviet economy; Marxism; Poverty)

Howard J. Sherman

Soviet economy's decline (*see* Decline of the Soviet economy)

Special drawing rights

The special drawing right (SDR) is an international financial asset created by the International Monetary Fund (IMF), which serves as an international unit of account, a means of payment among certain eligible official entities, and an international reserve asset. Allocations of SDRs augment IMF member countries' international reserves at a lower cost than does earning them with a balance-of-payments surplus or by borrowing. The IMF Articles of Agreement call upon IMF member countries to make the SDR the principal reserve asset of the international monetary system.

History

The Board of Governors of the IMF agreed at the 1967 annual meetings in Rio de Janeiro to create a new international monetary reserve asset to be named the Special

Drawing Right. The legal framework for their creation and allocation to member countries was established by the first amendment to the IMF's Articles of Agreement adopted in 1968. The second amendment (1978) provided for a considerable liberalization of the rules governing the use of the SDR. On January 1, 1970, the first distribution of 3.4 billion SDRs was made to IMF member countries. Subsequent distributions of 3 billion SDRs each were made in 1971 and 1972, and of SDR 4 billion in 1979, 1980, and 1981, bringing the total amount to SDR 21.4 billion.

Characteristics

Allocations of SDRs, which require the approval of IMF member countries having 85 percent of the voting strength of the total membership, are distributed to members in proportion to their quotas in the IMF. Members must pay a quarterly charge on their cumulative allocations and receive interest quarterly on the daily average balance of SDRs held. The rate of charge on allocations and the rate of interest on holdings are equal so that the system is self-financing. Members holding more SDRs than their cumulative allocation earn net interest, and those holding fewer SDRs than they were allocated pay net charges. The SDR interest rate is set weekly to equal a weighted average of short-term interest rates prevailing in the countries whose currencies are in the SDR's valuation basket (see p. 926).

The SDRs issued by the IMF can be used only in transactions among monetary authorities (central banks), certain international institutions, and the IMF. They may be used to purchase foreign currency and to settle financial obligations and in a variety of other financial operations (e.g. loans, swaps, and as collateral). SDRs have been used in recent years primarily in voluntary transactions among holders and in transactions and operations between members and the IMF.

The SDR's value in terms of other currencies is established daily by the IMF on the basis of the prevailing market value of the amounts of the five currencies in the SDR's valuation basket. A "designation" mechanism ensures that SDRs can be used at their official value. The IMF will meet requests by members with a balance-of-payments need to use their foreign exchange reserves, by designating stronger members to provide a freely usable currency in exchange for SDRs at the official exchange rate of the SDR for that currency. It has not been necessary to use this mechanism since mid-1987.

The exchange value of the SDR has been redefined several times. Initially, the value of the SDR was defined as equivalent to ⅟₃₅th of an ounce of gold. This value was the same as that of US$1, which also was pegged to gold. Since the breakdown of the par-value Bretton Woods system, the value of the SDR has been defined in terms of a currency basket. Effective July 1, 1974, the SDR's valuation basket consisted of the currencies of the 16 IMF member countries whose exports of goods and services exceeded 1 percent of world exports.

Since January 1, 1981, the valuation of the SDR has been based on the currencies of the five IMF member countries with the largest shares of exports. The valuation basket has been reviewed and adjusted every five years since. While the currencies in the basket were not changed as a result of subsequent reviews, the amount of each currency was adjusted to reflect its relative international importance based on the value of goods and services exported by the country issuing it and use of the currency as an international reserve asset. The amount and initial weight of the currencies in the basket established on January 1, 1991 are as follows:

Currency	Initial weight	%
U.S. dollar	0.572	40
Deutsche mark	0.453	21
Japanese yen	31.8	17
French franc	0.800	11
U.K. pound sterling	0.0812	11

Uses

To date, SDRs have been used primarily between the IMF and its members. Credits extended by the IMF have frequently been paid in SDRs (all IMF financial activities, including credits, are denominated in SDRs). All charges paid by members to the IMF for the use of its financial resources (interest) must be paid in SDRs and about one-quarter of all repayments of principle by members to the IMF are paid in SDRs. In addition, significant amounts are used by members to acquire currencies from other members or holders other than the IMF (about SDR 6 billion per year on average between 1987 and 1990). From 1984 through 1990 total uses of SDRs averaged roughly SDR 16 billion per year.

References

Coats, W, *Special Drawing Rights, Operations and Role in Development Finance,* Allied Publishers Limited, New Delhi, India, 1990; De Vries, M. G., *The International Monetary Fund 1966–1971: The System under Stress,* vol. 1, pts. I and II, International Monetary Fund, Washington, D.C., 1976; de Vries, M. G., *The International Monetary Fund 1972–1978: Cooperation under Trial,* vol. 1, pts. I and II, International Monetary Fund, Washington, D.C., 1985; International Monetary Fund, *Annual Report,* Washington, D.C.; International Monetary Fund, *Financial Organization and Operations of the IMF,* pamphlet series no. 45, 2d ed., Washington, D.C., 1991.

(*See also* Balance of international payments; Bretton Woods Conference; Foreign exchange rates; International economics, an overview; International Monetary Fund; Liquidity, international; Smithsonian Agreement)

Warren Coats and H. Robert Heller

Specialization (*see* Division of labor)

Speculating (*see* Commodity exchange; Futures)

Spillovers (*see* Externalities)

Stages theory of economic development

A stage theory of economic development describes economic growth by a succession of clearly defined takeoffs. Economic analysts generally seek to isolate the functional relationships which explain a nation's moving from low to higher incomes and from relatively simple to highly dependent means of production. The stages theory approach rationalizes the economic mechanism which links the introduction of new, sometimes radical innovation to changes in the structure and overall performance of economies. Almost all such relationships implicitly specify movement through gradual processes.

A stage theory must move progressively forward over time. The theory must correctly predict the successive stages. Any single stage must be clearly defined, with a limited number of characteristics distinguishing it from all other stages. The characteristics that distinguish stages must be observable, and, ideally, measurable. The takeoff stages must usher in demonstrable evidence of sustained growth. A stage theorist must be able to identify an economic system at a given stage and compare the states of development among nations.

Under the contemporary analytical approach to economic development, stage theories have been analyzed as incomplete treaties. The standard criticism levied against most stage schemata is their inability to finely distinguish the turning points as a nation leaves one stage and enters another. It is argued that the stagists have, in fact, outlined economic, sociological, and institutional stages with blurred endings and beginnings.

The earliest stage theories were reactions against the interpretation of economic change based on individual decision-making adjustments to market conditions. These stage theorists questioned marginalist theory and relied almost exclusively on empiricism and social change in interpreting economic growth. Although more contemporary stage analysts have incorporated the market action-reaction mechanism, they still heavily depend on historical socioeconomic changes to explain economic development.

Karl Bucher's Stages Theory

The first major works of stage theorists appeared in the late nineteenth century. Representative of the German historical school, Karl Bucher (1901) divided the economic growth of nations into three stages. The first stage is the closed household economy, characterized by the lack of any exchanges in the production of goods from raw material to final form. When exchanges take place between producer and consumer, the second stage, the town economy, has been attained. The transition from domestic to town economy, from nonexchange to exchange, is not abrupt and may take centuries to accomplish.

The third stage, the national economy, is characterized by the establishment of wholesale trade and markets—producer and consumer are estranged. The transition from town to national economy is based on the rise of political organization, permitting nation states.

Clark-Fisher Approach

Colin Clark (1940) and Allen G. B. Fisher (1939) viewed economic development through a triad of occupational stages. Nations beginning as initial primary goods producers (agriculture and fishing) move onto a higher level of development with the production of manufactured goods. This secondary stage comes through advancements in knowledge and skills. With the concomitant material accumulation, nations then seek greater welfare through forms of culture, and labor moves from a goods orientation to a service orientation. Representative of the tertiary stage is the growth in the transport, distribution, and public administration sectors. The highest levels of income are attained through nonmaterial output.

The Clark-Fisher stages approach has been criticized on two counts. Whereas the tertiary stage is last in their schema, for some low-income nations employment in the tertiary sector has exceeded the secondary sector's employment. Moreover, there is no theoretical basis to accept high employment in the service sector as representative of higher income levels. Conceivably the attainment of luxury manufacturers may be preferable to that of services or culture. However, the transition from primary to secondary employment has represented the development path of modern nations and is a good explanatory variable for income growth.

Marx's Stage Theory

A somewhat earlier, but unquestionably more influential, stage theorist is Karl Marx. Marx, as economic historian, provided the key variable bridging his various epochs. In Marx's theories, economic systems reach higher stages through the strained relations that run between the dynamic forces of production (knowledge and technological change) and the slower-evolving social and political organizations which permit production. The social, psychological, and economic forces that are continually at work between the accumulators and owners of capital and their workers generate the evolution from feudalism to capitalism to socialism.

Marx gave a demonstrable measure for the decline of capitalism: a falling rate of profit and a rising army of the unemployed. Marx also provided the foundation for the most influential modern stage theorist, Walter W. Rostow.

Walter Rostow's Stages

As a noncommunist manifesto, Rostow's *Stages of Economic Growth* (1960, 1971) is a foray into positioning the sweep of modern economic history under capitalism into neat and hopeful epochs. Similar to the assimilation of Marx's ideas, Rostow's language has entered our lexicon. Whereas Marx's "oppressed" and "exploited" are code words for revolutionary change, Rostow's terms "leading sectors," "takeoffs," and "drives to maturity" are hopeful banners of evolution.

Specifically, Rostow delegates the historical performance of modern industrial economies into stages of (1) the traditional, (2) the preconditions for takeoff, (3) the takeoff, (4) the drive to maturity, and, finally, (5) the age of mass consumption. Although it has a logical appeal to the historian, Rostow's five-stage schema is criticized for imprecisely defining the institutional and economic changes from stage to stage.

To Rostow's credit the most significant stage is set apart with concrete characteristics. The essential takeoff is marked by a doubling in rate of investment. Within this stage there also emerge leading industrial sectors and a political system which together fuel expansion.

Rostow's takeoff and the requisite performance of the investment variable spurred researchers to study the investment history of the high-income nations. In these investigations, a discernible jump of the investment ratio has not been universally detected, although a later rise in net capital formation at an intermediate point in the process provides useful evidence of improving economic growth. Moreover, the seemingly clear concept of leading sectors and their identification is seen as becoming mired in the links between industries under the impulse of growth.

Rostow (1990, p. 65), argues that "the relative degree of technological virtuosity is roughly related to the time of take off." Accordingly, stage theorists associate recent evidence of uneven growth and problems of distributional equity in newly developing nations with differences in the timing of takeoff's and differences in the size of their domestic markets. The general absence of institutional as well as organized administrative, technological, and managerial cohesion at the early stages of national sovereignty makes the process of economic development vulnerable to internal factionalism and external pressure.

Despite its lack of strict empirical verification, Rostow's work has provided the development economist with a receipt of the necessary ingredients for development. Economists have suggested that Rostow's stages would be better read as a prospectus rather than a treatise.

Alexander Gerschenkron's *Economic Backwardness in Historical Perspective,* published in 1962, studied the economic performance of nations in Eastern Europe. Gerschenkron establishes six propositions based on a nation's extent of backwardness as the key elements in its future development pattern. Although it received general acceptance, his work tends to explain the recent growth of selected nations rather than to establish a historical long-range set of defined stages.

Although no writer has presented a definitive stage theory of economic development, stage theorists have provided the development economist with avenues of research and with salient requirements for economic development. Whether the stage theorist can ever meet the strict tests drawn for a successful stage theory may be contemplated in light of Henry Bruton's remark (1960), "It must be recognized that in a long period analysis the distinction between 'economic' and 'non-economic' factors loses significance and . . . that economic growth must be seen as a special aspect of general social evolution rather than as a process which can be factored out of the social system and studied in isolation."

References

Bruton, Henry, "Contemporary Theorizing on Economic Growth," in B. Hoselitz (ed.), *Theories of Economic Growth,* Free Press, New York, 1960, pp. 297–298; Bucher, Karl, *Industrial Evolution,* S. M. Wickett (trans.), Toronto University Press, Toronto, 1901; Clark, C., *The Conditions of Economic Progress,* Macmillan, New York, 1940; Fisher, Allen G. B., "Production, Primary, Secondary and Tertiary," *Economic Record,* vol. 15, 1939, pp. 24–38; Fishlow, A., "Empty Economic Stages," *Economic Journal,* vol. 75, no. 297, March 1965, pp. 112–125; Gerschenkron, Alexander, *Economic Backwardness in Historical Perspective,* Harvard University Press, Cambridge, Mass., 1962; Kuznets, Simon, "Driving Force of Economic Growth: What We Learn from History," in Herbert Giersch (ed.), *Towards an Explanation of Economic Growth,* J.C.G. Mohr, Tubingen, 1981; Marx, Karl, and F. Engels, *The Communist Manifesto,* S. Moore (trans.), Washington Square Press, New York, 1964; Rostow, Walter W., *Stages of Economic Growth,* Cambridge University Press, Cambridge, 1971; Rostow, W. W., *History, Policy and Economic Theory,* Westview Press, Boulder, Colo., 1990.

(*See also* Economic growth; Infrastructure)

Rexford A. Ahene and Bernard S. Katz

Stagflation

Stagflation describes the condition of inflation's persistence and intractability when the economy's resources are utilized below its potential. The condition is puzzling in the perspective of conventional economic theory because inflation traditionally has been described as caused by too much money chasing too few goods, i.e., either an excess of money or an excess of demand over available supply pushes up the general level of prices in sustained fashion.

Two major variants may be found: first, Milton Friedman's declaration that "inflation is always and everywhere a monetary phenomenon," and second, in the alternative Keynesian expenditure-income approach, wherein an inflationary gap develops when the sum of money demands for goods and services is more than 100 percent of available or potential producible output, thereby generating rising prices. In the former approach, the causality of inflation lies primarily in an exogenously determined supply of money, in contrast with the latter's view that price levels are related to changes in aggregate demand while influenced by an at least partly endogenously determined money supply (and its velocity). In each case, however, the phenomenon of significantly rising prices is inconsistent with low, zero, or negative economic growth that, in combination, is the hallmark of stagflation.

In the United States, the coexistence of slack demand and rising prices has been registered not only in periods of slow economic growth but also in recessions. Indeed, the failure of prices to decline during recessions and an upward drift of the inflation floor at recession lows have become increasingly evident in the post–World War II period.

Varied Explanations

Explanations of stagflation are varied and, increasingly, depend on the expectational behavior of labor and business. Indeed, it is the initiating causes of inflation which feed expectations of ever-rising wages and prices that are said to be essential for and to precede the condition of stagflation.

Among the initiating causes are those related to money-supply changes and excess aggregate demand, as noted earlier. However, independently, expectations may also be supported by so-called cost-push inflation arising from imperfections in the factor and product markets where monopolistic or oligopolistic practices prevail; from imperfections resulting from shifts in the structure of demand whereby prices increase in sectors as demand rises without being accompanied by price declines in sectors where demand eases (because the mobility of resources is low); and from pricing behavior guided by long-run cost or rate-of-return considerations.

In the original classical-monetarist approach, stagflation could only be a transient phenomenon, because assumptions of flexible wages and prices precluded other possibilities. Departures from full employment would result in competitively dictated declines in both wages and prices, a situation which eventually would establish conditions of revived demand in factor and product markets. In the interim phase, unemployment would rise and competition for jobs would increase, so that wages would decline more than prices. The resultant fall in real wages would generate increased demand for labor (and reduced supply), which would eliminate any involuntary unemployment.

Monetarist Analysis

The modern monetarist analysis retains this inverse connection between changes in real wages and employment demand, while accepting the empirically established downward rigidity of wages and prices observed in the 1960s and 1970s. The modern monetarist also incorporates expectations in the theory of stagflation. Indeed, the expectations concept remains the basis for an explanation of the persistence of stagflation, possibly over several years, because that duration might be required for the dissipation of worker and company attitudes of resistance to lessened growth or to cuts in wages and prices. Thus, it is the doubt held by workers and companies that the condition of lessened aggregate demand is general and permanent which delays the wage and price reductions that would otherwise clear markets and restore equilibrium. As long as the more optimistic and irrationally held expectations are retained, both prices and employment rates may continue to rise.

Expansionary monetary policies might shorten the stagflation period but only at the cost of more inflation. If expectations of continuing high wage and price increases are validated by money-supply and demand growth, unemployment might be driven below the so-called natural rate—a so-called long-term sustainable level. The validation (through stimulated monetary growth) of successively higher expectations, as an alternative to stagflation, appears more politically palatable to governments and provides the basis for the accelerationist theory of inflation.

Momentum Theory

Allied but separately identifiable from the monetarist approach is the momentum theory of inflation and stagflation, which combines the elements of entrenched inflationary expectations with the sluggish response of manufacturing prices to short-run shifts in demand. Primarily reflecting market situations characterized by administered prices or competition among the few (which are said to predominate in manufacturing), the shared long-run interest of skilled workers and employers in continued employment relationships and in long-run sales and growth considerations looms more important than do short-run demand changes. This attitude thus leads to price strategies based on markups over unit costs of production at normal levels of output. Accordingly, prices may move higher during periods of slack demand in response to cost increases incurred previously during expansion periods but which as a matter of long-run company strategy were not at that time passed through into higher prices.

With wages and prices both geared to the long run, the acceleration of inflation which was associated with the demand-pull inflationary conditions of the late 1960s and early 1970s in the United States raised expectations of the magnitude of normal wage and price advances. This provided a momentum for expectations and inflation that extended into the middle 1970s, when aggregate demand was easing.

Under these circumstances, the economic policy prescription to thwart stagflation frequently is directed toward avoidance of overrobust expansion in economic growth for a period sufficiently long to lower expectations of inflation. However, this policy frequently has been characterized as neither politically acceptable nor feasible in the United States. Sometimes, the risk of large job losses over an extended period that this policy might cause by overdoses of fiscal and monetary restraint prompts proposals of an incomes policy to moderate wage and price increases that develop in an expanding economy.

Cost-Push Explanation

Related to situations where high demand does not prevail, cost-push is a more familiar classification in describing the concurrence of inflation and low or zero economic growth. The major pressure is said to be rising wage costs imposed by powerful unions which are passed on into higher prices especially under conditions of inelastic demand for labor, rivalry among unions, etc. Other elements on the cost or supply side in the last two decades have been both sharply higher prices caused by oil price increases mandated by the Organization for Petroleum Exporting Countries (OPEC) and rising food prices. These prompted labor on the basis of accelerated inflation to seek higher wage settlements, which in turn fed the wage-price (or, some say, the wage-wage) spiral. Keynesians aver that their analysis remains valid, needing only incorporation of asymmetry in wage and price response: large in booms, smaller in recessions, though still positive until expectations are changed, which may take several years.

An increase in costs ordinarily causes a reduction in output and employment in the standard case, unless validated by price advances via increases in the money supply. Under cost-push inflation, the macroeconomic policy recommendation of restraint in demand through fiscal and monetary means is said to be ineffective because its effects are concentrated more on reductions in production and employment than on the slowing of cost and price increases.

Closely allied with this is the view of Charles L. Schultze that changes in the structure of demand cause inflation in the United States. As shifts in demand for products and services develop, prices rise in industries experiencing increases but don't fall in industries where sales decreases are occurring. As a result, even the demand-deficient industries may be required to pay higher wages and prices for resources to maintain production. As a result, average prices for all industries tend to rise secularly.

Critics charge that cost-push based on the monopoly power of union labor and paucity of firms cannot serve as an independent initiator of inflation. The latter is a continuing process, it is said, and so the exercise of monopoly power by firms could result merely in one-time price increases to obtain maximum profits. Without changes in the money supply or other macroaggregate influences, increased claims for output in markets influenced by monopoly elements would be accompanied by reduced claims by competitive sectors—resulting in no change in average prices. Monetarists argue that only a steadily increasing degree of monopoly or oligopoly power could sustain the cost-push theory of inflation.

Nevertheless, cost-push does play an important though secondary role in the inflation theories of some monetarists. Price rises in slack markets are said to experience a step-by-step adjustment to a new equilibrium in a catch-up process following an initiating period of excess demand. Thus, continuously rising prices during slow economic growth or recession are said to reflect more a stretching out in time of the impact of the excessive demand in the preceding expansion phase of the business cycle. Accordingly, the policy prescription of the critics are centered on curbing aggregate demand in the expansion phase, especially by control of the money supply. In this theory, the root of the accelerated inflation in the 1970s was validation of unusual cost increases (e.g., energy and food in the mid- and late 1970s) through increases in the money supply.

Other Theories

In still another view, theories of the delayed effects of demand-pull or of cost-push as explanations of stagflation are said to have been inapplicable in the 1970s. In this approach, the equilibrium full-employment rate—the lowest rate without accelerating inflation—rose in the 1970s. Though the unemployment rate remained high during the business-cycle expansion that began in early 1975 (clinging to 5½ to 6 percent at the cyclical peak of 1978 to 1979 rather than returning to the low 4 percent rate of the 1950s), this did not reflect any deficiency of employment opportunities. Instead, such factors as increased search time for jobs, structural changes in the labor force, and involuntary unemployment supported a higher full-employment unemployment rate. Because income transfers such as unemployment benefits and other public welfare payments are more generous, job search times have become prolonged, especially because multiworker households have increased in number. Also, the structural factor reflects a higher proportion of women and young adults (both of whose unemployment rate is typically higher than average) in the labor force. Higher legislated minimum wage rates also tend to increase the unemployment rate for unskilled, newer workers. Accordingly, a natural rate of unemployment at full employment would need to be revised upward—in a sense, denying that stagflation exists in the customary way. The other side of this theory refers to the lowered potential real growth rate of the U.S. economy due to reduced productivity. Accordingly, measures to increase aggregate demand will generate inflation at lower economic growth rates than formerly in the post–World War II period.

In the rational expectations view, fluctuations in the economy represent departures (due to random supply, money or demand shocks) from a trend GNP close to potential—mainly generated by discretionary fiscal and monetary policy of a Keynesian persuasion. One area of agreement is the acceptance of price and wage rigidities which delay adjustment to trend.

References

Cagan, Phillip, *The Hydra-Headed Monster: The Problem of Inflation in the United States,* American Enterprise Institute for Public Policy Research, Washington, D.C., 1974; Gordon, R. J., "Recent Developments in the Theory of Inflation and Unemployment," *Journal of Monetary Economics,* vol. 2, 1976, pp. 185–219; Phelps, E. S., *Inflation Policy and Unemployment Theory: The Cost-Benefit Approach to Monetary Planning,* Norton, New York, 1972.

(*See also* Competition; Employment and unemployment; Expectations, Federal Reserve policy; Incomes policy; Inflation; Labor unions; Monetary policy; Money supply; Monopoly and oligopoly; Phillips curve; Rational expectations; Rigid prices; Velocity of circulation of money)

Herman I. Liebling

Standard of living

The concept of standard of living has been used extensively since the turn of the century by economists and laypeople alike. However, the concept has never had a precise meaning. In essence, it refers to a manner or way of living (i.e., level of living) that an individual or a society feels is important to attain (a standard).

At about mid-century, J. S. Davis (1945) sought to reform the careless use of this term by economists, state leaders, business executives, and the average individual. In his benchmark article, he drew a chief distinction between level (what is) and standard (level wanted and worked for), and between consumption (goods and services consumed) and living (consumption plus intangible conditions of life). Although standard and level of living can be the same under conditions of satisfaction, apathy, or hopelessness, this is an unusual use of standard of living. In 1954, an expert committee of the United Nations Economic and Social Council recommended that distinctions should be maintained between the "level" and "standard" of living. The Committee indicated that the concept "level of living" relates to the actual living conditions of a people, and the concept "standard of living" relates to aspirations or expectations of a people for living conditions they seek to attain or regain, or which they regard as fitting and proper for themselves to enjoy.

Standard of Living versus Family Budget

Nevertheless, journalists especially have continued to confuse the issue and have used the term usually as level of consumption or, less frequently, as level of living. Researchers in acknowledging that most people use the term in this sense have defined standard of living for respondents in their surveys. For example, Katona (1975) defined it as "managing to live on your income pretty much the same (as you are now)," whereas Hafstrom and Dunsing (1983) defined it as "the things you have and the way you are living now," and the North Central Technical Committee of the Agricultural Experiment Stations asked about satisfactions with present standards of living defined as "the goods and services consumed such as food, clothing, housing, transportation, etc." (Hafstrom 1983).

The definition and measurement of standard of living perhaps has provoked as much attention in social science as any other term. For example, expert committees in the United Nations and in the United States as well as individual authors have concerned themselves with this topic. Beginning in 1967, the Bureau of Labor Statistics developed standard-of-living budgets at designated lower, moderate, and higher levels for four-person families. These were an outgrowth of the earlier city worker's family budget developed for a modest but adequate living standard beginning in 1946.

Standard of living is used almost universally. It is included in the Charter of the United Nations as a general goal of international economic and social activity. It is used most often (in the sense of level of living) as a measure of progress in living conditions of nations at different points in time and for the comparison of these conditions in different nations at one point in time.

Higher or Lower Standard of Living

The rising standard of living has been one of the major goals of U.S. society. It also has been stressed in U.S. society to include continuous progress in the upgrading of many types of purchases (Katona, 1975). The idea embodied in this has led to criticism of Americans for being too easily manipulated, like puppets, by advertisers to buy more or better consumption goods, resulting in wasteful expenditures. Others, notably Katona, argue that the increase in expenditures for consumption goods brought about by the striving for a better standard of living results in consumer investment. Consumer investment itself acts, as does business investment, as a stimulus in the economy.

The threat of energy shortages, high unemployment, and worldwide inflation, partially stimulated by the aspirations of people throughout the world for a higher standard of living, has resulted in some serious questions concerning whether the standard of living should be lowered drastically to help solve these problems. It is argued that this solution would not work because it is the wanting and striving for improvement in private living standards that form the solid basis of U.S. prosperity (Katona, 1975).

Even more confusion has been added to the meaning of this term in recent years. Ideas such as quality of life and lifestyles have been equated with standard of living by some, while others have used standard of living as an influencing factor on quality of life and on lifestyles. Still other argue about the influence of quality of life and lifestyles on standard of living. As long as this confusion in the use of the term exists, it is important for economists to define standard of living in such a way that there will be no doubt as to its meaning.

References

Bureau of Labor Statistics, *Autumn 1978 Urban Family Budgets and Comparative Indexes for Selected Urban Areas,* Department of Labor Bulletin no. 79-305, 1979; Campbell, A., P. E. Converse, and W. L. Rodgers, *The Quality of American Life,* Sage, New York, 1976; Davis, J. S., "Standards and Content of Living," *American Economic Review,* vol. 35, no. 1, March 1945, pp. 1–15; Hafstrom, J. L., and M. H. Dunsing, "Level of Living: Factors Influencing the Homemaker's Satisfaction," *Home Economics Research Journal,* vol. 2, 1973, pp. 119–132; Hafstrom, J. L. (ed.), *Compendium of Quality of Life Research,* University of Illinois, Agricultural Experiment Station, Urbana, 1986; Hafstrom, J. L., "Satisfaction with Present Standard of Living: Predictions Using Various Statistical Techniques," in M. M. Dunsing (ed.), *Proceedings of the Symposium on Perceived Economic Well-Being,* University of Illinois, Agricultural Experiment Station, Urbana, 1983; Katona, G., *Psychological Economics,* Elsevier, New York, 1975; Sherwood, M. K., *The Measure of Poverty,* U.S. Department of Health, Education, and Welfare Technical Paper IV, Bureau of Labor Statistics (BLS), Family Budgets Program, Washington, D.C., 1977.

(*See also* Family budgets)

Jeanne L. Hafstrom

State and local government finance

State and local government finance deals with the revenues and expenditures of state and local governments. As shown in the table, state and local government revenues are substantial shares of total government revenues in the United States.

Government Revenues in the United States, 1988–1989 (millions of dollars)

	Federal	State	Local
Intergovernment from federal		108,235	17,588
Intergovernment from state	2,903		157,652
Property taxes		5,417	137,107
General sales and gross receipts taxes		93,414	19,183
Selective sales taxes	36,077	44,834	8,584
Individual income taxes	445,690	88,819	8,988
Corporate income taxes	103,291	23,861	2,060
Death and gift taxes	8,745	3,486	25
Severance taxes		4,147	
License taxes		17,666	713
Other general revenue taxes	22,050	2,523	7,818
Charges, miscellaneous general revenue	124,603	82,543	108,830
Utility and liquor store revenue		6,035	50,189
Insurance trust revenue	349,301	98,174	13,274
TOTAL REVENUE	**1,092,660**	**586,687**	**532,013**

SOURCE: U.S. Bureau of the Census, *Government Finances: 1988–89,* U.S. Government Printing Office, Washington, D.C., 1991.

Why should the study of state and local government finance require a special approach distinct from the analysis of taxes and expenditures at the national level? There are two major reasons: First, because of the smaller size of states and localities compared to the nation, their economies are inherently more *open;* the flows between localities and states of both goods and the factors of production—labor and capital—are proportionately larger than similar flows among nations. Second, state and local governments are constrained by different legal and constitutional restrictions from the national government.

Expenditures

State and local governments provide many goods and services, including education, highways, parks, and police and fire protection. A major concern in economics is whether expenditures for these functions will be at an efficient level, that is, whether the quantity of these goods and services will be increased to the point where the marginal benefits (valued according to the preferences of the individual members of society) are equal to the marginal costs.

Voting provides one means by which citizens express their preferences for public expenditures by all levels of government. At the local level, people may also express their preferences by moving to a community which offers the package of public services most appealing to their individual tastes. The efficiency of this "voting-with-your-feet" process has been a prominent topic in public finance since the seminal article by Charles Tiebout (1956).

One potential source of inefficiency is the existence of "spillover benefits" to non-residents from goods provided by a local government. For example, a city's treatment of its sewage benefits nonresidents by affecting the purity of their water supply. The city may fail to take these spillover benefits into account and provide suboptimal sewage treatment because nonresidents do not vote in municipal elections. Furthermore, the municipality may not be able to compel nonresidents to pay their share of the costs of locally provided public goods from which they benefit.

To correct the spillover problem, the state or national government may subsidize the local provision of goods with spillover benefits. Such subsidies provide the rationale for some of the intergovernment grants shown in the table. Another rationale for intergovernment grants is that "fiscal equalization grants" may be used to offset differences in the local tax base between rich and poor communities. Without such grants, poorer communities would provide lower-quality public services and/or impose higher tax rates on their residents. These differences in services and tax rates might distort individuals' choices of place of residence.

The mobility of population poses a problem for state or local governments attempting to redistribute income. If one locality offers more generous welfare benefits than others and finances this by higher taxes on its rich residents, it may experience an in-migration of poor people and an exodous of rich. For this reason, many experts have favored the federal government assuming full responsibility for programs involving the redistribution of income. However, actual practice in the United States since the 1930s has been a system in which welfare benefit levels are determined by the states, although the federal government pays a share of the cost.

Taxes

It is important to distinguish the "economic incidence" of a tax—how a tax affects the distribution of real income—from the "statutory incidence"—who has the legal obligation to pay the tax. For example, a tax on a business may be shifted forward to consumers through increased prices or shifted backward to employees through reductions in wages.

The openness of state and local economies has important effects on the incidence of state and local taxes. Consider a tax on capital such as the property tax or a corporate income tax. Many analyses of the incidence of such taxes at the national level assume that the nation is a closed economy and that the nation's total capital stock is fixed. These analyses conclude that the economic incidence of a tax on capital falls on the owners of capital because the tax reduces the aftertax rate of return. However, the incidence of a tax on capital imposed by a state or local government will not fall on the owners of capital in the long run because capital is mobile. In the long run the aftertax rate of return will be the same in all jurisdictions regardless of differences in local tax rates because investors would not invest where they received a lower rate of return than they could earn elsewhere. If capital is used to produce goods for sale in a national market, a local tax on capital cannot be shifted forward to buyers of the product because a firm would not be able to charge a higher price for its product than the price charged by competing firms located in jurisdictions with lower tax rates. Thus the burden of a local tax on capital must be shifted backward to less mobile complementary factors of production. By discouraging investment, local taxes on capital decrease the demands for land and labor, reducing land prices and—to the extent labor is less mobile than capital—wages.

The mobility of capital and labor make "supply-side" policies attractive to government officials. In the past experts have been skeptical of the influence of state and local taxes on business location, but many recent empirical studies have found a significant negative effect of tax burdens on state economic growth. However, studies have also found significant positive effects of public expenditures for functions such as education and transportation.

The "commerce clause" of the Constitution of the United States prohibits state policies which discriminate against interstate commerce and might reduce the openness of state economies. Obviously this prohibits states imposing "tariffs" on goods imported from other states, but the meaning of the commerce clause has also been an issue in cases challenging the constitutionality of aspects of other state taxes which might discriminate against out-of-state firms.

Government Borrowing

State and local government budgets distinguish capital spending from current operating expenses. Borrowing is considered an appropriate means of financing capital expenditures because future residents as well as current taxpayers will enjoy the benefits of these expenditures. It is thus equitable that future residents share in the costs through the taxes they will pay to service the debt used to finance capital improvement projects.

State constitutions and statutues generally prohibit state and local government borrowing to finance current operating expenses. When tax revenues fall during a recession, these governments are forced to raise tax rates and/or cut expenditures in order to maintain a balanced budget. This is the opposite of the countercyclical fiscal policy often recommended to national governments faced with a recession. In a recession, Keynesian economists would recommend that government spending be increased and/or taxes be cut to stimulate spending. The resulting increases in income would induce further increases in consumer spending, generating a "multiplier" effect bringing the economy out of the recession. However, the multiplier effect on a state economy from a countercyclical fiscal policy would be smaller than the multiplier effect at the national level because a large share of residents' spending is for goods "imported" from other states. Thus, even without constitutional restrictions on deficit financing, state governments would have little incentive to engage in countercyclical fiscal policy.

References

Aronson, J. Richard, and John L. Hilley, *Financing State and Local Governments*, Brookings, Washington, D.C., 1986; Fisher, Ronald C., *State and Local Public Finance*, Scott Foresman, Glenview, Ill., 1988; Ostrom, Vincent, Robert Bish, and Elinor Ostrom, *Local Government in the United States*, Institute for Contemporary Studies, San Francisco, 1988; Tiebout, Charles, "A Pure Theory of Local Expenditures," *Journal of Political Economy*, vol. 64, October 1956, pp. 416–424.

(*See also* Capital gains; Federal budget; Multiplier; Regional economics; Taxation, an overview; Urban economics)

John H. Beck

Static analysis

Static analysis refers generally to any analysis in which the passage of time does not play an essential role. A static analysis can be applied to flow variables (which are measured per unit of time) if the flows do not change any stocks which affect the equilibrium. In addition, a hybrid form of dynamic analysis uses the tools of static analysis to consider a sequence of short periods in which stocks change at the end of each period owing to flows within the period. With the notable exception of the *IS-LM* model, static analysis has been most fruitfully applied to microeconomic problems.

In a great many microeconomic problems, we can safely abstract from growth in the economy and deal with a model in which the equilibrium, once achieved, is unchanged period after period. Such an equilibrium is termed a "stationary state." Further, we are very frequently interested only in the final effects of some change in a parameter of the model—say, in a tax or a price. In such problems, we need to examine the equilibrium only at one arbitrary point in time, since the equilibrium is the same at any other time.

Two Types of Comparative Static Problems

Comparative static analysis examines the changes in the final equilibrium that result from some specified changes in the parameters of the model. Paul Samuelson (1947) observed that comparative static problems fall naturally into either of two types:

1. The first describes the optimizing behavior of individual economic agents (consumers, firms, or the like) as a function of the opportunities available to the agents. The solution of these problems normally involves finding a maximum or minimum of some objective function subject to the constraints which describe the opportunity set.

2. The second sort of problem studies an equilibrium involving the interaction (normally across markets) of a number of economic agents. In these cases, the equilibrium cannot be described as a maximum or minimum of some function. Instead, conditions for the stability of the equilibrium must be specified.

Samuelson's division of comparative static problems is fruitful because it focuses on the information required to make definite qualitative statements about the effects of a change in a parameter of the problem. It so happens that the ratio of the change in each endogenous variable to the change in the parameter generally can be expressed in terms of the determinants of certain matrices of partial derivatives. The conditions for achieving a maximum or minimum often restrict these determinants so that the sign of the ratio of changes can be inferred. The sign of this ratio indicates which direction the endogenous variable moves in response to a change in the parameter.

In the second sort of problem, Samuelson showed that a correspondence often exists between the conditions for stability of the equilibrium and conditions for definite results in a comparative static problem. This duality, called the "correspondence principle," allows one to find definite results for comparative static problems conditional upon observed stability or to infer stability given observed comparative static results. Thus, it is frequently imperative to carry out a formal analysis of the conditions for stability in order to obtain definite comparative static results.

A stability analysis examines whether, beginning from a point away from the equilibrium, the model moves to the equilibrium as times goes to infinity. One may consider any feasible starting point or only points near the equilibrium (local stability). Stability analysis is a sort of abbreviated dynamic analysis in which the only important question is whether the model converges to the stationary-state equilibrium.

Although static analysis has a long history in economics (for example, Marshall, 1920), the modern form using differential calculus was popularized by John Hicks (1939). Samuelson's *Foundations* clearly demonstrated the usefulness of formal techniques and introduced the correspondence principle to extend the range of problems for which definite answers may be obtained. Today a static analysis is standard operating procedure whenever the problem at hand can be analyzed in terms of the final effects on a stationary state.

References

Hicks, John R., *Value and Capital,* Oxford University Press, Oxford, 1939; Marshall, Alfred, *Principles of Economics,* 8th ed., Macmillan, New York, 1920; Samuelson, Paul A., *Foundations of Economic Analysis,* Harvard University Press, Cambridge, Mass., 1947.

(*See also* Economic models; General equilibrium; *IS-LM* model)

Michael R. Darby

Sticky prices (*see* Rigid prices)

Stochastic process (*see* Time series analysis)

Statistical methods in economics and business, an overview

Many statistical methods have been employed in analyzing economic and business problems. In the twentieth century, the field of econometrics emerged in which economic theory, statistical methods, data, and computers are employed to further understanding of economics and business and to produce statistical analyses and models which explain and predict economic and business behavior and are helpful in solving practical problems. Many results have been reported in economic, business, econometric, and statistical journals and texts.

To learn from past and current economic and business data and experience, a general objective of all sciences according to Pearson (1938) and Jeffreys (1988), researchers in economics and business, has been active in producing (1) data which measure and describe economic and business phenomena, (2) generalizations or models to explain past behavior and data and to predict as yet unobserved behavior and data, and (3) solutions to practical, private, and public economic and business problems. In each of these areas, statistical theory and methods have played a central role. For historical material and review articles on econometrics and statistical methods, see Epstein (1987) and Morgan (1990), Griliches and Intriligator (1983, 1984, 1986) and Granger (1990).

Statistical Methods in Measurement and Description

As regards statistical methods in measurement and description, much economic and business data which measure important economic variables such as output, employment, unemployment, prices, interest rates, income, and so on have been produced by use of censuses, surveys, and administrative records. Statistical procedures for conducting censuses and evaluating their results have been developed and applied in many countries. Such census data relating to population, employment, housing, and many other variables have been an important input to economic and business analysis. Similarly, scientifically designed statistical surveys have been employed by governments and business firms to generate useful data relating to unemployment, employment, consumer expenditures, etc. Much of these data have served as a basis for creating national income and product accounts for most countries of the world, data which are invaluable to economic and business analysts. Also, in recent years there have been a number of studies in which data have been produced by carrying out statistically designed experiments either in laboratories or in the field—see, e.g., Aigner and Morris (1979) and Hausman and Wise (1985).

The production of the data mentioned in the previous paragraph is a remarkable achievement in scientific statistical measurement that has been of great value to economics and business, especially since much of it is readily available in publications and computerized databases. Along with the use of statistical methods in the production of data, descriptive statistical methods have been employed to summarize the information in survey and time series data. A wide range of descriptive statistical measures, means, medians, modal values, index numbers, etc. have been employed as "measures of central tendency," and other statistical quantities have been put forward to measure dispersion, income inequality, poverty, industrial concentration, and other features of data in both univariate and multivariate settings, see, e.g., Engle and Rothschild (1992). Graphical techniques, such as box plots, faces, etc. have been developed to permit effective graphical presentation of data. For more on descriptive and graphical statistical methods, see entries under the words *exploratory data analysis* and *graphics* in annual issues of the *Current Index to Statistics,* published by the American Statistical Association and the Institute of Mathematical Statistics.

With respect to descriptive statistical methods for time series data, considerable work has described the components of time series data, for example monthly data on gross domestic product, employment, unemployment, and money supply measures. Generally, as in Burns and Mitchell (1946), there is a desire to describe various types of fluctuations or cycles and trends in the data. Many descriptive statistical methods are available for achieving these objectives; for example, statistical filtering techniques are embodied in the widely used U.S. Census X-11 computer program, which provides measures of seasonal, cyclical, trend, and noise components of series; see Zellner (1983) for articles describing and evaluating X-11 and other filtering methods. A related approach for descriptive "trend-cycle" analysis is trigonometric regression, which involves a least-squares fit of relationships containing periodic and trend terms. Last, the properties of time series data can also be studied in the frequency domain by use of statistical spectral methods, see, e.g., Priestley (1981, 1988). Analyses in the time and frequency domains can provide information about the kinds of systematic fluctuations or cycles that may be present in time series data. Also, in analyses involving two or more variables, it is possible to describe the lead-lag relationships existing between or among variables and the nature of the response of a particular variable or set of variables to changes in other variables. These statistical methods are helpful in discovering systematic relations, cycles, breaks in trends, and other interesting and unusual facts that often challenge economic and business theorists to provide explanations. See Box and Jenkins (1976) and Granger and Newbold (1977) for descriptions and applications of such methods. One famous example of the discovery of an unusual fact from simple, descriptive time series analysis was Kuznets's (1946) empirical finding that the percentage of income saved in the United States was relatively constant over the decades even though real per capita income had risen considerably, a fact that contradicted earlier theoretical results and led to the production of several new theories of consumption and saving; Friedman (1957), for example, used both cross-section and time series methods and data to test his new theory.

Although measurement and descriptive analyses are important and have provided many useful results, there is a need for analyses that lead to explanations of past data and experience and predictions of as yet unobserved data that are dependable. In approaching this range of problems, at least two approaches and their associated statistical methods have been used. First, many have utilized economic and business theory to formulate models to explain the variation of one, several, or many variables and then estimated their parameters and tested these models' ability to explain and predict using statistical methods and data [see, e.g., Griliches and Intriligator (1983, 1984, 1985)]. Others have used a statistical modeling approach to produce models which fit past data reasonably well and are successful in forecasting future data. Then an effort is made to use economic and business theory to explain why these empirical models work as well as they do and to improve them. Thus some have gone from economic and business theory to the data, and others have gone from empirical statistical models to economic and business theory. In both approaches statistical data and methods have been extensively employed. See Zellner (1979) for further discussion of this range of issues, Zarnowitz (1992) for data on the quality of economic and business forecasts, and Berndt (1990) for descriptions of applied analyses in several leading areas of economics and business. Roberts (1990) presents a perceptive discussion of how statistical methods are employed in businesses with attention given to quality management and improvement uses of statistical methods.

Statistical Modeling Methods

Statistical modeling methods have been utilized which involve the assumption that economic and business variables are generated stochastically and not deterministically. This is not to say that deterministic models are ruled out a priori, and, indeed, some in the chaos area have tested deterministic models against stochastic models. Use of stochastic models permits probabilistic modeling of phenomena and use of probability theory in mathematical and statistical analyses. A difficult problem is the initial formulation of a stochastic model for variables, such as daily stock returns or exchange rates. When little theory or knowledge is available relating to a phenomenon being studied, say the variation of stock prices, use of the hypothesis that all variation is random unless shown otherwise has been recommended as a point of departure for statistical modeling and causal analysis. For example, some have used random walk models for stock prices, exchange rates, real gross national product, etc. as initial, benchmark models. If y_t is a random variable under consideration, such a model is given by $y_t = y_{t-1} + \mu + e_t$, $t = 1, 2, \ldots, T$, for T time periods, where μ is a parameter with an unknown value and e_t is a random "error" or "disturbance" term that reflects the influence of factors that impinge on y_t. The e_t terms are nonobservable, and their introduction in the twentieth century was quite controversial—see Stigler (1986). However, their introduction has proven quite useful and successful in permitting the use of formal statistical inference methods.

In implementing the random walk model for y_t and many other models, assumptions are usually made about the properties of the random e_t terms or, equivalently, about the differences $y_t - y_{t-1}$, which reflect what an investigator knows or is willing to assume. For example, it might be assumed that the e_t terms are normally and independently distributed, each with zero mean and common variance σ^2 or equivalently, that the differences $y_t - y_{t-1}$, $t = 1, \ldots, T$, are independently and normally distributed, each with mean μ, and variance σ^2. Given these assumptions, the model is a Gaussian or normal random walk model with parameters μ and σ^2. Under this model, the sample space is $-\infty < y_t < \infty$, for $t = 1, 2, \ldots, T$, and the parameter space is $-\infty < \mu < \infty$ and $0 < \sigma^2 < \infty$. In statistical modeling in general, a model's form, its stochastic assumptions, sample space, parameters and parameter space, and distributional assumptions are key elements not only in terms of characterizing the underlying phenomenon under consideration but also in choice of appropriate statistical methods for data analysis and inference.

In general with respect to economic and business stochastic statistical models, including the above random walk model, statistical methods are available for (1) point and interval estimation, that is for using the observed values of variables to compute estimated values of and probabilistic intervals for parameters, such as μ and σ^2 of the random walk model; (2) testing a variety of hypotheses, e.g., $\mu = 0$ or $\mu > 0$, (3) point and interval prediction, that is using past data and a model to compute predicted values and probabilistic intervals for a future, as yet unobserved outcome; and (4) diagnostic checking and model comparisons, that is, using data to check assumptions of models and to evaluate alternative models. It should be recognized that the basic procedures mentioned have been utilized in analyses of a broad range of models, namely, univariate and multivariate time series models, univariate and multivariate regression models, univariate and multivariate models for discrete random variables, simultaneous equations models, semiparametric models. See Greene (1990) and Judge et al.

(1985) for descriptions of such models and statistical methods for analyzing them. These models have been employed in modeling consumer and firm behavior, markets, regional economies, national economies, and other entities.

In many cases, the models mentioned at the end of the last paragraph have been put forward to explain the past in a causal sense and to predict the future. On the quality of performance, some have compared the predictive performance of these models with that of random walk models. If the models are found not to predict better than random walk models, their usefulness in providing causal explanations and predictions is called into question. For more on the definition of causality and statistical methods for producing and testing for causality, see the articles and references in Aigner and Zellner (1988).

Statistical Methods for Estimation, Testing, Prediction, Model Selection, and Diagnostic Testing

With respect to statistical methods for estimation, testing, prediction, model selection, and diagnostic checking, it should be appreciated that several competing statistical paradigms lead to somewhat different procedures and rationalizations for them. Three major statistical approaches are the sampling theory approach, the likelihood approach, and the Bayesian approach. See, e.g., Berger (1985), Geisser et al. (1991), Judge et al. (1985), Press (1989), and Zellner (1984) for discussions of alternative approaches to statistical inference and their associated methods and justifications. In the sampling approach, usually a frequency concept of probability is employed—see Jeffreys (1988, chap. 7) for a discussion of alternative definitions of probability, and estimation, testing, and other statistical methods are rationalized or justified by their average performance in repeated actual or potential samples of data. For example, in terms of the random walk model introduced above, the sample mean $\hat{\mu} = \Sigma_{t=1}^{T} (y_t - y_{t-1})$ $/T$ is a possible estimate of μ. To evaluate $\hat{\mu}$ as an estimate of μ, sampling theorists analyze the properties of $\hat{\mu}$ in repeated theoretical samples of data, that is for many draws from the random walk process. Thus they view $\hat{\mu}$ to be a random quantity, a so-called estimator, and establish its properties. For example, the mean of this estimator is μ, and thus it is unbiased. Further this estimator can be shown to be a minimal variance unbiased estimator, that is the estimator which is unbiased and has minimal variance in the class of unbiased estimators. "Sampling theory" procedures for interval estimation, testing, prediction, etc. have been developed for many problems, although in some problems finite sample results are difficult to derive, and thus large sample or asymptotic approximations are employed, particularly in analyzing time series, nonlinear, and simultaneous-equation models. See Berndt (1990), Greene (1990), and Judge et al. (1985) for many examples illustrating sampling theory methods and their uses in applications.

In the "likelihood approach," emphasis is placed on analyzing properties of a model's likelihood function for the given sample data. For the Gaussian random walk model mentioned above, the joint probability density function for the T y_t terms, $y = (y_1, y_2, \ldots, y_t)$, given y_0 is

$$f(y \mid y_0, \mu, \sigma^2) = (2 \pi \sigma^2)^{-\frac{T}{2}} \exp \left\{ - \sum_{t=1}^{T} (y_t - y_{t-1} - \mu)^2 / 2\sigma^2 \right\}$$

This function, viewed as a function of μ and σ^2 for the given observations on the ys is, by definition, the likelihood function, denoted by $l(\mu, \sigma^2 \mid y, y_0)$. Maximizing this likelihood function with respect to μ and σ^2 yields the following maximum likelihood estimates (MLEs)

$$\hat{\mu} = \sum_{t=1}^{T} (y_t - y_{t-1})/T \quad \text{and} \quad \hat{\sigma}^2 = \sum_{t=1}^{T} (y_t - y_{t-1} - \mu)^2 / T$$

These values of the unknown parameters make the given sample "most likely" or "most probable" in the sense that the above probability density function $f(y \mid y_0, \mu, \sigma^2)$ attains its maximal value for the observations when $\mu = \hat{\mu}$ and $\sigma^2 = \hat{\sigma}^2$. Although some likelihood advocates do not emphasize sampling properties of their procedures, many others do. In the present problem, it is seen that the MLE estimate of μ is the minimum variance unbiased estimator. However the MLE estimator for σ^2 is somewhat biased in small samples but not in large samples. Further, with respect to other estimation criteria, for example mean squared error, which does not place as much weight on unbiasedness, the MLE estimator $\hat{\sigma}^2$ is somewhat better than the minimum variance unbiased estimator of σ^2, namely

$$s^2 = \sum_{t=1}^{T} (y_t - y_{t-1} - \hat{\mu})^2/(T-1)$$

The use of relevant estimation criteria is important. Further, it is shown in the literature that MLEs for parameters of a wide range of models have fine sampling properties when sample sizes are large in that under this condition they are normally distributed with the mean equal to the parameter being estimated and efficient in the sense that their large sample variance is smaller than or equal to that of any other asymptotically normally distributed estimators which are asymptotically unbiased. Maximum likelihood estimates have been computed for many models in economics and statistics. Their finite sample sampling properties have been compared with those of other asymptotically efficient estimators, say minimum chi-squared estimators for logit and probit models, two- and three-stage least-squares and Bayesian estimators for parameters of supply and demand and other econometric models, and Stein-shrinkage estimators for parameters of regression and other models. See Judge et al. (1985) for reviews of some of these analyses and references to the literature.

The Bayesian Approach

A third major approach to statistical inference and decision is the Bayesian approach—see, e.g., Berger (1985), Box and Tiao (1973), Leamer (1978), and Zellner (1971, 1984) and the references in these works. In this approach to estimation, testing, prediction, and control, use is made of probabilities that measure reasonable degrees of belief and Bayes' theorem as a learning model. The references cited above show that the Bayesian learning model can be used to combine sample information contained in a likelihood function with other available information; the references also show how to use the combined information to make statistical inferences about values of parameters, future, as yet unobserved data, and other quantities of interest. If $l(\theta \mid Y)$ is a likelihood function for the parameter vector θ based on data y, and an investigator's information about possible values of the parameter vector is represented by a prior probability density function (pdf), $\pi(\theta \mid I)$, $\theta \epsilon \Omega$ where I denotes the background or prior information and Ω the parameter space. Note that the prior pdf represents information about possible values of the parameters. For example, in the above random walk model, if μ represents a mean rate of return for a particular stock, an investigator may have information about its value that he or she can represent by a normal density function with a given mean, say 5 percent and standard deviation equal to 2 percent. This density, and others like it for different parameters, represents information that can be used in analyses and lead to improved estimates and predictions. This normal prior pdf is an example of an "informative" prior pdf. When little or no information is available regarding possible values of the elements of θ, or regarding μ and σ^2 in the random walk example, a "noninformative" or "ignorance" prior pdf is employed. In either case, Bayes' theorem yields the result that a posterior pdf for θ that incorporates both the sample information and the information in the prior pdf is proportional to the product of the prior pdf and the likelihood function. That is, with $g(\theta \mid D)$ where $D = (y, I)$ denoting the posterior pdf, Bayes' theorem yields, $g(\theta \mid D) = c\,\pi(\theta \mid I) \times 1(\theta \mid y)$, where c is a normalizing constant. Thus, in general, the posterior pdf is proportional to the prior density times the likelihood function, and it incorporates the sample and prior information. If the prior pdf is uniform, then the posterior pdf for θ is proportional to the likelihood function. In this case, the modal value of the posterior pdf, the most probable value of θ, is precisely equal to the MLE estimate, a result that gives a Bayesian rationale for the MLE estimate. Further, it is shown in the literature that the modal value of a posterior pdf is an optimal point estimate in the sense of providing minimal expected loss when a zero-one loss function is employed. However, if a quadratic loss function is employed, it has been shown that the mean of a posterior pdf is an optimal point estimate. For any specific convex loss function, it is generally possible to compute a point estimate that minimizes posterior expected loss or equivalently maximizes expected utility (negative loss). See Berger (1985), Leamer (1978), Poirier (1991), and Zellner (1971) for proofs of these results and economic and business applications. This optimality property is valid for the actual observations at hand and is not a "repeated sampling property."

As regards sampling or frequentist properties of Bayesian minimum expected loss estimates, it has been shown that they are rather good under a broad range of both finite sample and large sample conditions. Thus Bayesian estimates are optimal for a given sample of data and optimal in repeated samples. Various studies have been performed to appraise the robustness of Bayesian estimation and other procedures to errors in formulating likelihood and loss functions and prior densities [see Berger (1985)].

With a posterior pdf available, it is possible to compute the probability that a parameter, say μ of the random walk model, has a value between a and b, $Pr(a < \mu > b \mid D)$. Such probability statements are quite valuable. Further, the predictive pdf $p(y_f \mid D)$, where y_f is a future, as yet unobserved observation, say, next year's rate of growth of GDP, is obtained as follows

$$p(y_f \mid D) = \int f(y_f \mid \theta) g(\theta \mid D) d\theta$$

where $g(\theta \mid D)$ is the posterior pdf. Predictive pdf's have been computed for many different models and used to make forecasts and to compute predictive intervals for as yet unobserved observations. For example, the mean of a predictive pdf is an optimal point prediction in the sense of minimizing expected predictive loss for quadratic loss functions. Optimal point predictions which incorporate sample and prior information can be derived for a wide range of loss functions. Finally, Bayes' theorem can be employed to transform prior odds on alternative hypotheses or models into posterior odds which reflect the impact of both sample and prior information. See the references cited above and Poirier (1991) for analyses illustrating and applying these posterior odds procedures for evaluating and comparing alternative hypotheses and models.

Controversies have raged over the years about the above and other approaches to statistical inference and their associated statistical methods. Fortunately, much progress has been made in understanding the interrelations of the various approaches, and it appears that a synthesis or compromise will soon be attained; for discussion of one such effort to produce a Bayes/non-Bayes compromise, see Good (1992). He points out that many non-Bayesians put distributions on parameters in random parameter regression models, random effects models, state-space models, etc. that are similar to prior densities, and he sees in this a meeting ground for Bayesians and non-Bayesians. However, there still remains the question of an appropriate concept of probability to employ in using statistical methods and whether the Bayesian learning model is broad enough to analyze all problems successfully. Then too, many discussions of alternative approaches to statistical inference have not as yet considered the problem of model formulation adequately. One promising approach in this regard is the maximum entropy approach which has been successfully used in physics and chemistry to produce models for observations and prior distributions. See Jaynes (1983) and Zellner (1991) for further discussion and references to the literature. Maxent methods make the formulation of models and prior densities explicit and reproducible. While this is true, as is well known it is only through application and use of models and prior densities to explain past data and to predict as yet unobserved data that we can determine whether our statistical methods and models are successful in practice. Many applications of statistical models and methods in recent decades have been successful, and thus the rapid growth in the number of statisticians and econometricians in industry, government, and academia. In the last 50 years, the more widespread use of statistical methods in economics and business has helped to make these fields more scientific and productive.

References

Aigner, D. J., and C. Morris "Experimental Design in Econometrics," *Annals of the Journal of Econometrics,* vol. 11, 1979; Aigner, D. J., and A. Zellner, "Causality," *Annals of the Journal of Econometrics,* vol. 39, 1988; Berger, J. O., *Statistical Decision Theory and Bayesian Analysis,* Springer-Verlag, New York, 1985; Berndt, E. R., *The Practice of Econometrics,* Addison-Wesley, Reading, Mass., 1990; Box, G. E. P., and G. M. Jenkins, *Time Series Analysis, Forecasting and Control,* Holden-Day, San Francisco, 1976; Box, G. E. P., and G. C. Tiao, *Bayesian Inference in Statistical Analysis,* Addison-Wesley, Reading, Mass., 1973; Burns, A. R., and W. C. Mitchell, *Measuring Business Cycles,* National Bureau of Economic Research, New York, 1946; Engle, R. F., and M. Rothschild, "ARCH Models in Finance," *Annals of the Journal of Econometrics,* vol. 52, 1992; Epstein, R. J., *A History of Econometrics,* North-Holland, Amsterdam, 1987; Friedman, M., *A Theory of the Consumption Function,* Princeton University Press, Princeton, N.J., 1957; Geisser, S., J. S. Hodges, S. J. Press, and A. Zellner (eds.), *Bayesian and Likelihood Methods in Statistics and Econometrics,* North-Holland, Amsterdam, 1981; Good, I. J., "The Bayes/Non-Bayes Compromise: A Review," presented at 1991 American Statistical Association Meeting, Atlanta, Georgia, to be published in *Journal of American Statistical Association,* 1992; Granger, C. W. J. (ed.), *Modelling Economic Series,* Clarendon Press, Oxford, 1990; Granger, C. W. J., and P. Newbold, *Forecasting Economic Time Series,* Academic Press, New York, 1977; Greene, W. H., *Econometric Analysis,* Macmillan, New York, 1990; Griliches, Z., and M. D. Intriligator (eds.), *Handbook of Econometrics,* vols. 1, 2, and 3, North-Holland, Amsterdam, 1983, 1984, 1986; Hausman, J. A., and D. A. Wise (eds.), *Social Experimentation,* University of Chicago Press, Chicago, 1985; Jaynes, E. T., *Papers on Probability, Statistics and Statistical Physics,* ed. by R. D. Rosenkrantz, Kluwer, Dordrecht, 1983; Jeffreys, H., *Theory of Probability,* Oxford University Press, London, 1988; Judge, G. G., et al., *The Theory and Practice of Econometrics,* Wiley, New

York, 1985; Kuznets, S., *National Income: A Summary of Findings,* National Bureau of Economic Research, New York, 1946; Leamer, E. E., *Specification Searches,* Wiley, New York, 1978; Morgan, M. S., *The History of Econometric Ideas,* Cambridge University Press, Cambridge, 1990; Pearson, K., *The Grammar of Science,* Everyman Edition, London, 1938; Poirier, D. J., "Bayesian Empirical Studies in Economics and Finance," *Journal of Econometrics,* vol. 49, nos. 1 and 2, July-August 1991; Press, S. J., *Bayesian Statistics,* Wiley, New York, 1989; Priestley, M. B., *Spectral Analysis and Time Series,* Academic Press, New York, 1981; Priestley, M. B., *Non-Linear and Non-Stationary Time Series Analysis,* Academic Press, New York, 1988; Roberts, Harry V., "Applications in Business Economic Statistics: Some Personal Views," *Statistical Science,* vol. 5, no. 4, 1980, pp. 372–390; Stigler, Steven M., *The History of Statistics,* Harvard University Press, Cambridge, Mass., 1990; Zarnowitz, V., *Business Cycles: Theory, History, Indicators and Forecasting,* University of Chicago Press, Chicago, 1992; Zellner, A., *An Introduction to Bayesian Inference in Econometrics,* Wiley, New York, 1971; Zellner, A., "Statistical Analysis of Econometric Models," *Journal of American Statistical Association,* vol. 74, 1979, pp. 628–651; Zellner, A. (ed.), *Applied Time Series of Economic Data,* U.S. Bureau of the Census, Washington, D.C., 1983; Zellner, A., *Basic Issues in Econometrics,* University of Chicago Press, Chicago, 1984; Zellner, A., "Bayesian Methods and Entropy in Economics and Econometrics," in W. T. Grandy, Jr., and L. H. Schick (eds.), *Maximum Entropy and Bayesian Methods,* Kluwer, Dordrecht, 1991, pp. 17–31.

(*See also* Bayesian inference; Business cycles; Computers in economics; Cross-sectional analysis in business and economics; Data banks; Distributed lags in economics; Econometrics, Economic forecasting methods; Game theory, economic applications; Index numbers; Input-output analysis; Leading indicator approach to forecasting; Random walk hypothesis; Regression analysis in business and economics; Sampling in economics; Seasonal adjustment methods; Seasonal variations in economic time series; Secular trend; Simulation in business and economics; Simultaneous equations in business and economics; Time series analysis)

Arnold Zellner

Stock

Stock represents equity or ownership in a corporation. (In the United Kingdom, however, the term usually means debenture bonds issued by corporations or the government. The British use the term *shares* when they refer to stock.) In the United States, stock is classified as either common or preferred. Common stock gives the holder an unlimited interest in the earnings and assets of a corporation after all prior claims have been met. Preferred stock has preference over the common with respect to the payment of dividends and claims on residual assets in the event that the corporation liquidates.

History

It is uncertain as to when the corporate form of business organization was first established and stock issued to represent ownership. Late in the twelfth century, Italians devised a financial instrument that facilitated their trade at the fairs held in the northern French region of Champagne. The *commenda* was a piece of paper that described the agreement between the merchants who went to the fairs and the investors who remained in Milan, Venice, and other Italian cities. Some evidence indicates that mines in Italy and central Europe were jointly owned, and shares in them were traded by the early sixteenth century. In 1553, London capitalists provided £6,000 in £25 shares for "the discovery of the northern parts of the world. . . ." The Dutch East India Company was formed in 1602, followed a few years later by the English East India Company. From the outset, the Dutch company had a permanent capital structure, which financed forts and munitions to protect its trading activities.

The English company, however, financed voyages separately, splitting the profits, if any, after the ships returned home. However, by 1657 it was forced to raise permanent capital for reasons similar to those of the Dutch company.

Liabilities and Rights of Stockholders

Until the nineteenth century, the joint-stock company, or corporation, was used almost exclusively to undertake foreign ventures. However, the industrial revolution led to domestic business endeavors that required immense amounts of capital funds, amounts too large for the sole proprietorship or partnership to raise. Thus, the corporation evolved. The corporation has two major advantages that enable it to raise the necessary funds. First, since in the eyes of the law the corporation is a legal entity separate from its owners, the stockholders' liability is limited to the investment they make in the corporation. Their personal assets are protected. Second, ownership can be transferred relatively easily—with actively traded stocks, in a matter of minutes. These advantages make corporate stock attractive to investors, who have thus provided the large amounts of capital funds that have allowed the corporation to become the vehicle for economic expansion in all the industrial nations.

In the United States, the laws of the state that chartered the corporation and the provisions of the charter itself govern the rights that stockholders have. In general, as a group, common stockholders have rights that include the following: to adopt and amend the bylaws; to amend the charter; to elect the directors of the corporation; to change the amount of authorized stock; and to enter into mergers.

The most important right that the individual stockholder has is sharing in the corporation's earnings when dividends are declared. He or she has the right to vote. But, since most shareholders in major U.S. corporations do not attend annual meetings, provision has been made that allows them to vote by proxy—a written power of attorney (usually temporary) that the stockholder gives to another person (the proxy) to vote her or his shares. Stockholders have the right to share residual assets in the event of dissolution, but since they are the last claimants, this is a relatively weak right. They may sell their shares. And they may inspect the corporation's books, a right that is strictly limited. Obviously, a shareholder who works for a competing company would not be given carte blanche to look at all the books. In many corporations, stockholders have preemptive rights, which allow them to maintain their proportionate shares of ownership if new common stock is issued. For example, suppose a stockholder owns 100 shares of the outstanding 1000 shares of ABC Corporation. If ABC plans to issue an additional 1000 shares of common stock, the shareholder must have the first chance to purchase 10 percent, or 100 shares of the new issue.

Preferred versus Common Stock

Preferred stock is frequently referred to as a hybrid security, because it has some features similar to common stock and others that resemble bonds. Like common stock, the preferred represents ownership in a corporation—the holder is not a creditor. Preferred stock pays dividends, not interest, allowing the directors of the corporation to pass (to not declare) a dividend without the legal repercussions that would occur if they failed to meet interest payments on bonds. But like bonds, preferred stock pays fixed-dollar amounts in dividends, and most preferred shareholders do not have the right to vote for the directors of the corporation.

Many preferred stocks are cumulative, that is, they carry the provision that all passed dividends from previous years must be paid to the preferred shareholders before the directors may declare a dividend to the common stockholders. Another feature that many preferred stocks have is convertibility—the right the holders have to convert the stocks into the common stocks of the same corporation.

Issuing Stock

When corporations issue stock, most use the services of an investment bank, a financial institution that acts as an intermediary between the corporation and the investing public. Investment banks, or underwriters, perform three important functions: First, they offer financial advice to their clients. For instance, they help the company to decide what type of security to issue and what provisions it should contain. In many cases the financial counsel is continuing. Often the investment banker will sit on the board of directors of a client corporation. Second, acting as intermediary, the investment bank distributes the securities when a public offering is made. The underwriter has a marketing organization that presumably distributes the securities more efficiently than would be done if the corporation attempted to do it itself. Finally, and probably most important, investment banks bear the risk of price declines while the new issue of stock is distributed. Once an underwriting agreement is reached between the issuing corporation and the underwriter, the latter guarantees that a certain amount of money for the securities will be turned over to the corporation on a specified date. If the price of the stock falls while the investment bank is marketing the securities, the underwriter suffers the loss.

Regulation of the Securities Industry

Following investigations into the collapse of the stock market in 1929, Congress enacted several laws that regulate the securities industry. The Securities Act of 1933, for instance, governs the issuance of stock, covering all interstate public offerings. The major thrust of this law is to provide full disclosure of all relevant information regarding the stock being offered. This information and a record of representations are contained in a registration statement made to the Securities and Exchange Commission (SEC)—a government agency established by the Securities Exchange Act of 1934—and summarized in a prospectus, which must accompany the offering. If the SEC thinks that the information is inadequate or misleading, the SEC will stop or delay the offering. Furthermore, if an investor suffers a loss because of misinformation, the investor may sue any of the parties who prepared the statement.

The Importance of Stock to the Economy

Equity financing via common or preferred stock historically represented a major source of funds to corporations; in a broader sense, stocks are an instrument used to bring savers and investors together, which is crucial for economic expansion. Industrial nations are highly specialized, and the people and institutions that save (consume less than their incomes) are usually different from those who invest (produce capital goods that increase the output of goods and services). Financial intermediaries, such as commercial banks, credit unions, and investment banks, bring savers and investors together in the financial sense, using various instruments including common and preferred stocks to do so. Stocks, therefore, are vital to a growing economy.

References

Brigham, Eugene F., and Louis Capenski, *Financial Management Theory and Practice,* 6th ed., Dryden, Hinsdale, Ill., 1991; Weston, J. Fred, and Eugene F. Brigham, *Essentials of Managerial Finance,* 6th ed., Dryden, Hinsdale, Ill., 1976.

(*See also* Bond; Financial instruments; Securities and Exchange Commission; Stock exchange)

Henry C. F. Arnold

Stock exchange

A stock exchange is an organized marketplace in which securities, such as bonds and common and preferred stocks, are bought and sold. Because the origins of today's stock exchanges usually were informal gatherings of merchants and others who traded securities, when the first organized marketplace began operations is difficult to pinpoint. Beginning in 1611, merchants met in Amsterdam to trade shares in the Dutch East India Company and, thus, may have formed the first stock exchange, or bourse, even though this exchange was not formally organized into the Association for Promoting Trading in Securities until 1785. The Paris Bourse was established in 1724, and in 1775 London brokers, who had been transacting business at Jonathan's (a coffee house), moved to a room in Sweeting's Alley and formally named it The Stock Exchange, the beginnings of what is today the third largest stock exchange in the world. The Philadelphia Stock Exchange, begun in 1790, was the first organized marketplace in the United States, followed two years later by that historic meeting on May 17, 1792, when 24 merchants agreed to meet every day under an old buttonwood tree on Wall Street. The New York Stock Exchange (NYSE) traces its genesis to this agreement. Japan's first stock exchanges were established in 1878 in Tokyo and Osaka as places where public bonds could be traded. Today, the Tokyo Stock Exchange is the world's largest, having eclipsed the NYSE in the late 1980s. Today there are stock exchanges in virtually every industrial nation in the world, including those in Zurich, Frankfort, Milan, Melbourne, and Toronto.

Regional Stock Exchanges

Nine stock exchanges, which are registered with the Securities and Exchange Commission (SEC) as national securities exchanges, operate in the United States (NYSE, American, Boston, Cincinnati, Midwest, Pacific, Philadelphia, and Spokane Stock Exchanges and the Chicago Board Options Exchange). At the end of 1989, these stock exchanges had 2697 issues of common stock listed, 692 issues of preferred stock, and 3362 bond issues. The market value of the common stock totaled nearly $3 trillion, the preferred over $35 billion, and the bonds more than $1.4 trillion. The market value of the NYSE's listed securities dwarfs the combined total of all the other exchanges. At the end of 1989, the total value of the "big board's" listed common stock was nearly $2.9 trillion, almost 97 percent of that listed on all U.S. exchanges. Nearly 90 percent of the market value of all preferred stock was listed on the NYSE and over 98 percent of the market value of bonds. The NYSE also dominates trading activity. Over the past decade, the NYSE has accounted for slightly more than 80 percent of all shares and over 85 percent of the dollar amount of stock traded on organized exchanges in the United States.

Although trailing far behind the NYSE, the American Stock Exchange (AMEX), also located in New York City, is the second largest organized securities market (in terms of number of shares and dollar amounts listed) in the United States. Established in the 1850s, the AMEX was called the New York Curb Exchange, because trading literally took place outside on the curb, until 1921 when its operations moved indoors. The name was finally changed in 1953. At the end of 1989, the market value of listed common stock on the AMEX totaled almost $98 billion and preferred stocks slightly over $3 billion.

Of the remaining six regional exchanges, only the Boston and Pacific Stock Exchanges had listed stocks with a market value of more than $1 billion—$1.9 billion and $1.2 billion, respectively—at the end of 1989. The Cincinnati Stock Exchange had only three common and one preferred stocks listed with a total market value of under $40 million, and the Spokane Stock Exchange's listed stock's value was roughly $8 million.

New York Stock Exchange

Since all the exchanges are organized and operate similarly to the NYSE, that exchange will be described in more detail. The NYSE is a corporation governed by 21 directors: 10 chosen from the securities industry, 10 from outside that industry, and the presiding officer of the Board, who is selected by the directors. The NYSE does not own securities, buy or sell stocks, or influence their prices. It provides a centrally located place for its members to buy and sell securities. Membership in the exchange numbers 1366 individuals who have bought seats, which allow them to trade securities on the floor of the NYSE. The value of a seat has fluctuated sharply over the years, reaching a high of $1.5 million in 1987 and sinking to a low of $4000 in both 1876 and 1878. In early 1992, an NYSE seat sold for $470,000.

Members may be either general partners or holders of voting stock in one of the 530 member firms in existence as of late 1991. Members perform different functions. Approximately 60 percent are either commission or floor brokers. The former are partners or officers of commission houses that execute trades for the public for which they are paid commissions. Many of the larger firms have several commission brokers handling the public's trading on the exchange floor. The latter, popularly known as $2 brokers, because at one time that was their commission for handling a 100-share transaction, help commission brokers by executing the latter's buy-and-sell orders when trading activity is high. Another 35 or so members are registered traders, or Registered Competitive Market Makers, who buy and sell for their own account, hoping to profit from their speculations. Their transactions must meet exchange requirements and allegedly increase the market's liquidity.

Finally, about 30 percent of the members are specialists, who act as both dealers and brokers. As dealers, the specialists are charged with maintaining an orderly market in the stocks in which they specialize. In carrying out this responsibility, specialists should be trading against the market—that is, buying if the prices of their stocks are declining and selling if they are rising. The object in both cases is to maintain price continuity and minimize the impact of a divergence of supply and demand. As brokers, specialists record other brokers' buy-and-sell orders that are away from the market—different from the prevailing prices—in their stocks. If and when the price of a stock moves up or down to the price on the order, specialists execute it and receive a commission for their services.

A corporation must meet certain requirements—more stringent on the NYSE than any of the other exchanges—before the NYSE will accept its stock for listing. These requirements include demonstrated earning power, minimum numbers of shares outstanding and shareholders of round lots (100 shares), and a minimum total market value of shares outstanding.

NYSE Economic Function

The major economic function of securities markets is to help allocate capital resources efficiently—to direct these scarce resources to endeavors that offer the best return and to carry out this function at minimum cost. Organized securities exchanges presumably perform this function most efficiently because they closely resemble the classic textbook example of a purely competitive market. With numerous buyers and sellers transacting homogeneous financial claims and with information available to all, the theoretical outcome of pure competition should result; scarce resources should be allocated efficiently.

Although the evidence indicates that the stock exchanges have performed this function well, there have been some problems. For example, from its origins in 1792 until the 1970s, the NYSE both regulated the actions of its members and limited access to the trading floor. The NYSE maintained a schedule of fixed minimum commission rates, which led to a deleterious impact on the allocational efficiency of the exchange. Furthermore, NYSE members had to execute trades in listed stocks on the exchange floor unless they got permission—rarely given—from the governing authorities to use a regional stock exchange (which listed the stock) or the over-the-counter (OTC) market, the market for security transactions that are not made on an organized stock exchange.

Also, nonmember brokers and dealers had access to the exchange floor only through member firms. They had to pay the standard fixed commission that any other customer would pay, which obviously encouraged them to avoid the NYSE.

Another problem has been the growth of block trading, which represents trades of 10,000 shares or more. Block trades are privately negotiated and do not depend to any significant degree upon either the facilities or procedures of the stock exchange.

Major Changes

These monopolistic intrusions led to inefficiencies and distortions, the most important of which was a fragmentation of the stock market. At any given time, a given stock might be trading at different prices in the various components of the stock market (the NYSE, the regional stock exchanges, and the OTC market), and customers might be deprived of receiving the best price when buying or selling stock. These restrictive practices came under a barrage of attacks from financial institutions, the SEC, the Antitrust Division of the Department of Justice, and the Congress in the late 1960s and early 1970s. These complaints led to major changes, all designed to increase competition and improve the efficiency of the securities markets and eventually lead to a National Market System—which Congress ordered in 1975. In 1972, the SEC mandated a Consolidated Tape System, which now reports all stock transactions on the exchanges and the OTC market, providing up-to-date information to investors from all components of the stock market. Since May 1, 1975, commissions on all transactions, no matter what size, have been competitively negotiated. This action has benefitted institutional investors most but has also led to discount commission houses that attract small investors interested only in having their trades executed, not in the other services provided by the typical firm. The Composite Quotation System, initiated in 1978, provides bid and asked prices for all listed stocks from all components of the stock market, thus aiding brokers in getting the best price for their customers. Finally, in 1978 the Intermarket Trading System (ITS) began functioning. The ITS electronically links the NYSE, the AMEX, and several regional exchanges and probably represents the most important step on the road to a true National Market System. However, before that becomes a reality, rapid technological advances may result in a global stock market, which would overwhelm a U.S. National Market System. Already, several hundred U.S. stocks trade in London and a smaller number in Tokyo. British and other nations' stocks trade in the United States and elsewhere. U.S. financial institutions have interests in foreign securities firms and have offices in the world's principal financial centers. Foreign companies have financial interests in U.S. financial institutions. Fueled by technology, we seem to be moving toward a true global financial market in which anyone with access to a telephone may trade stocks, bonds, and other financial instruments, as well as commodities, at any time, in any financial market in the world.

References

Amling, Frederick, *Investments: An Introduction to Analysis and Management,* 6th ed., Prentice-Hall, Englewood Cliffs, N.J., 1989.

(*See also* Bond; Securities and Exchange Commission; Stock; Stock price averages and indexes)

Henry C. F. Arnold

Stock-flow analysis

A stock-flow good can be produced and held, and its services can be consumed. The half-life of a pure flow good approaches zero: it can be produced and consumed, but not held. A pure stock good cannot be produced—see Marshall's (1920) meteoric stones—but it may be an empty economic box. In a sense all goods are pure stock goods: no molecule is exactly like another; one molecule of a certain grade of crude oil differs from another. In another sense, no good is a pure stock good: Works of art can be replicated to some degree.

The mathematical paradigm defining elementary stock-flow analysis is embedded in the classical theory of differential equations:

$$\dot{\xi} = f(\xi)$$

The system's motion ($\dot{\xi}$) is a function of its state (ξ); the simplest stock-flow equilibrium is a state, $\bar{\xi}$, so that $f(\bar{\xi}) = 0$. This being understood, stock-flow analysis makes transparent a number of otherwise opaque policy issues.

Stock-flow equilibrium is typically badly specified. If state variables are defined—as they are by Archibald and Lipsey (1958)—as microcosms, any stock-flow equilibrium will be unobservable (and thus chimerical). But macroeconomic steady states (regular motions) are, in principle, observable, that is, steady states in the sense of Marshall (1920), Pigou (1935), and Burstein (1988, chap. 2).

Stock-flow analysis has had a rough passage in the pure theory of consumer choice, because hedonic analysis is so perplexing. Becker (1965) and Lancaster (1966) built models in which service streams, yielding utility, are defined by qualities common to many goods; commodity space transmutes into characteristics space. This approach may now overshadow the more explicit stock-flow analysis of Bushaw and Clower (1957).

Stock-flow analysis dominates study of the demand for consumer durables. Chow (1957) sets the pace in his study of automobile demand: Demand for new cars (having the dimension of a flow) is mapped from the disparity of actual from desired stocks. The studies published in Harberger (1960) push in the same direction: Burstein (refrigerators) and Griliches (automobiles) probe hedonics; and Richard Muth (housing) develops a theme going back at least as far as J. M. Clark's (1917) approach to investment—the more durable the good, the less important is replacement (flow) demand and the more important is investment (flow) demand. In the upshot, estimates of price elasticity of demand for consumer durables have been corrected, and investment in productive capital is seen to be the tail of the asset-portolio-decision dog—not the other way around.

Completing the exposition,

- Consumption must be distinguished from depreciation (a distinction clouded by such nomenclature as "capital consumption allowances"). Households might hold stock-flow goods that do not depreciate, but consumption occurs: The goods yield services.

- The widely known, but ill understood, problem of dimensionality is to be clarified.

Consumption versus Depreciation

The distinction of consumption from depreciation being made, consider a stock-flow good that does depreciate. Depreciation is part of the cost of holding (and utilizing) an asset, as are (explicit or implicit) interest charges, and service streams are a benefit. The schematization is suggested by chapter 17 of Keynes's (1936) *General Theory.*

The theories of stock-flow goods and user cost intersect. A beautiful object—fungible so that it is a stock-flow good—may deteriorate independently of how often it is viewed. Contrast such an object with candy: One cannot hold candy and eat it too.

Dimensionality

Stock demands (X) are for tons of steel or numbers of cars to be held at date t; flow demands (x) are time rates of change; x_r may be translated as purchase of the rth commodity at an annualized rate symbolized by x_r. So the numbers representing stock and flow demand are incommensurate.

Flow demand is made commensurate with stock demand by integration: x_{rt} is the value of $f(t)$ at $t = \tau$; $f(t)$ describes the purchase plan; $\int f(t)dt$ has the dimension of a stock.

Not enough information has been supplied to map stock demands into flows: Intertemporal asset accumulation programs must be defined relative to initial data, objective functions, and technological and market constraints; some variant of optimal control must be deployed—but early stock-flow theory ignored Hamiltonians.

In period analysis, both x and X have the dimension of a stock: x_r is the number of units of the rth commodity to be purchased during the day and is commensurate with X_r, the number of units to be held at the end of the day.

Integration of "Stock-Flow" with Other Theories

The Theory of the Isolated Market   Consider this simple model. Freight cars are to be hired out by source holders who make a market for used cars and acquire new cars from manufacturers. Carriers rent equipment from source holders and provide shipping services. Flow equilibrium requires that replacement plus investment demand equal production of new cars. Investment demand depends on the current stock of sources relative to stocks planned for future dates, which in turn are functions of expected rents, interest rates, and source prices. Plans formed in this way generate investment demand on an interval.

The stock of sources is predetermined in the process generating instantaneous flow equilibrium. In a special case of stock-flow equilibrium—the stationary state—investment demand is nil. Then source rents and source prices, together with the stock of sources, are such that source makers' desired rate of production is equal to replacement demand by source holders.

Disequilibrium in the Isolated Market   Flow disequilibrium is more straightforward than stock-flow disequilibrium (an elusive concept). If transactions occur in flow disequilibrium so that there is false trading (the only real-world trading), some transactors will be disappointed; not all expectations will be fulfilled. In flow equilibrium, *cum* stock disequilibrium, no offer to sell or bid to buy at market fails to be filled.

Rational Expectations

Stock-flow equilibrium has become subsumed by a deep theory of futures markets. And under rational expectations, transactors, knowing the structures of the economy and the subeconomies in which they operate, will optimize relative to efficient estimates of future data. In the usual formulations of stock-flow markets, transactors fail to optimize even in deterministic models; in the nonstochastic world of ordinary stock-flow theory, rational transactors would achieve an equilibrium at the onset of a process spanning the system's phase space. Insights of earlier stock-flow theory are supported, but the analysis requires a quite different paradigm of market behavior. Related discussion is found in Foley (1975), Turnovsky and Burmeister (1977), Karni (1979), and Harrison (1987).

The Stock-Flow Paradigm and Modern Theory

In each of the following cases, response to stock disequilibrium is confused with a fundamental functional relationship between "the" rate of interest and variables like investment or foreign exchange rates or between changes in money growth and interest rates.

Say that "the" real interest rate somehow falls. Common economic reasoning suggests that:

- Agents will plan to hold more physical capital.
- Global portfolio managers, sensitive to uncovered yield differentials between money centers, will plan to reduce the proportion their holdings of "our" securities bear to total holdings.

Or say there is an unexpected increase in the growth rate of "base money": The banking system will, along well-known lines, seek to expand its collective balance sheet.

Once stock adjustment has been accomplished, stimulus to capital goods demand or weakness in "our" currency or excess demand in the "money market" will dissipate. Changes in control levels perturb the system, so that, e.g., stimulus may be transiently supplied to one or more markets, but no persisting effect results—perturbations vanish when stock-flow equilibrium is restored.

The Stationary State

Proper stock-flow analysis must, like quantum physics, abandon "individual laws of elementary particles and state directly the statistical laws governing aggregations; its laws are for crowds and not for individuals" (Einstein and Infeld, 1942, p. 15). Marshall (1920) and Pigou (1935), anticipating this point, supply parsimonious microeconomic foundations for the theory of stock-flow equilibrium. Pigou (1935, p. 81) described three degrees of stationary states: "First, the system of industry as a whole may be stationary, while the several industries that compose it are in movement. Secondly (each) industry may be stationary, while the individual firms in it are in movement. Thirdly, individual firms, as well as individual industries may be stationary." The macroeconomic analyses of J. S. Mill, Marshall, and Pigou are confined to the "first degree." Marshall (1920, pp. 366–367) wrote, "this (stationary) state obtains its name from the fact that in it the general conditions of production and consumption, of distribution and exchange, remain motionless; but yet it is full of movement; for it is a mode of life. The average age . . . may be stationary; yet each individual is growing up towards his prime, or downwards to old age."

References

Archibald, G. C., and R. G. Lipsey, "Monetary and Value Theory: A Critique of Lange and Patinkin," *Review of Economic Studies,* vol. 26, October 1958, pp. 1–22; Becker, G. S., "A Theory of the Allocation of Time," *Economic Journal,* vol. 75, September 1965, pp. 493–517; Burstein, M. L., *Money,* Schenkman Pub. Col., Cambridge, Mass., 1963; Burstein, M. L., *Modern Monetary Theory,* St. Martin's Press, New York, 1986; Burstein, M. L., *Studies in Banking Theory, Financial History and Vertical Control,* St. Martin's Press, New York, 1988; Bushaw, D. W., and R. W. Clower, *Introduction to Mathematical Economics,* Irwin, Homewood, Ill., 1957; Chow, G., *The Demand for Automobiles in the United States,* North-Holland, Amsterdam, 1957; Clark, J. M., "Business Acceleration and the Law of Demand," *Journal of Political Economy,* vol. 25, 1917, pp. 217–235; Clower, R. W., "Stock-Flow Analysis," in D. L. Shills (ed.), *International Encyclopedia of the Social Sciences,* Macmillan & The Free Press, New York, vol. 15, pp. 273–277; Clower, R. W., and M. L. Burstein, "On the Invariance of Demand for Cash and Other Assets," *Review of Economic Studies,* vol. 28, 1960, pp. 32–36; Einstein, A., and L. Infeld, *The Evolution of Physics,* Simon & Schuster, New York, 1942; Foley, D. K., "On Two Specifications of Asset Equilibrium in Macroeconomic Models," *Journal of Political Economy,* vol. 83, 1975, p. 303; Harberger, A. C. (ed.), *The Demand for Durable Goods,* University of Chicago Press, Chicago, 1960; Harrison, G. W., "Stocks and Flows," in J. Eatwell, M. Milgate, and P. Newman (eds.), *The New Palgrave Dictionary of Economics,* Stockton Press, New York, 1987, vol. 4, pp. 506–509; Karni, E., "On the Specification of Asset Equilibrium in Macroeconomic Models: A Note," *Journal of Political Economy,* vol. 83, 1979, p. 171; Keynes, J. M., *The General Theory of Employment, Interest and Money,* Harcourt & Brace, New York, 1936; Lancaster, K. J., "A New Approach to Consumer Theory," *Journal of Political Economy,* vol. 74, 1966, pp. 132–157; Marshall, A., *Principles of Economics,* 8th ed., Macmillan, New York, 1920; Pigou, A. C., *The Economics of Stationary States,* Macmillan, New York, 1935;

Turnovsky, S. S., and E. Burmeister, "Perfect Foresight, Expectations, Consistency and Macroeconomic Equilibrium," *Journal of Political Economy,* vol. 85, 1978, p. 379.

(*See also* Firm theory; General equilibrium; Static analysis)

M. L. Burstein

Stock market crashes

The word *crash* is usually reserved for only the most sudden extreme stock market price drops, as drops exceeding 6 percent between successive trading days. By this definition, there have been 25 stock market crashes in the United States since 1928; 14 of these occurred in the years from 1929 to 1933. The two biggest one-day crashes occurred in 1929 and 1987. On Monday, October 28, 1929, the Standard and Poor's composite index of stock prices (S&P index) closed 12.34 percent below the close of the preceding Saturday and closed yet again 10.16 percent lower one day later. On Monday, October 19, 1987, the S&P index closed 20.46 percent below the close of the preceding Friday; most of this decline took place in a few hours, between 1:30 and 4:00 p.m. EDT.

Sometimes the word *crash* is used to refer to major declines in stock prices that occurred over intervals of time as long as a few years. By this definition, the U.S. stock market crash of 1929 might be defined as the 86.2 percent decline in the S&P index between its high of September 7, 1929, and low of June 1, 1932. And, by this definition we could include as important crashes such recent events as the 49.2 percent decline in the Nikkei index in Tokyo between its high of December 29, 1989, and low of October 1, 1990, or the 79.4 percent decline in the Taiwan stock market between its high on February 12, 1990, and its low on October 1, 1990.

The Pattern of Stock Price Changes

Prices in the stock market show a tendency for rare sudden breaks, where prices change drastically more than is characteristic of their normal day-to-day movements. One sees from the figure on page 958 that the normal day-to-day price change is no more than plus or minus 2 percent: In 93.7 percent of trading days the stock market moved up or down no more than 2 percent. In 99.3 percent of trading days the level of stock prices moved up or down no more than 5 percent. Moreover, since big stock price movements occurred only in the years of the Great Depression and in the late 1980s (from 1941 to 1986 inclusive there was no time where stock prices, as measured by the S&P index, changed more than 6.75 percent between successive trading days), many stock market participants have gone through entire careers never observing a one-day movement in prices much greater than 5 percent. One of these participants might well conclude, if decades of personal experience with the market encourages assurance, that one-day movements of 8 percent or more just cannot happen. Yet, as the longer-term historical record attests, they do in fact happen. During the 63-year period covered by the figure, there were ten daily decreases of more than 8 percent and thirteen daily increases of more than 8 percent. Point *A* represents one extreme decline— −20.46 percent on October 19, 1987; point *B* represents −12.34 percent on October 28, 1929; point *C* represents −10.16 percent on October 27, 1929;

point *D* represents −9.92 percent on November 6, 1929 and −9.27 percent on October 8, 1937; point *E* represents −8.88 percent on July 20, 1933, −8.70 percent on July 21, 1933, −8.28 percent on October 26, 1987, −8.20 percent on October 5, 1932, and −8.02 percent on August 12, 1932; point *F* represents increases of 8.14 percent on July 24, 1933, 8.27 percent on February 11, 1932, 8.29 percent on December 15, 1931, 8.37 percent on February 13, 1932, 8.59 percent on October 8, 1931, 8.86 percent on August 3, 1932, and 8.95 percent on November 14, 1929; point *G* represents 9.10 percent on October 21, 1987, 9.52 percent on April 20, 1933, and 9.63 percent on September 15, 1939; point *H* represents 11.81 percent on September 21, 1932; and point *I* represents 12.36 percent on October 6, 1931 and 12.53 percent, the other extreme, on October 10, 1929. Statisticians describe this tendency for extremely rare and extremely big events as a tendency for "outliers," indicating that the distribution of stock price changes (as seen in the figure) has "fat tails" relative to the normal bell-shaped curve.

There is not, however, any marked tendency in these enormous sudden price breaks for asymmetry between increases and declines. Looking at the figure, one sees little evidence that the largest one-day drops tend to be larger than the largest one-day increases. Indeed, until the 1987 crash the biggest one-day movement in stock prices ever observed since January 1928 was an increase, not a decrease. Many of the largest percentage increases occurred immediately after major stock market drops and might be regarded as corrections of such drops; this was true of the two biggest percentage price increases ever, point *I* on the figure. But still, there are many

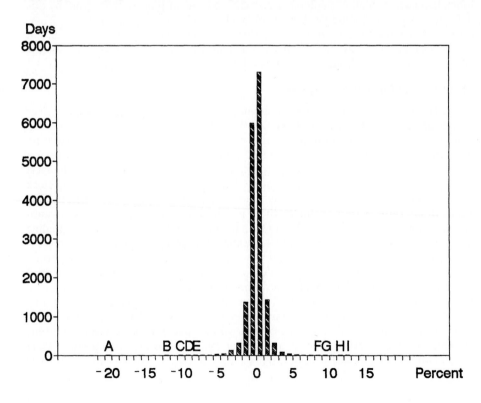

significant one-day increases that did not follow sharp one-day declines. The next three biggest one-day increases did not occur in close proximity to any sharp stock market decline: The S&P index rose 11.81 percent on Wednesday, September 21, 1932 (attributed by the news media to a reaction to rallies in wheat and cotton markets); the index rose 9.63 percent on Tuesday, September 5, 1939 (attributed to investors' deciding that a European war would help U.S. business, following Hitler's September 1 invasion of Poland); and the index rose 9.52 percent on Thursday, April 20, 1933 (attributed to news that President Roosevelt's controlled inflation program had been drafted).

Reasons for Concern about Crashes

There has been a great deal of public attention and concern about such crashes ever since the 1720 stock market crash in France and England associated with the collapse of share prices in the Mississippi Company and the South Sea Corporation. Crashes attract more attention than sudden price increases because crashes portend sudden and devastating economic hardship for some. People who borrowed money to buy stocks may be wiped out in a crash. Moreover, crashes tend to be followed by broader financial crises. In the century up to the crash of 1929, stock market crashes tended to be associated with banking crises as well. Moreover, the stock market crash of 1929 was followed by the great depression in economic activity of the 1930s, and many people have extrapolated that such crashes may be harbingers of depressions. However, we have had no other depressions of the severity of the 1930s, and only two crashes of the magnitude of 1929s, and hence we cannot know whether such crashes really portend economic depressions or whether the crash of 1929 only coincidentally preceded the depression. We do know that there is some tendency for smaller stock market downturns to precede the smaller recessions for which we have many examples. In 41 recessions from 1802 to 1990, 38 of them have been preceded or accompanied by declines of 8 percent or more in stock returns (Siegel, 1991). Still, the stock market declines often give false alarms, and the tendency for false alarms seems to have increased since World War II; notably the crash of 1987 produced no recession at all.

News and Crashes

Major stock price movements usually appear unrelated to any major economic news from outside the financial markets; there is usually no sensible reason for the crash. Moreover, big news days do not seem to correspond to especially large changes in stock prices. Cutler, Poterba, and Summers (1989) analyzed the most important news events, events that *The New York Times* carried as its lead story of the day, from 1941 to 1987. The typical change in stock prices on those 49 days, as measured by the standard deviation, was only 2.08 percent, only a little over twice the typical change (standard deviation of 0.82 percent) of all days in that period, hardly representative of the biggest movements in the stock market.

Popular accounts written after stock market crashes often attribute the crash to news events, but these news events are typically very minor or became known long before the crash. The October 1987 crash was attributed by some to remarks made over the preceding weekend by the U.S. Treasury secretary, by others to a proposed tax bill that became known five days before the crash. Such an event is possibly the disturbance that triggers an avalanche but cannot be sensibly regarded as its true cause.

The absence of news on days of big stock price changes has proved troublesome for theorists who think that financial markets are efficient and that every price movement must have a sensible cause. Some, e.g., Gennotte and Leland (1990), have proposed theories that the market rationally infers "news" about economic fundamentals from the price declines themselves.

Speculative Booms and Crashes

Many of the major stock market crashes occurred after booms, spectacular price runups to very high price-earnings ratios; certainly this is true of the 1929 and 1987 U.S. crashes and the Japanese and Taiwanese crashes referred to above. A popular interpretation of such crashes is that they occurred as a correction of investor over-enthusiasm. The enthusiasm for investing which sometimes precedes crashes could arise spontaneously in large populations by the same social processes that generate other social movements, processes that sociologists have studied extensively.

Sometimes booms may be understood in more economic terms using a feedback theory which asserts that price increases themselves may at certain times encourage increased investor demand among investors who extrapolate price changes and think that the past price increases portend future price increases. The investors may feel regretful that they were left out of the past price increases and fearful that they will miss future price increases. When these investors buy stocks, they tend to bid up prices yet more. A vicious circle is set up, creating an upward cycle of prices.

Investors do not always react this way to past price increases. What they do depends on the popular theories and models at the time. Investors try to guess what others are thinking and in turn what other investors think other investors are thinking. With investors trying to stay one step ahead of each other on such opinions and communicating rapidly with vast numbers of each other via price and via media accounts, views about the market may change dramatically and quickly.

Eventually, prices reach such a high level that they can be sustained only if there are very optimistic expectations for the market. At this time, many people begin to worry that the market is overpriced, and they begin to fear a crash. Any slight downward disturbance in the market, or some minor news event that provides a suggested point for concerted action, may then break the optimism, encourage investors to think the crash is imminent, and thus to try to sell, thereby bringing on the very crash that they feared.

During a speculative boom, many investors may be aware that there has been over-enthusiasm or that a feedback cycle is underway; that this is a distinct possibility may even be common knowledge. Many people may short stocks or buy puts, hoping to profit from the ultimate crash. Yet the effect of these people on the market may not be sufficient to stop the boom from developing. The amount these people are willing to risk is limited, and those who short stocks or buy puts stand to lose money if the stock market keeps going up; no one knows exactly when the crash will come.

Bates (1991) showed, based on the abnormally high prices of out-of-the-money puts then, that the market was unusually concerned about a crash in late 1986 and June through August 1987, although by his measure the fears appear to have become reduced just before the actual crash in October.

A U.S. survey taken right after the crash of October 19, 1987 (Shiller 1989) confirms that fears of a crash were very much on people's minds right before the crash. In answer to the question "Do you remember thinking or talking about events of 1929 on the few days before October 19, 1987?" 53.2 percent of a random sample of institutional investors and 35.0 percent of a random sample of high-income individual (nonprofessional) investors answered "yes." Most institutional and individual investors attributed the crash to investor psychology rather than to any theory of fundamentals such as profits or dividends. Professional economic forecasts of earnings or real interest rates show no sudden change at the time of the crash. What *did* remarkably change at the time of this crash was popular attention to the stock market: In the survey a remarkable 96.7 percent of the random sample of high-income individual investors reported that they heard about the crash on the day of the crash, 81.6 percent heard of it before 5:00 p.m. local time, therefore after the morning newspapers and before the evening news broadcasts. News of the crash spread largely by direct interpersonal communication as fast as news of the most severe national crises. The stock market crash of October 1987 appears to have been a time of heightened investor attention to the market, of sped-up reactions and hurried decisions, and of sudden concern about the psychology of other investors.

Policies to Reduce the Likelihood of Crashes

An unusually large amount of stock was held with margin credit just prior to the 1929 crash; this borrowing was widely held to have helped fuel the boom and the margin calls during the crash to have exacerbated it. The Securities Exchange Act of 1934 mandated margin requirements to reduce market volatility; whether these requirements had the intended effect remains controversial. The stock index futures markets that developed in the 1980s had lower margin requirements than did the stock markets themselves and thus weakened the effect of existing margin requirements. The introduction in the 1980s of portfolio insurance (trading strategies that respond automatically to price declines by selling in the stock index futures markets) and other program trading methods created automatic selling in reaction to price declines in 1987 that might have the same effect as the margin calls in 1929. The Presidential Task Force on Market Mechanisms, chaired by Nicholas Brady in response to a commission by President Ronald Reagan, recommended that margin requirements should be made consistent across markets and that circuit breaker mechanisms (such as price limits and coordinated trading halts) be implemented. The exchanges in fact adopted higher margin requirements on stock index futures and coordinated market halts and uptick rules that are triggered when prices change beyond certain announced thresholds.

Whether these policy measures will have a substantial effect on reducing the likelihood or severity of crashes remains controversial; there is certainly no assurance that these measures will prevent major crashes in the future.

References

Bates, David S., "The Crash of 87: Was It Expected? The Evidence from the Options Markets," *Journal of Finance,* vol. 46, no. 3, 1991, pp. 1009–1044; Cutler, David M., James M. Poterba, and Lawrence H. Summers, "What Moves Stock Prices?" *Journal of Portfolio Management,* Spring 1989, vol. 15, no. 3, pp. 4–12; Fisher, Irving, *The Stock Market Crash—and After,* Macmillan, New York, 1930; Gennotte, Gerard, and Hayne Leland, "Market Liquidity, Hedging, and Crashes," *American Economic Review,* vol. 90, no. 5, December 1990; Galbraith, John K., *The Great Crash,* Houghton Mifflin, New York, 1955; Hsieh, David A., and Merton H. Miller, "Margin Requirements and Stock Market Volatility," *Journal of Finance,* vol. 45, March 1990, pp. 3–29; Mitchell, Mark L., and Jeffry M. Netter, "Triggering the 1987 Stock Market Crash: Antitakeover Provisions in the Proposed House Ways and Means Tax Bill," *Journal of Financial Economics,* vol. 24, 1989, pp. 37–68; New York Stock Exchange, *Market Volatility and Investor Confidence: Report to the Board of Directors of the New York Stock Exchange, Inc.,* New York, 1990; Presidential Task Force on Market Mechanisms (Brady Commission), *Report,* U.S. Government Printing Office, Washington, D.C., January 1988; Shiller, Robert J., *Market Volatility,* MIT Press, Cambridge, Mass., 1989; Siegel, Jeremy J., "Does It Pay Stock Investors to Forecast the Business Cycle?" *Journal of Portfolio Management,* Fall 1991, pp. 27–34; U.S. Securities and Exchange Commission, Division of Market Regulation, *The October 1987 Market Break,* U.S. Government Printing Office, Washington, D.C., 1988.

(*See also* Great Depression; Leading indicator approach to forecasting)

Robert J. Shiller

Structural models (*see* Economic forecasting methods; Economic models)

Stock price averages and indexes

Arithmetic averages and indexes of selected stocks are designed to measure the level and trends of overall stock prices. Charles H. Dow, who founded the Dow-Jones Company, is reported to be the first person to have measured the general level of securities prices by calculating the average price of a few representative stocks. His first list in 1884 comprised 11 stocks, including 10 railroad companies, which were the leading business enterprises of that day. In 1897, Dow-Jones expanded the original list to a 20-stock rail average, which has continued to the present, although many of the stocks have been replaced, and the list's name has been changed to reflect the increasing importance of other means of transportation. In that same year, Dow-Jones introduced another average composed of 12 industrial stocks—the beginning of the Dow-Jones industrial average (DJIA). Since Dow-Jones' pioneering efforts, many firms, at one time or another, have computed and published stock price averages and indexes, but the DJIA has maintained its original prominence.

Major Averages and Indexes

Among those currently published on a daily basis in major newspapers are the following.

Dow-Jones Averages   These comprise four stock averages: The DJIA, consisting of 30 industrial stocks (8 stocks were added to the original 12 in 1916 and another 10 in 1926), which is the best-known and most popular measure of stock price trends; the transportation average of 20 stocks developed from the first of the Dow-Jones averages; the utility average of 15 stocks, which was introduced in 1929; and a composite average of the above 65 stocks. All stocks included in the Dow-Jones averages are listed on the New York Stock Exchange.

At the outset, the Dow-Jones averages literally represented the average price (arithmetic mean) of the stocks included in the group. But two major problems arose that distorted the averages. First, some companies included in the original list became less important, and others not on the list became more important. Consequently, the publishers periodically substituted stocks in their averages. However, unless they replace a stock with another selling at the same price (which is highly unlikely), price trends would be misrepresented because the average would rise or fall even if stock prices remained unchanged. Fortunately, substitutions were made infrequently. Second, stock splits and stock dividends, which occur far more frequently, distorted the averages unless the editors make adjustments. For example, suppose we have an average composed of three stocks whose prices per share are $25, $50, and $75, or an average of $50. If the company whose stock was selling at $75 decided to split the stock 5 for 1, the average would decline to $30—a 40 percent drop—obviously distorting stock price levels and trends.

Of the methods that could be used to prevent substitutions, stock splits, and dividends from affecting the averages, Dow-Jones uses the constant-divisor method. When computing the average after a split, for instance, they change the divisor so as to negate the distortion that would occur from the split. In the above example, before the split the average was 25 + 50 + 75 = 150, which, divided by 3, yields 50. After the split we get 25 + 50 + 15 = 90, which, if we divided by 3, would yield 30. Instead of dividing by 3, we solve the following equation so as to find that divisor that will keep the average unchanged, that is, at 50: $90/X = 50$, therefore, X equals 1.8, which is the new divisor. This divisor will be used until the next split, stock dividend, or substitution occurs. It should be stressed that the quotient computed is expressed in points, not dollars. The DJIA, for example, could rise 10 points without any of its 30 stocks increasing as much as a dollar.

Several criticisms have been leveled at the Dow-Jones averages. It is claimed that the number of stocks included in the averages is too small to be representative of the whole market. Furthermore, the stocks that are included are those of large, financially strong, blue-chip companies, whose stock price trends might differ markedly from those of other companies. Most important, the Dow-Jones averages (and other averages) are not weighted. The higher the price of the stock, no matter how large the corporation or its importance to the economy, the greater the weight it carries in the average. At one time, for instance, DuPont stock, because of its high price, influenced the DJIA more than the combined effect of the stock of United States Steel (now USX), General Motors, General Electric, and Westinghouse. Today, stocks like Merck and Disney weigh heavily in the DJIA. The Dow-Jones averages, even with these serious deficiencies, have moved in tandem with other more technically correct measures.

Standard & Poor's Indexes   The Standard & Poor's Corporation computes and publishes approximately 100 stock price indexes, individually covering various industries such as cement, copper, and chemicals. Better known however, are the seven S& P's indexes that are published in the daily newspapers: 400 industrial stocks; 20 transportation stocks; 40 utility stocks; 40 financial stocks; the composite index of the total 500 stocks above, probably the best known; the MidCap 400; and the 100 Stock Index, which comprises NYSE stocks that have options listed on the Chicago Board Options Exchange. The base for these indexes is the period 1941–1943 = 10, and they are weighted by the market value of the stocks. Standard and Poor's multiplies the price of each stock by the number of shares outstanding, adds the products and divides this sum by the value of the base period, and finally multiplies this quotient by ten. The result is a market-value-weighted index of stock prices.

NYSE Common Stock Index   In 1966, the New York Stock Exchange (NYSE) introduced a stock price index that covers all the common stocks listed on that exchange, currently those of over 1700 corporations. This index, too, is weighted by the market value of the stocks, and its base is December 31, 1965, equals 50. The NYSE calculates the index continuously during trading hours and releases the data every half hour. The exchange also computes and releases indexes for four major industry groups: industrial, transportation, utility, and finance.

AMEX Index   The American Stock Exchange also computes and publishes an index of the prices of its listed stocks. It was started on August 30, 1973, with a base equal to 100 (in July 1983 the base was adjusted to half that level) and includes approximately 800 stocks. Like the other indexes, it is weighted by the market value of the stocks included.

NASDAQ Index   The National Association of Securities Dealers Automated Quotations Index began in February 1971 and today includes some 3700 stocks that are traded over the counter. Its base is February 5, 1971, equals 100, and it is weighted by the market value of the issues included. Aside from the composite index, indexes for the following industry groups are also computed and published: industrial, financial, insurance, utilities, banks, and transportation.

Wiltshire 5000 Equity Index   Calculated by Wiltshire Associates of Santa Monica, California, the Wiltshire 5000 is the broadest measure of stock prices. It includes all NYSE, AMEX, and OTC stocks for which daily quotes are available. The index is weighted by market value and represents the total value of the 5000 stocks in billions of dollars. Changes are measured against a base market value for December 31, 1980.

Designed to Correct Deficiencies

As evident from the preceding description of the various stock price indexes, they are designed to correct the deficiencies of the Dow-Jones averages. All include many more stocks in their coverage, and, most important, all are weighted.

References

Brigham, Eugene F., and Louis Capenski, *Financial Management Theory and Practice,* 6th ed., Dryden Press, Hinsdale, Ill., 1991.

(*See also* Index numbers; Stock)

Henry C. F. Arnold

Subsidies

Ordinary economic transactions occur between two parties, a buyer and a seller. A subsidy is a grant of money from an outside third party to either the buyer or the seller in the transaction. Subsidies generally allow a buyer to receive a good or service for a lower price than would otherwise have been necessary. For example, in the United States payments to hospitals by government agencies allow many persons to receive medical care at charges below the cost incurred by the hospitals. The effects of a subsidy are, in general, the opposite of the effects of a tax on transactions, in that a subsidy encourages transactions whereas a tax restricts them.

A business firm will not stay in operation very long unless revenue is great enough to cover cost outlays plus a return on equity and on managerial effort as large as could be earned in other pursuits. If revenue from buyers is insufficient, a subsidy from an outside agency may keep the firm in operation. It does not matter in theory whether the subsidy is paid directly to the firm. If the subsidy goes to the buyer, then the subsidy raises the price that the buyer is willing to bid for a specified good. Even if a firm does not operate for profit, revenue from buyers plus subsidies from philanthropists or government must be sufficient to meet cost outlays and to replace deteriorating structures and equipment.

Principal Forms of Subsidy

A subsidy can affect both the equilibrium quantity and the price in transactions of a specified good. The actual results depend on the form of the subsidy, on whether firms behave competitively, and on the elasticities of supply and demand. The principal forms of subsidy are the flat grant and the matching grant. Flat grants are fixed sums of money that do not depend on an exact volume of production. This is most common in private charitable giving, such as religious contributions. Other examples are government grants to universities for research or for student financial aid in meeting tuition. Matching grants employ some formula relating the amount of subsidy to the amount of production or costs incurred. Allowance of various deductions from taxable income is an important type of matching subsidy for socially favored expenses.

A flat grant increases the quantity of a good produced under two conditions. In one case the firm or activity may otherwise cease to exist. This case is relevant in grants for basic research which produce valuable information but often with unenforceable property rights. In other cases, output and consumption are increased because the grant is combined with regulation to require that prices to consumers be low enough so that the activity just breaks even. A case of this sort is illustrated by local governments meeting the deficit of a mass-transit operator while requiring fares to be kept at some low level.

In the case of matching grants, we may assume that a government agency is set up to rebate to consumers some fraction of expense on a particular good. This is the same as offering a credit against income tax due from the individual (a refundable credit which would be received even if one were not to owe taxes). Demand for the good is increased because the net price—gross price less subsidy per unit—is less. If the supply is completely fixed, as may be the case in the short run, then the effect is to raise the income of producers. Potential buyers will bid against each other until the net price is restored to the preexisting gross price. If the supply is completely elastic with constant returns to scale and unchanging factor input prices and this may better characterize the long-run possibilities, then the subsidy increases output with a net price permanently reduced by the amount of subsidy per unit. Intermediate supply elasticities imply that both the output and the gross price rise from the preexisting equilibrium.

A subsidy has a distributional impact relative to the taxes needed to balance the budget of the government program. Suppose, for example, that the program is financed by a general proportional tax on all consumption. People with especially strong tastes for the subsidized good or people receiving external benefits from its production are relatively favored. Note that if the share of this good in total family consumption rises with family income, richer families are disproportionately benefited. If some resources are not supplied elastically to this industry, owners of these resources will have their incomes raised relative to others. The case of doctors supplying subsidized medical care is a primary example.

Rationale for Subsidy Programs Is Controversial

Economists (Milton Friedman, for example) distrustful of political power have warned that concentrated producer interests seek to capture favors in the political process from diffuse and unorganized taxpayers. Some subsidies clearly favor politically strong groups at a high cost to the rest of the taxpayers. Taxation specialists such as Joseph Pechman have also argued that many subsidies written into the tax laws erode the progressivity of the tax structure.

Martin Feldstein (1976) has articulated a more reassuring model of selection of subsidies. Suppose the production or consumption of some good generates positive externalities—where others in the community enjoy at little or no cost a good originally produced for another group—such that private markets are not induced to produce these goods in the appropriate quantity. Education, home ownership, and energy-producing inventions may be cited as candidates. Then a subsidy may be preferable to direct government production for several reasons: (1) There may be relatively less efficient managerial control in a bureaucratic agency than in a private corporation; (2) government may not produce the full variety and qualities of the good desired by individuals; and (3) the price elasticity of demand for the good may be greater than 1, in which case the revenue lost to the government is less than the private expenditures induced by the subsidy.

References

Feldstein, Martin, and Amy Taylor, "The Income Tax and Charitable Contributions," *Econometrica,* vol. 44, no. 6, November 1976, pp. 1201–1222; Friedman, Milton, *Capitalism and Freedom,* University of Chicago Press, Chicago, 1962, chap. 6; Musgrave, Richard, and Peggy Musgrave, *Public Finance in Theory and Practice,* 4th ed., McGraw-Hill, New York, 1984, chaps. 10, 11, 32; Pechman, Joseph, and Benjamin Okner, "Individual Income Tax Erosion by Income Classes," in *Economics of Federal Subsidy Programs,* U.S. Congress, Joint Economic Committee, 92d Cong., 2d Sess., 1972.

(*See also* Federal budget; Grants economics)

Bernard S. Friedman

Supply

Supply is a fundamental concept in both macro- and microeconomic analysis. In macroeconomic theory, aggregate supply is mainly a function of expected sales to consumers, businesses, and governments. In micro analysis, the subject of this entry, supply is mainly a function of prices and costs of production. A more complex view of the supply curve for a commodity is its relation between quantities forthcoming and the possible current prices of that commodity, its expected future prices, the prices of alternative goods and services, the costs of the producer, and time.

Opportunity Costs

Incorporated in the supply curve of goods and services are opportunity costs. Economists differ from accountants and from the Internal Revenue Service by including both explicit and implicit costs, or opportunity costs. Implicit costs are mainly business costs for wages, rents, and interest, whereas opportunity costs are the alternative costs of doing something else. A sole proprietor or the owners of businesses should calculate what they forgo in wages, rents, and interest by not working for someone else, or by renting the property they use to others, or by the possibility of converting plant and equipment to alternative investment projects.

The Shape and Position of Supply Curves

In competitive markets the shape, or elasticity of supply, reflects time in the production process, such as the immediate or market period, the short run, and the long run. Elasticity of supply is the relative change in price that induces a relative change in quantity supplied. The supply curve is a line on a diagram where the vertical axis measures price and the horizontal axis is quantity. Usually the coefficient of elasticity is positive, meaning that a rise in price induces an increase in the quantity supplied. In the immediate or market period, a given moment, time is defined as too short to allow for a change in output. The supply curve is vertical, and the coefficient of elasticity is zero. The short run is defined as a period sufficiently long to permit the producer to increase variable inputs, usually labor and materials, but not long enough to permit changes in plant and equipment. The supply curve in the short run is less inelastic or more elastic than in the immediate period. The long run permits sufficient time for the producer to increase plant and equipment. The longer the time, the greater the elasticity of supply.

Changes in supply are shifts in the position of supply curves. An increase in supply is a rightward movement of a supply curve, with more of the commodity being offered for sale at each possible price. Conversely, a decrease in supply shifts the supply to the left. An increase in supply can occur because sellers expect lower prices in the future, or, as in the agricultural sector, because of bountiful crops. The reverse is true of a decrease in supply. Over periods of time long enough for production processes to change, improvements in technology and changes in input prices and productivities are the main causes of changes in supply.

Short-Run Supply Curves

The short-run supply curve of a firm in pure competition is the marginal cost curve at a price equal to or greater than average variable cost, i.e, the producer can pay labor and materials bills. That marginal cost curve can permit economic losses (average revenue is less than average cost), or normal profits (average revenue equals average cost), or economic profits (average revenue is greater than average cost). The short-run supply curve of the industry is the horizontal addition of the marginal cost curves of all the firms in the industry. In monopolized markets, there is no supply curve. Rather, supply or output is one point, where marginal cost equals marginal revenue. If demand were to increase or decrease, a different unique output would materialize in equilibrium. A supply curve would not result from connecting these points.

Long-Run Supply Curves

By the definition of the long run, producers can expand or contract the sizes of their plants, everything being variable. The prices to be received for planned output must cover the producers' full costs, including opportunity costs and a normal profit. Until extensive research indicated otherwise, the view was that full costs per unit of output must increase with long-run expansion because of diminishing returns. Empirical findings strongly suggest the hypothesis that many long-run supply curves are flat over considerable ranges of output. The horizontal supply curves mean that the full cost per unit produced would remain constant if an industry were to double or quadruple in size. A horizontal supply curve for an industry is often assumed in applied theoretical work. That assumption bypasses many of the complications that pure theory delights in and is also probably quite realistic.

The Supply of Public Goods

When provided by government agents (federal, state, or local), the supply curve in the public sector is no different from that for the private sector. It is marginal cost. For equilibrium in the provision of pure public goods, the following condition holds: $MC = P = MU_A + MU_Z$. For equilibrium in the private sector, $MC = P = MU_A = MU_B$. However, collaborate private schemes can also provide pure public goods, i.e., goods that are shared by all participants. The consumers agree on the amount of the good to be provided, and then they agree on the cost-sharing arrangement among the volunteers. This kind of supply function typically relates to such shared facilities as private lakes, swimming pools, game reserves, and day care centers. A problem that arises with the provision of such cooperative public goods is that nonparticipants or "free riders" might use the facilities and contribute less than their true marginal benefits or contribute nothing at all.

Unusual Supply Curves

A number of unusual supply curves seem to exist. Most have one thing in common, a negative slope over some range of the supply curve. One such example is for the supply of blood. That curve can rise to the left so that less is supplied at higher prices. These higher prices tend to be relatively "low," and then, at prices higher than these "low" prices, the supply curve follows the usual rise to the right. The explanation is that some people are willing to donate blood and are not willing to sell blood for ethical reasons. After those individuals leave the market, others willing to sell blood at higher prices cause the supply-of-blood curve to assume its usual shape.

Another such curve is often called backward-sloping because its upper part, at high prices, has a negative slope, and its lower part, at low prices, has a positive slope. This curve can apply to the labor of an individual. At higher earning rates, the individual will work fewer hours than at lower rates. This is so if the income effect dominates the substitution effect in the individual's decisions. The higher earnings along with fewer hours are preferred to the combination of less leisure and the income provided by lower rates of earnings.

For very short periods, a negatively sloped supply curve can also describe the actions of speculators in an organized commodity market. They could be caught in a position where they desperately need cash. Then, faced with declining prices, they sell more as prices fall.

The final example is a supply curve surrounded by much theoretical controversy. It is the long-run supply curve for a competitive industry whose unit costs diminish as the industry expands. Depending on how they are coupled with their relevant demand curves (demand being more elastic than supply), these negatively sloped supply curves can indicate unstable equilibrium in the functioning of competitive markets.

Shortages and Surpluses

From time to time events in the economy bring about shortages of supply. These shortages occur when prices are at a level such that the quantities supplied are smaller than the quantities demanded at the same prices. These levels of prices exist under government price controls. Rent controls are an example. General price controls in periods of inflation can make shortages appear to be pervasive, even foreboding. Miniminum prices of the kind often imposed in periods of general economic contraction can be the cause of surpluses, gluts, and overproduction. When governments or producers' organizations (usually cooperatives in the dairy industry) establish minimum prices, the quantities supplied at those prices are nearly always greater than the quantities demanded at the same prices. The unsold quantities, the surpluses, may be destroyed or put into storage.

References

Buchanan, James M., "A Behavioral Theory of Pollution," *Western Economic Journal,* vol. 8, no. 4, December 1968, pp. 357–363; Hirschleifer, Jack, *Price Theory and Applications,* Prentice-Hall, Englewood Cliffs, N.J., 1988, chap. 7; Ireland, Thomas R., and James V. Koch, "Blood and American Social Attitudes," in Armen A. Alachthin (ed.), *The Economics of Charity: Essays on the Comparative Economics and Ethics of Giving and Selling, with Applications to Bloud,* Institute of Economic Affairs, London, 1973, pp. 152–153; Kohler, Heinz, *Intermediate Microeconomic Theory and Applications,* 3d ed., Scott, Foresman, Glenview, Ill., 1990, chap. 5; Watson, Donald S., and Mary A. Holman, *Price Theory and Its Uses,* 4th ed., Houghton Mifflin, Boston, 1977, chaps. 13, 14.

(*See also* Demand; Elasticity; Opportunity cost; Price theory; Production function; Scarcity)

Mary A. Holman

Supply-side economics

Supply-side economics emerged in the congressional policy process during 1975 to 1978 as an alternative to the demoralizing Phillips curve trade-offs, which had paralyzed U.S. economic policy by making economic growth synonymous with rising inflation. By the autumn of 1978, supply-side tax rate reductions, combined with limits on the growth of government spending, had passed both houses of Congress. These legislative initiatives were stymied by opposition from the Carter administration, but the growing influence of the supply-side approach to economic policy was reflected in the 1979 and 1980 *Annual Report* of the Joint Economic Committee of Congress.

In 1981 President Ronald Reagan succeeded in enacting a supply-side program. The implementation of the program was marred by a radical swing in monetary policy and by budget deficits that resulted from the unanticipated collapse in inflation, which, together with the 1981–1982 recession, removed $2.4 trillion from the five-year projected growth path of GNP.

Relative Prices

Supply-side economics restored the influence of fiscal policy by emphasizing relative price changes instead of income changes. Marginal tax rates affect the relative prices of leisure and current consumption in terms of forgone current and future income. The higher that marginal tax rates are, the cheaper leisure and consumption are in terms of forgone income.

In the Keynesian theory, tax-rate reductions boost aggregate demand and intensify inflationary pressures. In the supply-side theory, tax-rate reductions increase incentives and shift the aggregate supply curve. Thus, by leading directly to greater output, supply-side economics provided a way out of the Phillips curve conundrum. Supply-siders explained stagflation as the result of a policy mix that stimulated demand, while bracket creep, rising regulation, and other disincentives undercut the growth of aggregate supply. Hence, demand management had worsened inflation while reducing the rate of economic growth.

Initially, many economists objected to the emphasis on the relative price effects of fiscal policy. They argued that the incentives of lower tax rates would have perverse effects, because the income effect of a relative price change runs counter to and dominates the substitution effect. Thus, lower tax rates would allow people to reach their targeted levels of income and wealth with less work and a lower saving rate. Lester Thurow, for example, argued that the way to get people to work more was to impose a wealth tax, which would cause them to increase their effort in order to attain their desired posttax wealth.

The argument that the elasticities of response of work and saving to tax rates were zero or negative could hold for some individuals, but the argument could not be true for everyone in the aggregate. If the overall response to a tax-rate reduction was less labor supply, total production would fall. Once Keynesians realized that their own explanation of expansionary fiscal policy was undercut by their argument that people would take their tax cut in the form of increased leisure, they accepted the relative price effects of fiscal policy. Today economists realize that only the substitution effects are relevant in the aggregate.

Cost of Capital

Supply-side economists contributed the insight that marginal tax rates enter directly into the cost of capital. Investment opportunities that cannot earn a normal profit after covering tax and depreciation charges can be made profitable by a reduction in tax rates. This insight provided a more promising way of stimulating investment than the attempt to use monetary policy to drive market interest rates below the marginal return on plant and equipment. If markets clear, central banks cannot change the real interest rate independently of the tax, risk, and technological determinants of the cost of capital, as the U.S. experience in the 1970s demonstrates.

In post-Reagan years U.S. economic policy has again suffered from the misconception that interest rates determine the cost of capital. In practice, this view has led to increased taxation in attempts to reduce "crowding out" by the federal deficit and to spur capital investment by lowering deficits and interest rates. These attempts have failed. For example, the *Budget of the U.S. Government for Fiscal Year 1993* shows dramatic increase in the long-term structural deficit and deterioration in the economic growth path, despite the promises of the budget agreement that caused President George Bush to break his vow not to raise taxes. Supply-side economics explains this failure by observing that taxation (and regulation) also crowd out investment. "Crowding out" can be reduced only by cutting government expenditure and reducing disincentives.

From a supply-side perspective, the tax reform debate leading to the 1986 Tax Reform Act was not satisfactory. Although the 1986 Act further reduced the top tax rate, the debate emphasized the distortion of the choice of the investment mix caused by tax preferences. Reformers promised that increased efficiency from the elimination of these distortions would boost the economy. In contrast, supply-side economists stressed that a neutral tax system is one that excludes saving from the tax base. The nonneutral treatment of saving and investment results not only from tax preferences that distort the mix but also from the multiple taxation of saving that reduces the overall level of investment. From a supply-side perspective, tax preferences work to offset the multiple taxation of saving and to bring the individual's income from investment more in line with the economic return to society.

Empirical Basis

Various studies have provided empirical evidence that people respond to better incentives. For example, Michael Boskin (1978) found that saving responded to after-tax rates of return. Jerry Hausman (1981, 1983) found that direct taxes on earnings reduce labor supply and economic efficiency. Lawrence B. Lindsey (1990) found that the Reagan tax-rate reductions resulted in an increased willingness to hold dollars. This drop in velocity helped to break the back of inflation more rapidly than had been predicted. The decline in income velocity in the 1980s is proof that the long Reagan expansion was not a Keynesian demand phenomenon, because a recovery fueled by deficits would have raised the income velocity of money.

Laffer Curve

Supply-side economists have been accused of making a "Laffer curve" forecast and predicting that the 1981 Economic Recovery Tax Act would pay for itself with revenues from increased economic growth. However, no such prediction was made. The Reagan administration's budget and economic forecasts were based on the traditional Treasury Department static revenue forecast. Tables in the publicly available official documents show that the administration expected to lose a dollar of tax revenue for every dollar of tax cut.

Moreover, the Laffer curve does not predict that tax cuts pay for themselves. Rather, it is a pedagogic tool used to highlight the dynamic effects of tax policy in contrast with the static estimates that remain in use by policymakers. Both the Treasury and the Joint Taxation Committee of Congress assume that changes in taxation have no incentive effects. In the static forecasts that continue to be the basis for U.S. economic policy, an increase (or decrease) in tax rates raises (or lowers) revenue in strict proportion to the tax-rate change. Such a forecast lacks economic basis.

Internal Revenue Service data make it clear beyond any doubt that despite the large reduction in the top tax rate, upper-income taxpayers are paying a much larger percentage of the total income tax revenues than previously. The Treasury Department announced on November 2, 1990, that the data from the 1988 individual income tax returns showed a 54 percent increase in the share of federal income taxes paid by the top 1 percent of taxpayers (from 17.9 percent in 1981 to 27.6 percent in 1988). The share paid by the bottom half of taxpayers fell 23 percent (from 7.4 percent of the total in 1981 to 5.7 percent in 1988). Lindsey (1990) found that the marginal tax-rate reductions in the 1981 Act recovered more than one-third of the estimated direct revenue loss and that the reductions in the higher brackets more than paid for themselves. Others have found similar results. By making a static revenue forecast, the Reagan administration greatly overpredicted the revenue loss from the 1981 Economic Recovery Tax Act.

References

Anderson, Martin, *Revolution,* Harcourt Brace Jovanovich, New York, 1988; Boskin, Michael, "Taxation, Saving and the Rate of Interest," *Journal of Political Economy,* vol. 86, 1978, pp. 3–27; Hausman, Jerry, "Labor Supply," in H. J. Aaron and J. A. Pechman (eds.), *How Taxes Affect Economic Behavior,* Brookings Institution, Washington, D.C., 1981; Hausman, Jerry, "Taxes and Labor Supply," Working Paper no. 1102, National Bureau of Economic Research, Cambridge, Mass., 1983; Lindsey, Lawrence B., *The Growth Experiment,* Basic Books, New York, 1990; Lucas, R. E., Jr., "Supply-side Economics: An Analytical Review," *Oxford Economic Papers,* vol. 42, 1990, pp. 293–316; Robbins, A. E., G. A. Robbins, and Paul Craig Roberts, "The Relative Impact of Taxation and Interest Rates on the Cost of Capital," in R. Landau and Dale Jorgenson (eds.), *Technology and Economic Policy,* Ballinger, Cambridge, Mass., 1986; Roberts, Paul Craig, "The Breakdown of the Keynesian Model," *The Public Interest,* vol. 52, 1978, pp. 20–33; Roberts, Paul Craig, *The Supply-Side Revolution,* Harvard University Press, Cambridge, Mass., 1984; Roberts, Paul Craig, "What Everyone 'Knows' about Reaganomics," *Commentary,* February 1991, pp. 25–30; Ture, Norman B., "The Economic Effects of Tax Changes: A Neoclassical Analysis," in R. H. Fink (ed.), *Supply-side Economics: A Critical Appraisal,* University Publications of America, Frederick, Md., 1982.

(*See also* Federal Reserve policy; Fiscal policy; Keynesian economics; Laissez faire; Monetary policy; Say's law of markets)

Paul Craig Roberts

System of National Accounts

The System of National Accounts (SNA) is a set of international guidelines for recording estimates of transactions and stocks in macroeconomic accounts. As of the early 1990s, the SNA is followed by most countries; the United States plans to move toward it in the mid-1990s.

Development of the SNA

Reflecting growing interest in the field in the 1930s and early 1940s, a committee chaired by Sir Richard Stone laid the groundwork for an internationally comparable set of national accounts in a 1947 report prepared under the auspices of the League of Nations. The first SNA was drafted by an international committee of experts, again chaired by Stone, and was adopted by the U.N. Statistical Commission in 1953. A central feature was that it placed national income and product totals in an integrated system of economic transactions. It defined the economy essentially in terms of market transactions, and it presented consumption, investment, and saving measures in addition to the income and product totals. A revision in 1968 substantially extended the U.N. system to include input-output accounts, flow-of-funds accounts, and balance sheets.

Purposes of the SNA

The SNA has had two main purposes: to facilitate international comparisons and to serve as a guide to countries as they develop their own economic accounting systems. Most countries with market economies use the SNA as a guide. The European Community adopted a version of the SNA to be followed by its member countries beginning in 1970. Canada follows the broad outline of the SNA. Japan and Australia moved to the SNA after the 1968 revision.

Countries with centrally planned economies have followed a different system—the System of Balances of the National Economy, also called the material product system. This system accords with Marxist theory. Consistent with their transition to market-oriented economies, most of these countries have begun to move to the SNA.

The SNA as a System

The SNA is a framework that records the stocks and flows that are defined as part of the economy. That framework groups transactors and transactions in a way that is meaningful for economic analysis, forecasting, and policy.

For transactors, the SNA groups households, governments, and business enterprises (financial and nonfinancial) into sectors. However, some transactors have characteristics of more than one of these sectors, and the SNA deals with them either by treating them as a separate sector (as it does for nonprofit institutions serving households) or by combining them with one or more of the other sectors (as it does for unincorporated enterprises). Foreigners, to the extent that they have transactions with residents, are treated like a sector, called the "rest of the world." In a parallel presentation, the SNA groups producing establishments into industries.

The SNA groups transactions according to the major categories of economic activity—production, income and outlay, capital accumulation, and capital finance. The transactions—often referred to as "flows"—are supplemented by revaluations for price change; together the flows and revaluations "explain" the differences between the stocks shown in the opening and closing balance sheets.

Each group of flows and the stocks are arranged in a two-sided account in which the totals balance either by definition or by inclusion of a balancing item. When the transaction (and associated stock) accounts are set up for each transactor group, the result is a set of macroeconomic accounts for the nation and for the several sectors (and industries). The SNA aggregates—such as gross product, saving, and national wealth—are usually a total for an account or a balancing item.

Thus, the SNA provides a comprehensive framework: It includes measures of production, income, saving and investment, and wealth; it encompasses both domestic and foreign activities; it links financial and nonfinancial transactions; and it provides for both current and constant-price measures. Further, the SNA is an integrated system, that is, the several subsets of accounts use consistent definitions, classifications, and accounting conventions (valuation, time of recording, etc.).

Comparison of the SNA and the U.S. Economic Accounts

The SNA includes accounts that are separate systems in the United States. The national income and product accounts (NIPAs), prepared by the Bureau of Economic Analysis (BEA), cover the transactions that are grouped in the SNA as production, income and outlay, and capital accumulation. BEA's input-output accounts cover the production accounts by industry. The flow-of-funds accounts, prepared by the Federal Reserve Board, cover the financial transactions. Finally, the Federal Reserve Board also prepares revaluation accounts and balance sheets, but they only cover the private domestic sectors. (The SNA does not include balance-of-payments accounts.)

Compared with the U.S. economic accounts, the SNA is more comprehensive. The U.S. accounts do not include a complete set of either revaluation accounts or balance sheets. In addition, the SNA is more fully integrated. Most notable is that the NIPAs and the flow-of-funds accounts differ conceptually and statistically; they are not fully reconcilable.

The SNA's definitions, classifications, accounting structure, and accounting conventions differ to some extent from those used in the U.S. accounts. A reconciliation of gross national product and gross domestic product from the NIPA's and of gross domestic product as calculated for the SNA is shown for 1989 in the accompanying table.

	Billions of dollars
Gross national product, NIPAs	5,200.8
Less: Net factor income from abroad	37.6
Gross domestic product, NIPAs	5,163.2
Plus: Services of nonmilitary government structures and equipment	61.8
Less: Imputed financial service charges	103.2
Plus: Federal government pensions	10.2
Gross domestic product, SNA	5,132.0

In 1990 BEA announced a plan to modernize and extend its national accounts by moving toward the revised SNA. A shift to emphasize gross domestic product, rather than gross national product, as the primary measure of production beginning in 1991 anticipated the other steps to be taken in the mid-1990s.

Future of the SNA

A revision of the SNA begun in the early 1980s is intended to update the SNA to reflect new economic institutions, statistical developments, and analytical applications, to clarify and simplify its presentations, and to harmonize it with other international statistical guidelines. The revised SNA is expected to be presented to the U.N. Statistical Commission in 1993.

References

United Nations, *A System of National Accounts,* Studies in Methods, Series F, no. 2, rev. 3, New York, 1968; Carson, Carol S., and Jeanette Honsa, "The United Nations System of National Accounts: An Introduction," *Survey of Current Business,* vol. 70, June 1990, pp. 20–30.

(*See also* Bureau of Economic Analysis; Gross domestic product; National income accounting)

Carol Carson

Tableau economique (*see* Physiocrats)

Takeovers (*see* Mergers, takeovers, and corporate restructuring)

Taxation, an overview

Taxation is the compulsory means by which government finances its activities and expenditures. Government financing is also obtained through fees for specific services rendered and through borrowing, both of which are usually voluntary. At times, the distinctions among these three types of financing are narrow, and one country may label a tax what another categorizes as a fee.

Taxation is as old as government itself and has taken many forms. Since taxes must be assessed against some measurable base, tax systems and accounting systems have often grown hand in hand. In early civilizations, it was common for farmers or landowners to pay a portion of the measured produce from their land or the equivalent in coin or precious metal, to support government and church. Even the tithe, or giving of one-tenth of output, was often little different from a compulsory tax. With the growth in intercountry trade came the recording of transactions at borders—buyers and sellers wanted to ensure proper delivery of cargo. Tariffs were then assessed on the value of goods transferred. Throughout most of its early history, tariffs were the principal source of revenues for the U.S. government.

Modern governments rely mainly on the much more elaborate financial accounting systems made possible by the advent of the large organization and the corporation. To ascertain the profitability of different activities within an organization, the wages and income of different individuals and divisions must be determined and differentiated. Financial records must be detailed and precise. These records have allowed governments to assess taxes on measured wages of workers, profits of the organization, and value added (the value of output, less the cost of inputs) of the organization. Governments also depend upon the modern organization to withhold taxes and to report on payments (wages, interest) made to others. Because of the limited use of elaborate accounting systems, less developed market economies usually collect smaller percentages of output or income in taxes than do more developed market economies.

A distinction is often made between direct and indirect taxes. Direct taxes are assessed upon the tax-paying capacities of taxpayers such as their income or wealth. Indirect taxes are imposed upon objects or transactions regardless of the capacities of the taxpayer. Income taxes are the most important form of direct taxation, and sales taxes dominate the indirect tax category.

Many taxes cannot easily be categorized through this distinction. Social security taxes are based upon total levels of wages, but old age and disability benefits in many nations are adjusted upward in relationship to the amount of taxes paid. Social security taxes are also assessed directly upon employees and indirectly on employers according to the wages they pay employees.

In the United States, total taxes as a percentage of gross domestic product grew dramatically in World War II and more moderately since then (see figure on page 977). The most important source of growth after World War II was in social security taxes and in state and local taxes. Federal income taxes remained relatively constant, whereas corporate taxes and other federal taxes, mainly excise taxes, declined in relative terms.

The table on page 978 shows government receipts as a percentage of gross domestic product for the United States and an average for developed countries in the Organization for Economic Cooperation and Development. The United States differs from most other industrial countries in having fewer taxes on goods and services, mainly because it has no value-added tax. The states of the United States do collect consumption taxes through general sales taxes on goods, but usually not services, and federal, state, and local governments all impose selective excise taxes on particular sales such as alcohol, tobacco, and gasoline. The United States also relies less on gasoline taxes than most other developed nations. Social security contributions include taxes paid to old age, disability, medical, and unemployment insurance programs.

Relationship to Other Government Activity

Although taxes are used to cover the cost of government expenditures, governments often use means other than taxation to achieve expenditurelike goals. In particular, government may regulate activity without noting the costs of those regulations in government accounts. For example, a taxpayer may either be assessed a tax to pay for a government expenditure, or the taxpayer may be required directly to purchase a good or service. Employers may pay a tax on pollution, or they may be required to pollute less. Individuals may be required to contribute to a national insurance plan, or they may be required to purchase insurance directly.

Taxes and costs of government may also be hidden within the tax system itself. An individual could pay $10,000 in taxes and then receive $4000 in government expenditures. If those expenditures are made in the form of tax credits or other tax breaks, however, most government accounting systems would count taxes collected as only $6000 and expenditures as zero. Although the accounting is dramatically different,

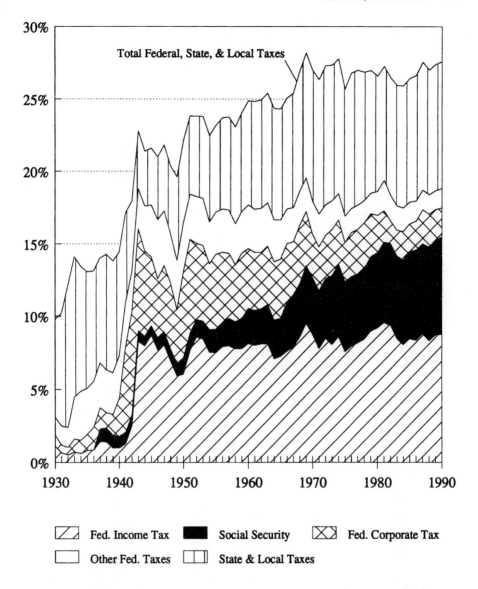

the economic effects of these two means of providing expenditures or subsidies may be exactly the same. Trading off "tax expenditures" for lower statutory rates of tax has been a basic component of many tax reform efforts around the world.

Purposes of Taxation

Although the primary purpose of taxation must always be to finance government, tax legislation has come to be used for a variety of other goals. Because taxes comprise a significant share of total income in the economy, attempts are often made to use taxes both to redistribute income and to influence the economic rate of growth.

Tax Receipts in Various Countries as a Percentage of GDP, 1987

	Total tax receipts % of GDP	Personal income tax	Corporate income tax	Social security contributions		Taxes on goods and services	Other taxes
				Employees	Employers		
United States	30.0	10.9	2.4	3.3	5.0	5.0	3.4
Japan	30.2	7.2	6.9	3.1	4.5	3.9	4.6
Australia	31.3	14.2	3.2	0.0	0.0	9.3	4.6
Switzerland	32.0	10.9	2.0	3.3	3.2	6.1	6.5
Canada	34.4	13.3	2.8	1.6	2.9	9.9	3.9
United Kingdom	37.5	10.0	4.0	3.1	3.5	11.8	5.2
Germany	37.6	10.9	1.9	6.1	7.2	9.6	2.0
Ireland	39.9	13.8	1.3	2.0	3.5	17.0	2.3
France	44.8	5.7	2.3	5.5	12.2	13.1	6.0
Netherlands	48.0	9.5	3.7	9.0	8.2	12.5	5.2
Sweden	56.7	21.1	2.3	0.0	13.2	13.7	6.4
EEC average*	40.6	10.7	3.0	4.1	6.8	13.2	3.9
OECD average*	38.8	11.9	3.1	3.1	5.5	11.8	4.2

* Unweighted. EEC = European Economic Community; OECD = Organization for Economic Cooperation and Development.

SOURCE: OECD (1990).

The distributive goals are usually sought through the use of progressive rate structures—the assessment of higher tax rates on those with greater ability to pay taxes. Higher tax rates on higher-income individuals may limit their accumulation of wealth and may also finance transfers to persons with lesser means. Lower tax rates on lower-income individuals correspondingly represent an attempt to provide them with government services at little cost.

The net effect of any redistributive policy requires examination of both the tax and expenditure side of the budget. Social security taxes in most countries, for instance, are mildly regressive: tax rates less than proportional to income because of limits on total wages subject to tax and the exemption of capital income from this form of taxation. The formulas by which social security taxes are determined, however, generally provide a much greater return on taxes paid by low-income individuals than by high-income individuals.

Many propose that taxes also be used to influence the economy. One goal is to dampen the size of a cyclical downturn or to promote growth. In the United States, tax cuts were used often in the post–World War II era to try to stimulate growth. The two principal examples were in the early 1960s, when the tax cuts were argued to stimulate demand by putting money in taxpayers' pockets, and in the early 1980s, when tax cuts were argued to provide incentives for work and saving. No downturn in the economy since World War II has occurred without at least a large public debate over whether and how tax cuts could "jump start" the economy. Even in absence of legislative action, tax policy is automatically countercyclical: Taxes go down when income goes down and go up when income goes up.

There is little consensus even in theory on the extent to which taxation should be used to achieve distributive and stabilization goals. Many believe, for instance, that taxes by themselves can only have modest effects on redistributing income or avoiding recessions.

More widespread agreement is obtainable, at least in theory, on the desirability of other goals or attributes of a good tax system: equity among equals, efficiency, and simplicity. Equity among equals means that those with equal ability to pay taxes, all other things being equal, should pay the same tax. In an income tax, for instance, this principle is used to argue that those with equal incomes should pay equal income tax. Efficiency implies that the distortive effects of taxation should be kept to a minimum. Efficiency often requires that taxes not arbitrarily be used to favor some form of consumption, income, or industry. A tax system should be simple so as to minimize waste and to limit the amount of time and resources extracted from taxpayers in compliance costs. Putting more resources into tax enforcement, moreover, prevents those resources from being more productive elsewhere.

Different weights are applied by different individuals to each of these goals, especially when they conflict. A simple tax system is not always efficient, and equity may require giving up some simplicity. The efficiency costs associated with raising taxes usually increase the higher the base from which the raises are made. For example, more inefficiency is created by increasing the rate of income taxation from 50 percent to 51 percent than from 10 percent to 11 percent.

Types of Taxes

Individual Income Taxes   The federal individual income tax is the best-known tax and largest source of revenues for the U.S. government. This tax's introduction in 1913 was influenced partly by a populist revolt against the use of tariffs. Originally the top rate was 7 percent, but this rate was quickly raised to 77 percent in World War I. Rates were lowered again in the 1920s, then raised during the Depression of the 1930s and World War II. During this latter war, the top rate reached 94 percent, exemptions were reduced, and withholding on wage income was introduced. A "class tax" was changed to "a mass tax."

Except for surtaxes in the Korean and Vietnam wars, there were almost no statutory increases in individual income taxes between World War II and 1982. Statutory tax cuts, however, were often offset by the influence of inflation and income growth, both of which tended to raise individuals' incomes and the rates at which they paid taxes. A tax act in 1981 both reduced individual rates once again and "indexed" or adjusted individual income tax brackets so that inflation would not automatically increase tax rates. After 1981, several tax bills attempted to raise individual taxes mainly through expansion of the tax base. The Tax Reform Act of 1986 represented a major watershed in individual income taxation. It involved the elimination and paring of more tax breaks than had been achieved in the entire history of the tax to that date.

At the state and local levels, meanwhile, individual income taxes became one of the fastest growing sources of revenue throughout the post–World War II era—partly because of expansion to more and more states and partly because inflation and real income growth were allowed to push taxpayers into higher tax brackets.

Corporate Income Taxes   The modern income tax in the United States began in 1909 with the taxation of corporate income at a rate of 1 percent. For many years, corporate taxes were larger than or equal in size to individual income tax collections. Many countries in the world now provide that when corporate taxes are paid, individual taxes will be reduced. For instance, a credit might be allowed for corporate dividends that derive from previously taxed corporate income. Although the United States does not "integrate" its corporate and individual income taxes in this manner, corporate tax receipts have declined in the United States because of lower rates and the availability of some tax breaks. Most important, a much greater portion of capital income earned within corporations has come to be paid as interest to bondholders. Interest income is not subject to corporate tax.

Payroll Taxes   Payroll taxes are assessed on employers and employees to cover the costs of many social insurance programs for the elderly, disabled, and unemployed. By far the largest of these programs in the United States are those administered by the Social Security Administration. Under the social security tax, employers and employees are assessed in equal amounts on a wage tax base, although employees are believed to bear the burden of the employer tax through lower cash wages. For many taxpayers now, the social security payroll tax is the largest tax that they pay.

Value-Added Taxes   Value-added taxes are applied in most developed countries and many underdeveloped countries. The tax base consists of the total sales price of a company's output, less the cost of purchases from other firms—that is, the company's value added. In practice, the company is usually assessed a tax on its sales, but a credit is given for taxes paid on its purchases. Even when a product goes through several layers of production, the final cumulative tax base should not equal more than the sales price of the final product.

The tax has several administrative advantages. Seldom are individuals required to pay the tax directly. If one company does not pay its tax, another company buying the products of the nonpaying company will receive less credit. Hence, the tax has both self-policing features and limited administrative costs. In practice, a number of exceptions from taxation make the tax much more complex than would be a flat tax on all forms of value added.

Value-added taxes are opposed by some who want smaller government and do not want to add another tax onto the existing system. Others believe that a value-added tax is regressive and favors capital owners, who do not pay the tax. However, many of those who favor a value-added tax would use it to substitute for another tax, such as the corporate tax or a portion of social security taxes.

Excise Taxes　In the United States, the principal taxes on goods and services are excise taxes. General sales taxes apply in most states to goods, but many services are exempt. Gasoline taxes are assessed by both federal and state governments, although many of these revenues are put into trust funds for highway construction. Airport and airway taxes have grown in importance with the expansion of air transportation, and several excise taxes are now assessed for environmental purposes. Alcohol and tobacco taxes, sometimes called "sin" taxes, have dwindled in relative size over the years. Selective excise taxes often become less important sources of revenue when consumers begin to devote greater portions of their income to new, often untaxed, goods and services and when inflation raises the price of taxed goods, but not the tax paid on those goods.

Estate, Gift, Inheritance, and Wealth Taxes　In the United States, very large estates are subject to taxation on the value of transfers. Some states assess a tax on inheritors rather than on the value of the estate. In practice, these taxes are only minor sources of funds to governments, and wealthy taxpayers attempt to avoid the tax through devices such as making transfers directly to grandchildren so that children will not pay the tax. Some European countries have attempted to assess wealth taxes on a more periodic basis, but these taxes have proven difficult to administer, especially for assets such as land for which there is often no easy way to determine valuation.

Property Taxes　Local governments depend largely upon the property tax, which mainly supports schools and local services such as police and fire. In a few states, some of those functions have been transferred partly to state government control. Historically, property taxes were first conceived as wealth taxes on all property, but during the twentieth century, the tax has come to be assessed mainly on land and buildings. A state and local tax revolt against the property tax lessened its relative importance in the late 1970s. Disputes over valuation of property are common, but governments have come to employ better data and techniques over the years. Urban areas typically face much higher property tax rates than rural areas, mainly because the cost of urban government is higher.

References

Bradford, David F., *Untangling the Income Tax,* Harvard University Press, Boston, 1986; Musgrave, Richard A., and Peggy B. Musgrave, *Public Finance in Theory and Practice,* McGraw-Hill, New York, 1984; Pechman, Joseph A., *Federal Tax Policy,* 5th ed., The Brookings Institution, Washington, D.C., 1987; Rosen, Harvey S., *Public Finance,* Irwin Press, Homewood, Ill., 1985; Steuerle, C. Eugene, *The Tax Decade: How Taxes Came to Dominate the Public Agenda,* The Urban Institute Press, Washington, D.C., 1992.

(*See also* Capital gains; Federal budget; Fiscal policy; State and local government finance; Value-added tax)

C. Eugene Steuerle

Technology

In the broadest sense, the term technology refers to the method of carrying out any activity that incorporates recurring acts, as well as the use of tools or implements. In a narrower and more common context, technology refers to the method of pursuing activities on a given minimum level of mechanical, engineering, or scientific sophistication. Accordingly, one may speak of technology of Stone Age endeavors in one extreme or of the high technology of modern-day undertakings in the other. Moreover, the technology concept can be used to describe a reservoir of knowledge, or it may be restricted to knowledge applied to actual procedures. In some countries, technology is used synonymously with or in lieu of engineering; hence, their schools of applied science are known as schools of technology.

The technology entity is commonly classified on any of the three following criteria: (1) the type of knowledge incorporated; (2) the type of broadly defined activity involved; or (3) the equipment used or narrowly defined type of activity involved. Examples of the first category include science-based, engineering, or chemical technologies. The second category includes industrial, agricultural, communications, laser, automotive, or even bolt-tightening technologies. In the last category, the concept of technology tends to become synonymous with the concept of technique.

Whereas the intermixing of the technology and technique concepts is not permissible in exacting treatments, the practice is nevertheless quite common in the literature. A clear line of distinction between the two concepts might be attempted on some criterion of sophistication differential, but specifying such criteria may be difficult, if possible at all. Alternatively, one might seek a distinction between technology and technique on the basis of the requirement for tools or implements. Hence, one may speak of techniques, but not technologies, of athletes or performing artists.

In economics, technology is a concept linked most commonly to the process of production, but there is also a smaller, more recent literature on the technology of consumption. Pertaining to production, the concept of technology is analytically expressed via the production function, i.e., the quantitative cause-and-effect relationship between material and human inputs into a process at one end and the resulting output (product) at the other. In the case of consumption, the use of the concept of technology is analogous, whereby a functional relationship is specified between inputs into and the results or output of consumptive activity.

Although technology as a static concept and as expressed through the production function is one of the cornerstones of traditional economic analysis, the critical importance of technology is lodged in the dynamic aspect of the concept, i.e., technological change. Technological change, viewed as a change in an existing production function or as the introduction of new types of production or of products, is commonly assumed to proceed in a forward direction, i.e., in the form of technological progress. Such progress, in turn, is usually assumed to bring about improvements when evaluated on criteria of efficiency, productivity, or welfare.

The phenomenon of technological change can be investigated on an individual, group, or aggregate scale. For example, if the change involves production functions, such functions can be postulated for the firm, the industry, or the economy as a whole. More generally, the phenomenon of technological change is always incorporated, in some form, in models of economic growth and development.

In economic history, important epochs of technological change have come to be associated with the key elements or ingredients of each case in point, such as mechanization, industrialization, or automation. In more focused historical contexts, one encounters the epoch of electrification, containerization, or computerization.

In the history of economic thought, technology and technological change have always had a place in the major writings. Adam Smith devoted considerable analytical interest to technology; John Stuart Mill regarded it primarily from a historical point of view; and Karl Marx made technological change one of the cornerstones of his system.

In the decades following World War II, economic interest in technological progress was probably the highest, throughout the entire history of economic thought. Until the late 1960s, or the early 1970s, the interest was focused on the causes of innovation; the economic impacts of different kinds of innovation; the deliberate promotion of progress in technology, primarily by the government; the spillover or fallout effect of a given type of new technology (e.g., military or space) on other types of endeavors; the promotion of domestic and international technology transfer via the exchange of know-how and materiel; and international differentials in technological potential known as the "technology gap."

By the 1970s, domestic and international events changed the picture dramatically. As a result of growing public opposition to U.S. military operations abroad that provided the stimulus for much of the government's technological initiative, technological progress as a social goal fell into widespread public disfavor. That disfavor also spilled over to the space effort. During the same period, the environmental protection movement sprang up and brought with it calls and legislation for "technology assessment," i.e., a study and determination of the undesirable side effects of technological progress. Technology assessment soon found its way into environmental economics. The inherent closeness of these subdisciplines to public sector economics spawned a surge of interest in technology policy during the decade of the 1980s. Some of the works published during that period resemble earlier policy treatises in their institutional-statistical orientation. Others, however, delved deep into micro- and macroeconomic theory, even game theory for their deliberations. Specifically, theories of taxation, government expenditures, and rational expectations have been used in this connection.

References

American Economic Association, *Papers and Proceedings of the Seventy-Eighth Annual Meeting,* Menasha, Wisc., May 1966; Fellner, William, "Trends in the Activities Generating Technological Progress," *American Economic Review,* vol. 60, no. 1, March 1970, pp. 1–29; Fusfeld, Herbert I., *The Technical Enterprise: Present and Future Patterns,* Ballinger, Cambridge, Mass., 1986; Landau, Ralph, and Dale Jorgenson, *Technology and Economic Policy,* Ballinger, Cambridge, Mass., 1986; National Science Foundation, *The Effects of International Technology Transfers on the U.S. Economy,* Washington, D.C., July 1967; Stoneman, Paul, *The Economic Analysis of Technology Policy,* Clarendon Press, Oxford, 1987; Terleckij, Nestor E., *Effects of R&D on the Productivity Growth of Industries: An Exploratory Study,* National Planning Association, Washington, D.C., December 1974.

(*See also* Automation; Economic growth; Innovation; Productivity; Research and development.)

Theodore Suranyi-Unger, Jr.

Theory of comparative advantage (*see* Comparative advantage theory)

Theory of interest (*see* Interest, economic theory of)

Theory of the consumer (*see* Consumer theory)

Theory of the firm (*see* Firm theory)

Thrift institutions: problems and challenges

Savings and loan associations, savings banks, and cooperative banks, commonly referred to as "thrift institutions," play an important role in the nation's financial services delivery mechanism. Together with commercial banks, they are known as depository institutions. They function as intermediaries between borrowers and lenders, gathering savings in the form of deposits and channeling the proceeds into productive investments.

Although the different types of thrift institutions originated concurrently during the early 1800s, they developed out of different needs and were intended to perform different functions. Over the years, however, they evolved into roughly similar types of institutions with distinct portfolio traits that have differentiated them from commercial banks. Traditionally, thrift institutions have relied on consumer passbook and small-time savings accounts as their primary source of funds and have used these funds predominantly for mortgages and other types of housing-related loans.

During the 1980s and early 1990s, high interest rates, excessive risk taking, lax supervision, and a collapse in real estate prices wreaked havoc on the thrift industry, reducing the number of institutions by almost half. In addition to the severe shrinkage, the legislative and regulatory response to this crisis blurred the portfolio distinctions among the different types of depository institutions and changed their respective roles.

Today, checking deposits of individuals and businesses appear among the liabilities of most thrift institutions, and consumer and small business loans figure prominently in their asset mix. Thus, in many ways thrift institutions are already operationally indistinguishable from many smaller commercial banks.

Savings Banks

The first savings bank in the United States was founded in Philadelphia, in 1816. Based on a concept developed in Europe centuries before, savings banks were designed as a means to encourage thrift by offering an investment option that was safe and provided a suitable return. The early savings banks received charters from their respective states and were organized as mutual institutions owned by the depositors and overseen by boards of trustees. These early institutions had broad investment authority and were operated as benevolent trusts distributing all earnings, except for additions to surplus, to the depositors.

Although savings banking spread rapidly in the northeastern United States, cultural distinctions and differing credit needs prevented savings banks from spreading westward. The number of savings banks peaked in the 1870s but has declined significantly since that time. As of June 30, 1991, there were 375 savings banks with $240 billion in assets.

Until the late 1970s, savings banks were chartered only by state authority and were organized strictly as mutual institutions. Beginning in 1977, however, savings banks first were given the option to convert to a federal charter and subsequently were allowed to convert to stock form of ownership. Legislative changes ultimately provided de novo entry under these new formats. Although many institutions have made use of the stock conversion option, very few institutions have exercised the federal chartering option. As of June 30, 1991, there were 153 stock institutions with $166 billion in assets and 222 mutual institutions with $73 billion in assets. All but 17 institutions are state chartered.

The operations of state-chartered savings banks are regulated by the state governments and by the Federal Deposit Insurance Corporation. The deposits of these institutions are insured by the Bank Insurance Fund administered by the FDIC.

Savings and Loan Associations

The first savings and loan association was founded in Frankford, Pennsylvania, in 1831. Also called "cooperative banks" and "building and loan associations," the purpose of these institutions was to pool funds to finance home ownership.

The early institutions were mutual institutions where the shareholders were also the owners and borrowers. These institutions operated within very narrow geographical limits and were designed to be self-liquidating. Once the original shareholders had received and repaid their loans, the institution terminated. As the number of associations grew, they evolved into a serial format, where new borrowers and shareholders were added periodically. Finally, a permanent form of organization was adopted, where shareholders and borrowers were independent.

For the first hundred years of their existence, all savings and loan associations were state chartered, and most associations remained mutually owned and operated. By the 1920s, their number had grown to over 12,000 institutions. The Great Depression triggered a number of savings and loan failures and raised concerns that the flow of funds to housing finance might be impaired. In response, Congress created a federal chartering authority in 1933 and established a dedicated industry lender, the Federal Home Loan Bank System.

Although all federally chartered savings and loan associations were originally mutual, legislative changes in the early 1980s created federally chartered stock institutions. These changes also permitted federally chartered savings and loan associations to call themselves "federal savings banks." As of June 30, 1991, there were 2216 savings institutions with $921 million in assets.

Currently, all savings and loan associations and all federally chartered savings banks are regulated by the Office of Thrift Supervision. The deposits of these institutions, with the exception of a handful of federal savings banks that are BIF-insured, are insured by the Savings Association Insurance Fund (SAIF) administered by the FDIC.

In addition to the SAIF-insured savings institutions, there are 91 cooperative banks, with over $7 billion in assets, located in the state of Massachusetts. Although they are operationally quite similar to savings and loan associations, their deposits are insured by the BIF.

Problems and Challenges

The last two decades have seen a remarkable change in the financial services industry in general and in the thrift industry in particular. The failure of about half of the savings and loan associations and a quarter of the savings banks has demonstrated the need to adapt to a changing market environment.

Although the first realization of trouble came with the high inflation and high interest rates of the early 1980s, the root of the problem extended back much further to the asset restrictions and tax incentives that fostered a rigid portfolio structure. Savings institutions were encouraged by legislation and regulation to confine their lending to illiquid fixed-rate mortgages while offering much shorter duration liabilities. This mismatch left the institutions' net worth vulnerable to interest rate increases.

Savings institutions were also limited in the interest rates they could pay on deposits. Although this restriction was intended to minimize costs, it impeded an institution's ability to attract funds when interest rates rose above the ceiling.

When interest rates rose sharply in the late 1970s, thrift institutions were unable to compete with unrestricted money-market instruments. To combat the ensuing disintermediation, Congress removed the deposit ceilings. This corrected the liquidity problem, but it created a severe profit squeeze.

Congress then addressed the profitability problems by removing many of the asset restrictions. Many institutions responded by acquiring higher-yielding but riskier assets. More important, the savings and loan regulators simultaneously embarked on a policy of official forbearance, reducing capital standards, debasing the accounting standards, encouraging rapid growth, and ignoring the increasing portfolio risk. Regulators also failed to uncover the fraudulent activities of a number of savings institution executives.

Despite the greater risk and the lack of appropriate supervision, the debacle in the savings and loan industry might have been avoided were it not for the untimely plunge in oil prices, the virtual disintegration of the oil-dependent economy of the Southwest, and the collapse of the real estate market.

Although the savings banks, located predominantly in the Northeast, hoped to escape a similar fate, a regional recession soon undercut real estate values in that area of the country and exposed a rash of questionable lending. The ensuing adjustments to loan values created severe losses, eroded the capital of many savings banks, and led to many failures.

In the end, the failure of so many thrift institutions caused the outright failure of one federal insurance agency, contributed to the insolvency of the other, and according to some estimates cost the U.S. taxpayer over $300 billion.

For the surviving thrift institutions, the challenge will be to remain financially viable in an environment in which the profitability of housing finance has been eroded by the growth of government-sponsored agencies, the costs of insurance and regulation have skyrocketed due to the widespread failures, and Congress appears to be unwilling to grant needed new powers.

References

Barth, James R., *The Great Savings and Loan Debacle,* The AEI Press, Washington, D.C., 1991; Ornstein, Franklin H., *Savings Banking: An Industry in Change,* Reston Publishing, Reston, Va., 1985.

(*See also* Banking system; Capital markets and money markets; Commercial banks: problems and solutions; Credit, an overview; Disintermediation; Financial institutions; Financial instruments; Interest rates; Mortgage credit; Saving)

Martin A. Regalia

Time series analysis

In business, economics, meteorology, engineering, and many other fields of sciences, observations are often taken in time order. Such observations are said to constitute a time series. Some examples are hourly temperature, daily stock price, weekly traffic volume, monthly consumer price index, and annual gross national product. Time series observations tend to exhibit patterns such as trends, seasonal fluctuations, irregular cycles, and occasional shifts in levels or variability. Statistically, this means that observations are serially dependent, which has led to the development of statistical theory and methods to handle the time-dependent structures.

Objectives of Time Series Analysis

In some problems, time series data may be available on a single variable of interest, and the objective of the analysis is to ascertain and extrapolate the pattern in the data for forecasting future observations or to assess the effect of known interventions. For example, one may have monthly data on the sales of refrigerators for the last five years and be asked to predict the sales for the next six months or to assess the impact of a major promotion campaign instituted five months ago. In other problems, time series data may be available on several related variables of interest. For instance, in studying demand for telephone, one may have data on monthly telephone installations, housing starts, and some index of business activity. As another example, to assess the trend in air pollution, time series data on air pollutants such as ozone and carbon monoxide, on input variables such as traffic counts and speed, and on meteorological variables including inversion height, temperature, wind speeds, and direction are usually collected. The main reasons for analyzing and modeling these series jointly are:

1. To understand the dynamic relationships among these series. They may be contemporaneously related, one series may lead the others, or there may be feedback relationships among some of the series. A better understanding of the dynamic structure could, for example, in an air pollution study, lead to the design of an appropriate control strategy to improve air quality.
2. To improve accuracy of forecasts. When there is information on one series contained in the historical data of other series, better forecasts will result when the series are modelled jointly.

Stochastic Structure

Let $\ldots, t-1, t, t+1, \ldots$ denote equally spaced time points and y_t the observation at time t. When there are k (>1) series under study, let $\mathbf{y}_t = (y_{1t}, \ldots, y_{kt})'$ denote the corresponding vector containing the k component observations. The probability model generating the series $\{y_t\}$ or $\{\mathbf{y}_t\}$ is called a *stochastic process,* and the available time series data are then a realization of the process. It is important to note a key distinction between time series observations and observations generated from designed experiments. For time series, there is usually one and only one realization y_t at a given time point t. However, because experiments can be repeated, there can be many realizations under the "same" experimental conditions. Thus, statistical inference on time series depends critically on the nature of the serial dependence of the stochastic process under study.

Stationary Process

When the joint probability distribution of any m observations $y_{t+1} \ldots , y_{t+m}$ from a stochastic process remains unchanged for different values of t, the process is said to be "stationary." In practice, this means that there is a state of equilibrium in which the overall behavior of the time series stays roughly the same over time. The theory of stationary process has been well developed and plays an important role in time series analysis. Although many of the series encountered in practice exhibit nonstationary behavior, often a suitable transformation such as differencing of the data will render them approximately stationary so that the theory of stationary process can be applied.

Linear Stochastic Models

For a single time series $\{y_t\}$, the serial dependence in the data can often be adequately approximated by a linear model of the form

$$y_t = c + \pi_1 y_{t-1} + \pi_2 y_{t-2} + \cdots + a_t \tag{1}$$

where c is a constant, $\pi_1, \pi_2, \ldots$ are parameters relating y_t linearly to its past values, and a_t is the error term. It is commonly assumed that $\{a_t\}$ is a series of identically and independently distributed normal random variables with zero means and common variance σ^2. At a given time origin T, the observations $y_T, y_{T-1}, \ldots$ are available. By putting $T + 1 = t$ in equation (1), it is easy to show that the best predictor of the observation one step ahead, y_{T+1}, is $\hat{y}_T(1) = c + \pi_1 y_T + \pi_2 y_{T-1} + \cdots$, and the associated forecast error is simply $y_{T+1} - \hat{y}_T(1) = a_{T+1}$ having variance σ^2. It is also straightforward to obtain from equation (1) predictors of observations l-steps ahead, y_{T+l}, $l = 2, \ldots$, as linear functions of $y_T, y_{T-1}, \ldots$ and their associated forecast errors.

   In practice, the model in equation (1) is not known and has to be built from available time series data. Since y_t can in principle relate to its remote past, for parsimonious representation of the model, it is useful to make the π's functions of a small set of parameters which can then be accurately estimated from the data. A widely used class of such models is the mixed autoregressive moving average (ARMA) models of orders (p, q) originally proposed by Yule and Slutsky,

$$y_t = c + \phi_1 y_{t-1} + \cdots + \phi_p y_{t-p} + a_t - \theta_1 a_{t-1} - \cdots - \theta_q a_{t-q} \tag{2}$$

This class of models has been found useful in representing a variety of stationary, nonstationary, and seasonal time series in diverse fields of sciences. By straightforward substitutions, one can readily derive the π's in equation (1) as functions of the finite parameter set $(\phi_1, \ldots , \phi_p; \theta_1, \ldots , \theta_q)$ in equation (2).

   To illustrate, consider first the case $p = 1$ and $q = 0$ in equation (2). We then have $y_t = c + \phi_1 y_{t-1} + a_t$, which is the first order autoregressive model frequently considered in the economics literature. For $-1 < \phi_1 < 1$, the model is stationary and the l-step ahead predictor will converge to the mean level of the series as the forecast horizon l increases. For $\phi_1 = 1$ and $c = 0$, this model is a nonstationary "random walk," widely believed to be appropriate for stock prices in an "efficient market." As another illustration, for $p = q = 1$, $c = 0$, and $\phi_1 = 1$, we have the model $y_t - y_{t-1} = a_t - \theta_1 a_{t-1}$. In this case, the l-step ahead predictor is, for all $l \geq 1$, $\hat{y}_T(l) = (1 - \theta_1) y_T + \theta_1(1 - \theta_1)y_{T-1} + \theta_1^2 (1 - \theta_1)y_{T-2} + \cdots$, which is an exponentially weighted average of current and past observations. Predictors of this kind which give more weights to recent information and less and less weights to information from the remote past seem intuitively appealing because time series data, especially those in business and economics, tend to exhibit unstable or nonstationary behavior over time. As a result, the "exponential smoothing" forecast discussed here has perhaps been the most widely applied forecasting technique in practice.

The model in equations (1) and (2) can be readily generalized to vector time series $\{y_t\}$ for which we have the vector ARMA model of orders p and q,

$$y_t = c + \phi_1 y_{t-1} + \cdots + \phi_p y_{t-p} + a_t - \theta_1 a_{t-1} - \cdots - \theta_q a_{t-q} \tag{3}$$

where c is a $k \times 1$ vector, the ϕ's and θ's are all $k \times k$ matrices, $a_t = (a_{1t}, \ldots, a_{kt})'$, and $\{a_t\}$ is now a series of identically and independently distributed random vectors from a multivariate normal distribution with a zero mean vector and a positive definite covariance matrix. To illustrate, supposing $k = 2$, $p = 1$, and $q = 0$, we have the bivariate first order autoregressive model

$$\begin{pmatrix} y_{1t} \\ y_{2t} \end{pmatrix} = \begin{pmatrix} c_1 \\ c_2 \end{pmatrix} + \begin{pmatrix} \phi_{11} & \phi_{12} \\ \phi_{21} & \phi_{22} \end{pmatrix} \begin{pmatrix} y_{1,t-1} \\ y_{2,t-1} \end{pmatrix} + \begin{pmatrix} a_{1t} \\ a_{2t} \end{pmatrix} \tag{4}$$

which shows that each component series is related to its own past and the past value of the other series. If $\phi_{12} = \phi_{21} = 0$, the two series are uncoupled in the sense that their relationship, if any, is coincidental via the correlation between a_{1t} and a_{2t}. If $\phi_{12} = 0$ but $\phi_{21} \neq 0$, then we have a unidirectional relationship that y_{1t} depends only on its own past but y_{2t} are affected by the past values of both. Thus y_{1t} is a leading indicator of y_{2t} by one period. Finally, if both ϕ_{12} and ϕ_{21} are nonzero, we have a general feedback relationship between these two series. We see, therefore, the class of vector ARMA model in equation (3) covers a wide spectrum of linear dynamic relationships among the component series.

Model Building

A useful way to build an ARMA model for the data at hand is to adopt an iterative process via (1) tentative model specification, (2) efficient estimation, and (3) diagnostic checking. For a single time series, computationally simple statistics such as the sample autocorrelation function and the sample partial autocorrelations have been widely used in the tentative model specification phase. The former is particularly useful in assessing the order of a moving average model, the latter that of a autoregressive model. The more recently proposed extended sample autocorrelation function approach has made it possible to specify directly the orders of the mixed ARMA models and hence further simplifies the procedure for model specification. Once a model is tentatively entertained, the parameters can then be efficiently estimated via the method of maximum likelihood. Finally, residuals calculated from the fitted model are then subject to various diagnostic checks to determine the overall adequacy of the entertained model and to search for directions of improvement. Of particular importance in this phase are procedures to detect existence of residual autocorrelations, outliers and structural changes such as level shifts, variance changes, and nonlinearities.

Much of the univariate time series modeling procedures can be extended to the vector case. Specifically, the pattern of the sample cross-correlation function and that of the sample partial autoregression matrix function (which is a direct generalization of the sample partial autocorrelation function) are useful for tentative specification of the orders of vector MA or AR models. Likewise, the model is then fitted by maximizing the likelihood function, and similar diagnostic procedures can be applied to the residuals.

Structural Analysis of Vector Model

For multiple time series analysis, when the number of components k in the y_t vector is moderately large, even small values for p and q in equation (3) can lead to a dauntingly large number of parameters to be estimated. This is because the ϕ's and θ's are all $k \times k$ matrices. Recently, a useful dimension reduction approach, called scalar component models (SCM), has been proposed. By considering linear transformations of y_t, the proposed procedure aims at searching for possible simplifications of the ϕ's and θ's matrices themselves. Other dimension reduction techniques include the reduced rank method, unobserved component models, and factor analysis. While much progress has been made, structural simplification remains an important research topic in linear multiple time series analysis.

Intervention Analysis

Time series observations are frequently subject to the influence of special events, or interventions, occurred at known time points, e.g., outbreak of wars, changes in fiscal policy, major sales promotions. It has been found useful to employ linear dynamic models of the form $Y_t = \delta_1 Y_{t-1} + \cdots + \delta_r Y_{t-r} + \omega_0 x_t - \cdots - \omega_s x_{t-s}$ where x_t is an indicator (dummy) variable for an intervention and Y_t represents its dynamic effect on the series. We can write the model for the observations as the sum of the intervention component Y_t and a noise component Z_t, $y_t = Y_t + Z_t$, where Z_t follows an ARMA model of the form in equation (2). The parameters in the intervention component and those in the noise component can then be jointly estimated to quantify the effects of these two components.

Time Series with Nonhomogeneous Variances

The model in equation (2) supposes that the variance of σ^2 of the innovations a_t remains constant over time. In reality, this variance homogeneity assumption is sometimes violated, especially in highly disaggregated financial data such as daily stock returns or exchange rates where we often see clusters of high volatility. Several models can be used to describe this kind of phenomenon. Denoting the variance of a_t as σ_t^2 one may employ a random step-change model in which there is a nonzero probability λ that σ_t^2 may change at any given point of time. Alternatively, one may relate σ_t^2 to past values of a_t. In particular, the model $\sigma_t^2 = \alpha_0 + \alpha_1 a_{t-1}^2 + \cdots + \alpha_r a_{t-r}^2$, which is called the autoregressive conditional heteroscedastic (ARCH) models, has been frequently considered in the analysis of financial time series.

Nonlinear Time Series Models

An extensive literature now exists on nonlinear time series models where y_t is related to its past values more generally by a nonlinear function. Such models are necessarily more complex, but they can represent phenomena such as time irreversibility and limit cycles which cannot be adequately described by linear models. For instance, it is well known that the dynamic behavior of economic indicators such as the gross national product (GNP) or the unemployment rate during a recession period is quite different from that when the economy is expanding. To describe this kind of nonhomogeneous behavior, one may adopt a piecewise linear model for different regimes of economic activity. For a simple illustration, let y_t represent the quarterly change in GNP. We may postulate a model of the form

$$y_t = \begin{cases} c^{(1)} + \phi^{(1)} y_{t-1} + a_t^{(1)} & \text{if} \quad y_{t-1} < 0 \text{ and } y_{t-2} < 0 \\ c^{(2)} + \phi^{(2)} y_{t-1} + a_t^{(2)} & \text{otherwise} \end{cases}$$

where $c^{(1)} \neq c^{(2)}$, $\phi^{(1)} \neq \phi^{(2)}$, and $a_t^{(1)}$ and $a_t^{(2)}$ have unequal variances. Here the region $(y_{t-1} < 0, y_{t-2} < 0)$ represents a period of economic decline, and the model says that the dynamic behavior of y_t is different for the two regions. This model is a special case of a class, known as the threshold autoregressive models, which have been applied to time series in various fields of sciences.

References

Box, G. E. P., and G. M. Jenkins, *Time Series Analysis, Forecasting and Control,* rev. ed., Holden-Day, San Francisco, 1976; Box, G. E. P., and G. C. Tiao, "Intervention Analysis with Applications to Economic and Environmental Problems," *Journal of the American Statistical Association,* vol. 70, 1975, pp. 70–79; Engle, R. F. "Autoregressive Conditional Heteroskedasticity with Estimates of the Variance of U.K. Inflation," *Econometrica,* vol. 50, 1982, pp. 987–1008; Tiao, G. C., and G. E. P. Box, "Modeling Multiple Time Series with Applications," *Journal of the American Statistical Association,* vol. 76, 1981, pp. 802–816; Tiao, G. C., and R. S. Tsay, "Model Specification in Multivariate Time Series" (with discussion), *Journal of the Royal Statistical Society,* series B, vol. 51, 1989, pp. 157–213; Tong, H. and K. S. Lim, "Threshold Autoregression, Limit Cycles, and Cyclical Data," (with discussion), *Journal of the Royal Statistical Society,* series B, vol. 42, 1980, pp. 245–292.

(*See also* Distributed lags in economics; Economic forecasting methods; Index numbers; Seasonal adjustment methods; Statistical methods in economics and business, an overview)

George C. Tiao

Transfer payments (*see* Poverty)

Underconsumption theories (*see* Juglar cycle)

Unemployment (*see* Employment and unemployment)

Unit management buyouts (*see* Going private and leveraged buyouts)

Urban economics

Producers and consumers, whose behavior are the main objects of economic inquiry, are not evenly spread throughout the land. Instead, they tend to be concentrated in places which are variously referred to as urban areas, cities, and metropolitan areas.

In urban economics, the fundamental assumptions and analytical tools of economics are employed to explain why such concentrations occur, how and why they vary in size and form, and how such concentrations generate both benefits and costs to their resident populations and industries and to the economy and nation at large.

Urban economics aims to improve the choice and design of public policies—federal, state, and local—to address the negative consequences of urbanization by enhancing our understanding of the underlying forces at work.

Urban Form

The heart of urban economics is the study of urban form, i.e., patterns of location and land use within metropolitan areas. The first step is descriptive: where households and private and public enterprises are currently located within the urban region and how much land they consume. Our ability to perform this task has been enhanced in recent years by the development of computer software for analyzing and displaying such data graphically.

The second task is to account for these patterns. For the urban economist, that means developing theories of how households and enterprises independently evaluate the positive and negative features of alternative places, in the light of their private interests, to arrive at their preferred locations.

Such theories (and models) generate hypotheses which are tested against observed patterns. Such theories form the foundation for the third step, which is to predict likely future patterns of land use and location, in the light of projected changes in the underlying determinants.

Residential Location Theory: The Model "T"

Early theories of residential choice focused on the trade-off between land costs and commuting costs in a monocentric urban region. It was assumed that enterprises would locate in that center and bid up land prices to the point where they would become prohibitive to all but the wealthiest and/or the smallest households. Other households would seek lower land prices away from the center, so they could afford more space for their homes, but that quest would be constrained by the cost of commuting to the center where all the jobs were located.

In this "model," rising affluence, reduced transportation costs, and the suburbanization of workplaces predictably disperse the population and lower average densities in the region as a whole.

Missing Realities

Like every good theory in its formative stages, the model "T" abstracted from some hard realities that ultimately could not be ignored. The urban riots of the 1960s focused public attention and stimulated research on the influence of racial discrimination on residential location patterns. The existence of "hardened" ghettos could not be explained simply in terms of the trade-off between land prices and commuting costs.

The other reality was and is the disparities within the urban area, among its many separate political jurisdictions, in the bundle of taxes and public services and in the socioeconomic composition of the population. It is reasonable to assume that households would choose locations in respect to these factors as well, particularly as the trade-off between land prices and commuting costs becomes increasingly tenuous with the suburbanization of employment, the emergence of the multicentered urban region, the increasing proportion of multiple-worker households, the ubiquity of access created by the rich transportation network, and the galloping rate of technological progress in communications.

Enterprise Location Decisions

Why do so many enterprises locate in the heart of an urban area where rents and congestion are at their maximums? This is perhaps the most intriguing question in urban economics. The answers to that question deal with the fundamentals of productivity and profit, thus providing a strong link between urban economics and mainstream economics.

One answer speaks to the historic advantages of the center as a location: access to shipping (water and rail), access to labor throughout the region, access to regionwide markets, access to city government. These factors underlie the logic of a single enterprise wanting to be in the center without reference to who else is there, but since many enterprises would be swayed by that logic, it inevitably leads to agglomeration.

The other answer speaks directly to the benefits to the individual enterprise which flow precisely from the simultaneous presence of many other enterprises in the same compact area: the economies that derive from agglomeration.

What are these economies of agglomeration? One set of economies has to do with the savings in transportation and communication costs resulting from proximity to suppliers, customers, and competitors. Another set has to do with Adam Smith's classic theorem, namely, that specialization is limited by the extent of the market. The great diversity of suppliers and vendors of highly specialized services is made possible by the existence of a large compact market for such services.

The continuing decentralization of employment in virtually all sectors of the economy and in all urban regions surely attests to the weakening of the logic of agglomeration as it applies to the historic center. However, urban economists continue to grapple with two imponderables: Will the historic center ultimately lose all its appeal as a site for agglomeration in competition with other centers throughout the region, or is the very logic of agglomeration being totally undermined by continuing rapid improvements in communication?

Problem and Research Agendas

As just suggested, the impact of communications technologies on urban form is clearly an emerging focus of research by urban economists. These technologies have implications for the organization and location of enterprises and the location of households within urban regions.

Urban transportation has long been on the problem and research agendas of urban economics. The dominance of the automobile as the preferred mode for moving about the urban region has been a source of concern for three reasons: traffic congestion, air pollution, and the handicapping of the "carless" population for whom mobility is reduced rather than enhanced by development patterns which assume automobile ownership.

Not surprisingly, therefore, the urban transportation research and policy agendas are long and complicated. Can we reduce auto dependency by encouraging more compact and mixed-use patterns of development? Should we aim for a better balance between the number of jobs and the number of housing units within subareas of the larger urban region? Can we influence modal choice by appropriate pricing policies and/or by subsidizing mass transit?

Growth Management

The urban transportation problem is currently being viewed in the larger context of the many actual and/or perceived negative consequences of unplanned or poorly planned urban growth which call for a response in the form of more aggressive management of urban growth.

Under the heading of growth management, urban economists are looking more intensively into the relation between patterns of land use and the costs they generate in the way of requirements for supporting infrastructure and public services, and into alternative strategies for mitigating and/or financing these costs. At the same time, there is considerable interest in the side effects of growth management, for example, on the price of housing.

The Urban Ghetto

The inner-city ghetto also remains firmly on the agenda of urban economics. In recent years, a new concept—the underclass—has emerged as a hypothesis for explaining the seemingly intractable nature of that problem.

References

Bradbury, Katherine L., Anthony Downs, and Kenneth A. Small, *Urban Decline and the Future of American Cities,* Brookings, Washington, D.C., 1982; Chinitz, Ben (ed.), *City and Suburb: The Economics of Metropolitan Growth,* Prentice-Hall, Englewood Cliffs, N.J., 1964; Heilbrun, James, and Patrick A. McGuire, *Urban Economics and Public Policy,* 3d ed., St. Martin's Press, New York, 1987; Meyer, John P., and Jose A. Gomez-Ibáñez, *Auto Transit and Cities,* A Twentieth Century Fund Report, Harvard University Press, Cambridge, Mass., 1981; Richardson, Harry W., *Urban Economics,* Penguin Books, 1971.

(*See also* Location theory; Microeconomics; Regional economics)

Benjamin Chinitz

U.S. business obsession with short-run performance

Although the term "short run" might encompass different time periods depending on how it is used, when applied to business strategies and practices, it generally refers to the next calendar quarter. For this is the frequency with which American companies report their sales and earnings results to the public (assuming the companies are publicly held). These periodic reports are essential if shareholders—usually absentee owners with little, if any, involvement in running the firm—are to have timely information regarding the state of their investment.

If these investors are satisfied, they will hold onto their shares of stock in the company—if not buy some more. Needless to say, this will bolster the price of the stock, making not just investors, but the company's managers, pleased. It is not too difficult to envision that part of a manager's compensation might depend on the performance of the company's stock. Indeed, most business schools "train managers to maximize shareholder return, and little in the corporate culture contradicts that lesson" (Eisenhart, 1989).

This has produced a system that tends to be geared toward short-term thinking, in the words of a principal of a major accounting firm. He further adds that "executives won't start to plan for the long term until incentives are strong enough to counteract the stimulant of the current situation, which is quarterly profits" (Eisenhart, 1989). In and of itself, this is not bad, however; as McGraw-Hill's *Business Week* recently put it, "managers . . . taking action that will buttress the stock price in the short-term . . . may sacrifice long-term returns" (Dobrzynski, 1991). To put it another way, few actions are undertaken that have no obvious short-run payoff.

In this regard, the captains of American industry are not very different from their brethren in the political arena. Elected officials face constant pressure to enact laws that will produce favorable results (more spending/lower taxes) quickly for their constituents, even if the economy might suffer in the longer run. Indeed, to a politician, the long run is the day after election day!

To be sure, most companies do have people who do long-range planning. Not surprisingly, most senior managers, if asked, will tell you they are operating under a long-range plan. As a matter of fact, in some industries, according to the Conference Board, long-range planning is essential to survival (Hirsch, 1990). Reference is made to such industries as pharmaceuticals and aerospace, where lead times of 9 years before new products begin to pay off are not unusual.

However, a recent poll of chief executives of American firms found that nearly nine out of ten thought business is generally too short-term-oriented. They evidently feel enormous pressure "to depart from these carefully laid long-range plans in order to maximize near-term profits." To counter this, the survey reports, some companies have changed their compensation plan to emphasize long-term results, rather than one-year performance (Quickle, 1989).

It is not difficult to understand why American businesspeople at least pay lip service to the notion of long-range planning. As Caspar Weinberger, publisher of *Forbes,* put it in his July 24, 1989, column "In an era when America urgently needs to become more productive and competitive, we can ill afford to neglect the advantages, indeed the necessity, of new infrastructures; new plants and machinery; new methods of production, distribution and communication; and new methods of using information. . . ." These, he says, are obtainable, but require large initial investments and a return on that capital that "sometimes takes several years."

Unfortunately, we seem to be too impatient. More than one observer of the American business scene has recalled John Maynard Keynes' observation that "in the long run we're all dead" and urged concentration on short-run objectives. All well and good, but when the short run becomes as short as the next calendar quarter, and the objective is simply maximizing short-run profits, many companies tend to lose their way; they lose sight of who they are and where they should be going. Robert Hayes (1985), a professor of management at the Harvard Business School, said: "Most companies select goals that are too short term . . . [a] series of short-term goals encourage episodic thinking . . . [they] also work to back companies into a mode of thinking that is based on forecasts (What do we think is going to happen?) rather than on vision (What do we want to happen?)."[1]

This fixation on the short run was carried even further in 1991, as the U.S. economy was struggling to emerge from its ninth postwar recession. Even as it was becoming apparent that the worst was over, and that a mild but noticeable recovery was getting under way, company after company suddenly started slashing payrolls. These layoffs would generally follow a disappointing earnings report.

This soon became a game of musical chairs, where each company was trying to improve its own fortunes at the expense of others. For, you see, these widespread layoffs, in turn, depressed confidence on the part of American consumers, as people became fearful for their jobs. Naturally, consumers cut down on their expenditures for big-ticket, postponable items like cars, houses, and household furnishings; and when they had to buy something, they opted for the least-expensive brand in the least-expensive store. As you might imagine, this cut into business sales and earnings—leading to yet another round of layoffs, and so on.

To save even more money, companies also began laying off relatively senior people. These older employees, of course, were paid more, and so their firing saved more dollars than the termination of an equal number of younger, lower-paid employees. The fact that the company lost highly skilled workers was rarely mentioned.

---

[1]From "Strategic Planning—Forward in Reverse," by Robert H. Hayes, *Harvard Business Review,* November/December 1985.

The irony of these tactics should not go unnoticed. Besides the vicious cycle just described, it appears that companies were trying to impress Wall Street with swift actions taken to boost profits in order to bolster the price of their stock. But the Wall Streeters these firms were trying to curry favor with were for the most part managers of the pension funds for the very employees who were losing their jobs!

Maybe the leveraged buyout movement was right after all. For private ownership definitely can take a longer-run approach to running a company; managers of publicly held firms must always worry about the next quarter's earnings.

References

Dobrzynski, Judith H., "How America Can Get the 'Patient' Capital It Needs," *Business Week,* October 1991, p. 112; Eisenhart, Tom, "Bush Pushes Long-Term Investment Goals," *Business Marketing,* April 1989, p. 40; Hayes, Robert H., "Strategic Planning—Forward in Reverse?" *Harvard Business Review,* November/December 1985, p. 113; Hirsch, Paul M., "Heroes of the Long Run," *Across the Board,* January/February 1990, p. 54; Quickle, Stephen W., "Companies in Crisis," *Business Month,* January 1989, p. 46; Weinberger, Caspar W., "The Importance of Long-Term Thinking," *Forbes,* July 1989, p. 31.

(*See also* Economic forecasts)

Irwin L. Kellner

User costs (*see* Opportunity cost)

Utility

After centuries of intellectual striving, economists have not yet settled on a definite meaning of utility. One difficulty stems from the fact that the term, taken from ordinary vocabulary, carries connotations that do not apply to the special area of economics, consumer behavior. On the other hand, its spread was enhanced by the fact that it was introduced, about 200 years ago, by Jeremy Bentham, propagandist and architect of modern utilitarianism. But Bentham blamed the French for the choice of the word "utility." Indeed, in French, there is no corresponding word for usefulness, which is covered by "utility." But the real snag was that also in ordinary English usage the two terms are virtually synonymous. The importance of this distinction for the study of consumer behavior was pointed out for the first time in an 1833 lecture by W. F. Lloyd, a Cambridge University economist.

Lloyd remarked that the usefulness of corn, for example, reflects its physicochemical properties, which are the same in time of famine as in a bumper-crop year. Eventually, utility acquired the meaning it has now in economics, which is that intended by Bentham: "a feeling of the mind" which, for everyone, varies with the circumstances but in the same manner for all. Yet even experts in the economics field may nowadays be caught speaking of the "utility of gold," for instance. We should not be surprised then that shortly before his death Bentham lamented that "utility was an unfortunately chosen word." Vilfredo Pareto proposed in his 1896 *Cours* to retain "utility" for usefulness—for the property of the object to produce pleasure—and to use "ophelimity" for subjective pleasure.

The importance of the concept of the Benthamite utility for economic science can hardly be overemphasized. To search for a cause of any phenomenon, especially one as important for human society as economic value, has been the main counsel of the ancient Greek philosophers. Plato, for example, argued that "each one of us has in his bosom two councilors, . . . we call one pleasure, and the other pain"—utility and disutility, in the present economic jargon.

We believe, with Aristotle, that all things that are exchanged one against another must possess one and the same homogeneous "essence." Millennia later, Karl Marx, just like Aristotle, argued that there is a common essence and it is labor for the production of goods and services. With its yearning for a monist explanation, the neoclassical school, while forcefully decrying Marx's idea, committed the very same sin, shifting one factor, labor, to another, utility. As one of the founders of the neoclassical school, W. Stanley Jevons, taught, "value in use equals total utility," a position shared by almost all members of that school.

Measuring Utility

It was Plato who first claimed that the feeling we call utility must have a measure; otherwise people would not be able to calculate their future pleasures. This idea was revived many centuries later by Bentham, who held that pleasure and pain must be cardinally measurable; that is, just as milk is measured in quarts and flour in pounds, utility is measurable in some proper units—in utils.

It was not surprising that eventually attempts were made at finding a way to measure utility. Both Irving Fisher (1927) and Ragnar Frisch (1932) proposed to measure the marginal utility of money with the aid of a directly useful commodity, such as sugar. The only result of their efforts was a controversy about the meaning of "measurability" that existed for some years thereafter.

In any case, they could not have satisfied Bentham, who had insisted that utility should be so measurable that the utilities of all persons of a community could be meaningfully added to express their total happiness. He even claimed that if the utilities of different persons cannot be meaningfully added, all political science must come to a standstill. But astounding as it may seem to us now, Bentham also professed that this was as absurd as summing apples and pears together.

Bentham's faith in a theoretical structure for political science was the basis for his belief that utility would ultimately be measured by a "moral thermometer." Because this idea tended to raise utilitarianism to the level of a theoretical science, it was subsequently defended by prominent writers, such as Francis Y. Edgeworth, who believed in an early invention of a "hedonimeter," and Frank Ramsey, who counted upon the possible designing of a "psychogalvanometer." However, their hopes have been officially abandoned. Nevertheless, current economic literature still includes arguments based on the Plato-Bentham principles, and some go so far as to attribute a utility to human life measurable in money.

The Principle of Decreasing Marginal Utility

The realization that subjective utility is an essential determination of economic value was hampered by the Aristotelian dogma that "the value of a thing lies in the thing itself," as Jean Baptiste Say insisted centuries later. The great appeal of that dogma stemmed from its corollary: in a just exchange of things, no party should gain or lose. Not only the scholastic doctors, but also classical economists, Karl Marx above all, were happy with it. David Ricardo explicitly dismissed the notion that the whims of people may influence economic value.

The opposition to the subjective basis of economic value lasted through the nineteenth century and was all the more intriguing since the role of consumer preferences had become obvious as a result of economic progress in several European urban communities. By 1750 Abbot Ferdinand Galliani clearly acknowledged, in his celebrated *Della Moneta (On Money),* the association of economic value with subjective utility. But the simple recognition of the subjective utility was not sufficient to spark a revolution in economic science. That occurred only when a specific law, now known as the principle of decreasing marginal utility (PDMU), was set forth.

However, that principle was first formulated a decade before Galliani's treatise by a famous mathematician and physicist, Daniel Bernoulli. He was led to it by a gambling paradox—the St. Petersburg paradox—in which the theoretical stake of the gambler playing against the bank is infinite. For its solution he introduced the idea that the "moral value" of an additional dollar is smaller for a millionaire than for someone not as rich (i.e., it produces less felicity for the former). However, because of its mathematical nature, Bernoulli's finding remained unknown to economists for more than 100 years. But it later became the main theoretical support for progressive taxation.

Around 1780, Bentham discovered the same principle, which he cast in a precise formulation. Rephrased, it states that successive units of wealth produce smaller and smaller additional utilities, all units of wealth being assumed equal. This formulation presupposes not only the measurability of utility but also the cardinal measurability of the object that produces felicity.

Great though Bentham's influence was, the economists of his time were still unable to perceive the theoretical importance of the PDMU. It was a German civil servant, Hermann Heinrich Gossen, who first related the principle to the behavior of an individual seeking to maximize happiness in life.

Even Gossen's volume, published in 1854, remained practically unknown for 36 years until W. Stanley Jevons learned of it by chance and praised it. The founding of utility theory is now customarily attributed to Jevons, Léon Walras, and Carl Menger, even though they only rediscovered Gossen's main idea.

Almost all economists have ignored a second law formulated by Gossen which states that the marginal utility of a commodity decreases if the same act of enjoyment of it is repeated too often. For example, it is well known that eating steak too often dulls the pleasure of eating it.

And another theorem proved by Gossen (improperly called Gossen's second law) shows the importance of the PDMU. It is as follows: In order to maximize the utility of a given budget confronted with given market prices, a person must spend income in such a way that the utility of the last penny spent on any item must be the same as that of other pennies spent during the same transaction. In other words, the marginal utility of money must be the same for all expenditures.

The Independence Axiom

Earlier writers, Gossen included, assumed that the utility of any commodity depends only on the amount of that commodity possessed by the individual in question, regardless of the amounts of other commodities the same individual may possess. According to this axiom, the utility U felt by a person I for the amount x_k of some commodity C_k is a simple function, $U_I(x_k)$. But when there is no danger of misunderstanding, it may be written U_x.

The utility of a marginal increment Δx then is $\Delta U = U(x + \Delta x)$, which, however, cannot serve as a theoretical definition of marginal utility: ΔU depends on the freely variable Δx. For this reason, marginal utility has come to be defined as the limit of the average marginal utility increment; i.e., the limits of $\Delta U / \Delta x$ for $\Delta x \rightarrow 0$. which is the first derivative, $U'(x)$, or $U(x)$. Therefore, the dimension of marginal utility is not utils, but a ratio of utils per amount of commodity. So it would not do to alter the paradox of value by saying instead that the marginal utility of diamonds is greater than that of water.

In diagrammatical analysis it is the representation of $U'(x)$, not $U(x)$, that is used. In such a diagram, the utility $U(x)$ is represented by the area shaded in Figure 1. Such an area may be infinite, in which case total utility, $U(x)$, would be infinite, too. But we should not demur at the idea of an infinite utility: in the last analysis all utilities felt by a person are infinite; the utility of drinking water to quench one's thirst, for instance, must be infinite because it includes the enjoyment of being alive. For the actions of any human, just as for those of a sea navigator, it does not matter how deep is the ocean of utility on which one sails while alive; only the height of the waves counts.

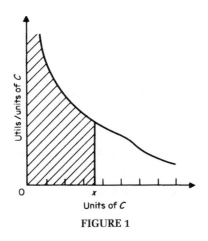

FIGURE 1

According to the independence axiom, the total utility of a bundle $(x_1, x_2, \ldots, x_n)$ of commodities $C_1, C_2, \ldots, C_n$ is the sum of the simple functions:

$$U_1(x_1) + U_2(x_2) + \cdots + U_n(x_n) \tag{1}$$

This unrealistic axiom was rejected by Edgeworth, who argued that total utility of that bundle is not expressed by (1) but by a function $U(x_1, x_2, \ldots, x_n)$ which rarely reduces to that of (1). The marginal utility of C_1 (say, of potatoes) is the limit of U/x_1 (in a simpler notation, U_1'), which also depends on the amounts of the other commodities in the bundle.

This brought up the issue of the relationship between commodities. As Edgeworth and, later, two Viennese bankers, R. Auspitz and R. Lieben, argued, if an increase in x_2 increases the marginal utility U_1'—as is the case for potatoes and butter, for example—C_1 and C_2 are complementary. But if an increase in x_2 decreases U_1', the two commodities are competitive, or rival, in use (potatoes and bread, for instance). Finally, if U_1' is independent of x_2, C_1 and C_2 are independent in use. Two commodities are thus complementary, competitive, or independent according to whether the second partial differential $\partial^2 U/\partial x_1 \partial x_2$ is greater than, less than, or equal to 0.

Isoutility Curves

Utility analysis could then no longer make proper use of a diagram such as that of Figure 1. As Edgeworth proposed, we may now visualize in the n-dimensional space an $(n-1)$-dimensional variety represented by $U(x_1, x_2, \ldots, x_n) = u$, with u being any given amount of utility. This variety is the loci of all bundles that produce the same amount of utility; it is an isoutility variety. For example, as shown in Figure 2, the commodity plane (for two commodities) is completely covered by a family of isoutility curves. Because of the crucial ideas illustrated by this particular figure, it now dominates a large number of economic arguments.

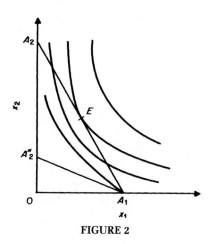

FIGURE 2

On this figure, the bundles (x_1, x_2) available to a budget of a given income, m, confronting market prices p_1 and p_2, are represented by

$$p_1 x_1 + p_2 x_2 = m \tag{2}$$

which is the equation of a straight line, such as $A_1 A_2$. The highest utility obtainable by that budget obviously corresponds to E, the point at which $A_1 A_2$ is tangent to an isoutility curve. The direction of a tangent to such a curve is given by

$$U_1 dx_1 + U_2 dx_2 = dU = 0, \tag{3a}$$

whereas for the direction of $A_1 A_2$ we have

$$p_1 dx_1 + p_2 dx_2 = 0 \tag{3b}$$

By comparing the last two equations it is seen that the coordinates of E must satisfy, in addition to (2), the familiar system

$$U_1'/p_1 = U_2'/p_2 \tag{4}$$

With some additions, ordinarily ignored, this is an equivalent statement of Gossen's theorem. The additions concern the fact that no actual individual ever buys every commodity available on the market—in the United States the rich would not buy ordinary hamburger, and the poor would not buy tenderloin. Hence, it is not correct to say that prices are proportional to the marginal utilities of everybody. For a simple illustration: If in Figure 2 the budget is $A_1A'_2$, the expenditure on commodity C_2 is nil and (4) no longer applies.

Theory of Binary Choice

After the publication of his *Cours*, Pareto kept moving toward an idea that was to revolutionize not only utility theory but also all social sciences. It consisted of replacing the fiction of cardinally measurable utility with a highly realistic theory sometimes called the "theory of choice," but more properly labeled the "theory of binary choice."

Pareto broached his new idea in several preparatory essays published in the famous, at that time, *Giornale degli Economisti,* where he spoke of choice (*scelta* in Italian), but he developed his new theory fully in 1906 in the *Manuale di Economia Politica.* However, he did not, not even in a later article in *Mathematical Encyclopedia,* cast his argument into an axiomatic framework. Thus, not all his assumptions were spelled out clearly—not even the key assumption of his new theory, which states: A person faced with the choice between two bundles of commodities is always able to tell which he or she prefers or whether it would not matter which bundle he or she might get, which is the case of indifferent bundles.

Pareto carried out an experiment by asking individuals to choose one bundle among virtually all possible pairs of bundles, one bundle being always a selected bundle *P.* On the basis of answers to this test, Pareto reasoned that commodity space may be divided into three distinct parts: (1) the domain of the bundles preferred to *P,* (2) the bundles such that *P* is preferred to the others, and (3) that of the indifferent bundles relative to *P.* He argued that domain (3) is an $(n - 1)$-dimensional variety, alias an Edgeworth isoutility variety containing *P.* Clearly, no measure of the propensity of a person is needed to reach this result, so that those varieties may be properly renamed "indifference" varieties.

It was on this seemingly simple argument that Pareto based his conclusion that complete comparability as in the binary choice, not cardinal measurability, is all that is needed to explain the behavior of consumers.

Eventually, the hidden assumptions in Pareto's argument, leading to the map of indifference varieties, were spotted and expressed in a suitable form:

1. The postulate of transitivity of choice, which states:
   An individual is rational (consistent) in choosing, which means that if he or she prefers *A* to *B* and *B* to *C,* then that person must prefer *A* to *C.* Or in a more comprehensive way, if a person may choose *A* from the pair (*A, B*) and *B* from the pair (*B, C*), the same person will not refuse *A* from the pair (*A, C*).

2. The indifference postulate, which states:
   Given any triplet of bundles *A, B, C,* such that *A* is preferred to *B* and *B* to *C,* on any continuous shift from *C* to *A,* there is a bundle *K* indifferent to *B.*

These two assumptions lead to a map identical to Figure 2, which Edgeworth obtained on the basis of cardinally measurable utility, but which Pareto achieved on a more creditable basis.

As Pareto proposed, we may assign a number to each indifference variety—any number, provided that in the geometrical order away from the origin, the higher variety should receive the higher number. This scale constitutes what Pareto called an ordinal measure, in this case, of ophelimity. Since the numbers of an ordinal scale, such as that just described, are arbitrary in that sense, then if ϕ (x, y) is an ordinal measure of a phenomenon determined by (x, y) and F is an arbitrary monotonous function, $F(\phi)$ also is an ordinal measure of the same phenomenon. For example, if xy is an ordinal measure of some phenomenon, so is $\log(xy)$. The difference between two ordinal measures has no meaning whatsoever. Clearly, two bundles may have the ordinal measures $(1, 59)$ on one scale and $(0, 10^{10})$ on another. This is the main difference between the ordinal and the cardinal scales.

According to Pareto's ordinal conception of consumer behavior, a person is able to tell when he was happier, say, when eating 10 plums or when drinking a glass of cola, but not by how much happier. This idea met with some incredulity among mathematicians, and the problem of comparability of differences became the subject of numerous essays. However, if the matter is examined critically, it is seen that the applicability of the ordinal scale to economic behavior does not rest on solid ground. The trouble spot is the indifference postulate, which requires not only that an individual have an uncommon ability for discrimination, perfect in comparison with material measuring instruments, but also that there always be bundles indifferent with respect to any given one.

It is unthinkable that the states of mind of an individual when confronted with two different situations would be identical. Therefore, the postulate of the existence of indifference emerges as a fallacy, the ordinalist fallacy. But we can drop it, too, by the negation: there are no indifferent bundles. In this case, any given bundle P divides the commodity space into three distinct categories, the singleton P and two domains, one of bundles preferred to P and one of bundles for which P is preferred. The variety that separates these two domains has the same properties as the Paretian indifference varieties. Referred to as the behavior varieties, they are represented by a map just like that of Figure 2 and with the same analytical properties. Choice is still completely ordered but is no longer measurable in any scale. E is still the optional allocation of A_1, A_2 because it is preferred to all others that are accessible.

A New Cardinalism for Utility

The craving for measure is so insatiable among modern scholars, especially among modern economists, that, Pareto's contribution notwithstanding, some have tried to provide utility with a pointer-reading measure, if not like the scale for measuring flour, for instance, at least like the scale for time or temperature. Utility would thus have a definite measure based on an arbitrary choice of the unit and of the origin of the scale. The seed of Daniel Bernoulli's solution of the St. Petersburg paradox, a gamble, in which the calculated stake was infinite for a finite gain, reappeared in a 1926 essay by Frank Ramsey and in 1944 in *Theory of Games and Economic Behavior* by Oskar Morgenstern and John von Neumann. Instead of a pointer-reading hedonimeter, these authors used as an instrument any individual who is supposed to be completely indifferent to a choice between some amount of ready cash, M, and a lottery ticket, which wins either M_1 with probability p or M_2 with probability $q = 1 - p$. If the individual tells us how much M must be to create this indifference, then we have the equality (in utils)

$$U(M) = pU(M_1) + qU(M_2) \tag{5}$$

If we choose the origin and the unit of the utility scale so that $U(M_1) = 0$ and $U(M_2) = 1$, then $U(M) = q$ utils. Varying all the parameters, we can determine the number of such utils of any M.

From a special viewpoint this scale is rather cardinal. Like time, utility (as already mentioned) has no condition corresponding to "nothing." But the differences of utility—of chronological time, too—are cardinally measurable. It seems in order to refer to this scale as weak cardinal. Not unexpectedly, the ordinalist camp has protested this utility theory, although cardinalism (strong or weak) merely extends the use of the ordinalist fallacy. Both positions are therefore open to the same criticism.

Revealed Preference

In a 1938 article, Paul A. Samuelson enunciated in essence the following behavioral axiom: If a person chooses P as the optimal distribution of his or her budget B, determined by some prices (p) and income I, when also Q may be chosen, the same person will never choose Q from any budget for which P is also available. This is now called the weak axiom of revealed preference, although the term "weak" is out of place in this context. The axiom is a significant landmark in analytical economics. It asserts in a simple and clear manner a test for the consistency of choice. Further, it explains the basic property of the indifference varieties, their convexity—an issue that previously had not been clarified satisfactorily.

However, this innovation has been criticized because of some weaknesses. The most important had its root in the overlooked essential difference between the Paretian and the Samuelsonian concepts. To wit, the algebra of the Paretian theory deals with the simplest possible relation, defined by just a pair, P and Q, and expressed by (PtQ) where t stands for "is preferred to" or "is indifferent to." The relation of the other algebra is compound $(PTQ):B$, where B stands for the budget that must be known for the specification of T. In the first algebra, given any pair (P, Q), t is determined, but not so in the second algebra, where for some pairs no T may exist. Consider also the symbolism that must be prepared for dealing with the validity of transitivity of revealed preference, which is $(PTQ):B$ and $(QT'R):B'$. No imperative reason exists in this theory for a T'' to exist for any given pair (P, R). In introducing his special preference idea, Samuelson did use a distinctive symbolism; yet he passed directly from the revealed preference relation to the binary one, thus implying that the individual by choosing P from a budget where Q was also accessible reveals that he prefers P to Q in the binary sense.

We may find it strange that because of that contention, the history of revealed preference has generated considerable discussion among economists. Presented by a mainstream economist, the idea of revealed preference became popular so quickly that it could hardly draw attention to its weakness. The fact that that measure cannot exist without transitivity was a point that was not appreciated in relation to the older problem of the paradox of integrability. As the simple relation of revealed preference does not always respond even to a pair of bundles, some analytical remodeling had to be imagined. It was the idea of a French mathematician, Jean Ville (1946, 1951–1952) and rediscovered by H. S. Houthakker (1950), known now as the strong axiom of revealed preference. Symbolically, that relation may be written

$$(PSQ):B_1B_2 \ldots B_n \tag{6a}$$

to stand for the sequence where the T's may also be "indifferent to"

$$(PTQ_1):B_1, [Q_1TQ_2:B_2, \ldots, (Q_{n-1}TQ_n)] \tag{6b}$$

which is transitive by its formal definition, but its factual validity is established by the strong axiom: for any two bundles, P and Q, either $(PSQ):B^*$ or $(PSQ:B_*)$, where B^* is some particular sequence of budgets and B_* is its inverse.

From Demand to the Ophelimity Map;
The Integrability Paradox

The connection between choice and the ordinary type of budget revived an old problem handled in 1886 and in 1896 by Giovanni Antonelli and better argued in 1906 by Pareto.

The problem was to derive the indifference map of the consumer from simple market data (prices and quantities bought). Pareto's solution involved a special piece of advanced calculus, namely, the representation of the indifference varieties by a total differential equation, the logic of which may be illustrated by Equations (3a) and (3b). He seemed to suppose that that equation is always integrable so as to yield by integration the corresponding ophelimity map. That solution was criticized by Fisher (1896), in his review of Pareto's *Cours*, and by Vito Volterra (1906), in the review of the *Manuale*. They both censored him for not being aware of the fact that, in Volterra's own words, "While a differential expression with two terms $Xdx + Ydy$ always admits an infinite number of integrating factors, a similar expression with three or larger number of terms need not have any."

Pareto, apparently intimidated, yielded in a footnote of the *Manuale* (App. S12), saying that "the observations and critics of a savant such as Mr. Volterra have a great value and are priceless for the progress of science." It was in this manner that a paradox known as the integrability problem was introduced into economics.

Nevertheless, Pareto's critics were wrong. In his *Cours* (App. I, S25), Pareto stated the integrability condition as clearly as possible. Besides, his critics used a concept of integrability inappropriate for the problem at hand. In correct mathematical usage, integrability is a point condition: one and only one differential planar satisfying the equation must pass through the point where the equation is said to be integrable.

For two dimensions then, any of the infinite number of available integrals (Vito Volterra had in mind) may not fulfill that particular condition in some points, isolated or not, called singular. Simple examples: $(y - b)dx + (x - a)dy = 0$ with the singular point (a, b) where two integral lines pass; or $(x - a)dx + (y - b)dg = 0$ with the same singular point through which no integral line passes; and finally $dx + 2Vxdy = 0$, $y/0$, for which $x = 0$ is a singular line. Such integrals cannot represent an ophelimity map usually because of the peculiarity of singularities. To be fit for that role, the integral must be a potential, that is, a function with a single value at every point at least over the pertinent commodity space. How delicate the problem set out by Pareto was is shown by the curious fact that the integral of the second example just mentioned is a potential even though it has a singular point.

The difficulties associated with singularities for the Paretian problem surfaced in connection with Volterra's misunderstanding as it was shown that the integrals of the intersection of a nonintegrable total differential equation in three dimensions with a budget plane necessarily involve some *bad* singularities (Georgescu-Roegen, 1936). Of these the most eye-catching was a map of spirals around a singular focus point, which explains why later it was maintained that any condition, such as the strong axiom of revealed preference, that would prohibit spirals would assure integrability (Houthakker, 1950; Samuelson, 1950). However, one of the greatest problems of classical mathematical analysis was unlikely to be solved that easily. A map with a new kind of singularity, a pole, proved that assertion wrong (Georgescu-Roegen, 1954).

In spite of the effort by many mathematical economists to clarify Pareto's path-breaking theory, his successors have held the conviction that the irremediable problem of that theory is the nonintegrability of demand functions. It is true that demand functions, in terms of income and prices, do not require integrability. But without the ophelimity map our understanding of consumer behavior would be poor. Instead of the clear structure of an indifference map in two dimensions, there would be a confusing map of demand curves intertwining with each other.

The blame for the misunderstanding of Pareto's theory of consumer behavior should go to the two scholars, Fisher and Volterra, for failing to recognize the logical soundness of his theory. Market demand may or may not be integrable, but under some assumptions concerning economic behavior, the same differential equation used by Pareto with community demand substituted for market demand is clearly integrable.

Volterra, particularly, ignored the fact that even if demand is integrable, the integrals have no ophelimity meaning unless it is known that the ophelimity map already exists (Georgescu-Roegen, 1975). And if it is known to exist, clearly it can always be reconstituted by integration from indirect (market) data.

Utility versus Wants

Physicists began their activity with the study of matter and energy in bulk and only much later came to consider their elementary constituents. Economists, on the other hand, started the study of human behavior with the elementary constituents: the wants. From Bentham on, until late in the nineteenth century, economists envisaged the consumer as a package of wants. They spoke of various laws of wants. But since these laws have a dialectical structure, they could not be subjected to strict mathematical treatment. With the unbelievable successes mathematicians had in the new astronomy, economists had to rethink their theories.

Just like Karl Marx, whom economists strongly criticized for maintaining in his theory of value that all concrete labors—carpenter, president, writer of *Capital*—are just some shapes of a jelly, abstract labor, neoclassical economists began to profess that all concrete wants are just some colorless jelly, the general and abstract want we call utility. As Jevons, the true founder of the new school, said in the opening of his opus, *The Theory of Political Economy* (1879), "Repeated reflection and inquiry have led me to the somewhat novel opinion, that value depends entirely upon utility." It may be too early to say whether the move in this direction has been helpful, but the fact is that the wants, not the unique want, utility, guide a consumer in the market.

Concrete wants are dialectical concepts with blurred, not sharply drawn, boundaries. Yet their structure is not completely amorphous. The terms are as flexible as they are appropriate. Wants are subject to various laws, the most important being their hierarchical order—a simple idea that goes back to Plato and is found with almost all modern greats, Carl Menger, Alfred Marshall, and Frank Knight. In general, wants are divided into three layers. The lowest layer, biological wants, consists of all fundamental wants and needs for survival. The next-higher layer consists of social wants, that is, of wants rooted in the social culture of an individual. By and large, these wants are ranked similarly for all members of the same society. The third layer includes all personal wants, rather desires, that can be satisfied by the upper crust in a land of plenty only after satisfying all lower wants. Leaving aside the ephemeral fashions, we find striking hierarchy even in this category.

The most important law of utility expresses this hierarchy. Indeed, no one has been able to justify the principle of decreasing marginal utility from facts without repeating the classic argument of Carl Menger about the way an isolated farmer would use his corn crop: the first bag for food, the second bag as fodder for his beasts of burden, and the very last to feed a pet.

There are some dynamic laws as well. The principle of the subordination of wants states more than their hierarchy. Set forth first by T. C. Banfield (1845) and embraced by Jevons, it says that the satisfaction of a want allows a higher want to manifest itself. To this Gossen added the principle of the satiable wants. Accordingly, no human would like to be loaded with too many automobiles or to be forced to eat one pound of caviar every day.

Another principle, "the irreducibility of wants," cuts through a most crucial dogma of neoclassical economics: that interpersonal comparison does not work. Its origin was a land of plenty where many people were able to satisfy a number of personal wants, satisfaction for which there is no workable hierarchy. Naturally, in these circumstances there can be no way to know who is happier, Paul with his camera or Paula with her golf clubs. Yet if other wants are considered, the irreducibility-of-wants principle instructs us differently. It is beyond question that no amount of food could save one from dying of thirst in a desert, nor can any splendid diamond save one from starving.

Because of the dialectical nature of the problem, the structure of wants had to be represented by a helpful diagram of the commodity space on which for every want there corresponds a particular domain. Such a diagram leads to an order which, like the behavior lines, is not measurable. The order of each bundle depends in this case on the hierarchy rank of the want and the rank of the bundle within the scope of the want of interest. It was from these factual considerations that it was found necessary to introduce in economics orders determined by more than one coordinate, like the order of words in a dictionary, known as the lexicographical order.

A Historical Footnote

There was a time, during the 1950s, when theory of utility dominated the thinking of many economists in the academic world. At the annual meetings of the American Economic Association, the session on any utility topic was scheduled in the grand ball room of the main hotel of the convention—and even there it opened with standing room. However, by the early 1970s a session on the latest topical idea, the lexicographical order, was put on the program only because one speaker was able to convince the chairman to do so, and the session was scheduled in an alcove in which there was room for a few chairs that were not all used.

A historian of economic thought may see that not all was in vain. As a consequence of World War II, the developed nations became aware of the immense world of undeveloped countries, while the true spirit of Pareto, a greater sociologist than an economist, was slowly imbuing economic thought. By extending the individual ophelimity to his famous welfare theorem and welfare index, Pareto, it should be noted, had perhaps unwittingly vindicated Bentham's tenet that political science cannot be meaningful without a "moral thermometer." Not only economists but almost every writer has become absorbed by the problem of developing the yet undeveloped, which would be an excellent preoccupation had it not turned into a promise second only to that of making every human immortal.

References

Spaceworks on Utility

Antonelli, G. B., "On the Mathematical Theory of Political Economy," in John S. Chipman et al. (eds.), *Preferences, Utility, and Demand,* Harcourt Brace Jovanovich, New York, 1971, pp. 333–360 (original work published 1886); Banfield, T. C., *Four Lectures on the Organization of Industry,* Taylor, London, 1845; Bentham, Jeremy, *The Principles of Morals and Legislation,* 1780, republished in vol. I of *The Works of Jeremy Bentham,* 11 vols., Tait, Edinburgh, 1838–1843; Bernoulli, Daniel, "Exposition of a New Theory on the Measurement of Risk," *Econometrica,* 1954, pp. 23–36 (original work published 1738); Lloyd, W. F., "A Lecture on the Notion of Value as Distinguished Not Only from Utility but Also from Value in Exchange," *Economic History,* 1927, pp. 179–182 (original work published 1833).

Modern Theory from Cardinal to Ordinal Utility

Edgeworth, F. Y., *Mathematical Psyciycs,* Kelley, New York, 1953 (original work published 1881); Gossen, Hermann Heinrich, *The Laws of the Human Relations and the Rules of Human Actions Derived Therefrom,* MIT, Cambridge, Mass., 1983 (original work published in German, 1854); Jevons, W. Stanley, *The Theory of Political Economy,* 5th ed., Kelley, New York, 1965 (1st ed., 1879); Marshall, Alfred, *Principles of Economics,* 8th ed., Macmillan, London, 1920 (1st ed., 1890); Menger, Carl, *Principles of Economics,* Free Press, Glencoe, Ill., 1951 (original work published in German, 1871); Pareto, Vilfredo, *Cours d'Economie Politique,* 2 vols., Rouge, Lausanne, 1896–1897; Pareto, Vilfredo, *Manuale di Economia Politica,* Libraria, Milan, 1906; Pareto, Vilfredo, *Manuel d'Economie Politique,* Girard, Paris, 1909 (English translation, *Manual of Political Economy,* Kelley, New York, 1971); Walras, Léon, *Elements of Pure Economics,* Allen & Unwin, London, 1954 (original work published in French, 1873).

Interpretative Account of Historical Developments

Collison Black, R. D., "Utility," *The New Palgrave Dictionary of Economics,* vol. 4, Macmillan, London, 1987, pp. 776–778; Georgescu-Roegen, Nicholas, "Utility," *The International Encyclopedia of the Social Sciences,* vol. XVI, Free Press, New York, 1968, pp. 236–267; Georgescu-Roegen, Nicholas, "Hermann Heinrich Gossen: His Life and Work in Historical Perspective," in H. H. Gossen *The Laws of the Human Relations and the Rules of Human Action Derived Therefrom,* MIT, Cambridge, Mass., 1983, pp. xi–cxlv; Stigler, George J., "The Development of Utility Theory," in J. J. Spengler and W. R. Allen (eds.), *Essays in Economic Thought: Aristotle to Marshall,* Rand-McNally, Chicago, 1960, pp. 606–665 (original work published 1950).

Contemporary Theory

Arrow, Kenneth J., "Utilities, Attitudes, Choices: A Review Note," *Econometrica,* 1958, pp. 1–23; Chipman, John S., "The Foundations of Utility," *Econometrica,* 1960, pp. 193–224; Georgescu-Roegen, Nicholas, *Analytical Economics: Issues and Problems,* Harvard University Press, Cambridge, Mass., 1966; Hicks, John R., *Value and Capital: An Inquiry into Some Fundamental Principles of Economic Theory,* 2d ed., Oxford, Clarendon, 1946 (1st ed., 1939); Hicks, John R., and R. G. D. Allen, "A Reconsideration of the Theory of Value," *Economica,* 1934, pp. 52–76, 196–219; Samuelson, Paul A., *Foundations of Economic Analysis,* Harvard University Press, Cambridge, Mass., 1947; Slutsky, Eugen, "On the Theory of the Budget of the Consumer," in American Economic Association, *Readings in Price Theory,* Irwin, Chicago, 1952, pp. 27–56 (original work published in Italian, 1915).

Measuring Utility

Fisher, Irving, "A Statistical Method for Measuring 'Marginal Utility' and Testing the Justice of a Progressive Income Tax," in J. H. Hollander (ed.), *Economic Essays,* Macmillan, New York, 1927, pp. 157–193; Frisch, Ragnar, *New Methods of Measuring Marginal Utility,* Mohr, Tuebingen, 1932.

Expectations and a New Measure for Utility

Friedman, Milton, and L. J. Savage, "The Utility Analysis of Choices Involving Risks," in American Economic Association, *Readings in Price Theory,* Irwin, Homewood, Ill., 1952, pp. 57–96 (original work published 1948); Georgescu-Roegen, Nicholas, "Choice, Expectations, and Measurability," *Quarterly Journal of Economics,* 1954, pp. 503–534 (reprinted in Georgescu-Roegen, Nicholas, *Analytical Economics: Issues and Problems,* Harvard University Press, Cambridge, Mass., 1966); Georgescu-Roegen, Nicholas, "The Nature of Expectation and Uncertainty," in Jean Bowman (ed.), *Expectation, Uncertainty, and Busibehavior,* Social Research Council, New York, 1958, pp. 11–29 (reprinted in Georgescu-Roegen, Nicholas, *Analytical Economics: Issues and Problems,* Harvard University Press, Cambridge, Mass., 1966); Marschak, Jacob, "Rational Behavior, Uncertain Prospects, and Measurable Utility," *Econometrica,* vol. 18, 1950, pp. 111–141; Neumann, John von, and Oskar Morgenstern, *Theory of Games and Economic Behavior,* Princeton University Press, Princeton, N.J., 1944; Ramsey, Frank P., *The Foundations of Mathematics and Other Logical Essays,* Humanity Press, New York, 1950.

The Integrability Paradox and Revealed Preference

Allen, R. D. G., "The Foundations of a Mathematical Theory of Exchange," *Economica,* 1932, pp. 197–226; Fisher, Irving, "V, Pareto, *Cours d'Economie Politique, Tome I,*" *Yale Review,* November 1896, pp. 325–328; Fisher, Irving, *Mathematical Investigations in the Theory of Value and Prices,* Yale University Press, New Haven, Conn., 1925 (1892 doctoral dissertation); Georgescu-Roegen, Nicholas, "The Pure Theory of Consumer's Behavior," *Quarterly Journal of Economics,* 1936, pp. 545–593 (reprinted in Georgescu-Roegen, Nicholas, *Analytical Economics: Issues and Problems,* Harvard University Press, Cambridge, Mass., 1966); Georgescu-Roegen, Nicholas, "Choice and Revealed Preference," *Southern Economic Journal,* 1954, pp. 119–130 (reprinted in Georgescu-Roegen, Nicholas, *Analytical Economics: Issues and Problems,* Harvard University Press, Cambridge, Mass., 1966); Georgescu-Roegen, Nicholas, "Vilfredo Pareto and His Theory of Ophelimity" (a paper presented in 1973), *Atti del Convegno Internazionale Vilfredo Pareto,* Academia Nazionale dei Lincei, Rome, 1975, pp. 223–265; Houthakker, H. S., "Revealed Preference and the Utility Function," *Economica,* 1950, pp. 150–174; Samuelson, Paul A., "A Note on the Pure Theory of Consumer's Behavior," *Economica,* 1938, pp. 61–71, 353–354; Samuelson, Paul A., "Consumption Theory in Terms of Revealed Preference," *Economica,* 1948, pp. 243–251; Samuelson, Paul A., "The Problem of Integrability in Utility Theory," *Economica,* 1950, pp. 355–385; Ville, Jean, "The Existence-Conditions of a Total Utility Function," *Review of Economic Studies,* 1951–1952, pp. 123–128 (original work published in French, 1946); Volterra, Vito, "Mathematical Economics and Professor Pareto's New Manual," in John S. Chipman (ed.), *Preferences, Utility, and Demand,* Harcourt Brace Jovanovich, New York, 1971, pp. 365–368 (original work published 1906).

(*See also* Classical school; Consumer theory; Neoclassical economics)

Nicholas Georgescu-Roegen

Value-added tax

The spread in popularity of the value-added tax (VAT) in the last 25 years has been one of the most astonishing phenomena of public finance. The tax is levied on the value added to inputs at each stage of production and distribution. In this way it avoids the disadvantages of the cascade turnover taxes. Value added can be computed either by deducting purchases from sales or by adding, basically, wages and profits. All VATs levied now are of the subtraction type. Further, the tax itself can be computed by subtracting the VAT content shown on all purchase invoices from the VAT liability on sales (the method used in most countries) or by using company accounts to subtract purchases from sales and apply the VAT rate to that figure (as in Japan). Although both methods give the same result, unless VAT content is shown on each invoice, only a single-rate VAT can be used.

The Tax Base

VATs have been applied sometimes only at the import and manufacturing stages but, in general, should apply to sales of all goods and services, including retail sales. The VAT on capital goods is, ideally, immediately creditable against any VAT liability on sales, and hence capital goods are untaxed. However, housing, as a retail sale, is fully liable to VAT, including the builder's and any agent's margins. It is difficult to identify on conventional invoice credit lines the value added on each service provided by financial institutions. Because of this, financial services are usually exempted from VAT. Exemption from VAT means only that the trader does not pay VAT, but, of course, the trader still pays VAT on any purchases and cannot claim credit against any VAT liability. Full exemption from VAT can only occur by using the zero rate. This is an actual rate of VAT against which credit for VAT paid on inputs can be claimed and thereby a full rebate obtained, for example, on exports (usually zero-rated).

Origins and Options

Various claims to have promoted the idea of VAT have been made (e.g., as early as 1911 in the United States), but the form in which we know it today originated in France in the period 1948 to 1968. The European Community adopted it as its general sales tax in 1968, largely because the tax content of exports and imports could be known precisely. Brazil had adopted a similar form in 1967; Korea did so in 1977, Hungary in 1988, and Canada in 1991. In 1992 it appears that most of the newly emerging countries of Eastern Europe and the Baltics are also adopting the VAT. Altogether, by 1993, some 70 countries throughout the world will be using VAT. In most countries it raises some 6 to 10 percent of gross domestic product in revenue.

The only serious competitor as a general consumption tax is the retail sales tax (RST). With equal coverage and rate, the yield of the RST and VAT would be identical (the sum of all the value-added fractions is equal to the retail value). Because the RST is a suspensive system where only the retail sale requires compliance with the tax authorities, less administration is needed. However, the VAT allows all tax to be removed on producer/capital goods, and this is difficult under an RST; it is easier to tax services under a VAT, and the audit trail is better and should lead to lower evasion (see discussions in Tait, 1991).

The United States has debated the adoption of a VAT frequently, most recently in the Treasury report of 1984, and a form of VAT was used in Michigan from 1953 to 1968. Recent large fiscal deficits have focused attention on the possibilities of a general federal VAT. In particular, much emphasis has been put on the potential to tax consumption and encourage savings by using a VAT. Recent estimates (1989) are that for each 1 percent rate of VAT, approximately $25 billion annually would be raised (a 10 percent VAT would yield $250 billion). Any federal VAT would have to be piggybacked or amalgamated with the states' RSTs. Some of these are 9 percent, and so a federal 10 percent VAT would lead to a tax of 19 percent on the retail sale. A federal VAT of 5 percent would still lead to a high combined VAT and retail sales tax. But the lower the VAT rate, the higher the costs of VAT administration as a proportion of the yield. The potential increase in U.S. federal bureaucracy needed for a VAT was estimated conservatively in 1984 at 20,000 persons. More realistically, on the basis of European figures, at least 50,000 might be needed for a U.S. VAT.

Rates

Most VATs use a standard rate that applies to the majority of goods and services. The EC has now set this rate at 15 percent or higher. The EC has also agreed that a rate equal to or lower than 5 percent can be applied to food, water distribution, pharmaceuticals, passenger transport, books, agricultural materials, and cultural events. Some countries have more rates (e.g., Turkey with five), but there are strong arguments in favor of using as few as possible. Problems of definition and borderline disputes are avoided, the tax base is not eroded, and consumer and producer choices are not distorted. The justification for using multiple rates is that in this way the regressivity of the VAT can be ameliorated. Of course, varying sales tax rates is an extremely blunt instrument to help low-income households; appropriately targeted public expenditures are much more efficient. The VAT is designed to yield large amounts of revenue, and that is what it does if it is kept simple. Equity is taken care of by other parts of the fiscal system.

References

Department of the Treasury, *Tax Reform for Fairness, Simplicity and Growth: Vol. 3 Value-Added Tax*, 1984; Organization for Economic Cooperation and Development, *Taxing Consumption*, Paris, 1988; Tait, Alan A., *Value-Added Tax: International Practice and Problems*, International Monetary Fund, Washington, D.C., 1988; Tait, Alan A. (ed.), *Value-Added Tax: Administrative and Policy Issues*, International Monetary Fund, Washington, D.C., 1991.

(*See also* Taxation, an overview)

Alan A. Tait

Value of the dollar

The dollar is the unit of currency and a measurement of economic value in the United States. It is also used as an unofficial currency in other parts of the world.

The value of a dollar in terms of some representative bundle of goods and services is always expressed in terms of changes in this value over some period of time. For example, in terms of the goods and services consumed by a typical American family, in June 1991 $1 purchased only 61 percent of what $1 purchased in 1980. Since the mixture of goods and services purchased by a typical family changes over time, comparisons such as this become more difficult the longer the period over which the comparison is made. But if we allow for this difficulty as best we can, $1 in 1990 purchased only 17 percent of what it purchased in 1939, just before World War II, and only 8 percent of what it purchased in 1914, just before World War I. This decline in value reflects the great price inflation that has taken place during the twentieth century, particularly immediately after the two world wars and during the 1970s. Only the Great Depression of the 1930s produced a significant interruption of this trend. It should be noted, however, that this decline in the value of a dollar does not imply a decline in American living standards. On the contrary, the standard of living of a typical American family has grown enormously during the twentieth century. Earnings have grown more than enough to compensate for the declining value of each dollar. For example, per capita disposable (i.e., aftertax) personal income in the United States, which was $324 in 1914 and $532 in 1939, had risen to over $15,600 by 1990.

Value of the Dollar Relative to Other Currencies

"Value of the dollar" has quite another meaning when the term is used to compare the dollar with other national currencies such as the British pound, the German mark (DM), or the Japanese yen. The history of each national currency is different, so that its value at any moment in terms of the U.S. dollar may vary greatly from one to another. For example, in mid-1991, one British pound was worth $1.63, whereas $1 was worth 1337 Italian lire. These numbers are basically conversion units such as 1 meter equals 3.3 feet or 1 kilogram equals 2.2 pounds. In particular, these conversion units do not mean that the British pound is stronger than the dollar or that the dollar is stronger than the Italian lira. Strength in currencies refers to whether economic factors are tending to push up or down the value of one currency relative to another.

These conversion units, which are called exchange rates, are important for travelers or traders because they indicate how much of another currency travelers and traders can buy for a unit of their own currency and, hence (given the prices in terms of foreign currencies), how much foreign goods or services cost in terms of their own currency. American travelers or traders can, thus, compare the dollar costs of foreign goods and services with what they would have to pay in the United States.

Unlike the conversion ratio between kilograms and pounds, the rate of conversion between currencies can change over time. For purposes of economic analyses, it is often of interest to compare how these external values of the dollar have changed. This can be done easily for a single foreign currency. For example, one British pound was worth $2.80 in 1965 and $1.63 in mid-1991; that is, the pound sterling depreciated relative to the dollar between 1965 and 1991. During the same period, in contrast, the German mark appreciated against the dollar, from $1 equals DM 4 to $1 equals DM 1.79. Since there are about 150 different currencies in the world, we need some method for averaging if we are to speak of the external value of the dollar in comprehensive terms. One way to average, which is especially useful if the focus is U.S. foreign trade, is to give a weight to each major foreign currency relative to the value of that country's merchandise in U.S. trade. Another method of averaging is to compare the value of the dollar with the value of a special drawing right (SDR). The SDR is an international unit of account managed by the International Monetary Fund and is a composite of five currencies, with the U.S. dollar having a weight of 42 percent.

The following table illustrates the external value of the dollar in terms of various units for selected years since 1960.

	1960	1965	1970	1975	1980	1985	1990
British pound ($/£)	2.80	2.80	2.40	2.22	2.33	1.30	1.80
German mark/$	4.20	4.00	3.66	2.46	1.82	2.94	1.62
Japanese yen/$	360	360	360	297	227	239	145
SDR ($/SDR)	*	*	1.00	1.21	1.30	1.02	1.36
U.S. trade-weighted index (15 currencies, 1980–1982 = 100)	112	112	113	97	91	127	87

* SDR was first created in 1970.

Changes in the external value of the dollar are caused by many factors. One of the most important is the change in the value of the dollar and of other currencies, in terms of goods and services (i.e., the rates of inflation in different countries). Thus, for the period 1970 to 1990 inflation in Germany was 112 percent, while inflation in the United States was 237 percent. During this period, the German mark appreciated against the U.S. dollar by 126 percent, thus compensating for the higher rate of inflation in the United States, for lower productivity gains, and for U.S. balance of payments problems. In this fashion, movements in exchange rates help to compensate for divergent movements in national rates of inflation and help correct trade imbalances.

References

Fisher, Irving, *The Purchasing Power of Money*, Macmillan, New York, 1912, rev. ed., 1926; Shapiro, Eli, Ezra Solomon, and William W. White, *Money and Banking*, 5th ed., Holt, Rinehart and Winston, New York, 1968.

(*See also* Consumer price index; Foreign exchange rates; Inflation; International Monetary Fund; Liquidity, international; Special drawing rights)

Richard N. Cooper

Variable annuity

A variable annuity is a contract in which the value of future periodic payments depends upon the investment performance of an underlying portfolio of securities, in return for a single payment or periodic payments that go into the buildup of the portfolio. Typically, the future annuitant builds the portfolio during the years spent working and receives annuity payments following retirement.

The main distinction between a variable annuity and the more common fixed annuity is implicit in the nomenclature. The present value of the variable annuity changes with current prices and earnings of the portfolio, while the fixed annuity is immune to such changes (through an insurance company's assumption of the investment risk). The two contracts share the common characteristic of an insurance arrangement insofar as the duration of the payment period is typically related to actuarial mortality tables.

An annuity may be variable only during the accumulation period, with a fixed annuity being purchased at retirement, or it may remain variable throughout the payout period. Defined-benefit corporate pension plans let employers invest in general or separate accounts of insurance companies despite the guarantee of a fixed benefit to the employee at retirement. Separate-account investment permits the employer to use equity, bond, or real estate portfolios during the accumulation period (thus perhaps reducing the cost of providing pensions), but a fixed annuity is purchased for each employee at retirement. Thus, corporate variable-payout pensions are rare, whereas individual variable annuities over the 1970s and 1980s have gained in popularity in both the accumulation and payout phase.

Characteristics of Variable Annuities

One's interest in a variable annuity is usually expressed in units, with an assumed starting value of $10. This method enables the contract holder and the funding agent to distinguish between the effects of cash flows and portfolio value changes. The purchaser acquires a given number of units at the then-prevailing unit price of the portfolio. The purchaser may later acquire additional units at then-current prices. Thus a periodic fixed payment will purchase a varying number of units, but the purchaser will always know how many units he or she holds, what the current price is (i.e., how the investment has performed), and what his or her total accumulated value is.

There is a close similarity between an annuity purchased through periodic payments and a dollar-averaging periodic purchase of a mutual fund. (A single-premium purchase of an annuity does not change the common characteristic with a mutual fund of the price link to an investment portfolio.) Both types of investments usually involve investment advisory and administrative charges to the purchaser. An annuity also carries mortality and expense charges because of the guarantee of the right to a life-expectancy-linked payment. Importantly, individual annuities have gained in attractiveness in the 1980s because the internal accumulation of earnings is tax-deferred until the payout period.

History and Growth of Variable Annuities

The development and growth of the variable annuity have been closely related to prevailing perceptions of common stocks as an inflation hedge. In a path-breaking study published in 1951, William Greenough of the Teachers Insurance and Annuity Association (TIAA) examined the performance over long accumulation and payment periods of pensions funded through fixed-income as against common-stock portfolios. (Fixed income refers primarily to long-term bonds and mortgages.) He concluded that "contributions to a retirement plan that are invested partly in debt obligations and partly in common stocks . . . offer promise of supplying retirement income that is at once reasonably free from violent fluctuations in amount and from serious depreciation through price level changes."

Consequently, TIAA established an affiliated College Retirement Equities Fund (CREF) and began to offer a split-funding plan under which future annuitants could choose the proportion of their retirement contributions that would go into fixed-income versus common-stock investments. During the early 1960s, numerous life insurance companies began to offer variable annuities both through group pension contracts and through their individual annuity marketing mechanisms. In the mid-1960s, self-employed and small-group employee participation in variable annuities was facilitated by the Keogh plan legislation; and in the mid-1970s, a further avenue for individual participation was granted via individual retirement account (IRA) legislation.

During the 1950s and 1960s, the variable annuity captured only a small share of the total retirement market. The IRA legislation opened an important tax-deferral door, and this feature of annuities became even more prominent with the gradual curbing of other tax shelters (such as passive real estate investment) during the 1980s. Annuity considerations paid to life insurance companies skyrocketed during the 1980s, raising the share of disposable personal income (DPI) paid to insurance companies for this product from about 1 percent in 1979 to over 3 percent in 1990.

Variable annuities played a considerable although still moderate role in the growth in recent decades of the annuity field as a whole. Of 14.6 million individual annuities in force with U.S. life insurance companies in 1989, over 2.7 million had a variable feature (but most of these annuities also had fixed features). Further, of the 42 million persons covered by group annuities, nearly 2.8 million had a variable feature in their pension plan.

IRA legislation and tax deferral of the "inside buildup" have been mentioned as key explanations of the recent rapid growth of annuities, including variable ones. In addition, strong equity performance in 1982–1991 and exceptionally high interest rates in the early and late 1980s should be mentioned. (Bond funds as well as equity funds can be a variable annuity funding vehicle.) Yield consciousness of an increasingly sophisticated public has led to much active searching for superior investment performance. This is perhaps especially true when one prepares for retirement, e.g., by buying an annuity.

References

American Council of Life Insurance, *Life Insurance Fact Book*, published biannually (with an annual update); Black, Kenneth, Jr., and Harold D. Skipper, Jr., "Annuity and Special-Purpose Benefits," *Life Insurance*, 11th ed., rev., Prentice-Hall, Englewood Cliffs, N.J., 1972, chap. 7; Greenough, William O., *A New Approach to Retirement Income*, Teachers Insurance and Annuity Association, New York, 1951; Toolson, Richard B., "Tax-Advantaged Investing: Comparing Variable Annuities and Mutual Funds," *Journal of Accountancy*, May 1991, pp. 71–77.

(*See also* Inflation; Interest rates; Pension funds)

Francis H. Schott

Velocity of circulation of money

The velocity of circulation of money was defined by Irving Fisher (1922) in *The Purchasing Power of Money* as money's rate of turnover. He preferred to estimate it by dividing the total payments effected by money in a year by the total amount of money in circulation in that year. In modern usage, velocity is more commonly defined as the ratio of total income to the quantity of money. In the second quarter of 1991, for example, the income velocity of M-1 in the United States (gross national product divided by the quantity of M-1) was 6.6. To put it another way, the total stock of M-1 (demand deposits and currency) was being spent, or turned over, at a rate of 6.6 times per year for the goods and services included in the gross national product.

Economists have been concerned with the velocity of circulation for several centuries because the effects of a given change in the quantity of money on incomes and prices will vary with changes in velocity. In short, it is necessary to account for the rate at which money will be used in attempting to predict how a change in the quantity of money will affect incomes and prices.

Between the second quarter of 1990 and the second quarter of 1991, for example, the stock of M-1 increased by 5.17 percent. But the income velocity of M-1 decreased by 1.9 percent in the same period. If income velocity had remained constant, GNP would have increased 5.17 percent instead of the 3.17 percent that it actually increased. Therefore, a decline in velocity offset nearly half of the effect of M-1 growth on GNP growth (5.17 percent − 1.9 percent − 1.9 percent of 5.1 percent = 3.17 percent).

Theories to Explain the Behavior of Velocity

The key issue in dispute among economists is the stability, or predictability, of velocity. Before the 1930s, Irving Fisher and other classical monetary economists believed that velocity was not affected by the rate of growth of the money supply or by changes in the volume of transactions and prices. They believed that velocity was determined by slowly changing institutional factors affecting payments practices, such as the frequency of receipts and disbursements, use of checks, density of population, and speed of transportation. In practice, they considered velocity to be virtually constant over short periods, although they recognized that changes in interest rates and other factors affecting the desirability of holding money could affect it. Subsequent experience demonstrated that they were too optimistic. Velocity does vary substantially over short periods, although over periods of a decade or so it is more stable.

During the 1930s, large velocity changes and the general rejection of classical monetary theory shifted economists' attention to other influences on velocity, including interest rates and the availability of substitutes for money. One early, pessimistic conclusion from this discussion was that velocity changes would tend to offset changes in the quantity of money, thus making monetary policy impotent. In an extreme version of this argument, an increase in the quantity of money would reduce interest rates, thus reducing the cost of holding money, and velocity would decline by enough to prevent the increase in quantity of money from inducing people to increase spending. When the income-expenditure theory of John Maynard Keynes became the predominant explanation of income and spending, many economists then assumed that velocity would adjust passively to income changes. In their view, velocity changes would enable a given quantity of money to accommodate the changes in income and spending induced by shifts in investment or government spending.

The emphasis on institutional factors affecting velocity reemerged in the discussion of new substitutes for money in the form of financial innovations and technological changes, such as credit cards and electronic funds transfer systems, in the 1960s, 1970s, and 1980s. This discussion raised the suspicion that financial innovations might make velocity so difficult to predict that the effectiveness of monetary policy would be impaired.

In modern quantity theory, often called the monetarist approach, velocity of circulation is determined by the factors that determine the demand for money. The demand for money, defined as the quantity people want to hold in relation to income, M/GNP, is simply the inverse of velocity, GNP/M. The factors determining velocity in this approach include wealth, interest rates, inflation expectations, and other factors influencing the desirability of holding money, such as the availability of money substitutes and technological changes in payments practices. An increase in people's wealth in relation to their current income would induce them to hold more money in relation to income and thus would reduce the velocity of circulation. Increases in interest rates or inflation expectations would raise the opportunity costs of holding money and so would increase velocity. Financial innovations which increase the speed of making payments also should tend to reduce the quantity of money people want to hold and, thus, should increase velocity.

There now is a large body of evidence that the velocity of circulation is stable, in the sense of being predictable from a few variables which can be observed. It should be possible, therefore, for a central bank or government to select a growth rate for the money supply that would contribute to stability in prices and economic activity. However, the difficulty of predicting velocity over particular short periods indicates that central banks are on shaky ground when they try to offset short-run swings in business activity with discretionary changes in monetary growth rates. The effects of short-run changes in money growth rates on income and economic activity tend to be reinforced by changes in velocity in the same direction, and so there is a risk of over-controlling (Schwartz, 1989).

Recent Behavior of Velocity in the United States

During each of the recessions since 1960, velocity of all the new and old monetary aggregates declined, or grew more slowly, from the cycle peak to the trough. During each of the expansions, velocity of all the new and old aggregates either grew more rapidly or declined more slowly than during the recessions. This tendency for velocity to fall in recessions and to rise in expansions has been observed in the United States ever since the Civil War. Therefore, there is no evidence that the cyclical behavior of velocity has changed radically in recent years.

The final interesting bit of evidence is that velocity of all the new and old aggregates either fell or grew more slowly in each of the periods in which growth rates of the aggregates declined. Velocity of all the aggregates also grew more rapidly, or declined more slowly, in each of the periods in which monetary growth rates accelerated. Therefore, there was no systematic tendency for velocity changes to offset changes in growth rates of the monetary aggregates. To the contrary, velocity changes systematically reinforced changes in monetary growth rates. Offsetting changes in velocity occurred for a quarter or two on several occasions in which there was a sudden, large change in growth rates of the money supply. These were soon followed, however, by changes in velocity in the same direction as the changes in monetary expansion rates.

Policymakers and outside observers were puzzled by a large fall of velocity in the early 1980s. Some argued that the fall was evidence that the old relationships between money and income had broken down. Counterarguments from monetarists stressed two main explanations for the apparent change in behavior. The first was that deregulation of the banking system had changed the attractiveness of holding money by making it possible for banks to pay interest on nearly all types of deposits (Carlson, 1991; Hetzel and Mehra, 1989). This would tend to reduce velocity as people built up their desired balances. A second explanation was that the success of the effort to reduce inflation after 1980 reduced people's inflation expectations and thus made them willing to hold more money. Recognition of changes in expectations makes the prediction of short-run velocity changes more difficult because it is not possible to observe people's expectations directly.

If people expect inflation to increase, they tend to hold less money. This increases velocity, as they, in effect, try to get rid of money. Because the U.S. price level was virtually unchanged between the end of the American Revolution and the beginning of World War II, the U.S. public did not expect much inflation except during wars. Wartime inflations had always been followed by deflations, until after World War II. Consequently, studies of the demand for money in the United States did not find much evidence of inflation-linked changes in velocity. The sharp inflation upsurge of the 1970s, however, apparently made Americans more inflation-conscious. This heightened awareness of inflation changes was reflected in velocity changes. William Gavin and William Dewald found in 1989 what they believe is a significant influence of shifts in monetary policy on inflation expectations and through these inflation expectations to velocity. Evidence from 80 years of U.S. experience and a 30-year cross section of 39 countries shows, they said, that velocity typically declines relative to trend when disinflation policies are adopted. By their calculations, a policy that reduced average inflation by 10 percentage points would be associated with an average 3 to 5 percentage-point reduction in velocity growth trends (Gavin and Dewald, 1989).

In sum, changes in the velocity of circulation of money can and do affect the influence of changes in money growth rates on incomes, prices, and other variables. However, monetarists believe that these changes in velocity can be predicted or offset well enough for control of the money supply to contribute to the achievement of stability in national incomes, price levels, interest rates, and exchange rates.

References

Campbell, Colin D., "The Velocity of Money and the Rate of Inflation: Recent Experience in South Korea and Brazil," in David Meiselman (ed.), *Varieties of Monetary Experience*, University of Chicago Press, Chicago, 1970, pp. 341–386; Carlson, John B., "Deregulation, Money, and the Economy," *Economic Commentary*, Federal Reserve Bank of Cleveland, March 1, 1991; Carlson, John B., and Sharon E. Parrott, "Understanding the Recent Behavior of M2," *Economic Commentary*, Federal Reserve Bank of Cleveland, June 15, 1991; Emery, Kenneth N., "Modeling the Effects of Inflation on the Demand for Money," *Economic Review*, Federal Reserve Bank of Dallas, March 1991, pp. 17–29; Fisher, Irving, *The Purchasing Power of Money*, 2d ed., 1922; reprinted in *Reprints of Economic Classics*, Kelley, New York 1963; Gavin, William T., and William G. Dewald, "The Effect of Disinflationary Policies on Monetary Velocity," *Cato Journal*, vol. 9, no. 1, Spring/Summer 1989, pp. 149–164; Hetzel, Robert L., and Yash P. Mehra, "The Behavior of Money Demand in the 1980s," *Journal of Money, Credit, and Banking*, vol. 21, no. 4, November 1989, pp. 455–462; Kenny, Lawrence W., "Cross-Country Estimates of the Demand for Money and Its Components," *Economic Inquiry*, vol. XXIX, October 1991, pp. 696–705; Schwartz, Anna J., "Monetarism and Monetary Policy," paper prepared for Southern Economic Association Annual Meeting, November 20, 1989; Selden, Richard T., "Monetary Velocity in the

United States," in Milton Friedman (ed.), *Studies in the Quantity Theory of Money,* University of Chicago Press, Chicago, 1956, pp. 179–275; Warburton, Clark, "Monetary Velocity, Monetary Policy, and the Rate of Interest," *Review of Economics and Statistics,* vol. 30, no. 4, November 1948, pp. 304–314, and vol. 32, no. 3, August 1950, pp. 256–257, reprinted in Clark Warburton, *Depression, Inflation and Monetary Policy, Selected Papers, 1945–1953,* Johns Hopkins Press, Baltimore, Md., 1966, pp. 258–278.

(*See also* Chicago school; Classical school; Federal Reserve policy; Federal Reserve System; Interest rates; Keynesian economics; Monetary policy; Money supply; Quantity theory of money)

A. James Meigs

Venture capital

"Venture capital" is a generic term used to refer to financing characterized by high risk, by the potential for substantial returns, and by the lack of short-term liquidity. The term is most often used to refer to the equity capital required to launch new commercial ventures and to finance their early-stage growth.

Returns to venture capital investors take the form of long-term capital gains. Consequently, the instruments used to structure venture capital financing typically are common stock, convertible preferred stock, convertible debentures, or long-term notes with warrants to purchase stock at nominal prices. All these instruments are forms of equity-type financing. Investors' returns are dependent upon the success of the venture. Debentures and notes typically are subordinated to the interests of other creditors, banks in particular.

Sources of Venture Capital

Sources of equity capital for new ventures can be divided into three broad categories: (1) founders, friends, and relatives, (2) high-net-worth individual investors (business angels), and (3) venture capital funds.

Founders, Friends, and Relatives

Over 90 percent of new ventures obtain their venture financing from founders, friends, and relatives. If these ventures succeed, they will provide a good income and often an appealing life-style for their founders. Due to the nature of the markets they serve or to the desires of the founder, these ventures seldom provide financial rewards sufficient to attract other sources of equity financing.

Business Angels

Business angels are self-made-net-worth individuals. They represent the largest source of both capital and entrepreneurial know-how in the United States. Angels usually invest in ventures related to the fields in which they have been successful themselves. Typically, they maintain close contact with the ventures they finance and can provide first-time entrepreneurs with invaluable know-how as well as capital. Angels are the primary source of seed and start-up financing for ventures with the prospect of becoming substantial businesses (at least $5 million in revenue) within a 5- to 10-year period. A round of angel financing typically is in the $100,000 to $1 million range raised from more than one investor. Over 50,000 companies per year raise capital from business angels.

Venture Capital Funds

The creation of venture capital funds and the venture capital industry is a post–World War II phenomenon. Approximately 600 U.S. venture funds manage about $35 billion. These funds are managed by full-time professionals and raise the capital they invest primarily from other institutions, e.g., pension funds, endowment funds, insurance companies, corporate investors, and, in some cases, wealthy individuals.

A typical round of financing from a group of venture capital funds is in excess of $2 million. These funds invest in ventures with the prospect of growing into companies generating $50 million or more in revenues within 5 to 7 years. Prospects for extraordinary growth are necessary since venture capital funds typically cash in their investments by selling the company to a large publicly traded corporation or by taking the company itself public, thereby creating a market for its shares. Most investments made by venture capital funds are post-start-up financing. About 2000 companies per year succeed in raising capital from venture capital funds.

Aspects of Venture Financing

Due Diligence   Due diligence refers to the process of investigating the merits of a prospective investment. Issues covered include the qualifications of the founding entrepreneurs, the size and growth characteristics of the venture's market, existing and potential competition, the technical feasibility of production and delivery systems, the potential for financial returns appropriate to the risks, and lack of liquidity of the investment. Preparation of a comprehensive, investor-oriented business plan is an essential step in raising venture capital. Once a potential investor has been identified, a period of several months typically elapses before an investment decision is made.

Cost of Venture Capital   The cost of venture capital is represented by the ownership percentage relinquished by the founders to their investors. The process of determining this percentage is as much art as it is science. The cost of venture capital depends upon investors' perceptions of risk. Seed and start-up financing is substantially riskier than later-stage financing. Consequently, for a given dollar investment, investors will demand a larger stake in the company for early-stage deals than for later-stage deals. Investors in early-stage rounds typically look for compound annual returns in the 40 to 60 percent range. They seldom earn these rates on their investments because very few ventures achieve the results projected in their business plans.

Exit Options   Venture capital is patient money. Realization of capital gains seldom occurs before 5 or 10 years from start-up. Nevertheless, venture investors need to know how and when they can expect to cash in their investments. The business plan should cover this issue in detail. Exit options include selling the company, turning it into a publicly held company, and buying back the investors' shares by the company itself or by its management team.

Conclusion

Raising venture capital is a complex, time-consuming process. Entrepreneurs are advised to start the search well ahead of their actual need for funds and to learn as much as possible about the process before beginning the search.

References

Ernst, and Young Staff, *Guide to Raising Venture Capital,* Wiley, New York, 1991; Gladstone, David, *Venture Capital Handbook,* Prentice-Hall, Englewood Cliffs, N.J., 1988; Henderson, James W., *Obtaining Venture Capital,* Lexington Books, Lexington, Mass., 1988; *Pratt's Guide to Venture Capital Sources,* Venture Economics, Boston, Mass., 1991; Rich, Stanley, and David Gumpert, *Business Plans That Win $$$,* Harper Row, New York, 1985; Schilit, W., Keith, *Dream Makers and Deal Breakers: Inside the Venture Capital Industry,* Prentice-Hall, Englewood Cliffs, N.J., 1991.

(*See also* Return on investment; Risk premium on investment)

William E. Wetzel, Jr.

Wage guidelines (*see* Incomes policy)

Wealth

The term "wealth" is used in two distinct but closely related senses. One usage relates to the tangible capital assets used in the process of production. The other concept is financial, equating wealth with net worth. The two concepts are the same for the total domestic economy, but they diverge with respect to individuals, organizations, and economic sectors.

Tangible wealth comprises the material means of production—land and other natural resources, structures, equipment, and inventory stocks. The term has also been extended to include the human factor of production, although balance sheets usually include only nonhuman capital goods that are bought and sold in organized markets, thus enabling an objective value to be assigned these goods. The economic value of human beings can be estimated only indirectly. But the inclusion of humans in the notion of tangible wealth means that they are part of the factors of production, representing capacity to produce income and product in the same sense as tangible capital. While most goods and services are sold to produce money income, some are not. Thus, owner-occupied dwellings and household durable goods represent wealth, although their services are rendered directly, as are the services of public infrastructure. The values of such nonmarket services may be imputed. And although wealth is tangible, its value reflects outlays for services designed to enhance its productivity—research and development in the case of nonhuman instruments, and education, for example, in the case of humans. The valuation of tangible wealth or capital reflects its expected future income, monetary or imputed. In the case of newly produced capital goods, the present value equals the purchase price, or cost of production including profit.

Net Worth

The concept of wealth as net worth represents the value of tangible assets plus intangible or financial assets, less liabilities. Balance sheets may, of course, be constructed for individuals or families, nonprofit organizations, firms, and governments—and combined, consolidated, or separately constructed for broad sectors: persons, business enterprises, and general government, as well as for the domestic or national economy. When the balance sheets of all sectors are consolidated, financial assets and liabilities wash out, and total domestic net worth equals the value of the productive tangible wealth. On a national basis, net worth equals the value of the domestic tangible wealth less the value of that portion owned by foreigners plus the claims by U.S. residents on foreign assets. In other words, national wealth (net worth) equals the value of domestic tangible wealth plus net foreign assets.

On a combined national balance sheet, the financial assets and liabilities are shown, but the difference equals the net foreign assets which, when added to the value of domestic tangible wealth, equal the net worth. Usually, balance sheets show only nonhuman wealth since human wealth is self-owned within the personal sector, and it is this sector to which labor compensation accrues.

For any one sector, net worth may be more (less) than the value of its tangible wealth to the extent that financial assets exceed (fall short of) liabilities. That is, the net worth of a sector, or of an individual or organization, equals the value of its tangible wealth plus its net financial claims on other sectors including the rest of the world. Thus, in an ultimate sense wealth represents tangible capital, either that owned by a sector or the net worth claimed, plus or minus, on the productive assets of other sectors. On a global basis wealth is productive capital since that is what produces income and product. The financial assets and liabilities are but evidences of ownership or indebtedness.

Valuation

On the balance sheets of firms, physical wealth is usually carried at original or acquisition cost. Accumulated depreciation reserves are also shown so that the net value may be computed. Balance sheets for the personal and government sectors have also been constructed using original cost valuation for comparability with the business sector. But for comparability with the national income and product accounts, in which market values are employed, it is necessary to revalue the various categories of physical wealth in terms of market prices, or proxies. For nonreproducible wealth, primarily land and natural resources (but also including art and other collectibles), market pricing is the direct approach, although appraisals or discounting actual and/or expected future income may be resorted to.

Inventory revaluations require adjustment for changes in prices between the times goods are acquired and are sold or else charged to expense, which depends on methods of inventory accounting. To revalue net depreciable assets, one must obtain estimates of the various types of structures and equipment carried on the books by year of acquisition and revalue them to current prices using appropriate price indexes. Since the indexes are based on price data for new items, the revalued estimates represent depreciated replacement costs which are only an approximation to market prices of used assets, many of which are not traded in organized markets. Because of the difficulty of obtaining book values of depreciable assets by type and age, the perpetual inventory method of estimation may be used. This involves deflating annual fixed investments by type, depreciating over the estimated lifetimes of the various types of structures and equipment, summing net investments of all vintages for each year, and then revaluing the net stocks to replacement costs by use of the same price indexes used to deflate the annual investments.

For the corporate business sector, an alternative approach is to take the market value of equities, add liabilities, and subtract financial asset values. The deviations of these values from depreciated replacement costs fluctuate considerably and are significant in indicating changes in the state of business confidence and expectations.

Cash and short-term financial instruments are usually carried at face value. Long-term debt may be restated to reflect changing market values. If equities are carried on the left-hand side of business-sector and combined national balance sheets, there should be an offsetting entry on the right-hand side so that net worth properly reflects the wealth of the property owners.

Since there is no market value of human beings, estimates may be made by determining the costs of rearing, educating, and training members of the labor force, revalued to current prices, or by discounting actual or projected future labor compensation to obtain present values. In the United States, the latter values significantly exceed the costs, suggesting a higher rate of return on human than on nonhuman wealth.

Historical Review

Ever since the time of Sir William Petty (the latter part of the seventeenth century) and later mercantilist writers, the notion of wealth as a stock of goods and natural resources required for the production of goods and services has been an important part of economics. One reason Adam Smith in *The Wealth of Nations* defined national product in material terms was that he thought only tangible goods could be accumulated to increase national wealth, which he perceived as the source of economic growth and development. His lead was followed by David Ricardo and Karl Marx, and the national income accounting systems of communist countries still revolve around the concept of material product. Ever since the writings of Alfred Marshall, economists in the West have recognized the production of services as part of national product, and that certain service outlays—notably for research, education, training, health, and mobility—contribute to immaterial capital, embodied in human beings. The growth of human capital or wealth is considered coordinate with the growth of nonhuman wealth in contributing to economic progress.

Occasional estimates of national wealth have been made by individual investigators in many advanced countries. In 1955, the Japanese government conducted its first sample survey of the components of wealth. In 1959, the Soviet Union conducted a complete inventory of its structures and equipment, with valuations based on engineering appraisals. The U.S. government conducted eight censuses of wealth between 1850 and 1922, when the procedure was dropped because of the ambiguity created by a mixture of valuations. Since then, occasional estimates and time series have been prepared by individual scholars, notably R. Doane, S. Kuznets, R. Goldsmith, and J. Kendrick.

In recent years, the National Income and Wealth Division of the Bureau of Economic Analysis in the U.S. Department of Commerce has published estimates of real stocks of reproducible capital for the business sector and is in the process of extending these to cover the other sectors. When the tangible wealth estimates are completed, they can be combined with estimates of financial assets and liabilities, prepared by the Federal Reserve Board since the late 1950s as part of its flow-of-funds statistics, to provide complete balance sheets for the nation, by sector. It is important that balance sheets and wealth statements be prepared as part of an integrated set of national economic accounts in view of the close relationship between the stock and flow estimates. Other nations are also moving toward official preparation of balance sheets to accompany their national income and product accounts. Estimates of human wealth, however, are still the work of individual investigators.

Significance of Wealth:
Relationship to Other Variables

Tangible wealth, as the value of the factors of production, is the source of income and product. Indeed, economic growth—the rate of increase in real national product—may be viewed as a process of capital formation and thus of the rate of increase in real national wealth, human and nonhuman. Actually, in the United States since 1929 real product has grown somewhat faster than real wealth owing to economies of scale and other variables affecting total productivity. In current prices, however, net national income in 1983 was approximately the same percentage of net national wealth as in 1929, reflecting an increase in the price deflator for wealth relative to that for product. Although the average rate of return was around 10 percent per annum, it was somewhat higher for human wealth than for nonhuman.

Wealth is also related to aggregate demand. Its age composition is a factor in replacement demand for durables. The structure of the balance sheets of which wealth data are a part influences demand as households and firms attempt to adjust portfolios toward desired proportions. Also wealth, as a major indicator of permanent income, is an important determinant of consumption expenditures.

In reciprocal fashion, the growth of income and its allocation between saving for capital formation and consumption determine the growth of wealth. The increase in real wealth between the beginning and end of a period equals the real net investment during the period. In current prices, however, changes in net worth reflect changes in prices of assets and liabilities, as well as the volume of saving and investment. Thus, a revaluation account is required to supplement the capital (flow-of-funds) account in order to explain changes in balance sheets and wealth. The revaluations, resulting in realized and unrealized capital gains or losses, themselves influence expenditure decisions.

References

Conference on Research in Income and Wealth, *Measuring the Nation's Wealth,* Studies in Income and Wealth, vol. 29, National Bureau of Economic Research, New York, 1964; Goldsmith, R. W., and R. E. Lipsey, *Studies in the National Balance Sheet of the United States,* 2 vols., National Bureau of Economic Research, Princeton University Press, Princeton, N.J., 1963; Kendrick, John W., *The Formation and Stocks of Total Capital,* National Bureau of Economic Research, New York, 1976; Lipsey, Robert E., and Helen S. Tice (eds.), *The Measurement of Saving, Investment, and Wealth,* Studies in Income and Wealth, vol. 52, University of Chicago Press, Chicago, 1989.

(*See also* Flow of funds; Saving)

John W. Kendrick

Welfare economics

Modern economics is divided into the two major areas of macroeconomics and microeconomics. Microeconomics, in turn, can be divided into the areas of positive microeconomics and normative microeconomics. The former deals with the explanation and prediction of actual resource allocation decisions made by consumers, producers, and government agencies. The latter deals with how those resource allocation decisions ought to be made: with the criteria for judging alternative resource allocations and with mechanisms for achieving them. Welfare economics, synonymous with normative microeconomics, is a collection of propositions and analytical devices useful for evaluating resource allocation decisions. Welfare economics should not be confused with government welfare programs. Although it can be used to evaluate such programs, as a scientific and politically neutral procedure it neither espouses nor opposes them. Welfare economics is the modern basis for economic policy analysis.

History

The distinction between welfare economics and positive microeconomics is a relatively modern convention. For the better part of the history of economic science, up until roughly the first quarter of the twentieth century, this distinction was not drawn. Welfare economics evolved gradually from the body of economic thought, and for this reason it is difficult to pinpoint its precise beginnings. Generally, the writings of such luminaries as Marshall, Edgeworth, Walras, Pareto, and Fisher can be thought of as containing the seeds of welfare economics. The publication of Pigou's *Economics of Welfare* in 1920 might be considered the point at which welfare economics assumed its present independent identity. From 1920 to roughly 1950, the theoretical foundations of welfare economics were fashioned by such writers as Pigou, Hicks, Kaldor, and Scitovsky. During the fifties and early sixties, welfare economics and general equilibrium theory developed jointly, bringing sophisticated mathematical tools into the economists' arsenal. Arrow and Debreu were path breakers in this period. More recently, welfare economics has developed an applied facet. That is, some recent developments have focused on applying welfare economic theory to the understanding and resolution of practical economic problems. Applied welfare economics is often done under the rubric of cost-benefit analysis.

Discussion

Welfare economics, as the term suggests, deals with the welfare, or well-being, of the members of a society. It addresses the issue of deciding which of several alternative economic states of affairs (resource allocations and income distributions) is best; and it addresses how well market (or other economic) systems perform. Much of the literature on welfare economics has dealt with exploring, proposing, and refining notions of what constitutes a better economic state; with exploring the performance of market systems; and more recently with exploring the implications of nonmarket social decision processes, such as various voting systems.

Welfare economics is founded on two postulates. First, the individual is the one and only judge of his or her own well-being, and, second, the welfare of society is influenced only by the welfare of each individual. These postulates reject the notion of an organic state independent of and greater than the sum of the individuals composing it, and they reject the notion that the individual exists to further the goals of the state. Rather, the postulates adopt the view that the economic system exists to serve the needs and desires of the individual. The "fundamental theorem" of welfare economics states that a perfectly competitive market system will achieve a "Pareto-efficient" allocation of resources.

Current Status

Some years ago it was fashionable to suggest that welfare economics was dead. At that time the field was mired in apparently fruitless explorations for new and tractable welfare criteria. Since then, however, the field has been invigorated by new developments: an emphasis on policy applications, the analysis of social (especially political) decision processes, an exploration of the implications of property rights, and an analysis of the effect of asymmetric information on markets. These new directions breathed life into the field, and there is little doubt that the death of welfare economics was greatly exaggerated. Today, welfare economics provides the theoretical basis and analytic tools for such dynamic areas as cost-benefit analysis, public-sector economics, social choice theory, and policy science. Actual problems in areas such as public-utility pricing, deregulation, farm policy, government R&D, airport location, economic development, pollution control, energy policy, and many others have been and are being addressed using welfare economics. On the theoretical front, the continued development of social choice theory and the study of asymmetric markets and property rights are providing fresh insights and are furthering the evolution of welfare economics. It is likely that welfare economics will find extensive use in both practical and theoretical analyses of the transition of Eastern Europe to market economies.

References

Arrow, K. J., *Social Choice and Individual Values,* Cowles Commission Monograph no. 12, Wiley, New York, 1951; Bator, F., "The Simple Analytics of Welfare Maximization," *American Economic Review,* vol. 47, 1957, pp. 22–59; Baumol, W. J., *Welfare Economics and the Theory of the State,* Harvard University Press, Cambridge, Mass., 1965; Coase, R. H., "The Problem of Social Cost," *Journal of Law and Economics,* vol. 3, 1960, pp. 1–44; Furubotn, E., and S. Pejovich, "Property Rights and Economic Theory: A Survey of the Recent Literature," *Journal of Economic Literature,* vol. 10, 1972, pp. 1137–1162; Lehn, K., "Information Asymmetries in Baseball's Free Agent Market," *Economic Inquiry,* 1984, pp. 37–44; Little, I. M. D., *A Critique of Welfare Economics,* 2d ed., Clarendon Press, Oxford, 1957; Mishan, E., *Welfare Economics,* Random House, New York, 1964; Pigou, A. C., *The Economics of Welfare,* 4th ed., Macmillan, New York, 1932; Rawls, J. A., *A Theory of Justice,* Harvard University Press, Cambridge, Mass., 1971; Sen, A. K., *Collective Choice and Social Welfare,* Holden-Day, San Francisco, 1970.

(*See also* Cost-benefit analysis; Externalities; Microeconomics; Normative economics)

Peter G. Sassone

World Bank

The World Bank is the world's foremost intergovernmental organization concerned with the external financing of the economic growth of developing countries. Officially known as the International Bank for Reconstruction and Development (IBRD), its Articles of Agreement were negotiated by the delegates, the British and the American in particular, from 44 nations at the Bretton Woods (New Hampshire) Conference in July 1944. The Articles of Agreement of the International Monetary Fund, substantially amended subsequently, were negotiated at the same time.

World Bank loans finance Bank-approved imports into developing countries. A small fraction of the funds loaned have actually been paid into the Bank (in freely convertible currencies) by member nations as a portion of their subscriptions. Much the greater part has been borrowed, however. Bonds are sold in the world's leading capital markets, that is to say, on the basis of the remaining portions of the member nations' subscriptions (guarantees). From time to time, as the uncommitted lending power has become scarce, member nations have been asked by the executive directors of the Bank to increase the amount of their subscriptions. (The countries with the largest subscriptions lead the way.) In 1946, total subscriptions to the Bank were, roughly, $10 billion. In 1991, agreement was reached to increase, over several years, the total from $90 billion to $174 billion.

Before recommending a Bank loan, the staff of the Bank must be reasonably satisfied that the productivity of the borrowing country will be increased and that the prospects for repayment are good. A country must be judged creditworthy. Engineering investigations are frequently carried out to determine the probable relation of a proposed project to benefits and costs. Increasingly, however, the Bank has shifted somewhat away from project lending (e.g., for a dam or a highway or a port); it has become concerned with education and other human services, the environment, and, through structural adjustment loans, the modification of governmental policies that are thought to have impeded long-run growth. The Bank has also paid increasing attention to the evaluation of previous lending. Recently, moreover, it has acceded to the requests of the American secretary of the treasury to help to ease the huge, outstanding, largely commercial-bank debt.

Voting power in the Bank (as well as in the Fund) is determined by the size of each member nation's subscription. Subscriptions, in turn, are based on a formula that takes into account such variables as the value of each nation's foreign trade and its total output. Ultimate power, through weighted voting, rests with the Board of Governors of the Bank (and the Fund). The governors meet annually in September. The day-to-day affairs of the Bank are determined, however, by executive directors who live permanently in Washington, D.C. They hire a president, who, in turn, hires a staff. By tradition, rather than law, the president of the Bank is an American, usually a banker, proposed by the President of the United States.

Because of the size of their subscriptions, five nations—the United States, Japan, Germany, the United Kingdom, and France—are entitled to appoint executive directors; the remaining seventeen directors are elected by some combination of the votes of the other nations. There are 156 member nations, but, with the independence of the Baltic states and the devolution of the Soviet Union into separate republics, the membership could increase to over 170, thereby including all the independent nations in the world. The Soviet Union was one of the forty-four governments whose representatives signed the original Bretton Woods agreements, but along with the other members of the Warsaw Pact, it chose not to join the Bank or the Fund when these organizations were formally incorporated in 1946. (Poland and Czechoslovakia joined the Bank and the Fund initially but withdrew when the cold war began in earnest and a loan to Poland was blocked by the United States.) In 1979 communist China replaced the Republic of China.

World Bank Group

In 1954, an International Finance Corporation was established to supplement the World Bank by participating in equity financing in member countries, and in 1960, a third organization, the International Development Association (IDA), was created. These three organizations constitute the World Bank Group. The IDA has the same officers and staff as the World Bank, but its separate charter enables it to offer loans to low-income member countries repayable at 0.75 percent interest over 50 years (including 10 years' grace). (The World Bank per se charges ½ percent over the cost to it of borrowing—about 8½ percent.) Soft or concessionary assistance is made possible by contributions to (replenishments of) the IDA by the governments of high-income (industrial) countries. The management of the World Bank Group is thus enabled to offer rates of interest and loan maturities which take into account the nature of the projects financed and the presumed ability of borrowing governments to service their debt. The initial capitalization of IDA for the 5 years 1960 to 1964 was less than $1 billion in hard currencies. By 1992, the ninth replenishment for 3 years will be over $11 billion.

The Presidents

The Bank Group has had seven presidents, the last of whom was Barber Conable, a former congressman who helped to arrange the recent large increase in subscriptions to the Bank as well as the ninth replenishment of IDA.

Eugene Meyer (1946), publisher of the *Washington Post* and first president of the World Bank, resigned because he did not feel he had sufficient power relative to the executive directors. His successor, John J. McCloy, accepted the presidency only after President Truman assured him that he would be fully in charge of the Bank, rather like the chief executive officer in a private American business corporation, a condition that came gradually to be altered only after governments began periodically to replenish the International Development Association in 1964. McCloy left after two years to become high commissioner to Germany.

The third president, Eugene Black (1949–1962), who came to the Bank initially from the Chase Manhattan Bank as executive director for the United States, developed the market for the bonds the Bank sought to sell and arranged Bank lending for infrastructure: dams, roads, irrigation systems, and so on. For balance of payments reasons, George Woods (1963–1968), the fourth president and former chairman of the board of the First Boston Corporation, was impeded by the virtual closing of the security markets of the United States and the unwillingness of the American Congress to contribute as much to IDA as Woods wished. He succeeded in greatly expanding lending for agriculture (the green revolution) and education, however. Eugene Black and George Woods were both concerned about the problem of Third World debt. Woods even sought to make IDA lending more important than World Bank lending, but he was unsuccessful.

It was former Secretary of Defense Robert McNamara (1968–1981) who succeeded in loosening the financial constraints so that Bank lending could be expanded across the board. He also turned his attention to poverty in the low per capita income nations of the world. During McNamara's first 10 years as president, the lending commitments of the World Bank increased from less than $1 billion a year to well over $5 billion, and the size of the staff almost kept pace. By 1990, Bank lending commitments had risen to over $15 billion a year.

A. W. (Tom) Clausen (1981–1986) followed McNamara. He had been president of the Bank of America, a position to which he returned after he completed his term with the World Bank. Cofinancing with governments and private institutions became more important under Clausen's leadership. He also succeeded in developing as a separate organization a Multilateral Guarantee Investment Agency which will insure private investors against certain noncommercial political risks. By that time, however, the power of the executive directors had been substantially reestablished, and the staff of the Bank had become so large that it had a momentum of its own. Barber Conable (1986–1991) sought to change this but had relatively little success.

Today, the World Bank Group is a far cry from what it was when the World Bank began in 1946 under President Eugene Meyer—with three floors of rented office space at 1818 H Street NW and a few dozen employees. Even in the final days of the presidency of George Woods, in 1968, the group had fewer than 1500 employees and four buildings. As of August 31, 1991, however, on the eve of the accession to the presidency of Lewis Preston, former chairman of the board of J. P. Morgan & Co., the World Bank Group had 3 senior vice presidents, 14 vice presidents, and 6500 employees scattered through 18 separate buildings in Washington, D.C.; 2 large offices in Paris and Tokyo; and 50 regional offices.

The Record

The World Bank Group has had a significant positive effect on the flow of capital to the poorer countries of the world, both directly and indirectly, and knowledge of Third World problems has increased enormously. Still, the record of growth is spotty. In much of East Asia, per capita income is rising rapidly, but in Africa south of the Sahara, in South Asia, and in much of Latin America, the growth of per capita income has been discouragingly slow.

References

Annual Reports, The World Bank, Washington, D.C.; Ayres, Robert L., *Banking on the Poor,* MIT Press, Cambridge, Mass., 1983; *The Bank's World,* published monthly by the World Bank Group, Washington, D.C.; *Finance and Development,* published quarterly by the International Monetary Fund and the International Bank for Reconstruction and Development, Washington, D.C.; Mason, Edward M., and Robert Asher, *The World Bank since Bretton Woods,* Brookings, Washington, D.C., 1973; Oliver, Robert W., *International Economic Cooperation and the World Bank,* Macmillan, London, 1975; *World Development Reports,* Oxford University Press, New York, published for the World Bank.

(*See also* Bretton Woods Conference; International economics, an overview; International Monetary Fund)

Robert W. Oliver

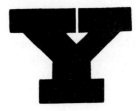

Yield curve

The yield curve is a smoothly drawn curve that depicts the functional relationship between yield-to-maturity and years-to-maturity of fixed-income securities at a given point in time. Isolation of this relationship requires that all other factors affecting yield—risk of default, liquidity, cost of acquisition, and so on—be held constant; thus, yield curves are drawn only for securities that are identical except for maturity. For example, the most frequently used are those for U.S. Treasury securities because these debt obligations are available in a wide range of maturities, from a few days to more than 20 years, and are virtually identical in all other respects.

Varying economic conditions result in yield curves that have one of three basic shapes: A flat curve means that yields on short, intermediate, and long maturities are almost the same, suggesting that the supply of and demand for loanable funds are roughly in balance throughout the market. An upward-sloping curve indicates that yields are higher on longer maturities and suggests that the demand for short-term funds relative to supply is greater than it is for long-term funds. Finally, a downward-sloping curve shows that yields are higher on shorter maturities, indicating that the demand for longer-term funds relative to supply is greater than that for short-term funds.

Usefulness of Yield Curves

Yield curves are useful because they show geometrically the term structure of interest rates. Since yield curves assume flat, upward, and downward slopes at different times, the question arises: Why does the term structure of interest rates differ so markedly on different dates? Economists have put forth three major hypotheses to explain the pattern of interest rates.

The Liquidity Preference Hypothesis   This hypothesis states that investors place a premium on liquidity, that is, the ability to convert an asset into cash quickly without loss. Since shorter maturities are somewhat more liquid than longer ones, they will command higher prices and, therefore, lower yields than longer maturities. However, scant evidence, if any, exists that liquidity-seeking investors dominate the fixed-income securities markets. In fact, investors might actually prefer paying a premium for an assured long-term rate rather than confronting the uncertainty of what rate they will receive on funds reinvested each time the short-term obligations mature. Furthermore, and more damaging, although this hypothesis could explain what some people feel is a normal yield curve—upward sloping—it obviously fails to account for the other two basic shapes.

The Market Segmentation Hypothesis (Preferred Habitat)   This hypothesis asserts that there are separate markets for short- and long-term fixed-income securities and that demand and supply in each determine yields on short and long maturities. Because the market is segmented, any pattern of yields could result depending upon the demand for and supply of short-term funds relative to that for long-term debt obligations. Thus this hypothesis can explain why yield curves come in a variety of shapes. But it denies that capital funds might be mobile among different maturities. In other words, it states that portfolio managers will only hold short- or long-term maturities and that governments and corporations will not vary the maturities of their debt issues. The evidence overwhelmingly argues against this position. Although perfect substitutability among various maturities does not exist, portfolio managers do alter the maturity composition of their portfolios, and governments and corporations behave similarly when issuing new debt claims, each responding to changing differentials between short- and long-term yields.

The Expectations Hypothesis   This hypothesis holds that investor expectations about future short-term rates determine the relationship between short- and long-term yields. If investors expect short-term rates to increase, the yield curve will slope upward; if they anticipate falling short-term rates, the curve will slope downward; and if they believe that these rates will remain at the same level, the curve will be flat. For example, suppose that you plan to invest funds for 2 years and that you have a choice between a 1- and a 2-year Treasury security, each yielding 6 percent. If you expect short-term rates to rise to, say, 8 percent, you would buy the 1-year security. Then, 1 year hence when it matures, you would reinvest the funds at 8 percent, raising your average annual rate of return above what you would have received on the 2-year security. Relatively greater demand for short-term securities will tend to push up their prices, reduce their yields, and result in a yield curve that slopes upward. The opposite occurs if you expect falling short-term rates. You would purchase the 2-year obligation, prices of longer maturities would tend to increase, their yields would decline, and a downward-sloping yield curve would result. Finally, if you expect short-term rates to remain unchanged, you would be indifferent about a choice between the two securities and demand would be roughly even throughout the market, resulting in a flat yield curve.

The expectations hypothesis can also explain different yield curve patterns. But its fundamental assumption is opposite that of the market segmentation hypothesis: all maturities are perfect substitutes; that is, no market segmentation whatsoever exists. However, the evidence indicates otherwise. Some investors (e.g., commercial banks) tend to favor shorter maturities, while others (e.g., life insurance companies) tend to prefer longer-term obligations. Critics have also attacked the assumptions that investors can accurately forecast short-term interest rates and that they all will agree with the predicted direction and magnitude of movements. Obviously these assumptions are too emphatic.

Empirical studies suggest, however, that the expectations hypothesis, with modifications that take the criticisms noted into account, best explains the term structure of interest rates and, therefore, the various yield curve patterns.

References

Shiller, Robert, and J. Houston McCullock, "The Term Structure of Interest Rates," National Bureau of Economic Research, Working Paper no. 2341, August 1987; Van Horne, James C., *Financial Market Rates and Flows,* Prentice-Hall, Englewood Cliffs, N.J., 1984.

(*See also* Interest rates)

Henry C. F. Arnold

Z

Zero population growth

Zero population growth (ZPG) is a concept that has been popularized mainly by those who are convinced that the world has reached a stage at which it has become imperative that human population growth be halted as soon as possible. Indeed, most adherents of ZPG as a policy goal believe that populations are now excessive in a large majority of the world's nations. They would encourage these nations to take steps not merely to stabilize their populations, but gradually to reduce them over the next several generations.

The first widely read portrayal of the dire consequences of unchecked population growth came from the economist Thomas Malthus, who published in 1798 his theory that the growth rate of population must inevitably outstrip the growth rate of food production. Malthus expected that ZPG would be reached in most countries at a relatively early date, certainly within a hundred years. A limited ability to expand food supply would choke population growth off by malnutrition, disease, and outright starvation. He visualized a high birthrate–high death rate world in which population would level off at the maximum number supportable, at a bare subsistence level, by inexorable constraints on food output.

Malthus, in 1798, was unable to imagine the enormous increase in agricultural productivity and the astounding advances in science and technology during the nineteenth and twentieth centuries which made it possible for industrializing nations to support rapidly growing populations at rising levels of per capita real consumption. Malthus came to be seen by most economists as a grossly overpessimistic theorist whose gloomy forecasts helped to saddle on economics the epithet of "the dismal science."

In the late twentieth century, there was a broad consensus among economists that a slowing of population growth rates would be beneficial for the poorer nations of Asia,

Africa, and Latin America, but only a very small minority of economists were endorsing the goal of worldwide ZPG. Among the few well-known contemporary economists who could arguably be claimed to be ZPG advocates were Kenneth Boulding, Nicholas Georgescu-Roegen, Robert Heilbroner, E. J. Mishan, and Joseph J. Spengler.

By the 1960s, however, alarm over population growth was reviving. The world's population swelled from an estimated 2 billion in 1930, to 3 billion by 1960, to 4 billion by 1975, and to more than 5 billion by 1990. If maintained—assuming it to be maintainable—the recent rate of growth would bring world population to almost 10 billion by the year 2025 and to near 15 billion by 2050.

Within the academic community, expressed fear over population growth and advocacy of ZPG have come largely from natural scientists, particularly biologists. Their concern with population growth in the relatively rich countries of North America and Western Europe has not arisen from any expected shortfall of food supplies. They fear, rather, damage to the natural environment and to the general quality of human existence. As more and more human beings are crowded into a fixed geographical space—e.g., the continental United States—the advocates of ZPG believe it will become increasingly difficult, if not impossible, to maintain a low level of environmental pollution. They have a vision of ever-higher levels of human congestion: more densely populated urban areas, intolerable traffic congestion, the overcrowding by humanity of the seashore, lakes, and state and national parks. They argue that a stabilized—preferably, reduced—population would be able to maintain over a longer time period a standard of living based upon our current high per capita consumption of such nonrenewable resources as fossil fuels and minerals. We would thereby gain time in which to develop new and less polluting technologies, such as solar energy, which would draw upon nonexhaustible resources.

Since the early 1980s there have been developments both discouraging and encouraging to the proponents of ZPG. Apprehension has risen over the depletion of the ozone layer, the possibility that a "greenhouse effect" is being created by the burning of a growing volume of fossil fuels, and the rapid depletion of forests in the Amazon basin and elsewhere. Concern has grown over acid rain, the fouling of beaches by garbage dumped in the ocean, and the disposal of toxic wastes. Meanwhile, immigration into the United States—both legal and illegal—has continued at a rate that is far above that which is acceptable to supporters of ZPG. They see no possibility of stabilizing the U.S. population unless the inflow of immigrants is drastically reduced. As the black and Hispanic proportions of the U.S. population rise, with their birthrates higher than that of the white population, some advocates of ZPG have become less hopeful that the overall national birthrate can be reduced to the level required for population stability. In a number of Western European nations also, a continuing flow of legal and illegal immigration, mainly from the Middle East and North Africa, has alarmed those who consider Europe to have pushed already above an optimum population level. Admittedly, in both Western Europe and the United States, many of the supporters of limited and rigorously controlled immigration are motivated less by a fear of population growth than by the desire to maintain a predominantly white population. In France and Germany, especially, open expression of hostility toward nonwhite immigrants grew in the 1980s and early 1990s.

On the positive side, from the perspective of ZPG supporters, technological developments have improved the prospects for a policy of population control—should such a policy eventually be adopted. Improvements have been made in surgical techniques for sterilization of both men and women. The "abortion pill," RU-486, offers cheaper and less traumatic abortions. It can be expected to become available throughout most of the world, although as of the end of 1992 it cannot be legally prescribed in the United States. The surgically implantable contraceptive (Norplant, reportedly effective for a 5-year period) promises a great potential gain in reducing the number of undesired pregnancies.

Among the larger nations, Japan appears the most likely candidate to first achieve ZPG, in combination with a high material standard of living. Japan's birthrate has been greatly reduced from its pre–World War II level. The Japanese are well aware of the space limitations of their islands, and have evidently abandoned their former ambitions to escape those limitations by seizing territory from other nations. Their determination to preserve their racial and cultural homogeneity is reflected in Japanese unwillingness to accept more than a small trickle of legal immigration. And in marked contrast to the United States, the island nation of Japan is in an excellent position to defend itself against illegal immigration.

In the tragic Malthusian scenario, ZPG is reached by the death rate rising to the high level of an unrestrained birthrate. If this scenario is someday to be played out anywhere in the world, it seems likely to first appear in sub-Saharan Africa. During the 1980s, most African nations made little, if any, progress toward establishing more effective governments, encouraging birth control and family planning, and raising the educational attainments of their people. In much of Africa, per capita food production fell slightly in the 1980s.

Pessimists and Optimists

Like Malthus in his day, those who advocate ZPG can be categorized as pessimists. They are frightened of the prospects for humanity within the not-so-distant future, the next 50 to 100 years. They look upon the earth as having a limited maximum sustainable carrying capacity for the human population. Although world population might rise above, and remain above, this limit for a period of time, the result will be such damage to the environment that the planet's long-run sustainable carrying capacity will ultimately be lowered. An overpopulated world will greatly increase the grave environmental harms inflicted by conversion of arable land to urban use; deforestation through excessive lumbering; lowering of water tables through overreliance upon irrigation; creation of dust bowls from overgrazing and plowing of semiarid lands; depletion of ocean and fresh-water fisheries from overfishing and the buildup of water pollution; loss of topsoil from strip-mining; reduction of crop yields from soil erosion, air pollution, and rapid depletion of nonrenewable sources of fertilizers; accelerated rates of exhaustion of recoverable deposits of fossil fuels and minerals; probable radioactive poisoning of some local areas from accidents in nuclear power plants; the pollution of underground water aquifers by seepage from garbage dumps; and the increasing difficulty of finding acceptable sites for the disposal of toxic waste, especially radioactive waste. By the early 1990s the environmental threat that had come to attract the greatest attention and controversy was the greenhouse effect, which many scientists feared must inevitably be brought on by the increasing discharge of heat, fossil fuel residues, and other pollutants into the atmosphere. In the worst-case scenarios, the greenhouse effect was projected to cause such catastrophic climatic changes in some parts of the world that it would become impossible for the present levels of population to be maintained in those areas.

Proponents of ZPG call upon economists to embrace, in Kenneth Boulding's phrase, an "economics of spaceship earth." Humanity must be brought to recognize and accept the inescapable necessity of achieving a steady-state equilibrium between the world's population and its productive capacity from renewable resources. Time is short—world population, at its current growth rate, will soon be pressing upon the limits of the earth's carrying capacity.

In contrast to the ZPG advocates, most professional economists can be described as optimists. They do not fear an imminent crisis. One of the strongest proponents of an optimistic viewpoint is Julian Simon, who describes human beings as constituting the "ultimate resource." Human scientific genius, and the myriad other manifestations of human ingenuity, can assure us of a continuing rise in the standard of living for the reasonably foreseeable future. Advancing science and technology almost certainly will not only enable a greatly enlarged human population to live on the earth, but also allow our descendants to enjoy an increase in real material consumption per capita. While ZPG advocates consider world population, now approaching 6 billion. to have already arrived at a level that may threaten human living standards, the more optimistic among the economists see no insuperable obstacles to an eventual world population of at least 20 billion, with per capita consumption of food and other goods and services generally above current levels. From an optimist's perspective, the adherents of ZPG are alarmists who persist in crying wolf, when the wolf has yet to appear above the horizon.

Optimism about population growth rests upon the foundations of faith in humankind's problem-solving capacities and the view that earth's potentially exploitable reservoir of resources is vast. Even for those resources conventionally described as exhaustible, a well-functioning market price system can satisfactorily regulate their rate of consumption over time. As and when the relative prices of such resources rise, adequate incentives will thereby be provided to discover new supplies, reduce the costs of resource extraction, and develop substitutes. (Julian Simon has pointed out that the real, inflation-adjusted prices of most "exhaustible" mineral resources actually fell during the 1980s.) World reserves of petroleum and coal are ample to give scientists enough time to develop abundant supplies of energy from alternative sources, both nuclear and solar. Technological innovation and a sophisticated use of such economic incentives as taxes on the discharge of pollutants will enable humankind to hold pollution down to a tolerable level, even with growth in both the human population and real industrial output per capita.

Most of those economists who acknowledge that humanity, to some degree, may be facing a potential population problem are also optimistic that this problem will be satisfactorily solved over time. In the advanced industrialized nations, the age-old economic incentives to produce children in order to provide labor for the family farm and support for parents in old age have almost vanished. Expanded opportunities for employment of women outside the home have greatly raised the opportunity cost of having children. In some European countries, net reproduction rates have fallen below unity. Plausible demographic projections indicate that ZPG might well be attained within one or two generations by the combined total population of that area of the globe occupied by the United States, Canada, Western Europe, the non-Asiatic regions of the former Soviet Union, and the Soviet's former Eastern European satellite countries—provided, however, that the peoples inhabiting this area of the world embrace the Japanese model of immigration restriction and take whatever steps that may be required to choke off further net inflows of immigrants from the relatively impoverished regions of the world.

In the poorer, less-developed nations of Asia, the Middle East, Africa, and Latin America, birthrates generally continue to be well above death rates. Their rising populations have understandably generated a great increase in the late twentieth century in the numbers of their people who desperately seek, by legal or illegal means, entry into the richer countries of North America and Western Europe. Many economists remain optimistic, however, that birthrates in these less-developed countries will be reduced over the next 50 to 75 years to levels not far above those in the industrialized nations. Their hopes ride largely upon the extent to which the governments of these countries will prove willing and able to carry out policies to increase literacy and education, raise real incomes, persuade their people to accept contraceptive techniques, and establish old-age security programs to reduce the incentive to have children.

Coercion?

Can humanity achieve a state of worldwide ZPG in the absence of governmental coercion? Men and women cherish their traditional unfettered freedom to decide upon the number of children they wish to have. China is the only nation currently attempting to force married couples to produce fewer children than many couples would prefer. Those in the Western world who advocate ZPG are reluctant to praise China as a model. If one is attempting to convince others of the necessity of ZPG, it is inexpedient to alienate many potential converts by an explicit endorsement of governmentally imposed restrictions on childbearing. Nevertheless, a large proportion—probably a majority—of ZPG supporters doubt that world population growth can be brought to a halt if all human beings are allowed complete freedom of choice with respect to the number of new humans they bring into this world.

Since the earth is finite, it is impossible for an infinite number of human beings to live upon this planet. There must come a time when earth's human population reaches a number that it will never exceed. In that sense, zero population growth is inevitable.

The more impassioned advocates of ZPG argue that since ZPG must come eventually, we should make a deliberate and intelligent attempt to achieve it as soon as possible, if necessary by the imposition of rigid population-control measures. We must do this in order to escape the human suffering and the environmental damage that will result should ZPG arrive, instead, through the Malthusian controls of disease and famine.

Those who see no need for a ZPG policy have more confidence that people will continue to find the means to support a growing population over many years into the future, and that the world's rate of population growth will gradually subside without the adoption of coercive techniques to control human reproduction.

References

Brown, Lester R., *Building a Sustainable Society,* Norton, New York, 1981; Daly, Herman E. (ed.), *Toward a Steady-State Economy,* Freeman, San Francisco, 1973; Ehrlich, Paul R., and

Anne H. Ehrlich, *The Population Explosion,* Simon and Schuster, New York, 1990; Malthus, Thomas R., in Philip Appleman (ed.), *An Essay on the Principle of Population,* Norton, New York, 1976; Olson, Mancur, and Hans Landsberg (eds.), *The No-Growth Society,* Norton, New York, 1973; Simon, Julian L., *The Economics of Population Growth,* Princeton University Press, Princeton, N.J., 1977; Simon, Julian L., *The Ultimate Resource,* Princeton University Press, Princeton, N.J., 1981; Spengler, Joseph J., *Facing Zero Population Growth,* Duke University Press, Durham, N.C., 1978.

(*See also* Malthusian theory of population)

Robert E. L. Knight

Name Index

Subject Index

About the Editor in Chief

Douglas Greenwald is one of this country's best-known economic consultants to government and business. Formerly Vice President/Economics of the McGraw-Hill Publications Company, Dr. Greenwald is also the editor in chief of the prestigious *McGraw-Hill Dictionary of Modern Economics* and the coauthor (with Dexter Keezer) of *New Forces in American Business*. He has testified many times before congressional committees on the economic outlook, prospects for capital expenditures, and the industrial operating rate. Dr. Greenwald is a fellow of the National Association of Business Economists and the American Statistical Association as well as a member of the American Economic Association and the Atlantic Economic Society.